THIRD EDITION

UNDERSTANDING PSYCHOPATHOLOGY

SOUTH AFRICAN PERSPECTIVES <<<<<

Burke
Austin
Bezuidenhout
Botha
Du Plessis
Jordaan
Lake
Makhafula
Makhubela
Moletsane
Nel
Pillay
Stein
Ure
Von Krosigk
Vorster

OXFORD
UNIVERSITY PRESS

SOUTH AFRICA

OXFORD
UNIVERSITY PRESS

Oxford University Press is a department of the University of Oxford.
It furthers the University's objective of excellence in research, scholarship,
and education by publishing worldwide. Oxford is a registered trade mark of
Oxford University Press in the UK and in certain other countries.

Published in South Africa by
Oxford University Press Southern Africa (Pty) Limited

Vasco Boulevard, Goodwood, N1 City, Cape Town, South Africa, 7460
P O Box 12119, N1 City, Cape Town, South Africa, 7463

Psychopathology: South African Perspectives 3e

ISBN 978 0 19 072256 2

First impression 2019

Typeset in Minion Pro 10pt on 12.5pt
Printed on 70 gsm wood-free paper

Acknowledgements
Publishing Manager: Alida Terblancge
Publisher: Marisa Montemarano
Development Editor: Jeanne Maclay-Mayers
Editor: Vivian O'Neill
Proofreader: Angela Voges
Indexer: Clifford Perusset
Cover Designer: Judith Cross
Cover Image: theromb, Shutterstock
Spec Designer: Yaseen Baker
Typesetter: Chris Leo
Printed and bound by: ABC Press, Cape Town
11987

The authors and publisher acknowledge the following parties for the images used in this book:
Cover: theromb, Shutterstock; p. 8a: Andrea Danti, Shutterstock; p. 8b: Designua, Shutterstock; p. 8c: Designua,
Shutterstock; p. 9: Designua, Shutterstock; p. 52: Natata, Shutterstock; p. 53: Natata, Shutterstock; p. 85: paintings,
Shutterstock; p. 91: Kheng Guan Toh, Shutterstock; p. 129: Foto24, Getty; p. 134: Jen Watson, Shutterstock; p. 169a:
Everett-Art, Shutterstock; p. 169b: Vuyile Voyiya; p. 171: Duplass, Shutterstock; p. 181: karenfoleyphotography,
Shutterstock; p. 194: Designua, Shutterstock; p. 223: Blamb, Shutterstock; p. 262: Blamb, Shutterstock; p. 284:
NatthapongSachan, Shutterstock; p. 300a: Suttha Burawonk, Shutterstock; p. 300b: Zephyr, Science Photo Library;
p. 391: Peter Hermes Furian, Shutterstock; p. 393: CP DC Press, Shutterstock; p. 417: Debby Wong, Shutterstock;
p. 423: Juice Team, Shutterstock.

CONTENTS

Foreword   xiii
Preface   xv
Contributors   xvi

PART 1: THE BIG PICTURE   1

CHAPTER 1: ORIGINS AND CAUSES OF PSYCHOPATHOLOGY   3

Karel Botha, Mokgadi Moletsane, Malose Makhubela & Alban Burke

Introduction   5
Equifinality and multifinality   6
Biomedical perspectives   7
    Genetic predisposition   7
    Abnormal functioning of neurotransmitters   8
    Endocrine dysregulation   11
    Structural abnormalities   12
Psychological perspectives   12
    Psychodynamic approaches   12
    Behavioural/learning perspectives   14
    Cognitive-behavioural perspective   15
    Humanistic and existential perspectives   16
Social perspectives   17
    Community psychology perspective   17
    Political perspective   19
    Cultural psychology and cross-cultural psychology perspectives   19
Religious perspectives   25
    Mental illness from the perspective of African Traditional Religion   25
    Mental Illness from the perspective of Islam   28
    Mental Illness from the perspective of Christianity   29
Integrated perspectives   30
    The biopsychosocial model   31
    The diathesis-stress model   31
    The ecological systems theory   37
    Towards a universal schema in the context of globalisation   38
Conclusion   41

CHAPTER 2: DESCRIBING AND CLASSIFYING ABNORMAL BEHAVIOUR — 44

Tracey-Lee Austin & Dan J. Stein

Introduction   46
A brief history of psychopathology   51
   Psychopathology in South Africa   54
   Global perspectives   55
   Critical perspectives   55
Contemporary classification of mental disorder   56
   The *Diagnostic and Statistical Manual of Mental Disorders* (DSM)   58
   The *International Classification of Diseases* (ICD)   67
   Comparison and critique   71
Conclusion   73

CHAPTER 3: PSYCHOLOGICAL ASSESSMENT AND PSYCHO-DIAGNOSTICS — 77

Tracey-Lee Austin & Gale Ure

Introduction   79
Basic steps in the diagnostic process   79
Interviewing and observations   80
   The clinical interview   80
   Mental Status Examination (MSE)   81
   Behavioural assessment   82
Physiological assessments   84
   Physical examination   84
   Neuro-imaging   85
   Psycho-physiological assessment   86
Psychological testing   86
   Culture and assessment   88
   Intelligence tests   88
   Personality inventories   89
   Projective tests   90
   Neuropsychological assessment   93
   False positives, false negatives, and malingering   95
   Arriving at a diagnosis: The use of diagnostic classification systems   95
Conclusion   96

CHAPTER 4: ABNORMAL PSYCHOLOGY FROM A MENTAL WELLNESS PERSPECTIVE 98

Karel Botha & Edwin du Plessis

Introduction   100
A brief history of mental wellness and positive psychology   101
Different perspectives on mental wellness   103
    Individual perspectives   103
    Sociocultural and sociopolitical perspectives   104
Mental illness from a well-being perspective   106
    Mental illness according to Keyes' Mental Health Continuum   106
    Mental illness as impaired levels of psychological well-being   107
    Mental illness as the absence, opposite, or exaggeration of
      psychological strengths   108
Strengths that protect against mental illness   110
    Cognitive strengths   110
    Positive affect and emotional intelligence   111
    Self-regulation   112
    Coping   113
    Resilience   114
    Post-traumatic growth   115
    Interpersonal strengths   116
    Religiosity and spirituality   117
Treatment from a wellness perspective   118
    Treatment of the mentally ill person   118
    Support for the family of the mentally ill person 119
    Promoting well-being in communities   121
Conclusion   123

CHAPTER 5: LEGAL AND ETHICAL ISSUES IN MENTAL DISORDERS 125

Christiaan Bezuidenhout

Introduction   127
Core ethical values and standards   127
Legal perspective   128
    Human rights in South Africa   129
    The Mental Health Care Act (No. 17 of 2002) and the Mental Health Care
      Amendment Act (No. 12 of 2014)   131
    The Traditional Health Practitioners Act (No. 22 of 2007)   133
    The state of mental healthcare in South Africa   136
History of the South African ethical code for psychologists   136

Ethical behaviour   **138**
   Statutory control over ethical behaviour   139
   Challenges to ethical behaviour   142
   Ethical dilemmas   145
Specific ethical issues for mental healthcare professionals   **145**
   Confidentiality and reporting to third parties   146
   Dangerousness   147
   Suicide and euthanasia   152
   Committing a client   154
Consequences of unethical conduct   **155**
Conclusion   **157**

PART 2: A CLOSER LOOK   159

CHAPTER 6: ANXIETY, OBSESSIVE-COMPULSIVE, AND TRAUMA-RELATED DISORDERS   161

Karabo Makhafula & Melanie Lake

Introduction   **166**
Fear, anxiety, stress, and worry   **167**
   Fear   167
   Anxiety   167
   Stress   168
   Worry   168
History of anxiety and panic disorders   **168**
Anxiety disorders   **170**
   Separation anxiety disorder   170
   Specific phobias   170
   Panic disorder   172
   Agoraphobia   174
   Social anxiety disorder (social phobia)   175
   Generalised anxiety disorder   178
Obsessive-compulsive and related disorders   **180**
   Obsessive-compulsive disorder   180
   Body dysmorphic disorder   182
   Hoarding disorder   183
   Trichotillomania   184
   Excoriation (skin-picking) disorder   184
Trauma and stressor-related disorders   **184**
   Reactive attachment disorder   185
   Disinhibited social engagement disorder   185
   Posttraumatic stress disorder   186
   Acute stress disorder   189
   Adjustment disorders   189
Cross-cultural and African perspectives   **190**

Epidemiology   192
Aetiology   192
  Biological processes   192
  Psychological perspectives   194
  Psychosocial stressors   198
  Integrated perspectives   199
Conclusion   199

CHAPTER 7: MOOD DISORDERS   **201**

Karabo Makhafula & Alban Burke

Introduction   206
History of mood disorders   207
Epidemiology   208
Life course   209
Clinical picture   209
Depressive disorders   210
  Major depressive disorder (MDD)   211
  Persistent depressive disorder (dysthymia)   213
  Premenstrual dysphoric disorder   213
  Disruptive mood dysregulation disorder   214
  Substance/medication-induced depressive disorder 215
  Depressive disorder due to another medical condition 215
Bipolar and related disorders   216
  Bipolar I and bipolar II disorders   216
  Cyclothymic disorder   218
Symptoms of mood disorders   219
Cross-cultural and African perspectives   220
Aetiology of mood disorders   221
  Stress and environmental factors   221
  Biological factors   222
  Genetics   222
  Integrative model   224
Conclusion   225

**CHAPTER 8: SCHIZOPHRENIA SPECTRUM AND OTHER
PSYCHOTIC DISORDERS**   **227**

Elsabe Jordaan

Introduction   232
Psychosis and the psychotic disorders   233
Diagnosing schizophrenia spectrum and other psychotic disorders 234
Schizophrenia   238
  History of schizophrenia   238
  Prevalence and course   239

Clinical picture	**241**
Schizophrenia	241
Positive symptoms	244
Negative symptoms	248
Schizophrenia subtypes in the ICD-10	249
Other schizophrenia spectrum and psychotic disorders	253
Violence risk and mortality risk	254
Cross-cultural and African perspectives	**256**
Aetiology	**258**
Biological factors	258
Psychological factors	265
Sociocultural factors	270
Integration of aetiological factors	272
Controversial issues in the diagnosis and management of schizophrenia	**273**
Should the diagnosis continue to be used?	273
'Normality' and 'abnormality'	274
Labelling	274
De-institutionalisation	275
Conclusion	**275**

CHAPTER 9: NEUROCOGNITIVE DISORDERS

CHAPTER 9: NEUROCOGNITIVE DISORDERS	**279**

Basil Joseph Pillay

Introduction	**284**
The classification of neurocognitive disorders	**286**
History of neurocognitive disorders	**289**
Delirium	**290**
Clinical picture	290
Epidemiology	291
Aetiology	292
Treatment and management of delirium	292
Neurocognitive disorder (dementia)	**293**
Clinical picture	294
Epidemiology	297
Aetiology	298
Treatment and management of neurocognitive disorder (dementia)	304
Amnestic disorders	**305**
Clinical picture	305
Epidemiology	306
Aetiology	306
Treatment and management of amnestic disorders	307
Assessment of neurocognitive disorders	**308**
Contextual and cross-cultural perspectives	**311**
Conclusion	**313**

CHAPTER 10: DISSOCIATIVE, SOMATOFORM, AND RELATED DISORDERS 317

Revised by Gale Ure

Introduction   322
Dissociation, somatising, and stress   322
  What is dissociation?   322
  What causes dissociation?   323
  Compartmentalisation   324
  Detachment   326
  Early adversity and future pathology   328
Dissociative disorders and their comparative nosology   329
  Dissociative amnesia   331
  Dissociative fugue   335
  Dissociative identity disorder   336
  Depersonalisation/derealisation disorder   339
  Trance and possession disorders   344
  Ganser's syndrome   345
  Related conditions in South Africa   347
  Related conditions in other cultures   348
  Epidemic hysteria   350
Somatoform disorders and their comparative nosology   352
  Conversion disorder   353
  Somatic symptom disorder   360
  Persistent somatoform pain disorder   365
  Illness anxiety disorder   369
  Psychological factors affecting other medical conditions   372
Factitious disorder and malingering   373
  Factitious disorder   373
  Malingering   376
Conclusion   381
  Pathogenesis   382
  Symptom expression   382

CHAPTER 11: CONDITIONS RELATED TO SEXUAL HEALTH AND PARAPHILIC DISORDERS 385

Juan A. Nel & Melanie Lake

Introduction   390
History of medicalisation of sexuality and gender   396
Clinical picture   400
Conditions related to sexual health   400
  Sexual dysfunctions   401
  Male and female sexual dysfunctions   403
  Sexual interest/arousal disorders   405

Orgasmic disorders   411
Sexual pain disorders   414
Gender dysphoria/gender incongruence   **416**
Issues with gender identity   420
Paraphilic disorders   **422**
Cross-cultural and African perspectives   **427**
Aetiology   **434**
Biological factors   434
Psychological factors   435
Social and interpersonal factors   437
Conclusion   **438**

**CHAPTER 12: SUBSTANCE-RELATED AND ADDICTIVE
DISORDERS**   **441**

Gale Ure

Introduction   **446**
Historical perspective   **447**
Theories of addiction   **448**
The disease model   448
Moral theory   448
Psychoanalytic theories   449
Behavioural theories   449
Types of addiction   **449**
Clinical picture   **451**
Substance-induced disorders   **452**
Substance intoxication and withdrawal   452
Substance/medication-induced psychotic disorder   453
Substance use disorders   **455**
Non-substance-related disorders   **458**
Gambling disorder   458
Internet gaming disorder   459
South African perspectives on specific substances   **460**
Alcohol (dop)   460
Cannabis (dagga/zol)   462
Methamphetamine (tik/crystal meth)   463
Nyaope (whoonga)   464
Cocaine (coke)   465
Heroin (smack)   465
MDMA (ecstasy)   466
Prescription and over-the-counter medications   466
Aetiology   **467**
Biological factors   467
Psychological and social factors   470
Conclusion   **472**

CHAPTER 13: EATING AND FEEDING DISORDERS   475

Elsabe Jordaan

Introduction   479
History of eating disorders   480
Types of feeding and eating disorders   482
   Pica   482
   Rumination disorder   482
   Avoidant/restrictive food intake disorder   482
   Anorexia nervosa   483
   Bulimia nervosa   489
   Binge-eating disorder   494
   Other specified feeding or eating disorder   497
   Unspecified feeding or eating disorder   498
Aetiology   499
   Biological factors   499
   Psychological factors   503
   Sociocultural factors   511
Cross-cultural perspectives   518
   South African perspective   520
Stress, risk, and vulnerability   523
Conclusion   524

CHAPTER 14: PERSONALITY DISORDERS   527

Beate von Krosigk

Introduction   532
History of personality disorders   535
Clinical picture   539
Cluster A personality disorders   542
   Paranoid personality disorder   543
   Schizoid personality disorder   545
   Schizotypal personality disorder   547
Cluster B personality disorders   548
   Borderline personality disorder   548
   Histrionic personality disorder   551
   Narcissistic personality disorder   552
   Antisocial personality disorder   553
Cluster C personality disorders   555
   Avoidant personality disorder   555
   Dependent personality disorder   556
   Obsessive-compulsive personality disorder   557
Comorbidity   559

Aetiology   560
 Biological factors   561
 Intra- and interpersonal factors   565
 A holistic perspective for understanding the development of personality
   functioning/dysfunction   573
Problems and controversies   575
Conclusion   578

CHAPTER 15: NEURODEVELOPMENTAL AND OTHER
CHILDHOOD DISORDERS   581

                                                                          Adri Vorster

Introduction   586
Developmental psychopathology   586
History of developmental psychopathology   587
Contextualising developmental psychopathology in South Africa   588
Childhood disorders and stigma   590
The classification of childhood disorders   591
Intellectual disability (intellectual development disorder)   592
 Aetiology of intellectual disability   597
Autism spectrum disorder   600
 Aetiology of autism spectrum disorder   605
Elimination disorders   606
 Enuresis   606
 Encopresis   608
 Aetiology of elimination disorders   609
Externalising disorders   612
 Attention-deficit/hyperactivity disorder   613
 Conduct disorders   619
 Aetiology of externalising disorders   624
Internalising disorders   627
 Depression   628
 Anxiety   629
 Aetiology of internalising disorders   631
Conclusion   634

ANSWERS TO MULTIPLE-CHOICE QUESTIONS   637

REFERENCES   638

GLOSSARY   698

INDEX   716

FOREWORD

One of the primary ways in which readers are likely to engage with this text is to view it as a foundational academic resource as they seek further education and training, and perhaps even in the pursuit of a formal qualification. While this focus on the text as a resource would not be an inaccurate characterisation, it does belie the complex intellectual drivers and the multiplicity of uses of a text such as this within the extant knowledge base today.

But this type of comprehension of the text should not detract from a range of more invisible questions that it is attempting to be responsive to. Any text on psychopathology is fundamentally also addressing the quintessential questions of what constitutes normality and abnormality at a given point in our history; whether this range, normality to abnormality, is static or fluid; to what degree such syndromes are adaptive or maladaptive; and the extent to which the genesis of psychopathology can be thought of as being located within society or within aspects of intrinsic human development. These are questions that are likely to be asked in some iteration or another, by laypersons and professionals alike – by children, by parents, by teachers and by mental healthcare providers. What the text is ultimately therefore engaged with are the existential, philosophical, ethical, political, and historical dimensions of what constitutes normality and abnormality within the human condition in our society today.

But beyond this, readers will encounter a social scientific analysis of psychopathology in context. Rather than approaching the field as a set of fixed syndromes, there is deep recognition of the contextually contingent nature of psychopathology. Furthermore, reading theorists such as Freud alongside Fanon, for example, provides for varied perspectives on how to assess the complex relationships between psychopathology and context.

In so doing, the text is of course also directly attuned to current debates on the psychosocial – the seamless relationship between individuals and society and the mutually reinforcing ways in which they interact and shape each other. What it is being attentive to is the long-established social scientific debates on structure versus agency and individual-social dualism – both of which are fundamentally attempting to unpack the extent to which psychosocial life (and, in this instance, psychopathology) is primarily determined by the agency of the individual or is directed by society.

Of course, recent deliberations within the higher education sector across the world have highlighted matters of curriculum transformation, decolonising the curriculum and offsetting the dominance of Western and northern paradigms, epistemic justice, and knowledge that is produced within southern contexts, as central to more equitable forms of knowledge production and distribution. Again, this text attempts to engage both mainstream and alternative perspectives on psychopathology, and is interested in determining how well constructs travel across space, time, and history. In so doing, it is not concerned with jettisoning one archive for another, or replacing one canonical set of texts and theorists with others, but is interested in the expansion of the knowledge archive to include both dominant and historically subordinated forms of knowledge on psychopathology.

This text has a remarkable scope, covering aetiological understandings, classificatory systems, psychodiagnostics, and the specificities of clinical syndromes from childhood through to adulthood. The range of authors with specific skill sets and expertise is a further value-add to the text, often involving prominent practitioners, academics, researchers, and scientists. Not only is the text user-friendly for students, but the ancillary materials available will no doubt also enhance the educational experience across the teaching and learning sphere. Now in its third edition, I have no doubt that the text will be of immense academic value to students, will offer laypersons a glimpse into the complex relationship between the mind and society, will serve as a quick reference guide for mental healthcare practitioners, will contribute to the extant knowledge base for those conducting scientific research, and will also stand as a historical marker of one of the ways in which psychopathology was being conceptualised in South Africa at the beginning of the 21st century.

Prof. Garth Stevens
President: Psychological Society of South Africa (PsySSA)

PREFACE

The authors would like to thank the users of the first and second editions for their valuable feedback. We tried, as far as possible, to address all the comments.

As was the case with the previous editions, this book is the product of collaboration between practitioners and experienced academics from various universities.

We have included as much South African research as possible, and present a South African, cross-cultural view on the various pathologies. We also present the South African code of conduct, the legislation regarding mental healthcare, and aspects of the South African Constitution, as these are relevant to our readership.

With an awareness that many of the students at South African universities come from the wider African region, and with an acknowledgement of what the region as a whole is offering in terms of relevant research, we also refer to recent African studies throughout the book.

In addition, we have included diagnostic criteria from both the American Psychiatric Association's *Diagnostic and Statistical Manual of Mental Disorders* (DSM) and the World Health Organization's *International Classification of Diseases* (ICD). We adopted this dual approach because both classification systems add to our understanding of disorders. Throughout the book, we compare these two classification systems, pointing out similarities and differences between them. This should enable students to move between the two systems in both research and practice. (While most clinicians rely on the DSM, the ICD system is used for medical aid claims.)

We have also referred to both the tenth and the eleventh versions of the ICD system. The tenth version (ICD-10) was published in 2016, and is currently still in use. The eleventh version was released in 2018 to allow WHO member states to prepare for its implementation. These states will report to the WHO using this version from the beginning of 2020. By referring to both versions of the ICD system, we hope to allow students the opportunity to start preparing for the implementation of ICD-11, while still being able to function in an environment that uses the ICD-10.

However, owing to space constraints, not every disorder in each framework could be dealt with. A survey was done to establish the disorders covered in the undergraduate curricula at the different South African universities, and we include only disorders that appear in these curricula. Similarly, we could not provide every detail of the disorders that are covered in this book. We rely on lecturers to provide students with further information, and on students to read beyond the contents of the book.

We hope that this book serves as a good introductory text for undergraduate students, and that it introduces a wide variety of theories. We have tried to keep it as simple as possible, without compromising important facts and terminology. To assist students we provide a glossary of important terms, case studies, and helpful hints. In addition there are, at the end of each chapter, multiple-choice questions and paragraph and essay questions that will help students assess their understanding and prepare for examinations.

Ancillary material for lecturers prescribing the textbook is available on the OUPSA website, www.oxford.co.za. Students may download the solutions to the end-of-chapter multiple-choice questions from the same website.

We trust that you will find the book interesting and informative.

The authors

CONTRIBUTORS

Burke, Alban MA (Psychology) DLitt et Phil (Psychology): Director: Centre for Psychological and Career Services, University of Johannesburg

Austin, Tracey-Lee MA (Psychology) DLitt et Phil (Psychology): Clinical Lead: Khiron House

Bezuidenhout, Christiaan DPhil (Criminology): Professor: Department of Social Work and Criminology, University of Pretoria

Botha, Karel MA (Clinical Psychology) PhD (Psychology): Professor: School of Psychosocial Behavioural Sciences, North-West University

Du Plessis, Edwin MA (Clinical Psychology) PhD (Psychology): Principal Clinical Psychologist/Senior Lecturer: Department of Psychiatry, University of the Free State

Jordaan, Elsabe MA (Clinical Psychology): Clinical psychologist in private practice

Lake, Melanie MA (Clinical Psychology) DLitt et Phil (Psychology): Clinical Lead Psychology: Waikato District Health Board

Makhafula, Karabo MA (Clinical Psychology): Clinical Psychologist: Centre for Psychological and Career Services, University of Johannesburg

Makhubela, Malose MA (Clinical Psychology) PhD (Psychology): Associate Professor: Department of Psychology, University of Johannesburg

Moletsane, Mokgadi MEd (Educational Psychology) PhD (Educational Psychology): Associate Professor: Department of Educational Psychology, University of the Western Cape

Nel, Juan A MA (Clinical and Research Psychology) DLitt et Phil (Psychology): Research Professor: Department of Psychology, University of South Africa

Pillay, Basil MA (Clinical Psychology) PhD (Med): Head: Department of Behavioural Medicine, University of KwaZulu-Natal

Stein, Dan J FRCPC (Psychiatry) PhD (Clinical Neuroscience) DPhil (Philosophy): Head: Department of Psychiatry and Mental Health, University of Cape Town

Ure, Gale MA (Psychology) DLitt et Phil (Psychology) MScMed (Bioethics and Health Law) PHD (Bioethics and Health Law): Research Specialist, Life Healthcare

Von Krosigk, Beate MA (Psychology), DLitt et Phil (Psychology): Senior Lecturer: Department of Psychology, University of South Africa (retired)

Vorster, Adri MEd (Educational Psychology): Lecturer: Department of Psychology, University of the Witwatersrand

PART 1 | THE BIG PICTURE

CHAPTER 1   Origins and causes of psychopathology   3
CHAPTER 2   Describing and classifying abnormal behaviour   44
CHAPTER 3   Psychological assessment and psycho-diagnostics   77
CHAPTER 4   Abnormal psychology from a mental wellness perspective   98
CHAPTER 5   Legal and ethical issues in mental disorders   125

1

ORIGINS AND CAUSES OF PSYCHOPATHOLOGY

Karel Botha, Mokgadi Moletsane, Malose Makhubela & Alban Burke

CHAPTER CONTENTS

Introduction
Equifinality and multifinality
Biomedical perspectives
    Genetic predisposition
    Abnormal functioning of neurotransmitters
    Endocrine dysregulation
    Structural abnormalities
Psychological perspectives
    Psychodynamic approaches
    Behavioural/learning perspectives
    Cognitive-behavioural perspective
    Humanistic and existential perspectives
Social perspectives
    Community psychology perspective
    Political perspective
    Cultural psychology and cross-cultural psychology perspectives
Religious perspectives
    Mental illness from the perspective of African Traditional Religion
    Mental Illness from the perspective of Islam
    Mental Illness from the perspective of Christianity
Integrated perspectives
    The biopsychosocial model
    The diathesis-stress model
    The ecological systems theory
    Towards a universal schema in the context of globalisation
Conclusion

LEARNING OUTCOMES

After studying this chapter, you should be able to:
- Review some of the current perspectives in psychopathology.
- Explain the role of neurotransmitters in disorders.
- Describe the psychological defence mechanisms.
- Understand the importance of cultural awareness and sensitivity in the field of psychology.
- Critically analyse and interpret the African personality model.
- Explain indigenous African understandings of the aetiology of mental illness.
- Understand the use of the biopsychosocial model and the diathesis-stress model as multidimensional approaches to understanding psychopathology.

PERSONAL HISTORY CASELET

'Why do they do it, Tambu', she hissed bitterly, her face contorting with rage, 'to me and to you and to him? Do you see what they've done? They've taken us away. Lucia. Takesure. All of us. They've deprived you of you, him of him, ourselves of each other. We're grovelling. Lucia for a job, Jeremiah for money. Daddy grovels to them. We grovel to him'. She began to rock, her body quivering tensely. 'I won't grovel. Oh no, I won't. I'm not a good girl. I'm evil. I'm not a good girl'. I touched her to comfort her and that was the trigger. 'I won't grovel, I won't die', she raged and crouched like a cat ready to spring.

The noise brought Babamakuru and Maiguru running. They could do nothing, could only watch. Nyasha was beside herself with fury. She rampaged, shredding her history book between her teeth ('Their history. F*cking liars. Their

bloody lies'.), breaking mirrors, her clay pots, anything she could lay her hands on and jabbing the fragments viciously into her flesh, stripping the bedclothes, tearing her clothes from the wardrobe and trampling them underfoot. 'They've trapped us. They've trapped us. But I won't be trapped. I'm not a good girl. I won't be trapped'. Then as suddenly as it came, the rage passed. 'I don't hate you, Daddy', she said softly. 'They want me to, but I won't'. She lay down on her bed. 'I'm very tired,' she said in a voice that was recognisably hers. 'But I can't sleep. Mummy will you hold me?'. She curled up in Maiguru's lap looking no more than five years old. 'Look what they've done to us', she said softly. 'I'm not one of them but I'm not one of you.' She fell asleep.

Source: Dangaremba, 1991, pp. 200–201.

INTRODUCTION

Psychopathology is the scientific study of psychological disorders, and a central question in psychopathology concerns *why* people develop psychological disorders.

The study of the causes of disorders is known as aetiology, literally meaning the study of origination or causation. This is an extremely important area of knowledge in psychology, psychiatry, and medicine, as it helps us to understand which factors contribute to the development of a disorder and how these factors operate.

Understanding aetiology guides the clinician in understanding a patient's symptoms and making decisions regarding treatment. In a broader sense, it may influence preventative measures and thus help to prevent the onset of disorders. However, aetiology does not provide us with direct answers about the causes of disorders, because:

- Human behaviour is highly complex.
- Disorders are more often than not caused by multiple factors.
- Causal factors change over the lifespan.
- Different causal routes exist for the same disorder.
- The same causal route may develop into different disorders.

Nevertheless, there are a number of reasons why the study of the aetiology of disorders is important. These include:

- Treatment and management of disorders is often, if not always, informed by the aetiology of the disorder.
- A better understanding of aetiology can also inform categorisation and classification of disorders.
- Studies of aetiology stimulate further research. (You will notice that for many disorders, such as autism, the causes are still not fully understood.)

When studying the aetiological models in this chapter, it is important to remember that not any one of these models is better than the others as, in most cases, each model offers explanations from different perspectives.

Given the fact that psychiatry dominates the discourse in psychopathology, we can expect that the medical model will dominate both the classification and explanations of the aetiology of disorders. Throughout the book, we will investigate the biomedical explanations of the causes of disorders, but focusing on these factors only would provide a limited and one-dimensional view of psychopathology.

Jaspers (1962) argues that it is essential to understand abnormal behaviour in its totality. This statement implies that one has to go further than 'mere' biological descriptions, in that one must also investigate all of the factors that contribute to the clinical picture and to the development and maintenance of disorders. For this reason, it is important to describe both macro (e.g. psychodynamic, cognitive-behavioural, behavioural, and humanistic) and micro (uni- and multivariate) psychological understandings of disorders.

One could argue that both the medical and psychological explanations focus quite strongly on intrapersonal factors, and may exclude external factors. You will notice, however, that for most disorders, there are also external factors that influence the development of these disorders. It is therefore important to consider social factors, such as socio-economic, sociopolitical, and cultural factors. Failing to do so will lead to a very superficial understanding of abnormal behaviour. Indeed, one of the aims of this book is to familiarise readers with a cross-cultural, (southern) African view of abnormal behaviour.

EQUIFINALITY AND MULTIFINALITY

The field of psychopathology is a complex one, and disorders may develop due to multiple factors, and the interaction between these factors. The contribution of multiple factors is confounding, because in some instances, different factors in different people may all lead to the same disorder.

Cicchetti and Rogosch (1996) use the term 'equifinality' when sets of differing circumstances lead to the same disorder.

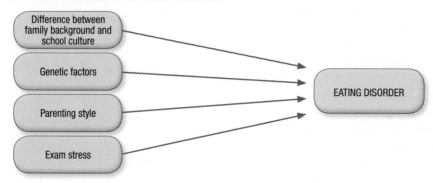

Figure 1.1: Differing circumstances leading to the same disorder

Source: Created by OUP.

In other instances, the same causal factor may lead to different disorders in different people. Cicchetti and Rogosch (1996) use the term 'multifinality' when sets of similar beginnings lead to different disorders.

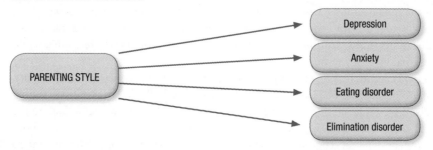

Figure 1.2: Similar beginnings leading to different disorders

Source: Created by OUP.

From the above, one can conclude that there are individual differences in terms of our reaction to circumstances, as well how similar circumstances can lead to different outcomes.

BIOMEDICAL PERSPECTIVES

The biomedical model claims that all mental illnesses have a biological cause. Modern neuro-imaging methods have enabled relatively non-invasive in vivo studies of brain structure and function. There are many studies that report abnormalities in shape, size, and function in multiple anatomical regions of the brain, particularly related to the so-called neuropathology of the different disorders; however, structural and functional cerebral abnormalities in most of these disorders are at best subtle rather than gross (Chua & McKenna, 1995).

Unfortunately, from this perspective, other factors such as social pressures, type of parenting, or additional environmental factors are seen as secondary in the precipitation of mental disorders (Cartwright, 2008).

Biological abnormalities are understood to occur mainly in four different areas: genetic predisposition, abnormal functioning of neurotransmitters, endocrine dysregulation, and structural abnormalities in the brain.

Genetic predisposition

We inherit our genetic predisposition from our parents. Genes, or chemical units, are arranged in a specific order along chromosomes, and they are responsible for determining things such as the physical appearance (e.g. eye colour, hair colour) and the sex of an individual. Most of us have 46 chromosomes.

Some researchers have found that abnormalities in genetic makeup can predispose some individuals to particular mental illnesses. A great deal of the research in this area has been done on twins because of the genetic makeup they have in common (Cartwright, 2008). It has been found, for instance, that monozygotic twins (twins with the same genetic makeup – 'identical' twins), whose mother has a mental disorder, have a greater likelihood of both developing mental illness.

However, this is not the case with twins who do not share exactly the same genetic makeup (dizygotic twins). Cartwright (2008), citing the works of Gottessman (1991), McGuffin and Katz (1993) and McGue (1993) argue that there is evidence that genetic predisposition plays a role in the development of mental illnesses such as mood disorders (see Chapter 7), schizophrenia (see Chapter 8), and alcoholism (see Chapter 12).

However, a common mistake is to simply blame genetic transmission when mental illness seems to run in families. Twin studies and adoption studies are regarded as 'natural experiments' that enable an estimate to be made of the extent to which traits are familial because of shared genes, shared environment, or a combination of both. In the late 1900s, a confusing and apparently contradictory array of studies reported links with various genes in schizophrenia (Moldin, 1997). In contrast, the identification and cloning of genes and the clarification of chromosomal abnormalities have led to progress in understanding the molecular biology of genetic neuropsychiatric disorders. Multigene (polygenetic) models of inheritance are still commonly regarded as the best model of familial transmission of schizophrenia (Tsuang, Stone, & Faraone, 2000).

There is speculation that the mapping of the human genome will help to develop better treatments for psychiatric illness, and to make discrimination against people with mental disorders a thing of the past (McGuffin & Martin, 1999). However, despite the hype, accurate prediction may never be possible because of the complexity of the genetics of common disorders (Holtzman & Marteau, 2000). Scepticism about the current over-enthusiasm for genetic explanations is required.

Abnormal functioning of neurotransmitters

Neurotransmitters are chemical substances in the brain and are responsible for the communication of nerve impulses among the brain cells (Cartwright, 2008). Figure 1.3 shows the endings of two nerve cells, and the gap between them across which the neurotransmitters pass. This gap is called a synapse.

There are two main types of neurotransmitters that are implicated in most psychiatric disorders, namely monoamine neurotransmitters and amino acid neurotransmitters. The four monoamine neurotransmitters are as follows (with C being carbon, H hydrogen, N nitrogen and O oxygen):

- epinephrine/adrenaline ($C_9H_{13}NO_3$)
- norepinephrine/noradrenaline ($C_8N_{11}NO_3$)
- dopamine ($C_8H_{11}NO_2$)
- serotonin ($C_{10}H_{12}N_2O$).

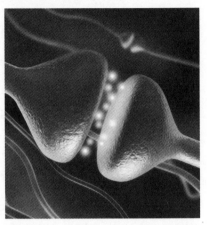

Figure 1.3: Synaptic transmission in the human nervous system

Monoamine neurotransmitters are derived from aromatic amino acids (e.g. phenylalanine, tyrosine and tryptophan) and contain one amino (–NH2) group that is connected to an aromatic ring by a two-carbon chain (–CH2–CH2–). As can be seen in the diagrams below, these monoamine neurotransmitters all contain a 'flat' ring. The atoms in this ring are held together by stable bonds.

Figures 1.4 and 1.5 show the neurotransmitters epinephrine (adrenaline) and norepinephrine (noradrenaline), which are associated with the body's response to stress.

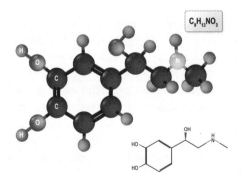

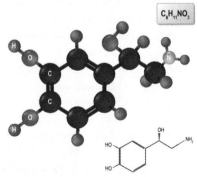

Figure 1.4: An illustration of an epinephrine (adrenaline) molecule

Figure 1.5: An illustration of a norepinephrine (noradrenaline) molecule

Figures 1.6 and 1.7 show the neurotransmitters dopamine and serotonin, which have been found to be associated with a number of psychiatric illnesses.

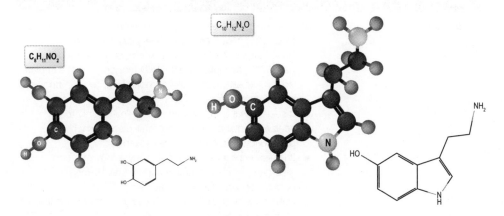

Figure 1.6: An illustration of a dopamine molecule

Figure 1.7: A diagram of a serotonin molecule

 ACTIVITY

In what way is the structure of the four monoamine neurotransmitters similar?

Theories of neurotransmitter dysfunction arose following the introduction of psychotropic drugs at a time when few neurotransmitters had been discovered. Despite the subsequent discovery of a vastly more complex neurotransmitter network, psychiatrists still use such simplistic notions as a 'chemical imbalance' when they explain mental illness in their everyday management of patients. For example, the dopamine hypothesis of schizophrenia (dopamine overactivity in schizophrenic brains) arose because neuroleptic drugs, such as chlorpromazine, appear to act via an inhibition of dopamine receptors.

However, measurements of dopamine metabolites *in vivo*, or of the transmitter and its receptors in post-mortem brain tissue, do not provide unequivocal evidence of a hyperactivity of dopaminergic neurotransmission in the disease; this may be because it is difficult to disentangle the iatrogenic (caused by medical treatment) effects of the drugs themselves (Reynolds, 1989). Moreover, many of the newer drugs do not appear to work by dopamine antagonism, raising the question of the nature of atypical antipsychotic medication.

Table 1.1 is a recent summary of what we know about the role that neurotransmitters play in psychological disorders.

Table 1.1: Summary of role of neurotransmitters in disorders

Neurotransmitter	Pathology
Dopamine	■ Over-secretion seems to play a role in schizophrenia. ■ Dopamine hypothesis was initially derived from observations that drugs that block dopamine receptors have anti-psychotic results, AND that drugs that stimulate dopamine activity induce psychotic symptoms in people who do not suffer from schizophrenia. ■ It seems as if over-secretion is not limited only to schizophrenia, but is present in all disorders where psychotic symptoms may be present. ■ It is also implicated in the pathophysiology of mood disorders, where dopamine activity may be low in depression and high in mania. ■ Substance and addictive related disorders are also linked to dopamine activity.
Serotonin	■ Depression is associated with too little serotonin and mania with too much serotonin. ■ According to the permissive hypothesis, serotonin seems to work in conjunction with norepinephrine, where low levels of serotonin permit abnormal levels of norepinephrine to cause depression and mania. ■ Eating disorders (anorexia nervosa and bulimia nervosa) are also linked to low serotonin.
Norepinephrine and epinephrine	■ Norepinephrine, in conjunction with serotonin, may play a role in the pathophysiology of depression. ■ Anxiety and mania have also been linked with activity of these neurotransmitters.
Amino acid neurotransmitters (glutamic acid and gamma-aminobutyric acid [GABA])	■ Play an important role in the pathophysiology of a variety of psychiatric disorders such as anxiety disorders (e.g. panic disorder), schizophrenia, depression, Alzheimer's disease and bipolar disorder.
Neuropeptides	■ Neuropeptides can act as neuromodulators, neurohormones or neurotransmitters. ■ Neuropeptidergic systems have been linked with major disorders including mood disorders, dementia, psychoses and autism spectrum disorders.
Acetylcholine	■ The most common association is between degeneration of cholinergic neurons and dementia. ■ It may also be involved in mood and sleep disorders.
Novel neurotransmitters (e.g. nitric oxide, carbon monoxide, and endocannabinoids)	■ Ascribed neurotransmitter status/function in the early 1990s and are mostly atypical. ■ Implicated in schizophrenia, anxiety, and mood disorders.

Source: Sadock, Sadock, & Ruiz, 2015.

 **ACTIVITY**

Using the Internet, research the medicine Largactil, and say which neurotransmitters are affected by this medicine.

Endocrine dysregulation

According to Sadock et al. (2015), pathological alterations (e.g. abnormal regulation) in the functioning of neuro-endocrine (hormonal messaging) axes are implicated in the pathophysiology of some psychiatric disorders such as mood disorders and schizophrenia (see Table 1.2).

Table 1.2: The link between selected hormonal axes and disorders

Hormonal axis	Pathophysiology of disorders
Hypothalamic-Pituitary-Adrenal	■ This axis responds to stress by increasing the secretion of cortisol which helps us adapt to stress. ■ Linked to mood disorders, posttraumatic stress disorder, dementia of the Alzheimer's type and substance use disorders.
Hypothalamic-Pituitary-Thyroid	■ Absence of thyroid hormone in early infancy leads to mental retardation (cretinism). ■ Administration of thyroid hormone has a brief mood-elevating response in depression. ■ Anxiety, mania, and psychoses can be induced by thyroid disorders.
Hypothalamic-Pituitary-Gonadal	■ Growth hormone dysregulation may be implicated in mood disorders, ADHD, and schizophrenia.
Growth hormone	■ Growth hormone dysregulation may be implicated in mood disorders, eating disorders, and schizophrenia.
Prolactin	■ Release of prolactin is dependent on dopamine release and therefore may be implicated in negative symptoms of schizophrenia, depression, and anxiety.
Melatonin	■ Involved in the regulation of circadian rhythms and has been implicated in the pathophysiology of depression.
Insulin	■ Involved in the pathophysiology of Alzheimer's and depression.
Oxytocin	■ Linked to socialisation in autistic children.

Source: Adapted from Sadock et al., 2015.

Structural abnormalities

The Swiss psychiatrist Adolf Meyer, who worked in the USA in the early 1900s, was fond of seeing his philosophical approach to psychiatry, with its emphasis on the person, as an advance over the mechanistic approach that arose in Europe in the 1800s. However, his work was largely neglected, as the biomedical discourse in describing and explaining disorders became progressively more dominant. It seems as if reducing a person to merely a brain makes disorders easier to describe and treat, with the result that the philosophical debate around the relationship between mind and brain has dwindled.

The discovery, however, that the adult brain is capable of extensive reorganisation has necessitated a radical revision of traditional notions of anatomical fixity, and has sparked interest and research into the concept of brain plasticity (Castillo, 1998; Eisenberg, 1995). Research has also moved beyond the role of neurotransmitters to the role of neuromodulators, and it is becoming abundantly clear that the brain is biochemically able to modify its own responsiveness to incoming stimuli. This implies that the human brain seems to be socially constructed in the literal sense that brain cell architecture itself is fashioned by input from the social environment.

Traditionally, structural abnormalities occurring in the brain have also been associated with various disorders. It has been well established that different parts of the brain regulate different aspects of human functioning (see Chapter 9). For instance, it has been found that the limbic system serves to regulate emotional reactions such as fear, aggression, and sexual expression. Thus, injuries to these parts of the brain could impair a person's emotional control (Cartwright, 2008). Structural abnormalities in the brain may be caused by a wide variety of factors and may result in a number of disorders (see Chapter 9).

PSYCHOLOGICAL PERSPECTIVES

It is particularly in the field of abnormal behaviour that opposing theoretical paradigms meet head to head. At the one extreme, we have the medical paradigm that maintains that the causes of most of the disorders are biological or physiological in nature. This theoretical approach bases its argument on the fact that there is increasing evidence of the heritability of disorders as well as the efficacy of pharmacological treatments of disorders. At the other extreme, we have the theorists who believe that all disorders are caused by psychosocial factors. The approach in this textbook is that there is room for both these arguments; therefore, it is necessary to investigate psychological theories of disorders.

Psychodynamic approaches

Contemporary psychodynamic approaches are derived from the theory of psychoanalysis produced by the Austrian neurologist Sigmund Freud in the late 1800s. Those who work from a psychoanalytic point of view believe that the way in which we relate to others and ourselves is largely influenced by internal forces that exist outside consciousness. Freud believed that sexual and aggressive instincts, and the associated thoughts and feelings, become repressed and unconscious once they are perceived to be forbidden by society.

Freud believed that, although such thoughts and feelings are forced into the unconscious, they are still able to exert partial control over the individual by expressing themselves through symptoms. He viewed the formation of psychological symptoms as a compromise between the expression of forbidden wishes and their total repression (Cartwright, 2008).

Freud viewed the personality as being divided into three parts: the id, the ego, and the superego. He used the term 'id' to refer to instincts and drives, the term 'ego' to refer to the part of the psyche that attempts to control the expression of the id, and the term 'superego' to refer to a person's conscience and the ability to distinguish between right and wrong. Freud believed that the formation of these mental structures was strongly influenced by early childhood experiences and the quality of the child's relationship with their parents (Cartwright, 2008).

According to Cartwright (2008), this paradigm understands psychopathology to occur for two main reasons. First, psychological disorders emerge when conflict between the id, the ego, and the superego give rise to distressing symptoms. Second, mental disorders emerge when deficiencies in the ego hinder the individual's ability to repress instinctual drives. In both cases, the individual makes use of psychological defence mechanisms (see Table 1.3) in an attempt to ward off excessive psychological pain and repressed fears.

Table 1.3: Examples of psychological defence mechanisms

Defence mechanism	Description
Displacement	One way to avoid the risk associated with feeling unpleasant emotions is to displace them, or put them somewhere other than where they belong. You may be angry with a lecturer for a poor mark but be unable to express it, so you go home and get angry with your mother instead. This is an example of displacement.
Sublimation	Sublimation is the healthy redirection of an emotion. For example, when receiving a bad mark, you may choose to direct more energy into your studies rather than getting angry with your mother.
Projection	Projection is something we all do. It is the act of taking something of ourselves and placing it outside us, onto others. Sometimes we project positive and sometimes negative aspects of ourselves. Sometimes we project things we don't want to acknowledge about ourselves (e.g. 'I have not made a mistake; it is you who are critical of me and everything I do').
Intellectualisation	Intellectualisation involves removing the emotion from emotional experiences, and discussing painful events in detached, uncaring, sterile ways. Individuals may know all the words that describe feelings, but have no idea what they really feel like.
Denial	Denial is the refusal to acknowledge what has happened, is happening, or will happen (e.g. when a man's wife is having an affair but he says she is not).
Repression	Repression involves unconsciously putting painful thoughts and memories out of our minds and forgetting about them.

Defence mechanism	Description
Suppression	Suppression involves consciously trying to put painful thoughts and memories out of our minds and forget about them.
Reaction-formation	When we have a reaction that is too painful or threatening to feel (such as intense hate for someone with power over us), we turn it into the opposite (intense liking for that person). Another example of reaction-formation would be if you were behaving very badly towards someone because you really liked them.

Source: Cartwright, 2008, p. 462.

In contemporary psychodynamic thinking, the fundamental ideas remain the same as in the original psychoanalytic theory: human actions and experiences are seen to be strongly influenced by unconscious processes (Frude, 1998). However, the psychodynamic model has developed in many diverse ways over the years (Frude, 1998). For instance, the work of the Austrian-British psychoanalyst Melanie Klein in the early 1900s emphasised the importance of internalised object relations in the development of the personality.

Internal objects are essentially mental representations that are formed when significant others (or external 'objects') are 'internalised' by the individual, adding to the nature of the personality. Object-relations theorists believe that early relationships, particularly with the mother (or primary caregiver), shape the personality and lay the foundation for other relationships in the person's life (Cartwright, 2008).

Early trauma and/or deprivation are also understood to be key factors in the development of psychopathology. An example of this approach is the attachment theory of the British psychiatrist John Bowlby (1980), who emphasised bonding between a caregiver and a child, and the long-term effects that the quality and nature of this bond have on relationships (Frude, 1998).

In this way, contemporary psychodynamic approaches, such as the object-relations approach, emphasise the role that emotional relationships and the surrounding environment play in the formation of the personality. The contemporary approaches place less emphasis on the role of instinctual drives than the traditional Freudian approach (Cartwright, 2008).

Behavioural/learning perspectives

The behavioural perspective is mainly influenced by the experimental work of the Russian physiologist Ivan Pavlov (in the late 1800s and early 1900s) and the American psychologists John B. Watson and B. F. Skinner (in the early 1900s). The fundamental viewpoint is that behaviour is learned through a number of different processes and mechanisms, such as habituation, sensitisation, conditioning, and modelling.

Habituation refers to the process whereby a person ceases to respond to a stimulus after repeated presentations. It is thus a gradual adaptation to a new situation or stimulus. Although it has an adaptive function, it may also cause maladaptive behaviour, for example, drug addiction. Habituation does not require the person to be aware of the process; it may occur naturally and unconsciously.

Sensitisation, in contrast, refers to an extreme response to a stimulus that holds significant consequences. It is a learning process wherein we become sensitive to pain, sound, smell, and other senses. While sensitisation is a good adaptive learning process of an organism, it can also lead to a maladaptive process when the organism is 'sensitised' with harmful stimuli, for example, fear or anxiety.

The process through which a person manages these two opposite influences is called conditioning. Classical conditioning refers to the learning process in which an individual initially associates a stimulus with another (neutral) stimulus, and later responds to the associated stimulus in its absence. For example, when you react nervously to the neighbour's aggressive dog (stimulus), your response is expected and therefore unconditioned (unlearned). However, when another neutral stimulus is paired with the unconditioned stimulus, it may elicit a conditioned response. For example, if the only time you see the dog is when the neighbour opens a screeching garden gate (neutral stimulus) to take her for a walk, you could start to act nervously whenever you hear the screeching gate, even if the dog is not in sight. Your nervous reaction is now conditioned by the screeching gate.

Another example is posttraumatic stress disorder (PTSD) (see Chapter 6), which is often characterised by classically conditioned responses to stimuli such as sounds present at the time of the traumatic event (Charney, Deutsch, Krystal, Southwick, & Davis, 1993). This is why PTSD sufferers tend to avoid situations that remind them of their traumatic experience.

Operant conditioning refers to how an individual gradually learns to achieve a specific goal. A critical factor in this type of conditioning is reinforcement, which can either be obtained by a positive stimulus or reward, or by avoidance of a negative stimulus. If you avoid going outside every time you hear the neighbour's screeching gate, you soon learn that in doing so you don't have to confront the dog. By avoiding the negative stimulus, you are conditioned to stay indoors whenever you hear the screeching gate.

Finally, modelling, based on the work of Albert Bandura, refers to learning that takes place through observation alone, without directly experiencing an unconditioned stimulus or a reward. Through a number of experiments, Bandura demonstrated that children learn and imitate behaviours they have observed in other people through a process of (i) attention – noticing something; (ii) retention – remembering what was noticed; and (iii) reproduction – producing an action that is a copy of what was noticed. From this point onwards, other processes like conditioning may play a role that changes the probability of the behaviour being executed again.

Thus, according to the behavioural perspective, dysfunctional behaviour develops because an individual learns ineffective or dysfunctional responses, or fails to learn appropriate, adaptive behaviour. A number of therapeutic approaches based on the behavioural perspective have been developed, for example, behaviour modification, behaviour therapy, systematic desensitisation, and biofeedback.

Cognitive-behavioural perspective

Central to the cognitive-behavioural perspective is the idea that mental disorders are caused by aspects of the content of thoughts (e.g. biases in thinking) as well as information-processing factors (e.g. biases in perception, cognitive distortions, etc.). There are many variations of this theory, for example, the theories of helplessness (Seligman, 1975) and hopelessness (Beck, 1972), as well as the rational-emotive theory of Ellis (1995). These theorists believe that irrational beliefs and automatic thoughts are primarily responsible for the development of psychopathology (Beck, 1972; Ellis, 1995; Glasser, 1984).

This perspective may explain some types of disorders better than others (see, for example, Chapters 6 and 7). An example would be the American psychiatrist Aaron Beck's (1976) cognitive theory of depression. He suggested that negative automatic thoughts (e.g. 'nobody likes me') trigger a negative process that includes cognition, affect, and behaviour. After developing such distorted thoughts, a person would look for ways to confirm these thoughts through adopting negative behaviours (e.g. not learning for a test or behaving badly in class). These would, in turn, impact on the person's emotions, making them feel more depressed. This sets up a vicious cycle as the more depressed the individual feels, the more negatively they perceive themselves, the world, and the future. This is commonly referred to as the 'cognitive triad' of depression (Beck, 1976). Chapter 7 in this textbook illustrates how cognitive factors play an important role in the development and maintenance of mood disorders.

Humanistic and existential perspectives

A so-called third force in psychology emerged during the middle of the 1900s, opposing the determinism of both the psychodynamic and behaviourist approaches. This force consists of two broad approaches, the humanistic and existential perspectives.

The principal figures in developing a humanistic approach to psychology were the American psychologists Carl Rogers and Abraham Maslow. The humanistic perspective believes in a person's free will and their ability to choose how to act in different contexts. According to Rogers, each human being lives in a world of his or her own creation and has a unique perception of the world, also known as their phenomenal field (Gross, 2010). It is this perception of external reality that shapes life, and not the external reality itself.

The most significant element within the phenomenal field is the sense of self, which, according to Rogers, is constantly in the process of forming and reforming. Maslow, in turn, saw self-actualisation as being at the peak of a hierarchy of human needs. According to the humanistic perspective, a fully functioning person has achieved self-actualisation, whereas psychopathology develops when a person is blocked from realising his/her potential.

The existential perspective emphasises the uniqueness of each individual, the quest for values and meaning, and the existence of freedom for self-direction and self-fulfilment (Butcher, Mineka, & Hooley, 2010). Although it also emphasises free will and the ability to choose, it is less optimistic than the humanistic approach as it indicates that the sociopolitical context is often alienating and dehumanising.

The American psychologist Rollo May specifically pointed out that the growth in science and technology – think in terms of today's digital age, the Internet and social networks – poses a social and emotional threat to the individual, which, if not managed constructively, may easily develop into anxiety and, eventually, psychopathology. The Scottish psychiatrist R. D. Laing was another existentialist who was against what he called the dehumanising science of psychiatry and the focus on medication as a form of treatment.

SOCIAL PERSPECTIVES

Community psychology perspective

Psychologists who are actively involved in the community define community psychology in many ways. For Orford (1992), it means understanding people within their social worlds, while Edwards (1998, p. 70) defines it as 'psychology of, with, and for the people'.

Community psychology focuses on preventing rather than treating dysfunction. According to some writers, sensitivity to under-represented groups, such as those previously disadvantaged, is critical in understanding the community perspectives. Louw and Edwards (1993) have criticised the way most South African psychology students are trained according to an American–European model of education, and they argue that this needs to be seriously considered by institutions that train psychologists. This concern is echoed by many writers (e.g. Pillay, 2003) who call for training that focuses on prevention and mass intervention and thus prepares mental healthcare workers to function according to the needs of the South African community.

Based on the definitions stated above, community psychologists would argue that broad social factors need to be considered if we are to fully understand the development of psychological problems. This would include factors such as the socio-economic status of the community, access to resources, and the nature of social interaction within the community. All these factors impact on the mental health of the individual. From this perspective, problems like violence and sexual abuse cannot be understood unless the social context of the community is also considered.

Community psychology is therefore interested in understanding psychopathology from within the context of the community. As Ahmed and Pretorius-Heuchert (2001, p. 19) state, 'this means that community psychology regards whole communities, and not only individuals, as possible clients. There is an awareness of the interaction between individuals and their environments, in terms of causing and alleviating problems'. Thus, the emphasis here lies on the importance of the social, political, and cultural context in understanding, identifying, and treating psychological problems (Cartwright, 2008).

Many authors (e.g. Castillo, 1998) argue that an individual's actions always take place within a cultural context. How someone experiences distress or makes sense of psychological problems depends on deeply ingrained cultural beliefs and practices. Castillo (1998) maintains that we cannot truly explain a person's normal behaviour (or what is considered in some cultures to be abnormal behaviour) if we do not have an understanding of that individual's cultural background.

For example, Cartwright (2008) cites the examples of Zulu- and Xhosa-speaking communities, where *ukuthwasa* is a psychological state associated with an ancestral calling to become a traditional healer. Individuals experiencing this condition endure states of emotional turmoil and hear voices (of the ancestors calling the individual to become a traditional healer) which from a typical Western psychiatric perspective would be considered to be symptoms of schizophrenia (see Chapter 8). They also experience bouts of depression and mania (i.e. symptoms of a mood disorder; see Chapter 7). If we view this behaviour in isolation (i.e. without taking the person's cultural beliefs into account), we run the risk of making an incorrect diagnosis. This would mean that the individual would not receive the most appropriate treatment.

This should not be taken to mean that mental illness is non-existent in non-Western communities (see Table 1.4). A number of studies using epidemiological research have indicated that psychiatric disorders do exist in non-Western communities (e.g. Asuni, Schoenberg, & Swift, 1994; Swartz, 1998). Understanding how mental illness is experienced and treated in different cultures is also inextricably linked to appreciating concerns about access to treatment (Castillo, 1998). We know, for instance, that traditional healers from within a particular community are able to reach communities in ways that Western forms of medicine cannot (Swartz, 1998). As well as helping patients gain better access to treatment, community psychologists concern themselves with the prevention of mental illness (and other social problems) by facilitating social change and empowerment in the community.

Table 1.4: Four myths about mental illness in non-Western countries

Mental illness does not exist in developing countries.
Mental illness is not recognised as pathological in non-Western communities.
Mental illness is accepted in non-Western communities in an unstigmatised manner.
All mental disorders can be cured by indigenous healers.

Source: Cartwright, 2016, p. 504.

Another community aspect relates to violence and trauma. Reports indicate that post-apartheid South Africa has extremely high rates of violent crime, sexual violence, and domestic abuse. For example, some surveys have found that South Africa has among the highest incidences of murder, armed robbery, and intimate partner violence (Kaminer, Grimsrud, Myer, Stein, & Williams, 2008). These authors examined the relative risk for posttraumatic stress disorder (PTSD) associated with political, domestic, criminal, sexual, and other forms of assault in the South African population. They found that over one-third of the South African population has been exposed to some form of violence. Among men, political detention, torture, criminal assault, and childhood abuse were the forms of violence most strongly associated with a diagnosis of PTSD, while rape and intimate partner violence had the strongest association with PTSD among women.

Given these problems, community psychologists in South Africa see their role as extending beyond the traditional consulting room to include such diverse practices as consciousness-raising, advocacy, and social upliftment (Gibson & Swartz, 2008). They position themselves in identification with the concerns of the socially and politically disadvantaged members of any society and have the potential to challenge social phenomena that lie at the heart of human unhappiness. Gibson and Swartz (2008) further argue that community psychologists must attempt to resist pathologising and medicalising human problems. According to them, the problems are inevitably intertwined with a particular social or political environment.

Political perspective

Political factors impact on our mental health, as highlighted by the black Caribbean psychiatrist Frantz Fanon, who practised in the French colony of Algeria between 1953 and 1956. In his 1956 letter of resignation from the Psychiatric Hospital of Blida-Joinville, Fanon objected to how the colonised Arab people 'live in a state of absolute depersonalisation' (Fanon, 1967a, p. 53). In his later book *Black Skin, White Masks*, Fanon examines the psychological effects of a racially unequal society and writes, '[t]he Negro enslaved by his inferiority, the white man enslaved by his superiority alike behave in accordance with a neurotic orientation' (1967b, p. 60).

Fanon's writings about colonial societies had deep resonances with what was happening in apartheid South Africa. Many research reviews and reports (Foster, Freeman, & Pillay, 1997; Holdstock, 1981; Lambley, 1980; Nzimande, 1986; Swartz, 1987; Van der Spuy & Shamley, 1978) highlight the discriminatory and abusive effects of apartheid, which was often called 'colonialism of a special type'.

Mental healthcare during the apartheid era was conducted within the discriminatory context of apartheid laws and did not confront the underlying structural societal conditions. This resulted in psychology being seen as maintaining and perpetuating an oppressive economic–political system (Bulhan, 1985; Lazarus, 1988), and psychologists being labelled as the servants of power and more specifically as 'servants of apartheid' (Webster, 1986).

Fanon's writings are also relevant in our post-1994 context. As Gibson and Beneduce (2017) observe, Fanon saw the end of colonialism as a necessary requirement for mental health, but also acknowledged that the journey of healing mental disorders would only begin at liberation and would be complicated by postcolonial dilemmas: 'the upheavals and fratricidal conflicts; the hypocrisies and hucksterism of national elites; and above all the sufferings of the men and women, and indeed of entire communities and generations, who have been indelibly marked by the violence to which they have been subjected, and whose very future is compromised' (Gibson & Beneduce, 2017, p. 13).

In 2011, South Africa was said to be experiencing 'decolonisation of a special type' (Lee, 2011). Although it had achieved democracy, many communities, especially black communities, remained poor, landless, and lacking access to services. In 2015, the South African economist Haroon Bhorat noted that the country was 'one of the most consistently unequal countries in the world'.

It is unsurprising then that critical psychology is becoming increasingly popular in South Africa, where it is generally considered as part of a global agenda of resistance to applying Western-based approaches across cultures of diversity. The approach challenges dominant perspectives in psychology, aiming to redress injustice. Although the critical psychology movement began in the 1970s, while Fanon had already died in 1961, his ideas are popular among critical psychologists (Bulhan, 2015; Hook, 2001; Painter & TerreBlanche, 2004).

Cultural psychology and cross-cultural psychology perspectives

Culture is an extremely important construct in defining, describing, and explaining abnormal behaviour. It refers to the way much of our behaviour is shared and to how learned behaviour is transmitted from one generation to the next.

The American psychologist R. H. Dana (2000) states that culture is not like any other variable; this is because it comprises the context for the operation of all the other variables. In his model, Dana (2000) maintains that culture has provided a centralised role in understanding behaviour.

Psychologists have for some time argued that behaviour can be viewed as a function of the interaction between people and their environment. Culture plays an important role in many prominent macro-theories of human development, such as ecological systems theory, sociocultural theory, social learning theory, and the eco-cultural model. In each of these models, psychological outcomes, both positive (see Chapter 4) and negative, are influenced by culture in highly complex and interactive ways.

Within abnormal behaviour, it is important to note that, although certain sociocultural conditions may contribute to a higher occurrence of mental disorders, this doesn't really suggest that those conditions aetiologically cause mental disorders; they may merely facilitate or render some groups of people more susceptible to psychopathology. So, in which specific ways does culture influence psychopathology? According to Tseng (2001), culture's contribution to psychopathology is multifaceted. Culture defines normality and it sanctions idioms of distress. According to Makhubela (2016), Tseng (2001, in Bhugrah & Bhui, 2007), and Viswanath and Chaturvedi (2012), its effects can also be seen to be:

- pathogenic (directly causing mental disorders)
- pathofacilitative (promoting the incidence of certain mental disorders)
- pathoselective (influencing the reaction patterns that result in mental disorders)
- pathoplastic (shaping the symptoms of mental disorders)
- patho-elaborating (exaggerating behaviour associated with mental disorders)
- pathoreactive (influencing society's reaction to mental disorders).

In addition, it is worth noting that the aforementioned cultural effects on mental disorders are contingent on the category of disorders or the nature of the psychopathology (Tseng, 2001). In the main, mental disorders that are largely caused by biological factors (e.g. genetics and neurobiology) are less likely to be influenced by cultural factors, and any cultural impact present would be ancillary. On the other hand, mental illness with psychological causes is largely attributed to cultural factors. This primary distinction is essential when discussing the ways culture may influence psychopathology.

Schizophrenia is a good example of a mental disorder that has no pathogenic effects of culture (i.e. because it is predominantly caused by biological-hereditary factors); however, it has pathoplastic, pathoreactive, and pathofacilitating influences of culture. On the other hand, personality disorders provide a good example of mental disorders where culture exerts all levels of influence (i.e. pathogenic, selective, plastic, elaborating, facilitating, and reactive). Defining (ab)normality of personality is a culture-relative enterprise, whose boundaries mirror the specific ideals, social norms, resources, philosophies, and social structure of the society (Foulks, 1996).

Cultural psychology as a sub-discipline began with the study of the behaviour of people in widely diverse and previously unfamiliar cultures that were conspicuously different from the investigator's own culture. It rapidly evolved into the systematic exploration of the different experiential histories of people reared in different cultures. Essentially, the current field of cultural psychology represents recognition of the cultural specificity of all human behaviour, through which basic psychological processes may result in highly diverse performance, attitudes, self-concepts, and world views in members of different cultural populations.

Cultural differences can become cultural handicaps when the individual moves out of the culture or subculture in which he or she was reared and endeavours to function, compete, or succeed within another culture. However, it is these very contacts and interchanges between cultures that often stimulate the advancement of civilisations (Anastasi & Urbina, 1997).

The contribution of culture is being increasingly recognised and integrated in all fields of psychology from research and theory on lifespan development, social behaviour, emotion, or thinking, on the one hand, to the practice of industrial/organisational, clinical or counselling psychology, on the other (Anastasi & Urbina, 1997).

Given the fact that humans are extremely mobile and that, due to many social forces (e.g. wars, emigration, etc.), they move to and settle in different societies and communities, there are very few, if any, societies that have not become culturally diverse. It is therefore safe to assume that mental health professionals across the world will be in regular contact with people who are from different cultures. If they are to deal effectively with these people they will need special skills. According to Kazarian and Evans (1998, in Kekae-Moletsane, 2004), skills and knowledge for multicultural assessment include:

- recognising cultural diversity
- understanding the role of culture, ethnicity, and race in the sociopolitical and economic development of diverse ethnic and cultural populations
- understanding the significant impact of socio-economic and political factors on the psychosocial, political, and economic development of groups
- helping clients to understand, maintain, and/or resolve their own sociocultural identification
- understanding the impact of the interaction of culture, gender, and sexual orientation on behaviour and needs.

In South Africa, there has been concern over the failure of mental health professionals to adequately meet the needs of a culturally diverse society. Most psychologists in South Africa are still white and middle class, and many struggle to communicate in an African language. In addition, the nature of the mental health services has been criticised for being Eurocentric in its derivation, value base, and orientation (Naidoo, 1996; Wouters, 1993); in addition, the focus on individual curative therapy may not be culturally appropriate or comfortable for all sectors of South African society, especially for those cultures that are more group-oriented (Naidoo, 1996). According to Kazarian and Evans (1998, in Kekae-Moletsane, 2004), there is also a lack of adequate measures of culture in psychological assessment.

Cross-cultural challenges may also extend to diagnosis, which may be racially skewed (see Freeman, 1992). While things might have improved, the cultural congruence problems of mental health services in South Africa still persist (Petersen & Lund, 2011).

There could be various explanations for these challenges. One of the main reasons could be the cultural insensitivity of the clinician. Making an accurate diagnosis or offering adequate clinical service (see Chapter 2) relies on intricate processes and an understanding of the finer nuances of languages and culture. Cultural insensitivity could arguably lead to a crude diagnostic process in which a clinician may make a diagnosis based on only a few obvious symptoms (e.g. hearing voices, in the case of *ukuthwasa*), leading to misdiagnosis.

Furthermore, access to mental health services, especially in rural areas, is limited, which may lead to 'minor disorders' (such as anxiety and depression) not being recognised or treated (see Chapter 5).

One of the main hurdles in dealing with people from different cultures is ethnocentrism. Ethnocentrism refers to judging other people from within one's own cultural perspective. All people are, to a greater or lesser extent, ethnocentric; however, a problem arises when one views one's own culture as superior to other cultures. Typically, ethnocentric individuals will judge other people relative to their own particular ethnic group or culture, basing this on language, behaviour, customs, and religion.

Cross-cultural psychology, according to Berry, Poortinga, Segall, and Dasen (2002), attempts to reduce ethnocentrism by:

- recognising the limitations of our current knowledge
- seeking to extend our data and theory through the inclusion of other cultures
- reducing the culture-bound nature of the discipline.

An example of ethnocentrism is the tendency in Western medicine to discredit the methods of the traditional African healer, even though a comprehensive understanding of some types of psychopathology is found among the traditional healers in African societies.

However, some psychologists and psychiatrists who have studied and worked closely with traditional healers have developed empathetic understandings of their methods, and have acknowledged the healing that they achieve (Buhrmann, 1986; Edwards, 1982; Kottle, 1988, all in Louw & Edwards, 1993).

Traditional beliefs and practices concerning illness and health are still widely followed, especially in rural areas of South Africa (Louw & Edwards, 1993). These beliefs and practices form a coherent system that has maintained individual and social equilibrium for generations. According to Moodley and Sutherland (2010), traditional healing methods are also re-emerging alongside modern Western clinics in several large metropolitan cities.

Since the traditional healers are easily available and represent the same cultural group as the clients, they are trusted and perceived as well trained. In addition, some of the older people in African communities, who are not traditional healers, acquired knowledge of indigenous healing from the past generations and are therefore familiar with traditional prevention, diagnosis, prognosis, and medicine.

These are usually wise older women and men who give advice to the community members. They can be regarded as indigenous community counsellors. Out of these traditional beliefs and practices has come an African understanding of aetiology. The study conducted by Moletsane (2011) highlights these African aetiological explanations (see Table 1.5). When assisting clients from an African cultural background, it is crucial to have an understanding of these aetiological explanations.

Table 1.5: Indigenous African aetiological explanations

Cause of illness	Explanation
Boloi (Sesotho) or *ubuthakathi* (isiZulu): to be bewitched	It can be described as sorcery/witchcraft or use of superpower to harm or even kill someone, usually an enemy.

Cause of illness	Explanation
Go roula (Sesotho)	A widow has to wear black clothes for 12 months to show that she is mourning for her husband. This only applies to wives, not husbands. If this practice is not properly followed, it can cause illness.
Sefifi/senyama (Sesotho) or *isinyama* in isiZulu	A widow is regarded as contagious as she has *senyama* or *sefifi* which means bad luck due to her husband's death. The bad luck can be cured if the widow and the youngest child in the family are cleansed by bathing with a herb concoction as recommended by the traditional healer or a traditional community counsellor after the death of her husband. A person who is menstruating or who had sex that day is also regarded as having *sefifi*. Such people are not allowed to enter the same room as a new-born baby or a sick person because they might pass their bad luck or illness to the baby or aggravate the condition of the sick person.
Makgome (Sesotho)	After the death of the husband, a widow is prohibited from having a sexual relationship with anyone. Widows are supposed to abstain from sexual activities for a period of one year. If this practice is ignored, they can cause serious illness to themselves and to anyone who has sexual contact with them.
Go tlola (Sesotho) or *ukudlula* in isiZulu	When a widow fails to abstain from sex during the mourning period, this can cause compulsion neurosis (the uncontrollable impulse to perform stereotyped irrational acts).
Go lahla maseko/setso (Sesotho) or *ukulahla amasiko* in isiZulu	This is the failure to perform the traditional practices. For example, due to Western cultural influence, people might not believe in African rituals. This might anger the ancestors which will cause ill health or other types of problems in a person's life.
Ba fase ba re furaletse/ba fase ba re lahlile (Sesotho) or *abaphansi ba si fulathele* (isiZulu)	This means the ancestors have turned their backs on a person. This usually happens when people experience problems either with relationships, work, finance, health, etc., and they then think that the ancestors are angry with them.
Go thwasa (Sesotho) or *ukuthwasa* (isiZulu) (calling)	The calling by the ancestors to become a traditional healer. If ignored, it can cause illness or even death.
Sejeso (Sesotho) or *isidliso* (isiZulu)	Growth or pain in the stomach due to sorcery/witchcraft.
Tokolosi (Sesotho) or *tokoloshe* (isiZulu)	Witchcraft through an animal-like witch. The witches can send *tokolosi* to take part in bewitching another person.
Letswalo (Sesotho) or *uvalo* (isiZulu)	Anxiety attributed to witchcraft or sorcery.
Go gatiswa/mohlala (Sesotho) or *umeqo* (isiZulu)	A disorder attributed to stepping on a concoction of herbs of sorcery. This can cause pain and swollen feet for the person who stepped on the concoction.
Mafofonyane (Sesotho) or *amafufunyane* (isiZulu)	Spirit possession as a result of witchcraft or sorcery.

Source: Created by author Moletsane. (Adapted from Moletsane, M. K. (2011). Indigenous African personality and health theories. Paper presented at a seminar, at the University of Western Cape, Department of Psychology.)

According to Lesolang-Pitje (2003), South Africa in the post-apartheid era recognises traditional healing as part of the health system (see also Chapter 5). The process of consultation with traditional healers' associations started in 1995. According to Bojuwoye (2003), traditional healers are acknowledged for their extraordinary knowledge of histories, religions, philosophies, institutions, and other bodies of knowledge and language of their culture. They are experts in the use of their cultural languages to accurately construct, explain, and communicate what is culturally believed to be fundamentally true about the world people live in.

Nevertheless, patients should not be assigned a specific type of treatment simply based on their cultural roots. Makhubela (2016) warns of 'ultra-essentialist theorising, by some African psychologists' saying that it is 'redolent of a relativism that reifies culture as the only determinant of behaviour and its psychological variants' (p. 6).

Fanon was also against 'cultural chains', although 'he attempted to use meaningful cultural referents in his sociotherapy programs' (Cherki, 2017, p. xii). As Fanon's ex-colleague, Cherki remembers:

> … even if he concluded that reference points and markers that had been destroyed by the dominant culture had to be restored in order to enable subjects to reconstitute their symbolic space, he did not think, like many ethnopsychiatrists do, that liberation would come from assigning subjects to their alleged culture of origin. He was a tenacious militant for culture in motion, constantly altered by new situations. (2017, p. xii)

In South Africa, in a 1998 study of Xhosa-speaking schizophrenic patients, Swartz and Lund note that 'while patients frequently described their condition in terms of "amafufunyana" or "nerves", they reported that their preferred mode of treatment had shifted from consultation with traditional healers to use of psychiatric services'.

 ACTIVITY

The following extract comes from the same Zimbabwean novel, *Nervous Conditions*, as the extract at the start of the chapter. This novel was first published in 1988. Which of the themes from this extract are relevant to psychopathology in South Africa today?

By ten o'clock we were on our way to the city, arriving there before twelve because Babamukuru drove like an August wind. Maiguru and I talked to Nyasha constantly all the way, to keep her with us, to prevent her mind from wandering too far.
In the city Maiguru's brother immediately made an appointment with a psychiatrist. We felt better—help was at hand. But the psychiatrist said that Nyasha could not be ill, that Africans did not suffer in the way we had described. She was making a scene. We should take her home and be firm with her. This was not a sensible thing to say in front of my uncle, who found these words vastly reassuring and considered going back to Umtali at once, turning a deaf ear to Nyasha when she begged to see an African psychiatrist. Nyasha's uncle, though, with the authority of seven years of learning to recognise suffering when he saw it, was able to persuade my uncle to wait.

There were no black psychiatrists, but she was persuaded to see a white one. This man was human. She needed to rest, he said. So Nyasha was put into a clinic, where she stayed for several weeks. Slowly, with the aid of doses of Largactil and the practical attention of her aunts who lived in the city, my cousin's condition improved...

Source: Dangaremba, 1991, pp. 201–202.

RELIGIOUS PERSPECTIVES

The Indian psychiatrist Dinesh Bhugra considers the division between psychiatry and religion as an artificial one and that there is 'much room for understanding the same phenomena from different perspectives' (1997, p. i). While not everyone will agree, and while Motlana (1988) warns of the 'tyranny of superstition', it is clearly useful to have an understanding of a patient's spiritual framework when trying to understand that patient.

Mental illness from the perspective of African Traditional Religion

According to African Traditional Religion there is a powerful being which supersedes all of us. This supreme power is invisible and can be seen as God or more than one god. According to Bojuwoye (2003), God is the supreme being and the ultimate source of life energy.

Below this supreme being are the ancestors, as indicated in Figure 1.8. Ancestors are people who have died but whose spirits are still alive and are among the living. The ancestors are watching and protecting their living relatives. It is believed that the ancestors play a crucial role in people's lives by communicating with God on behalf of the living. The ancestors use dreams, signs, or traditional or spiritual healers to deliver the messages from God (or the gods) to those who are alive. Holdstock (1982, in Louw & Edwards, 1993) states that the relationship with the ancestors (and through the ancestors, with God) permeates all beings.

In Figure 1.8, the person is represented as 'the body'. The outer layer of the body is like a cover or container of the human's

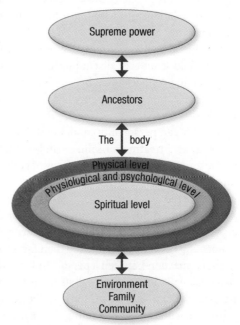

Figure 1.8: African model of personality

Source: Moletsane, 2011.

body. The body needs to be active in order to be in a good physical shape. There are other levels of functioning, such as the physiological, which focuses on the body's physiological functioning, and the psychological, which focuses on the stability of a person's mind. The physiological and psychological levels of a person are important; for the body to survive and to be healthy, it needs good nutrition and a stable mind.

The spiritual part is the inner part or the seed of a person. The spirit is regarded as the seed because it does not die even after the body has died. Sow (1977, in Berry et al., 2002) also regards the inner layer as the 'spiritual principle', which represents a soul that can never perish. It can leave the body during sleep and during trance states (see Chapter 10) and leaves definitively upon death. Sow (1977, in Berry et al., 2002) further states that the spiritual principle does not give life to the body; rather, it has an existence of its own, belonging to the sphere of the ancestors and representing that sphere in each person.

Every person has a connection or relationship with their environment; hence, people adapt to their own environment. If people do not adapt to their environment, they get sick. This happens because their state of equilibrium is weak. The arrows in Figure 1.8 represent the firm connections between the gods or the supreme power, the ancestors, a person, the environment, the family, and the community. This bond or connection also represents the state of equilibrium. Thus, the state of equilibrium is represented by the lines that join the different levels together.

If the different levels are held together firmly (the levels being the supreme power; ancestors; physical, physiological and psychological; and spiritual), then there is a state of equilibrium in a person's life. In that state, a person is healthy and happy, or satisfied with life in general. This can be because the ancestors are satisfied that the person has a strong bond and good relationships with his or her family or they take good care of the elderly people in the family, etc.

On the other hand, if one or more (or all) of the levels is/are not held firmly, then the person is in a state of disequilibrium. While in a state of disequilibrium, the person is unhappy and gets sick often because the relationships or bonds between the levels are weak. For example, this can happen when a person has angered the ancestors by not performing rituals.

The African personality model described above helps to provide an explanation of the aetiology and treatment of illness and mental disorder (see also Table 1.5). Thus, illnesses and disorders happen when the lines of connection are disturbed. In order to diagnose the illness or disorder, one has to establish where in these lines of connection the disturbances have occurred.

According to Sow (1977, in Berry et al., 2002), a rupture of the connection between a person and their ancestors leads to serious chronic psychotic states, a rupture of the connection between a person and their family leads to organic illness, while a disequilibrium in the connection between a person and their community leads to more benign organic and psychosomatic illnesses as well as neurotic states. Once the site and nature of the rupture have been identified, the person's equilibrium can then be restored by means of therapy or other indigenous ways of healing. Thus, healing occurs when there is resolution of conflict with community, family, and/or ancestors, because by doing so, the connection lines will become firm again and the connection will not be disturbed.

✅ ACTIVITY

Discuss how the African Traditional Religion concepts of disequilibrium and rupture can be used to find the origins of Mandla's mental illness.

Mandla's mother passed away recently. He feels guilty because he feels he did not give his mother enough support while she was still alive. His mother suffered a stroke and on several occasions Mandla refused to transport her to the hospital for regular check-ups, saying that he was too busy. He used to go to parties with friends, and now that his mother is no longer alive, he feels bad that he did not give her all the support she deserved and he did not take the chance to tell her that he loved her. Mandla is now experiencing severe headaches and sleepless nights. He often dreams about his mother being angry with him. Based on Mandla's scenario, explain:

■ the consequences of disequilibrium and rupture of connection between Mandla and his mother, who has passed away

■ the reason why firm connection and good relationship between different levels of the African personality model are crucial for a person's health.

Traditional Africans believe that a sickness, especially one that is emotional or psychological in nature, originates from a disruption in the connections between people, the gods, and the ancestors. In response to these disruptions, traditional healers work with clients and their families, rather than on an individual basis with the client alone. Traditional healers also work with gods and ancestors in the healing process.

According to Bojuwoye (2003), traditional African healthcare delivery approaches are said to be active and directive. The process moves through three main stages, which include establishing a relationship; identification and discussion of the problem; and the problem-solving stage. Certain principles guide the decisions, choices, and actions that take place in these stages. Some of them are:

■ *The principle of education or information:* The traditional healer helps the patient understand the different elements contained in the universe, for example, the connection between the different levels that constitute a person, according to African personality theory (see Figure 1.8). This helps the patient understand how their illness or misfortune may be caused by their state of disequilibrium (see Figure 1.8).

■ *The principle of interconnectedness or the phenomenal world:* This principle is found in the African world view, which states that people are interconnected. For instance, if a mother is sick or not happy, her situation will affect other people such as family members, neighbours, colleagues at work, etc.

■ *The principle of social contact and interpersonal relationship:* This principle ensures harmony within the universe. Problems are dyadic in nature, and using relationships to address some of them may be a good strategy. Activities such as ritual ceremonies are regarded as important for interpersonal growth.

■ *The principle of personal empowerment:* By performing rituals, a person is empowered. If a person is empowered, the power is transferred to other people. For example, if someone is healthy and positive about life, the positive energy spreads to people around them.

- *The principle of psychological arousal:* During the ritual ceremony, through the vigorous exercise of singing and dancing, the spirits are lifted and this process arouses people psychologically and emotionally. It is a space where people can express their emotions.
- *The principle of ritualistic support:* Participating in vigorous body movements during the ritual ceremony is therapeutic. During these ceremonies, people are made aware that they are not alone but their problems and grief are shared with others.

These therapeutic components do not necessarily follow a sequence but can be applied interchangeably during sessions. Traditional healing models are holistic and treat the 'whole' person, employing interventions targeted at all forces responsible for ill health including both symptoms and causes of ill health (Bojuwoye & Sodi, 2010). Furthermore, traditional healing is comprehensive and concerned with illness prevention, health promotion, and/or cure (Bujowoye & Sodi, 2010).

The African healing model is related to both the Islamic and Christian perspectives in terms of its focus on spiritual healing.

Mental illness from the perspective of Islam

Written by Tasneem Bulbulia and Sumaya Laher (2013) and initially published in the *South African Journal of Psychiatry*.

Islamic perspectives on illness have been developing for centuries (Wan Hazmy, Zainur, & Hussaini, 2003) and can be traced to the Quran itself (Okasha, 2001). Within the Quran, four components are mentioned that have come to be viewed as a holistic model of the self (Al-Issa, 2000). This model is based on the interrelation between the *ruh* (soul), the *qalb* (connection between the soul and the body), the *aql* (intellect), and the *nafs* (drives or desires) merging through the *dahmeer* (consciousness) (Al-Issa, 2000; Okasha, 2001; Laher & Khan, 2011).

In order to be healthy, all four aspects of the self need to be balanced. An imbalance in any aspect results in physical, mental, and/or spiritual illness (Ally & Laher, 2008). Islamic understandings of mental and physical illness correspond to currently accepted diagnostic classifications as described in the DSM-IV-TR1 and the ICD-10 (World Health Organization, 1993). Islam, however, acknowledges an additional category of illnesses: spiritual illnesses, which are broadly divided into two types, *sihr* (black magic) and *nazr/ayn al husood* (evil eye) (Ally & Laher, 2008).

Jinn, spirit possession, and bewitchment all fall under the category of *sihr*. *Nazr*, on the other hand, is when a person looks at another person with an 'evil eye' or with envy. When a person has *nazr* they suffer from certain symptoms. For example, things do not seem to work out for them in personal or business ventures, or they undergo changes in appetite. However, people who suffer from spiritual illnesses caused by *sihr* present with more severe symptoms, leading to more profound and destructive disturbances in physical, mental, and spiritual well-being. *Sihr* needs to be treated by traditional healers (Ally & Laher, 2008).

Treatment of illnesses in Islam

Ally and Laher (2008) say that within the Islamic religion, moulanas and/or sheikhs are considered the traditional source of healing. Asefzadeh and Sameefar (2001) emphasise that even in countries with practising physicians, Muslims continue to consult Islamic traditional healers.

Islamic traditional healing practices cover a wide range of remedies. Treatments for medical conditions include herbal remedies, massage therapy, and cupping (Al-Issa, 2000). Treatments for mental illness may include herbal remedies, massage therapy, *taa'weez* (amulets with Quranic verses), water over which verses of the Quran are read, and special *zikr* and *duas* (prayers).

Treatment for spiritual illnesses includes *taa'weez*, water over which verses of the Quran are read, special *zikr* and *duas* (prayers), burning *lobaan* (frankincense) or other natural substances, and/or using herbal remedies to ease physical symptoms (Ally & Laher, 2008).

Ally and Laher (2008) state that Islamic traditional healers try to treat spiritual aspects of illness by removing the effects of *sihr* or *nazr* using any combination of treatments mentioned above. However, they also noted that if psychological or medical symptoms are present, assistance from a psychologist or doctor may be necessary. Islamic traditional healers have value in that they contribute to the treatment of physical, mental, and spiritual illness, and thus to mental health and well-being.

 ACTIVITY

> The Muslim psychologist G. Hussein Rassool explains the condition of *Waswâs al Qahri*, which he describes as 'akin to pathological obsessive-compulsive disorder' (2019, p. 147). Summarise what he is saying about this condition.
> *Waswâs* is the whispering of the devil of the devil's insufflations (*Waswâs-il-Khannas*, Qur'an, p. 114) over and over again, as *Waswâsah* by itself suggests repetition. This evil suggestion is to test the believer in having thoughts of disbelief, obsession related to purification, and the fear of losing control in acts of worship. All believers are subjected to these thoughts and whispers from Satan or *Jinn* but, for some, it becomes an obsession and compulsion. *Waswâs al Qahri* is a complex psycho-spiritual problem found in Muslim populations.
>
> **Source:** Hussein Rassool, 2019, p. 147.

Mental illness from the perspective of Christianity

In the Christian tradition, mental disorders have often been attributed to spiritual-supernatural causes (i.e. demonic possession, immorality/sinfulness, and spiritual failure), and spiritual social support has always been the preferred mode of treatment. These beliefs, despite being contentious among mainstream mental health practitioners, have implications for understanding mental illness in ethno-religious communities because they remain prevalent till today (Leavey, 2010).

According to the American psychologist Amber Martinez-Pilkington, since the advent of psychology, 'many psychologists and pastors have been mutually sceptical of each other', with each accusing the other of 'denying an important aspect of the human person' (Martinez-

Pilkington, 2007, p. 203). However, by the turn of the last century, Christian psychiatrist Dan Blazer was seeing the relationship between Christianity and psychiatry as 'a comfortable accommodation', with each allowing a large territory to the other (Kramer, 1999, p. 327).

The practice of Sacramental Confession that is part of the Catholic tradition is particularly interesting from a psychological point of view. Martinez-Pilkington (2007) observes that psychologists claim that confession 'breeds unnecessary guilt from which their patients must recover'. However, the Swiss psychiatrist Carl Jung wrote that the 'Catholic Church possesses a rich instrument (in the form of confession) that can be utilised as a ready-made pastoral technique' (Worthen, 1974, p. 275).

 ACTIVITY

Consider the following extract from the Christian Bible. If you accept that the man in this story did stand up, why do you think he was able to?

Jesus heals a paralytic

17 One day, while He was teaching, Pharisees and teachers of the law were sitting nearby (they had come from every village of Galilee and Judea and from Jerusalem); and the power of the Lord was with Him to heal. 18 Just then some men came, carrying a paralysed man on a bed. They were trying to bring him in and lay him before Jesus; 19 but finding no way to bring him in because of the crowd, they went up on the roof and let him down with his bed through the tiles into the middle of the crowd in front of Jesus. 20 When He saw their faith, He said, "Friend, your sins are forgiven you." 21 Then the scribes and the Pharisees began to question, "Who is this who is speaking blasphemies? Who can forgive sins but God alone?" 22 When Jesus perceived their questionings, He answered them, "Why do you raise such questions in your hearts? 23 Which is easier, to say, 'Your sins are forgiven you,' or to say, 'Stand up and walk'? 24 But so that you may know that the Son of Man has authority on earth to forgive sins"—He said to the one who was paralysed—"I say to you, stand up and take your bed and go to your home." 25 Immediately he stood up before them, took what he had been lying on, and went to his home, glorifying God. 26 Amazement seized all of them, and they glorified God and were filled with awe, saying, "We have seen strange things today."

Source: Luke 5:17–26, The New Revised Standard Version

INTEGRATED PERSPECTIVES

As indicated in the introduction to this chapter, psychological disorders are most often caused by multiple factors acting in complex and dynamic ways. The biopsychosocial model, the diathesis-stress model, and the ecological systems theory discussed here provide us with broad theoretical frameworks that allow a number of different perspectives to be used, thus demonstrating the multidimensional nature of understanding and treating psychopathology.

The biopsychosocial model

According to the biopsychosocial model (see Figure 1.9), behaviour is too complex to be understood from one perspective only. It takes the view that psychological disorders are caused by multiple biological, psychological, and social factors in interaction with each other.

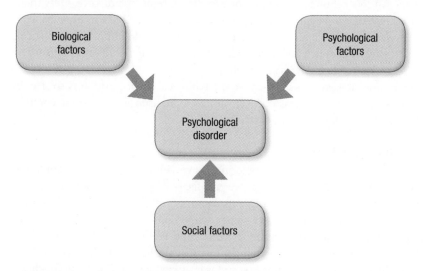

Figure 1.9: The biopsychosocial model

For example, Isaac is diagnosed with depression. Biologically, a contributing factor could be his neurophysiological vulnerability to producing unhealthy levels of stress hormones when experiencing stress. On a psychological level, Isaac has observed that his parents are extremely negative and avoidant when things go wrong, and so he has developed irrational beliefs regarding uncertainty (e.g. 'I can't cope with uncertainty'). On a social level, Isaac, who is part of a minority group, has been discriminated against in his school, which has contributed to a feeling of helplessness. Thus, factors from all three dimensions interact to contribute to his depression.

The diathesis-stress model

The diathesis-stress model was first introduced by Meehl (1962). He suggested that some people inherit or develop biological predispositions (diathesis) to psychopathology. In this situation, mental disorders will not emerge until environmental stressors or biological stressors become intense enough to convert predispositions into actual psychological disorders (see Figure 1.10).

Figure 1.10: The diathesis-stress model

Thus, there is an interaction between the diathesis (a biological predisposition to a disorder) and a stressor, which together cause a disorder to develop. A biological predisposition on its own is therefore usually not sufficient to develop a psychological disorder. For example, when a person has a biological vulnerability to developing depression, this may lie dormant until the person is exposed to a significant stressor, for example, a traumatic divorce. Only then is the predisposition to develop depression triggered and actualised. This also explains why not all people develop disorders after experiencing stressors (they do not have a biological predisposition), or why all people with biological predispositions do not develop a disorder (they have not been exposed to a significant stressor).

There are exceptions, however; in some cases, the biological predisposition is so strong that a disorder develops without a stressor. Also, without a predisposition, a strong enough stressor may lead to the development of a psychological disorder.

Risk and vulnerability

The previous section discussed the way people may have vulnerabilities to developing a mental disorder; these vulnerabilities can involve risk factors in a number of areas. These include social, family, individual, and life-events factors (see Table 1.6). Social factors include socio-economic status and minority status, while family factors include parental pathology and parenting style, as well as family dynamics and expressed emotion. Individual factors include gender, cognitive ability, and temperament, while life events that may present risk include individual events, natural disasters, and war or civil unrest. (Look out for these aetiological risk factors in Chapters 6–15.)

Table 1.6: Risk factors at social, family, individual, and life-events levels

Level	Factor	Examples
Social	Socio-economic status (SES)	Social drift: Mental illness and poverty are considered to interact in a negative cycle; that is, not only is the risk of mental illness among people who live in poverty higher, but so too is the likelihood that those living with mental illness will drift into or remain in poverty.
		Social stress: The lower the SES, the greater the stress, i.e. stress associated with social deprivation increases risk for disorders.
		Lack of resources: Limited financial, psychological, social and environmental resources
		Neighbourhood: Lower socio-economic areas are often associated with high levels of crime, violence, substance abuse, etc., as well as a lack of infrastructure. Poor housing or living conditions, for example, may be seen by children as shameful or degrading, may reduce opportunities for productive learning and social interaction, or may increase their exposure to disease and injury.

Level	Factor	Examples
Social	Minority status	Gender: Women encounter more role strain than men and are at greater risk for physical and sexual assault than men. The socially defined role of women in many societies exposes them to greater stresses, which, together with other factors including family violence and abuse, leads to higher rates of depression and anxiety.
		Prejudice and discrimination: Discrimination based on race, ethnicity, culture, nationality, sexual orientation, religion and gender. Racism or discrimination towards a particular group in society, for example, raises that group's exposure to social exclusion and economic adversity, thereby placing them at a higher risk of stress, anxiety and other common mental disorders.
		Cultural transition: Stress due to adopting or rejecting some of the norms of one's own or other cultures.
Family	Parental pathology	Children with a parent who has a mental illness or substance use disorder are placed at a high risk of experiencing family discord and psychiatric problems. The intergenerational transfer of mental disorders is the result of interactions between genetic, biological, psychological, and social risk factors occurring as early as pregnancy and infancy.
	Parenting styles	Authoritarian parenting (harsh, controlling, and abusive) may place children at risk for developing conduct disorders, and permissive parenting may lead to interpersonal problems.
	Family dynamics	Family violence or conflict, persistent beating, severe bullying, and parental loss or abuse can cause a level of trauma that may have a long-term effect on a person's life.
	Expressed emotion	Family members with high expressed emotion are hostile, critical, and intolerant.
Individual	Gender	Certain genders are more at risk for some disorders than others.
	Cognitive ability	Limited cognitive abilities are directly or indirectly associated with more frequent negative outcomes.
	Temperament	Difficult temperament, as characterised by poor emotional regulation, low impulse control, and hostility, is often associated with some disorders
Stressful/ adverse life events	Personal	Divorce, unemployment, etc. may lead to a variety of disorders.
	Natural disasters	Floods, fires, earthquakes, etc. may lead to trauma- or stressor-related disorders.
	Civil unrest/war	Exposure to extreme life-threatening events may lead to trauma- or stressor-related disorders.

Figure 1.11 presents a graphic matrix showing how risk factors interact across different settings and at different levels to influence a person's mental health over their life course (World Health Organization, 2012).

Setting	Home/family	School	Media/information	Work	Community/home
Culture			Discrimination/social inequalities		
	Low socioeconomic status	Adverse learning environment	Adverse media influences		Social exclusion
Community			Neighbourhood violence/crime		Poor civic amenities
	Poor housing/living conditions	Peer pressure		Job intensity or insecurity	
Family	Parental mental illness	Difficulties at school	Family violence or conflict	Unemployment	
	Substance use in pregnancy				Debt/poverty
		Trauma or maltreatment	Criminal or anti-social behaviour		Bereavement
Individual	Insecure attachment	Poor nutrition	Psychoactive substance use	Harmful alcohol use	Elder abuse
	Malnutrition				
	Low self-esteem	Physical ill health		Physical ill health	

| Prenatal period and early children | Childhood | Adolescence | Adulthood | Older adulthood |

Figure 1.11: Schematic overview of risks to mental health over the life course

Figure 1.12 (World Health Organization, 2010) shows how risk and vulnerability factors interact in a circular way to lead to poor mental health conditions. Increased vulnerability may arise from violence, abuse, and lack of access to opportunities, amongst others. These may lead to worsened mental health, which in turn may worsen vulnerability to mental conditions. Similarly, obstacles to development such as poverty, inequality, and reduced social capital also interact with worsened mental health in a bidirectional way, to present an increased risk for mental conditions.

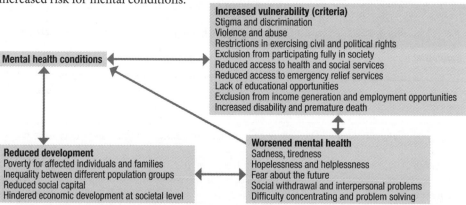

Increased vulnerability (criteria)
Stigma and discrimination
Violence and abuse
Restrictions in exercising civil and political rights
Exclusion from participating fully in society
Reduced access to health and social services
Reduced access to emergency relief services
Lack of educational opportunities
Exclusion from income generation and employment opportunities
Increased disability and premature death

Mental health conditions

Reduced development
Poverty for affected individuals and families
Inequality between different population groups
Reduced social capital
Hindered economic development at societal level

Worsened mental health
Sadness, tiredness
Hopelessness and helplessness
Fear about the future
Social withdrawal and interpersonal problems
Difficulty concentrating and problem solving

Figure 1.12: Vulnerabilities, mental disorders, and adverse developmental outcomes

Protective factors

As with the risk and vulnerability factors discussed in the previous section, protective factors can operate at a number of levels and across diverse contexts or settings. Table 1.7 gives examples of such protective factors at the community, social, family, and individual levels. These factors provide protection against the risk of developing mental disorders.

Table 1.7: Examples of protective factors at various levels

Level	Factor
Community	Effective schooling
	Organisations, clubs, support groups
	Higher SES neighbourhoods with good infrastructure
	High levels of public safety
	Good emergency and healthcare services
Social	Prosocial, supportive peers and friends
Family	Close relationships with family members
	Authoritative parenting
	Organised home environment
	Socio-economic advantages
	Low expressed emotion (supportive and criticism is reserved)
Individual	Good cognitive abilities
	Positive self-perceptions
	Positive outlook on life
	Good sense of humuor
	Good emotional regulation
	High impulse control

ACTIVITY

Read the following extract from *Nervous Conditions*, which describes an event that occurs earlier in the story. Based on this extract, identify the risk factors and protective factors for Nyasha's mental health.

'Don't push me too far,' Babamukuru pleaded. Mustering up his courage, Chido tried to help.
'They were only talking for a few minutes, Dad,' he said, and was ordered to be silent.
'You, Chido, keep quiet,' Babamuluru snapped. 'You let your sister behave like a whore without saying anything. Keep quiet.'
'Babawa Chido,' began Maigure, but was silenced immediately. Nyasha grew uncharacteristically calm at times like this. 'Now why,' she enquired of no particular person, 'should I worry about what people say when my own father calls me a whore?' She looked at him with murder in her eyes.
'Nyasha, be quiet,' Chido advised.
'Chido, I have told you to keep out of this, reminded Babamakuru, gathering within himself so that his whole weight was behind the blow he dealt Nyasha's face. 'Never,' he hissed. 'Never,' he repeated, striking her other cheek with the back of his hand, 'speak to me like that.'

Source: Dangaremba, 1991, p. 114.

Stress and coping

As will be seen in Chapter 6, stress is common in people's lives today. Stress is an unpleasant state of tension that occurs when people experience demands either from within, or from the external environment, which exceed their capacity to cope. This puts physical and mental strain on a person, leading to vulnerability to mental disorder. In the Transactional Model of Stress and Coping (Lazarus & Folkman, 1984), stressful experiences are understood as transactions between the person and their environment. How the person responds depends on how they perceive and appraise these stressors. Coping refers to the ways in which people try to deal with the stress they experience (see Chapter 4 for more on coping).

ACTIVITY

Read the following extract from *Nervous Conditions*, and discuss what is happening in Nyasha's life at this point, using the terms 'stress' and 'coping' to help you.

Nyasha regarded her plate malevolently, darting anguished glances at her father, drained two glasses of water, then picked up her fork and shoveled the food into her mouth, swallowing without chewing and without pause except to sip between mouthfuls from a third glass of water. Maiguru ate steadily and fussed over me, placing another chunk of meat, another spoonful of vegetables on my plate and making cheerful conversation about my lessons, my friends and the food at Sacred Heart. When Nyasha's plate was empty they relaxed and the atmosphere returned almost to normal. Nyasha excused herself immediately. I thought she had gone to the bedroom to read but when I followed her there the room was empty. I could hear retching and gagging from the bathroom.

She returned silently to her books, a mathematics exercise this time, and was still working when I rolled over to sleep at eleven o'clock. In the early hours of the morning something prodded me awake. It was Nyasha.

'Can you help me?' she asked timidly. 'I can't get the right answer. I ought to be able to, but I keep getting it wrong.' It was not a difficult problem. She had made a careless mistake. 'Silly me,' she said when I found her mistake. 'I'm not concentrating hard enough.'

Source: Dangaremba, 1991, p. 198.

The ecological systems theory

Urie Bronfenbrenner was a Russian-American psychologist who developed the ecological systems theory to illustrate the impact of different factors on the development of an individual. He introduced his theory by saying, 'The ecological environment is conceived as a set of nested structures, each inside the next, like a set of Russian dolls' (1979, p. 3). By 1989, Bronfenbrenner had conceived of six systems that impacted on the development of the person (1979, 1989):

- the microsystem (the people with whom the developing person interacts, and the connections between these people)
- the mesosystem (the interrelations between the settings in which the developing person participates)
- the exosystem (the settings that interact with the mesosystem, but where the developing person does not actively participate)
- the macrosystem (the culture, subculture, beliefs, and ideology in which the microsystem, mesosystem, and exosystem exist)
- the chronosystem (the dimension of time and its impact on bodies, relationships, and society).

It is the interaction within and between the systems that are key to this theory (see Figure 1.13 below).

Bronfenbrenner originally developed this model to explain factors that influence human development, but it also provides a useful theoretical framework to understand all the possible factors that may contribute to the development of pathology.

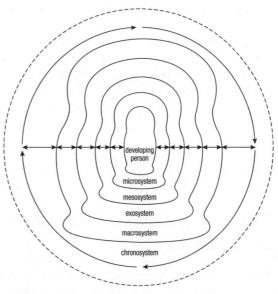

Figure 1.13: An illustration of Bronfenbrenner's ecological systems theory

According to Hepworth, Rooney, Dewberry Rooney, Strom-Gottfried, and Larsen (2010), this model organises a wide range of information that enables us to understand the reciprocal relationships between people and their environment. According to this theory, there are multiple nested systems that influence our development (Berk, 2000):

- **The individual (intrapersonal)** with her or his own physical, biological, and psychological characteristics.
- **The microsystem (interpersonal)**, which encompasses the relationships and interactions people have with their immediate surroundings (e.g. peer groups).
- **The mesosystem** provides the connections between the structures of the person's microsystem (e.g. parent–teacher meetings).
- **The exosystem** can be described as the larger social system that has an indirect impact on a person's functioning, by means of interactions with the microsystem (e.g. events that occur in the parent's workplace).
- **The macrosystem** is the outermost layer, which consists of cultural values, customs, and laws (e.g. the rituals that accompany reaching puberty).

All of these layers are embedded within the **chronosystem**, which incorporates both the historical context within which the individual is situated and the personal life events in that individual's life (e.g. reaching puberty).

 ACTIVITY

Read this final extract from *Nervous Conditions*, which comes earlier in the story than all the other extracts, and is where Nyasha talks to the narrator about the time she and her brother spent with their parents in England when they were young. Explain how the other systems have affected Nyasha's microsystem and the individual that she is.

'We shouldn't have gone,' Nyasha was saying, looking disheartened. 'The parents ought to have packed us off home. They should have, you know. Lots of people did that. Maybe that would have been the best. For them at least, because now they are stuck with hybrids for children. And they don't like it. They don't like it at all. It offends them. They think we do it on purpose, so it offends them. And I don't know what to do about it, Tambu, really I don't. I can't help having been there and grown into the me that has been there. But it offends them – I offend them. Really, it's very difficult.'

Source: Dangaremba, 1991, p. 78.

Towards a universal schema in the context of globalisation

How do we understand mental illness in the context of globalisation, where cultures always intermix and create amalgams, and also in settings of hyperdiversity, where hybrid forms of identity proliferate? How do we define what mental health and illness are in contexts of pluralism, where people are at once traditional and modern? Do we seek recourse in the supposedly universal biomedical paradigms of psychopathology? Or do we defer to traditional conceptions of mental illness? Or do we do both? These questions lead on to other questions about the universality or relativity of psychopathology and attendant treatment practices.

The biopsychosocial model (discussed earlier in detail) was advanced to solve the problem of focusing solely on the biomedical paradigm in psychopathology. It was also intended to solve the rift between biological reductionist and cultural relativist approaches. A relativist approach includes the notion that one's views, ideals, and practices should be understood based on one's own culture, and not be judged against the standards of another culture.

Advocates of the biopsychosocial model argue that each of the above-mentioned outlooks alone was insufficient, but together they were complementary. Their perspective was reflected in the increased emphasis on gene–environment interactions in the aetiology of mental disorders. Of course, the biopsychosocial model itself is not without its detractors, with concerns centring around the supposed over-emphasis on biology and the supposed under-emphasis on culture.

Although cultural variations in the presentation of mental illness are long-standing, culture has received increased attention from formal psychiatric nosology (Alarcon, 2001; Mezzich et al., 1996). Both the DSM-5 (American Psychiatric Association, 2013) and the ICD-11 (World Health Organization, 2018a) have been revised to include culture as a feature in diagnosis, while they have also expressly committed themselves to assuming a theoretically neutral position on the subject of aetiological factors.

The uncovering of distinctive psychopathologies among different cultural groups stimulated Western practitioners' focus on culture's contribution to mental disorders. These so-called exotic syndromes (from a Western perspective), beyond the boundaries of the recognised (Western) psychopathology classification system, were later to be grouped together and branded 'culture-bound syndromes' in the DSM-IV. These conditions could not easily be identified according to existing psychiatric classifications, because 'official' psychopathology nosology is based on clinical accounts of commonly observed mental illnesses in Western societies; thus, they pay less attention to infrequently encountered psychiatric conditions, especially those from diverse cultures outside of their sphere of concern (Tseng, 2001).

While still in common use in some psychiatric nosology (e.g. DSM-5), views about the cultural boundedness of these unique psychopathologies have been challenged by cross-cultural studies (Sumathıpala, Sırıbadanna, & Bhugra, 2004). This research shows that, while the so-called culture-specific disorders may be closely related to certain ethnic features, they are not necessarily tied to any particular cultural group or society. In addition, they have been reported historically in other cultures (i.e. developed societies) outside of the societies where they were thought to occur. Also, many commentators have called for these cultural syndromes to be abandoned because they are seen as a product of a problematic colonial history within mental health practice and study.

It would seem that, in negotiating the tension between accepting a set nosological standard and acknowledging the role of culture and context in mental disorders, standard psychopathology paradigms are not just commanding tools for clinical diagnoses any more. Instead, they have also become sites of inquiry in the reconsideration of the validity of the biological aetiology and the universality of mental illness.

Illness explanatory models (i.e. people's own explanations of illness that may or may not be independent of their own culture's conceptions of illness) have been suggested as an option to manage concerns about what is seen as the undue prominence of biology (at the expense of psychological and social factors) in the biopsychosocial model. For instance, Kleinman (1977) argued that, instead of assuming the universality of psychiatric categories and psychological modes of expressing illness, attention should be moved to the social and cultural contexts of illness and healing.

This flows from the argument that assumptions about the universality of psychopathology suffer from 'category fallacy', the flawed belief that conceptual categories that work well in one cultural setting will necessarily have similar salience and efficacy in another. For Littlewood (1990), category fallacy arises from confounding professional Western explanatory models of mental illness with universal concepts of psychopathology.

The import of the illness explanatory model for clinical assessment was manifestly acknowledged under the cultural formulation by the American Psychiatric Association (APA) in Appendix 1 of the fourth edition of the *Diagnostic and Statistical Manual of Mental Disorders*, (DSM-IV) (American Psychiatric Association, 1994; Lewis-Fernández, 2009) and the *Outline for cultural formulation* in the DSM-5 (American Psychiatric Association, 2013).

This part of the DSM-IV makes mention of another feature of cultural assessment, that of culture-bound syndromes (termed 'cultural concepts of distress' in the DSM-5) (Aggarwala, Nicasio, DeSilva, Boiler, & Lewis-Fernández, 2013). As mentioned above, these syndromes also speak to a local configuration of illness, but are more broadly related to the conceptualisation of an illness entity. On the contrary, the illness explanatory model is largely concerned with individual explanations of the manifestation of the disorder, and this may or may not be consistent with fixed illness entities (i.e. official disorders or local culture-bound syndromes). That is, there is an acknowledgement within formal diagnostic systems that, within each culture, people may carry their own explanations of illness, and these may not be influenced by their culture (Weiss & Somma, 2007, in Bhugrah & Bhui, 2007).

This progress notwithstanding, there is a persistent legacy of colonialism in contemporary psychopathology perspectives; this can be seen in the ongoing flirtation/preoccupation with exoticism (in the form of culture-bound syndromes), as well as with the reification and essentialisation of culture as reflecting individual traits, and the penchant for creating hierarchies between traditional and modern societies.

The existence of discrete national mental illness classification systems across countries (i.e. the DSM in the United States and a variety of national mental disorder categories in the ICD for other countries) reveals that the field is still in the era of 'national psychopathologies'. It is only when we can fashion a single international diagnostic schema (as in other disciplines), that we can truly say we have an international/universal science (or whatever we choose to call it). It is worth mentioning, though, that there is greater (and increasing) consensus between the two dominant systems than in the past. The benefits of integrating, relating, and accommodating diverse notions of mental illness in a globalising world and in multicultural societies should never be lost on us.

CONCLUSION

In South Africa, it is important that we embrace a more critical perspective on abnormal behaviour. This not only implies that students in psychology and psychiatry need to be trained from a more critical and culturally sensitive perspective, but also that society as a whole needs to be better educated in terms of what it could and should expect from these professions. In addition, citizens need to be educated about their rights in this regard, consistent with the international trend of involving users and user groups in decision-making and accountability.

Furthermore, there needs to be a more holistic understanding of patients. The lack of a whole-person way of understanding mental health problems originates in medical training that focuses on physical disorder. In particular, reductive causal analyses do not necessarily help us understand the full range of normal and abnormal human behaviour. To achieve this understanding, there needs to be less emphasis on a natural scientific perspective of basic biological processes.

Despite the many failings of a positivist approach to abnormal behaviour, its attraction is that it seems to avoid the complexities and uncertainties of psychological and social perspectives. This seduces students and clinicians alike with the idea that experimental natural science is an adequate discourse for a description of what is normal and abnormal; this may lead to their adopting a mechanistic view in their treatment of patients.

In South Africa, we also need to go a step further due to our culturally diverse society. Cultural beliefs and the traditional African way of living in South Africa are not well known to most mental health professionals, especially those socialised within Western culture. It is imperative that, when psychological interventions (any type of therapy, counselling, diagnosis, or psychological test) are conducted with indigenous African people the psychologist concerned is familiar with traditional African cultural beliefs and ways of living. In that way, the risk of misdiagnosis will be reduced, if not eliminated, and clients will be appropriately and ethically treated.

MULTIPLE-CHOICE QUESTIONS

1. The chemicals that allow transmission of signals between neurons are called:
   a) reuptake inhibitors
   b) hormones
   c) neurotransmitters
   d) genes
2. From a psychoanalytic perspective, psychopathology occurs when:
   a) conflict between the id, the ego, and the superego gives rise to distressing symptoms
   b) deficiencies in the ego hinder the individual's ability to repress instinctual drives
   c) instinctual drives take over the superego
   d) both a and c

3. You failed your last psychology test but you put this out of your mind while you study for your next test. Which defence mechanism are you using?
   a) reaction-formation
   b) denial
   c) projection
   d) repression

4. The goals of community psychology include the following:
   a) prevention (rather than just treatment) of mental illness
   b) understanding of people within their social worlds
   c) understanding psychopathology from within the context of community
   d) all of the above

5. Which of the following is NOT a myth about mental illness in non-Western countries?
   a) All mental disorders can be cured by indigenous healers.
   b) Mental illness is not recognised as pathological in non-Western communities.
   c) Mental illness is accepted in non-Western communities in an unstigmatised manner.
   d) Mental illness does not exist in non-Western countries.

6. Which of the following is a consequence of apartheid?
   a) The population of psychologists in South Africa is predominantly black, middle-class, and male.
   b) Psychologists serve predominantly black patients.
   c) The mental health needs of black South Africans and the disadvantaged community have been largely neglected.
   d) All of the above are consequences of apartheid.

7. Which of the following is incorrect in terms of the skills and knowledge required for multicultural assessment?
   a) ability to recognise cultural uniformity
   b) ability to help clients to understand, maintain, and resolve their own sociocultural identification
   c) understanding of the interactive effects of culture, gender, and sexual orientation on behaviour and needs
   d) none of the above

8. Ethnocentrism refers to:
   a) misjudging other people within from one's own cultural system
   b) judging other people from within their own cultural system
   c) judging other people from within one's own cultural system
   d) b and c

9. According to the African personality model, a rupture between the person and their ancestors leads to:
   a) organic illness
   b) a serious chronic psychotic state
   c) a mild psychotic state
   d) none of the above

10. The following is not considered an integrated approach to mental disorder:
    a) the cognitive-behavioural perspective
    b) the biopsychosocial model
    c) the diathesis-stress model
    d) the ecological systems theory

PARAGRAPH AND ESSAY QUESTIONS

1. What is serotonin, and what do we know about how it works?
2. Explain the importance of cultural awareness and sensitivity in therapy. Give practical examples.
3. Traditional beliefs and practices are still respected, especially in rural areas. Describe the causes of illness and their explanation according to the indigenous African aetiological explanation.
4. Critically explain and analyse the African personality theory, emphasising the importance of the firm connections between different levels.
5. Which religious traditions believe in the possibility of spirit possession, and how will this affect how a psychiatrist works with people who belong to these religions and religious traditions?
6. Analyse the challenges faced by mental health professionals in a multicultural and multilingual South Africa and give your own recommendation as to how they can better serve their clients in a diverse society.
7. Explain the ways in which sociopolitical factors can have an impact on our mental health, according to community psychologists.

2 DESCRIBING AND CLASSIFYING ABNORMAL BEHAVIOUR

Tracey-Lee Austin & Dan J. Stein

CHAPTER CONTENTS

Introduction
A brief history of psychopathology
Psychopathology in South Africa
Global perspectives
Critical perspectives
Contemporary classification of mental disorder
The *Diagnostic and Statistical Manual of Mental Disorders* (DSM)
The *International Classification of Diseases* (ICD)
Comparison and critique
Conclusion

LEARNING OUTCOMES

After studying this chapter, you should be able to:

- Explain how abnormal behaviour has been defined using the criteria of statistical deviance, maladaptiveness, and personal distress.
- Briefly review the history of psychopathology as it has evolved through a number of eras.
- Describe broader political and sociocultural factors that influence our perceptions of abnormality and normality.
- Describe the contemporary classification of mental disorders, particularly the use of the *Diagnostic and Statistical Manual of Mental Disorders* and the *International Classification of Diseases.*

PERSONAL HISTORY CASELET

Bulumko was only 18 when he was recruited by Umkhonto we Sizwe, as part of the struggle against against apartheid, and only 19 when he was captured and tortured by the security police. Although he suffered greatly, he believed fully in the cause, and when he was released from jail, he continued with his clandestine activities. He was overjoyed when Nelson Mandela was released from jail, and when freedom came to South Africa, and he celebrated his 26th birthday by voting in the first democratic elections. A few years later, he was working as a bank teller, and an armed robbery took place at his workplace. During the robbery he was threatened at gunpoint, and was convinced that he was going to die. For weeks afterwards, he had recurring images of the robbery, he felt unsafe, particularly at work, and he had trouble concentrating and sleeping. These symptoms were accompanied by a great deal of distress, and he was unable to do the work that he had long done so well. During this period, he also started having intrusive memories of the time when he had been tortured in jail. He decided to seek professional help, and he was diagnosed with posttraumatic stress disorder. He embarked on a course of psychotherapy, and was given a medication to assist him with his symptoms. Several weeks later, he felt much better; he had far fewer symptoms, and he was able to function effectively at work.

INTRODUCTION

It seems obvious: mental disorders are a crucially important focus of psychology because they are associated with so much distress and impairment, and because they contribute so much to the global burden of disease. However, it turns out that the question of how best to define and conceptualise mental disorders is far from resolved. Indeed, a discussion of mental disorders raises a range of deep conceptual questions.

Consider, for example, the contrasting views of Sigmund Freud, the Viennese father of psychoanalysis, and of Frantz Fanon, a Caribbean-born psychiatrist and philosopher who worked in Algeria. For Freud, unconscious conflict explained a great deal of behaviour, including a range of 'neurotic' behaviours, and these could be resolved by the 'talking therapy'. For Fanon, on the other hand, people with mental disorders were individuals who had become strangers to their environment, and so political action was called for (Gibson & Beneduce, 2017).

The case of Bulumko outlined above may also be viewed from a range of different perspectives. From a clinical perspective, his symptoms might well be consistent with the diagnosis of posttraumatic stress disorder. However, there is a range of other considerations; it is notable that this diagnosis did not begin during his first exposure to trauma, but rather after a subsequent trauma. A full understanding of trauma seems to require an appreciation of social and political context.

This chapter provides an introduction to the description and classification of mental disorders. We will consider some of the debates about definitions of these conditions, review some of the history of how the conditions have been conceptualised, and discuss contemporary approaches to nosology (the science of disease classification and description). We will contextualise nosological debates with some examples from South Africa.

Common terms in psychiatric nosology include *abnormal behaviour*, *psychopathology* and *psychological or mental disorders* (see Box 2.1 for some definitions of these terms). The description of choice may reflect the paradigm or epistemology of the person using it, reflecting stances on:

■ *How the person who 'suffers', or is 'diagnosed', with a disorder is viewed:* For example, use of the term *psychiatric disorder* may suggest that a *patient* is diagnosed with a disorder. In contrast, use of the term *psychological disorders*, may suggest that a *client* is coping with adverse life events in such a way that it causes distress for the client and those people directly involved with them. Similarly, the term *disease* emphasises the mechanisms that underlie symptoms, while the term *illness* emphasises the experience of symptoms.

> **NOTE**
> Although one preferred way of referring to a person who is a recipient of mental healthcare services is 'mental healthcare user', many practitioners, depending on their perspective, refer to such a person as either a patient or a client. These terms will be used interchangeably throughout this book.

- *The cause(s) of the disorder:* For example, in the case of *psychiatric disorders*, one may emphasise biopsychosocial factors, whereas in the case of *psychological disorders*, one may emphasise psychosocial factors. The term *mental disorder* is often used by both psychiatrists and psychologists, and proponents of this term may argue that it is neutral with respect to underlying aetiology.
- *Treatment:* In the case of *psychiatric disorders*, one may emphasise medical treatment (e.g. cognitive-behavioural psychotherapy, medication, ECT, etc.), whereas in the case of *psychological disorders*, one may emphasise psychological treatment (e.g. psychotherapy, marital therapy, family therapy, etc.). These kinds of contrasts are increasingly difficult to defend, however, given data that psychotherapy alters brain function, and that pharmacotherapy alters psychological function.

For the purposes of this book, we will take an integrative approach that recognises that a comprehensive appreciation of psychopathology requires an understanding of both mechanism (i.e. disease) and meaning (i.e. illness). In addition, an integrative approach accepts that discussion about mental disorder entails a consideration of both facts and values and appreciates that, while mental disorders are socially constructed (like all health conditions), they also are real entities that are underpinned by biological, psychological, and social structures and processes. We will mainly use the terms *psychopathology* and *mental disorders*.

BOX 2.1: DEFINITION OF TERMS

Abnormal behaviour	Any behaviour that deviates from social and statistical norms, and that is maladaptive and causes personal distress (Barlow & Durand, 2005).
Psychopathology	Derived from the words 'psyche', meaning mind or soul, and 'pathology', meaning disease or illness. In essence, then, the term may be understood as referring to the study of 'mind illnesses' or psychological disorders (Barlow & Durand, 2005).
Psychological or mental disorder	A psychological dysfunction within an individual that is associated with distress or impairment in functioning and a response to this which deviates from the person's culture (Barlow & Durand, 2005).

When making a decision about whether a person is suffering from a mental disorder, we first need to establish defining criteria that separate such disorders from normal behaviour. These criteria have been argued to include **statistical deviance**, **maladaptiveness** and **personal distress**.

- *Statistical deviance:* One of the ways in which psychopathology can be defined is by making use of statistical norms of behaviour and experience to determine what is 'normal'. Anything that falls far from the norm would be considered 'abnormal'

(Barlow & Durand, 2005). From this perspective, infrequently occurring behaviours, such as violence, public nudity, or hallucinations (such as hearing voices that do not exist) are seen as abnormal or as a sign of mental disorder.

One potential shortcoming of this definition, however, is that the norm, or what is considered 'normal' behaviour, will be influenced by our **cultural or social perspectives**. For example, the 'abnormal' behaviours just mentioned, namely, hearing voices and some forms of public nudity, may be considered normal in some African cultures and may be instrumental in giving cultural meaning to particular life events (Cartwright, 2008). Perhaps more relevant to criticising a reliance on statistical deviation are modern data demonstrating the extraordinarily high prevalence of mental disorders. This is not limited to mental health; many people have dental caries (i.e. they are extremely common), but tooth decay is nevertheless pathological.

Furthermore, just because a particular behaviour is considered to be 'normal', this does not necessarily mean that it is also healthy or socially appropriate. It has been suggested that entitlement and narcissism have increased in recent times; while these may be the norm in some segments of society, it is not clear that these are healthy or acceptable. In other words, abnormality and statistical deviance cannot always be equated, and the context in which the individual lives needs to be taken into consideration.

A more accurate way of understanding deviance may be to look at the extent to which cultural norms or ideological perspectives have been breached. However, even within a particular cultural context, equating deviance with abnormality is problematic because such a criterion does not distinguish between **positive and negative behaviours** that deviate from the norm. For example, deviations from the norm may be due to characteristics such as being a genius or some form of outstanding achievement. These could hardly be viewed as pathological (Cartwright, 2008). Similar considerations apply to deviations of physical traits.

Table 2.1: Some myths about mental illness

Myth	Fact
People with psychological disorders behave in odd or bizarre ways.	The behaviour of patients with mental disorders is most often indistinguishable from that of 'normal' people.
Mental patients are unpredictable and dangerous.	A typical patient with a mental disorder is no more dangerous than a 'normal' person.
Mental disorders are caused by fundamental mental deficiencies and are therefore shameful.	Everyone shares the potential for becoming disordered and behaving abnormally.
Abnormal and normal behaviour are qualitatively different.	Few abnormal behaviours are unique to patients with mental disorder. Abnormality usually occurs when there is a poor fit between behaviour and the situation in which it is enacted.

Source: Cartwright, 2016, p. 492.

- *Maladaptiveness:* Focusing on the degree to which certain behaviours or experiences are maladaptive to the self or others is another way of defining psychopathology. Behaviours that prevent the individual from adapting or adjusting for the good of the individual or group are defined as abnormal. This criterion is grounded in the belief that individuals need to evolve and adapt for the good of the self, as well as to ensure the survival of the individual and the broader community. Common indications of psychopathology such as fatigue, depression, and suicide would fit this criterion because they hinder the individual's personal growth and actualisation. Similarly, impairment in social, occupational, or family function may point to the presence of mental disorder.

  The criterion of maladaptiveness is, however, relative to the particular culture within which it is being examined; for example, in some African countries, there are certain rituals that could be considered to be strange or 'barbaric' to people from other countries. One such example would be trance states (see Chapter 10). Barlow and Durand (2005) quote an example of an East African woman, who heard voices and then killed a goat with her bare hands. If this behaviour is observed out of context, it would seem as if this person suffers from a mental disorder; however, seen within the cultural context, her actions form part of an important ritual. In the South African context, it is important to differentiate between *ukuthwasa* – the process of being summoned by the ancestors to be a healer – and mental illness.

  One of the main problems with the criteria of both maladaptiveness and statistical deviance is that they attempt to assess abnormality from a position outside the individual's own experience of the apparent problem. This has led many researchers to prefer the criterion of personal distress over the above-mentioned criteria when it comes to defining psychopathology (Cartwright, 2008). On the other hand, the person's perception may not be accurate; they may not be aware, for example, of how their symptoms are impairing them. You will notice that, where possible in this textbook, sections that describe cross-cultural variations of the disorders have been included in the chapters, in order to sensitise the reader to cultural variations in the presentation of disorders.

- *Personal distress:* Psychological disorders are very often accompanied by distress and suffering. In cases where anxiety and depression are the prominent symptoms, people often struggle with intolerable negative thoughts about themselves and their world (Cartwright, 2008). In these instances, it is appropriate that personal distress is considered when deciding what constitutes a mental disorder. However, there are exceptions; for example, people who suffer from personality disorders often do not show overt signs of distress.

  The absence of distress is, however, not limited to personality disorders. One could therefore conclude that distress alone is not sufficient to define abnormality. Furthermore, one must also keep in mind the fact that the presence of distress alone does not imply abnormality, as all people can and will experience distress at some stage of their lives. Distress is often a healthy response to adverse life situations (Barlow & Durand, 2005). Examples of normal distress are grief after the loss of a significant person in one's life, being a victim of a violent crime, or retrenchment.

From the above discussion, it is clear that distinguishing between normality and abnormality is not as easy as it first seems. This is an issue which has been, and still is, debated in psychology and other fields. A further complication in this debate is that cultures, societies, and communities are dynamic and that norms, values, and rituals change over time. What could once have been described as abnormal may be considered to be normal later. For instance, up until quite recently, homosexuality was a diagnosable mental disorder. It is only since 1973 that homosexuality has ceased to be regarded as a mental disorder; this because there was no clear link to be found between mental disorders, abnormality, and homosexuality (see Chapter 11). Such empirical data, as well as broader political and sociocultural forces, have been shown to have a significant impact on how we view mental disorders (Cartwright, 2008).

Current approaches to defining mental disorder often rely on a combination of the features mentioned above, highlighting the presence of distress and impairment (Stein et al., 2010). They also draw a distinction between the underlying dysfunction that is suggested (i.e. the mechanisms that produce symptoms), and the evidence of symptom severity or chronicity or ensuing distress or impairment that points to such underlying dysfunction (i.e. the expression and the experience of symptoms).

One influential account of the nature of mental disorder has proposed that mental disorders are characterised by harmful dysfunction. This view recognises that presence of disorder is more than just dysfunction; depending on the sociocultural context, such dysfunction may or may not be associated with distress and impairment. Similarly, current approaches often emphasise that the construct of mental disorder involves both assessment of facts and value judgements (as indicated by the term 'harmful'), and that it is important to have ongoing investigation of these facts and values in order to continue to advance nosology (Stein et al., 2010).

A related issue is the question of the specificity versus universality of mental disorders. A classical approach has argued that mental disorders have universal forms, and that only the content of symptoms differs from place to place and time to time. Thus schizophrenia is characterised by hallucinations (reflecting underlying universal biomedical processes in this disorder), but what the voices might say differs from culture to culture.

A more critical approach has argued that the expression and experience of mental disorders differs from place to place and time to time; psychiatric entities are socially constructed and culture bound (and symptoms have meaning within a particular context – they may be idioms of distress). We would suggest that an integrative position is again useful: a full appreciation of symptoms of mental disorders requires both a knowledge of underlying biopsychosocial structures and processes, as well as an understanding of the particular individual's circumstances and their psychosocial context; mental disorders involve both mechanism and meaning.

BOX 2.2: ATTITUDES TOWARDS PSYCHOLOGY, PSYCHIATRY AND MENTAL ILLNESS

Aim: Stones (1996) conducted a study to explore attitudes towards psychology, psychiatry, and mental illness.

Method: Stones (1996) used a self-report questionnaire survey. He conducted his study among a large sample of university students as well as among smaller groups of healthcare professionals, patients, and the general public.

Results: Some of the main findings of this study included the following:

- The extent of the individual's knowledge of mental illness, and the degree of contact with mental-health professionals, significantly influenced the person's perception of mental illness.
- Members of the public were found to be more optimistic about the efficacy of psychological treatment than psychologists.
- Although psychologists and other healthcare professionals were viewed positively, the general public still preferred to consult a friend rather than a psychologist in times of personal distress.

Conclusion: Attitudes towards mental illness and its treatment are influenced by knowledge and understanding of mental illness and its treatment.

A BRIEF HISTORY OF PSYCHOPATHOLOGY

Mental disorders have been, and sometimes still are, ascribed to supernatural causes. Mental illness is sometimes seen as a punishment for sins committed or as a form of demonic possession. However, this perspective has been repeatedly challenged, such as when, in 1584, the English politician Reginald Scot published *The Discovery of Witchcraft,* in which he contended that so-called possessions were medical illnesses and not visitations from evil spirits (Cartwright, 2008).

During this time in Europe, the institutionalisation of the mentally ill was on the increase. Yet asylums became well known for their inhumane treatment of mental patients, as these institutions were more like prisons than hospitals (Barlow & Durand, 2005). The treatment of these patients included restraining them for long periods of time, placing them in dark cells, and subjecting them to torture-like treatments.

However, in the late 1700s, these kinds of treatments were gradually challenged as humanitarian reforms emerged. In France, Philippe Pinel (1745–1826) put forward the idea that kindness and consideration towards mental patients (moral therapy) was necessary for their recovery (Barlow & Durand, 2005). Pinel argued that their chains should be removed and that, instead of being incarcerated in dungeons, they should be placed in sunny rooms, be permitted to do exercise, and partake in other constructive activities. Many patients were reported to have completely recovered from their mental illnesses once they were treated in a humane fashion. Gradually, trained nurses and other professionals were introduced to help in the treatment of patients with mental disorders.

Recent histories of mental illness have emphasised the contributions of non-Western cultures, and have also critiqued the way in which history often treats key role-players with excessive respect. Nevertheless, it is important to emphasise the significant advances that have occurred in our understanding and treatment of mental disorders over time. Contemporary perspectives emphasise the range of biopsychosocial risk and resilience factors (see Chapter 1) that contribute to the emergence and maintenance of mental disorders; these range from genetic factors through to social determinants.

Towards the end of the 1800s in Europe, there were many significant factors that emphasised biological risk factors for mental disorders. One key factor was the observation that syphilis (a sexually transmitted disease caused by bacteria infiltrating the brain) produces the same symptoms as a mental disorder, for example, delusions of persecution or grandeur (see Chapter 8), as well as other bizarre behaviours (Barlow & Durand, 2005).

This encouraged the search for other biological causes that might be associated with mental illness and formed the foundation of modern-day psychiatry. Many other developments, supported and encouraged by the American psychiatrist John P. Grey, occurred during this era, in an attempt to identify, understand, and treat different forms of psychopathology. In 1854, Grey maintained that mental disorders are always caused by physical factors; therefore, these patients should be treated as if they are physically ill (Barlow & Durand, 2005).

In 1883, the German psychiatrist Emil Kraepelin observed that certain symptoms occurred with specific types of mental disease. Based on this observation, he developed a classification system for a number of disorders, most notably *dementia praecox* (known today as schizophrenia, see Chapter 8) and manic-depressive psychosis (known today as bipolar disorder, see Chapter 7). Kraepelin's views about classification were revolutionary and served as a precursor to the *Diagnostic and Statistical Manual of Mental Disorders* that is currently used to make a diagnosis.

The scientific era has also been characterised by the development of many different psychological theories and treatments. Some of the theories that are used in the field of abnormal behaviour are quite complex, in different ways, and so cannot be fully outlined in this introductory chapter. However, we briefly note the relevance of psychoanalysis, community psychology, and cognitive-behavioural theories of psychopathology and its treatment.

In the late 1800s, Freud developed a theory, named psychoanalysis, which attempted to explain almost all areas of the human psyche. One aspect of his theory also attempted to explain how mental disorders develop. At the basis of this explanation is Freud's understanding of the structure of personality (i.e. the id, ego, and superego), as well as defence mechanisms (Barlow & Durand, 2005). According to Freud, unconscious conflict, as well as over-reliance on certain defence mechanisms, gives rise to different forms of disorders.

Figure 2.1: Sigmund Freud

A more politically aware perspective of mental disorders was introduced by Frantz Fanon in the mid-1900s. A Caribbean-born psychiatrist working in the French colonies in North Africa, Fanon was critical of colonial psychiatry and focused on enabling patients to use 'authentic speech by re-establishing an environment that allows each subject to take up again the traces of real or psychical events' (Cherki, 2017, p. xi). To

do this, Fanon, together with Charles Géronimi, established a psychiatric day hospital in Tunis that was attached to Charles-Nicolle General Hospital. In line with his idea that 'care for madness requires a returning of freedom to the mad' (Gibson & Beneduce, 2017, p. 13), the patients at this hospital were free to come and go. This allowed 'the possibility that the caregiver-patient relationship could be an encounter of two freedoms' and that no 'rupture with the day-to-day environment was involved' (Cherki, 2017, p. xi). Community psychology has continued to emphasise the importance of providing services where people live, and of a focus on recovery.

Figure 2.2: Frantz Fanon

Another important school of thought in the field of abnormal behaviour is behaviourism, which gained prominence in the 1950s. The theoretical roots of this school of thought can be traced back to theorists such as the Russian physiologist Ivan Pavlov (1890) and the American psychologist John Watson (1878–1958), who was of the opinion that psychology should follow more stringent scientific research methods, such as those used by the natural sciences (Barlow & Durand, 2005). This opinion differed from psychoanalysis and its claims that psychopathology had its genesis in psychological conflict caused by instinctual drives (Cartwright, 2008).

Influential theorists such as the American psychologist B. F. Skinner (operant conditioning) and the South African psychiatrist Joseph Wolpe (systematic desensitisation) built on Watson's initial theory. These behaviourists believed that psychopathology could be better understood by the observation of how abnormal behaviour is learned and reinforced by the external environment (Cartwright, 2008; Rachman, 2000).

Numerous other forms of psychological treatments have emerged in the past 50 years, many of them claiming to have a better understanding of the human condition and abnormal behaviour. Existential psychotherapy, logotherapy, gestalt psychotherapy, and cognitive-behaviour therapy are but a few of the treatments developed in this era (Cartwright, 2008).

Over the years, there has been a great deal of conflict about which treatments are more effective, and this has often led to some treatments being favoured over others, without a clear reason being given. Often, the choice of treatment method simply depends on the therapist's chosen theoretical orientation, rather than on the evidence base. There is increasing effort aimed at determining the common factors across different psychotherapies that determine treatment outcome, and at expanding and consolidating the evidence base (Cartwright, 2008).

The introduction of psychotropic (mood-altering) drugs in the 1950s has also been heralded as an important landmark in the history of mental disorder. Drugs such as lithium, chlorpromazine, and imipramine were hailed as miracle drugs because, for the first time, symptoms associated with mania, psychosis, and depression could be controlled through the use of medication. This made it possible for many patients to be discharged from, or altogether avoid admission to, psychiatric institutions. Many patients were able to maintain normal productive lives under continuing medication.

In this way, psychopharmacological treatment was able to provide a cost-effective way of managing patients without having to resort to lengthy stays in psychiatric hospitals (Cartwright, 2008). There is ongoing debate about the possible over-medicalisation of behavioural conditions. However, particularly in low- and middle-income countries, where the majority of the world's population lives, the evidence shows that there is under-diagnosis and under-treatment of mental disorders.

Psychopathology in South Africa

Psychology was first established as a formal academic discipline in South Africa during the 1920s, which was a time of class ordering, labour problems, and racial oppression (Foster, 1993). It suited those in power to adopt the dominant social scientific discourse of the time, which was one of racial differences and racial inferiority (Gould, 1981), an idea reinforced by the fact that the psychometric tests being used in South Africa were designed mainly for the white population. These culturally biased tests were used to endorse racial oppression, ill-treatment, substandard education, misdiagnosis, exclusion from various services and opportunities, and neglect. For example, a study conducted by Freeman (1992) found that black patients were more likely to be diagnosed with a psychotic disorder such as schizophrenia, whereas white patients were more likely to be diagnosed with a mood disorder (see Chapter 1 for more on this).

Colonial psychiatry saw itself as drawing on European principles of humaneness; for example, early psychiatric hospitals in South Africa aimed to provide patients with a caring environment. However, such hospitals were racially segregated, and amenities for black patients were significantly inferior. The rationale for differential treatment of psychiatric patients based on race was based on arguments in anthropology, psychiatry, and psychology; none of these arguments are, however, are based on good evidence (Burke, 2010; Szasz, 1974). Human rights violations and health disparities were an important focus of the Truth and Reconciliation Commission in South Africa, and a commitment to equitable mental health services remains an important goal of mental advocates in South Africa.

The above-mentioned structural conditions of the past, particularly the racial discrimination propounded by the apartheid-era governments, continue to underlie health disparities in South Africa, including in mental health. South Africa is unfortunately still contending with the legacy left by the colonial and apartheid eras, while at the same time having to deal with newer public health threats such as the human immunodeficiency virus (HIV) and acquired immunodeficiency syndrome (Aids) epidemic, and the growing burden of disease from chronic non-communicable diseases. Although research on mental disorders in South Africa has long been underfunded, after the establishment of democracy in the country, a range of work has been funded, including the first nationally representative epidemiological survey of mental disorders in Africa, and development of locally relevant psychometric measures, as well as study of a range of psychotherapeutic interventions.

Global perspectives

There are other views and histories of psychopathology that differ from the dominant Western approach (see Chapter 1). In China and India, for example, there are traditions of healing that do not share the Western tradition of trying to separate physical from mental illnesses. In southern Africa, alongside the biomedical or Western perspective of psychopathology, there are other important traditions. Indigenous theories of illness, including theories of psychopathology, commonly see personal problems as being caused by difficulties in social relationships. These relationships may be both with living people and with ancestors or shades, who continue to play an important part in social life even after death. Religious healing is also very common in southern Africa, and some churches, most notably the Zionist Church, practise a form of religion that combines indigenous beliefs with Christianity, often in charismatic forms (Cartwright, 2008).

In addition to psychologists and psychiatrists (of whom there are relatively few on the African continent), people in southern Africa may consult an *isangoma* or *igqira* (indigenous healers), *inyanga* or *ixhwele* (herbalists), or *umprofethi* (prophet in the Zionist church). Different frameworks lead to a range of explanatory models of mental disorder. Importantly, people may hold multiple coexistent explanatory models, seeing mental disorders at times as caused by genetics, and at other times as caused by ancestors. Such complexity is not limited to any particular population group; other South African groups may, for example vacillate between using allopathic, homeopathic, and spiritual explanations.

The question of whether different forms of interventions are effective, and of how and whether practitioners from different healing traditions can and should work together, is an interesting and complex one. Cross-cultural psychiatrists such as Lewis-Fernández and Kleinman (1995) have argued that psychopathological investigations need to consider the social world in their research paradigms if we are to better understand the sources and consequences of mental disorders.

With the emergence of the discipline of global mental health, there has been increased attention to social determinants of mental disorder, and to developing feasible and acceptable interventions in low- and middle-income countries. Such interventions need to consider an individual's context and perspective, including explanatory models (Cartwright, 2008). This is relevant in the South African context, given the important role that culturally derived understandings of mental disorder may play in the expression and experience of mental disorders, and in the negotiation of a treatment plan. You will see that, in chapters on different disorders in this volume, a South African perspective has been included in order to develop a better understanding of the manifestation of these disorders in different cultures.

Critical perspectives

A discussion of mental disorders needs to include the view of those who are critical of this construct, arguing that 'mental disorders' are socially constructed entities or that 'treatment' is a form of social control. This kind of argument gained particular traction during the 1960s, when a range of criticisms of the 'establishment' were formulated. The term 'anti-psychiatry' was introduced by the South African-born psychiatrist David Cooper (1967). Some in the anti-psychiatry movement argued that the construct 'illness' (in its broadest sense) refers to abnormalities in physical functioning and therefore cannot be applied to a psychological disorder that has no evidence of physical pathology.

Proponents of this movement have further argued that doctors tend to view the mentally ill as blameless victims of brain diseases, and that they uncritically accept the idea of physiological bases for mental illness, ignoring important social determinants. Some in this movement argue that this view has led to the inhumane treatment of patients as though they are objects (Johnstone, 2000). This opposition to the standard view of mental disorders may lead to an anti-authoritarian position that argues against the use of psychiatric diagnosis, drug treatments, electroconvulsive treatments, and involuntary hospitalisation.

This early form of anti-psychiatry lost its momentum for a number of reasons. First, some of its main proponents were ultimately more interested in personal authenticity than in carrying through their ideas in clinical practice. Second, there were many different and often opposing views within the movement, as is illustrated by the disagreement between the Hungarian-American psychiatrist Thomas Szasz and the Scottish psychiatrist R. D. Laing, who were both proponents of the anti-psychiatry movement. For example, Szasz (1976) was quite scathing in his censure of Laing, as Laing never denied the reality of mental turmoil, merely contending that so-called mental illness was more understandable than is generally assumed. Szasz (1976), however, was unrelenting in his stance. He stated, for example, that '[it] places psychiatry in the company of alchemy and astrology and commits it to the category of pseudoscience. The reason for this is that there is no such thing as "mental illness"' (Szasz, 1974, p. 1).

Nevertheless, much of this debate continues in different forms in the 2000s. Even though the discipline of global mental health builds on work in cross-cultural and community psychiatry, and though it emphasises social determinants, human rights, and the importance of adapting interventions to suit the local context, it has been criticised for exporting Western constructs of mental disorder to the rest of the world.

Some of the critique may be useful in that it encourages a focus on both disease mechanisms and on illness meanings, as well as on how mental disorders have components that are both universal and contextually bound. Furthermore, it encourages researchers and practitioners to consistently reflect on whether their own perspectives carry cultural bias or further health inequities. However, some criticisms of psychiatric disorders, such as those of Scientology (and the allied Citizens Commission on Mental Health Rights) seem to be conceptually incoherent, with no supporting empirical evidence, and they inappropriately ignore the universal aspects of mental disorders and the very real suffering that they bring.

CONTEMPORARY CLASSIFICATION OF MENTAL DISORDER

By now it should be clear that the study of abnormal behaviour is not as simple as it may have seemed to begin with. From the definition of abnormal behaviour, as well as from the history of mental illness, it can be seen that there have been many controversies and debates. These controversies and debates have also found their way into the classification of different disorders. It is a typical human characteristic to try to create order out of chaos by classifying observations into categories. This is also a characteristic that underlies science. In line with this, and also in an attempt to make the field of psychopathology more scientific, there have been attempts to classify the different disorders according to their observable characteristic signs and subjectively reported symptoms.

As with many other domains in the study of abnormal behaviour, there are both major and more subtle disagreements in terms of the classification of disorders. This is exemplified in some of the differences in the two main classifications of disorders in current use.

The *International Classification of Diseases* (ICD) is produced and published by the World Health Organization (WHO); includes a section on mental, behavioural, and neurodevelopmental disorders; is aimed at primary care practitioners; and is mandated for use worldwide. A draft version of the eleventh edition (ICD-11) has recently been released.

The *Diagnostic and Statistical Manual of Mental Disorders* (DSM), produced and published by the American Psychiatric Association (APA), is solely focused on mental disorders, is widely used by psychiatrists, and has been particularly important in research. It is currently in its fifth edition (DSM-5, published in 2013).

The intention of diagnostic manuals is to develop reliable and clinically useful categories and criteria, and to optimise healthcare and health statistics. DSM-III was particularly important because it established diagnostic criteria for mental disorders; this then gave impetus to a great deal of research, including work in psychiatric epidemiology. Importantly, DSM-III aimed to be neutral with regard to aetiology; the DSM gradually moved away from psychoanalytically informed terms such as 'neurosis', replacing them with descriptive terms.

Both the DSM-5 and ICD-11 do, however, acknowledge aetiology to some extent – for example, using shared aetiology (such as exposure to trauma) as a criterion for categorising disorders. Chapter V of the ICD-10, the Classification of Mental or Behavioural Disorders, 'is intended for general clinical, educational and service use' (World Health Organization, 1992, p. 1). The DSM-5 (American Psychiatric Association, 2013, p. xli) is more specific, indicating that 'this edition of DSM-5 was designed first and foremost to be a useful guide to clinical practice'. This includes:

- providing a means by which the profession **communicates** briefly and clearly within itself (and with other professionals) about clinically recognisable conditions for which it has professional responsibility for diagnosis, care, or research
- facilitating the objective assessment of the presentation of symptoms in a wide variety of clinical settings
- outlining information about the likely **outcome** (prognosis) of psychiatric disorders with and without treatment
- summarising what is known of **aetiology** (causes) or patho-physiological processes
- providing a structured way in which to understand and diagnose mental disorders.

Despite the stated intentions of the DSM-III and DSM-IV, they were not as atheoretical and problem-free as was envisaged. Thus, for example:

- DSM diagnostic categories can be considered to be based on particular psychiatric theories and data, and the systems are therefore not simply theory-neutral descriptions.
- The borders between DSM diagnostic categories and normality can be fuzzy, and particular diagnostic entities can often be specified by numerous possible combinations of symptoms (so they are heterogenous).

- Many of the DSM categories overlap in symptomatology or occur together, so that patients may often be diagnosed with a number of comorbid disorders (which may be the result of the system).

DSM and ICD diagnoses are widely used by clinicians, researchers, administrators, and medical aid providers in many countries. We will describe the development of each in some more detail.

The *Diagnostic and Statistical Manual of Mental Disorders* (DSM)

Background and history

As the fields of psychiatry and psychology developed, the need arose for a more systematic way of classifying and diagnosing disorders. In 1952, the APA published the first *Diagnostic and Statistical Manual of Mental Disorders* (DSM-I). Since then, the system has been regularly updated. DSM-II was relatively short, consisting of only 119 pages. However, this changed with DSM-III, which was 494 pages long and included 265 sub-categories of disorder. DSM-III (American Psychiatric Association, 1980), led by Robert Spitzer, was particularly important because it provided diagnostic criteria for each disorder. DSM-IV took a very similar approach, but updates were based on reviews of the literature and the emergent evidence base.

As described above, it is notable that, with DSM-III, there was a movement away from psychoanalytically informed terms such as 'neurosis', and towards more descriptive terms such as 'anxiety disorders'. DSM-III claimed to be neutral with regard to aetiology, but for some the rationale for the classification system was based on biological findings (e.g. panic disorder and generalised anxiety disorder were separated out, based on supposed differences in response to pharmacotherapy). This shift coincided with shifts in academic psychiatry in the United States in the late 1970s and early 1980s. Prior to that time, psychiatric thinking and treatment were heavily informed by psychoanalysis; DSM-III was influenced by and gave impetus to a shift to a more neuroscientifically informed psychiatry.

The focus on diagnostic reliability in DSM-III was in response to a number of issues. First, there was evidence that diagnostic practices differed significantly between the United States and the United Kingdom; for example, in the United States, there was a much lower threshold for the diagnosis of schizophrenia. Second, there was a need to counter criticism of psychiatry as non-scientific, by both the anti-psychiatry movement of the 1960s and researchers who wanted to develop a scientific foundation for psychiatry (see Box 2.3). DSM-III and DSM-IV largely succeeded in this aim: the manual was quickly adopted around the world, clinicians used it to diagnose their patients in a uniform way, educators used it to teach about diagnosis, and researchers used it for many purposes, including treatment trials (limited, for example, to those who met DSM criteria for a particular condition) and epidemiological studies (with questionnaires closely based on DSM symptoms). These are important contributions.

Table 2.2: Overview of development of the DSM classification system

Year	Revision	Underlying paradigm
1952	The APA published the first edition of the DSM (DSM-I), replacing the collection of diagnoses endorsed by the APA in 1933	■ DSM-I was heavily influenced by: 　▸ psychoanalytic theory 　▸ Adolf Meyer's emphasis on individual failures of adaptation to biological or psychosocial stresses as the cause of psychiatric illness. ■ The diagnoses enumerated in DSM-I indicate a major enlargement in the ways in which a psychotic illness could be experienced and named.
1968	DSM-II	■ The proportion of psychiatrists following psychodynamic tenets rose to one-third by the late 1950s, and to half by the early 1970s. ■ Psychoanalysis and psychodynamics dominated the curriculum of medical schools and residency programmes, as well as the orientation of many academic departments, through the mid-1960s. ■ Like DSM-I, DSM-II presented a psychosocial view of psychiatric illness. ■ Psychiatric illnesses were reactions to stresses of everyday living, not discrete disease entities that could easily be demarcated from one another or even from normal behaviour or experience. ■ From this perspective, naming a disease was of much less significance than understanding the underlying psychic conflicts and reactions that gave rise to symptoms.
1980	DSM-III	■ Reflected American psychiatry's embrace of a biomedical model of disease, complete with discrete illness categories that were distinct both from one another and from that which qualified as 'normal'. ■ The whole of medicine had experienced a cultural shift, one that was characterised by: 　▸ reliance on standardised knowledge rather than clinical expertise 　▸ statistical knowledge based on groups rather than individuals 　▸ an increasing knowledge of the biological basis of disease, including the psychobiology of mental disorders. ■ The diagnostic manual that grew out of this transition from psychodynamics to biopsychiatry was explicitly 'atheoretical' with regard to aetiology, but most of the diagnostic categories enumerated in the DSM-III were arguably underpinned by an implicit assumption that biology and not psychological conflict was their primary cause.

Year	Revision	Underlying paradigm
1994	DSM-IV	■ DSM-IV built upon the research generated by the empirical orientation of DSM-III. By the early 1990s, most psychiatric diagnoses had an accumulated body of published studies or data sets. ■ Publications until the end of 1992 were reviewed for DSM-IV, which was published in 1994. ■ Conflicting reports or lack of evidence were addressed by literature reviews, data re-analyses and field trials. ■ The National Institute of Mental Health sponsored 12 DSM-IV field trials together with the National Institute on Drug Abuse (NIDA) and the National Institute on Alcohol Abuse and Alcoholism (NIAAA). ■ The field trials compared the diagnostic criteria sets of DSM-III, DSM-III-R, ICD-10 (which had been published in 1992), and the proposed criteria sets for DSM-IV. ■ The field trials recruited subjects from a variety of ethnic and cultural backgrounds, in keeping with a concern for cross-cultural applicability of diagnostic standards. ■ In addition to its inclusion of culture-specific syndromes and disorders, DSM-IV represented much closer cooperation and coordination with the experts from WHO who had worked on ICD-10.
2000	DSM-IV-TR	■ DSM-IV-TR did not represent either a fundamental change in the basic classification structure of DSM-IV or the addition of new diagnostic entities. ■ The textual revisions that were made to the 1994 edition of DSM-IV fall into the following categories: ▸ correction of factual errors in the text of DSM-IV. ▸ review of currency of information in DSM-IV. ▸ changes reflecting research published after 1992, which was the last year included in the literature review prior to the publication of DSM-IV. ▸ improvements to enhance the educational value of DSM-IV. ▸ updating of ICD diagnostic codes, some of which were changed in 1996.
2013	DSM-5	■ Reordering of disorders into a revised organisational structure. ■ Increased representation of developmental, gender, and cultural issues related to diagnosis. ■ Attempted to integrate the latest scientific findings in genetics and neuro-imaging. ■ Rigorous process of scientifically reviewing proposed changes to the nosology. ■ Employed a broad consultative process.

Source: Adapted from https://www.encyclopedia.com/history/dictionaries-thesauruses-pictures-and-press-releases/psychology-and-psychiatry

At the same time, the DSM-III and DSM-IV received significant criticism. First, some argued that, by reducing diagnosis to 'checkbox menus' and so a 'cookbook approach', clinicians overlooked the specific details and circumstances of each patient. This criticism is not entirely fair, as DSM does not aim to replace comprehensive assessment and evaluation, only to provide reliable diagnostic criteria. Second, when DSM is used, it is common for individuals to have significant comorbidity, arguably suggesting that this this is an artefact of a suboptimal system. Nevertheless, comorbidity may simply reflect the complexity of clinical reality. Third, it has been argued that the DSM system, which entails multiple heterogenous disorders, does not reflect psychobiological realities, which are often dimensional in nature: a symptom like insomnia is found in a range of categorical diagnoses (e.g. depression, posttraumatic stress disorder), and it is more likely, for example, that severe insomnia has a specific psychobiology than, say, depression. Still, while it is true that DSM-defined depression can vary in character, it is not clear that the psychobiology of insomnia is necessarily simple or unidimensional.

Over time, perhaps the largest perceived limitation of the DSM was that it was not sufficiently consistent with a neuroscientific approach to psychiatry; diagnosis did not rely on biomarkers, did not reflect growing understanding of the neurobiological aetiology of mental disorders, was not sufficiently dimensional, and did not sufficiently predict response to pharmacological intervention. The DSM-5 explicitly aimed to incorporate neuroscientific findings into the nosology, with the hope that new research on the aetiology of mental disorders would lead to more valid categories and criteria. Thus, for example, the new chapter on obsessive-compulsive and related disorders builds on research indicating that the disorders in this chapter have overlapping phenomenology and psychobiology, and fall on a spectrum of conditions. However, it turned out that this goal was overambitious; the DSM-5 does not represent an entirely new approach, but rather is best viewed as an incremental iteration, incorporating a range of new evidence.

A number of specific incremental advances in the DSM-5 are worth pointing out. First, all changes from DSM-IV to DSM-5 were thoroughly reviewed, and had to be justified with reference to the evidence base in general, and with respect to whether they advanced diagnostic validity in particular. A range of systematic reviews and empirical research was specifically undertaken as part of the revision process. Second, committee members came from different professions and countries, and there was broad consultation during the revision process, including with ICD-11 leaders and with mental health users.

Third, a range of subtle changes were made to reflect biological realities. For example, DSM-5 is organised on developmental and lifespan considerations, beginning with disorders that first manifest in early childhood, followed by disorders that manifest in adolescence and early adulthood, and ending with disorders relevant to adulthood and later life (American Psychiatric Association, 2013). Fourth, the manual carefully attempts to delineate the way in which gender and culture impact on diagnosis. DSM-5 includes, for example, a cultural formulation interview (CFI) that operationalises the process of data collection to make a cultural formulation. Like other changes in DSM-5, the CFI is evidence-based, incorporating a great deal of cross-cultural research (see Table 2.3).

Despite many criticisms levelled at the DSM classification system, many practitioners, educators, and researchers find this classification system useful. Given the large audience for this system, as well as the wide variety of paradigms and epistemologies that are supported by different people in this audience, it is unlikely that a single approach will satisfy everybody's opinions. Furthermore, the DSM is not a static system, as there is a constant process of trying to improve it. The DSM-5 is testimony to this constant attempt to improve the system, as well as of the ongoing debate and critique that suggestions for change produce.

Table 2.3: DSM-5 Cultural Formulation Interview (CFI)

Supplementary modules used to expand each CFI subtopic are noted in parentheses.	
GUIDE TO INTERVIEWER	**INSTRUCTIONS TO THE INTERVIEWER ARE ITALICISED**
The following questions aim to clarify key aspects of the presenting a clinical problem from the point of view of the individual and other members of the individual's social network (i.e. family, friends, or others involved in current problem). This includes the problem's meaning, potential sources of help, and expectations for services.	*INTRODUCTION FOR THE INDIVIDUAL:* I would like to understand the problems that bring you here so that I can help you more effectively. I want to know about *your* experience and ideas. I will ask some questions about what is going on and how you are dealing with it. Please remember there are no right or wrong answers.
CULTURAL DEFINITION OF THE PROBLEM	
CULTURAL DEFINITION OF THE PROBLEM (Explanatory Model, Level of Functioning)	
Elicit the individual's view of core problems and key concerns. *Focus on the individual's own way of understanding the problem.* *Use the term, expression, or brief description elicited in question 1 to identify the problem in subsequent questions (e.g., 'your conflict with your son').*	1. What brings you here today? *IF INDIVIDUAL GIVES FEW DETAILS OR ONLY MENTIONS SYMPTOMS OR A MEDICAL DIAGNOSIS, PROBE:* People often understand their problems in their own way, which may be similar to or different from how doctors describe the problem. How would you describe your problem?
Ask how the individual frames the problem for members of the social network.	2. Sometimes people have different ways of describing their problem to their family, friends, or others in their community. How would you describe your problem to them?
Focus on the aspects of the problem that matter most to the individual.	3. What troubles you most about your problem?
CULTURAL PERCEPTIONS OF CAUSE, CONTEXT, AND SUPPORT	
CAUSES (Explanatory Model, Social Network, Older Adults)	
This question indicates the meaning of the condition for the individual, which may be relevant for clinical care.	4. Why do you think this is happening to you? What do you think are the causes of your [PROBLEM]?

Note that individuals may identify multiple causes, depending on the facet of the problem they are considering.	PROMPT FURTHER IF REQUIRED: Some people may explain their problem as the result of bad things that happen in their life, problems with others, a physical illness, a spiritual reason, or many other causes.
Focus on the views of members of the individual's social network. These may be diverse and vary from the individual's.	5. What do others in your family, your friends, or others in your community think is causing your [PROBLEM]?

STRESSORS AND SUPPORTS (Social Network, Caregivers, Psychosocial Stressors, Religion and Spirituality, Immigrants and Refugees, Cultural Identity, Older Adults, Coping, and Help Seeking)	
Elicit information on the individual's life context, focusing on resources, social supports, and resilience. May also probe other supports (e.g. from co-workers, from participation in religion or spirituality).	6. Are there any kinds of support that make your [PROBLEM] better, such as support from family, friends, or others?
Focus on stressful aspects of the individual's environment. Can also probe, e.g., relationship problems, difficulties at work or school, or discrimination.	7. Are there any kinds of stresses that make your [PROBLEM] worse, such as difficulties with money, or family problems?

ROLE OF CULTURAL IDENTITY (Cultural Identity, Psychosocial Stressors, Religion and Spirituality, Immigrants and Refugees, Older Adults, Children, and Adolescents)	
	Sometimes, aspects of people's background or identity can make their [PROBLEM] better or worse. By *background* or *identity*, I mean, for example, the communities you belong to, the languages you speak, where you or your family are from, your race or ethnic background, your gender or sexual orientation, or your faith or religion.
Ask the individual to reflect on the most salient elements of his or her cultural identity. Use this information to tailor questions 9–10 as needed.	8. For you, what are the most important aspects of your background or identity?
Elicit aspects of identity that make the problem better or worse. Probe as needed (e.g. clinical worsening as a result of discrimination due to migration status, race/ethnicity, or sexual orientation).	9. Are there any aspects of your background or identity that make a difference to your [PROBLEM]?
Probe as needed (e.g. migration-related problems; conflict across generations or due to gender roles).	10. Are there any aspects of your background or identity that are causing other concerns or difficulties for you?

CULTURAL FACTORS AFFECTING SELF-COPING AND PAST HELP SEEKING

SELF-COPING
(Coping and Help Seeking, Religion and Spirituality, Older Adults, Caregivers, Psychosocial Stressors)

Clarify self-coping for the problem.	11. Sometimes people have various ways of dealing with problems like [PROBLEM]. What have you done on your own to cope with your [PROBLEM]?

PAST HELP SEEKING
(Coping and Help Seeking, Religion and Spirituality, Older Adults, Caregivers, Psychosocial Stressors, Immigrants and Refugees, Social Network, Clinician-Patient Relationship)

Elicit various sources of help (e.g. medical care, mental health treatment, support groups, work-based counselling, folk healing, religious or spiritual counselling, other forms of traditional or alternative healing). *Probe as needed (e.g. 'What other sources of help have you used?').* *Clarify the individual's experience and regard for previous help.*	12. Often, people look for help from many different sources, including different kinds of doctors, helpers, or healers. In the past, what kinds of treatment, help, advice, or healing have you sought for your [PROBLEM]? *PROBE IF DOES NOT DESCRIBE USEFULNESS OF HELP RECEIVED:* What types of help or treatment were most useful? Not useful?

BARRIERS
(Coping and Help Seeking, Religion and Spirituality, Older Adults, Psychosocial Stressors, Immigrants and Refugees, Social Network, Clinician–Patient Relationship)

Clarify the role of social barriers to help seeking, access to care, and problems engaging in previous treatment. *Probe details as needed (e.g. 'What got in the way?').*	13. Has anything prevented you from getting the help you need? *PROBE AS NEEDED:* For example, money, work or family commitments, stigma or discrimination, or lack of services that understand your language or background?

CULTURAL FACTORS AFFECTING CURRENT HELP SEEKING

PREFERENCES
(Social Network, Caregivers, Religion and Spirituality, Older Adults, Coping and Help Seeking)

Clarify individual's current perceived needs and expectations of help, broadly defined. *Probe if individual lists only one source of help (e.g., 'What other kinds of help would be useful to you at this time?').*	Now let's talk some more about the help you need. 14. What kinds of help do you think would be most useful to you at this time for your [PROBLEM]?

Focus on the views of the social network regarding help seeking.	15. Are there other kinds of help that your family, friends, or other people have suggested would be helpful for you now?
CLINICIAN–PATIENT RELATIONSHIP **(Clinician–Patient Relationship, Older Adults)**	
Elicit possible concerns about the clinic or the clinician–patient relationship, including perceived racism, language barriers, or cultural differences that may undermine goodwill, communication, or care delivery. *Probe details as needed (e.g. 'In what way?').* *Address possible barriers to care or concerns about the clinic and the clinician–patient relationship raised previously.*	Sometimes doctors and patients misunderstand each other because they come from different backgrounds or have different expectations. 16. Have you been concerned about this and is there anything that we can do to provide you with the care you need?

Source: *Diagnostic and Statistical Manual of Mental Disorders,* fifth edition (DSM-5), 2013, https://www.psychiatry.org/File%20Library/Psychiatrists/Practice/DSM/APA_DSM5_Cultural-Formulation-Interview.pdf.

BOX 2.3: ON BEING SANE IN INSANE PLACES

Aim: Rosenhan (1973) conducted a famous study that attempted to explore the validity of psychiatric diagnoses.

Method: A form of participant observation was used in the study whereby eight psychologically healthy individuals were admitted to different psychiatric units after claiming to have been 'hearing voices'. These individuals were instructed by the researcher as to how they should act and what they should say (i.e. they were the research confederates in the study). No other symptoms or problems were discussed with the hospital staff. After gaining admission, all subjects acted their normal selves and no longer claimed to be hearing voices.

Findings: Once the admission to the hospital had taken place, Rosenhan found that, no matter what these individuals did, they were perceived as being psychologically ill by the staff in the hospital.

Conclusion: The validity of making a psychiatric diagnosis is questionable as the staff in the hospital failed to distinguish between healthy individuals and those who were genuinely mentally ill.

Source: Rosenhan, 1973.

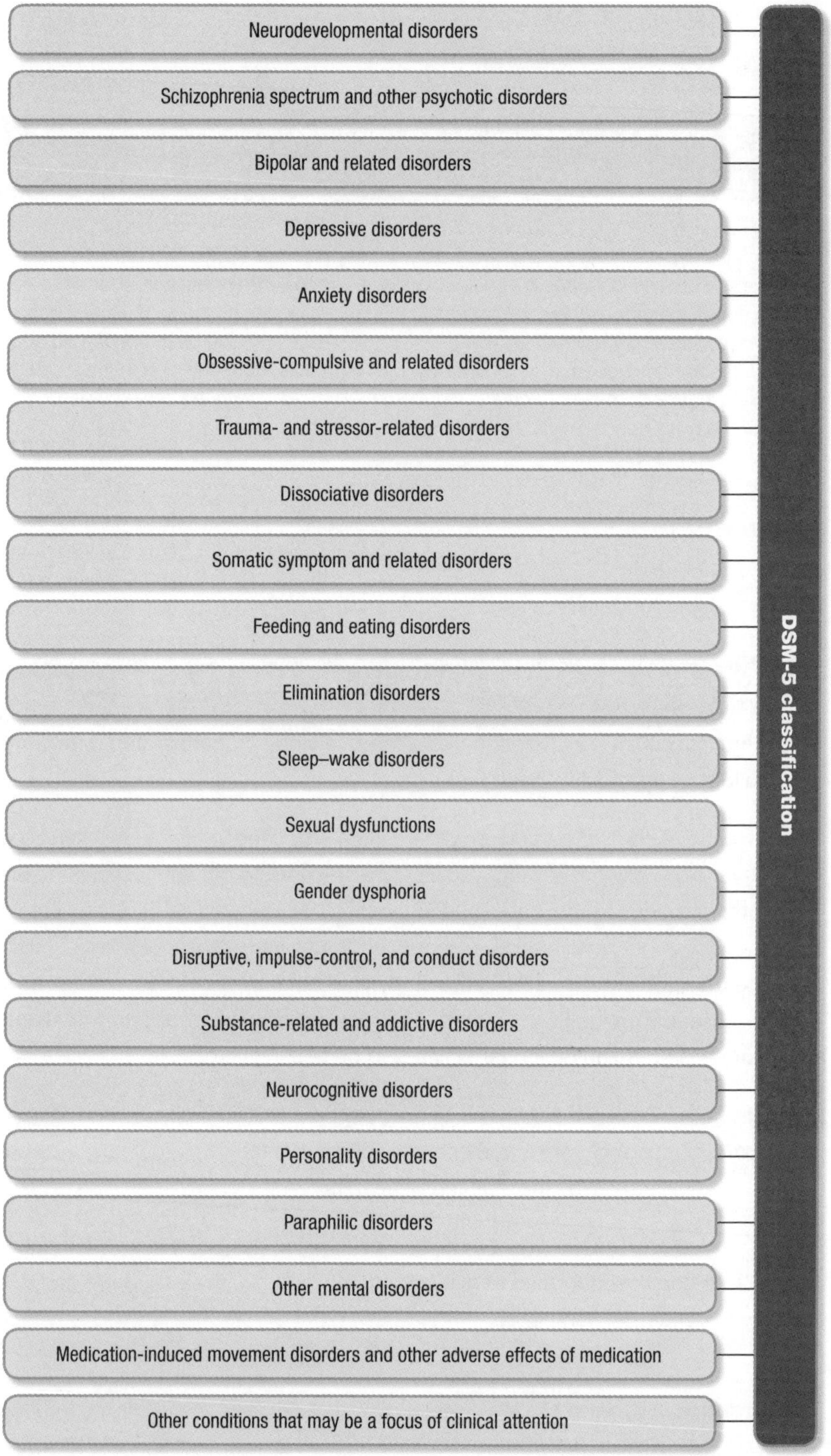

Figure 2.3: The American Psychiatric Association DSM-5 categorises mental disorders as shown above.

Source: Figure created by OUP reflecting information found in *Diagnostic and Statistical Manual of Mental Disorders*, fifth edition (DSM-5), 2013.

DSM-5 classification

- Neurodevelopmental disorders
- Schizophrenia spectrum and other psychotic disorders
- Bipolar and related disorders
- Depressive disorders
- Anxiety disorders
- Obsessive-compulsive and related disorders
- Trauma- and stressor-related disorders
- Dissociative disorders
- Somatic symptom and related disorders
- Feeding and eating disorders
- Elimination disorders
- Sleep–wake disorders
- Sexual dysfunctions
- Gender dysphoria
- Disruptive, impulse-control, and conduct disorders
- Substance-related and addictive disorders
- Neurocognitive disorders
- Personality disorders
- Paraphilic disorders
- Other mental disorders
- Medication-induced movement disorders and other adverse effects of medication
- Other conditions that may be a focus of clinical attention

The *International Classification of Diseases* (ICD)

Background and history

According to Hammond and Richeson (2012, p. 362), the French physician, Jacques Bertillon, 'introduced the *Bertillon Classification of Causes of Death* at the International Statistical Institute in Chicago' in 1893. This system was adopted by a number of countries, including Canada, Mexico, and the United States (Hammond & Richeson, 2012). These adoptions were recommended by the American Public Health Association (APHA), which also recommended that the system should be revised every ten years to ensure that the system remained current. Consequently, in 1900, the first international conference was held to revise the *Bertillon Classification of Causes of Death*; thereafter, revisions occurred every ten years (Holzinger, 2014). The first edition comprised a single volume, which was small compared with current coding texts.

The following revisions had only minor changes; however, the sixth revision (1948) was expanded to two volumes and included morbidity and mortality conditions. This revision carried a new title: *Manual of International Statistical Classification of Diseases, Injuries and Causes of Death* (ICD). Prior to the sixth revision, responsibility for ICD revisions fell to the Mixed Commission, a group composed of representatives from the International Statistical Institute and the Health Organization of the League of Nations. In 1948, 'the World Health Organization (WHO) assumed responsibility for preparing and publishing the revisions to the ICD every ten years' (Bowie & Schaffer, 2014) (see Table 2.4). Following this, the name of the ICD changes every ten years (Bowie & Schaffer, 2014).

It was only in the early 1960s that the Mental Health Programme of the World Health Organization (WHO) became actively engaged in a programme aiming to improve the diagnosis and classification of mental disorders. In order to do so, the World Health Organization convened a series of meetings to review knowledge, actively involving representatives of different disciplines, various schools of thought in psychiatry, and all parts of the world in the programme. As a result of these meetings, research was stimulated on criteria for classification, and reliability of diagnosis. Numerous proposals to improve the classification of mental disorders resulted from this extensive consultation process, and these were used in drafting the eighth revision of the *International Classification of Diseases* (ICD-8). A glossary defining each category of mental disorder in ICD-8 was also developed (World Health Organization, 1993).

Table 2.4: Historical development of the International Statistical Classification of Diseases

Year	Revision
1893	Jacques Bertillon introduces the *Bertillon Classification of Causes of Death* at the International Statistical Institute in Chicago.
1900	The first international conference to revise the *International Classification of Causes of Death* convenes.
1910–1940	American Public Health Association revises the system every ten years.

Year	Revision
1948	ICD-6: World Health Organization assumes responsibility for the ICD system. Mental and behavioural disorders are introduced for the first time.
1957	ICD-7.
1968	ICD-8.
1977	ICD-9.
1983–1994	Greater cooperation between DSM-IV and ICD panels in order to bring the two classification systems in line with each other.

Source: ICD-10 *Classification of Mental and Behavioural Disorders: Diagnostic Criteria for Research*. World Health Organization (WHO), Geneva, 2007.

As a result of scientific progress in the broader field of medicine, and more specifically psychiatry, the 1970s saw further interest in improving psychiatric classification worldwide. Several major research efforts were undertaken. One of these, a collaboration between the World Health Organization and the United States Alcohol, Drug Abuse, and Mental Health Administration (ADAMHA), tested for reliability and acceptability in research centres around the world. This effort was aimed at the development of the Composite International Diagnostic Interview based on both DSM and ICD diagnostic criteria.

Other projects focused on developing an assessment instrument suitable for use by clinicians (Schedules for Clinical Assessment in Neuropsychiatry), and an instrument for the assessment of personality disorders in different countries (the International Personality Disorder Examination). For the World Health Organization, the outcome of this work was a clear set of criteria for ICD-10 and assessment instruments that were able to produce data necessary for the classification of disorders according to the criteria included in Chapter V (F) of the ICD-10 (World Health Organization, 1993).

Although the ICD-10 developed alongside and was strongly influenced by the American Psychiatric Association's DSM-III, and although the two manuals sought to use the same codes and diagnostic categories, there were still some differences. Similarly, although there were consultations between the developers of the DSM-5 and the ICD-11, and although the DSM-5 was an influential document, there are important differences between the DSM-5 and the ICD-11. While some may argue that such differences reflect weaknesses in nosological science, the DSM-5 and the ICD-11 have different audiences and different aims, and classification systems need to be 'fit for purpose', so it is unsurprising that they do not fully overlap.

The World Health Organization aims at reaching a global audience and improving global health, and must therefore be suitable for use by primary care and non-specialist practitioners in low- and middle-income countries where the vast majority of the world's population lives. The ICD-11 therefore provides diagnostic guidelines for each disorder, and tries to avoid overly precise diagnostic criteria. The rationale is that any loss of reliability

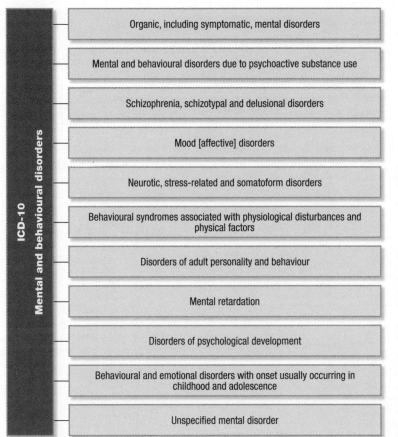

Figure 2.4: The World Health Organization ICD-10 categorises mental and behavioural disorders as shown above.

Source: *International Statistical Classification of Diseases and Related Health Problems*, tenth revision (ICD-10), 2016.

is more than justified by the clinical utility of the system. Other strengths of the ICD-11 include very wide consultation with experts from around the world, and extensive literature reviews and empirical research, including a global clinical practice network that undertook careful testing of draft diagnostic guidelines, and rigorous field trials of diagnostic guidelines in centres around the world.

A notable feature of the ICD-11 is that it has several innovations in areas where the DSM-5 appeared to be at an impasse: for example, there has long been dissatisfaction with the classification of personality disorders; the DSM-5 proposed new approaches but ultimately simply replicated the DSM-IV, while the ICD-11 developed a novel approach to personality disorder. Arguably, the DSM-5 was constrained by perceptions that American psychiatry is influenced by the pharmaceutical industry and has over-medicalised problems of everyday living, while the World Health Organization is perceived as an unbiased institution that aims to improve global health. Whether or not such factors played a role, it is interesting that, in direct contrast to the DSM-5, the ICD-11 has included controversial diagnostic entities such as gaming disorder and compulsive sexual behaviour disorder.

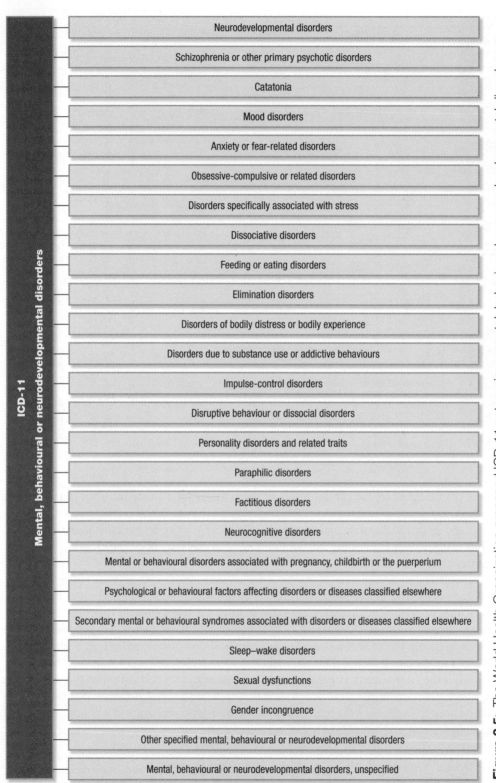

Figure 2.5: The World Health Organization proposed ICD-11 categorises mental, behavioural or neurodevelopmental disorders as shown above.

Source: *International Classification of Diseases for Mortality and Morbidity Statistics*, eleventh revision (ICD-11), 2018.

Comparison and critique

As has been previously mentioned, the format and use of current classification systems are not free from criticism. Indeed, the operationalisation of diagnostic criteria in the DSM-III was partly in response to criticisms of earlier psychiatric classification (Blashfield, 1984). The primary motivation of these standardised, criterion-based definitions was to make diagnosis more consistent and reliable, initially for research purposes (Feighner et al., 1972). Classification systems have continued to develop via the various editions of the DSM and ICD, most recently the DSM-5 (American Psychiatric Association, 2013), which includes a focus on diagnostic validity, and the ICD-11 (World Health Organization, 2018a), which focuses a great deal on clinical utility.

However, even the most reliable of diagnostic criteria are not necessarily valid in the sense of measuring what they are supposed to measure. While there have been ongoing advances in understanding the nature of mental disorders, these constructs remain somewhat fuzzy and quite complex. Fuzziness emerges at the borders between different disorders (say between bipolar disorder and schizophrenia), and between normality and psychopathology; these continue to be a matter of clinical judgement (e.g. taking into account impairment and distress), rather than easily resolved with diagnostic biomarkers (i.e. the boundary problem).

Even important and widely used diagnoses such as schizophrenia are currently very heterogenous, and may ultimately turn out to represent multiple conditions. Advances in neuroscience, such as genome-wide association studies (GWASs) have shed light on the genetic architecture of mental disorders. Consistent with fuzziness, these data indicate, for example, that there is significant overlap in genetic risk factors for different mental disorders (e.g. between bipolar disorder and schizophrenia); consistent with complexity, multiple genes contribute to the risk of any single mental disorder.

From a clinical perspective, one key issue is whether a diagnosis is helpful or not. On the one hand, it may be argued that a diagnosis is key for treatment planning. Certainly, data on the epidemiology of mental disorders have shed light on the huge burden of mental disorders, and have encouraged advocacy and destigmatisation in order to address the under-diagnosis and under-treatment of mental disorders. It is notable that consumer advocates have strongly argued for inclusion of particular entities in the DSM-5 and ICD-11 in order to ensure that they are brought to the attention of clinicians, and that health systems provide appropriate services for their treatment.

On the other hand, the act of diagnosis may have problematic aspects. First there is the risk of over-medicalisation and inappropriate focus on interventions targeting individuals (rather than targeting social determinants). Similarly, a single-word diagnosis is quite different from a comprehensive understanding of a person's problems. Furthermore, a diagnosis may itself stigmatise individuals or discourage them from taking responsibility for changing their behaviours. It is also possible that diagnoses shape and strengthen particular idioms of distress; it is notable, for example, that the diagnosis of posttraumatic stress disorder is more common in societies where there is a high awareness of this entity, and less common in regions where trauma prevalence is higher (Johnstone, 2000). These debates are unlikely to be easily resolved and, for the foreseeable future, clinicians need to be wary of both under-diagnosis and over-diagnosis.

From the perspective of some clinical neuroscientists, a key problem for the field is that the DSM and ICD are not sufficiently biological in their approach. The National Institute of Mental Health in the United States has developed a framework, called the Research Domain Criteria (RDoC), that attempts to provide a more biologically grounded approach to assessment and evaluation, particularly for research purposes. The RDoC domain of negative valence, for example, includes constructs such as acute threat and sustained threat. Each of these can be assessed by dimensional measures, and are underpinned by specific neural circuits and molecular pathways, which can be further studied in the laboratory setting. While potentially useful for researchers, this approach should not be seen to represent a paradigm shift (it builds incrementally on prior work), does not yet resolve the boundary problem, and is not well-suited for day-to-day clinical use, particularly in primary care settings.

A range of different solutions have been put forwards to address problems in nosology. Examples of these include:

- **The dimensional model:** The dimensional approach recognises that mental disorders lie on a continuum ranging from disturbed to normal behaviour, and that mental disorders may evolve over time through various stages of the disorder. For example, the personality disorders are increasingly regarded as extreme variants of common personality characteristics. Although the DSM-5 has expanded the number of specifiers and subtypes in an effort to increase its dimensional approach (Regier, Kuhl, & Kupfer, 2013), a categorical approach remains dominant in both the DSM-5 and the ICD-11. In the dimensional model, a patient would be identified in terms of their position on a specific dimension of cognitive or affective capacity, rather than placed in a categorical 'box'. Categories and dimensions are not, however, mutually exclusive constructs; any dimension can be cut at particular point, to create a category.

- **The holistic model:** The holistic approach to mental disorders considers pharmacological treatments, and social and spiritual treatments, on a similar level. Certainly, there is growing research interest in so-called alternative approaches to intervention. For example, a number of African traditional medicines have psychotropic properties. Nevertheless, decisions to use such approaches should be made on the basis of the relevant evidence base (there is a growing database of rigorous controlled trials of these agents). Furthermore, provision of a diagnosis is not necessarily reductionistic. As argued throughout this chapter, it is important to recognise the biopsychosocial underpinnings of disorders – and the role of context in expressing and experiencing symptoms – and to target these in an integrated way.

- **The Johns Hopkins model (the perspectival model):** This model, which is consistent with an integrative approach to nosology, was developed at Johns Hopkins University and is based on the work of American psychiatrists Paul McHugh and Phillip Slavney (Peters & Chisolm, 2017). This model argues that different mental disorders have different natures (Peters & Chisolm, 2017). The model identifies four broad 'perspectives' that can be used to identify the distinctive characteristics of mental disorders, which may be obscured by the categorical classifications. The four perspectives are:
  - *Disease:* This perspective emphasises the role of general medical illnesses or structural damage to the brain that produce psychiatric symptoms. It may be useful for disorders such as Alzheimer's disease or schizophrenia.

- *Dimensions:* This perspective emphasises symptoms due to cognitive or emotional vulnerability in a particular person, and a life experience that precipitates symptoms in the context of this vulnerability. It may be useful, for example, in addressing depressive symptoms in the context of loss.
- *Behaviours:* This perspective emphasises disorders that emerge from maladaptive patterns of behaviour (alcoholism, drug addiction, eating disorders, etc.) that have become a dysfunctional way of life.
- *Life story:* This perspective emphasises disorders related to life experiences, such as traumatic events that have injured hopes and aspirations.

The Johns Hopkins model can, for example, be applied to the case of Bulumko. On the one hand, we know that exposure to severe trauma can lead to brain changes, thought to underlie a diagnosis of posttraumatic stress disorder. On the other hand, a severe stressor may also lead to a spectrum of anxiety and depressive symptoms, particularly in someone with a history of prior traumatisation. Finally, while Bulumko's early exposure to the stress of imprisonment was meaningful for him, it was difficult for him to make any sense of the robbery. The Johns Hopkins model is consistent with the biopsychosocial models that have long been advocated in medicine and psychiatry. However, it may also be argued that each of these four dimensions can be applied to a range of conditions, with many mental disorders involving biopsychosocial processes, and necessitating an appreciation of both mechanisms and meanings.

The ongoing controversies and debates about mental disorders are entirely appropriate, given that diagnostic decisions reflect not only the presence of particular signs and symptoms, but also societal values. At any particular junction in historical or geographical space, theoretical constructs in both medicine and psychiatry reflect the context of that time and space. Nevertheless, this is not to say that diagnosis is merely about social control; the iterative improvements in the DSM and ICD reflect rigorous debate about both the relevant facts and values. It is particularly important to realise that diagnosis is only one aspect of individual and public healthcare; a comprehensive and integrated approach to services is needed not only to assist particular mental health users, but also to advance global mental health.

CONCLUSION

Abnormal behaviour has been defined using the criteria of statistical deviance, maladaptiveness, personal distress, and underlying dysfunction. In addition to these criteria, broader political, sociocultural, and historical factors are important in understanding the nature of normality or abnormality; our classification systems are both theory-bound and value-laden. The classification of mental illnesses is a complex task, and only one step on the path to a full appreciation of the pathogenesis of psychological problems and mental disorders. Such an appreciation likely requires both a knowledge of underlying mechanisms (including psychobiological and evolutionary mechanisms) and an understanding of relevant meanings (e.g. the idioms of distress).

Classification systems raise deep philosophical questions (Table 2.5). A classical view of science and diagnosis emphasises that diagnoses have invariant necessary and sufficient criteria, that diagnoses are useful in describing the world 'out there', and that closer observation will ultimately advance science and medicine. A critical perspective on science and diagnosis emphasises that diagnoses change from time to time and place to place, that diagnoses are social constructs used to control deviance, and that alternative models of health care are needed (Stein, 2008).

An integrative perspective draws on the strengths of each of these views while avoiding their weaknesses (e.g. classical scientism, critical relativism) (see Table 2.5). It argues that, while diagnoses are both theory-bound and value-laden, we can progressively improve our diagnostic classifications. It notes that classifications address key questions about human nature, and must necessarily be fit for purpose, so that it is appropriate to be constantly critical of our classifications, and to attempt to improve them over time. It argues that a full appreciation of clinical problems and disorders requires both knowledge of mechanisms and understanding of meanings (Stein, 2013).

An integrative perspective on classification may self-reflexively note that the language of diagnosis draws on specific medical metaphors. In one common medical metaphor, for example, disease is an enemy that attacks, and medications are in turn an 'arsenal' that defends. However, a range of other metaphors are useful in clinical practice. For example, a moral metaphor that emphasises that it is the duty of an individual to take responsibility for their health may be useful in encouraging patients to alter their behaviour.

The medical metaphor is easily applicable to typical diseases (e.g. pneumonia), where patients are allowed to assume the sick role. However, in atypical conditions (e.g. alcoholism, gaming disorder), there is much more contention about whether the sick role is appropriate. Hence the debate, for example, about whether substance use disorders are best conceptualised as 'brain disorders' or, for example, as problems in learning.

In South Africa, where classifications were for many years laden with the theory of apartheid, it is arguably relevant to draw on the strengths of the critical perspective. At the same time, given growing recognition of the links of appropriate diagnosis and treatment of mental disorders to sustainable development, it is arguably important to draw on the strengths of the classical view. An integrative perspective may, however, be particularly valuable in avoiding the relativism of an outright critical view and the scientism of an outright classical view: we need to appreciate how diagnosis is theory-bound and value-laden, how clinical work requires a holistic understanding of the individual and their context, and how public mental health relies on recognising human rights (see Chapter 5) and addressing social determinants contributing to disorders.

In the clinical context, an integrative perspective may be useful in addressing the twin dangers of under-diagnosis and over-diagnosis. In low socio-economic groups in South Africa, there is overwhelming evidence of under-diagnosis and under-treatment, and of the need to scale up diagnosis and treatment. In view of the links to sustainable development, it is appropriate to advocate for vastly increased resources for mental health services. In high socio-economic groups, however, there is anecdotal evidence of over-diagnosis and over-medicalisation in some cases. It is crucial to be aware of the range of factors (pharmaceutical advertising, ignoring the adaptive value of mental symptoms) that may drive such phenomena.

In the research context, an integrative perspective may be useful in ensuring attention to both mechanisms and meaning, and to both discovery science and implementation science. A strong critical voice in South Africa has appropriately resonated with the view that it is less important to understand the world than to change it. At the same time, in the current context, it is important that South Africa also stay abreast of discovery science, while simultaneously undertaking implementation science to scale up effective and cost-efficient diagnostic practices and treatments. Indeed, perhaps a key take-home message of this chapter is the complexity of diagnosis and clinical practice, and the need therefore to adopt non-reductionist and integrative approaches.

Table 2.5: Classical, critical, and integrative approaches

	Classical	Critical	Integrated
Philosophical influences	Plato, logical positivists, early Wittgenstein	Vico, Herder, much continental philosophy	Aristotle, Bhaskar, Lakoff
View of categories	Categories can be defined using necessary and sufficient criteria	Categories reflect human practices	Categories reflect both human practices and real underlying structures/mechanisms
View of psychiatric disorders	Disorders can be defined using necessary and sufficient criteria	Psychiatric classifications reflect human practices	Nosologies reflect both human practices and real underlying structures/mechanisms
Is disorder x in category or spectrum y?	Research the relevant necessary and sufficient components	Answers reflect practices inside medicine (clinical utility) and outside	Debate both the relevant underlying psychobiology and the clinical utility

Source: Stein, 2008.

MULTIPLE-CHOICE QUESTIONS

1. According to the criteria of statistical deviance, a behaviour is abnormal when it deviates from:
   a) previous family patterns
   b) the norms of a specified social or cultural group
   c) maladaptiveness
   d) personal distress

2. DSM-5 makes use of _____ to inform new groupings of related disorders within the existing categorical framework.
   a) brain scans
   b) scientific indicators
   c) educated guesswork
   d) social indicators

3 DSM-5 is organised on:
   a) developmental and lifespan considerations
   b) medical considerations
   c) socio-economic considerations
   d) personality structure considerations

4. DSM-5 utilises a/an _____ documentation of diagnosis.
   a) axial
   b) categorical
   c) non-axial
   d) non-dimensional

5. DSM-5 is based on a _____ classification system.
   a) dimensional
   b) categorical
   c) prototypical
   d) psychoanalytic

PARAGRAPH AND ESSAY QUESTIONS

1. Why do we need a classification system for mental illness?
2. Describe how the DSM and ICD classifications differ.
3. This chapter mentions obsessive-compulsive disorder. Look at Figures 2.3, 2.4, and 2.5 and suggest under which category this disorder would be placed in the DSM-5, ICD-10, and ICD-11.
4. This chapter started off with a person who experienced posttraumatic stress disorder. Looking at Figures 2.3, 2.4, and 2.5, suggest under which category it would be placed in the DSM-5, ICD-10, and ICD-11.
5. What is your first impression of how the DSM-5, ICD-10, and ICD-11 systems categorise mental disorders? Do you think your opinion might change? Give reasons for your answer.
6. Choose a behaviour that you consider abnormal. Using the criteria of maladaptiveness, statistical deviance, and personal distress, consider which criterion best fits the chosen behaviour.

3 PSYCHOLOGICAL ASSESSMENT AND PSYCHO-DIAGNOSTICS

Tracey-Lee Austin & Gale Ure

CHAPTER CONTENTS

Introduction
Basic steps in the diagnostic process
Interviewing and observations
    The clinical interview
    Mental Status Examination (MSE)
    Behavioural assessment
Physiological assessments
    Physical examination
    Neuro-imaging
    Psycho-physiological assessment
Psychological testing
    Culture and assessment
    Intelligence tests
    Personality inventories
    Projective tests
    Neuropsychological assessment
    False positives, false negatives, and malingering
    Arriving at a diagnosis: The use of diagnostic classification systems
Conclusion

LEARNING OUTCOMES

After studying this chapter, you should be able to:

- Describe the nature and function of clinical assessment and the concepts that determine the value of assessment (reliability, validity, and standardisation).
- Describe the purpose of the clinical interview, physical examination, and formal behavioural assessment in the evaluation process.
- Compare and contrast projective tests, personality inventories, and neuropsychological tests for the purpose of psychological evaluation.
- Explain how medical techniques such as PET, CAT, and MRI scans are appropriate tools for assessing psychological disorders, including limitations of such methods.
- Explain the nature and purposes of psychiatric diagnosis and how the DSM and ICD are used to help therapists and counsellors make an accurate psychiatric diagnosis.

PERSONAL HISTORY CASELET

When Catherine's son got sick, it was usually one of two things: he usually got a high temperature and started vomiting, or he just got a high temperature. Catherine noticed that when she took her son to the doctor because he had a high temperature and was vomiting, the doctor said it was a bacterial infection and prescribed medicines to treat the illness directly. However, when she took her son to the doctor just because he had a high temperature, the doctor would say he had a virus, and that he could not treat the virus but only the symptoms, and that Catherine should just give her son medicine to control his temperature and give him plenty of fluids.

Because both money and time were in short supply, Catherine stopped taking her son to the doctor when he simply had a temperature, even though this made her feel like a bad mother. Although she worried about whether she was making the right call, she just gave him medicine to keep his temperature down and waited for him to get better. While she was waiting she noticed that when her son seemed to have a virus, he did not sweat even though his temperature was high. Then suddenly his temperature would drop and he would start to sweat like he normally did. Catherine assumed this was what was meant by the term 'the fever broke'. She always felt relieved when this happened, and started to feel there was a pattern to his illnesses.

Catherine didn't go to the doctor much herself, until she realised that her anxiety was growing so bad that it was stopping her functioning, and her ability to parent. Going out became difficult. She kept on having to sit down or lie down. She assumed that what she was experiencing was what was meant by the term 'a nervous breakdown'. When she did then see a doctor about this, Catherine sensed that he was looking for pattern, in a similar way to when he was trying to decide whether her son's illness had been a bacterial infection or a virus. He was asking questions to work out what symptoms she did or did not have, so that he could work out what kind of mental illness it was and what the prognosis was likely to be. She was surprised that the discussion about her anxiety was so similar to the discussion about her son's illnesses.

INTRODUCTION

Inherent in the study of psychopathology and in the treatment of psychological disorders is the process of clinical assessment and diagnosis (Sadock, Sadock, & Ruiz, 2017). Clinical assessment is the evaluation and measurement of psychological, biological, and social factors in individuals who present with possible psychological disorders (Sadock, Sadock, & Ruiz, 2017). Diagnosis is the process whereby the clinician determines whether the particular problem with which the individual presents meets all the criteria for a psychological disorder as described in either the DSM-5 (American Psychiatric Association, 2013) or the ICD-10 (World Health Organization, 2016).

To the untrained eye, it would seem relatively unproblematic to make an accurate diagnosis. However, from what you have read in the earlier chapters, it should be relatively clear that this is not as simple as it first seems. We have already alluded to some of the problems related to diagnostic systems, which form the basis of a diagnosis, but we have also discussed how culture and social forces impact on the experience and presentation of mental disorders. Given this, it is usual for the clinician to begin an assessment by collecting a wide range of information in order to determine where the source(s) of the problem might lie and then to focus on areas that appear to be most relevant. There are three basic concepts that help to establish the value of assessments:

- *Reliability:* The degree to which a measurement is **consistent**, that is, two or more assessors will get the same results when using the same assessment tool; this also refers to how stable the results of the assessment are over time.
- *Validity:* The degree to which the tool or technique assesses or measures what it is supposed to assess or measure.
- *Standardisation:* The process of determining specific **norms** and requirements for an assessment technique to make certain that it is used in a consistent manner across assessment situations. This includes administration instructions, evaluation of the results, and comparison of these with data for large numbers of people (Anastasi, 1988).

There are a number of procedures that can be used during a clinical assessment in order to help the clinician to obtain the information needed to both understand and assist patients. These procedures include a clinical interview, which normally includes a Mental Status Examination (MSE), a physical examination, behavioural observation and assessment, and psychological tests (Sadock, Sadock, & Ruiz, 2017).

BASIC STEPS IN THE DIAGNOSTIC PROCESS

The first step towards making a diagnosis is to ask the patient what is wrong, in order to establish the **presenting problem**. Often, patients present with more than one problem. If this happens, the diagnostician will rank these from the most important to the least important, and deal with them in sequence in this order. A full history of the presenting condition(s) and other relevant facts should then be taken.

During the interview, the diagnostician will focus not only on the content of a patient's history, but also on observable signs (e.g. tone of the patient's voice, eye contact, etc.).

Both the DSM-5 and the ICD-10 (and ICD-11) systems stipulate that the diagnosis of a psychological or psychiatric disorder cannot be made if there is evidence of a medical condition that could explain the problem. In these cases, it is essential that a **medical examination** be carried out to rule out the possibility of a medical condition. This examination is done by a qualified medical practitioner. This medical examination would focus specifically on the presenting symptoms. The general physical examination consists of:

- basic observations, such as the person's gait, skin tone, voice intonation, and ability to hold a normal conversation
- taking the blood pressure and checking for basic signs of disease such as anaemia or swelling of the legs
- examining the various organ systems of the body: the heart, lungs, bowels, etc.

It may also be important that a **neurological examination** is performed by a medical specialist. This examination gives an understanding of the well-being of the person's central and peripheral nervous systems, as well as the musculoskeletal, endocrine, and vascular systems. It is the tool that physicians use to identify structural and psychiatric abnormality.

The next step would be an examination, usually by a psychiatrist or a clinical psychologist, to determine the individual's mental condition. This involves investigating the individual's abilities regarding orientation to time, place, and person (in other words, do they know what the date and time are, where they are, and who they are), attention span, concentration, and memory. Any psychopathology must also be identified, for example, abnormalities in perception of stimuli, thought content, speed of thought, and logical thinking. It must be kept in mind that patients do not verbalise a diagnosis, but they describe their problem in terms of symptoms; thus they give a subjective description of what they feel, experience, and observe (e.g. feeling depressed, a change in appetite, etc.). During the interview, the diagnostician will focus not only on the content of a patient's history, but also on observable signs (e.g. tone of the patient's voice, eye contact, etc.).

Often the above-mentioned steps result in only a **provisional** or tentative diagnosis, and further investigations such as psychological tests may be conducted in order to refine the diagnosis, or in order to rule out a diagnosis such as mental retardation.

Using all of the available evidence, the diagnostician is then able to make a firm diagnosis (see Figure 3.1). From a list of the possible diagnoses based on the symptoms and signs, the diagnostician identifies the most likely diagnosis (e.g. clinical conditions, personality disorders, as well as physical diseases) through a process of identification and elimination.

INTERVIEWING AND OBSERVATIONS

The clinical interview

The clinical interview is a very important part of the assessment process. It is always the first step of the process and is used by most mental health professionals. It allows the diagnostician to obtain:

- a detailed description of the presenting problem or chief complaint, in other words, the reason for the patient having presented or been brought in

- detailed history of the patient's life, his or her current situation (including work, habits, and relationships), and social history
- information about attitudes, emotions, and current and past behaviour
- family history
- information about when the problem started, as well as whether any significant events occurred at about the time that the problem started.

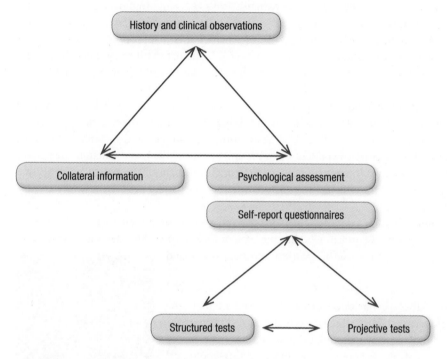

Figure 3.1: Triangulation in the diagnostic process

Source: Created by author Burke.

The Mental Status Examination (MSE) is often used to help organise the information gathered during the clinical interview.

Mental Status Examination (MSE)

The MSE involves a systematic observation of the patient's behaviour and is usually structured and detailed. It is generally performed quite quickly by an experienced interviewer during the course of assessing the patient. The MSE encompasses five categories (Soltan & Girguis, 2017):

- ***Appearance and behaviour:*** The clinician observes the patient for any overt physical behaviours, dress, posture, appearance, and facial expression. For example, if the patient appears to be listening to or conversing with an imaginary person, this may indicate the presence of hallucinations.

- *Thought processes:* The patient's conversation can give a very good indication of their thought processes. One would note the rate and flow of speech (very fast or very slow), as well as continuity of speech (does the patient make sense when talking or are his or her ideas presented in a disconnected manner?). Attention is also given to the content of the patient's speech. Here one would note the presence of delusions and/or hallucinations.
- *Mood and affect:* Mood is subjective, that is, how the patient feels most of the time. Affect is what the clinician observes as the patient speaks (i.e. laughing, frowning, or crying). Here one would note whether the patient's affect is appropriate (i.e. the patient seems sad when talking about something sad), or whether it is inappropriate (i.e. the patient laughs while talking about something very sad). If the patient displays very little or no affect while speaking, one would also note this. The affect would then be called 'blunted' or 'flat'.
- *Intellectual functioning:* It is possible for a clinician to make a rough estimate of a patient's intellectual functioning simply by talking to him or her. The clinician would note whether the patient is able to talk in abstractions and understand metaphors (as most of us can do), whether the patient has a reasonable vocabulary, and whether the patient has a good, average, or poor memory. The rough estimate of the patient's intellectual functioning helps the clinician to conclude whether the patient is above or below average in intelligence.
- *Sensorium:* This term denotes a person's general awareness of their surroundings. Here the clinician would confirm whether the patient knows what the date and time are, and who, and where, they are (orientation to time, person, and place).

HELPFUL HINT

Mental Status Examination

- A (Appearance and behaviour)
- T (Thought processes)
- M (Mood and affect)
- I (Intellectual functioning)
- S (Sensorium)

The aim of these behavioural observations is to enable the diagnostician to establish which areas of the patient's behaviour and condition (if any) should be assessed in more detail and more formally. If there is a possibility of a psychological disorder being present, then the clinician would be able to hypothesise about which disorder it might be, and this in turn would provide more focus for further assessment.

It is important to conduct the clinical interview in an empathic manner that will put the patient at ease and gain his or her trust, because it is only when the patient feels understood that he or she is likely to divulge very personal and important information. It is not possible for clinicians to hypothesise about a possible diagnosis if they have only some of the necessary information.

Behavioural assessment

This process makes use of **direct observation** in order to assess formally an individual's thoughts, feelings, and behaviour in a specific context. This process may be more appropriate when a clinician assesses individuals who are not old enough or who are unable (due to the nature of their disorder or cognitive deficits) to report their problems and/or experiences (Greene & Ollendick, 2000). This type of assessment can be conducted by going to the patient's workplace or home (or school, in the case of young children), or by setting up a role-play simulation in a clinical setting to observe how the individual might behave in similar situations.

In a behavioural assessment, one would identify the specific behaviour one wants to observe (the **target behaviour**) in order to determine what influences it. One would focus on the antecedent (what happened just before the behaviour), then one would focus on the behaviour itself, and then on the consequences (what happened directly after the behaviour) (Greene & Ollendick, 2000).

EXAMPLE CASE

Behavioural assessment
Mr Grant complains that his daughter is naughty. Upon observing, one would see that Mr Grant asks his daughter to complete her homework (antecedent). His daughter then proceeds to scream and run out of the house to hide in the garden, where she continues to scream at her father (behaviour). Mr Grant tries to placate his daughter and offers her all kinds of treats if she will just do some of her homework (consequence). One can see that the request to do homework triggers the behaviour and the consequence encourages (reinforces) rather than stops the behaviour.

People can also observe their own behaviour using a technique called **self-monitoring** (Haynes, 2000). Here the individual can, for example, record the number of sweets he or she eats on a particular day and note what occurred before the sweet eating in order to identify what triggers the sweet-eating behaviour.

Behaviour-rating scales can also be used in order to assess behaviour and then to assess changes in the person's behaviour. For example, the Brief Psychiatric Rating Scale assesses 18 areas of concern and can be completed by hospital staff (Lezak, 1995).

One needs to note that awareness of being observed (reactivity) can distort any observational data. Any time one observes how people behave, one's presence can cause them to alter their behaviour. The same is true when people observe their own behaviour.

 **ACTIVITY**

Behaviour diary
Pick a certain behaviour that you would like to change, and then monitor it according to the following example.

Example: Not getting enough sleep (insomnia). In this example, it becomes clear how anxiety and behaviour affect the person's sleep pattern. If one keeps a diary such as the one below, it often becomes easy to identify patterns, and possible causes, of behaviour.

	Hours of sleep	Activities before bedtime	Thoughts and feelings when going to bed
Monday	6	Watched television till 23h00. Drank 3 cups of coffee while watching television.	Thinking about Psychology test on Friday.
Tuesday	5	Studied until 22h00. Drank 500 ml carbonated cold drink.	Worried about test and that I'm not getting enough sleep.
Wednesday	5	Studied until 22h00. Drank 500 ml carbonated cold drink.	Worried about test and that I'm not getting enough sleep.
Thursday	3	Studied until 03h00. Drank 1 l carbonated cold drink, 3 cups of coffee and other energy drinks.	Keep worrying that I have not studied enough and keep going through the work in my mind.
Friday	10	Had supper and a hot shower and then went to bed.	None – too tired.

PHYSIOLOGICAL ASSESSMENTS

Physical examination

Many medical conditions can mimic the symptoms of a psychological disorder, and a psychiatrist or neurologist may request a physical examination to rule these out. For example, an overactive thyroid can produce symptoms common in most anxiety disorders. It is thus important to rule out a medical condition before making a psychological or psychiatric diagnosis which may lead to an incorrect treatment programme (Sadock, Sadock, & Ruiz, 2017).

Neuro-imaging

This technique allows us to take accurate pictures of the brain's structure and function. When looking at the **structure** of the brain, we look at the size or shape of the various parts and whether there is any damage. When looking at the function, we look at metabolic activity and blood flow (Linden & Fallgatter, 2009).

The first technique for examining **brain structure** was developed in the early 1970s and made use of multiple X-rays of the brain taken from different angles. These X-rays are attenuated differentially by tissues of different densities, and the degree of attenuation is picked up by detectors. A computer then reconstructs pictures of 'slices' of the brain. This procedure takes about 15 minutes and is called a **Computerised Tomography** (CT) scan (see Figure 3.2). A CT scan is non-invasive and may be useful for locating brain tumours and injuries. CT scans are not routinely used in psychiatry, as they cannot be justified unless there are clear indications for their use (Chhagan & Burns, 2017).

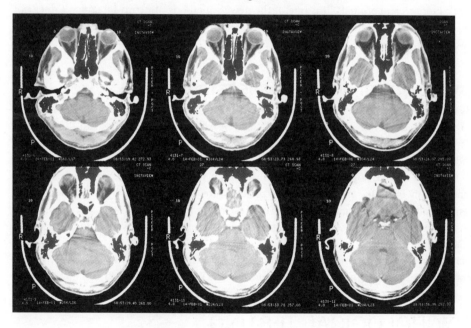

Figure 3.2: Computerised Tomography (CT) scan

A more recent procedure that gives greater resolution without the risk of radiation is nuclear **Magnetic Resonance Imaging** (MRI). Here a patient's head is put in a high-strength magnetic field through which radio frequency signals are then transmitted. These signals alter the protons in the hydrogen atoms and the alteration is measured, together with the time taken for the protons to return to normal. This procedure is expensive and cannot be used if the patient suffers from claustrophobia (Andreasen & Swayze, 1993).

In order to measure **brain function**, several procedures can be used. The first procedure is known as the **Positron Emission Tomography** (PET) scan. Here the individual is injected with a tracer substance attached to radioactive isotopes. This substance then interacts with glucose, blood, or oxygen. When any part of the brain becomes active, the glucose, blood, or oxygen flow to these areas of the brain and detectors can identify the location of the isotopes. In this way, we can see which parts of the brain are working and which parts are not. PET scans are useful for supplementing MRI and CAT scans in localising sites of trauma. The PET scan can also be used to identify varying patterns of metabolism that might be associated with different disorders (Andreasen & Swayze, 1993).

Another procedure used to assess brain function is known as **Single Photon Emission Computed Tomography** (SPECT). It is similar to a PET scan, but a different tracer substance is used. It is less accurate than a PET scan; however, it is less expensive than a PET scan and therefore is used more often (Andreasen & Swayze, 1993).

A **functional MRI** (fMRI) is an advanced and rapid technique used to take pictures of the brain at work and to record changes in the brain from one second to the next (Andreasen & Swayze, 1993). An fMRI is a specialised type of MRI scan. It measures the dynamic regulation of the blood flow in the brain, which is related to neural activity in the brain or spinal cord of both humans and animals. It is one of the newest methods of neuro-imaging. It does not expose the patient to radiation, and is minimally invasive and widely available. For this reason, it has come to be the preferred means of brain mapping (Andreasen & Swayze, 1993).

Psycho-physiological assessment

This refers to the measurement of changes in the nervous system that may reflect emotional or psychological events. The measurements can be taken either directly from the brain or from other parts of the body. There are several different ways of measuring these changes (Andrasik, 2000):

- An electro-encephalogram (EEG) measures brain wave activity. This can be done while the person is awake or asleep. EEG patterns are often affected by psychological or emotional factors and can be an index of these reactions.
- An individual's heart rate, electrodermal activity (sweat gland activity), and respiration can also be measured.

Psycho-physiological approaches are increasingly being used to understand psycho-pathological processes (Infantolino, Crockers, Heller, Yee, & Miller, 2016).

PSYCHOLOGICAL TESTING

Psychological tests are used to determine emotional, behavioural, or cognitive responses that could be associated with a specific disorder. Generally, the topic of assessment elicits suspicion and confusion in the minds of many due to the racially tainted history of psychological assessment in South Africa. This is mainly due to the fact that, in the past, very few of the tests were normed on diverse cultural groups in South Africa. This led to the inappropriate use of norms for certain subgroups, which contributed to discriminatory thinking (Louw & Allen, 1996). The criticism and suspicion of psychological assessment is, in many instances, not unwarranted. The misuse of assessment by both trained and untrained people is significant, and many serious injustices have been perpetrated in assessment processes (Saunders, 2008).

Although there are many forms of assessment and many different contexts within which assessment occurs, we will be focusing only on testing in clinical environments (i.e. those settings where one assesses in order to make an accurate diagnosis). In these contexts, many different assessment methodologies apply, and each of these may require different qualifications and skills (Eabon & Abrahamson, 2019).

All behavioural and personality-based assessments must be carried out by a registered psychologist with skills and experience in assessment in a cross-cultural context, as this is the nature of the assessment environment in South Africa (Saunders, 2008). Although psychological testing falls mainly in the realm of psychology, many other mental healthcare professionals (e.g. social workers, nurses, and occupational therapists) may make use of some tests. It must be stressed, however, that the use of psychological tests is regulated by legislation and, in some instances, it is stipulated that only trained and registered psychologists may use certain tests, as specified by the Health Professions Council of South Africa (HPCSA).

One may well ask why the use of tests is so strictly legislated, but the answer is actually quite simple. Assessment is not an exact science, and tests are not always bound by procedure. This means that sometimes the test instructions and, especially, the interpretation of results, are not reliant on specific formulae or techniques, but rather depend on a great deal of skill and experience being exercised by a trained expert. If used incorrectly, tests may produce **false negatives** or **false positives** (these concepts will be discussed in more detail later in this chapter).

According to Saunders (2008), advanced tests in particular require substantial skill and expertise. These advanced tests include intelligence tests, personality tests, and projective and other diagnostic tests, and they should only be carried out by:

- *Registered psychologists:* These are trained professionals, registered with the HPCSA, who are required to use their knowledge and specialist expertise to select, use, and interpret the required assessment instruments. These professionals rely on their knowledge and understanding of the theory of human behaviour.
- *Psychometrists:* A psychometrist is a person who has received training in psychology with an emphasis on tests and measurement. The basic function of a psychometrist is to administer and score psychological tests under the direct supervision of an appropriately registered psychologist. Psychometrists are also required to record responses accurately and score tests using appropriate norms. Psychometrists keep note of test behaviour, especially any behaviours that might affect test results. Psychometrists must be competent in the use of a variety of tests in order to assess intelligence, personality, aptitude, achievement, comprehension, memory, perception, and motor skills. They should be aware of ethical issues regarding patient confidentiality, protection of test security, and constraints on dual relationships with patients.
- *Trained allied professionals:* Social workers, occupational therapists, and nurses are allowed to be involved in the administrative elements of some instruments. These include test administration and the scoring and recording of results. These professionals ought to be trained, supervised, and mentored by a qualified, registered psychologist, due to the fact that the principles and ethics of assessment are the same regardless of what element of competence is being assessed.

Psychological tests have to be reliable as well as valid in order for the results to be of any use to the clinician. There are a number of different types of psychological tests, including intelligence tests, personality inventories, projective tests, and neuropsychological tests.

Culture and assessment

One of the major challenges to psychological testing is the influence of cultural factors on test results. In order to overcome these problems, psychologists aim to construct culture-free or culture-fair tests (Anastasi & Urbina, 1997). A **culture-free test** is a test that aspires to minimise the effects that culture may have on a person's performance on the test. Although this is the ideal, it seems difficult, if not impossible, to construct a test that is not affected by culture. Furthermore, it is often difficult to determine whether such a test is truly culture-free.

A **culture-fair test** is designed to be free of cultural bias, as far as possible, so that no one culture has an advantage over another. The test is designed so as not to be influenced by verbal ability, cultural climate, or educational level. The purpose of a culture-fair test is to eliminate any social or cultural advantages, or disadvantages, that a person may have due to his or her upbringing. The test can be administered to anyone, from any nation, speaking any language. A culture-fair test may help identify learning or emotional problems (Anastasi & Urbina, 1997; Van der Vijver & Rothmann, 2004).

Culture-fair tests are designed to assess intelligence, personality, attitudes, interests, and a multitude of other attributes, without relying on knowledge specific to any individual cultural group. They rely largely on non-verbal questions, in order to accommodate English-additional-language speakers. An important issue for assessment of these people is that they are likely to lack familiarity both with the English language and with Western culture. Culture-fair testing is a timely issue, given current debate over bias in intelligence and educational testing. This is so because such testing particularly affects students who can speak and write English, but who are unfamiliar with Western, middle-class culture (Anastasi & Urbina, 1997; Van der Vijver & Rothmann, 2004).

Bias in intelligence testing has a historical precedent in early tests that were designed to exclude people from schools, universities, professions, and jobs on the grounds of intellectual abilities. Critics of current tests claim that they discriminate against some ethnic groups in similar ways, in that the tests call for various types of knowledge unavailable to those outside the middle-class cultural mainstream. Although culture-fair tests do reduce differences in performance between Western people and non-Western people who are members of minority groups, the latter still lag behind on the standard tests for predicting success in school, suggesting that in their quest for academic success, members of minority groups must overcome cultural barriers that extend beyond those encountered in IQ tests (Van der Vijver & Rothmann, 2004; Groth-Marnat & Jordan Wright, 2016).

Intelligence tests

Wechsler considered intelligence to be a global concept involving the ability to act with purpose, to think in a rational manner, and to deal with the environment in an effective way (Groth-Marnat, 1999). Most definitions of intelligence include the following areas: abstract thinking; learning from experience; solving problems through insight; adjusting to new situations; and focusing and sustaining the ability to achieve a desired goal (Coulacoglou & Saklofske, 2017; Groth-Marnat & Jordan Wright, 2016).

Intelligence Quotient (IQ) tests are very good predictors of academic performance, and intelligence tests are quite accurate in predicting future behaviour such as educational achievement, job performance, and earning potential. Intelligence tests also provide clinicians with baseline measures that can be used to determine the degree of change that has occurred in an individual over time, or to determine how the individual compares with other people in a certain area or ability (Groth-Marnat & Jordan Wright, 2016). However, one needs to be careful not to see individuals simply as their IQ score; people are capable of more cognitive abilities than can be measured on intelligence tests (Frederiksen, 1986). In addition, aspects like emotional intelligence are important for successful functioning in society (Coulacoglou & Saklofske, 2017).

In order to assess intellectual functioning or intellectual disability, the clinician can make use of the **Wechsler Adult Intelligence Scale** (WAIS). The current edition of this test is the WAIS-IV, which has norms for use with South Africans. This instrument contains four index scales (Verbal Comprehension, Perceptual Reasoning, Working Memory, and Processing Speed), which measure a range of skills. These include knowledge of facts, vocabulary, verbal reasoning skills, short-term memory, abstract thinking ability, psychomotor ability, ability to learn new relationships, planning ability, and non-verbal reasoning (Tulsky, Zhu, & Prifitera, 2000; Coulacoglou & Saklofske, 2017).

When an individual does not have functional language or is from a culture for which there is no appropriate instrument, one can make use of a non-verbal test such as the **Raven's Standard Progressive Matrices** (RSPM) (Groth-Marnat, 1999). This test emphasises non-verbal tasks and assesses abstract thinking ability and ability to reason, as well as giving an IQ score. Thus, this test can also be used to supplement findings from the WAIS (Bilker et al., 2012).

Personality inventories

The basic components of personality are called traits, which the DSM-5 defines as enduring patterns of perceiving, relating to, and thinking about the environment and oneself that are exhibited in a wide range of social and personal contexts (American Psychiatric Association, 1994). There is an assumption that, if one is able to typify someone's personality, then it will be possible to identify the causes of, as well as predict, that person's future behaviours (Reid, 2011; Conard, 2006). Linked to this assumption is the notion that a personality disorder (see Chapter 14) is a mental illness with consequences similar to those of other major psychiatric disorders such as schizophrenia (Angleitner & Ostendorf, 1994).

It is possible to evaluate an individual's personality by a detailed clinical interview (as described above) and by administering a personality test. It is beyond the scope of this section to review the large number of tests that can be used, so we will focus on two that have gained wide acceptance, the **Minnesota Multiphasic Personality Inventory-2** (MMPI-2) and the **Millon Clinical Multiaxial Inventory III** (MCMI-III).

Minnesota Multiphasic Personality Inventory-2 (MMPI-2)

The MMPI-2 is a standardised questionnaire that draws out a broad range of self-descriptions that are then scored to give a quantitative assessment of an individual's level of emotional adjustment and attitude toward test-taking (Groth-Marnat & Jordan Wright, 2016).

The MMPI-2 can be administered to individuals who are 16 years old or older. The MMPI-2 consists of 567 statements that can be answered as true or false, based on whether or not the individual agrees with the statement. However, the individual responses are not examined; rather, the pattern of responses is evaluated to see whether it resembles patterns from groups of individuals who have specific disorders. Each group is represented on separate standard scales. These scales represent measures of personality traits rather than diagnostic categories (Groth-Marnat & Jordan Wright, 2016).

The content for most of the questions is quite obvious as they deal with psychological, neurological, psychiatric, and physical symptoms (Groth-Marnat, 1999). Some of the questions are obscure in the sense that the underlying process they are assessing is not intuitively obvious (Groth-Marnat & Jordan Wright, 2016). The MMPI-2 is extremely reliable when it is interpreted according to standardised procedures, and its validity with a wide range of psychological problems has been attested to by a large number of studies (Wise, Streiner, & Walfish, 2009).

Millon Clinical Multiaxial Inventory-IV (MCMI-IV)

The MCMI-IV is a standardised self-report questionnaire which comprises statements that can be answered as true or false, based on whether or not the individual agrees with the statement. As with the MMPI-2, it is the pattern of responses that is evaluated in order to determine whether it bears a resemblance to patterns from groups of individuals who have specific disorders. Scoring the instrument produces 25 scales that are divided into six categories, namely, Modifying Indices, Random Response Indicators, Clinical Personality Patterns, Severe Personality Pathology, Clinical Syndromes, and Severe Clinical Syndromes. These scales are closely associated with Millon's theory of personality (Pincus & Krueger, 2015), and are aligned with the DSM-5 and ICD-10.

The MCMI-IV can be administered to individuals who are 18 years old or older, and it is used to assess a broad range of information related to an individual's personality, emotional adjustment, and attitude towards taking tests. This instrument is distinctive in that it focuses on personality disorders together with symptoms that are normally associated with these disorders (Groth-Marnat & Jordan Wright, 2016; Pincus & Krueger, 2015).

The MCMI-IV can be used as an alternative to the MMPI-2 or to complement it, as both these instruments cover an extensive range of adult pathology (clinical symptomatology and chronic personality patterns).

Projective tests

Our unconscious processes have the ability to influence psychological disorders (Sadock, Sadock, & Ruiz, 2017). Some way of assessing these unconscious thoughts and feelings was needed, and so assessment measures known as projective tests were developed. Projective tests either present a wide variety of ambiguous stimuli to an individual who is asked to describe what they see, or they ask the individual to draw something. The theory behind these techniques is that people tend to project their own personality and fears onto other people and objects, in this case onto the ambiguous stimuli or drawing, without realising that they are doing so (Watkins, Campbell, Nieberding, & Hallmark, 1995). Although there are many different projective techniques, the most widely used ones include the **Rorschach Inkblot Test**, the **Thematic Apperception Test**, the **Draw-A-Person Test**, and the **Kinetic Family Drawing Test**. The first two of these are described in more detail below.

Rorschach Inkblot Test

The test consists of ten cards, each with a bilaterally symmetrical inkblot printed on it (see Figure 3.3). The individual is simply asked to tell the clinician what they see. The aim of using this technique is to assess the structure of the personality, paying particular attention to how the individual constructs their experience (cognitive structuring) and what meaning they assign to their perceptual experience. The idea behind this instrument is that individuals organise environmental stimuli according to their specific needs, motives, and conflicts (Groth-Marnat & Jordan Wright, 2016).

When confronted by ambiguous stimuli, the need for organisation becomes greater. Hence individuals make use of their own internal ideas, images, and relationships in order to create a response. The manner in which individuals organise their responses to the inkblots is representative of how they will confront any other ambiguous situation. Scoring and interpreting the Rorschach is extremely complex and requires extensive training (Groth-Marnat & Jordan Wright, 2016). The test is based on psychoanalytic theory, and the inkblots have changed several times since the test was developed.

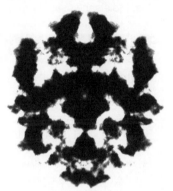

Figure 3.3: Example of Rorschach-type inkblot

Supporters of the Rorschach Inkblot Test believe that the subject's response to an ambiguous and neutral stimulus can provide insight into his or her thought processes, but it is not clear how this occurs. There is still considerable controversy around the use of this instrument (Wood, Nezworski, Lilienfeld, & Garb, 2003). The criticisms relating to this test are based mainly on quantitative psychometric theory and include, inter alia, aspects such as the subjectivity of the interpretation of results, and the reliability (more specifically, the inter-rater reliability) and validity of the test (Di Nuovo & Castellano, 2016).

The Exner Scoring System has addressed many of these criticisms with an extensive body of research (Exner, 2002). This system of scoring (also known as the 'Comprehensive System') is meant to address problems related to the validity of the test, and has become the scoring system of choice; however, disagreements about the test's validity remain.

Wood et al. (2003) maintain that, despite the criticisms, there is substantial research supporting the usefulness of some of the scores on this test. For example, there is some evidence that the Deviant Verbalisations scale relates to bipolar disorder. Further examples of its usefulness include:

- Several scores correlate well with general intelligence.
- Validity has also been shown for detecting such conditions as schizophrenia and other psychotic disorders, thought disorders, and personality disorders.

One of the major threats to the reliability of the Rorschach is in the detail of the testing procedure, such as:

- where the tester and subject are seated
- any introductory words
- verbal and non-verbal responses to subjects' questions or comments
- how responses are recorded.

Although Exner has published detailed instructions, Wood et al. (2003) cite many instances where the proper prescribed testing and scoring procedures have not been followed.

 ACTIVITY

In 2004, Mokgadi Kekae Moletsane adjusted the standard administration procedures when using Rorschach cards with black South African learners to accommodate cultural differences and in this way enable these learners to give sufficient responses.

The table below summarises the differences between the presentation of the test instructions during the Rorschach Comprehensive System (RCS) administration procedures and the Adjusted Rorschach Comprehensive System (ARCS) administration procedures that Moletsane used. How do they differ?

RCS	ARCS
Instructions of the test ■ Greetings (not as emphasised as in ARCS) ■ Side-by-side seating is emphasised ■ The researcher passes the first block and asks: 'What might this be?' ■ If, despite of the pre-test preparation the participant comments, 'It's an inkblot,' the researcher should counter with an acknowledgement plus a restatement of the basic instruction such as: 'That's right. This is an inkblot test, and what I want you to tell me is: what it might be.'	**Presentation phase (P phase)** ■ Introduction: 'Good morning/Good afternoon (greetings are emphasised). My name is (…). I am not a teacher or school inspector, but a psychologist. I work with people in order to know them better. Today I am looking forward to working with you. At the end of the sessions I hope to know you better.' ■ Explanation of Rorschach test: 'Please relax. This test is not a typical school test and it has got nothing to do with your school performance. There are no correct and incorrect answers. This test will give me an idea of how you see things around you. Your answers will help me to know you better.' ■ Presentation of inkblots: 'I am going to show you ten cards. I will start with the first one and I want you to tell me what this might be. I will show you all the cards one by one.' **Re-emphasising phase (RE-phase)** ■ In order to make sure that the participant understood the instructions the researcher should say: 'I have just said that I am going to show you ten cards. I will start with the first one. I want you to tell me what this might be. Let me make sure that you understand. After I have given you a card you must please tell me what it might be. Do not feel embarrassed to tell me because nothing is embarrassing to me. Did you understand? Please feel free to ask any questions before we start.'

Source: Moletsane, 2004, pp. 167–168.

Thematic Apperception Test (TAT)

This instrument consists of a series of 20 cards, 19 of which have pictures and one of which is blank. The individual is asked to tell a story about what he or she thinks is happening in each picture, as well as what the characters might be thinking and feeling. The purpose of the TAT is to reveal the emotions, sentiments, drives, and conflicts of the individual being assessed (Morgan, 1995). The TAT presents more structured stimuli than the Rorschach and hence tends to elicit more complex and organised responses (Groth-Marnat & Jordan Wright; 2016). The TAT also looks at the individual's current life situation rather than the underlying personality structure (Morgan, 1995).

The findings on the TAT can provide valuable information supplementary to other psychological test results, due to the fact that the TAT is able to elicit rich, varied, and multifaceted information, as well as personal data that the individual may consciously resist divulging. Owing to the fact that interpretation of the TAT stories is more qualitative than quantitative, and therefore also quite subjective, it is difficult to determine this instrument's reliability. The reliability improves, however, if one uses the quantitative scoring methods that are available (Groth-Marnat & Jordan Wright, 2016).

Neuropsychological assessment

One very important area in clinical practice is the screening for, and assessment of, possible neuropsychological impairment or brain dysfunction (Goldstein, 2000). This type of screening might be necessary when an individual has suffered some kind of head injury and the extent of damage to the brain needs to be assessed. This may be done in order to determine eligibility for workmen's compensation, a disability grant and/or compensation from the Road Accident Fund.

There are other situations where a neuropsychological screening or assessment might be useful. These would include: determining whether an individual is suffering from depression or organically based dementia; determining why an individual is performing badly at work or school; working with someone who has been abusing drugs or alcohol; and so forth.

When preparing to do a neuropsychological assessment, the clinician has two options. One option is to administer one of the existing, standardised batteries such as the **Luria-Nebraska Neuropsychological Battery** or the **Halstead-Reitan Neuropsychological Battery** (Lezak, 1995). Both of these offer a complex and comprehensive battery of tests to assess a variety of skills. Alternately, clinicians can compile their own battery of neuropsychological tests, based on the functions that they want to assess.

The Luria-Nebraska Neuropsychological Battery (LNNB)

The LNNB is based on Russian neuropsychologist Alexander Luria's theory of higher cortical functioning (Luria, 1966). Luria's examination techniques were originally organised into a battery by the Danish neuropsychologist Anne-Lise Christensen (1979) and, subsequently, items from this battery were selected by Golden, an American, based on whether they were able to discriminate between normal individuals and neurologically impaired patients (Golden et al., 1985). The LNNB produces eleven scores, namely: Motor Functions, Rhythm, Tactile Functions, Visual Functions, Receptive Speech, Writing, Reading, Arithmetic, Memory, and Intellectual Processes; optional scales are Spelling and Motor Writing (Lezak, 1995).

In order to determine whether or not there is brain damage, an individual's score on each of the battery's eleven clinical scales is compared to a critical level appropriate for that person's age and education level. For example, if the individual has five to seven scores above the critical level, he or she most likely has some sign of neurological impairment. If the individual has eight or more scores above the critical level, this indicates a clear history of neurological disorder (Lezak, 1995).

There is controversy surrounding the LNNB's reliability and validity. The LNNB has been criticised by some researchers on the grounds that it tends to overestimate the degree of neuropsychological impairment (i.e. it gives false positives); in other cases, it has failed to detect neuropsychological problems (i.e. it gives false negatives) (Adams, 1984). Another criticism is that the Intellectual Processes scale has not been found to correspond well with other measures of intelligence, such as the Wechsler Adult Intelligence Scale (WAIS) (Crosson & Warren, 1982). Other research, however, has found the LNNB to be a useful measure for distinguishing between brain-damaged individuals and non-brain-damaged individuals with psychiatric problems (Lezak, 1995).

The Halstead-Reitan Neuropsychological Battery (HRNB)

The Halstead-Reitan Neuropsychological Battery (HRNB) began as a battery of seven tests that were apparently able to discriminate between individuals with frontal lobe lesions, individuals with other lesions, and normal individuals. The HRNB is able to evaluate a wide range of nervous system and brain functions, including: visual, auditory, and tactual input; verbal communication; spatial and sequential perception; the ability to analyse information, form mental concepts, and make judgements; motor output; and attention, concentration, and memory. The battery also provides useful information regarding the cause of damage (e.g. closed head injury, alcohol abuse, Alzheimer's disease, stroke, etc.), which part of the brain was damaged, whether the damage occurred during childhood, and whether the damage is getting worse, staying the same, or getting better. Information regarding the severity of impairment and areas of personal strengths can be used to develop plans for rehabilitation or care. The HRNB consists of the Category Test, the Tactual Performance Test, the Rhythm Test, the Speech Sounds Perception Test, the Finger-Tapping Test, the Trail-Making Test, and the Aphasia Screening Test (Lezak, 1995).

Due to its complexity, the HRNB needs to be administered by a professional examiner and interpreted by a trained psychologist. Test results can be affected by the examinee's age, education level, intellectual ability, and, to some extent, gender or ethnicity, which should always be taken into account in interpretation. Owing to the fact that the HRNB is a fixed battery of tests, some unnecessary information may be gathered, or some important information may be missed. Overall, the battery requires five to six hours to complete. There is controversy surrounding the HRNB's reliability and validity, and the battery has also been criticised because it does not include specific tests of memory; rather, memory is evaluated within the context of other tests (Lezak, 1995).

False positives, false negatives, and malingering

For any assessment strategy, one has to bear in mind that there may be times when the test results indicate a problem when there is no problem (**false positives**) and times when the results indicate that there is no problem when actually some difficulty does exist (**false negatives**). False results are particularly worrying when one is assessing for brain dysfunction because important medical problems that need to be treated might go unnoticed (Boll, 1985). Because neuropsychological tests are mainly used as screening devices, they should be paired with other assessments in order to improve the likelihood that problems will be identified.

Complicating the process of diagnosis, there will also be times when a person deliberately falsifies their results in the hope that a problem will be diagnosed so that they can gain something (**secondary gain**). This may include getting out of court appearances, receiving monetary compensation, receiving attention from relatives, and so forth (Sadock, Sadock, & Ruiz, 2017). When malingering is suspected, the clinician can make use of the Rey 15-item test and the Forced Choice test, both of which are good indicators of malingering (Lezak, 1995) (see also Chapter 10).

Arriving at a diagnosis: The use of diagnostic classification systems

The ultimate goal of an assessment would be to arrive at a **diagnosis** by using either the DSM or the ICD classification systems. The purpose of the aforementioned techniques is both to generate a list of signs and symptoms and to rule out other disorders that could better explain the symptoms with which the person is presenting. This list can then be compared with the diagnostic criteria of either classification system. There are, however, some important points to remember when one arrives at the point of making a diagnosis:

- Both classification systems specify the minimum number of symptoms that need to be present. If the minimum **number of symptoms** is not present, one cannot make the diagnosis (see Figure 3.4).
- In conjunction with the above, both systems specify the minimum **duration of the symptoms** (how long these symptoms must be present for before the diagnosis can be made). Once again, if the symptoms have not been present for the minimum time, one cannot make the diagnosis (see Figure 3.4).
- In many cases, there are overlaps between the symptoms in disorders, or a person may display symptoms of more than one disorder. In these cases, the diagnostician will make a **differential diagnosis**; that is, the diagnostician will list all the possible disorders.
- Often, the differential diagnosis will include disorders that naturally occur together. We refer to these as comorbid disorders.
- The classification systems also list the epidemiology of disorders (age of onset, gender, and cultural statistics), as well as the prognosis (expected outcome or course of a disorder).
- The final diagnosis is used to communicate information about the person to other professionals, and this information informs professionals about the treatment or management of the person, as well as the expected course and outcome of the disorder.

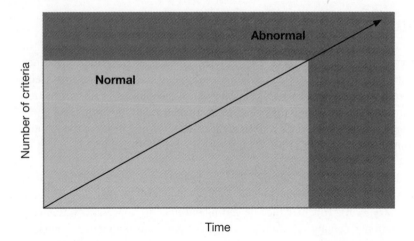

Figure 3.4: The interaction between number of criteria and duration of symptoms

Source: Created by author Burke.

CONCLUSION

The assessment and diagnostic process involves complicated, and often time-consuming, procedures. It is also not a purely mechanistic process in which a set series of steps are followed. It requires a certain amount of investigative and deductive reasoning, technical skills, and sensitivity to the person's cultural and social background. It is for this reason that only qualified psychologists and medical professionals may make a diagnosis. A diagnosis is important to inform the professionals about treatment and prognosis; however, a diagnosis (especially a misdiagnosis) may also cause a lot of harm. It is therefore important that diagnosticians abide by a strong set of ethical principles (see Chapter 5).

MULTIPLE-CHOICE QUESTIONS

1. Which of the following factors is typically NOT part of a clinical assessment?
   a) psychological
   b) social
   c) biological
   d) astrological
2. In terms of psychological assessment, which of the following describes the concept of validity?
   a) Two or more 'raters' get the same answers.
   b) An assessment technique is consistent across different measures.
   c) Scores are used as a norm for comparison purposes.
   d) An assessment technique measures what it is designed to measure.

3. Which of the following describes an intelligence test?
    a) It determines the possible contribution of brain damage to the person's condition.
    b) It uses imaging to assess brain structure and/or function.
    c) It assesses long-standing patterns of behaviour.
    d) It ascertains the structure and patterns of cognition.
4. As part of a psychological assessment, a mental status exam is used to find out how a person thinks, feels, and behaves; its primary purpose, however, is to determine:
    a) which areas of the patient's condition may need more assessment
    b) what type of treatment should be used
    c) which medication would be most effective
    d) whether the individual also has a medical condition
5. Use of the Rorschach test has long been considered controversial because of all of the following concerns EXCEPT:
    a) the test is based on psychoanalytic theory
    b) there is little or no data regarding its reliability or validity
    c) subjective interpretation of the results
    d) until recently there were no standardised procedures for administering the test

PARAGRAPH AND ESSAY QUESTIONS

1. In two paragraphs, explain what the Mental Status Examination is.
2. Explain the differences between the Rorschach Inkblot Test and the Luria-Nebraska Neuropsychological Battery (LNNB).

Karel Botha & Edwin du Plessis

CHAPTER CONTENTS

Introduction
A brief history of mental wellness and positive psychology
Different perspectives on mental wellness
    Individual perspectives
    Sociocultural and sociopolitical perspectives
Mental illness from a well-being perspective
    Mental illness according to Keyes' Mental Health Continuum
    Mental illness as impaired levels of psychological well-being
    Mental illness as the absence, opposite, or exaggeration of psychological strengths
Strengths that protect against mental illness
    Cognitive strengths
    Positive affect and emotional intelligence
    Self-regulation
    Coping
    Resilience
    Post-traumatic growth
    Interpersonal strengths
    Religiosity and spirituality
Treatment from a wellness perspective
    Treatment of the mentally ill person
    Support for the family of the mentally ill person
    Promoting well-being in communities
Conclusion

LEARNING OUTCOMES

After studying this chapter, you should be able to:
- Demonstrate understanding of what we can benefit from approaching abnormal psychology from a psychological well-being perspective.
- Describe the history of mental wellness and positive psychology.
- Explain mental wellness in terms of the mental health continuum, impaired psychological well-being, as well as deficits in character strengths.
- Describe different strengths that buffer against the development of mental illness.
- Provide an overview of different wellness-based psychotherapies.

PERSONAL HISTORY CASELET

Depression has been shown to promote traits of realism and empathy. Mildly depressed individuals tend to see the world more as it is and are realistic enough to see painful truths, whereas many 'normal' people suffer from positive illusion – an inflated sense of false control. Obsessive-compulsive disorder (OCD) is known to encourage traits of perfectionism and meticulousness. Many people with OCD have enhanced organisational skills and a heightened ability to foresee sequences of events necessary for categorisation and planning. The hypomania stage of bipolar disorder supports traits of energy, creativity, and confidence. When channelled to higher tasks, these qualities can result in outstanding productivity in some people.

ADHD sustains traits of hyperfocus, hyperspeed, and risk-taking behaviours. The stimulated brains of ADHD individuals allow them to effortlessly multitask, quickly process information, and have an increased capacity for multiplex vision to solve problems outside the box during crisis situations. There are other mental diseases with useful traits that aren't covered here. The goal is to illustrate that mental illness can be harnessed and redirected to beneficial use. And mental health treatments today are more effective than ever before to achieve this end.

'What doesn't destroy me makes me stronger.' – *Nietzsche*
This is a credo I live by. So true that I even have it inked onto my shoulder. Mental illness doesn't make you crazy or weak. I've had my own personal battle with OCD since childhood. For me, once I was able to manage the unhealthy part of my mental disease, the beneficial traits of OCD shined. I can't say that I would have reached my successes today without these attributes. However, I can say that my weakness was the force that drove my strength.

Source: Jenny C. Yip https://www.psychologytoday.com/us/blog/the-ocd-monster/201207/what-doesnt-destroy-me-makes-me-stronger

INTRODUCTION

In the typical description of abnormal behaviour, there seems to be an emphasis on the negative (i.e. what is or has gone 'wrong'). But focusing only on negative factors leads to a rather one-dimensional view of abnormal behaviour; as the American psychologist Martin Seligman (2005) pointed out, psychology is not only the study of disease, weakness, and damage, but also the study of strength and virtue.

This chapter, in contrast to the rest of the book, focuses on mental illness from a strength-and-wellness point of view. The aim of the chapter is to improve your understanding of abnormal psychology, emphasising the strengths available to individuals and communities in adversity, how these strengths may prevent pathology and promote psychological well-being, and finally, how a strengths-based approach may be used in treating abnormal behaviour.

But first, let us discuss some reasons why we need to look at abnormal psychology from a wellness perspective:

- *Normality and abnormality are not different in kind:* Maddux (2005) states that both adaptive and maladaptive psychological functioning are acquired and maintained through the same processes, and differ in degree rather than in quality. Supporting this idea, Manderscheid et al. (2010) remind us that mental health and mental illnesses can both cause and be influenced by positive or negative social determinants of health, for instance, income, housing, stress, early childhood experiences, education level, social support, and access to resources. Therefore, Wood and Tarrier (2010) argue that it is not logical to study either negative or positive functioning in isolation. This is because any designation of a characteristic as positive or negative is simplistic and inaccurate, because any trait can be positive or negative, depending on the situation.

- *Abnormal psychology is limited and narrows our focus:* According to Maddux (2008), clinical psychology, with its focus on abnormal behaviour, has to a large extent narrowed our focus onto what is weak and defective about people to the exclusion of what is strong and healthy. Although clinical psychology has produced many successes in treating psychopathology, and has built an extensive understanding of mental illness, Ryff and Singer (1998) believe that psychology should be more than a 'repair shop' for broken lives. In this regard, Wright and Lopez (2005) argue that it is a common error in professional psychology to make important decisions based primarily on the deficiencies of the person, instead of giving serious consideration to his or her deficits and strengths. Being problem oriented, the clinician easily concentrates only on pathology and dysfunction, neglecting the discovery of available strengths that could be drawn upon in problem-solving efforts.

- *Understanding strengths may help us to understand and treat mental disorders:* In support of the growing perception that psychotherapy should be more about amplifying strengths than repairing weaknesses, there is an increasing interest in building human strengths in different psychotherapeutic strategies. For example, Ruini and Fava (2004) proposed that psychological well-being needs to be incorporated into the definition of recovery, while Seligman (2008) believes that the promotion of well-being may be one of the best ways to alleviate mental disorder. These authors support the belief that absence of well-being creates vulnerability to adversity, and that the route to long-term recovery lies in facilitating the positive, rather than on exclusively treating the negative.

Even though these reasons are primarily theoretically motivated, they make an important statement that needs to be explored further. To start with, we will explore the concept of psychological well-being.

> **EXAMPLE CASE**
>
> *Imagine that you are a clinical psychologist with a strong focus on abnormality only, in other words, with what is wrong with clients. A 30-year-old client, John, experienced shock and fear when he was a victim of a hijacking and has been referred to you. By taking a one-sided perspective focusing on abnormality only, there is a risk that you (i) are biased into thinking that something must be wrong with John; and (ii) focus on signs and symptoms that confirm the diagnosis of, say, posttraumatic stress disorder. The possibility exists, however, that John's behaviour is a natural, healthy response to the trauma, and/or that his response to the trauma fits a category in the DSM called 'additional conditions that may be a focus of clinical attention'. This category describes conditions that led to contact with the mental healthcare system, but without sufficient evidence to justify a diagnosis of a mental disorder. Taking this abnormality perspective risks a missed opportunity or, at best, limited ability to recognise and facilitate the strengths John might have.*

A BRIEF HISTORY OF MENTAL WELLNESS AND POSITIVE PSYCHOLOGY

The scientific study of human strengths and mental wellness is not a new venture. William James, in the late 1800s, made a significant contribution to the science of psychology in general, but also to a first understanding of positive functioning, in particular (Hefferon & Boniwell, 2011). Most of the prominent early psychologists (see Table 4.1) described human potential to some extent, despite the fact that they mainly focused on abnormal behaviour.

According to Abraham Maslow (1987), for example, a person is healthy and shows mental wellness when his or her potential is actualised, rather than blocked. For Maslow, human motivation depended on a five-level hierarchy of needs:

- physiological needs
- safety needs
- belongingness and love needs
- esteem needs
- self-actualisation needs.

Table 4.1: Some early psychologists' views on human strengths

Psychologist	Concept of mental wellness
Gordon Allport	Maturity
Carl Jung	Balance

Psychologist	Concept of mental wellness
Carl Rogers	The fully functioning person
Erich Fromm	Productivity
Abraham Maslow	Self-actualisation
Viktor Frankl	Self transcendence

Source: Adapted from Peterson, 2006, p. 36.

In 1958, the Austrian-British psychologist Marie Jahoda was amongst the first to attempt to operationalise psychological well-being, when she listed six criteria she argued were needed to establish positive mental health (Compton, 2005). In addition, the humanistic movement, led by the American psychologists Abraham Maslow and Carl Rogers, criticised traditional psychology for primarily focusing on negative aspects of human behaviour (Baumgardner & Crothers, 2009). These theorists saw human nature as basically positive, and proposed that the goal of psychology should be to study and promote the achievement of productive and healthy lives.

In a world-wide explosion of interest and research on psychological well-being during the 1990s, significant contributions were made by South African researchers such as D. J. W. Strümpfer (1995) who extended Antonovsky's construct 'salutogenesis' (the origins of health) to 'fortigenesis' (the origins of strengths), and by Marié Wissing and Chrizanne Van Eeden (1997), who proposed the term 'fortology' (the study of strengths). However, these terms were not adopted and, in 1998, Seligman (then president of the American Psychological Association) made a plea for a major shift in psychology's focus to what became known as 'positive psychology'. Seligman's intention was that this would broaden the scope of psychology to promote the study and understanding of healthy human functioning.

Positive psychology is defined in a number of ways. However, the following definition is particularly relevant to this chapter as it emphasises the integration between positive and negative aspects of human functioning. According to Linley, Joseph, Harrington, and Wood (2006, p. 8), positive psychology is 'the scientific study of optimal human functioning, which aims to redress the imbalance in psychology, integrating the positive aspects of human functioning and experience with our understanding of the negative aspects of human functioning and experience'.

Positive psychology studies what people do right and how they manage to do it (Compton, 2005). However, it complements, rather than replaces, our understanding of how positive and negative life events and emotions are interconnected (Baumgardner & Crothers, 2009). Wong (2011) indicates that positive psychology has effectively changed the language and landscape of mainstream psychology and it continues to grow exponentially in terms of teaching, research, and applications.

However, it is also important to realise that, despite its popularity and widespread interest, positive psychology has been criticised for being hegemonic in its strong North American and European influence. This resulted in the placement of the individual as the primary focus in research, excluding real issues related to historical, cultural, political, and societal context (Becker & Marecek, 2008; Christopher & Hickinbottom, 2008).

Harrell (2014) indicates that, with respect to social justice, positive psychology research, to date, has paid little attention to 'positive' concepts and processes such as empowerment, liberation from oppression, bridging differences, equality, loyalty, social interest, and collective identity. There is therefore a strong need to decentre Western, particularly North American, positive psychology, and make visible contributions across the world. According to Marujo and Neto (2014), for positive psychology to become a constructive force for social change, it needs theoretical flexibility and a view to real-life social issues.

Nevertheless, when Eloff, Achouri, Chireshe, Mutepfa, and Ofovwe (2008) interviewed psychologists in six African nations, 'several participants linked positive psychological constructs to indigenous practices, rather than Western knowledge', suggesting that 'positive psychological constructs developed from the grassroots can help acknowledge and tap into local knowledge, and provide answers to society's issues in ways that are relevant, relatable, and practical' (Rao, Donaldson, & Doiron, 2015, p. 68)

DIFFERENT PERSPECTIVES ON MENTAL WELLNESS

Individual perspectives

Generally, mental wellness or psychological well-being has been conceptualised within the positive psychology approach from two related, but different, traditions, namely hedonic and eudaimonic well-being.

Hedonic well-being relates to subjective experiences of pleasure and life satisfaction, and most research work in this regard has focused on the concept of happiness. Diener (2000) indicates that happiness is a form of subjective well-being, which he defined as life satisfaction, characterised by the subjective presence of positive affect, and a relative absence of negative affect.

> **HELPFUL HINT**
> - Hedonic well-being is about happiness, pleasure, and life satisfaction.
> - Eudaimonic well-being is about meaning, purpose, and engagement.

Seligman (2008), in formulating the conceptual framework for positive psychology, broke the term 'happiness' down into three quantifiable aspects. The first, positive emotion (the *pleasant* life), reflects the emphasis on understanding the determinants of happiness as a desired state. The other two aspects relate more to eudaimonic well-being, characterised by meaning, purpose, and the realisation of one's potential. In this regard, Seligman (2008) describes happiness as being a result of engagement (the *engaged* life), which refers to active and meaningful involvement in activities and relationships with others, and purpose (the *meaningful* life), which is about going beyond our own self-interests and preoccupations and being involved in something larger than oneself.

The work of the American psychologist Carol Ryff on eudaimonic well-being is probably the most influential in this area. According to Ryff, positive functioning consists of six basic elements, which together she calls psychological well-being (Ryff & Keyes, 1995). Each element is important in the striving to become a better person and to realise one's potential. The six elements are:

- **Self-acceptance:** A positive and accepting attitude towards aspects of self in past and present
- **Purpose in life:** Goals and beliefs that affirm a sense of direction and meaning in life
- **Autonomy:** Self-direction as guided by one's own socially accepted internal standards
- **Positive relations with others:** Having satisfying personal relationships in which empathy and intimacy are expressed
- **Environmental mastery:** The capability to manage the complex environment according to one's own needs
- **Personal growth:** The insight into one's own potential for self-development.

Apart from the few approaches to psychological well-being mentioned here, other notable perspectives, not discussed in this chapter, include flow theory (Csikszentmihalyi, 1990), self-determination theory (Ryan & Deci, 2000), and the broaden-and-build theory of positive emotions (Fredrickson, 2013).

Sociocultural and sociopolitical perspectives

Although eudaimonic well-being includes positive relations with others, research in this regard primarily focusses on how it impacts on individual fulfilment. Keyes (1998) initiated a move to understanding well-being from a social perspective. He provided a conceptual analysis of social well-being that consists of five dimensions; these describe a person who is functioning optimally in society. These dimensions are social coherence, social acceptance, social actualisation, social contribution, and social integration. According to Keyes (1998), well-being thus consists of emotional well-being (happiness/hedonic well-being), psychological well-being (the six dimensions by Ryff), and social well-being.

The South African researchers Wissing and Van Eeden (2002), Wissing and Temane (2008), Khumalo, Wissing, and Temane (2008), and Khumalo, Temane, and Wissing (2013) made a powerful contribution to a better understanding of well-being as strongly rooted in sociocultural context. More specifically, well-being seems to be dependent on the community in which an individual lives. Du Toit, Wissing, and Khumalo (2014) refer to community as a group of people sharing common values and knowledge, and who may be differentiated from other communities by geographical localisation, as well as race, socio-economic status, and cultural identity.

Du Toit et al. (2014) put forward convincing literature evidence that well-being within communities is often based on the quality of the relationships between community members, including aspects like overcoming conflict with others, the building of strength and resilience through collaborative efforts, and harmony in diversity. Individuals and groups should therefore experience a sense of community, in which they feel that they belong, that they matter, that their needs are met, and finally, that they have a shared history.

Strongly related to community is the notion of cultural identity, specifically because culture is defined as the values, beliefs, and behaviour shared by a group of people (Khumalo, 2014, in reference to Matsumoto, 1996). As different cultures are diverse and complex, it is no surprise that well-being and happiness differ quite substantially between cultural communities (Khumalo, 2014). Wissing and Temane (2008) and Khumalo et al. (2008), for example, found that relatedness, a sense of community, and interpersonal trust and integrity in group contexts seem to be more important to black South Africans, while competency and agency may be more important to white South Africans.

Research further suggests that well-being is higher in wealthier countries, in those individuals with employment, in those communities with higher social capital – that is, communities or societies characterised by trust, freedom, and equality (Khumalo, 2014) – and in those who are politically stable and where people feel safe and secure (Tiliouine, 2017).

In this regard, Marujo and Neto (2014) indicate that positive psychology has yet to make a significant contribution to burning social issues such as poverty and inequality. South Africa, in particular, is an interesting case in point. Bookwalter (2012) indicates that the apartheid system generated massive inequality in both opportunity and income, and although the end of apartheid in the early 1990s brought a large increase in reported happiness in both black and white South Africans, much needs to be done to improve the lives of all citizens. One reason for this is that South Africa still has one of the most unequal distributions of income and wealth in the world, largely corresponding to race.

However, according to Bookwalter (2012), income only matters in small ways. Even the poorest South Africans are also able to enjoy better subjective well-being when they have access to better infrastructure and service delivery. This is supported by Veenhoven (2012) who indicates that happier nations are those with positive economic development, freedom, rule of law, and good governance.

 ACTIVITY

The following extract is written by a group of authors led by the social worker and academic Alean Al-Krenawi, senior lecturer at Ben Gurion University of the Negev in Israel. It makes interesting observations regarding the relationship between emotional burnout and political ideology during times of political violence. What observations does it make, and how do you feel about these?

Political ideology serves as a lens through which a person understands and interprets political events, and therefore, has an effect on the psychological reaction to these events. The importance of examining political ideology is suggested by terror management theory. According to this theory, our awareness of human vulnerability and mortality leads to the development of cultural institutions that provide order and meaning, and thereby ensure literal or symbolic immortality. The protective effect of culture is especially salient when awareness of human vulnerability and death is enhanced, as it is in times of war and political conflicts. Under such circumstances, people tend to cling to their cultural beliefs or ideology, embracing individuals who are similar to them (the in-group), and rejecting those who are different (the out-group). It seems that when the awareness of death increases, the role of ideology becomes more salient as it serves as a buffer, providing order in the chaos, meaning, predictability, and even symbolic immortality, thus reducing the pathogenic effect of stressors. In this way, social or political world views and actions give meaning to traumatic experiences.

Studies demonstrate that the first Intifada had a different effect on Israeli right- and left-wing political activists. For example, Jewish left-wing activists reported higher levels of emotional burnout than their right-wing counterparts. These findings reveal that the Intifada is incongruent with former political beliefs regarding the Israeli–Palestinian conflict, resulting in greater emotional burnout. In addition, this highlights the significant role played by the political ideology of Israeli children/youth who have been confronted with political violence associated with the Israeli–Palestinian conflict.

Source: Al-Krenawi et al., 2011.

MENTAL ILLNESS FROM A WELL-BEING PERSPECTIVE

In this section, we will describe three different well-being perspectives on mental illness:

- mental illness according to Keyes' Mental Health Continuum
- mental illness as impaired levels of psychological well-being
- mental illness as the absence, opposite, or exaggeration of psychological strengths.

Mental illness according to Keyes' Mental Health Continuum

Keyes (2002) proposed a mental health continuum in which mental health is viewed as a complete state consisting of the presence and/or absence of mental illness and mental health symptoms. Later, Westerhof and Keyes (2010) described this as a two-continuum model where one continuum indicates the presence or absence of mental health, and the other shows the presence or absence of mental illness. Both are related but distinct dimensions, so that the absence of mental illness does not equate to the presence of mental health, or vice versa. Thus, for each individual, there is, at any point in time, an independent indication on both these continua of the level of mental health and of mental illness. Four levels of well-being are identified in this way (see Table 4.2).

Table 4.2: The mental health continuum

		Mental health	
		High	Low
Mental illness	High	Struggling	Floundering
	Low	Flourishing	Languishing

Source: Adapted from Keyes & Lopez, 2005, p. 50.

These four levels of well-being can be described as follows:

- *Flourishing:* Characterised by high levels of mental health, as well as the absence of recent mental illness. People in this category are in a state of complete mental health.
- *Languishing:* Those without mental illness, but who also have low levels of well-being, are in a state of incomplete mental health.
- *Struggling:* Those who have a mental illness, but who also present with aspects of well-being, are in a state of incomplete mental illness.
- *Floundering:* Those who present with mental illness, as well as an absence of well-being, are in a state of complete mental illness.

According to Keyes and Lopez (2005), the ability to diagnose complete and incomplete states of mental illness and health may lead to more effective prevention and treatment programmes. For example, incomplete mental health (languishing) may be a 'way station' at which individuals find themselves prior to the onset of depression, or a place where many people are left following traditional psychotherapeutic treatment. Preventatively, the diagnosis of languishing among youth may be used to identify individuals who require interventions to elevate well-being and prevent development of mental illness.

In a group of South African adolescents from various ethnic backgrounds, Van Schalkwyk and Wissing (2010) found 42% to be flourishing, with 53% moderately mentally healthy, and 5% languishing. Thus, nearly 60% are not functioning optimally. Lower psychological well-being was characterised by meaninglessness, impaired relations, identification with dysfunctional outsiders, self-incompetence, destructive behaviours, negative emotions, and helplessness. The adolescents understood and experienced *flourishing* as purposeful living, being a role model, having positive relations, self-confidence and self-liking, a constructive lifestyle, constructive coping, and positive emotions.

Mental illness as impaired levels of psychological well-being

Ruini and Fava (2004), in developing well-being therapy (WBT) (see later in chapter), provide an interesting perspective on mental illness. Their approach is motivated by the observation that, among others, Ryff's model of psychological well-being provides a useful description of specific impairments of patients with mood disorders. In support of the idea that well-being and distress are not mutually exclusive, and that well-being could thus not be attained simply from the removal of distress, they had to demonstrate impaired levels of psychological well-being in a clinical population to justify therapeutic efforts aimed at increasing psychological well-being.

Rafanelli and colleagues (Ruini & Fava, 2004) found that patients with anxiety and mood disorders displayed significantly lower levels in all six dimensions of Ryff's psychological well-being model compared to healthy subjects. Individuals are therefore at risk of mental illness when they show impaired levels of the six dimensions in the following way (Ruini & Fava, 2004, p. 376):

- *Impaired self-acceptance:* Feels dissatisfied with self; is disappointed with what has occurred in past life; is troubled about certain personal qualities; wishes to be different from what he or she is.

- *Impaired purpose in life:* Lacks a sense of meaning in life; has few goals, lacks a sense of direction, does not see purpose in past life; has no outlooks or beliefs that give life meaning.
- *Impaired autonomy:* Over-concerned with the expectations and evaluation of others; relies on judgement of others to make important decisions; conforms to social pressures to think or act in certain ways.
- *Impaired positive relations with others:* Has few close trusting relationships with others; finds it difficult to be open and is isolated and frustrated in interpersonal relationships; is not willing to make compromises to sustain important ties with others.
- *Impaired environmental mastery:* Difficulties in managing everyday affairs; unable to change or improve surrounding contexts.
- *Impaired personal growth:* A sense of personal stagnation; lacks a sense of improvement or expansion over time; bored and uninterested with life; unable to develop new attitudes or behaviours.

This framework provides us with a new way of looking at mental illness. For Ruini and Fava (2004), the most important benefit is that it provides a clear goal for well-being therapy, which is to move impaired levels of psychological well-being to optimal levels of functioning.

Mental illness as the absence, opposite, or exaggeration of psychological strengths

For Park, Peterson, and Seligman, character strengths are positive traits that are reflected in feelings, thoughts and behaviours (2004). They exist in degrees and can be measured as individual differences. As an initial step toward specifying important positive traits, the Values in Action (VIA) Classification of Strengths was developed to complement the *Diagnostic and Statistical Manual of Mental Disorders* (DSM) (see Chapter 2) by focusing on what is right about people (Peterson, 2006). The VIA categorises and describes 24 character strengths with reference to six broad virtue classes, namely, wisdom, courage, humanity, justice, temperance, and transcendence.

Peterson (2006) indicates that the VIA classification identifies ways of doing well and, by implication, it also identifies ways of doing poorly. As all character strengths are on a continuum between deficiency and excess, disorders may thus be generated from both of these, thus adding another dimension to the understanding of abnormal psychology. The classification is therefore approached from the existence of strengths and disorders in degrees along a continuum ranging from *opposite* through *absence* to *strength*, and finally *exaggeration*. Table 4.3 shows the six virtues, with one example each of a character strength, and Peterson's (2006) classification thereof in terms of psychological disorder.

Table 4.3: Adapted version of the VIA: A well-being and mental illness perspective

Psychological well-being		Psychological disorder		
Virtue	Character strength	Absence	Opposite	Exaggeration
Wisdom: Cognitive strengths	e.g. Creativity	Conformity	Triteness	Eccentricity
Courage: Emotional strengths	e.g. Persistence	Laziness	Helplessness	Obsessiveness
Humanity: Interpersonal strengths	e.g. Kindness	Indifference	Cruelty	Intrusiveness
Justice: Civic strengths	e.g. Citizenship	Selfishness	Narcissism	Chauvinism
Temperance: Self-control strengths	e.g. Self-regulation	Self-indulgence	Impulsivity	Inhibition
Transcendence: Meaning strengths	e.g. Hope	Present orientation	Pessimism	Pollyannism

Source: Adapted from Peterson, 2006, p. 39.

Absence of the strength creativity is *conformity*, for example. According to Peterson (2006), this is probably not a significant problem for any given individual; however, for an entire group or society it means stagnation. The opposite of creativity is *triteness*, or unoriginality, and Peterson (2006, p. 41) indicates this as a disorder as it is an 'aesthetic offence' and causes people to follow fads blindly. Finally, exaggeration of creativity, *eccentricity*, is in essence referring to a person who is out of touch with the reaction of others. Peterson refers to exhibitionism as an example, but one could just as well include schizotypal and histrionic personality disorders (see Chapter 14).

Another good example would be the character strength of persistence. The absence of persistence, *laziness*, is probably not a disorder in itself, but may put people at risk later on of developing disorders. Its opposite, *helplessness*, may be associated with mood disorder (see Chapter 7), while exaggeration of persistence, *obsessiveness*, may be associated with obsessive-compulsive disorder (see Chapter 6).

According to Peterson (2006), this approach creates a new language from which we can better understand psychological disorders. For example, when we examine depression in terms of its association with such difficulties as disinterest, indifference, helplessness, isolation and loneliness, pessimism, and alienation, then we can readily understand when and why depression is a psychological problem.

STRENGTHS THAT PROTECT AGAINST MENTAL ILLNESS

The previous section put abnormal psychology in a different light, and helped us to better understand the complex relationship between mental illness and mental wellness. Although a large number of strengths/protective factors are described in the literature, this section focuses on how a selected few cognitive, emotional, and interpersonal strengths buffer/ protect against the development of mental illness.

Cognitive strengths

Many forms of psychopathology are related to cognitive dysfunctions. Anxiety and mood disorders, for instance, are often precipitated and maintained by pessimism, irrational beliefs, hopelessness, and mindlessness. This section discusses optimism and mindfulness.

Optimism

Optimists, in contrast to pessimists, are people who expect good things to happen to them (Carver & Scheier, 2005). They have high levels of positive expectancy – a sense of confidence about the attainability of a goal, even when things are difficult. Optimism and pessimism are basic qualities of personality, and influence people's subjective experiences when confronting problems, as well as the actions people engage in to try to deal with these problems. Optimists tend to be more hopeful; they believe, according to Snyder, Rand, and Sigmon (2005), that they can find pathways to desired goals and become motivated to use those pathways.

Optimism protects against the development of psychopathology in a number of ways. Optimists are more proactive in that they take active steps to ensure the positive quality of their future. They also use more problem-centred coping and, when this is not a possibility, they turn to strategies such as acceptance, humour, and positive reframing (Carver & Scheier, 2005). Kasayira and Chireshe (2010) indicate that individuals affected by poverty and HIV/ Aids in sub-Saharan Africa who ascribe more positive meaning to their situation report higher levels of psychological well-being and lower levels of depressed mood. An example of this is seeing their situation as creating opportunities for personal growth,

The motivational component in hope is agency, which is the perceived capacity to use one's pathways to reach desired goals. Hope enhances confidence, effective future thinking, and flexibility in finding alternative goals when goal blockages are experienced (Snyder at al., 2005). In a South African study, Maree, Maree, and Collins (2008) found that hope, among others, fosters energy to pursue goals.

Mindfulness

Mindfulness refers to paying attention to the world around us in a way that allows openness and flexibility (Langer, 2005). It is the ability to refine one's perspective in the face of new circumstances, thus keeping multiple perspectives about the same phenomenon 'alive' at any given moment. Mindfulness includes qualities like *non-judging* (the ability to recognise that things are not inherently equal to how we judge them), *patience* (the ability to allow events to unfold in their own time rather than always pushing, wishing, or working to make things happen according to our present desires), and *non-striving* (the ability to let go of preconceived ideas of what should happen) (Kabat-Zinn, 1990).

Langer (2005) indicates that mindfulness is the opposite of mindlessness, a state of consciousness marked by little awareness of what is going on in the present moment, in which a person is governed by rule and routine, habit, and automatic behaviour.

Mindfulness helps in dealing with uncertainty as it helps the individual to accept that things change and that change need not be feared. When uncertain, mindfulness leads to engagement with the task at hand (Langer, 2005).

Positive affect and emotional intelligence

Our evolutionary heritage and life learning have given us the capacity to experience a rich array of emotions. We can feel sad, happy, anxious, surprised, bored, exhilarated, scared, disgusted, or disappointed, to name just a few emotions (Baumgardner & Crothers, 2009). The exact number of basic human emotions varies from seven to ten depending on the theorist; however, the various lists show a fair amount of agreement (Compton, 2005; Ekman, 1993).

Positive psychologists typically measure people's emotional experience in terms of both the positive and negative affective dimensions. This two-dimensional assessment and summary follows from research suggesting that, despite their diversity, if we evaluate emotions by their psychological and physiological effects, we see that emotions come in two basic forms, namely positive and negative affect (Baumgardner & Crothers, 2009). Positive affect refers to emotions such as cheerfulness, joy, contentment, and happiness while negative affect refers to emotions such as anger, fear, sadness, guilt, contempt, and disgust.

Emotions can serve a very useful function if 'used' properly (Compton, 2005). The ability to use emotions wisely might be considered a type of intelligence. Over the past few decades, a number of theorists have developed the concept of emotional intelligence (Compton, 2005). Emotional intelligence involves the ability to monitor one's own and others' feelings and emotions, to discriminate among them, and to use the information to guide one's thinking and actions (Salovey & Mayer, 1990).

People who are high in emotional intelligence have the ability to use their emotions wisely, and they appear to have a deeper understanding of their emotional lives (Salovey, Mayer, & Caruso, 2002); as a consequence, they are happier and more successful in their lives (Chamorro-Premuzic, Bennett, & Furnham, 2007; Murphy & Janeke, 2009).

Several studies have pointed out that a higher level of emotional intelligence correlates with more adaptive ways of coping (Salovey, Bedell, Detweiler, & Mayer, 1999; Salovey, Stroud, Woolery, & Epel, 2002); contributes to the achievement of better academic results (Parker, Summerfeldt, Hogan, & Majeski, 2004; Van der Zee, Thijs, & Schakel, 2002); is associated with better interpersonal relations (Mayer, Caruso, & Salovey, 1999); and is a protective factor in both physical and mental health (Austin, Saklofske, & Egan, 2005; Tsaousis & Nikolaou, 2005).

Self-regulation

According to Vohs and Baumeister (2004) and Baumeister, Vohs, and Tice (2007), every major personal and social problem, including drug addiction, eating disorders, excessive spending, crime and violence, emotional problems (such as depression), underachievement in work and school, procrastination, and sexually transmitted diseases, involves some kind of failure of self-regulation.

Self-regulation is defined by Maes and Karoly (2005, p. 269) as 'a systematic process of human behaviour that involves setting of personal goals and steering behaviour toward the achievement of established goals'. It includes 'self-corrective adjustments, originating within the person, that are needed to stay on track for whatever purpose is being served' (Carver, 2004, p. 10). Self-regulation unfolds in at least three phases (Botha, 2013):

- Goal establishment
- Goal implementation
- Adjustment.

In the first phase, goal establishment gives direction to how goals are put into action. During this phase, motivational aspects like self-efficacy beliefs and intrinsic motivation play a vital role in establishing goals that will be easier to self-regulate. In the second phase, during goal implementation, the individual aims to promote positive outcomes and prevent negative outcomes. To do this, one needs to focus attention on the task at hand, control and regulate internal and external distractions, and monitor one's own behaviour by comparing it with personal goals and standards, in an effort to get feedback about the success of one's behaviour.

Finally, if a difference between an intended and real outcome is anticipated, or actually occurs, the individual needs to make appropriate adjustments. According to Brandtstädter and Rothermund (2002), adjustment is possible through adaptive flexibility; this is the ability to flexibly switch between different means of reaching a goal, whether persevering, changing, or even disengaging from a goal, depending on what would be most appropriate or effective in any given situation.

Kuhl, Kazén, and Koole (2006) state that self-regulation is an immensely adaptive capacity, as effective self-regulation fosters health-promoting behaviours, positive psychological well-being, and high job performance. This adaptive capacity has been supported by a number of South African studies, for example, in:

- black South African students, in which self-regulation correlates positively with positive affect and subjective well-being (Khumalo et al., 2008);
- children in the Durban area, who regulate themselves in an attempt to adopt a position of care and concern for those who are living with HIV (Bhana, 2008); and
- street youths in the Free State and Gauteng who cope by being able to regulate themselves by adjusting their behaviour, for example, by demonstrating respect for the community's values, even if different from their own, and asking forgiveness when appropriate (Malindi & Theron, 2010).

Coping

The ability to cope with the stress associated with daily living plays an important role in determining the mental wellness of an individual. Coping can be defined as 'constantly changing cognitive and behavioural efforts to manage specific external and/or internal demands that are appraised as taxing or exceeding the resources of a person' (Lazarus & Folkman, 1984, p. 141). These cognitive and behavioural efforts are directed at mastering, tolerating, reducing, and/or minimising environmental and internal demands and conflicts that strain an individual's resources (Schafer, 2000).

Lazarus and Folkman (1984) have proposed that the way individuals appraise situations they are faced with largely determines the level of stress they experience. Coping, however, is not just related to the demands of the situation, but is also determined by the extent of the resources available to a person (Compton, 2005; Frydenburg, 1997).

There are a large number of coping styles; these can be grouped into three subtypes: (i) those in which a person attempts to change negative emotions; (ii) those in which a person attempts to change the situation that caused the stress; and (iii) those that just seek to avoid the problem. These are called emotion-focused coping, problem-focused coping, and avoidance, respectively (Compton, 2005).

According to Lazarus and Folkman (1984, p. 150), emotion-focused coping is 'directed at regulating emotional responses to problems'. The goal is to release the tension, forget the anxiety, eliminate worry, or just release the anger. Research suggests that emotion-focused coping might be effective in the initial stages of coping; however, the beneficial effects of these strategies are usually short-lived, with levels of renewed anxiety and stress returning as stressful circumstances persist (Reineke, 2006).

Another coping style, problem-focused coping, involves the use of realistic strategies that could make a tangible difference in the situation that causes stress (Compton, 2005). The use of problem-focused coping strategies has been reported to increase the likelihood of positive outcomes, which then allows individuals to be hopeful and improve their levels of motivation and satisfaction (Lewis & Frydenburg, 2002).

Examples of problem-focused coping strategies include situational coping, self-restructuring, and accessing social support. These types of coping strategies are associated with good problem-solving skills, cognitive and behavioural restructuring, seeking help or advice and information regarding the problem, and establishing plans and steps that should be taken to deal with a stressful situation (Wong, Reker, & Peacock, 2006).

Of course, in many instances, people combine the above two types of coping. For instance, if a person consistently takes work problems home to their spouse, but the discussions help the person to decide on a course of action that could change the situation, then he or she has combined emotion-focused and problem-focused coping to help solve the problem.

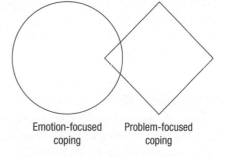

Emotion-focused coping   Problem-focused coping

Figure 4.1: A person's approach to coping with a particular problem can combine emotion-focused coping and problem-focused coping.

Source: Created by OUP.

Lastly, another way of dealing with stressors is to simply use avoidance (Compton, 2005). Here, a person attempts to run away from stress, refuses to confront difficulties presented by life events, or attempts to deny their impact and importance. Under most circumstances this strategy is not very adaptive.

Cultural and gender differences may also influence the type of coping used. Possible differences between the coping strategies employed by individuals from collectivist cultures and those from more individualist cultures have been noted (Hashim, 2003; Mann et al., 1998). People from mainly individualistic cultures are more inclined to demonstrate more active forms of coping such as emotion-focused and problem-focused coping, while people from collectivist cultures are more inclined to utilise avoidance coping (Hashim, 2003; Mann et al., 1998). Although very little research is available with regard to ethnic differences and coping within the South African context, George (2009) reported a higher usage of avoidance coping strategies amongst black and coloured adolescents than white adolescents.

Frydenburg (1997) found that boys (more than girls) use avoidance as a coping mechanism. Boys tend to get involved in alternative activities, such as sport, to reduce their stress, and in this way they suppress or ignore the problem more than girls do. Girls, however, are more inclined to use social support, rely on others for approval, and appraise events as more complex and negative; thus, they are more affected by stressful situations than boys (Frydenburg, 1997; Frydenburg, 2008; Seiffge-Krenke, 2006). In a South African study involving adolescents, Wissing, Claassens, and Du Toit (1998) found that female participants more often used emotion-focused coping strategies such as seeking social support and emotional discharge to deal with stress.

A good example of coping within a social context comes from the study by Roos, Chigeza, and Van Niekerk (2012), on older adults in a rural, drought-stricken community in the North West province of South Africa. Coping strategies seemed to be primarily interpersonal: first, the older adults proactively planned in collaboration with others, specifically regarding how to deal with food shortages. Second, the participants strove to be innovative in securing additional income, for example, doing extra work, being involved in saving schemes, and by sharing resources. All these actions were used to the benefit of the community, which implies a strong sense of shared responsibility. Roos and colleagues concluded that the findings reveal a strong interdependence in this specific community, with members being able to maintain their functioning due to the collective mobilisation of resources, despite the drought.

Resilience

Adverse life events such as family violence, the loss of a loved one, traumatic experiences, and sexual molestation often result in mental health problems. However, what is surprising is that many of the individuals exposed to these adverse life events turn out to be quite well adjusted (Baumgardner & Crothers, 2009). After a brief period of disturbance, some people quickly return to competent and healthy functioning. Like a rubber band that is stretched, but does not break, resilient individuals are able to regain their composure and confidence, and move forward with their lives.

As suggested above, the underlying concept of resiliency is the belief that some people emerge from stressful conditions as competent, well-adapted individuals (Peterson, 2006;

Phan, 2006). Masten (2001) defines resilience as a phenomenon characterised by good outcomes in spite of serious threats to adaptation or development. Similarly, Ryff and Singer (2003, p. 20) define resilience as 'maintenance, recovery, or improvement in mental or physical health following challenge'.

Resilience is often operationalised as the positive end of the distribution of developmental outcomes in a sample of high-risk individuals. Risk and resiliency research is traditionally part of the field of developmental psychopathology. In other words, resilience is a construct that emerged from the field of child and adolescent psychology, and which surfaces here as the contrast of psychopathology (Masten, 2001; Phan, 2006).

It is important to note that the descriptions of resilient responses or resilient individuals are judgement calls (Baumgardner & Crothers, 2009). For a judgement of resilience to be made, a person must first face a significant threat or risk that has the potential to produce negative outcomes. Without a demonstrated risk, there is no resilience. The second part of resilience requires judgement of a favourable or good outcome. The standards for judging outcomes may be defined by the normative expectations of society for the age and situation of the individual. Finally, as suggested above, Masten (2001) notes that some researchers have defined resilience as an absence of problem behaviours or psychopathology following adversity. Children of alcoholic, mentally ill, or abusive parents may be judged resilient if they do not develop substance abuse problems, suffer mental illness, become abusive parents themselves, or show symptoms of poor adjustment.

Studies suggest various adaptive systems as explanations of resilience, focusing on processes acting at multiple levels from childhood to old age, which promote and protect human development across the lifespan (Carrey & Ungar, 2007; Lerner, 2006; Masten & Obradovic, 2006). From a family resilience perspective, Greeff (2012, p. 288) provided a comprehensive review and concluded that 'a family's ability to have a sense of control over the outcome of events, while using an active approach in dealing with crises' can be considered a general resilience quality. However, more research needs to be done to understand what resilience entails in a wider variety of family forms and structures, and pertaining to more specific life crises.

Post-traumatic growth

A growing body of empirical literature reveals that many people find meaningful life lessons, a renewed appreciation for life, and increased feelings of personal strength as a result of traumatic experiences (see Affleck & Tennen, 1996; Nolen-Hoeksema & Davis, 2002; Tennen & Affleck, 2002, for reviews). Previously, this area of study has been referred to as benefit-finding, positive changes, growth from adversity, thriving, and psychological growth (Lechner, 2009; Tennen & Affleck, 2002), but this phenomenon is now known as post-traumatic growth (Hefferon & Boniwell, 2011).

Drawing on the work of the existential psychiatrist Viktor Frankl (1976), post-traumatic growth captures the main theme of research showing the potential for growth and enhancement that may result from personal suffering (Baumgardner & Crothers, 2009). Frankl argued that a will to find meaning was a basic motivational force in people's lives. He thought that people need an overarching sense of purpose, meaning, and direction to sustain them through life's journey.

A meaningful life is expressed in people's goals and ambitions that, in turn, direct their energy towards the future. When traumatic experiences shatter or disrupt these goals and purposes, life may be perceived as meaningless. Under such conditions, people are highly motivated to restore a sense of meaning and purpose to their lives. Such circumstances present opportunities for personal growth, as people develop and commit themselves to new goals, ambitions, and purposes that re-establish their sense of meaning and direction (Baumgardner & Crothers, 2009).

Between the initial traumatic event and the subsequent experience of post-traumatic growth, the individual needs to engage in appropriate cognitive work (Triplett, Tedeschi, Cann, Calhoun, & Reeve, 2011). Thus, a significant factor in the path from cognitive threat to growth is assumed to be the degree to which the person engages in repeated thinking about the event. Meaning-making seems to be an important aspect of this process. Meaning-making refers to an active process of reappraisal and revision of how an event might be interpreted or what it might signify (Baumeister & Vohs, 2002).

Researchers have focused on two forms of meaning-making following a traumatic event: making sense of the event and finding benefits or positive outcomes from the event (Nolen-Hoeksema & Davis, 2002). Sense-making refers to making the event comprehensible in terms of a person's assumptions or beliefs about how the world operates (Baumgardner & Crothers, 2009; Janoff-Bulman, 1992).

The second form of meaning-making is called benefit-finding (Baumgardner & Crothers, 2009). This involves finding benefits or positive outcomes in trauma and loss. Research consistently finds that people report positive benefits from adversity. For example, Nolen-Hoeksema and Davis (2002) found that, six months after losing a loved one to terminal illness, 73% of bereaved people reported at least some positive outcomes. Eighteen months later, 77% reported some benefit from their loss.

Interpersonal strengths

One of the most important risks for the development of abnormal behaviour relates to interpersonal deficits, for instance, lack of effective interpersonal skills, aggression, revenge, unresolved conflict, neglect, and abuse. In this section, we will briefly discuss altruism, empathy, humility, and forgiveness as interpersonal strengths.

Altruism and empathy

Altruism is a form of prosocial behaviour intended to benefit others. It is motivated by internal motives such as concern for others or by internalised values, goals, and self-rewards rather than by the expectation of concrete or social rewards or the avoidance of punishment (Eisenberg & Ota Wang, 2003).

In the Nguni culture, this deep social obligation is understood through the saying *umuntu ngu umuntu ngabantu*, which literally means 'a person is a person through others'. This expression, generally known as *ubuntu*, refers to humane care, dignity, and cultured humanity, developed through processes of mutuality, humanisation, socialisation, and communal spirituality (Edwards, 2010).

The source of altruistic motivation, according to Batson, Ahmad, Lishner, and Tsang (2005, p. 496), is empathy, defined as 'an other-oriented emotional response elicited by and congruent with the perceived welfare of someone else'. San rock art is a visual history of such transpersonal patterns (Edwards, 2010).

Humility and forgiveness

The capacity to tolerate and understand people different from ourselves is necessary for peaceful coexistence and cooperation among people from various cultures and racial or ethnic backgrounds (Eisenberg & Ota Wang, 2003). Critical ingredients and prerequisites of tolerance and understanding are humility and forgiveness. Tangney (2005) indicates that humility is:

- the ability to keep one's talents and accomplishments in perspective
- to have a sense of self-acceptance
- an understanding of one's imperfections
- to be free from both arrogance and low self-esteem.

Tangney (2005) further emphasises that humility is an increase in the valuation of others, rather than a decrease in the valuation of oneself. Indeed, Tangney argues that, to a certain extent, humility is the opposite of narcissism (a pathological form of self-focus – see Chapter 14), while it also inhibits anger and aggression, and fosters forgiveness.

McCullough and Van Oyen Witvliet (2005, p. 446) define forgiveness as 'an approach whereby people suppress their natural negative responses to transgressors and become increasingly motivated to enact positive ones instead'. According to Van Dyk (2008), given our country's history of conflict and violence, there is a great need for forgiveness between ethnic and racial groups. McCullough and Van Oyen Witvliet (2005) argue, however, that the tendency to retaliate or seek retribution after being victimised is deeply ingrained in the biological, psychological, and cultural levels of human nature.

This is costly, Van Dyk (2008) indicates, as lack of forgiveness is related to, among others, higher levels of depression and health complaints; obsession with power, stereotypes, and paranoia; lower self-esteem; and power struggles. It makes sense, therefore, that one of the aims of the Truth and Reconciliation Commission in South Africa was healing through forgiveness, preventing further pathology developing from the adverse consequences of apartheid.

Religiosity and spirituality

Religion and spirituality are central to the lives of many people, and it is no surprise that there has been a recent resurgence of interest in the role both play in well-being. Religiosity can be defined as one's relationship with a particular faith tradition or doctrine about a divine other or supernatural power (Reich, Oser, & Scarlett, 1999, in Abdel-Khalek, 2012). Spirituality may form part of being religious, and refers to the connection with the mystical or something larger than oneself. Although it is a universal experience, no adequate definition exists (Diener & Biswas-Diener, 2008)

Religion and spirituality can be evidenced by diverse practices and beliefs, including extrinsic religiosity (outward signs of religious activity, such as church-going) and intrinsic religiosity (inward depth of feeling). However, Allport (1950, 1959, in Abdel-Khalek, 2012) and Diener and Biswas-Diener (2008) also remind us that religion can unfortunately be divisive. While it can lead to tremendous generosity, it often leads to intense animosity as well. Generally, though, research seems to indicate that religion is beneficial to a sense of personal well-being and overall adjustment, and even though it depends on where people live, religious people are on the whole happier than the non-religious (Abdel-Khalek, 2012; Diener & Biswas-Diener, 2008; Kim-Prieto & Diener, 2009).

Why would this be? According to Diener and Biswas-Diener (2008), some common 'active ingredients' exist:

- **Comforting beliefs:** Most, if not all, religions offer tremendous psychological comfort regarding questions about death and the afterlife.
- **Social support:** Organised religion provides important emotional benefit in terms of the social support and sense of belonging for members of congregations or religious communities.
- **A sense of meaning:** Religion helps people to understand the world and gives a broad purpose to life.
- **Stable families:** Most often, a religious upbringing provides a sense of community, security, and harmonious family environments.
- **Experience of ritual:** Ritual is part of most religions, and the sights, smells, and sounds are an attractive appeal to the senses that both attract and reinforce allegiance with religion.
- **Experience of positive emotions linked to spirituality:** People often experience an increase in positive emotions like love, gratitude, awe, and transcendence when spiritually engaged in a religious activity.

However, Diener and Biswas-Diener (2008) admit that, because religious beliefs and practices also have led to intolerance, war, and even genocide, much more research needs to be done to exactly understand the dynamic interplay between religion, spirituality, and well-being.

TREATMENT FROM A WELLNESS PERSPECTIVE

Treatment of the mentally ill person

In traditional clinical psychology, the primary goal has been symptom reduction in mental illness, whereas from a wellness perspective, symptom reduction should only be one component in treatment (Keyes & Lopez, 2005). The objective in positive psychology treatment is to promote levels of well-being or build upon a person's existing strengths. More specifically, Joseph and Linley (2004) argue that the positive psychotherapist's task is to facilitate the client's inherent tendency towards actualisation.

Moreover, if psychological problems are seen as deficits in the tendency towards actualisation, the therapist, in working to facilitate the actualising tendency, is both helping to alleviate problems and to promote well-being. In this way, ill-being and well-being are understood as a continuum of experience rather than as distinct categories. Joseph and Linley (2004) recognise, however, that the medical approach need not be rejected altogether, and some disorders should still be treated within the medical field by psychiatrists.

A number of psychotherapeutic models have been developed from the positive psychology perspective. For example, solution-focused therapy (De Shazer & Berg, 1997) places the focus on solutions rather on problems. Within a collaborative therapist–client relationship, strengths that have been used to solve similar problems in the past are rediscovered, and realistic goals for newer healthy behaviours are set. The focus is thus clearly on what is right and what works in the person's functioning, rather than on what is wrong.

Positive psychotherapy (Peseschkian, 1997, in Compton, 2005) hypothesises that each person has inherent but under-utilised capabilities for dealing with problems. The task of the therapist is to assess the person's abilities, possibilities, and problems, and to enhance a person's under-utilised strengths and capabilities.

Hope therapy (Lopez, Floyd, Ulven, & Snyder, 2000) is based on the idea that hope is characterised by pathways thinking (see earlier in this chapter). The aim is thus to help people to identify and develop clear goals; to facilitate the belief that they have the capacities and resources to reach those goals; to identify numerous paths to those goals; and to summon the energy and commitment to reach those goals.

Finally, **well-being therapy** (WBT) (Ruini & Fava, 2004) is a structured, directive, short-term psychotherapeutic strategy based on Ryff's model of psychological well-being. The purpose of well-being therapy is to move people from impaired to optimal functioning in the six dimensions of psychological well-being (Ruini & Fava, 2004). For example, if we take the well-being dimension *purpose in life*, the aim is to move the client from lacking a sense of meaning and goal-directedness in life to having goals, aims, and objectives for living, and a sense of directedness, meaning, and purpose in life.

Well-being therapy's effectiveness may be based on two distinct clinical phenomena: (i) an increase in psychological well-being may have a protective effect in terms of vulnerability to chronic and acute life stresses (cf. Ryff & Singer, 1998); and (ii) the inverse correlation between positive and negative affects contributes to the fact that changes in well-being may induce a decrease in distress and vice versa. Therefore, an increase in psychological well-being may decrease residual symptoms, which direct strategies like cognitive therapy or pharmacology would be unlikely to affect. It is important, however, to remember that well-being therapy is still at a developmental stage, and more validation studies are required to further elucidate its specific role in clinical and health psychology.

Support for the family of the mentally ill person

When a person is mentally ill, this often creates a significant burden for his or her family. In 2015, the South African researchers Masego C. Mokgothu, Emmerentia Du Plessis, and Magdalena P. Koen examined the strengths of South African families who were supporting family members with mental illness. Following the hierarchical model of Maslow, these authors produced guidelines for psychiatric nurses to follow in supporting families with mentally ill members. These guidelines are provided in the extract in Box 4.1 because they offer a concise strengths-based approach to helping the caregivers of the mentally ill.

BOX 4.1: RECOMMENDATIONS FOR PSYCHIATRIC NURSES ON HOW TO SUPPORT FAMILIES IN SUPPORTING MENTALLY ILL FAMILY MEMBERS

The guidelines follow Maslow's framework, as the findings and conclusions illustrated similarities with this approach. The recommendations below are formulated to fall in line with Maslow's framework.

Physiological needs

Psychiatric nurses should use educational programmes to encourage families to continue to maintain the physiological needs of the mentally ill family members in order to improve their quality of life. Psychiatric nurses should furthermore acknowledge the strengths of families to explain the importance of treatment to the mentally ill family member and avoidance of habits (such as use of substances) and should collaborate with families to prevent relapse. Psychiatric nursing should furthermore encourage families to continue to be involved in supportive activities, such as to recognise signs and symptoms of mental illness and to take the mentally ill family member to the hospital or clinic.

The need for safety and security

Psychiatric nurses should empower families to maintain the good health of a mentally ill family member by conducting psycho-education on the nature of the disease, treatment and management, side-effects of prescribed medication, signs and symptoms of relapse, coping skills and appropriate available community resources for dealing with a crisis situation. Psychiatric nurses should furthermore acknowledge families' strengths with regard to support of the mentally ill family member, to obtain support from external sources, to supervise the mentally ill family member, to use calming techniques, to keep him or her busy and to protect him or her. By acknowledging these strengths, psychiatric nurses and families can explore, reflect on and improve on such strengths as ways to support the mentally ill family member.

The need for love and a feeling of belonging

Mentally ill family members' needs for love and belonging might be met when families provide support in the form of prayer, involving support from neighbours and traditional healers and by conveying caring through ensuring that the mentally ill family member obtains treatment and by using calming techniques. These strengths can be acknowledged by the psychiatric nurse and the psychiatric nurse should, in turn, make families aware of these strengths and explore with them the unique ways in which they meet these needs of their mentally ill family members. Psychiatric nurses should also empower families by encouraging them to join support groups as this can help them to express their own feelings. Listening to others can foster a sense of hope and enhance emotional, physical and psychological wellbeing. In addition, talking to people with similar problems promotes a sense of belonging.

Esteem needs

Psychiatric nurses should empower families by helping them to acknowledge their strengths in meeting the esteem needs of mentally ill family members and to strengthen their communication skills, such as understanding and praise, conflict management skills and maintaining a respectful attitude. This can be done by means of psycho-education and case management.

Self-actualisation

From the findings and conclusions it is evident that families do give attention to the self-actualisation needs of mentally ill family members by praying with them and by exercising their faith and cultural practices. Psychiatric nurses should explore these strengths with families and, if acceptable to the family and mentally ill family member, encourage prayer, faith and acceptance. Families can be advised to engage in prayer meetings and church activities as this might promote self-actualisation and strengthen the family's ability to support their mentally ill family member.

In addition, psychiatric nurses should collaborate with the South African Police Force with regard to involuntary hospitalisation of a mentally ill family member. This will provide families with further support in terms of managing aggressive and violent family members who are mentally ill. Further support to families include that psychiatric nurses should help them by means of training sessions that teach families about sharing tasks and household chores, so that they are able to relieve one another when caring for a mentally ill family member.

Source: Mokgothu, Du Plessis, & Koen, 2015.

Promoting well-being in communities

According to Marujo and Neto (2014), the usefulness of positive psychology to society in general needs a stronger concern for real-life social issues before it can become a constructive force for social change. Even though positive psychology is linked to indigenous knowledge systems, Eloff et al. (2008) found that, as a science and practice, it is still emerging in Africa, especially outside South Africa. They hypothesised that this is due to the contradiction in adhering to a 'positive approach' while many countries experience profound socio-economic challenges like unrest, war, and poverty.

Although these findings are based on a study more than a decade ago, in 2019 there is still no clear evidence that positive psychology has moved closer to making a significant impact in promoting well-being on a large social scale. Marujo and Neto (2014) take this African challenge into account when they propose a '*Felicitas Publica*' – an Italian concept referring to civil society based on different forms of relationships, where equity and efficacy are the key role-players.

The model defends a type of happiness that promotes: (i) economic development centred on the dignity of everyone; (ii) civil virtuousness and practice of the civil good; and (iii) shared and relational goods through an investment in social capital. 'Relational goods' refer to the affective non-instrumental side of interpersonal relationships, for example, friendship or trust in a work context. The relationship itself constitutes the 'good', either in family relations, friendship, love, or neighbourhood and community social ties.

The best chance we have, therefore, according to Marujo and Neto (2014), is to start by changing the focus of researchers to, among others, move intentionally (i) from the intrapersonal to the community and public domains; (ii) from the privileged to the underprivileged groups; (iii) from culture-insensitive interventions to tailor-made procedures, co-created by the participants in local areas; and (iv) from rigour in terms of numbers to a complementary rigour with words and dialogue. What these authors advocate is a psychology of liberation and of collective well-being that is less preoccupied with its scientific and social status, and more concerned with real problems of people in need.

 ACTIVITY

In 2012, during the 'Arab Spring', António Guterres was the UN High Commissioner for Refugees. He observed that as violence erupted in Libya in late February, 'border points with Tunisia that had formerly received 1,000 persons a day were getting that many in an hour'. Guterres went on to write:

> *The response from ordinary Tunisians was remarkable in its altruism. I witnessed villagers sharing their homes and land while others drove for miles to provide sandwiches for those stuck in the crowds at the border. That Tunisia maintained an open border is also noteworthy as it was still emerging from its own 'Arab Spring' turmoil.*

Suggest why Guterres chose to write about the events from this positive angle.

CONCLUSION

Although there is some critique that positive psychology is nothing more than a trend with a short lifespan, Baumgardner and Crothers (2009) indicate that positive psychology has generated a large amount of research and theory, and achieved scientific respectability to promote the study and understanding of healthy human functioning. According to Peterson (2006), positive psychology does have something to say about abnormal psychology, specifically in providing a lens of normality through which to view abnormality.

Peterson (2006) proposes that, as positive psychology is about the presence of strengths, the absence of these strengths should be used as the hallmark of 'real' psychological disorder. In support of Seligman (2006), who proposed that positive psychology is not intended as a replacement for clinical psychology, Peterson (2006) further indicates that this approach might expand what clinical psychologists most helpfully do.

In this regard, both Maddux (2008) and Wood and Tarrier (2010) propose a new approach to abnormal psychology, called positive clinical psychology, which should:

- be more integrated and reject the illness ideology
- predict disorders above and beyond the presence of negative characteristics
- promote resilience in non-clinical populations
- foster positive characteristics to treat clinical disorder
- have the potential to expand the knowledge base of clinical psychology rapidly.

In conclusion, we would like to support Sheldon and King (2001, p. 216) who said that 'positive psychology is an attempt to urge psychologists to adopt a more open and appreciative perspective regarding human potentials, motives and capacities'.

MULTIPLE-CHOICE QUESTIONS

1. According to Martin Seligman, psychology is not just the study of disease, weakness, and damage, but also:
   a) the study of relationships
   b) the study of mental illness
   c) the study of strength and virtue
   d) the study of human beings
2. Generally, well-being has been conceptualised within the positive psychology approach from two related, but different, traditions, namely:
   a) wisdom and courage
   b) hedonic and eudaimonic
   c) coping and resilience
   d) psychoanalytic and clinical

3. Which of the following is NOT an example of a protective factor against the development of mental illness?
   a) optimism
   b) emotional intelligence
   c) denial
   d) resilience
4. Emotional intelligence involves the ability to:
   a) know what other people are thinking before they do
   b) monitor one's own and others' feelings and emotions, to discriminate among them, and use the information to guide one's thinking and actions
   c) set personal goals and steer behaviour towards the achievement of established goals
   d) none of the above
5. According to the theory on coping (Compton, 2005) described in this chapter, three types of coping styles can be identified. They are:
   a) emotion-focused coping, problem-focused coping, and avoidant coping
   b) emotion-focused coping, behaviour-focused coping, and denial-focused coping
   c) emotion-focused coping, relationship-focused coping, and solution-focused coping
   d) none of the above

PARAGRAPH AND ESSAY QUESTIONS

1. Discuss the six basic elements of positive functioning as proposed by the work of Carol Ryff.
2. Compare and contrast the different forms of coping. Make sure to note similarities and differences.
3. Explain why it is in important, in a country like South Africa, to take the broader sociopolitical context into account when trying to understand how psychological well-being is experienced and maintained in community context.
4. Describe the different psychotherapeutic models that have been developed from the positive psychology perspective. Provide a brief description, as well as the specific aim, of each model.

5 LEGAL AND ETHICAL ISSUES IN MENTAL DISORDERS

Christiaan Bezuidenhout

CHAPTER CONTENTS

Introduction
Core ethical values and standards
Legal perspective
    Human rights in South Africa
    The Mental Health Care Act (No. 17 of 2002) and the Mental Health Care Amendment
      Act (No. 12 of 2014)
    The Traditional Health Practitioners Act (No. 22 of 2007)
    The state of mental healthcare in South Africa
History of the South African ethical code for psychologists
Ethical behaviour
    Statutory control over ethical behaviour
    Challenges to ethical behaviour
    Ethical dilemmas
Specific ethical issues for mental healthcare professionals
    Confidentiality and reporting to third parties
    Dangerousness
    Suicide and euthanasia
    Committing a client
Consequences of unethical conduct
Conclusion

LEARNING OUTCOMES

After studying this chapter, you should be able to:
- Critically highlight the prerequisites for ethical conduct.
- Outline the concept 'ethical behaviour'.
- Explain the role of the Health Professions Council of South Africa in ensuring ethical conduct in the health and behavioural medicine disciplines.
- Critically debate the different circumstances under which a therapist can divulge client information to a third party.
- Explain the possible consequences unethical conduct could have for a practitioner.
- Explain in your own words certain unique factors to consider in the South African context, to ensure ethical conduct at all times.

PERSONAL HISTORY CASELET

Takalani Home was overcrowded when Ms Boitumelo Mangena's brother went there to find his mother. He was asked to wait for her to be brought to him but the first person they brought was not his mother, although the woman was wearing his mother's name tag. He was then told to walk through the hall to find his mother. He reported that the circumstances were 'extremely devastating'. The place was overcrowded and some people were sitting on the floor. The patients were still in their Life Esidimeni uniforms. Ms Mangena's brother did not recognise his mother at first because of the amount of weight she had lost. He had to walk around the hall a second time before he found her. She was sitting in a corner shivering, without any socks or jersey. Her feet were swollen and she was extremely hungry. The nurse with whom Ms Mangena's brother spoke was new and had no experience caring for mental healthcare users. The patients at Takalani were receiving the same medication despite having different mental health conditions. If mental healthcare users could not walk or talk for themselves, they would not get what they needed, including their food and medication. Ms Mangena's brother insisted on seeing where his mother slept. There were not enough beds for all the patients. Some of the mental healthcare users slept on benches or on the floor without mattresses. He was taken to a bed, but he knew that it was not his mother's bed because there were pictures of another person's family on the wall by the bed (Moseneke, 2018, p. 33).

INTRODUCTION

Most people who suffer from a mental disorder are extremely vulnerable, and when we deal with vulnerable people, we must always make sure that their rights, dignity, and safety are addressed. The 'Life Esidimeni Tragedy' (which is described in the caselet at the start of this chapter, and explained further below) is the most notorious recent event where there was a failure to address the rights, dignity, and safety of the mentally ill. However, this incident is not the only incident where the mentally ill have been failed in South Africa. People with mental disorders are killed in some communities after being accused of witchcraft, while in other communities, psychologists break the law by discussing the private details of patients in social situations.

The purpose of this chapter is to provide the reader with an understanding of the legal rights of people who have been diagnosed with a mental disorder and the legal framework that lays out the ethical standards health professionals should adhere to when they interact with their clients.

CORE ETHICAL VALUES AND STANDARDS

The core ethical values and standards required of healthcare practitioners include the following (Health Professions Council of South Africa [HPCSA], 2008, p. 2):

1. *Respect for persons:* Practitioners should respect patients as persons, and acknowledge their intrinsic worth, dignity, and sense of value.
2. *Best interests or well-being (non-maleficence):* Practitioners should not harm or act against the best interests of patients, even when the interests of the latter conflict with their own self-interest.
3. *Best interests or well-being (beneficence):* Practitioners should act in the best interests of patients even when the interests of the latter conflict with their own personal self-interest.
4. *Human rights:* Practitioners should recognise the human rights of all individuals.
5. *Autonomy:* Practitioners should honour the right of patients to self-determination to make their own informed choices and to live their lives by their own beliefs, values, and preferences.
6. *Integrity:* Practitioners should incorporate these core ethical values and standards as the foundation for their character and practice as responsible healthcare professionals.
7. *Truthfulness:* Practitioners should regard the truth and truthfulness as the basis of trust in their professional relationships with patients.
8. *Confidentiality:* Practitioners should treat personal or private information as confidential in professional relationships with patients – unless over-riding reasons confer a moral or legal right to disclosure.
9. *Compassion:* Practitioners should be sensitive to, and empathise with, the individual and social needs of their patients and seek to create mechanisms for providing comfort and support where appropriate and possible.
10. *Tolerance:* Practitioners should respect the rights of people to have different ethical beliefs as these may arise from deeply held personal, religious, or cultural convictions.

11. *Justice:* Practitioners should treat all individuals and groups in an impartial, fair, and just manner.

12. *Professional competence and self-improvement:* Practitioners should continually endeavour to attain the highest level of knowledge and skills required within their area of practice.

13. *Community:* Practitioners should strive to contribute to the betterment of society in accordance with their professional abilities and standing in the community.

LEGAL PERSPECTIVE

The Universal Declaration of Human Rights was adopted by the United Nations General Assembly in France on 10 December 1948. This declaration emerged following the atrocities that took place before and during the Second World War. Its aim was to ensure that all humans on earth should have the same basic rights, purely because they are human. In this Universal Declaration, it is stated that 'all human beings are inherently entitled' to basic rights. In Article 1 of the Declaration it is declared that: 'All human beings are born free and equal in dignity and rights. They are endowed with reason and conscience and should act towards one another in a spirit of brotherhood.'

Similarly, basic human rights became a very important aspect in South Africa after apartheid was toppled. The new Constitution was promulgated to ensure human rights for all human beings in South Africa.

However, between 2016 and 2017 at least 142 mentally ill people died in what is today seen as one of the most serious human rights abuse cases ever in South Africa. Mentally ill patients who were living in Life Esidimeni, a professionally managed and privately owned institution, were transported to non-profit facilities after the state closed down the private facility without clear reasons. These patients died as a direct result of the transfers from the Life Esidimeni facility to the 27 unlicensed non-government organisations (NGOs) (Masinga, 2017). These patients were 'transported [using] inappropriate and inhumane modes of transport' in ways that 'were most negligent and reckless and showed a total lack of human dignity, care and human life' (Makgoba, 2017, p. 2). Patients experienced 'extreme neglect, insufficient or rotten food, exposure to cold, lack of medication, overcrowding [and] abuse', and their 'bodies were stacked upon each other in morgues' (Bornman, 2017).

Although health professionals and families requested the state to reconsider their idea to close down Life Esidimeni, the state still proceeded with their plan. In their haste to move the mentally ill patients, they lost medical records, medical prescriptions, and medicines. In an article in *The Economist* (How 143 mentally ill South Africans were sent to their deaths, 2018), it is claimed that 'so chaotic was the move that the authorities lost track of many of the patients: 59 are still missing, and nine of the dead have not been identified'. Since this tragedy, many other stories have surfaced about the failing health services and especially services for the mentally ill. Specific reasons for this tragedy are still lacking, while the then leaders in government treated this incident with impunity (Makgoba, 2017).

Human rights in South Africa

When dealing with people with mental disorders, it is important to remember that, no matter how severe their disorder, one is first and foremost dealing with another human being and, as such, this person has certain human rights. This person is protected by the Constitution of the Republic of South Africa, and practitioners should be acutely aware of the constitutional rights of their clients (see Table 5.1).

Figure 5.1: Former Deputy Chief Justice Dikgang Moseneke during the Life Esidimeni arbitration hearing at Emoyeni Conference Centre, Parktown, on 9 October 2017 in Johannesburg, South Africa.

Table 5.1: Relevant excerpts from the Constitution of the Republic of South Africa, 1996

Founding provisions

1. The Republic of South Africa is one, sovereign, democratic State founded on the following values:
   (a) Human dignity, the achievement of equality and the advancement of human rights and freedoms.
   (b) Non-racialism and non-sexism.
   (c) Supremacy of the constitution and the rule of law.

Rights

7. (1) This Bill of Rights is a cornerstone of democracy in South Africa. It enshrines the rights of all people in our country and affirms the democratic values of human dignity, equality, and freedom.

Equality

9. (1) Everyone is equal before the law and has the right to equal protection and benefit of the law.
   (2) Equality includes the full and equal enjoyment of all rights and freedoms. To promote the achievement of equality, legislative, and other measures designed to protect or advance persons, or categories of persons, disadvantaged by unfair discrimination may be taken.
   (3) The state may not unfairly discriminate directly or indirectly against anyone on one or more grounds, including race, gender, sex, pregnancy, marital status, ethnic or social origin, colour, sexual orientation, age, disability, religion, conscience, belief, culture, language, and birth.
   (4) No person may unfairly discriminate directly or indirectly against anyone on one or more grounds in terms of subsection (3). National legislation must be enacted to prevent or prohibit unfair discrimination.
   (5) Discrimination on one or more of the grounds listed in subsection (3) is unfair unless it is established that the discrimination is fair.

Human dignity

10. Everyone has inherent dignity and the right to have their dignity respected and protected.

Life

11. Everyone has the right to life.

Freedom and security of the person

12. (1) Everyone has the right to freedom and security of the person, which includes the right:
    (a) not to be deprived of freedom arbitrarily or without just cause;
    (b) not to be detained without trial;
    (c) to be free from all forms of violence from either public or private sources;
    (d) not to be tortured in any way; and
    (e) not to be treated or punished in a cruel, inhuman, or degrading way.
    (2) Everyone has the right to bodily and psychological integrity, which includes the right:
    (a) to make decisions concerning reproduction;
    (b) to security in and control over their body; and
    (c) not to be subjected to medical or scientific experiments without their informed consent.

Privacy

14. Everyone has the right to privacy, which includes the right not to have:
    (d) the privacy of their communications infringed.

Health care, food, water, and social security

27. (1) Everyone has the right to have access to:
    (a) health care services, including reproductive health care;
    (3) No one may be refused emergency medical treatment.

Access to information

32. (1) Everyone has the right of access to:
    (b) any information that is held by another person and that is required for the exercise or protection of any rights.

Source: Extracted from the Constitution of the Republic of South Africa, 1996

Despite the increased focus on a rights-based approach, mistreatment of people with mental disorders continues. In recent years (consider the Life Esidimeni incident), there have been many media reports of abuse of patients by the State, institutions, or individuals. The South African Constitution states very clearly that all people must be treated with dignity and respect. Further pertinent issues, for the purposes of this chapter, include the right to privacy and the right to information. This implies that all mental healthcare practitioners must respect the privacy of their clients and also that they may not withhold any information from their clients.

Further aspects of importance are those of forced detention and treatment of psychiatric patients. Previously, it was relatively easy to have a patient certified and admitted to a psychiatric hospital without their consent and against their will. However, in order to protect the legal rights of patients in this regard, the Mental Health Care Act (No. 17 of 2002) has stipulated the exact procedures that need to be complied with regarding the admitting of patients to psychiatric and rehabilitation institutions. Furthermore, any treatment and research has to comply with the Constitution. Finally, all laws, Acts, and professional codes of conduct must adhere to the Constitution.

The Mental Health Care Act (No. 17 of 2002) and the Mental Health Care Amendment Act (No. 12 of 2014)

It was envisaged that many past ethical abuses against individuals with mental disorders would be corrected by the Mental Health Care Act (No. 17 of 2002) (MHCA) (implemented in 2004). The Mental Health Care Amendment Act (No. 12 of 2014) made a small amendment to the 2002 MHCA regarding the 'delegation of powers'; however, the rest of the content stayed the same. The MHCA sought to bring mental healthcare practices in line with those of the World Health Organization (WHO), and to promote the human rights of people with mental disorders in South Africa.

The purpose of the Mental Health Care Act (No. 17 of 2002) is:

> To provide for the care, treatment, and rehabilitation of persons who are mentally ill; to set out different procedures to be followed in the admission of such persons; to establish Review Boards in respect of every health establishment; to determine their powers and functions; to provide for the care and administration of the property of mentally ill persons; to repeal certain laws; and to provide for matters connected therewith.

The Act covers, inter alia, the following:
■ Designation of health establishments administered under the auspices of the State as psychiatric hospitals or as care and rehabilitation centres
■ Provision of mental healthcare, treatment, and rehabilitation services at health establishments
■ Respect, human dignity, and privacy
■ Consent
■ Determinations concerning mental health status
■ Disclosure of information
■ Knowledge of rights
■ Appointment of an administrator for care and administration of property of the mentally ill person or person with severe or profound intellectual disability.

One way of viewing this Act is that it operationalises the terms of the Constitution as they apply to patients with a mental disorder. The Act also clearly defines different mental health professionals and their roles and responsibilities (see Table 5.2). Any person who acts outside of these makes him- or herself guilty of a crime.

Table 5.2: Relevant definitions from the Mental Health Care Act (No. 17 of 2002)

Term	Definition
Assisted care, treatment, and rehabilitation	The provision of health interventions to people incapable of making informed decisions due to their mental health status and who do not refuse the health interventions.

Term	Definition
Assisted mental healthcare user	A person receiving assisted care, treatment, and rehabilitation.
Care and rehabilitation centres	Health establishments for the care, treatment, and rehabilitation of people with intellectual disabilities.
Health establishment	Institutions, facilities, buildings, or places where people receive care, treatment, rehabilitative assistance, diagnostic or therapeutic interventions, or other health services. Includes facilities such as community health and rehabilitation centres, clinics, hospitals, and psychiatric hospitals.
Involuntary care, treatment, and rehabilitation	The provision of health interventions to people incapable of making informed decisions due to their mental health status and who refuse health intervention but require such services for their own protection or for the protection of others.
Involuntary mental healthcare user	A person receiving involuntary care, treatment, and rehabilitation.
Medical practitioner	A person registered as such in terms of the Health Professions Act (No. 56 of 1974).
Mental healthcare practitioner	A psychiatrist or registered medical practitioner or a nurse, occupational therapist, psychologist, or social worker who has been trained to provide prescribed mental healthcare, treatment, and rehabilitation services.
Mental healthcare provider	A person providing mental healthcare services to mental healthcare users and includes mental healthcare practitioners.
Mental healthcare user	A person receiving care, treatment, and rehabilitation services or using a health service at a health establishment aimed at enhancing the mental health status of a user, State patient, or mentally ill prisoner, or where the person concerned is below the age of 18 years or is incapable of taking decisions, and in certain circumstances may include: (i) prospective user; (ii) the person's next of kin; (iii) a person authorised by any other law or court order to act on that person's behalf; (iv) an administrator appointed in terms of this Act; and (v) an executor of that deceased person's estate.
Mental illness	A positive diagnosis of a mental health-related illness in terms of accepted diagnostic criteria made by a mental healthcare practitioner authorised to make such diagnosis.

Term	Definition
Psychiatric hospital	A health establishment that provides care, treatment, and rehabilitation services only for users with mental illness.
Psychiatrist	A person registered as such in terms of the Health Professions Act (No. 56 of 1974).
Psychologist	A person registered as such in terms of the Health Professions Act (No. 56 of 1974).
Social worker	A person registered as such in terms of the Social Services Professions Act (No. 110 of 1978).
Voluntary care, treatment, and rehabilitation	A provision of health interventions to a person who gives consent to such interventions.

Source: Adapted from www.hpcsa.co.za

Moosa and Jeenah (2010, p. 125) state that the Act was intended to 'remove distinctions between health professionals, in that any registered medical practitioner or psychiatrically trained nurse/occupational therapist/psychologist/social worker (defined as a "mental health care practitioner") is allowed to provide mental health care, treatment, and rehabilitation (CTR) services'.

In addition, the National Health Act (No. 61 of 2003) (NHA) refers to categories of workers in more general terms as 'healthcare providers', where a 'health practitioner or provider' is a person providing health services in terms of any law such as the Allied Professions, Health Professions, Nursing, Pharmacy, and Dental Technicians Acts. The NHA is meant to be one of the legislative measures that will facilitate the progressive realisation of the right to health. This Act also refers to the fact that everyone in South Africa should have access to healthcare services.

The Traditional Health Practitioners Act (No. 22 of 2007)

South Africa is a diverse country where many people believe in indigenous medicines and religious ways of curing illness. It is not uncommon for black South Africans to consult with a traditional healer when they feel emotionally disturbed in some way. Traditional healers are an important source of psychiatric support in South Africa. Two types of traditional healers exist, namely a *sangoma* and an *inyanga*. A *sangoma* uses traditional medicines, but relies primarily on divination and communication with the ancestors for healing powers/purposes (see Chapter 1). The *inyanga* is a herbalist who is concerned with medicines made from plants and animals.

The World Health Organization (WHO) defines a traditional health practitioner (THP) as 'a person who is recognised by the community where he or she lives as someone competent to provide healthcare by using plant, animal, and mineral substances and other methods based on social, cultural and religious practices' (Zuma, Wight, Rochat, & Moshabela, 2016, p. 2). These authors also state that some researchers believe that eight in ten black South

Africans utilise traditional healers exclusively or in conjunction with Western medicine. In this regard, McFarlane (2015) claims that more than 200 000 traditional healers care for more than half of the South African population. The estimated South African population is about 58 million people (http://www.statssa.gov.za/), which means that at least 28 million people are still making use of the services of traditional healers (Zuma et al., 2016).

Since traditional healers are a diverse population, it is difficult to predict the number of traditional healers and their ratio to the general population accurately. In South Africa, traditional healing consists of a combination of healing practices such as divining, herbalism, and spiritualism. Zuma et al. (2016, p. 2) posit in this regard that those healers who are 'registered under the South African Traditional Health Practitioners Act include herbalists (izinyanga or amaxhwele), diviners (izangoma, umthandazi or amagqirha), traditional surgeons (iingcibi) who mainly do circumcisions, and traditional birth attendants (ababelethisi or abazalisi)'.

It is discussed in Chapter 10 how some indigenous diagnoses (e.g. *amafufunyana* and *ukuthwasa*) have symptoms that may be seen as evidence of schizophrenia (Bezuidenhout & Klopper, 2011; Zabow, 2007). Based on this, it became evident that the human rights of the client and the traditional healer needed to be protected through a legal mandate. In this context, the purpose of the Traditional Health Practitioners Act (No. 22 of 2007) was to:

- Establish the Interim Traditional Healers Council of South Africa.
- Provide for the registration, training, and practice of traditional healers.
- Serve and protect the interests of the public who use the services of traditional health practitioners.

The need for this Act was precipitated by the significant political and social changes that have occurred in South Africa since 1994 (Janse van Rensburg, 2009). Since democratisation, a very high premium is placed on human rights, which entail the equal, just, and fair treatment of all people. Cross-cultural diagnosis and treatment present serious challenges in this context; thus, mental health professionals need to be trained to recognise and accommodate diverse customs and practices, and to support people with a variety of needs. A *Government Gazette* promulgation made some of the sections of the Act, which regulates South Africa's traditional health sector, effective on 1 May 2014; most sections of the Act became binding after the 2008 proclamation (Tshehla, 2015).

Figure 5.2:
A traditional healer

Table 5.3: Psychologists actively registered with the HPCSA per ethnic group as of 2 August 2018

Ethnicity of psychologist	Number	% of registered psychologists
African	1 269	14.47
Chinese	9	0.1
Coloured	471	5.37
Indian	591	6.75
White	5 731	65.35
No information	698	7.96
TOTAL	8 769	100

Source: Electronic mail from Yvette Daffue (17 August 2018), IT Department (Statistics & Data Analysis), Health Professions Council of South Africa.

In addition, as a result of historically privileged access to training, most psychologists practising in South Africa are white and from a Western background (see Table 5.3). Burke, Harper, Rudnick, and Kruger (2007) observe that psychologists in South Africa face the following challenges:

- The use of Western texts in an African context
- Racism that has remained after apartheid
- Cultural differences between African and Western world views
- Language barriers.

The challenge lies in the ability to understand other cultures and ethnic groups. In professional practice, when a client from a different ethnic background, who is in need of assistance, approaches a psychologist, the psychologist is obliged to serve the client with a high level of professionalism and ethical standards. In some cases, this may be difficult because of language problems and differences in belief systems. Some African cultures or ethnicities, for example, lack separate words for manifestations of depression or panic attacks (SADAG Conference, 2011). In many cases, depression or panic attacks will be seen as 'madness' because the behaviour is out of context and most often not understood. If no indigenous concepts exist for a symptom or condition, how can Western definition and interpretation of it make sense?

If necessary, professionals should acknowledge their incapacity to treat someone and, in this case, they should refer a client to a suitable therapist, colleague, or traditional healer. Incompetence or the inability to understand the genuine need of the client can make the client vulnerable to many varieties of unethical actions by the practitioner. The MHCA and a dialogue about different disorders should contribute to more ethical actions and an increased culture of understanding. This is because 'patients see no conflict in seeking both allopathic and traditional African healing for their ailments, as doctors diagnose and treat the pathology while traditional healers establish what is wrong with the body-mind complex and importantly who or what (mostly harmful spirits) made the person ill (done mainly by isangomas)' (Peltzer, 2009). Notwithstanding this, many role-players are not enthusiastic in terms of integrating the two systems as many feel the traditional system lacks research and scientific proof.

The state of mental healthcare in South Africa

Despite South Africa's progressive mental health legislation, ongoing barriers to the financing and development of mental health services exist. These result in: (i) psychiatric hospitals remaining outdated, falling into disrepair, and often being unfit for human use; (ii) serious shortages of mental health professionals; (iii) inability to develop vitally important tertiary level psychiatric services (such as child and adolescent services, psychogeriatric services, neuropsychiatric services, etc.); and (iv) community mental health and psychosocial rehabilitation services remaining undeveloped, so that patients end up institutionalised, without hope of rehabilitation back into their communities. This state of affairs remains unchanged despite the legislated commitments to reform mental healthcare in the 2002 MHCA.

However, the MHCA has not yet brought about the envisaged changes to ensure fair, just, and ethical treatment of all patients. Many facilities and psychiatric hospitals are still delivering substandard services. Patients are still being housed in dilapidated buildings with poor infrastructure. Ramlall, Chipps, and Mars, (2010, p. 669) state in this regard that 'in such conditions, the shortage of specialist facilities, admission beds, and staff trained in psychiatry is of concern'.

HISTORY OF THE SOUTH AFRICAN ETHICAL CODE FOR PSYCHOLOGISTS

According to Pettifor and Sawchuk (2006), codes of ethics for psychologists were established about 50 years ago. In 1953, the American Psychological Association set the tone when it published a provisional code of ethics for acceptable professional conduct. The main aims of the code were to ensure respect, confidentiality, and doing no harm to a patient.

The global professionalisation of psychology escalated rapidly after the Second World War. In 1948, the first professional association in South Africa was formed, namely the South African Psychological Association (SAPA). This was the first body in South Africa that discussed a possible list of regulations or ethics for psychologists.

In 1955, SAPA eventually accepted a set of ethical standards that was largely based on the ethical standards that the American Psychological Association had proposed in 1953. This was called Ethical Standards of Psychologists, Summary of Ethical Principles. Prior to this, no action could be taken when a complaint was lodged against a member of SAPA. Although membership of SAPA was voluntary, this code allowed for the termination of membership in cases of misconduct.

Although SAPA ceased to exist in 1982, and a new body, the Psychological Association of South Africa (PASA), was established in 1983, the ethical standards set by SAPA were adhered to until 1985. PASA then set new ethical standards until this association was replaced by the Psychological Society of South Africa (PsySSA) in 1994. It must be noted that, although SAPA, PASA, and PsySSA were or are all professional bodies, they do not have any statutory powers. In South Africa, the statutory power over health professionals is held by the Health Professions Council of South Africa (HPCSA), which was established in 1999, having previously been known as the South African Medical and Dental Council (SAMDC) (Scherrer, Louw, & Möller, 2002). Guided by the Medical, Dental and Supplementary Service Professions Act (No. 56 of 1974), the name of this statutory body was changed to acknowledge psychology and other supplementary health professions.

In an endeavour to make psychology more formalised and structured in South Africa, a Professional Board for Psychology was set up in 1974. This was done in terms of the Medical, Dental and Supplementary Service Professions Act (No. 56 of 1974). The Professional Board for Psychology is currently one of the 12 professional boards under the auspices of the HPCSA. Since 1974, the HPCSA has been charged by the above Act to register people who want to use the title 'psychologist' and to practise as psychologists (Louw, 1997a). The Professional Board for Psychology ensures that psychologists register with the Council before they can enter professional practice. The Board also ensures that people who request official registration as psychologists have sufficient professional training (Scherrer et al., 2002).

The Professional Board for Psychology developed a set of rules during 1977 that can be seen as the first official code of conduct for psychologists in South Africa. Although the professional bodies or associations (e.g. SAPA, PASA, and PsySSA) had voluntary membership, and each association had its own set of rules and regulations, registration as a practising psychologist could (and can) only take place through the Professional Board for Psychology. Thus, practising psychologists (and psychometrists) do not have to be members of professional associations as long as they are officially registered with the Professional Board for Psychology. The Professional Board for Psychology is furthermore responsible for disciplinary actions if a registered psychologist is accused of unprofessional behaviour (Louw, 1997b).

The American Psychological Association has been the global leader with regard to ethical standards for psychologists and is required to update the code of ethics regularly to adhere to social changes and demands internationally. In this regard, Canter, Bennett, Jones, and Nagy (1994, p. xv) reported that 'to address the many changes that have occurred in recent years as the profession of psychology has evolved, the APA, ... developed a new code of ethics, titled Ethical Principles of Psychologists and Code of Conduct (1992)'.

However, following this, suggestions have been forthcoming from the global psychology community to develop an international code of ethical principles for psychologists. These suggestions were answered when the International Union of Psychological Science passed a resolution in 2002 that urged member societies to enact codes of ethics and to take action against members who were guilty of human rights abuses. This endeavour 'denounced all practices that were inconsistent with the high moral standards required for psychologists to conduct scientific and professional activities' (Pettifor & Sawchuk, 2006, p. 217).

Gobodo-Madikizela and Foster (2005, p. 344) assert that 'every person should be accorded a sense of value, worth, and dignity, and that every person should be protected from infringements and abuses of these fundamental rights'. Mental illness or abnormality is something that is different from what is expected or usual; it is usually different in such a manner that it is worrying, harmful, or not understood by others, especially if they think from an 'ableism' frame of mind.

It would be ideal if there was a clear dividing line between what is considered normal and what abnormal behaviour is, but ever-increasing evidence does not allow for such a clear-cut line; rather abnormality and normality fall on a continuum, which challenges the notion of labelling and treating a mentally ill person differently (Nolen-Hoeksema, 2013).

HELPFUL HINT

Considering the different legal acts as well as the different approaches to describing abnormality or insanity, contemporary judgement of what is abnormal is influenced by the interaction of four aspects, known as the 4Ds. These include:

- **Dysfunction**
- **Distress**
- **Deviance**
- **Dangerousness.**

Dysfunctional behaviours refer to those thoughts, feelings, and behaviours that interfere with a person's ability to function in everyday life (e.g. holding a job or building and keeping close relationships). These people tend to lose touch with reality, and that makes it difficult for them to function in general society. Behaviours and feelings that are distressing to both themselves and others are also considered when contemplating what is abnormal. Deviant behaviours, thoughts or feelings are those that diverge from the norm, such as hearing voices or seeing people who are not there. The final element is dangerousness. Some behaviours can lead to excessive aggression or suicidal gestures, and this is also vital in determining whether the behaviour is normal or not.

There is no sharp line between normality and abnormality, and thus all four the elements lie on a continuum (Nolen-Hoeksema, 2013).

The aim of the following section is to address the complex and sometimes poorly understood phenomenon of ethical conduct in the behavioural sciences. Apart from being a human rights abuse, unacceptable conduct with a client or research participant during any interaction has the potential to result in disciplinary action or a legal encounter. Knowledge gained from this section should enable learners and practitioners to understand clearly the complex challenges to maintaining acceptable professional conduct.

ETHICAL BEHAVIOUR

Ethics are 'moral principles' that a mental health practitioner should uphold at all times. According to Burke et al. (2007), the word 'ethics' is derived from the Greek word *ethos* (character). It refers to a set of moral principles that define what is acceptable and unacceptable and which appeal to a person's moral responsibility to act within the acceptable boundaries of humanity. Zabow and Kalsiki (2006, p. 357) assert that 'ethical principles and the law frequently interact'.

According to Pope and Vasques (2007), it is important that practitioners are aware of the ethical code that applies to their profession; however, this awareness alone is not sufficient. According to these authors, a code of ethics cannot be followed in a thoughtless, rote manner, as ethical codes merely prompt, guide, and inform a practitioner's ethical deliberations. Professional conduct requires an ethical character first and foremost, and also requires an active, thoughtful, and creative approach, for the following reasons (Pope & Vasques, 2007):

- Each client or patient is unique; therefore, one cannot make ethical judgements based only on similarities with other clients. In each new case, the practitioner must apply his or her mind anew to the ethical considerations.
- Related to the above, each situation is unique, and ethical codes, no matter how thorough they are, cannot prescribe for all situations that a practitioner may encounter.
- Ethical codes may, in different situations and with different clients, provide us more or less clarity regarding the types of ethical considerations that may be significant, but often the code provides only broad guidelines that are open to interpretation by practitioners.

In the context of professional practice, ethical behaviour refers to a set of behavioural expectations that need to be adhered to by psychologists when they interact with clients, so as to avoid causing harm to these clients. They should respect and honour the emotions and opinions of others, and they should never exploit or abuse these (Alvesson & Sköldberg, 2000; Becker, 1992).

The essence of ethical behaviour is to act in a way that is always in the best interest of the client (principle of beneficence), for example, by making sure that the client always receives the best possible treatment. In addition, the professional should not take any action that can be damaging to the client (principle of non-maleficence). Ethical behaviour is nested in a set of values that every behavioural and healthcare professional should internalise.

Statutory control over ethical behaviour

One of the distinctions between a profession and an occupation is that all professions have codes of ethics, and there is always a statutory body that takes the responsibility for setting up and implementing an ethical code of behaviour for a particular profession. As described earlier, in South Africa, the Health Professions Council of South Africa (HPCSA) is the statutory body that performs this function for all health and allied professions. The HPCSA is the overarching body that is made up of professional boards of all the professions that fall under its auspices.

The Professional Board for Psychology is responsible for setting up and implementing the ethical code for psychologists. The ethical code for psychologists is an extensive document that covers a wide range of professional conduct (see Table 5.4). It must be remembered, however, that the field of ethics and ethical conduct is complicated and, given the fact that this book focuses mainly on abnormal behaviour, this section cannot cover the ethical code in its entirety. The most recent ethical rules for psychologists were promulgated by the Professional Board for Psychology in August 2006, and are available on the HPCSA website.

The code of conduct for psychologists was guided and developed from a generic set of ethical and professional standards of the HPCSA. This is because each discipline is confronted with unique ethical challenges that differ in intricacy and relevance (Zabow & Kaliski, 2006). However, codes of conduct all have one thing in common, namely, to ensure that a set of standards or rules is established, and that the members or individuals who are associated with the body or organisation that prescribes these codes or rules should adhere to them. If an individual breaches the prescribed code of behaviour or expectations, sanctions of some kind should be forthcoming.

Table 5.4: Excerpts from the ethical code for psychologists as it relates to abnormal behaviour

Broad area	Examples of sub-areas
Professional competence	Competency limits Maintaining competence Adding new competencies
Professional relations	Respect for human rights and for others Informed consent Unfair discrimination Sexual and other harassment Avoiding harm Conflict of interest Multiple relationships Exploitative relationships Cooperation with other professionals
Privacy, confidentiality, and records	Rights to confidentiality Limits on intrusions on privacy Legally dependent clients Release of confidential information
Assessment activities	Appropriate use of assessment methods Informed consent in assessments Communication of results Scoring, interpreting, and explaining assessment results
Therapeutic activities	Informed consent to therapy Interruption of therapy Terminating therapy

 ACTIVITY

The American psychologist Gerald Corey and the South African psychologists Lionel Nicholas and Umesh Bawa write that '[i]nformed consent involves the right of clients to be informed about their therapy and to make autonomous decisions relating to it'. They also note that informed consent 'establishes a basic foundation for creating a working alliance and a collaborative partnership between the client and the therapist' (Corey, Nicholas, & Bawa, 2017, p. 37). Explain what the authors mean by this second statement.

With regard to the formulation of board-specific ethical codes, Burke et al. (2007, p. 113) maintain that the many levels at which a practitioner can be registered pose an additional challenge. According to these authors, an ethics manual will probably be more useful than a specific code of ethics. As more and more practitioners with different levels of training are being allowed to do therapeutic work, for example, debriefing and play therapy, different levels of registration should guide the future development of the proposed manual.

As of May 2018, the community of practitioners and prospective practitioners registered under the auspices of the Professional Board for Psychology was as follows: psychologists, intern psychologists, student psychologists, registered counsellors, psychometrists, student psychometrists, psychotechnicians and student registered counsellors. There are also five specific categories of registration for psychologists: clinical, counselling, educational, industrial, and research psychology. In addition, there are gazetted scopes of practice for neuro-psychologists and forensic psychologists. Although many categories of mental healthcare workers exist, the number of registered mental health workers in relation to the South African public is worrisome.

Table 5.5: Professional Board for Psychology registered practitioners

Registration name	Registration code	Total
Psychotechnician	PM	19
Psychometrist	PMT	2 124
Registered counsellor	PRC	2 482
Psychologist	PS	8 800
Intern psychologist	PSIN	934
Student psychometrist	PMTS	769
Student psychologist	PS S	1 398
Psychology visiting student	PS V	3
Student registered counsellor	SRC	2 862
Total		**19 391**

Source: Adapted from: http://www.hpcsa.co.za/Publications/Statistics

In addition to the board's efforts to guide, ensure ethical behaviour, and protect information, the Protection of Personal Information Act (POPI) was enacted in November 2013 (No. 4 of 2013). This act aims to address data and information, and it also applies to the health professions. In short, the POPI Act promotes transparency with regard to what information is collected and what is processed. POPI contains eight conditions for lawful processing of personal information that need to be adhered to by health practitioners:

- accountability
- processing limitation
- purpose specification
- further processing limitation
- information quality
- openness
- security safeguards
- data subject participation.

Practitioners work with clients' data and perhaps share this data with colleagues. In some situations, administrators are privy to very sensitive information or they deal with personal files haphazardly. This places a significant burden on practitioners to ensure that they deal with personal data very carefully, as the Act clearly specifies that three elements of potential liability are involved when dealing with client information and data:

- civil liability (negligence plays an important part here)
- criminal liability (intentionally misappropriating a client's information)
- administrative liability (where the office administration processes are key).

The challenge with the POPI Act is that the concept of 'personal information' is extremely broad and includes anything related to biometric or biographical information (e.g. an identity number, birthdate, contact details, race, gender, marital status, sexual orientation, ethnic origin), photos, voice and video recordings (typical in a therapeutic environment), criminal record, and physical and mental health information (Berry, 2015). Inappropriate use of any information of a client may lead to a fine, a criminal record, and even a prison sentence.

In concluding this section, it is clear that the appropriate governing or administrative body with the legal mandate to represent its registered members should ensure that a code of conduct is developed and that its members adhere to it. The Professional Board for Psychology used these guidelines to develop a board-specific code of conduct. The relevant code of conduct must always incorporate the core values of integrity, trust, and honesty. After a proper investigation, a confirmed breach of the code of conduct by the members should be punished in accordance with the level of unethical behaviour. The fairly new POPI Act adds additional security measures to the protection of clients and their information, to ensure that personal information is dealt with in a highly professional and secure manner.

Challenges to ethical behaviour

Regardless of the current legal dilemmas and the relevant legislation and standing of a professional or statutory body, its 'watchdog' role over practitioners in the mental health and medical sciences and the proper implementation of the POPI Act cannot be overemphasised; annually, a number of practitioners are found guilty of misconduct. The HPCSA Annual Report (2017/2018, p. 48) shows that, during the 2017/2018 financial year, a total of 2 608 complaints of a varying nature (e.g. wrong billing information, fees charged, fraud, unethical behaviour, etc.) were received by the HPCSA with regard to all the professional boards. A total of 798 (30.59%) complaints were mediated; a total of 243 (30.45%) of the complaints were finalised; 24 (3%) of the cases were referred for preliminary investigation. The Medical and Dental Board received 724 complaints, while the Psychology Board received 15 complaints.

However, the full extent of unethical conduct is unknown and inadequately understood. Although many complaints are lodged against psychologists, 'organised statistics on the exact scope of these complaints are not readily available. This is both odd and regrettable since complaints against psychologists in South Africa are not uncommon' (Scherrer et al., 2002, p. 55). The most common issues that can lead to a complaint are as follows (Louw, 1997b; Psychological Society of South Africa, 1994):

- *Professional disrespect:* Derogatory statements between psychologists about each other's training and skills.
- *Breaches of confidentiality:* A breach of confidentiality occurs when the psychologist tells someone the content of therapy sessions or divulges the diagnosis of a client without the client's permission.
- *Confidentiality and forensic reports:* When a psychologist is doing an interview for court work (forensic) purposes, the interviewee should be informed at the outset that confidentiality is not possible as the psychologist is going to write a report of the findings for the court and is most probably going to testify in court about the findings. The interviewee cannot complain about the contents of the report if the information was given voluntarily and if the psychologist explained to the interviewee that confidentiality was not possible.
- *Inappropriate relationships with clients:* A therapist should not enter non-professional relationships with his or her clients, and he or she should refrain from socialising with clients where possible. This includes any sexual relationships with clients.
- *Selection assessments:* A psychologist who evaluates a person for selection procedures for employment placement should obtain written consent from the candidate to divulge information to the employer.
- *Fees:* Overcharging and inflated fees can be seen as fraud. The psychologist should charge a patient strictly according to the actual duration of the therapy session and according to the agreed fees.
- *Advertising:* There are strict guidelines about appropriate advertising for professional services. For example, it would be inappropriate for a psychologist to announce his or her name and contact details during a school assembly.
- *Competence:* Professionals should be careful not to act outside their level of competence as this may lead to harm to the client. In particular, psychologists may misuse psychological tests, or use inappropriate tests, which can contribute to an incorrect diagnosis of a client's problem.

In addition to this, mental healthcare practitioners should be meticulous when they safeguard client information, and about the way client files are stored, who is allowed to have access to the information, and sharing information with colleagues or friends. Even video and audio recordings should be secured at all times. The fact that cyber-crime is rife, and hackers make it their business to hack personal information, means that practitioners must ensure that they install the best firewalls and spyware on their information technology systems. If not, they could run the risk of either carelessly and unintentionally disclosing client information or becoming the reason why client information is breached. Some hackers such as cyber-bullies (Bartol & Bartol, 2017) or vengeance cyber-hackers can steal sensitive client information to either request a ransom or share it in the public domain. Considering the POPI Act, a mental health practitioner can end up in jail simply because of the negligent safeguarding of client information.

CASE STUDY

Crystal, a 20-year-old female client, has been consulting with Dr B, a male psychologist, for six months. During the consultations, the client has disclosed her feelings of incompetence and her low self-esteem to her therapist. This has become a discussion point during every consultation. She also disclosed to the therapist that she stays at home over weekends as she does not have any male friends, and she feels too shy to go out on her own. Eventually, she tells Dr B that she feels safe with him and that she does not feel incompetent when she interacts with him. During a consultation, Dr B suggests that she go out with her female friends, as group socialisation may help her to feel more confident to go out over weekends. Crystal then suggests to Dr B that he should take her out one weekend, as she feels safe with him. During the therapeutic session, Dr B declined this offer. However, later that evening after he consulted with his last client he checked Crystal's file that was lying on his table and called her on her mobile phone, indicating that he would accept her offer to go out and suggesting they go to a night club.

Discussion

In this context, an appropriate and ethical response would be to treat the suggestion in a professional manner without hurting the client's feelings. Clearly, Dr B should not accept the invitation to take Crystal out. It would be inappropriate and unethical behaviour for Dr B to enter into a social relationship with his client. Dr B should always act in such a way that he helps the client with her problem, but he should refrain from getting involved with her on a personal level. It is also very unprofessional to leave her file on his desk while consulting with other clients. If one considers the POPI Act, Dr B could be liable should any information about Crystal get into the public domain.

As is indicated above, practitioners may be guilty of a wide range of misbehaviours that include unacceptable marketing practices, harmful interventions, inappropriate relationships with clients (see the case study of Dr B), professional sabotage or malicious gossip, sexual harassment, overcharging of medical schemes and patients, and breaking confidentiality through careless discussions about clients in public settings (see the case study of Dr C).

'Interesting' clients are sometimes mentioned in social discussions. Practitioners may mask the individual's name and gender but provide enough information in the conversation to allow an educated guess to be made about who the person may be. The casual sharing of the client's information to make conversation or to sound informed and astute is a serious breach of client–therapist confidentiality.

In the human sciences, a scrupulous respect for human dignity is required; however, it is often challenging to adhere to the code of conduct relevant to the discipline because it is human nature to inquire, to experiment, and to bend the rules. Thus, as previously mentioned, some professionals do act outside the prescribed boundaries of the code of conduct. However, all professionals who are bound by their relevant code of conduct should always act ethically and strive towards a shared commitment to their profession's vision, principles, and ethical standards of behaviour.

Ethical dilemmas

Sometimes, practitioners are faced with two or more ethical principles from the code of conduct that are in direct conflict with one another. Practitioners then have to use their personal discretion to decide which principle to prioritise and abide by. According to Burke et al. (2007, p. 111), not many ethical codes give criteria that help practitioners decide which principle is more important in cases of such conflict, yet the practitioner must make a decision. However, the practitioner is required to make the judgement'. This supports the suggestion that a manual for practitioners should be developed, with best-practice examples and real-life dilemmas, and added discussions around the issues involved.

SPECIFIC ETHICAL ISSUES FOR MENTAL HEALTHCARE PROFESSIONALS

A basic premise of mental healthcare is confidentiality. This means that the professional commits to keeping what the client tells them confidential. However, there are some exceptions to this in that information can be divulged in certain situations. For example, a practitioner may be confronted by a visibly aggressive client who clearly does not want to calm down even if asked politely to do so, or a person who divulges information about their terrorist cell which plans to blow up the Union Buildings, or a person who describes his fantasies about killing his estranged girlfriend or a person who has given up hope and threatens to commit suicide. Is there cause to divulge information in these cases? It is not within the scope of this chapter to explore all these debates. However, in the following sections, four aspects will be addressed to answer some of these difficult questions in mental health intervention. These include breaches of confidentiality and reporting to third parties, dangerous clients, suicidal clients, and the committing of a client.

CASE STUDY

During a soccer game Dr C bumped into a female client at the cold-drink stand. After he greeted the client, Dr C and his friend made their way to their seats. Dr C's friend asked him about the woman he had greeted. His friend was very inquisitive and asked Dr C several questions about the woman. Dr C replied 'professionally' by saying, 'She is a client and unfortunately I cannot tell you anything about her.' However, after the game, Dr C and his friend went to a pub to have a few drinks and to celebrate their team's victory. The friend once again enquired about the woman they saw earlier at the soccer. Dr C, now under the influence of alcohol, told his friend that her previous boyfriend had drugged and raped her, and had taken intimate photographs of her and posted them online.

Discussion

There are several ethical issues here. First, Dr C should not have revealed that the woman in question was a client (principle of privacy). Second, this kind of discussion with friends is forbidden according to the code of conduct, as it betrays the client's confidentiality. If the client or another professional learn about this, they can report Dr C to the HPCSA and the Professional Board for Psychology. The HPCSA will then investigate the matter and will deal with Dr C according to its prescribed mandate.

Confidentiality and reporting to third parties

Athough the HPCSA prescribes certain guidelines, the onus still lies on the professional to decide whether or not to break confidentiality by divulging information to a third party. The premise of ethical conduct is based on the professional's respect for, and dedication to, the client. This means that they do not tell anyone else what the client has said or done (see the case study of Dr C). However, the HPCSA allows a registered practitioner to break confidentiality in the following instances (Health Professions Council of South Africa, 2007):

1. A practitioner shall divulge verbally or in writing information regarding a patient which he or she ought to divulge only:
   a. In terms of a statutory provision;
   b. At the instruction of a court of law; or
   c. Where justified in the public interest.
2. Any information other than the information referred to in subrule (1) shall only be divulged by a practitioner:
   a. With the express consent of the patient;
   b. In the case of a minor under the age of 14 years, with the written consent of his or her parent or guardian; or
   c. In the case of a deceased patient, with the written consent of his or her next of kin or the executor of such deceased patient's estate

In Rule 30 of the Professional Board for Psychology regarding 'Rules of Conduct Pertaining Specifically to Psychology', it is stated in Chapter 2 that a psychologist may release confidential information 'upon court order or to conform to legal imperatives or upon the written authorisation of the client, parent of a minor client, or legal guardian'.

Dangerousness

To complicate the challenges of ethical conduct and keeping confidentiality, therapists sometimes consult with dangerous or high-risk individuals who may talk about their intense anger and frequent violent thoughts. A question that arises from this is whether a therapist is obligated to warn others (authorities or a third party, e.g. the intended victim) that the client has indicated to them that they have fantasies of acting dangerously, or they intend to, or have already, acted dangerously (see discussion of the Tarasoff Case in Box 5.1).

BOX 5.1: THE TATIANA TARASOFF CASE

The Tarasoff Case has been highly publicised since the early 1970s and is regularly used to support discussions on dangerousness, the assessment of risk, and the divulging of patient information (as in the 2002 article by Herbert and Young). Prosenjit Poddar, who was an outpatient at the University of California's Berkeley campus clinic, revealed to his psychiatrist his desires to harm or kill a girl he had met at a dance. Poddar had dated this young woman (Tatiana Tarasoff) for a short time after he met her. After their brief relationship ended, Poddar became highly distressed and paranoid. After Poddar threatened to blow up Ms Tarasoff's house, a friend persuaded Poddar to seek therapy at the campus clinic. However, after eight sessions, Poddar discontinued his therapy after the psychiatrist warned that he would restrain Poddar if he continued to make threats against his ex-girlfriend. The psychiatrist consulted his supervisor and together they decided to inform the university campus police about Poddar's threats and to ask for their assistance in admitting Poddar to hospital.

The campus police investigated the case and subsequently questioned Poddar; they reported that he appeared quite rational during the interview and that he had promised to stay away from his ex-girlfriend. He also promised that he would never harm Tatiana. The clinic director instructed his staff not to pursue efforts to hospitalise Poddar. Poddar kept a low profile after the arrest and, for some time, complied with his promise not to contact or hurt Tatiana. However, two months after this event, he went to Tatiana's home and stabbed her to death.

Although the clinic initiated the contact with the campus police, they never contacted Tatiana Tarasoff to warn her of any potential danger. Her parents subsequently sued the Berkeley Clinic on the grounds of negligence. They were of the opinion that the psychiatrist who treated Poddar had been negligent in not warning Tarasoff (or them) of the danger she was in. The case was dismissed by the lower courts, but when the Tarasoff parents took the case to the Supreme Court of California, it confirmed that therapists have a duty to break confidentiality to warn of potential harm. This decision has been controversial and was later amended to say that therapists need to take measures to protect intended victims.

Discussion

It is good practice for psychologists to warn clients at the beginning of their therapy that there may be circumstances under which confidentiality could be broken. These would include the threat of harm to themselves (suicide) or to others (assault or homicide).

In view of the rules (described in the previous section) that regulate the instances when a counsellor can breach the confidentiality clause, the following questions arise: How does one determine which cases should be shared with the authorities because this is justified as acting in the public interest? If a client reveals information that indicates possible aggressive or dangerous behaviour in the future, should the therapist inform the authorities, considering that a 'false alarm' would constitute a breach of confidentiality?

In this situation, the professional has to balance the risk of harm to others against adhering to the ethical code of conduct by maintaining confidentiality. However, it is very difficult to make an accurate prediction of dangerousness and violence. To illustrate some of the problems with the prediction of dangerousness, the potential physical and/or emotional harm caused by a client, and the role of the practitioner in this context, read the case study of Sipho.

CASE STUDY

During a visit to his lecturer, who is also a clinical psychologist, Sipho shares the following information with his lecturer. He explains to her that his academic performance is suffering because his girlfriend has recently ended their three-year relationship, and she immediately started seeing someone new. The lecturer convinces Sipho to come and see her in her capacity as a clinical psychologist to address his emotional distress. After four counselling sessions, Sipho shares enough detail of his post-relationship behaviour with the lecturer for her to make the following conclusions: Sipho is obsessed with his ex-girlfriend, he shows self-mutilating behaviour, stalks his ex-girlfriend, photographs her against her wishes, telephones her repeatedly, and makes threats to commit suicide after he has killed her. This type of behaviour can clearly be categorised as potentially harmful to others. Depending on the personality of the ex-girlfriend and her knowledge of Sipho, she may see his behaviour either as childish and a nuisance or as posing a serious threat to her and other community members. If she is distressed by his behaviour, and feels that it has a negative effect on her well-being, she may believe that she is being harmed emotionally.

Sipho is diagnosed as suffering from a borderline personality disorder. However, this diagnosis and the ex-girlfriend's distress do not enable a professional to predict accurately the level of dangerousness the behaviour poses. Thus, the lecturer has a dilemma. Should Sipho be referred for further therapy or should he be admitted to a mental hospital for both his own and for his ex-girlfriend's protection? Many individuals (male and female) show 'dangerous tendencies' follow the break-up of a love relationship or something similarly traumatic. What should the lecturer do?

Discussion

First, the lecturer should have referred Sipho to another professional, as, by seeing him as a client, she entered into a dual relationship with him (as lecturer and counsellor). Second, the practitioner's present dilemma is whether she should inform the authorities of Sipho's behaviour before something destructive takes place. The counsellor is bound by a code of ethical conduct to keep the client's information to herself. However, there seems to be a real risk of harm to her client and his ex-girlfriend. In cases like these, counsellors are guided by their own discretion, but they are also guided by the Tatiana Tarasoff Case (see Box 5.1).

The case study of Sipho clearly illustrates an ethical dilemma that some practitioners face from time to time. According to the HPCSA criteria (see Table 5.4), a client has the right to confidentiality; however, in this case, the client's fantasies had a direct impact on the safety of another person. These kinds of situations force practitioners to make a judgement as to the seriousness of the matter and to what extent it is anticipated that clients will act on their fantasies, delusions, or hallucinations. In the Tarasoff Case, it is quite clear that the practitioner judged that there was a real threat, otherwise the campus police would not have been notified. Notifying the police was clearly a breach of confidentiality; the question is, was this justified? In addition, the question needs to be asked as to why the victim was not notified.

Dangerous acts and violent behaviour towards others carry negative consequences for the entire community. To determine or predict that someone is a dangerous person who poses a threat to others or society is therefore a daunting task. It is usually agreed that behaviour that causes physical injury and/or damage to property can be deemed dangerous. However, not only physical actions may be regarded as dangerous or destructive; boundaries start to blur when it comes to psychological injury or property damage.

Psychological injury can have irreversible consequences for the emotional well-being of a person (Bartol & Bartol, 2017). Thus, in some cases, the court accepts that actions causing psychological or emotional damage are also characteristic of dangerous behaviour. The legal definition is, however, largely focused on physical or tangible harm and does not really accommodate psychological or emotional damage (Bartol, 2002; Bartol & Bartol, 2005; Bartol & Bartol, 2011; Bartol & Bartol, 2017; Blackburn, 1993).

One of the difficulties illustrated by the Tarasoff Case is that some people who seem to pose no threat to society may indeed be dangerous, while others regarded as dangerous may show no such behaviour following release from care. The MacArthur Risk Assessment Study in the United States (see Table 5.6), which is hailed as one of the most prominent studies in connection with dangerousness, showed that in a significant number of cases, people were incorrectly judged to be dangerous. It seems that clinicians are not able to predict with accuracy the probability of harm occurring, nor can they accurately specify the type of violence or severity of harm an individual may cause.

The tendency amongst clinicians is to over-predict a person's level of dangerousness. Some studies suggest that two out of every three (66%) predictions are 'false positives' (Bartlett & Sandland, 2003; Bartol & Bartol, 2011; Walker, 1996). A false positive refers to the situation when a person is labelled dangerous but does not exhibit dangerous behaviour after the prediction. However, Ashworth (2000) refers to other prediction studies which found 50% accuracy in prediction of dangerousness. Ashworth (2000, p. 180) also states that no 'significant improvements [in prediction] have been reported in recent years'.

Prediction thus remains unreliable in the determination of dangerousness. In support of this, Kaliski (2006, p. 117) claims that 'the sad reality is that few experts, regardless of their professional backgrounds, can provide reliable predictions of future violence'. Some psychologists believe that they can predict dangerousness with relative certainty, while others are not so confident.

Because of this difference in opinion and haziness surrounding the prediction of dangerous behaviour, the 'prediction' of dangerousness became known as 'risk assessment'. Risk assessment implies that psychologists can assess the probability that an individual is likely to act in a dangerous way but not predict outright that a person will surely act in a dangerous manner towards others or him- or herself.

The risk assessment of dangerous or violent behaviour is a daunting task as incorrect prediction can carry grave consequences for the individual, the psychologist, and the community. Dangerous persons can be deemed harmless and released into society only to act in a violent way while others can be predicted to be non-violent but then turn violent after the diagnosis.

Because of this, a thorough violence risk assessment (prediction of dangerousness) is often a required element of a clinical or forensic evaluation (by order of the court) (e.g. determining whether a person should be acquitted for their misdeed; whether they are not guilty by reason of insanity (NGRI); or whether they are suitable candidates for release into the community (and perhaps become an outpatient at a mental hospital).

Rosenfeld et al. (2017) argue in this regard that clinicians often have little or no guidance on how to make the decision to utilise a risk assessment instrument or which one to use. More and more research on violence and dangerousness risk assessment is readily available but, to be able to do a thorough violence risk assessment, considerable time and resources are needed. It is also difficult to determine when a person will act dangerously, as any human being has the ability to act violently and dangerously in a certain situation.

There are different types or techniques to predict dangerousness. Styles to risk prediction include unaided/unstructured clinical risk assessment; actuarial methods; and structured clinical judgement.

Unstructured risk assessment refers to the assessment of risk that is solely based on clinical judgement (Dolan & Doyle, 2000) and has no statistical foundation (Bartol & Bartol, 2017). This approach is very subjective, based purely on the expertise and experience of the clinician. There are no guidelines as to what factors should be studied; therefore, the factors that are accounted for are unknown. Finally, this approach has little empirical support (Bartol & Bartol, 2017).

Actuarial methods use algorithms along with a small number of predetermined factors which allow for coding. This is more broadly defined as a method that utilises a combination of empirical risk factors that correspond to a probability of re-offending (Mills & Gray, 2013). Its weaknesses lie in a number of factors:

- The small number of risk factors cannot always account for individual differences and variations in risk.
- The measures were originally developed to fit a specific population, and this makes generalisation difficult.
- The definition of violence is restricted in the fact that it cannot address frequency, severity or duration.
- Due to the strict adherence to the actuarial tool, the clinician has no professional input in terms of judgement (Bartol & Bartol, 2017).
- There exists no theoretical basis for the factors that are included (Churcher, Mills, & Forth, 2016).

Following actuarial approaches, the next development involved structured clinical/professional judgement (SPJ); this developed from combining both clinical and actuarial approaches (Bartol & Bartol, 2017). Thus, SPJ is the combination of empirical knowledge and professional expertise (Dolan & Doyle, 2000). This approach has emerged more recently; therefore, it has not been adequately researched yet. With SPJ, the clinician speculates on what circumstances might contribute to violent acts; thus, there still exists a degree of subjectivity (Bartol & Bartol, 2017).

The difference between SPJ and unstructured clinical judgement is that SPJ includes risk factors that have theoretical relevance and that have been statistically proven to be linked to re-offending. The combination of these factors is used to help clinicians come to conclusions regarding risk. The offenders are then rated on numerous different risk factors and, according to their rating, placed in a category (e.g. low, average or high risk) (Churcher et al., 2016).

The core difference between clinical risk assessment and actuarial risk assessment lies in the fact that the clinical method is based on the professional's subjective, clinical methods, whereas an actuarial approach is rooted in statistical assessment. Clinicians collect information pertaining to the individual's background, including risk and protective factors related to the individual who is being assessed.

Table 5.6: Factors that can contribute to risk of violent behaviour

Factor	Contribution to risk of violent behaviour
Gender	Slight difference in terms of gender, with men being slightly more prone to violence than women.
Prior violence	A history of violent behaviour seems to be strongly related to future violence.
Childhood experiences	A history of serious and frequent physical abuse and a father with a criminal record or with a history of substance abuse predict subsequent violent behaviour.
Neighbourhood and race	Race is not a factor as different race groups from the same disadvantaged neighbourhoods had the same rates of violence.

Factor	Contribution to risk of violent behaviour
Diagnosis of mental disorder	A diagnosis of schizophrenia is associated with a lower rate of violence than a diagnosis of certain personality or adjustment disorders. A co-occurring diagnosis of substance abuse is strongly predictive of violence.
Delusions	The presence of delusions is not associated with violence; however, a generally 'suspicious' attitude toward others seems to be related to later violence.
Hallucinations	Hallucinations in general do not seem to be related to violence with the exception of where voices specifically commanded a violent act.
Violent thoughts	Thinking or daydreaming about harming others was associated with violence, particularly if the thoughts or daydreams were persistent.

Source: Adapted from http://www.macarthur.virginia.edu/risk.html

Whether or not one has a statutory or ethical duty to warn or protect, many practitioners regard the Tarasoff ruling as the 'standard of practice' with regard to potentially dangerous clients (Bartol & Bartol, 2008). However, others do not agree with the Tarasoff ruling in therapeutic situations where an individual divulges their intention to hurt another person. For example, Bersoff (2002, p. 570) is of the opinion that the Tarasoff Case should be seen as 'bad law, bad social science, and bad social policy'. Bersoff insists that Poddar was an outpatient and not under the control of a mental hospital and therefore not eligible for involuntary commitment. This means that there was no legal duty on the psychiatrist to protect private third parties from harm.

Suicide and euthanasia

Mental health practitioners are often confronted by individuals who express their intent to take their own lives because of some form of distress. Although this is very difficult to determine, the World Health Organization (2014b) estimates that, world wide, approximately 800 000 people die each year because of self-death or suicide (intentionally causing your own death). Suicide rates differ by gender and age. Men account for roughly three times the number of suicides of women, and this gender disparity is even greater in high-income countries. It is estimated that there were 12.3 deaths by suicide for every 100 000 people in South Africa in 2015 (Wilkinson, 2017). Social factors such as unemployment and economic hardship, combined with the lack of suicide prevention and intervention services, all contribute to South Africa's suicide rate.

In conjunction with the many factors and influences that could contribute to suicidal behaviour or tendencies, some comorbid disorders can also lead to suicide. Two of the most common underlying disorders that are related to suicide are schizophrenia and depression. The suicide incidence among people suffering from schizophrenia is at least 20 times higher than the incidence amongst the general population. Alcoholism and substance addiction also often correlate with suicidal behaviour.

Suicide is common in most cultures of the world, and it occurs at all social levels and amongst all races in South Africa. Meyer, Teylan, and Schwartz (2014) insist that a history of mental disorders, in particular mood and substance use disorders, presents a major risk factor in those who attempt suicide. Additional suicide risk factors include family discord, childhood trauma, quality of attachment to significant others, as well as abuse, peer conflict and bullying. It is important that one considers the complex interaction of certain social, emotional, and psychological factors with the genetic and other biological dispositions of individuals who consider suicide.

Due partly to the fact that there are so many myths about suicide, it can be very difficult to predict whether a client or patient who expresses his or her will to die will actually go through with his or her intention. The mental health practitioner should always consider a suicide threat to be serious and should treat a suicidal person ethically and with dignity. Anyone expressing suicidal feelings needs immediate attention. However, it is often difficult to intervene, and to prevent suicide, because of the level of distress suicidal clients manifest with. The client usually does not realise the limitations and irrationality of his or her thought processes. Many insist that it would be better if they take their own life. In addition, it is difficult to distinguish between those who will attempt suicide and those who only consider suicide (Klonsky & May, 2013).

This opens up the question whether any person has the right to intervene if another human being decides to take his or her own life. The Constitution states that we have a right to life but the same argument can be put forward for death. We have a right to die and probably a right to die as we wish to die. For example, one might ask whether an aged person with a terminal illness has the right to insist on suicide or assisted suicide (euthanasia). This becomes a very controversial issue since healthcare practitioners are trained to save lives and to help humans. This issue continues to be the subject of fierce legal and moral debate.

Although euthanasia has been legalised in a few countries, in South Africa it is illegal to assist a person to take his or her own life, even on request. It is also vital for mental health practitioners to act according to the current legal guidelines; otherwise, they could face serious criminal charges such as accessory to murder or murder. In addition, should a practitioner treat a suicidal client inappropriately or neglect to take reasonable steps to assist a suicidal person, he or she could be charged with unethical behaviour by the HPCSA. Neglecting this duty can have very serious mental health implications for clients (Bhamjee, 2010; Egan, 2008; Hoffmann, Myburgh, & Poggenpoel, 2010; Lippi, Smit, Jordaan, & Roos, 2009; Prinsloo & Louw, 1989; Sneiderman & McQuoid-Mason, 2000).

The two underlying principles of the ethical code, namely beneficence (acting in the best interest of the client) and non-maleficence (minimising harm) are relevant here. On the one hand, one could argue that the decision to break confidentiality 'on behalf of the client' could be deemed by the client to be an act of maleficence; clients could argue that the practitioner is not treating them with the necessary respect and dignity.

However, suicidal clients may be very vulnerable and unable to make a rational decision for themselves. In this situation, it may be in the client's best interest (beneficence) to make a decision to protect him or her from harm. In this case, the beneficence outweighs any potential maleficence. Allan (1997, p. 80) states that 'where a client is in immediate and real danger of serious harm but is incapable of giving consent, or refuses, and where there is no reasonable alternative to the course of action considered ... contacting the person's relatives or the police may be justified'. Others would say that this action is not only justified but an obligation of professional ethical behaviour.

In addition, family murders are increasing in South Africa amongst all cultural and ethnic groups (known as murder-suicide or extended suicide). Extended suicide occurs when the parent carefully plans the murder and tries to prevent the victims from experiencing any pain. Murder-suicide is likely to be preceded by a pathological possessiveness of the husband in respect of his wife and children, especially his wife. Males who view their family members as property are more likely to commit an impulsive family murder or murder-suicide. It is difficult for the practitioner to decide whether the client who raises a possible family murder during therapy will commit either one of these types of family murder. The question arises whether this intention provides enough grounds to inform the other members of the family and the authorities.

In addition to all the factors discussed above, in the case of psychologists, their decision about possibly breaking confidentiality about these matters is often influenced by their own values as well as their therapeutic modality.

Committing a client

Committing or referring a client for observation has considerable implications for both parties. Mere admission to a psychiatric institution can be stigmatising and potentially degrading. Referral for observation is a commonly used mental health intervention whereby the referred individual is monitored or treated for specific behaviour. It is essential to adhere to guidelines for good medical practice during the referral process, as incomplete assessment and poor quality of referral could have detrimental consequences for both the health professional referring the person as well as for the practitioner receiving the patient in the facility. Poor quality of referrals to mental health service providers should be seen as a serious infringement of human rights. Typical infringements include unclear referrals and breaches of patient confidentiality (Struwig & Pretorius, 2009).

Should it become evident that a client needs to be committed, a health professional is obliged to discuss with the client the possibilities for treatment and the possible effects of non-treatment (e.g. distress, injury and, in extreme cases, death). Other options such as medication should also be discussed. This is important especially if the person has the capacity to make informed decisions about his or her care. In cases where a person poses a risk, the person should be informed that a risk assessment is needed and that it should be considered as an attempt to reduce harm.

Some individuals with a severe mental illness may lack the capacity to recognise the presence of a disorder, to consider advice regarding the risks and benefits of treatment, or to make an informed choice about their condition and the best option for treatment. Swanepoel (2010) proposes that three factors should be considered when confronted with the ethics of decision-making regarding a client/patient:

- Psychologists always have choices they can select from as they make decisions.
- The consequences of each of the different choices should be taken into account.
- The context of the specific ethical dilemma must be considered as it will have an effect on the eventual decision.

The healthcare professional could, where possible, obtain a second opinion if uncertain about aspects of the person's condition.

Although the legal capacity of a person can be assessed quite accurately, we should stay mindful of our limitations in terms of predicting dangerousness. Should a person lack the capacity to make a decision on his or her commitment, the healthcare professional should discuss the person's condition with other relevant role-players such as a spouse or other direct family members, and take immediate action. This swift action could reduce risks in cases where a person has a severe mental condition or poses a safety risk to others.

In this case, the patient should be committed to ensure immediate proper care and to reduce any form of risk (Ryan, Nielssen, Paton, & Large, 2010). However, Zabow (2008, p. 62) warns practitioners not to be over-enthusiastic about committing clients. He mentions the issues of personal liberty and autonomy, which have to be weighed against the intention to restore mental health and the provision of care.

CONSEQUENCES OF UNETHICAL CONDUCT

The HPCSA will investigate any written allegations submitted to it regarding the violation of the code of ethical behaviour by a mental healthcare practitioner.

If a client wishes to lodge a complaint of unethical behaviour against a psychologist, he or she should direct a letter describing the complaint to the HPCSA. The complainant could also be a colleague or an ordinary member of society.

Following receipt of a complaint, the Professional Board will notify the accused that a complaint has been lodged and request him or her to submit an explanation in defence of the alleged malpractice. The defence or explanation is put before the Committee for Preliminary Inquiry. This committee deals with all matters, within current policy parameters, relating to preliminary enquiries regarding complaints, determination of accounts, and fines, in terms of the Medical, Dental and Supplementary Health Service Professions Act (No. 56 of 1974) and reports to the Board about these.

The Committee for Preliminary Inquiry will decide whether the complaint warrants further investigation. If a satisfactory explanation is given by the practitioner, it is usually accepted and no further action is taken.

However, the accused can be called to meet with the committee if it is not satisfied with the justification. If the explanation is not accepted, an inquiry by the Disciplinary Committee will follow.

Corrective actions for confirmed breaches of ethical conduct by members of the HPCSA are described in the disciplinary policies. The legal implications that can be expected when a member breaches the Code of Conduct or behaves unethically are stipulated on the official website of the HPCSA (www.hpcsa.co.za).

If the transgression is minor, for example advertising services inappropriately, the practitioner will be warned or fined. If the transgression is of a more serious nature, the practitioner can be put on probation, suspended for a specified time, or struck off the roll. In very serious cases, where criminal charges are laid against the professional, a prison sentence may be imposed by the court. The complainant can also lodge a civil case against the practitioner.

Even if psychologists are successful with their defence of the complaint, they are likely to suffer as the complaint itself may damage their reputation. In addition, the process may have severe financial implications, both directly in terms of legal costs and indirectly in terms of loss of income (Scherrer et al., 2002).

In addition to the process described above, from September 2005, the HPCSA appointed an ombudsman to assist in investigating and settling complaints referred by the legal services department of the Committee for Preliminary Inquiry. The ombudsman addresses complaints against registered practitioners and determines their nature and validity in terms of the Medical, Dental and Supplementary Health Service Professions Act (No. 56 of 1974). The Office of the Ombudsman also renders a mediation service and endeavours to resolve matters amicably, if at all possible.

This regulatory framework therefore governs the disciplinary processes when a complaint is lodged against a practitioner. The HPCSA also follows a policy of transparency by posting on their website all the cases that they investigate, the names of the offending parties, and their punishment, to ensure that the public is protected from similar malpractice in the future.

CASE STUDY

Dr A is a well-known psychiatrist who falsely claims from medical schemes for 'consultations with patients' he sees on a weekly basis. He also overcharges some patients and claims for chronic depression medicines that he 'prescribes and provides' for them on a monthly basis. Through these actions, Dr A is fraudulently claiming thousands of rand from medical schemes for fictitious 'patients' with behavioural disorders.

In a severe case of unethical behaviour like this, the following needs to be considered: Dr A's actions are premeditated and harmful, but he did not hurt his patients directly (either physically or psychologically). However, his actions run the risk of exhausting the patients' medical funds. The primary victims in this context are the medical schemes. The secondary victims are the patients because their capacity to get treatment when they indeed need it is damaged.

Discussion

Should Dr A get a warning, with the requirement that he pay the medical schemes back what he owes them, or should Dr A get a fine? Or should he be suspended from practice for a period of time? In a case like this, Dr A would probably be required to pay back the fees to the medical schemes, he would probably have to pay a fine, and he would most likely be removed from the register for a period of time. In addition, depending on the extent of the fraud, he may face criminal charges.

CONCLUSION

When dealing with people with a mental disorder, we must always remind ourselves that we are dealing with people who are vulnerable. Swanepoel (2010, p. 853) argues that 'making ethical or moral decisions, like any other decision in healthcare, is not a precise art but a learned skill'. Furthermore, in this context, it is evident that mental health professionals are in a position of power in relation to their clients; therefore, they should be very careful not to abuse this position or to harm the client in a therapeutic environment.

Professional behaviour is expected at all times, partly 'because of the essentially private, highly personal, and sometimes intensely emotional nature of the relationship' (Zabow & Kaliski, 2006, p. 360). Practitioners should always ensure that they act professionally in a clinical or therapeutic situation, and they should guard against any situation or action that can be deemed unprofessional or unethical. It goes without saying that the practitioner should never fuel or encourage a situation that could lead to unethical behaviour.

This chapter has provided a brief overview of important elements regarding legal and ethical issues concerning the management of people with a mental disorder. Any mental health professional must have a working knowledge of the relevant legal Acts and ethical codes to ensure that their conduct is above reproach at all times. This chapter should, however, have made it abundantly clear that ethical decisions are not always as clear-cut as they may seem at first glance. Practitioners, relying on their own ethical character, their knowledge of relevant laws, and their knowledge of the ethical codes, need to navigate themselves through any difficult situations they may encounter. Failure to do this successfully makes them vulnerable to litigation and disciplinary action.

MULTIPLE-CHOICE QUESTIONS

1. Beneficence is the ethical value whereby:
   a) practitioners should not harm or act against the best interests of patients, even when the interests of the latter conflict with their own self-interest
   b) practitioners should act in the best interests of patients even when the interests of the latter conflict with their own personal self-interest
   c) practitioners should honour the right of patients to self-determination to make their own informed choices and to live their lives by their own beliefs, values, and preferences
   d) practitioners should treat personal or private information as confidential in professional relationships with patients – unless overriding reasons confer a moral or legal right to disclosure.
2. The following professionals do not operate under the auspices of the Professional Board for Psychology:
   a) life coaches
   b) registered counsellors
   c) psychometrists
   d) psychotechnicians

3. The Mental Health Care Act that is currently binding was published in ___ and amended in ___:
   a) 1982 and 2000
   b) 1992 and 2011
   c) 2002 and 2014
   d) 2012 and 2017
4. A mental health service provider should always refrain from:
   a) breaking confidentiality
   b) an actuarial approach
   c) condoning euthanasia
   d) dual relationships.
5. According to Swanepoel (2010), when confronted with an ethical dilemma a psychologist should:
   a) embark on the process of gaining informed consent
   b) consult a traditional healer from the client's context
   c) take the consequences of the different options into account
   d) take out professional insurance.

PARAGRAPH AND ESSAY QUESTIONS

1. Critically discuss the prerequisites for ethical conduct in a therapeutic context.
2. Define ethical behaviour in your own words.
3. Examine the role of the Health Professions Council of South Africa in ensuring ethical conduct in the health and behavioural disciplines.
4. Explain why it is important to accommodate indigenous belief systems in modern psychology.
5. Critically explain the different circumstances under which a therapist can divulge client information to a third party. Illustrate your answer with a case study.
6. Distinguish between the different types of prediction with regard to dangerousness.
7. Debate the possible consequences that unethical conduct can have for a practitioner.
8. Explain the legal implications that unethical conduct can have for a practitioner.
9. Explain in your own words which unique factors need to be considered in the South African context in order to ensure ethical conduct at all times.

PART 2 | A CLOSER LOOK

CHAPTER 6	Anxiety, obsessive-compulsive, and trauma-related disorders	161
CHAPTER 7	Mood disorders	201
CHAPTER 8	Schizophrenia spectrum and other psychotic disorders	227
CHAPTER 9	Neurocognitive disorders	279
CHAPTER 10	Dissociative, somatoform and related disorders	317
CHAPTER 11	Conditions related to sexual health and paraphilic disorders	385
CHAPTER 12	Substance-related and addictive disorders	441
CHAPTER 13	Eating and feeding disorders	475
CHAPTER 14	Personality disorders	527
CHAPTER 15	Neurodevelopmental and other childhood disorders	581

Karabo Makhafula & Melanie Lake

CHAPTER CONTENTS

Introduction

Fear, anxiety, stress, and worry

Fear

Anxiety

Stress

Worry

History of anxiety and panic disorders

Anxiety disorders

Separation anxiety disorder

Specific phobias

Panic disorder

Agoraphobia

Social anxiety disorder (social phobia)

Generalised anxiety disorder

Obsessive-compulsive and related disorders

Obsessive-compulsive disorder

Body dysmorphic disorder

Hoarding disorder

Trichotillomania

Excoriation (skin-picking) disorder

Trauma and stressor-related disorders

Reactive attachment disorder

Disinhibited social engagement disorder

Posttraumatic stress disorder

Acute stress disorder

Adjustment disorders

Cross-cultural and African perspectives

Epidemiology

Aetiology

Biological processes

Psychological perspectives

Psychosocial stressors

Integrated perspectives

Conclusion

LEARNING OUTCOMES

After studying this chapter, you should be able to:

- Show a general understanding of the anxiety disorders and be able to distinguish the anxiety disorders from other mental disorders.
- Be able to distinguish the anxiety disorders from each other.
- Be able to distinguish fear from anxiety.
- Describe the history of the anxiety disorders.
- Describe generalised anxiety disorder.
- Describe the panic disorders.
- Describe the phobic disorders.
- Describe obsessive-compulsive disorder.
- Describe the stress disorders.
- Describe the additional diagnoses of anxiety.
- Discuss cross-cultural differences and, more specifically, South African particulars, in terms of variations in the presentation of the anxiety disorders.
- Formulate an aetiological model of the anxiety disorders and discuss the integrated model of aetiology.

PERSONAL HISTORY CASELET

You don't really have to learn to float. A block of wood can float, and so can a person. What you might have to learn is how to not get in your own way, how to simply let floating happen.

The block of wood doesn't have to make it happen, it just floats, as long as it's in water. People will float too, if they just lay down on the water.

But people, unlike blocks of wood, often find it hard to let go and trust in their body's natural ability to float. Their mistrust and apprehension will lead them to 'do things' to try and stay afloat.

That's not floating, that's sinking! To teach someone to float, you might have to give them a few instructions – lay back, lay your head on the water, lay your arms and legs out, lie still – but the most important part of the 'technique' of floating is ... do nothing, let go, and let time pass.

Float versus swim

When anxious clients come to me for help in dealing with anxiety, they usually expect that I will offer them the swimming kind of help: lots of specific ways for coping with anxiety, and many techniques to keep them 'afloat'.

But what they really need is more the floating kind of help. They need to learn to let go, rather than to make something happen, or prevent something from happening. That's the surest path to anxiety relief.

Source: David Carbonell (2019) *Claire Weekes: Float Through Anxiety*. https://www.anxietycoach.com/claire-weekes.html

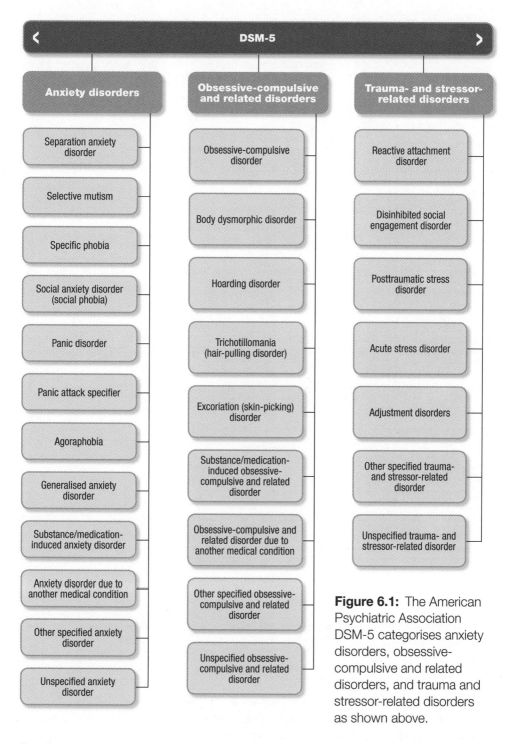

Figure 6.1: The American Psychiatric Association DSM-5 categorises anxiety disorders, obsessive-compulsive and related disorders, and trauma and stressor-related disorders as shown above.

Source: Figure created by OUP reflecting information found in *Diagnostic and Statistical Manual of Mental Disorders*, fifth edition (DSM-5), 2013.

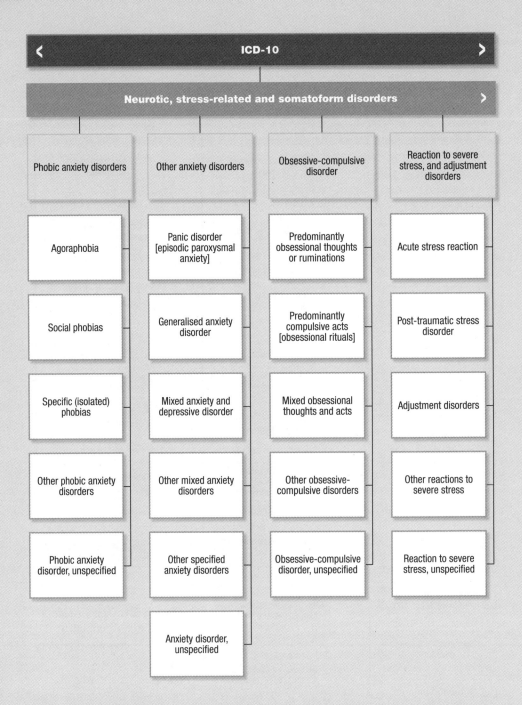

Figure 6.2: The World Health Organization ICD-10 categorises phobic anxiety disorders, other anxiety disorders, obsessive-compulsive disorder, reaction to severe stress, and adjustment disorders as shown above.

Source: *International Statistical Classification of Diseases and Related Health Problems*, tenth revision (ICD-10), 2016.

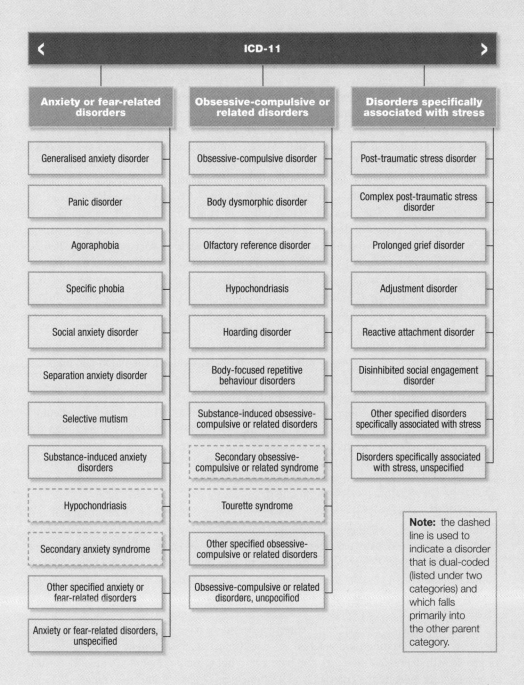

Figure 6.3: The World Health Organization proposed ICD-11 categorises anxiety or fear-related disorders, obsessive-compulsive and related disorders, and disorders specifically related to stress as shown above.

Source: *International Classification of Diseases for Mortality and Morbidity Statistics*, eleventh revision (ICD-11), 2018.

INTRODUCTION

The word 'anxiety' originates from the Latin *anxietas*, meaning to choke, throttle, and upset, and it is frequently used in everyday language to refer to an emotion that is evoked in a wide range of situations. Many communities around the world are plagued with the reality of crime, terrorism, motor vehicle accidents, natural disasters, and other potential threats that create a social climate of fear and anxiety. More commonly, anxiety develops as a result of everyday pressures such as finances, relationship stressors, work-related pressures, etc.

The South African Stress and Health Study (SASH) identified anxiety disorders as the most prevalent class of mental disorders in South Africa (8.1%), with panic disorder having the greatest number of severe cases (66%) (Herman et al., 2009). Anxiety is also used to describe a specific cluster of disorders that share core features of excessive fear and anxiety, and related behavioural disturbances (American Psychiatric Association, 2013). People with anxiety disorders describe a sense of worry that is either present most of the time, or only present in specific situations. Anxiety encompasses physiological, cognitive, affective, and behavioural responses. When an individual is in an anxiety-provoking situation, the autonomic nervous system induces physiological arousal that is characterised by sweating, palpitations, headache, shortness of breath, and tachycardia (rapid heart rate). This reaction results in negative cognitions (thoughts), unpleasant feelings, and tension, and a feeling of apprehension or foreboding. Once this reaction has been induced, the individual prepares to either confront or avoid the situation.

Research suggests that most anxiety disorders have an earlier age of onset compared to many other classes of psychiatric disorders. They have been found to be more prevalent in females than males, with the prevalence rate being twice as high in females. The median age of onset varies between specific anxiety disorders. Anxiety symptoms are widespread across communities, and they have high frequency in the global population. In the short term, anxiety can help drive performance, but if excessive and persistent, it can have a potentially substantial negative impact on an individual's functioning.

Anxiety disorders can present alone but they are often comorbid with other mental and medical conditions, and they may also be comorbid among themselves. The association between anxiety and pain has been documented extensively, as physical symptoms are exacerbated by anxiety or are comorbid with anxiety disorders (Jordan & Okifuji, 2011). Somatic complaints (physical symptoms) are a common feature of anxiety disorders and may include gastrointestinal symptoms, headaches, and muscle tension. They may also lead to substance use.

The coexistence of anxiety and depressive disorders has been extensively recorded in literature and is a common presentation in clinical practice. Studies indicate that up to 70% of people with depressive disorders also have comorbid anxiety symptoms, with 40% to 70% simultaneously meeting the criteria for at least one type of anxiety disorder (Zhiguo & Fang, 2014). The comorbidity of these two disabling conditions presents a treatment challenge in that individuals are more functionally impaired than those who present with either disorder alone.

There is a distinction between state anxiety, trait anxiety, and anxiety disorders (Pérez-Edgar & Fox, 2005). State anxiety refers to a measure of an individual's immediate or acute level of anxiety, whereas trait anxiety refers to the long-term tendency of an individual to show anxiety responses to environmental events. At the other end of the spectrum lie anxiety disorders; these are disabling and limit an individual's ability to engage freely and effectively with their environment. The distinction between state and trait anxiety, and anxiety disorders, is in the degree of functional impairment that results (Pérez-Edgar & Fox, 2005).

Based on the commonality between their neurobiological, genetic, and psychological features, anxiety disorders are split into three categories in the DSM-5:

- anxiety
- obsessive-compulsive and related disorders
- trauma- and stressor-related disorders.

Selective mutism and separation anxiety disorder are currently classified with 'other anxiety disorders' whereas, in the DSM-IV, they were included in the disorders diagnosed in infancy, childhood, and adolescence.

FEAR, ANXIETY, STRESS, AND WORRY

The DSM-5 distinguishes between fear, anxiety, stress, and worry. These terms will be discussed in this section.

Fear

Fear is a commonly experienced and basic emotion felt by all species. It is defined as an emotional response to real or perceived imminent threat (American Psychiatric Association, 2013). It is not necessarily unreasonable or unwarranted. In fact, in many instances, the experience of fear helps us to survive by assisting us to respond to actual threats in our environment. When faced with a threat, our priority is to escape that threat, or to fight, if escape is not an option. This reaction is associated with autonomic arousal that is necessary for the 'fight-or-flight' reaction, which is the body's physiological response to fear. In the world we live in today, we are often faced with threats of possible future harm. It is unfortunate that violent crime, personal injury, and traumatic exposure have become a part of our daily reality.

Fear is a response to an immediate threat, and this distinguishes it from anxiety. Anxiety is an emotion that is associated with worrying about future events that may or may not happen, such as whether one will cope under a particular set of circumstances, and worrying about interpersonal difficulties or specific upcoming events.

Anxiety

As a system that helps us prepare for the future, anxiety is functional and adaptive at a normative level. Many people experience anxiety in different ways, with different durations and degrees of intensity. It allows people to ready themselves to face future situations, and the continuum between worry, anxiety, and panic operates as an alarm system that is aimed at protecting us from harm. Using information gathered from our past experiences helps us to avoid certain consequences or to brace ourselves in certain situations.

When we are unable to prepare for the future in an effective and efficient manner, this results in uncertainty, which contributes to anxiety (Grupe & Nitschke, 2013). As explained by Meyerbröker and Powers (2015), when this system is triggered even in relatively safe environments, it can result in us fearing the alarm system itself, which can be disabling. Pathological anxiety results when our danger detection system is triggered in a non-adaptive way.

Cognitive theory describes a 'catastrophic cognition' as a primary mechanism for anxiety disorders. This model proposes the misinterpretation of bodily sensations, which gives rise to bodily arousal, resulting in a panic attack (Beck & Emery, 1985; Clark, 1986). These catastrophic cognitions (thoughts) include physical, emotional, mental, behavioural, and social catastrophes (Austin & Richards, 2001).

Stress

Stress is a common occurrence and is synonymous with the lives that many people lead today. During periods of stress, bodily systems are put under strain in order to cope with excessive demands in the environment. At times, people are able to manage their stress and continue to live healthy lives in spite of their stressors. Stressors are perceived as qualitatively positive or negative. The effects of negative events can lead to physical illness and psychological disorders such as anxiety disorders, mood disorders, substance abuse, or physical illness. Stress often has a negative effect on quality of life, resulting in weight changes, insomnia, changes in mood, and mental fatigue.

The General Adaptation Syndrome (GAS) is a three-stage process that refers to the different stages of stress that the body goes through during a stressful reaction. Fear and the 'alarm response' are considered to be the first phase of the stress response. This involves the 'fight-or-flight' reaction during which the body prepares to fight or to flee from a perceived dangerous situation. During this phase, the body releases adrenalin, the heart rate increases, and the adrenal glands release cortisol. Phase two is called the 'resistance stage'. During this stage, certain coping actions occur, and these are aimed at returning the body to its pre-stress state. During the resistance stage, the body repairs itself by normalising the functions that were elevated during the alarm response stage. The final stage, called the 'exhaustion stage', occurs when the resistance stage is continuous and prolonged, and it can result in chronic stress. This can have a negative impact on the immune system, resulting in physical illness. It can also lead to psychological distress.

Worry

The term 'worry' is also mentioned in the DSM-5, referring to the cognitive aspects of apprehensive expectation (American Psychiatric Association, 2013).

HISTORY OF ANXIETY AND PANIC DISORDERS

In the second half of the 1800s and the early 1900s, the Austrian neurologists Sigmund Freud and Moritz Benedikt, the German psychiatrist Carl Friederich Otto Westphal, and the French psychotherapist Pierre Janet all made contributions to this emerging field. Freud proposed that anxiety is caused by defence mechanisms that are triggered in response to threatening impulses. Benedikt described a condition he called '*platzschwindel*' ('place dizziness') (Balaban & Jacob, 2001; Hinton, Nathan, Bird, & Park, 2002), which Westphal then termed '*agoraphobie*', and which we now call agoraphobia (Callard, 2006; Sinnott, Jones, & Fordham, 1981), probably from the Greek words for 'open space' and 'fear'. Westphal also described how obsessive images could overcome the will of a sane and insightful person, contributing to research on what later became known as obsessive-compulsive disorder (De Haan et al., 2013). Janet studied the relationship between memory and trauma.

The emergence of PTSD as a clinical diagnosis resulted from observations made of the psychological distress incurred by combatants and concentration camp survivors of World Wars I and II. Following this, the negative impact of traumatic exposure related to other life stressors also received growing recognition in research literature in later years.

A lot of the discussion around anxiety and panic disorders surrounded the presence or absence of cues, and what did, or did not, constitute a distinct disorder. For example, in 1980, the DSM-III recognised panic disorder without agoraphobia and panic disorder with agoraphobia as distinct disorders. In the DSM-5, the anxiety disorders, the obsessive-compulsive and related disorders, and the trauma- and stressor-related disorders were considered distinct enough to be placed in three separate chapters. The ICD-10 instead uses four categories, because it makes a distinction between the more specific 'phobic anxiety disorders' and the more general 'other anxiety orders'. However, the ICD-11 has three sets of disorders, which are very similar to the DSM-5 categories.

Figure 6.4: *The Scream* (1895) by Edvard Munch is seen as an early depiction of anxiety experienced by the artist when outside in nature.

Figure 6.5: *Black and Blue 1* by Vuyile Voyiya was inspired by a South African man who had been beaten by the apartheid regime, and continued to try to fend off attackers even when no one was there.

 **ACTIVITY**

Compare the two artworks that both show people who suffer from disorders described in this chapter. How are they similar? How are they different?

ANXIETY DISORDERS

Separation anxiety disorder

Individuals who experience separation anxiety disorder (see also Chapter 15) have inappropriate and excessive worry about being separated from their home, or from significant attachment figures. This results in significant distress when the individual faces the prospect of, or has the experience of, leaving a significant attachment figure, which is often followed by excessive worry about losing the attachment figure through injury, illness or other forms of harm. The individual may refuse or be reluctant to leave the home as a result of this excessive worry. As a result, symptoms of separation anxiety often lead to significant distress in daily functioning and may also result in somatic (physical) complaints, which often present when separation is anticipated or experienced (American Psychological Association, 2013), as well as nightmares involving the theme of separation.

The restructuring of some sections of the DSM-5 brought about a reclassification of separation anxiety disorder into the anxiety disorders category. In previous versions of the DSM, this disorder was listed under the section 'disorders usually first diagnosed in infancy, childhood, or adolescence'. This was because this disorder was considered to typically develop in childhood, and was diagnosed in adults only if the onset was before 18 years of age. Although the vast majority of diagnoses are made during childhood, the current classification acknowledges that separation anxiety disorder may be diagnosed throughout the entire lifespan. Therefore, even if appearing in childhood, separation anxiety disorder may persist into adulthood.

Specific phobias

Fear is understood as an adaptive and healthy response to environmental threats and, as discussed earlier, it is a useful response that prepares individuals to respond to threatening stimuli in their immediate environment. When there is an extreme manifestation of fear towards objects or situations in the absence of danger that warrants such fear, the fear may be described as maladaptive.

Specific phobia (previously referred to as 'simple phobia') is marked by persistently excessive or unreasonable fear when anticipating, or in the presence of, a specific object or situation. When individuals with specific phobia encounter the feared object or situation, they may experience intense fear or anxiety, which may also result in a panic attack. The fear or anxiety frequently results in avoidance behaviour, or it is endured with extreme discomfort or dread.

To varying degrees, specific phobia may cause an individual to lead a restricted lifestyle, and it can have a significant impact on quality of life. Examples of specific phobias include animal phobias such as fear of dogs or spiders, or blood-injection-injury phobias such the fear of injections or being close to needles. This condition frequently emerges in childhood, with a mean onset of between the ages of seven and nine. Specific phobias tend to persist for several years and they are strongly predictive of anxiety and mood disorders, as well as substance use disorders (Eaton, Bienvenu, & Miloyan, 2018).

Early discussions about the aetiology of specific phobias attributed these conditions to evolution, in that the feared stimuli reflected the dangers of our prehistoric environment. The fear of these evolutionary dangers became genetically encoded as a result of natural selection. Consequently, people would still possess the innate fear of certain stimuli; for example, a fear of heights may cause someone to drive long distances in order to avoid flying. However, in other cases, people develop adaptive mechanisms to certain fears; for example, air crew may be trained to experience less anxiety when flying.

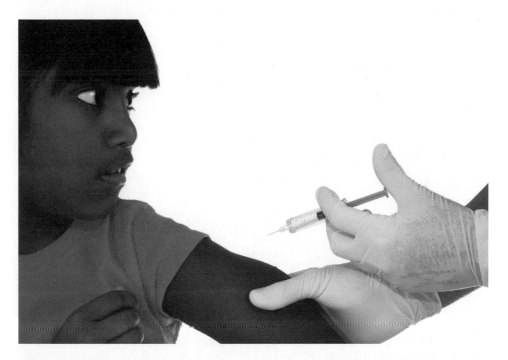

Figure 6.6: People with needle-related fear and needle phobia tend to have extreme vasovagal responses (sudden, rapid drop in heart rate and blood pressure, often resulting in fainting). This condition (also known as trypanophobia), affects an individual's functioning. It may result in avoidance of healthcare settings.

Table 6.1: Diagnostic criteria for specific phobia from the DSM-5 and ICD-10

DSM-5	ICD-10
A. Marked fear or anxiety about a specific object or situation (e.g. flying, heights, animals, receiving an injection, seeing blood). Note: In children, the fear or anxiety may be expressed by crying, tantrums, freezing, or clinging. B. The phobic object or situation almost always provokes immediate fear or anxiety. C. The phobic object or situation is actively avoided or endured with intense fear or anxiety. D. The fear or anxiety is out of proportion to the actual danger posed by the phobic object or situation and to the sociocultural context. E. The fear, anxiety, or avoidance is persistent, typically lasting for six months or more. F. The fear, anxiety, or avoidance causes clinically significant distress or impairment in social, occupational, or other important areas of functioning. G. The disturbance is not better explained by symptoms of another mental disorder, including fear, anxiety, or avoidance of situations associated with panic-like symptoms or other incapacitating symptoms (as in agoraphobia); objects or situations related to obsessions (as in obsessive-compulsive disorder); separation from home or attachment figures (as in separation anxiety disorder) or social situations (as in social anxiety disorder).	■ A disorder in which anxiety is provoked only, or predominantly, in certain highly specific situations. ■ These situations may include proximity to particular animals, heights, thunder, darkness, flying, closed spaces. ■ The specific phobic object or situation is the characteristically avoided or endured with dread. ■ The triggering situation is often discrete. ■ Contact with the triggering situation can evoke panic attacks.

Source: Reprinted with permission from the *Diagnostic and Statistical Manual of Mental Disorders*, fifth edition (DSM-5), American Psychiatric Association (APA), 2013, p. 197, and the ICD-10 *Classification of Mental and Behavioural Disorders: Diagnostic Criteria for Research*, World Health Organization (WHO), Geneva, 2007.

Panic disorder

Panic disorders were first included in the DSM-III, where they were described as spontaneous episodes of intense anxiety. Panic disorder is represented by recurrent (i.e. more than one), unexpected panic attacks (i.e. there is no obvious cue or trigger at the time of the occurrence). Panic attacks are a particular type of fear response, and they occupy a prominent space in the anxiety disorders cluster (Hanson & Modiba, 2017). The DSM-5 defines a panic attack as an abrupt surge of intense fear or intense discomfort that reaches a peak within minutes, and during which time there is the presence of four or more of a list of 13 somatic (physical) and cognitive symptoms.

Following at least one attack, there is a period of at least one month (or more) where the individual worries that another attack may occur and/or the attack may be followed by a pattern of maladaptive behaviours related to the attacks. The symptoms of panic attacks are provoked unexpectedly and have no obvious trigger. Panic disorder is said to affect 3% to 4% of the general population and is most prevalent in women. Panic attacks are not limited to anxiety disorders and can also feature in other mental disorders.

Table 6.2: Diagnostic criteria for panic disorder from the DSM-5 and ICD-10

DSM-5	ICD-10
A. Recurrent unexpected panic attacks. A panic attack is an abrupt surge of intense fear or intense discomfort that reaches a peak within minutes, and during which time four (or more) of the following symptoms occur: Note: the abrupt surge can occur from a calm state or an anxious state. (1) Palpitations, pounding heart, or accelerated heart rate. (2) Sweating. (3) Trembling or shaking. (4) Sensations of shortness of breath or smothering. (5) Feelings of choking. (6) Chest pain or discomfort. (7) Nausea or abdominal distress. (8) Feeling dizzy, unsteady, light-headed, or faint. (9) Chills or heat sensations. (10) Paresthesias (numbness or tingling sensations). (11) Derealisation (feelings of unreality) or depersonalisation (being detached from oneself). (12) Fear of losing control or 'going crazy'. (13) Fear of dying. Note: Culture-specific symptoms (e.g. tinnitus, neck soreness, headache, uncontrollable screaming or crying) may be seen. Such symptoms should not count as one of the four required symptoms. B. At least one of the attacks has been followed by one month (or more) of one of the following: (1) Persistent concern or worry about additional panic attacks or their consequences (e.g. losing control, having a heart attack, 'going crazy'). (2) A significant maladaptive change in behaviour related to the attacks (e.g. behaviours designed to avoid having panic attacks, such as avoidance of exercise or unfamiliar situations). C. The disturbance is not attributable to the physiological effects of a substance (e.g. a drug of abuse, a medication) or another medical condition (e.g. hyperthyroidism, cardiopulmonary disorders).	■ The essential feature is recurrent attacks of severe anxiety (panic), which are not restricted to any particular situation or set of circumstances and are therefore unpredictable. As with other anxiety disorders, the dominant symptoms include sudden onset of palpitations, chest pain, choking sensations, dizziness, and feelings of unreality (depersonalisation or derealisation). There is often also a secondary fear of dying, losing control, or going mad. Panic disorder should not be given as the main diagnosis if the patient has a depressive disorder at the time the attacks start; in these circumstances the panic attacks are probably secondary to depression.

DSM-5	ICD-10
D. The disturbance is not better explained by another mental disorder (e.g. panic attacks do not occur only in response to feared social situations, as in social anxiety disorder; in response to circumscribed phobic objects or situations, as in specific phobia; in response to obsessions, as in obsessive-compulsive disorder; in response to reminders of traumatic events, as in posttraumatic stress disorder, or in response to separation from attachment figures, as in separation anxiety disorder).	

Source: Reprinted with permission from the *Diagnostic and Statistical Manual of Mental Disorders*, fifth edition (DSM-5), American Psychiatric Association (APA), 2013, p. 208, and the ICD-10 *International Statistical Classification of Disease and Related Disorders*, World Health Organization (WHO), Geneva, 2016.

Agoraphobia

The term 'agoraphobia' stems from the Greek '*agora*' which refers to large, open spaces, such as marketplaces. The classic description of agoraphobia is credited to C. F. Westphal, who, in the 1800s, described it as a phobia of large, open spaces. This paved the way for what became described in literature as a common and upsetting phobic disorder (Wittchen, Gloster, Beesdo-Baum, Fava, & Craske, 2010). Agoraphobia is marked by intense fear or anxiety that is triggered by real or anticipated exposure to a wide range of situations. The classification of agoraphobia as a primary diagnosis, with or without recurrent panic attacks, was included in the DSM-III and, since its publication in 1980, agoraphobia has gained much attention. In the DSM-IV-TR, panic disorder was diagnosed with or without agoraphobia, and agoraphobia without history of panic disorder.

Table 6.3: Diagnostic criteria for agoraphobia from the DSM-5 and ICD-10

DSM-5	ICD-10
A. Marked fear or anxiety about two (or more) of the following five situations: (1) Using public transportation (e.g. automobiles, buses, trains, ships, planes). (2) Being in open spaces (e.g. parking lots, marketplaces, bridges). (3) Being in enclosed places (e.g. shops, theatres, cinemas). (4) Standing in line or being in a crowd. (5) Being outside of the home alone.	■ The essential feature is recurrent attacks of severe anxiety (panic). ■ The panic attacks are not restricted to any particular situation or set of circumstances and are therefore unpredictable. ■ The dominant symptoms include: ▸ sudden onset of palpitations, chest pain, choking sensations, dizziness, and feelings of unreality (depersonalisation or derealisation).

DSM-5	ICD-10
B. The individual fears or avoids these situations because of thoughts that escape might be difficult or help might not be available in the events of developing panic-like symptoms or either incapacitating or embarrassing symptoms (e.g. fear of falling in the elderly; fear of incontinence). C. The agoraphobic situations almost always provoke fear or anxiety. D. The agoraphobic situations are actively avoided, require the presence of a companion, or are endured with intense fear or anxiety. E. The fear or anxiety is out of proportion to the actual danger posed by the agoraphobic situation and to the sociocultural context. F. The fear, anxiety, or avoidance is persistent, typically lasting six months or more. G. The fear, anxiety, or avoidance causes clinically significant distress or impairment in social, occupational or other important areas of functioning. H. If another medical condition (e.g. inflammatory bowel disease, Parkinson's disease) is present, the fear, anxiety, or avoidance is clearly excessive. I. The fear, anxiety, or avoidance is not better explained by the symptoms of another mental disorder – for example, the symptoms are not confined to specific phobia, situational type; do not involve only social situations (as in social anxiety disorder) and are not related exclusively to obsessions (as in obsessive-compulsive disorder), perceived defects or flaws in physical appearance (as in body dysmorphic disorder), reminders of traumatic events (as in posttraumatic stress disorder), or fear of separation (as in separation anxiety disorder). Note: Agoraphobia is diagnosed irrespective of the presence of panic disorder. If an individual's presentation meets criteria for panic disorder and agoraphobia, both diagnoses should be assigned.	▪ There is often a secondary fear of dying, losing control, or going mad.

Source: Reprinted with permission from the *Diagnostic and Statistical Manual of Mental Disorders*, fifth edition (DSM-5), American Psychiatric Association (APA), 2013, p. 217, and the ICD-10 *International Statistical Classification of Disease and Related Disorders*, World Health Organization (WHO), Geneva, 2016.

Social anxiety disorder (social phobia)

In the DSM-5, social anxiety disorder has been recognised as the principal name for the diagnosis, where previous versions of the DSM named this diagnosis 'social phobia'. This change was intended to convey the pervasive and significant impairment that results from the disorder. The DSM-5 recognises that the fear felt by people with social anxiety disorder is out of proportion to the actual threat, and it should represent a deviation in terms of the individual's cultural context.

Social anxiety disorder frequently emerges during adolescence or early adulthood, and involves excessive and persistent fear of negative evaluation in social and/or performance situations. According to the DSM-5 criteria for social anxiety disorder, the feared social situation must almost always provoke fear and anxiety, and the situation is avoided or endured with fear and anxiety. The individual fears facing possible scrutiny by others due to fears that he or she may behave in ways that will be negatively evaluated, resulting in rejection.

Social anxiety disorder is accompanied by associated behaviours that are aimed at reducing the anxiety. These include avoiding eye contact, holding a glass tightly, limiting conversation, or remaining quiet in social conversations. People with social anxiety disorder tend to exaggerate small mistakes into anxiety-inducing events and may even ruminate on events after they have occurred, with unpleasant thoughts and feelings. They are excessively concerned about others' judgements and perceptions of them.

Therefore, social anxiety disorder is a risk factor for substance use, depression, and suicide. It also has a negative impact on the individual's ability to function in social contexts and, because people with social anxiety disorder do not develop adequate social skills, it can have a negative effect on the individual's life in the long term.

Many people may be described as shy, but the difference between the two is that, while people who are shy tend to feel uncomfortable in the presence of others, those with social anxiety disorder experience **extreme** anxiety in social situations, and they tend to actively avoid such situations. Exposure to people and social situations usually provokes anxiety in people with social anxiety disorder, and they tend to avoid such situations or they endure them with intense fear or anxiety. They are usually aware that the fear and anxiety are excessive or unreasonable.

Figure 6.7: Common fears associated with social anxiety disorder

Table 6.4: Symptoms of social anxiety disorder are illustrated below

Cognitive	Physiological	Behavioural
Self-consciousness	Sweating	Avoidance
Social inferiority	Blushing	Poor eye contact
Negative self-appraisal	Tremor	Speaking in a soft/inaudible tone
Awareness that feelings and thoughts are irrational		

Epidemiological studies indicate that the prevalence rates for social anxiety disorder range from 3% to 16% in the global population (Seedat, 2013). In general, more females than males present with social anxiety disorder. The median age of onset for this disorder is 13 years, and late onset (after age 30) is uncommon (Schneier & Goldmark, 2015). It may develop as a result of a childhood history of social inhibition and shyness. Children who experience negative social events such as bullying, or being ridiculed or laughed at while speaking in front of a group, may remember the impact of that stressful situation and be prone to developing social anxiety. Children tend to be concerned with being able to make friends, and being able to initiate conversations. When these social functions are not adequately accomplished, the child may develop social anxiety disorder. In other cases, the disorder may develop slowly, following several social interactions and over a long period.

Table 6.5: Diagnostic criteria for social anxiety disorder from the DSM-5 and ICD-10

DSM-5	ICD-10
A. Marked fear or anxiety about one or more social situations in which the individual is exposed to possible scrutiny by others. Examples include social interactions (e.g. having a conversation, meeting unfamiliar people), being observed (e.g. eating or drinking), and performing in front of others (e.g. giving a speech). Note: In children, the anxiety must occur in peer settings and not just during interactions with adults. B. The individual fears that he or she will act in a way or show anxiety symptoms that will be negatively evaluated (i.e. will be humiliating or embarrassing; will lead to rejection or offend others). C. The social situations almost always provoke fear or anxiety. Note: In children, the fear or anxiety may be expressed by crying, tantrums, freezing, clinging, shrinking, or failing to speak in social situations.	■ A disorder in which anxiety is provoked only, or predominantly, in the situation of possible scrutiny by other people. ■ Certain social situations are then characteristically avoided, or endured with dread. ■ More pervasive social phobias are usually associated with fear of criticism and low self-esteem. ■ Secondary manifestations may include blushing, hand tremor, and nausea. The patient is sometimes convinced that these signs are the primary problem. ■ Symptoms may progress to panic attacks.

DSM-5	ICD-10
D.　The social situations are avoided or endured with intense fear or anxiety. E.　The fear or anxiety is out of proportion to the actual threat posed by the social situation and to the sociocultural context. F.　The fear, anxiety or avoidance is persistent, typically lasting for six months or more. G.　The fear, anxiety, or avoidance causes clinically significant distress or impairment in social, occupational, or other important areas of functioning. H.　The fear, anxiety, or avoidance is not attributable to the physiological effects of a substance (e.g. a drug of abuse, a medication) or another medical condition. I.　The fear, anxiety, or avoidance is not better explained by the symptoms of another mental disorder, such as panic disorder, body dysmorphic disorder, or autism spectrum disorder. J.　If another medical condition (e.g. Parkinson's disease, obesity, disfigurement from burns or injury) is present, the fear, anxiety, or avoidance is clearly unrelated or is excessive.	

Source: Reprinted with permission from the *Diagnostic and Statistical Manual of Mental Disorders*, fifth edition (DSM-5), American Psychiatric Association (APA), 2013, p. 202, and the *ICD-10 Classification of Mental and Behavioural Disorders: Diagnostic Criteria for Research*, World Health Organization (WHO), Geneva, 2007.

Generalised anxiety disorder

Generalised anxiety disorder (GAD) is characterised by excessive anxiety and worry (apprehensive expectation) about a number of events or activities. Typically, people with this disorder describe a sense of persistent worrisome thinking that is difficult to control and causes distress in their daily lives. To meet the criteria for generalised anxiety disorder, an individual must experience three (or more) of a possible six symptoms which cause significant distress or impairment in the individual's social, occupational, or other important area of functioning.

People with generalised anxiety disorder worry excessively about many everyday events. The age of onset is broad, with many reporting that they have felt anxious and nervous throughout their lives. The symptoms tend to fluctuate throughout the lifespan, with excessive worry and anxiety being more intense at different periods. In younger children, generalised anxiety disorder often presents as school-related concerns, whereas older individuals tend to be more concerned with their well-being or that of others.

Females are more susceptible to generalised anxiety disorder than males, as are individuals from more developed countries in comparison with those from less-developed countries. Anxiety disorders have emerged as the most prevalent mental disorders in the general population, with patients often seen in the primary healthcare setting. The incapacity that results from generalised anxiety disorder is suggested to be as significant as that which results from other chronic medical illnesses (Hofmann, Dozois, & Smits, 2014).

Table 6.6: Diagnostic criteria for generalised anxiety disorder from the DSM-5 and ICD-10

DSM-5	ICD-10
A. Excessive anxiety or worry (apprehensive expectation), occurring more days than not for at least six months, about a number of events or activities (such as work or school performance). B. The individual finds it difficult to control the worry. C. The anxiety and worry are associated with three (or more) of the following six symptoms (with at least some symptoms having been present for more days than not for the past six months): Note: Only one item is required in children. (1) Restlessness or feeling keyed up or on edge. (2) Being easily fatigued. (3) Difficulty concentrating or mind going blank. (4) Irritability. (5) Muscle tension. (6) Sleep disturbance (difficulty falling or staying asleep, or restlessness, unsatisfying sleep). D. The anxiety, worry, or physical symptoms cause clinically significant distress or impairment in social, occupational, or other important areas of functioning. E. The disturbance is not attributable to the physiological effects of a substance (e.g. a drug of abuse, a medication, or another medical condition (e.g. hyperthyroidism). F. The disturbance is not better explained by another mental disorder (e.g. anxiety or worry about having panic attacks in panic disorder, negative evaluation in social anxiety disorder [social phobia], contamination or other obsessions in obsessive-compulsive disorder, separation from attachment figures in separation anxiety disorder, reminders of traumatic events in posttraumatic stress disorder, gaining weight in anorexia nervosa, physical complaints in somatic symptom disorder, perceived appearance flaws in body dysmorphic disorder, having a serious illness in illness anxiety disorder, or the content of delusional beliefs in schizophrenia or delusional disorder).	■ A disorder in which the manifestation of anxiety is the major symptom. ■ The anxiety is generalised and persistent and not restricted to, or even strongly predominating in, any particular environmental circumstances (i.e. it is 'free-floating'). ■ The dominant symptoms are variable, but include: complaints of persistent nervousness, trembling, muscular tensions, sweating, light-headedness, palpitations, dizziness, and epigastric discomfort. ■ Fears that the patient or a relative will shortly become ill or have an accident are often expressed. ■ Depressive and obsessional symptoms, and even some elements of phobic anxiety, are often present, provided that they are clearly secondary or less severe.

Source: Reprinted with permission from the *Diagnostic and Statistical Manual of Mental Disorders*, fifth edition (DSM-5), American Psychiatric Association (APA), 2013, p. 222, and the ICD-10 *Classification of Mental and Behavioural Disorders: Diagnostic Criteria for Research*, World Health Organization (WHO), Geneva, 2007.

OBSESSIVE-COMPULSIVE AND RELATED DISORDERS

Obsessive-compulsive disorder (OCD) was included in the chapter on anxiety disorders in earlier versions of the DSM. The disorder was characterised by the presence of both obsessions and compulsions; however, it was later found that a number of disorders are characterised by only obsessions or compulsions, rather than both. The new category introduced in the DSM-5 has been named 'Obsessive-compulsive and related disorders'. OCD, together with a number of new disorders, namely body dysmorphic disorder, hoarding disorder, trichotillomania (hair-pulling disorder), and excoriation (skin-picking) disorder form this separate chapter in the DSM-5. This new category includes disorders with obsessions, compulsions or both.

Obsessive-compulsive and related disorders, or other symptoms characteristic of these disorders, may be induced by the use of a substance or medication. The symptoms of this disturbance are triggered as the direct result of using the substance or medication, or exposure to certain toxins; the symptoms develop during or soon after exposure to the substance or medication, and the substance/medication must be capable of producing such an effect. Once the substance/medication is discontinued, the symptoms usually improve or remit over a certain period (depending on the half-life of the substance/medication).

Obsessive-compulsive disorder

The hallmarks of obsessive-compulsive disorder (OCD) include obsessions, which are recurrent and persistent thoughts, urges, or images that are experienced as intrusive and unwanted, and/or compulsions, which are the repetitive behaviours or mental acts that an individual feels driven to perform in response to an obsession or according to rules that must be applied rigidly. The repetitive thoughts, images, impulses or actions are distressing and impact negatively on the individual's daily functioning. They are also time-consuming.

The obsessions and compulsions vary. Some obsessions include religious or somatic concerns, as well as concerns about symmetry, hoarding, and sexually intrusive thoughts. Compulsions, aimed at reducing these recurrent and persistent thoughts, include counting, washing, repeating, checking, ordering, and conducting mental rituals.

This is often a debilitating condition as it substantially influences an individual's daily functioning. OCD can have an adverse effect on an individual's relationships, ability to perform their work, and on their overall quality of life. The potential level of impairment to an individual's functioning warrants its classification as a disorder. OCD has a world-wide prevalence of 1.5% to 3%. The onset of OCD is during childhood for one-third to one-half of individuals (Camprodon, Rausch, Greenberg, & Dougherty, 2016). OCD is associated with an increased risk of suicidal ideation and suicidal behaviour.

Figure 6.8: People with OCD perform certain acts repeatedly. These acts are aimed at reducing the anxiety associated with uncontrollable thoughts, impulses or images.

Table 6.7: Diagnostic criteria for obsessive-compulsive disorder from the DSM-5 and ICD-10

DSM-5	ICD-10
A. Presence of obsessions, compulsions, or both: Obsessions are defined by (1) and (2): (1) Recurrent and persistent thoughts, urges, or images that are experienced, at some time during the disturbance, as intrusive and unwanted, and that in most individuals cause marked anxiety or distress. (2) The individual attempts to ignore or suppress such thoughts, urges, or images, or to neutralise them with some other thought or action (i.e. by performing a compulsion). Compulsions are defined by (1) and (2): (1) Repetitive behaviours (e.g. hand washing, ordering, checking) or mental acts (e.g. praying, counting, repeating words silently) that the individual feels driven to perform in response to an obsession to according to rules that must be applied rigidly. (2) The behaviours or mental acts are aimed at preventing or reducing anxiety or distress, or preventing some dreaded event or situation; however, these behaviours or mental acts are not connected in a realistic way with what they are designed to neutralise or prevent, or are clearly excessive.	■ The essential feature of this disorder is recurrent obsessional thoughts or compulsive acts. ■ Obsessional thoughts are ideas, images, or impulses that enter the patient's mind again and again in a stereotyped form. ■ Obsessions are almost invariably distressing and the patient often tries, unsuccessfully, to resist them. ■ Obsessions are recognised as own thoughts, although they are involuntary and often repugnant. ■ Compulsive acts or rituals are stereotyped behaviours that are repeated again and again. ■ Compulsions are not inherently enjoyable, nor do they result in the completion of inherently useful tasks. ■ Compulsions function to prevent some objectively unlikely event, often involving harm to or caused by the patient, that he or she fears might otherwise occur.

DSM-5	ICD-10
B. The obsessions or compulsions are time-consuming (e.g. take more than one hour per day) or cause clinically significant distress or impairment in social, occupational, or other important areas of functioning. C. The obsessive-compulsive symptoms are not attributable to the physiological effects of a substance (e.g. a drug of abuse, a medication) or another mental condition. D. The disturbance is not better explained by the symptoms of another mental disorder (e.g. excessive worries, as in generalised anxiety disorder; preoccupation with appearance, as in body dysmorphic disorder; difficulty discarding or parting with possessions, as in hoarding disorder; hair pulling, as in trichotillomania [hair-pulling disorder]; skin picking as in excoriation [skin-picking disorder] disorder; stereotypies, as in stereotypic movement disorder; ritualised eating behaviour, as in eating disorders; preoccupation with substances or gambling, as in substance-related and addictive disorders; preoccupation with having an illness, as in illness anxiety disorder; sexual urges or fantasies, as in paraphilic disorders; impulses, as in disruptive, impulse-control, and conduct disorders; guilty ruminations, as in major depressive disorder; thought insertion or delusional preoccupations, as in schizophrenia spectrum and other psychotic disorders; or repetitive patterns of behaviour, as in autism spectrum disorder).	■ The patient usually recognises that this behaviour is pointless or ineffectual, and repeatedly makes attempts to resist. ■ Anxiety is almost invariably present. ■ If compulsive acts are resisted, the anxiety gets worse.

Source: Reprinted with permission from the *Diagnostic and Statistical Manual of Mental Disorders*, fifth edition (DSM-5), American Psychiatric Association (APA), 2013, p. 237, and the ICD-10 *Classification of Mental and Behavioural Disorders: Diagnostic Criteria for Research*, World Health Organization (WHO), Geneva, 2007.

Body dysmorphic disorder

Body dysmorphic disorder is characterised by a preoccupation with an imagined flaw or 'defect' in one's appearance. This perceived defect is not observable to others or appears as slight. Alternatively, where there is a slight flaw in the individual's appearance, the individual's response to that flaw is markedly excessive. Enrico Morselli introduced the term *dysmorphophobia* over a century ago. He defined this disorder as 'the sudden onset and subsequent persistence of an idea of deformity: the individual fears he has become, or may become deformed, and feels tremendous anxiety of such an awareness' (Fava, 1992, p. 117).

Body dysmorphic disorder often causes significant distress and impairment in the individual's daily functioning, involves time-consuming rituals such as gazing in the mirror for extended periods, attempts at concealing or improving the perceived flaw, and constantly making comparisons between one's own appearance and that of others. These individuals often undergo a variety of medical consultations and procedures (often involving dieting), which are aimed at correcting the perceived defect.

Individuals with body dysmorphic disorder often struggle to maintain social relationships and, as a result, are often socially isolated. They are also often subjected to scrutiny and judgement by others, as they are seen as being obsessed with their appearance. This impacts on their development of social competence, and they often lack confidence as they believe that they are constantly being negatively evaluated by people. The individual's preoccupation may involve any part of the body, although it typically involves the skin, hair, and facial features. The preoccupation may also be on more than one area of the body. Common preoccupations in body dysmorphic disorder involve concerns around symmetry (a feeling that the body features are out of proportion), acne, wrinkles, scars, and extremes of complexion.

In the case of muscle dysmorphia, individuals become excessively preoccupied with the idea that their body is too small or insufficiently lean or muscular. This disorder involves males almost exclusively. Muscle dysmorphia is a form of body dysmorphic disorder.

Hoarding disorder

The core symptoms of hoarding disorder differ from those of other obsessive-compulsive and related disorders. Freud was instrumental in introducing the concept of what became known as hoarding, with his concept of the anal character. He described the anal character as having a combination of three peculiarities, namely orderliness (referring to body cleanliness and paying excessive attention to detail even in petty/minor duties), obstinacy (i.e. being defiant, even to the point of vindictiveness), and parsimony (i.e. an extreme unwillingness to spend money or use resources; this could be exaggerated to the extent of extreme greed for material wealth). Other voices contributed to broadening our understanding of this disorder. Several observations emerged that posited that hoarding and other OCD symptoms are distinct conditions (Fontenelle & Grant, 2014).

Hoarding disorder is described as difficulty discarding or parting with possessions, regardless of their actual value. It involves excessive accumulation of items or possessions, an accumulation of clutter, and difficulty disposing of the possessions. Usually, as a result of hoarding, the living areas become so cluttered that use of the space is severely circumscribed. Individuals with hoarding disorder are often restricted in their homes because they are unable to live in or use sections of their houses.

Often these accumulated possessions may pose a physical danger and possibility of personal injury to the individual and others living in the home. If the living areas are uncluttered, it is usually due to the assistance of a third party. Frequently hoarded items include newspapers, papers, and clothing items, regardless of whether these items are of value or not. Understandably, hoarding disorder often impacts negatively on relationships, resulting in strain in the individual's family and interpersonal relationships. People with hoarding disorder may also acquire items excessively by, for instance, collecting free items.

Trichotillomania (hair-pulling disorder)

Trichotillomania is characterised by the recurrent pulling out of one's hair, leading to significant hair loss. The sites from which hair is pulled may vary over time; these sites may be from any area of the body where hair grows, although the scalp is the most common site. This disorder causes marked distress as well as social and occupational impairment. The excessive hair-pulling may result in an irreversible lack of hair growth, as it can endure for months and even years.

Hair-pulling appears to be relatively common (to different degrees) in the general population; however, when it is excessive and meets the criteria for trichotillomania, interventions should be considered (Grant & Chamberlain, 2016). There is evidence for a genetic vulnerability to trichotillomania, and the typical age of onset is usually 10–13 years, across different cultural settings. Hair-pulling triggers may be sensory (e.g. hair thickness, length, and location), emotional (e.g. feeling anxious, bored, angry, or tense), and cognitive (e.g. thoughts about one's hair and appearance) (Grant & Chamberlain, 2016).

Excoriation (skin-picking) disorder

The DSM-5 has included excoriation (skin-picking) disorder as a new disorder in the obsessive-compulsive and related disorders category. The core feature of this disorder is recurrent picking at one's own skin, despite repeated efforts to stop, resulting in skin lesions and causing significant distress and impairment in social, occupational, and other important areas of functioning. The skin-picking is not limited to a particular body site and may involve picking, scratching, pinching, squeezing, scrubbing, biting, or digging the skin. It often involves rituals, as people affected by this disorder feel compelled to perform these actions. People affected by this disorder use fingertips or instruments such as tweezers and needles to pick the skin, resulting in tissue damage. The individual is often aware of the harmfulness of their behaviour but struggles to resist the urge. The skin-picking is usually triggered by an emotional state (e.g. anxiety), and the disorder is often associated with other obsessive-compulsive and related disorders.

TRAUMA AND STRESSOR-RELATED DISORDERS

Trauma and stressor-related disorders represent a new chapter in the DSM-5 in which exposure to a traumatic or stressful event is an explicitly listed diagnostic criterion across all disorders in this category. Disorders listed in this category include reactive attachment disorder, disinhibited social engagement disorder, posttraumatic stress disorder (PTSD), acute stress disorder, and adjustment disorders.

Both reactive attachment disorder and disinhibited social engagement disorder are disorders of attachment resulting from psychological distress experienced by a child during infancy or childhood. Both result from instances of insufficient care, thus limiting the child's ability to form healthy attachments. Healthy attachment relationships are necessary throughout our lives. Infants are primed to have a close bond with their primary caregiver, and there is an inherent dependence on their caregiver for survival. When the infant's primary needs are met, and when they are able to look to the attachment figure for cues about the environment, then a healthy bond is created.

The infant's physiological needs are met through the physical contact that the infant maintains with their caregiver. When atypical events that disrupt this process occur, they disrupt the infant's potential to form this important bond, and so the infant's ability to form a healthy internal working model for relationships is disrupted. This tends to have a significant impact on interpersonal relationships throughout the person's life. Early attachment relationships influence how we later relate to others, how we perceive ourselves in relation to others, and how we view others. Thus, the quality of our attachment relationships provides the groundwork for later interpersonal relationships.

Due to the similarity in their aetiology, the DSM-IV considered reactive attachment disorder and disinhibited social engagement disorder as two subtypes of reactive attachment disorder. These disorders have since been separated in the DSM-5, due to the distinct differences in their symptomatology and course.

Reactive attachment disorder

Reactive attachment disorder is limited to infancy (at least nine months) or early childhood (evident before the age of five years); it is characterised by a pattern of markedly disturbed and developmentally inappropriate attachment behaviours. The disorder develops as a result of extremes of insufficient care such as social neglect or deprivation, repeated changes of primary caregivers, or contexts where there are limited opportunities to form stable attachments. Children with reactive attachment disorder rarely turn to or seek an attachment figure for comfort, support, protection or nurturance.

Early emotional and attachment experiences affect the developing brain, and thus, early childhood trauma alters the structure and neurochemicals in the brain. Ideally, infancy is a time during which the infant and caregiver share attachment experiences from which the developing infant forms a secure attachment relationship with the caregiver. In the absence of this experience, the infant later develops into a child who lacks the skill to self-soothe, regulate emotions, and engage in healthy relationships with others. These difficulties are often pervasive and extend to adulthood, where the individual struggles to engage in healthy relationships. The child with reactive attachment disorder experiences persistent social and emotional disturbances, limited positive affect, and periods of unexplained irritability, sadness or fearfulness (American Psychiatric Association, 2013).

Disinhibited social engagement disorder

Disinhibited social engagement disorder (DSED) describes a pattern of disinhibited behaviour in which a child approaches and interacts with unfamiliar adults in a manner that is over-familiar (i.e. a verbal or physical violation of culturally sanctioned social boundaries). As with reactive attachment disorder, this condition primarily results from extreme neglect or insufficient care or deprivation occurring before the age of two years. Children with DSED tend to venture away from their caregivers, even to unfamiliar settings and, on returning, they often do not check in with the caregiver. These children are also willing to venture off with unfamiliar people with little or no hesitation and express a readiness to accept things from unfamiliar people (e.g. toys, hugs, food).

Posttraumatic stress disorder

The shift in location of posttraumatic stress disorder (PTSD) from anxiety disorders (in the DSM-IV) into the new 'trauma and stressor-related disorders' chapter of the DSM-5 has placed significant emphasis on tightening the definition of trauma. PTSD entails multiple emotions that fall outside of the fear/anxiety spectrum (Pai, Suris, & North, 2017), hence its removal from the anxiety disorders. This has resulted in the inclusion of more diagnostic criteria and specifiers, as well as explanation of the behavioural symptoms that result from PTSD. Psychologists who specialise in the treatment of PTSD are generally supportive of these changes, as they are now much more in line with therapy goals. These include overcoming avoidance; restructuring excessively negative beliefs about the traumatic event, self, and symptoms; as well as resolving the common but 'stuck' PTSD emotions of guilt, shame, and anger (Resick, Monson, & Chard, 2017).

PTSD presents in varied ways and results in several possible symptom patterns. It involves exposure to a traumatic event or an intensely threatening experience, which culminates in aberrant fear responses to reminders of the trauma over a period of time. Type-I trauma PTSD typically develops after one significantly stressful Criterion A event, whereas complex PTSD (C-PTSD) may develop after what we call Type-II traumas (Cloitre, Courtois, et al., 2011). This latter type is considered repeated or prolonged traumas, often interpersonal, and from which escape was not possible, including being a victim of childhood sexual or physical abuse, domestic violence, sex trafficking, or slave trade, for instance.

Table 6.8: Diagnostic criteria for posttraumatic stress disorder from the DSM-5 and ICD-10

DSM-5	ICD-10
A. Exposure to actual or threatened death, serious injury, or sexual violence in one (or more) of the following ways: (1) Directly experiencing the traumatic event(s). (2) Witnessing, in person, the event(s) as it occurred to others. (3) Learning that the traumatic event(s) occurred to a close family member or close friend. In cases of actual or threatened death of a family member or friend, the event(s) must have been violent or accidental. Note: In children, learning that the traumatic event(s) occurred to a parent or caregiving figure. (4) Experiencing repeated or extreme exposure to aversive details of the traumatic event(s) (e.g. first responders collecting human remains; police officers repeatedly exposed to details of child abuse). Note: Criterion A4 does not apply to exposure through electronic media, television, movies, or pictures, unless this exposure is work-related.	■ Disorder arises as a delayed or protracted response to a stressful event or situation (brief or long in duration) of an exceptionally threatening or catastrophic nature, likely to cause pervasive distress in almost anyone. ■ Typical features include: ▸ Episodes of repeated reliving of the trauma (in intrusive memories, 'flashbacks' dreams, or nightmares). ▸ Persisting backgrounds of sense of 'numbness' and emotional blunting (detachment from other people, unresponsiveness to surroundings, anhedonia) as well as avoidance of activities and situations reminiscent of the trauma.

DSM-5	ICD-10
B. Presence of one (or more) of the following intrusion symptoms associated with the traumatic event(s), beginning after the traumatic event(s) occurred: (1) Recurrent, involuntary, and intrusive distressing memories of the traumatic event(s). Note: In children older than 6 years, repetitive play may occur in which themes or aspects of the traumatic event(s) are expressed. (2) Recurrent distressing dreams in which the content and/or affect of the dream are related to the traumatic event(s). Note: In children, there may be frightening dreams without recognisable content. (3) Dissociative reactions (e.g. flashbacks) in which the individual feels or acts as if the traumatic event(s) were recurring. (Such reactions may occur on a continuum, with the most extreme expression being a complete loss of awareness of present surroundings.) Note: In children, such trauma-specific reenactment may occur in play. (4) Intense or prolonged psychological distress at exposure to internal or external cues that symbolise or resemble an aspect of the traumatic event(s). (5) Marked physiological reactions to internal or external cues that symbolise or resemble an aspect of the traumatic event(s). C. Persistent avoidance of stimuli associated with the traumatic event(s), beginning after the traumatic event(s) occurred, as evidenced by one or both of the following: (1) Avoidance of or efforts to avoid distressing memories, thoughts, or feelings about or closely associated with the traumatic event(s). (2) Avoidance of or efforts to avoid external reminders (people, places, conversations, activities, objects, situations) that arouse distressing memories, thoughts, or feelings about or closely associated with the traumatic event(s). D. Negative alterations in cognitions and mood associated with the traumatic event(s), beginning or worsening after the traumatic event(s) occurred, as evidenced by two (or more) of the following: (1) Inability to remember an important aspect of the traumatic event(s) (typically due to dissociative amnesia and not to other factors such as head injury, alcohol, or drugs).	‣ A state of autonomic hyperarousal and hypervigilance (enhanced startle reaction and insomnia). ■ Anxiety and depression are commonly associated with the above signs and symptoms, and suicidal ideation is not infrequent. ■ Onset follows the trauma with a latency period that may range from a few weeks to months. ■ Course is fluctuating, but recovery can be expected in the majority of cases. ■ In a small proportion of cases, the condition may follow a chronic course over many years, with eventual transition to an enduring personality change.

DSM-5	ICD-10
(2) Persistent and exaggerated negative beliefs or expectations about oneself, others, or the world (e.g. 'I am bad', 'No one can be trusted', 'The world is completely dangerous', 'My whole nervous system is completely ruined'. (3) Persistent and exaggerated cognitions about the cause or consequence of the traumatic event(s) that lead the individual to blame himself/herself or others. (4) Persistent negative emotional state (e.g. fear, horror, anger, guilt, or shame). (5) Markedly diminished interest or participation in significant activities. (6) Feelings of detachment or estrangement from others. (7) Persistent inability to experience positive emotions (e.g. inability to experience happiness, satisfaction, or loving feelings). E. Marked alterations in arousal and reactivity associated with the traumatic event(s), beginning or worsening after the traumatic event(s) occurred as evidenced by two (or more) of the following: (1) Irritable behaviour and angry outbursts (with little or no provocation) typically expressed as verbal or physical aggression toward people or objects. (2) Reckless or self-destructive behaviour. (3) Hypervigilance. (4) Exaggerated startle response. (5) Problems with concentration. (6) Sleep disturbance (e.g. difficulty falling or staying asleep or restless sleep). F. Duration of the disturbance (Criteria B, C, D and E) is more than 1 month. G. The disturbance causes clinically significant distress or impairment in social, occupational, other important areas of functioning. H. The disturbance is not attributable to the physiological effects of a substance (e.g. a medication, alcohol) or another medical condition.	

Source: Reprinted with permission from the *Diagnostic and Statistical Manual of Mental Disorders*, fifth edition (DSM-5), American Psychiatric Association (APA), 2013, p. 271, and the ICD-10 *Classification of Mental and Behavioural Disorders: Diagnostic Criteria for Research*, World Health Organization (WHO), Geneva, 2007.

Acute stress disorder

Acute stress disorder is marked by the development of characteristic symptoms following exposure to one or more traumatic event(s). The symptoms last for a period of between three days and one month following traumatic exposure, and they do not extend beyond a period of four weeks. Thus, acute stress disorder symptoms occur in the early post-trauma period and could potentially result in a later presentation of PTSD. However, this is not always the case because, in many instances, the traumatic symptoms remit naturally. Acute stress disorder typically presents as an anxiety response that includes some form of re-experiencing of, or reactivity to, the traumatic event(s) (American Psychiatric Association, 2013). The clinical presentation may also vary, as in the case of PTSD.

Acute stress disorder was introduced in the DSM-IV to describe people who were exposed to a traumatic event and presented with symptoms consistent with PTSD but had not yet fulfilled the criteria for duration of disturbance. This diagnostic category was meant to identify individuals who were at risk of developing PTSD. This sparked much discussion and debate, as questions related to whether it is a reliable predictor of PTSD arose, as well as whether it pathologises what is considered to be a normal stress reaction. In the DSM-IV, the diagnostic criteria for acute stress disorder were the same as those for PTSD, except a shorter duration of time was specified for acute stress disorder. The diagnostic criteria for acute stress disorder have changed significantly with the publication of the DSM-5.

Adjustment disorders

Adjustment disorders result from a maladaptive response to stressful life events. They occur in response to an identifiable stressor, and are experienced as distressing and have a negative impact on an individual's daily functioning. Adjustment disorders occur within three months of the onset of the stressor and do not represent bereavement. Once the stressor has been resolved, the symptoms do not persist beyond a period of six months.

The stressor may be an individual event or it may be recurrent, as in the case of ongoing domestic abuse with increasing intensity. The level of distress experienced is out of proportion to the severity and intensity of the stressor. For the first time, these disorders form part of the trauma and stressor-related disorders chapter of the DSM-5, and they continue to be recognised in the ICD-10. In previous versions of the DSM, adjustment disorders were positioned between the V-codes (problem level conditions) and Axis 1 disorders. The DSM-5 diagnostic criteria for adjustment disorders are listed in Table 6.9.

Table 6.9: Diagnostic criteria for adjustment disorders from the DSM-5 and ICD-10

DSM-5	ICD-10
A. The development of emotional or behavioural symptoms in response to an identifiable stressor(s) occurring within three months of the onset of the stressor(s).	■ States of subjective distress and emotional disturbance, usually interfering with social functioning and performance, arising in the period of adaptation

DSM-5	ICD-10
B. These symptoms or behaviours are clinically significant, as evidenced by one or both of the following: (1) Marked distress that is out of proportion to the severity or intensity of the stressor, taking into account the external context and the cultural factors that might influence symptom severity and presentation. (2) Significant impairment in social, occupational, or other important areas of functioning. C. The stress-related disturbance does not meet the criteria for another mental disorder and is not merely an exacerbation of a preexisting mental disorder. D. The symptoms do not represent normal bereavement. E. Once the stressor or its consequences have terminated the symptoms do not persist for more than an additional six months.	to a significant life change or a stressful life event. The stressor may have affected the integrity of an individual's social network (bereavement, separation experiences) or the wider system of social supports and values (migration, refugee status), or represented a major developmental transition or crisis (going to school, becoming a parent, failure to attain a cherished personal goal, retirement). Individual predisposition or vulnerability plays an important role in the risk of occurrence and the shaping of the manifestations of adjustment disorders, but it is nevertheless assumed that the condition would not have arisen without the stressor. The manifestations vary and include depressed mood, anxiety or worry (or a mixture of these), a feeling of inability to cope, plan ahead, or continue in the present situation, as well as some degree of disability in the performance of daily routine. Conduct disorders may be an associated feature, particularly in adolescents. The predominant feature may be a brief or prolonged depressive reaction, or a disturbance of other emotions and conduct.

Source: Reprinted with permission from the *Diagnostic and Statistical Manual of Mental Disorders*, fifth edition (DSM-5), American Psychiatric Association (APA), 2013, p. 286, and the ICD-10 *International Statistical Classification of Disease and Related Disorders*, World Health Organization (WHO), Geneva, 2016.

CROSS-CULTURAL AND AFRICAN PERSPECTIVES

Anxiety disorders are widespread across all communities and have been shown to be of increasing prevalence and a common cause of disability globally. These disorders have been associated with substantial healthcare costs, as people with anxiety tend to make frequent use of health services (Costa e Silva, 1998). The World Mental Health Survey conducted from 2002–2004 (Kessler et al., 2009) indicated that a lifetime diagnosis was found in at least one-third of South African respondents. In addition, Stein et al. (2007) indicated that South Africa has the sixth highest prevalence of anxiety disorders compared with 14 other countries.

Unfortunately, insufficient attention has been given to examining the impact of sociocultural factors on the manifestation of anxiety disorders in particular societies and cultures. This is especially relevant in South Africa, where there has been a paucity of research aimed at exploring the culture-related clinical patterns of anxiety disorders. Cross-cultural studies of anxiety provide critical information about the presentation and manifestation of the disorders across different cultures. This is essential as it sheds light on the interplay of biological, psychological, and social factors that impact on the expression of anxiety disorders. While anxiety has been identified across different cultures on a global scale, the context in which it is experienced shapes how it is interpreted and the responses given to it.

Cultural beliefs tend to influence how an individual processes and interprets anxiety-provoking stimuli in the environment. In the Middle East, for instance, panic disorder usually involves the fear of the afterlife, rather than of dying, as people fear possible punishment and torture after death, if their wrongdoings on earth outweigh their good deeds (Mosotho, Louw, & Calitz, 2011b). Perceptions about mental illness, coping styles and support from family, friends, and the community may influence an individual's help-seeking behaviours. The clinician's own culture and beliefs may also influence the clinician's approach to treatment.

The DSM has identified certain culture-bound syndromes (see Chapter 10) that are specific to a particular culture and are recognised as an illness within the context of that culture. The brain fag syndrome has been described in the DSM as a cluster of somatic complaints (consisting of pains and burning sensations around the head and neck), cognitive impairments (including inability to grasp the meaning of written and sometimes spoken words, inability to concentrate, and poor retention), sleep-related complaints (consisting of fatigue and sleepiness despite adequate rest), and other somatic impairments (e.g. blurring, eye pain, and excessive tearing) (American Psychiatric Association, 2013). This psychiatric condition was first studied among African students in the 1960s, and it represents a highly researched aspect of anxiety disorders.

Although anxiety is a universal phenomenon, and the manifestation of different anxiety disorders is seen across different cultures, there are significant cross-cultural differences in the description and experience of anxiety (Guarnaccia et al., 2005). For example, the word 'anxiety' is not used in many African cultures and languages.

Traditionally, African people view personhood from a systemic, communal, and socio-centric perspective, in which the individual is part of a bigger whole. An individual's social and cultural context plays a significant role in how the individual interprets and copes with traumatic events that could potentially result in the onset of PTSD. The African perspective of trauma is based on the view that trauma is based on one's interaction with society and culture over a period of time (Motsi & Masango, 2012).

 ACTIVITY

The Ugandan psychiatrist Seggane Musisi has written, 'It behoves all African scholars, and health workers in particular, to research and publicise the causes, effects, and sequels of mass trauma on our peoples and to find appropriate solutions both for prevention and treatment. These are the areas in need of extensive research by researchers possessing trans-cultural and transdisciplinary competence' (2004, p. 82).
Suggest why Musisi calls for a focus on 'mass trauma'.

EPIDEMIOLOGY

Anxiety disorders are chronic and result in significant impairment in functioning across multiple contexts. Many people with anxiety disorders suffer for many years, although the prevalence decreases in older age. The lifetime prevalence of anxiety disorders is said to vary between 14% and 29% in Western countries; three out of four people with an anxiety disorder experience at least one other mental disorder in their lifetime (Michael, Zetsche, & Margraf, 2007). Social anxiety disorder and specific phobia are suggested to be the most common lifetime anxiety disorders, and both disorders commonly present with comorbid mental disorders, including mood disorders and other anxiety disorders (Rudaz, Ledermann, Margraf, Becker, & Craske, 2017).

Depression and anxiety are said to be more prevalent among women than men, and they account for the most significant causes of disease burden globally. This burden has been recognised over the years. There is sufficient evidence to suggest that anxiety disorders result in increased morbidity and mortality globally. It has also been noted that people with anxiety tend to make greater use of healthcare services, which has enormous financial implications and a negative impact on productivity.

AETIOLOGY

A number of aetiological causes have been offered to explain the complexity and heterogeneity of anxiety disorders. Earlier theoretical models emphasised the role of biological and behavioural aspects of anxiety disorders, while contemporary theories comprise biopsychosocial models that include cognitive, behavioural, genetic, and environmental aspects of anxiety disorders. These models have made a significant contribution in advancing our understanding of anxiety disorders from various approaches.

Biological processes

The English biologist Charles Darwin made a significant observation that there are common characteristics in the expression of emotion in humans and animals. Animal research on stress responding and fear responses has provided some insights into the biological mechanisms of anxiety in humans, although they do not replicate all features of specific anxiety disorders. Animals have an intrinsic response to certain noxious stimuli in the environment, for instance, sights, sounds and odours of their predators. These sounds and odours naturally elicit a sense of fear in the animal.

When an organism experiences fear, it results in heightened awareness and reactivity to the aversive event or threat. Fear has been described as a natural, evolutionarily developed response to environmental threats, and it involves specific endocrine and autonomic changes aimed at protecting the organism. The autonomic changes associated with fear allow the organism to prepare to act in a particular way in the face of an environmental threat. When the fear response is activated, associated defensive behaviours such as fighting, fleeing or freezing occur (Shiromani, Keane, & LeDoux, 2009).

Fear and anxiety involve behavioural, autonomic, and endocrine changes aimed at increasing an organism's chances of survival (Shiromani et al., 2009). Through our senses, we take in information from the environment, and certain information is subsequently selected for further processing, which guides our behaviour. Several specific phobias have been identified as originating as natural survival mechanisms rather than pathological conditions (Bandelow et al., 2016).

Neurochemistry

Multiple neurotransmitters have been found to play a role in fear and anxiety behaviour. Neurotransmitters implicated in anxiety disorders include serotonin, glutamate, GABA (gamma-amino butyric acid), and norepinephrine (also known as noradrenaline). Serotonin enhances fear and anxiety, and its anxiogenic (anxiety-causing) effects respond to selective serotonin reuptake inhibitors (SSRI), selective serotonin-norepinephrine reuptake inhibitors (SNRI), and other classes of pharmacological drugs. Norepinephrine neurons are projected to different areas of the brain by a structure called the locus coeruleus. These neurons regulate mood, cognition, and sleep.

Brain structure and functioning

Several neural circuits have been found to work differently in people with anxiety disorders. The amygdala and insula have been identified as two structures that seem to be overly responsive in the brains of people with high levels of anxiety. The amygdala is a complex structure whose function is poorly known. It has been associated with the storage of emotional memories, processing fear and other aspects of emotional and social behaviour. Studies suggest that the amygdala is central in instigating anxiety responses. This structure plays a critical role in mediating emotions, such as anxiety. Functional neuro-imaging has shown elevated amygdala activity in the brains of healthy anxious individuals. Functional and anatomical changes in the amygdala also occur following acute and chronic stress.

The limbic system refers to a group of interrelated structures that lie on both sides of the thalamus, beneath the cerebrum. This system comprises a loop of cortical structures surrounding the corpus callosum and thalamus, and is made up of the cingulate gyrus, parahippocampal gyrus, hippocampus, amygdala, and hypothalamus. The hypothalamus mediates the stress response, while the hippocampus is responsible for encoding memories (Hanson & Modiba, 2017). Other structures of the brain are, at times, considered also to form part of the limbic system. A critical function of the limbic system is mediating autonomic, emotional, and behavioural responses to threat, and it also plays a significant function in the storage of emotional memories. Some of these limbic structures are suggested to be hyper-responsive in anxiety-prone individuals (Hanson & Modiba, 2017).

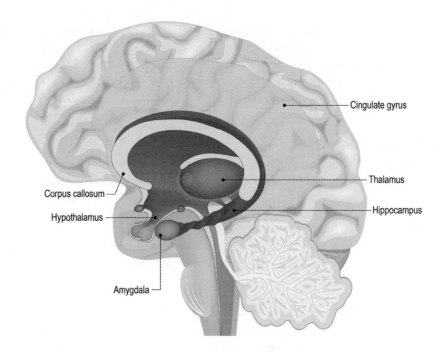

Figure 6.9: Schematic diagram of the areas of the brain forming the limbic system that are involved in anxiety.

Genetics

Genetic factors play a role in anxiety disorders; however, the specificity of the genetic predisposition is unclear (Pérez-Edgar & Fox, 2005). The heritability estimates of anxiety disorders suggest a moderate level of clustering of certain traits within a family (Shimada-Sugimoto, Otowa, & Hettema, 2015), which may result in a temperament that later increases one's risk of developing an anxiety disorder. These heritability estimates suggest that anxious traits and anxiety disorders share a moderate heritability.

Psychological perspectives

Psychodynamic models

The traditional psychoanalytical work of Freud and contemporary psychodynamic theorists has provided a range of views on the nature of the self. Psychodynamic conceptualisation posits that psychopathology stems from an impoverished relationship with parental figures. Children experience a void-like state in the absence of emotional proximity, mirroring, and containment by key relational figures. This triggers a state of anxiety followed by the activation of a defence. These defences are triggered in an attempt to prevent a dangerous intrapsychic situation from becoming traumatic (Slavin-Mulford & Hilsenroth, 2012). If this anxiety state is unable to activate adequate defences, this results in traumatic anxiety and a state of internal tension that is described as anxiety. The primary anxieties or psychological threats faced by children are usually related to abandonment or the loss of an object, loss of the object's affection, castration anxiety, and superego anxiety (guilt) (Wolitzky & Eagle, 1997).

Behavioural models

Behavioural/learning models were the prominent empirical theoretical framework of anxiety disorders from the 1920s until the 1970s (Mineka & Zinbarg, 2006). Fear conditioning theories have shaped our understanding of the acquisition and persistence of phobic behaviours through a process of associated learning. These models describe how pathological anxiety and phobias are acquired through traumatic exposure and aversive classical conditioning. Through the process of Pavlovian fear conditioning, a non-threatening object or environmental stimulus (conditional stimulus) is paired with a fear-producing (dangerous and threatening) stimulus, resulting in a phobic reaction.

As a result of this exposure, the non-threatening object/stimulus elicits a new set of responses aimed at increasing the organism's chances of survival. Once an individual experiences an anxiety episode, it results in increased vigilant fear of future anxiety attacks. This anticipatory state can cause physiological arousal for the vulnerable individual, who becomes sensitive and hypervigilant to environmental stimuli. In this way, future anxiety attacks may be triggered by a wide variety of events.

Through a process of operant conditioning, pathological fears are maintained. Operant conditioning involves a process of reinforcement, in which the phobic person actively undertakes to avoid the feared object. This avoidance results in a reduction in anxiety (negative reinforcement), which serves to maintain the fear.

Behavioural models also provide a useful frame for understanding the development of PTSD, using the learning theory principles of classical conditioning. Although many individuals are exposed to traumatic events, not all go on to develop PTSD. Keane and Barlow (2002) proposed a triple vulnerability model, aimed at explaining how PTSD develops. This model is based on the theoretical descriptions of fear and anxiety (Keane, Marshall, & Taft, 2006). Based on this model, an individual's vulnerability towards PTSD is determined by pre-existing psychological variables (i.e. pre-existing psychological factors related to the individual), factors related to the traumatic event (e.g. one's immediate response to the trauma), and events that occur following the trauma. These factors may not be considered causative, but rather as risk factors that predispose an individual to PTSD.

The authors also explain that exposure to a traumatic event triggers intense basic emotions, which serve as true alarms. Such basic emotions include rage, disgust, and distress, as well as other emotions that are brought about by the overwhelming effect of the traumatic event. Exposure to events that resemble or trigger an aspect of the traumatic event tend to evoke the true alarm response, and from this a learned alarm develops. Learned alarms include anniversaries of the traumatic event, memories, and other cues related to the trauma. This may result in persistent avoidance of stimuli related to the trauma, as in the case of a phobic reaction. Anxiety disorders may result in an individual living a progressively restricted life, which limits their opportunities to master their fears.

Although useful, early behavioural/learning models did not account for why, after exposure to the same aversive or distressing stimulus, some people develop phobias while others do not. Nor do they explain why some go on to develop anxiety in the absence of such a stimulus (e.g. a fear of snakes without being in contact with one) and why some stimuli were more likely to elicit a greater sense of fear compared with others. Vicarious conditioning in phobia can account for those people who acquire strong, phobic-like reactions after observation of others experiencing a trauma or behaving fearfully.

Individual life experiences may also account for why some people develop a vulnerability or an invulnerability to certain phobias. The process of conditioning may be affected by the level of control that an individual has over a traumatic event (e.g. the ability to escape the situation), while other events can impact on the strength of the conditioned fear over a period of time (e.g. a fear that becomes reinforced following the experience of another related or unrelated traumatic event) (Mineka & Zinbar, 2006).

Cognitive models

Cognitive models have been a prominent frame for affective disorders such as anxiety and depression. These models propose that cognitive processes determine the way we select, interpret, and process information from the environment, and that cognitive processes mediate all emotional and behavioural responses. This system for processing information from the environment is necessary for our survival as we select, encode, store, and retrieve information in order to deal with potential dangers (Beck & Clark, 1988).

The American psychiatrist Aaron Beck developed a cognitive theory of anxiety and depression that provides a conceptual framework for anxiety. It is based on the assumption that, while cognitive appraisal of environmental threat is necessary for survival, anxious individuals incorrectly overestimate the degree of this threat and they underestimate their ability to cope. Anxiety disorders involve the perceived physical and psychological danger.

Beck and the Canadian psychologist David Clark (1988) explain that we process information from the environment through schemas. Stimuli that are consistent with existing schemas are encoded and stored, while those that are inconsistent are disregarded and forgotten. However, in psychopathological states, maladaptive schemas dominate the information-processing system, and they are rigid, impermeable, and concrete. When an individual encounters a particular environment, these maladaptive schemas are triggered, resulting in an anxiety episode.

Cognitive approaches propose an interactional model that examines how relevant life stressors interact with cognitive vulnerability. These models assist the phobic person to readjust maladaptive and distorted patterns of thinking and replace these with healthy and functional cognitions. Beck (1976) also proposed that emotions are triggered by dysfunctional thoughts, beliefs, and attitudes, and that these beliefs lead to avoidant behaviour. A person with social phobia may believe that he or she will be negatively evaluated or scrutinised by others, which may result in anxiety, apprehension, and fear, which may cause the individual to avoid social interactions. Avoidance of social interactions serves to maintain the individual's anxiety.

Humanistic and existential models

Humanistic and existential theories posit that people have a need to survive and to live as fully as possible. These approaches place emphasis on the individual's subjective experience, self-awareness, and positive growth. Humanistic approaches view human behaviour as fundamentally good, and the approach is based on the assumption that people have the potential to maintain healthy relationships and to act in their own and others' best interests.

Anxiety results when people fail to win the approval of others and/or do not meet their own internal harsh standards for an ideal self. An existential approach views psychological difficulties as stemming from anxiety over existential issues of life such as the meaninglessness of life (experienced as isolation, loneliness, and despair) and the finality of death.

Family systems theory

General systems theory is based on the premise that systems are made up of interrelated parts that each perform a specific function in maintaining the whole. A change in one part of the system impacts on the system as a whole. Murray Bowen, an American psychiatrist, developed a family systems theory that views the family as an emotional unit in which members are able to impact each other's thoughts, feelings, and behaviours in significant ways. This refers to the family's level of interdependence, which varies from family to family. The degree of family cohesion, emotional support, and warmth serves as a protective factor against anxiety disorders.

Conversely, negative experiences in one's family of origin (such as family abuse or violence) may result in an individual having poor emotion regulation, and difficulty balancing individuality and togetherness in relationships, which may manifest as anxiety (Priest, 2015). While a child may have a genetic predisposition towards anxiety, the environment in which that child is raised often plays an additional role in exacerbating their anxiety. A child may also have a learned fear response as a result of witnessing such responses in other family members.

Developmental perspectives

Developmental theories emphasise the role of personality and temperament, the family context, and parenting styles in the development of anxiety. For example, children of parents who display a controlling and overprotective style of parenting are prone to developing anxiety disorders. In addition, when parents reinforce an avoidant style of interaction in their children, this may also lead to the children developing anxiety disorders. Children whose parents are indifferent, or show rejection towards their children, also show a greater vulnerability to anxiety disorders. A child's temperament (inherited emotional and behavioural responsiveness) may also attract a particular style of parenting. For instance, a child who is shy may elicit overprotectiveness. This interplay between temperament and parenting styles influences the child's vulnerability to anxiety disorders through its negative impact on the child's independence and sense of agency.

Psychosocial stressors

An interplay between neurobiological factors and psychosocial stressors has been postulated to form the basis of anxiety disorders. Psychosocial stressors such as traumatic experiences occurring during the course of an individual's life are a significant contributor to anxiety disorders. PTSD is understood to be related to exposure to one or more severe traumatic event(s); however, a range of factors are required to account for the pathogenesis of the disorder, since not everyone who has been exposed to a traumatic event(s) will develop PTSD. People who have a strong support network are less likely to develop PTSD following a traumatic event. Social support from family, friends, and community members plays an important role in preventing the onset of PTSD. Healthy coping mechanisms, such as active problem-solving, are also significant in preventing PTSD.

Several studies have linked social and psychological factors with anxiety disorders. A wide range of factors such as living alone, discontentedness with partner situation, dissatisfaction or unhappiness at work, and loneliness and poor quality of life have been identified as significant predictors of anxiety disorders for both men and women (Flensborg-Madsen, Tolstrup, Sørensen, & Mortensen, 2012). Negative life events that occur during childhood (e.g. parents' divorce) may increase a child's vulnerability to anxiety disorders.

In the case of acute stress disorder and PTSD, the stressor is the predominant causal factor resulting in these disorders. These stress disorders may be regarded as maladaptive responses to severe or continued stress, and in the absence of the stressors, the conditions would not exist.

 ACTIVITY

PTSD is commonly experienced by groups of people who experience war and forced migration, as is the case in many parts of Africa. In 2004, the journal *African Health Sciences* published the article 'Traumatic events and symptoms of post-traumatic stress disorder amongst Sudanese nationals, refugees and Ugandans in the West Nile'. This was written by Indian doctor Unni Krishnan Karunakara and the German psychotherapist Frank Neuner, along with co-authors Margarete Schauer, Kavita Singh, Kenneth Hill, Thomas Elbert, and Gilbert Burnha. Read the extract below and explain which of their expectations was not corroborated by their findings.

'Regression analyses show that traumatic events experienced in the preceding year were more predictive than traumatic events ever experienced. Contrary to our expectations, witnessed events turned out to be more significant in predicting symptoms of PTSD than experienced events. An explanation could be that the refugees continue to be in an insecure state and that witnessing increases anxiety levels and the expectation that the same could happen to them. Whereas, having survived a violent act may have a limiting effect on levels of anxiety in some of the survivors. On the other hand, it could also be that respondents were unwilling to admit being a victim of a worst type of traumatic experience like sexual violence. These survivors may inaccurately report having witnessed, rather than experienced, the traumatic event.'

Source: Karunakara et al., 2004.

ACTIVITY

In 2011, South African researchers L. I. Zungu and N. G. Malungu produced a draft report: 'Post Traumatic Stress Disorder in the South African Mining Industry'. When studying the claims submitted by mineworkers for PTSD, they found that 'the majority (87.8%) of PTSD claimants witnessed the traumatic mine accidents compared to a minority (12.2%) who were reported to be the victims of such accidents' (p. 75). How does this observation relate to the extract above by Karunakara et al.?

Integrated perspectives

Current research suggests that anxiety disorders should be viewed from an integrated, biopsychosocial perspective, which requires an understanding of the complex interaction of brain, body, and environment. This integrated approach advances efforts to develop a more comprehensive understanding of anxiety disorders. Anxiety disorders usually result from a combination of the factors below:

- *Biological factors* (e.g. genetic vulnerability, an oversensitive fear network, neurochemistry).
- *Psychological factors* (e.g. maladaptive cognitive appraisals, cognitive distortions, and lack of perceived control over stressful life events).
- *Social factors* (e.g. dysfunctional learned responses or conditioning).

The biopsychosocial model of anxiety recognises that biological and/or psychological (i.e. temperamental) vulnerability plays a role in influencing the extent to which an event is viewed or experienced as traumatic. In addition, environmental stressors sensitise the individual who is biologically predisposed to an overactive alarm response. An integrated model of anxiety considers the convergence between the oversensitised biological system, psychological vulnerability, learning processes, and disrupted attachment and separation.

CONCLUSION

The paradoxical function of anxiety has been extensively noted in literature. As an adaptive response, it is essential in preparing an organism to respond to future threats; however, if excessive, it may result in various forms of psychopathology. Changes in the DSM categorisation of anxiety disorders have advanced our understanding of these disorders over time. Culture influences the epidemiology, phenomenology, and treatment outcome of people who suffer from anxiety. The significance of certain anxiety-related symptoms, and the meaning assigned to these, is also influenced by the sociocultural context of the treating clinician. Therefore, it is essential to develop a model that assumes an integrated framework of anxiety disorders.

MULTIPLE-CHOICE QUESTIONS

1   Which of the following statements would **not** be considered true for people with an anxiety disorder?
   a) Severe distress that ultimately results in the reduction of the quality of life.
   b) Chronic anxiety, or sufficient and frequent anxiety, is enough to lead to impaired functioning.
   c) Simple reaction of 'fight or flight' as a survival function.
   d) Disproportionate reaction to the possibility danger of a threat.
   e) The symptoms of fear continue to be experienced long after the legitimately fear-producing situation had passed.

2.   Worry and ruminations are considered to be _____ symptoms of anxiety
   a) Emotional   b) Cognitive
   c) Somatic   d) Behavioural
   e) None of the above

3   Obsessions are:
   a) Persistent, non-intrusive, normal thoughts
   b) Normal impulses, but abnormal responses
   c) Inappropriate behaviour
   d) Nearly excessive worries
   e) Persistent, intrusive, and anxiety-provoking thoughts

4.   Compulsions are:
   a) Mental behaviours the individual can decide to perform, or not to perform
   b) Repetitive mental acts or behaviours the individual feels compelled to perform
   c) Behaviours or mental acts that increase distress
   d) Behaviours that are realistically connected to the preceding thought
   e) None of the above

5.   The three categories: anxiety or fear-related disorders; obsessive-compulsive or related disorders; and disorders specifically associated with stress, all come from:
   a) DSM-IV-TR   b) DSM-5
   c) ICD-10   d) ICD-11

PARAGRAPH AND ESSAY QUESTIONS

1.   Distinguish between fear and anxiety, as well as between 'normal' and 'pathological' anxiety.
2.   Define generalised anxiety disorder. Compare and contrast generalised anxiety disorder with the other anxiety disorders.
3.   Give an integrated explanation of the aetiology of generalised anxiety disorder.
4.   People suffering from obsessive-compulsive disorder are generally considered to be insightful regarding their condition. In what way is this helpful, and how can it be unhelpful in certain circumstances?
5.   Drawing on what you know of South Africa, give five common psychosocial stressors that could contribute to the onset of acute stress disorder or PTSD in our context.

7 MOOD DISORDERS

Karabo Makhafula & Alban Burke

CHAPTER OUTLINE

Introduction
History of mood disorders
Epidemiology
Life course
Clinical picture
Depressive disorders
    Major depressive disorder (MDD)
    Persistent depressive disorder (dysthymia)
    Premenstrual dysphoric disorder
    Disruptive mood dysregulation disorder
    Substance/medication-induced depressive disorder
    Depressive disorder due to another medical condition
Bipolar and related disorders
    Bipolar I and bipolar II disorders
    Cyclothymic disorder
Symptoms of mood disorders
Cross-cultural and African perspectives
Aetiology of mood disorders
    Stress and environmental factors
    Biological factors
    Genetics
    Integrative model
Conclusion

LEARNING OUTCOMES

After studying this chapter, you should be able to:

- Show a general understanding of mood disorders and be able to distinguish mood disorders from other disorders.
- Describe the history of mood disorders.
- Understand the problems relating to the nosology of mood disorders.
- Describe a major depressive episode.
- Describe a manic episode.
- Describe and distinguish between major depression (unipolar depression), persistent dysthymic disorder, bipolar disorder, and cyclothymia.
- Identify cross-cultural and, more specifically, South African variations in the presentation of mood disorders.
- Formulate an aetiological model of mood disorders.

PERSONAL HISTORY CASELET

Yi, a 20 year-old woman who lives in Gauteng, is seriously distressed. She is having difficulty sleeping; she has lost her appetite; and she lacks interest in her studies. Yi also says that she has little energy and is having a difficult time balancing school and family obligations. Although she does not spontaneously use emotional terms to describe how she feels, when asked she agrees that she is unhappy and anxious. All these symptoms are consistent with the DSM criteria for major depressive disorder (American Psychiatric Association, 2013).

Yet Yi reports other symptoms that are not typically associated with major depression. She describes bodily aches and pains, especially in her stomach and liver. She has become particularly concerned about what other people think of her, making it hard for her to get along with her family. Finally, she reports that, at night, the spirit of a disgruntled ancestor visits her, right before she is about to fall asleep. These encounters sap her energy. Although she says that she knows other people who have been visited by spirits, she is nonetheless concerned about experiencing these visits herself.

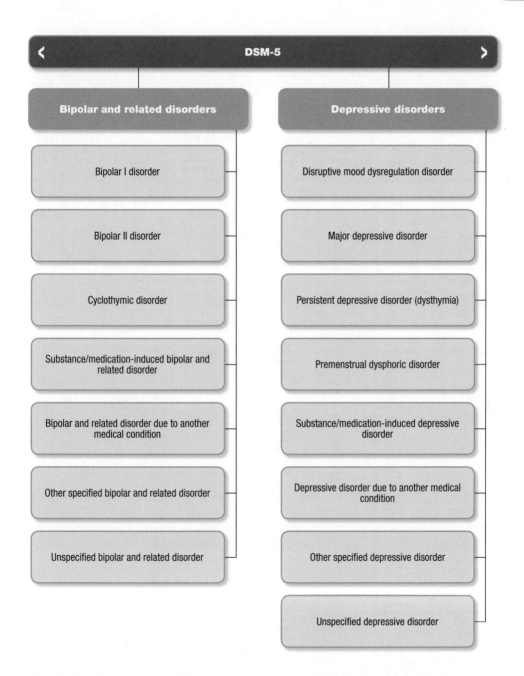

Figure 7.1: The American Psychiatric Association DSM-5 categorises bipolar and related disorders and depressive disorders as shown above.

Source: Figure created by OUP reflecting information found in *Diagnostic and Statistical Manual of Mental Disorders*, fifth edition (DSM-5), 2013.

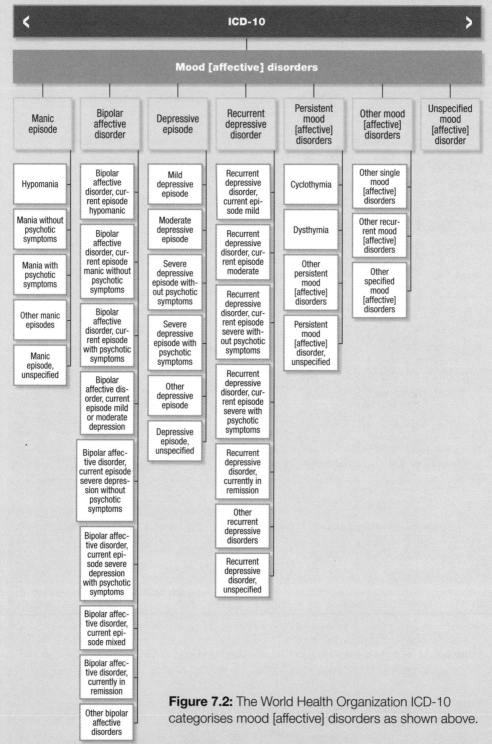

Figure 7.2: The World Health Organization ICD-10 categorises mood [affective] disorders as shown above.

Source: *International Statistical Classification of Diseases and Related Health Problems*, tenth revision (ICD-10), 2016.

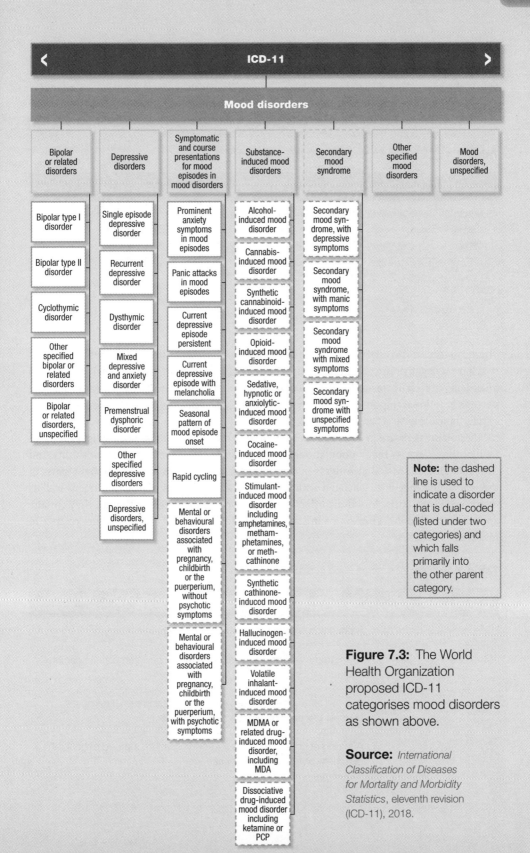

Figure 7.3: The World Health Organization proposed ICD-11 categorises mood disorders as shown above.

Source: *International Classification of Diseases for Mortality and Morbidity Statistics*, eleventh revision (ICD-11), 2018.

INTRODUCTION

While the term 'mood' may be used interchangeably with the term 'emotion' in everyday language, these terms refer to different aspects in the fields of psychology and medicine. Key definitions of these and related terms are given in Table 7.1.

Table 7.1: Common terms used in relation to moods

Term	Definition
Emotion	A reaction that occurs when an organism encounters a meaningful stimulus.
Feeling	An experience of emotion that influences our behaviour.
Affect	The outward expression of an emotional state.
Mood	A sustained emotional state (the overall affective state).

The term 'mood disorders' is used to describe disorders that affect a person's mood and that have a negative impact on daily functioning. Mood disorders (also known as affective disorders) are characterised by persistent dysregulation of mood. This means that the person's emotional responses are poorly modulated. Mood disorders are also associated with psychomotor (physical) and cognitive changes.

These disorders are recognised as one of the most commonly occurring groups of mental illness across many populations, and they are a significant cause of morbidity and disability globally. Mood disorders are considered a major health concern in many parts of the world, and they are associated with a risk of suicide and loss of functioning, as well as major economic costs. Mood disorders can affect people of all ages, although they usually appear during adolescence or young adulthood. Table 7.2 explains key terms related to mood disorders.

Table 7.2: Common terms used in relation to mood disorders

Term	Definition
Syndrome	A condition characterised by a set of symptoms.
Mood disorder	A syndrome that has depressive or manic symptoms as its primary feature.
Depression	A mood state characterised by feelings of sadness, loneliness, despair, low self-esteem, and self-reproach.
Dysphoria	A feeling of unpleasantness and/or discomfort; a mood of general dissatisfaction and restlessness

Mania	A mood state characterised by an abnormally elevated, euphoric, or irritable mood.
Hypomania	A mood state with the qualitative characteristics of mania but somewhat less intense.
Chronic illness	An illness that persists for a long time or constantly recurs.
Episode of an illness	A period of illness that occurs over a restricted time (the illness may comprise a sequence of such episodes).
Unipolar mood disorder	A mood disorder characterised by episodes of depression only.
Bipolar disorders	Disorders characterised by the presence of mixed episodes, manic episodes or hypomanic episodes

The DSM-5 discusses mood disorders in two separate chapters: namely 'Bipolar and related disorders' and 'Depressive disorders'. However, both the ICD-10 and the ICD-11 group these disorders together. While the ICD-10 names this category 'mood [affective] disorders', in the ICD-11 this has been shortened to just 'mood disorders'. This chapter discusses both depressive and bipolar disorders, as they share a common feature of mood disturbance. Depressive disorders are discussed first. These disorders are characterised by low, empty or irritable mood, with associated somatic and cognitive changes. Bipolar disorders are discussed in the second part of the chapter. The core feature of these disorders is a fluctuation in mood and energy that represents a change in daily functioning.

HISTORY OF MOOD DISORDERS

> *The people ought to know that the brain is the sole origin of pleasures and joys, laughter and jests, sadness and worry as well as dysphoria and crying. Through the brain, we can think, see, hear, and differentiate between feeling ashamed, good, bad, happy. ... Through the brain we become insane, enraged, we develop anxiety and fears, which can come in the night or during the day, we suffer from sleeplessness, we make mistakes and have unfounded worries, we lose the ability to recognise reality, we become apathetic and we cannot participate in social life. ... We suffer all those mentioned above through the brain when it is ill ...*
> *(Hippocrates, in Marneros & Angst, 2007, p. 1)*

The scientific investigation of mood disorders began after Phillipe Pinel, a French doctor, published *Philosophical nosography or the method of analysis applied to medicine* (*Nosographie philosophique ou méthode de l'analyse appliquée à la médecine*) in 1798. In this publication, Pinel proposed four categories of mental illness, one of which was melancholia (depression) and another mania (by which he meant madness). Jean-Étienne-Dominique Esquirol, a student of Pinel's, went on to study both melancholia and mania.

In 1851 Jean-Pierre Falret, another French psychiatrist, then described a mental state that laid the basis for what was called 'circular insanity' (*folie circulaire*), which presented as successive and regular reproduction of a manic state, a melancholic state, and a prolonged lucid interval (Yatham & Maj, 2010). This came to be called 'manic-depressive insanity'.

At the end of the 1800s, by examining not just the symptoms but also the patterns of symptoms, the German psychiatrist Emil Kraepelin made this category of manic-depressive insanity narrower, by proposing that *dementia praecox* (which is now called schizophrenia) be considered a separate disorder. Kraepelin also described the phenomenon of mania as periods of 'increased busyness' with marked changes of energy or activity. The work done by Kraepelin was fundamental in shaping modern psychiatry.

In the first half of the 1900s, another German psychiatrist, Karl Kleist, encouraged psychiatrists to view mood disorders as either unipolar or bipolar. When the DSM-III was published in 1980, the term 'manic depressive disorder' was changed to 'bipolar disorder'.

The DSM-5 defines mania as being 'a distinct period of abnormally and persistently elevated, expansive, or irritable mood and abnormally and persistently increased activity or energy' (American Psychiatric Association, 2013, p.124). A manic episode usually results in changes in behaviour that represent a change from an individual's usual functioning. These include increased energy, engaging in risky behaviour such as breaking the law, spending money excessively, or engaging in risky sexual behaviour. This may continue for several weeks, and it is likely to cause a significant disruption in the individual's life. Some people are able to mask these symptoms for a period of time; however, this becomes more difficult over time as the illness progresses.

There are currently several pharmacological alternatives for treating bipolar disorder. These include lithium carbonate, antipsychotics, and mood stabilisers. The management of bipolar disorder usually involves a combination of medication and psychotherapy.

The ICD-10 characterises depressive disorders according to their severity (mild, moderate, severe, and psychotic depressive disorder). The category *recurrent depressive disorder* is used when there is more than one episode of depressive disorder. Bipolar disorder is classified according to the experience of repeated (two or more) episodes of depression and mania or hypomania. The ICD-10 defines mania and hypomania as a period of significantly disturbed mood and a change in the quantity and speed of (physical and mental) activity. A diagnosis of bipolar disorder is given when there are recurrent episodes of mania as these resemble bipolar disorder in their course and prognosis.

EPIDEMIOLOGY

Mood disorders are a major health concern in the global population, and they result in a significant decline in quality of life. The World Health Organization (WHO) has recognised depressive and bipolar illnesses as the most burdensome and disabling of the world's medical conditions (Murray & Lopez, 1996). In addition, the increased risk of suicide associated with mood disorders presents a daunting clinical challenge.

Mood disorders commonly co-occur with chronic medical conditions and can have a negative effect on the outcome of those comorbid conditions. Chronic illnesses that frequently co-occur with mood disorders include cancer, cardiovascular disease, HIV/Aids, and neurological disorders. The functional impairment associated with mood disorders also adds to the economic burden associated with chronic diseases. In particular, there is a complex, bidirectional relationship between depression and chronic illness. Medical illness is a risk factor for major depression, and this in turn affects the outcome of the medical condition. Depression may also be a prominent feature in the development and course of medical conditions.

Research on gender differences in depression suggest that, across cultures and across the world, women are more susceptible to depression compared to men, at a ratio of 2:1 (Ngcobo & Pillay, 2008), although equal prevalence rates have been found before puberty (Hirschfeld & Weissman, 2002). There is also a growing body of evidence that suggests that mood disorders are prevalent among children and adolescents, which increases the risk of lifelong disability. Research suggests that depression, mania, and mania-like symptom clusters are common among children and adolescents in the general population (Kessler, Avenevoli, & Merikangas, 2001).

There is limited research on the epidemiology of mood disorders in South Africa although the South African Stress and Health Study (SASH) (Herman et al., 2009) showed a greater prevalence of major depressive episode among females compared with males, and a greater lifetime prevalence of major depressive episode associated with low levels of education. Those aged between 40 and 49 years were also found to have a greater risk of major depressive episode than other age groups. In South Africa, socio-demographic disparities contribute significantly to the complex problem of mental health.

LIFE COURSE

Adolescence is a high-risk period for the onset of many psychiatric disorders (Duffy, 2015) including mood disorders. Mental disorders that manifest during this stage tend to persist into adulthood. Adolescent mood disorders are associated with an increased risk of premature death and suicide.

Genetic risk factors predicting the onset of mood disorders in young people are variable. Although a confirmed positive family history of mood disorders in a first-degree family member is a significant and robust risk factor predicting the onset of mood disorders in offspring, those with such a family history do not always go on to develop mood disorders.

Mood disorders tend to persist over a long period of time, and people who have one major depressive episode tend to become vulnerable to recurrent episodes and intermittent, subclinical episodes. However, there are instances where people recover after a single, major depressive episode. This is usually the case when there is an acute stressor.

CLINICAL PICTURE

People with mood disorders experience pervasive alternating episodes of mania (or hypomania), depressive episodes, or mixed episodes (a combination of mania/hypomania and depressive episode). This dysregulation of mood often interrupts their daily life. This is often accompanied by some degree of cognitive disturbances (such as poor attention and concentration) and a change in psychomotor activity. Mood disorders tend to impact on most areas of functioning.

When a diagnosis of major depressive episode is made, it is essential to establish whether the episode is part of a major depressive disorder or another mental disorder. Mood disorders are commonly comorbid with medical illnesses, and therefore this is an essential aspect to consider when diagnoses are made. In addition to this, major depressive disorder must be differentiated from normal sadness or bereavement. In the context of bereavement, a diagnosis of major depressive disorder is only made if the symptoms persist beyond a certain period of time.

DEPRESSIVE DISORDERS

Most people have gone through periods of low mood or sadness at some point in their lives. This is transient and it is sometimes in response to an identifiable event or a particular set of circumstances. On the other hand, depressive disorders are a group of clinical disorders characterised by the presence of sad, empty, or irritable mood, with somatic or cognitive changes (American Psychiatric Association, 2013). These symptoms have a significant impact on an individual's ability to perform his or her daily functions. It may be difficult to sleep, eat, work, study, and engage with family and friends.

Owing to its impact on millions of people around the world, depression is considered to be 'the common cold of mental illness'. The World Health Organization (WHO) recognises depression as one of the most prevalent disorders – one that affects an estimated 4.4% of the world's population and is the single largest contributor to disability worldwide (Whiteford et al., 2013). It is also associated with an increased risk of suicide.

Many people with this disorder are treated in primary care settings, while others require hospitalisation. Major depression is the fourth leading cause of disease burden in the world in people aged between 15 and 44 years (Costello et al, 2002).

In South Africa, the accuracy of the prevalence rates is limited, as much of the data is collected in clinic settings, which introduces a potential bias (Tomlinson, Grimsrud, Stein Williams, & Meyer, 2009); this is because this does not account for those who do not seek treatment, or those who seek treatment in different places.

In the DSM-5, the depressive disorders category includes:

- major depressive disorder
- persistent depressive disorder
- premenstrual dysphoric disorder
- disruptive mood dysregulation disorder
- substance/medication-induced depressive disorder
- depressive disorder due to another medical condition.

The first four of these are described below, while the other two are mentioned more briefly.

Major depressive disorder (MDD)

Major depressive disorder (MDD) is distinguished from a transient mood state that is experienced by many people at some stage in their lives. Major depressive disorder is a clinical syndrome characterised by a depressed mood or loss of interest or pleasure in nearly all activities, which is present for most of the day, nearly every day. People with this disorder also experience cognitive, physical (somatic), behavioural, and perceptual changes, as well as disturbances in neuro-vegetative functions (e.g. appetite and sleep disturbances). For diagnosis, these symptoms must have persisted for a duration of two weeks, but they can also last longer.

Major depressive disorder is a lifelong, episodic disorder with multiple recurrences, averaging one episode in every five-year period (Fava & Kendler, 2000). It also has a variable course (in terms of chronicity and remission), with a high probability of recurrence (Thomas & Seedat, 2018). The adapted DSM-5 diagnostic criteria for major depressive disorder are listed in Table 7.3 (American Psychiatric Association, 2013; Thomas & Seedat, 2018):

Table 7.3: Diagnostic criteria for major depressive disorder from the DSM-5 and major depressive episode from the ICD-10

DSM-5 Major depressive disorder	ICD-10 Major depressive episode
A Five (or more) or the following symptoms have been present during the same two-week period and represent a change from previous functioning; at least one of the symptoms is either (1) depressed mood or (2) loss of interest or pleasure. (1) Depressed mood most of the day, nearly every day, as indicated by subjective report (e.g. feels sad, empty, or hopeless) or observation made by others (e.g. appears tearful). (Note: In children or adolescents, can be irritable mood.) (2) Markedly diminished interest in pleasure in all, or almost all, activities most of the day, nearly every day (as indicated by either subjective account or observation). (3) Significant weight loss when not dieting or weight gain (e.g. a change of more than 5% of body weight in a month), or decrease or increase in appetite nearly every day. (Note: In children, consider failure to make expected weight gain.) (4) Insomnia or hypersomnia nearly every day (5) Psychomotor agitation or retardation nearly every day (observable by others; not merely subjective feelings or restlessness or being slowed down.) (6) Fatigue or loss of energy nearly every day. (7) Feelings of worthlessness or excessive or inappropriate guilt (which may be delusional) nearly every day (not merely self-reproach or guilt about being sick).	■ In typical depressive episodes of all three varieties (mild, moderate, and severe), the individual usually suffers from: ‣ Depressed mood. ‣ Loss of interest and enjoyment. ‣ Reduced energy leading to increased fatigability and diminished activity. ‣ Marked tiredness after only slight effort is common. ■ Other symptoms include: ‣ Reduced concentration and attention. ‣ Reduced self-esteem and self-confidence. ‣ Ideas of guilt and unworthiness.

DSM-5 Major depressive disorder	ICD-10 Major depressive episode
(8) Diminished ability to think or concentrate, or indecisiveness, nearly every day (either by subjective account or observed by others). (9) Recurrent thoughts of death (not just fear of dying), recurrent suicidal ideation without a specific plan, a suicide attempt, or a specific plan for committing suicide. B. The symptoms cause clinically significant distress or impairment in social, occupational, or other important areas of functioning. C. The episode is not attributable to the physiological effects of a substance or to another medical condition. Note: Criteria A–C represent a major depressive episode. Note: Responses to a significant loss (e.g. bereavement, financial ruin, losses from a natural disaster, a serious medical illness or disability) may include the feelings of intense sadness, rumination about the loss, insomnia, poor appetite, and weight loss noted in Criterion A, which may resemble a depressive episode. Although such symptoms may be understandable or considered appropriate to the loss, the presence of a major depressive episode in addition to the normal response to the significant loss should be carefully considered. This decision inevitably requires the exercise of clinical judgement based on the individual's history and the cultural norms for the expression of distress in the context of loss. D. The occurrence of the major depressive episode is not better explained by schizoaffective disorder, schizophrenia, schizophreniform disorder, delusional disorder, or other specified or unspecified schizophrenia spectrum or other psychotic disorder. E. There has never been a manic episode or a hypomanic episode. Note: This exclusion does not apply if all of the manic-like or hypomanic-like episodes are substance-induced or are attributable to the physiological effects of another medical condition.	▸ Bleak and pessimistic views of the future. ▸ Ideas or acts of self-harm or suicide. ▸ Disturbed sleep. ▸ Diminished appetite.

Source: Reprinted with permission from the *Diagnostic and Statistical Manual of Mental Disorders*, fifth edition (DSM-5), American Psychiatric Association (APA), 2013, p. 160, and the *International Statistical Classification of Diseases and Related Health Problems*, tenth revision (ICD-10), World Health Organization (WHO), Geneva, 2007.

While grief can, on the surface, appear similar to a major depressive episode (MDE), in the case of grief the predominant feeling is of emptiness and loss, with occasional positive emotions and humour. This differs from the depressed mood and inability to anticipate happiness or pleasure that is associated with a major depressive episode (American

Psychiatric Association, 2013). During grief, there is a period of dysphoria that varies in intensity and is often associated with thoughts or reminders of the deceased, whereas the depressed mood associated with a major depressive episode is more pervasive and persistent (American Psychiatric Association, 2013).

Feelings of worthlessness are frequently present in a major depressive episode, whereas self-esteem is usually preserved during grief, and thoughts of death are usually in response to longing for the deceased (American Psychiatric Association, 2013). On the other hand, in the case of a major depressive episode, such thoughts are often focused on ending one's own life (American Psychiatric Association, 2013).

Persistent depressive disorder (dysthymia)

Persistent depressive disorder (dysthymia) is a syndrome characterised by a chronically depressed mood lasting for at least two years. It differs from major depressive disorder in that it is a chronic illness with generally less severe depressive symptoms.

The essential feature is a depressed mood that occurs for most of the day, for more days than not, as indicated by either subjective reports or observation by others, for a period of at least two years. In children and adolescents, the mood can be irritable, and the duration must be at least one year.

Other symptoms of the disorder include changes in appetite, sleeping patterns, low energy, low self-esteem, poor concentration or difficulty making decisions, and feelings of hopelessness. Any symptom-free period does not last longer than two months at a time. During or preceding this time, the criteria for major depressive disorder may be continuously present.

Because of the persistent nature of this disorder, people who experience these symptoms may consider them as 'normal', and therefore not report them unless they are directly prompted.

Premenstrual dysphoric disorder

Premenstrual symptoms commonly affect women of reproductive age, resulting in mild to moderate psychological symptoms, including cognitive and behavioural changes. These symptoms usually resolve by the end of menstruation and are followed by a symptom-free interval after menstruation and before ovulation (Walsh, Ishmaili, Naheed, & O'Brien, 2015).

Premenstrual dysphoric disorder (PMDD) represents a new category in the DSM-5 although premenstrual changes had been identified in literature long before this addition. In 1931, premenstrual change was termed 'premenstrual tension' (PMT) and later renamed 'premenstrual syndrome' (PMS), which was then included in the DSM-IV.

Women with premenstrual dysphoric disorder experience fluctuations in mood, as well as irritability, dysphoria, anxiety, and somatic (physical) symptoms that are present during the majority of their menstrual cycles. The symptoms usually peak and then remit around the onset of the menses, and resolve shortly thereafter (American Psychiatric Association, 2013).

Disruptive mood dysregulation disorder

Disruptive mood dysregulation disorder is characterised by a series of severe, recurrent temper outbursts that occur at least three times per week. These include verbal rages and/or physically aggressive behaviours toward people or property that are grossly out of proportion in intensity or duration to the situation, and are inconsistent with the individual's developmental level (American Psychiatric Association, 2013). This diagnosis is reserved for children and youth aged 6–18 years (although the typical age of onset is before the age of 10 years), who display chronic, severe, persistent, non-episodic irritability, accompanied by severe temper outbursts (Roy, Lopes, & Klein, 2014). The diagnostic criteria for disruptive mood dysregulation disorder (as adapted from the DSM-5) are illustrated in Table 7.4 (American Psychiatric Association, 2013).

Table 7.4: Diagnostic criteria for disruptive mood dysregulation disorder from the DSM-5

DSM-5
A. Severe recurrent temper outbursts manifested verbally (e.g. verbal rages) and/or behaviourally (e.g. physical aggression towards people or property) that are grossly out of proportion in intensity or duration to the situation or provocation.
B. The temper outbursts are inconsistent with developmental level.
C. The temper outbursts occur, on average, three or more times per week.
D. The mood between temper outbursts is persistently irritable or angry most of the day, nearly every day, and is observable by others (e.g. parents, teachers, peers).
E. Criteria A–D have been present for 12 or more months. Throughout that time, the individual has not had a period lasting three or more consecutive months without all of the symptoms in Criteria A–D.
F. Criteria A and D are present in at least two of three settings (i.e. home, school, with peers) and are severe in at least one of these.
G. The diagnosis should not be made for the first time before age 6 or after age 18 years.
H. By history or observation, the age of onset of Criteria A-E is before 10 years.
I. There has never been a distinct period lasting more than one day during which the full symptom criteria, except duration, for a manic or hypomanic episode have been met. **Note:** Developmentally appropriate mood elevation, such as occurs in the context of a highly positive event or its anticipation, should not be considered as a symptom of mania or hypomania.
J. The behaviours do not occur exclusively during an episode of major depressive disorder and are not better explained by another mental disorder (e.g. autism spectrum disorder, posttraumatic stress disorder, separation anxiety disorder, persistent depressive disorder [dysthymia]). **Note:** This diagnosis cannot coexist with oppositional defiant disorder, intermittent explosive disorder, or bipolar disorder, although it can coexist with others, including major depressive disorder, attention-deficit/hyperactivity disorder, conduct disorder, and substance use disorders. Individuals whose symptoms meet criteria for both disruptive mood dysregulation disorder and oppositional defiant disorder should only be given the diagnosis of disruptive mood dysregulation disorder. If an individual has ever experienced a manic or hypomanic episode, the diagnosis of disruptive mood dysregulation disorder should not be assigned.
K. The symptoms are not attributable to the physiological effects of a substance or to another medical or neurological condition.

Source: Reprinted with permission from the *Diagnostic and Statistical Manual of Mental Disorders*, fifth edition (DSM-5), American Psychiatric Association (APA), 2013, p. 156.

Disruptive mood dysregulation disorder was introduced as a diagnostic category to address the problem of the over- or misdiagnosis of bipolar disorder in children. The diagnosis of severe, chronic, and irritable mood in children has been a challenge for clinicians due to the symptom overlap between mood, anxiety, and disruptive behaviour disorders (Roy et al., 2014). Table 7.5 below shows the key differences between disruptive mood dysregulation disorder and bipolar mood disorder (which is discussed later in this chapter).

Table 7.5: Key differences between disruptive mood dysregulation disorder and bipolar mood disorder

Disruptive mood dysregulation disorder	Bipolar mood disorder
Chronic irritability	Episodic irritability (representing a change from the individual's usual state)
Mood is consistently irritable and angry	Mood varies across periods of normal mood, depression, and mania

Source: Adapted from: Roy, Lopes, & Klein, 2014.

Substance/medication-induced depressive disorder

A diagnosis of substance/medication-induced depressive disorder is made when depressive disorder symptoms appear during or within one month after the use of a substance, and where there is confirmation from the individual's history, physical examination, or laboratory findings of the use/abuse of a substance. The symptoms must have developed during or soon after the substance intoxication or withdrawal, or after being exposed to a medication. In addition, the substance or medication must be able to cause the depressive symptoms.

Depressive disorder due to another medical condition

In the process of making a diagnosis of depressive disorder, clinicians have to rule out other medical conditions and ensure that the symptoms are not caused by the use of prescription medicines (see previous section). Certain medical conditions, such as hypothyroidism (an underactive thyroid), can trigger psychiatric symptoms. These secondary causes are viewed as distinct from major depressive disorder in terms of their recurrence and neurobiological underpinnings (Thomas & Seedat, 2018).

BIPOLAR AND RELATED DISORDERS

Bipolar mood disorder, bipolar affective disorder, and manic-depressive disorder are all terms that have been used interchangeably (Zilesnick, 2014). The core feature of bipolar disorder is a fluctuation between abnormally high moods (mania or hypomania) and abnormally low moods (depressive episode) (Zilesnick, 2014) as well as a fluctuation in energy levels.

The DSM-5 refers to this group of disorders as 'bipolar and related disorders', and these are presented as a separate chapter in the DSM-5. The three main sub-categories of this chapter of the DSM-5 are:

- bipolar I disorder
- bipolar II disorder, and
- cyclothymic disorder.

While the ICD-10 does not differentiate between bipolar I disorder and bipolar II disorder, the ICD-11 does. The ICD-11 has also brought cyclothymic disorder into the same group as bipolar I and bipolar II disorders, and is therefore very similar to the DSM-5 in its categorisation of these disorders.

Bipolar I and bipolar II disorders

Bipolar disorder is described as a recurrent, cyclical, episodic illness, with episodes of mood changes and periods of normal mood (euthymia) (Rodseth, 2011). Bipolar I and bipolar II disorders are distinguished by the severity of the highs and the duration of the episodes (Miric, 2015). Bipolar I category is characterised by at least one lifetime experience of a manic episode *with or without* associated depressive symptoms. The bipolar II category involves at least one lifetime experience of a hypomanic episode *with one or more* major depressive episode.

The diagnosis of bipolar disorders is complicated, and patients are often first diagnosed with unipolar depression before a diagnosis of a bipolar disorder is made. Establishing whether an individual has had previous or current experiences of manic or hypomanic episodes is essential in distinguishing bipolar disorder, as it is necessary to meet the criteria for a manic episode before a person can be diagnosed with bipolar I disorder. According to the American Psychiatric Association (2013, p. 123), '[t]he manic episode may have been preceded by and may be followed by hypomanic or major depressive episodes'. The diagnostic criteria for a manic episode are described in Table 7.6.

Table 7.6: Diagnostic criteria for a manic episode from the DSM-5

DSM-5
A.   A distinct period of abnormally and persistently elevated, expansive or irritable mood and abnormally and persistently increased activity or energy, lasting at least one week and present most of the day, nearly every day (or any duration if hospitalisation is necessary)
B.   During the period of mood disturbance and increased energy or activity, three (or more) of the following symptoms (four if the mood is only irritable) are present to a significant degree and represent a noticeable change from usual behaviour: (1) Inflated self-esteem or grandiosity.

DSM-5

(2)   Decreased need for sleep (e.g. feels rested after only three hours of sleep).
    (3)   More talkative than usual or pressure to keep talking.
    (4)   Flight of ideas or subjective experience that thoughts are racing.
    (5)   Distractibility (i.e. attention too easily drawn to unimportant or irrelevant external stimuli), as reported or observed.
    (6)   Increase in goal-directed activity (either socially, at work or school, or sexually) or psychomotor agitation (i.e. purposeless non-goal-directed activity).
    (7)   Excessive involvement in activities that have a high potential for painful consequences (e.g. engaging in unrestrained buying sprees, sexual indiscretions, or foolish business investments).
C.   The mood disturbance is sufficiently severe to cause marked impairment in social or occupational functioning or to necessitate hospitalisation to prevent harm to self or others, or there are psychotic features.
D.   The episode is not attributable to the physiological effects of a substance (e.g. a drug of abuse, a medication, or treatment) or to another medical condition.
    Note: A full manic episode that emerges during antidepressant treatment (e.g. medication, electroconvulsive therapy) but persists at a fully syndromal level beyond the physiological effect of that treatment is sufficient evidence for a manic episode and, therefore, a bipolar I diagnosis.
Note: Criteria A–D constitute a manic episode. At least one lifetime manic episode is required for the diagnosis of Bipolar I disorder.

Source: Reprinted with permission from the *Diagnostic and Statistical Manual of Mental Disorders*, fifth edition (DSM-5), American Psychiatric Association (APA), 2013, p. 124.

The diagnostic criteria for a hypomanic episode are described in Table 7.7.

Table 7.7: Diagnostic criteria for a hypomanic episode from the DSM-5

DSM-5

A.   A distinct period of abnormally and persistently elevated, expansive, or irritable mood and abnormally and persistently increased activity or energy, lasting at least four consecutive days and present most of the day, nearly every day.
B.   During the period of mood disturbance and increased energy or activity, three (or more) of the following symptoms (four if the mood is only irritable) have persisted, represent a noticeable change from usual behaviour, and have been present to a significant degree:
    (1)   Inflated self-esteem or grandiosity.
    (2)   Decreased need for sleep (e.g. feels rested after only three hours of sleep).
    (3)   More talkative than usual or pressure to keep talking.
    (4)   Flight of ideas or subjective experience that thoughts are racing.
    (5)   Distractibility (i.e. attention too easily drawn to unimportant or irrelevant external stimuli), as reported or observed.
    (6)   Increase in goal directed activity (either socially, at work or school, or sexually) or psychomotor agitation.
    (7)   Excessive involvement in activities that have a high potential for painful consequences (e.g. engaging in unrestrained buying sprees, sexual indiscretions, or foolish business investments).

DSM-5

C. The episode is associates with an unequivocal change in functioning that is uncharacteristic of the individual when not symptomatic.
D. The disturbance in mood and the change in functioning is observable by others.
E. The episode is not severe enough to cause marked impairment in social or occupational functioning or to necessitate hospitalisation. If there are psychotic features, the episode is, by definition, manic.
F. The episode is not attributable to the physiological effects of a substance (e.g. a drug of abuse, a medication, or treatment).
Note: A full hypomanic episode that emerges during antidepressant treatment (e.g. medication, electroconvulsive therapy) but persists at a fully syndromal level beyond the physiological effects of that treatment is sufficient evidence for a hypomanic episode diagnosis. However, caution is indicated so that one or two symptoms (particularly increased irritability, edginess, or agitation following antidepressant use) are not taken as sufficient for diagnosis of a hypomanic episode, nor necessarily indicative of a bipolar diathesis.
Note: Criteria A–F constitute a hypomanic episode. Hypomanic episodes are common in bipolar I disorder but are not required for the diagnosis of bipolar I disorder.

Source: Reprinted with permission from the *Diagnostic and Statistical Manual of Mental Disorders*, fifth edition (DSM-5), American Psychiatric Association (APA), 2013, p. 124.

The peak incidence of bipolar disorder is between the ages of 12 and 30 years, and the symptoms are pervasive. Bipolar disorder is associated with a high rate of relapse, which sometimes occurs even when treatment is adhered to. The median age of onset of bipolar disorder is around 20 years (Weissman & Gamerof, 2008, in Aiyelero, Kwanashie, Sheikh, & Hussaini, 2011).

Biological and psychosocial factors have been found to influence the aetiology and course of bipolar disorder (Buickians, Miklowitz, & Kim, 2007). Bipolar disorders are associated with various comorbid medical conditions such as cardiovascular diseases, auto-immune diseases, and metabolic disorders. Psychiatric comorbidities include attention-deficit/hyperactivity disorder (ADHD), and anxiety, personality, and substance use disorders, which further complicate the clinical picture.

People diagnosed with bipolar disorder usually have difficulty in interpersonal relationships and they often report high levels of conflict with family and friends. These interpersonal difficulties may also present in other areas of the individual's functioning, such as in the workplace. This often results in people with bipolar disorder feeling rejected and isolated. Bipolar disorder often has a negative impact on social, school or occupational functioning and on interpersonal relationships.

Cyclothymic disorder

Cyclothymic disorder could be regarded as a less severe disorder than either bipolar I or bipolar II disorder. The essential feature of this disorder is a chronic, fluctuating mood disturbance that is characterised by numerous periods of hypomanic symptoms (that do not meet the full criteria for a hypomanic episode) and periods of depressive symptoms (that do not meet the full criteria for a major depressive episode).

During the initial two-year period, the symptoms are persistent, and there is no symptom-free period lasting longer than two months (American Psychiatric Association, 2013). This is a chronic subtype of bipolar disorder that is often associated with moodiness and irritability (Van Meter & Youngstrom, 2012). Although the symptoms of cyclothymic disorder are mild and 'sub-threshold', they may be a precursor to bipolar I or II disorders. The progression from 'childhood moodiness' into cyclothymic disorder or bipolar I and II disorders is a developing area of research.

SYMPTOMS OF MOOD DISORDERS

Table 7.8: Core signs and symptoms of mania and depression

Sign/symptom	Mania	Depression
Appearance	■ Colourful, strange, garish style	■ Loss of interest in personal appearance and grooming
Mood	■ Prolonged elation and euphoria ■ Excessive optimism ■ Cheerfulness ■ Heightened irritability	■ Feelings of sadness ■ Low mood ■ Pessimism ■ Suicidal ideation
Speech	■ Rapid loud speech ■ Difficult to interrupt	■ Slowed speech ■ Monotonous and monosyllabic
Activity	■ Restlessness ■ Impulsivity ■ Risk-taking behaviour	■ Difficulty initiating tasks ■ Low energy ■ Loss of interest in activities ■ Psychomotor slowness
Sleep	■ Decreased need for sleep	■ Insomnia: (early morning waking), or hypersomnia
Cognition	■ Difficulty planning and reasoning ■ Distractible	■ Reduced ability to concentrate ■ Poor memory
Self-perception and thinking	■ Exaggerated self-confidence ■ Grandiose thinking	■ Low self-esteem ■ Feelings of guilt and worthlessness ■ Sense of hopelessness

CROSS-CULTURAL AND AFRICAN PERSPECTIVES

South Africa's cultural diversity exposes us to different ways of understanding phenomena, alternative ways of learning about the world and about each other, and variations in help-seeking behaviours. It represents an important aspect of health, illness, and healing and, as such, the cultural context of the community concerned is an important aspect of the management of various health conditions (Sodi, 2011).

In the field of psychology, there exists a need for us to expand our understanding of the cultural expressions of emotions, as we are often interacting with people of different cultures. The relationship between mental health and culture has generated growing research interest in recent years. Culture influences many aspects of mental health. It can account for how certain symptoms are expressed, how individuals interpret those symptoms, the expression of distress, and attitudes towards treatment.

Mood disorders are a universal phenomenon; however, culture influences their expression and manifestation. There are also multiple world views and cultural conceptualisations of illness and health, and therefore, multiple cultural healthcare systems may be used to understand illness and health (Sodi, 2011). As a result, a culturally appropriate response to a stressor is not considered a mental illness, and symptoms must be understood from within the context in which they occur. These factors add a level of complexity to the assessment and management of mood disorders.

The process of diagnostic assessment and intervention is shaped by the culture of the clinician, the client, and the context in which they operate. In the case of major depressive disorder, somatic complaints are a common presenting complaint across many cultures, as are insomnia and loss of energy (American Psychiatric Association, 2013).

If we think about the case study of Yi at the beginning of this chapter, we can see that she exhibits certain core symptoms of depression that are consistent across cultures (even while they may vary in terms of manifestation, prevalence, and intensity). However, Yi describes being visited by the spirit of a disgruntled ancestor, which is a commonly described expression of depression among African people, who may also describe possession and poisoning.

It is also important to consider how language affects the way in which certain symptoms are described and perceived. According to Baloyi (2008, p.), '[i]n most African languages emotive concepts cannot simply be captured by a single concept because in many instances these concepts have different meanings depending on the context'. Baloyi (2008) cautions against directly translating feelings from English to African languages in a way that may alter or misrepresent the meaning. There may also be distinct differences in the description and experience of mood disorders across cultures, and the use of cultural idioms of distress is particularly common in many African cultures.

Nevertheless, there are core clinical features that are stable across cultures and contexts, and these include a depressed mood or the loss of interest or pleasure in nearly all activities.

 **ACTIVITY**

Alemayehu Negashm is an Ethiopian researcher who wrote *Bipolar disorder in rural Ethiopia: Community-based studies in Butajira for screening, epidemiology, follow-up, and the burden of care* (2009). It is available online at: http://www.diva-portal.org/smash/get/diva2:211781/FULLTEXT01.
Read pages 31–38 of this article and consider how this context is different from and also similar to the American context that is the basis of the DSM-5.

AETIOLOGY OF MOOD DISORDERS

Hugo, Boshoff, Traut, Zungu-Dirwayi, and Stein (2003) observe that South Africans view the main cause of orders such as depression as 'weak character'. However, while personal vulnerabilities and psychosocial factors have been implicated in the onset of mood disorders, mood disorders are attributed to multiple risk factors, including stress and environmental factors, biological factors, and genetic factors. Researchers remain unclear about the exact causal dynamics that explain how these interrelated factors trigger the onset of mood disorders, although integrative research is under way.

The age of onset of mood disorders is an important consideration. An earlier age of onset is associated with a worse course of illness. This leads to a greater incidence of recurrence, relapse, chronicity, and functional impairment.

Stress and environmental factors

The association between stressful life events and mood disorders has been extensively reported in the literature. Financial difficulties, separation and divorce, exposure to violence, health problems, and loss of employment are just some of the challenges that many adults face at certain points in their lives. These stressors often lead to distress and can be triggers for depressive episodes. Life events that occur during childhood or adolescence may also be precursors to mood disorders. The number and severity of stressful life events increase the risk, severity, and chronicity of mood disorders such as depression (Otte et al., 2016).

Stressful life events tend to affect individuals differently and this variation is based on individual biological and psychological adaptations to environmental factors. When an individual faces a stressor, cognitive processes determine how the individual appraises the stressor and their potential to cope. Neural structures are also activated in response to the stressor, including sensory pathways that convey information to the central nervous system (CNS), resulting in an endocrine response and activation of the autonomic nervous system (ANS) and hypothalamic-pituitary-adrenal (HPA) axis (Tafet & Nemeroff, 2016). Stressful life events can affect the individual, family, and community, potentially increasing the risk of mood disorders.

Biological factors

There is relatively little known about the aetiology of mood disorders, and there is still much reliance on diagnostic categories rather than biological markers. Clinical studies have uncovered the biological causes of mood disorders and the related biochemical and endocrine (hormone) changes. Multiple interconnected neurotransmitter circuits (circuits of interconnected neurons that carry signals between brain cells) have been implicated in the development of mood disorders.

Mood disorders are associated with a dysregulation of specific neurotransmitters that play a part in the regulation of sleep, appetite, sexual function, endocrine function, arousal, and emotional states. Monoamine signalling and disruption in the hypothalamic-pituitary-adrenal (HPA) axis are also integral to both major depressive disorder and bipolar disorder (Manji et al, 2003). It is for these reasons that pharmacological interventions work to target these neurotransmitter pathways in order to normalise mood and other associated symptoms of major depressive disorder and bipolar disorder.

Antidepressants, such as selective serotonin reuptake inhibitors (SSRIs), inhibit the reuptake or reabsorption of serotonin and other neurotransmitters (such as dopamine and norepinephrine) by neurons in the brain, making greater levels of these neurotransmitters available in the synapse (the small gap between neurons that allows direct communication between neurons) (see Figure 7.4).

Another essential causal factor of mood disorders is altered biological rhythms. When an individual has a mood disorder, there is commonly a fluctuation or variation in mood states throughout the day. Disrupted circadian rhythms (an internalised, 24-hour biological cycle that regulates daily functions such as sleeping, waking, and eating) often underlie mood disorders. A disruption in the sleep–wake cycle has an impact on mood states, and researchers have highlighted that the manipulation of the sleep cycle can have a positive effect on mood. Globally, sleep deprivation has been used as an alternative treatment for mood disorders in what has come to be known as 'wake therapy' (Wirz-Justice, 2008).

Genetics

Genetic factors have been linked to all major psychiatric disorders. The exact genetic factors involved in mood disorders are not known. Meta-analyses have shown an estimated heritability for major depressive disorder at 37% with a higher prevalence rate for women than men (Flint & Kendler, 2014). Genetic studies have also shown that there is a strong genetic basis in both bipolar I and bipolar II disorder, with evidence indicating that up to 80% of patients diagnosed with bipolar I disorder have a family history of mood disorders (Zilesnick, 2014). Genetic studies suggest that the risk of major depressive disorder is threefold higher in first-degree relatives.

In general, individuals with mood disorders often have a history of these disorders in their immediate families, although this is not always the case. In cases of parental depression, it is not only the presence of psychopathology in the parent that results in psychopathology in the child, but rather the processes that result from the disorder (for instance, biological predisposition, including genetics, negative parenting, or stressful parent-child dynamics) that link the risk factor with unfavourable outcomes (England & Sim, 2009). Genetic risk factors rely greatly on exposure to environmental stressors and adverse circumstances.

Therefore, a person's genetic predisposition to a mood disorder does not necessarily result in the manifestation of a mood disorder.

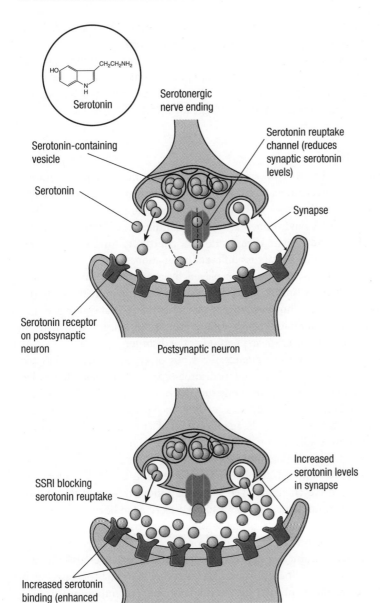

Figure 7.4: This diagram illustrates how selective serotonin reuptake inhibitors function.

 **ACTIVITY**

Consider the following quotation from child psychiatrist, Daniel Siegel, and early childhood expert, Mary Hartzell. Which message are these authors conveying?

'It is not just inheritance that determines human development. Genes determine much of how neurons link up with each other, but equally important is that experience activates genes to influence this linkage process. How we treat our children changes who they are and how they develop ... Nature needs nurture' (Siegel & Hartzell, 2004, p. 34).

Integrative model

Each of the aetiological models discussed above forms part of a specific domain of causative factors. Developing an integrative model is useful in providing a more comprehensive and inclusive formulation that will further enhance our understanding of mood disorders across the lifespan. An individual's environmental context, culture, developmental history, cognitive style, and biological and genetic composition all contribute towards the onset, course, and expression of mood disorders across different populations.

The diathesis-stress model focuses on the role played by genetic and environmental factors in the expression of a mental disorder. According to this model, an individual inherits a predisposition to a mental disorder; however, it is stressful life events that can trigger the expression of that disorder. In an individual with a high level of resilience, it may take an extremely stressful life event(s) to trigger the expression of the disorder.

Emotion regulation refers to how we influence the types of emotions we experience and when these emotions are experienced. In depressive disorders, particularly major depressive disorder, emotion dysregulation may be a central construct (Mehrabi et al., 2014). People who struggle to regulate their emotions in their daily lives are likely to experience longer and more severe periods of distress, which may result in the manifestation of a mood disorder (Mehrabi et al., 2014). Deficits in emotion regulation underlie a number of psychological disorders, and it would seem that this is a significant aetiological factor for mood disorders.

On the other hand, socio-economic factors such as poverty and unemployment may trigger a mood disorder, as can life-changing events such as childbirth – as in the case of postpartum depression. Postpartum depression has also been ascribed to hormonal changes during pregnancy, when levels of oestrogen, progesterone, and cortisol drop dramatically in the 48 hours following delivery. Psychosocial stressors such as acute life events (e.g. divorce, forced migration, etc.), chronic stress, and past traumatic experiences also interact to contribute to the development of mood disorders. At times, even normal life events (such as changes in a family's life cycle) may present significant emotional difficulties for some.

A growing body of evidence suggests that an individual's environmental context is a significant determinant in the onset, course, and expression of mood disorders. Studies highlighting the role of recent life events and social support have suggested that individuals with mood disorders experience increased stressful life events prior to the onset or subsequent episodes of their disorder. Social support is also linked with a positive course of illness.

These factors focus on the external environment in which the mood disorder is experienced, but it is important to understand that there are also internal factors that influence the expression of mood disorders. In addition to the complex neurobiological causes of mood disorders, there are also other psychological factors, such as emotion regulation, discussed earlier in this section, which may trigger a mood disorder. How an individual makes sense of or derives meaning from a particular life stressor determines his or her response to it (see also Chapter 4). This is also an important consideration in our search for an integrative model of mood disorders.

CONCLUSION

Despite the progress made on the classification of mood disorders, there is still a need to explore the causes of these disorders further. There are also distinct differences in the presentation of mood disorders that require further study. For instance, while some individuals experience a pervasive pattern of clinically significant mood disorder symptoms, others are able to respond to the challenges and losses of everyday life in a manner that does not constitute a clinical presentation. The question arises about why some people are more resilient to adversity; thus a comprehensive understanding of the different causal mechanisms of mood disorders is necessary.

MULTIPLE-CHOICE QUESTIONS

EXAMPLE CASE

Read through the following case study, and then answer the multiple choice questions: Ruth is a 24-year-old woman who recently gave birth to a baby. Although her baby is healthy, Ruth has been very tearful since the birth. The nursing sisters in the ward have become worried about her, as she has become very withdrawn and tends to sleep through the day, and she shows little interest in the baby. She refuses to get out of bed, claiming that she is very tired. Her appetite is poor, and even when encouraged, she does not finish her meals. These symptoms started in the final weeks of her pregnancy. The nursing staff have also noticed that she never has any visitors and that not even the father of the baby has come to visit. Ruth has told one of the nursing sisters that she is concerned as she does not know how she will care for the baby as she lives in an informal settlement and is unemployed. According to Ruth, the father of the baby denies that it is his child, and tends to become verbally and physically abusive when she insists that it is his child. The only solution that she sees to the problem is to kill herself and the baby. When confronted about this by the doctor, she insists that a voice told her that she is bad, and needs to be punished for having a child that she cannot take care of. She is convinced that this is the voice of her mother who passed away a year ago.

1. The most appropriate diagnosis for Ruth would be:
   a. persistent depressive disorder (dysthymia)
   b. bipolar I disorder
   c. bipolar II disorder
   d. major depressive disorder

2. When considering your diagnosis, which one of the following factors influenced your diagnosis the most?
   a. the auditory hallucination (i.e. the voice she heard)
   b. a physically abusive partner
   c. poor appetite, fatigue, and oversleeping
   d. suicidal thoughts
3. The fact that Ruth is very tearful and suicidal is an indication of a _____ mood.
   a. euphoric
   b. euthymic
   c. bipolar
   d. dysphoric
4. The voice telling Ruth that she is bad and needs to be punished is an example of a(n):
   a. mood-congruent hallucination
   b. mood-incongruent hallucination
   c. illusion
   d. mood-congruent delusion
5. If you had to explain the cause of Ruth's disorder from a cognitive perspective, you would say that her disorder could have been caused by:
   a. low levels of serotonin
   b. high levels of monoamine oxidase
   c. negative perceptions of herself, the world, and the future
   d. a lack of social support
6. From a psychosocial perspective, the disorder may been caused by:
   a. low social support; high perceived control
   b. high social support; low perceived control
   c. high social support; high perceived control
   d. low social support; low perceived control

PARAGRAPH AND ESSAY QUESTIONS

1. Distinguish between a major depressive episode and a manic episode in terms of:
   a. emotional symptoms
   b. cognitive symptoms
   c. behavioural symptoms
   d. physical symptoms
2. Describe the difference between unipolar and bipolar disorders.
3. List and describe the symptoms of major depression.
4. Give a brief description of the biological causes of depression.
5. Describe how social factors may cause or maintain depression.
6. Explain how cyclothymia and dysthymia are classified in the ICD-10, and compare this to how the DSM-5 and ICD-11 classify the equivalent disorders.

8 SCHIZOPHRENIA SPECTRUM AND OTHER PSYCHOTIC DISORDERS

Elsabe Jordaan

CHAPTER CONTENTS

Introduction
Psychosis and the psychotic disorders
Diagnosing schizophrenia spectrum and other psychotic disorders
Schizophrenia
History of schizophrenia
Prevalence and course
Clinical picture
Schizophrenia
Positive symptoms
Negative symptoms
Schizophrenia subtypes in the ICD-10
Other schizophrenia spectrum and psychotic disorders
Violence risk and mortality risk
Cross-cultural and African perspectives
Aetiology
Biological factors
Psychological factors
Sociocultural factors
Integration of aetiological factors
Controversial issues in the diagnosis and management of schizophrenia
Should the diagnosis continue to be used?
'Normality' and 'abnormality'
Labelling
De-institutionalisation
Conclusion

LEARNING OUTCOMES

After studying this chapter, you should be able to:

- Define schizophrenia and explain the difference between schizophrenia and psychosis.
- Describe the history of schizophrenia, including the work of Kraepelin and Bleuler.
- Show a general understanding of schizophrenia and distinguish schizophrenia from other disorders.
- Distinguish between and describe the positive and negative symptoms of schizophrenia.
- Describe the intra- and interpersonal aspects of the aetiology of schizophrenia.
- Identify cross-cultural and, more specifically, South African, aspects that impact on the presentation of schizophrenia.
- Describe the clinical characteristics and major subtypes of schizophrenia: paranoid, catatonic, disorganised, undifferentiated, and residual.
- Describe the aetiology of schizophrenia, including the potential genetic, neurobiological, developmental, and psychosocial influences and risk factors.
- Describe what is known about abnormalities in neuro-cognitive and biological functioning, and their relation to the symptom clusters of schizophrenia.
- Identify the factors influencing the prevalence, onset, and course of schizophrenia (e.g. poor vs good premorbid factors) and explain why they are important.
- Describe how expressed emotion influences in the course of schizophrenia, particularly in terms of relapse risk.

PERSONAL HISTORY CASELET

George is a 22-year-old man who went to London a year ago, where he worked at various casual jobs. He also found a place to stay in a commune where he started interacting with other people of his age who introduced him to clubs and drugs.

After about eight months in London, George's behaviour started changing and, one night, he woke to see a bright light and heard the voice of God. The voice told him that he was the 'chosen one'. This voice constantly gave him instructions.

George also discovered that he could communicate with world leaders via telepathy. He would often go into long conversations with them, suggesting ways and means for bringing about world peace.

George started to sleep very little and his personal hygiene deteriorated. He withdrew into his room and became socially isolated. As a result, he lost his job and became dependent on the other people in the commune for food and financial support.

The other people in the commune became concerned about George and realised that something was wrong. They coerced him into going to hospital, where he was finally admitted to the psychiatric ward. Here a diagnosis of paranoid schizophrenia was made.

As soon as George's symptoms stabilised, he was discharged, and his father was able to fetch him and bring him back to South Africa.

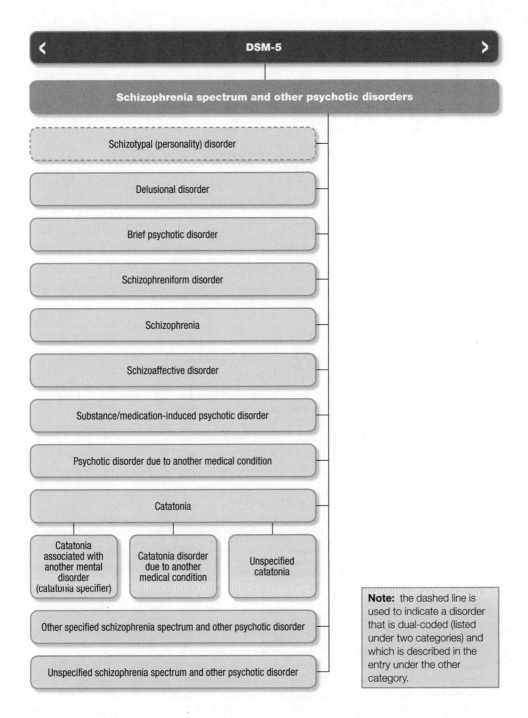

Figure 8.1: The American Psychiatric Association DSM-5 categorises disorders on the schizophrenia spectrum and psychotic disorders as shown above.

Source: Figure created by OUP reflecting information found in *Diagnostic and Statistical Manual of Mental Disorders*, fifth edition (DSM-5), 2013.

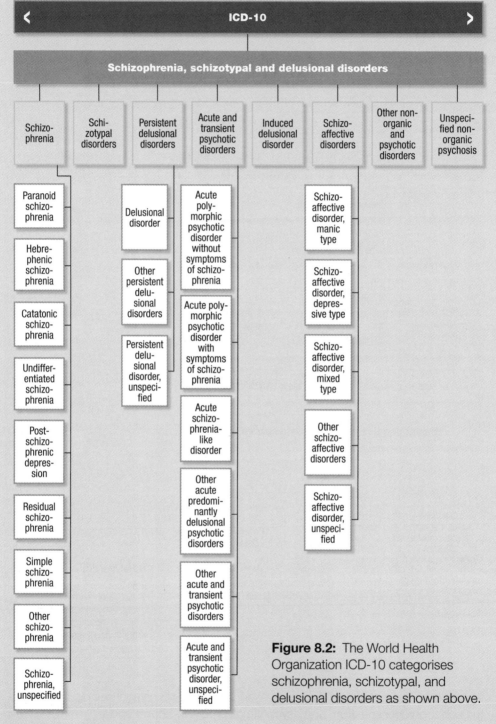

Figure 8.2: The World Health Organization ICD-10 categorises schizophrenia, schizotypal, and delusional disorders as shown above.

Source: *International Statistical Classification of Diseases and Related Health Problems*, tenth revision (ICD-10), 2016.

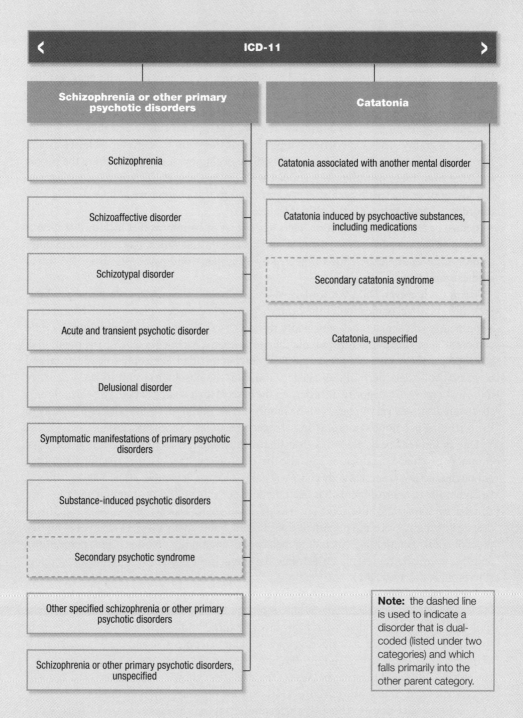

Figure 8.3: The World Health Organization proposed ICD-11 categorises schizophrenia or other primary psychotic disorders, and catatonia as shown above.

Source: *International Classification of Diseases for Mortality and Morbidity Statistics*, eleventh revision (ICD-11), 2018.

INTRODUCTION

In the previous chapters (i.e. anxiety and mood disorders), we have dealt with disorders that could be considered to be 'milder' disorders. What is meant by this is that people suffering from those disorders, despite the severity of the disorder and irrational thoughts, are usually still able to function relatively normally. The main reason for this is that they are still 'in touch with reality'. They experience symptoms that they can, to a greater or lesser extent, recognise as abnormal. In this chapter, we will be dealing with disorders where the people suffering from these disorders lose contact with reality. In scientific language, we refer to this losing of contact with reality as *psychosis*, and in this chapter we will be dealing with disorders where psychosis is the central feature.

It must be stressed that psychosis refers to a cluster of symptoms that include disruptions in mood, thoughts, perception, language, and behaviour, and which may be present in other disorders, for example, psychosis triggered by a substance and psychosis associated with a medical condition.

There are, however, DSM-5 disorders where psychosis is the primary symptom (see Table 8.2). The DSM-5 classification of the primary psychotic disorders places these disorders on a spectrum, with schizotypal personality disorder (see Chapter 14) representing the mild end of the spectrum and schizophrenia the more severe (Arciniegas, 2015). The mention of schizoptypal personality disorder in the DSM-5's chapter titled 'Schizophrenia spectrum and other psychotic disorders' in this category indicates the nosological shift in DSM-5, where there was a move to categorise disorders on the basis of their shared aetiology. Schizophrenia spectrum disorders vary in terms of the number, type, duration, complexity, and severity of their defining psychotic symptoms and associated features (Arciniegas, 2015).

Due to limited space, we will be dealing mainly with schizophrenia, as it is the most common psychotic disorder. It can also be regarded as the 'classic' psychotic disorder, although this view is increasingly controversial (Guloksuz & van Os, 2018; Kaplan, Sadock, & Grebb, 1994). Schizophrenia has been the focus of a great deal of attention and research, and yet we have very little solid knowledge about many aspects of the disorder. This is despite it being a severe and persistent condition that potentially involves all areas of human psychological functioning (including behaviour, cognition, emotion, and perception), and that it usually represents an extreme deviation from normal health and functioning (Picchioni & Murray, 2008).

The impact of this syndrome on the lives of the affected individuals and their families is often disastrous; schizophrenia usually results in lifelong impairment and disability. The individual and their families often bear direct financial and emotional costs. The costs to society are also significant, considering the loss of human potential, and the financial impact of treatment, hospitalisation, and the disability pension payments that result. Schizophrenia can also be considered 'extreme' because of the absence of known causes, objective diagnostic criteria, specified course, and effective treatments for this category of disorders.

Due to the fact that psychosis is the central symptom, it makes sense to start with a description of what psychosis is and what it entails, before moving on to the details of the disorders that have psychosis as a central theme.

 ACTIVITY

Watch the film *A Beautiful Mind*. It is a story about a brilliant mathematician, John Nash, who lived with schizophrenia. The film provides a good portrayal of what it is like for a person to experience schizophrenia.

PSYCHOSIS AND THE PSYCHOTIC DISORDERS

The word 'psychosis' has its roots in the Greek *psyche* (mind or soul) and *-osis* (abnormal condition), therefore referring to an 'abnormal condition of the mind' (Sommer, 2011). Psychosis usually describes a break in the individual's contact with reality. There is a range of definitions of the concept of psychosis. Restrictive definitions may refer only to the presence of hallucinations in the absence of insight that the experiences are not 'real', while the widest definitions focus on the extent of functional impairment that a person experiences. The DSM-5 use of the term refers to the presence of specific symptoms. Table 8.1 summarises the central features that define the psychotic disorders.

Table 8.1: Definition of terms

Terminology	Definition
Delusion	Fixed false belief that does not change despite evidence to contrary.
Hallucination	Perception that occurs in absence of external stimulus.
Disorganised speech	Impaired verbal communication to point of incomprehensibility. Also known as formal thought disorder.
Disorganised behaviour	Difficulties in any form of goal-directed behaviour, including daily living activities; may range from 'silliness' to agitation or even catatonia.
Negative symptoms	Decreases in normal behaviour, including diminished emotional expression, decreased speech output, decreased self-initiated behaviours, decreased socialisation with others, and diminished ability to experience activities as pleasurable.

In schizophrenia, schizophreniform disorder, schizoaffective disorder, and brief psychotic disorder, psychosis indicates the presence of delusions, hallucinations, disorganised thinking (speech), and disorganised abnormal motor behaviour (including catatonic behaviour) or negative symptoms. In the case of delusional disorder, 'psychotic' refers to the presence of delusions (American Psychiatric Association, 2013).

In summary, individuals experiencing psychosis may have difficulty recognising which of their sensory experiences are real, and which are not; in other words, they experience hallucinations. They may also have difficulty assessing whether their thoughts are based on reality (delusions). They may struggle to organise their own thoughts and their speech (disorganised speech), and their emotions. Their behaviour may also be unusual and without an obvious goal (disorganised behaviour).

They may also experience the relative absence of behaviour that is usually taken for granted (negative symptoms), such as decreased speech output, decreased social interaction, as well as possible reductions in goal-directed behaviour and reduced experiences of pleasure. An observer may describe the psychotic person's speech, emotional expression, and behaviour as 'illogical' or 'confused'.

It is highly probable that experiencing a psychotic episode will severely disrupt individuals' lives, and they may struggle to function as they did before, at home, school, or at work. Individual experiences of psychosis may differ; despite having similar diagnoses, people may experience their symptoms differently, or experience a different combination of symptoms (American Psychiatric Association, 2013).

The notion of 'insight' is also relevant in a discussion of psychosis and the psychotic disorders. In psychology and psychiatry, 'insight' refers to a person's awareness and recognition of his or her own illness. The dimensions of this awareness include acknowledging the consequences of behaviour as a result of one's condition, as well as admitting to a need for treatment (Markov & Berrios, 1992).

While some disorders are typically associated with 'good insight' (e.g. phobias), schizophrenia and the psychotic disorders are usually associated with 'poor insight' (i.e. the person has little awareness that anything is wrong with him or her) (Markov & Berrios, 1992).

DIAGNOSING SCHIZOPHRENIA SPECTRUM AND OTHER PSYCHOTIC DISORDERS

The DSM-5 acknowledges the cultural context of mental disorders as the framework for individual expression and for understanding the behaviour, signs, and symptoms that constitute diagnostic criteria; the DSM-5 states that the diagnostic process should assess whether the experiences, symptoms, and behaviours of an individual are in contrast to the norms of his or her specific culture of origin and cause adaptation difficulties for the person in his or her culture of origin. Section III of the DSM-5 provides an outline for cultural formulation that involves a systematic assessment of the cultural aspects of individual mental health presentations. All the schizophrenia spectrum and other psychotic disorders categories include specific culture-related diagnostic issues that should be taken into account when making a diagnosis (American Psychiatric Association, 2013).

Psychotic symptoms may also arise as the physiological consequences of a substance (e.g. medication, drug of abuse or toxin), or of another medical condition. It should also be noted that, although psychosis is the central element of the schizophrenia spectrum disorders, it also presents in other conditions. These include, most notably, the mood disorders, where it could be associated with either a manic or depressive episode in bipolar disorder or a depressive episode in major depressive disorder (American Psychiatric Association, 2013; Arciniegas, 2015).

For these reasons, extensive neuropsychiatric assessment is key to the evaluation and management of psychosis. This process involves gathering information about the individual's medical history (including general, psychiatric, and neurologic history), as well as the person's use of medications and/or substances that are potentially causative of psychosis. Medical examinations and investigations (such as blood and urine tests) should be performed to exclude delirium or other non-psychiatric origins of psychotic symptoms. The order of priority for excluding other causes before diagnosing schizophrenia spectrum and other psychotic disorders is the following: delirium (including delirium associated with substance intoxication/withdrawal), psychosis secondary to neurologic, medical or substance use disorder, and mood disorder with psychotic features (Arciniegas, 2015).

The DSM-5 presents the schizophrenia spectrum and other psychotic disorders along a gradient of severity. In making a diagnosis, clinicians should first exclude conditions that may not meet the full criteria for a psychotic disorder or that are limited to a single sphere of pathology. The second step is to consider conditions that are time-limited. Lastly, other conditions that could be associated with psychosis must be excluded before a diagnosis of schizophrenia spectrum disorder can be made (American Psychiatric Association, 2013).

In the initial phases of a first episode of psychosis, it may be difficult to establish with which type of psychotic disorder the person is presenting. This is because some of the criteria used to diagnose the type of psychotic disorder may not be yet known (e.g. duration and severity of symptoms). A description of the psychotic disorders enumerated in the DSM-5 is shown in Table 8.2.

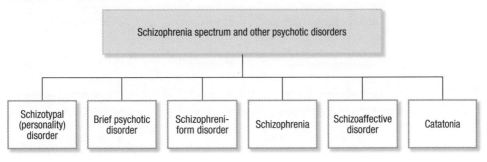

Figure 8.4: Schizophrenia spectrum and other spectrum disorders

Source: Figure created by author Jordaan reflecting information found in *Diagnostic and Statistical Manual of Mental Disorders*, fifth edition (DSM-5), 2013.

Table 8.2: Schizophrenia spectrum and other psychotic disorders in DSM-5

Diagnosis	Diagnostic features	Duration	Subtype/Specifiers
Schizotypal (personality) disorder	Listed in this category, but discussed in the section of personality disorders in the DSM-5 (see Chapter 14 of this book)		
Delusional disorder	One (or more) delusion(s)	1 month	Subtypes: Erotomanic Grandiose Jealous Persecutory Somatic Mixed Unspecified Specifier: ■ With non-bizarre content
Brief psychotic disorder	One (or more) of following symptoms: ■ Delusions ■ Hallucinations ■ Disorganised speech ■ Grossly disorganised or catatonic behaviour	Change from non-psychotic to psychotic within 2 weeks, and episode lasts for at least 1 day, but less than 1 month	Specifiers: ■ With/without marked stressors ■ With postpartum onset ■ With catatonia
Schizophreniform disorder	Two or more of the following: ■ Delusions ■ Hallucinations ■ Grossly disorganised or catatonic behaviour ■ Negative symptoms ■ No functional decline	1–6 months	Specifiers: ■ With good prognostic features ■ Without good prognostic features ■ With catatonia
Schizophrenia	Two or more of the following: ■ Delusions ■ Hallucinations ■ Disorganised speech ■ Grossly disorganised or catatonic behaviour ■ Negative symptoms	Minimum of 6 months; minimum of 1 month of active phase symptoms	A number of specifiers relating to course of disorder

Diagnosis	Diagnostic features	Duration	Subtype/Specifiers
Schizoaffective disorder	Uninterrupted period of illness during which there is a major mood episode concurrent with symptoms of schizophrenia	Minimum of 2 weeks of same period of illness of hallucinations or delusions with absence of mood symptoms; mood episode present for substantial portion of active and residual periods of illness	Specifiers: ■ Bipolar type ■ Depressive type ■ With catatonia A number of specifiers relating to course of disorder
Catatonia associated with another mental disorder	Three (or more) typical symptoms of catatonia (e.g. stupor, catalepsy, echolalia, echopraxia, etc.)		Indicate the name of the associated mental disorder
		No specifiers	Chronic where no intervention
		No specifiers	Variable (do not always fully remit if medical condition is treated)
		No specifiers	Variable

Source: Reprinted with permission from the *Diagnostic and Statistical Manual of Mental Disorders*, fifth edition (DSM-5), American Psychiatric Association (APA), 2013.

The conditions included in the schizophrenia spectrum require consideration of number, complexity, and duration of the psychotic symptoms necessary for diagnosis to increase from the mild to the severe end of the schizophrenia spectrum (American Psychiatric Association, 2013; Arciniegas, 2015). The DSM-5 also offers an eight-item Clinician-Rated Dimensions of Psychosis Symptom Severity scale in Section III that rates the severity of the defining symptoms of the schizophrenia spectrum disorders. It also rates possible cognitive and mood symptoms with a view to predicting aspects of the condition (e.g. cognitive and neurological deficits) and to assist with prognosis, treatment planning, and tracking symptoms over time (American Psychiatric Association, 2013; Arciniegas, 2015).

Schizophrenia spectrum or the other psychotic disorders are potentially serious and stigmatising diagnoses, and care should be taken when such diagnoses are made. The diagnostic process is complicated by issues such as psychotic symptoms potentially occurring in an array of physical and mental disorders, high degrees of intra-individual and inter-individual variability in symptom presentation over time, and the embeddedness of labelling behaviour as problematic or symptomatic in culture and in time (Gaebel & Zielasek, 2015; Hayes, Osborn, Lewis, Dalman, & Lundin, 2017; Singh, Mattoo, & Grover, 2016).

SCHIZOPHRENIA

History of schizophrenia

The earliest descriptions of the schizophrenic disorders were made in the early 1800s, when John Haslam (Haslam, 1809/1976) and Phillipe Pinel (Pinel, 1801/1962) described some of the symptoms as part of what Haslam termed 'a form of insanity'. It was noted that the disorder tended to have an early age of onset, typically in adolescence (Berrios, Luque, & Villagrán, 2003).

By the end of the nineteenth century, a German psychiatrist, Emil Kraepelin, translated the original French term to *dementia praecox*, again pointing out the characteristic cognitive aspects (*dementia*) and age of onset (*praecox*) of the condition. Kraepelin also described the characteristic course of the disorder, which involves deterioration over a period of time. Very importantly, he distinguished between this condition and manic (bipolar) psychosis.

Kraepelin's second major contribution was the idea that various manifestations of the condition (e.g. catatonia and paranoia), which were earlier regarded as being distinct disorders in themselves, were variations of *dementia praecox*. Kraepelin distinguished hallucinations, delusions, and a decline in cognitive functioning as symptoms of the disorder. He ascribed the condition to a type of organic decline and considered the prognosis to be poor (Cranco & Lehman, 2000).

Eugen Bleuler was a Swiss psychiatrist who first coined the term schizophrenia in 1911. This term replaced *dementia praecox*. Bleuler's definition of schizophrenia was wider than that of Kraepelin. This was because he regarded both the age of onset and the course of the disorder as being more fluid. Bleuler also differed from Kraepelin in that he believed that schizophrenia did not always imply a course marked by deterioration.

Bleuler used the term 'schizophrenia' ('split mind') to allude to the break between thought, emotion, and behaviour that characterises the disorder (Cranco & Lehman, 2000; Daubenton & Van Rensburg, 2001). The 'splitting' refers to the split between intellect, emotion, behaviour, and external reality, rather than the 'split' or multiple personalities seen in dissociative identity disorder (see Chapter 10).

Bleuler described four fundamental or primary symptoms of schizophrenia (the four A's): autism (self-focus), associations ('loose' or unconnected ideas), affective disturbances (emotional inappropriateness), and ambivalence (lack of resolve over actions). Bleuler regarded hallucinations and delusions as secondary symptoms of the disturbance, differing again from Kraepelin, who viewed delusions and hallucinations as distinguishing features (Cranco & Lehman, 2000; Daubenton & Van Rensburg, 2001).

Internationally, a discrepancy arose in the diagnosis of the schizophrenic disorders, since practitioners in the United States tended to follow Bleuler's broader approach, while European practitioners utilised Kraepelin's view. Before the publication of the DSM-III, this resulted in almost twice as many diagnoses of schizophrenia in the United States compared to Europe (Cranco & Lehman, 2000). The DSM-I and DSM-II utilised the four A's and Bleuler's approach. The DSM-III thus moved towards a more restrictive definition of the disorder. This trend continued in the DSM-III-R (Cranco & Lehman, 2000; Daubenton & Van Rensburg, 2001) and has also continued in the DSM-5.

One of the biggest changes in the classification of this disorder, from DSM-IV-TR to

DSM-5, was the elimination of the subtypes of schizophrenia (i.e. paranoid, disorganised, catatonic, undifferentiated, and residual types). This was done because the subtypes were demonstrated to have limited diagnostic stability, low reliability, and poor validity, and did not show differences in treatment responses, nor in terms of the course of the disorders. Rather than distinguishing between different subtypes, the DSM-5 adopts a more dimensional approach where the symptoms are rated in terms of severity (American Psychiatric Association, 2013).

Prevalence and course

Schizophrenia has a similar prevalence worldwide, which appears to be in the 0.3%–0.7% range for the adult population (American Psychiatric Association, 2013). The prevalence is somewhat greater in men, particularly in instances where sampling emphasises longer duration and negative symptoms, whereas similar sex ratios for males and females are found when samples allow for the inclusion of mood-related symptoms and brief presentations. Some variations in prevalence appear to exist across race/ethnicity, country, and country of origin for immigrants and their children (American Psychiatric Association, 2013).

The manifestation of schizophrenia can be gradual or rapid. In the majority of cases, there appears to be a gradual onset (prodromal phase) characterised by the appearance and escalation of symptoms (see Figure 8.5). The typical age of onset is in the early to mid-20s for males and in the late 20s for females. An early age of onset is associated with a generally poor prognosis, although this effect may be gender-related, with generally worse premorbid functioning and outcomes for males, whereas females are more at risk for late onset (onset after 40 years of age).

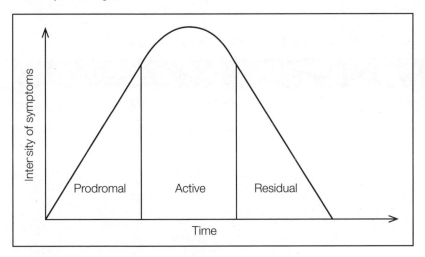

Figure 8.5: Pathway of development of a psychotic episode

Source: Created by author Burke.

The onset of distinct psychotic symptoms characterises active-phase schizophrenia. The course of the disorder appears to differ between individuals, with some presenting with relapses and remissions, while others remain chronically ill. Remission occurs when a person's symptoms reduce and their condition improves. In addition, some individuals remain relatively stable, while others progressively decline. It appears that the negative symptoms persist and become gradually more obvious in some individuals during the course of the disorder (American Psychiatric Association, 2013).

The predictors of the course and outcome of schizophrenia are largely unknown, and only about 20% of those diagnosed with this disorder show a favourable outcome. Although psychotic symptoms may diminish with age, cognitive impairments persist (American Psychiatric Association, 2013). The length of duration of psychosis has been increasingly emphasised as a factor that impacts the course of the disorder. Indications are that a longer duration of untreated psychosis is associated with a poorer treatment response. A shorter duration of untreated psychosis usually predicts a better response to antipsychotic medication, and consequently less severe overall psychopathology, fewer positive symptoms, fewer negative symptoms, and better functioning (Perkins, Gu, Boteva, & Lieberman, 2005).

Schizophrenia in childhood has the same central features as in adulthood, but diagnosis is more difficult, and symptoms such as delusions and hallucinations should be distinguished from normal fantasy play. Similarly, some symptoms frequently occur in other disorders with childhood onset, such as disorganised speech (e.g. in autism spectrum disorder) and disorganised behaviour (e.g. in attention-deficit/hyperactivity disorder), and these conditions should be duly considered in the diagnostic process. Non-specific emotional-behavioural difficulties, as well as challenges in the areas of motor, language, and intellectual development, are more likely to precede a diagnosis of schizophrenia in childhood (American Psychiatric Association, 2013).

Table 8.3: Distribution of outcome categories of chronic and acute onset

Chronic onset	Acute onset
Complete remission: 0%	Complete remission: 33%
Partial remission: 18%	Partial remission: 27%
No remission: 82%	No remission: 40%

Source: Adapted from Eggers & Bunk, 1997.

CLINICAL PICTURE

Schizophrenia

CASE STUDY

Schizophrenia

Gina is a 32-year-old woman who is currently admitted in a psychiatric hospital. She was hospitalised after she left home suddenly in the middle of the night after a disagreement with her mother. Her family were alarmed because she had not left the house unaccompanied in the last three years. She drove around aimlessly for hours and was found in a dangerous part of the city, confused about where she was. Gina had been a top student at university and had several high-paying jobs in the information technology field until a few years before her hospitalisation. She struggled to remain in any position for long, however. She blamed her managers, who were 'too demanding', as well as her colleagues, who were 'out to get her'. She believed that her manager at her last place of employment had devised ways to listen in on her conversations, film her at work, and had even installed cameras in her home. She had to undress in the dark for fear that her image would be broadcast on the Internet by her former manager.

Gina had become increasingly religious, although she was no longer motivated to attend church. She heard the voices of angels and demons and believed that she was being singled out for attack by demons. She sometimes sent former acquaintances and colleagues long rambling messages about her powers and the spiritual messages that she received in the early morning hours from her pet cat's eyes. Her sisters found it difficult to follow conversations with Gina because she tended to go off on tangents that were unrelated to their original topics. She also had a habit of making up her own words to express herself. Gina had gained 40 kilograms and had become unrecognisable since her days at university. As a student she had a fashionable 'funky' hairstyle, wore colourful outfits, and enjoyed experimenting with make-up; however, in recent years she only bathed or washed her hair when forced to do so by her mother. Gina's family were generally supportive. Her father was a stern and withdrawn man who rarely spoke or smiled and her mother a tired-looking, but kindly, woman who worried that Gina was becoming 'just like her mad aunt'.

The symptoms of schizophrenia impact the cognitive, behavioural, and emotional functioning of an individual, including thought, perception, attention, motor behaviour, affect, emotion, and life functioning. These effects typically result in gross impairment in the areas of occupational and social functioning. Although a great variety of symptoms are possible in individuals with schizophrenia, it is rare for one person to display all of these difficulties at once.

Unlike most of the diagnostic categories discussed in this text, the diagnosis of schizophrenia does not have an essential or core symptom that is required in order to make the diagnosis (American Psychiatric Association, 2013). However, as highlighted in the case study of Gina, schizophrenia is regarded in DSM-5, ICD-10 (World Health Organization, 2007), and ICD-11 (World Health Organization, 2018c) terms as a psychotic disorder, implying the presence of hallucinations, delusions, disorganised speech, and/or disorganised behaviour (see Table 8.4).

Table 8.4: General diagnostic criteria for schizophrenia from the DSM-5 and ICD-10

DSM-5	ICD-10
A. Two (or more) of the following, each present for a significant portion of time during a one-month period (or less if successfully treated). At least one of these must be (1), (2), or (3): (1) Delusions. (2) Hallucinations. (3) Disorganised speech (e.g. frequent derailment or incoherence). (4) Grossly disorganised or catatonic behaviour. (5) Negative symptoms (i.e. diminished emotional expression or avolition). B. For a significant portion of time since the onset of the disturbance, level of functioning in one or more major areas, such as work, interpersonal relations, or self-care, is markedly below the level achieved prior to the event (or, when the onset is in childhood or adolescence, there is failure to achieve expected level of interpersonal, academic, or occupational functioning). C. Continuous signs of the disturbance persist for at least six months. This six-month period must include at least one month of symptoms (or less if successfully treated) that meet Criterion A (i.e. active-phase symptoms) and may include periods of prodromal or residual symptoms. During these promodal or residual periods, the signs of the disturbance may be manifested by only negative symptoms or two or more symptoms listed in Criterion A present in an attenuated form (e.g. odd beliefs, unusual perceptual experiences).	■ The normal requirement for a diagnosis of schizophrenia is that a minimum of one very clear symptom (and usually two or more if less clear-cut) belonging to any one of the groups listed as (a) to (d) below, or symptoms from at least two of the groups referred to as (e) to (h), should have been clearly present for most of the time during a period of one month or more. ■ Conditions meeting such symptomatic requirements but of duration less than one month (whether treated or not) should be diagnosed in the first instance as acute schizophrenia-like psychotic disorder and are classified as schizophrenia if the symptoms persist for longer periods: (a) thought echo, thought insertion or withdrawal, and thought broadcasting; (b) delusions of control, influence, or passivity, clearly referred to body or limb movements or specific thoughts, actions, or sensations; delusional perception; (c) hallucinatory voices giving a running commentary on the patient's behaviour, or discussing the patient among themselves, or other types of hallucinatory voices coming from some part of the body; (d) persistent delusions of other kinds that are culturally inappropriate and completely impossible, such as religious or political identity, or superhuman powers and abilities (e.g. being able to control the weather, or being in communication with aliens from another world);

DSM-5	ICD-10
D. Schizoaffective disorder and depressive or bipolar disorder with psychotic features have been ruled out because either: 1) no major depressive or manic episodes have occurred concurrently with the active-phase symptoms, or 2) if mood episodes have occurred during the active-phase symptoms, they have been present for a minority of the total duration of the active and residual periods of the illness. E. The disturbance is not attributable to the physiological effects of a substance (e.g. a drug of abuse, or medication) or another medical condition. F. If there is a history of autism spectrum disorder or a communication disorder of childhood onset, the additional diagnosis of schizophrenia is made only if prominent delusions or hallucinations, in addition to the other required symptoms of schizophrenia, are also present for at least one month (or less if successfully treated).	(e) persistent hallucinations in any modality, when accompanied either by fleeting or half-formed delusions without clear affective content, or by persistent over-valued ideas, or when occurring every day for weeks or months on end; (f) breaks or interpolations in the train of thought, resulting in incoherence or irrelevant speech, or neologisms; (g) catatonic behaviour, such as excitement, posturing, or waxy flexibility, negativism, mutism, and stupor; (h) 'negative' symptoms such as marked apathy, paucity of speech, and blunting or incongruity of emotional responses, usually resulting in social withdrawal and lowering of social performance; it must be clear that these are not due to depression or to neuroleptic medication; (i) a significant and consistent change in the overall quality of some aspects of personal behaviour, manifest as loss of interest, aimlessness, idleness, a self-absorbed attitude, and social withdrawal. ■ The diagnosis of schizophrenia should not be made in the presence of extensive depressive or manic symptoms or if it occurs in the presence of overt brain disease or during states of drug intoxication or withdrawal.

Source: Reprinted with permission from the *Diagnostic and Statistical Manual of Mental Disorders* (DSM), fifth edition, American Psychiatric Association (APA), 2013, p. 99, *and Classification of Mental and Behavioural Disorders: Diagnostic Criteria for Research*, tenth revision (ICD-10), World Health Organization (WHO), Geneva, 2007.

Up to now, we have referred to psychosis as the main feature of schizophrenia; however, we need to remember that psychosis refers to a number of symptoms (or, in some cases, clusters of symptoms), and that not all the symptoms of psychosis are present in all people. In fact, the different subtypes of psychotic disorders are characterised by different signs and symptoms of psychosis; that is, different disorders have different symptoms and, within these, individuals show variation in their symptom presentation. One approach to these symptoms is to divide them into two broad categories: positive symptoms (active symptoms) and negative symptoms (the absence or decrease of normal functions).

Positive symptoms

The positive symptoms of schizophrenia have an active presentation and can be seen as an excess or distortion of behaviour. These symptoms are characteristic of the active or acute phase of the disorder. The positive symptoms comprise hallucinations and delusions, as well as grossly disorganised behaviour (including catatonia) and disorganised speech (American Psychiatric Association, 2013).

Hallucinations

Hallucinations are sensory events that take place in the absence of environmental stimuli. Hallucinations can therefore be regarded as distortions of perception (see Table 8.5).

Table 8.5: Summary of types of hallucinations

Sense	Hallucination	Associated with	Description
Hearing	Auditory hallucination	Most common in many psychiatric disorders such as schizophrenia	False perception of sound most commonly, but not limited to, voices.
Vision	Visual hallucination	Most common in medical disorders	False perception of images which may be formed (e.g. people) or unformed (e.g. flashes of light).
Taste	Gustatory hallucination	Most common in medical disorders	False perception of (unpleasant) taste.
Smell	Olfactory hallucination	Most common in medical conditions (e.g. epilepsy)	False perception of smell.
Touch	Tactile (haptic) hallucination	Psychotic disorders such as schizophrenia	False perception of touch or surface sensation (e.g. phantom limb after an amputation or sense of insects crawling on or under skin).
	Somatic (kinaesthetic) hallucination	Psychotic disorders	False perception of things occurring to or in the body.

Source: Kaplan et al., 1994, p. 307.

Although any of the senses may be affected, auditory hallucinations (hearing sounds or voices that other people cannot hear) are the most common hallucination in schizophrenia (Sartorius, Shapiro, & Jablonsky, 1974) and often involve the hearing of voices. The voice may appear to come from either inside or outside one's head; a voice coming from outside the person's head is generally considered more severe. The voices may be male or female, recognised as the voice of someone familiar or not recognised as familiar, and may be critical or positive. The content of what the voices say is usually unpleasant and negative.

Typically, the voices are heard conversing and/or commenting. When the voices comment, the comments are usually about the person's behaviour or thoughts, typically in the third person (such as, 'Isn't she stupid?'). Sometimes the voices provide a 'running commentary' on the person's behaviour as it occurs ('She is cooking.'). At other times, the voices may instruct the person to do something, and these are commonly known as 'command' hallucinations. These experiences can be very frightening and upsetting to the individual experiencing them.

Research utilising brain imagery to observe brain activity of people experiencing auditory hallucinations implicates the speech centre of the brain, Broca's area, in the generation of auditory hallucinations, and not Wernicke's area, the area of the brain involved in language comprehension (Cleghorn et al., 1992; McGuire, Shah, & Murray, 1993). This implies that auditory hallucinations involve listening to one's own thoughts, rather than hearing the voices of others.

Delusions

Delusions are beliefs that are firmly held contrary to reality and contrary to what most members of a society would regard as reality. Garety (1991) defines delusions as false personal beliefs that are firmly and consistently held despite logic or experiences to the contrary.

Several types of delusion were first described by a German psychiatrist, Kurt Schneider (1959). These are:

- *Delusions of persecution:* A belief that others are plotting against, mistreating, or even attempting to murder you; the belief that others are 'out to get you'
- *Delusions of thought broadcasting:* The belief that others know what you are thinking
- *Delusions of control:* The belief that an outside agency is attempting to influence or control you
- *Delusions of grandeur:* The belief that you are a powerful or famous person
- *Delusions of reference:* The belief that all that is happening involves or alludes to yourself
- *Thought withdrawal:* The belief that your thoughts are being removed from your mind by an external force.

Since the work of Schneider (1959) a number of additional delusions have been identified (see Table 8.6).

Table 8.6: Summary of delusions

Type	Subtype	Description
Nihilistic		The self, others, or the world are non-existing or ending.
Poverty		One either has no material possessions or one will be deprived of them.

Type	Subtype	Description
Somatic		Beliefs about one's body functions (e.g. 'My brain is rotting.'). Not to be confused with somatic hallucination.
Paranoid	Persecution	One is being persecuted or victimised.
	Grandeur	Exaggerated sense of own worth, powers, or identity.
	Reference	Events or others' behaviour has a significant, negative meaning.
Self-accusation		Feelings of remorse or guilt for events for which one cannot possibly be responsible.
Control	Thought withdrawal	Belief that one's thoughts are being extracted by others.
	Though insertion	Belief that thoughts are being planted into one's head by others.
	Thought broadcasting	Belief that one's thoughts are being broadcasted so that others are can know them.
	Thought control	Other people have control over one's thoughts.
Infidelity		Extreme pathological jealousy.

Source: Adapted from Kaplan et al., 1994, pp. 305–306.

Of the types of delusion discussed above, delusions of persecution are the most common to schizophrenia (Sartorius et al., 1974). Research suggests that delusions may differ in the impact they have on a person's life in that they vary in strength and disruptiveness (Brett-Jones, Garety, & Hemsley, 1987; Howard, 1992). The delusions of individuals with a diagnosis of schizophrenia are typically of a more bizarre (highly implausible) nature than those of other diagnostic categories (Junginger, Barker, & Coe 1992).

CASE STUDY

Example of a delusion

Thandi believes that she has been admitted to a psychiatric ward because the chief psychiatrist is secretly conspiring with a political organisation that wants to know what she is thinking. In order to read her mind, 'they' inserted a device under the nail of her left big toe. This device enables 'them' to listen in on her thoughts.

Disorganised thinking (speech)

This set of symptoms was first described by Bleuler in 1911 and is also known as 'formal thought disorder'. This is regarded as characteristic of schizophrenia. Disorganisation of speech can be defined as verbal communication in the known language of the individual which does not conform to the linguistic rules that govern the language. It is not due to intellectual, educational, or cultural disadvantage.

These unusual patterns of speech and writing result in verbal communication that holds little or no meaning for others. The listener experiences conversations with these individuals as illogical, and they may rapidly move between topics. People with schizophrenia usually lack insight into their condition (i.e. they are unaware of the problem themselves). Disorganised speech in schizophrenia can take on various forms:

- *Loosening of associations:* This is also referred to as cognitive slippage or derailment. Loosening of associations entails the person moving between unrelated ideas in conversation. Speech may be incoherent and responses may be bizarre and idiosyncratic. The presence of loosening of associations is regarded as one of the most valuable diagnostic distinctions in the diagnosis of schizophrenia.
- *Problems with attention:* This involves an inability to direct sustained focus to a single aspect of the environment or to organise environmental inputs (Cranco & Lehman, 2000).
- *Neologisms:* The speech of some people with a diagnosis of schizophrenia may contain new words that are combinations of words in common usage.

> **EXAMPLE CASE**
>
> **Interviewer:** Sam, can you tell me why you were admitted to hospital?
> **Sam:** I don't have time to be in hospital. The time has come for me. When time is right ... Time waits for no man!
> *Note that Sam did not answer the question asked. Going off on a tangent and not answering the question is called 'tangentiality'. He also suddenly shifted between topics in the conversation, talking about unrelated areas. This is called 'loosening of associations' or 'derailment'.*
> **Interviewer:** I believe that your mother has been to visit you?
> **Sam:** Mom was here. Here today, gone tomorrow. Mom and I enjoy baking cakes together. Mom is going to take me shopping. We'll buy up a storm, and bake up a storm and shake up a storm. Our cakes are fabulicious. There was a cake sale at church. The sermon on Sunday was about the Lion and the Lamb. The Lion and the Lamb shall be together ...
> *Sam again did not answer the question. It is not clear whether he did not understand the question, struggled to focus his attention, or did not want talk about his mother. Sam's use of the word 'fabulicious' is an example of a neologism, a combination of 'fabulous' and 'delicious'.*

Disorganised or catatonic behaviour

The activity levels (motor functions) of some people with a diagnosis of schizophrenia may range from unusually high or unusually low, to the bizarre. Manifestations may include agitation, catatonia, or stereotyped movements. Agitation is shown when a person paces about rapidly, talking fast and non-stop, with arms swinging. Catatonia involves remaining in unusual physical postures for extended periods of time. Inappropriate affect, the display of emotions that are unrelated or inappropriate to those expected in a given situation, may also be present (Cranco & Lehman, 2000).

Negative symptoms

Negative symptoms have long been acknowledged as a core component of schizophrenia (Marder & Galderisi, 2017). The negative symptoms of schizophrenia refer to the absence of behaviours generally expected in a person. This term therefore refers to a deficit in usual behaviours such as social interaction with others and the display of emotions. The presence of negative symptoms is generally associated with reduced everyday functioning and a poor prognosis. The five constructs that comprise the negative symptoms of schizophrenia are reduced emotional expression (blunted affect), poverty of thought and speech (alogia), reduced ability to experience emotions (anhedonia), social and emotional withdrawal (asociality), and apathy (avolition) (Carpenter, 1992; Marder & Galderisi, 2017). These are described below.

Blunted affect

This feature of schizophrenia is also referred to as 'emotional blunting', with the term 'flat affect' referring to the extreme end of the range of reduced emotional expression. Blunted affect is an absence of the spontaneous emotional reactions usually expected from people. This includes a lack of facial expression, poor eye contact, a toneless voice, and an absence of emotional responses to the events in the person's environment (Marder & Galderisi, 2017).

Alogia

Alogia refers to a restriction in the amount or content of spontaneous speech a person produces. The term is derived from the Latin *a* (without) and *logica* (reason). People who display this symptom may be very brief and monosyllabic in their responses in conversation. Their responses may also be slow or delayed, and they appear to have little interest in the conversation. Alogia is also sometimes referred to as 'poverty of speech' (Marder & Galderisi, 2017).

Anhedonia

Anhedonia is a reduced ability to experience pleasure or pleasant emotions. Anhedonia is a central element of both depression and schizophrenia. It comprises both the reduction in capacity to experience pleasure from ongoing activities and a decreased ability to anticipate pleasure in future. These deficits may be related to some aspects of motivation (Marder & Galderisi, 2017).

Asociality

Asociality is a decreased need for close relationships with others, which leads to reduced social initiative and a reduction in motivation for social interactions. Asociality is often present before the onset of schizophrenia and is also found in schizoid personality disorder and in autism (Marder & Galderisi, 2017).

Avolition

Avolition is a reduction in initiation and persistence of goal-directed behaviour, in other words, a difficulty in starting and continuing actions. These actions include aspects of everyday life that are usually taken for granted by most people (e.g. self-care and personal hygiene). The person appears to lack the motivation or ability to engage in self-directed behaviour (Marder & Galderisi, 2017).

EXAMPLE CASE

Interviewer: Do you have brothers or sisters?
Zandile: Yes.
Interviewer: How many brothers or sisters do you have?
Zandile: Two.

The example above illustrates the brief answers and apparent lack of interest in the conversation associated with alogia. A more usual response would be: 'Yes, I have one brother and one sister. I am the middle child. My brother lives in Durban and my sister has passed away.'

Schizophrenia subtypes in the ICD-10

Although the DSM-5 no longer differentiates between subtypes of schizophrenia, the ICD-10 does. The ICD-10 classification places the diagnosis in the 'schizophrenia, schizotypal, and delusional disorders' category. The ICD-10 requirements are that a diagnosis should meet the general criteria for schizophrenia (Table 8.4) and specifies course subtypes (World Health Organization, 1992). The ICD-10 lists the subtypes of schizophrenia as the following: paranoid schizophrenia; hebephrenic schizophrenia; catatonic schizophrenia; undifferentiated schizophrenia; post-schizophrenic depression; residual schizophrenia; simple schizophrenia; other schizophrenia and schizophrenia, unspecified (World Health Organization, 2016). These subtypes relate to the most prominent symptoms present in an individual at the time of diagnosis.

Paranoid schizophrenia

This subtype appears to be the most prevalent form of schizophrenia. The ICD-10 describes the most salient features of this subtype as the presence of significant delusions and auditory hallucinations with relatively intact affective and cognitive functioning (see Table 8.7).

In the case of delusions, these may be multiple, but typically share a common theme. In paranoid schizophrenia, the content of hallucinations usually relates to the theme of the delusions (World Health Organization, 1992, 2016).

Hebephrenic schizophrenia

This subtype is characterised by a disorganisation in speech, thought, and behaviour; in addition, flat or inappropriate affect and severe disintegration and regression to disinhibited, unorganised behaviour are associated with this subtype. Hallucinations and delusions, if present, are characterised by shifting themes and fragmented content (Cranco & Lehman, 2000; World Health Organization, 2016).

Catatonic schizophrenia

Catatonia includes a wide range of psychomotor impairments. These disturbances can range from extreme activity to complete immobility. Seemingly involuntary movements, echolalia, and echopraxia may be present. Echolalia presents as the senseless and parrot-like repetition of a phrase just uttered by another person, while echopraxia involves imitating the movements of others (American Psychiatric Association, 2000; World Health Organization, 2016).

Undifferentiated schizophrenia

This subtype is diagnosed in individuals who clearly meet the general criteria for schizophrenia, but where a mixed presentation excludes them from the paranoid, catatonic, and disorganised subtypes (World Health Organization, 2016).

Post-schizophrenic depression

This subtype is diagnosed in the presence of a depressive episode arising from schizophrenic illness where persisting symptoms of schizophrenia remain, but do not overshadow the clinical presentation (World Health Organization, 2016).

Residual schizophrenia

Residual schizophrenia is diagnosed in the chronic phase of schizophrenia where the person has a history of psychosis, but is presenting currently with negative symptoms (World Health Organization, 2016).

Simple schizophrenia

Simple schizophrenia has prominent negative symptoms that present early and is marked by rapid deterioration in functioning. This is a rare subtype characterised by the features of the residual subtype in the absence of clear episodes of psychosis (World Health Organization, 2016).

Other schizophrenia

This subtype includes cenesthopathic schizophrenia (characterised by the experience of unusual bodily sensations) and schizophreniform disorder not otherwise specified (World Health Organization, 2016).

Unspecified schizophrenia

Symptoms of Schizophrenia are present, but do not meet the criteria of any of the schizophrenia subtypes (World Health Organization, 1992).

The ICD-10 will remain in use until 2022, when it will be replaced by the ICD-11. The ICD-11 replaces the ICD-10 category of 'schizophrenia, schizotypal and delusional disorders' with a category termed 'schizophrenia and other primary psychotic disorders', where 'primary' is indicative of psychosis as the central feature (Reed et al., 2019). The most important difference between ICD-10 and ICD-11 is the elimination of the schizophrenia subtypes as a result of their low predictive and treatment selection utility. The symptoms of schizophrenia remain largely the same as for the ICD-10, but dimensional descriptors are included. The dimensional descriptors in ICD-11 include positive symptoms, negative symptoms, depressive mood symptoms, manic mood symptoms, psychomotor symptoms, and cognitive symptoms (Reed et al., 2019).

The ICD-11 introduces a new diagnostic grouping for catatonia, acknowledging that catatonia is associated with a range of mental disorders; this is in contrast to ICD-10, which included catatonia as a schizophrenia subtype and as 'organic catatonic disorder', one of the organic disorders grouping (Reed et al., 2019).

Table 8.7: Diagnostic criteria for paranoid schizophrenia from the ICD-10

ICD-10

■ The general criteria for a diagnosis of schizophrenia must be satisfied. The clinical picture is dominated by relatively stable, often paranoid, delusions, usually accompanied by hallucinations, particularly of the auditory variety, and perceptual disturbances. Disturbances of affect, volition, and speech, and catatonic symptoms, are not prominent.
■ Examples of the most common paranoid symptoms are:
  ▸ delusions of persecution, reference, exalted birth, special mission, bodily change, or jealousy;
  ▸ hallucinatory voices that threaten the patient or give commands, or auditory hallucinations without verbal form, such as whistling, humming, or laughing;
  ▸ hallucinations of smell or taste, or of sexual or other bodily sensations; visual hallucinations may occur but are rarely predominant.
■ Thought disorder may be obvious in acute states, but if so, it does not prevent the typical delusions or hallucinations from being described clearly. Affect is usually less blunted than in other varieties of schizophrenia, but a minor degree of incongruity is common, as are mood disturbances such as irritability, sudden anger, fearfulness, and suspicion. 'Negative' symptoms such as blunting of affect and impaired volition are often present but do not dominate the clinical picture.

Source: Reprinted with permission from the *Classification of Mental and Behavioural Disorders: Diagnostic Criteria for Research*, tenth revision (ICD-10), World Health Organization (WHO), Geneva, 2007.

Table 8.8: Diagnostic criteria for hebephrenic schizophrenia from the ICD-10

ICD-10

■ A form of schizophrenia in which affective changes are prominent, delusions and hallucinations fleeting and fragmentary, behaviour irresponsible and unpredictable, and mannerisms common. For a confident diagnosis of hebephrenia, a period of two or three months of continuous observation is usually necessary, in order to ensure that the characteristic behaviours are sustained.
  ▸ The mood is shallow and inappropriate and often accompanied by giggling or self-satisfied, self-absorbed smiling, or by a lofty manner, grimaces, mannerisms, pranks, hypochondriacal complaints, and reiterated phrases.
  ▸ Thought is disorganised and speech rambling and incoherent.
  ▸ There is a tendency to remain solitary, and behaviour seems empty of purpose and feeling.
■ In addition, disturbances of affect and volition, and thought disorder are usually prominent. Hallucinations and delusions may be present but are not usually prominent.

ICD-10
▪ Drive and determination are lost and goals abandoned, so that the patient's behaviour becomes characteristically aimless and empty of purpose. ▪ A superficial and manneristic preoccupation with religion, philosophy, and other abstract themes may add to the listener's difficulty in following the train of thought.

Source: Reprinted with permission from the ICD-10 *Classification of Mental and Behavioural Disorders: Diagnostic Criteria for Research*, World Health Organization (WHO), Geneva, 2007.

Table 8.9: Diagnostic criteria for undifferentiated schizophrenia from the ICD-10

ICD-10

▪ Conditions meeting the general diagnostic criteria for schizophrenia but not conforming to any of the above subtypes, or exhibiting the features of more than one of them without a clear predominance of a particular set of diagnostic characteristics. This rubric should be used only for psychotic conditions (i.e. residual schizophrenia and post-schizophrenia depression are excluded) and after an attempt has been made to classify the condition into one of the three preceding categories.
▪ Diagnostic guidelines: This category should be reserved for disorders that:
  ▸ meet the diagnostic criteria for schizophrenia;
  ▸ do not satisfy the criteria for the paranoid, hebephrenic, or catatonic subtypes;
  ▸ do not satisfy the criteria for residual schizophrenia or post-schizophrenia depression

Source: Reprinted with permission from the ICD-10 *Classification of Mental and Behavioural Disorders: Diagnostic Criteria for Research*, World Health Organization (WHO), Geneva, 2007.

Table 8.10: Diagnostic criteria for catatonic schizophrenia from the ICD-10

ICD-10

▪ The general criteria for a diagnosis of schizophrenia must be satisfied. Transitory and isolated catatonic symptoms may occur in the context of any other subtype of schizophrenia, but for a diagnosis of catatonic schizophrenia one or more of the following behaviours should dominate the clinical picture:
  ▸ stupor (marked decrease in reactivity to the environment and in spontaneous movements and activity) or mutism;
  ▸ excitement (apparently purposeless motor activity, not influenced by external stimuli);
  ▸ posturing (voluntary assumption and maintenance of inappropriate or bizarre postures);
  ▸ negativism (an apparently motiveless resistance to all instructions or attempts to be moved, or movement in the opposite direction);
  ▸ rigidity (maintenance of a rigid posture against efforts to be moved);
  ▸ waxy flexibility (maintenance of limbs and body in externally imposed positions); and
  ▸ other symptoms such as command automatism (automatic compliance with instructions), and perseveration of words and phrases.

Source: Reprinted with permission from ICD-10 *Classification of Mental and Behavioural Disorders: Diagnostic Criteria for Research*, World Health Organization (WHO), Geneva, 2007.

Other schizophrenia spectrum and psychotic disorders

Schizotypal personality disorder

Although this is a personality disorder (see Chapter 14), the DSM-5 notes it in this category as it considers it to be part of the schizophrenia spectrum disorders (American Psychiatric Association, 2013). Schizotypal personality disorder represents the less severe end of the schizophrenia spectrum disorders and is defined by a pervasive pattern of interpersonal and social deficits associated with a reduced capacity for or intense discomfort with close relationships.

Cognitive distortions, such as ideas of reference, odd beliefs, magical thinking, and paranoia, as well as perceptual disturbances such as bodily illusions, may be present. Eccentricities of behaviour and appearance, 'odd' thinking and speech, inappropriate or constricted affect, an absence of close friends, and increased social anxiety that persists even with familiarity may also be present (American Psychiatric Association, 2013; Arciniegas, 2015).

Delusional disorder

The essential feature of this disorder is the presence of one (or more) delusions that persists for at least a month without prominent hallucinations. If hallucinations occur, these are related to the theme of the delusion. The DSM-5 specifies erotomanic, grandiose, jealous, persecutory, somatic, mixed, and unspecified subtypes (American Psychiatric Association, 2013).

Brief psychotic disorder

The essential features of this disorder are that it involves the sudden onset of positive symptoms of psychosis (i.e. delusions, hallucinations or disorganised speech), or abnormal psychomotor behaviour (such as catatonia). The psychosis develops suddenly (a shift from a non-psychotic state to a psychotic state in a period of two weeks), without a prodromal phase, and lasts at least a day, but not more than a month, with full recovery of premorbid functioning. The DSM-5 includes as specifiers the presence of marked stressors (brief reactive psychosis), the absence of stressors, and the presence of catatonia (American Psychiatric Association, 2013).

Schizophreniform disorder

The symptoms of this disorder are identical to those of schizophrenia, with the main difference between the two disorders being duration, with schizophreniform disorder lasting at least one month, but no longer six months. This disorder follows the same pattern as that of schizophrenia (i.e. prodromal, acute, and residual phases). As with brief psychotic disorder, a specifier for the presence of comorbid catatonia has been added in DSM-5 (American Psychiatric Association, 2013).

Schizoaffective disorder

This disorder can best be understood as an overlap between schizophrenia and a mood disorder. Although this disorder requires that the person displays symptoms of schizophrenia, the symptoms of a major mood episode (depressive or bipolar) must be present for the majority of the total duration of the disorder (American Psychiatric Association, 2013).

Other specified schizophrenia spectrum and other psychotic disorders

This sub-category provides for the diagnosis of conditions where the symptoms characteristic of the schizophrenia spectrum and other psychotic disorders cause significant distress or functional impairment, but do not meet the full diagnostic criteria. The DSM-5 specifies four conditions that require the 'other specified' designation:

- persistent auditory hallucinations
- delusions with significantly overlapping mood episodes
- attenuated psychosis syndrome
- delusional disorder in a partner of an individual with delusional disorder (American Psychiatric Association, 2013).

Unspecified schizophrenia spectrum and other psychotic disorders

This diagnosis is made in presentations of symptoms characteristic of the schizophrenia spectrum and other psychotic disorders that cause clinically significant distress and functional impairment that do not meet the full criteria for other diagnoses in this category or where more information is required before a more specific diagnosis can be made (American Psychiatric Association, 2013).

Violence risk and mortality risk

As for many other aspects related to the presentation of schizophrenia, the issue of violence risk (suicide and violence towards others) in people diagnosed with schizophrenia is potentially controversial and far from clear cut.

The issue of violence risk, particularly to others, in people with schizophrenia is coloured by media portrayals of people with mental illness. Media often depict people with mental illness as being prone to violence, and more dangerous than the rest of the population. These portrayals are not always accurate reflections of reality, since research evidence on this issue is mixed (Lindquist & Allebeck, 1990; Steadman & Ribner, 1980). Issues of stigma are also exacerbated by public perceptions that people diagnosed with schizophrenia are aggressive or violent (Torrey, 2011). It should be noted that people living with schizophrenia are also more likely than the general population to be subjected to violent victimisation (Latalova, Kamaradova, & Prasko, 2014).

It is difficult to predict when or how a person with a diagnosis of schizophrenia will act in a dangerous or violent way towards to others (see Chapter 5). Individuals with a diagnosis of schizophrenia do pose a greater potential risk for violence than many other categories of disorder (Cranco & Lehman, 2000). There is an association between schizophrenia and other psychotic conditions, and violence and violent offending, especially homicide. However, the elevated risk appears to be strongly associated with substance abuse comorbidity (Fazel, Gulati, Linsell, Geddes, & Grann, 2009).

Those diagnosed with paranoid delusions may pose a particular risk, since they may act rapidly and unpredictably in response to a delusion or a perceived threat. The risk is greater in individuals whose functioning remains intact enough to be able to create and execute plans of attack. This would not typically be true of people with disorganised behaviour symptoms, for instance, because they are unlikely to be able to organise their thoughts and behaviour sufficiently to carry out a planned attack (Cranco & Lehman, 2000).

Persons with a schizophrenia diagnosis have a significantly elevated risk for premature death, both from natural and unnatural causes. In the United States, adults diagnosed with schizophrenia pass away at a rate that is 3.5 times greater than that of the general population (Olfson, Gerhard, Huang, Crystal, & Stroup, 2015). The reduction of life expectancy for people diagnosed with schizophrenia is 10 to 25 years (Laursen, Munk-Olsen, & Vestergaard, 2012).

The rates for medical illness and mortality in patients with schizophrenia are also significantly higher than those in the general population (Goff et al., 2005). Elevated risk of accidental death and increased risk of death by suicide contribute to the increased mortality rate due to unnatural causes, with 28% of the increased mortality rate being associated with suicide, and accidents accounting for 12% of the elevation. The remainder of the mortality rate is associated with the range of conditions that cause death in the general population (Brown, 1997; Olfson et al., 2015).

When considering suicide risk, it should be noted that up to 20% of individuals with this diagnosis attempt suicide more than once, and 5%–6% of people with a schizophrenia diagnosis die by suicide. Many others experience significant suicidal ideation (American Psychiatric Association, 2013). Approximately 10% of individuals diagnosed with schizophrenia complete suicide within the first ten years of their diagnosis (Cranco & Lehman, 2000). Risk factors for suicide include being younger, male, of white race/ethnicity, unemployed, and having comorbid substance use.

Schizophrenia-related risk factors that appear to be of importance are the number of previous suicide attempts, as well as the presence of depressive symptoms or feelings of hopelessness, and active hallucinations and delusions (American Psychiatric Association, 2013; Hor & Taylor, 2010; Olfson et al., 2015). Command hallucinations to harm oneself or others may trigger suicidal behaviour. Risk is elevated in the time period following a psychotic episode or discharge from hospital (American Psychiatric Association, 2013).

The only consistent protective factor for suicide in schizophrenia is effective treatment. Prevention of suicide in patients with schizophrenia relies on identifying those at risk and providing the best available treatment for psychosis, as well as for comorbid depression and substance use (Hor & Taylor, 2010). The question remains whether suicide prevention interventions early in the illness could reduce this risk.

Despite the increased suicide risk, death due to natural causes accounts for most of the excess mortality associated with schizophrenia, with cardiovascular disease and respiratory diseases posing the highest threats (Olfson et al., 2015). The medical illness risk associated with schizophrenia may be modifiable. The top six global modifiable mortality risk factors in the general population are hypertension, smoking, raised glucose levels, physical inactivity, obesity, and high blood cholesterol levels. Patients with schizophrenia are exposed to all of these risk factors (Wildgust & Beary, 2010).

The highest rates of cigarette smoking are found among schizophrenic patients in that up to 83% of these patients smoke daily (De Leon, Diaz, Rogers, Browne, & Dinsmore, 2002; Smith, Singh, Infante, Khandat, & Kloos, 2002). Increased risk in schizophrenia patients is specifically for cardiovascular disease due to cigarette smoking, and increasingly due to diabetes and obesity. Schizophrenia patients also have higher rates of infection with HIV and infectious hepatitis. Interventions that have been applied successfully to the general population can be applied to individuals with schizophrenia, potentially improving their health (Goff et al., 2005).

CROSS-CULTURAL AND SOUTH AFRICAN PERSPECTIVES

Any discussion of cultural considerations in relation to schizophrenia is fraught with difficulty. Cross-cultural comparisons have been criticised on the basis of reflecting diagnostic errors (see Chapter 1). For example, greater sociocultural and/or class differences between clinician and patient are more likely to result in errors in diagnosing schizophrenia. Misdiagnosis may also be the result of racial bias and stereotyping (see Chapter 3) (Sue et al., 2006).

The validity of applying diagnostic criteria developed for a white, middle-class population to other cultures has also been questioned (Adebimpe, 1981). In the United States and England, for example, proportionately more people from ethnic minority groups are diagnosed with schizophrenia. This may reflect misdiagnosis, rather than cultural prevalence differences (Jones & Gray, 1986; Lindsey & Paul, 1989). Some authors suggest that differences between ethnic groupings dissolve when the groups are matched in terms of socio-economic factors and education (Carson, Butcher, & Coleman, 1988).

Cultural differences in schizophrenia symptomatology have been described by a variety of researchers; however, the core symptoms of appear to exhibit stability across cultures. However, there is cultural plasticity in terms of content of delusions and hallucinations (Campbell et al., 2017; Sue & Morishima, 1982). More visual hallucinations have been described in people from Mexico and Kenya, and more hallucinations of all types have been described in people from West Indian and Asian cultures (Krassoievitch, Perez-Rincon, & Suarez, 1982; Ndetei & Singh, 1983; Ndetei & Vadher, 1984). Wig (1983) describes a greater incidence in developing countries of brief psychotic disorders (characterised by sudden onset, limited duration, and good prognosis), usually in reaction to an extreme psychosocial stressor.

Cultural differences in the clinical presentation of schizophrenia in the South African context have been described. In the South African setting, the initial presentation is often acute (as opposed to insidious) (Daubenton & Van Rensburg, 2001). Visual hallucinations are more common in the indigenous populations of Africa, and this is also the case in the South African population (Daubenton & Van Rensburg, 2001).

In South Africa, the symptom presentation may also vary across cultures (Daubenton & Van Rensburg, 2001). The core symptoms of schizophrenia and the presence of positive and negative symptoms appear to remain the same across South African cultural groupings (Emsley et al., 2001). However, significant differences in the clinical presentation of non-core symptoms of schizophrenia have been found between Xhosa-speaking and English-speaking South Africans. The differences reported include higher prevalence of aggressive and disruptive behaviour in the Xhosa-speaking patients. In addition, Xhosa-speaking patients also appear to experience more symptoms of a persecutory, sexual, and fantastic nature, as well as more self-neglect and irritability.

The content of the positive symptoms also appears affected by culture in the South African context (Maslowski, Janse van Rensburg, & Mthoko, 1998). Specifically, the content of delusions is often associated with the life experience and culture of the patient. In South Africa, these themes often centre on traditional belief systems, political realities, and famous individuals. A typically South African example is that patients with schizophrenia regularly claim to be Nelson Mandela, or to be related to him (Daubenton & Van Rensburg, 2001).

These findings have been supported by the findings of a study conducted by Mosotho, Louw, and Calitz (2011a), which investigated the clinical presentation of schizophrenia among Sotho speakers. These authors found little variation in the core symptoms of schizophrenia among Sotho speakers. However, as with the studies described above, the content of hallucinations and delusions was found to be strongly influenced by cultural aspects. The participants in this study reported frequent somatic symptoms such as headaches, palpitations, dizziness, and excessive sweating. Similarly, the delusional content of Xhosa-speaking South Africans contained more persecutory content, with beliefs of jealousy-induced witchcraft as causal in their condition (Campbell et al., 2017). In South Africa, the clinical presentation of schizophrenia is often complicated by the use of substances such as cannabis (see later in this chapter), alcohol, and Mandrax, used in various combinations (Daubenton & Van Rensburg, 2001).

Schizophrenia shares a number of symptoms with some indigenous forms of 'illness' in South Africa, such as *ukuthwasa* (ancestral calling) and *amafufunyana* (spirit possession) (see Chapter 10). This has led to much debate around whether to understand these presenting symptoms from within the context of the indigenous healing system (where traditional healers such as an *inyanga* or an *isangoma* would be used), or from the perspective of the biomedical model, where the individual showing the symptoms would be diagnosed with schizophrenia.

Attitudes and beliefs about schizophrenia may differ substantially from Western assumptions in patients, family members, and mental healthcare workers in South Africa (Mbanga et al., 2002). Tensions exist in the interface between Western mental healthcare and traditional healing in the South African context (Kahn & Kelly, 2001). Campbell et al. (2017) emphasise that greater knowledge of indigenous explanatory systems will enhance understandings of treatment needs and the usefulness of assessment tools that are culturally sensitive, for instance the DSM-5 cultural formulation.

Challenges in treatment and care of South Africans who live with severe mental illness such as schizophrenia were brought sharply into awareness with the Life Esidimeni tragedy in 2015/2016, when 143 people at psychiatric facilities in Gauteng, South Africa, died of causes including starvation and neglect. This occurred after an outsourced care contract was terminated with a private service provider (Life Esidimeni) in an apparent 'de-institutionalisation' and cost-saving bid. Inquiries into the circumstances of the tragedy have served to underscore the inequity that exists between general healthcare and mental healthcare, as well as between community- and hospital-based mental healthcare (Robertson et al., 2018).

The challenges to delivery of treatment to people with a diagnosis of schizophrenia in the South African context are chronic under-resourcing of mental health services (Lund, Kleintjes, Kakuma, Flisher, & the MHaPP Research Programme Consortium, 2010), and the consequences of de-institutionalisation policies (also see Chapter 5), specifically the rise of the revolving-door phenomenon (service users who are hospitalised frequently) (Botha et al., 2010; Robertson et al., 2018).

Relapse is considered a general problem among South Africans with this diagnosis. Relapse has many potentially negative consequences, such as hospitalisation, the development of treatment resistance, progressive structural brain damage and consequent cognitive impairment, personal distress, incarceration, and financial implications. Factors associated with relapse among South Africans with a diagnosis of schizophrenia are a comorbid depressed mood, and poor treatment compliance due to limited insight on the part of the patient and to unpleasant medication side effects. South African relapse and rehospitalisation rates remain relatively high and suggest that a more robust health system is required to prevent revolving-door phenomena (Kazadi, Moosa, & Jeenah, 2008; Tomita & Moodley, 2016).

South African authors have added their voices to those questioning the view that schizophrenia is associated with better outcomes in developing countries. The political, social, and economic challenges of life in countries in Africa, Latin America, and Asia pose psychosocial stressors that, together with limited mental health services in these regions, impact negatively on outcomes for people with schizophrenia in the developing world (Burns, 2009).

Some intriguing research findings on the aetiology of schizophrenia are coming out of South Africa. These will be included in the discussion in the following section.

AETIOLOGY

Schizophrenia is arguably the mental disorder that has generated the most research (MacDonald & Schulz, 2009). Despite this bewildering body of work, we are far from understanding the causality of this category of disorders. Earlier in this chapter, difficulties in even attempting to define this condition were discussed. What does appear clear from the available information is that the causality of schizophrenia is complex and characterised by multiple causes (or vulnerabilities) interacting with one another.

In the following discussion of the aetiology of schizophrenia, possible biological factors represent a convenient starting point. Psychological and social factors will also be discussed. This section will conclude with an integrative description of the aetiology of the disorder.

Biological factors

When the biological or medical dimensions in the aetiology of schizophrenia are considered, three aspects are typically in the forefront. These are genetics, physiological vulnerabilities and development, and neurochemistry.

Genetics

The hereditary component to the causality of schizophrenia appears to be undisputed (Gottesman 1991; Ubell, 1989). Unfortunately, however, no single gene can be identified that is directly linked to the aetiology of schizophrenia, and the evidence regarding genetics indicates that multiple genes are involved. These genes give rise to an inherited vulnerability for developing the disorder (Gottesman, 1991). Possible ways to research a genetic component to the causality of schizophrenia include family, twin, adoptee, offspring of twins, and linkage studies.

Schizophrenia does appear to run in families (Ayano, 2016). When considering family studies, research indicates that relatives of a person diagnosed with schizophrenia are at an increased risk for the disorder, when compared to the general population. The degree of the genetic relationship influences the risk: the closer the genetic relationship with the person with schizophrenia, the greater the risk (Gottesman, 1991).

The schizophrenia risk in first-degree relatives of someone with the diagnosis is 10%. This risk increases to 40% in cases where both parents have schizophrenia (Ayano, 2016). It also seems that the relatives of people with this diagnosis are also at an increased risk for other disorders, most notably schizotypal personality disorder. Schizotypy refers to a personality trait that includes positive, negative, and disorganised elements and that is stable over time (Steffens, Meyhöfer, Fassbender, Ettinger, & Kambietz, 2018). Schizotypy may represent a genetic vulnerability for schizophrenia spectrum disorders (Barrantes-Vidal, Grant, & Kwapil, 2015). The drawback of family studies is that there is no control for the influence of environment in this data.

Twin studies assume that, theoretically, the concordance rate for monozygotic (identical) twins should be 100%. If the development of schizophrenia in an individual is solely due to genetic influences, both monozygotic twins should always develop the disorder since they share 100% of their genetic material. Similarly, the concordance rate for dizygotic (fraternal) twins should be 50%, since they share 50% of their genetic material. Research indicates that the concordance rate for identical twins is around 40%–50%, while the concordance rate for fraternal twins appears to be about 10%–17% (Ayano, 2016; Gottesman, 1991).

Thus, twin studies appear to confirm a genetic component to the causality of schizophrenia; however, it is clear that a large part of the variance is not explained by genetics. Work by Dworkin, Lenzenweger, and Molin (1987) indicates a stronger genetic component for negative symptoms than for positive symptoms. Difficulties in interpreting twin studies include the fact that twins share a common environment, including from the antenatal environment to the family system. Conversely, even identical siblings can have very different social and physical childhood experiences.

Adoption studies eliminate the role of environment, as they study children who were adopted at a very young age and who were born to mothers who were diagnosed with schizophrenia. These studies often span many years. The general conclusion that can be drawn from studies with this approach is that children of parents with a diagnosis of schizophrenia, who were raised in families without schizophrenia, have a higher risk for the disorder than the general population. Thus, risk for schizophrenia is increased for biological relatives of persons with schizophrenia, but not for adopted relatives (Ayano, 2016; Kety et al., 1994).

One approach that has produced some of the most compelling evidence for a genetic component in the causality of schizophrenia is investigating the offspring of twins. This research investigates the possibility of individuals being 'carriers' of a genetic predisposition even when they do not display symptoms of the disorder themselves. Evidence from this research indicates that children of a non-symptomatic identical twin of parents with a diagnosis of schizophrenia have the same risk for the disorder as the children of the twin with the diagnosis (17%), again suggesting a genetic component to the disorder (Gottesman, 1991).

Consensus regarding the genetic aspect of the causality of schizophrenia (and other psychological disorders) currently appears to be that some genetic involvement can be inferred from the available information. As suggested above, no single gene involved in the causation of schizophrenia (or any other psychological disorder) has been identified to date. It seems there is polygenetic involvement (i.e. a vulnerability to the disorder is due to a number of genes scattered throughout our chromosomes) (Gottesman, 1991). One current hypothesis is that a range of rare genetic variations combine and manifest in a common clinical presentation (Ayano, 2016). Environmental interactions and interactions with the rest of the genome also contribute to the ultimate clinical presentation, but meta-analysis of twin studies indicates that genetic factors represent about four-fifths of the increased risk for schizophrenia (Sullivan, Kendler, & Neale, 2003).

South African research is making some notable contributions to the research into the genetic component of the aetiology of schizophrenia. In order to study rare genetic mutations that are associated with the genetics of psychiatric disorders, an international collaborative research project which spanned twelve years utilised a sample of Afrikaner families afflicted with schizophrenia. The Afrikaner population is a genetically relatively isolated population, characterised by close-knit family structures for which detailed medical and ancestral records are available. This facilitated the family-based genetic study and offered reliable discrimination between familial and non-familial forms of the disorder. This research served to confirm the role of new genetic mutations in non-familial cases of the disease, as well as the presence of rare inherited structural mutations that affect many genes in familial schizophrenia (Xu et al., 2009). This research has been described as 'offering the first clear view of the genetic landscape of schizophrenia' (Karayiorgou & Gogos, 2011, p. 2).

Brain structure

As discussed in the section on the history of the disorder, brain abnormality has been suspected as a causal factor in schizophrenia since the earliest descriptions of the condition. Evidence indicates that abnormal neurological findings are more common in people with a diagnosis of schizophrenia. The role of brain structure in schizophrenia has been investigated through brain-imaging techniques and post-mortem analyses of people with schizophrenia, as well as investigating cognitive markers through utilising neuropsychological assessment techniques. Advances in brain-imaging technologies have contributed to knowledge of the macroscopic changes in the brain associated with schizophrenia, including the typical ventricular enlargement, reductions in grey matter volume as well as overall brain volume, and white matter abnormalities (Bakhshi & Chance, 2015).

An aspect of brain structure that has been extensively investigated is the ventricular system. Ventricles are cavities in the brain filled with cerebrospinal fluid that cushions the brain and spinal cord. Evidence for enlarged ventricles comes from a variety of sources, including post-mortem inspection (Dwork, 1997; Heckers, 1997), CT scans, and MRI studies (Andreasen et al., 1990; Nopoulos, Flaum, & Andreasen, 1997). Enlarged ventricle size is important because it implies that brain cells have either been lost, or never developed in the first place.

A relationship appears to exist between enlarged ventricle size and the negative symptoms of schizophrenia (Crow, 1985; McGlashan & Fenton, 1991). Ventricular enlargement in people with schizophrenia is associated with poor premorbid adjustment, decreased response to drug treatment, and impaired scores on neuropsychological assessment (Andreasen et al., 1992). Findings of a twin study conducted by Suddath et al. (1990) imply that ventricular enlargement in people with a diagnosis of schizophrenia may not have a genetic origin. However, the abnormal structural changes in schizophrenia, such as enlarged lateral and third ventricles, have largely been taken as strong evidence of a neurodevelopmental origin of schizophrenia (Kim, 2016).

Decreased activity in the frontal lobes (hypofrontality) also appears to be linked to schizophrenia. The frontal lobes are responsible for thinking, reasoning, planning, memory, experiencing reward, and social behaviour. A relationship appears to exist between hypofrontality and the negative symptoms of schizophrenia (Andreasen, Olsen, Dennert, & Smith, 1982).

Post-mortem studies have found prefrontal cell abnormalities and hippocampal cell abnormalities associated with schizophrenia (Lewis et al., 2003). Medial temporal lobe structures (including the hippocampus, the superior, frontal and prefrontal cortices, and the thalamus) appear to be smaller in schizophrenic patients (Davidson & Heinrichs, 2003). A number of brain systems, including the prefrontal cortex and the temporal cortex, as well as subcortical structures, appear to experience functional abnormalities in schizophrenic patients (Van Snellenberg, Torres, & Thornton, 2006).

Neurochemistry

As with theories regarding brain abnormalities and schizophrenia, neurochemistry as a possible causative factor has a long history and has been the subject of much research. No biochemical theory has been conclusively proven to date. Numerous biochemical pathways are likely involved in schizophrenia, rather than a single abnormality (Ayano, 2016). Current research focus is on various neurotransmitters, including dopamine, serotonin, GABA (g-aminobutyric acid), and glutamate. Neurotransmitter hypotheses are mostly based on the responses that patients exhibit to psychoactive agents and by post-mortem evidence (Ayano, 2016).

One of the most enduring theories relating to biochemical factors in the causality of schizophrenia is the dopamine hypothesis (Davis, Kahn, Ko, & Davidson, 1991). The dopamine hypothesis states that schizophrenia is linked to an excess of dopamine activity at some synaptic sites (see Figure 8.6). The dopamine hypothesis is based on the fact that drugs that reduce dopamine activity in the brain reduce the symptoms of schizophrenia. Conversely, drugs that increase the levels of dopamine in the brain have side effects that resemble the symptoms of schizophrenia. An excess of dopamine is therefore assumed to cause some of the symptoms of schizophrenia.

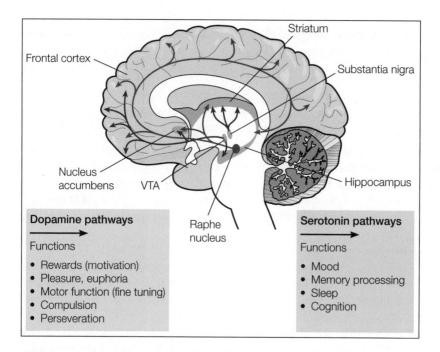

Figure 8.6: Illustration of dopaminergic pathways

Research on the use of three different types of drugs has provided support for the dopamine hypothesis. The three types of drugs in question have the effect of either decreasing or increasing the levels of dopamine in the brain. The drugs that decrease dopamine activity are called dopamine antagonists, while drugs that increase dopamine activity are called dopamine agonists. The three types of drugs that have received the most attention in research on the dopamine hypothesis are the phenothiazines, L-dopa, and the amphetamines.

Phenothiazines are drugs that decrease dopamine activity (dopamine antagonists) in the brain by blocking the brain's use of dopamine in dopamine receptor sites in post-synaptic neurons (Davis et al., 1991). When used in the treatment of schizophrenia, these drugs improve symptoms such as thought disorders, hallucinations, and mood symptoms.

The drug L-dopa is used in the treatment of the symptoms of Parkinson's disease such as tremors, and muscle and limb rigidity. L-dopa is converted to dopamine in the body, thereby increasing dopamine levels in the brain. In some cases, use of this drug can create schizophrenia-like symptoms. Conversely, the phenothiazines (dopamine antagonists) can create side effects that are similar to the symptoms of Parkinson's disease (Davidson et al., 1987).

Amphetamines are stimulant drugs that elevate the brain's levels of the neurotransmitters norepinephrine and dopamine. Doses of amphetamines induce symptoms like those of acute paranoid schizophrenia in non-schizophrenic people (Nielsen, Lyon, & Ellison, 1983). Amphetamines also increase the severity of psychotic symptoms when administered to people with the diagnosis of schizophrenia (Van Kammen, Docherty, & Bunney, 1982).

In summary, drugs known to decrease dopamine activity (antagonists) have the effect of decreasing schizophrenia-like symptoms, while drugs known to elevate dopamine activity (agonists) have the effect of elevating schizophrenia-like symptoms. It is therefore possible to conclude that the causality of schizophrenia is linked to elevated levels of dopamine. In addition, the dopamine antagonists appear to block one specific group of dopamine receptors, the D2 receptors. The suggestion is therefore that schizophrenia in some individuals is caused by increased dopamine activity at the D2 receptors (Davis et al., 1991).

Technological advances for the study of neural functioning and neurochemicals have focused on the receptor sites for dopamine in the brain, rather than only on dopamine levels. This research has led to the idea that an oversensitivity of the dopamine receptors, or an increased number of dopamine receptors, could be a causal factor for schizophrenia, rather than simply an excess of dopamine (Goldsmith, Shapiro, & Joyce 1997).

Evidence contradicting the dopamine hypothesis has emerged, however. Antipsychotics in the form of dopamine antagonists are not useful in the treatment of all people with the diagnosis of schizophrenia, neither are they effective for the treatment of all schizophrenia symptoms. The negative symptoms, in particular, appear relatively unresponsive to these drugs (Davis et al., 1991).

In considering the effects of the various drugs on positive and negative symptoms, it is useful to study the neural pathways that utilise dopamine. The mesolymbic dopamine pathway (see Figure 8.6) appears to be involved in the positive symptoms of schizophrenia. It also appears to be the site where the therapeutic effects of antipsychotics take place by blocking dopamine receptors.

The prefrontal cortex appears to be implicated in the negative symptoms of schizophrenia. This proposition would account for the presence of positive and negative symptoms in the same person, and account for the ineffectiveness of antipsychotics for the negative symptoms, since it is known that they have little impact on the dopamine neurons in the prefrontal cortex (Davis et al., 1991).

The dopamine hypothesis has also involved studying the relationship between serotonin and dopamine. The advent of the drug clozapine (a weak dopamine antagonist, but effective in treating schizophrenia) has given rise to the dopamine–serotonin relationship being investigated as a causal factor for schizophrenia symptoms. Clozapine is a serotonin antagonist in addition to being a weak dopamine antagonist, and may be involved in blocking several neurotransmitter systems at once (Kahn et al., 1993).

The effects of clozapine and other second-generation antipsychotic agents have given rise to the serotonin hypothesis, implicating excessive serotonin as a cause of both the positive and negative symptoms of schizophrenia. Clozapine is effective in treating positive symptoms in chronic schizophrenia, which serves as evidence for the serotonin hypothesis (Ayano, 2016).

G-aminobutyric acid (GABA) is involved in the regulation of dopamine activity and may be involved in the pathophysiology of schizophrenia. Reduction of GABA-releasing neurons that inhibit dopamine activity may in turn be involved in hyperactivity of dopaminergic neurons (Ayano, 2016; Taylor & Tso, 2015).

The glutamate hypothesis originated from abnormal reductions of glutamate receptors found post-mortem in the brains of people with a previous schizophrenia diagnosis. Ingestion of glutamate antagonists (such as ketamine) causes an acute reaction that resembles schizophrenia and that mimics the cognitive difficulties associated with schizophrenia (Ayano, 2016).

The glutamate and the dopamine hypotheses are the most important neurochemical theories for schizophrenia aetiology. Both views originally emerged from indirect pharmacological evidence supported by post-mortem studies. Improvements in neuro-imaging techniques have provided updated findings on glutamate and dopamine abnormalities and suggest an integrated model for interactions between the glutamate and dopamine systems in schizophrenia (Howes, McCutcheon, & Stone, 2015).

Our current understanding of the complex relationships between neurotransmitter systems, and the relationship between these systems and schizophrenic symptomatology, is incomplete. Advanced and complex research utilising new technologies holds the possibility of increasing our knowledge of biochemical interactions, as well as our understanding of the causality of schizophrenia and the development of new treatment options.

Neurodevelopmental factors

Increasing evidence of genetic factors in the aetiology of schizophrenia has stimulated interest in the role of neurodevelopmental processes in schizophrenia. The neurodevelopment view links the influence of genetics, adverse environmental exposure, and pathogenic events (Kim, 2016). Perinatal environmental exposure such as maternal viral infection, foetal malnutrition or very premature birth are associated with neurological abnormalities, and they present evidence for a neurodevelopmental aetiology of schizophrenia (Kim, 2016)

A number of studies have linked schizophrenia and the influenza virus. Although the evidence is somewhat inconsistent (Westergaard, Mortensen, Pedersen, Wohlfahrt, & Melbye, 1999), studies of populations exposed to influenza epidemics indicate that individuals with antenatal exposure to the virus during the second trimester were at higher risk of developing schizophrenia (Cannon, Barr, & Mednick, 1991; Mednick, Huttonon, & Machon, 1994). Post-mortem evidence suggests that viral infection may influence foetal brain development. Cell migration appears to be disrupted in a critical period for cortical growth during this stage of pregnancy (Akbarian et al., 1995).

Other early neurological insults, most notably birth complications, may be associated with increased risk for developing schizophrenia (Boog, 2004). Reports of an accumulation of adverse events during the pre- and perinatal periods, and the presence of behavioural and cognitive symptoms during childhood and adolescence, support the hypothesis of a neurodevelopmental aetiology for schizophrenia.

Recent interpretations of the combination of genetic and environmental factors view this interaction as potentially disrupting a normal developmental course in early life. The resultant alternative developmental paths are thought ultimately to give rise to schizophrenia in individuals (Lewis & Levitt, 2002). Bakhshi and Chance (2015) suggest that, taken in combination, investigations of childhood-onset schizophrenia and outcomes of neuro-anatomical studies provide evidence for a progressive neurodevelopmental model of altered neuroplasticity in schizophrenia.

South African research findings support the neurodevelopmental origin of schizophrenia and offer possible insight into specific times of neurodevelopmental insult during antenatal development. Research conducted in the Eastern Cape by Koen, Niehaus, De Jong, Muller, and Jordaan (2006) found links between minor physical abnormalities in schizophrenia in a Xhosa population, as compared to control groups. In addition to lending support to the neurodevelopmental view of schizophrenia aetiology, this research also may offer a means of subtyping schizophrenia for future genetic research.

Psychological factors

In the absence of conclusive evidence implicating an entirely biological explanation of the aetiology of schizophrenia, psychological and environmental aspects must be considered in terms of aetiology. A recent meta-analysis of 44 studies (Fusar-Poli et al., 2017) compared persons with ultra-high risk for psychosis with control populations and found that obstetric complications, lower child and adolescent functioning, lower educational level, childhood trauma (including emotional abuse or physical neglect), higher perceived stress, affective comorbidities, and male gender presented ultra-high risk. In addition, tobacco use, single status, physical inactivity, and unemployment were identified as ultra-high risk factors. This discussion of psychological factors will begin with a focus on individual factors and factors involving the family, followed by a consideration of broader social aspects.

Individual factors
Studies of high-risk children

In the 1960s, Danish researchers (Mednick & Schulsinger, 1968) followed up a group of 207 children who were identified as 'high risk' for developing schizophrenia, on the basis of their mothers having been diagnosed with the condition. A matched control group of 104 children was utilised. The children in the study were followed up for more than ten years.

Several aspects were identified in this study that served as predictors for the onset of schizophrenia. These included pregnancy and delivery complications, which were implicated in negative symptom presentations, and family instability, which was implicated in positive symptom presentations.

Predictors that were identified in similar studies in the United States and Israel were attentional dysfunction, low IQ scores, poor concentration, poor verbal ability, and poor motor abilities (Cornblatt & Erlenmeyer-Kimling, 1985; Marcus et al., 1987). Early developmental delays in achievement of motor milestones (sitting, standing unsupported, and walking) were found to be associated with adult onset schizophrenia (Filatova et al., 2017). Currently it seems that the clear developmental risk factors for schizophrenia spectrum (and for the affective psychoses) are obstetric complications, childhood psychopathology, markers of cognitive difficulties, and motor dysfunction (Laurens et al., 2015).

Psychological trauma and stress

Despite much data supporting an indirect link between childhood trauma (during childhood, experiencing a very distressing event or situation beyond one's control or capacity for coping) and adult psychosis, the role and underlying mechanisms of childhood trauma in the causality of psychosis remain poorly understood (Aakre, Brown, Benson, Drapalski, & Gearon, 2014; Conus, Cotton, Schimmelmann, McGorry, & Lambert, 2010; Mayo et al., 2017; Şahin et al., 2013).

Trauma has been found to be predictive of the onset of psychosis in high-risk samples, with childhood sexual abuse, followed by physical abuse, constituting the highest risk factors for later transition to psychosis (Bechdolf et al., 2010; Conus et al., 2010; Mayo et al., 2017). Some findings also suggest that a history of childhood trauma, particularly emotional abuse, is independently associated with poorer response to treatment with antipsychotic medication (Misiak & Frydecka, 2016).

Beside the impact of narrowly defined traumatic events, the cumulative impact of stressful life events has been linked to adulthood onset of psychosis (Whitfield, Dube, Felitti, & Anda, 2005; Mayo et al., 2017), but the role of stressful life events in adulthood has not received the same research attention as accumulated childhood trauma (Beards et al., 2013). However, there is evidence that exposure to adult stressful life events increases risk for psychosis and onset of positive symptoms of schizophrenia (Beards et al., 2013; Gallagher, Jones, & Pardes, 2016).

Similar results were found in a study that investigated the factors that predict relapse in people with a diagnosis of schizophrenia (Ventura, Nuechterlein, Lukoff, & Hardesty, 1989). Although people with a diagnosis of schizophrenia appeared to be impacted by the stress of their entire life situation (Forgus & DeWolfe, 1974), a number of research studies have indicated that stress associated with difficulties in close personal relationships is a precipitating factor for a schizophrenia episode (Birley & Brown, 1970; Forgus & DeWolfe, 1974; Schwartz & Myers, 1977).

South African research findings have suggested a link between exposure to trauma and the clinical presentation of first-episode psychosis in South Africa. More specifically, these researchers found that previous traumatic experiences are associated with positive and affective symptoms in patients experiencing a first psychotic episode (Burns, Jhazbhay, Esterhuizen, & Emsley, 2010). Furthermore, childhood trauma was found to be associated with white matter changes in first-episode schizophrenia (Asmal et al., 2018).

Research on moderating factors in the link between childhood trauma and premorbid adjustment in first-episode schizophrenia in a South African cohort confirmed an association between childhood trauma and premorbid adjustment in persons ultimately diagnosed with schizophrenia. However, the research results are suggestive of a complex interplay of risk factors, rather than merely an accumulation of adversity (Kilian et al., 2017).

Faulty learning and cognitive mechanisms

The association between trauma and the psychotic disorders has been explained from behavioural and cognitive-behavioural angles, and several cognitive mechanisms appear to be involved in this interplay (Mayo et al., 2017).

The faulty learning aspect may be related to the child being conditioned into believing that the world is an unfriendly and threatening place. This happens through being exposed to early traumatic experiences, such as disruptions in parenting. Faulty learning could result from disturbed social interaction, learning from observing role models behaving in grossly inappropriate ways, and from efforts to meet inappropriate parental expectations. Such faulty learning manifests in faulty assumptions about reality, difficulties regarding a sense of self and self-worth, emotional immaturity, and a lack of effective coping skills (Carson et al., 1988).

Similarly, early adversity has been hypothesised to lead to the formation of negative schemas, which in turn lead to an external locus of control or increased paranoid symptoms. Childhood trauma may also be linked to faulty information processing, such as excessive focus on irrelevant or threatening environmental information inputs (Gibson, Alloy, & Ellman, 2016; Mayo et al., 2017).

Cannabis use

Cannabis use appears to be an independent risk factor for schizophrenia (Andréasson, Engström, Allebeck & Rydberg, 1987). High consumers of cannabis appear to be at greater risk of developing schizophrenia (Ayano, 2016). Cannabis use also seems to be associated with poor outcome in existing schizophrenia and may trigger psychosis not only in vulnerable individuals, but also in people who do not have a prior history of difficulties (Andréasson et al., 1987; Henquet, Murray, Linszen, & Van Os, 2005; Smit, Bolier, & Cuijpers, 2004).

Cannabis use is thought to interact with genetic and environmental risk factors to cause psychotic illness (Kuepper et al., 2011). However, the association between cannabis use and the onset of psychosis has not been conclusively shown to be causal, and it remains unclear whether cannabis use triggers psychosis or whether individuals with a high risk for psychosis are also more likely to use cannabis (Ayano, 2016). Increased public awareness of this interplay, and the potential risks for developing a psychotic illness as a result of cannabis use, may play a role in the prevention of schizophrenia and psychotic illness.

Family influences

Various theoretical constructs have come into play in considering the role of the family in the aetiology of schizophrenia. In the families of people diagnosed with schizophrenia, the following have been studied:

- the 'schizophrenogenic' (schizophrenia-inducing) mother
- faulty communication patterns
- destructive marital interactions
- pseudo-mutuality and pseudo-hostility
- undermining of personal authenticity.

The 'schizophrenogenic mother' is a psychoanalytic concept first used by Frieda Fromm-Reichmann (1948). This term was also utilised in the early days of family therapy. This concept refers to a style of parenting which could serve to hinder childhood ego development. The behaviours and attitudes of schizophrenogenic mothers were typically described as being cold, rejecting, dominating, overprotective, and insensitive to the needs of others. This description was often linked particularly to the relationship between mother and son. However, this notion has been criticised on the basis that it lacks validating data and is gender biased, and it has fallen into disuse (Roff & Knight, 1981).

The family systems approach emerged in the 1950s and made a major impact on how the causality of schizophrenia is viewed. The family systems view emerged from research into the interaction and communication patterns of families with a member diagnosed with schizophrenia. This research identified communication patterns that appeared to be typical of families with a family member with schizophrenia. This typical communication pattern was called 'double-bind' communication; this refers to communication patterns containing 'mixed messages'.

According to Bateson (1959), the families of people with schizophrenia are characterised by communications that present the identified patient (diagnosed family member) with mixed messages that put them in a no-win situation. For example, a mother pays a surprise hospital visit to her son diagnosed with schizophrenia. When he sees her, he is excited and puts his arms out to greet her. She stiffens and draws back from him. He in turn, draws back from her. She responds by asking if he is not going to greet her and whether he is not happy to see her. Together with the mixed verbal message, there are also subtle non-verbal messages that prohibit the identified patient from either commenting on the situation or leaving it. Thus, double-bind communication usually takes place on both the verbal and non-verbal levels.

The double-bind theory was extremely important to the development of family systems therapy because it represented a coherent and sophisticated explanation for the link between abnormal behaviour and underlying family processes or patterns of interaction.

The family systems approach has contributed much to our understanding of the causality of schizophrenia and other mental disorders. One major contribution is that it sees the causality as having interpersonal aspects as opposed to purely intrapersonal aspects (i.e. the pathology is inherent to the person, as in the biological view). Thus, this perspective regards the seat of pathology as being between people, rather than located within the individual.

Another of the major contributions of this approach has been the notion of mutual causality or circular causality (reciprocal cause and effect). This means that patterns that are part of the cause of psychopathology are seen as vicious circles, where the interactions form a loop such that they continuously affect each other.

Other theorists who contributed to our understanding of family dynamics associated with the development and maintenance of schizophrenia were Theodore Lidz and Lyman Wynne in the United States and R.D. Laing in the United Kingdom. Lidz described two types of problematic marital relationship patterns in families of people with a diagnosis of schizophrenia (Lidz, Fleck, & Cornelison, 1965). These are 'marital schism' and 'marital skew'.

Marital schism occurs when constant undermining of one parent by the other takes place, with expressions that children resemble the undermined parent. Marital skew takes place when the family maintains stability by accepting as normal the destructive and often extremely domineering behaviour of one or more of the members. In both these types of families, the parents constantly compete for the children's loyalty, with the result that the children experience being torn between their parents (Lidz et al., 1965).

Wynne described families with a diagnosed schizophrenic member as having unusual and problematic emotional transactions, boundaries, and communication styles. The emotional transactions and role structure in these families were described by Wynne and his co-workers as reflecting either 'pseudo-mutuality' or 'pseudo-hostility' (Wynne, Ryckoff, Day, & Hirsch, 1958). With pseudo-mutuality, the role structure in families of people with schizophrenia is characterised by rigidity and conflict, while a pretence or mask of openness and mutual understanding is being maintained. This has the effect of hampering the children of the family in their attempted moves towards emotional maturity.

In the case of pseudo-hostility, there are overt expressions of conflict, with very rigid underlying coalitions between some family members. Wynne and his colleagues described the boundaries of these families as a 'rubber fence' because they allow professionals to have superficial contact with them, but resist any change to the family dynamics. The families of schizophrenics also exhibited communication deviance in that they struggled to remain focused when attempting to discuss solutions to problems (Wynne et al., 1958).

R. D. Laing, a Scottish psychiatrist who was heavily influenced by the existentialist movement, also emphasised the role of the family. He regarded schizophrenia as a sane response to an insane situation. Laing used the term 'mystification' (coined by Marx) to describe the process that he observed in the parents of children diagnosed with schizophrenia. In this process, parents denied, distorted, or relabelled their children's experiences to fit in with their own expectations. Laing argued that mystification as a result of these processes caused the development of an overtly displayed false self and a privately experienced real self. Laing (1969) believed that schizophrenia developed when the split between these selves became too big.

The contributions of the family systems model in particular have been criticised for methodological problems. One of these points of critique is that family interactions become the focus of study only after the diagnosis of a family member. Another related issue is a lack of use of control groups (or families) for the purposes of comparison by the family systems approach. These two issues present difficulties because conclusions are drawn about the family interactions, but whether these types of interactions will always give rise to the same types of pathology remains unclear.

Expressed emotion

Negative affective communication variables have also been the focus of research into the family dynamics associated with the development and maintenance of schizophrenia. 'Negative affective communication' refers to the emotional tone of family interactions and attitudes. The main variable that has been distinguished is expressed emotion (EE). Studies on these variables have mostly focused on the maintenance of schizophrenia in families once the disorder has been diagnosed.

Expressed emotion refers to a pattern of communication which is characterised by statements expressing criticism, hostility, and over-involvement. Initial research in this area was done by Brown, Bone, Dalison, and Wing (1966), and Brown, Birley, and Wing (1972). This research divided families of people diagnosed with schizophrenia into 'high-EE families' and 'low-EE' families. In a nine-month follow-up of discharged patients living with their families, high relapse rates were found in the high-EE families. Thus, it appears that this aspect of the family environment also impacts on the person with a diagnosis of schizophrenia.

High-EE families also make more negative comments regarding the symptoms of schizophrenia displayed by the patient. The negative symptoms appeared more likely to elicit negative comment, and the family members making negative comments were more likely to regard the symptoms as being within the control of the patient. In addition, unusual thoughts expressed by the patient elicited more critical comments from family members in high-EE families. In turn, an increased number of critical comments appeared to trigger a higher number of unusual thoughts in the person diagnosed with schizophrenia. A circular (bi-directional) relationship therefore appears to exist between expressed emotion and unusual thoughts in people diagnosed with schizophrenia and their families (Lopez, Nelson, Snyder, & Mintz, 1999; Weisman et al., 1998).

In terms of causality and expressed emotion, a number of issues prevent us from drawing the conclusion that high EE is a causal factor, rather than merely a precipitating factor, in schizophrenia. High EE communication patterns appear to be present not only in the families of people with a diagnosis of schizophrenia, but also in families where a member has been diagnosed with depression, bipolar disorder, and eating disorders (Kavanagh, 1992). Cultural differences also appear to exist in terms of high-EE communication, with Western families displaying more high EE communication. Despite this finding for Western families, the incidence of schizophrenia appears to be relatively stable at about 1% across cultures (Leff et al., 1990).

Issues such as variability across cultures, high EE not being specific to families with a member with a diagnosis of schizophrenia, and a possible bi-directional relationship between EE and symptoms of schizophrenia imply that, for the moment, the concept of EE may be more useful in the prevention of relapse than in understanding the aetiology of schizophrenia. Recent statistical analysis of studies investigating EE in families of persons living with schizophrenia has confirmed EE as a 'robust and valuable predictor of relapse in schizophrenia' (Weintraub, Hall, Carbonella, Weisman de Mamani, & Hooley, 2017, p. 346). A model that was developed to decrease expressed emotion in families with a member with schizophrenia, the family psycho-education approach, has proved to be one of the most consistent relapse prevention interventions available (McFarlane, 2016).

EXAMPLE CASE

Mary was discharged from hospital three weeks ago. Her mother is frustrated that Mary is so inactive. The following two examples show what Mary's mother might say, depending on her level of expressed emotion:

High expressed emotion
'I think if Mary just got some exercise, or did something constructive, she would feel much better. Just do something active … but she won't listen to me, I am just her mother …'

Low expressed emotion
'I try to let Mary go at her own pace. I accept that she will take some kind of action when she feels ready.'

Sociocultural factors

The effects of social class

Gottesman (1991) maintains that one of the most unchanging outcomes of research on schizophrenia is that it is most prevalent among people who live in the poorest, often central, sections of large cities, who inhabit the lowest socio-economic levels, and who are employed in occupations with the lowest status. Two explanations have been put forward to make sense of this phenomenon, the sociogenic hypothesis and the social selection theory.

The sociogenic hypothesis views the stressors of a low socio-economic status as causing, or contributing to, the development of schizophrenia. The sociogenic hypothesis regards possible sources of stress as being either environmental factors or biological factors. The environmental factors that could be associated with low socio-economic status include mistreatment and disrespect from others, lack of education, low-grade employment, and low levels of rewards and opportunities. An example of the biological factors is poor nutrition during pregnancy (Gottesman, 1991).

Gallagher et al. (2016) found that onset of positive symptoms is often preceded by environmental stressors, but only for persons with low socio-economic status of origin, leading the researchers to hypothesise that these participants exhibit a heightened reactivity to stressors that is related to 'the human toll of impoverishment' (Gallagher et al., 2016, p. 101).

Social selection theory can also be described as downward drift theory. In this view, people who are in the process of developing the disorder and people with the diagnosis tend to move or drift to the poorest areas of cities due to their decreased functioning, which in turn decreases their employment opportunities and earning capabilities (Gottesman, 1991).

In attempts to clarify these issues, researchers have examined the possible downward trend in occupational status in people diagnosed with schizophrenia (Keith, Regier, & Rae, 1991). Another research strategy has been to compare the occupational status of people diagnosed with schizophrenia with that of their fathers. The downward drift tendency across generations was confirmed in several studies with this approach (Gottesman, 1991). Social drift is generally regarded as frequent in the psychotic disorders, and those living with psychotic conditions are more likely to be part of the lower social classes (Ventriglio et al., 2016). Social drift is linked to increased suicide risk, depression, and hopelessness at first clinical presentation (Ventriglio et al., 2016).

Somewhat more evidence appears to exist for the downward drift theory than for the sociogenic hypothesis. This should not be taken to imply that the social environment plays no role in the causality of schizophrenia, however. Some evidence suggests that the stressors associated with low socio-economic status contribute to the development of schizophrenia in some individuals (Gottesman, 1991). An explanation that includes both views is probably more accurate.

The effects of migrant status

A great deal of data is available on the incidence of schizophrenia. One of the areas of substantial variation in incidence is migrant status (McGrath et al., 2004). A variety of studies have indicated an elevated risk for psychiatric disorder, and particularly psychotic disorders, for first-generation adult immigrants. Members of ethnic minorities residing in neighbourhoods that create relative isolation have an additionally elevated risk. Most of these studies have been conducted in Europe (Menezes, Georgiades, & Boyle, 2011).

Despite not all studies supporting this association, systematic reviews of the data appear to indicate that, in general, migrant groups are significantly more at risk of developing schizophrenia than native-born populations (McGrath et al., 2004). A more recent systematic review of available research on the incidence of schizophrenia and other psychotic disorders has found increased risk for both ethnic minority groups and migrant groups across four continents. Meta-analyses found that first- and second-generation migrants have a risk of schizophrenia that is 2–4.5 times greater than that of the the majority population (Tortelli et al., 2015).

Some theories that have been suggested to explain this tendency emphasise psychosocial variables, such as socio-economic disadvantage, exposure to racism, and discriminatory practices, as well as factors related to family and community responses to psychiatric disorders in migrant populations (Jarvis, 1998). Other theories put forward environmental causes such as obstetric complications and perinatal infections as aetiological models (Eagles, 1991). The convergence of risk factors, such as vulnerability based on exposure to novel viruses, abnormal immunological responses, obstetric complications, and differential foetal survival have also been suggested in an attempt to explain this data (Harrison, 1990).

A meta-analysis conducted by Tortelli et al. (2015) attempted to control for methodological bias and confirmed increased risk for non-affective and affective psychotic disorders in black Caribbean descendants of migrants and other ethnic minority groups in England. These authors concluded that this phenomenon is best explained by higher exposure to economic and social disadvantage in a post-migratory context.

Integration of aetiological factors

One way we can integrate the seemingly disjointed factors described above is to view them as predisposing, precipitating, and maintaining factors, respectively. Predisposing factors imply an underlying (usually biological) vulnerability to the disorder. In the case of schizophrenia, genetics and brain structure (including biochemical aspects) represent this biological vulnerability. Precipitating factors are the life circumstances of an individual that trigger the underlying vulnerability, thereby causing symptoms of the disorder to manifest. These factors may be either intrapersonal or interpersonal in nature. Examples of possible precipitating or triggering factors for schizophrenia from the discussion above are psychological stress, cannabis use, faulty learning, and possibly the impact of the family system.

Once the disorder has been triggered, remission of symptoms is hindered by maintaining factors. Thus, the maintaining factors complicate and extend the course of the disorder. Factors in the discussion above that may act as maintaining factors include family dynamics and the presence of high expressed emotion in the family, cannabis use, and sociocultural factors such as social class and migrant status. Again, maintaining factors may include intra- or interpersonal aspects.

As with all the other facets of this much-researched but puzzling disorder, an attempt to view the aetiology of schizophrenia in an integrated way is far from clear-cut, with some factors playing both precipitating and maintaining roles. The strong arguments for the biological basis of the disorder (and, most recently, the neurodevelopmental views) would place less emphasis on the triggering events than with other disorders, such as the mood disorders.

Perhaps the metaphor of schizophrenia as a biological time bomb is most apt. While some disorders, such as the mood disorders, can be likened to landmines, which can remain dormant for many years and that require a trigger to manifest, schizophrenia is probably more like a time bomb ticking towards its inevitable explosion. Precipitating factors such as psychological stress and cannabis use probably serve to hasten the inevitable, while the maintaining factors, such as high expressed emotion, merely worsen the devastation left in the wake of the bomb's explosion.

CONTROVERSIAL ISSUES IN THE DIAGNOSIS AND MANAGEMENT OF SCHIZOPHRENIA

Various authors have acknowledged that schizophrenia is probably one of the most researched, yet most confusing and most contested, of the psychological disorders (Carson, 1985; Guloksuz & Van Os, 2018). A number of controversies have been associated with the diagnosis, management, and treatment of schizophrenia. Some of these issues will be highlighted in this section, including the question of whether the concept 'schizophrenia' remains valid, the views of the anti-psychiatrists, as well as current trends towards de-institutionalisation and the impact of this on people diagnosed with schizophrenia and their families.

Should the diagnosis continue to be used?

The two main classification systems that are used when making a diagnosis of schizophrenia (the DSM and ICD systems), and the very notion of 'schizophrenia', may be problematic when it comes to research and treatment of schizophrenia (Guloksuz & Van Os, 2018). Although schizophrenia accounts only for approximately 30% of a broader psychotic condition, it has become the lens through which all 'psychotic' symptoms are viewed (Guloksuz & Van Os, 2018). Both research and recovery-directed clinical practice are stymied by the conflagration of 'schizophrenia' and psychosis (a multidimensional variation with highly unpredictable intra- and interpersonal variations).

McCarthy-Jones (2017) points out that, despite much research and advances in treatment, the recovery rate for schizophrenia has not improved over time, and he speculates that this is attributable to the conceptual difficulties implied in the term 'schizophrenia'. One of the main difficulties is that 'schizophrenia' is conceptualised as a single biological disease entity, which in turn allows for research designs that fail to differentiate between risk for onset and risk for poor outcome (Guloksuz & Van Os, 2018). The conceptual issue is that, if schizophrenia is conceptualised in purely medical terms, that is, as a biological dysfunction causing a physiological disease, then a diagnosis of a single entity, 'schizophrenia', is possible.

However, there is a lack of clear diagnostic markers to aid in the diagnosis of schizophrenia (Carson, 1985; Guloksuz & Van Os, 2018), and it appears that the evidence has 'fatally undermined' the notion of schizophrenia as a discrete entity (Murray, 2017, p. 256). The prevailing view currently is that schizophrenia represents the severe end of a psychosis spectrum of disorders (Guloksuz & Van Os, 2018; Murray, 2017), and the concept of 'schizophrenia' will ultimate be broken down and replaced with more useful diagnostic terms (Green, 2018; Guloksuz & Van Os, 2018; Murray, 2017). However, for the moment, the term remains in use because it continues to refer accurately to some aspects of reality in some settings, and because, at the moment, there is no coherent or agreed-upon alternative to replace it (Green, 2018).

'Normality' and 'abnormality'

When one tries to look at schizophrenia in a critical way, one of the central themes is that of 'normality' versus 'abnormality'. Two main strands make up this theme. This first is that of the anti-psychiatry movement (see Chapter 2), which queried whether mental illness exists at all. The second strand of the argument queries whether mental health professionals are able to distinguish between those with and those without mental illness.

A different but related question is that of labelling. Labelling theorists are interested in how psychiatric diagnoses (or labels) become self-fulfilling prophesies for those who are 'labelled'. This will be discussed in the following section.

What if 'schizophrenia' does not exist at all? This is the view of the anti-psychiatrists (Laing, 1969; Szasz, 1961), who contest the very existence of schizophrenia and other mental illnesses. The anti-psychiatry movement holds that the act of diagnosing, as well as the diagnostic categories, are influenced by values, morals, and political considerations within society. Psychiatry can be seen as a form of social control. This social control is achieved by medicalising behaviour that breaks social rules. This means that any behaviour that makes other people uncomfortable, is irritating, or that questions the status quo is approached as if it were an illness with a physical cause, needing to be diagnosed and treated (Szasz, 1970; Ussher, 1991).

The anti-psychiatrists do not agree with conventional models of psychiatric classification and diagnosis. They also disagree with the generally accepted use of an analogy between medical and mental disorders. The reason for this is that, while the characteristics of medical disorders are usually objective, the features of mental disorders are usually more a question of subjective interpretation on the part of the clinician. Szasz (1961) sees the problematic behaviours of the 'mentally ill' as 'problems of living' rather than as symptoms of underlying brain disease. While he acknowledges that the difficult behaviours of those people who would usually be described as 'mentally ill' could be strange, irritating, or even deviant, he feels that individuals should take responsibility for their actions.

In Chapter 2 (Box 2.3), reference is made to the famous Rosenhan experiment (1973). In this experiment, eight 'pseudo-patients' (research assistants) were admitted to mental hospitals after simulating a major symptom of mental illness (only hallucinations: hearing voices). All were admitted, and all (but one) were discharged with diagnoses of 'schizophrenia in remission'. In some cases, the pseudo-patients were kept in hospital for several weeks. This study therefore questions the reliability and usefulness of psychiatric diagnosis and even whether mental health professionals are able to distinguish those who are 'normal' from those who are 'abnormal'.

Labelling

A related concept is that of labelling. This refers to a tendency to view the label ascribed to a person as a description of the person as a whole, rather than merely a description of his or her behaviour. This creates expectations about how the person will act for both the labelled person and for the people around him or her (including clinical staff). According to Rosenhan (1973), one of the consequences of the psychiatric labels ascribed to the pseudo-patients who took part in his experiment was that ordinary behaviours exhibited by the pseudo-patients (such as taking notes or pacing up and down) were seen as signs of mental illness by psychiatric staff.

The label in this way becomes a self-fulfilling prophecy. In our use of language, the person becomes the disorder, for example, 'Margaret is a schizophrenic', as opposed to 'Margaret has a diagnosis of schizophrenia'. This is also true for the person's own view of himself or herself.

De-institutionalisation

As seen above, the practice of institutionalising people with a diagnosis of schizophrenia has been critiqued by the anti-psychiatrists as a method of social control of people who do not conform to the behaviours expected by society. The other side of the coin is the practice of de-institutionalisation, which has had significant and controversial consequences.

In the 1980s in the United States (and in the early 2000s in South Africa), changes in legislation and policies took place that severely restricted psychiatric hospital beds. These changes also affected the possible length of stay in such facilities, as well as placing limitations on who could be committed involuntarily (Mental Health Care Act, No. 17 of 2002) (see Chapter 5). Contrast this approach to statements earlier in this chapter regarding the impact of schizophrenia on the independent functioning of some people with this diagnosis. The aims of these policies in the United States and in South Africa were to move the mentally ill, and their care, from institutions into communities and community care structures.

In the United States, de-institutionalisation is regarded as a failure, since it resulted in a large number of people with mental illnesses (schizophrenia, in particular) becoming homeless. An additional consideration is the unpredictable dangerousness to self (and, in some cases, to others) which characterises this population (Cranco & Lehman, 2000). In South Africa, the consequences of policies leading to de-institutionalisation are acknowledged in the National Mental Health Policy Framework and Strategic Plan 2013–2020, which states that de-institutionalisation in South Africa took place at a rapid rate in the absence of the required development of community-based psychiatry services, leading to high levels of homelessness, people living with mental illness in prison, and revolving-door care for South African mental health service users (National Department of Health, South Africa, 2012). This situation has also been linked to the Life Esidimeni tragedy, mentioned earlier in this chapter.

CONCLUSION

This chapter has attempted to give an overview of schizophrenia and other disorders associated with psychosis as a cluster of disorders. Psychosis is a very serious psychiatric symptom, and schizophrenia can be regarded as the 'classic' psychotic disorder. The introduction described schizophrenia as an 'extreme' disorder. The impact of this group of disorders and behaviours on diagnosed individuals, their families, and on the broader society is indeed extreme in terms of its emotional and financial costs.

Despite schizophrenia being one of the most researched disorders, we still cannot make conclusive statements regarding the causes of schizophrenia, the course of schizophrenia, possible effective treatments of schizophrenia, and, least of all, the diagnosis of schizophrenia itself. Even the management of people with schizophrenia is fraught with difficulties. It appears that this cluster of behaviours, which has fascinated and puzzled mental health researchers for more than 200 years, will continue to do so for some time to come.

MULTIPLE-CHOICE QUESTIONS

1. Which of the following is *not* a typical symptom of schizophrenia?
   a) delusions
   b) inappropriate emotions
   c) disorganised speech and behaviour
   d) refusal to maintain minimum body weight
2. Which of the following is the definition of catatonia?
   a) silly and immature behaviour
   b) *dementia praecox*
   c) immobility or agitated excitement
   d) delusions of grandeur
3. Which of the following is the definition of paranoia?
   a) silly and immature behaviour
   b) anhedonia
   c) alternating immobility and agitated excitement
   d) delusions of persecution
4. The main symptoms of psychosis are:
   a) hallucinations and delusions
   b) delusions and disorganised behaviour
   c) disorganised behaviour and hallucinations
   d) hallucinations, delusions and disorganised behaviour
5. The most common type of hallucination experienced by schizophrenic patients is:
   a) visual
   b) auditory
   c) tactile
   d) olfactory
6. Flat affect can be described as:
   a) inability to initiate and persist in activities
   b) inability to experience pleasure
   c) lack of emotional response; blank facial expression
   d) lack of speech content and/or slowed speech response
7. Through deductive reasoning, which of the following scenarios supports the dopamine hypothesis of schizophrenia?
   a) Antipsychotic drugs (neuroleptics) act as dopamine agonists, increasing the amount of dopamine in the brain.
   b) Antipsychotic drugs (neuroleptics) are also used to treat Parkinson's disease (a disorder due to insufficient dopamine).
   c) The drug L-dopa, a dopamine agonist, is used to treat symptoms of schizophrenia in patients with Parkinson's disease.
   d) Amphetamines, which activate dopamine, can increase psychotic symptoms in people with schizophrenia.

8. Which one of the following is *not* a schizophrenia risk factor:
   a) history of childhood trauma.
   b) birth complications
   c) developmental delays motor functioning
   d) legal trouble as a result of giving in to peer group pressure as an adolescent (excluding involvement with substances)

9. There seems to be evidence of neuro-anatomical causes for schizophrenia as seen by which one of the following?
   a) All patients with schizophrenia have smaller ventricles in their brains.
   b) In some schizophrenia patients there is an excess amount of 'grey matter' in the cerebral cortex.
   c) The majority of schizophrenia patients have enlarged ventricles in their brains.
   d) Many patients with schizophrenia have increased activity in the frontal lobes of their brains.

10. Which of the following is not listed under 'schizophrenia or other primary psychotic disorders' in the ICD-11?
    a) schizophrenia
    b) catatonic schizophrenia
    c) schizotypal disorder
    d) schizoaffective disorder

PARAGRAPH AND ESSAY QUESTIONS

1. Describe the 'positive' and 'negative' symptoms of schizophrenia. Explain what is meant by these terms and how they relate to prognosis and outcome.
2. Discuss the similarities and differences between schizotypal disorder and schizophrenia in terms of diagnostic considerations and DSM-5 criteria for diagnosis.
3. Discuss some of the causative factors of schizophrenia, including genetic influences, neurotransmitter imbalances, prenatal viral exposure, and psychological stressors.
4. Define 'expressed emotion' and describe how this would impact on relapse risk in a person with schizophrenia.
5. Schizophrenia is associated with increased risk for mortality. Discuss this statement, indicating which risk factors may be modifiable.

9 NEUROCOGNITIVE DISORDERS

Basil Joseph Pillay

CHAPTER CONTENTS

Introduction
The classification of neurocognitive disorders
History of neurocognitive disorders
Delirium
  Clinical picture
  Epidemiology
  Aetiology
  Treatment and management of delirium
Neurocognitive disorders (dementia)
  Clinical picture
  Epidemiology
  Aetiology
  Treatment and management of neurocognitive disorder (dementia)
Amnestic disorders
  Clinical picture
  Epidemiology
  Aetiology
  Treatment and management of amnestic disorders
Assessment of neurocognitive disorders
Contextual and cross-cultural perspectives
Conclusion

LEARNING OUTCOMES

After studying this chapter, you should be able to:
- Show a general understanding of neurocognitive disorders.
- Distinguish between the different neurocognitive disorders.
- Provide a clinical description of each disorder.
- Understand the problems relating to the classification of these disorders.
- Understand the way in which neurocognitive disorders are assessed.
- Identify cross-cultural and, more specifically, South African, concerns associated with neurocognitive disorders.

PERSONAL HISTORY CASELET

Mrs G is 89 years old and lives with her family in Durban. There has been a gradual change in her personality and behaviour over the past ten years. Mrs G loved cooking, baking, reading, and knitting. Everyone who knew her always spoke fondly of her cooking and baking skills. However, her family noticed that she was not managing to cook and bake as before. She began forgetting the family's favourite recipes that she had made for years from memory, and sometimes she omitted essential ingredients. On one occasion she had mistakenly used cinnamon powder instead of cocoa when making a chocolate cake. Although her family found it amusing, she was very embarrassed and felt offended. She frequently became sensitive to criticism and was defensive when corrected about her behaviour, which was not in keeping with her personality.

She loved knitting and had knitted some beautiful and intricate garments for her children and grandchildren. As the years went by, she found it increasingly difficult to complete knitting and sewing projects. In more recent years, she would repeatedly undo her knitting and start over again without completing the task or making substantial progress.

Mrs G was also an avid reader. More recently, her family observed that she would begin reading a book and return to the first page each day because she could not remember what she had read the previous day. Although she read the text fluently, her understanding and comprehension were poor. She had become increasingly forgetful, misplaced things and repeated herself in daily conversations.

Of late, her memory for recent events had declined – they were forgotten in minutes, resulting in her asking the same thing over and over again. She frequently became disoriented and did not know where she was. At times, she could not recall whether members of her family were living or dead, and at other times, she confused her children with her grandchildren or siblings.

Surprisingly, she recalled and recounted events of her early years, especially about her granny, father, and siblings who had been deceased for many years. Her confusion and disorientation became worse at dusk and when she was in unfamiliar surroundings, for example, in shopping malls or visiting family or friends. Mrs G also had difficulty sleeping at night and frequently complained of body aches and pains. Her family and friends considered her changes as part of her aging process.

Recently, Mrs G developed a mild paralysis on the right side of her body. She was diagnosed has having had a mild stroke, and she was in cardiac failure. Her brain CT scan and MRI revealed a picture of vascular dementia.

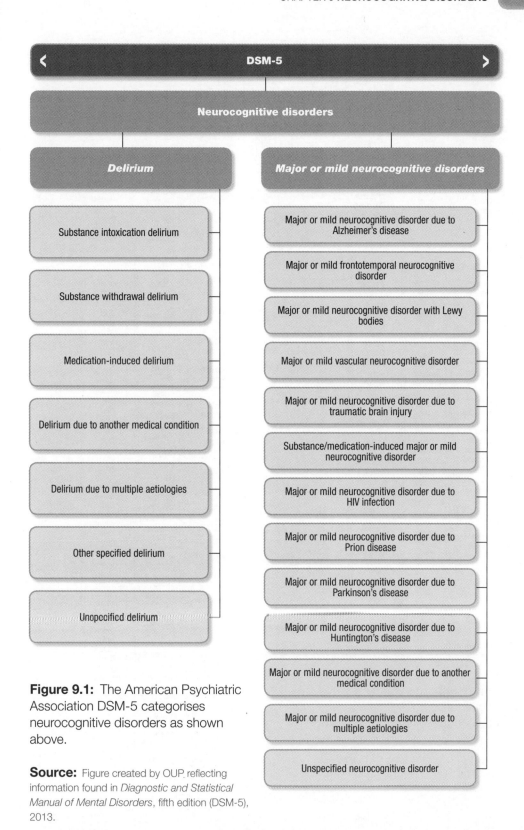

Figure 9.1: The American Psychiatric Association DSM-5 categorises neurocognitive disorders as shown above.

Source: Figure created by OUP, reflecting information found in *Diagnostic and Statistical Manual of Mental Disorders*, fifth edition (DSM-5), 2013.

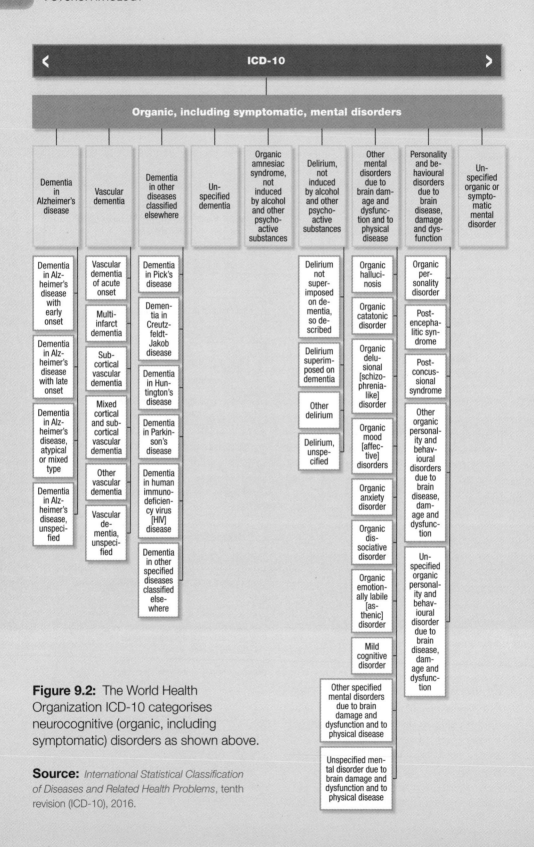

Figure 9.2: The World Health Organization ICD-10 categorises neurocognitive (organic, including symptomatic) disorders as shown above.

Source: *International Statistical Classification of Diseases and Related Health Problems*, tenth revision (ICD-10), 2016.

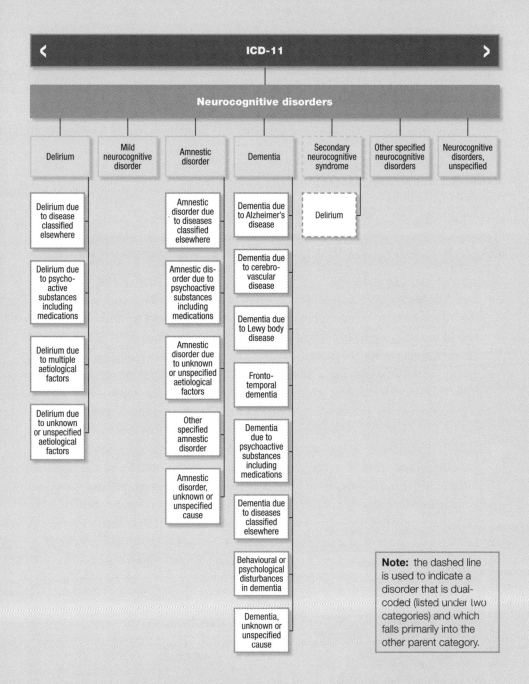

Figure 9.3: The World Health Organization proposed ICD-11 categorises neurocognitive disorders as shown above.

Source: *International Classification of Diseases for Mortality and Morbidity Statistics*, eleventh revision (ICD-11), 2018.

INTRODUCTION

We all rely on our cognitive abilities daily. We think about issues or events, solve problems, make decisions, remember things (such as telephone numbers or what we have to do), or we are just in a state of awareness (i.e. where we are, what time it is, what day or month it is). Have you ever had the experience of not being able to do these things? Can you recall a situation where you were unable to remember an important date, or not able to recall a person's name, or where you had left your phone? If you have, you will know that it is usually quite embarrassing and sometimes frightening. Imagine what it would be like if this happened all the time. We would not be able to function or perform simple, routine tasks we take for granted. This is what neurocognitive disorders are all about.

BOX 9.1: BASIC NEUROANATOMY

Together, the brain and spinal cord form the central nervous system (CNS). The brain is divided into two hemispheres (referred to as the left and right hemisphere) which are connected by the corpus callosum. The folded or wrinkled area is referred to as the cerebrum or cortex and is actually a continuous sheet folded into rises (gyri) and troughs (sulci). The cerebrum comprises four lobes: the frontal, parietal, occipital, and temporal lobes. The frontal lobe is the most anterior lobe and is important for planning, organisation, abstract thought, etc. (referred to as executive functioning), as well as motor control, memory, and many other functions. The parietal lobe is posterior to (behind) the frontal lobe and dorsal (towards the back of the brain) and is important for spatial processing, cognitive processing, motor control, memory, and other functions. The occipital lobe is most posterior and is mainly associated with visual processing. The temporal lobe is on the ventral surface (towards the bottom) of the brain and is important for auditory and visual processing, language, memory, and many other functions. Below the cortex are the subcortical areas. These structures include the hypothalamus (which supports homeostatic functions, including regulation of food intake); thalamus (important for perception and cognition), and brain stem, made up of the midbrain, pons, medulla, and cerebellum (plays an important role in motor function).

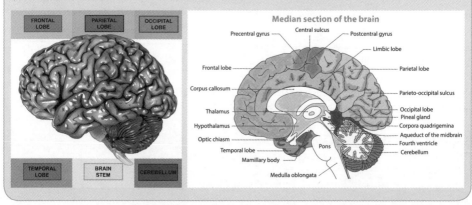

The word 'cognition' is the broad term used to refer to tasks that include memory, language, orientation, judgement, problem-solving, planning, the ability to have interpersonal relationships, and to perform actions (referred to as **praxis**). When a person has significant, regular trouble in these areas of cognition, which disrupts their daily functioning, it may be due to a neurocognitive disorder.

These disruptions in cognition can be the result of many causes. These include: head injury (e.g. following a motor vehicle accident or a gunshot to the head, or from a fall); a medical condition (e.g. HIV/Aids); or the misuse or abuse of substances (e.g. alcohol, cannabis, cocaine, etc.). Aging can also produce these cognitive problems, and in some instances, like Alzheimer's disease, it can be very distressing for the sufferer and the family.

In this chapter, we will focus on the common neurocognitive disorders by explaining:

- how they are classified
- how the disorders present themselves
- the main differences between the different types of neurocognitive disorders
- their aetiology (cause)
- their assessment, treatment, and management.

Finally, the chapter will close with some comments on contextual and cultural issues.

As you can see, neurocognitive disorders are closely related to the brain and brain functioning. The structures of the brain and their functions are provided in Box 9.1 to help you understand some of the terminology used in this chapter (and elsewhere in this textbook), and to identify the areas to which we refer. Box 9.2 provides explanations for anatomical terms of direction used in this chapter.

BOX 9.2: ANATOMICAL TERMS OF DIRECTION

Medial	Towards the midline of the body
Lateral	Away from the midline of the body
Proximal	Towards a reference point (extremity)
Distal	Away from a reference point (extremity)
Inferior	Lower or below
Superior	Upper or above
Anterior	Towards the front
Ventral	Beneath; underside
Posterior	Towards the back
Dorsal	Posterior

THE CLASSIFICATION OF NEUROCOGNITIVE DISORDERS

Depending on the classification used, neurocognitive disorders can be organised into two (DSM-5) or three (ICD-10) broad areas. The DSM-5 distinguishes between delirium and major or mild neurocognitive disorders, and the ICD-10 between delirium, dementia, and amnestic disorders. Within each group, there are further subgroups, which are organised according to their aetiology. In the ICD-11, the classification of neurocognitive disorders is harmonised with the DSM-5.

Table 9.1 lists the *Diagnostic and Statistical Manual of Mental Disorders* (DSM-5) (American Psychiatric Association, 2013) and the *International Classification of Diseases* (ICD-10) (World Health Organization, 1993) classifications of neurocognitive disorders.

Table 9.1: Classification of neurocognitive disorders as adapted from the DSM-5 and ICD-10

DSM-5	ICD-10	ICD-11
Delirium		
■ Delirium due to a general medical condition ■ Substance-induced delirium ■ Delirium due to multiple aetiologies ■ Delirium not otherwise specified	■ Delirium not induced by alcohol and other psychoactive substances ■ Delirium, not superimposed on dementia, so described ■ Delirium, superimposed on dementia, so described ■ Other delirium ■ Delirium, unspecified	■ Delirium due to disease classified elsewhere ■ Delirium due to psychoactive substances including medications ■ Delirium due to multiple etiological factors ■ Delirium due to unknown or unspecified aetiological factors
		■ Mild neurocognitive disorder
		Amnestic disorder ■ Amnestic disorder due to diseases classified elsewhere ■ Amnestic disorder due to psychoactive substances including medications ■ Amnestic disorder due to unknown or unspecified aetiological factors ■ Other specified amnestic disorder ■ Amnestic disorder, unspecified

DSM-5	ICD-10	ICD-11
Dementia		

■ Major and mild neurocognitive disorders
■ Major or mild neurocognitive disorder due to Alzheimer's disease
■ Major or minor frontotemporal neurocognitive disorder
■ Major or mild neurocognitive disorder with Lewy bodies
■ Major or mild vascular neurocognitive disorder
■ Major or mild neurocognitive disorder due to:
  ▸ Traumatic brain injury
  ▸ HIV infection
  ▸ Prion disease
  ▸ Parkinson's disease
  ▸ Huntington's disease
  ▸ Another medical condition
  ▸ Multiple aetiologies
  ▸ Unspecified neurocognitive disorder
	■ Dementia in Alzheimer's disease
	■ Dementia in Alzheimer's disease with early onset
	■ Dementia in Alzheimer's disease with late onset
	■ Dementia in Alzheimer's disease, atypical or mixed type
	■ Dementia in Alzheimer's disease, unspecified
	■ Vascular dementia
	■ Vascular dementia of acute onset
	■ Multi-infarct dementia
	■ Subcortical vascular dementia
	■ Mixed cortical and subcortical vascular dementia
	■ Other vascular dementia
	■ Vascular dementia, unspecified
	■ Dementia in other diseases classified elsewhere
	■ Dementia in Pick's disease
	■ Dementia in Creutzfeldt-Jakob disease
	■ Dementia in Huntington disease
	■ Dementia in Parkinson's disease
	■ Dementia in human immunodeficiency virus (HIV) disease
	■ Dementia in other specified diseases classified elsewhere
	■ Unspecified dementia
	■ Amnestic disorders
	■ Organic amnestic syndrome, not induced by alcohol and other psychoactive substances
		■ Dementia due to Alzheimer's disease
		■ Dementia due to cerebrovascular disease
		■ Dementia due to Lewy body disease
		■ Frontotemporal dementia
		■ Dementia due to psychoactive substances including medications
		■ Dementia due to diseases classified elsewhere
		■ Behavioural or psychological disturbances in dementia
		■ Dementia, unknown or unspecified cause

DSM-5	ICD-10	ICD-11
Other mental disorders due to brain damage and dysfunction and to physical disease		
	■ Organic hallucinosis ■ Organic catatonic disorder ■ Organic delusional (schizophrenia-like) disorder ■ Organic mood (affective) disorder ■ Organic anxiety disorder ■ Organic dissociative disorder ■ Organic emotionally labile (asthenic) disorder ■ Mild cognitive disorder ■ Other specified mental disorders due to brain damage and dysfunction and to physical disease ■ Unspecified mental disorders due to brain damage and dysfunction and to physical disease	
Personality and behavioural disorders due to brain disease, damage, and dysfunction		
	■ Organic personality disorder ■ Post-encephalitic syndrome ■ Post-concussional syndrome ■ Other organic personality and behavioural disorders due to brain disease, damage, and dysfunction	
Other cognitive disorders		
■ Unspecified neurocognitive disorder	■ Unspecified organic or symptomatic mental disorder	■ Other specified neurocognitive disorders ■ Neurocognitive disorders, unspecified

Source: Information from the *Diagnostic and Statistical Manual of Mental Disorders*, fifth edition (DSM-5), American Psychiatric Association (APA), 2013, *ICD-10 Classification of Mental and Behavioural Disorders: Diagnostic Criteria for Research*, World Health Organization (WHO), Geneva, 2007, and *International Classification of Diseases for Mortality and Morbidity Statistics*, eleventh revision (ICD-11), 2018.

In the DSM-II and previous editions of the DSM, these disorders were referred to as 'organic mental disorders' or organic brain disorders, because they are linked to an identifiable pathology such as a brain tumour or a cerebral disease. In the DSM-5, the term 'organic mental disorder' was replaced with cognitive disorders because the previous term incorrectly implies that disorders *not* in this group of disorders (i.e. the so-called non-organic or functional mental disorders, like depression) do not have a biological basis. You will notice from Table 9.1 that the ICD-10 still retains the use of the word 'organic'.

The DSM-5, however, went a step further and renamed this category 'neurocognitive disorders', which clearly indicates these 'cognitive disorders' have a clearly delineated neurological aetiology.

HISTORY OF NEUROCOGNITIVE DISORDERS

'Dementia' was a term first used by the French doctor Philippe Pinel in the late 1700s. Initially, this was a very wide term used for people suffering intellectual deficit, but the term narrowed during the 1800s to refer to people who suffered a decline in cognitive ability (DementiaTalk, 2017).

In the second half of the 1800s, the Russian neuropsychiatrist, Sergei Sergeievich Korsakoff, studied the loss of memory owing to alcohol. The syndrome he identified was sometimes called alcoholic dementia, but is more commonly called Korsakoff syndrome. At the end of the 1800s, the Czech psychiatrist Arnold Pick was examining the brains of patients who had died from dementia, and found unusual bodies in the brain tissue. This led to this form of dementia being named Pick's disease; this form affects personality and memory.

At the start of the 1900s, for people to be diagnosed with different types of dementia, the age of onset was considered an important factor. For people to be diagnosed with what was then called 'senile dementia', they needed to be over 65. Therefore, when the German psychiatrist Alois Alzheimer studied similar conditions in younger patients, he used the term 'presenile dementia' to refer to dementia with onset before the age of 65. His colleague, Emil Kraepelin, used the term 'Alzheimer's disease' to refer to this condition in 1910, and this name is still used today.

Significant research on the role of proteins in dementia took place in Germany in the 1920s, with the work of the neurologists Hans Gerhard Creutzfeldt and Alfons Maria Jakob, and in the 1930s, with the work of Friedrich Heinrich Lewy (who later became Frederic Henry Lewey after emigrating).

In 1970, the British psychiatrist Martin Roth questioned how useful it was to use the age of onset to distinguish between Alzheimer's disease ('presenile dementia') and senile dementia of the Alzheimer's type (Ellison, n.d.). Then, in 1976, the American neurologist Robert Katzmann examined 'countless autopsies from patients across the age spectrum and found that the pathological changes described by Alzheimer were indeed a common feature in all of them' (Sontheimer, 2015, p. 101).

'Delirium', as a term, has existed for far longer than 'dementia', but it was only in the latter half of the 1900s that there was significant agreement on what should be referred to as 'delirium'. In 1987, the Polish psychiatrist Zbigniew J. Lipowski considered it a disorder of acute confusion that primarily affected older people (Lipowski, 1987). Adamis, Treloar, Martin, and Macdonald observe that '[n]ot until the twentieth century was it thought that delirium was marked by a full recovery among survivors, and this was probably due to the desire for a clear distinction from dementia' (2007, p. 467).

DELIRIUM

Clinical picture

Delirium is usually seen as a temporary state of mental confusion with fluctuating consciousness. It usually occurs rather suddenly and is characterised by mental confusion, the inability to pay attention, and the inability to think clearly. This condition is generally reversible. In addition, it is accompanied by anxiety, disorientation, and incoherent speech. Delirium is an abnormal mental state and not a disease. It is sometimes also referred to as an 'acute confusional state' or 'acute brain syndrome'.

The main feature of the disorder is the impairment in consciousness. By consciousness, we mean awareness that can vary from being fully alert to being comatose (unconscious) – see Figure 9.4 for a graphical representation of how the levels of consciousness are rated. In order to diagnose delirium, there are specific features that must be present. See Table 9.2 for the DSM-5 and ICD-10 diagnostic criteria for delirium.

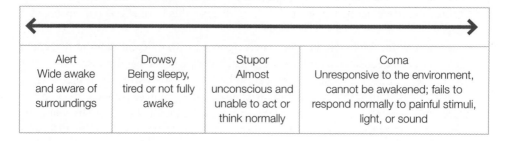

Alert	Drowsy	Stupor	Coma
Wide awake and aware of surroundings	Being sleepy, tired or not fully awake	Almost unconscious and unable to act or think normally	Unresponsive to the environment, cannot be awakened; fails to respond normally to painful stimuli, light, or sound

Figure 9.4: Levels of consciousness

The cognitive changes in delirium include memory impairment, disorientation, and language and perceptual disturbance. In addition, emotional disturbances commonly occur. There may be anxiety, fear, depression, irritability, anger, euphoria (excitement or elation), and apathy, all of which can occur rapidly and with unpredictable shifts from one emotional state to another.

Epidemiology

According to the DSM-5 (American Psychiatric Association, 2013), delirium is likely to occur in about 0.4% of the adult general population between the ages of 18 and 55 years, and in about 1.1% of those 55 years and older. In medical inpatients, it is more common and ranges from 10% to 31%, increasing significantly in the elderly. The incidence of new delirium per admission ranges from 3% to 29%, and occurrence rate per admission varies between 11% and 42%.

Table 9.2: Diagnostic criteria for delirium from the DSM-5 and ICD-10

DSM-5	ICD-10
A. A disturbance in attention (i.e. reduced ability to direct, focus, sustain, and shift attention) and awareness (reduced orientation to the environment). B. The disturbance develops over a short period of time (usually hours to a few days), represents a change from baseline attention and awareness, and tends to fluctuate in severity during the course of a day. C. An additional disturbance in cognition (e.g. memory deficit, disorientation, language, visuospatial ability, or perception). D. The disturbances in Criteria A and C are not better explained by another preexisting, established, or evolving neurocognitive disorder and do not occur in the context of a severely reduced level of arousal, such as coma. E. There is evidence from the history, physical examination, or laboratory findings that the disturbance is a direct physiological consequence of another medical condition, substance intoxication or withdrawal (i.e. due to a drug of abuse or to a medication), or exposure to a toxin, or is due to multiple aetiologies.	For a definite diagnosis, symptoms, mild or severe, should be present in each one of the following areas: ■ Impairment of consciousness and attention (on a continuum from clouding to coma; reduced ability to direct, focus, sustain, and shift attention); ■ Global disturbance of cognition (perceptual distortions, illusions, and hallucinations – most often visual; impairment of abstract thinking and comprehension, with or without transient delusions, but typically with some degree of incoherence; impairment of immediate recall and of recent memory but with relatively intact remote memory; disorientation for time as well as, in more severe cases, for place and person); ■ Psychomotor disturbances (hypo- or hyperactivity and unpredictable shifts from one to the other; increased reaction time; increased or decreased flow of speech; enhanced startle reaction); ■ Disturbance of the sleep–wake cycle (insomnia or, in severe cases, total sleep loss or reversal of the sleep–wake cycle; daytime drowsiness; nocturnal worsening of symptoms; disturbing dreams or nightmares, which may continue as hallucinations after awakening); ■ Emotional disturbances, e.g. depression, anxiety or fear, irritability, euphoria, apathy, or wondering perplexity. The onset is usually rapid, the course is diurnally fluctuating, and the total duration of the condition less than six months.

Aetiology

Delirium is further classified according to its aetiology. For example, if the aetiology of the delirium is a consequence of a general medical condition (i.e. a seizure or renal failure), then 'delirium due to a general medical condition' is diagnosed. If it is a consequence of a drug misuse or abuse, then 'substance intoxication delirium' or 'substance withdrawal delirium' is diagnosed. The category 'delirium due to multiple aetiologies' is used when there may be several causes for the delirium, or 'delirium not otherwise specified' is considered when the aetiology is not established or not known. There are several common causes of delirium (see Table 9.3).

Table 9.3: Some common causes of delirium

Central nervous system	Epilepsies and seizures, migraine, head trauma, brain tumour, stroke
Metabolic disorder	Diabetes
Systemic illness	Infection (malaria, sepsis, viral, syphilis), dehydration, nutritional deficiency, burns, heat stroke
Medical conditions	Cardiac failure or surgery, leukaemia, renal failure, hepatitis, etc.
Medications	Pain medication, antibiotics, antivirals, antifungals, steroids, cardiac medication
Over-the-counter (OTC) medications	Herbal remedies and nutritional supplements
Drugs of abuse	Intoxication and withdrawal from drugs such as alcohol, cannabis (dagga), MDMA (Ecstasy), Crystal meth (Tik), cocaine, heroin, etc.
Toxins	Intoxication and withdrawal from aluminium, pesticides, etc.

Source: Adapted from Sadock & Sadock, 2007.

Treatment and management of delirium

The symptoms of delirium usually develop suddenly (e.g. after a head injury) or they can develop over hours to days. Delirium is dangerous and is sometimes fatal, especially in the elderly. Since delirium is often associated with an underlying physical cause, recovery is to be expected if it is treated appropriately. Recovery from the delirium may occur in a few hours to days, or symptoms may persist for weeks to months, this being common in the elderly or those with coexisting dementia.

The management of delirium involves identifying and correcting the underlying problem and symptomatically managing any behavioural or psychiatric symptoms. If the underlying aetiological factor is promptly treated, recovery is usually quick and likely to be complete. Recovery is also related to premorbid cognitive and physical abilities. If a person had good cognitive and physical functioning before the illness, he or she has better recovery from delirium. Those with previous episodes of delirium may be at increased risk for recurrent symptoms.

Although most individuals recover fully, delirium may progress to stupor, coma, seizures, or death, especially when the underlying cause is untreated. However, in the elderly, full recovery is less likely. Even when there is recovery in the elderly, there are often persistent cognitive deficits. In the medically ill, delirium is associated with more medical complications and higher mortality.

So-called environmental interventions are generally recommended for patients with delirium. These interventions are designed to reduce or eliminate environmental factors that exacerbate delirium. They include providing an optimal level of environmental stimulation, reducing sensory impairments, and making environments more familiar. In addition, cognitive-emotional support provides patients with reorientation and reassurance. In particular, information concerning delirium may reduce fear or discouragement. Doctors may also use certain drugs (e.g. antipsychotic drugs) to control agitation in the patient.

 ACTIVITY

Read the following information about delirium in Ugandan intensive-care units, then suggest how physicians could screen for delirium in these settings.

A mechanical ventilator is a machine that assists a patient to breathe. In 2015, Kwizera et al. published a study on the prevalence of delirium in mechanically ventilated patients in four Ugandan intensive care units (ICUs). The authors of the study found that delirium, in these contexts, was associated with a history of mental illness, anaemia, sedation, endotracheal tube use, and respiratory acidosis.

They noted that, due to increasing access to critical care, the number of mechanically ventilated patients is increasing, and therefore more patients are at risk of experiencing delirium in the ICU setting. They also noted that few of the ICU physicians are aware of delirium or test for it in their patients.

Source: Kwizera et al., 2015.

NEUROCOGNITIVE DISORDER (DEMENTIA)

The DSM-IV-TR and the ICD-10 refer to these disorders as dementia. However, the DSM-5 and the ICD-11 use the term 'neurocognitive disorders' instead. The American Psychiatric Association (2013) states that, while the term 'dementia' is a customary description of degenerative disorders for older adults, the term 'neurocognitive disorders' is more inclusive as it includes neurocognitive disorders that affect younger people as well. In order to accommodate both the DSM-5 and ICD-10 descriptions of these disorders, we will refer to them as neurocognitive disorder (dementia) in the rest of this chapter.

The American Psychiatric Association (2013) views these disorders as unique when compared to the other DSM-5 categories, as the underlying pathology and aetiology can be easily determined. The primary diagnosis would be major or mild neurocognitive disorder, followed by an aetiological subtype (e.g. Alzheimer's disease, Parkinson's disease, HIV infection, etc.) (see Table 9.1).

To understand the clinical picture of these disorders, it is necessary to note which neurocognitive domains are affected. The DSM-5 describes these domains as follows (American Psychiatric Association, 2013):

- **Complex attention:** Sustained, divided, and selective attention, as well as processing speed.
- **Executive functioning:** Planning, decision-making, working memory, error detection and correction, inhibition, and mental flexibility.
- **Learning and memory:** All memory registers (e.g. short-term, semantic, autobiographical) and implicit learning.
- **Language:** Expressive and receptive language.
- **Perceptual-motor:** This includes visual perception, visuo-constructional abilities, and perceptual-motor praxis and gnosis.
- **Social cognition:** Recognition of emotions and theory of mind.

Clinical picture

In neurocognitive disorder (dementia) there is the gradual loss of mental abilities or cognitive skills such as thinking, remembering, and reasoning, which results in a person not being able to do simple, everyday activities, such as getting dressed or eating. They may lose their ability to solve problems, experience difficulty controlling their emotions, and undergo a personality change. They may sometimes become agitated or hallucinate (i.e. see or hear things that are not there). Memory loss is a common symptom of neurocognitive disorder (dementia). However, many different diseases can cause dementia (Sadock & Sadock, 2007). Table 9.4 lists the DSM-5 criteria for major neurocognitive disorder and ICD-10 criteria for dementia, and Table 9.5 lists the DSM-5 criteria for mild neurocognitive disorder.

Table 9.4: Diagnostic criteria for major neurocognitive disorder from the DSM-5 and dementia from the ICD-10

DSM-5 Major neurocognitive disorder	ICD-10 Dementia
A. Evidence of significant cognitive decline from a previous level of performance in one or more cognitive domains (complex attention, executive function, learning and memory, language, perceptual-motor, or social cognition) based on: (1) Concern of the individual, a knowledgeable informant, or the clinician that there has been a significant decline in cognitive function; and	The primary requirement for diagnosis is evidence of the following: ■ There is a decline in both memory and thinking which is sufficient to impair personal activities of daily living, as described above. ■ The impairment of memory typically affects the registration, storage, and retrieval of new information, but previously learned and familiar material may also be lost, particularly in the later stages.

DSM-5 Major neurocognitive disorder	ICD-10 Dementia
(2) A substantial impairment in cognitive performance, preferably documented by standardised neuropsychological testing or, in its absence, another quantified clinical assessment. B. The cognitive deficits interfere with independence in everyday activities (i.e. at a minimum, requiring assistance with complex instrumental activities of daily living such as paying bills or managing medications). C. The cognitive deficits do not occur exclusively in the context of a delirium. D. The cognitive deficits are not better explained by another mental disorder (e.g. major depressive disorder, schizophrenia).	▪ Dementia is more than dysamnesia; there is also impairment of thinking and of reasoning capacity, and a reduction in the flow of ideas. ▪ The processing of incoming information is impaired, in that the individual finds it increasingly difficult to attend to more than one stimulus at a time, such as taking part in a conversation with several persons, and to shift the focus of attention from one topic to another. The above symptoms and impairments should have been evident for at least six months for a confident clinical diagnosis of dementia to be made.

Source: Reprinted with permission from the *Diagnostic and Statistical Manual of Mental Disorders*, (DSM), fifth edition, American Psychiatric Association (APA), 2013, p. 602, and the ICD-10 *Classification of Mental and Behavioural Disorders: Diagnostic Criteria for Research*, World Health Organization (WHO), Geneva, 2007.

Neurocognitive disorder (dementia) is an extremely common condition among the elderly. However, it must not be confused with the normal decline in cognitive functioning that occurs with aging. The diagnosis of neurocognitive disorder is made when there is greater memory and other cognitive impairment than would be expected due to normal aging and when the symptoms cause considerable impairment in the person's everyday functioning (Sadock & Sadock, 2007).

Table 9.5: Diagnostic criteria for mild neurocognitive disorder from the DSM-5

DSM-5
A. Evidence of modest cognitive decline from a previous level of performance in one or more cognitive domains (complex attention, executive function, learning and memory, language, perceptual-motor, or social cognition) based on: (1) Concern of the individual, a knowledgeable informant, or the clinician that there has been a significant decline in cognitive function; and (2) A substantial impairment in cognitive performance, preferably documented by standardised neuropsychological testing or, in its absence, another quantified clinical assessment. B. The cognitive deficits do not interfere with capacity for independence in everyday activities (i.e. complex instrumental activities of daily living such as paying bills or managing medications are preserved, but greater effort, compensatory strategies, or accommodation may be required).

DSM-5
C.   The cognitive deficits do not occur exclusively in the context of a delirium.
D.   The cognitive deficits are not better explained by another mental disorder (e.g. major depressive disorder, schizophrenia).

Source: Reprinted with permission from the *Diagnostic and Statistical Manual of Mental Disorders*, (DSM), fifth edition, American Psychiatric Association (APA), 2013, p. 605.

As described before, there are several areas of cognitive disturbance that may occur. One of the critical ones is memory impairment, which is understood to be a prominent early symptom and is required to make the diagnosis of neurocognitive disorder (dementia). The person is not able to learn new things or forgets previously learned information. As a result, the person will lose or forget things, such as wallets, keys, or the food cooking on the stove, or he or she may become lost in unfamiliar surroundings. In the advanced stages of the disorder, the person may actually forget his or her occupation, schooling, birthday, family members, and sometimes even his or her name.

Another area of potential deterioration is that of language function (aphasia). The person may have difficulty naming people and objects. Speech may become vague, long-winded, and repetitive with excessive use of non-specific words such as 'thing' and 'it'. In the advanced stages of dementia, the person may even be mute or have a deteriorated speech pattern characterised by echolalia (i.e. echoing what is heard) or palilalia (i.e. repeating sounds or words over and over).

A further area of potential deterioration is the failure to recognise or identify objects despite there being intact sensory function (agnosia). The person may not be able to recognise familiar objects, such as a table or a pen. As the dementia progresses, the person may be unable to recognise family members or even his or her own reflection in the mirror.

Common in neurocognitive disorder (dementia) are problems with the ability to plan, organise, sequence, and abstract (referred to as executive functioning), which is associated with frontal lobe functioning. Patients with this disorder may also become spatially disorientated, have difficulty with spatial tasks, and have poor judgement and insight. They may not be aware of their memory loss or other cognitive deterioration and may do things that are not in keeping with their actual abilities, for example, driving a car erratically, or making huge purchases or sales.

They may demonstrate disinhibited behaviour. This may include tactless, rude, or even offensive actions that do not follow the usual social rules about what to say or where to do something. This includes things like making inappropriate jokes, neglecting personal hygiene, or being inappropriately familiar with strangers. Sometimes people with neurocognitive disorder (dementia) may become violent and harm others. Depression and suicidal behaviour commonly occur in dementia. Some individuals may also have motor disturbances, resulting in an unsteady gait, which may contribute to falls that result in injuries with serious consequences and complications (Sadock & Sadock, 2007).

 **ACTIVITY**

Watch these movies about dementia, and its impact on sufferers, their family and community. Bear in mind that movies do not always capture the full impact of the disorder and often sensationalise the content. However, these movies do provide some valuable insight and understanding of dementia.

Still Alice (2014)
This movie is based on Lisa Genova's 2007 bestselling book of the same name. Julianne Moore plays Alice Howland, a professor diagnosed with early-onset Alzheimer's disease.

Away From Her (2007)
In *Away From Her*, Julie Christie was nominated for a Best Actress Oscar for her portrayal of Fiona, a woman with Alzheimer's who voluntarily enters a long-term care facility to avoid being a burden to her husband.

The Savages (2007)
Laura Linney (nominated for an Oscar) and Philip Seymour Hoffman play siblings in this tragic comedy about adult children caring for a parent with dementia.

The Notebook (2004)
This movie is based on the best-selling novel by Nicholas Sparks, and features James Garner as Noah, the loving husband of Allie (Gena Rowlands), who is in a nursing home due to Alzheimer's disease.

Iris: A Memoir of Iris Murdoch (2001)
This movie tells the true story of how English novelist Iris Murdoch's succumbed to Alzheimer's disease. It is based on the book *Elegy for Iris* by John Bayley, who was Murdoch's partner for 40 years, and it depicts his unconditional love for her.

Epidemiology

The prevalence of neurocognitive disorder (dementia) depends on age and the extent of the cognitive impairment. There is a rise in prevalence as a result of the growing aging population. Major neurocognitive disorder (dementia) is present in about 1–2% of the general population that is older than 65 years, and 30% of the general population older than 85 years (American Psychiatric Association, 2013). Prevalence of minor neurocognitive disorder varies from 2–10% at age 65 and 5–25% by age 85 (American Psychiatric Association, 2013).

Very few studies on prevalence of neurocognitive disorder (dementia) have been carried out in Africa. A series of studies from Ibadan, Nigeria, have produced consistently low rates for neurocognitive disorder (dementia), especially for Alzheimer's disease (Hall, 1994). More recent studies reveal rather higher rates, but still lower than surveys carried out elsewhere (Ineichen, 2000).

The sub-Saharan Africa (SSA) regional estimate of age-specific dementia prevalence in people aged 60 years and over is now 6.38%, doubling with every 7.2 year increment in age. It is estimated that 2.13 million people were living with dementia in SSA in 2015. This number will reach 3.48 million by 2030, and 7.62 million in 2050, with the most important increases in eastern and central SSA (Alzheimer's Disease International, 2017)

There are several possible reasons for these findings, including differential survival rates, the hiding of cases by relatives because of stigma, reluctance to seek medical assistance as it is considered inappropriate, poor access to medical care, the feeling that the old person has come to the end of his or her useful life, as well as defective case-finding techniques (Ineichen, 2000).

The statistics on prevalence of neurocognitive disorder (dementia) in developing societies are incomplete but the estimate of people suffering with neurocognitive disorder (dementia) in developing countries is 6.8% (Brodrick, 2002). The prevalence of different causes of neurocognitive disorder (dementia) (e.g. infections, nutritional deficiencies, traumatic brain injury, endocrine conditions, cerebrovascular diseases, seizure disorders, brain tumours, substance abuse, etc.) varies substantially across cultural groups.

Aetiology

The neurocognitive disorders (dementias) are sub-categorised according to presumed aetiology (see Table 9.1). For the purposes of this book, only some of the aetiological subtypes will be discussed.

Neurocognitive disorder (dementia) due to Alzheimer's disease

Alzheimer's disease is the most common cause of neurocognitive disorder (dementia), occurring in 50% or more of all cases. Factors that are considered major risks are family history of Alzheimer's disease, genetic factors (e.g. links to chromosomes 1, 14, and 21, multiple E4 genes, and amyloid deposits), and head injury. While there are variations or subtypes of Alzheimer's disease, generally speaking the onset is subtle in that there are initial symptoms of memory impairment and a general and gradual deterioration in cognitive abilities (Sadock & Sadock, 2007). The pathology is associated with the parietal and temporal regions of the brain.

Neurocognitive disorder (dementia) due to vascular disease

Cerebrovascular disease, which affects blood vessels in the brain, is considered to be the second-most common cause of neurocognitive disorder (dementia). Mainly small and medium-size vessels may undergo infarction, which is death or damage as a result of obstruction to the local blood supply. This results in multiple lesions, involving changes to structures in the brain. These infarctions may be due to injury or disease in the brain.

Neurocognitive disorder (dementia) associated with cerebrovascular disease usually has an abrupt onset and fluctuating course. The risk factors associated with this neurocognitive disorder (dementia) are hypertension, diabetes, advanced age, stroke, alcoholism, and other cardiovascular risk factors such as smoking and obesity. This disorder tends to be more common in men. Compared to Alzheimer's disease, patients with vascular neurocognitive disorder (dementia) are more like to have depression, affective changes, disturbance of gait, and confusion, which is often more noticeable in the evenings (Sadock & Sadock, 2007).

Neurocognitive disorder (dementia) due to Parkinson's disease

Parkinson's disease is a disorder that affects nerve cells in the part of the brain controlling muscle movement, that is, the substantia nigra in the basal ganglia. Nerve cells in this part of the brain are responsible for producing a chemical called dopamine, which acts as a messenger between the parts of the brain and nervous system that help control and coordinate body movements. Damage or death of these nerve cells results in reduced dopamine, and the part of the brain controlling movement fails to work as it should. The loss of nerve cells is a slow process, and Parkinson's disease usually only starts to develop when around 80% of the nerve cells in the substantia nigra are lost.

The sufferer typically demonstrates slow and abnormal movements. These include: a tremor, or shaking, which usually begins in a limb, and often the hand or fingers; slowed movements (bradykinesia); muscle stiffness; impaired posture and balance; decreased ability to perform unconscious movements, including blinking, smiling or swinging the arms during walking; and changes in speech and writing. This neurocognitive disorder (dementia) is commonly associated with depression.

The causes of Parkinson's disease are unknown, but several factors appear to play a role. These include genetics, pesticides and herbicides used in farming, traffic or industrial pollution, medication (drug-induced Parkinsonism), other progressive brain conditions, and cerebrovascular disease

Researchers have noted that changes that occur in the brains of people with Parkinson's disease include the presence of Lewy bodies; that is, clumps of specific substances within brain cells are microscopic markers of Parkinson's disease. Researchers believe that these Lewy bodies hold an important clue to the cause of Parkinson's disease (see neurocognitive disorder dementia due to Lewy body disease below).

Neurocognitive disorder (dementia) due to Huntington's disease

Huntington's disease results from genetically influenced degeneration of brain cells in subcortical areas of the brain (brain stem, thalamus, basal ganglia, or tracts connecting these areas to the frontal lobe). Huntington's disease is passed genetically from parent to child. Each child of a Huntington's disease parent has a 50–50 chance of inheriting the Huntington's disease gene. If a child does not inherit the gene, they will not develop the disease and cannot pass it on to subsequent generations. A person who inherits the gene will sooner or later develop the disease.

The neurocognitive disorder (dementia) associated with this disease is characterised by more motor abnormalities (slow or uncontrolled motor movement) and fewer language abnormalities. This degeneration also causes loss of intellectual abilities and emotional disturbance. The person with this disease has difficulty with complex tasks.

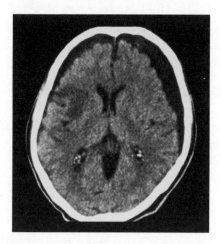

Figure 9.5: MRI image – demonstrates bilateral atrophy of the head of the caudate nuclei and compensatory ventricular dilatation of the frontal horns bilaterally suggestive of Huntington's disease

Major or mild frontotemporal neurocognitive disorder (dementia)

This disorder was previously referred to as dementia due to Pick's disease, but this has changed in the DSM-5 to reflect the neuroanatomical area that is affected, rather than the underlying aetiology. This disorder is characterised by atrophy or shrinking of the frontal and temporal regions of the brain (see Figure 9.6). In the early stages of this disorder, there is some executive dysfunction, but personality and behavioural changes are prominent, with cognitive functions remaining intact.

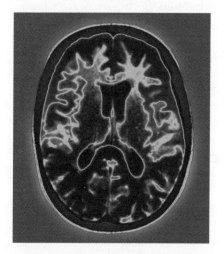

Figure 9.6: CT scan of Pick's disease

Neurocognitive disorder (dementia) due to Lewy body disease

Lewy body disease is a neurocognitive disorder (dementia) associated with Lewy inclusion bodies found in the cerebral cortex (see Figure 9.7). Lewy bodies are round deposits that contain damaged nerve cells. It is believed that they are formed as the cells try to protect themselves from attack. This disorder presents in a similar way to Alzheimer's but is more rapid; it is characterised by greater deficits in attention, psychomotor speed, and verbal fluency. Other features are hallucinations, Parkinsonian-type and other motor features, and extrapyramidal signs (abnormal involuntary movements, alterations in muscle tone, and postural disturbances).

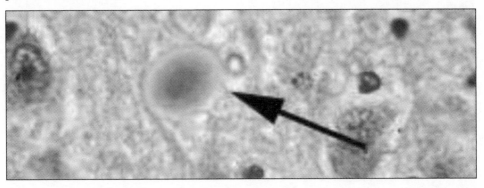

Figure 9.7: Microscopic image of a Lewy body

Source: U.S. National Library of Medicine. http://www.nlm.nih.gov/medlineplus/images/lewybody.jpg.

Neurocognitive disorder (dementia) due to Prion disease

This disorder includes neurocognitive disorders due to a group of sub-acute spongiform encephalopathies (e.g. Creutzfeldt-Jakob disease, which is more commonly known as 'mad cow disease') (American Psychiatric Association, 2013). The disorder has an insidious onset with rapid progression of impairment (from minor to major impairments within six months) (American Psychiatric Association, 2013). Motor symptoms, such as ataxia (abnormal movements) are prominent in this disorder.

Neurocognitive disorder (dementia) due to HIV infection

The human immunodeficiency virus (HIV) is a virus that spreads through certain body fluids and attacks the body's immune system. A compromised immune system makes it harder for the body to fight off infections and other diseases. Opportunistic infections and certain cancers then take advantage of a very weak immune system, and this signals that the person has acquired immunodeficiency syndrome, or Aids. Unlike some other viruses, the human body cannot get rid of HIV completely, even with current treatment. So, once you get HIV, you have it for life.

HIV/Aids contributes substantially to the burden of disease in developing countries and in sub-Saharan Africa in particular. There are an estimated 25 million individuals living with HIV across Africa (UNAIDS/WHO, 2006). See Box 9.3 for HIV/Aids figures for South Africa.

Neurocognitive disorder (dementia) that is associated with direct HIV infection of the central nervous system is typically characterised by forgetfulness, slowness, poor concentration, and difficulties with problem-solving. Behavioural manifestations most commonly include apathy and social withdrawal. Occasionally, these may be accompanied by delirium, delusions, or hallucinations. Neurocognitive disorder (dementia) in association with HIV infection may also result from accompanying central nervous system tumours (e.g. primary central nervous system lymphoma) and from opportunistic infections (e.g. tuberculosis and syphilis).

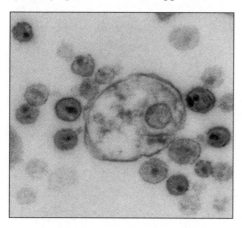

Figure 9.8: HIV particles adhering to a CD4 lymphocyte

Source: Courtesy of Optics and Imaging Centre Nelson R Mandela School of Medicine, University of KwaZulu-Natal.

BOX 9.3: HIV/AIDS IN 2018

	Number of people living with HIV in 2018	New infections in 2018	Change in Aids-related deaths since 2010
Worldwide	37.9 million	1.7 million	–33%
In South Africa	7.52 million	270 000	–43%

For more information, see https://www.statssa.gov.za/publications/P0302/ P03022018.pdf and https://www.unaids.org/sites/default/files/media_asset/ UNAIDS_FactSheet_en.pdf

Source: Table created by OUP based on information from Statistics South Africa (2018); UNAIDS (2018); UNAIDS (2019).

Neurocognitive disorder (dementia) due to traumatic brain injury

The prevalence of head trauma is extremely high in South Africa given the high rate of motor vehicle accidents (MVAs) (see Box 9.4) and high level of violence (see Box 9.5).

BOX 9.4

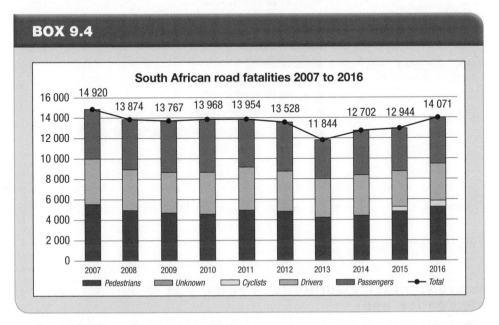

Source: Automobile Association of South Africa, RTMC Calendar report, 2016.

BOX 9.5: SA CRIME STATS, 1 APRIL 2017 TO 31 MARCH 2018

Category	Number
Contact crimes	601 366
Contact-related crimes	115 361
Property-related crimes	507 975
Other serious crimes	438 113
Total	**1 662 815**

Contact crimes include murder, attempted murder and sexual offences, as well as common assault and robbery.

Source: Businesstech, 2018.

Head injury-related neurocognitive disorder (dementia) is characterised by emotional lability, dysarthria (speech impairment), and impulsivity.

The worldwide burden of traumatic brain injury is presented in Figure 9.9.

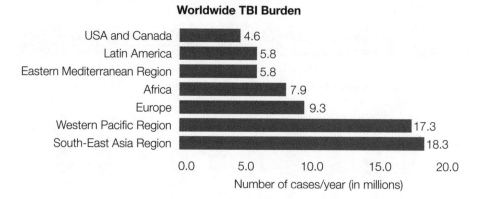

Figure 9.9: Graph showing the worldwide traumatic brain injury burden

Source: Dewan et al., 2018. p. 8.

Neurocognitive disorder (dementia) due to substance/medication use

This disorder results from the abuse of drugs or medication, or from toxin exposure. Such substances include alcohol, inhalants, sedatives, hypnotics, or anxiolytics (medication for the treatment of anxious states).

Treatment and management of neurocognitive disorder (dementia)

As with delirium, treating the underlying cause of neurocognitive disorder (dementia) is necessary although the condition most often is not reversible. However, by understanding the aetiology of the neurocognitive disorder (dementia), it may be possible to arrest or reverse the process. In some cases, especially in neurocognitive disorder (dementia) due to vascular disease, preventative measures may be possible. Preventative measures may include changes in diet and exercise, as well as blood-pressure monitoring. Changes in cognitive function significantly affect sufferers, who can benefit immensely from supportive and educational psychotherapy. In addition, assistance in dealing with loss and grief is also important for both the individual and his or her family.

 **ACTIVITY**

Read the following study on the prevalence of neurocognitive impairment among HIV-positive individuals in Botswana. What are the authors suggesting might decrease the prevalence of neurocognitive impairment in this context, and how could this idea be tested?

In 2010, Lawler et al. published their study of the prevalence of neurocognitive impairment among HIV-positive individuals in Botswana, where they used the International HIV Dementia Scale (IHDS) to assess participants. The authors found that despite the fact that 97.5% of participants were receiving highly active antiretroviral therapy (HAART), 38% met criteria for dementia on the IHDS, and 24% were diagnosed with major depressive disorder.

In their conclusion, Lawler et al. stated that the 'prevalence of neurocognitive impairment in HIV-positive individuals in Botswana is higher than expected, especially since almost all of the subjects in this study were prescribed HAART. This suggests the need to reconsider the timing of introduction of antiretroviral therapy in developing countries where HAART is generally not administered until the CD4 cell count has dropped to 200/mm3 or below'.

Source: Lawler et al., 2010.

AMNESTIC DISORDERS

Historically, the DSM made provision for a group of disorders known as amnestic disorders. Although the DSM-5 no longer has this category, the ICD-10 does.

Clinical picture

An amnestic disorder is characterised by memory impairment in the absence of other significant accompanying cognitive impairments. The syndrome is characterised by the inability to learn new information (anterograde amnesia), and the inability to recall knowledge stored from before the onset of the disorder (retrograde amnesia). Short-term and recent memory is usually affected. Patients often cannot remember what they had for breakfast or the name of their doctor.

The onset can be sudden (e.g. when the cause is trauma, cerebrovascular events, or toxic substances) or gradual (e.g. cerebral tumours). Amnestic disorders are also sub-categorised according to presumed aetiology: amnestic disorder due to a general medical condition (such as head injury), substance-induced persisting amnestic disorder (induced by, for example, excessive alcohol consumption or carbon monoxide poisoning), or amnestic disorder not otherwise specified (Sadock & Sadock, 2007). The ICD-10 criteria for amnestic disorders are specified in Table 9.6.

Table 9.6: Diagnostic criteria for amnestic disorders from the ICD-10

Amnestic disorders
The primary requirements for this diagnosis are: ■ Memory impairment as shown in impairment of recent memory (learning of new material); disturbances of time sense (rearrangements of chronological sequence, telescoping of repeated events into one, etc.). ■ Absence of defect in immediate recall, of impairment of consciousness, and of generalised cognitive impairment. ■ History or objective evidence of chronic (and particularly high-dose) use of alcohol or drugs. ■ Personality changes, often with apparent apathy and loss of initiative, and a tendency towards self-neglect may also be present, but should not be regarded as necessary conditions for diagnosis. ■ Although confabulation may be marked, it should not be regarded as a necessary prerequisite for diagnosis.

Source: Reprinted with permission from the ICD-10 *Classification of Mental and Behavioural Disorders: Diagnostic Criteria for Research*, World Health Organization (WHO), Geneva, 2007.

Epidemiology

There are no adequate studies on the incidence and prevalence of amnestic disorders. They are most commonly found in association with excessive use of alcohol and traumatic head injury. We would imagine the prevalence to be significantly high in South Africa given the high levels of head injury due to motor vehicle accidents and other violence (e.g. armed assaults, grievous bodily harm, and domestic violence). This violence is often complicated or exacerbated by irresponsible use of alcohol.

Aetiology

The main brain areas that are implicated in the amnestic disorders are the temporal lobes, midline nuclei of the thalamus, hippocampus, mammillary bodies, and the amygdala. The left hemisphere is more implicated than the right.

Some symptoms associated with the frontal lobes are usually seen in amnestic disorders. These symptoms include confabulation (fabrication of detailed, plausible experiences and events to cover gaps in memory) and apathy. There are several possible causes for amnestic disorders.

These include (Sadock & Sadock, 2007):
■ systemic conditions (such as thiamine or vitamin B1 deficiency)
■ hypoglycaemia (low blood sugar)
■ brain-related conditions like hypoxia (low oxygen)
■ seizures and epilepsies
■ surgical procedures to the brain
■ infections (e.g. herpes simplex encephalitis)
■ tumours

- cerebrovascular diseases
- substance-related conditions (related to e.g. alcohol, neurotoxins, sedatives, and many over-the-counter drugs).

Some of these causes are discussed in more detail below:
- *Cerebrovascular diseases:* These usually affect the hippocampus and involve the posterior cerebral and basilar arteries and their branches. Infarctions rarely involve only the hippocampus; more commonly, they also affect the occipital and parietal lobes.
- *Multiple sclerosis:* Memory disorder is the most common cognitive complaint in patients with multiple sclerosis.
- *Korsakoff syndrome:* This is an amnestic syndrome caused by thiamine deficiency; it is commonly associated with chronic alcohol abuse. The neglect of proper eating by chronic alcohol abusers is the cause for the thiamine deficiency. Individuals with Korsakoff syndrome also demonstrate personality changes and a lack of initiative, spontaneity, and general interests. Confabulation, apathy, and passivity are also common.
- *Alcoholic blackouts:* Individuals with severe alcohol abuse may present with memory loss of the events that occurred while they were intoxicated.
- *Head injury:* Amnesia is a common symptom in head injury. Usually the amnesia is retrograde and includes the actual traumatic event.
- *Transient global amnesia:* This syndrome is characterised by the abrupt loss of the ability to recall recent events or to remember new information. It is associated with mild confusion, lack of insight, and the inability to perform previously learned complex tasks. The condition usually last for 24 hours.

Treatment and management of amnestic disorders

As in all of the cognitive disorders, the primary approach to treatment of the amnestic disorders is to treat the underlying cause. Thus, the initial treatment is directed to the underlying pathological process.

If the underlying cause is primary, systemic, or cerebral, the treatment may include the use of thiamine, antiretroviral medication, or aspirin. Sometimes, drugs that seem to improve memory in patients with Alzheimer's disease may be used. However, despite the variety of pharmaco-therapeutic trials that have been undertaken, no drug treatments have been proved effective in amnestic disorder (Sadock & Sadock, 2007).

For mild cases of amnesia, rehabilitation may involve teaching memory techniques and employing the use of memory tools, such as calendars, lists, notes, timers, and association techniques. These memory exercises and retraining can be very useful. Helpful prompting of the date, time, and location is also known to reduce anxiety.

Patients with amnestic disorder also experience considerable difficulty in their social and occupational functioning. To help such patients, emotional and social support may be necessary. They may also require supervised living conditions to ensure that appropriate feeding and care occurs. Many patients do slowly recover over time, and sometimes they may even recover memories that were formed before the onset of the amnestic disorder. It is useful, particularly after the remission of the amnestic episode, to provide psychotherapy or counselling in order to help the individual adjust to their period of illness and to aid their recovery.

ASSESSMENT OF NEUROCOGNITIVE DISORDERS

The assessment usually begins with a review of the clinical notes of doctors or information recorded in the hospital or clinic files. This is followed by clinical interviews, observation, and basic screening tests.

Several simple screening tests and/or rapid assessments are undertaken by the clinician. The most common is the Mini Mental Status Examination (MMSE), which is a quick way to evaluate cognitive function. The test has a set of questions and tasks that assess orientation, memory, attention, concentration, calculation, language, and consciousness (see Table 9.7). The MMSE has been traditionally used to screen for cognitive impairment in a variety of dementia illnesses, including HIV-associated dementia.

Table 9.7: Mini Mental Status Examination

Task	Instructions
Date orientation	'Tell me the date?'
Place orientation	'Where are you?'
Register three objects	Name three objects slowly and clearly. Ask the patient to repeat them.
Serial sevens	Ask the patient to count backwards from 100 by 7. Stop after five answers. (Or ask them to spell 'world' backwards.)
Recall three objects	Ask the patient to recall the objects mentioned above.
Naming	Point to your watch and ask the patient 'What is this?' Repeat with a pencil.
Repeating a phrase	Ask the patient to say 'no ifs, ands, or buts'.
Verbal commands	Give the patient a plain piece of paper and say 'Take this paper in your right hand, fold it in half, and put it on the floor.'
Written commands	Show the patient a piece of paper with 'CLOSE YOUR EYES' printed on it.
Writing	Ask the patient to write a sentence.
Drawing	Ask the patient to copy a pair of intersecting pentagons on a piece of paper.

Source: Adapted from Folstein, Folstein, & McHugh, 1975.

Probably the most widely used test to quantify the level of consciousness is the Glasgow Coma Scale (GCS). Performance on the GCS total score is used to establish the level of consciousness. It is simple and correlates well with outcome following severe brain injury. Scores are given for:

- eye-opening response (e.g. whether the patient does not open their eyes, or opens their eyes spontaneously, or opens their eyes to a painful stimuli or to light),
- verbal response (e.g. whether the patient makes no sounds, makes incomprehensible sounds, utters inappropriate words, or responds normally to questions),
- motor response (e.g. whether the patient makes no movement, responds to painful stimuli by withdrawing, or obeys a command to perform a motor activity).

Another simple and commonly used test is the Clock Drawing Test (CDT). The CDT is used to assess cognitive functioning in psychiatric and neurological settings. The patient is asked to draw the face of a clock with all the numbers on it. The patient is then asked to draw the hands pointing to ten past eleven. The drawing is scored for accuracy of the representation of the clock face, the layout of numbers, and the position of the hands. Total cut-off scores are used to indicate whether the drawing is suggestive of dementia. The test is used as a clinical screening task for visuo-spatial and constructional disabilities, and can be useful as a dementia screening device (Spreen & Strauss, 1991). For examples of the deterioration on the CDT see Figures 9.10 and 9.11.

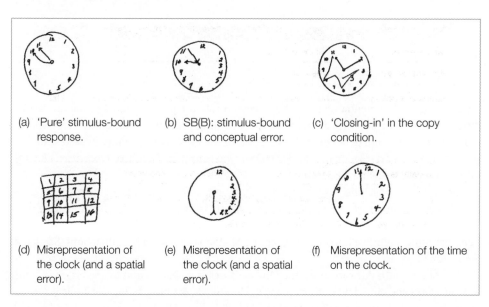

(a) 'Pure' stimulus-bound response.

(b) SB(B): stimulus-bound and conceptual error.

(c) 'Closing-in' in the copy condition.

(d) Misrepresentation of the clock (and a spatial error).

(e) Misrepresentation of the clock (and a spatial error).

(f) Misrepresentation of the time on the clock.

Figure 9.10: Examples of stimulus-bound and conceptual errors on the Clock Drawing Test

Source: Rouleau et al., 1996. Reprinted from *Brain and Cognition*, 32(1), Rouleau, I., Salmon, D. P., Butters, N. Longitudinal analysis of clock drawing in Alzheimer's disease patients, pp. 17–34. © 1996, with permission from Elsevier.

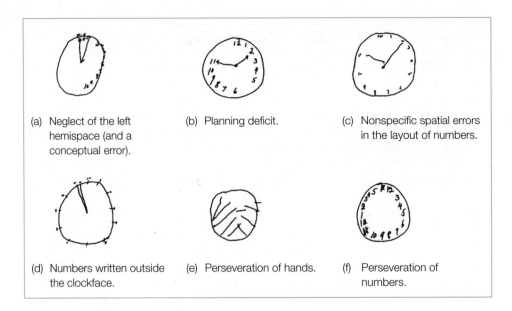

(a) Neglect of the left hemispace (and a conceptual error).

(b) Planning deficit.

(c) Nonspecific spatial errors in the layout of numbers.

(d) Numbers written outside the clockface.

(e) Perseveration of hands.

(f) Perseveration of numbers.

Figure 9.11: Examples of spatial and/or planning deficits in the layout of numbers and perseverative errors on the Clock Drawing Test

Source: Rouleau et al., 1996. Reprinted from *Brain and Cognition*, 32(1), Rouleau, I., Salmon, D. P., Butters, N. Longitudinal analysis of clock drawing in Alzheimer's disease patients, pp. 17–34. © 1996, with permission from Elsevier.

There are several dementia scales that are used to rate the patient's functioning on various criteria. Some of these scales are rated by the attending practitioner or family/caregivers so that the clinician is not dependent on the report of the ill patient. Commonly used scales are the International HIV Dementia Scale (HDS), Deterioration Cognitive Observee (DECO), or the Clinical Dementia Scale (CDS).

The HDS was developed as a bedside evaluation test to differentiate patients with HIV-associated dementia from those who are cognitively normal. A South African study found that the HDS correlates positively with the MMSE and that it identified more participants demonstrating cognitive impairment than the MMSE (Ganasen, Finchama, Smit, Seedat, & Stein, 2007).

In another South African study, the DECO scores were also found to correlate well with MMSE scores and clinicians' ratings (Lenger, De Villiers, & Louw, 1996). See Table 9.8 for an example of a few items from the DECO (Ritchie & Fuhrer, 1992; 1994).

Table 9.8: Instructions and sample of DECO items

We would like you to tell us how your relative was a year ago. The following questions ask about a number of everyday situations. We would like you to tell us whether in these situations he or she is doing about the same, not as well, or much worse, than a year ago. Put a cross in the square to show your reply.

	Better or about the same	Not as well	Much worse
Does he or she remember as well as before which day and which month it is?			
When he or she goes out of the house, does he or she know the way as well as before?			
Have there been changes in his or her ability to remember his or her own address or telephone number?			

Source: Ritchie & Fuhrer, 1994.

There are more sophisticated neuropsychological assessments, which are usually done after the initial screening tests indicate a cognitive disorder. Such neuropsychological assessments are usually administered and conducted by experienced psychologists and those specialising in neuropsychology. These neuropsychological tests may be administered individually or as a complete battery. See Chapter 3 for a more detailed discussion of these tests.

Other useful and also necessary assessments are the neuro-imaging techniques (discussed in Chapter 3) such as X-rays, Magnetic Resonance Imaging (MRI), Functional Magnetic Resonance Imaging (fMRI), and Positron Emission Tomography (PET) scans, as well as other laboratory tests. These are extremely helpful in the diagnosis of cognitive disorders but are extremely expensive and not always readily available.

CONTEXTUAL AND CROSS-CULTURAL PERSPECTIVES

Individual and group beliefs and attitudes influence health behaviour. Therefore, all disorders and illness behaviours are strongly influenced by cultural and contextual factors. Furthermore, cultural and social beliefs, and environment, also influence the way healthcare facilities are used (Pillay, 1996). Although Western medicine plays a dominant role in the mass control of disease, traditional or folk medicine continues to play an important role in the healthcare of communities. People possess unique attitudes, values, and beliefs about health and illness, which integrally influence their health behaviour. When working in multicultural settings, it is important to be aware of the cultural and language differences that can influence a diagnosis of cognitive disorders.

In addition to culture and social background, educational background and environmental factors must be taken into consideration when one evaluates an individual's mental capacity or disorders (Jinabhai et al., 2004; Ngcobo & Pillay, 2008; Pillay, 2000). In South Africa, past inequalities in education, and the consequent lack of facilities and resources, significantly impact on the evaluation and understanding of individuals with cognitive disorders.

In South Africa, no equivalent term for dementia is identified in any local languages, and there is a general lack of awareness of dementia among the community. The most prominent belief regarding the underlying cause of dementia is that it is part of normal ageing, and people with dementia are routinely referred to as 'childlike' (Alzheimer's Disease International, 2017). According to this review, in some instances when people with dementia are perceived to be witches, the fear inevitably results in discrimination, isolation, and instances of violence.

Some of the symptoms associated with cognitive disorders, such as disorientation, changes in consciousness, forgetfulness, amnesia, seizures, dissociation, delusions, or changes in behaviour and personality, may be accounted for differently by different indigenous world views. For example, according to traditional African views, some of these symptoms may be explained as:

- *Ukuthwasa*, the calling to be a traditional healer whose role is to help in the caring and healing process of the whole person, addressing the condition, and also restoring balance by addressing the alleged causes of the illness.
- *Ukufa kwabantu*, which broadly means 'the illnesses of the people' and is not recognised by the patient as an illness or disease per se, but as a disturbance caused by breaking a taboo or displeasing an ancestor, or due to a spell that has been cast on the patient. These include:
  - *Indiki*, *ufufunyane*, or *izizwe* (spirit possession)
  - *Umnyama* (pollution or contamination)
  - *Ubuthakathi* (bewitchment or sorcery)
  - *Ukuphonsa* (curses or spells)
  - *Umkhondo*/*umeqo*/*idliso* (some form of poisoning).

BOX 9.6

Ubuthakathi is the 'direct' use of traditional herbs or ointments or medicines which can be either sprinkled over someone else's food or yard or applied anywhere in order to come into physical contact with the person. It always has evil intentions.

Ukuphonsa is 'indirect'. Literally translated as 'throwing', it implies distance. It can be done even when there is no way of actually coming into contact with the medicine that is used. It may have good intentions, e.g. to gain the love of someone.

All cultures and religious groups have traditional explanations for 'abnormal behaviour'. In Islam, magic, sorcery, and witchcraft all fall under the term '*sihr*'. Belief in demonic possessions and the existence of *jinn* also form part of the culture of Islam.

According to Hussain and Cochrane (2002), *jinn* are a separate 'race' that can appear in different forms and can cause harm by possessing a human. *Jinn* can also cause physical illness, anger, or sadness. They can be used by sorcerers to wreck marriages, cause mental illness, and inflict constant pain in the body or even epilepsy (Abdussalam-Bali, 2004; Hussain & Cochrane, 2004; Karim, Saeed, Rana, Mubbashar, & Jenkins, 2004). *Jinn* possession also manifests with bizarre, multiple behaviours, and odd movements. Similar explanations about spirit possession are common in other Eastern religions, as well as among some Christian groups.

It seems that Western patients rely mainly on answers from technological medicine whereas more traditional cultures or religious groups seek divination from a healer who can restore the equilibrium of their lives. About 80% to 90% of people from developing societies rely on traditional healing for healthcare. The DSM-5 uses the term 'culture-bound syndrome' for many of these conditions; this refers to 'recurrent, locality-specific patterns of aberrant behaviour and troubling experience that may or may not be linked to a particular DSM-5 diagnostic category'.

Meyer, Moore, and Viljoen (2002) argue that it is essential to consider a patient's cultural context when they present in a healthcare setting. Ignoring (or being ignorant of) a patient's cultural context and their belief system risks misdiagnosis, the application of inappropriate therapeutic techniques, and great distress and pain for the patient.

Further, most neuropsychological and psychological assessments were developed in Western contexts but are widely used in South Africa and other developing countries, where the contexts are very different. In addition, level of education significantly contributes to the variations in the scores on these tests (Brodrick, 2002; Lenger, De Villiers, & Louw, 1996), and cultural differences in cognitive and perceptual information-processing are known to influence performance even on the nonverbal tests.

In addition, individuals from some backgrounds may not be familiar with the information used in certain tests of general knowledge (e.g. names of presidents, geographical knowledge), memory (e.g. date of birth in cultures that do not routinely celebrate birthdays), or orientation (e.g. sense of place and location may be conceptualised differently in some cultures). Thus, in some populations (such as immigrants), attributing low scores to pathological processes rather than to other factors can result in diagnostic error and/or over-diagnosis of significant morbidity, as well as over-prescribed treatment (Klimidis & Tokgoz, n.d.).

CONCLUSION

Increasing longevity as a result of better health, diets, and living conditions, as well as changes in lifestyle, contribute to the steady increase of the prevalence of cognitive disorders. Depending on the classification system being used, cognitive disorders may be divided into three main groups: delirium, dementia, and amnestic disorders. In each category, the aetiology of the disorder influences the onset, course, treatment, and outcome of the disorder. Symptoms of different cognitive disorders also occur in other medical conditions. This, as well as the influence of beliefs, and cultural and contextual factors, makes diagnosis and treatment of these disorders complicated and difficult.

MULTIPLE-CHOICE QUESTIONS

1. The three categories of cognitive disorders in the ICD-10 are:
    a) delirium, dementia, and amnestic disorders
    b) delirium, dementia, and Alzheimer's
    c) Alzheimer's, delirium, and amnestic disorders
    d) Alzheimer's, organic, and amnestic disorders
2. The symptoms of delirium tend to develop:
    a) very slowly, over the course of several years
    b) very quickly, over the course of a few hours to a few days
    c) moderately slowly, over the course of several months
    d) either very quickly or very slowly, depending on the cause
3. The gradual deterioration of brain functioning that affects judgement, memory, language, and other cognitive processes, is called:
    a) major or mild neurocognitive disorders (dementia)
    b) delirium
    c) amnestic disorder
    d) mental retardation
4. Neurocognitive disorders that are caused by HIV appear to be due to:
    a) side effects of neurotransmitters
    b side effects of antiretroviral treatment
    c) opportunistic infections that occur in HIV patients
    d imbalances in the neurotransmitters
5. Compared to most disorders, Huntington's disease is very unusual because it is:
    a) the result of one gene
    b) influenced by many genes
    c) always a cause of dementia
    d) associated with subcortical impairment
6. The main impairment in amnestic disorders is an inability to:
    a) transfer information from the short-term memory into long-term memory
    b) remember significant events from the distant past
    c) perform basic arithmetic
    d) remember one's own name
7. Pick's disease is now known as the following in the DSM-5:
    a) major or mild frontocerebral neurocognitive disorder
    b) major or mild frontotemporal neurocognitive disorder
    c) major or mild tempovascular neurocognitive disorder
    d) major or mild cerebrovascular neurocognitive disorder
8. The ICD-11 has a category named:
    a) mild neurocognitive disorder
    b) major neurocognitive disorder
    c) mild or major neurocognitive disorder
    d) none of the above

9. The age on onset for Alzheimer's disease is:
   a) 45
   b) 55
   c) 65
   d) none of the above
10. The deterioration in cognitive skills that are a result of dementia includes all of the following except:
    a) palilalia
    b) aphasia
    c) ataxia
    d) echolalia

PARAGRAPH AND ESSAY QUESTIONS

1. Define 'neurocognitive disorders'.
2. Name five types of dementias.
3. Name the main types of neurocognitive disorders as described in the ICD-10 and describe how each of these disorders are sub-classified.
4. Provide a description of the main domains of neurocognitive functions.
5. Write an essay on the clinical picture, epidemiology, aetiology and treatment of neurocognitive disorders.
6. Distinguish between delirium and neurocognitive disorder (dementia).
7. With reference to the ICD-10, how are amnestic disorders different from delirium and dementia?
8. Describe the aetiological subtypes of neurocognitive disorders.
9. Briefly explain Korsakoff's syndrome.
10. What are the common assessments used in establishing a neurocognitive disorder?
11. Write a brief essay on the assessment of neurocognitive disorders.
12. Neurocognitive disorders (like all mental disorders and illness behaviours) are strongly influenced by cultural and contextual factors. Explain this statement.

Revised by Gale Ure

CHAPTER OUTLINE

Introduction
Dissociation, somatising, and stress
  What is dissociation?
  What causes dissociation?
  Compartmentalisation
  Detachment
  Early adversity and future pathology
Dissociative disorders and their comparative nosology
  Dissociative amnesia
  Dissociative fugue
  Dissociative identity disorder
  Depersonalisation/derealisation disorder
  Trance and possession disorders
  Ganser's syndrome
  Related conditions in South Africa
  Related conditions in other cultures
  Epidemic hysteria
Somatoform disorders and their comparative nosology
  Conversion disorder
  Somatic symptom disorder
  Persistent somatoform pain disorder
  Illness anxiety disorder
  Psychological factors affecting other medical conditions
Factitious disorder and malingering
  Factitious disorder
  Malingering
Conclusion
  Pathogenesis
  Symptom expression

*The original version of this chapter was written by Conrad Visser and Larise du Plessis. Third edition version revised by Gale Ure.

LEARNING OUTCOMES

After studying this chapter, you should be able to:

- Describe the concepts of dissociation and somatising.
- Discuss the association between early adversity, trauma, dissociation, and somatising.
- Provide an overview of the psychological processes of compartmentalisation and detachment.
- Provide an overview of current nosological approaches to dissociative and somatoform disorders.
- Describe the aetiology, pathogenesis, epidemiology, clinical features, and differential diagnoses of dissociative and somatic symptoms and related disorders, as classified by the DSM-5.
- Describe conditions other than the dissociative disorders that are characterised by prominent dissociation.
- Describe culture-specific conditions with strong dissociative phenomena.
- Discuss *amafufunyana* and *ukuthwasa* in relation to dissociation.
- Describe Ganser's syndrome.
- Discuss psychological factors affecting other medical conditions.
- Describe factitious disorder.
- Define malingering and give an approach to the detection of deceit in clinical practice.

PERSONAL HISTORY CASELET

Claudia Z lives in a small coastal town in the Eastern Cape. She is a 27-year-old single mother of two young children, one of whom is intellectually disabled. Since her father's death three years ago, she has been responsible for supporting her ailing mother, working as a packer at a small supermarket in town. A few weeks before the collapse, she met a police officer on secondment from Port Elizabeth. A romantic relationship developed but was soon spoiled by mistrust, resentment, and physical violence. One Monday, Claudia collapsed at work and was taken to the local hospital.

She was found to be fully conscious and able to give an adequate account of herself and recent events. She described a sudden and complete loss of sensation in her lower limbs, and she could no longer move. Her general examination was unremarkable. She was unable to lift her legs off the bed, let alone stand. On examination, her clinical signs were normal. She also demonstrated a dense sensory loss affecting both lower limbs, but not conforming to any known neurological distribution. She was transferred to Port Elizabeth where detailed special investigations failed to uncover any focal neurological lesions. A psychiatrist who consulted her while she was in Port Elizabeth commented that she appeared childlike and displayed a glib disregard for her apparently grave neurological condition. During her stay in hospital, she received regular visits by the hospital clinical psychologist who provided supportive therapy. Exactly a week after the sudden onset of paralysis and sensory loss, Claudia stood up and discharged herself from hospital.

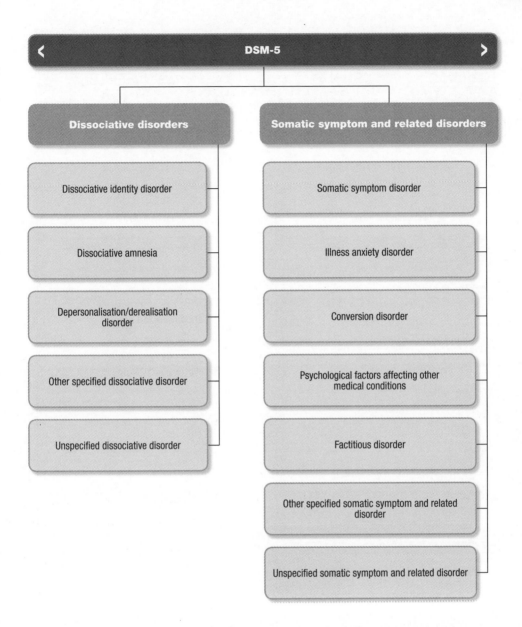

Figure 10.1: The American Psychiatric Association DSM-5 categorises dissociative disorders and somatic symptom and related disorders as shown above.

Source: Figure created by OUP reflecting information found in *Diagnostic and Statistical Manual of Mental Disorders*, fifth edition (DSM-5), 2013.

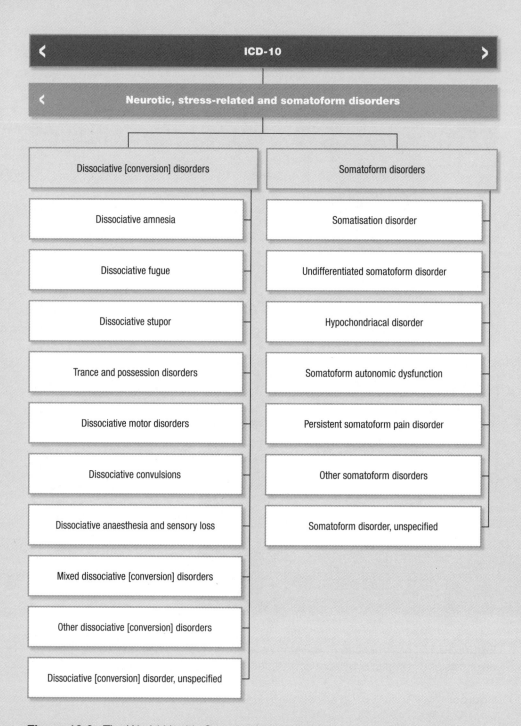

Figure 10.2: The World Health Organization categorises dissociative [conversion] disorders and somatoform disorders as shown above.

Source: *International Statistical Classification of Diseases and Related Health Problems*, tenth revision (ICD-10), 2016.

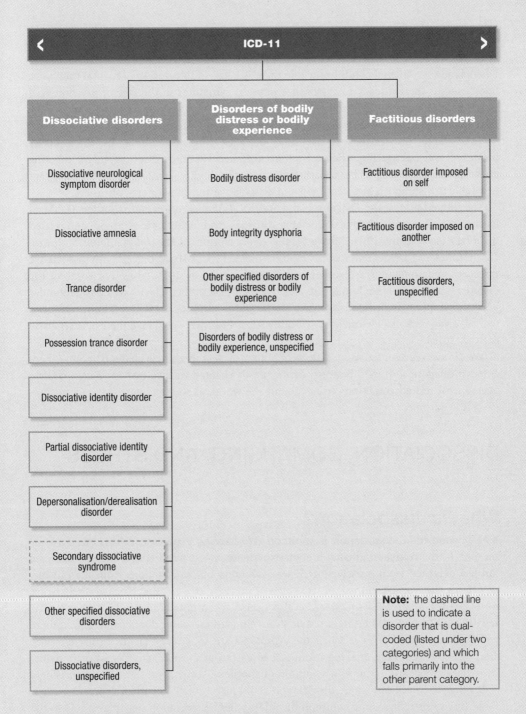

Figure 10.3: The World Health Organization categorises dissociative disorders, disorders of bodily distress or bodily experience, and factitious disorders as shown above.

Source: *International Classification of Diseases for Mortality and Morbidity Statistics*, eleventh revision (ICD-11), 2018.

INTRODUCTION

Dissociation is a mental condition where there is a loss of integration of mental functions. Somatising is the tendency to experience physical symptoms in the face of psychological distress. This chapter deals with both dissociative and somatoform disorders because of the neuroscientific and clinical similarities exhibited by the two categories.

This chapter also deals with factitious disorder, where symptoms are intentionally produced, and malingering, where symptoms are faked. Factitious disorder and malingering are dealt with in this chapter because they may present as bodily symptoms, and it is important to be able to distinguish between them and dissociative and somatoform disorders.

The fifth edition of the *Diagnostic and Statistical Manual of Mental Disorders* (DSM-5) has two separate categories for dissociative disorders and for somatic symptom and related disorders (see Figure 10.1). Similarly, the tenth edition of the *International Statistical Classification of Diseases and Related Health Problems* (ICD-10) also deals with dissociative disorders and somatoform disorders separately (see Figure 10.2). However, some of the disorders that are classified under dissociative disorders in the ICD-10 are classified under 'somatic symptom and related disorders' in the DSM-5. In the new ICD-11, both categories will fall away, and a single category – 'bodily stress disorder' – will take their place (Gureje & Reed, 2016).

We discuss representative conditions of both disorders in a single chapter, because there is much categorical overlap between them. In this chapter, we also provide a comparative overview of related conditions from around the world, as well as South African culture-specific syndromes.

DISSOCIATION, SOMATISING, AND STRESS

What is dissociation?

As a phenomenon, dissociation is common. We have all experienced it in one form or another. In the course of normal human experience, when faced with a major threat, we can feel detached from ourselves, as if we look upon our own actions from the outside, experience the world as unreal, or have little or no recall of a trauma. Normal dissociation is not limited to stressful situations; it also occurs when bored, engaged in monotonous activities, and when meditating, tired or sleepy. In extreme cases, dissociation can become pathological in itself. This is when the symptoms are so severe that they interfere with the person's functioning, making it difficult to carry out normal activities of daily living. Dissociation may also occur as a symptom of another disorder, and there is a surprisingly wide range of conditions where dissociation could play a role in a patient's clinical picture, Table 10.1 summarises some common disorders where dissociation may play a role in the patient's diagnosis.

Table 10.1: Examples of clinical conditions where dissociation might be observed as a symptom

Mental disorders
Dissociative disorders
Panic attack (partially mediated by metabolic effects of hyperventilation)
Acute stress disorder and post-traumatic stress disorder
Borderline personality disorder
Somatoform disorders
Schizophrenia and other psychotic states
Somnambulism ('sleepwalking')
Dementia and delirium

Substance-related disorders
Alcohol
Cannabis (dagga)
Sedative-hypnotics (e.g. benzodiazepines like diazepam; older antihistamines like cyclizine)
Hallucinogens (e.g. lysergic acid diethylamide – LSD; phencyclidine and ketamine)
Opiates (morphine-like)
Steroids
Antipsychotic agents
Lithium
Anticholinergic agents

Neurological and general medical conditions
Hypoxia (insufficient oxygen supply to brain)
Metabolic disturbances (e.g. alkalosis, hypoglycaemia, hyponatraemia, hypocalcaemia)
Organ failure (kidney and liver)
Hypertensive encephalopathy
Cerebral infections (e.g. herpes simplex encephalitis, falciparum malaria)
Cerebral neoplasms (e.g. astrocytoma, glioblastoma multiforme, metastases)
Post-concussion
Stroke (especially if it involves brain stem, basal forebrain, thalamic and medial attentional structures)
Transient global amnesia
Wernicke-Korsakoff syndrome (vitamin B1 deficiency)
Epilepsy (e.g. temporal lobe epilepsy)
Migraine
Post-operative states (unique combination of stress response and fluid, electrolyte, and metabolic changes)

What causes dissociation?

The Mexican academic, Etzel Cardeña, produced an overview of dissociation in 1994. This provides a simple model of dissociation, and a practical point of departure for understanding how dissociation relates to threat. He viewed dissociation as comprising three distinct features, which act in the following way:

- *Suspended integration of mental modules (mental systems or information streams):* This initiates when, in a time of high trauma and stress, and unable to exit the environment, the person effectively removes the association between the themselves and the event, and in so doing, removes the threat from their consciousness.
- *An altered state of consciousness occurs:* The person has effectively negated the trauma and stress by shifting it, 'becoming' someone else to whom the frightening events make no difference. This is because the person does not exist, in the case of dissociative identify disorder, or by ignoring the fact that the event(s) ever happened.
- *A defence mechanism:* The person has successfully deflected the bad feelings by allowing themselves to experience the trauma as if it has been observed rather than felt. It is therefore as if the trauma has never had an effect on them.

Recent insights into the neural mechanisms at play in dissociation highlight these very features. Mindful of this, the expression of dissociation in animals, and the fact that dissociation is not limited to stressful situations, we propose to restate Cardeña's model to broaden its conceptualisation: Dissociation is a genetically endowed trait, adapted as a defence to threat that suspends the integration of mental systems and alters consciousness by narrowing the traumatic event into a context that the person can survive. As a defence mechanism, it partners 'fight and flight'. It operates throughout the animal kingdom and, by virtue of the survival advantage it confers, is preserved across generations.

Cardeña further conceptualised dissociation to involve two distinct psychological processes: compartmentalisation and detachment. Each process possesses its own distinct neural circuitry.

Compartmentalisation

Compartmentalisation refers to subconscious brain activity that acts as a defence mechanism to counteract feelings of cognitive dissonance. Cognitive dissonance occurs when a person has internal conflicting emotions about certain experienced situations or events that cause psychological discomfort and anxiety. The person then separates himself or herself from his or her personal feelings, beliefs, values, and cognitions about a situation in order to continue to coexist with it. This inhibition prevents explicit acknowledgement of the situation. An example would be a doctor who has strong feelings about abortion having to assist a woman to terminate a pregnancy.

Compartmentalisation allows these conflicting ideas to coexist by inhibiting all direct or explicit acknowledgement and interaction between the distinctly compartmentalised states of one's self. Compartmentalised processes continue to function in spite of their disconnection from the person's consciousness and other mental processes. Compartmentalisation can manifest as amnesia, as well as other deficits like psychogenic blindness, loss of tactile sensation, and paralysis.

Anatomically and functionally, the brain's cortex is arranged hierarchically. Primary cortical regions are devoted to single operations and are subordinate to higher-order or association cortical regions. Compartmentalisation relies on this top-down regulation of subordinate cortical regions responsible for sensory or motor processing by the higher-order cortices.

If the motor system is involved, paralysis results, without any demonstrable pathology of the apparatus of movement. With paralysis, it is as if the primary motor cortex, responsible for transmitting the final command for the contraction of a muscle group, had been 'taken off-line', its activity suspended by higher-order motor cortex like the prefrontal cortex. Evidence for this exists in functional brain imaging. If it involves modality-specific sensory systems, the patient becomes blind or deaf, or loses the sense of touch. The 'lesion' responsible for this dissociation is not anatomical, but functional.

This apparently bizarre situation is one expression of the fear response and confers survival advantage on animals possessing the trait. In the animal kingdom, paralysis is a common defensive behaviour. We have all heard of an animal rolling over and 'playing dead'. In neuroscientific terms, 'playing dead' is called 'freezing', or 'tonic immobility'. The immobile prey survives a possible death as it escapes detection by its predator. The sensory equivalent can result in anaesthesia and analgesia, with diminished tactile sensation and dampened experience of pain. Freezing and anaesthesia partner 'fight and flight' as behavioural phenomena characteristic of the fear response. Figures 10.4 and 10.5 illustrate compartmentalisation.

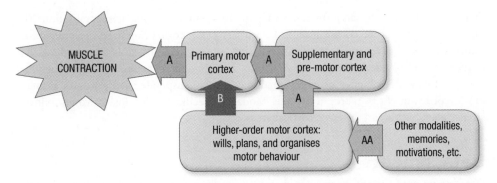

Figure 10.4: The hierarchical arrangement of motor integration and information flow in the brain

Source: Created by author Visser.

Figure 10.4 depicts the hierarchical arrangement of motor integration and information flow in the brain. Sensory and other information is fed to higher-order motor cortices (prefrontal cortex and cingulate gyrus), represented by Process AA. Process A indicates hierarchical flow of information from the highest- to lowest-order motor cortex (i.e. prefrontal to primary), from where the final instruction is passed onto the appropriate muscles to contract. Process B indicates the modulating influence of higher-order cortex over subordinate cortex – an example of top-down regulation.

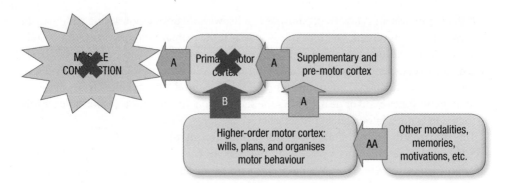

Figure 10.5: Motor integration and information flow in the brain where the higher-order association cortex inhibits the primary motor cortex

Source: Created by author Visser.

Figure 10.5 depicts the same process as Figure 10.4, but with compartmentalisation. The higher-order association cortex inhibits the primary motor cortex via Process B, interrupting information passage for further motor-processing. The result of this compartmentalisation is a failure to 'will' or release the motor behaviour. Despite an intact neural network, functional paralysis follows. The higher-order association cortex has suspended activity of the primary motor cortex, in effect 'taking it off-line'. Modality-specific sensory losses would follow a similar plan, but recruit different cortical areas.

Detachment

Detachment corresponds to an altered state of consciousness. Subjectively, it involves the experience of alienation of the self from the world outside. Emotional experiences are numbed, or blunted, and the person may experience depersonalisation or derealisation. The altered state of consciousness interferes with encoding of traumatic information, disturbing the memory trace of the event. The person also fails to integrate the emotional with the contextual aspects of the experience.

As memory is state dependent, these weakly integrated traces can be brought into conscious experience when the person is faced with a new stressful event in the present. As a result, aspects of the trauma can be re-experienced, like the 'flashbacks' of post-traumatic stress disorder (see Chapter 6). Detachment can also snuff out emotional experience when, for example, the right prefrontal cortex inhibits activity in the limbic system. Likewise, parts of the parietal cortex can be inhibited, resulting in disturbances in the internal representation of the self and its relation to the external world. The person then experiences depersonalisation and derealisation. Figures 10.6 and 10.7 illustrate the process of detachment.

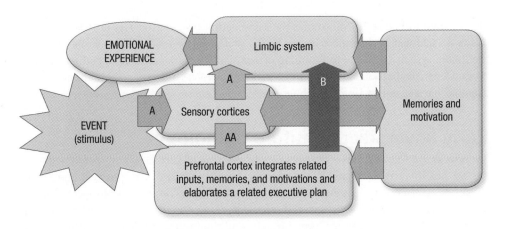

Figure 10.6: The flow of information when experiencing an event

Source: Created by author Visser.

The diagram in Figure 10.6 illustrates the flow of information when experiencing an event. Process A indicates incoming sensory information. Process AA represents passage of integrated sensory experience to the prefrontal executive cortex. The limbic system mediates the emotional experience of the event and is reliant on integrated sensory information. Process B sets the sensitivity of limbic information-processing.

Like compartmentalisation, detachment may also confer survival advantage on a person in the face of extreme threat. By reducing the adverse emotional aspects of the stress response, the brain's finite attentional capacity is rationed and can remain focused on the primary task at hand, thereby averting threat.

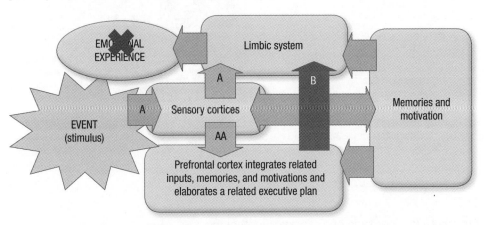

Figure 10.7: The flow of information when experiencing an event showing detachment of the limbic system by the prefrontal cortex inhibiting it

Source: Created by author Visser.

The diagram in Figure 10.7 illustrates the same neural system as in Figure 10.6. Process B shows detachment of the limbic system by the prefrontal cortex inhibiting it. Inhibition of the limbic system gives rise to numbing of emotional experience related to the traumatic event. Depersonalisation follows a similar path, but involves different areas of the cortex, for example, parietal cortex (inferior lobule).

Early adversity and future pathology

So, how can a once-adaptive system become the seat of such disabling pathology? The answer lies in early adversity. When exposed to severe threat, like physical and sexual abuse, or severely inconsistent attachment, a child may respond defensively through compartmentalisation or detachment. If repeatedly traumatised, the dissociative response is strengthened in a use-dependent way through conditioning, and becomes established as the preferential response to threat.

In other words, the more a neural process – in this case, dissociation – is used, the more efficient it becomes and the more easily it is engaged. Later, when faced with a significant psychosocial threat, dissociation is engaged as the preferential response and produces symptoms like blindness, paralysis, amnesia, attentional narrowing, disturbed personal identity, and alienation. Somatising phenomena may also include sensory disturbances of various kinds that point towards dissociation: pain, sensory loss, dizziness, and abdominal discomfort are examples that come to mind. Figure 10.8 summarises the origin of dissociative pathology.

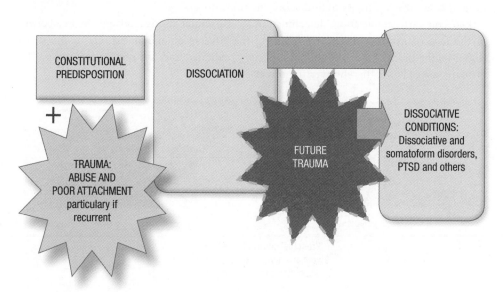

Figure 10.8: The origin of dissociative pathology

Source: Created by author Visser.

A likely pathogenetic explanation for pathological dissociation is given in Figure 10.8. In vulnerable individuals, early adversity leads to dissociation as expression of the fear response. Given the salience of the traumatic event, the patient becomes conditioned to respond automatically with dissociative phenomena if faced with significant psychosocial stressors. As a result, the prospect of perceived future trauma unleashes dissociative phenomena and sets the scene for the emergence of dissociative and somatoform disorders, as well as related conditions like acute stress disorder.

DISSOCIATIVE DISORDERS AND THEIR COMPARATIVE NOSOLOGY

According to the DSM-5, dissociative disorders are typically characterised by 'a disruption of and/or discontinuity in the normal integration of consciousness, memory, identity, emotion, perception, body representation, motor control and behavior' (American Psychiatric Association, 2013, p. 291). What follows are descriptions of the individual conditions included under the category of dissociative disorders.

The DSM-5 recognises three dissociative disorders: dissociative amnesia (with dissociative fugue as a specifier), dissociative identity disorder, and depersonalisation/derealisation disorder.

The ICD-10 offers a longer list of dissociative disorders: dissociative amnesia, dissociative fugue, dissociative stupor, dissociative trance and possession disorders, dissociative motor disorders, dissociative convulsions, dissociative anaesthesia and sensory loss, mixed dissociative [conversion] disorders, and other dissociative [conversion] disorders (World Health Organization, 2016). By considering conversion as a dissociative condition, the ICD-10 takes a somewhat different view on dissociative conditions from the DSM-5.

Table 10.2 compares how the two texts classify dissociative disorders. The shaded rectangles indicate similarity between the different classifications.

> **HELPFUL HINT**
>
> **Common features of dissociative disorders**
>
> - Constitutional predisposition
> - History of childhood trauma
> - Symptoms emerge following psychosocial stressor
> - Symptoms include amnesia, identity disturbance, and alterations in sensory experience

Table 10.2: Comparative nosology of dissociative disorders

DSM-5	ICD-10
Dissociative amnesia	Dissociative amnesia Dissociative fugue

DSM-5	ICD-10
Depersonalisation/derealisation disorder	Depersonalisation/derealisation disorder*
Dissociative identity disorder	Dissociative trance and possession disorder
Other specified dissociative disorders Unspecified dissociative disorders	Dissociative [conversion] disorder, unspecified
	Dissociative stupor** Dissociative motor disorders** Dissociative convulsions** Dissociative anaesthesia and sensory loss** Mixed dissociative [conversion] disorders**
	* Listed under other neurotic disorders ** Conforms to DSM-5 conversion disorder and functional neurological disorder where they are considered somatoform/somatic symptom disorders

As can be seen in Table 10.2, the dissociative motor disorders, dissociative convulsions, dissociative anaesthesia and sensory loss, and mixed dissociative [conversion] disorders are equivalent to the conversion disorder in the DSM-5, which is classified under 'somatic symptom and related disorders'.

It should also be noted that depersonalisation/derealisation disorder is not listed in the ICD-10 as a dissociative [conversion] disorder but is instead listed in the ICD-10 under 'other neurotic disorders'.

Diagnosis of dissociative disorders using the ICD-10 approach requires the fulfilment of the general criteria for dissociative disorders as well as those for the specific disorders, but this requirement does not apply to depersonalisation/derealisation disorder (which the ICD-10 does not classify as a dissociative disorder). Table 10.3 lists the ICD-10 general criteria for dissociative disorders.

Table 10.3: General criteria for dissociative disorders (ICD-10)

G1. There must be no evidence of a physical disorder that can explain the characteristic symptoms of this disorder (although physical disorders may be present that give rise to other symptoms).
G2. There are convincing associations in time between the onset of symptoms of the disorder and stressful events, problems, or needs.

Source: Reprinted with permission from the ICD-*10 International Statistical Classification of Diseases and Related Health Problems*, World Health Organization (WHO), Geneva, 2016.

Dissociative amnesia

Amnesia, or the inability to recall, is common to almost all dissociative disorders and is prominent in dissociative amnesia and dissociative identity disorder. However, when amnesia is the predominant mode of presentation, a diagnosis of dissociative amnesia is most appropriate.

Dissociative amnesia shows the following characteristics:

- The amnesia involves episodic memory, with loss of autobiographical recollection of events and important personal information.
- The amnesia is not the result of failure to encode, store, or retrieve information as occurs in Wernicke-Korsakoff syndrome, stroke, or other lesions involving the medial memory structures. As a consequence, it is possible to recover lost memories, and deficits are usually reversible.
- Commonly, the amnesia involves a discrete period and does not involve vagueness or poor retrieval. Instead, a full range of information is simply not accessible. Uncommonly, people are unable to recall any personal information, and they are then said to experience generalised amnesia. Systematised, or selective, amnesia concerns the failure to recall certain, but not all, events during a relatively short period.
- The amnesia is predominantly retrograde. Retrograde amnesia refers to amnesia for past events, or events before an index event (such as trauma). Anterograde amnesia refers to the inability to form new memories following an index event and is the most pronounced aspect of amnesia of physical origin like concussion (see Chapter 9). In dissociative amnesia, new information can still be learnt and anterograde amnesia is unusual, except for a very brief period following the index trauma.
- The amnesia involves events of a stressful or traumatic nature like incidents of child abuse. Other events, like the death of a spouse, can also trigger dissociative amnesia.
- It is not uncommon to experience amnesia for many events.
- Patients with dissociative amnesia appear normal in other respects; memory for general information is intact as are non-declarative memory (including procedural memory for tasks like riding a bike or changing gears) and other cognitive functions.
- The amnesia is too expansive for ordinary forgetfulness to have been the cause.
- Occasionally, if associated with minor head trauma, the trauma is too slight to have physiological consequences on memory function matching what is observed.
- Although uncommon, travel away from familiar surroundings can occur in dissociative amnesia. Currently, travel is the defining feature of dissociative fugue. However, in a move away from previous DSM classifications, where dissociative fugue was considered to be a distinct disorder, the DSM-5 has included dissociative fugue as a specifier, rather than a distinct disorder in dissociative amnesia.

HELPFUL HINT

Clues to dissociative amnesia

- Blackouts or time losses of discrete duration
- Reports of behaviour patient cannot account for
- Appearance of unexplained possessions
- Unexplained changes in relationships
- Wandering away
- Unexplained changes in abilities, tastes, knowledge
- Incomplete recall of life events
- Episodes of mistaken identity.

Source: Adapted from Hales, Yudofsky, & Gabbard, 2008.

EXAMPLE CASE

Thandiwe (18 years old) had recently moved to a well-known South African university town to commence studies in journalism. One night during orientation week, she was found sitting outside the university's administration block by a patrolling police officer. She was crying and looked anxious. Concerned, the officer took her to the nearby provincial hospital where she was able to give her name, age, and a few other personal particulars but she could remember none of the events of that day. With gentle persuasion from the casualty officer, she eventually related how she could recall a 'dream-like' image of 'two dark figures'. Following the recommendations of the casualty officer, she admitted herself to the local mental health facility the next morning. She continued to be amnesic for recent events, but was able to recount her life story. She was also able to learn new information and easily adapted to the hospital milieu. Although aware of her amnesia, she seemed detached and indifferent to it.

Thandiwe's family history was as follows: She grew up in an abusive home. Her father, a wealthy businessman in Cape Town, was well known as a 'sex addict' and often cheated on Thandiwe's mother. He often arranged lavish receptions at their home where people 'partied hard'. Once, Thandiwe was drawn into a sexual orgy involving her father, two unknown women, and her brother. Her father eventually committed suicide when investigated for molesting the daughter of his personal assistant.

Thandiwe related how her move from Cape Town to study at university had been particularly stressful. She found some comfort with her new boyfriend and appeared to have become heavily dependent on him. Despite his apparent support, she felt increasingly anxious, inadequate, and fearful. She experienced ever-more-frequent headaches and insomnia. A res mate of hers later indicated that on the day she was found roaming the streets, she had walked in on her boyfriend 'making out' with another girl. She apparently ran out of the residence, screaming. A friend found her a short while later, sitting outside, looking dazed and saying nothing. The friend suggested that they seek help from the university counselling centre, but Thandiwe objected and walked off. Thandiwe has never used drugs, and a casualty drug screen was clear. She had no medical history.

Within days of admission, she made a complete recovery and was able to relate events leading to the amnesic episode. After discharge, she was referred for psychotherapy.

Epidemiology

Dissociative amnesia is considered the most common of the dissociative disorders, but as is common with dissociative disorders in general, epidemiological data are limited. Dissociative amnesia appears to be more common in women than men and in young, rather than older, adults. Its incidence rises during war and social unrest and seems to correlate with natural and human-made disasters. A direct relationship appears to exist between the severity of trauma and the incidence of amnesia.

Aetiology and pathogenesis

In keeping with the general model for dissociation, faced with significant trauma, patients with dissociative amnesia fail to integrate the emotional aspects of an experience with its context and story. A constitutional predisposition or diathesis is a likely added risk factor.

Diagnosis, clinical features, and course

Table 10.4 lists comparative diagnostic criteria for dissociative amnesia.

Table 10.4: Diagnostic criteria for dissociative amnesia from the DSM-5 and ICD-10

DSM-5	ICD-10
A. An inability to recall important autobiographical information, usually of a traumatic or stressful nature, that is inconsistent with ordinary forgetting. Note: Dissociative amnesia most often consists of localised or selective amnesia for a specific event or events; or generalised amnesia for identity and life history. B. The symptoms cause clinically significant distress or impairment in social, occupational, or other important areas of functioning. C. The disturbance is not attributable to the physiological effects of a substance (e.g. alcohol or another drug of abuse, a medication) or a neurological or other medical condition (e.g. partial complex seizures, transient global amnesia, sequelae of a closed head injury/traumatic brain injury, or other neurological condition). D. The disturbance is not better explained by dissociative identity disorder, posttraumatic stress disorder, acute stress disorder, somatic symptom disorder, or major or mild neurocognitive disorder.	■ The general criteria for dissociative disorder must be met. ■ There must be amnesia, either partial or complete, for recent events or problems that were or still are traumatic or stressful. ■ The amnesia is too extensive and persistent to be explained by ordinary forgetfulness (although its depth and extent may vary from one assessment to the next) or by intentional simulation.

Source: Reprinted with permission from the *Diagnostic and Statistical Manual of Mental Disorders*, fifth edition (DSM-5), American Psychiatric Association (APA), 2013, p. 298, and ICD-10 *Classification of Mental and Behavioural Disorders: Diagnostic Criteria for Research*, World Health Organization (WHO), Geneva, 2007.

Most cases have their onset following an emotionally stressful event (as in the case study of Thandiwe). Onset is usually abrupt, but this is not a diagnostic requirement.

Most patients are aware of the memory loss; some appear upset about it, others indifferent. Infrequently, patients may wander away from familiar surroundings. Rarely, patients may also assume new identities. The extent and depth of amnesia may vary across clinical encounters. Other cognitive functions are unaffected. Patients are usually alert before and after the onset of amnesia, but clouding of consciousness surrounding the traumatic events can be apparent. Anxiety and depression commonly co-occur with the amnesia and stressful event. The end of an amnesic episode is usually abrupt and complete. Dissociative amnesia is common, as it can occur as a component of other mental health conditions. These can include posttraumatic stress disorder, anxiety disorders, acute stress disorder, etc.

The diagram in Figure 10.9 shows an example of the time taken from the traumatic event with retrograde memory loss to recovery. The second arrow depicts anterograde memory loss and the time taken to regain the ability to recall these memories. Amnesia for antecedent events constitutes the retrograde amnesia; the period of amnesia following the insult constitutes the anterograde amnesia. The gradual return of memory following a brain insult outstrips the period of memory loss predating it.

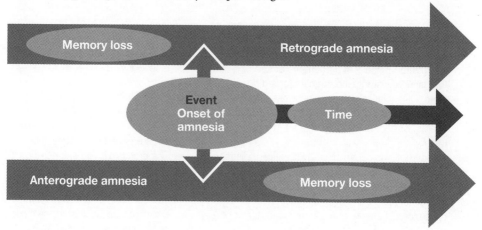

Figure 10.9: The temporal pattern of amnesia as a result of acute derangement of brain function

Source: Created by author Ure based on Weiten (2007), p. 286.

Differential diagnosis

Conditions listed in Table 10.2 must be considered when making a diagnosis of dissociative amnesia. Cognitive decline due to advanced age or disease, for example, should also be considered. Aiding differentiation, the cognitive deficits of dementia and delirium (see Chapter 9) are readily apparent and extend well beyond memory. Loss of personal information in dementia usually indicates advanced disease when obvious other signs of dementia are apparent. Post-concussion amnesia involves both retrograde and anterograde elements. The retrograde component is typically short and always shorter than the anterograde amnesia (see Figure 10.9). History and physical evidence of head trauma further support a diagnosis of post-concussion amnesia. There are a number of physical conditions that should be excluded, for example, physical trauma, cerebrovascular accidents (CVA), epilepsy, and long-term substance abuse-related symptoms.

Epilepsy commonly interrupts recall. A seizure can result in precipitous memory impairment. While epileptic patients are prone to increased seizure activity during periods of emotional stress, seizures are typically associated with other predictable and stereotypic phenomena. These include convulsive movements, incontinence, tongue-biting, aimless stereotypies (repetitive behaviours like plucking at clothes, fumbling with an object, smacking of the lips, and fluttering of eyelids), unresponsiveness, and a glazed look during a non-convulsive seizure. A history of epileptic aura characterised by emotional changes, memory aberrations like déjà vu, and aberrant sensory experiences like smelling burning rubber is often noted as well.

Although sleepwalking, or somnambulism, may resemble a dissociative state, it occurs during sleep and usually at night. In contrast to the sleepwalker's glazed look and lack of responsiveness, patients with dissociative amnesia appear normal to casual observers and do not let on that anything is amiss.

Acute and posttraumatic stress disorders are characterised by dissociative symptoms and memory disturbances. Hyperarousal, psychic numbing, phobic avoidance, and depression are also more prominent. Factitious disorders and malingering must be considered if the presentation is atypical. Where gain is suspected, like escaping trial, malingering must be a prime consideration.

Dissociative fugue

As mentioned before, in the DSM-5 dissociative fugue is considered to be only a specifier for dissociative amnesia, and not a distinct disorder; however, it is listed as a distinct disorder in ICD-10. Although rare, dissociative fugue is an apt reminder of the adaptive origins of dissociative conditions. Fight and flight are the archetypical defensive behaviours among animals. 'Fugue', derived from the Latin *fugare* meaning 'to flee', refers to the 'flight' behaviour characteristic of the fear response; travel from a person's customary home or place of work indeed defines dissociative fugue. Amnesia of important aspects of personal identity is another prerequisite. Patients may adopt a new identity during a fugue episode, although this is uncommon.

Epidemiology

Dissociative fugue is believed to be rare and is encountered during periods of high stress, such as war, civil unrest, natural disasters, and following intense interpersonal conflict.

Aetiology and pathogenesis

Like dissociative amnesia, the pathogenesis of dissociative fugue conforms to the general model for dissociation. Patients with mood disorders and certain personality disorders, notably borderline, histrionic, and schizoid personality disorder, are at greater risk of responding with fugue-like behaviour following trauma. Marital, financial, and occupational stress, violence, and war experiences serve as the trigger in most instances. Other risks include the presence of depression, previous suicide attempts, substance abuse, and brain injury.

Diagnosis, clinical presentation, and course

In the aftermath of a traumatic life event, the patient with dissociative fugue wanders away from home, work, or their usual social environment, often for days on end. During an episode, sufferers have complete amnesia of personal information and past experiences, and they are characteristically unaware that something is amiss with their ability to recall information. During the fugue, the patient functions otherwise normally and can even secure employment and earn a living. Like dissociative amnesia, very little attracts the attention of the casual observer to its existence. Once resolved, patients can recall events preceding the fugue but are amnesic for events during it. A fugue is usually short-lived, lasting mere hours to a few days, with spontaneous recovery occurring as abruptly as its onset. Rarely, fugues may last months and involve distant travel. Recurrence is rare. Table 10.5 lists the ICD-10 diagnostic for dissociative fugue.

Table 10.5: Diagnostic criteria for dissociative fugue from the ICD-10

ICD-10
■ The general criteria for dissociative disorder must be met.   ■ The individual undertakes an unexpected yet organised journey away from home or from the ordinary places of work and social activities, during which self-care is largely maintained.   ■ There is amnesia, either partial or complete, for the journey which also meets Criterion C for dissociative amnesia.

Source: Reprinted with permission from the ICD-10 *Classification of Mental and Behavioural Disorders: Diagnostic Criteria for Research*, World Health Organization (WHO), Geneva, 2007.

Differential diagnosis

Wandering is not an unusual behavioural manifestation of psychopathology. It is not unusual to read a newspaper headline about a patient who has strayed from a hospital ward and gone missing. Such wanderings usually involve acute psychosis, mania, delirium, or dementia. While the travel in dissociative fugue is purposeful and organised in its execution, the wanderings of a demented or delirious patient are aimless. Other cognitive impairments are usually obvious in dementia and delirium (see Chapter 9).

Wandering may be encountered in complex partial epilepsy. Dissociative amnesia occasionally involves travel. In dissociative identity disorder, the new identities or 'alters' are more completely established than the new identity in dissociative fugue, and switching between identities dominates the clinical picture.

Dissociative identity disorder

Conceptually, dissociative identity disorder represents a chronic dissociative disorder characterised by the existence of two or more distinct identities or personalities. It typically follows childhood sexual or physical abuse and is considered the most serious of the dissociative disorders.

Benjamin Rush, the father of American psychiatry, described a syndrome not unlike dissociative identity disorder in the early 1800s. Jean-Martin Charcot, a French neurologist, and Pierre Janet did likewise in France, and Sigmund Freud in Austria and Eugen Bleuler in Switzerland also recognised it and described its symptoms. In the 1970s and 1980s, following the attraction of the films *Sybil* and *The Three Faces of Eve*, the condition, then called multiple personality disorder, entered pop culture. Incorporation of the condition into the DSM-III in 1980 cemented the condition's status.

However, because of its apparent rarity outside the United States, dissociative identity disorder is sometimes considered an example of an American culture-bound syndrome. Golub (1995) showed that more than 60 per cent of cases worldwide emanated from the United States. It has even been suggested that the condition is non-existent in Great Britain, Russia, India, and South East Asia. Studies in Iran, Germany, Australia, Sweden, and the Netherlands have yielded a wide incidence range (2 to 17%) among psychiatric patients (Hales et al., 2008).

Nevertheless, with our ever-deepening understanding of the pathogenic mechanisms underlying the dissociative disorders in general, the set of phenomena now known as dissociative identity disorder does possess neuroscientific validity. It remains listed in the DSM-5 as a distinct disorder, and appears in the ICD-10 under 'other dissociative [conversion] disorders'.

Epidemiology

A full understanding of the incidence and prevalence of dissociative identity disorder has not been achieved, and estimates range widely. The overwhelming majority of cases are female, with onset commonly in adolescence and a mean age of onset of thirty. There appears to be an inherited basis to the condition – first-degree relatives of probands diagnosed with dissociative identity disorder have a greater risk of developing the condition than the population at large.

Aetiology and pathogenesis

As a dissociative condition, dissociative identity disorder shares its pathogenic mechanism with other dissociative conditions. It is recognised that nearly 100% of cases involve a traumatic event during childhood – usually physical or sexual abuse, the latter often incestuous. Lack of emotional support surrounding the trauma and poor attachment add to the risk. Other traumatic events, like the death of loved one, may also prove sufficient as risk factors.

Diagnosis, clinical presentation, and course

The DSM-5 diagnostic criteria for dissociative identity disorder requires the presence of at least two or more distinct personalities or an experience of possession (American Psychiatric Association, 2013), and the absence of a general medical condition, such as certain epilepsies and the exclusion of effects of psychotropic substances. Table 10.6 lists the DSM-5 criteria for dissociative identity disorder and the ICD-10 diagnostic criteria for multiple personality disorder.

Table 10.6: Diagnostic criteria for dissociative identity disorder from the DSM-5 and for multiple personality disorder from ICD-10

DSM-5 Dissociative identity disorder	ICD-10 Multiple personality disorder*
A. Disruption of identity characterised by two or more distinct personality states, which may be described in some cultures as an experience of possession. The disruption in identity involves marked discontinuity in sense of self and sense of agency, accompanied by related alterations in affect, behaviour, consciousness, memory, perception, cognition, and/or sensory motor functioning. These signs and symptoms may be observed by others or reported by the individual. B. Recurrent gaps in the recall of everyday events, important personal information, and/or traumatic events that are inconsistent with ordinary forgetting. C. The symptoms cause clinically significant distress or impairment in social, occupational, or other important areas of functioning. D. The disturbance is not a normal part of a broadly accepted cultural or religious practice. Note: In children, the symptoms are not better explained by imaginary playmates or other fantasy play. E. The symptoms are not attributable to the physiological effects of a substance (e.g. blackouts or chaotic behaviour during alcohol intoxication) or another medical condition (e.g. complex partial seizures).	In this residual code, the general criteria (G1 AND G2) for dissociative [conversion] disorders must be met. ■ Two or more distinct personalities exist within the individual only one being evident at a time. ■ Each personality has its own memories, preferences, and behaviour patterns, and at some time (and recurrently) takes full control of the individual's behaviour. ■ There is inability to recall important personal information, which is too extensive to be explained by ordinary forgetfulness. *Other dissociative [conversion] disorder

Source: Reprinted with permission from the *Diagnostic and Statistical Manual of Mental Disorders*, fifth edition (DSM-5), American Psychiatric Association (APA), 2013, p. 292, and ICD-10 *Classification of Mental and Behavioural Disorders: Diagnostic Criteria for Research*, World Health Organization (WHO), Geneva, 2007.

The average number of personalities ranges from five to ten but only two or three are usually evident at diagnosis. Transitions between personalities can occur gradually, but more frequently occur rapidly and quite dramatically. While possessing one personality, the patient is amnesic of the others. Occasionally, one personality retains awareness of another's qualities. Classically, each alter has a well-developed set of attributes.

Patients may appear coy or seductive, look depressed or anxious, but mental state examination is usually normal. It is rare for a switch between alters to occur during a clinical encounter. Sometimes patients report hallucinations. Conversion symptoms may also be present, typically non-epileptic seizures. Different alters may exhibit different conversion or other somatic symptoms.

In children, the condition may look more trance-like. During adolescence, dissociative identity disorder can take two forms. In the first, symptoms are similar to those of borderline personality disorder or a rapid-cycling bipolar condition, with unstable moods, impulsivity, risk-taking, and self-injury. In the second form, adolescent patients are socially withdrawn and reason in a childlike manner. Although rare, adolescent males can display prominent antisocial behaviour.

Dissociative identity disorder can emerge as early as three years of age. The earlier the onset, the worse the prognosis is likely to be. Severity is determined by early age of onset, chronicity, the number of alters, and the coexistence of other mental conditions. Mood, anxiety, and substance use disorders are commonly diagnosed as co-morbid conditions, as is borderline personality disorder. Prognosis is typically guarded and recovery incomplete.

Differential diagnosis

Dissociative amnesia is an obvious differential diagnosis of dissociative identity disorder. However, in dissociative amnesia the adoption of different identities does not occur and tends to run an acute course, while dissociative identity disorder is chronic. In schizophrenia and other psychotic disorders, patients may adopt a new identity as expression of a delusional state. But schizophrenia's typical affective incongruence, and the presence of delusions and formal thought disorder, make for ready differentiation. In both rapid-cycling bipolar conditions and borderline personality disorder, the absence of distinct personalities distinguishes them from dissociative identity disorder.

Complex partial epilepsy may be confused for dissociative identity disorder, but is associated with typical phenomena suggesting epilepsy. Factitious disorders and malingering should always be considered. However, atypical presentations and, in the case of malingering, the identification of an obvious external motivation for the behaviour, steers diagnosis away from dissociative identity disorder.

Depersonalisation/derealisation disorder

Depersonalisation is a feeling that the body or self is altered and not real, while derealisation involves the perception that the external world is not real. The experiences of depersonalisation and derealisation are collectively referred to as alienation. Although depersonalisation and derealisation experiences are not recognised as separate diagnostic entities by either the DSM-5 or the ICD-10, the distinction between them is useful inasmuch as it provides for a better account of a patient's personal experience.

Depersonalisation is conceptualised by the DSM-5 as a persistent or recurrent alteration in the perception of self, resulting in the suspension of a person's sense of their own personal reality (American Psychiatric Association, 2013). Experientially, depersonalisation states include feelings of estrangement from the self, being like a machine, dead, in a dream, or being detached from the body. In derealisation, individuals or objects are experienced as unreal, dreamlike, or visually distorted. The person experiences a sense of unreality or detachment with respect to their surroundings. Patients maintain intact reality-testing and experience depersonalisation or derealisation with full awareness of its abnormality.

Symptoms of depersonalisation or derealisation are usually transient. They often occur at the same time as anxiety states. Depersonalisation or derealisation are common in panic attacks.

Instead of 'depersonalisation/derealisation disorder', the ICD-10 uses the term 'depersonalisation-derealisation syndrome'. It views this not as a dissociative [conversion] disorder but under the rubric of 'other neurotic disorders', where it finds itself in the motley company of neurasthenia, the Asian culture-specific syndromes of *latah*, *koro* and *dhat*, psychaesthenia, psychaesthenic neurosis, psychogenic syncope (fainting), and occupational neurosis (e.g. writer's cramp).

Epidemiology

Depersonalisation and derealisation are common and occur from time to time in up to 70% of otherwise healthy individuals. The sexes are equally affected. Depersonalisation or derealisation is particularly common during adolescence. Onset is usually between the ages of 15 and 30, but can occur as young as 10.

There is limited data available on the occurrence of pathological depersonalisation/derealisation. A recent community-based study in the United States found a prevalence of depersonalisation disorder of 0.8% (Johnson, 2006). Surveys in the United Kingdom and Canada have revealed one-month prevalence rates between 1.2% and 1.7% (Hales et al., 2008) The prevalence of depersonalisation/derealisation in the psychiatric population is substantially higher, occurring most notably with posttraumatic stress disorder, major depressive disorder, panic disorder, schizophrenia, and substance-use disorders.

Aetiology and pathogenesis

The general pathological mechanism involved in depersonalisation/derealisation involves dissociative detachment. Detachment is the subjective experience of an altered state of consciousness characterised by alienation of the self or the external world. Detachment arises during periods of stress and represents an adaptive response whereby the expression of anxiety mediated by the limbic system is inhibited in a top-down fashion by the prefrontal cortex. As a result, anxiety is kept in check, freeing the brain to devote processing capacity to averting extreme threat. Depersonalisation/derealisation can be likened to a soldier persevering with combat despite sustaining otherwise debilitating wounds. The soldier remains focused, and performance is not curtailed by pain that would normally cause incapacitation. Table 10.7 lists common conditions and substances typically associated with the emergence of depersonalisation/derealisation.

Table 10.7: Causes of depersonalisation/derealisation

CAUSES OF DEPERSONALISATION/DEREALISATION			
Mental	**Substances of abuse**	**Medical**	**Other**
Panic attack Generalised anxiety disorder Phobias Obsessive-compulsive disorder Posttraumatic stress disorder Acute stress disorder Major depressive episodes Mania Schizophrenia Somatoform disorders Conversion disorder Other dissociative disorders	Alcohol intoxication and withdrawal Cannabis Opioids Hallucinogens Stimulants Solvents **Medicinal substances** Anticholinergic agents Antihistamines Barbiturates Benzodiazepines Beta-blockers	Botulism Cardiac arrhythmias Cerebral infections Cerebral ischaemia Cerebral neoplasm Cerebral trauma Epilepsies Huntington's disease Hypocalcaemia Hypoglycaemia Hyponatraemia Hypoxia Hypothyroidism Lupus erythematosus Migraine Multiple sclerosis Myocardial ischaemia	Boredom Electrical stimulation Emotional trauma Exhaustion Sensory deprivation
Borderline personality disorder Histrionic personality disorder Schizoid personality disorder Schizotypal personality disorder Dementia Delirium	Digoxin Neuroleptic agents Opiate analgesics Scopolamine	Spinocerebellar degeneration Hemi-depersonalisation Right (non-dominant) parietal cortical lesions	

Diagnosis, clinical features, and course

Table 10.8 gives the DSM-5 diagnostic criteria for depersonalisation/derealisation disorder, and the ICD-10 diagnostic criteria for depersonalisation-derealisation syndrome (which is classed as a non-psychotic neurotic disorder).

Table 10.8: Diagnostic criteria for depersonalisation/derealisation disorder from the DSM-5 and depersonalisation-derealisation syndrome from the ICD-10

DSM-5 (Depersonalisation/derealisation disorder)	ICD-10 (Depersonalisation-derealisation syndrome)
A. The presence of persistent or recurrent experiences of depersonalisation, derealisation, or both: (1) **Depersonalisation:** Experiences of unreality, detachment, or being an outside observer with respect to one's thoughts, feelings, sensations, body, or actions (e.g. perceptual alterations, distorted sense of time, unreal or absent self, emotional and/or physical numbing). (2) **Derealisation:** Experiences of unreality or detachment with respect to surroundings (e.g. individuals or objects are experienced as unreal, dreamlike, foggy, lifeless, or visually distorted). B. During the depersonalisation or derealisation experiences, reality-testing remains intact. C. The symptoms cause clinically significant distress or impairment in social, occupational, or other important areas of functioning. D. The disturbance is not attributable to the physiological effects of a substance (e.g. a drug of abuse, medication) or another medical condition (e.g. seizures). E. The disturbance is not better explained by another mental disorder, such as schizophrenia, panic disorder, major depressive disorder, acute stress disorder, posttraumatic stress disorder, or another dissociative disorder.	For a definite diagnosis, there must be either or both of A and B, plus C and D: ■ Depersonalisation symptoms, i.e. the individual feels that his or her own feelings and/or experiences are detached, distant, not his or her own, lost, etc.; ■ Derealisation symptoms, i.e. objects, people, and/or surroundings seem unreal, distant, artificial, colourless, lifeless, etc.; ■ An acceptance that this is a subjective and spontaneous change, not imposed by outside forces or other people (i.e. insight); ■ A clear sensorium and absence of toxic confusional state or epilepsy.

Source: Reprinted with permission from the *Diagnostic and Statistical Manual of Mental Disorders*, fifth edition (DSM-5), American Psychiatric Association (APA), 2013, p. 302, and ICD-10 *Classification of Mental and Behavioural Disorders: Diagnostic Criteria for Research*, World Health Organization (WHO), Geneva, 2007.

Patients with depersonalisation/derealisation do not cease to have bodily experiences and remain aware of the external world. However, the quality of experience is changed. Alienation results in body parts taking on a foreign feel. Commonly, body parts, particularly the extremities, are experienced as changing shape or size.

Occasionally, patients may experience a sense of removal from their own body, as if the conscious self has been evacuated from the confines of the physical body. Autoscopy is one example of this, where patients feel as if they are viewing themselves from the outside, often from above and a short distance away. These out-of-body or extracorporeal experiences are often encountered in accounts of near-death experiences and in paranormal literature.

With reduplication phenomena, patients have the experience of being duplicated and present in two different places at once. For example, patients may confirm their presence in the consulting room while, at the same time, believe that they are at home. The patient may be at pains to convince the doctor of the reality of the experience. Reduplication is also experienced in active psychosis, dementia, delirium, seizures, migraine, and focal lesions involving the parietal cortex.

Derealisation often partners depersonalisation. However, during childhood or adolescence, it is not uncommon for derealisation to occur in isolation, divorced from any depersonalisation. Frequently, anxiety, even panic, accompanies depersonalisation, underscoring their commonality as stress responses. During an episode, a patient may appear preoccupied and dysphoric. Reality-testing remains intact. When depersonalisation is experienced frequently, patients start ruminating about their experiences, and phobic avoidance towards situations that may cue depersonalisation may ensue. Often, depersonalisation symptoms make a sudden first appearance, accompanied by intense anxiety and hyperventilation.

In more than half of cases, depersonalisation/derealisation disorder tends to be a chronic condition. For most patients, symptom intensity remains fairly constant and symptoms cluster in episodes separated by periods of remission. Like other dissociative conditions, depersonalisation or derealisation tend to occur during periods of increased psychosocial stress. However, relaxation, boredom, and use of medicinal substances can also precipitate spells of depersonalisation or derealisation.

Differential diagnosis

As Table 10.7 demonstrates, causes of depersonalisation/derealisation are many and varied. Depersonalisation/derealisation may occur in major depressive episodes, schizophrenia, and other experiences of psychotic alienation, but a meticulous history and mental state examination should provide enough information to make the diagnostic distinction. Enquiry must be made into the use of psychoactive substances – even the unsuspecting use of medicinal agents like colic remedies are known to produce depersonalisation/derealisation phenomena.

The occurrence of isolated depersonalisation/derealisation in the absence of other psychopathology should warn of the possibility of serious physical pathology like cerebral neoplasm or central nervous system infection, and this warrants thorough neurological examination, including brain imaging.

Classically, epilepsy is considered the archetypal physical or non-psychiatric cause of depersonalisation/derealisation. The abrupt onset of a seizure and its predictable accompaniments like convulsive movements, stereotypies, disturbed consciousness, and amnesia assist with accurate differentiation.

Depersonalisation/derealisation can occur during a migrainous aura. In migraine, the aura comprises primarily sensory disturbances that announce the imminent onset of headache. The migrainous aura is differentiated from depersonalisation/derealisation disorder by the presence of severe, classically one-sided and pulsatile (throbbing) headache, photosensitivity, hyperacusis (heightened sensitivity to sound), nausea, and vomiting. Migraine equivalents, where aural phenomena occur in the absence of the typical headache, are cause for serious diagnostic challenge.

Trance and possession disorders

Trance and possession disorders have been a source of debate for a number of years. Both the DSM-5 and the ICD-10 describe the phenomenon in similar terms – that it is transient, involuntary, that it impairs functioning, and that it is upsetting. It is a worldwide occurrence, but appears to be more prevalent in ethnic communities, and where the ethnic group is in a minority, it may be linked to acculturation problems. Research tends to indicate that there is a very strong link between trance, possession, and both traumatic and psychological events (Gureje & Reed, 2016).

Biomedical science has limited jurisdiction over trance and possession, with its very Western thinking, as these are universal to non-Western cultural groups. There are difficulties with diagnosis, and these have often been listed in both the DSM and ICD as 'for further study' because of this. The most important feature of these disorders is that they cause a loss of personal identity. Symptoms are often culture-bound – that is, they are specific to a specific culture. They are often in response to situations where the person feels out of control of their surrounds and the events which may be occurring at the time. Linked to the person's sense of personal agency, the concept of possession may offer the possessed person a way of intentionally explaining and regaining control over their own feelings of being out of control. A cross-cultural approach seems necessary for a better understanding of the disorder as well as to increase the validity of diagnosis and efficacy of management.

A trance is a mental condition based on a narrowed focus of attention, where surroundings that are outside this focus of attention are lost to consciousness. Observing trance and possession states around the world yields remarkable similarities. Shamans are common in sub-Saharan Africa, the Middle East, Latin America, South East Asia, Japan, the Pacific Islands and India. Typically, a medium or shaman may preside over a séance-like event. When the shaman enters a dissociative state, an entity from another realm or spirit world takes over conscious awareness and influences behavior. Catholic exorcisms, directed at driving out a demon that possesses the sufferer, are also considered dissociative states (Ferracuti, 1996). Trance and possession states are only considered to indicate a trance and possession disorder if the state is involuntary or unwanted, and if it occurs outside religious or culturally accepted situations (World Health Organization, 2016).

The ICD-10 considers trance and possession disorders as a distinct category under dissociative [conversion] disorders. In the DSM-5, dissociative trance disorder is no longer a distinct disorder as it was in the previous edition. Instead, it is under 'Other specified dissociative disorders'.

The most common features are amnesia, emotional disturbance, and loss of personal identity (Spiegel, 1997), features that bear resemblance to DSM-5's dissociative identity disorder. Altered states of consciousness, stereotyped motor behaviour, short duration, fatigue in the aftermath, normal behaviour between trances, onset before age 25, limited education, low socio-economic status, and having witnessed a trance previously have all been found in relation to this condition (Kua, 1986).

Table 10.9 provides the ICD-10 criteria of trance and possession disorders.

Table 10.9: Diagnositic criteria for trance and possession disorders from the ICD-10

ICD-10

The general criteria for dissociative disorder must be met.
■ Either of the following must be present:
  ▸ Trance. There is temporary alteration of the state of consciousness, shown by any two of:
    ☐ loss of the usual sense of personal identity;
    ☐ narrowing of awareness of immediate surroundings, or unusually narrow and selective focusing on environmental stimuli;
    ☐ limitation of movements, postures, and speech to repetition of a small repertoire.
  ▸ Possession disorder. The individual is convinced that he or she has been taken over by a spirit, power, deity, or other person.
■ Both (1) and (2) of criterion B must be unwanted and troublesome, occurring outside or being a prolongation of, similar states in religious or other culturally accepted situations.
■ Most commonly used exclusion clause: The disorder does not occur at the same time as schizophrenia or related disorders, or mood (affective) disorders with hallucinations or delusions.

Source: Reprinted with permission from the ICD-10 *Classification of Mental and Behavioural Disorders: Diagnostic Criteria for Research*, World Health Organization (WHO), Geneva, 2007.

> **HELPFUL HINT**
> **Trance and possession disorders**
> ■ Trance and possessed states are common
> ■ Encountered in all peoples of the world
> ■ Onset often before age 25
> ■ Often follows psychosocial trauma
> ■ Amnesia is characteristic
> ■ Loss of personal identity is common
> ■ Marked emotional disturbance
> ■ Dissociative identity disorder probably related
> ■ Can be normal or pathological
> ■ Travel, wandering from familiar surroundings
> ■ Assumption of new identity.
>
> Source: Adapted from Hales et al., 2008

Worldwide, predictable psychosocial stressors have been identified as precipitants of trance states. In South Africa, Szabo (2005) identified major depressive episodes and bereavement as triggers.

Ganser's syndrome

Ganser's syndrome is also known as the 'syndrome of approximate answers' or 'twilight hysteria'. This disorder was first described by Sigbert Ganser in 1898. In a paper entitled *Concerning an Unusual Hysterical Confusional State (Über einen eigenartigen hysterischen Dämmerzustand)*, Ganser described his observations of a behavioural syndrome found among young men freshly admitted to a Dresden prison. The pre-eminent feature of the condition is paralogia, or the giving of approximate answers.

The paralogic phenomenon, known by the German *vorbeireden*, is illustrated by the following examples: When asked to do a simple calculation like '3 + 1', the patient may answer '5'; asked to name a pencil, the patient responds with 'pen'. Believed to be common, such so-called Ganserian phenomena occur on a continuum of severity. Unusual psychosocial stress and neurological factors have been implicated in its causation. Its pathogenesis is likely dissociative in nature. However, patients often have antisocial or histrionic premorbid personalities, and the condition is frequently encountered in prisoners facing trial, fuelling the sceptics' argument against its existence (Allen, Postel, & Berrios, 2000; Sadock & Sadock, 2000).

It is appealing to speculate about a possible pathogenic mechanism. A constitutionally vulnerable young male, of low intellect and a background of social adversity, is faced with a severe threat, like incarceration. An example of this can be seen in research done into the stresses experienced by people who are immigrating. Alteration in the person's sense of self, brought about by the changes in circumstances, and being in a different country, may bring about dissociative symptoms. The commonalities appear to be persons in their forties, after they have lived in the new country for between seven and 22 years. The dissociative symptoms may be accompanied by a number of somatic complaints (Staniloiu, Borsutzky, & Markowitsch, 2010). Dissociation of some kind likely ensues, with attentional impairment, disorientation, amnesia, hallucinations, conversion, somatising, and paralogia. The argument for Ganser's syndrome being a form of transient, even schizophrenic, psychosis or a delirium remains unsettled. Recent research also indicates that there may be a link between Ganser's syndrome and the presence of organic brain lesions (Anupama, Nagaraja Rao, & Dhananjaya, 2006).

In the ICD-10, Ganser's syndrome is listed under 'other dissociative [conversion] disorder' along with multiple personality disorder. In terms of the DSM-5, Ganser's syndrome would be considered as an 'unspecified dissociative disorder'.

BOX 10.1: FEATURES OF GANSER'S SYNDROME

1. Sense of space and time is disorganised.
2. The patient tends to 'suspend' information at his or her disposal and gives 'I don't know' answers.
3. Clouding of consciousness.
4. Despite intact understanding of a question, the patient displays a psychogenic inability to answer.
5. Answers are true to the semantic sphere of the question. Ganser referred to this phenomenon as *vorbeireden* (to talk past the point) and exemplified it thus: When at a railway station, '… a railway employee gave you a ticket at random rather than the ticket you asked for; the point being that he did not give you a bucket of water or a cup of tea'.
6. The patient may hallucinate and re-enact, in a hallucinatory manner, certain traumatic experiences.
7. General or partial analgesia that can migrate across the body.
8. Even innocuous questions like 'What is your name?' may cause difficulty and trigger vorbeireden.
9. Symptoms appear all at once and leave in a staggered manner, leaving a 'mode of being' similar to the personality before onset of the twilight state.
10. Later, when told about the behaviour, the patient expresses surprise.

Source: Allen, Postel, & Berrios, 2000.

EXAMPLE CASE

A 45-year-old South African man was admitted to a neurology ward with a partial weakness on his left side (left hemiparesis) and a four-day history of amnesia and wandering. Physical examination was unremarkable, but a urine toxicology screen was positive for both cannabis and ecstasy. During admission his consciousness fluctuated, and although extensive investigation revealed no organic cause for his symptoms he was given a course of intravenous acyclovir to treat possible encephalitis. After three weeks he was referred for psychiatric assessment. He was able to give a rational account of himself, disclosing that as a young man, he had fought in the Rhodesian War, where he had been personally involved in the murder and torture of the civilian population. After the war he had become a teacher, emigrating to the UK in 2002. He then developed several symptoms related to his time in the Rhodesian Army. He reported intrusive visual hallucinations that gave a 'snapshot' of his experiences during the war, he became hypervigilant, and his performance at work began to suffer. He was unable to give any account of his activities for the four-day period that correlated with his wandering, but did recall his admission to hospital. On examination of his mental state, the only notable abnormality was his giving of approximate answers. When asked to spell WORLD backwards, he replied 'EBOLG'. When asked to recall the words honesty, window, and lace, he replied 'modesty, house, shoes'. The request to write a complete sentence was met with the words 'Where I'm I going to …'. With the history of visual hallucinations, conversion symptoms, approximate answers, and clouding of consciousness, a diagnosis of Ganser's syndrome was made. His symptoms subsequently improved with no specific intervention, and he was discharged.

Source: Dwyer & Reid, 2004.

Related conditions in South Africa

Among South Africa's black population, the occurrence of demon possession and the role of shamans or mediums are well known (Heap, 1991). *Amafufunyana* is found among the Xhosa-, Zulu- and Tswana-speaking peoples of southern Africa. Translated, *amafufunyana* means 'evil spirits'. *Ukuthwasa* refers to a person 'arising', upon his or her calling, to become a diviner or traditional healer. While it is apparent that *amafufunyana* and *ukuthwasa* overlap with schizophrenia (Niehaus, 2004), they also conform to the construct of dissociative trance disorder with possession.

Traditional beliefs about the causation of *amafufunyana* understand it to be a manifestation of ancestral anger, causing angry spirits to enter the mind of an affected person. Bewitchment is a frequent explanatory theme, or cause. Other causes are failure to observe a traditional ritual, stepping over a dangerous track, evil spirits, poisoning with soil and ants from the grave, and a variety of witch-familiars like the river snake, *impundulu* (evil lightning bird) or *tokoloshe* (dwarf-like creature with baboon-like facial features). The Xhosa people in the Cape Peninsula believe 'nerves', relationship problems, drug or alcohol abuse, and the Lord's Will to cause *amafufunyana*. But, the most widely held belief among the Xhosa about its causation is that it is multifactorial, with spiritual, social, interpersonal, and other influences (Ensink, 1996; Kruger, 2007).

The earliest warning of impending *amafufunyana* is social withdrawal. Listlessness, poor appetite, grunting, falling down, and overt aggression may follow. Vocalisations may emerge, believed to be the *amafufunyana* or evil spirits speaking through the person once they have seized control of his or her mind. The vocalisations can be in a foreign language or sound like those of an entirely different person, even of the opposite gender. Communication disturbances are present, with incoherence and neologisms that can take the guise of formal thought disorder. During the acute phase, the person may also thrash around wildly and walk on all fours. Outlandish movements, not unlike convulsions, may occur. After effects include an inability to recall events during the affliction, and feeling dazed and tired. Cataloguing the phenomenology of *amafufunyana* highlights conspicuous similarities between it and syndromes like *amok, pibloktoq* and the exaggerated startle, or hyperekplexia, of *latah* and Jumper Disease of Maine.

Ukuthwasa concerns a calling from ancestors for a person to undergo diviner or *thwasa* training and usually follows on misfortune befalling the person. Clinical manifestations of *ukuthwasa* are varied and include anxiety, labile moods, loss of appetite, 'confused' feelings, and auditory and visual hallucinations. Somatic complaints, most typically involving the joints, emerge. The affected person can become restless and wander, sometimes disappearing from home. Personal hygiene is neglected, and social isolation sets in. Sexual desire may be heightened or lost, with infertility supervening. Antisocial behaviour, violence, and aggression have been noted in *ukuthwasa* (Buhrman, 1984; Ensink & Robertson, 1999). The prominence of dreams in *ukuthwasa* is noteworthy with water the near-universal theme. Dreams often involve an attraction for rivers and other bodies of water, as well as the urge to be submerged. Other common themes concern forests and animals.

Symptoms do not remit until the call for training is accepted. If not heeded, 'madness' and death may follow. If *thwasa* training is not completed, the original *ukuthwasa* may be transformed into *ukuphambana*, a Xhosa word for unspecified insanity (Ensink, 1996). Interestingly, in their survey of Xhosa-speakers in the Cape Peninsula, Ensink and Robertson (1999) found that most respondents viewed alcohol or drug abuse as the principal cause of *ukuphambana*.

The bewildering variety of symptoms associated with *ukuthwasa* allows for its placement within several diagnostic categories. The interpretation of spiritual influence, or being under the spell of an external agency, aligns it with dissociative trance disorder with possession or dissociative identity disorder, as proposed in DSM-5. However, when hallucinations and social withdrawal are present, schizophrenia or other psychotic states must be considered. *Amafufunyana* and *ukuthwasa* affect adults and children alike (Ensink, 1996). It appears that the majority of patients with *amafufunyana* had experienced an earlier episode of amafufunyana, while few reported previous *ukuthwasa*. A family history of schizophrenia or another psychiatric disorder was more common for those with *ukuthwasa* than *amafufunyana*.

Related conditions in other cultures

In Latin America, a common condition is *ataque de nervios*, a dissociative-like state characterised by a dramatic display of negative emotions and somatic symptoms in the wake of a psychosocial stressor. Coexistence of *ataque de nervios* with major depression and anxiety disorders correlates with a history of childhood abuse.

In China, the diagnosis of *yi-ping*, meaning hysteria, typically affects women with histories of interpersonal conflict, illness, or following the death of a loved one. The symptoms of *yi-ping* appear not unlike the general schema for dissociative disorders: memory disturbance, loss of personal identity, lessened awareness of surroundings, and excessive emotionality.

It is not difficult to align the so-called 'running syndromes' with dissociative amnesia, fugue, or trance disorders. Amok is the prototypical 'running syndrome' and is found in Malay men. It produced the expression 'to run amok'. A man so affected enters a trance-like state and, imbued with a mysterious energy, runs or takes flight, a behaviour he can sustain for long hours on end. In its wake he remembers very little, if anything; he experiences fatigue and could commit suicide. *Amok* is attributed to interpersonal conflict, personal abuse, intolerable embarrassment, slight, shame, and loss of honour. Running *amok* is seen as a way to seek revenge and restitution for a perceived insult to a man's dignity. The person running *amok* is not regarded as possessing responsibility for his actions as he is believed to be spirit-possessed. The amnesia is also regarded as prejudicial to sufferers when called to account.

Another much-debated condition from the Malaysian peninsula and Indonesian archipelago is *latah*. *Latah* can be normal or pathological and is characterised by exaggerated startle responses. Sufferers habitually jump violently when startled, something they find most unpleasant. Trance-like states with automatic obedience may occur. The sufferer may feel compelled against his will to imitate the speech and behaviour of others (echolalia and echopraxia) (Eisenberg, 1959; Ropper, 2001; Tanner, 2001; World Health Organization, 1992). Coprolalia, or the compulsive-like, irresistible utterances of profanities, is not uncommon. Behaviours continue even if the sufferer realises that his tormentors, believed to be controlling him, want to ridicule and degrade him. *Myriachit* is an identical condition found in the Arctic regions of Siberia. *Latah* is listed under 'other neurotic disorders' in ICD-10.

Pibloktoq is a typical running syndrome recognised by the Inuit peoples of the Arctic. (*Pibloktoq*, itself a transliteration, is variously spelt *pibloktok* and *pivloktoq* and sometimes erroneously referred to as 'Arctic Psychosis'). *Pibloktoq* is characterised by prodromal listlessness, fatigue, dysphoria, and mental 'confusion'. A 'seizure' of disruptive behaviour ensues during which sufferers strip off their clothing and embark on a spell of frenzied running and rolling in the snow. Echolalia and echopraxia emerge, along with destructive behaviours directed at objects, not people. Episodes are brief, often lasting mere minutes, and followed by loss of consciousness. Afterwards, the person has no recollection of the episode. Interpersonal stress is a likely precipitant.

From the tropics and Arctic, we move to New England and Canada where Jumper Disease of Maine, a condition much in the vein of *latah*, is found. Jumper Disease of Maine is also known as 'Jumping Frenchmen of Maine', 'Jumpers', 'Shakers', and 'Barkers'. The 'Jumpers' were members of an isolated, socially backward Francophone community in the Goosey Lake area of Northern Maine. They were descendants of a deviant Methodist sect that settled in New England four hundred years ago. 'Jumpers' are so called for their fierce startle response, with violent jumping and twisting. When startled, they also display echolalia and echopraxia. As a religious service reaches rapture, 'Jumpers' would jump and roll around in ecstasy, crawl about on all fours while making barking noises and emitting incoherent utterances understood by fellow worshippers as speaking in tongues (Eisenberg, 1959;

Ropper, 2001). Speaking in tongues or glossolalia is considered normal and even desirable in certain Pentecostal churches. In the early nineties, genetic linkage analyses demonstrated that point mutations in the gene coding for the glycine receptor are present in patients with hyperekplexia, or excessive startle, as found in Jumpers. Glycine is an amino acid neurotransmitter and modulates neural stimulation (Ropper, 2001; Shiang, 1993).

In Iran, Egypt, Sudan, Ethiopia, and Somalia, people experience dissociative episodes, which they term 'zar'. This is when a person believes that he or she is possessed by a spirit. Such people may laugh, talk to themselves, cry, and sometimes harm themselves. In the society where such people live, they are considered to be be afflicted, but not necessarily ill. In local cultures, zar is not considered to be pathological, but if it becomes severe, may be indicative of more severe mental illness, for example, schizophrenia (Staniloiu et al., 2010).

Whereas the neural mechanism of dissociation is universal, its appearance depends on the prevailing cultural context. Among Africans and East Asians, where communalism is more prominent, the dissociation readily manifests with possession of the patient by an external agency – a demon, a deity, or another person. In the West, particularly North America, where individual and personal experience are primary, dissociation in the form of dissociative identity disorder manifests with competing versions of the self.

Epidemic hysteria

It is not unheard of for a collection of people, usually participating in a single activity, to exhibit dissociative-like behaviour and report experiences of dissociation, somatising, or anxiety. Epidemic hysteria is strictly defined as a constellation of symptoms suggestive of bodily illness, but without identifiable cause, that occurs between two or more people who share beliefs in those symptoms (Philen, Kilbourne, McKinley, & Parrish, 1989). Rather than viewing the phenomenon as a group of people each with an individual dissociative disorder, Boss (1997) suggests that epidemic hysteria should be viewed as a social phenomenon involving otherwise healthy people.

Two characteristic patterns of epidemic hysteria are recognised. In the first, the anxiety variant, abdominal pain, headache, dizziness, fainting, nausea, and hyperventilation are the most common symptoms. In the second type, or motor variant, frenetic dancing, convulsions, laughing, and loud utterances are noted (Boss, 1997). Characteristically, girls are more affected than older women, boys, or men. It is also recognised among young performers, at schools, and religious gatherings (Small, 1991; Wittstock, 1991).

Symptom propagation is believed to occur through social networks, mediated, at least in part, by sight and sound. Observing a friend become sick is a good predictor of the development of symptoms (Small, 1991), but multiple psychological and physical mechanisms most likely contribute to outbreaks. The case vignette, concerning a widely-reported event at a school in Mthatha, is illustrative.

EXAMPLE CASE

For over a week in late May 1999, a group of girls attending St. John's College, a church school with over a thousand pupils in Mthatha (formerly Umtata) in the Eastern Cape Province of South Africa, started behaving strangely: they screamed, foamed at the mouth, fainted, and jerked. Newspaper reports spoke of an 'outbreak of hysteria'. No boys were affected. While initially sceptical, fearing the looming June examinations had precipitated a large-scale hoax, the principal was eventually obliged to appeal to the church to intervene.

The Anglican Archdeacon called upon was frustrated at his first attempts at exorcism and noted that 'the spirit was moving from one girl to another' where they had been gathered in one classroom. Subsequently, he set about doing individual exorcisms. Shortly thereafter, thirty-two girls were admitted to the provincial hospital. Twenty-five were effectively sedated and discharged home, four were observed in casualty, two admitted to the internal medicine unit for suspected but unspecified 'illness', and one was referred to the psychiatric unit. A hospital spokesman described the girls as being in a 'very hysterical state'. The school was closed for a week following the exorcism. Although newspapers reported this phenomenon as possession by evil spirits, they also reflected the public's ambivalence regarding the supernatural. An alternative context soon emerged, one that was sociological and secular. It highlighted the tense relationship between religion and mental health in a context of rapid social change and the transition from traditional society to the often confusing urbanised, competitive Western culture.

Source: Parle, 2003.

Soccer crowds, audiences at pop concerts, and protestors can all display so-called mass hysteria. Public protest can transform into collective rampage with wanton destruction and looting. In another manifestation of group behaviour, more than 900 followers of the charismatic Reverend Jim Jones committed suicide in November 1978 at the People's Temple Agricultural project, referred to as Jonestown, in Guyana. Reminiscent of Jonestown was the behaviour of the Branch Davidians, followers of David Koresh, in 1993 in Waco, Texas, and the North Korean Sun Myung Moon Cult. Stage hypnotists draw capacity audiences who witness or keenly participate in group hypnosis, another manifestation of group dissociation.

Although influenced by many external factors, crowd behaviour at soccer stadium disasters, like Hillsborough in the United Kingdom in 1989, and the Orkney and Ellis Park tragedies in South Africa in 1991 and 2001 respectively, may have been partially influenced by dissociative-like group behaviour.

SOMATOFORM DISORDERS AND THEIR COMPARATIVE NOSOLOGY

Somatising lies at the heart of these disorders. It refers to a tendency to experience bodily, or somatic, distress in the face of psychological stress. While intuitively logical, robust evidence for a causal link between stress and somatising is still lacking. In the DSM-5 (American Psychiatric Association, 2013), the diagnosis is made on the basis of positive symptoms and signs (i.e. distressing somatic symptoms along with abnormal thoughts, emotions, and behaviours in response to these symptoms), rather than the absence of medical reasons for these symptoms.

Seven types of somatoform disorder are recognised in DSM-5. These are: somatic symptom disorder, illness anxiety disorder, conversion disorder (functional neurological symptom disorder), psychological factors affecting other medical conditions, factitious disorder, other specified somatic symptom and related disorder, and unspecified somatic symptom and related disorder (American Psychiatric Association, 2013).

The ICD-10 takes a distinctly different approach. The most noteworthy differences are the absence of conversion disorder (which is considered a dissociative disorder) and body dysmorphic disorder (which is subsumed under hypochondriacal disorder). Listed disorders are: somatisation disorder, undifferentiated somatoform disorder, hypochondriacal disorder, somatoform autonomic dysfunction, persistent somatoform pain disorder, other somatoform disorders, and somatoform disorder, unspecified.

Table 10.10 lists disorders of the different nosologies. It also shows how the DSM-5's somatic symptom disorder is a wider category than the ICD-10's somatisation disorder, and how the ICD-10 classes neither conversion disorder nor factitious disorder as somatoform disorders.

The DSM-5's somatic symptom disorder and the ICD-10's somatisation disorder, undifferentiated somatoform disorder, and persistent somatoform pain disorder all have persistent pain as a joint symptom. The differences between the two systems are more that they are arranged differently rather than that they differ in concept. The use of the word 'disorder' tends to indicate a shift away from providing a 'diagnosis', instead suggesting that there may be another complaint causing the disorder. The rationale for this is that somatoform disorders are perceived to be disorders of behaviour – in this case, acting out a sick role and illness behaviour to convey other, more internalised issues.

Table 10.10: Comparative nosology of somatoform disorders

DSM-5	ICD-10
Somatic symptom disorder	Somatisation disorder
	Undifferentiated somatoform disorder
Specifier: with pain as predominant symptom	Persistent somatoform pain disorder
Illness anxiety disorder	Hypochondriacal disorder

DSM-5	ICD-10
Conversion disorder (functional neurological symptom disorder)	
Factitious disorder	
Other specified somatic symptom and related disorder	Somatoform autonomic dysfunction
	Other somatoform disorders
Unspecified somatic symptom and related disorder	Somatoform disorder, unspecified
Psychological factors affecting other medical condition	

Conversion disorder

Conversion disorder (functional neurological symptom disorder) is a syndrome characterised by pseudoneurological (dissociative and somatoform) symptoms. In the case of Claudia Z, at the beginning of the chapter, the paralysis which she exhibited on admission to hospital, which was due to her converting her feelings of being overwhelmed and being unable to cope with the pressures and trauma of her life, resolved as soon as she no longer felt overwhelmed. Once considered a dissociative disorder by the DSM, conversion disorder was reclassified as a somatoform disorder in the DSM-III (American Psychological Association, 1980) and remains so till today.

In the DSM-5, it retains its location under the category 'somatic symptom disorder' (American Psychiatric Association, 2013). This recognises its primary presentation as somatic while avoiding inferences about a pathogenic mechanism. In contrast, ICD-10 continues to consider conversion disorder as a group of dissociative disturbances. Although neuroscientific evidence for a dissociative neural mechanism in its expression is suggested (Spitzer, 2006), a precise understanding of the pathogenesis of conversion disorder continues to elude us.

History

Conversion has been recognised since antiquity. The concept of 'hysteria' was first introduced by Egyptian physicians around 1900 BCE, who regarded the emergence of symptoms to be the result of a 'wandering uterus'. Hysteria is derived from the ancient Greek word '*hyster*' meaning 'uterus'. The term is attributed to the ancient Greek physician Hippocrates.

In the 1800s, consideration of this disorder was revived. A French physician, Paul Briquet, proposed

> **HELPFUL HINT**
>
> **Conversion disorder: Rules of thumb**
>
> - Affects females more than males
> - Psychologically unsophisticated
> - History of childhood trauma
> - Symptoms associated with psychosocial stressor
> - Mono-symptomatic and pseudo-neurological
> - Symptoms: sensory, motor, seizure, and mixed
> - Usually brief course
> - Coexistence of other neurological illness common.

that the disorder resulted from brain dysfunction following stressful environmental events acting on the 'affective part of the brain'. Charcot evoked and manipulated signs of hysteria through hypnosis. He also proposed that the disorder arose in individuals predisposed by heredity; once exposed to a traumatic event, a 'functional' or 'dynamic' brain lesion resulted. Janet viewed hysteria as a disturbance in selective attention (Black, 2004; Ford, 1985).

It was Sigmund Freud who first introduced the term 'conversion' to medicine. In psychoanalysis, conflict exists between instinctual impulses, such as aggression or sexuality, and the prohibition of their expression. Conversion involves the repression of unconscious intrapsychic conflict and the consequent conversion of the associated anxiety into a physical, or somatic, symptom. As a consequence, the patient avoids conscious confrontation of unacceptable, intolerable impulses. The resolution of intrapsychic conflict is considered the primary gain. But, in communicating a need for special treatment through the expression of the conversion symptom, the patient may derive additional benefits from others, bringing about the so-called secondary gain that can be seen as a way of nonverbally manipulating others and the environment (Ford, 1985; Sadock & Sadock, 2000). However, despite the logical appeal provided by the psychoanalytic understanding of conversion, clinical experience has failed to show convincingly that any gain is derived.

Over the ensuing decades, other aetiological theories emerged, including theories relating to social, communication, and behavioural aspects. The ascent of neuroscience in the late 1900s saw a resurgence of interest in the biological mechanisms at play in conversion disorder. Clinical experience, neuropsychological evidence, and advances in neuro-imaging and neuro-physiological techniques have yielded insightful and practical pathogenic theories of conversion and conversion disorder.

Epidemiology

Mild conversion symptoms not needing medical attention occur in as many as one-third of all people. Among psychiatric patients, the incidence of conversion symptoms is between 5% and 15%. Females outnumber males by up to five to one. In men, conversion symptoms mainly relate to occupational accidents, military service, being on trial, and serving a prison sentence. Onset can be at any age, but is most common in adolescence. Conversion disorder is most common in the youngest child in a family, in lower socio-economic classes, sub-average intelligence, educational underachievement, rural domicile, and exposure to war and combat (Ford, 1985).

Conversion disorder is universal but the type of symptoms depends on sociocultural contexts. In Nigeria and India, the most common pseudo-neurological complaints are feelings of heat, peppery and crawling sensations, numbness, burning hands, and a hot peppery sensation in the head. 'Brain fag', a condition originally described in Nigerian university students and believed not uncommon in South Africa, presents with the aforementioned symptoms. Pseudo-neurological symptoms are also common in *ataque de nervios* and include heat rising to the head, numbness of extremities, and pseudo-seizures (Escobar, 2004).

Aetiology and pathogenesis

To facilitate understanding of its pathogenesis, we need to explore the important clinical manifestations of conversion disorder. Conversion involves the emergence of a single symptom, or set of symptoms, referable to the nervous system. This mode of presentation is called 'monosymptomatic' and 'pseudo-neurological' and can affect any aspect of neurological function, including abnormal movements, paralysis, gait disturbances, non-seizural convulsions, mutism, urinary retention, hallucinations, pain, blindness, deafness, analgesia, and disequilibrium symptoms like giddiness and a sense of lurching.

On neurological examination, inconsistencies abound: simultaneous contraction of opposing agonist-antagonist muscle groups, fluctuating weakness, sensory losses that do not follow anatomical boundaries, and dramatic and implausible movement and gait disturbances. *La belle indifférence* (the flippant lack of concern for the apparently serious neurological handicap shown by the patient) reminds of lesions involving the non-dominant parietal cortex. When a stroke affects the non-dominant parietal cortex, the patient tends to neglect, or deny the existence of, the opposite part of the body; this is called hemi-neglect.

The patient may also seem unaffected by the affliction and carry on as if there is nothing wrong at all, a phenomenon called anosognosia, meaning 'failure to recognise disease'. Because the left side of the body is represented mainly in the right hemisphere of the brain, the preponderance of left-sided symptoms in conversion disorder further implicates non-dominant hemispheric involvement because, in most people, the non-dominant hemisphere is located on the right. Alexithymia and anxiety are also common in conversion disorder.

Slater (1965) found that more than 50% of patients with a current diagnosis of conversion disorder proceed to develop a recognisable neurological condition within ten years of original diagnosis. Although this claim has become controversial, the presence of conversion disorder does not rule out concurrent or future neurological disease. Likewise, actual neurological disease does not exclude conversion disorder (Black, 2004).

Ludwig (1972) posited that sensory information feeding into the cortex is inhibited by other cortical regions thereby barring somatic information from consciousness. Findings suggesting bi-frontal and right parietal dysfunctions (as suggested by *la belle indifférence* and the preponderance of left-sided symptoms) supported this notion (Flor-Henry, 1965, cited in Black, 2004). In addition, subtle verbal imprecision, impaired vigilance and memory, affective incongruence, and disordered processing of endogenous somatic percepts (internal sensory and experiential representations of the body) are also demonstrable and support left-dominant impairments. Impaired inter-hemispheric communication further compounds the picture (Black, 2004; Sadock & Sadock, 2000).

Functional neuro-imaging findings provide more support for the neurological basis of conversion disorder. For example, activation of the anterior cingulate gyrus and association motor cortices (areas concerned with the initiation and planning of movements), and inactivity of the primary motor strip (the area of cortex that transmits the final signal for muscle contraction), have been demonstrated in conversion paralysis (refer to Figure 10.4). Right inferior parietal dysfunction is also demonstrable on functional imaging.

Unlike the primary sensory cortices (the first cortical area to receive incoming sensory information), the body is not conformally mapped onto the inferior parietal cortex. In this instance, conformal mapping means that bodily features are represented in the cortex in a manner that their relationships and relative sizes are maintained. It is analogous to a map drawn of Africa, faithfully showing South Africa at the tip of the continent embracing a much smaller land-locked Lesotho and showing that the much larger Congo, with which it shares no border, lies to its north. In higher-order cortices, conformity is not maintained and the bodily representation is distorted. As a consequence, dysfunction in a higher-order sensory cortex, like the inferior parietal cortex, may explain the disregard for anatomical constraints so characteristic of sensory conversion symptoms.

Since the 1800s, most observers have noted the universality of early trauma as a predictor of conversion disorder. The earlier the trauma and the longer its duration, the more severe conversion symptoms are likely to be. Incestuous experiences appear to confer additional risk. Although specific details of abuse may be questionable, patients probably experienced significant problems with attachment, impaired object relations, and a dysfunctional family system (Krahn, 2008).

Conversion disorder appears to be the result of dynamic restructuring of neural networks leading to the disconnection of volition, sensory experience, and movement. In the absence of an identifiable anatomical lesion, the disconnection is considered 'functional' and emerges as a result of dissociative compartmentalisation related to early adverse experience. While primary perception and motor control are intact, integration of sensory percepts and motor planning is not. As a result, when disruption occurs at the level of preconscious motor planning, paralysis ensues; when modality-specific attention is disrupted, sensory losses like blindness and anaesthesia follow (Black, 2004; Krahn, 2008; Mailis-Gagnon & Israelson, 2003; Sierra, 1998; Spence, 2000). Disturbances of right fronto-parietal networks may cause disturbances in self-recognition and the sense of 'selfhood' (Black, 2004; Sierra, 1998). The well-documented occurrence of 'negative affectivity' most likely relates to non-dominant frontal disturbances (Black, 2004). Our current understanding of conversion as an evolutionary adaptation underlies its existence as a brain response type.

Diagnosis, clinical presentation, and course

Conversion symptoms fall into four broad categories: sensory, motor, seizure, and mixed. Conventionally, diagnosis has been one of exclusion, but the nature of conversion symptoms alone can alert the doctor to their presence. Conversion symptoms do not observe neurological constraints and tend to demonstrate incongruence and internal inconsistencies. Tables 10.11 and 10.12 provide diagnostic criteria for conversion disorder of DSM-5 and ICD-10 respectively. Examples of incongruent and inconsistent symptoms are provided in the discussion on individual symptom categories.

Table 10.11: Diagnostic criteria for conversion disorder (functional neurological symptom disorder) from the DSM-5

DSM-5
A. One or more symptoms of altered voluntary motor or sensory function.
B. Clinical findings provide evidence of incompatibility between the symptom and recognised neurological or medical conditions.
C. The symptom or deficit is not better explained by another medical or mental disorder.
D. The symptom or deficit causes clinically significant distress or impairment in social, occupational, or other important areas of functioning or warrants medical evaluation.

DSM-5
Specify symptom type: **(F44.4) With weakness or paralysis** **(F44.4) With abnormal movement** (e.g. tremor, dystonic movement, myoclonus, gait disorder) **(F44.4) With swallowing symptoms** **(F44.4) With speech symptom** (e.g. dysphonia, slurred speech) **(F44.5) With attacks or seizures** **(F44.6) With anaesthesia or sensory loss** **(F44.6) With special sensory symptom** (e.g. visual, olfactory, or hearing disturbance) **(F44.7) With mixed symptoms**

Source: Reprinted with permission from the *Diagnostic and Statistical Manual of Mental Disorders*, fifth edition (DSM-5), American Psychiatric Association (APA), 2013, p. 318.

Table 10.12: Diagnostic criteria for dissociative equivalents of conversion disorder from the ICD-10

DISSOCIATIVE MOTOR DISORDERS
■ The general criteria for dissociative disorder must be met. ■ Either of the following must be present: ▸ Complete or partial loss of the ability to perform movements that are normally under voluntary control (including speech). ▸ Various or variable degrees of incoordination or ataxia, or inability to stand unaided.

DISSOCIATIVE CONVULSIONS
■ The general criteria for dissociative disorder must be met. ■ The individual exhibits sudden and unexpected spasmodic movements, closely resembling any of the varieties of epileptic seizure, but not followed by loss of consciousness. ■ The symptoms in Criterion B are not accompanied by tongue-biting, serious bruising or laceration due to falling, or urinary incontinence.

DISSOCIATIVE ANAESTHESIA AND SENSORY LOSS
■ The general criteria for dissociative disorder must be met. ■ Either of the following must be present: ▸ Partial or complete loss of any or all of the normal cutaneous sensations over part or all of the body (specify: touch, pinprick, vibration, heat, cold). ▸ Partial or complete loss of vision, hearing, or smell (specify).

Source: ICD-10 *International Statistical Classification of Diseases and Related Health Problems*, World Health Organization (WHO), Geneva, 2016.

A history of physical or sexual abuse is sometimes reported. A psychological trauma that precedes onset of the index conversion symptom is usually identifiable, although it remains unclear whether this is a prerequisite for symptom development. Over and above the conversion symptom, history and mental state examination will often reveal a person of low intellect who is psychologically unsophisticated. Patients may come across as depressed or anxious. Alexithymia, or the inability of a patient to 'read' his or her own mood, is common during the conversion episode and is an enduring trait in patients prone to conversion (Grabe, 2000). About 50% of patients display *la belle indifférence*. Cognitive deficits are not clinically conspicuous, although very slight verbal expressive difficulties may be noted. Insight is often poor. Personality styles commonly associated with conversion disorder are passive-aggressive, dependent, antisocial, and histrionic. Conversion patients are at heightened risk of suicide and self-harm (Black, 2004; Ford, 1985; Krahn, 2008; Sadock & Sadock, 2000).

Regarding sensory symptoms: anaesthesia (loss of sensation) and paraesthesia (abnormal sensations like 'pins and needles') are common in conversion disorder and tend to involve the extremities. Anaesthesia often follows a 'glove and stocking' distribution uncharacteristic of peripheral neuropathy, or spinal cord or brain pathology. Likewise, hemi-anaesthesia (loss of sensation over one half of body) strictly observing the patient's midline with perfect demarcation of anaesthetic skin and normal skin suggests conversion disorder or feigning.

All sensory modalities fall prey to conversion disorder, including the organs of special sensation: blindness, tunnel vision, monocular diplopia (double vision in one eye only), deafness, and loss of smell and taste. Careful neurological examination usually uncovers normal sense organs and intact pathways; for example, pupils respond appropriately to light, and 'blind' patients can negotiate obstacles without help.

Regarding motor symptoms, weakness, paralysis, abnormal movements, and gait disturbances are all encountered. In a paralysed limb, muscle tone and reflexes remain normal. Wasting is usually absent, except in cases of chronic conversion paralysis where disuse atrophy sets in. Fasciculations – small ripple-like contractions in a muscle indicative of loss of innervation to the muscle – are absent. Hoover's sign may be observed, where the heel of an ostensibly paralysed limb presses down onto the doctor's hand when the patient is asked to raise the other leg.

Conversion paralysis involving one side of the body is contradicted by a patient's failure to turn his or her head to that side when instructed. Movement disturbances are often grotesque and involve the extremities, trunk, head, and face. Swaying, rhythmical tremors, tic-like and choreiform (dance-like) movements occur. Bobbing of the head on the trunk is a strong indicator of conversion disorder. Abnormal movements typically worsen when attention is drawn to them. Astasia-abasia – an outrageous gait with a general wildness uncharacteristic of true ataxia – is typical of conversion disorder. Patients with astasia-abasia rarely fall, and when they do, rarely hurt themselves. As with sensory disturbances, weakness and other motor abnormalities tend to fluctuate from examination to examination.

Regarding seizures: pseudo-seizures are convulsive events resembling true seizures. To complicate matters, nearly one-third of patients with pseudo-seizures have confirmed epilepsy. Certain pseudo-seizures may have their origins in the expression of a complex learnt response to stress that recruits the same or similar neural networks to those usually active during a true seizure. Predating the onset of pseudo-seizures, an epileptic patient might have responded to a psychological trauma with a true seizure. Conforming to a dissociative mechanism, this 'seizure response' becomes the preferential response to future trauma. When challenged again by similar trauma, neural networks behave as is usual during a seizure. This produces the observable phenomena without demonstrable seizural electrical activity.

Clinically, then, the patient shows behaviour indistinguishable from a true seizure, but without the occurrence of an electrophysiological storm. Indicators for the occurrence of pseudo-seizures include the absence of injuries during falls, no tongue-biting, absence of urinary incontinence, intact light and gag reflexes, and no rapid increase in serum prolactin concentration. Prolactin is a hormone released by the pituitary and promotes lactation; a seizure stimulates sudden release of prolactin into the bloodstream. A most useful aid in diagnosing pseudo-seizures is constant video EEG telemetry.

Regarding other symptoms, communication disturbances, usually of an expressive kind, range from mutism to bizarre and changeable disturbances of articulation. Aphonia, or the inability to produce the necessary voice on which words are grafted through articulation, is also encountered. Conversion aphonia is distinguished from true aphonia (e.g. damage to the recurrent laryngeal nerve or resection of the larynx) by the retained ability to vocalise while coughing or sneezing. Globus hystericus, or 'lump in the throat', common in states of anxiety and experienced by normal people, is likely to be a mixed sensory and motor cnversion phenomenon.

Non-physiological and fanciful symptoms tend to occur in least educated patients. Conversion patients' proneness to suggestion adds to the difficulty in securing reliable symptoms (American Psychiatric Association, 2000). False memories, particularly of childhood physical and sexual abuse, are now considered conversion phenomena (Krahn, 2008) but are not accommodated by DSM-5 or ICD-10 schemata. The concept is also at odds with the DSM's declared stance on limiting phenomena encountered in somatoform disorders, the category to which conversion disorder belongs in the DSM-5, to the bodily aspects. That said, conversion hallucinations, or pseudo-hallucinations, differ from psychotic hallucinations, hallucinations found in delirium, and those associated with posttraumatic stress disorder, acute stress disorder, and dissociative trance disorder. Pseudo-hallucinations may take on a useful, supportive quality, like a distressed girl hearing the voice of her boyfriend comforting her. They may also contain magical and childlike imagery. Insight into their 'unreality' is mostly retained (Hales et al., 2008).

As regards the course of this disorder, in 90% to 100% of cases, conversion symptoms resolve within a few days. One in four patients experiences recurrence of conversion during periods of psychosocial stress. Good premorbid psychosocial adjustment, sudden onset of symptoms following a clearly identifiable stressor, no comorbid psychiatric or medical

> **HELPFUL HINT**
>
> **Conversion disorder symptoms**
>
> - Mono-symptomatic and pseudo-neurological
> - Symptoms do not adhere to neurological constraints and are incongruent and internally inconsistent
> - Sensory: blindness, tunnel vision, hearing loss, loss of sensation over skin (e.g. glove-and-stocking)
> - Motor: paralysis, abnormal movements, gait disturbance (astasia-abasia)
> - Pseudo-seizures
> - Common: weakness, blindness, sensory loss, and mutism
> - Extravagant symptoms correlate with psychological naivety.

conditions, and the absence of civil or criminal litigation improve prognosis. The longer conversion symptoms remain present, the worse the outcome. The delayed emergence of a neurological condition always remains likely, necessitating meticulous examination and rigorous surveillance.

Differential diagnosis

It stands to reason that neurological conditions involving sensory and motor symptoms, as well as seizures, are differential diagnoses. The range of candidate pathologies is wide, including cerebrovascular disease, cerebral neoplasia, infection, neuro-degenerative conditions, epilepsies, and dementias. Other conditions include myasthenia gravis (progressive muscle weakness, worsened by fatigue, caused by auto-immune destruction of the junction of motor nerves onto muscles) and other myopathies (muscle diseases).

Multiple sclerosis (an auto-immune inflammation and destruction of white matter in the central nervous system degrading nerve conduction) can mimic sensory and motor conversion symptoms. Affective disturbances often accompany both multiple sclerosis and conversion disorder. A related condition, optic neuritis (inflammation of the retina and optic nerve) causing visual loss can be misdiagnosed as conversion disorder. Other conditions with confusing symptoms include Guillain–Barré syndrome, a condition involving the spinal cord and causing progressively ascending paralysis involving more and more of the body.

Schizophrenia, depression, and anxiety conditions can also be associated with strange bodily phenomena. Somatic symptom disorder can have pseudo-neurological symptoms. The presence of other somatic symptoms and their chronicity sway diagnosis in the direction of somatic symptom disorder. Hypochondriasis concerns a preoccupation with disease and patients do not focus on specific symptoms. Malingering and factitious disorders remain the greatest diagnostic challenge when faced with a patient presenting with atypical or implausible symptoms.

Somatic symptom disorder

Somatic symptom disorder (somatisation disorder) is a state when fluctuating pain, and anxiety about the pain, persist, even when no physical cause for the pain can be found. This disorder has been observed for a long time. In England, in the 1600s, physician Thomas Sydenham recognised that 'antecedent sorrows' (psychosocial stressors) were involved in the pathogenesis of the condition. In France, in the mid-1800s, Paul Briquet recognised the involvement of multiple organ systems and noted the condition's chronicity. The disorder is still also known as Briquet's syndrome.

In the 1970s, in the USA, John Feighner and other psychiatrists produced a comprehensive list of diagnostic criteria for the syndrome that were very influential. The 'Feighner criteria' are still considered the gold standard against which to measure somatic symptom disorder. However, they are complex and unwieldy, deterring doctors from adopting them for everyday practice. Dauntingly, Feighner identified 59 criteria spread across ten groups. Positive diagnosis required the presence of 25 criteria, representing nine of the ten groups.

The term 'somatisation disorder' was introduced for the first time in the DSM-III in 1980. Although simpler than Feighner's, the DSM criteria were also complex. Despite attempts at truncating and simplifying the criteria, most psychiatrists continue to find them difficult to use, and the diagnosis is often rejected in favour of simpler criteria, and often physical clinical indications are used (Hales et al., 2008).

The DSM's somatic symptom disorder is related the ICD-10's somatisation disorder, persistent somatoform pain disorder (discussed below) and undifferentiated somatoform disorder.

Epidemiology

Somatic symptom disorder is believed common in primary healthcare and general medical practice, affecting as many as 10% of patients and, because of the difficulties with diagnostic criteria as discussed above, is probably under-diagnosed. The condition predominantly affects females with an incidence five-fold that for males. The higher-than-expected incidence in men of Greek and Puerto Rican extraction implicates cultural factors modifying the sex ratio (American Psychiatric Association, 2000). Somatic symptom disorder mainly affects people of low socio-economic standing and limited education. By definition, the onset has to be before age 30; most commonly, onset is in adolescence.

Aetiology and pathogenesis

Psychoanalytic theories about the causation of somatic symptom disorder suggest that symptoms are substitutes for repressed unacceptable impulses of a sexual or violent nature. As a social communication, it is seen to produce secondary gain through avoiding work and garnering sympathy and support. Parental teaching may also play a role. The presence of significant psychosocial trauma, particularly in childhood, appears important to its development. Functional neuro-imaging studies have implicated the frontal and non-dominant parietal lobes in the neural dysfunctions of somatic symptom disorder. Decreased blood flow has been demonstrated in the cerebellum, frontal and temporo-parietal regions, as well as reduced metabolism and size of sub-cortical structures, notably the caudate nucleus. Distractibility, poor habituation to repetitive stimuli, and circumstantial associations are neuropsychological abnormalities shown in the disorder. Evoked potential studies have shown abnormal sensory-processing.

An appealing but unproven theory holds that cytokines play a role in the expression of symptoms in somatic symptom disorder. Cytokines are signalling molecules that mediate communication between different cells involved in the immune response. Serum concentrations of cytokines, particularly Interleukins 1, 2, and 6, as well as Tumour Necrosis Factor α, are raised during infections, notably the influenza-A virus. Cytokines are believed responsible for the constitutional symptoms of lethargy, depression, poor sleep, and lack of appetite characteristic of systemic infection and certain cancers. Although supporting data are lacking, abnormal cytokine production may account for some of the symptoms of somatic symptom disorder. Cytokine abnormalities are also associated with major depression and schizophrenia (see Chapters 7 and 8).

Data suggest that somatic symptom disorder is at least partly genetically determined. For example, it occurs in up to 20% of first-degree female relatives of somatic symptom disorder probands. Interestingly, both substance abuse and antisocial personality disorder are over-represented in families of female somatic symptom disorder probands (Cloninger & Yutzy, 1993). In contrast, relatives of male probands cluster with anxiety disorders. We could argue that males and females manifest with somatic symptom disorder of different aetiology or pathogenesis (Hales et al., 2008). A 29% concordance for somatic symptom disorder in monozygotic twins, as well as suggestive evidence from adoption studies, lends further credence to a genetic basis for the condition.

Diagnosis, clinical presentation, and course

In summary, the defining feature of somatic symptom disorder is the occurrence of multiple bodily symptoms emanating from multiple organ systems. Symptoms include pseudo-neurological ones. The condition is further characterised by cognitive distortions about the symptoms, anxiety about them, and dysphoria. Early psychosocial adversity (mostly in childhood) is reported by patients, and time of onset is related to trauma. The specific presence of histrionic or borderline personality traits, conversion and dissociative phenomena, sexual difficulties, menstrual irregularities, and strained relationships assist with recognition (Hales et al., 2008).

Table 10.13 lists the DSM-5 and ICD-10 diagnostic criteria for this disorder. Somatic complaints can be grouped according the structure provided by Criterion B of the DSM-5 or ICD-10 diagnostic criteria. Examples of specific symptoms are provided in the diagnostic criteria of the ICD-10.

> **HELPFUL HINT**
>
> **Somatic symptom disorder: Rules of thumb**
>
> - Affects predominantly females
> - Psychologically unsophisticated, lower socio-economic standing and education
> - History of childhood trauma
> - Symptoms related to psychosocial trauma
> - Poly-symptomatic, multiple organ systems
> - Chronic course.

Table 10.13: Diagnostic criteria for somatic symptom disorder from the DSM-5 and the ICD-10

DSM-5 Somatic symptom disorder	ICD-10 Somatisation disorder
A. One or more somatic symptoms that are distressing or result in significant disruption of daily life. B. Excessive thoughts, feelings, or behaviours related to the somatic symptoms or associated health concerns as manifested by at least one of the following:	■ There must be a history of at least two years of complaints of multiple and variable physical symptoms that cannot be explained by any detectable physical disorders. (Any physical disorders that are known to be present do not explain the severity, extent, variety, and persistence of the physical complaints, or the associated social disability.) ■ If some symptoms clearly due to autonomic arousal are present, they are not a major feature of the disorder in that they are not particularly persistent or distressing. ■ Preoccupation with the symptoms causes persistent distress and leads the patient to seek repeated (three or more) consultations or sets of investigations with either primary care or specialist doctors. In the absence of medical services within the financial or physical reach of the patient, there must be persistent self-medication or multiple consultations with local healers.

DSM-5 Somatic symptom disorder	ICD-10 Somatisation disorder
(1) Disproportionate and persistent thoughts about the seriousness of one's symptoms. (2) Persistently high level of anxiety about health or symptoms. (3) Excessive time and energy devoted to these symptoms or health concerns. C. Although any one somatic symptom may not be continuously present, the state of being symptomatic is persistent (typically more than 6 months).	■ There is persistent refusal to accept medical reassurance that there is no adequate physical cause for the physical symptoms. (Short-term acceptance of such reassurance, i.e. for a few weeks during or immediately after investigations, does not exclude this diagnosis.) ■ There must be a total of six or more symptoms from the following list, with symptoms occurring in at least two separate groups: **Gastrointestinal symptoms** (1) abdominal pain; (2) nausea; (3) feeling bloated or full of gas; (4) bad taste in mouth, or excessively coated tongue; (5) complaints of vomiting or regurgitation of food; (6) complaints of frequent and loose bowel motions or discharge of fluids from the anus; **Cardiovascular symptoms** (7) breathlessness without exertion; (8) chest pains; **Genito-urinary symptoms** (9) dysuria or complaints of frequency of micturition (10) unpleasant sensations in or around the genitals; (11) complaints of unusual or copious vaginal discharge; **Skin and pain symptoms** (12) blotchiness or discolouration of the skin; (13) pain in the limbs, extremities, or joints; (14) unpleasant numbness or tingling sensations. ■ Most commonly used exclusion clause: Symptoms do not occur only during any of the schizophrenic or related disorders, any of the mood (affective) disorders, or panic disorder.

Source: Reprinted with permission from the *Diagnostic and Statistical Manual of Mental Disorders*, fifth edition (DSM-5), American Psychiatric Association (APA), 2013, p. 311, and the ICD-10 *Classification of Mental and Behavioural Disorders: Diagnostic Criteria for Research*, World Health Organization (WHO), Geneva, 2007.

Although similar in content, the approach adopted by ICD-10 differs from that of the DSM-5 in a number of important ways. The DSM-5 approach is primarily concerned with examples of somatic symptoms associated with significant distress and impairment. The ICD dwells more on the process of the condition, as well as peculiarities of its course and natural behaviour. For example, attention is drawn to the chronicity of the disorder and the variable nature of symptoms.

The quality of psychological distress and related behaviours are also described in ICD-10 and include: preoccupation, anxiety, and resultant increased utilisation of resources (e.g. 'repeated consultations') and use of alternative resources, including traditional healers, where logistical constraints prevail. The ineffectiveness of reassurance by professionals (and others) is emphasised. Somatic symptoms listed in ICD-10 differ qualitatively from those in DSM-5, including, for example, 'bad taste' and 'excessively coated tongue'. ICD-10 does not list pseudo-neurological symptoms, thus emphasising the distinction between somatisation disorders and conversion disorders. Dissociative symptoms are also not specified.

While still untested in large clinical settings, the leaner approach of DSM-5 appears practical. DSM-5 recognises that somatic symptom disorder, illness anxiety disorder, and undifferentiated somatoform disorder share the following characteristics: multiple somatic symptoms or health concerns referable to different organ systems, the presence of related cognitive distortions, chronicity, dysfunction, and reduced quality of life. In previous editions of the DSM, pain disorder was described as a separate disorder, but in DSM-5, pain is included as a specifier for somatic symptom disorder.

DSM-5 also addresses the major criticisms of the previous somatoform disorder (DSM-IV-TR), namely over-reliance on counting physical symptoms to reach diagnostic threshold and lack of any substantial psychological criteria. DSM-5 somatic symptom disorder emphasises symptoms that are singularly psychological: cognitive distortions, high health-related anxiety, disproportionate and persistent concerns about the seriousness of symptoms, and excessive time and energy devoted to their symptoms and health concerns.

Patients recount frequent visits to doctors, clinic sisters, and casualty departments. Interpersonal conflict, chronic distress, anxiety, and depression are not uncommon. Acts of deliberate self-harm and threats of suicide are also not unusual. Female patients may dress in a seductive manner or appear demure in consultation – an observation not unfamiliar in borderline or histrionic personality disorder (see Chapter 14). Patients also tend to be self-absorbed, display an external locus of control, seek praise, behave dependently, and manipulate interpersonal situations. On examination, it becomes apparent that patients often present their complaints in an exaggerated manner, peppered with colourful descriptions. Accounts of their multiple bodily complaints can be vague and ineffectual. The historical description of their symptom careers is often faulty, and patients sometimes fail to distinguish between current, recent, and past symptoms in their convoluted stories.

The nature and occurrence rates of symptoms vary across different cultures. Burning sensations in extremities, the feeling of worms crawling in the head, and formication (the feeling of ants crawling under the skin) are pseudo-neurological phenomena more common in Africa and South Asia than North America. In parts of the world where concern about semen loss is rife, symptoms referable to the genitalia are more common (American Psychiatric Association, 2000). In India, this syndrome is known as *dhat*. A whitish discharge in urine is interpreted by patients as semen loss. Both men and women are afflicted as females are also thought to secrete semen. A similar condition, known as *shen-k-uei*, is found in Taiwan (World Health Organization, 1992).

Somatic symptom disorder is a chronic, disabling condition. Increases in symptom severity coincide with periods of heightened psychosocial stress. Symptoms come in spurts, lasting around six to nine months. Relatively symptom-free periods last around six months; it is rare for a patient to be free of symptoms for more than a year. Common comorbid psychiatric conditions are major depressive disorder, personality disorders, substance-related disorders, generalised anxiety disorder, and phobias. The most serious complication of somatic symptom disorder is iatrogenic ('iatrogenic' literally means 'caused by the doctor' – *iatros* is doctor in Greek) and involves the risks of invasive diagnostic procedures, medication side effects, and repeated surgery.

Differential diagnosis

It stands to reason that the differential diagnoses of somatic symptom disorder include general medical and neurological illness. Conditions with non-specific, transient, and fluctuating clinical manifestations present as the most likely candidates. As for conversion disorder, multiple sclerosis and myasthenia gravis are primary considerations. Systemic lupus erythematosus, acute intermittent porphyria, and porphyria variegata (also known as South African porphyria, most commonly encountered among certain Afrikaans families), hyperthyroidism, hyperparathyroidism, and haemochromatosis, or haemosiderosis (excessive deposition of iron in tissues) must be considered. Hyperparathyroidism, a surprisingly common condition among the elderly, causes sustained high concentrations of serum calcium, or hypercalcaemia, the consequences of which are manifold and affect many organ systems.

Whereas syphilis was known as the 'great mimicker' in the pre-antibiotic era, acquired immune deficiency syndrome (Aids) is its modern-day counterpart. Given its variable manifestations, Aids warrants inclusion on the list of differential diagnoses. In older patients, particularly over the age of 40, the onset of multiple bodily symptoms must alert the doctor, or psychologist, to the possible presence of a medical condition. Obvious psychiatric differentials for somatic symptom disorder are illness anxiety disorder, conversion disorder, and pain disorder. Other psychiatric conditions presenting with unexplained physical symptoms notably include schizophrenia, where psychotic bodily experiences and beliefs, like kinaesthetic (bodily) hallucinations, are surprisingly common. Somatic complaints, even psychotic ones, occur in major depressive disorder. Panic attacks are also defined by many bodily sensations.

> **HELPFUL HINT**
>
> **Features suggestive of somatic symptom disorder rather than physical disease**
>
> - Association with psychosocial stressor
> - Involvement of multiple organ systems
> - Absence of characteristic findings on examination and laboratory investigations
> - Absence of structural abnormalities.

Persistent somatoform pain disorder

The International Association for the Study of Pain (Merskey & Bogduk, 1986, p. 209) defines pain as 'an unpleasant sensory and emotional experience associated with actual or potential tissue damage, or described in terms of such damage'. This definition stresses the subjective nature of pain. Chronic pain is defined as 'pain that persists beyond the normal time of healing' (Merskey & Bogduk, 1986, p. 209).

Acute pain is a cardinal adaptive response to tissue damage, initiated by nociception (stimulation of nerves conducting pain) and accompanied by behaviours that limit tissue damage. Chronic pain, on the other hand, involves layers of pain experience, suffering, and pain behaviour, and is a dysfunctional remnant of a once-adaptive behaviour. Pain behaviour encompasses a patient's efforts to avoid factors that may precipitate or aggravate pain, such that restrictions in behaviour adversely affect all experience. The maintenance of pain is mediated through several mechanisms located in the peripheral and central nervous systems. In addition, emotional and motivational aspects exert their influence through conditioning. Although pain experienced in persistent somatoform pain disorder may have had a definite nociceptive origin, psychological factors are foremost in its persistence.

The validity of this disorder has been questioned since its first incarnations as somatoform pain disorder in the DSM-III-R (American Psychiatric Association, 1987). Pain without nociceptive origin is unusual, and separating the psychological and physical aspects of chronic pain is nearly impossible. In the DSM-5, pain is a specifier of somatic symptom disorder. The DSM-5 emphasises the psychological aspects of the disturbance with reference to cognitive distortions and emotional impacts, supporting 'pain behaviour' as a manifestation of chronic pain. In the ICD-10, persistent somatoform pain disorder is limited to chronic pain without any demonstrable nociceptive origin.

Epidemiology

Pain is the commonest complaint in all of medicine. The general practitioner will attest to this, with frequent encounters with patients complaining of lower back pain, joint pains, and headaches. In the developed world, estimates of the occurrence of chronic pain range between 25% and 30% of the general population. Thousands of people are given disability benefits each year because of chronic pain. In the Netherlands, it is estimated that 10 000 new cases of chronic pain are added annually, with substantial burden on the fiscus (Verhaak, Kerssens, Dekker, Sorbi, & Bensing, 1998). Persistent somatoform pain disorder is diagnosed twice as commonly in women as in men. Onset is usually in the fourth or fifth decade of life. Demographically, persistent somatoform pain disorder is associated with lower educational achievement and lower socio-economic standing.

Aetiology and pathogenesis

Chronic pain can have multiple origins, but a physiological predisposition is likely. First-degree relatives of persistent somatoform pain disorder probands are at increased risk of developing it. Developmental risks include childhood adversity such as parental separation, alcohol abuse in the home, quarrelling parents, and lack of physical affection towards the child. An association between chronic pain and depressive conditions has long been reported, yet its neural mechanism remains elusive. The conscious experience of pain is modulated by the cerebral cortex through descending inhibitory pathways using serotonin as neurotransmitter.

Endorphins also modulate the expression and experience of pain. Endorphins are opioid-like molecules that occur naturally in the central nervous system. A primary lesion in one of these

> **HELPFUL HINT**
> **Chronic physical pain**
> - Pain fluctuates
> - Patients can be distracted from pain experience
> - Analgesics provide relief
> - Examples:
>   - Neuropathies (e.g. diabetic)
>   - Neuralgia (e.g. trigeminal, post-herpetic)
>   - Neuroma (e.g. arising from severed nerve)
>   - Cancer (especially pancreatic carcinoma)
>   - Arthritis (e.g. rheumatoid, osteoarthritis)
>   - Peripheral vascular disease.

modulatory systems could result in true persistent somatoform pain disorder, as opposed to a disorder characterised by chronic pain co-occurring with another mental condition such as depression or emerging on the back of actual tissue damage and nociceptive pain.

Kindling is the systematic amplification of a nerve's responsiveness following repeated low-grade or sub-threshold stimulation of a post-synaptic nerve. Kindling, through long-term potentiation and other forms of neural plasticity, is considered an essential mechanism in the formation of memory. In the development of chronic pain, kindling may be active in neural networks that relay pain-related information between the cortex and limbic system (Rome, 2000).

In the spinal cord and peripheral nervous system, further mechanisms can maintain pain in the absence of tissue damage (Dworkin & Wilson, 1993; Shipton, 2008). These include taking over non-nociceptive nerves to mediate pain (e.g. nerves that characteristically conduct fine touch now come to relay pain), sensitisation (increased responsivity), and amplification (increased nerve signal intensity).

Psychodynamic theories of chronic pain relate to patients symbolically expressing intrapsychic conflicts by means of the body. Others may regard emotional suffering as weakness, thus displacing the problem to the body. Pain can also function as a mechanism for obtaining love and nurturance, as well as for averting responsibilities. These secondary gains reinforce pain and maintain the pain-related behaviour. Intractable pain has also been conceptualised as a means to manipulate others and to gain the upper hand in tense interpersonal situations, like a strained marriage.

EXAMPLE CASE

Frans, 42, is a machine operator at a bottling plant outside Pretoria. He is divorced and has two teenage children living with his ex-wife. His general practitioner referred him to the specialist psychiatric clinic of a local teaching hospital for evaluation and further management. Five years ago, Frans injured his neck when he was knocked over by a forklift. He sustained what appeared to be a minor sprain to his neck muscles with no fracture or dislocation. Due process for lodging an injury-on-duty claim was followed. But, after a protracted dispute and escalating tension between Frans and his employer, his claim for compensation was rejected. In the ensuing months, Frans found it increasingly hard to work. He was always in pain and struggled to move his neck. Eventually, he went on an extended sick leave. For the past six months, Frans has been on unpaid leave of absence and has struggled to make ends meet.

When examined by the attendant clinical psychologist, Frans came across as miserable. He struggled to describe his feelings and repeatedly brought the conversation back to his intractable pain, his suffering, and inability to enjoy life the way he used to before the injury. He stopped playing club rugby after the accident, gave up fly-fishing, no longer tinkers in the garage, and has even stopped visiting friends. Never free of pain, he has resorted to a daily intake of over-the-counter analgesics, often taking excessive amounts causing unpleasant side effects and occasional withdrawal symptoms. His alcohol intake has also escalated. Recently, he was convicted for driving under the influence of alcohol. The embarrassment of the conviction and the relentless pain made him contemplate suicide for the first time. He implored the psychologist to do his best, for he claimed that were it not for the pain, his life would be 'back on track'.

Diagnosis, clinical presentation, and course

The ICD-10 diagnostic criteria for persistent somatoform pain disorder are provided in Table 10.14. The ICD-10 criteria for persistent somatoform pain disorder draw attention to the all-consuming nature of the disorder, where pain-related behaviours have superseded adaptive functioning and ruined experience. DSM-5 considers pain as a somatic symptom, regardless of origin. When pain is the focus of presentation, and the patient's psychic life is fashioned around it, it becomes a disorder in its own right. In stark contrast, chronic nociceptive pain, without negative modification by psychological factors, is not a mental disorder; this includes, for example, chronic cancer pain, post-herpetic neuralgia (pain following reactivation of chickenpox), and peripheral vascular disease in an otherwise well-adjusted individual with good premorbid psychosocial adaptation.

In persistent somatoform pain disorder, all kinds of pain can be present: lower back pain, facial pain, headache, or pelvic pain. Any pathological process can be responsible for the initiation of pain – trauma, surgery, or degeneration. The pain experience is all-consuming and colours every aspect of the patient's world. Patients can become utterly preoccupied with the pain and blame all their miseries and misfortunes on it (see the case study of Frans). If not for the pain, an idealised life is imagined. Patients may deny any other causes of distress.

> **HELPFUL HINT**
> **Persistent somatoform pain disorder: Rules of thumb**
> - Pain is focus of presentation
> - Feelings, motivations, and behaviours become subordinate to pain experience
> - Pain behaviour is demonstrated with cognitive distortions and depression
> - Chronic course.

On history and examination, evidence of depression is present in nearly all patients. Typical depressive phenomena are anhedonia, lack of energy, decreased libido, insomnia, weight loss, psychomotor retardation, and irritability.

Persistent somatoform pain disorder is often complicated by substance abuse, commonly painkillers and alcohol. Common comorbid conditions are major depressive disorder – present in 25-50% of cases – and dysthymic disorder. Persistent somatoform pain disorder usually runs a chronic, unremitting, and disabling course. Antecedent personality pathology, marked passivity, substance abuse, and a long pain history predict a guarded outcome. Litigation and potential compensation predict a poorer prognosis.

Differential diagnosis

The following characteristics of nociceptive pain help to differentiate it from persistent somatoform pain disorder: physical pain fluctuates and is sensitive to emotions and contextual factors; distraction is usually possible and analgesics provide relief. Persistent somatoform pain disorder may be difficult to distinguish from somatic symptom disorder, but in the latter, multiple systems are involved and non-pain symptoms are present. Illness anxiety/hypochondriasis is characterised by a preoccupation about being ill, as opposed to the presence of pain. Conversion disorder is typically short-lived and symptoms are limited to a single pseudo-neurological set. Pain, by definition, is also not considered a manifestation of conversion disorder.

Factitious disorders provide a diagnostic challenge. Malingering typically occurs in a context where external motivations, like avoiding prosecution or obtaining compensation, are identifiable. However, diagnosis is made difficult because persistent somatoform pain disorder patients may well be motivated to malinger given the prospect of financial reward through disability compensation or the payment of damages.

Table 10.14: Diagnostic criteria for persistent somatoform pain disorder from the ICD-10

ICD-10
■ There is persistent severe and distressing pain (for at least six months, and continuously on most days), in any part of the body, which cannot be explained adequately by evidence of a physiological process or a physical disorder and which is consistently the main focus of the patient's attention.   ■ Most commonly used exclusion clause: This disorder does not occur in the presence of schizophrenia or related disorders, or only during any of the mood (affective) disorders, somatisation disorder, undifferentiated somatoform disorder, or hypochondriacal disorder.

Source: Reprinted with permission from the ICD-10 *Classification of Mental and Behavioural Disorders: Diagnostic Criteria for Research*, World Health Organization (WHO), Geneva, 2007.

Illness anxiety disorder

In ordinary speech, the term 'hypochondriac' is used to refer to a person who is constantly describing illness symptoms that he or she is experiencing, when the symptoms are not present. Hypochondriasis (as it was previously known in the DSM-IV-TR), in its current conceptualisation as illness anxiety disorder in the DSM-5, concerns the morbid preoccupation with a disease conviction which involves the fear of contracting, or the belief of having, a serious disease. Exaggerated awareness and frankly inaccurate interpretation of bodily symptoms and functions give rise to the erroneous beliefs and fears.

The ancient Greeks attributed the syndrome to visceral disturbances in the 'hypochondrium' (*hypo* refers to below, *chondrium* to cartilage), or the area of abdomen below the cartilaginous border of the ribcage. In the 1800s, hypochondriasis referred specifically to unexplained conditions limited to the anatomical hypochondrium.

Illness anxiety disorder, or hypochondriacal disorder as it is called in the ICD-10, has virtually always been subservient to another mental disorder, like an anxiety disorder or major depression. Since its induction into the modern nosologies, its validity as a separate condition has been questioned. The location of this disorder within the somatoform disorders has also been the topic of debate.

Symptoms of this disorder often occur in depressive and anxiety disorders. In addition, it is not unusual for it to exist comorbidly with these conditions. This observation has led to it being conceptualised as a symptom dimension, rather than a diagnostic category. Symptom dimensions recognise the occurrence of clusters of symptoms across different disorders, but do not regard the clusters as diagnostic entities in their own right. For example, fever is a typical symptom dimension in general medicine: we recognise its occurrence in many conditions but do not talk of 'fever disorder'.

Epidemiology

In a general medical population, the six-month prevalence of this disorder ranges between 4% and 6%, although a wide range has been found by various studies (Escobar et al., 1998). Information from Africa about its prevalence and other epidemiological characteristics is negligible. In contrast with somatic symptom disorder and conversion disorder, the sexes are equally affected. Age of onset is typically in the twenties, although the condition can start at any age. Social class, education, and marital status appear not to affect its expression.

Aetiology and pathogenesis

Extensions of psychoanalytic theory explain this disorder as disturbed object relations, displacement of repressed hostilities to the body in order to better communicate anger – albeit indirectly – and an interplay between masochism, guilt, conflicted dependency, and the need for suffering and receiving love. Defences against low self-esteem, inadequacy, and conditioned reinforcement of the sick role have also been considered causative. The most compelling evidence points toward it as a variant expression of other mental conditions, notably anxiety disorders and depression. It seems these conditions establish a hypervigilant state which is biased towards the detection of harm, including probable noxious signals originating from the person's own body. It is like an over-sensitive smoke detector, raising the alarm for evacuation on detecting the smoke of a single cigarette wafting in from an office balcony. If this hypothesis holds sway, disturbances in the neural substrate of fear are implicated in the condition's pathogenesis.

> **HELPFUL HINT**
> **Illness anxiety/ hypochondriasis: Rules of thumb**
>
> - Preoccupation with having a disease
> - Absence of demonstrable pathology
> - Anxious disposition
> - Reassurance not helpful
> - Symptoms correlate with psychosocial stress.

Diagnosis, clinical presentation, and course

Table 10.15 lists the DSM-5 diagnostic criteria for illness anxiety disorder and the ICD-10 criteria for hypochondriacal disorder. The most notable difference between the DSM-5 and ICD-10 diagnostic approaches is the latter's integration of body dysmorphic disorder with hypochondriacal disorder (Criterion A (2)). In contrast, DSM-5 explicitly excludes body dysmorphic disorder in Criterion F, and has included body dysmorphic disorder in the obsessive-compulsive disorders. ICD-10 also specifies schizophrenia as a primary differential diagnosis.

Table 10.15: Diagnostic criteria for illness anxiety disorder (DSM-5) and hypochondriacal disorder (ICD-10)

DSM-5 Illness anxiety disorder	ICD-10 Hypochondriacal disorder

A. Preoccupation with having or acquiring a serious illness.
B. Somatic symptoms are not present or, if present, are only mild in intensity. If another medical condition is present or there is a high risk for developing a medical condition (e.g. strong family history is present), the preoccupation is clearly excessive or disproportionate.
C. There is a high level of anxiety about health, and the individual is easily alarmed about personal health status.
D. The individual performs excessive health-related behaviours (e.g. repeatedly checks his or her body for signs of illness) or exhibits maladaptive avoidance (e.g. avoids doctor appointments and hospitals).
E. Illness preoccupation has been present for at least six months, but the specific illness that is feared may change over that period of time.
F. The illness-related preoccupation is not better explained by another mental disorder, such as somatic symptom disorder, panic disorder, generalised anxiety disorder, body dysmorphic disorder, obsessive-compulsive disorder, or delusional disorder, somatic type.
	■ Either of the following must be present:
	  ▸ a persistent belief, of at least five months' duration, of the presence of a maximum of two serious physical diseases (of which at least one must be specifically named by the patient)
	  ▸ a persistent preoccupation with a presumed deformity or disfigurement (body dysmorphic disorder)
	■ Preoccupation with the belief and the symptoms causes persistent distress or interference with personal functioning in daily living and leads the patient to seek medical treatment or investigations (or equivalent help from local healers).
	■ There is persistent refusal to accept medical reassurance that there is no physical cause for the symptoms or physical abnormality. (Short-term acceptance of such reassurance, i.e. for a few weeks during or immediately after investigations, does not exclude this diagnosis.)
	■ Most commonly used exclusion clause: The symptoms do not occur only during any of the schizophrenic and related disorders or any of the mood (affective) disorders.

Source: Reprinted with permission from the *Diagnostic and Statistical Manual of Mental Disorders*, fifth edition (DSM-5), American Psychiatric Association (APA), 2013, p. 315, and the ICD-10 *Classification of Mental and Behavioural Disorders: Diagnostic Criteria for Research*, World Health Organization (WHO), Geneva, 2007.

The heterogeneity of patients with a DSM-5 diagnosis of illness anxiety disorder is widely recognised. Around one-quarter of patients with this disorder display 'classical' illness anxiety, or fear of having a serious medical condition, but do not report somatic symptoms. The rest display a mix of illness anxiety and somatic symptoms.

This disorder commonly coexists with a depressive or anxiety disorder. The illness concerns fluctuate and typically intensify during periods of increased psychosocial stress, most notably the death of a loved one or serious illness affecting a person important to the patient. The disorder follows an episodic course with symptomatic episodes lasting months to years. Periods of remission are of similar duration. Significant long-term improvement is expected in one-third of cases. Predictors of good prognosis are: high socio-economic status, sudden onset of symptoms following a distinct stressor, the absence of significant personality pathology, no serious medical illness, and treatment-responsive anxiety or depression.

Differential diagnosis

As health concerns are about bodily disease, this disorder must be differentiated from general medical conditions. Like somatic symptom disorder, medical conditions with ill-defined, transient, and fluctuating phenomena present as primary candidates for differential diagnosis. Examples of these include multiple sclerosis and systemic lupus erythematosus, while occult neoplasms (present but undetected cancers) are good examples in this regard.

The distinction between illness anxiety disorder and somatic symptom disorder depends on the focus of the patient's concern: in the former, the concern is the presence or risk of developing a specific *disease*; in the latter, the patient complains of identified symptoms, not disease entities. Illness anxiety disorder patients mostly list no or fewer symptoms than do patients with somatic symptom disorder. The latter also involves multiple bodily systems.

Conversion disorder can be distinguished from illness anxiety disorder by the preponderance of female patients and the sudden and dramatic onset of pseudo-neurological symptoms. *La belle indifférence* also points toward conversion disorder. Body dysmorphic disorder – considered a variant of hypochondriasis by the ICD-10 – involves preoccupation with an anatomical abnormality, not illness anxiety. If illness concerns are of delusional intensity, psychotic disorders must be considered. Anxiety and depressive disorders often coexist with illness anxiety disorder and hypochondriacal complaints are not infrequent in these conditions.

Psychological factors affecting other medical conditions

This diagnostic category is included in this chapter for the sake of completeness. Where psychological factors are adjudged to adversely affect the expression of established physical illness, this diagnosis is justified. Psychological factors are considered ways of responding to stress, interpersonal style, maladaptive coping, denial, and non-compliance. By contrast, a psychological reaction to a physical condition is best considered an adjustment disorder. Obviously, physical illness can precipitate any psychiatric disorder.

FACTITIOUS DISORDER AND MALINGERING

Factitious disorder and malingering are considered to be illness-endorsing behaviours, and they involve the volitional and untruthful presentation of phenomena suggestive of illness or impairment. A good understanding of their clinical nature is also an invaluable aid to the process of diagnosis. Illness-endorsing behaviours show a professed belief in something that is untrue, where efforts are directed at endorsing the truth of a claimed illness. Any symptom, or combination of symptoms, whether physical or psychological, can be presented. Factitious disorder and malingering are disorders involved in such illness-endorsing deception.

Deceit involves a subject about which the person chooses to deceive, the deceptive distortion introduced into the subject, and a behaviour that communicates this untruth to the target of deceit. For example, in an effort to avoid being punished by his school teacher for not handing in his homework, a boy fabricates a story that his dog has eaten it. Here, the homework constitutes the subject of deceit, the alleged behaviour of his dog the distortion, and the boy's account of events is the behaviour. In illness-endorsing behaviours, the subject of deceit concerns a chosen illness, and the distortion lies in the manifestations of the chosen illness as displayed by the person carrying out the deception. The behaviour involves this person's attempts at convincing the examiner, or target of deceit, of the reality of the illness.

In malingering, the ruse involves the intentional endorsing of a false illness to avert threat or receive unfair advantage. An accused person may pretend to be psychotic so as to avoid trial. Another may feign chronic pain to obtain disability benefits. In malingering, the motivation is external and the malingerer is aware of it. In factitious disorder, the motivation is internal, or intrapsychic, and the patient unaware of it. In both malingering and factitious disorder, the deception is volitional and occurs with full awareness. The behavioural aspect of deceit concerns the quality of perpetration or how the deception is 'pulled off'.

The success of deceit rests on two pillars: familiarity with the subject of deceit and a style of communication that avoids raising suspicion. Deceitful communication succeeds if it appears natural and targets an unsuspecting audience. Deceitful communication is a skill honed through practice. Anxiety is its greatest foe. Suspicion is more often raised by the nature of the communication than by factual errors about the subject of deceit. While factual knowledge is a necessity to test the truth of any claim, recognising the presence of deceit also rests on keen observation and familiarity with human nature. In both factitious disorder and malingering, the untruthfulness of a claim exists on a continuum: deceitful symptoms may involve exaggeration of current ones, displacement of symptoms from one site or system to another, mislabelling innocuous experiences as symptoms, reporting past symptoms, and outright fabrication (Du Plessis, 2003).

Factitious disorder

DSM-5 departs from the previous approaches to factitious disorders by relocating them to the 'somatic symptom disorder category'. This move highlights the importance of differentiating factitious disorder from other disorders characterised by somatic symptoms. DSM-5 also draws attention to the objective identification of deceit, or recognition of a 'pattern of falsification'.

According to DSM-5, factitious disorder involves the intentional production or feigning of physical or psychological symptoms in order to assume the sick role. Not only do patients deceive in their reporting of symptoms, they misrepresent their medical histories, and often their lives. The ICD-10 takes a similar approach.

DSM-5 identifies two kinds of factitious disorder, the first being factitious disorder imposed on self (see Table 10.16 for the diagnostic criteria). The second is factitious disorder imposed on another, also called Münchhausen by proxy. This is a disturbing situation where a caregiver, usually a mother, intentionally induces or feigns signs and symptoms in a person entrusted to their care, usually a child, to meet their own needs for attention. Münchhausen by proxy can be potentially deadly for the child. There are challenges with diagnosing this disorder, however. All of the potential indicators that a parent may be trying to get attention for are the same behaviours that a parent with a child with a rare illness may demonstrate in order to get help for their sick child.

Aetiology, pathogenesis, and epidemiology

The aetiology is unknown. Men are more often affected than women. It is believed that many factitious patients suffered childhood abuse, poor attachment, and perceived their parents as rejecting. Frequent contact with doctors and nurses and repeated hospitalisation may have been seen as a source of care and nurturance and an escape from harsh familial environments. This care and nurturance received may have served as reward, in turn reinforcing the illness-endorsing behaviour. Yet, such patients appear to provoke repeated rejection, at first by a parent, then later by doctors and other caregivers. Rejection is thus re-enacted with masochistic regularity. Patients who present with predominantly psychological features have often had first-hand experience of living with, or taking care of, a relative with a mental disorder. Patients often have above-average medical or psychological knowledge, gained from relatives or their own training and employment as laboratory technicians or nurses. Statistical data on factitious disorder are limited.

Diagnosis, clinical presentation, and course

Patients with factitious disorder challenge the doctor–patient relationship in that the patient enters the relationship from a position of intentional deceit and destruction of trust. It is very difficult as a healthcare professional not to feel betrayed and angry, and to be tempted towards punitive behaviour. However, this must be strenuously resisted. Confrontation, exposure at all costs, and blaming attitudes are not helpful and may even precipitate severe personality disintegration, impulsive acts of self-harm, and outright psychosis.

Factitious disorder imposed on others is popularly known as Münchhausen syndrome, after the extravagant Karl Friedrich Hieronymus Freiherr von Münchhausen (1720–1797) from Bodenwerder, now in Germany. A retired German cavalry officer and storyteller, he was renowned for his lavishly exaggerated tales of conquest and travel. He claimed, for instance, to have extracted himself from a swamp by his own hair and to have ridden a bisected horse into battle. Like the Baron, patients can present with pseudologia phantastica (pathological or compulsive lying), which is an elaborate, often fancifully overstated account of a person's exploits, where limited factual material is seamlessly mixed with outright fantasy. The patient also appears to believe his or her patently untrue stories.

Factitious disorder patients can present with a bewildering array of signs and symptoms and become remarkably adept at manipulating laboratory tests and clinical techniques (see the case study of Pule). Their symptoms can cover the entire spectrum of internal medicine, surgery, and other disciplines. In time, patients become experts at symptomatology. Combined with oft-rehearsed performances in front of various medical specialists, some patients can turn even the doubters among these professionals into believers, strengthening and perpetuating the patient's dependency on healthcare. These patients submit themselves to repeated dangerous diagnostic procedures. The so-called washboard or gridiron abdomen is well known in surgical wards and speaks of repeated abdominal surgery.

Comorbid conditions like borderline personality disorder and depression are common. Factitious psychotic symptoms are more likely with borderline patients and those with a close relative who is mentally ill. Such patients have a prognosis worse than bipolar I or schizoaffective disorder (Sadock & Sadock, 2000). Factitious disorder runs a chronic, mostly unremitting, course. Morbidity is presumed high because of exposure to multiple diagnostic and therapeutic interventions. In spite of the deceitful nature of their presentations, patients with factitious disorder are distressed and dysfunctional. Often, factitious disorder is an even stronger reason for intervention than the fallacious presenting condition. Factitious disorder also does not provide patients with immunity from other illnesses.

Table 10.16: Diagnostic criteria for factitious disorder imposed on self from the DSM-5

DSM-5
A. Falsification of physical or psychological signs or symptoms, or induction of injury or disease, associated with identified deception.
B. The individual presents himself or herself to others as ill, impaired, or injured.
C. The deceptive behaviour is evident even in the absence of obvious external rewards.
D. The behaviour is not better explained by another mental disorder, such as delusional disorder or another psychotic disorder.

Source: Reprinted with permission from the *Diagnostic and Statistical Manual of Mental Disorders*, fifth edition (DSM-5), American Psychiatric Association (APA), 2013, p. 321.

Differential diagnosis

As factitious disorder is almost always a diagnosis of exclusion, the differential diagnosis involves any conceivable condition. Psychiatric differential diagnoses include somatic symptom disorder, illness anxiety disorder/hypochondriacal disorder, persistent somatoform pain disorder, borderline, antisocial, and histrionic personality disorder, schizophrenia, and malingering. Ganser's syndrome must be considered because of similarities in response style (e.g. *vorbeireden* or talking past the point).

> **EXAMPLE CASE**
>
> *Pule, a single man of thirty, presented to a well-known Johannesburg surgeon. Pule has a confirmed Bachelor's degree in biochemistry and had been employed as a laboratory technician at a private pathology laboratory until his retrenchment a year earlier. In the interim, he had worked as a waiter in Melville. He informed the surgeon that, for the past year, he had been experiencing repeated spells of light-headedness and fainting after meals. Pule produced a pile of reports from special investigations suggesting that he had experienced periods of sustained hypoglycaemia (low blood sugar). The surgeon immediately considered the possibility of insulinoma – an insulin-secreting tumour of the pancreas. As an earlier dedicated arteriogram of the pancreas had failed to demonstrate a tumour, the surgeon organised admission for a repeat arteriogram and other investigations.*
>
> *While examining Pule, the surgeon noticed that he must have undergone many laparotomies (major abdominal surgery) and remarked about his 'grid-iron abdomen'. Pule admitted to this, listing appendectomy, cholecystectomy (removal of the gall bladder), and several exploratory laparotomies. Curiously, Pule could not provide any documentary evidence of the previous operations and was hesitant to divulge the names of previous doctors and details of admissions. Pule described how, as a youngster, he had been sickly and often in hospital for 'months at a time'. He claimed to have spent weeks in ICU, requiring cardiopulmonary resuscitation on four occasions. Pule further related how, after graduating, he had worked for Medécins sans Frontières in the Congo and Darfur, was involved in an exchange programme with a Libyan university, taught English in Taiwan, travelled across Tibet, met the Dalai Lama, played as a jazz saxophonist in Cape Town, worked as a clerk at the South African embassy in Guatemala, and spent three years in exile in the former East Germany.*
>
> *Pule's very full life and improbable experiences left the surgeon uneasy and suspicious. In the first two days in hospital, Pule experienced three episodes of severe hypoglycaemia, culminating on one occasion in a grand mal seizure. For reasons she could not explain, an experienced nurse on the eve of retirement became suspicious of his presentation. When Pule had another hypoglycaemic attack, she decided to inspect the drawer of his bedside table. Perhaps not unsurprisingly, she discovered several half-empty blister packs of metformin, an oral treatment for diabetes and the most likely explanation for Pule's hypoglycaemic spells. With the surgeon's support, she approached Pule, gently enquiring about the tablets. Enraged, he accused both of them of criminal negligence and threatened litigation. But, minutes later, Pule fled the hospital, never to be seen again.*

Malingering

Malingering is not a mental disorder. Cunnien (1997) framed malingering as a conscious and deliberate behaviour that constitutes a form of pretence, fabrication, or feigning in the presence of an objectively identifiable goal. Rogers (1988) offered a similar understanding, but added that malingering can coexist with true illness. Turner (1997) emphasised that malingering per se is neither symptom nor illness, but behaviour.

Unrelated to Münchhausen by proxy, malingering by proxy involves the reporting of untruthful symptoms in another and is motivated by an identifiable external incentive, like securing a child support grant (Hales et al., 2008). Extended malingering involves the co-opting of others to endorse the index malingerer's deceitful claims. Dysfunctional malingering syndrome involves the continuation of ongoing attempts at malingering despite the malingerer's realisation of its lack of success. In the ICD-10, a malingerer is defined as a 'person feigning illness (with obvious motivation)' (2016). The ICD-11 goes further and gives a description of malingering (which is given in Table 10.17).

Table 10.17: The description of malingering from the ICD-11

ICD-11
Malingering is the feigning, intentional production or significant exaggeration of physical or psychological symptoms, or intentional misattribution of genuine symptoms to an unrelated event or series of events when this is specifically motivated by external incentives or rewards such as escaping duty or work; mitigating punishment; obtaining medications or drugs; or receiving unmerited recompense such as disability compensation or personal injury damages award.

Source: Reprinted with permission from the ICD-11 *Classification of Mental and Behavioural Disorders*, World Health Organization (WHO), Geneva, 2018d.

Epidemiology, clinical presentation, and assessment

Malingering is surprisingly common. In a general psychiatric population, Rogers et al. (1998) found its incidence among people undergoing evaluation in personal damages suits at close on 50%, and 21% in those undergoing assessment in criminal matters. In South Africa, the occurrence of malingering is not well studied. The clinical picture of malingering is rightly confusing, and differential diagnoses embrace all of medicine and psychology. Its proper detection requires an alertness to inconsistency and a healthy dose of scepticism, all without sacrificing compassion.

Exposing malingering is both satisfying and annoying, but it is humbling for professionals to realise their vulnerability to being deceived. The literature is replete with psychological tests tailored for the assessment of malingering. By virtue of their design and the predictable manner in which test-takers respond, most psychometric and neuropsychological tests are de facto malingering screening devices. Most clinicians rely on their pattern-recognition ability to unmask malingering and do not employ systematic protocols; however, novice practitioners lack this experience.

Aware of the novice's needs and potential benefits of a systematic model, Du Plessis (2003) developed the Expert Model for the clinical detection of malingering (see Tables 10.18, 10.19, and 10.20). The Expert Model is synthesised from clinical approaches taken by experts in forensic psychiatry. As it is generic and systematic, the Expert Model can assist the practitioner in any branch of clinical medicine.

Expert Model for the detection of malingering

The Expert Model follows a three-step approach:

- Suspicion – formation of the initial malingering hypothesis
- Iterative hypothesis testing – the deductive stage
- Clinical confirmation.

Table 10.18: Expert Model: Step-wise approach

STEP 1 – SUSPICION
1. Raised by context.
2. Raised by symptomatology and/or assessment behaviour dimension.
3. Psychological testing, laboratory investigations, and information from third parties.
STEP 2 – ITERATIVE HYPOTHESIS TESTING
1. Reviewing the domain or domains in which suspicion originally raised.
2. Examining other domains (symptomatology and assessment behaviour) for supportive evidence.
3. Strengthened by formal psychological testing, laboratory investigations, information from third parties.
STEP 3 – CLINICAL CONFIRMATION
1. Presentation is implausible or impossible.
2. Sufficient iterations, rigorous cross-referencing to amass sufficient evidence.
3. Confession.
4. Direct observation of production of symptoms.
5. Escape from assessment not accounted for by another reason.

Table 10.19: Expert Model: Symptomatology dimension – domains and examples

SYMPTOMATOLOGY DIMENSION
Explanatory notes
Requires expert knowledge and appraisal of symptoms.
Can be least labour and resource intensive, relying mainly on the clinical interaction, nursing, and incidental interactions.
Special investigations can add valuable information when least expected. Behaviour during test-taking or when undergoing laboratory procedures is often revealing (e.g. no anxiety in MRI tunnel in person claiming claustrophobia).
The dimension has four domains: Atypicality, Incongruence, Fluctuation-Variability, and Longitudinal.

Domains with examples
Atypicality domain Psychopathological phenomena are mostly stereotypical and reflect pathological functioning in neural systems. Memory impairments conform to impairments in attentional, learning, and memory systems and have predictable features (i.e. anterograde and retrograde components). Likewise, disturbances in language, praxis, and gnosis have typical manifestations. Psychotic phenomena are surprisingly stereotypical in presentation.
Incongruence domain It is most unusual for a disease or disorder to be characterised by a single phenomenon: 'orphan' symptoms draw immediate attention to their improbability. Symptoms typically keep predictable company and occur in predictable clusters, referred to as syndromes. Malingering is often characterised by the occurrence of orphan symptoms or arbitrary clustering of symptoms not conforming to any known, or likely, pathophysiological process.
Fluctuation-Variability domain Disease processes run a course that is mostly predictable. For example, daily fluctuations are characteristic of mood disturbances: depression is typically worse in the mornings, or afternoons, but not stable. Sleep disturbances display typical patterns. By virtue of their neurobiological origins, typical psychotic hallucinations are worse when alone or at night; hallucinating while having a conversation is most unusual. This is the first point of departure of this assessment domain: the clinician must appraise whether expected changes across time and contexts are observed. Second, the malingerer may be unable to maintain the deceit over time. He or she may also present differently across contexts: while being interviewed by the psychiatrist, the malingerer may display a certain set of symptoms and behaviours, yet, when in the dining hall, observed by nurses, his or her guard may be down and symptoms disappear. 'Fluctuation' refers to unusual, unexpected, and atypical changes in presentation over time, and 'variability' to changes across contexts.
Longitudinal domain Whereas the aforementioned domains rely heavily on clinical interaction, nursing observation, observation during psychological testing, and other activities, the Longitudinal domain taps into the malingerer's behaviour and mental state outside the assessment context. Reports by relatives, friends, colleagues, police officials, prosecutors, correctional service members, teachers, and previous doctors and psychologists may be invaluable in shedding light on a person's behaviour, mental state, and adaptation before the assessment. Pathological conditions have natural histories and conditions often take months to resolve. In certain conditions, signs and symptoms of disturbance are always present (e.g. mental retardation, dementia, and schizophrenia). A person's history should support the current presentation. Discrepancies between psychiatric history, reported mental state, and adaptive functioning with assessment findings raise suspicion.

As a form of deceit, malingering is detectable along two dimensions: errors of fact and errors of communication. Errors of fact involve the subject of deceit (e.g. the illness, like psychosis) and the distortion introduced by the malingerer (factors adjudged by the malingerer to create the guise of psychosis, like fake delusions). Errors of fact concern symptomatology and are amenable to clinical assessment, provided the assessor is sufficiently familiar with the field's symptomatology. Special investigations, neuropsychological measures, and information from third parties may assist in detecting false symptoms.

Errors of communication concern the manner in which the malingerer communicates the deception; these are also amenable to clinical appraisal. Both error dimensions are composed of domains designed to assist the doctor or psychologist with the detection of malingering. In the Expert Model, errors of fact are appraised in the 'symptomatology dimension' (so named because the subject of deceit and deceitful distortion concern symptoms). The communicative behaviour always plays out in an assessment context and is thus represented by the 'assessment behaviour dimension'. Table 10.18 summarises the three steps employed by the Expert Model in the detection of malingering. Tables 10.19 and 10.20 explain and list examples of symptomatology and assessment behaviour.

Table 10.20: Expert Model: Assessment behaviour dimension

ASSESSMENT BEHAVIOUR DIMENSION
Explanatory notes
This dimension of assessment does not rely on expert knowledge of a specific discipline, but on keen observation.
Least labour and resource intensive, relying mainly on the clinical interaction, nursing reports, other incidental interactions.
Consists of eight domains: interactional style, response style, paralingual, affective display, motoric behaviour, autonomic phenomena, temporo-contextual inconsistency and general deceitfulness.
Assessment behaviour is in operation across all contexts where the subject of an elaborate assessment process interprets the contexts as scrutiny. The more naturalistic a setting, like when mixing with patients in the courtyard of a ward or during dinner time, the less likely the person will react with overt assessment behaviour. But, we should be mindful that assessment is stressful and many sincere people, normal or mentally ill, react to assessment with awkward affectedness.
Domains and examples
Interactional style
Unduly familiar, obsequious or unduly formal.
Bland and insincere.
Lack of cooperation: unwilling to answer, contrariness, sarcasm.
Response style
Directing focus of conversation: either towards, or away from a topic.
Unexpected shifts: from specifics to generalities, or vice versa.
Requests for clarifications or repetitions: 'pardon', 'I did not get that', 'can you repeat that?'.
Qualifiers/modifiers: 'but', 'however', 'ordinarily', 'essentially', 'specifically'.
Expanded contractions: 'cannot', 'did not', 'were not', 'will not' instead of 'can't', 'weren't', 'won't'.
Covert denials of lying: 'frankly', 'obviously', 'to tell the truth', 'honestly, believe me' …
Bamboozlers
Q: 'Have you phoned the client?'   A: 'I have not managed to get through to her.'
Q: 'Isn't this room a bit damp?'   A: 'The owner used to use it as a studio.'
Communication errors, changes of thought in mid-cadence, unexpected grammatical errors.
Stilted language.

Domains and examples

Paralingual
Pause fillers: 'Uh', 'err', 'ah', 'eissh'.
Pregnant pauses.
Prosodic changes: increased pitch, speaking with a clenched jaw ('lying through his teeth'), slower pace, response delays.
Stuttering and throat clearing.

Affective display domain
Forced, unnatural smiling: linear smile, absence of canthic creases.
Smiling, laughing, and giggling: increased frequency, often incongruent and insincere.
Affective responses following utterance: affect always precedes awareness and utterance.
Unexpected affective responses.

Motoric behaviour
General agitation: psychomotor restlessness, hand-wringing, handling objects, lower limbs restless.
Posture: more leaning and postural shifts.
Gestures: less finger pointing, fewer hand gestures but more pronounced shoulder shrugs.
Emergence of movement disorders.
Ward-off: hand obscuring face, hand-to-face movements, facial grooming, touching nose, crossing arms, closing hands, interlocking fingers.

Autonomic
Breathing: sighs, deep or shallow breathing, 'discordant breathing'.
Decreased saliva: dry mouth sound, drinking, swallowing, throat clearing.
Tremor: wavering phonation, manipulating objects, may tend to hide hands.
Sweaty palms.

Temporo-contextual inconsistency
Marked inconsistencies in behaviour, interaction, and performance across different contexts, e.g. no interaction during consultation with psychiatrist but engages freely with nurses and others on ward, playing darts and serving at meal times.

General deceitfulness

Doctors and psychologists are trained to relieve suffering, rehabilitate, and restore dignity. We tend to trust our patients. Forensic evaluations fight against the grain of what the healing professions are about. Entering a consultation with the presumption that the patient is malingering is cynical and dark. However, naively believing everything a patient reports is playing with fire. Striking that delicate balance is what the art of medicine and psychology is about.

CONCLUSION

At first glance, the dissociative and somatoform disorders appear complex with an unsettled classification and often unwieldy diagnostic criteria. Management is frequently difficult and a strained therapist–patient relationship not uncommon. The fact that a single biopsychosocial model eludes us further compounds things.

Despite these difficulties, we can get to grips with these conditions. What follows is a summary of what we do know about dissociative and somatising conditions, which highlights their differentiating features. To keep things clear, matters of classificatory contention are not considered in the summary.

Pathogenesis

Dissociative and somatoform disorders mostly follow a similar pathogenic process:

- Early adversity or trauma: Child abuse, trauma, serious illness, and poor attachment.
- Constitutional predisposition exists.
- Dissociation is expressed as a defensive response to trauma and is associated with fight and flight.
- Detachment and compartmentalisation are neural information processes at play.
- Dissociative compartmentalisation and detachment operate to produce predictable disturbances in:
  - Memory
  - Sensory experience
  - Motor behaviour
  - Representation of the self and the external world.

Symptom expression

- Emergence, exacerbation, or maintenance of symptoms follows, or is related to exposure to trauma or adversity.
- Symptoms consist of a variable mix of dissociative phenomena and somatising.
- A mix of mental and bodily symptoms is the norm.
- Somatic symptoms can occur in almost any bodily system or affect almost any function.
- Negative affects and limited capacity to describe experienced feelings are common co-occurrences.
- Somatic symptoms do not yield to medical explanation.
- Course is often chronic.

Using the psychopathological mode of presentation and the course of the condition as parameters, Table 10.21 provides a useful guide to recognising and differentiating conditions.

Table 10.21: Primary mode of presentation and course of dissociative and somatoform disorders

Category	Disorder	Subtype/ specifier	Primary mode of presentation	Course
Dissociative disorder	Dissociative identity disorder		Disturbed personal identity	Recurrent, chronic
	Dissociative amnesia		Amnesia	Transient, brief
		Fugue	Amnesia, travel, disturbed personal identity	Transient, days to months
	Depersonalisation/ derealisation disorder		Alienation from self	Recurrent, brief

Category	Disorder	Subtype/ specifier	Primary mode of presentation	Course
Somatic symptom and related disorders	Somatic symptom disorder		Multiple symptoms in different organ systems	Chronic
		Pain	Pain overwhelms all experience and behaviour	Chronic
	Illness anxiety disorder/ hypochondriasis		Preoccupation with disease, not specific symptoms	Chronic
	Conversion disorder		Sensory, motor disturbance, pseudo-seizures	Transient, can be chronic

Dissociation and somatising as symptom dimensions

- Dissociation is not limited to the dissociative disorder construct. It occurs across a wide spectrum of psychiatric and medical conditions:
  - Acute stress disorder
  - Posttraumatic stress disorder
  - Panic attack
  - Other anxiety disorders
  - Schizophrenia and other psychotic disorders
  - Depressive disorders
  - Borderline personality disorder.
- Somatising and somatic phenomena also occur across a wide spectrum of mental conditions:
  - Depressive disorders
  - Schizophrenia and other psychotic disorders
  - Panic attack
  - Generalised anxiety disorder and other anxiety disorders.
- In these instances, dissociation and somatising occur as fairly predictable symptom clusters, or dimensions but do not define the conditions.
- In posttraumatic stress disorder, obsessive-compulsive disorder, and borderline personality disorder, prominence of dissociative symptoms predicts a poorer long-term outcome.
- Both dimensions are not infrequent in a variety of conditions usually considered as 'culture-bound syndromes' in the current classificatory systems (e.g. running syndromes, spirit possessions, etc.).

MULTIPLE-CHOICE QUESTIONS

1. Dissociation:
    a) is a phenomenon only encountered in mental disorders
    b) involves severance of connection between one's sense of identity, feelings, thinking, and behaviour
    c) comprises the psychological processes of containerisation and detachment
    d) cannot occur during bereavement
2. Somatising:
    a) is dominated by fear and perplexity
    b) involves mental anguish sublimated into meditation-like dissociation
    c) is encountered in a broad spectrum of mental disorders
    d) is an uncommon finding in patients with depression and anxiety disorders
3. Dissociative disorders:
    a) are characterised by recurrent episodes of brief psychosis
    b) may involve disturbances in memory, personal identity, and perception
    c) are very rare in developed Western societies
    d) are noted for their insidious onset without identifiable stressors
4. Indicate the true statement:
    a) As it is a mental condition, persistent somatoform pain disorder is not associated with morbidity.
    b) Hypochondriasis is defined as the occurrence of many symptoms, referable to different organs.
    c) Somatic symptom disorder is typically brief in duration.
    d) Conversion disorder may occur in epileptic patients.
5. Indicate the true statement:
    a) In factitious disorders, the patient does not deliberately feign or exaggerate symptoms.
    b) Dissociative fugue concerns the fabrication of symptoms in the presence of a clear, identifiable external motivation.
    c) Malingering is not a mental disorder.
    d) As there is no true pathology, patients with factitious disorders experience no distress.

PARAGRAPH AND ESSAY QUESTIONS

1. Describe dissociation with reference to the fear response and the processes of compartmentalisation and detachment. Mention how symptoms correlate with the two constructs.
2. Give an account of *amafufunyana*, *ukuthwasa*, and selected culture-specific syndromes from the rest of the world, with reference to dissociation and somatising.
3. Describe the aetiology, epidemiology, clinical presentation, and differential diagnosis of dissociative amnesia, conversion disorder, and illness anxiety disorder/hypochondriasis.
4. Compare and contrast malingering and factitious disorders.
5. Explain why conversion disorder is classed under 'dissociative [conversion] disorders' in the ICD-10 and under 'somatic symptom and related disorders' in the DSM-5.

Juan A. Nel & Melanie Lake

CHAPTER OUTLINE

Introduction
History of medicalisation of sexuality and gender
Clinical picture
Conditions related to sexual health
    Sexual dysfunctions
    Male and female sexual dysfunctions
    Sexual interest/arousal disorders
    Orgasmic disorders
    Sexual pain disorders
Gender dysphoria/gender incongruence
    Issues with gender identity
Paraphilic disorders
Cross-cultural and African perspectives
Aetiology
    Biological factors
    Psychological factors
    Social and interpersonal factors
Conclusion

LEARNING OUTCOMES

After studying this chapter, you should be able to:

- Show a general understanding of conditions related to sexual health (namely, sexual dysfunctions and gender dysphoria), and be able to distinguish them from paraphilic disorders, based on the most recent scientific evidence and human rights considerations.
- Describe the history of the medicalisation of sexuality and gender.
- Understand the problems relating to the nosology of conditions related to sexual health and paraphilic disorders.
- Describe, and distinguish between, sexual dysfunctions, gender dysphoria, paraphilias, and paraphilic disorders.
- Identify cross-cultural and, more specifically, South African, variations in the presentation of sexual dysfunctions and gender dysphoria.
- Formulate an aetiological model of conditions related to sexual health (i.e. sexual dysfunctions and gender dysphoria).

PERSONAL HISTORY CASELET

There is nothing that excites Tshepiso more than anticipating commuting between Parktown station and Soweto in the overloaded train carriages. A great deal of effort is made to find the one woman in the crowd that he finds most appealing. The next challenge is to get up close enough to her as she makes her way onto the platform and train, so that he can push himself up against her, rubbing his penis against her body. All the while, his stance is one of minding his own business, an 'unawareness' of how this may be experienced by the woman who is, indeed, the focus of his attention – his victim. The thrill lies in that it is his secret. These encounters fuel Tshepiso's fantasies during masturbation. While rubbing himself against the woman, he visualises having a significant sexual bond, at times leading to him reaching orgasm.

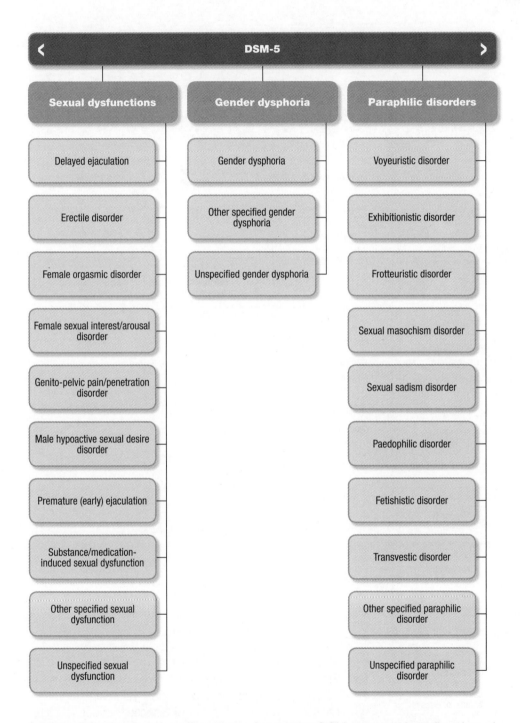

Figure 11.1: The American Psychiatric Association DSM-5 categorises disorders of sexual dysfunctions, gender dysphoria, and paraphilic disorders as shown above.

Source: Figure created by OUP reflecting information found in *Diagnostic and Statistical Manual of Mental Disorders*, fifth edition (DSM-5), 2013.

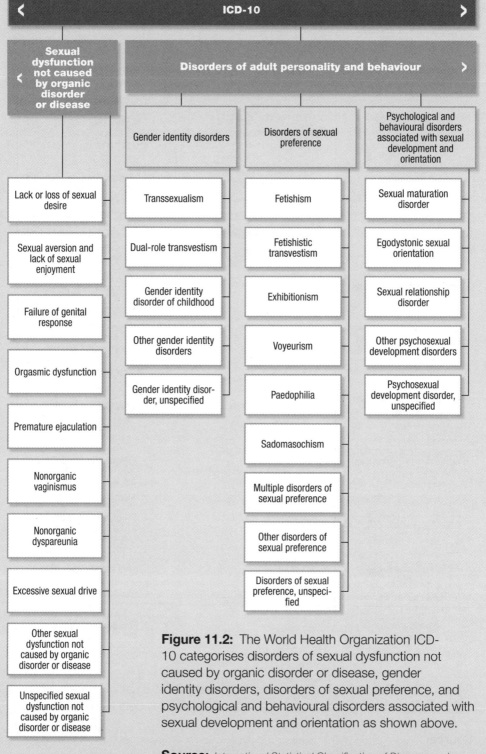

Figure 11.2: The World Health Organization ICD-10 categorises disorders of sexual dysfunction not caused by organic disorder or disease, gender identity disorders, disorders of sexual preference, and psychological and behavioural disorders associated with sexual development and orientation as shown above.

Source: *International Statistical Classification of Diseases and Related Health Problems*, tenth revision (ICD-10), 2016.

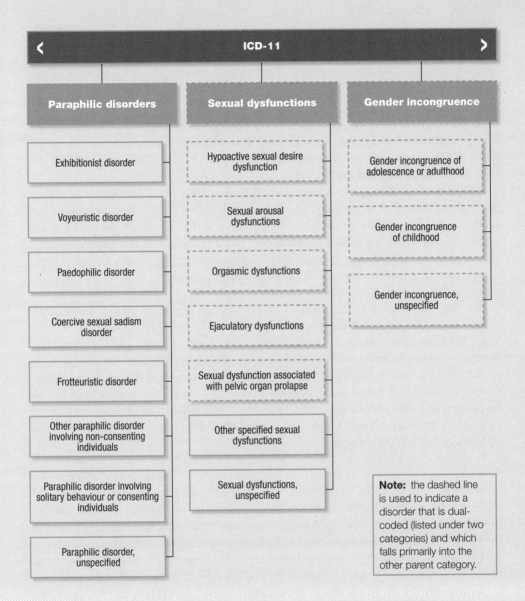

Figure 11.3: The World Health Organization proposed ICD-11 categorises paraphilic disorders, sexual dysfunctions, and gender incongruence as shown above.

Source: *International Classification of Diseases for Mortality and Morbidity Statistics*, eleventh revision (ICD-11), 2018.

INTRODUCTION

This chapter deals with the fascinating aspects of human functioning: sexuality and gender. We will be exploring the diagnostic criteria and aetiology of two groups of conditions related to sexual health: firstly, sexual dysfunctions and gender dysphoria or gender incongruence, and secondly, paraphilic disorders (such as the example at the beginning of this chapter). While conditions related to sexual health are no longer classified as mental health disorders in the ICD-11, and neither are the paraphilias per se, paraphilic disorders most certainly are, both within the DSM-5 and the ICD-11.

As you progress through this chapter, it will become clear that the distinction between 'normal' and 'abnormal' sexual and gender behaviour is not too clear. This is a very important point that needs special emphasis here. To contextualise this discussion, we return to our earlier definitions of abnormality as behaviours that are statistically rare (atypical), cause intense personal distress and impairment in global functioning or psychological dysfunction (breakdown in cognitive, emotional, or behavioural functioning), and/or are culturally inappropriate or not expected (see Chapter 1).

The very definition of some sexual and gender behaviours as disordered or abnormal is not only contentious, but also theory dependent and value laden (Campbell, Artz, & Stein, 2015). Sexuality remains a sensitive and emotive issue in most societies, including South Africa, and for many it is still a taboo subject. However, the importance of people's sexual selves, as well as healthy sexual functioning and expression, is undisputed (Chou, Cottler, Khosla, Reed, & Say, 2015). In many somewhat conservative modern homes, even discussions on healthy sexual functioning may be out of the question. One can imagine the extra layers of embarrassment and secrecy that might accompany the experience of sexual and gender diversity and/or sexual dysfunction.

From the study of both physical and psychological human functioning, we know that sexuality is a powerful driving force (Pigg & Adams, 2005). At the same time, it is typically regulated by a host of social conventions. Societal norms and values tend to prescribe, and often prohibit, the sexual behaviours from which we may choose. This can result in a conflict of interests between individual freedom and the pressure to conform to the expectations of the masses. Moreover, sexual standards and acceptable practices can change (and certainly have changed) according to the particular society or culture, religion, language group, and/ or historical context in which people find themselves. In fact, in the past few decades there have been major shifts in related social attitudes and in policies, laws and human rights standards (Reed et al., 2016). See the case study below for a related example.

Something as biologically and physiologically determined as the classification of a person as being male or female or intersex is likely to be accompanied by different sets of sexual expectations or privileges. Thus, the abnormality criterion of 'culturally inappropriate or not expected' may exert a lot of influence when it comes to the sexual dysfunctions and gender dysphoria that together are placed in the ICD-11 under 'conditions related to sexual health', rather than 'mental health disorders', effective from 2022 (World Health Organization, 2018c).

An important criticism levelled at this criterion is that it is inappropriate, because social norms and values are merely constructions; they do not exist in any absolute sense outside this context (that is, people merely agree to agree on them), and social constructions run the risk of being reified (made into 'real' objects or accepted as 'truth'). In this regard, consider the fact that the *National Geographic* (2017) published a special edition with the title *Gender Revolution* – looking at the cultural, social, biological, and personal aspects of gender – to reflect the shifting landscape of gender globally and the extent to which the once intensely private aspect of gender identity has in recent years entered the public sphere. This entire issue is available online at www.natgeo.com/genderrevolution.

Indeed, use of the term 'pathology' in reference to diverse sexual behaviours is problematic (Campbell et al., 2015; Hekma, 2009; Pan-American Health Organization & World Health Organization [PAHO & WHO], 2000). Long-standing controversies regarding terminology relate to whether to refer to these sexual behaviours as 'variations', 'preferences', 'deviations', or 'diseases' (Psychological Society of South Africa [PsySSA], 2017; Seligman & Rosenhan, 1998). It is important to bear in mind that, while the medical community is interested in the consequences of unusual sexual practices for health, many psychologists consider paraphilias to be compulsive behaviours.

Figure 11.4: Symbols reflecting sexual and gender diversity

However, many people who practice diverse sexual behaviours, including bondage and discipline and sadomasochism (BDSM) and/or kink, do not feel that they fall into either of these categories. For these 'kinky' individuals, there are only two non-negotiable issues when it comes to human sexual behaviour: that coercion of others (especially children and adolescents) into sexual activities is never permissible, and that people must not be led by their sexual urges into regrettable, dangerous, detrimental, or mutilating practices (Love, 1995; Moser, 1999). For kink folk, the operative terms are 'safe', 'sane', and 'consensual' (PsySSA, 2017).

It is important to note that the (mental) health fraternity is increasingly acknowledging the substantial shifts that have occurred in how sexual and gender diversity is perceived. This can, amongst others, be seen in the significant changes to diagnostic criteria applied to paraphilias in the DSM-5 (American Psychiatric Association, 2013), and those proposed for the ICD-11 (World Health Organization, 2018c), which, among other aspects, clearly distinguish paraphilias from paraphilic disorders.

This significant shift is also visible in the launch in 2017 by the Psychological Society of South Africa (PsySSA) of the landmark South African practice guidelines for psychology professionals working with sexually and gender-diverse people (PsySSA, 2017). This 85-page document contains 12 practice guidelines, each providing a review of current knowledge, globally and particularly locally, followed by potential application in psychological practice. It constitutes a first of its kind on the African continent. See https://docs.google.com/viewerng/viewer?url=http://www.psyssa.com/wp-content/uploads/2018/04/PsySSA-Diversity-Competence-Practice-Guidelines-PRINT-singlesided.pdf&hl=en_US

Figure 11.5: South African practice guidelines for psychology professionals working with sexually and gender-diverse people

Source: PsySSA, 2017.

Sexual dysfunctions and gender dysphoria remain contentious issues because sexual functioning and gender are sensitive topics. Other historical and ongoing controversy and/or debates in the area include:

DISORDERED OR JUST DIFFERENT?

A young male psychology student who has been living quite happily with his mild PVC (polyvinyl acetate, a common plastic) clothing fetish, a paraphilia, for the last few years may experience no personal distress. If his family does not know of his choice, while a few close friends accept it and his girlfriend loves it, he may encounter no problems in social functioning. If he is doing well in his studies and looking forward to his working years, we might not find impairment in his academic and/ or occupational contexts either. His PVC fetish may very well be less frequently encountered in the general population than the more common sexual arousal patterns, but this criterion alone is not enough to consider him disordered. The only problem that this young man experiences might be the prejudice of the less well informed in society, who would consider him a pervert, or even dangerous, if they were to find out.

- Sexually diverse groups, such as bisexual people, who may suffer the broader societal expectation of heteronormativity (which suggests that heterosexuality is the only 'normal' way), or even pressure from people with a same-sex sexual orientation to 'make up their minds'.
- Women's liberation groups that have issues with psychological theories, such as Freudian psychoanalysis, which holds that certain types of sexual functioning in women (vaginal orgasm) are 'mature', whereas others (clitoral orgasm) are 'immature'.
- Transgender activists who have come to mistrust psychologists as healthcare providers (given a lack in affirmative psychological practice) while needing them, for instance, for assessments and motivations for gender-affirming surgery (previously referred to as 'sex change' or 'sex reassignment surgery').
- Heterosexual men and women who have had difficulties accepting the historically male constructions of sexual norms or roles (such as that only the man should initiate sex).

When people in positions of power (such as psychologists, politicians, and religious leaders) get to judge the sexual and gender diversity of others, including sexual orientation, gender identity or expressions, the effects of their disapproval can be devastating in terms of the associated neglect, deprioritisation, marginalisation, exclusion, discrimination, and victimisation (Nel, 2009; PsySSA, 2017).

Gender is also a highly politicised concept. In recent years, feminist scholars have successfully challenged the status quo and contributed to a body of knowledge that suggests that any consideration of human sexuality is incomplete unless it takes 'masculinity' and 'femininity' to be cultural concepts (PAHO & WHO, 2000; PsySSA, 2017). In the context of this chapter, the difference between biological sex (the classification of a person as male or female) as fixed and gender (including gender roles) as flexible is of paramount importance.

In human beings, there are two distinct biological sexes, male and female. Men possess male gonads and various other male anatomical features, whereas women possess female gonads and other recognisable female anatomical features. The vast majority of people will be easily distinguishable as either one or the other.

However, this is not the case with the very small percentage of individuals who are intersex, a term referring to a variety of conditions (genetic, physiological or anatomical) in which a person's sexual and/or reproductive features and organs do not conform to dominant and typical definitions of 'female' or 'male' (PsySSA, 2017). It has been said that the prevalence of intersex (also known in the DSM-5 as disorder of sex development or, more affirmatively, as diversity of sex development) in South Africa is amongst the highest in the world. A famous intersex South African is, of course, middle-distance runner and 2016 Olympic gold medalist, Caster Semenya (see https://en.wikipedia.org/wiki/Caster_Semenya), around whose continued participation in women's events there has been considerable controversy.

Figure 11.6: Caster Semenya (far right) at the 2016 Olympic Games

Extrapolating from international figures, which estimate that between one in 500 and one in 1 000 are affected to a significant degree, at the very least 45 000 to 90 000 South Africans are intersexed to a significant degree (Thoreson, 2013). Medical practitioners observing anatomical sexual ambiguity at birth have often treated the situation as an emergency, immediately performing surgery. Depending on the mix of characteristics, such babies have often been 'assigned' to one or other sex and given medical and psychosocial treatments considered supportive of that gender. Much criticism has been levelled at the medical practice of 'deciding' such an important part of an individual's identity in such cases (Barlow & Durand, 2011; PsySSA, 2017; Samelius & Wägberg, 2005). Increasingly, surgery is only considered as a last resort, and implications for a specific psychological gender identity are borne in mind.

The complexity of human sexual functioning can be seen in the reality that biological or anatomical sex does not necessarily relate in a direct sense to one's sexual orientation, or, for that matter, to one's gender identity. Also, 'sexuality is not reducible to a body part or a drive; it must be understood as integral to an entire matrix of social, economic, cultural, and relational forces; it is constructed rather than given' (Petchesky, 2008, p. 12). Sexuality, like gender, is complex and multidimensional. In practice, this implies that what people do sexually (their behaviour) may differ from both their sexual orientation and desire (i.e. object choice or fantasy), and also their sexual identity. Their sexual identity, in fact, may or may not correspond with their behaviour or their desire. As Petchesky (2008) emphasises, all three of these aspects are again distinct from gender expression, gender orientation, and gender identity.

A comparison of studies involving large samples of adults across the United Kingdom, France, and the United States suggests that the overwhelming majority of people have engaged only in heterosexual behaviour (sexual relationships with members of the opposite sex). In addition to vaginal intercourse being a near universal experience, with 25% of males and females in the United States having had vaginal intercourse by age 15, 75% of American men have engaged in oral sex and only one-fifth report having engaged in anal sex (Barlow & Durand, 2011; Barlow, Durand, Du Plessis, & Visser, 2017).

Population-based surveys in the United States and elsewhere increasingly include questions that allow for an estimate of the size of the lesbian, gay, bisexual, and transgender (LGBT) population. Accordingly, it is estimated that 3.5% of adults in the United States identify in terms of their sexual orientation as lesbian, gay or bisexual; of these, slightly more identify as bisexual. An estimated 0.3% of adults in the United States are transgender in terms of their gender identity, thus bringing the estimate of the size of the LGBT population in the United States to 3.8%. Women are considerably more likely than men to identify as bisexual. If same-sex attraction is taken into consideration in addition to behaviour, almost 11% of Americans acknowledge at least some same-sex sexual attraction, while 8.2% report they have engaged in some same-sex sexual behaviour in their lifetime (Gates, 2011).

Earlier reviews of prevalence studies (Gonsiorek & Weinrich, 1991) concluded, however, that the rate of same-sex sexuality in the United States is between 4% and 17% (depending on whether bisexuals are included and how same-sex sexuality is defined). It is important to note that, nowadays, same-sex sexual orientation (most often called gay or lesbian) and bisexual orientation are seen as normally occurring sexual diversity or variations rather than as problems, and are *not* considered to be indications for treatment (American Psychiatric

Association, 2013; PsySSA, 2017; World Health Organization, 2018c). Nonetheless, the majority of people engage in heterosexual vaginal intercourse within a relationship with one partner.

Due to some of the issues of contention described above, sexuality has been an under-researched area. Therefore, both nationally and internationally, reliable and valid data on both the common and less common sexual practices is lacking (Campbell et al., 2015). It does, however, seem that sexual practices and what constitutes sexual satisfaction, is increasingly similar globally (Barlow et al., 2017). Nonetheless, the body of scientific knowledge on sexuality is growing, and various aspects are relevant here. Internationally, research on sexuality issues is mainly the domain of the humanities and social sciences, most notably within the disciplines of history, literature, ethnology, sociology, and social anthropology (Pigg & Adams, 2005). Interestingly, psychology is not at the forefront of related research.

Sexology is the scientific study of human sexuality, including sexual interests, behaviours and functioning (Southern African Sexual Health Association [SASHA], 2015) and is a rather small, but growing, field. Clinical sexology is that sub-discipline of sexology where registered psychologists and social workers with further training and qualification in sexology focus on the prevention and treatment of sexual problems. These problems pertain to sexual dysfunctions, compulsive sexual behaviours, and syndromes following sexual victimisation, while also engaging with gender dysphoria (PAHO & WHO, 2000; SASHA, 2015).

Sexual health concerns and problems refer to life situations related to sexuality that impact on wellness and quality of life. For this reason, they require interventions by individual health practitioners, often medical doctors and psychologists, and/or society in the form of awareness-raising. These concerns and problems include, amongst others, sexual dysfunctions, sexual violence, and the HIV/Aids pandemic.

Although there are gender differences in sexual behaviour, the sexes are drawing closer in terms of their sexual attitudes and behaviours (Barlow et al., 2017). The previous societal 'double standard' (found, for instance, in the outdated idea that viewed promiscuous men in a positive light and promiscuous women in a negative light) has all but disappeared in Western societies. This outdated idea had the effect of socialising a number of women to develop conservative, embarrassed, self-conscious, or behaviour-inhibiting sexual self-schemas, whereas many other women developed schemas including passion, romance, and openness to sexual experience (Andersen & Cyranowski, 1994; Barlow & Durand, 2011). On the other hand, men were found not to develop negative core beliefs about sex (Andersen, Cyranowski, & Espindle, 1999).

There are a number of gender differences in sexual behaviour. For example, a much higher percentage of males than females report masturbating (Barlow et al., 2017). This is the largest gender difference in sexual behaviour, and may be because masturbation is more anatomically convenient for men or more socially permissible, although women have been encouraged to self-explore sexually for years. Males also express more permissive attitudes and behaviours towards casual and premarital sex than do females. Females report having had fewer sexual partners than males and a lower frequency of intercourse. Women tend to desire more intimacy and demonstrations of love during sex, while men tend to emphasise arousal (Nel, 1999).

College students and young adults engage in alarmingly high rates of sexual risk behaviour (Caico, 2014; Sarason & Sarason, 1993). The number of partners and types of sexual activity practised by college women has remained fairly constant since 1975, although the use of condoms has increased (Barlow et al., 2017; Nel, 1999). While more than 53% of males and 62% of females of all ages report no more than one sexual partner over the previous five years (Barlow et al., 2017), Barlow and Durand (2011) report that more than 23% of American men have had 20 and more sexual partners.

Sexual activity can, and does, continue into old age for many. Sexual behaviour can continue past the age of 80 for some. Barlow and Durand (2011) report that 50% of men and 36% of women aged 75 to 79 are sexually active; 39% of men and 17% of women in the United States aged 75 to 85 are sexually active (Barlow et al., 2017). The decreases in sexual activity that are found in some ageing people may be related to more general decreases in mobility and overall health. Various diseases of old age, and the treatments given for them, may have vasocongestive response effects and arousal-reducing effects that interfere with sexual behaviour. Ageing males may have a difficult time achieving or maintaining an erection, and ageing women may experience a reduction in vaginal lubrication. Overall, high levels of both physical and mental health, and good relationship quality, have been found to be the best predictors of sexual wellbeing (Laumann et al., 2006).

There are four categories of sexual dysfunctions with, in most instances, differences between how they manifest in males and females. These are sexual desire disorders, sexual arousal disorders, orgasmic disorders, and sexual pain disorders. There are eight major paraphilic disorders described in the DSM-5 (American Psychiatric Association, 2013) and numerous less common ones that have been the topic of specific studies and dedicated research (Money, 1984, 1988). Advocacy by social movements for recognition of, respect for, and the protection of the rights of sexually and gender-diverse persons and communities has contributed greatly to sexual dysfunctions and gender dysphoria/incongruence being declassified as mental health disorders in both the DSM-5 (American Psychiatric Association, 2013) and ICD-11, released in 2019, but effective from 2022 (World Health Organization, 2018c); they have been moved to a section of the ICD-11 now named conditions related to sexual health, thus separating them from paraphilic disorders into stand-alone categories.

HISTORY OF MEDICALISATION OF SEXUALITY AND GENDER

In the 1960s you were sick if you liked being a homosexual; now you are sick if you do not like being a homosexual.

MacDonald, 1976, in Steffens & Eschmann, 2001, p. 7.

The distinction between sex and gender in the English language was only emphasised in the 1950s and 1960s by British and American psychiatrists and other medical professionals working with intersex and transgender people (Esplen & Jolly, 2006).

Same-sex sexual orientation was deemed to be psychopathology within the biomedical model and treated as a mental disorder until quite recently (Nel, 2009). Classified as a disorder by the American Psychiatric Association in 1953, homosexuality was declassified in 1973 (Shidlo & Schroeder, 2002), an action that was supported by the American Psychological Association in 1975, when a related resolution was passed, also encouraging professionals to work against the prevailing idea that same-sex sexuality was 'perverse' (Goldfried, 2001).

The American National Association of Social Workers followed suit in 1977. In their first policy statement related to same-sex sexuality issued in 1977, it was emphasised that the Association's position of non-discrimination and equal status for all, regardless of sexual orientation, best served the mental health and welfare interests not only of affected individuals, but also of society as a whole (Tully, 2000). The 'expert' opinion of same-sex sexuality as undesirable, along with research aimed at 'converting' same-sex sexual behaviour to that of the mainstream, however, persisted until the late 1970s (Nel, 2009).

From the early 1970s, the term 'homosexual' was increasingly rejected as pathologising and replaced with the term 'gay' by activists and affirmative healthcare practitioners alike. Gonsiorek (1988) reported that 'ego-dystonic homosexuality', an incomprehensible diagnosis, unpopular with many mental health professionals who did not agree with it, was excluded from the revision of the DSM-III in 1987. Ego-dystonic homosexuality was understood as having a same-sex sexual orientation or attraction that is at odds with one's idealised self-image as heterosexual, causing anxiety and a desire to change one's homosexual orientation.

While the American Psychiatric Association's DSM classification system declassified homosexuality as pathology in 1973, the ICD only delisted homosexuality in 1999. Now 'officially' seen as mere sexual diversity rather than a problem, same-sex sexual orientation, itself, is no longer deemed a 'condition' to be treated. Accordingly, ICD-11 recommends the removal of all ICD-10 categories of sexual orientation (Reed et al., 2016; World Health Organization, 2018c). See Table 11.1 for a brief overview of the history of sexual dysfunctions and gender dysphoria.

Table 11.1: Summary of history of scientific study of sexuality and gender (adapted from Nel & Lake, 2005)

Dates	Theorist	Description
1856–1939	Sigmund Freud (Austrian, neurologist; founder of psychoanalysis)	The father of psychoanalysis, Freud developed theories regarding the effect of sexual development on behaviour in a period when others steered away from sexuality-related research or discussions.

EXAMPLE CASE

Henry is a 45-year-old psychologist in private practice. He started smoking cigarettes at university. He can't really say why, except that the rest of his classmates were doing it, and he felt it made him look cool. He stopped smoking in the house twice, while his wife was pregnant with each of their two children. He reports that he does not have any health issues related to his smoking, but does tell an amusing story about almost passing out and having to be carried down a flight of stairs when there was a fire drill at his practice. He is unable to walk quickly, or to exercise. He has tried numerous medications to stop, but feels that his 'head needs to be in the right place' before he will really get it right. He has stopped smoking on occasion, but not for longer than three months. He has used a patch, chewed nicotine gum, and used sprays, but feels embarrassed when he uses them in front of colleagues.

He has changed to a lighter cigarette with less nicotine, because this is healthier, but admits that he has started smoking more. He puts this down to stress at work. Sitting down and having a relaxing cigarette makes him feel good, and he feels happy when he smokes. His favourite times to smoke are when he has a beer, and after dinner.

He is not permitted to smoke in the house or in the car when his wife is with him, as she says that she can feel the difference in her breathing when she is in close contact with smokers. She is a non-smoker. She has suggested that he vape, but he says that he may get addicted to it, as he has heard that there are sometimes illegal substances mixed into the liquids. The couple has not been out for a romantic night out to movies or dinner for some time, as he cannot go without a cigarette for longer than 30 minutes. His wife has tried to get him to go for hypnotherapy and cognitive behaviour therapy, but he insists that it is a waste of money as he is a professional himself, and that he will stop when he is ready. She feels that it is affecting their intimate life – she does not enjoy kissing him, his breath is bad and he smells of smoke.

His doctor has indicated that he needs to stop smoking as he has early-onset emphysema, a chronic lung disease. While he is aware that stopping will significantly reduce his risk of death, he is reluctant to stop smoking, saying that he knows that he should, and will stop after the Christmas holidays, or his birthday, or a difficult client at work, or sometime soon.

 ACTIVITY

There are many memes on social media that show desperate people craving coffee. We laugh at these, and sometimes even identify with the dozy person who needs his or her morning coffee fix. Kyle feels that he is one of those people. If he does not have a cup of coffee to start his day, and then another 12 to 14 during the day, he feels dysfunctional. He reports that he cannot wake up, cannot be creative (he works in an advertising agency) and is not able to function socially before he has had his caffeine hit.

Caffeine is used in combination with painkillers for treating both mild pain and migraines. In increased doses it is considered a banned substance in sport. Caffeine is used in some skin creams, and is used in the treatment of acute medical conditions. Kyle does not feel that he is self-medicating. He feels that, as coffee makes him a nicer person, it has value for him. Is Kyle a substance abuser?

Dates	Theorist	Description
1859–1939	Havelock Ellis (British, physician)	Ellis introduced sexual information and outlooks that were revolutionary and polemic (Godow, 1982). Made up, primarily, of a series of six research volumes from the years 1896 to 1910 on Studies in the Psychology of Sex, these findings convinced Ellis that the norm in human sexuality was variability, both across and within cultures. He found so much variability in human sexual expression that a definitive appraisal of what was 'normal' was extremely difficult to make. Ellis introduced a number of highly progressive ideas for his time, including the contention that heterosexuality and homosexuality are not absolutes, but instead manifested in terms of varying degrees on a continuum. Ellis propagated a tolerant attitude towards individual sexual choices.
1868–1935	Magnus Hirschfeld (German; physician)	Informed by his travels in Africa, Hirschfeld was convinced that puritanical European society had inflicted unnecessary sexual mores on people in the process of colonisation. He also first discovered that hormones influenced sexual behaviour and that irregularities in development 'caused' sexual deviance (Tully, 2000).
1872–1922	Iwan Bloch (German; dermatologist and psychiatrist)	Author of among others, *Psychopathia Sexualis*, Bloch suggested that sexual problems could not be understood based exclusively on theology, medicine, law, or anthropology. He considered biological observation and cultural research as the two fundamental pillars of sexual investigation, which required a restricted, independent rigorous science.
1948	Alfred Kinsey and associates (Alfred Kinsey; American; biologist, professor of entomology and zoology, and sexologist)	Released findings from 16 000 interviews in the book *Sexual Behaviour in the Human Male* (Kinsey, Pomeroy, & Martin, 1948). A few years later, the book *Sexual Behaviour in the Human Female* (Kinsey, Pomeroy, Martin, & Gebhart, 1953) followed. These pioneering works offered findings that surprised many people, most notably the report that roughly 10% of people engaged in same-sex sexual relationships. This data has since been presumed to be inaccurate due to the less sophisticated sampling procedures of his day and the contradictory findings of many recent studies (Barlow & Durand, 2011).
1952	Copenhagen University Hospital	Christene Jorgensen had the first successful gender affirming surgery in Denmark (Tully, 2000).
	DSM-III	'Ego-dystonic homosexuality' included in the DSM-III.

Dates	Theorist	Description
1966	William H. Masters and Virginia E. Johnson (American; gynaecologist, American; sexologist)	Conducted research in couple's sex therapy and published their pioneering work in the book Human Sexual Response. This was based on 13 years of experience in treating infertility problems in their St Louis laboratory during the 1950s and 1960s. They identified four distinct stages during sexual activity: arousal (or excitement), plateau, orgasm, and resolution (Masters & Johnson, 1976). They also proposed three female sexual disorders, namely dyspareunia, vaginismus, and orgasmic dysfunction.
1979	Harry Benjamin (German-American; endocrinologist and sexologist)	The Harry Benjamin International Gender Dysphoria Association releases the first version of the standards of care, specifying the minimum requirements for proper care and protection of both the person with gender dysphoria and the professionals who provide treatment.
1921–2006	John Money (New Zealander-American); psychologist, sexologist and author)	First formulated and defined the concepts of gender role and gender identity. Amongst others, his clinical contributions include gender affirming treatments in transgender persons and extensive work with the paraphilias (Money, 1984, 1988).
2003	The New Definitions Committee	The New Definitions Committee (Basson et al., 2003, in Brotto & Klein, 2007) provides new definitions and diagnostic criteria for female sexual dysfunctions, including sexual desire disorders in women.
1987	DSM-III-R	'Ego-dystonic homosexuality' excluded from revised DSM-III (DSM-III-R).
1998	Pfizer	First oral treatments of male sexual dysfunction become available, contributing to a significant increase in related scientific research.
1999	ICD	ICD delists homosexuality as psychopathology.
2001	Rosemary Basson (Clinical professor at the University of British Columbia)	Rosemary Basson is involved in the Consensus Report, which problematises the inclusion of female sexual dysfunction in the DSM-III.
2003	Roy Moynihan (journalist)	Roy Moynihan questions whether researchers are building markets for new medications in the article 'The making of a disease: female sexual dysfunction' (Moynihan, 2003).
2017	Psychological Society of South Africa	Launch of the landmark South African practice guidelines for psychology professionals working with sexually and gender-diverse people.

Dates	Theorist	Description
2018	ICD-11	Effective from 2022, ICD-11 introduces substantial changes related to sexuality and gender identity, reflective of major shifts in social attitudes and policies, laws and human rights standards since the last ICD revision in 1990.

Scientific interest in sexual dysfunctions and their treatment has soared since 1998, when oral treatments for male sexual dysfunction first became available (Brotto & Klein, 2007). The availability of effective and safe medications not only to improve, but also to modify, the sexual functioning of individuals has similarly brought about renewed interest in the prevalence and consequences of compulsive sexual behaviour (PAHO & WHO, 2000) (also see Chapter 12). For example, use of anti-androgen medication, for example Androcur, is associated with the hypothesis that the higher prevalence of paraphilias in males is due to increased androgens. Another example is the use of selective serotonin reuptake inhibitors (SSRIs) and other antidepressants to treat premature ejaculation and compulsive forms of sexual behaviours (PAHO & WHO, 2000).

CLINICAL PICTURE

In previous editions of the DSM, sexual dysfunctions, gender identity disorder, and paraphilias were all categorised under sexual and gender identity disorders. Although still residing under mental and behavioural disorders, the DSM-5 differentiates between three distinct categories, i.e. sexual dysfunctions, gender dysphoria, and paraphilic disorders (see Figure 11.1) and deals with them in different sections. It is important to note that the DSM constitutes only one of several classification systems, with others including the ICD and indigenous knowledge systems (IKS). Reflecting this, as well as the views of the authors of this chapter, who themselves are critical of the view of some sexual and gender behaviours being disordered or abnormal, this chapter is divided into two. In accordance with the ICD-11, it refers to the first section as conditions related to sexual health (that is, sexual dysfunctions and gender dysphoria/gender incongruence). As some paraphilias are still considered as disorders in both the DSM and the ICD, paraphilic disorders are discussed separately.

CONDITIONS RELATED TO SEXUAL HEALTH

This section has been named in accordance with the ICD-11 which embodies a more integrated approach to sexual health by bridging the mind/body split which has long been a defining feature of medical care related to sexual dysfunction (World Health Organization, 2018a). This section of the chapter contains two parts: sexual dysfunctions and gender dysphoria.

Sexual dysfunctions

The World Health Organization defines sexual health as a state of physical, emotional, mental, and social well-being in relation to sexuality and not merely as the absence of disease, dysfunction or infirmity. Accordingly, sexual health requires an affirming approach to sexuality and sexual relationships, as well as the possibility of having pleasurable and safe sexual experiences, free of coercion, discrimination, and violence. Furthermore, for sexual health to be attained and maintained, the sexual rights of all persons must be respected, protected, and fulfilled (World Health Organization, 2002). For a brief overview of the views on sexual health of the American Sexual Health Association, see https://www.youtube.com/watch?v=Fm7IDARpz6Y

Reflecting its development from a medical rather than social model, the DSM classification of sexual dysfunction does not include what have been termed 'sexual difficulties' (McConaghy, 2005). Such difficulties may relate to the emotional tone of sexual relations, an inability to relax, too little foreplay before intercourse, disinterest, partners choosing an inconvenient time, being 'turned off', and being attracted to people other than an intimate partner (McConaghy, 2005).

If we accept that it may be very difficult to ask the question of what constitutes 'normal' sexual behaviour, we may need to rephrase our question. The question – 'What makes sexual behaviour that differs somewhat from the norm a disorder?' – makes more sense and acknowledges many of the issues raised above. It would probably be the question asked by a mental health practitioner sensitive to these issues. It is important to note that anyone may experience aspects of these difficulties occasionally, which may fall within so-called normal parameters. Experiencing occasional problems with one's sexual functioning is extremely common (Nolen-Hoeksema, 2013). These difficulties are diagnosed as dysfunctional only when they are enduring, cause the person significant emotional distress, and interfere with intimate relationships.

In light of this point, sexual dysfunctions are understood to exist when an individual persistently finds it difficult to function adequately while having sex. This set of disorders involves people having trouble engaging in sexual relationships with others and enjoying a sexual act to the point of sexual satisfaction. In order to examine what adequate sexual functioning might be, we must name and understand the phases of the human sexual response.

As indicated above, sex researchers Masters and Johnson (1976) identified four distinct phases during sexual activity: arousal (or excitement, which refers to a subjective sense of sexual pleasure and physiological signs of arousal), plateau (the brief period before orgasm), orgasm (in males, feelings of the inevitability of ejaculation followed by ejaculation, and in females, involuntary contractions of the walls of a section of the vagina), and resolution (the decrease in arousal after orgasm has occurred, especially in men).

BOX 11.1

Sexual dysfunctions may occur in people, regardless of their relationship status, sexual orientation, gender identity, and/or any other such factor.

A fifth stage, the 'desire phase' (when sexual urges occur in response to sexual cues or fantasies), that precedes the arousal phase, was suggested by Kaplan (1979); this has been the topic of research and psychotherapeutic interventions ever since (Talmadge & Talmadge, 1986; Verhaege, 1998). This has important implications for the study of sexual dysfunctions, as one disorder category refers specifically to inadequate desire-phase functioning.

'Sexual dysfunction' refers to some inadequacy in functioning at one of the phases of desire, arousal, and/or orgasm. Strictly speaking, no sexual dysfunction can occur during the phases of plateau or resolution. An inability to feel sexual desire, to become sufficiently aroused to have sex, or to achieve orgasm would be considered sexual dysfunctions. These are typically sexual problems related to the sexual response cycle or to pain. The stages of sexuality (desire, arousal, and orgasm) are each associated with specific dysfunctions. Impairment may be experienced in only one of the three areas of sexuality, or in two or in all three. The DSM-5 categories of sexual dysfunction are shown in Table 11.2.

Table 11.2: Sexual dysfunctions in males and females, according to DSM-5

Sexual dysfunction	Males	Females
Sexual interest/arousal disorders	Male hypoactive sexual desire disorder Erectile disorder	Female sexual interest/arousal disorder
Orgasmic disorders	Delayed ejaculation Premature (early) ejaculation	Female orgasmic disorder
Orgasmic sexual pain disorders		Genito-pelvic pain/penetration disorder

Source: Reprinted with permission from the *Diagnostic and Statistical Manual of Mental Disorders*, fifth edition (DSM-5), American Psychiatric Association (APA), 2013.

Diagnoses also indicate specifiers, including: lifelong (i.e. the person has always had the problem) versus acquired (i.e. new in onset), and generalised (i.e. experienced in all situations and with all partners) versus situational (i.e. the difficulty is experienced in selected situations or with certain partners) (American Psychiatric Association, 2013).

There are numerous biological factors that can cause and maintain various sexual dysfunctions. These include vascular and hormonal abnormalities, undiagnosed diabetes, and the use and/or abuse of certain drugs. For this reason, a thorough psychological assessment, with the intention of diagnosing and treating a sexual dysfunction, should be preceded by a physiological examination by a medical doctor or specialist. The purpose of this is to exclude any physiological factors before a psychologist conducts the assessment to look for psychological factors that may be playing a role in the sexual dysfunction. General medical conditions and other physiological problems may be the primary cause of the problem, as well as being much easier to treat than psychological problems. Many medical drugs are available nowadays that promise effective treatments.

The psychological factors that may cause and maintain various sexual dysfunctions include certain psychological disorders (depression or schizophrenia) and maladaptive attitudes and cognitions. Closely related are the sociocultural factors such as relationship problems, traumatic experiences, and cultural taboos against sex (such as from one's cultural upbringing or society). These aetiological factors will be discussed in more depth later in the chapter. Aetiology is important to identify as this is likely to guide treatment options available to a patient or client. However, when making clinical judgements about the presence of a sexual dysfunction, clinicians should always give recognition to an individual's ethnic, cultural, religious, and social background in so far as they may influence sexual desire, expectations, and attitudes about performance (American Psychiatric Association, 2013).

Male and female sexual dysfunctions

BOX 11.2

It should be noted that premature (early) ejaculation only occurs in men, while genito-pelvic pain/penetration disorder only occurs in women.

Males may experience a dysfunction in terms of lack of desire for sex or they may experience sexual aversion, the inability to attain and/or maintain an erection, the inability to control or delay ejaculation (early ejaculation), or the inability to ejaculate at all. Females may experience a dysfunctional level of desire for sex or they may experience sexual aversion, an inability to become sexually aroused, an inability to become aroused enough to achieve orgasm, or an inability to tolerate vaginal penetration. Below we will work through both the male and female versions of the disorders of sexual desire, arousal, orgasm, and sexual pain. Female and male sexual dysfunctions can have a major impact on quality of life and interpersonal relationships. They are multicausal and multidimensional problems, combining biological, psychological, and interpersonal determinants.

The lack of sexual desire and impaired physical excitement, in what would typically be considered arousing situations, is known as sexual unresponsiveness (previously called 'frigidity'). Unresponsiveness and difficulty reaching orgasm are the most common sexual dysfunctions in women. The most common sexual dysfunctions in men are ejaculating too quickly, and impaired excitement, known as erectile dysfunction (previously called 'impotence') (Brotto & Klein, 2007).

EXAMPLE CASE

Sexual dysfunction in Nigerian women
In 2007, Benjamin Fajewonyomi, Ernest Orji, and Adenike Adeyemo published a research study on the prevalence of sexual dysfunction in women in Ile-Ife, Nigeria. The 384 female respondents had been recruited from out-patient clinics. The authors reported the following:

Of 384 female patients interviewed, 242 (63%) presented with sexual dysfunctions. Types of sexual dysfunction included disorder of desire (n=20; 8.3%), disorder of arousal (n=13; 5.4%), disorder of orgasm (n=154; 63.6%), and painful coitus (dyspareunia) (n=55; 22.7%). The peak age of sexual dysfunction was observed among the age group of 26–30 years. Women with higher educational status were mostly affected. The reasons for unsatisfactory sexual life mainly included psychosexual factors and medical illnesses, among which included uncaring partners, present illness, excessive domestic duties, lack of adequate foreplay, present medication, competition among wives in a polygamous family setting, previous sexual abuse, and feelings of guilt among infertile women due to previous pregnancy termination. The culture of male dominance in the local environment, which makes women afraid of rejection and threats of divorce if they ever complain about sexually-related matters might perpetuate sexual dysfunction among the affected Individuals. (p. 101)

The authors were surprised at the high rate of sexual dysfunction among the respondents, but linked it to the patriarchal system in Nigeria and women's lack of control over their sexual lives. They recommended 'a broader-based study at the community level' to 'further elucidate the cause, effect, and magnitude of these problems among couples in the African setting' (p. 105).

The Masters and Johnson four-stage human sexual response cycle, which informs the classification system of sexual dysfunctions, has been criticised with regard to its lack of generalisability for women (Brotto & Klein, 2007). This model may describe male sexual functioning well but that of women less so. It has also been suggested that sexual difficulties in women have been over-diagnosed and medicalised, and that the designation 'dysfunction' is unhelpful (Brotto & Klein, 2007).

This criticism is what informs many of the changes made in the classification and diagnosis of sexual dysfunctions in women, in particular. It is purported that the previous standard for diagnosing a sexual dysfunction often resulted in inflated estimates of the proportion of women meeting criteria for sexual dysfunction. To improve precision regarding duration and severity criteria compared with DSM-IV-TR, and to reduce the likelihood of over-diagnosis, all of the sexual dysfunctions (except substance-/medication-induced sexual dysfunction) now require a minimum duration of approximately six months, as well as more precise severity criteria. This provides useful thresholds for making a diagnosis and distinguishes transient sexual difficulties from more persistent sexual dysfunction (American Psychiatric Association, 2013).

Going forward, the presence of more symptoms relating to women's sexual functioning, the reporting of distress, as well as revised duration and severity criteria, will help to ensure that short-term, and possibly even adaptive, changes in sexual functioning are not labelled as a dysfunction (American Psychiatric Association, 2012b). Nonetheless, in terms of the DSM-5, both men and women may experience the full scope of sexual disorders, and, as indicated, people of heterosexual, bisexual, and same-sex sexual orientations are also all prone to these problems. Difficulties with and/or the inability to become aroused or reach orgasm are as common in same-sex as in heterosexual relationships (Barlow & Durand, 2011).

Sexual interest/arousal disorders

As is indicated in Table 11.2, three conditions are placed under the category of sexual interest and arousal disorders, namely, female sexual interest/arousal disorder, erectile disorder, and male hypoactive sexual desire disorder.

Female sexual interest/arousal disorder and male hypoactive sexual desire disorder

A man or woman with this disorder has a level of interest in sexual activities that is so low as to be considered abnormal. The person typically does not imagine sexual activity or fantasise, does not wish for more sexual activity, and does not seek out actual sexual relationships. This may be the case even during times of being in a romantic relationship with a potential sexual partner or someone with whom they used to have sex.

Hypoactive sexual desire is difficult to define in absolute terms (such as, how often one wants to have sex in one month), given the lack of reliable population norms. However, the definition emphasises the persistent lack or deficiency of well-accepted 'markers' of desire, such as sexual thoughts or fantasies, as well as absent or deficient receptivity to sexual initiation by a partner. The definition also requires that the man or woman be significantly distressed by this deficiency in desire and/or experience significant interpersonal (romantic relationship) difficulties due to it.

Table 11.3: Diagnostic criteria for hypoactive sexual desire disorders from the DSM-5 and the ICD-10

DSM-5 (female sexual interest/ arousal disorder)	DSM-5 (male hypoactive sexual desire disorder)	ICD-10
A. Lack of, or significantly reduced, sexual interest/arousal, as manifested by at least three of the following: (1) Absent/reduced interest in sexual activity. (2) Absent/reduced sexual/erotic thoughts or fantasies. (3) No/reduced initiation of sexual activity, and typically unreceptive to a partner's attempts to initiate. (4) Absent/reduced sexual excitement/pleasure during sexual activity in almost all or all (approximately 75–100%) sexual encounters (in identified situational contexts or, if generalised, in all contexts).	A. Persistently or recurrently deficient (or absent) sexual/erotic thoughts or fantasies and desire for sexual activity. The judgement of deficiency is made by the clinician, taking into account factors that affect sexual functioning, such as age and general and sociocultural contexts of the individual's life. B. The symptoms in Criterion A have persisted for a minimum duration of approximately six months.	▪ The subject is unable to participate in a sexual relationship as they would wish. ▪ The dysfunction occurs frequently, but may be absent on some occasions. ▪ The dysfunction has been present for at least six months. ▪ The dysfunction is not entirely attributable to any of the other mental and behavioural disorders in ICD-10, physical disorders (such as endocrine disorder) or drug treatment.

DSM-5 (female sexual interest/ arousal disorder)	DSM-5 (male hypoactive sexual desire disorder)	ICD-10
(5) Absent/reduced sexual interest/arousal in response to any internal or external sexual/erotic cues (e.g. written, verbal, visual). (6) Absent/reduced genital or nongenital sensations during sexual activity in almost all or all (approximately 75– 100%) sexual encounters (in identified situational contexts or, if generalised, in all contexts). B. The symptoms in Criterion A have persisted for a minimum duration of approximately six months. C. The symptoms in Criterion A cause clinically significant distress in the individual. D. The sexual dysfunction is not better explained by a non-sexual mental disorder or as a consequence of severe relationship distress (e.g. partner violence) or other significant stressors and is not attributable to the effects of a substance/ medication or another medical condition.	C. The symptoms in Criterion A cause clinically significant distress in the individual. D. The sexual dysfunction is not better explained by a non-sexual mental disorder or as a consequence of severe relationship distress or other significant stressors and is not attributable to the effects of a substance/ medication or another medical condition	■ There is a lack or loss of sexual desire, manifest by diminution of seeking out sexual cues; thinking about sex with associated feelings of desire or appetite; or sexual fantasies. ■ There is a lack of interest in initiating sexual activity either with partner or as solitary masturbation, at a frequency clearly lower than expected, taking into account age and context, or at a frequency very clearly reduced from previous much higher levels.

Source: Reprinted with permission from the *Diagnostic and Statistical Manual of Mental Disorders*, fifth edition (DSM-5), American Psychiatric Association (APA), 2013, pp. 433, 440, and the *International Statistical Classification of Diseases and Related Health Problems*, tenth revision (ICD-10), World Health Organization (WHO), Geneva, 2007.

This diagnosis is subtyped as: lifelong or acquired, generalised or situational. Sexual desire disorders that are exclusively physical (organic) in origin would not be considered to be psychological disorders. A full diagnosis must first exclude the possibility of organic origin and be based on the best available evidence from the medical history, laboratory tests, and physical examinations done on the patient.

A number of factors are well known to have an impact on men's and women's general sexual desire, also sometimes called libido (one's sex drive). (In the original Freudian terminology, the libido referred to an instinctual pressure for gratification of sexual desires.)

So-called positive factors tend to increase levels of sexual desire whereas negative factors tend to decrease these levels. Table 11.4 highlights some of the physiological, psychological, and sociocultural factors on both sides.

Table 11.4: Factors that affect libido

Positive factors	Negative factors
Good health	Disease
Effective stimulation	Stress
Good body image	Fatigue
High self-esteem	Lactation in women
Privacy	Alcohol and other substances (use and abuse)
Security	Medical drugs (e.g. antidepressants)
Trust	Dyspareunia (genital pain with intercourse)
Affection	Depression or other psychological difficulties
Good relationship(s)	Anxiety or anger
Good communication	Inhibitions
	Traumatic experience(s)

Source: Compiled by author Juan Nel.

Changes brought about in the DSM-5 follow from research that indicates that sexual response is not always a linear, uniform process, and that the distinction drawn between certain phases (for example, desire and arousal) may be artificial. In the sexual experiences of women, in particular, desire and (at least subjective) arousal overlap substantially. Also, it is purported that, in some women, desire precedes arousal, while in other women it follows. There are variations in how women define desire, ranging from a focus on sexual behaviour as an indicator of desire, to spontaneous sexual thoughts and fantasies, with others emphasising the responsive nature of women's desire (American Psychiatric Association, 2013).

In the same vein, the New Definitions Committee (Basson et al., 2003, in Brotto & Klein, 2007) provided new definitions and diagnostic criteria for female sexual dysfunctions, including sexual desire disorders in women, which were subsequently incorporated in the DSM-5. For diagnosis with female sexual interest/arousal disorder, a woman must present with: the persistent or recurrent deficiency (or absence) of sexual thoughts, fantasies, and/ or desire for, or receptivity to, sexual activity, which causes personal distress. This move may help to counter the pathologising of women who merely experience lower sexual desire than their partners do, or than some expected 'norm'. Some women report experiencing low sexual drive but may not be distressed by this and may not be motivated to change it.

The two important elements in the new definition are the persistent lack of desire and resulting personal distress. Thus, the definition would not apply to the woman who lacks desire only in some circumstances (for example, during periods of marital conflict) or at certain times (for example, before or during menstruation) (Basson et al., 2003, in Brotto & Klein, 2007). Similarly, even if sexual desire was persistently lower than that of the partner or women of comparable age and socio-economic status, the definition would not apply in the absence of personal distress in response to the situation.

As far as the arousal component of this disorder is concerned, women with this disorder would experience recurrent or persistent inability to achieve or maintain the necessary physical responses (lubrication and swelling) of sexual excitement while engaging in sexual behaviours. Moreover, the disorder must cause the woman to experience a significant level of emotional distress and/or interpersonal (intimate relationship) problems. Female sexual arousal disorder is associated most strongly with difficulty becoming aroused during penile sexual intercourse. The woman's desire for sexual activities may be strong but she typically finds her body becoming unresponsive during the sexual act (see Table 11.3).

Female sexual interest/arousal disorder may be lifelong or acquired and may be generalised across sexual activities or situational (depending upon the partner, and/or circumstances). Prevalence rates are harder to estimate for women with female sexual interest/arousal disorder because they may be less likely than men to seek treatment for this condition.

Male hypoactive sexual desire disorder

EXAMPLE CASE

Male hypoactive sexual desire disorder
A 45-year-old male business executive presents at a clinic with the problem of fatigue for the past four months and, related to that, he has noticed that his desire for intimacy and sexual intercourse has decreased.

On further inquiry, it is ascertained that he holds a senior position at work and that he is always under pressure to meet deadlines. Because of this, he continuously feels anxious and angry, and he feels depressed if he does not meet some of his deadlines. He does take alcohol, but does not think that he has a drinking problem.

DISCUSSION
This client presents with low sexual desire. His main problem, however, is fatigue, resulting from his heavy schedule at work. Typically, the psychologist or doctor always has to ask about sexual function because, if not asked, most clients or patients will not volunteer such information.

Many may believe that such a problem will either get better with time or that the psychologist or doctor will be uncomfortable discussing it.

In this particular client, we find that there are a few factors that put him at risk of developing erectile dysfunction as well, and these are the following:

- *Anxiety*
- *Anger*
- *Alcohol*
- *Ageing.*

In others, there may also be the following risk factors:

- *Drugs*
- *Deliberate control*
- *Dissociation (past negative experiences)*
- *Depression.*

Note: These are popularly known as the '4As' and the '4Ds'.

Diagnosis of this disorder must be based on two critical aspects: a low/absent desire for sex as well as the absence of sexual thoughts or fantasies (see Table 11.3) (American Psychiatric Association, 2013). This disorder may often be associated with, or caused by, other sexual or non-sexual disorders (e.g. erectile disorder, major depression, etc.). Men with this disorder report that they do not initiate sexual activity, or that they are unresponsive to partner's attempts to initiate such activity (American Psychiatric Association, 2013).

Sexual aversion disorder

While still in the ICD-10, the diagnosis of sexual aversion disorder has been removed from the DSM-5 due to infrequent use and lack of supporting research. As opposed to a person with hypoactive sexual desire disorder described above, a person (man or woman) with sexual aversion disorder may be interested in sex and even enjoy sexual fantasising. He or she is also quite likely to enjoy and practise masturbation to the point of orgasm. However, the individual is repulsed by the notion of engaging in the actual sex act (or parts thereof) with another person. The most important difference between these first two disorders is that individuals with hypoactive sexual desire disorder seem to have no interest in sexual activity, whereas individuals with sexual aversion disorder associate sexual thoughts and activities with fear, panic, and/or disgust.

Sexual aversion disorder, then, is characterised by the active dislike and avoidance of genital contact with a would-be sexual partner. This dislike and avoidance must also cause the individual emotional distress and/or interpersonal (romantic relationship) problems. Some people may experience a generalised dislike and avoidance of all sexually intimate behaviours, whereas others dislike and avoid only specific facets of sexual activity between people (such as vaginal penetration). This diagnosis is subtyped as: lifelong or acquired, generalised or situational.

Table 11.5: Diagnostic criteria for sexual aversion disorder from the ICD-10

ICD-10

■ The subject is unable to participate in a sexual relationship as they would wish.
■ The dysfunction occurs frequently, but may be absent on some occasions.
■ The dysfunction has been present for at least six months.
■ The dysfunction is not entirely attributable to any of the other mental and behavioural disorders in ICD-10, physical disorders (such as endocrine disorder), or drug treatment.
■ Sexual aversion:
  ▸ The prospect of sexual interaction with a partner produces sufficient aversion, fear, or anxiety that sexual activity is avoided, or, if it occurs, is associated with strong negative feelings and an inability to experience any pleasure.
  ▸ The dysfunction is not due to performance anxiety (reaction to previous failure of sexual response).
■ Lack of sexual enjoyment:
  ▸ Genital response (orgasm and/or ejaculation) all occur during sexual stimulation, but are not accompanied by pleasurable sensations or feelings of pleasant excitement.
  ▸ There is an absence of manifest and persistent fear or anxiety during sexual activity.

Source: Reprinted with permission from the *International Statistical Classification of Diseases and Related Health Problems*, tenth revision (ICD-10), World Health Organization (WHO), Geneva, 2007.

Erectile disorder

A man with erectile disorder (or erectile dysfunction – ED) would experience the recurrent, partial or complete inability to achieve or maintain an erection while engaging in sexual behaviours. This must also cause the man emotional distress and/or interpersonal (intimate relationship) problems. The man may still retain an active interest in sexual behaviours, and may even engage in them with a flaccid penis but with less intense pleasure than would be experienced with an erection. The inability to achieve or maintain an erection sufficient for satisfactory sexual 'performance' has historically or colloquially been called 'impotence', but the term 'erectile dysfunction' is preferable.

Male erectile disorder is said to have either an organic or psychogenic origin (McConaghy, 2005). Organic origin would refer to an onset not related to life events, with previously normal functioning and the man's libido intact. Here, the aetiology is most likely to be post-operative, vascular, neuropathic, or metabolic in nature, or due to drugs, dyspareunia, ageing, or physical trauma. Psychogenic origin would refer to a man with fully turgid morning erections and/or erections with masturbation, and otherwise intact neurological, circulatory, and endocrine systems, as well as genitalia. The aetiology here is most likely life events or other psychosocial factors.

Table 11.6: Diagnostic criteria for erectile disorder from the DSM-5 and the ICD-10

DSM-5	ICD-10
A. At least one of the three following symptoms must be experienced in almost all or all (approximately 75–100%) occasions of sexual activity (in identified situational contexts or, if generalised, in all contexts): (1) Marked difficulty in obtaining an erection during sexual activity. (2) Marked difficulty in maintaining an erection until the completion of sexual activity. (3) Marked decrease in erectile rigidity. B. The symptoms in Criterion A have persisted for a minimum duration of approximately six months. C. The symptoms in Criterion A cause clinically significant distress in the individual. D. The sexual dysfunction is not better explained by a nonsexual mental disorder or as a consequence of severe relationship distress or other significant stressors and is not attributable to the effects of a substance/medication or another medical condition.	■ The subject is unable to participate in a sexual relationship as he would wish. ■ The dysfunction occurs frequently, but may be absent on some occasions. ■ The dysfunction has been present for at least six months. ■ The dysfunction is not entirely attributable to any of the other mental and behavioural disorders in ICD-10, physical disorders (such as endocrine disorder) or drug treatment. ■ Erection sufficient for intercourse fails to occur when intercourse is attempted. The dysfunction appears as one of the following: ‣ Full erection occurs during the early stages of lovemaking but disappears or declines when intercourse is attempted (before ejaculation, if it occurs). ‣ Erection does occur but only at times when intercourse is not being considered. ‣ Partial erection, insufficient for intercourse, occurs, but not full erection. ‣ No penile tumescence occurs at all.

Source: Reprinted with permission from the *Diagnostic and Statistical Manual of Mental Disorders*, fifth edition (DSM-5), American Psychiatric Association (APA), 2013, p. 426, and the *International Statistical Classification of Diseases and Related Health Problems*, tenth revision (ICD-10), World Health Organization (WHO), Geneva, 2007.

Male erectile disorder is associated with difficulty becoming physically aroused, although desire may be strong. Arousal disorders may be lifelong or acquired and may be generalised across sexual activities or situational depending upon the partner and/or circumstances. Arousal disorders may be considered a greater impairment by men than by women. The prevalence of male erectile disorder is high. Definitive worldwide prevalence data is lacking, but it is believed that percentages range from 7% to 58% of men (Brotto & Klein, 2007).

Orgasmic disorders

Research increasingly suggests that women's sexual excitement varies greatly. In the DSM-5, an attempt is made to reduce the normative stance in relation to how orgasms are perceived and what may constitute a 'normal excitement phase', especially in women. Also, it is increasingly recognised that orgasm is not an 'all-or-nothing' phenomenon. As indicated, severity and duration criteria have also been adopted to avoid pathologising normal variations and short-term changes in sexual functioning.

In the current DSM-5, however, the diagnosis of orgasmic disorders in both women and in men refers to the recurrent absence of orgasm or the unacceptable delay in orgasm following sexual excitement. This condition is also called 'anorgasmia' and refers to inhibited orgasm or the inability to achieve orgasm despite desire and arousal. In women, this is called female orgasmic disorder, and it is a common complaint in women seeking sexual therapy (Brotto & Klein, 2007). In the case of men, there are two disorders that can be considered orgasmic disorders: delayed ejaculation and premature (early) ejaculation. The partner variables and relationship functioning are furthermore emphasised in the DSM-5 (American Psychiatric Association, 2012b).

Table 11.7: Diagnostic criteria for female orgasmic disorder from the DSM-5 and the ICD-10

DSM-5	ICD-10 (orgasmic disorder)
A. Presence of either of the following symptoms and experienced in almost all or all (approximately 75–100%) occasions of sexual activity (in identified situational contexts or, if generalised, in all contexts): (1) Marked delay in, marked infrequency of, or absence of orgasm. (2) Marked reduced intensity of orgasmic sensations. B. The symptoms in Criterion A have persisted for a minimum duration of approximately six months.	■ The subject is unable to participate in a sexual relationship as he or she would wish. ■ The dysfunction occurs frequently, but may be absent on some occasions. ■ The dysfunction has been present for at least six months. ■ The dysfunction is not entirely attributable to any of the other mental and behavioural disorders in ICD-10, physical disorders (such as endocrine disorder) or drug treatment. ■ Orgasmic dysfunction (either absence or marked delay) appearing as one of the following: ▸ Orgasm has never been experienced in any situation.

DSM-5	ICD-10 (orgasmic disorder)

C. The symptoms in Criterion A cause clinically significant distress in the individual.
D. The sexual dysfunction is not better explained by a non-sexual mental disorder or as a consequence of severe relationship distress (e.g. partner violence) or other significant stressors and is not attributable to the effects of a substance/ medication or another medical condition.
	▸ Orgasmic dysfunction has developed after a period of relatively normal response.
	■ General: Orgasmic dysfunction occurs in all situations and with any partner.
	■ Situational:
	  ▸ For women: Orgasm does occur in certain situations (e.g. when masturbating or with certain partners).
	  ▸ For men, one of the following can apply: Only during sleep, never during the waking state. Never in the presence of a partner. In the presence of a partner but not while inserted.

Source: Reprinted with permission from the *Diagnostic and Statistical Manual of Mental Disorders*, fifth edition (DSM-5), American Psychiatric Association (APA), 2013, p. 429, and the *International Statistical Classification of Diseases and Related Health Problems*, tenth revision (ICD-10), World Health Organization (WHO), Geneva, 2007.

Premature (early) ejaculation

The most common male sexual disorder is premature ejaculation (PE), also known as early ejaculation. As indicated earlier, this is also one of the two gender-specific disorders, in that it only occurs in males. Genito-pelvic pain/penetration disorder, that is discussed later is the second gender-specific disorder and only occurs in females. Premature ejaculation is a dysfunction of the orgasm phase, as based on the classical theories of Masters and Johnson.

The DSM-5 diagnostic criteria for premature ejaculation are those most often used, and they refer to persistent or recurrent onset of orgasm and ejaculation with minimal sexual stimulation before, upon, or shortly after penetration and before the person wishes it. The disorder is also marked by emotional distress or interpersonal (romantic relationship) difficulty. The disorder should not be exclusively due to the direct effects of a substance, such as opiate withdrawal.

The DSM-5 cautions that mediating factors such as age, novelty of the situation or partner, and frequency of sexual activity need to be considered before making this diagnosis. Several features helpful in determining the severity of the problem are incorporated in the DSM-5 diagnostic parameters. These include the onset or duration (lifelong or acquired/episodic), and the context as generalised (global or all situations) or situational (some circumstances) (American Psychiatric Association, 2013).

Table 11.8: Diagnostic criteria for premature (early) ejaculation from the DSM-5 and the ICD-10

DSM-5	ICD-10

A. A persistent or recurrent pattern of ejaculation occurring during partnered sexual activity within approximately one minute following vaginal penetration and before the individual wishes it.
Note: Although the diagnosis of premature (early) ejaculation may be applied to individuals engaged in non-vaginal sexual activities, specific duration criteria must not have been established for these activities.
B. The symptom in Criterion A must have been present for at least six months and must be experienced in almost all or all (approximately 75–100%) occasions of sexual activity (in identified situational contexts or, if generalised, in all contexts).
C. The symptoms in Criterion A cause clinically significant distress in the individual.
D. The sexual dysfunction is not better explained by a non-sexual mental disorder or as a consequence of severe relationship distress or other significant stressors and is not attributable to the effects of a substance/medication or another medical condition.
	▪ The subject is unable to participate in a sexual relationship as he would wish.
	▪ The dysfunction occurs frequently, but may be absent on some occasions.
	▪ The dysfunction has been present for at least six months.
	▪ The dysfunction is not entirely attributable to any of the other mental and behavioural disorders in ICD-10, physical disorders (such as endocrine disorder) or drug treatment.
	▪ Inability to delay ejaculation sufficiently to enjoy the sexual interaction manifests as either:
	  ▸ Occurrence of ejaculation before or very soon after entry (before or within 15 seconds of entry) or
	  ▸ Ejaculation in absence of sufficient erection to make entry possible.
	Note: Not due to prolonged abstinence of sexual activity.

Source: Reprinted with permission from the *Diagnostic and Statistical Manual of Mental Disorders*, fifth edition (DSM-5), American Psychiatric Association (APA), 2013, p. 443, and the *International Statistical Classification of Diseases and Related Health Problems*, tenth revision (ICD-10), World Health Organization (WHO), Geneva, 2007.

Delayed ejaculation

Men with this disorder are either unable to reach ejaculation or, in cases where they do, this is often delayed (American Psychiatric Association, 2013). There is a problem with the concept of delayed ejaculation as there is no real norm for what a normal time period before reaching ejaculation is or should be (American Psychiatric Association, 2013). Rather than defining this disorder in terms of time, the essential feature is rather to describe it in terms of a man's report that he has the inability to ejaculate, despite adequate stimulation and the desire to ejaculate (American Psychiatric Association, 2013).

Table 11.9: Diagnostic criteria for delayed ejaculation from the DSM-5

DSM-5
A. Either of the following symptoms must be experienced in almost all or all (approximately 75–100%) occasions of partnered sexual activity (in identified situational contexts or, if generalised, in all contexts), and without the individual desiring delay: (1) Marked delay in ejaculation. (2) Marked infrequency or absence of ejaculation. B. The symptoms in Criterion A must have persisted for a minimum duration of approximately six months. C. The symptoms in Criterion A cause clinically significant distress in the individual. D. The sexual dysfunction is not better explained by a non-sexual mental disorder or as a consequence of severe relationship distress or other significant stressors and is not attributable to the effects of a substance/medication or another medical condition.

Source: Reprinted with permission from the *Diagnostic and Statistical Manual of Mental Disorders*, fifth edition (DSM-5), American Psychiatric Association (APA), 2013, p. 424.

Sexual pain disorders

In previous editions of the DSM, there were two disorders that could be considered to be sexual pain disorders: dyspareunia and vaginismus. Dyspareunia was a disorder that could be made in either men or women, while vaginismus was gender specific. The DSM-5 does not distinguish between these disorders, and they are now considered to be one disorder – genito-pelvic pain/penetration disorder – and this disorder is limited to women only, making it the second of two gender-specific disorders (American Psychiatric Association, 2013). The ICD-10, however, does distinguish between these disorders, retaining criteria for dyspareunia and vaginismus.

Genito-pelvic pain/penetration disorder

This disorder is characterised by genital pain during sexual intercourse. The essential feature of this is the persistent or recurrent experience of genital pain before, during, or after engaging in sex (American Psychiatric Association, 2013). In women, this is experienced as vaginal pain that is either shallow or deep. People with this disorder do experience sexual desire and arousal, but the severe pain that is associated with this will in all likelihood disrupt their sexual behaviour.

Table 11.10: Diagnostic criteria for genito-pelvic pain/penetration disorder from the DSM-5 and dyspareunia from the ICD-10

DSM-5	ICD-10 (dyspareunia)

A. Persistent or recurrent difficulties with one (or more) of the following:
(1) Vaginal penetration during intercourse.
(2) Marked vulvovaginal or pelvic pain during vaginal intercourse or penetration attempts.
(3) Marked fear or anxiety about vulvovaginal or pelvic pain in anticipation of, during, or as a result of vaginal penetration.
(4) Marked tensing or tightening of the pelvic floor muscles during attempted vaginal penetration.
B. The symptom in Criterion A have persisted for a minimum duration of approximately six months.
C. The symptoms in Criterion A cause clinically significant distress in the individual.
D. The sexual dysfunction is not better explained by a non-sexual mental disorder or as a consequence of severe relationship distress (e.g. partner violence) or other significant stressors and is not attributable to the effects of a substance/medication or another medical condition.
	■ The subject is unable to participate in a sexual relationship as he or she would wish.
	■ The dysfunction occurs frequently, but may be absent on some occasions.
	■ The dysfunction has been present for at least six months.
	■ The dysfunction is not entirely attributable to any of the other mental and behavioural disorders in ICD-10, physical disorders (such as endocrine disorder) or drug treatment.
	■ In addition, for women:
	  ▸ Pain during sexual intercourse, experienced at the entry of the vagina, throughout or only when deep thrusting of the penis occurs.
	  ▸ Not attributable to vaginismus or failure of lubrication; dyspareunia due to organic pathology should be classified according to the underlying disorder.
	■ In addition, for men:
	  ▸ Pain or discomfort during sexual response. Careful recording should be established of the timing of the pain and the exact localisation.
	  ▸ Absence of local physical factors. If found, the dysfunction should be classified elsewhere.

Source: Reprinted with permission from the *Diagnostic and Statistical Manual of Mental Disorders*, fifth edition (DSM-5), American Psychiatric Association (APA), 2013, p. 437, and the *International Statistical Classification of Diseases and Related Health Problems*, tenth revision (ICD-10), World Health Organization (WHO), Geneva, 2007.

Another feature of the disorder is the persistent or recurrent involuntary contraction of the muscles surrounding the opening of the vagina, thus preventing intercourse. This action is a spasm of muscles that closes the vagina and can occur as a result of attempted penetration with a penis, finger, tampon, or even a speculum (as in a medical examination). In the normal human sexual response cycle, a woman typically experiences a relaxing of the vaginal muscles with sexual arousal. A woman with this disorder, however, would experience a closing of these muscles that is involuntary, or not under her control. It can be diagnosed with reports of involuntary muscle spasms in the outer third of the vagina when intercourse or other types of vaginal penetration are attempted (McConaghy, 2005). The problem affects 1% to 6% of women (Hersen, Turner, & Beidel, 2007).

Table 11.11: Diagnostic criteria for vaginismus from the ICD-10

ICD-10
■ The subject is unable to participate in a sexual relationship as she would wish.
■ The dysfunction occurs frequently, but may be absent on some occasions.
■ The dysfunction has been present for at least six months.
■ The dysfunction is not entirely attributable to any of the other mental and behavioural disorders in ICD-10, physical disorders (such as endocrine disorder) or drug treatment.
■ Spasm of the perivaginal muscles is sufficient to prevent penile entry or make it uncomfortable.
■ The dysfunction appears as one of the following: ▸ Normal response has never been experienced. ▸ Vaginismus has developed after a period of relatively normal response.

Source: Reprinted with permission from the *International Statistical Classification of Diseases and Related Health Problems*, tenth revision (ICD-10), World Health Organization (WHO), Geneva, 2007.

EXAMPLE CASE

Female sexual dysfunction in female genital mutilation (FGM)
The impact of female genital mutilation on the lives of women and girls is enormous, as it often affects both their psychology and physical being. Among the complications that are often under-reported and not always acknowledged is female sexual dysfunction. This presents with a complex of symptoms including lack of libido, arousability, and orgasm. This often occurs in tandem with chronic urogenital pain and anatomical disruption due to perineal scarring.

To treat female sexual dysfunction in women with FGM, each woman needs specifically directed holistic care, geared to her individual case. This may include psychological support, physiotherapy and, on occasion, reconstructive surgery. In many cases the situation is complicated by symptoms of chronic pelvic pain, which can make treatment increasingly difficult, as this issue needs a defined multidisciplinary approach for its effective management in its own right.

Source: Elneil, 2016.

GENDER DYSPHORIA/GENDER INCONGRUENCE

Previous editions of the DSM referred to gender identity disorder that was under 'sexual and gender identity disorders', but DSM-5 refers to gender dysphoria as a new diagnostic class; this is reflective of a change in how the defining features of the disorder are conceptualised (American Psychiatric Association, 2013). As such, the phenomenon of 'gender incongruence' is emphasised, rather than the cross-gender identification. DSM-5 also recognises that gender dysphoria is a unique condition, given that, while mental health professionals make the diagnosis, the treatment is mostly endocrinological and surgical (American Psychiatric Association, 2013).

The essential feature of the condition is a psychological dissatisfaction with one's gender assigned at birth. 'Gender dysphoria refers to the distress that may accompany the incongruence between one's experienced or expressed gender and one's assigned gender. Although not all individuals will experience distress as a result of such incongruence, many are distressed if the desired physical interventions by means of hormones and/or surgery are not available' (American Psychiatric Association, 2013, p. 451).

People with gender dysphoria may dress in the clothes of the opposite gender simply in order to wear the clothes of the gender to which they feel they truly belong. This differs from the cross-dressing of transvestites. A transvestite man will wear women's clothing because this advances his sexual arousal and satisfaction, but someone assigned male at birth who experiences gender dysphoria (also known as a transwoman) would dress as a woman, with no sexual arousal aims but because they feel that they are (or should be) 'a she', a woman.

Figure 11.7: Laverne Cox, an American transgender celebrity

'Transgender' is:

> *A term for people who have a gender identity, and often a gender expression that is different to the sex they were assigned at birth by default on account of their primary sexual characteristics. It is also used to refer to people who challenge society's view of gender as fixed, unmoving, dichotomous and inextricably linked to one's biological sex. Gender is more accurately viewed as a spectrum, rather than as a polarised, dichotomous construct. (PsySSA, 2017, p. 63)*

Importantly, the term 'transgender' is used in reference to, among others, transsexuals, genderqueers, people who are androgynous, and those who defy what society tells them is appropriate for their gender. It is similarly important to distinguish a transgender identity from sexual orientation and that transgender people could be heterosexual, bisexual, same-sex attracted or asexual (PsySSA, 2017).

A fundamental component of most people's self-concept is their gender identity, or their sense of themselves as either male or female. This differs from their gender role, which instead refers to how they believe they should behave in society as either a male or female. Gender identity should also, importantly, be clearly distinguished from a person's sexual orientation, which is the emotional, romantic, and/or sexual attraction for either a male or female sexual partner. Also, someone assigned male at birth with gender dysphoria differs from the same-sex sexual arousal patterns of a gay male with so-called effeminate behaviour. People with gender dysphoria also differ from intersex individuals (previously known as hermaphrodites).

Depending on the biological sex of the individual in question, gender dysphoria results in an attraction to partners of either the same or opposite sex. For example, it is possible for someone assigned male at birth to experience gender dysphoria (in this instance, viewing themself as a transwoman), and feel convincingly that she is in the 'wrong body' as her sense of gender identity is strongly female, while still conforming to the historical masculine gender roles of pursuing a competitive career and playing aggressive sports, and also having a man as her romantic and sexual partner. (Note: the appropriate pronouns to employ in addressing a transgender person would be determined by themselves.)

The DSM-5 acknowledges the developmental stages of a person with gender dysphoria, and how this manifests differently in children and adolescents/adults, by describing different criteria for these age groups (see Table 11.12).

Table 11.12: Diagnostic criteria for gender dysphoria (DSM-5) and gender identity disorder (ICD-10)

DSM-5 (gender dysphoria in children)	DSM-5 (gender dysphoria in adolescents)	ICD-10 (gender identity disorder)
A. A marked incongruence between one's experienced/expressed gender and assigned gender, of at least six months' duration, as manifested by at least six of the following (one of which must be Criterion A): (1) A strong desire to be of the other gender or an insistence that one is the other gender (or some alternative gender different to one's assigned gender).	A. A marked incongruence between one's experienced/expressed gender and assigned gender, of at least six months' duration, as manifested by at least two of the following: (1) A marked incongruence between one's experienced/expressed gender and primary and/or secondary sex characteristics (or in young adolescents, the anticipated secondary sex characteristics).	■ Desire to live and be accepted as a member of the opposite sex, mostly accompanied by the wish to transform one's body to resemble, as closely as possible, that of the preferred sex through surgery and hormonal treatment. ■ Presence of the transsexual identity for a minimum of two years persistently.

DSM-5 (gender dysphoria in children)	DSM-5 (gender dysphoria in adolescents)	ICD-10 (gender identity disorder)
(2) In boys (assigned gender), a strong preference for cross-dressing or simulating female attire; or in girls (assigned gender), a strong preference for wearing only typical masculine clothing and a strong resistance to the wearing of typical feminine clothing. (3) A strong preference for cross-gender roles in make-believe play or fantasy play. (4) A strong preference for the toys, games, or activities stereotypically used or engaged in by the other gender. (5) A strong preference for playmates of the other gender. (6) In boys (assigned gender), a strong rejection of typically masculine toys, games, and activities and a strong avoidance of rough-and-tumble play; or in girls (assigned gender), a strong rejection of typically feminine toys, games and activities. (7) A strong dislike of one's sexual anatomy. (8) A strong desire for the primary and/or secondary sex characteristics that match one's experienced gender. B. The condition is associated with clinically significant distress or impairment in social, school, or other important areas of functioning.	(2) A strong desire to be rid of one's primary and/or secondary sex characteristics because of marked incongruence with one's experienced/expressed gender (or, in young adolescents, a desire to prevent the development of the anticipated secondary sex characteristics). (3) A strong desire for the primary and/or secondary sex characteristics of the other gender. (4) A strong desire to be of the other gender (or some alternative gender different to one's assigned gender). (5) A strong desire to be treated as the other gender (or some alternative gender different to one's assigned gender). (6) A strong conviction that one has the typical feelings and reaction of the other gender (or some alternative gender different to one's assigned gender). B. The condition is associated with clinically significant distress or impairment in social, occupational, or other important areas of functioning.	■ Not a symptom of another mental disorder, such as schizophrenia, or associated with chromosome abnormality.

Source: Reprinted with permission from the *Diagnostic and Statistical Manual of Mental Disorders*, fifth edition (DSM-5), American Psychiatric Association (APA), 2013, p. 452, and the *International Statistical Classification of Diseases and Related Health Problems*, tenth revision (ICD-10), World Health Organization (WHO), Geneva, 2007.

Issues with gender identity

The evolution of the social and legal position on same-sex sexual orientation from that of 'sick' to just another aspect of human diversity is important to emphasise here, as it seems that a similar process is occurring with gender dysphoria, as well as with transgender identities more broadly. However, gender dysphoria, previously referred to as gender identity disorder and/ or as 'transsexuality', is still firmly considered psychopathology and included as a diagnostic category in the DSM-5 (American Psychiatric Association, 2013). Similarly, the ICD-10 lists 'transsexualism' and gender identity disorder as sexual deviations and disorders of adult personality and behaviour (Ministerial Advisory Committee on Gay and Lesbian Health, 2002).

However, many progressive psychotherapists who affirm lesbian, gay, bisexual, transgender, and intersexual (LGBTI) individuals do not consider transgender identification, per se, to be a mental illness (see the discussion of the abbreviation LGBTIQA+ in the section on cross-cultural and African perspectives). Recent criticisms against labelling gender dysphoria as mental illness have proposed that gender identity perception is a right. Critics argue that psychology and other health fields, for that matter, do not help people by pathologising what may be viewed as a normal variant of human sexuality and gender roles.

Most people (including transgender people) feel that having a recognised gender identity accords with their sense of self. However, Dreger (2006) challenges the notion that everyone has a true, core, single, unchanging gender identity. Dreger suggests that, just as physical sexual anatomies do not come in only two types that never change, neither do gender identities. A libertarian view of legal gender or sex identity advocates that, instead of the state adjudicating on a person's identity in terms of sex and gender, people ought to have their own say about their genders, regardless of their anatomy (Dreger, 2006).

Accordingly, LGBTIQA+-affirmative therapists believe that transgender identity is not a mental illness and that there is no need for psychotherapeutic treatment for transgender people per se (Nel, 2007; PsySSA, 2017; Victor, Nel, Lynch, & Mbatha, 2014). It should also be noted that, in the case of South Africa, the law allows a person to change, under certain conditions, their sex as recorded in the population registry – see the Alteration of Sex Description and Sex Status Act (No. 49 of 2003) (Republic of South Africa, 2003).

While the World Health Organization's ICD-10 also refers to gender identity disorder (as was the case with the DSM-IV-R), the ICD-11 uses 'gender incongruence' to refer to people whose gender identity is different from the gender they were assigned at birth. Importantly, gender incongruence has been moved out of the mental disorders chapter of the ICD and into the sexual health chapter, effective from 2022.

The World Health Organization is of the view that the change is expected to improve social acceptance among transgender people, while still making important health resources available (World Health Organization, 2018c). This is so because the ICD is used by countries to define eligibility and access to healthcare, in the formulation of relevant laws and policies, and also by health professionals as a basis for conceptualising health conditions, treatments, and outcomes (Chou et al., 2015).

Transitioning from one gender to another is often a complex and phased process. This involves adopting the appearance of the desired gender (that is, in clothing and grooming, gender-affirming treatment with cross-sex hormones, and surgical alteration of secondary sex characteristics). For instance, the hormone Depo-Testosterone is prescribed for transmen, transmasculine, and gender-diverse people who are assigned female at birth and later diagnosed with gender dysphoria. For many transmasculine people, using testosterone enables them to live their authentic self (McLachlan, 2019), as testosterone enables a transman/transmasculine person to experience masculinisation and this often decreases, alleviates, and, at times, even resolves the gender dysphoria.

Many individuals experiencing gender dysphoria, who have health insurance that would fund it or who can afford it themselves, may seek gender-affirming surgery (previously known as sex-reassignment surgery or 'sex-change operations'). This involves the procedure and treatments that aim to alter the genitals surgically (someone assigned female at birth with gender dysphoria may request that the uterus and ovaries be removed), with other sex-typing physical characteristics (breasts and facial hair) being changed with the therapeutic use of medicines and hormones.

Transgender people have, more often than not, been misunderstood and misdiagnosed by their caregivers, who have frequently allowed personal prejudice to affect their judgements adversely (World Professional Association for Transgender Health [WPATH], 2011). In recognition of the scarcity of so-called qualified gender specialists, standards of care for gender dysphoria were established as early as 1979, by WPATH (formerly known as the Harry Benjamin International Gender Dysphoria Association),with the assistance of professionals in both the medical and psychological sciences.

The standards of care, which are currently in their seventh version (WPATH, 2011), specify the minimum requirements for proper care and protection of both the person with gender dysphoria and the professionals who provide treatment. The standards of care articulate WPATH's professional consensus regarding the psychiatric, psychological, medical, and surgical management of gender dysphoria. Included are requirements for determining a patient's suitability for hormone therapy and gender-affirming surgery. Note, the overall goal of treatment, whether psychotherapeutic, endocrine, or surgical therapy, for people with gender dysphoria is lasting personal comfort with the gendered self, in order to maximise overall psychological well-being and self-fulfilment (WPATH, 2011).

Importantly, in this seventh version of the standards of care, gender dysphoria is considered gender diversity, which is not pathological. The idea of mental healthcare is minimised, and reparative therapies are considered unethical. The standards of care promote a client-centred and health-focused (rather than clinician-centred) approach. Access to healthcare for medical treatment ought not to be reliant on a diagnosis, unless gender-affirming surgery is required (WPATH, 2011).

In accordance with the above, PsySSA released a position statement on sexual and gender diversity in 2013 (Victor et al., 2014) that preceded the PsySSA affirmative practice guidelines (PsySSA, 2017). Both these documents encourage usage of relevant international practice guidelines, such as the standards of care, in the absence of South African-specific guidelines. They also caution against interventions aimed at changing a person's sexual orientation or gender expression, such as 'reparative' or conversion therapy, and oppose the withholding of best practice gender-affirming surgery and treatment, and best practice transgender healthcare.

Lastly, while separate from gender dysphoria and transgender identification, intersex people are marginalised in the extreme and may become almost totally invisible in society, being regarded mostly as abnormal (Council of Europe, 2015; Samelius & Wägberg, 2005). The standard protocol on the treatment of intersex children has been gender-affirming surgery and altering the genitals of the person in order to assign them to one of the two recognised biological sexes: male and female.

Internationally, a small but growing intersex movement is lobbying against this practice, which it considers to be discriminatory, disrespectful, and at risk of causing both physical and psychological harm (Council of Europe, 2015; Samelius & Wägberg, 2005). Increasingly, advocacy and lobbying efforts aim to ensure such choices are left to intersex individuals themselves, to be made at a time when they can do so in an informed manner. In this regard, see what intersex Belgian model Hanne Gaby Odiele has to say about wanting to break the taboo (http://www.dailymail.co.uk/news/article-4147844/Belgian-model-Hanne-Gaby-Odiele-reveals-s-intersex.html?ito=email_share_article-bottom). The Australian Psychological Society has similarly made a useful information sheet available on children born with intersex variations (see https://www.psychology.org.au/getmedia/2d12b9c7-4a99-4c0b-9ee2-7079c6be3ba8/Children_born_with_intersex_variations.pdf).

PARAPHILIC DISORDERS

Some people find numerous creative ways of enhancing their sexual satisfaction or fulfilling their sexual needs and desires. Most of the time, this can be done within the social limitations on sexual behaviour. Judgements about what sexual behaviours are acceptable have differed across historical periods and cultures and continue to be subjective and socioculturally constructed. Socially unacceptable sexual behaviours are those that are prohibited by modern cultural norms, and sometimes even by laws, in which case they become criminal.

'Paraphilia' is the term used to describe sexual interests in which sexual arousal, behaviours, and satisfaction occur in the context of unusual or inappropriate objects, including either non-human objects (or body parts, activities, or situations), and/or non-consenting adults or children (Love, 1995) (see Table 11.13 for an overview of the paraphilias). Paraphilias may include suffering or humiliation of self, partner, or children.

The meaning of paraphilia, coined by Stekel in 1923, is 'love' for, or an attraction to, something beyond the usual (para: besides, going beside or beyond, amiss; philia: love or attachment to). Paraphilias are also, amongst other common terms, referred to as 'deviances', 'perversions', or 'sexual aberrations' (Love, 1995). It ought to be noted that the ICD-10 refers to disorders of sexual preference, instead of referring to a paraphilia (WHO, 2007).

Reflective of significant global social and legal changes, and also informed by human rights frameworks, the ICD-11 distinguishes between conditions relevant to public health and clinical psychopathology and those that are considered private behaviour and are thus not relevant to clinicians (Reed et al., 2016); the same applies to paraphilias.

The paraphilias can be divided into those that involve consenting others (such as sadomasochism) or non-consenting others (such as in exhibitionism). They can also be divided into those that involve contact with others (such as frotteurism) or no contact with others (such as in some fetishes). These distinctions are important in making sense of which paraphilias are deemed a disorder and those that are not. Arousal patterns related to solitary behaviours or consenting adults are only included under paraphilic disorders in the ICD-11 should significant risk of injury or death or marked distress be present. Importantly, this distress must extend beyond mere rejection or feared rejection by others (World Health Organization, 2018c).

The DSM-5 uses the term 'paraphilic disorders' to designate those atypical sexual behaviours that are considered to be disorders. When people with a paraphilic disorder also violate laws, they would additionally be considered sex offenders or criminals. People with paraphilic disorder rarely present voluntarily (American Psychiatric Association, 2013), until their actions attract the attention of law-enforcement agencies.

Figure 11.8: Fetish gear

Although the paraphilias are often associated with sexual offending by the general public, this is not always the case. Those convicted of sexual offences represent the more severe end of the spectrum of the atypical sexual behaviours. Fetishism and transvestic fetishism are mostly considered benign, whereas sadism and masochism (S&M), although often practised between consenting adults, are less benign as they may result in injury. Frotteurism, voyeurism, and exhibitionism are not considered benign as they involve non-consenting others who may feel that they became 'victims'. Lastly, paedophilic disorder is considered the most severe of the paraphilias and is clearly a punishable offence.

Several of the more recently written psychopathology textbooks have begun to acknowledge that the inclusion of atypical sexual behaviour in the DSM is a contentious issue. As argued earlier in this chapter, the distinction between 'normal' and 'abnormal' sexual behaviour is a difficult one. Norms regarding sexual practices change considerably over time, because of the influence of changing cultural and religious beliefs and values (see the example of same-sex sexuality above). Norms regarding sexual practices also vary across and within cultures. For example, in Western cultures, women's breasts are eroticised, and revealing them is considered sexually arousing, while in many other cultures, breasts are viewed purely as a means to feed babies.

Amongst many other norms, societal expectations for sexuality have changed with regard to masturbation and the virtuousness of suppressing sexual arousal. For example, in stark contrast to earlier times and their mores and values, the absence of sexual desire is today considered a clinical disorder. Also, we know the extent to which premarital heterosexual sexual behaviour has in recent years become culturally acceptable in many parts of the world.

In response to the above-mentioned criticisms, the DSM-5 made two broad changes that affect several of the paraphilia diagnoses, in addition to various amendments to specific diagnoses. The first broad change follows from consensus that paraphilias are not per se psychiatric disorders. The DSM-5 makes a distinction between 'paraphilias' and 'paraphilic disorders', and notes that there are a number of paraphilias that are not listed under paraphilic disorders (American Psychiatric Association, 2013). The implication is that a paraphilia, in and of itself, would not automatically justify or require psychiatric intervention. A paraphilic disorder, on the other hand, is a paraphilia that causes distress or impairment to the individual or harm to others.

A paraphilia is recognisable according to the nature of the associated urges, fantasies, or behaviours, but a paraphilic disorder is diagnosed on the basis of distress and impairment. In this conception, having a paraphilia would be a necessary but not sufficient condition for having a paraphilic disorder (American Psychiatric Association, 2012b). According to the Paraphilias Subworkgroup, the above-mentioned approach leaves intact the distinction between normative and non-normative sexual behaviour, which could be important for researchers, but resists automatically labelling non-normative sexual behaviour as psychopathological (American Psychiatric Association, 2012b).

The second broad change applies to paraphilias that involve non-consenting persons, such as voyeuristic disorder, exhibitionistic disorder, and sexual sadism disorder. In these instances, especially for uncooperative patients, it is suggested there be a minimum number of separate victims for diagnosing the paraphilia. Research indicates that a substantial proportion – perhaps a majority – of patients referred for assessment of paraphilias are referred after committing a criminal sexual offence. Such patients are typically neither truthful nor forthcoming about their sexual urges and fantasies. The criteria have therefore been modified to lessen the dependence of diagnosis on patients' self-reports regarding urges and fantasies (American Psychiatric Association, 2012b).

In an attempt to obtain similar rates of false positive and false negative diagnoses for all the paraphilias, the suggested minimum number of separate victims varies for diagnosis of the different paraphilias in the DSM-5. For example, three different victims are required for a diagnosis of voyeuristic disorder, but only two different victims for a sexual sadism disorder diagnosis. This is informed by the rationale that paraphilias differ in the extent to which they resemble behaviours in the typical adult's sexual repertoire (American Psychiatric Association, 2012b).

In the DSM-5, to be deemed a disorder, the associated recurrent, intense sexual urges, fantasies, or behaviours must bring about clinically significant distress or impairment in personal, social, academic, or occupational functioning, or in other important domains of an individual's life. To qualify for such a diagnosis, a person would also need to have acted on the urges and/or fantasies, or to have experienced marked distress or interpersonal difficulties as a result of them (American Psychiatric Association, 2013).

Table 11.13: Summary of paraphilias

TYPE	DESCRIPTION
Fetishism	The use of inanimate objects as the preferred or exclusive source of sexual arousal. Fetishism may also refer to being sexually attracted to inanimate objects (or just a single body part) or a source of specific tactile stimulation (Love, 1995). People with a fetish most often focus their sexual activities on non-human objects and thus do not impose their desires on other people and may go unnoticed. Fetish objects include clothing (in particular, underwear), footwear, certain materials or fabrics (including leather, plastics, diapers, and gloves). Fetish behaviours commonly include fondling, smelling, and licking the object(s), but where the individual needs to acquire the object secretly from someone else (such as women's worn panties), they may also include having to steal the object(s).
Transvestic fetishism	In transvestic fetishism, sexual arousal in heterosexual men is associated with the act of cross-dressing in women's clothes (American Psychiatric Association, 2013). This cross-dressing, ranging from using only one item of women's clothing to completely dressing as a woman with make-up and a wig, can go on to become the man's primary means of becoming sexually aroused. This condition also indicates a sexual attraction to the clothing of the opposite sex, but once orgasm occurs, sexual arousal typically declines and the man is strongly motivated to remove the items of women's clothing.
Sexual sadism	Sexual sadism involves the recurrent urge or behaviour to inflict (real, not simulated) pain or humiliation on a sexual partner for sexual arousal (American Psychiatric Association, 2013). The person typically achieves their sexual satisfaction from inflicting pain and/or humiliation on a sexual partner. Sexual sadism often includes certain rituals (such as binding and handcuffing the partner) and clearly recognisable props (such as leather zip masks and whips) to be used in such encounters. More males than females engage in sadist and masochist sex, and females not engaged in commercial sex work may become involved only in response to a male's wishes or as non-consenting victims.
Sexual masochism	Sexual masochism involves the recurrent urge or behaviour of wanting to be made to suffer (real, not simulated) pain or humiliation for sexual arousal (American Psychiatric Association, 2013). It can be considered, to a great extent, to be the reverse of sexual sadism. In sexual masochism, an individual will also gain sexual gratification by having a sexual partner cause them to suffer pain and or humiliation.

TYPE	DESCRIPTION
Voyeurism	Voyeurism refers to the act of watching an unsuspecting individual undressing, naked, engaging in sex, or bathing, in order to become sexually aroused. The watching is done in secret, most often by a man, who may masturbate while watching the scene or shortly thereafter. The person being watched, most often a woman, must be unaware of the peeping and would be very distressed were she to find out; in other words, the woman is not a cooperative sexual partner, nor is the act consensual. While many people may engage in such behaviours at some point or another in their lives, they become a problem for individuals when the voyeurism develops into their primary sexual outlet or when these individuals clash with law-enforcement agencies as a result (Love, 1995).
Exhibitionism	The recurrent urge or behaviour to gain sexual arousal from shocking others (most often unsuspecting strangers) by exposing one's genitals (American Psychiatric Association, 2013). It can be considered, to a great extent, to be the reverse of voyeurism. There are many different degrees or levels of exhibitionism as well as reasons or benefits believed to be obtained from exposing. The observers are typically strangers who are quite involuntarily made witness to the exhibitionist's display. In almost all cases, a man will exhibit himself to a surprised woman. The exhibitionist's sexual arousal typically comes from observing the victim's response in terms of surprise, fear, or disgust or even from the fantasised notion that the woman was aroused by his actions. The viewer's reactions must provide sufficient perceived ego boost, novelty, embarrassment, defilement, or other discomfort to produce the high level of stimulus required for the exhibitionist's orgasm (Love, 1995).
Frotteurism	Frotteurism is the recurrent urge to or behaviour of touching or rubbing against a non-consenting person (American Psychiatric Association, 2013). This leads to sexual arousal and will also result in sexual gratification through the pressing up against a stranger or even fondling parts of his or her body. The frotteur's behaviours are often opportunistic in nature, with the setting playing an important role. When many people are packed together in a crowded place, such as an underground subway, a train, elevator, or a queue, the frotteur's bumping or rubbing against another person may not be identified as sexual. Quite often the target or victim will not realise that the contact has anything to do with sexual behaviours (Love, 1995).

TYPE	DESCRIPTION
Paedophilic disorder	Paedophilic disorder, often erroneously understood to be synonymous with child molestation, involves sexual attraction to prepubescent or peri-pubescent children, most often girls (Love, 1995). People with paedophilic disorder (who are typically adults, but are required to be at least 16 years of age in order to make the diagnosis) are sexually attracted to children (required to be less than 13 years of age, and at least 5 years younger than the perpetrator). Most troubling about this disorder is that it is the most common of the paraphilias and the non-consenting others are young people. The sexual acts that paedophiles most often engage in with children are those of exposing or touching the child's genitals, or oral and even penetrative sex.
Paraphilias not otherwise specified	Other paraphilias not otherwise specified include: ■ telephone scatalogia (obscene phone calls) ■ necrophilia (sexual attraction to corpses) ■ partialism (exclusive focus on one part of the body) ■ zoophilia (sex with animals) ■ coprophilia (sexual attraction to faeces) ■ urophilia (sexual attraction to urine).

Source: Table compiled by author Nel.

CROSS-CULTURAL AND AFRICAN PERSPECTIVES

In this section, an overview of the needs and rights of the sexually and gender diverse in South Africa, and in particular, lesbian, gay, bisexual, transgender, intersex, queer (LGBTIQA+) people and communities, provides a lens through which to comment on this specific context, and on the sexuality and gender 'landscape'. Note, the + indicates, as per current practice, an openness to additional categorisation and self-claimed descriptors of sexually and gender-diverse persons and communities (PsySSA, 2017).

Sexuality and gender touch upon some of the most intimate and personal aspects of human existence. Sexuality is a core value and is central to self, identity, culture, and nation (Pigg & Adams, 2005). Issues of sexuality and gender, moreover, carry much cultural weight and are, therefore, vulnerable to exploitation for political means (Academy of Science of South Africa, 2015). Rape as an act of war is but one example of such exploitation. Most societies attempt to control the sexual behaviour of their members in some way or other (Goodwach, 2005). Sexuality is thus recognised as a powerful domain, in terms of both general social prejudice and stigmatisation, and, more specifically, the pathologising of minority groups or 'deviant' categories of people (Hook, 2002).

The values, beliefs, and stereotypes of a psychotherapist (or researcher on sexual and gender functioning) are central in working with sexuality and sexual minorities. These values will directly influence the way in which problems are defined, formulated, and evaluated, as well as the types of intervention that may be offered. While some experts understand sexuality as universal, there are others who view sexuality as context specific in terms of meaning, practice, and outcome (Pigg & Adams, 2005).

However, sex and sexuality are often universalised in the name of health and well-being. Patriarchal Westernised ways of defining sexual 'norms', sexual orientation, and gender identity make the assumption that biological sex (which is essentially fixed) forms the basis for people's identities and determines their sexual expression (Pigg & Adams, 2005). The medical model is interested in objective knowledge that is unaffected by the healthcare recipient's values and meanings. Similarly, the contextual aspects of sex, race, and culture also do not feature significantly in the medical model. Thus, within the medical model, the assumption is that an expert can 'diagnose' objectively and apply a clearly linked solution (Hook, 2002).

Yet human sexuality is powerfully influenced by the specific sociocultural and temporal context within which it is found. Apartheid South Africa, for instance, was notorious for having been a particularly repressive society (Nel, 2005b; Seedat, Duncan, & Lazarus, 2001). Until the early 1990s, strong emphasis was placed on the legal restriction of sexuality, with several laws regulating sexual behaviour. For instance, sex 'across the colour line' was prohibited, sex between men was criminalised until as recently as 1996, and there were laws against all forms of pornography (Nel, 2005b). Sex work is still illegal in South Africa, but in recent years there have been several proposals to legalise it.

The freedom of political association, of speech, and of sexual expression that now exists in South Africa is new. Sexuality-related issues often elicit strong (negative) emotional responses, including feelings of guilt and shame, and are considered 'private' and 'personal', and 'not to be discussed'. The sexual behaviours of others still tend to be viewed in strict and rigid terms of 'rightness' or 'wrongness', and those behaviours departing from the norm are severely criticised. For these reasons, sexuality has more often than not been veiled in secrecy. However, following decades of Calvinist rule, the multibillion-rand South African sex industry (including upmarket entertainment venues, strip clubs, several chains of sex shops, house parties, and sex work) that has emerged post-1994 suggests that a sexual revolution has occurred.

Nonetheless, hetero- and cisnormative assumptions remain a core characteristic of contemporary South African culture. These assumptions and attitudes are pervasive in the media, religious teachings and practices, legal discourses, education, and healthcare. Neglect or deliberate exclusion of LGBTIQA+ people in gender analyses and policy discussions reflect the pervasiveness of hetero- and cisnormative assumptions (PsySSA, 2017; Samelius & Wägberg, 2005). The silencing of same-sex sexuality that occurs in this manner implies a taboo and undesirability, and perpetuates prejudice (Eliason, 1996).

Sexually and gender-diverse persons and communities in South Africa also have to contend with homo- and transphobia (PsySSA, 2017). Being lesbian or gay in South Africa has often been considered a 'sickness', a 'sin', 'criminal', or un-African. Today, there are restrictions against the public expression of these opinions. However, religious condemnation, harassment in the workplace and other places, public statements of homoprejudice, and violence towards LGBTIQA+ people are still rife. Moreover, internalised oppression is prevalent within many LGBTIQA+ people (Nel, 2005a).

In an overview of LGBTIQA+ identities in South Africa, Nel (2007) emphasises significant differences along the designated 'racial' categories of black, 'coloured', Asian, and white. As a legacy of the South African history of apartheid and patriarchy, the most visible and vocal subsection of the LGBTIQA+ community was, until recently, white and predominantly male, many of whom are well positioned in the workplace and are affluent in comparison to other sectors of society (Nel, 2007). This group has been the most researched and is often considered the least vulnerable. However, this group is not a true reflection of the community as a whole. The vast majority of LGBTIQA+ individuals in South Africa are black, unemployed, and poor, and have low literacy levels (Reid & Dirsuweit, 2002).

Intersectional understanding is vital (PsySSA, 2017). Indeed, owing to the multiplicity of contributions to their minority status in terms of gender, sexual orientation, socio-economic status, and race, under-resourced black lesbians are assumed to be the most vulnerable subsection of the community (Reid & Dirsuweit, 2002). For a variety of reasons, this subsection of the community is also severely under-researched (Nel, 2007). However, recent research indicates disproportionately high levels of risk of victimisation, including 'corrective rape' (Mitchell & Nel, 2017; Polders, 2006; Reid & Dirsuweit, 2002).

Nel (2007) asserts that, as in Europe and America, and for very much the same reasons, use of the abbreviation LGBTIQA+ in reference to sexual minorities is common practice in South African activist circles. Use of this abbreviation is, however, not a true reflection of representation or inclusion in decision-making. In fact, participation of bisexual, transsexual, and intersexual people in the so-called LGBTIQA+ sector or movement is very limited, partly because numbers are relatively small. As a consequence, knowledge of issues related to bisexual, transgender, and especially intersex people is also very limited.

In particular, the paucity of referenced accounts of bisexual life (specifically) in South Africa, and the under-representation of bisexual concerns in lesbian and gay organisations in general, remains a striking feature, even today. Bisexual people's greater invisibility, as well as the preconceived ideas that bisexual people are fence-sitters and fearful of disclosing their sexual orientation, has been suggested as a possible reason (Nicholas, Daniels, & Hurwitz, 2001, in Francoeur, 2001).

Internationally, activism within the LGBTIQA+ community attaches a very high premium to the notions of inclusion and representation. Use of the abbreviation LGBTIQA+ in reference to sexual minorities, not only on the basis of alternative sexual orientation but also gender non-conformity and biological variance, is an indication of this inclusive stance (Nel, 2007). Such a stance is very much informed by the need for corrective measures in response to lifelong experiences of marginalisation, exclusion, and disqualification; it is also politically informed by the need for solidarity among sexually and gender-diverse persons and communities in the face of discrimination at the hands of a vast majority (Nel, 2007).

However, in terms of academic research, the abbreviation LGBTIQA+ minimises theoretical distinctions drawn between biological variance, gender, and sexual orientation. This may not be helpful in either research endeavours or psychosocial intervention programmes (Nel, 2009). Importantly, as the transgender community in South Africa becomes more organised, they are also resisting being clustered together with the LGB community (GenderdynamiX, n.d.).

The formal training of psychologists and psychology professionals is currently not sufficiently inclusive of the issues and needs of the sexually and gender diverse. It is inexcusable for professionals not to counteract consciously notions of same-sex sexuality as psychopathology or criminal behaviour. Representatives at a 2007 South African conference on teaching psychology at universities, held at the University of the Free State, acknowledged that content related to sexual orientation and gender identity is often restricted to sub-fields such as social and abnormal psychology (Nel, 2007).

The 2007 conference referred to above considered the substantial challenges in addressing these issues. These challenges include an inherent conservatism and patriarchy in South Africa, as well as resistance to addressing themes of sexuality and gender within the profession of psychology. In addition, related terminology, such as sexual orientation, gender identification, LGBTIQA+, MSM (men who have sex with men), WSW (women who have sex with women), and homosexuality versus same-sex sexuality, is often confusing, poorly understood, and controversial. Conventional labelling and stereotypes require careful 'unpacking' in terms of meaning, as well as problematisation that acknowledges fluidity instead of linear descriptions (Nel, 2007).

 ACTIVITY

The Sexuality and Gender Division (SGD) is a division of the Psychological Society of South Africa. Read about it online at:

https://www.psyssa.com/wp-content/uploads/2019/04/PsySSA-Sexuality-and-Gender-Division-flyer-2018_fin.pdf

Figure 11.9: Postgraduate student attendees at a South African LGBTIA+-affirmative practice workshop in 2019.

Large parts of Africa have been devastated by the effects of sexual ill-health and suffering brought about by, amongst other things, a lack of sexual rights and education, a culture of sexual coercion, and limited access to professional sexual healthcare. South Africa is no exception in this regard. While South Africa has one of the most progressive constitutions in the world, which includes freedom of sexual orientation in its Bill of Rights, unfortunately, the incidence of rape in South Africa is one of the highest in the world; indeed, South Africa is 'second only to India with regard to the endemic prevalence of HIV/Aids' (Nel, 2007, p. 133).

In South Africa, the field of sexology is poorly developed, and specialised healthcare, including sex therapy, is available only to a select few, almost exclusively at private healthcare facilities in urban centres. Until recently in South Africa, very limited funds and support were made available for research and education on sexuality issues. Only a limited number of medical professionals, psychologists, and other therapists can consider themselves to be well-versed sexologists, and most have no recognised formal qualification in this speciality (Nel, 2007).

The arrival of oral treatments for erectile dysfunction changed the lack of funding for sexuality research in South Africa. Pharmaceutical companies that produce related treatments, such as Viagra, Cialis, and Levitra, have prioritised the provision of credible information and education on sexual health issues from a multidisciplinary perspective. This information is made available to the general public, the media, and healthcare professionals. Yet, a recent systematic review of South African research on sexual dysfunction disorders published in peer-reviewed journals reveals that, despite growing awareness of the importance of sexual health, South African-based scientific research on sexual dysfunction is limited (Campbell & Stein, 2014).

The impact of HIV/Aids and other sexually transmitted infections on sexual dysfunction in the South African context similarly remains an unexplored area, as does the influence of interpersonal violence and intimate partner violence on sexual health and functioning. Domestic violence has been identified as a considerable contributor to the burden of disease in South Africa, and high rates of sexual and domestic violence significantly contribute to the increased vulnerability of South African women to sexually transmitted diseases and HIV infection (Campbell & Stein, 2014).

The endemic prevalence of HIV/Aids, as well as of rape of women and child abuse (De la Rey & Eagle, 1997), may be partly related to the lack of sexuality education and inadequate understandings of gender issues. Until the mid-1990s, very little emphasis was placed on sexual rights, and it is only recently that public campaigns and debates on sexuality issues, and the responsibilities that go with freedom, have been introduced. Despite strong recommendations in this regard, sex education and gender awareness are yet to be comprehensively introduced in schools (Bhana, 2012).

South Africa is a signatory of the international agreement reached at the Fourth World Conference on Women held in Beijing in 1995 and subscribes to the rights contained in the Sexual Health Charter; it is therefore obliged to ensure that the sexual rights of all people are respected, protected, and fulfilled. Furthermore, several sexual and reproductive rights are included as human rights in the South African Constitution. These include the right to expression of sexual orientation without interference from others, equality and equity for all, the right to make choices free from gender-based discrimination, freedom from sexual violence or coercion, and the right to privacy (Nel, 2007).

However, the relentless HIV pandemic and also the very high levels of rape, domestic violence, incest, and teenage pregnancy in South Africa suggest that many people are not able to claim their sexual and reproductive rights; indeed, the country is far from translating these 'paper rights' into practice (Nel, 2007).

BOX 11.3: WHAT ARE SEXUAL RIGHTS?

Sexual rights derive from human rights (see Chapter 5) that are already recognised in national, regional, and international human-rights documents and other consensus documents and in national laws. Sexual rights protect all people's rights to fulfil and express their sexuality and enjoy sexual health, while being mindful of the rights of others. They include the right of all persons, free of coercion, discrimination, and violence, to the following:

1. The right to sexual freedom.
2. The right to sexual autonomy, sexual integrity, and safety of the sexual body.
3. The right to sexual privacy.
4. The right to sexual equity.
5. The right to sexual pleasure.
6. The right to emotional sexual expression.
7. The right to sexually associate freely.
8. The right to make free and responsible reproductive choices.
9. The right to sexual information based upon scientific inquiry.
10. The right to comprehensive sexuality education.
11. The right to Sexual Health care.

Source: Adapted from PAHO & WHO, 2000. Promotion of sexual health: Recommendations for action. Proceedings of a regional consultation convened by Pan-American Health Organization (PAHO) and World Health Organization (WHO), in collaboration with the World Association for Sexology (WAS), Antigua, Guatemala, May 19–22, 2000, pp. 37–38. Available online: http://www.paho.org/english/hcp/hca/promotionsexualhealth.pdf.

HIV and Aids have contributed significantly to the current state of the public healthcare system in South Africa being overstretched, with state hospitals bearing the brunt as they attempt to accommodate people suffering from HIV/Aids-related illnesses (South African National AIDS Council, 2018). However, affirmative healthcare for the sexually and gender diverse, including LGBTIQA+ issues, remains virtually non-existent in the Department of Health (DoH), and also in HIV prevention and care. Similarly, reports on HIV transmission mostly do not adequately differentiate between male-to-male and male-to-female modes of transmission (Samelius & Wägberg, 2005).

As indicated, HIV-prevention and treatment programmes initiated by the government insufficiently recognise the diversity of sexual expressions, behaviours, and needs of LGBTIQA+ groups and generally target only the mainstream population. It is only with the 2005–2011 South African National Strategic Plan (NSP) for HIV/Aids and STIs that the vulnerabilities of LGBTIQA+ people and men who have sex with men (MSM) were recognised. Even more so, the South African National LGBTI HIV Plan, 2017–2022, that was released in 2018, is deemed a milestone in the country's response to HIV, Aids, STIs, and TB for LGBTIQA+ persons (South African National AIDS Council, 2018).

Assumptions of sameness, rather than a respect for differences or diversity, seem to characterise current practices in mainstream healthcare in South Africa (Nel, 2007). Nel (2007) furthermore argues that it goes without saying that everyone has the right to be treated as equal and to healthcare services that adhere to the minimum standards. However, because of the diverse people who inhabit South Africa, it is erroneous and inappropriate to believe that 'one size fits all'. While the LGBTIQA+ sector in South Africa (including organisations such as OUT LGBT Well-Being, Triangle Project, and Anova Health4Men) renders (sexual) health and psychosocial services, recognition is seldom given to LGBTIQA+ clients in government and civil society initiatives.

No specific healthcare service for LGBTIQA+ clients is provided by government. Increasingly, clients demand the services of affirming healthcare workers, and although the number of these providers has significantly increased in recent years, not many qualify as affirmative of sexual and gender diversity when the American Psychological Association guidelines (2011) or home-grown PsySSA guidelines for affirmative practice (PsySSA, 2017) are used as a yardstick. As the uptake of the PsySSA guidelines for affirmative practice increases, one can reasonably expect that change, for the better, is afoot in the delivery of competent services that recognise diverse needs.

BOX 11.4: TRANSGENDER RIGHTS

The first specifically transgender organisation on the continent, Gender DynamiX, located in Cape Town, South Africa, was launched only in 2005. While transgender rights are now protected, and it is possible legally to change gender on birth certificates and in identity documents (Samelius & Wägberg, 2005; Thoreson, 2013), bureaucratic procedures and state official ignorance and prejudice render many of these rights useless.

Figure 11.10: Gender Dynamix is a non-profit organisation that supports the development of the trans and gender diverse movement(s) in southern Africa

AETIOLOGY

Scientific enquiry to establish causality is an enduring feature of conventional psychology. This also applies with regard to conditions related to sexual health and paraphilic disorders. Ongoing debates highlight 'nature' on the one hand and 'nurture' on the other, or suggest a combination of both. Inherent qualities, such as biochemistry and the prenatal influences of hormones and nutrition, feature in the biological theories of causality or predisposition that support nature as cause. The psychological theories suggest that intrapsychic factors, such as early childhood experiences or belief systems, can cause disorders. The social and interpersonal theories of causality would then look to interpersonal relationships and the impact of the social environment on a person.

Sexual and gender identity-related problems are usually associated with other presenting symptoms as well. Thus, most sexual dysfunctions include a combination of both physical and psychological causes. An individual's specific biological predispositions may interact with psychological factors to produce a dysfunction in what we call the diathesis-stress model (see Chapter 2). This model proposes that it takes both a predisposition (or vulnerability) to a disorder and a life stressor (or trigger) to create the disorder.

Vulnerabilities may be found in various biological factors (genes or brain anomalies), psychological factors (maladaptive beliefs, poor skills, or unconscious conflicts), and social factors (maladaptive upbringing, poor relationships, or chronic stress). Stressors may include biological triggers (onset of a disease or exposure to toxins), psychological triggers (violation of trust or perceived loss of control), and social triggers (major loss or traumatic event).

Clinical assessment of sexual behaviour consists of interviewing, medical evaluation, psychological assessment, and physiological assessment. Clinicians must be sensitive to patients' discomfort with discussing sexual issues and a possible lack of understanding of clinical terminology. Physiological assessment may include techniques such as use of a penile plethysmograph (penile strain gauge) for men or a vaginal photoplephysmograph for women. Measurements of arousal may be taken concurrently with exposure to erotic stimuli. Measurement of nocturnal penile tumescence may also be useful in showing whether erection can occur.

Biological factors

A number of biological factors may play a role in either predisposing an individual to conditions related to sexual health, in particular sexual dysfunctions, or triggering these conditions. These include organic factors (such as diabetes; neurological, vascular, thyroid, pituitary, renal or liver disease; depression; and fatigue), medications (such as antihypertensive and psychotropic drugs), and the use or abuse of other substances (such as alcohol and drugs).

In terms of organic factors, neurological diseases and chronic illness may interfere with sexual functioning. Vascular disease, such as arterial insufficiency and venous leakage, has been associated with erectile problems in males (McConaghy, 2005). The use of certain drugs, recent surgery, and other medical conditions may all affect sexual functioning. Drug and alcohol abuse suppresses sexual arousal. In addition, a major physical cause of sexual dysfunction is the use of antihypertensive or antidepressant medications (SSRIs) and tranquillisers.

Biological mechanisms of sexual arousal and orgasm in women are poorly understood at present (Brotto & Klein, 2007). For example, the neurophysiology of the female sexual response has not been adequately studied. This includes the role of neurotransmitters and local vaso-active substances in determining vascular smooth muscle tone, vasodilatation, and vaginal lubrication. Likewise, the role of steroid hormones in the modulation of sexual desire and arousal in women is not well understood. The effects of ageing and menopause on female sexual functioning are important areas for further research.

Another good example of the many organic causal factors behind a sexual dysfunction is that of premature or early ejaculation. Among the numerous organic conditions that may lead to abnormalities of emission and ejaculation are acute or chronic polyneuropathy, endocrine disorders, serological disorders, and the side effects of other drug therapies (McConaghy, 2005). In the aetiology of gender dysphoria, exposure to certain hormones at critical periods *in utero* has been suggested as an important contribution to the development thereof (McConaghy, 2005).

If we refer back to the distinctions in orgasmic disorder as being either primary (having never experienced an orgasm) or secondary (had previous orgasms), we see that secondary orgasmic disorder is more frequently due to underlying organic disease or medication (and, at times, underlying relationship difficulties) (Sarason & Sarason, 1993).

More attention should also be focused on aetiology of sexuality issues in the ageing. Risk factors such as the normal ageing process, chronic illness, a history of surgery or physical trauma, drugs, and other modifiable factors may be important in sexual dysfunction in the elderly. Other risk factors include chronic illness, and systemic diseases such as atherosclerosis, diabetes, cardiovascular disease, and renal and liver failure. Neurogenic conditions such as Alzheimer's disease, multiple sclerosis, tumours, and brain trauma may also play a role in sexual dysfunctions. Psychiatric disorders such as depression and anxiety, as well as endocrine disorders such as hyper- and hypothyroidism, hypogonadism, and hyperprolactinaemia, have similarly been implicated.

As biological factors are strongly implicated in some sexual dysfunctions, effective medical treatments have been developed for some of them, for example erectile dysfunction. Vaso-active therapy involves injection of papaverine into the penis immediately before intercourse, which facilitates erection. However, this method may cause discomfort or pain, and studies have reported high attrition rates. Penile implants and vascular procedures are surgical alternatives. Also, vacuum device therapy creates a vacuum that draws blood into the penis, which is then trapped by placing a ring around the base of the penis.

Psychological factors

Psychological factors can play a major role in causation, with anger, stress, and anxiety frequently implicated in the sexual dysfunctions. Current theory suggests that cognitive processes are heavily involved in sexual problems (Sarason & Sarason, 1993). Learning theory implicates early learning or 'erotophobia' in sexual dysfunctions. Within the individual, dysfunctional attitudes (such as sexual guilt), past experience, and traumatic experiences (such as rape or incest) may become problematic for sexual functioning.

The aetiology of vaginismus provides us with examples of fear and trauma factors that can play a role in sexual dysfunction. Sexual traumas such as rape, incest, molestation, and painful, coercive, or unsatisfactory first sexual intercourse experience can lead to this. More general fears of pregnancy or infertility, sexually transmitted infections (including HIV), intimacy, penetration, or loss of control, and other factors such as misinformed beliefs that a woman is 'too small', or that sex results in pain, may be problematic. Poor body image or poor self-esteem and performance anxiety may also lead to difficulties in sexual functioning. Given embedded assumptions of heteronormativity in society, an individual who experiences sexual orientation-related distress may also be more at risk of sexual dysfunction.

Ignorance of sexual functioning and even basic ignorance of anatomy may lead to sexual problems. For example, a very young or uninformed individual may believe that he may 'get lost' in his sexual partner, and that this may result in losing his penis. Much in the way of societal faulty beliefs regarding sex and sexual functioning may be carried over to the individual in myths and misinformation from any number of sources. This can result in unrealistic expectations that serve only to impede the individual's sexual functioning and satisfaction. On the other hand, the fear of losing control of feelings and behaviour, in someone who is sexually responsive, is often at the core of the problem. The resulting defensive behaviour of 'holding back' and over-control may prevent some women letting go to orgasm. Fear of losing control over bladder function, or fear of losing consciousness if becoming too highly aroused, may further inhibit and prevent orgasm.

Sigmund Freud contributed an important example in the way of myth or unrealistic expectations with his views on vaginal versus clitoral orgasm, with the former being considered the preferable, and only 'mature', form of sexual pleasure for women. Today it is accepted that there is no superior form of orgasm. The epidemiological data varies, but it is accepted that more than 50% of women need direct clitoral stimulation to orgasm (Brotto & Klein, 2007). Unfortunately, this medical knowledge is not always carried over to the beliefs held in society. Many media sources, such as popular men's and women's magazines, still back the idea that some forms of sexual expression are 'must-do' and are readily achievable by anyone, if they just try hard enough.

A further myth is that of the simultaneous orgasm. In modern sexology, this is seen as a sign of dominance or control instead of a sign of couple closeness. Such expectations create performance pressure in the female partner that would definitely further inhibit sexual enjoyment and freedom to orgasm. Many popular sexual myths in heterosexual relationships (some of which are more strongly held in some population groups) include the following, among others:

- Men know everything about sex.
- Men are always in the mood.
- A person who does not enjoy sex does not love his or her partner.
- Women should not ask for what they want.
- The man will know best how to please the woman.

Body-image problems might be a reason for primary anorgasmia, but could also be present in the woman who is orgasmic with solo masturbation but not in the presence of a partner. As suggested above, a related factor is that of performance anxiety. In women who have normal sexual arousal but fail to orgasm, performance pressures and anxieties are very often to blame. Regardless of whether these pressures are self-imposed or due to scrutiny from their partner, the result is often a pattern of 'spectatoring' (that is, detailed self-monitoring during sexual activity). This leads to a loss of spontaneity and inhibits sexual responsiveness in both women and men. This inhibition leads to further sexual 'failure', thereby reinforcing expectation in a self-perpetuating cycle.

Masters and Johnson (1970) revolutionised sex therapy with a brief, direct, therapeutic programme that first excluded physical or organic causes of dysfunction (which would be treated medically if indicated) and offered the psychological and interpersonal treatment strategies for which they are still well known today. The therapy includes basic education about sexuality and emphasises improving communication and reducing performance anxiety. The methods of 'sensate focus' and non-demand pleasuring are also used. The success of the programme is widely documented (Sarason & Sarason, 1993), and sex therapies have evolved and expanded upon these pioneering methods.

Social and interpersonal factors

Interpersonally, we need to look to social issues such as sexual myths and misinformation, covered extensively in the previous section, as well as interpersonal factors such as relationship failure and poor communication, as causal factors in sexual dysfunctions. Current theory suggests that numerous social and interpersonal factors are likely to interact in contributing to sexual function problems (Sarason & Sarason, 1993). The distinction between primary and secondary orgasmic disorder can be a useful example in understanding this, and we see that primary orgasmic disorder is often the result of sexual guilt due to a strictly conservative sexual upbringing, for instance.

In the aetiology of vaginismus, social and interpersonal factors may cause problems for an individual. These include socially learned sexual inhibitions or sexual aversion due to conflict or trauma, as well as guilt, which may be due to religious orthodoxy or negative parental attitudes to nudity, masturbation, or sex in general (Sarason & Sarason, 1993).

Script theory postulates that behaviours are demonstrated in accordance with scripts that reflect social and cultural expectations (McConaghy, 2005). Sexual guilt can play havoc with otherwise healthy people and their otherwise healthy sexual functioning. The origins of sexual guilt are numerous and often complex. Very often, such guilt is the result of religious or cultural upbringing that portrays sex in a negative light. Many anorgasmic women were brought up to feel that sex is inherently sinful and bad, that their genitals are dirty, and that masturbation is evil or perverted (McConaghy, 2005). A further, closely linked, contributor is that persons with negative attitudes towards sex typically feel that sexual fantasies are improper, and they actively fight off such fantasies when they occur. This creates an impediment to natural sexual arousal and release.

Deterioration in personal relationships and poor social skills may also play a role. Although tensions in relationships are quite normal and do not necessarily result in sexual dysfunction, it is striking that anorgasmia can be a sign of underlying relationship problems. Common problems are power struggles, poor communication and conflict resolution, gender-role conflicts, jealousies, or retribution for real or perceived injustices between partners. It is not difficult to see why physical or emotional abuse may prevent a person from relaxing sexually in order to orgasm. Even minor issues in a relationship, however, can create resentment or frustration that interferes with sexual enjoyment.

The aetiology of the paraphilias often includes learning and experiences with others in an interpersonal setting. The development of unusual or inappropriate sexual arousal patterns may occur in the context of other sexual and social difficulties, although not all adults with sexual and social difficulties develop unusual or 'deviant' sexual patterns (McConaghy, 2005). Early experience and the nature of an individual's sexual fantasies appear to play a role. According to an operant conditioning paradigm, a learning process may occur (often in early childhood psychosexual development) in which a deviant sexual behaviour is reinforced through association with pleasure. An alternative theory is suggested by those who believe that 'unusual' sexual attraction patterns are acquired, often in later life, and are indicative of sexual sophistication, and not pathology (Baldwin, 2003; Moser, 1999), as is now also increasingly acknowledged in the DSM and ICD.

There is no convincing evidence for any particular explanation for gender dysphoria (McConaghy, 2005). Researchers with a biological orientation provide explanations pointing to genes or sex hormone fluctuations duing intrauterine development. Researchers with other orientations implicate social and interpersonal learning experiences. In developmental terms, the period between approximately 18 months and three years of age may be critical for gender identity development, and 'learning' of gender roles may furthermore be influenced by family experiences (McConaghy, 2005).

 ACTIVITY

In 2018, Ahmed E. Arafa and Shaimaa A. Senosy studied female sexual dysfunction in Egyptian women with anxiety disorder. They concluded that female sexual dysfunction was 'highly prevalent in patients with anxiety' and that 'higher anxiety scores inversely correlated with the patients' sexuality' (p. 545).

In these cases, do you think the sexual dysfunctions would have been caused by biological, psychological, social, and/or interpersonal factors? (You may wish to refer to anxiety disorders in Chapter 6.)

CONCLUSION

It is important to bear in mind some of the challenges and concerns regarding the conditions related to sexual health (that is, sexual dysfunctions and gender dysphoria) as raised by activists, academics, and researchers who in their work prioritise the needs and rights of females, and the sexually and gender diverse. The responsiveness of the compilers of the DSM and also the ICD to these issues, as is evident from recent revisions, is to be welcomed.

This chapter makes it apparent that there is a large degree of variability in the diagnostic features and presumed aetiologies of the sexual dysfunctions in men and women. As complaints tend to be highly comorbid within an individual, and between partners in a couple, a comprehensive biopsychosocial assessment of both partners may be required for accurate diagnoses with the aim of effective treatment.

Furthermore, the DSM now clearly acknowledges that transgender people do not necessarily have a mental disorder and the ICD-11 even more strongly asserts this position.

Gender dysphoria as a diagnosis is only applicable when someone with a transgender identity has marked clinical distress and/or impairment. It is all-important to consider the impact of stigma, prejudice, discrimination, and victimisation in all walks of life on the sexually and gender diverse, and how this may account for much of the distress witnessed in clinical contexts.

The clear distinction between paraphilias and paraphilic disorders in the DSM and ICD is also important and, indeed, may change society's understandings of sexual diversity that does no harm to others.

MULTIPLE-CHOICE QUESTIONS

1. Which of the following do not negatively affect men's libido?
    a) fatigue
    b) antidepressants
    c) dyspareunia
    d) lactation
2. Gender dysphoria is diagnosed when:
    a) a person's gender assigned at birth is inconsistent with the person's gender identity
    b) a person's gender assigned at birth is consistent with the person's gender identity
    c) an individual is born with ambiguous genitalia
    d) all of these are correct
3. Paraphilia is defined as:
    a) a dysfunction
    b) an attraction to inappropriate individuals or objects
    c) an attraction to machines
    d) a desire that dominates the personality
4. The main feature of sexual arousal disorders is:
    a) lack of desire for sex despite normal physical sexual response
    b) sexual arousal to inappropriate stimuli
    c) the experience of pain during sex
    d) lack of desire or interest in sexual activity
5. Which of the following do not appear in the ICD-10 but do appear in the ICD-11?
    a) gender identity disorder of childhood
    b) gender incongruence
    c) transsexualism
    d) dual-role transvestism

PARAGRAPH AND ESSAY QUESTIONS

1. a) What is the Masters and Johnson four-stage human sexual response cycle?
   b) What are its advantages and disadvantages?
2. Name three gender differences that exist in sexual attitudes and sexual behaviours.
3. Describe the impact of culture on the definition of a condition related to sexual health. What cross-cultural evidence suggests that 'normal' sexual behaviour is culturally defined?
4. Describe the symptoms of three different forms of paraphilia. What do all paraphilias have in common and how does one distinguish between paraphilias and a paraphilic disorder?
5. Is female sexual dysfunction a mental disorder in the DSM and ICD categorisation systems? Discuss.

12 SUBSTANCE-RELATED AND ADDICTIVE DISORDERS

Gale Ure

CHAPTER CONTENTS

Introduction
Historical perspective
Theories of addiction
The disease model
Moral theory
Psychoanalytic theories
Behavioural theories
Types of addiction
Clinical picture
Substance-induced disorders
Substance intoxication and withdrawal
Substance/medication-induced psychotic disorder
Substance use disorders
Non-substance-related disorders
Gambling disorder
Internet gaming disorder
South African perspectives on specific substances
Alcohol (dop)
Cannabis (dagga/zol)
Methamphetamine (tik/crystal meth)
Nyaope (whoonga)
Cocaine (coke)
Heroin (smack)
MDMA (ecstasy)
Prescription and over-the-counter medications
Aetiology
Biological factors
Psychological and social factors
Conclusion

LEARNING OUTCOMES

At the end of this chapter, you should be able to:

- Identify the difference between use, dependence, withdrawal, intoxication, and addiction.
- Identify groups of substances by type.
- Explain the aetiology of substance abuse and the potential for addiction.
- Explain substance use in the South African context.
- Explain the similarities between addiction to substances and addiction to behaviours.

PERSONAL HISTORY CASELET

Siphamandla lies under the bridge on the outskirts of town, high on nyaope after sharing a 'blue train' with his friends. He had been feeling physically ill, suffering from stomach cramps and nausea because he had been unable to score nyaope for a while. He feels like the drug is healing him, the cramps recede, the nausea abates, and he is able to face the day. 'I feel powerful,' he says, over and over again.

Siphamandla has been on the street for several years now and has lost all interest in 'getting clean'. His family will not allow him to return to the house, as he stole his mother's TV and watch to sell to buy the drug. He no longer feels hungry and cannot remember when last he ate. He is thin and malnourished, but says he isn't sick. A few his friends have died on the street, some from Aids, and some because their immune systems have broken down due to malnutrition.

Siphamandla started using about five years ago, when he was fourteen; he only used the drug once – and he was hooked. He was given his first hit by his cousin, who had been using for about a year. Most of the unemployed men in his street use the drug. He has broken the law many times to score nyaope, and has committed acts of assault, prostitution, and theft.

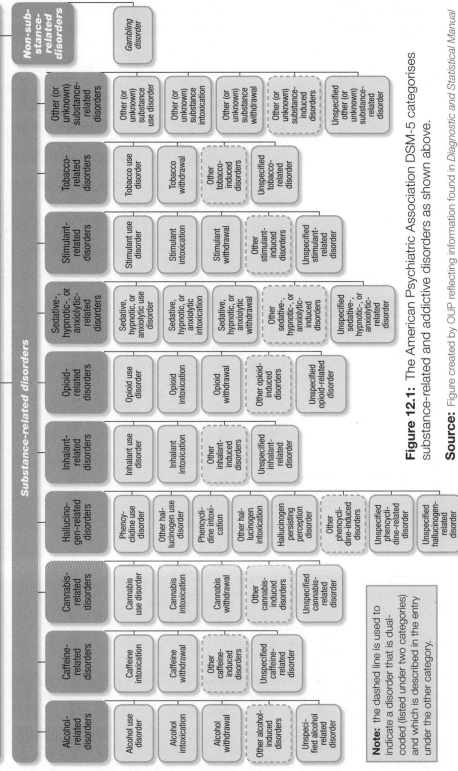

Figure 12.1: The American Psychiatric Association DSM-5 categorises substance-related and addictive disorders as shown above.

Source: Figure created by OUP reflecting information found in *Diagnostic and Statistical Manual of Mental Disorders*, fifth edition (DSM-5), 2013.

Note: the dashed line is used to indicate a disorder that is dual-coded (listed under two categories) and which is described in the entry under the other category.

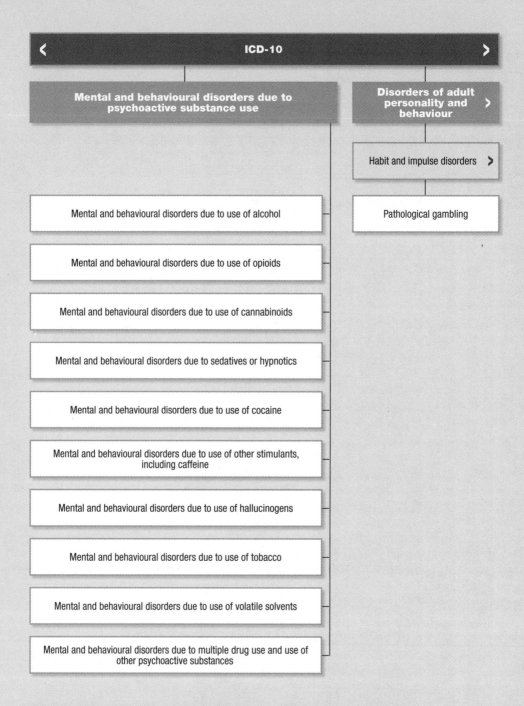

Figure 12.2: The World Health Organization ICD-10 categorises mental and behavioural disorders due to psychoactive substance use, and habit and impulse disorders, as shown above.

Source: *International Statistical Classification of Diseases and Related Health Problems*, tenth revision (ICD-10), 2016.

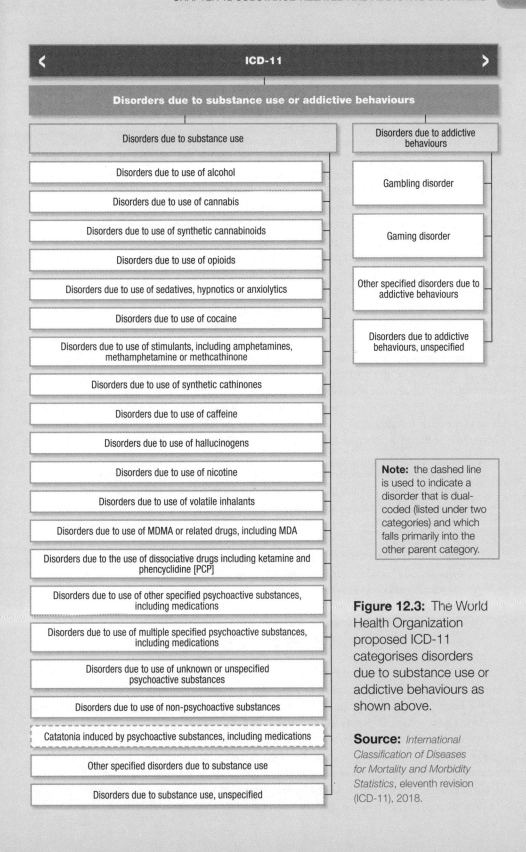

Figure 12.3: The World Health Organization proposed ICD-11 categorises disorders due to substance use or addictive behaviours as shown above.

Source: *International Classification of Diseases for Mortality and Morbidity Statistics*, eleventh revision (ICD-11), 2018.

INTRODUCTION

When you think about addiction, what comes into your mind first – a picture of a skinny young woman injecting heroin or a celebrity baring his soul on television about his treatment programme?

The most common reaction to hearing the word 'addiction' is to think of *substance* use and abuse, but substances are not always involved. Addictions that are of sufficient clinical concern presently fall under the DSM-5 and ICD-10 categories of impulse-control disorders. These addictions include those involving food (see Chapter 13), the Internet, pathological gambling, and, since the World Health Organization has recently declared it a mental disorder, sex. Disorders categorised in the DSM-5 under 'disruptive, impulse-control, and conduct disorders' sometimes have components of addictive behaviour listed in the ICD-10, for example, kleptomania and pyromania (fire-starting) (see Chapter 15), as do some of the eating disorders (American Psychiatric Association, 2000).

Disorders of this nature have as their specific identifier the compulsive failure to control impulses or extreme difficulty in controlling impulses, despite the negative consequences that may be attached to acting on them. This can include the failure to stop gambling even if one realises that not doing so will result in a significant negative consequence, for example, that one's wife could leave. This failure to control impulses can also refer to the impulse to engage in violent or destructive behaviours (e.g. road rage, sexual behaviour, fire starting, stealing, and self-abusive behaviours) (Lemonick & Alice, 2007).

The most significant recent development in medical thinking around addiction has been a formal position statement from the Board of the ASAM (American Society of Addiction Medicine, 2011) which formalised the following definition of addiction:

> Addiction is a primary, chronic disease of brain reward, motivation, memory, and related circuitry. Dysfunction in these circuits leads to characteristic biological, psychological, social, and spiritual manifestations. This is reflected in an individual pathologically pursuing reward and/or relief by substance use and other behaviours.
>
> Addiction is characterised by inability to consistently abstain, impairment in behavioural control, craving, diminished recognition of significant problems with one's behaviours and interpersonal relationships, and a dysfunctional emotional response. Like other chronic diseases, addiction often involves cycles of relapse and remission. Without treatment or engagement in recovery activities, addiction is progressive and can result in disability or premature death.

This definition does not necessarily provide a revolutionary explanation of addiction, but it does cement medicine's acceptance of addiction as a disease. It does this by noting the role of the brain in the aetiology and prognosis of the disease. It also attempts to consolidate previous psychological, behavioural, moral, and biological models under one umbrella interpretation. This formalisation of the definition appears to be in response to the difficulties that surfaced in the development of the DSM-5, and which were the cause of a number of obstacles in the interpretation of addiction (Robinson & Wilson, 2011). It is hoped that incorporation of all the elements in a formal definition will provide a holistic picture of how to provide appropriate treatment and resources.

HISTORICAL PERSPECTIVE

The acceptability of substance use, as well as the types of substances that have been declared substances of abuse, changes over time. For example, cannabis or dagga (from the Khoi word *daXab*) has been used in southern Africa for centuries, but the Sotho king Moshoeshoe cautioned people about its use, and John Dube, the ANC's first president, was a campaigner against the use of this substance (Du Preez, 2018).

Despite this situation being echoed around the world in relation to a variety of different substances, there was no formalised concept of addiction until the 1914 Harrison Narcotics Tax Act in the USA (Clausen, 1957; Reid & Sheeby, 1990). Then, descriptions of addiction were linked to the social notion that behavioural excesses were related to morbid (or a symptom or sign which is indicative of disease) appetites, vices, or habits. Cannabis was made illegal in many states of the USA around this time, and only recently has become legal in a few of these states again.

Similarly, South Africa made the possession of cannabis illegal in 1922, and this restriction lasted until 2018, when it was decriminalised for personal use. The South African Constitutional Court found that the ban on the use of the plant infringed on the Bill of Rights, which gives all citizens the right to privacy. Persons may therefore cultivate, possess, and smoke cannabis in private. It is, however, illegal to smoke it outside your own home, deal in marijuana, or sell it to other people.

At present, the government still needs to decide on what the age restriction will be for smoking cannabis and how much is considered as constituting 'personal use' (African News Agency, 2018). People who work with heavy machinery, or where they may put the public at risk through this usage, will not be permitted to use the drug, and may be subjected to on-the-job testing (Jorge & Adams, 2019). Medical marijuana may be produced and used in South Africa, as a valid clinical choice ('Medical marijuana given green light', 2017).

Alcohol has been illegal in many Muslim countries for centuries, and it remains illegal in some today, including Somalia and Libya. It was briefly illegal in the USA in the 1920s, but this period of prohibition did not last.

There are no formal references to tobacco use before the 1400s, although it is generally acknowledged that it was used for medicinal purposes in America, as well as being smoked. From the 1500s, after Christopher Columbus had introduced the leaves to Europe, the use of tobacco increased throughout the world. From the 1930s to the 1950s, the health benefits were advertised by doctors – one slogan being: 'More doctors smoke Camels than any other cigarette'. In the 1950s, however, the link between bronchogenic cancer and smoking was discovered. As research into the health issues caused by smoking increased, the health risks over time became obvious and costly (Markel, 2007). Governments in many countries have acted to reduce tobacco use in their citizens. Smoking has been banned in public places in South Africa since 1993.

Lysergic acid diethylamide (LSD), accidentally discovered in 1943 by the Swiss scientist Albert Hofmann, was for a while treated as a wonder drug. In the 1960s in the USA, it was legally used in psychedelic psychotherapy, and also to treat alcoholics (Hofmann, 1980). However, it was made illegal there in 1968, and is now illegal in most countries. Yet the interest in LSD has not subsided; in the past few years, there has been a resurgence of experimentation into the properties of the drug, which has been identified as potentially being of therapeutic value in the treatment of depression (Dutton, 2018).

THEORIES OF ADDICTION

The disease model of addiction is a popular way of conceiving of addiction, while other conceptions include moral theory, behavioural theories, psychological theories, and combinations of these.

The disease model

The American disease model has been in existence since 1935 (Reid & Sheeby, 1990) and has not changed substantially since then (see the Board of the American Society of Addiction Medicine definition in the Introduction to this chapter). This addiction model describes the origins of this disease as having genetic, biological, environmental, and neurological predisposing factors. To be considered a disease, the traditional medical model of disease only needs an atypical disorder to exist, that causes discomfort, loss of functionality, or concern to the sufferer. Criticism of this model has always been that medicalising the label 'addict' prevents people from taking responsibility for exercising self-control and causes stigma.

The liquor industry has been supportive of this model as it suggests that only *some* people will become alcoholics and the rest of the population is able to drink without long-term consequence. This model has resulted in more benevolent treatment of substance users, diversion from prison into rehabilitation facilities, and less rejection by the community.

However, a substantial amount of the literature from the late 1960s until well into the 1980s rejected outright this medical (disease) model of mental illness, as well as the usefulness of hospitalisation and medication for addiction. Use of clinical diagnostic criteria to identify addiction was seen as medicalisation of violations of social norms rather than recognition of real clinical symptoms (Levine & Troiden, 1988).

Moral theory

This model has its foundations in the social thinking that certain people either have deficits in their ability to take personal responsibility for their lives and/or they lack spiritual strength to deal with events in their lives. While this thinking may seem old-fashioned and quite blaming, many present-day spiritually based programmes rely on this maxim, including those of Alcoholics Anonymous and Narcotics Anonymous (Alcoholics Anonymous World Services, Inc, 2012; Narcotics Anonymous, Inc., 2012). A spiritual guide or religious teacher is required to assist the person back to the right moral path.

The judicial system takes a similar position. Substance use is not a justifiable defense for a crime, and individuals are held accountable for their actions. This means that using substances – or not attempting to get help in controlling an addiction – is regarded as 'willful misconduct' and requires law enforcement to punish offenders. For example, driving under the influence of alcohol is a crime, regardless of whether or not the person is diagnosed as an alcoholic (Maatz, 2005; Reid & Sheeby, 1990). Correctional services intervention may be required to ensure that the person remains accountable and to impose punitive consequences, if considered necessary.

Psychoanalytic theories

Models of addiction based on individual character trait differences came into being after World War II and were grounded in psychoanalytic understandings of people. Psychoanalysis postulated that addiction was the result of a person's developmental stasis (being stuck) at a significant stage of their personality development. In the case of addiction, this has been regarded as being at the oral phase. This has been linked over time to sex-role conflicts, latent homosexuality, and low self-esteem (Meyer, Moore, & Viljoen, 1993; Reid & Sheeby, 1990), amongst others.

Contemporary psychoanalytic theory views addiction to be a result of an individual's attempts to reduce anxiety (Thombs, 2006). Use of substances and/or the continuous use of pornography, for example, are ways for the person to protect him- or herself against debilitating and painful emotions such as loneliness and depression. In this situation, intervention by a trained professional is required (Gumbiner, 2010).

Behavioural theories

In the past, the term 'addiction' referred exclusively to the use of substances. Today, it has come to include all behaviors that are habitual. Addiction can also be described as compulsive participation in pleasurable behaviors that becomes pathological, for example, pathological gambling. Thus, addictions can be seen as persistent and repetitive behaviours in the face of negative consequences (National Institute on Drug Abuse, 2018). An addiction could be considered to be a persistent behavior pattern characterised by:

- a powerful desire to continue the activity, which places it out of voluntary control
- a tendency to increase the frequency, duration, or amount of the activity over time
- a psychological or physical dependence on the gratification that is derived from participating in the activity
- a potentially detrimental effect on both the individual and society. For example, if a person steals money from his or her family to sell and/or purchase drugs, the family may become economically deprived by the loss of funds, a sense of trust may be lost, etc.

TYPES OF ADDICTION

Typically, in the past, addiction to substances was thought of as being the only form of addiction. The DSM-5 views addiction as extending beyond substances alone to include a wide array of other behaviours, both in the current classification (i.e. gambling disorder), as well as in the section that includes conditions that require further study (i.e. Internet gaming disorder, sex addiction).

The ICD-10, however, does not list or describe non-substance-related addictions. The ICD-11 allows for both gambling and gaming disorders, under the heading of 'other specified disorders due to addictive behaviours', and for addictive disorders that are unspecified, but which include any behaviours that follow an addictive pattern. The comparison between the DSM-5, ICD-10, and ICD-11 disorders is represented in Table 12.1

Table 12.1: Summary of substance- and non-substance related disorders in DSM-5 and ICD-10

DSM-5		ICD-10	ICD-11
Category	**Disorders**		
Substance-related disorders	Alcohol	Mental and behavioural disorders due to use of alcohol	Disorders due to use of alcohol
	Caffeine	Note: ICD-10 lists this as a stimulant	Disorders due to use of caffeine
	Cannabis	Mental and behavioural disorders due to use of cannabinoids	Disorders due to use of cannabis Disorders due to synthetic cannabinoids
	Cocaine	Mental and behavioural disorders due to use of cocaine	Disorders due to use of cocaine
	Hallucinogen	Mental and behavioural disorders due to use of hallucinogens	Disorders due to use of hallucinogens
	Inhalant	Mental and behavioural disorders due to use of volatile solvents	Disorders due to use of volatile inhalants
	Opioid	Mental and behavioural disorders due to use of opioids	Disorders due to use of opioids
	Sedative, hypnotic or anxiolytic	Mental and behavioural disorders due to use of sedative hypnotics	Disorders due to use of sedatives, hypnotics or anxiolytics
	Stimulants	Mental and behavioural disorders due to use of other stimulants, including caffeine	Disorders due to use of stimulants, including amphetamines, methamphetamine or methcathinone; disorders due to use of synthetic cathinones
	Tobacco	Mental and behavioural disorders due to use of tobacco	Disorders due to use of nicotine

DSM-5		ICD-10	ICD-11
Category	**Disorders**		
	MDMA/MDA and related	Not included as a specific category	Disorders due to use of MDMA or related drugs, including MDA
	Dissociative		Disorders due to use of dissociative drugs including ketamine and phencyclidine (PCP)
	Other/unknown	Mental and behavioural disorders due to multiple drug use and use of other psychoactive substances	
Non-substance-related	Gambling	No provision for behavioural addictions as an independent spectrum of mental disorders.	Disorders due to addictive behaviours: Gambling disorder
	Conditions for further study: Caffeine use disorder; Internet gaming disorder; sex addiction; exercise addiction	No provision for behavioural addictions as an independent spectrum of mental disorders.	Disorders due to addictive behaviours: Gaming disorder; other specified disorders due to addictive behaviour; disorders due to addictive behaviours, unspecified.

CLINICAL PICTURE

The description of this category of disorders has become complicated since the introduction of the DSM-5 and the upcoming ICD-11. This is largely due to the ongoing debates regarding the constructs that underlie these disorders, such as dependence, addiction, use, and abuse. In the past, only substance-related disorders were included in this category, whereas the DSM-5 and ICD-11 also make provision for non-substance-related addictions. Furthermore, in the past, the DSM made a distinction between *abuse* and *dependence*, whereas the DSM-5 does not make this distinction. In addition, the DSM-5 now describes the substance-related disorders in terms of use, intoxication, and withdrawal, and the ICD-10 describes them in terms of acute intoxication, harmful use, dependence, and withdrawal.

The ICD-11 classifies patterns of use that may require clinical attention; that includes harmful patterns of use, dependence, intoxication, and withdrawal, and psychotic conditions which may be caused by use of the substance. These can be either specified or unspecified. The 'addictive' component of substance-related disorders is subsumed in the diagnostic criteria of both the DSM 5 and the ICD-11, where reference is made to 'craving' or 'a strong desire or urge to use a substance' (American Psychiatric Association, 2013). A further way in which this is addressed is by means of severity specifiers (i.e. mild, moderate, or severe).

This group of disorders can be divided into three categories, i.e. substance-induced disorders, substance use disorders, and non-substance-related disorders.

SUBSTANCE-INDUCED DISORDERS

This section includes intoxication, withdrawal, and other substance/medication-induced disorders (e.g. psychotic, bipolar, depressive, anxiety, obsessive-compulsive, sleep, and neurocognitive disorders, as well as sexual dysfunctions and delirium) (American Psychiatric Association, 2013).

Substance intoxication and withdrawal

In previous editions of the DSM, general criteria for intoxication and withdrawal were provided; however, due to the differences between these states for different substances, the DSM-5 has opted to include them within the substance-specific sections. The ICD-10 provides general criteria for these states. The ICD-11 provides specific reference to withdrawal, intoxication, and psychosis under each substance. Due to practical constraints, only the general criteria for substance intoxication and withdrawal will be discussed.

Acute intoxication is the state that follows administration, ingestion, or exposure to a psychoactive substance. The administration results in changes and disturbances in consciousness, cognition, perception, mood, or behaviour. These cause maladaptive changes in behaviour or psychological states and responses that are of clinical significance. These can be, for example, belligerence, mood disturbance, cognitive impairment, impaired judgement, and impaired social or occupational functioning. These changes can be directly attributed to the immediate pharmacological effects of the substance and will resolve over time.

These symptoms are reversible and differ between substances. There is usually a complete recovery, except in cases of long-term use, where there is residual damage, for example, to brain structure or where complications may have been caused. Consequences of substance intoxication may include delirium, coma, trauma, convulsions, and vomiting (American Psychiatric Association, 2000; World Health Organization, 2016).

Table 12.2: Diagnostic criteria for substance intoxication from the ICD-10

ICD-10
■ A transient condition following the administration of alcohol or other psychoactive substance, resulting in disturbances in level of consciousness, cognition, perception, affect, or behaviour, or other psychophysiological functions and responses.
■ This should be a main diagnosis only in cases where intoxication occurs without more persistent alcohol- or drug-related problems being concomitantly present. Where there are such problems, precedence should be given to diagnoses of harmful use, dependence syndrome, or psychotic disorder.

Source: Reprinted with permission from the ICD-10 *Classification of Mental and Behavioural Disorders: Diagnostic Criteria for Research*, World Health Organization (WHO), Geneva, 2016.

After prolonged and persistent use of a substance, there might be an attendant group of symptoms that develop when the person either terminates the use of the substance completely, or when the drug is reduced. These symptoms may vary in intensity and severity. These symptoms are time-limited, that is, they last for a specific period of time that is related to the type of substance and dosage being utilised immediately before the reduction or termination of use. These symptoms cause clinically significant distress or impairment in functioning. Convulsions and delirium are relatively common during cessation of use of a substance (American Psychiatric Association, 2000; World Health Organization, 2016).

Table 12.3: Diagnostic criteria for substance withdrawal from the ICD-10

ICD-10
■ A group of symptoms of variable clustering and severity occurring on absolute or relative withdrawal of a substance after repeated, and usually prolonged, and/or high-dose use of that substance. Onset and course of the withdrawal state are time limited and are related to the type of substance and the dose being used immediately before abstinence. The withdrawal state may be complicated by convulsions.
■ Withdrawal state is one of the indicators of dependence syndrome and this latter diagnosis should also be considered.
■ Withdrawal state should be coded as the main diagnosis if it is the reason for referral and sufficiently severe to require medical attention in its own right.
■ Physical symptoms vary according to the substance being used. Psychological disturbances (e.g. anxiety, depression, and sleep disorders) are also common features of withdrawal. Typically, the patient is likely to report that withdrawal symptoms are relieved by further substance use.

Source: Reprinted with permission from the ICD-10 *Classification of Mental and Behavioural Disorders: Diagnostic Criteria for Research*, World Health Organization (WHO), Geneva, 2016.

Substance/medication-induced psychotic disorder

Psychosis caused by substance use may also mimic some of the psychiatric disorders; for example, substance abuse psychosis can be confused with schizophrenia. Substance use psychosis includes a group of symptoms that may occur following psychoactive substance use and which are not merely symptoms of intoxication produced by that substance. These symptoms also do not form part of a withdrawal state. Hallucinations are typically present, and these, while most often auditory, can also be found in more than one sensory modality. There may be delusions (which are often paranoid), perceptual disturbances, psychomotor disturbances, and abnormal mood (World Health Organization, 2016).

Table 12.4: Diagnostic criteria for substance/medication-induced mental disorders (DSM-5) and substance-induced psychotic disorder (ICD-10)

DSM-5 Substance/medication-induced mental disorders	ICD-10 Substance-induced psychotic disorder
A. The disorder represents a clinically significant symptomatic presentation of a relevant mental disorder. B. There is evidence from the history, physical examination, or laboratory findings of both of the following: (1) The disorder developed during or within one month of a substance intoxication or withdrawal or taking a medication; and (2) The involved substance/medication can produce the mental disorder. C. The disorder is not better explained by an independent mental disorder (i.e. one that is not substance- or medication-induced). Such evidence of an independent mental disorder could include the following: (1) The disorder preceded the onset of severe intoxication or withdrawal or exposure to the medication, or (2) The full mental disorder persisted for a substantial period (e.g. at least one month) after the cessation of acute withdrawal or severe intoxication or taking the medication. This criterion does not apply to substance-induced neurocognitive disorders or hallucinogen persisting perception disorder, which persist beyond the cessation of acute intoxication or withdrawal. D. The disorder does not occur exclusively during the course of a delirium. E. The disorder causes clinically significant distress or impairment in social, occupational, or other important areas of functioning.	■ A cluster of psychotic phenomena that occur during or immediately after psychoactive substance use and are characterised by vivid hallucinations (typically auditory, but often in more than one sensory modality), misidentifications, delusions and/or ideas of reference (often of a paranoid or persecutory nature), psychomotor disturbances (excitement or stupor), and an abnormal affect, which may range from intense fear to ecstasy. The sensorium is usually clear but some degree of clouding of consciousness, though not severe confusion, may be present. The disorder typically resolves at least partially within one month and fully within six months. ■ Psychoactive substance-induced psychotic disorders may present with varying patterns of symptoms. These variations will be influenced by the type of substance involved and the personality of the user. For stimulant drugs such as cocaine and amphetamines, drug-induced psychotic disorders are generally closely related to high dose levels and/or prolonged use of the substance. ■ A diagnosis of psychotic disorder should not be made merely based on perceptual distortions or hallucinatory experiences when substances having primary hallucinogenic effects (e.g. lysergic acid diethylamide (LSD), mescaline, cannabis at high doses) have been taken. In such cases, and also for confused states, a possible diagnosis of acute intoxication should be considered. ■ Particular care should also be taken to avoid mistakenly diagnosing a more serious condition (e.g. schizophrenia) when a diagnosis of psychoactive substance-induced psychosis is appropriate. Many psychoactive substance-induced psychotic states are of short duration provided that no further amounts of the drug are taken (as in the case of amphetamine and cocaine psychoses). False diagnosis in such cases may have distressing and costly implications for the patient and for the health services.

Source: Reprinted with permission from the *Diagnostic and Statistical Manual of Mental Disorders*, fifth edition (DSM-5), American Psychiatric Association (APA), 2013, p. 488, and ICD-10 *Classification of Mental and Behavioural Disorders: Diagnostic Criteria for Research*, World Health Organization (WHO), Geneva, 2016.

SUBSTANCE USE DISORDERS

The pattern of substance use in these disorders is maladaptive, leading to clinical impairment or distress as described below. These maladaptive patterns continue for a period of twelve months or more, and are demonstrated by one or more of the following:

- Ongoing use that results in a failure to meet important role obligations as required by home, work, or school. This can include being repeatedly absent from work or school, poor work performance, suspensions, expulsions from school, and neglect of children or household, all of which are directly attributable to the substance use.
- Recurrent use of substances in places where this could be hazardous. This would include driving a car while under the influence or operating heavy machinery, for example.
- Legal problems that may arise because of substance use. These can include being arrested for disorderly conduct or for criminal behaviours, for example, petty theft due to substance use.
- Continued use of the substance, despite experiencing problems in interpersonal or vocational situations that are either caused, or made worse, by using substances. These problems may include arguments and physical fights with a spouse about consequences of intoxication (American Psychiatric Association, 2000).

Furthermore, substance use encompasses a group of behavioural, cognitive, and physiological phenomena that occur after a period of repetitive and prolonged substance use. It involves a difficulty in controlling the use of a substance and an associated desire to continue its use. There are a number of symptoms that would indicate dependence:

- 'Tolerance' describes the need for ever-increasing amounts of a substance to produce intoxication or the desired effect. Use of increased amounts of the substance can sometimes cause tolerance to levels that would be lethal to a non-user.
- 'Withdrawal' is the development of a substance-specific syndrome due to the termination of, or reduction in, substance use that has been heavy and prolonged. It is a maladaptive behavioural change that occurs in the blood and cells when use of a substance of dependence is terminated. These changes can be either physical or cognitive, or both, and are acute and unpleasant.

   Depending on the substance being removed, they can include convulsions, shaking, difficulty sleeping, and perceptual difficulties. Delirium, confusion, and hallucinations may also occur. In alcohol withdrawal, delirium tremens may occur. There is a time limit to the period of withdrawal, and this is related to the type and the amount of substance being used at the time of removal. The person is likely to resume using the substance to relieve or reduce the symptoms.

- 'Compulsive use' describes the pattern of taking the substance in larger amounts or over a longer period than was originally intended, for example, if a person decides to have one or two drinks when socialising but instead ends up drinking until they are intoxicated.

- There are often numerous and unsuccessful attempts to decrease or discontinue use. The person continues to express a desire to stop or cut down on the use of the substance.
- There is a time component, where the person's life is taken over by substance-related activities. There would be, for example, excessive time spent on:
  - acquiring the substance
  - using the substance
  - recovering from its effects.
- A person may, for example, take leave from work on days when he or she has a hangover from excessive alcohol consumption the night before.
- The person's life begins to revolve around the use of the substance. There is a corresponding reduction in other activities of daily life, for example vocational activities, sport, and socialising.
- Psychological and physiological symptoms that can be directly attributed to use of the substance, for example depression, do not contribute to a desire or attempts to stop. This occurs even if the cause of the problem is directly related to substance use, for example, damage to organs due to alcohol use (American Psychiatric Association, 2000; World Health Organization, 2016).

Table 12.5: Summary of general symptoms of substance dependence (ICD-10)

ICD-10
<ul><li>A definite diagnosis of dependence should usually be made only if three or more of the following have been present together at some time during the previous year:<ul><li>A strong desire or sense of compulsion to take the substance.</li><li>Difficulties in controlling substance-taking behaviour in terms of its onset, termination, or levels of use.</li><li>A physiological withdrawal state when substance use has ceased or been reduced, as evidenced by: the characteristic withdrawal syndrome for the substance or use of the same (or a closely related) substance with the intention of relieving or avoiding withdrawal symptoms.</li><li>Evidence of tolerance, such that increased doses of the psychoactive substances are required to achieve effects originally produced by lower doses (clear examples of this are found in alcohol- and opiate-dependent individuals who may take daily doses sufficient to incapacitate or kill intolerant users).</li><li>Progressive neglect of alternative pleasures or interests because of psychoactive substance use; increased amount of time necessary to obtain or take the substance or to recover from its effects.</li><li>Persisting with substance use despite clear evidence of overtly harmful consequences, such as harm to the liver through excessive drinking, depressive mood states consequent to periods of heavy substance use, or drug-related impairment of cognitive functioning. Efforts should be made to determine that the user was, or could be expected to be, aware of the nature and extent of the harm.</li></ul></li></ul>

Source: ICD-10 *Classification of Mental and Behavioural Disorders: Diagnostic Criteria for Research*, World Health Organization (WHO), Geneva, 2016.

NON-SUBSTANCE-RELATED DISORDERS

In addition to the substance-related disorders, the DSM-5 also considers other forms of addiction, such as gambling disorder (American Psychiatric Association, 2013). During the development of the DSM-5, excessive behavioural patterns, such as Internet gaming disorder, sex, exercise, and shopping addiction were also considered for inclusion; however, due to a lack of scientific evidence, these disorders were not included. However, Internet gaming disorder was included in the section for disorders that need further investigation. The reason for considering the behavioural addictions is due to evidence that suggests that certain repetitive behaviours activate the reward systems like those activated by drugs, and that the resulting behaviours are comparable to those produced by substance use disorders (American Psychiatric Association, 2013).

Gambling disorder

For most people, gambling is a form of recreation, but for some, gambling becomes an addiction with far-reaching personal and social consequences. Compulsive gambling affects people from all cultures, ethnicities, ages, genders, and socio-economic groups. A definition of compulsive gambling would be as follows:

> Compulsive gambling, also called gambling disorder, is the uncontrollable urge to keep gambling despite the toll it takes on your life. Gambling means that you're willing to risk something you value in the hope of getting something of even greater value.
>
> Gambling can stimulate the brain's reward system much like drugs or alcohol can, leading to addiction. If you have a problem with compulsive gambling, you may continually chase bets that lead to losses, hide your behavior, deplete savings, accumulate debt, or even resort to theft or fraud to support your addiction.
>
> Compulsive gambling is a serious condition that can destroy lives. Although treating compulsive gambling can be challenging, many people who struggle with compulsive gambling have found help through professional treatment. (https://www.mayoclinic.org/diseases-conditions/compulsive-gambling/symptoms-causes/syc-20355178)

South Africa has a well-developed research entity run by the Casino Association of South Africa, which monitors gambling behaviours in the national context. Findings of this group demonstrate that only 12% of the gambling population use regulated gambling institutions, while 19% gamble in informal venues. The gambling population is also analysed according to socio-economic status: more people in low to middle socio-economic groups choose to gamble in informal venues. Informal gambling is linked to problem gambling on a larger scale than formal gambling (Casino Association of South Africa, 2011).

Table 12.6: DSM-5 criteria for gambling disorder

DSM-5
A. Persistent and recurrent problematic gambling behaviour leading to clinically significant impairment or distress, as indicated by the individual exhibiting four (or more) of the following in a 12-month period: (1) Needs to gamble with increasing amounts of money to achieve the desired excitement. (2) Is restless or irritable when attempting to cut down or stop gambling. (3) Has made repeated unsuccessful efforts to control, cut back, or stop gambling. (4) Is often preoccupied with gambling (e.g. having persistent thoughts of reliving past gambling experiences, handicapping or planning the next venture, thinking of ways to get money with which to gamble). (5) Often gambles when feeling distressed (e.g. helpless, guilty, anxious, depressed). (6) After losing money gambling, often returns another day to get even ('chasing' one's losses). (7) Lies to conceal the extent of involvement with gambling.
(8) Has jeopardised or lost a significant relationship, job, or educational or career opportunity because of gambling. (9) Relies on others to provide money to relieve desperate financial situations caused by gambling. B. The gambling behaviour is not better explained by a manic episode.

Source: Reprinted with permission from the *Diagnostic and Statistical Manual of Mental Disorders*, fifth edition (DSM-5), American Psychiatric Association (APA), 2013, p. 585.

The symptoms, as described in Table 12.6 usually have an onset during adolescence or early adulthood but may have a first onset during later adulthood (American Psychiatric Association, 2013). Typically, the disorder has a slow onset that gradually increases over time (interestingly, more rapidly in women than men), and the gambling patterns may either be regular or episodic (American Psychiatric Association, 2013). An interesting phenomenon is that most individuals with this disorder report one or two types of gambling; however, some individuals participate in a wide range of gambling activities.

There is some evidence of a genetic component in this disorder; this is supported by the fact that it is more frequent in monozygotic than dizygotic twins and first-degree relatives. It also has a high comorbidity with antisocial personality disorder, depressive and bipolar disorders, and other substance use disorders (American Psychiatric Association, 2013).

Internet gaming disorder

Internet addicts display similar brain changes to those seen in substance users and other impulse-control disorders. This is one of the findings of a series of MRI scans done by a group of Chinese researchers on 35 participants (Briggs, 2012). The scans indicated that there was a disruption to white matter connections in the orbital frontal cortex, the same areas as those involved in substance use (Fowler, Volkow, Kassed, & Chang, 2007). These white matter connections are the bridge between regions of the brain involved in generating emotion, executive functioning (e.g. sustaining attention), cognition, self-control, and decision-making. Comparable similarities have been found in video game addicts.

SOUTH AFRICAN PERSPECTIVES ON SPECIFIC SUBSTANCES

Alcohol (dop)

It has been stated, erroneously, that South Africa is ranked as the country with the highest alcohol consumption in the world. However, this does not mean that South Africa does not have a serious alcohol problem amongst its population. Global statistics place South Africans as having one of the highest per capita rates of consumption of alcohol (30th out of 195 countries), at a rate of 11 litres per person per annum. South Africa also carries the shameful title of being the country with one of the highest number of drunk drivers, with as many as 58% of road fatalities attributable to the consumption of alcohol ('South Africa Worst', 2015). Belarus is the number one country with consumption of 17 litres per person per year. Out of 195 countries, South Africans came in at 59th place for heavy, episodic drinking amongst people who drink (Bhardwaj, 2018).

Alcohol consumption has a number of negative consequences, for example, foetal alcohol spectrum disorders, where a foetus is affected by the mother's intake of alcohol during pregnancy. This may cause physical and intellectual disabilities, and behavioural disturbances. Cardiac defects and sight problems are also common. Alcohol abuse also poses a risk to the economy of the country, as the healthcare costs linked to the physical effects of long-term abuse include liver, kidney, and brain damage are high (Mokolobate, 2017; Peltzer, Davids, & Njuho, 2010). Alcohol abuse is also a contributing factor in unemployment, sexual risk behaviours, crime, breakdown in family life, violence, aggression, and malnutrition (Setlalentoa, Pisa, Tehkisho, & Loots, 2009).

South Africa's relationship with alcohol is complex and is linked to both the political and socio-economic history of the country. Traditional beer (*utshwala* or *mqombothi*) was usually made from sprouted corn, maize meal, and water, which were all easily available and grown in rural areas for food. This beer's effect was mild as it had a low alcohol content, and it formed the foundation of traditional community celebrations.

During the colonial period, wine-making was introduced in the Cape. The workers on the wine-producing farms were provided with alcohol instead of wages. This was called the 'dop system', and it promoted the excessive and ongoing use of alcohol as a functional norm.

From the late 1800s, alcohol imported from Mozambique and bottled in Pretoria was one of the most important sources of income for the growing population of the Transvaal. This population provided hospitality services for the influx of miners drawn to the province by the dream of gold and instant wealth (Van Onselen, 1982).

During apartheid, a traditional South African institution, the shebeen, came into being. The operation of shebeens was illegal, as black South Africans were prohibited from making and using alcohol (Olivier, Curfs, & Viljoen, 2016). The 'concoctions' that were sold there often had additions such as methylated spirits – which is poisonous – to increase the intoxication potential. This beer's effect was more intoxicating than that of rural beer, and its effects could sometimes be lethal (SA History Online, 2008).

The operation of licenced shebeens is now legal. However, these facilities are seldom regulated. For example, the cheap beer *mbamba* is often spiced with other things such as spirits or even battery acid to give it extra kick (Masipa, 2015).

It should be noted that many South African drink only in moderation or not at all. However, compared to people in the rest of Africa, South Africans on average drink a lot of alcohol (see Figure 12.4).

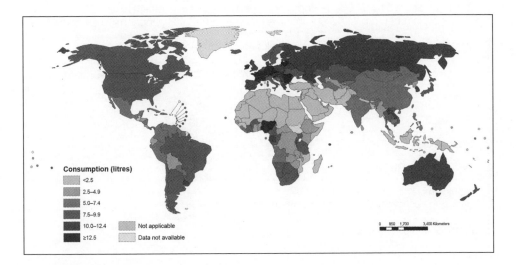

Figure 12.4: Total alcohol per capita (15+ years) consumption, in litres of pure alcohol, 2016

Source: World Health Organization, 2018e.

The Global Information System on Alcohol and Health (GISAH) monitors trends in the use of alcohol, and its effect on populations of countries around the world. It covers the areas of consumption and the harm that alcohol causes. Worldwide, alcohol causes the death of around 3.3 million people annually. Sixty different diseases have been identified where alcohol plays a causal role (World Health Organization, 2014a).

 **ACTIVITY**

Study the table below, and decide what is the most valuable point that you would take away from it.

South Africa

Total population: 51 452 000 ➤ Population aged 15 years and older (15+): 70%
Population in urban areas: 62% ➤ Income group (World Bank): Upper middle income

Prevalence of alcohol use disorders and alcohol dependence (%), 2016*

	Alcohol use disorders**	Alcohol use disorders**
Males	12.4	4.2
Females	1.8	0.7
Both sexes	7.0	2.4
WHO African Region	3.7	1.3

* 12-month prevalence estimates (15+).
** including alcohol dependence and harmful use of alcohol.

Source: Adapted from World Health Organization, 2018e.

Cannabis (dagga/zol)

The effects of cannabis are varied and can differ from person to person. Some people may feel relaxed and happy, others may giggle. Music and colours may appear to be more intense, and it may cause an increase in appetite. There are also negative effects. It can affect memory, and it may cause psychosis, where a person may feel paranoid, hallucinate or have panic attacks. It can cause nausea and lethargy. Long-term use can interfere with a person's ability to concentrate and may demotivate a person to the extent that they may not be able to maintain work or complete their education.

Cannabis (or marijuana) has, for a very long time, carried the label of being a gateway drug (Secades-Villa, 2015), that is, a drug that precedes use of more illicit and potentially more dangerous drugs. More recently, however, there has been debate, and an ongoing and increasing amount of research that indicates that this is not the case, and that most people who will try the drug will not go on to use stronger drugs, or become addicted to any substance. People are more likely to use alcohol or nicotine preceding hard drug use (Centers of Disease Control and Prevention, 2018; National Academies of Sciences, Engineering and Medicine (NAP), 1999).

Marijuana has historically been the 'soft porn' of drugs when it comes to first-time-user experimentation with illegal substances, because the consequences for use, while being illegal, are perceived to be less risky, both socially and physiologically, than, for example, cocaine or heroin. These drugs, which are seen as being 'harder', have an increased risk of addiction and negative effects across functioning. They also carry a greater legal penalty for their use if caught.

Criminalisation of the use of cannabis in South Africa has raised numerous arguments in recent years, not the least of which being that the threat of criminal action has not reduced the rate of first-time marijuana use, and therefore, by association, has not reduced hard drug use. This has also been the finding of the majority of international drug research efforts (National Institute on Drug Abuse, 2017). Research has also demonstrated that use of the drug is less harmful than the use of alcohol (Lachenmeier & Rehm, 2015; Sewell, Poling, & Sofluogo, 2009), for example, which is legal.

As indicated above, there are documented health risks associated with cannabis use. These range from cognitive and motor impairments to memory loss, psychosis, paranoia, and the potential precipitation of schizophrenia. Long-term use causes physical effects, for example, coughing and wheezing, and lung and immune system impairment in some individuals (Silver, 2017).

There are, however, also health benefits associated with the drug. The use of cannabis to alleviate – whether physically or psychologically – the symptoms of epilepsy, multiple sclerosis, cancer, and chronic pain, has served to push it into the spotlight as perhaps needing a less stigmatising 'makeover', and a more thorough investigation of the positive aspects, which appear to outweigh the negatives.

A declaration by the High Court in the Western Cape in March 2017 (Evans, 2017) that the criminalisation of the drug when used in the privacy of one's own home was unconstitutional was based on the question of whether government was entitled to prescribe what people do in their own homes. This in turn raised the issue of whether criminalising private use could be seen as an infringement of the right to privacy. The question of what legitimate rights the State has to regulate what a person may or may not do in his or her own private space was raised in this matter, and the High Court found the government's position was not justifiable.

From a clinical perspective, the lifting of the legal sanctions for private use will provide some benefit to those using the drug for medicinal reasons, as they will be permitted to grow and use the plant in their own homes. While it is still too soon to determine long-term effects of legalising the drug, reports from international research where marijuana has been legalised show no marked differences in public healthcare usage in the short to medium term. Will South Africa be the same? Watch this space.

Methamphetamine (tik/crystal meth)

Methamphetamine (or 'crystal meth') is an 'upper', which means that, initially, users feel euphoric, confident, and energetic when they use the drug. These feelings of well-being are produced by dopamine, a neurotransmitter produced in the brain. Initial use of the drug produces up to two-thirds more dopamine than the body produces naturally. However, with sustained use, tolerance is built up. This tolerance forces the body to seek more and more of the drug to achieve the feelings of well-being that were experienced at the first use of the drug. Eventually, the body stops producing dopamine altogether, which plunges the user into depression. The body's ability to restore its dopamine production systems may be impaired or permanently damaged by ongoing use of methamphetamine.

Methamphetamine is an inexpensive drug and is three-and-a-half times more powerful than cocaine. The duration of the high is from six to twelve hours, compared to the half an hour to three hours of some other substances like cocaine. The drug fills the user with a feeling of euphoria, and the addiction is caused by users continually attempting to recreate that first feeling. The associated psychotic behaviour, memory loss, aggressions and violent behaviour have led to its use and sale being a major factor in gang violence in the Cape Flats In the Western Cape (Caelers & Bailey, 2006).

'Meth Mouth' is an identifying feature of long-time meth users. Users suffer from tooth loss due to decay. The decay is caused by meth's capacity to impede the flow of saliva in the mouth. Meth addicts also commonly do not keep themselves adequately hydrated, and this causes natural acids and bacteria to build up around the base of the teeth, eating away at the gums and the enamel of the teeth. Poor hygiene, and a corresponding lack of oral care, exacerbate the problem (Castro, 2006).

Methamphetamine can be made in a normal domestic kitchen. It is used by people of all ages in all communities. It is also more common in rural environments which are not commonly associated with substance use, although use is spreading rapidly to major centres around the world. It was estimated that, in 2006, 26 million people globally were using the drug (Castro, 2006).

Nyaope (whoonga)

Nyaope, also known as whoonga, is a uniquely South African township drug. It is a combination drug principally made up of low-grade heroin and cannabis (dagga), and a mixture of other substances, which can include a mishmash of anti-retroviral drugs, detergents, milk powder, rat poison, bicarbonate of soda, and pool cleaner, amongst others. Users of the drug often have burnt index fingers and thumbs, and burns on their lips, because the nyaope is smoked right down to the end of the cigarette. This is because, while it is an inexpensive drug, its users come from an environment of poverty and crime, and every molecule of the drug is precious.

The effects of the drug, however, do not last long. Because of this, and the expense of the drug, users turn to unconventional methods of getting high. One way is to 'bluetooth', which involves a group of users injecting themselves with the blood of a person who is high from the drug. HIV is spread rapidly using this method, as a user's immunity is usually low. This is because users do not eat regularly, as the drug prevents them from feeling hunger. Experts say that a user cannot get high from 'bluetoothing', and that it only has a placebo effect (Sifile, 2017).

Nyaope users, who often come from stable homes in the community, go from being hardworking and caring individuals to stealing from their family members and friends to fund their habit. Street drugs like nyaope are feared by communities, as they watch the future of their youth being destroyed. Rehabilitation for these users is expensive, as they are weaned off nyaope onto methadone, a heroin substitute. Withdrawal is extremely unpleasant. Nyaope was declared an illegal drug in South Africa in 2014 and carries a hefty 15-year jail sentence for its possession (Ephrahim, 2014; Health24, 2014; Maseko, 2015).

 **ACTIVITY**

Watch https://www.youtube.com/watch?v=qD0w36VRkg8 – The Nyaope 'Bluetooth' craze caught on camera
Watch https://www.youtube.com/watch?v=1q441LKR268 – Nyaope wreaks havoc in the lives of young women

Cocaine (coke)

Cocaine use in South Africa sits at around 0.3% of reported drug users, compared to 4.0% of the adult, substance-using population's use of cannabis (Peltzer & Phaswana-Mafuya, 2018). Of these cocaine users, only around 5% are likely to develop addiction. If the total drug-taking population is thought to be an estimated 12% of the general population, cocaine users are a minority, in spite of its being considered highly addictive.

The drug is a party drug for the most part. A cocaine high leaves the user feeling more confident, chatty, and creative. It also acts as an aphrodisiac, and being a stimulant, is also energising, making it a sought-after drug for its sexually stimulating effects. After prolonged use, however, it may begin to have the opposite effect.

Cocaine is expensive, and out of the recreational range of most people. It is known as the 'rich man's drug' because the intense high is short-lived, and more of the drug is required to satisfy the psychological craving, sometimes costing thousands of rand a night (Crossroads Recovery Centre, 2019; Delphi Health Group, 2019).

There are several physical conditions associated with long-term use. Arteriosclerosis (hardening of the artery walls), heart and lung disease, high blood pressure, depression, and schizophrenia are all potential negative health consequences of use (Anonymous, 2016).

Heroin (smack)

Heroin use has been increasing in South Africa, largely due to gang involvement, organised crime, and corruption within the police force. It is estimated that there are around 100 000 users in South Africa. The eastern seaboard of South Africa is a recognised heroin transit route for shipments of the drug to Europe and North America (Haysam, 2019).

Heroin can be sniffed, smoked, inserted rectally, or injected intravenously. The drug gives users a feeling of warmth and detachment, makes them relax, and reduces anxiety. It has strong sedative and analgesic properties, which make both physical and psychological pain simply fade away.

However, use of heroin can cause negative effects. These can include nausea, respiratory depression, lowered blood pressure, and constipation. Once the high has faded, the physical symptoms of withdrawal appear. These can include fever, vomiting, sweating, and can potentially cause seizures. People who abuse heroin will have difficulty terminating use because of the physical withdrawal symptoms associated with terminating (Drug Policy Alliance, 2019).

MDMA (ecstasy)

Methylenedioxymethamphetamine or MDMA is commonly known as ecstasy or E. It is a recreational psychoactive drug. Its use is associated with raves and electronic dance music. The effects range from increases in energy, pleasure, and physical sensations. The effects of the drug can last for between three and six hours. Some of the drug's side effects are rapid heartbeat, paranoia, sleeplessness, visual impairment, and sweating.

Deaths related to the drug have been caused by increased body temperature and dehydration (McCann, 2014). Although MDMA has no approved medical use, research is being carried out to ascertain whether it is effective in the treatment of treatment-resistant PTSD (Philipps, 2016).

Prescription and over-the-counter medications

Some medications used to treat chronic pain can be addictive; these can include both prescribed and over-the-counter products. These are members of the opioid group of substances. Codeine, oxycodone, and morphine are all substances that have been linked to abuse and addiction. People who use these substances for an extended period may build up tolerance to the drug, needing more and more to get the same effect, and may perhaps even become dependent on it physically (Lynch, 2013).

Non-medical use of other prescription medications, for example, tranquilisers, stimulants, and sedatives is reported to be on the increase in the United States and other developed countries. The incidence of prescription opioid overdose has quadrupled from 2002 to 2014 (Compton, Jones, & Baldwin, 2016). In South Africa, these figures are not available.

EXAMPLE CASE

Lindi is a ballet dancer. She fell and hurt her foot while performing on stage about a year ago. She was in real pain, but the show had to go on, and her doctor prescribed her very strong painkillers to help her get through three shows a day. A year later, she is addicted to the painkillers, only now her doctor isn't prescribing them for her any more, because he explained to her that they are addictive, and that she should only use them for a short time. She has started using about double the amount that her doctor had prescribed initially.

To get her pills, Lindi goes to doctors, usually different ones every time, and tells each of them a different story. She has stolen prescription pads and written her own prescriptions. She also goes from pharmacy to pharmacy and pays cash for her medication. She does not believe that she has a problem. It is the doctor's fault for not understanding that she cannot perform without the pills, and that she is in constant pain. She believes that, if she does not take the pills, she will be in too much pain to perform, which is unacceptable. She does not believe that she needs to go to rehabilitation, because she is not addicted. They 'simply help her get through her job'.

AETIOLOGY

Despite wide coverage in the media and many psycho-educational programmes, substance use and addiction continue to be psychosocial problems. Internationally, governments have tried to curb smoking in public, and in many countries cigarette advertising has been banned. The use and distribution of many substances have been outlawed in many countries. Furthermore, many people are aware of the negative effects of short- and long-term use of substances; however, none of this seems to prevent people from starting or continuing to use substances. To understand this, we must take a closer look at the causes of substance use, as this may offer some explanation as to why preventive strategies have been largely unsuccessful.

Substance use is problematic because it poses many health problems, and it is seen as a challenge across many areas of social and community life. This means that treatment needs to include many varied aspects, some not necessarily directly related to healthcare, but which might be required to assist the person recover. An example would be vocational training, amongst others.

As suggested earlier, there has been much discussion around what could cause substance use and addiction, and whether the causes indicate or affect what treatment should be used. In the past, there have been two prominent theories: the first is that substance use is an illness and needs to be medically treated, and the second is that it is a habit and needs willpower to be cured.

Biological factors

Genetic predisposition

There is a growing body of evidence that genetic factors play a significant role in both substance use and substance dependence. Scientists believe that these may influence as much as 40% to 60% of a person's predisposition to addiction (American Society of Addiction Medicine, 2011). While there is no obvious Mendelian gene transmission, it would not be unreasonable to assume that addictions may be polygenic (determined or influenced by many genes), which would certainly increase the possibility of addiction heritability (Genetic Science Learning Center, University of Utah, 2013).

According to gene studies, addictions are moderately to highly hereditable. A person's risk is mediated by the degree of relationship to an addicted relative (Bevilacqua & Goldman, 2009). This means that, if an immediate family member has an addiction to a substance, the children will be significantly more prone to addictive behaviour (Kreek, Nielsen, Butelman, & Laforge, 2005; National Institute on Drug Abuse, 2016).

People with a predisposition to a mental disorder also appear to run a significantly higher risk of substance use and addiction than the broader populace. This is possibly because of the attendant lack of insight that is symptomatic of several psychiatric disorders like schizophrenia, for example (National Institute on Drug Abuse, 2018).

The influence of environmental and social factors that interact with this biological inheritance will affect how much these genetic factors will be expressed in a person's life. Nurture factors, for example, parenting and life experiences, will affect the person's resilience, and will have a direct influence on whether or how these indications of addiction will appear (National Institute on Drug Abuse, 2016). Resilience (Akst, 2011; Wallace, 1999) and cultural factors will also play a role in how addiction manifests in people with a genetic susceptibility (Rodgers, 1994) (see Chapters 1 and 4). Environmental and genetic variables combine to trigger, firstly, the initial use of an addictive agent, and secondly, to press the transition from use to addiction.

Brain structures

The structures of the brain affected by addiction are those generally associated with reward. These structures, which include the nucleus accumbens, anterior cingulate cortex, basal forebrain, and amygdala, are all part of the motivational hierarchy and are modified by the addiction. Over-arousal of these areas, which reward our normal behaviors, produces the euphoric results that are constantly being sought by people who use substances. This cycle teaches them to repeat the behaviour.

Other biological variances may also influence addictions. Stress has been shown to increase the desire for drugs. Hormones also play a role in addictions. Research has shown, for example, that some women crave nicotine more during certain phases of their menstrual cycle (National Institute on Drug Abuse, 2018).

Brain-imaging studies have been valuable in identifying neurobiological effects of substance addiction. They have also been useful in providing explanations for vulnerability and have been able to provide insight into users' struggles with recovery, as well as their subjective experiences.

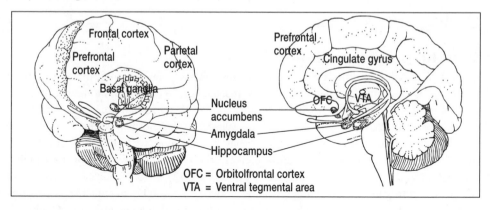

Figure 12.5: Major brain regions with roles in addiction. The prefrontal cortex is the focal area for cognition and planning. The ventral tegmental area (VTA) and nucleus accumbens (NAc) are key components of the brain's reward system. The VTA, NAc, amygdala, and hippocampus are major components of the limbic system, which coordinates and drives emotions and memories.

Source: Fowler et al., 2007.

Neurotransmission and interconnection between the hippocampal and cortical systems, which are brain reward structures, are also affected by addiction. When there has been a previous experience of reward, be it food, sex, alcohol, or other substances, these structures will trigger cravings for the substance and for the subsequent participation in addictive behaviours (Fowler et al., 2007).

Long-term use of substances may disturb the way important brain structures cooperate to influence behaviour, particularly that which is linked to the substance use. Continuous use may lead to tolerance of a substance. Tolerance to a drug means that the user will need to take more and more of the substance to recreate the original dopamine high (National Institute on Drug Abuse, 2018). Thus, increased dosages are required to produce the same intoxication effect.

In turn, brain changes might lead to addiction – or the need to seek out substances and to take them compulsively. Addiction removes a person's ability to maintain control over his or her own behaviour. It also reduces his or her ability to make appropriate decisions, while at the same time producing intense pressure to take the substance.

The neurobiological component of addiction goes far beyond being simply the neurochemistry of reward (see next section). Altered impulse control, impaired judgement, and the pathological quest for rewards are all the result of dysfunction of memory, motivation, and reward functions of the white matter connections between the frontal cortex and reward circuits. The ability to delay gratification and control impulsivity is housed in the frontal lobes. Early-life exposure of the frontal lobe and connective tissue, and their functioning, to substance use while these structures are maturing plays a significant role in the development of addiction.

Neurotransmitters

The rewards produced by substances are often more pleasurable than those produced naturally. When some substances are used, this can lead to the release of two to ten times the quantity of dopamine than from a natural reward. If the substance is inhaled during smoking, or injected straight into a vein, the resulting high is also virtually immediate, and the effects can be sustained for extended periods, unlike those of many natural rewards which produce pleasure, like eating and sex. The brain remembers this pleasure, as the extreme nature of the high leaves an enduring memory of the experience. This memory drives the person to seek the same pleasure over and over, and this compulsion is effectively addiction (National Institute on Drug Abuse, 2018).

The brain operates using chemicals and, as substances are chemicals, they work along with the brain's neurotransmitters to disrupt normal functioning. The chemical makeup of some substances, for example marijuana and heroin, closely resembles that of neurotransmitters naturally found in the brain. This allows these substances to initiate neurotransmitter activity. However, these triggers are not the same as normal activation, and the neurons then convey aberrant information to various brain centres (National Institute on Drug Abuse, 2018).

This close resemblance in structure tricks the receptors and permits the substance to attach to and activate the nerve cells 'under false pretences'. Deviant messages are then sent via the neural network. Methamphetamine and cocaine are two substances that trigger neurons to release excessive quantities of naturally produced neurotransmitters, or which alter the usual reuptake process that manages these chemicals. This interference can lead to vastly amplified neural messages. These messages then disturb the usual communication pathways. The magnitude of the altered effect is comparable to the difference between having someone sit in the dark with candlelight and someone sitting in a room with a halogen searchlight (National Institute on Drug Abuse, 2018).

There are numerous physical effects that can be experienced when substances are used continuously and in the long term. The same processes that are involved in producing tolerance to a substance can cause structural changes, which in turn alter brain function. These changes may lead to irreversible damage and deterioration in the long term. Glutamate, a neurotransmitter also found in the brain, aids in the process of learning and is also affected by changes to the reward system. When the amount of glutamate in the brain is changed by the use of substances, attempts by the brain to counterbalance the changes can lead to impairment of cognitive processes (National Institute on Drug Abuse, 2018).

Ongoing use can also lead to changes in habits or subconscious memory systems, for example, conditioning. This type of learning, during which contextual triggers are associated with the pleasurable substance experience, can lead to cravings. These cravings are then activated when the person is exposed to the triggers, even if the substance is not always associated directly with them. This learned response is long-lived and can resurface after long periods of abstinence (National Institute on Drug Abuse, 2018).

Psychological and social factors

A basic human desire is to feel good. Substances of misuse produce overwhelming feelings of pleasure and well-being. Once this euphoria has died away, however, it is usually followed by other, often negative, effects. These may vary from substance to substance. Cocaine, a stimulant, is one such example. The initial 'high' is accompanied by feelings of power, increased self-confidence, and improved energy levels. In a different drug cluster, the results may be radically different. The exhilaration caused by an opiate, for example heroin, is usually followed by the sensation of calm. Clearly, it would not make sense to become addicted to a substance which initially produces unpleasant effects (National Institute on Drug Abuse, 2018).

In addition, people may want to make themselves feel less anxious or more capable in circumstances they believe are difficult. People who are shy and nervous in social situations may use substances to give them courage and to reduce their social anxiety. Furthermore, stress has been identified as a key factor in initiating substance use, maintaining substance use, and causing relapse in people attempting to rehabilitate from addiction. Those who suffer from stress and related disorders, and those who suffer from depressive illness, may begin abusing substances to reduce their general feelings of being unable to cope (National Institute on Drug Abuse, 2018).

People may also want to improve their performance in work, social, sexual, or sporting spheres. The increasing demands that are put on individuals to achieve in all spheres of human life may create a need in some people to utilise substances just to keep up with the rest of humanity. In addition, they may use these to augment or increase their sporting or mental performance beyond their natural talent. This pressure to perform above one's capacity can play a role both in initiating experimentation with substances and in maintaining substance use behaviour (National Institute on Drug Abuse, 2018; Urban & Gao, 2014).

Curiosity and peer pressure add a further social dimension. Adolescents and young people are particularly susceptible to the significant effects of peer pressure and media exposure. This exposure tells people that they should not be anything other than thin (hence the use of chemical appetite suppressants), 'cool' (add the use of alcohol and/or drugs when socialising), and fashionable (smoking was seen as being very sophisticated right up to the 1980s). These behaviours are driven by the person's own need to fit in with others of the same age and social groups. These people are more prone to participate in dangerous and risk-taking behaviours when they are with others, for example, speeding while driving a vehicle, or having unprotected sex with strangers while intoxicated (National Institute on Drug Abuse, 2018).

Many people experiment to see what effect substances will have on them, and they do this with little coercion. When substance use becomes the sole focus of a person's life, however, it reduces a person's capacity for containing his or her desires and exercising self-control. Because there are physical changes to the brain in individuals addicted to substances (see previous section), their ability to make appropriate judgements and decisions may be impaired. Studies also show that this damage results in a reduction in the ability to learn and remember, and in the ability to control and moderate behaviour. These changes are believed to modify the way the brain functions in the long term and may go a long way towards explaining the apparently irrational, obsessive, and detrimental patterns of behaviour that are seen in addiction (National Institute on Drug Abuse, 2018).

However, not all substance use, or even ongoing use, can be diagnosed as pathological or clinically significant. This means that not all people using a substance will require professional assistance to reduce or terminate use of the substance. These people may show little or no visible interference or alteration in their level of functioning. Thus, even if the person uses the substance regularly, it does not reduce their ability to work, to bring up a family, or to behave appropriately in social interactions.

For example, many people drink heavily on weekends, or utilise sleeping pills to sleep, sometimes for their whole lives; others smoke dagga (cannabis) every day but they appear to experience no marked side effects. Other useful examples are smoking cigarettes and drinking coffee, both of which are considered substances of use, but neither of which is considered to impact on normal daily functioning. Long-term health disruption and the harm done, if any, may become clinically significant only once physical consequences like emphysema or cancer occur.

Social and environmental factors can have a compounding effect on the likelihood of substance use. A lack of parental supervision that provides appropriate discipline and structure, and contact with friends or social situations where drugs are freely available and in open use, may desensitise one to the potential harm of substance use. Early aggressive behaviours and poor social skills may also predispose a person to future substance problems. Conversely, people who exhibit personal self-control, who have positive relationships with their families, and who are academically competent are less likely to turn to substances. Attending schools with firm anti-substance policies and monitoring processes may also prevent early exposure to substance use.

Substance use is a significant community problem because it has an observable impact on the social environment. A substantial amount of research in the United States has linked substance use to crime (National Institute on Drug Abuse, 2018); there is no current research available to gauge the scale of this link on the African continent. Research findings have reported loss of ability to work, harm to self and others while under the influence of alcohol, and loss of inhibitions, which might lead to indiscriminate sexual practices (Strong, Bancroft, Carnes, Davis, & Kennedy, 2005), or to self-harm behaviours

(Roy, 2001). Communities with high levels of poverty, and which may be marginalised from participating in community structures, pose more risk to their members than those with strong neighbourhood connections and inclusion.

 ACTIVITY

Read the following text and discuss whether you agree that exercise addiction could be a valid form of addiction.

Jane*, who cannot sleep if she has not completed her exercise targets for the day, will get out of bed to run in circles around her lounge in the middle of the night so that she can make her daily steps goal on her health rewards programme. Jason* sneaks out of work to go to the gym to push heavier and heavier weights to increase the size of his muscles, which are already disproportionately large. He is trying to find a doctor who will provide him with steroids to increase his muscle size even further.

Repetitive behaviors are now being recognised as having the potential to become behavioral addictions (Grant, Potenza, Weinstein, & Gorelick, 2010). The urge to exercise, and the resulting patterns of behavior that cause clinically significant distress or disability and loss of function, have been identified as the new behavioural addiction of the 21st century. There is also some indication that the same medications used in the treatment of addiction can be effective in the treatment of 'exercise addiction'.

CONCLUSION

While there are limited sources of information from South Africa, international statics are indicating that substance use is implicated in around 50% of diagnoses of psychotic mental illness in other countries, for example, schizophrenia (Drake, Mueser, & Brunette, 2007; Mueser, Yarnold, & Levinson, 1990). This is a very sobering thought (Saban et al., 2014). However, if people have the right to autonomy, and the right to control their bodies, should they not be able to choose what to put into them?

Similarly, gambling, gaming, smartphone, and sex addictions are all examples of how, in our modern society, it is easy to become hooked on social media, pornography, and gambling, because they are so easily available – they are on the phone. We don't need to connect to people any longer – we can feel good by using technology to give us our highs (De Lange, 2013). The more isolated we get, the more necessary it is to find something to make us feel good, and so we get addicted to the easy fix. There are even apps available to cure our addictions to social media (Dvorak, 2015). In the modern world, we are becoming lonelier (Gonchar, 2017), poorer (Joseph, 2017), and less able to cope with the demands of our lives, and both substances and other addictions may offer us a chance to escape.

There are many discussions that can arise out of the social context of substance use and addictions. What we should bear in mind at the end of this chapter is that there is a very human story behind each incidence of substance use or addiction.

MULTIPLE-CHOICE QUESTIONS

1. In terms of substance-related disorders, the word *addiction* is most closely associated with:
   a) substance use
   b) intoxication
   c) substance dependence
   d) polysubstance abuse
2. The ICD-10 category of habit and impulse-control disorders includes:
   a) gaming disorder
   b) exercise addiction
   c) non-voluntary non-substance-use disorder
   d) pathological gambling
3. According to which of these is addiction seen as a person's attempt to reduce anxiety?
   a) the disease model
   b) moral theory
   c) psychoanalytic theories
   d) behavioural theories
4. According to the ICD-10, substance withdrawal may include:
   a) unsteady gait
   b) garbled speech
   c) tics
   d) convulsions
5. Medication-induced psychotic disorder can mimic the symptoms of:
   a) schizophrenia
   b) cyclothymic disorder
   c) delirium
   d) hallucinogen-persisting perception disorder

PARAGRAPH AND ESSAY QUESTIONS

1. Which four reasons are given to explain why people use substances?
2. Describe the general effects of each of the following:
   a) cannabinoids
   b) opioids
   d) stimulants
   e) hallucinogenics
3. Name six negative results of alcohol use in South Africa today.
4. List three harmful effects that substance abuse can have on others.
5. Describe the physical signs that may be present if a person is using:
   a) Tik
   b) Nyaope
6. Name the brain structures that are involved in the process of addiction.
7. List four behaviours that are commonly associated with addiction.
8. Describe how neurotransmitters interfere with normal functioning of the brain in relation to addiction.
9. Will further legalisation of cannabis in South Africa increase the number of people who become addicted to 'harder' drugs? Explain your answer.
10. Should exercise addiction be considered for inclusion into the next version of the ICD? Why?

Elsabe Jordaan

CHAPTER CONTENTS

Introduction
History of eating disorders
Types of feeding and eating disorders
   Pica
   Rumination disorder
   Avoidant/restrictive food intake disorder
   Anorexia nervosa
   Bulimia nervosa
   Binge-eating disorder
   Other specified feeding or eating disorder
   Unspecified feeding or eating disorder
Aetiology
   Biological factors
   Psychological factors
   Sociocultural factors
Cross-cultural perspectives
   South African perspective
Stress, risk, and vulnerability
Conclusion

LEARNING OUTCOMES

After studying this chapter, you should be able to:

- Show a general understanding of feeding and eating disorders, and distinguish the disorders from each other.
- Distinguish between anorexia nervosa subtypes.
- Describe the intrapersonal aspects of the aetiology of the eating disorders.
- Describe the role of cultural and gender features in the aetiology of the eating disorders.
- Identify cross-cultural and, more specifically, South African, aspects that are relevant to the prevalence of eating disorders.

PERSONAL HISTORY CASELET

My life is fear and food, but mostly fear. I am terrified of being fat and I am always thinking of ways to become thinner. I measure my waist and thighs at least three times per day, and I look in the mirror as often as I can, just to make sure than I don't look any fatter. I become really desperate if I look bigger or I haven't managed to lose at least a few grams. I hate my fat thighs and I hate feeling fat. When I lose weight, I feel elated and proud of myself. This causes a lot of stress at home because my parents are getting very paranoid about my weight. Ever since my gymnastics coach refused to allow me to train because I am too thin, my parents have been taking me to doctors and dieticians to try to get me to stop losing weight.

Actually, it all started at gymnastics practice, when the coach said that I was too heavy to be any good on the beam. I decided that I was going to lose at least two kilograms before my next gymnastics practice, and I did! At first everyone complimented me, saying that I was looking good. My mom was proud of my weight loss and showed me off to her friends. I kept at it and I lost twelve kilograms in three months.

I have always tried to make my parents proud and to live up to their expectations. I am a top-ten student in my grade, am on the school debating team and have provincial colours for cross-country running. Even though I tell everyone what they want to hear, I know that I can't give in to food. I tell my mom that I am still menstruating, even though it stopped months ago. I am always hungry and I love reading recipe books and baking, but I can't eat any of those disgusting, fattening cakes or biscuits. My mom and dad have started fighting about my eating. My mom is trying to be strict and forcing me to eat fattening food, but my dad says he is happy if I eat salad; at least I am eating something…

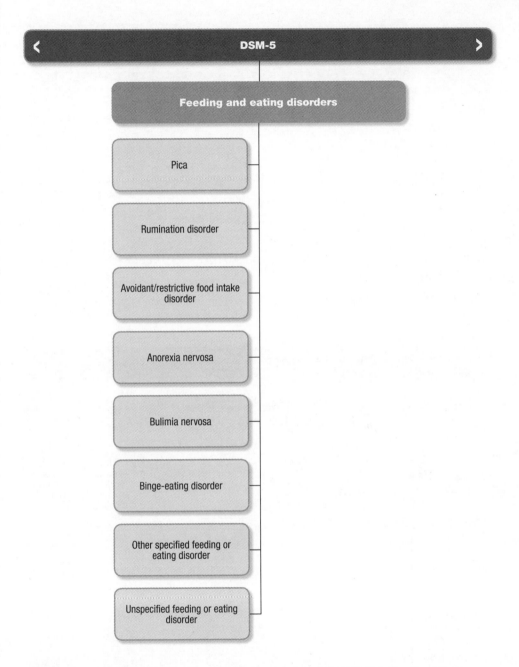

Figure 13.1: The American Psychiatric Association (2013) DSM-5 categorises feeding and eating disorders as shown above.

Source: Figure created by OUP reflecting information found in *Diagnostic and Statistical Manual of Mental Disorders*, fifth edition (DSM-5), 2013.

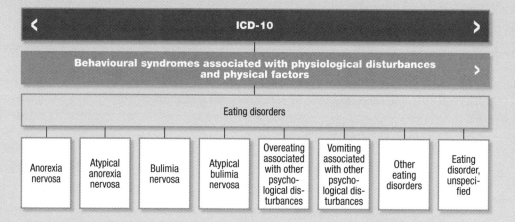

Figure 13.2: The World Health Organization (2016) ICD-10 categorises eating disorders as shown above.

Source: *International Statistical Classification of Diseases and Related Health Problems*, tenth revision (ICD-10), 2016.

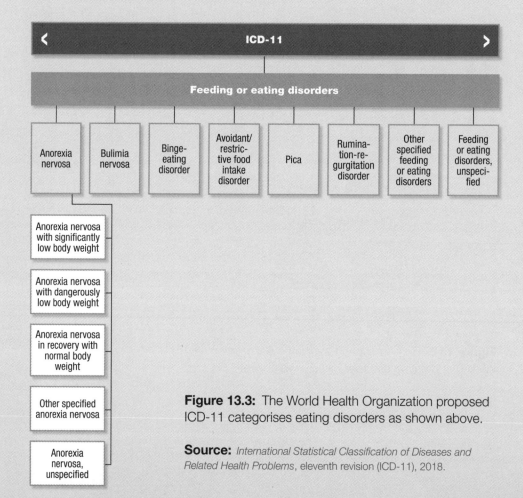

Figure 13.3: The World Health Organization proposed ICD-11 categorises eating disorders as shown above.

Source: *International Statistical Classification of Diseases and Related Health Problems*, eleventh revision (ICD-11), 2018.

INTRODUCTION

The discussion in this chapter will focus on one of the aspects of human physiology that is a basic requirement for our survival (and well-being), namely, eating. This is something that most of us take for granted, but for some, eating can become disordered. The major eating disorders are serious and chronic conditions with relatively negative outcomes and the highest mortality rate of all the mental health disorders (Micali, Hagberg, Petersen, & Treasure, 2013).

Extreme disruptions in eating behaviour characterise the feeding and eating disorders. The DSM-5 expanded on this section from previous editions by including binge-eating disorder, pica, rumination disorder, and avoidant/restrictive food intake disorder, in addition to the more traditional eating disorders of anorexia nervosa and bulimia nervosa (American Psychiatric Association, 2013). Anorexia nervosa is characterised by a notably low body weight as a consequence of limiting the intake of energy relative to energy needed, the extreme fear of weight gain, and a disturbed self-perception of body shape or weight (American Psychiatric Association, 2013).

Bulimia nervosa comprises recurrent episodes of binge eating and associated compensatory behaviours that are inappropriate attempts to avoid weight gain. With bulimia nervosa, the evaluation of self is disproportionately affected by body weight and shape (American Psychiatric Association, 2013). Examples of compensatory behaviours are excessive exercise and the misuse of laxatives to purge. In both anorexia and bulimia nervosa, the person's experience and perception of their own body weight and shape appear to be disturbed. Both these disorders are associated with an extreme drive to be thin.

In the DSM-5 the name of the eating disorders diagnostic category was changed to 'Feeding and eating disorders'. This change reflects the inclusion of the feeding disorders associated with infancy, childhood, or adolescence.

Obesity is the accumulation of body fat that is excessive to the extent that it represents a health risk, according to the World Health Organization (2018b). After much contemplation and debate, obesity was not included in the DSM-5, since it has not been linked to a consistent psychological or behavioural syndrome. Simple obesity is included as a general medical condition in the *International Classification of Diseases* (ICD-10) (World Health Organization, 2016).

The ICD-10 classification will be in use until 2022, when the ICD-11 will be adopted. The ICD-11 category is called 'Feeding and eating disorders' and includes binge-eating disorder and avoidant/restrictive food intake disorder as new entities. The ICD-11 also updates some of the criteria of anorexia nervosa and bulimia nervosa, to reflect recent research (Reed et al., 2019). The ICD-11 includes 'with dangerously low body weight' and 'with significantly low body weight' as subtypes of anorexia nervosa (Luciano, 2015). Binge-eating disorder is characterised by excessive eating in a short period of time, and people with this disorder report a sense of lack of control during an episode (American Psychiatric Association, 2013).

Although anorexia nervosa has been described in Western culture since the eleventh century, both anorexia nervosa and bulimia nervosa have shown dramatic increases in Western countries from the 1930s up to the end of the last century (Hoek, 2017). However, recent studies suggest that this trend has shifted and that the overall incidence of anorexia nervosa has been stabilising, with the exception of the high-risk group comprising girls between the ages of 15 and 19 years (Smink, van Hoeken, & Hoek, 2012). However, it appears that bulimia nervosa may have been decreasing since the early 1990s and into the 21st century (Hoek, 2017; Smink et al., 2012).

While eating disorders occur comparatively infrequently in the general population (with incidence rates so low that they are difficult to research), anorexia nervosa continues to occur more often in young women (Hoek, 2017; Smink et al., 2012). The 12-month prevalence of anorexia nervosa among young women is about 0.4%, about 1%–1.5% for bulimia nervosa, and binge-eating disorder prevalence is approximately 0.8% for adult males and 1.6% for adult females In the United States (American Psychiatric Association, 2013). In the South African context, eating disorders have been described in the white female population since the 1970s. They were first reported in black females in 1995, and at the time, an increase in the prevalence of eating disorders was noted, particularly among sections of the population that espouse Western values (Delport & Szabo, 2008; Szabo, 1998). However, the current South African prevalence of eating disorders is not known due to the lack of follow-up and epidemiological research (Revelas, 2013).

A defining aspect of anorexia and bulimia nervosa is that these disorders seem to be highly population specific. Initially, these disorders appeared to be almost exclusive to young females and to Western groups (or groups that have assimilated Western values). However, the idea that the eating disorders are exclusive to Western groups is not supported by data (Lake, Staiger, & Glowinski, 2000). Nevertheless, these disorders seem to have a very strong sociocultural aetiological component (Revelas, 2013).

Data that includes the entire age span puts the gender ratio at between 1:29 and 1:10 of male to female, but small-scale studies of clinical populations of children suggest that as many as 19%–30% are boys (Wenar & Kerig, 2006). People from a higher socio-economic class were also thought to be more at risk; however, more recent research suggests that the spread of eating disorder symptoms is relatively equal across socio-economic status levels (Mulders-Jones, Mitchison, Girosi, & Hay, 2017).

The eating disorders and obesity have a significant impact on human life and well-being. All the eating disorders are associated with an increased mortality risk, with the mortality rate for anorexia nervosa being the highest of all the psychological disorders (Miller & Golden, 2010; Smink et al., 2012). A woman with anorexia nervosa is twelve times more likely to die than a woman of the same age in the general population without anorexia nervosa (Miller & Golden, 2010). The mortality rates for anorexia nervosa are between 5% and 18%, while obesity is associated with increased morbidity and mortality (Kaplan et al., 1994; Schwartz & Brownell, 2007).

HISTORY OF EATING DISORDERS

The first case descriptions of self-starvation were documented in the second half of the seventeenth century. An 18-year-old English girl by the name of Martha Taylor was described by John Reynolds, an English doctor who visited her on behalf of the Royal Society. She refused all solid food, had stopped menstruating, and became emaciated. Reynolds wrote at that time that most young women who fell into this state were between 14 and 20 years of age; this implies that the condition was known even then. At about the same time, Richard

Morton, a 17th-century English physician, described two cases with symptoms typical of anorexia nervosa, and distinguished them from consumptive disease (tuberculosis) (Halmi, 2000; Treasure, 2013).

In France, in the nineteenth century, French psychiatrist Louis-Victor Marcé described cases of 'young girls' who carried their refusal to eat to 'the utmost limits' (Halmi, 2000). In 1873, two papers were published virtually simultaneously by British physician William Gull and French neuropsychiatrist Ernest Charles Lasèque, discussing the description and treatment of 'hysterical anorexia'. Common usage of the term 'anorexia nervosa' arose after the publication of Gull's work (Halmi, 2000; Vandereycken & Van Deth, 1989).

In the early twentieth century, pituitary insufficiency and anorexia nervosa were confused with one another. The pituitary gland and the hypothalamus are brain areas involved in the control of eating behaviour. Destruction of these areas results in emaciation and starvation (Kaplan et al., 1994). However, endocrine studies, together with the clinical histories and psychological descriptions of anorexia nervosa, showed pituitary insufficiency and anorexia nervosa to be different disorders (Halmi, 2000).

By the 1950s, Hilde Bruch, a German-American psychoanalyst, described the central psychological aspect of anorexia nervosa as a sense of inadequacy that pervades the person's behaviour and cognition. She also described methods for intervening in the cognitive processes of these patients, creating a foundation for cognitive therapy with this disorder (Halmi, 2000; Skårderud, 2009).

Bulimia nervosa was first described as a distinct syndrome in 1979 by British psychiatrist, Gerald Russell (Halmi, 2000; Vandereycken, 2002) and was first recognised as a disorder in 1980 in the DSM-III (American Psychiatric Association, 1980).

Although night-eating syndrome and binge eating were both first described in the 1950s by Albert Stunkard, an American psychiatrist who pioneered obesity research, psychiatry has been concerned with eating and overeating since the middle of the 19th century, when it viewed dietary moderation as essential to mental well-being and overeating as a moral shortcoming (Allison, Lundgren, & Wadden, 2016; Occhiogrosso, 2008). By the early 20th century, this view gave way to descriptions of neurological and psychiatric conditions associated with overeating, such as frontal lobe impairment and schizophrenia. During this time, influenced by Freudian psychoanalysis, overeating was portrayed as 'excessive orality' (Occhiogrosso, 2008, p. 270). The 1970s and 1980s saw increased focus on overeating symptoms, and binge eating was first mentioned in the DSM in 1987 as a feature of bulimia nervosa. Binge eating was included as a possible feature of 'eating disorder not otherwise specified' in DSM-IV in 1994, while binge-eating disorder was included as a disorder in DSM-5 in 2013 (American Psychiatric Association, 2013; Occhiogrosso, 2008).

In Africa, there was not a focus on eating disorders until the end of the 1900s. In 1988 the Nigerian psychiatrist Oluwole Famuyiwa wrote about anorexia nervosa that: 'The relatively low prevalence of the disorder that has been observed might be due to: the protective influence of the Nigerian extended kinship system, the customary passion for plumpness as an attribute of physical attractiveness, carbohydrate diet "resistance" and the non-inclusion of cases in hospital records because of consultation with unorthodox healers' (p. 550). However, he also said that the 'general trend of increasing prevalence calls for more diagnostic vigilance' in developing countries (Famuyiwa, 1988, p. 550).

This vigilance was observed by researchers in both Kenya and Nigeria. In 2004, the

Kenyan psychiatrists Frank Njenga and Rachel Kengethe stated, on the basis of their research, that 'anorexia nervosa is a rare disorder in Africa' (p. 188). However, in 2017 the Nigerian researcher Betty-Ruth Iruloh noted that both anorexia nervosa and binge eating occurred amongst Nigerian university students, and called for parents, educational institutions, and the government to 'wake up to their responsibilities' to teach about eating disorders (Iruloh, 2017, p. 76).

TYPES OF FEEDING AND EATING DISORDERS

In this section, we will be exploring all the disorders that are characterised by a persistent disturbance of eating, or eating-related behaviours, that impact on physical health and/ or psychosocial functioning. The epidemiology of the first three disorders is relatively unknown. Avoidant/restrictive food intake disorder is newly defined in the DSM-5 and is speculated to be the most common of the feeding disorders (Hoek, 2017).

Pica

This disorder typically has a childhood onset, but may occur during childhood, adolescence or adulthood. The essential feature of the disorder is the eating of one or more non-nutritional or non-food substances (e.g. soil, paper, chalk, etc.). The non-nutritional substances that are eaten must be developmentally and culturally inappropriate; typically, there is no aversion to normal or healthy food (American Psychiatric Association, 2013). One would not diagnose this disorder before the age of two years, as children before this age often eat non-food substances as part of their exploration of their world. This disorder is often associated with other mental disorders such as intellectual disabilities, autism spectrum disorders or schizophrenia (American Psychiatric Association, 2013).

Rumination disorder

Rumination disorder may occur at any stage of human development, but the onset is usually between the ages of 3 and 12 months. It is characterised by the repeated regurgitation of food after feeding or eating which is characterised by previously digested or swallowed food being brought up into the mouth. This occurs in the absence of nausea, retching or disgust, and is not due to any identifiable medical reason. Although the disorder frequently remits spontaneously it may, in severe cases result in medical emergencies and may even be fatal, especially during infancy (American Psychiatric Association, 2013). As with pica, rumination disorder occurs more frequently in association with intellectual disability (Hoek, 2017).

Avoidant/restrictive food intake disorder

This disorder usually develops in infancy or early childhood; it may persist into adulthood. The main diagnostic feature is the avoidance, or restriction, of food intake to such an extent that healthy nutritional requirements are not met (American Psychiatric Association, 2013).

The key features of this disorder include (American Psychiatric Association, 2013, p. 334):
- Significant weight loss
- Significant nutritional deficiency
- Dependence on enteral feeding or nutritional supplements
- Marked interference with psychosocial functioning.

The symptoms of this disorder occur in the absence of any clear medical reasons, cultural practices or excessive concern about body weight. It seems as if in many cases the restriction may be based on the characteristics of food such as appearance, colour, smell, texture or taste. Given that the restriction may be due to the sensory characteristics of food, it should not come as a surprise that it is often associated with disorders, such as autism, where heightened sensory sensitivities are a characteristic (American Psychiatric Association, 2013). The DSM-5 (American Psychiatric Association, 2013) suggests that the food restriction may present differently during different developmental stages. For instance, very young infants may appear too sleepy, agitated or distressed to feed, whereas infants and young children may not engage with their caregiver around feeding and hunger, or may be distracted by other activities. In older children and adolescents, general emotional problems that do not meet the diagnostic criteria for anxiety or mood disorders may be related to the avoidance or restriction of food intake (American Psychiatric Association, 2013).

Anorexia nervosa

Prevalence and course

The DSM-5 describes the prevalence of anorexia nervosa as about 0.4% among females, while the prevalence among males appears to be in the vicinity of one-tenth of that in females (American Psychiatric Association, 2013).

The incidence of anorexia nervosa has been increasing since the 1930s and studies from different Western countries have reiterated this trend (Halmi, 2000; Hoek, 2017; Jones, Fox, Babigan, & Hutton, 1980; Lucas, Beard, O'Fallon, & Kurlan, 1991; Willi & Grossman, 1983). However, recent studies suggest that the incidence of anorexia nervosa has stabilised in past decades, with the possible exception of the so-called high-risk cohort of females between the ages of 15 and 19 years. It has been speculated that this pattern could be ascribed to either an earlier age of onset or to early diagnosis (Micali et al., 2013; Smink et al., 2012).

The onset of anorexia nervosa is usually during adolescence or early adulthood. Onset may be associated with a life stressor, and onset after 40 years of age appears to be rare (American Psychiatric Association, 2013). In terms of course and outcome, a high degree of variability appears to characterise anorexia nervosa. In many individuals, a period of altered eating behaviour may precede meeting the full anorexia nervosa criteria. Some individuals make a full recovery subsequent to one episode; others exhibit a pattern of weight gain and relapse, while for a third group, the course appears to be chronic over many years (American Psychiatric Association, 2013).

The eating disorders are notable for the great deal of diagnostic overlap that occurs between categories of disorder. Miller and Golden (2010) estimate that 30% of patients with a diagnosis of anorexia nervosa on intake will cross over to bulimia nervosa, but are also likely to relapse into anorexia nervosa. A smaller group (about 14%) are likely to cross over from an intake diagnosis of bulimia nervosa to anorexia nervosa.

While anorexia nervosa will remit within five years of first presentation in most individuals, hospitalisation may be necessary to restore weight and to treat medical complications. Overall remission rates may be lower for individuals with a history of hospitalisation (American Psychiatric Association, 2013).

While the DSM-5 rates long-term mortality associated with anorexia nervosa as about 5%, due to medical complications or suicide, some studies indicate that this figure may be as high as 20% (American Psychiatric Association, 2013; Ratnasuriya, Eisler, Szmukler, & Russell, 1991). Suicide accounts for up to half of these mortalities (Agras, 1987).

Specific cultural, gender, and age features

The eating disorders are arguably the group of disorders where age, culture, and gender features come together in the most obviously significant way. The occurrence of anorexia nervosa is almost exclusively in females (approximately 90%). It is most prevalent in post-industrialised and high-income countries, and in cultures and settings where high value is placed on thinness; however, there is uncertainty about incidence in low- and middle-income countries (American Psychiatric Association, 2013).

Clinical picture

The term 'anorexia nervosa' means 'nervous loss of appetite'. It is distinguished by three core criteria, namely: (1) persistent restriction of energy intake; (2) a great fear of becoming fat; and (3) disturbance in self-perception of body shape or size (American Psychiatric Association, 2013; Halmi, 2000).

Table 13.1: Diagnostic criteria for anorexia nervosa from the DSM-5 and the ICD-10

DSM-5	ICD-10
A. Restriction of energy intake relative to requirements, leading to a *significantly low body weight* in context of age, sex, developmental trajectory, and physical health. Significantly low weight is defined as weight that is less than minimally normal or, for children and adolescents, less than that minimally expected. B. Intense fear of gaining weight or of becoming fat, or persistent behaviour that interferes with weight gain, even though at a significantly low weight.	■ For a definite diagnosis, all of the following are required: ▸ Body weight is maintained at least 15% below that expected (either lost or never achieved), or Quetelet's body-mass index is 17.5 or less. Prepubertal patients may show failure to make the expected weight gain during the period of growth. ▸ The weight loss is self-induced by avoidance of 'fattening foods' and one or more of the following: self-induced vomiting; self-induced purging; excessive exercise; use of appetite suppressants and/or diuretics. ▸ There is body-image distortion in the form of a specific psychopathology whereby a dread of fatness persists as an intrusive, over-valued idea and the patient imposes a low weight threshold on himself or herself.

DSM-5	ICD-10
C. Disturbance in the way in which one's body weight or shape is experienced, undue influence of body weight or shape on self-evaluation, or persistent lack of recognition of the seriousness of the current low body weight.	▸ A widespread endocrine disorder involving the hypothalamic-pituitary-gonadal axis is manifest in women as amenorrhoea and in men as a loss of sexual interest and potency. (An apparent exception is the persistence of vaginal bleeds in anorexic women who are receiving replacement hormonal therapy, most commonly taken as a contraceptive pill.) There may also be elevated levels of growth hormone, raised levels of cortisol, changes in the peripheral metabolism of the thyroid hormone, and abnormalities of insulin secretion. ▸ If onset is prepubertal, the sequence of pubertal events is delayed or even arrested (growth ceases; in girls the breasts do not develop and there is a primary amenorrhoea; in boys the genitals remain juvenile). With recovery, puberty is often completed normally, but the menarche is late.

Source: Reprinted with permission from the *Diagnostic and Statistical Manual of Mental Disorders*, fifth edition (DSM-5), American Psychiatric Association (APA), 2013, p. 338, and the ICD-10 *Classification of Mental and Behavioural Disorders: Diagnostic Criteria for Research*, World Health Organization (WHO), Geneva, 2007.

EXAMPLE CASE

Mary is a fifteen-year-old girl who is currently an inpatient in a private hospital that has a special unit for the treatment of eating disorders. Mary was admitted to the unit urgently because her body weight had dropped to dangerously low levels. At the time of her admission, Mary was a promising ballet dancer, who was planning to make this her career.

It transpired that Mary was severely restricting her intake of food. She was allowing herself half a can of creamed corn every second day. Mary was proud of her ability to control her appetite. Although an attractive girl, Mary's problems with eating and weight were affecting her appearance. Her hair was dull and thinning. She wore several layers of shapeless clothing, and she always seemed to be cold. Mary's skin was also dull and breaking out in a rash. Mary was painfully thin. She admitted that she might be a little underweight, but the staff at the unit had the feeling that she was just saying this to pacify them. While being in the unit, Mary got into trouble several times for breaking the unit rules. Once, she was found in the bathroom drinking a lot of water before she was due to be weighed, and on another occasion, she was discovered quietly doing push-ups in her room in the middle of the night.

Mary's treatment was complicated by the fact that the staff on the unit were at their wits' end about how to deal with Mary's mother. Mary's mother was extremely demanding with all the staff members on the unit. She repeatedly told the treating team that she loved her daughter and had her best interests at heart. According to Mary's mother, she knew exactly what was best for Mary. Her mother felt that Mary had to get back to ballet as soon as possible, because she was such a gifted dancer. This meant that she had to gain some weight so that she could be discharged and attend ballet practice with a top teacher. Mary's mother once showed the team a picture of the cabinet that she had specially ordered for all her daughter's awards. Mary's mother regularly telephoned Mary's psychotherapist after sessions to tell the therapist what Mary had thought of the session, and to inform the therapist whether it had been a useful session or not. Her mother also insisted on attending all Mary's consultations with the dietician. The treatment team never met Mary's father, who frequently worked away from home. He had a high-paying job which supported the family's very comfortable lifestyle. The treatment team got the impression that the relationship between Mary's parents was strained, but this was never openly acknowledged. Mary's mother described their family as loving, caring, and 'very close'.

Mary had a sister who was three years younger. Both girls were being home-schooled by their mother at the time of Mary's admission. All of the family members claimed that an extremely positive and close relationship existed between Mary and her sister. Mary's sister accompanied her mother on most visits to the unit. On two occasions, they were dressed in very similar outfits.

During a session with her therapist, Mary said that Victoria Beckham was her idol. She also stated that her problem with eating started during a gymnastics practice session three years ago when her instructor told her that she was three kilograms overweight, and that she had to lose the weight before the next practice session in four days' time, if she wanted to be any good at the sport at all.

Criterion A specifies that body weight is significantly low. In adults this is below minimum normal weight in terms of the individual's sex, age, and physical health, whereas in children and adolescents, weight is less than the minimum expected in terms of their developmental trajectory. In adults, sustaining a low body weight (Criterion A) is often noted after a period of significant weight loss, but in children and adolescents, there may be a failure to make weight gains expected in relation to their growth and physical development, for instance weight maintenance despite growing in height. Gauging the significance of an individual's weight may be complicated by the range of normal weight and by conflicting published definitions of thinness. The DSM-5 recommends using Body Mass Index (BMI) to determine thinness in conjunction with physiological indicators and clinical history. BMI is calculated as weight in kilograms/height in metres^2. In adults, a BMI of between $17 \, kg/m^2$ and $18.5 \, kg/m^2$ may be rated as significantly low, while BMI-for-age below the 5th percentile in children and adolescents is usually considered to be underweight. Both clinical information (build, history, and the presence of physiological disturbance) and numerical indicators should be used in the assessment of Criterion A (American Psychiatric Association, 2013).

The intense fear of weight gain or 'becoming fat' experienced by these individuals (Criterion B) continues despite successful weight loss, and may increase in intensity even as weight decreases. Fear of gaining weight may not be recognised or acknowledged by younger persons or by some adults, and may have to be deduced from clinical information such as observation, collateral history, physical and laboratory findings, and course of weight loss over time (American Psychiatric Association, 2013).

The self-esteem of individuals diagnosed with anorexia nervosa depends greatly upon their weight and body shape. Their experience of their own body shape is typically unrealistic, in that they invariably see themselves as 'fat', even when they appear very thin to an objective observer (Criterion C). They also tend to have unrealistic views about the significance of weight fluctuations. Weight loss is regarded as a great achievement, while weight gain is seen as unacceptable and a loss of self-control (American Psychiatric Association, 2013).

Denial and lack of insight are often associated with a diagnosis of anorexia nervosa. People with this diagnosis may verbalise an acknowledgement of being too thin, but do not believe this within themselves. They often deny the medical consequences of their state of starvation. Indeed, people with a diagnosis of anorexia nervosa seldom seek help or medical attention of their own accord, and seldom complain of weight loss. It is more likely that pressure from family will bring the person to seek medical help.

The person with anorexia nervosa may be unreliable when it comes to the history of the problem, and it is advisable for practitioners to obtain collateral information (Agras, 1987; American Psychiatric Association, 2013). The 'lack of insight' associated with anorexia nervosa can also be seen in the phenomenon of 'pro-ana' websites, discussed later in this chapter.

In the case of Mary described above, she restricted her food intake to just half a can of creamed corn per day. She also used restricting behaviours in that she exercised in the middle of the night. In the case study, Mary appears to lack insight into her condition, since she violates rules designed to help her gain weight, and she attempts to deceive unit staff into thinking that she has gained weight, which was not the case.

Serious medical conditions that have the potential to be life threatening can arise as a result of starvation, and these features are associated with anorexia nervosa. Most major organ systems are potentially compromised by the nutritional deficits caused by starvation, and signs of physical abnormalities such as compromised vital signs and cessation of menstruation (amenorrhea) are often found (American Psychiatric Association, 2013).

Undernutrition and very low body weight are associated with depressive and obsessive-compulsive symptoms in persons with anorexia nervosa. Depressive symptoms such as low mood, social withdrawal, increased irritability, sleep difficulties, and decreased interest in sex may arise as a physiological consequence of semi-starvation, but may also be severe enough to result in the diagnosis of major depressive disorder (American Psychiatric Association, 2013).

Obsessive-compulsive features either related or unrelated to food are often noted. Preoccupations and symptoms that are food related, such as hoarding food, collecting recipes, and thinking constantly of food and cooking may be worsened by nutrition deficits. Obsessive-compulsive signs and symptoms unrelated to food, weight, and body shape could warrant an added diagnosis of obsessive-compulsive disorder (American Psychiatric Association, 2013).

Other aspects associated with anorexia nervosa include a strong need for control and perfectionism, issues relating to eating in public, a rigid thinking style, feelings of being ineffective, as well as limited social and emotional expressiveness (American Psychiatric Association, 2013). Some of these personality aspects are illustrated in the case study of Eva.

EXAMPLE CASE

Eva is an attractive woman in her early forties. She takes care of her appearance, even though she looks too thin. When Eva was in her mid-teens, she was diagnosed with anorexia nervosa. Eva denies that she is currently anorexic; however, she continues to exhibit some of the behaviours associated with this condition. Eva works seven days a week, even though her job as an estate agent is not that demanding. She insists on doing everything perfectly and spends long hours in the office to achieve this. Eva's hobby is cake-baking and decorating. She even gets special requests for functions and parties. Eva has many acquaintances, but few friends. Eva has never been married and is not in a relationship currently. She claims that her single status is due to the fact that she is only attracted to tall, blue-eyed men between the ages of 20 and 30 years.

Anorexia nervosa subtypes

The DSM-5 describes two subtypes of anorexia nervosa: restricting type and binge-eating/purging type. These subtypes are identified according to the presence or absence of binge-eating and purging behaviour during an episode of anorexia nervosa (American Psychiatric Association, 2013).

Restricting type

Weight loss in this subtype is typically achieved by means of restricting food intake or engaging in excessive exercise. Binge-eating or purging behaviour has not been present in the three months preceding the current episode (American Psychiatric Association, 2013).

Binge-eating/purging type

This subtype is characterised by the use of purging techniques such as self-induced vomiting, the use of laxatives (medication that relieves constipation), diuretics (medication that increases the frequency of urination so that the body loses fluids), or enemas, subsequent to ingesting any amount of food; these behaviours have has been present during the previous three months (American Psychiatric Association, 2013).

BOX 13.1: ANOREXIA NERVOSA IN KENYA

In 2004, the Kenyan psychiatrists Frank Njenga and Rachel Kengethe published a study on anorexia nervosa in Kenya because emerging evidence was suggesting 'a real lack of occurrence' in Africa, despite the problem that it presented in the West.

The article was based on a series of interviews undertaken in 2001, where 26 psychiatrists practicing in Kenya were interviewed and asked if they had ever dealt with cases of anorexia nervosa in Kenya. The respondents had dealt with a total of thirteen cases. Of these, six patients were 'Asians' or 'Caucasians', who made up 'no more than 0.25% of the Kenyan population', while only seven of the patients were 'Africans'.

Njenga and Kengethe (2004) investigated the abilities of the psychiatrists in the study to diagnose anorexia nervosa and concluded that, '[t]here is no doubt that Kenyan psychiatrists were well able to recognise the disorder' (p. 193). Njenga and Kengethe (2004) concluded that 'anorexia nervosa is indeed rare in Kenya, despite an increasing degree of Westernisation in urban areas' (p. 193).

Nevertheless, Njenga and Kengethe (2004) also recorded the following disturbing information: '[t]wenty-five percent of the patients did not receive any treatment after the diagnosis. The psychiatrists did not feel they could help this type of patient' (p. 191).

Source: Based on information in Njenga & Kangethe, 2004.

Bulimia nervosa

EXAMPLE CASE

Sindi is a 19-year-old student who presented at the student counselling centre of the large university where she is a first-year student in the Commerce faculty. She is a pretty girl of slightly above average weight. The problems that she describes to her counsellor are a low mood, feelings of self-disgust, and being out of control. Sindi describes herself as 'fat, worthless, and pathetic'.

Sindi confides in her counsellor that she has problems in maintaining her weight. She has picked up a lot of weight since the beginning of her first year at university. Sindi discloses to her counsellor that she sometimes resorts to self-induced vomiting in order to control her weight.

Sindi describes her introduction to university life as a shock. She initially experienced being away from home as very difficult, but she describes the situation back at home as problematic. She says that she often feels guilty because she has left her two younger siblings to cope on their own. Sindi's mother suffers from bipolar disorder, and her mood sometimes affects her ability to cope with the two younger children. Sindi's father tries his best, but he just can't stand up to her mother when she gets 'into one of her states'.

Sindi describes her pattern of eating and vomiting as occurring more and more often. Sometimes food is all she can think about. She spends large amounts of money on junk food such as ice cream, cakes, and burgers. She usually can't wait to get to her room so that she can eat all the food at once. She then induces vomiting to get rid of the large amount of food that she has consumed. After this she weighs herself to make sure that she hasn't gained any weight from her session of overeating.

Prevalence and course

Bulimia nervosa appears to exhibit a prevalence of approximately 1%–1.5% of females in industrialised countries, while the prevalence among males appears to be one-tenth of that in females (American Psychiatric Association, 2013; Halmi, 2000). Smink et al. (2012) suggest that the occurrence of bulimia nervosa may have been declining since the early 1990s.

The course of bulimia nervosa typically has its onset in late adolescence or early adulthood, often during or after a period of dieting, and may be triggered by an accumulation of stressful life events (American Psychiatric Association, 2013). The pattern of disturbed eating appears to be maintained for several years. The course could either be chronic or could be marked by remissions and relapses into binge-eating behaviour. Over the longer term, the symptoms appear to resolve to an extent. Remissions of a year or longer appear indicative of a better long-term prognosis (American Psychiatric Association, 2013). There appears to be some potential for diagnostic crossover from bulimia nervosa into anorexia nervosa (in about 10–15% of cases), and into binge-eating disorder in individuals who continue to engage in binge eating in the absence of compensatory behaviours (American Psychiatric Association, 2013).

Specific culture- and gender-related diagnostic issues

The incidence of bulimia nervosa appears to be similar for most industrialised countries. As with anorexia nervosa, at least 90% of cases are female. In addition, as with anorexia nervosa, the group in which this disorder occurs appears to be mainly white, although cases from other ethnic groups have been reported (American Psychiatric Association, 2013).

In terms of specific culture-related issues, the historical conceptualisation has been that young, Caucasian, high-income females are at a greater risk of developing anorexia nervosa or bulimia nervosa, or both (Pike, Hoek, & Dunne, 2014). However, the cultural backdrop of the eating disorders, and bulimia nervosa in particular, may be shifting. This is suggested by apparently decreasing bulimia nervosa incidence rates in Caucasian North American and Northern European groups and increasing bulimia nervosa rates in North American in Hispanic and black American groups (Pike et al., 2014).

Clinical picture

The literal translation of 'bulimia' is 'ox hunger', which means any great, ravenous hunger; the term refers to the binging behaviour associated with this disorder (Ambrose & Deisler, 2010). The three pivotal aspects of the diagnosis of bulimia nervosa can be described as: (i) recurrent episodes of overeating or 'binging'; (ii) evading weight gain by means of compensatory behaviours such as self-induced vomiting and/or purgative use; and (iii) self-evaluation that overemphasises body weight and shape (American Psychiatric Association, 2013). The use of purgatives could include abusing laxatives or diuretics.

A binge can be defined as eating an amount of food that is more than most people would eat in a similar situation, in a restricted period of time (typically less than two hours) (American Psychiatric Association, 2013; Vitousek & Gray, 2005). In addition, the eating behaviour is out of control during a binging episode, typified as being unable to stop eating once one has started (American Psychiatric Association, 2013). In the early stages of this disorder, the lack of control may manifest as ravenous eating. As the disorder progresses, a lack of control of behaviour, such as irresistible impulses to binge or inability to stop the course of the binge, appear to become evident. Some individuals report dissociative experiences as part of the binge-eating episode, as well as during the post-binge period (American Psychiatric Association, 2013).

Binge eating is most commonly triggered by an experience of negative affect, but may also be preceded by interpersonal stressors, negativity around body shape, weight or food, dieting behaviour or boredom. Binge-eating episodes are typically concealed, as individuals with bulimia nervosa often feel shame related to their difficulties with eating. The kind of food eaten during binging varies greatly between individuals and between individual episodes, but often involves food that would otherwise be avoided. The binge eating typically stops only once the individual is full to the point of discomfort or pain. The binge-eating episodes often have the short-term effect of alleviating the feelings associated with the triggers, but later consequences are emotional discomfort and negative self-evaluation (American Psychiatric Association, 2013).

The inappropriate compensatory behaviours to avoid gaining weight involve purging, most commonly by means of self-induced vomiting, although laxative, diuretic, insulin or thyroid hormone misuse, enemas, fasting or excessive exercise may also be employed. Some individuals utilise more than one purging technique. The vomiting behaviour typically has the effect of immediately relieving the physical discomfort and fear of weight gain, and this relief becomes a goal in itself in some cases. In some individuals, vomiting occurs even after a small amount of food has been consumed (American Psychiatric Association, 2013).

Table 13.2: Diagnostic criteria for bulimia nervosa from the DSM-5 and the ICD-10

DSM-5	ICD-10
A. Recurrent episodes of binge eating. An episode of binge eating is characterised by both of the following: (1) Eating, in a discrete period of time (e.g. within any two-hour period), an amount of food that is definitely larger than what most individuals would eat in a similar period of time under similar circumstances. (2) A sense of lack of control over eating during the episode (e.g. a feeling that one cannot stop eating or control what or how much one is eating). B. Recurrent inappropriate compensatory behaviours in order to prevent weight gain, such as self-induced vomiting; misuse of laxatives, diuretics, or other medications; fasting; or excessive exercise.	■ For a definite diagnosis, all of the following are required: ▸ There is a persistent preoccupation with eating, and an irresistible craving for food; the patient succumbs to episodes of overeating in which large amounts of food are consumed in short periods of time. ▸ The patient attempts to counteract the 'fattening' effects of food by one or more of the following: self-induced vomiting; purgative abuse, alternating periods of starvation; use of drugs such as appetite suppressants, thyroid preparations or diuretics. When bulimia occurs in diabetic patients they may choose to neglect their insulin treatment.

DSM-5	ICD-10
C. The binge eating and inappropriate compensatory behaviours both occur, on average, at least once a week for three months. D. Self-evaluation is unduly influenced by body shape and weight. E. The disturbance does not occur exclusively during episodes of anorexia nervosa.	▸ The psychopathology consists of a morbid dread of fatness and the patient sets herself or himself a sharply defined weight threshold, well below the premorbid weight that constitutes the optimum or healthy weight in the opinion of the physician. There is often, but not always, a history of an earlier episode of anorexia nervosa, the interval between the two disorders ranging from a few months to several years. This earlier episode may have been fully expressed, or may have assumed a minor cryptic form with a moderate loss of weight and/or a transient phase of amenorrhoea.

Source: Reprinted with permission from the *Diagnostic and Statistical Manual of Mental Disorders*, fifth edition (DSM-5), American Psychiatric Association (APA), 2013, p. 345, and the ICD-10 *Classification of Mental and Behavioural Disorders: Diagnostic Criteria for Research*, World Health Organization (WHO), Geneva, 2007.

In terms of impact on body weight, purging is not an effective way in which to restrict the intake of calories, since vomiting results in a reduction of only about 50% of calories consumed, while laxative use has very little impact on weight (Kaye, Weltzin, Hsu, McConaha, & Bolton 1993). People with a diagnosis of bulimia nervosa are usually within the range of normal weight to overweight. Individuals diagnosed with bulimia nervosa appear to tend to restrict their food intake ('diet') between binges and thus avoid food that they regard as 'fattening' or that is likely to trigger a binging episode (American Psychiatric Association, 2013).

In the case of Sindi, she is described as being slightly overweight and she overemphasises the aspects of weight and appearance when describing herself to her counsellor. Binging behaviour is present in her buying large amounts of junk food and consuming it in a short period of time. Sindi vomits to purge herself of the food, and her fear of gaining weight is illustrated by her weighing herself after every binging and purging session.

Features associated with bulimia nervosa are potentially serious medical consequences such as fluid and electrolyte imbalances. Gastrointestinal symptoms are common, and frequent laxative abuse can lead to intestinal problems such as permanent colon damage or severe constipation. Tearing of the oesophagus or the stomach and heart arrhythmias are rare, but potentially deadly, medical problems that may result from purging behaviours.

Amenorrhea or menstrual irregularity is common in females with bulimia nervosa, although it remains unclear whether this is caused by fluctuating weight, nutritional deficiency or psychological distress. Diagnostic markers include enlarged salivary glands in chronic bulimia nervosa (which, ironically, result in a 'chubby' facial appearance) and electrolyte imbalances. With vomiting, the dental enamel of the teeth may be eroded, and calluses on the fingers or backs of the hands may develop as a result of stimulating the gag reflex (American Psychiatric Association, 2013).

The presence of a wide range of comorbid conditions is common, and these include increased mood and anxiety symptoms. There is also an increased likelihood of substance abuse or dependence involving alcohol or stimulants (used to suppress appetite). A significant number of people (between 28% and 77%) diagnosed with bulimia nervosa meet the criteria for one of the personality disorders, most frequently borderline personality disorder (American Psychiatric Association, 2013; Halmi, 2000).

Table 13.3: Comparison of eating disorders

ANOREXIA NERVOSA	BULIMIA NERVOSA	BINGE-EATING DISORDER
Age of onset: 14	Age of onset: 18	Age of onset: early 20s
Excessive thinness	Average or overweight	Overweight or obese
Disturbance In body Image	Self-evaluation unduly impacted by weight	Self-evaluation unduly impacted by weight
Amenorrhea	Normal menstruation	Normal menstruation
Voluntary food restriction, binging and purging in binge-eating/purging subtype	Binging and purging	Binging
Family enmeshment, rigid, overprotective, poor conflict resolution	Family history of psychological problems, substance abuse, family discord, overt hostility	Mothers show less warmth and higher expressed emotion, over-involvement and criticism (Schmidt, Tetzlaff, & Hilbert, 2015).
Not interested in sex	Sexually active with little enjoyment	Lower frequency, lower enjoyment than controls (Castellini et al., 2010)
Over-controlled	Emotionally labile	Emotional dysregulation, avoidance of negative emotion (Leehr et al., 2015)
Comorbid with depression and anxiety disorders (including social phobia and OCD)	Comorbid with depression, anxiety, substance abuse, and personality disorders	Comorbid with bipolar, depressive, anxiety and to lesser degree, substance abuse disorders (American Psychiatric Association, 2013)
Maternal history of anorexia	Family history of obesity	Family history of binge-eating disorder and obesity (Lydecker & Grilo, 2017)
Ego-syntonic	Ego-dystonic	Ego-dystonic

Source: Information on anorexia nervosa and bulimia nervosa adapted from Wenar & Kerig, 2006, p. 378.

Binge-eating disorder

Binge-eating disorder (BED) is characterised by episodes of binge eating that cause significant distress for the individual, but the person does not engage in compensatory behaviours. This disorder was included in the DSM-5 as a new disorder.

> **EXAMPLE CASE**
>
> *Simone is a 48-year-old woman who presented for treatment at a specialised ward for eating disorders. She is visibly overweight, but very well groomed and well dressed. Simone has risen through the ranks to the position of manager at her place of employment where she started as an administrative assistant 13 years ago. She also takes excellent care of her husband, her two primary-school daughters from her previous marriage, and her elderly parents who live with her. Her husband works abroad and is home infrequently. Simone describes spending large amounts of money on food or snacks, which she consumes in her car after work. She says this usually happens on her way home from a busy day at work when she feels guilty because she knows that her children need her at home to help them with their homework and to prepare the evening meal. She then stops off at an expensive shop to buy the food or snacks (doughnuts are her favourite). Simone then eats all the food or snacks while parked in the parking lot. She does this very fast and is terrified that someone might notice or recognise her. She then drives home, feeling devastated by guilt and remorse. What makes it worse is that her husband, when he is at home, comments on how much weight she has gained and complains that she is not physically attractive to him any more. Simone feels that he may leave her because of this. She is desperate not have another failed marriage and presented for treatment for this reason. Her episodes of binge eating became much worse after her husband decided to renew his work contract abroad for another five years.*

Prevalence and course

Binge-eating disorder is both the most common of the eating disorders and the most prevalent eating disorder among males (Guerdjikova, Mori, Casuto, & McElroy, 2017). The prevalence of binge-eating disorder is 1.6% of women and 0.8% of men over a 12-month period among adults in the United States. Both the gender ratio and the prevalence among diverse ethnic and minority groups appear more evenly distributed in binge-eating disorder. There is a greater prevalence of binge-eating disorder among people who require treatment for weight loss than in the general population (American Psychiatric Association, 2013).

Binge-eating disorder often has its onset in adolescence or young adulthood, but may also manifest later. Stice, Marti, and Rohde (2013) place the age of onset of binge-eating disorder at 18–20 years, about one to two years later than for anorexia and bulimia nervosa. There is little information available about the development of the disorder, but both episodic binge eating and loss-of-control eating may mark the prodromal phase of the eating disorders.

Binge-eating disorder appears to follow a similar course to bulimia nervosa and can continue into middle age, but may have higher remission rates than either anorexia nervosa or bulimia nervosa (American Psychiatric Association, 2013). In contrast to bulimia nervosa, where dieting behaviour precedes onset, dieting is common after the onset of binge-eating disorder. There seems to be little risk of crossover between binge-eating disorder and the other eating disorders (American Psychiatric Association, 2013; Guerdjikova, O'Melia, Mori, McCoy, & McElroy, 2012).

Comparisons between binge-eating disorder, anorexia nervosa, and bulimia nervosa have found a number of similarities. For example, for all three disorders, there is typically distress on the part of the 'sufferer', as well as a decrease in quality of life and a similar pattern of comorbidity. However, binge-eating disorder seems to be associated with an older age of onset, as well as with a greater prevalence in males than the other eating disorders. The course of binge-eating disorder is also distinctive. While anorexia nervosa and bulimia nervosa are characterised by frequent crossover between the two disorders during the course of the disturbance, binge-eating disorder appears less likely to shift in symptomology (Wonderlich, Gordon, Mitchell, Crosby, & Engel, 2009).

Table 13.4: Diagnostic criteria for binge-eating disorder from the DSM-5

DSM-5
A. Recurrent episodes of binge eating. An episode of binge eating is characterised by both of the following:
(1) Eating, in a discrete period of time (e.g. within any two-hour period), an amount of food that is definitely larger than what most individuals would eat in a similar period of time under similar circumstances.
(2) A sense of lack of control over eating during the episode (e.g. a feeling that one cannot stop eating or control what or how much one is eating).
B. The binge-eating episodes are associated with three (or more) of the following:
(1) Eating much more rapidly than normal.
(2) Eating until feeling uncomfortably full.
(3) Eating large amounts of food when not feeling physically hungry.
(4) Eating alone because of feeling embarrassed by how much one is eating.
(5) Feeling disgusted with oneself, depressed, or very guilty afterwards.
C. Marked distress regarding binge eating is present.
D. The binge eating occurs, on average, at least once a week for three months.
E. The binge eating is not associated with the recurrent use of inappropriate compensatory behaviour as in bulimia nervosa and does not occur exclusively during bulimia nervosa or anorexia nervosa.

Source: Reprinted with permission from the *Diagnostic and Statistical Manual of Mental Disorders*, fifth edition (DSM-5), American Psychiatric Association (APA), 2013, p. 350.

Clinical picture

Recurrent binge-eating episodes constitute the central aspect of binge-eating disorder, where a 'binge' is characterised by eating more food in a specified time period than most other people would eat in a similar situation and a simultaneous experience of the eating being out of control. The sense of lack of control is specified as the feeling of being unable to control eating or stop eating once started. The binge eating also has to be associated with at least three of the following experiences: eating significantly faster than usual, eating large amounts of food in the absence of hunger until uncomfortably full, and eating alone due to embarrassment about the amount of food consumed and feelings of self-disgust, depression or guilt afterwards.

The type of food eaten varies between individuals and between individual binge-eating episodes. As with bulimia nervosa, triggers are typically negative affective states, interpersonal stressors, dieting behaviour, negative self-evaluation of body weight or shape, negative feelings related to food or boredom, which may be briefly alleviated by the binging episode; the episode is typically followed by negative affective states and negative self-evaluation (American Psychiatric Association, 2013).

In the case study of Simone, the pattern of rapid eating is clearly present, as is the aspect of eating alone because of embarrassment, as well as the feelings of guilt after an episode of binging.

Features associated with binge-eating disorder are overweight and obesity, particularly in those who seek treatment. The distinction between binge-eating disorder and obesity should be noted, however. Individuals with obesity do not typically engage in a pattern of binge eating. Individuals with binge-eating disorder typically display higher functional impairment, lower quality of life, more subjective distress, and increased psychiatric comorbidity in comparison with those with obesity (American Psychiatric Association, 2013).

As with anorexia nervosa and bulimia nervosa, comorbidity commonly occurs with the personality disorders and the mood and anxiety disorders, and somewhat with the substance use disorders (American Psychiatric Association, 2013).

Summary of outcomes for anorexia nervosa over a six-year period

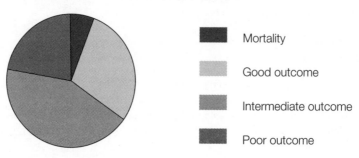

- Mortality
- Good outcome
- Intermediate outcome
- Poor outcome

Summary of outcomes for bulimia nervosa over a six-year period

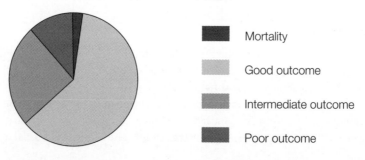

- Mortality
- Good outcome
- Intermediate outcome
- Poor outcome

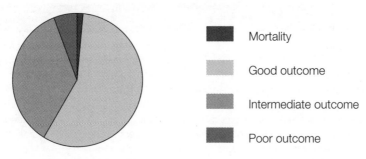

Summary of outcomes for binge-eating disorder over a six-year period

- Mortality
- Good outcome
- Intermediate outcome
- Poor outcome

Figure 13.4: Summary of outcomes for anorexia nervosa, bulimia nervosa and binge-eating disorder after a six-year follow-up

Source: Fichter & Quadflieg, 1997; 1999; Fichter, Quadflieg, & Gnutzmann, 1998.

Other specified feeding or eating disorder

The DSM-5 provides the category of 'Other specified feeding or eating disorder' for disordered eating that does not meet the full criteria of any of the feeding or eating disorders. Cases where all the criteria for anorexia nervosa are met, with the exception that the person's weight remains in the normal range despite significant weight loss, are diagnosed in this category as atypical anorexia nervosa. This diagnosis process also applies when all the criteria for bulimia nervosa are met, except the frequency or duration criteria (American Psychiatric Association, 2013).

Another disorder in this category is purging disorder, where a person displays recurrent purging behaviour, in the absence of binge eating, in order to influence body weight or shape (American Psychiatric Association, 2013). The last disorder in this category is referred to as night-eating syndrome, where a person either eats after awakening from sleep, or where the person continues to eat excessively after an evening meal (American Psychiatric Association, 2013).

The introduction of the 'Other specified feeding or eating disorder' category in DSM-5 as a replacement for the 'Eating disorder not otherwise specified' category has resulted in decreased reported prevalence of this category, compared to the previous catch-all diagnosis, which was a 'poorly defined and heterogeneous residual category representing the majority of DSM-IV ED cases' (Dahlgren, Wisting, & Rø, 2017, p. 56). However, since this new category does not include strict diagnostic criteria, researchers and clinicians are cautioned that they should diligently note the characteristics, particularly the significant distress and impairment component of the diagnosis, to avoid labelling an eating disturbance as an eating disorder (Dahlgren et al., 2017). The epidemiology, risk factors, and aetiology of this new category remain largely unknown. In the case of sub-threshold anorexia nervosa or bulimia nervosa, similar aetiological and risk factors as for the full diagnoses are likely to apply (Lock, La Via, & AACAP, 2015).

Table 13.5: Diagnostic criteria for Other specified feeding or eating disorder from the DSM-5

DSM-5
This category applies to presentations in which symptoms characteristic of a feeding and/or eating disorder that cause clinically significant distress or impairment in social, occupational, or other important areas of functioning predominate but do not meet the full criteria for any of the disorders in the feeding and eating disorders diagnostic class. The other specified feeding or eating disorder category is used in situations in which the clinician chooses to communicate the specific reason that the presentation does not meet the criteria for any specific feeding and eating disorder. This is done by recording 'other specified feeding and eating disorder' followed by the specific reason (e.g. 'bulimia nervosa of low frequency').

Examples of presentations that can be specified using the 'other specified' designation include the following:

1. **A typical anorexia nervosa:** All of the criteria for anorexia nervosa are met, except that, despite significant weight loss, the individual's weight is within or above the normal range.
2. **Bulimia nervosa (of low frequency and/or limited duration):** All of the criteria for bulimia nervosa are met, except that the binge eating and inappropriate compensatory behaviours occur, on average, less than once a week and/or for less than three months.
3. **Binge-eating disorder (of low frequency and/or limited duration):** All of the criteria for binge-eating disorder are met, except that the binge eating occurs, on average, less than once a week and/or for less than three months.
4. **Purging disorder:** Recurrent purging behaviour to influence weight or shape (e.g. self-induced vomiting; misuse of laxatives, diuretics, or other medications) in the absence of binge eating.
5. **Night-eating syndrome:** Recurrent episodes of night eating, as manifested by eating after awakening from sleep or by excessive food consumption after the evening meal. There is awareness and recall of the eating. The night eating is not better explained by external influences such as changes in the individual's sleep–wake cycle or by local social norms. The night eating causes significant distress and/or impairment in functioning. The disordered eating pattern is not better explained by binge-eating disorder or another mental disorder, including substance use, and is not attributable to another medical disorder or to an effect of medication.

Source: Reprinted with permission from the *Diagnostic and Statistical Manual of Mental Disorders*, fifth edition (DSM-5), American Psychiatric Association (APA), 2013, p. 353.

Unspecified feeding or eating disorder

The DSM-5 provides the category of unspecified feeding or eating disorder for disordered eating that does not meet the full criteria of an eating or feeding disorder, but that causes significant distress or impairment in social, occupational or other important areas of functioning. This category is often used in situations where insufficient information is available to the clinician to make a more specific diagnosis (American Psychiatric Association, 2013).

AETIOLOGY

Much debate exists about the kind of explanations applicable to the eating disorders, with biopsychiatric approaches emphasising the elements of personality and cognition that seem to spring from neural circuitry and/or genetics, whereas the sociocultural proponents focus on cultural aspects such as media and peer influences (Smolak & Levine, 2015). The relatively circumscribed prevalence rates in young, white, middle-class females from industrialised societies is suggestive of the sociocultural aspects that must be considered in the aetiology of these disorders. As in the case of other psychopathologies, it appears unlikely that a single causal factor can give rise to these disorders. Issues that will be considered in this discussion of the aetiology of the eating disorders include intrapersonal aspects such as genetics, biological and psychological functioning, as well as interpersonal considerations, such as cultural expectations, the changing role of women in Western society, the role of the media, and the impact of family dynamics.

Biological factors

In the past three decades, the biological underpinnings of the eating disorders have been increasingly emphasised, but understanding the biological bases of the eating disorders is still in its early stages (Lock & Le Grange, 2015; Madden et al., 2015). When considering the biological or medical dimensions in the aetiology of the eating disorders, two aspects are typically in the forefront. These are genetics and neurophysiological considerations.

Genetic factors

Relatively little is understood of the genetic component of the aetiology of the eating disorders (Lock & Le Grange, 2015). Approaches to investigating the genetic contribution to the development of the eating disorders include family studies, twin studies, molecular genetics and genome-wide association studies (Lock & Le Grange, 2015). Anorexia nervosa, bulimia nervosa, and binge-eating disorder appear to run in families. This is demonstrated in twin and adoption studies across a variety of populations and using a range of methods; these have found moderate-to-high heritability for these disorders (Culbert, Racine, & Klump, 2015).

Relatives of persons with eating disorders are four to five times more likely to develop an eating disorder than the general population (Strober, Freeman, Lampert, Diamond, & Kaye, 2000). Female family members of individuals with anorexia nervosa are 11 times more likely to be affected by anorexia nervosa themselves, and those who have a relative with anorexia nervosa or bulimia nervosa are more at risk for either disorder, indicating a possible genetic correlation between anorexia and bulimia nervosa (Yilmaz, Hardaway, & Bulik, 2015). In addition, twin studies have found significantly higher concordance rates for monozygotic than for dizygotic twins in both anorexia nervosa and bulimia nervosa (Fichter & Naegel, 1990; Holland, Hall, Murray, Russell, & Crisp, 1984; Kendler et al., 1991).

Although molecular genetic data has produced some promising results, no strong predisposing genes have been conclusively located to date from either genetic linkage studies or candidate gene studies (Mayhew, Pigeyre, Couturier, & Meyre, 2018). There have been no genome-wide association studies investigating either bulimia nervosa or binge-eating disorder, and the genome-wide association studies of anorexia nervosa were insufficient in sample size to yield significant findings (Baker, Janson, Trace, & Bulik, 2015).

Recently, the field of epigenetics has gripped public imagination. Health registry data linked the so-called Hunger Winter mass starvation of the population in occupied areas of the Netherlands in WW II with epidemiological information that documented the long-lasting and cross-generational effects of starvation on subsequent generations; for example, granddaughters of women who endured starvation tended to be heavier.

An explanation put forward for these effects is the epigenetic impact of starvation (Monosson, 2015). Epigenetics is 'the study of changes in organisms brought about by gene expression, rather than by alteration of the genetic code in the form of DNA' (Launer, 2016, p. 183). In anorexia nervosa, starvation is the kind of environmental condition likely to cause epigenetic changes (Mayhew et al., 2018). The best known epigenetic mechanism is DNA methylation (Launer, 2016). Mayhew and colleagues (2018) suggest that, taken as a whole, the available findings on changes in DNA methylation patterns in subjects with anorexia nervosa and bulimia nervosa point to effects on a range of behaviour- and affect-regulation systems, maintenance of body weight, and nutritional sensitivity, as possible pathways to development of eating disorders.

A general vulnerability to psychological difficulties associated with eating disorders is suggested by several studies. Genetic factors appear to play a role in the disordered eating behaviours and problematic eating attitudes that are typical of the eating disorders (Yilmaz et al., 2015). Rutherford, McGuffin, Katz, and Murray (1993) found genetic influences on eating attitudes in a normal female twin population. A greater frequency of mood disorders and anxiety disorders, specifically obsessive-compulsive disorder, was found in first-degree relatives of people diagnosed with eating disorders, when compared to first-degree relatives of the control participants (Halmi, 2000).

Similarly, there has been speculation about the nature of the heritable genetic predisposition to eating disorders. Researchers such as Hsu (1990) suggest that more general aspects of personality, such as poor impulse control and emotional instability, may constitute the heritable aspects involved in the causality of eating disorders. The implication is that an inherited disposition to react to any source of stress in a particular way represents the genetic vulnerability associated with the eating disorders. These reactions include heightened emotionality in response to stress and engaging in impulsive eating behaviour as a way of alleviating the experience of stress and anxiety. Strober and Bulik (2002) speculate that eating disorders represent the exaggerated expression of heritable personality traits and biological processes that underpin the regulation of behaviour.

Overall, the available research suggests a general genetic predisposition. This, of course, still needs to be clarified by more, and more sophisticated, research.

Neurobiological factors

There has been increasing use of neuro-imaging and neuropsychological assessment to uncover changes in brain function that potentially increase vulnerability for developing an eating disorder (Madden, 2015).

Eating is a biological function. The hypothalamus is the part of the brain associated with the regulation of hunger and eating. It appears obvious therefore to look to this area when considering biological possibilities in the causation of eating disorders. Hypothalamic lesions in animals are associated with weight loss in these animals, but they do not parallel what we know of the clinical picture of anorexia nervosa. The animals in question become indifferent to food, whereas anorexia nervosa is characterised by both hunger and an interest in food (Hoebel & Teitelbaum, 1966).

Structural neuro-imaging research has found general cerebral atrophy both in individuals with anorexia nervosa and those with bulimia nervosa, albeit to a lesser extent in the latter. While full restoration was observed with weight recovery in some instances, there have been studies where no restoration has been noted. In bulimia nervosa patients, enlarged ventricles were noted regardless of normal weight, indicating a possibly predisposing factor (Von Hausswolff-Juhlin, Brooks, & Larsson, 2015). Studies using neuro-imaging have not yet yielded consistent results on the brain areas that are most affected in the eating disorders (Von Hausswolff-Juhlin et al., 2015).

In terms of biochemistry, the neurotransmitter systems that move through the hypothalamus have been investigated, and the levels of some hormones (e.g. cortisol and norepinephrine) regulated by the hypothalamus are found to be abnormal in people diagnosed with anorexia nervosa, although these abnormalities may be the result, rather than the cause, of self-starvation (Doer, Fichter, Pirke, & Lund, 1980; Kaye, 2008; Liebowitz, 1983).

The role of serotonin, and specifically lower serotonin levels in the eating disorders, has been of particular interest to researchers, as this is the neurotransmitter system most often implicated in the eating disorders. Serotonin is involved in the modulation of appetite in that increased serotonin causes feelings of satiety while starvation decreases serotonin activity. In addition, increased serotonin levels are associated with anxiety. The hypothesis is therefore that individuals with innately high levels of serotonin experience high levels of anxiety and employ excessive dieting as a strategy to reduce anxiety (Kaye et al., 2003). These researchers experimentally reduced serotonin levels in groups of anorexics and non-anorexic controls and were able to confirm this hypothesis.

Bulimia nervosa is, in turn, hypothesised to be associated with insufficient serotonin levels. Smith, Fairburn, and Cowen (1999) utilised the same procedure as Kaye et al. (2003) to deplete serotonin levels in a group of recovered bulimics and a normal control group. They found that lowered serotonin levels in the group of recovered bulimics caused depressive symptoms, difficulties with body image, and fear of losing control of eating behaviour.

Some research has found low levels of serotonin metabolites in people diagnosed with bulimia nervosa, as well as decreased responses to serotonin agonists, again implicating an underactive serotonin system (Jimerson, Wolfe, Metzger, Finkelstein, & Cooper, 1997). Finally, antidepressant medications that boost serotonin levels have met with some success in the treatment of bulimia nervosa. From the available information, serotonin appears to be implicated in bulimia nervosa, at least to a certain extent.

Neuro-imaging has found differences in serotonergic binding in the brains of individuals with binge-eating disorder as compared to healthy controls, with increased serotonergic binding in the parieto-occipital cortical regions and simultaneous decreases in the nucleus accumbens, inferior temporal gyrus, and lateral orbitofrontal cortex. These findings support the addiction model of binge eating (Majuri et al., 2017). Disrupted serotonin signalling has also been implicated in the link between a tendency to impulsive binge-eating behaviour (Stutz, Anastasio, & Cunningham, 2015).

Dopamine is a neurotransmitter that plays a major role in the reinforcing effects of food, with low dopamine levels increasing hunger and high dopamine levels increasing satiety (Bello & Hajnal, 2010; Lee & Lin, 2010). The relationship between dopamine and the experience of appetite has been used to explain differences between responses to food stimuli in participants with bulimia nervosa, who were more attentive to food stimuli compared to those with anorexia nervosa (Brooks, Prince, Stahl, Campbell, & Treasure, 2011). Similarly, individuals with decreased dopamine levels may require higher quantities of food or other substances to experience pleasure

Endogenous opioid peptides (EOPs) are also hypothesised to be involved in a vicious cycle related to the starvation-binge behaviour of people with an eating disorder diagnosis (Marrazzi & Luby, 1986). More specifically, EOPs occur naturally within our bodies and are produced by the body as a response to starvation. The opiate system is involved in decreasing the body's experience of pain, and the EOPs are involved with the experience of pleasure in eating. The theory put forward by some researchers is that people diagnosed with eating disorders become 'addicted' to the body's opiates during a period of self-starvation, and that patterns of starvation-binging stimulate EOP production in the body. In addition, opioids are increased by the pattern of excessive exercise present in some people with an eating disorder diagnosis (Davis, 1996).

An addiction model has also been proposed for binge-eating disorder. In the case of binge-eating disorder, neuro-imaging studies have found corticostriatal changes comparable to those found in substance abuse. Genetic and animal studies imply that binge-eating behaviour is related to maladaptation in dopaminergic and opiodergic neurotransmitter systems. Despite the neuropathological process of binge-eating disorder remaining relatively unknown, available data suggests neurophysiological changes in circuitry involved in motivation and impulse control, comparable to other 'impulsive/compulsive disorders' (Kessler, Hutson, Herman, & Potenza, 2016, p. 223).

In other words, responses to rewards on a neural level, and to food specifically, may be disordered and related especially to binge-eating symptomology (Kober & Boswell, 2017). However, evidence for an addiction model for the eating disorders has to be further established and findings replicated in larger samples (Kober & Boswell, 2017; Marrazzi & Luby, 1986; Wilson, 1991).

In terms of neurobiological factors and the eating disorders, there have been increasing attempts to understand the neurobiological underpinnings of the eating disorders, and it has been shown that changes occur in the neurobiology of individuals with eating disorders. However, many of the neurobiological regions, receptors, and chemicals that are implicated in the eating disorders, are also involved in other mental disorders. Improved knowledge of the neurobiology of the eating disorders is likely to result in improved interventions for these and other mental illnesses (Von Hausswolff-Juhlin et al., 2015).

However, biopsychiatric approaches are not able to account for some of the aspects that are unique to the eating disorders, such as the highly specific population involved. In order to gain some understanding of aspects that could influence these factors, we will look to the psychological and interpersonal aspects discussed in the following section.

Innate excessive serotonin → Anxiety → Dieting → Lowered serotonin → Temporary decreased anxiety
Dieting → Lowered serotonin → Depressed mood and urge to binge → Binge and purge
Disrupted serotonin → Depressed mood and lower impulse control → Binge → Temporary decreased distress

Figure 13.5: The possible role of serotonin in anorexia nervosa, bulimia nervosa and binge-eating disorder

Source: Adapted from Wenar & Kerig, 2006; Majuri et al., 2017.

Psychological factors

The discussion in this section will focus on individual factors. These individual factors are described in the context of the developmental demands associated with adolescence. The section on factors involving the family is also contextualised by the adjustments that families have to make when children enter adolescence. The broader social aspects that impact individuals will be discussed in the following section.

Developmental factors

Adolescence can be regarded as a time of great transition. The shift from childhood to adulthood brings with it changes in every sphere of a person's life (Ebata, Peterson, & Conger, 1990). The arena for this transition is the body itself. The physical changes that happen during adolescence include the development of mature size and body shape, hormonal changes, and the start of adult sexuality (Wenar & Kerig, 2006). Because of the physical changes that occur during adolescence, the adolescent's body image (psychological representation of the body) becomes much more central than during childhood (Wenar & Kerig, 2006).

Adolescence also marks a time during which a person experiences further cognitive development. Society increases its demands during this time, and a person is expected to take responsibility for decisions about his or her future (most importantly regarding romantic relationships and career choice). Relationships with peers also take on increased importance during this developmental phase (Wenar & Kerig, 2006).

The main developmental task of adolescence can be seen as finding the answer to the question, 'Who am I?' In terms of Erik Erikson's theory of human development, this stage represents the struggle between 'identity' and 'role confusion', and it occurs from the age of about eleven years through to the end of adolescence. Erikson viewed this stage as a time during which a person struggles to develop ego identity (a sense of inner sameness or continuity). Difficulties during this stage result in role confusion (not having a sense of self or one's place in the world). The ability to separate from the parent and leave home represents important challenges during this stage. Many of the disorders of adolescence can be linked to identity confusion, for example, conduct disorder and the psychotic disorders (Kaplan et al., 1996).

The family system also becomes an arena where change plays out, because parents are required to adapt their expectations and their parenting styles to accommodate the increased needs for independence and autonomy that adolescence brings (Wenar & Kerig, 2006).

The eating disorders typically emerge during adolescence up to early adulthood (in the case of binge-eating disorder). However, there are few studies that have produced data that view the eating disorders from a developmental perspective (Steiner & Lock, 1998). Some theorists regard the eating disorders as normative developmental processes 'gone awry' (gone wrong) (Wenar & Kerig, 2006, p. 360).

A few of the psychological theories and social factors discussed in the following sections describe how normative developmental processes 'go awry' in the areas of body image and emerging sexuality (Bruch's psychoanalytical theories), cognitive styles (cognitive-behavioural theories), the personality, and the family (the family systems approach). The consequences of these skewed developmental processes play out in the bodies of people diagnosed with an eating disorder.

Emotion reactivity and dysregulation

'Emotion reactivity' refers to the duration and intensity of an emotional reaction to a stimulus (Nock, Wedig, Holmberg, & Hooley, 2008), whereas 'emotional dysregulation' indicates deficits in the ability to tolerate and/modulate negative emotional states (Dvir, Ford, Hill, & Frazier, 2014). Human beings have the ability to moderate both the positive and negative experience of emotions through conscious or unconscious strategies, which in turn either promotes or inhibits behavioural goal attainment (Dvir et al., 2014). Emotions and their regulation represent an intersection of the biological, psychological, and interpersonal spheres and involve numerous interdependent processes (Dvir et al., 2014). There is an apparent link between emotion reactivity and psychopathology, and emotional dysregulation is implicated in many mental disorders. Deficits in emotional regulation have been posited as a central element in the eating disorders (Brockmeyer et al., 2014; Gross & Jazaieri, 2014).

Emotion reactivity has been put forward as a notable mechanism in disordered eating, particularly in binge-eating disorder. Leehr et al. (2015) found evidence that the experience of unpleasant emotion triggered binge eating in patients with binge-eating disorder.

It seems that at least a subgroup of individuals with eating disorders struggle to endure the experience of any negative or unpleasant emotions and attempt to regulate their emotions (minimise distress or anxiety) by doing something that they perceive as helpful in avoiding weight gain, such as binging, inducing vomiting or exercising (Haynos & Fruzzetti, 2011).

Lavender et al. (2014) found an association between disordered eating symptoms and emotional dysregulation in bulimia nervosa, and deficits in the recognition and regulation of emotions were noted in patients with anorexia nervosa (Harrison, Sullivan, Tchanturia, & Treasure, 2009). Both anorexia nervosa and bulimia nervosa appear to be characterised by a broad pattern of difficulties in emotional regulation, and it may be that more specific patterns of dysregulation distinguish the disorders (Lavender et al., 2014).

Emotional dysregulation may represent the core feature of binge-eating disorder (Kober & Boswell, 2017). Binge-eating disorder has been linked to impaired emotional regulation compared to normal and overweight control groups (Brockmeyer et al., 2014). The use of emotional suppression as a maladaptive strategy to regulate emotion in individuals with binge-eating disorder was described by Svaldi, Griepenstroh, Tuschen-Caffier, and Ehring (2012), as well as Danner, Sternheim, and Evers (2014).

It appears that eating-disordered individuals generally experience problems with emotional regulation. However, much research is required to clarify the specific types of emotional regulation difficulties, and the role of comorbid conditions involved with emotional regulation (e.g. depression and anxiety), in the different types of eating disorder (Danner et al., 2014).

Psychological theories

The various psychological theories regarding the aetiology of anorexia nervosa, bulimia nervosa, and binge-eating disorder centre on:

- psychoanalytic and psychodynamic formulations
- cognitive and learning approaches
- views of the family dynamics
- descriptions of personality functioning.

Aspects regarding family dynamics will be discussed in the section on interpersonal causal factors.

Initial psychoanalytic and psychodynamic theories of anorexia nervosa and obesity emphasised hunger as an innate drive, and food as a symbol of unconscious desires, such as love, hate, sexuality, and pregnancy. Anorexia nervosa was seen as a fear of food that was connected to unconscious fears of adulthood and sexuality or of oral impregnation (Vemuri & Steiner, 2007). These views on the causality of anorexia nervosa focused on phobic mechanisms. According to this view, the physical changes associated with puberty cause sexual and social tension. Anorexia nervosa is described as a phobic avoidance of food as a consequence of these tensions.

In this view, the tensions described are usually characterised by feelings of aggression and ambivalence towards the mother (as the primary supplier of food), while the relationship with the father is characterised as seductive and dependent. The fathers are themselves warm, but passive. All of these dynamics result in the anorexia sufferer experiencing guilt (Halmi, 2000). These dynamics are evident in the case study of Mary, described earlier in this chapter, where her mother appears to be over-involved in her daughter's life, while her father is often away from home.

Other psychodynamic views describe eating disorder symptoms as a need fulfilment; for example, the experience of success in dieting bolsters the individual's experience of personal efficacy. Avoiding sexual maturation and its consequences by maintaining a childlike body shape through dieting is also a psychodynamic view (Goodsitt, 1997).

Hilde Bruch (1904–1984) was considered a world authority on the eating disorders. She theorised that anorexia nervosa and bulimia nervosa were psychologically similar phenomena. Her view of the aetiology of the eating disorders was that individuals with this diagnosis have an underdeveloped sense of personal effectiveness and personal power, which they attempt to rectify through their symptoms by being 'different' and 'independent'. In her view, a sense of personal helplessness and powerlessness is fostered by an approach to parenting in which the wishes and views of the parent are imposed on the child.

In this approach, the parents fail adequately to take into account the child's actual needs. For instance, the parents decide when the child is hungry or tired. Individuals brought up in this manner fail to learn to recognise their own internal states and do not develop independence from others. The developmental demands of adolescence, including developing a sense of identity and achieving independence (as discussed above), push the person towards the societal values of being thin. The individual uses dieting as a means to experience a sense of personal control, power, and independence.

Psychodynamic views of bulimia nervosa describe food as symbolic of a chaotic mother–daughter relationship. In this view, the daughter does not develop an adequate sense of self and thus expresses ambivalence towards her mother in binging (bringing her closer) and purging (rejecting her) (Goodsitt, 1997).

An object relations understanding proposes that, in all the eating disorders, food is symbolic of the desirable early object. Binge eating represents the desire to secure the object by devouring it. Bulimic behaviour originates from the same process, but incorporates the fear that the object was destroyed by consuming it. This fear prompts the need to save the object by expelling it. The intensity of the craving to devour the object may be so extreme that it threatens ego loss, which in turn creates a fear of the desired object and a resulting 'stubborn' defence against the object; the defence against the longing to consume the object manifests as anorexia nervosa (Summers, 2014, p. 59).

Attachment theory emphasises the importance of early relationships for later psychological functioning. The nature of the attachment formed by an infant is determined by the interactions between the caregiver and the infant. The infant learns to regulate emotional experiences on the basis of the caregiver's sensitivity and responsiveness to the infant's communication behaviours (e.g. clinging and crying). Attachment theory postulates a connection between disrupted attachment and the development of an eating disorder (O'Shaughnessy & Dallos, 2009).

Women with eating disorders often report disrupted attachments. Extreme separation anxiety and unresolved loss and trauma have been identified as issues of concern in the treatment of eating disorders, from the perspective of attachment theory. However, conflicting data complicates attempts to find associations between subgroups of eating disorder and attachment style.

The link between food cue reactivity, craving, and binge-eating disorder represents a behavioural understanding of binge-eating disorder (Kober & Boswell, 2017). Conditioned responses to food cues in humans, similar to Pavlovian conditioned responses, including elevations in heart rate, and in gastric and neural activity, have been shown (Boswell & Kober, 2016). Food cue exposure also induces the experience of food craving ('the strong desire to eat') (Kober & Boswell, 2017, p. 34). Some individuals may be more sensitive and react more intensely to food cues, and thus also to stronger food craving. Furthermore, food craving has consistently been shown to trigger binge eating and overeating in binge-eating disorder (Kober & Boswell, 2017; Ng & Davis, 2013).

Cognitive-behavioural views of the aetiology of the eating disorders regard weight loss and the experience of successful dieting as strong reinforcing factors. These, in turn, are motivated by fear of weight gain and faulty perceptions of body image. Dieting and successful weight reduction are positively reinforced since they become associated with feelings of control, while dieting behaviours are negatively reinforced because they are associated with decreased anxiety about gaining weight (Fairburn, Shafran, & Cooper, 1999). Faulty perceptions of body image, and an extreme desire to be thin, also appear to be linked to experiences of negative comments about weight by parents or peers (Paxton,

Schutz, Wertheim, & Muir, 1999; Thompson, Coovert, Richards, Johnson, & Cattarin, 1995).

The cognitive-behavioural view of the aetiology of bulimia nervosa involves a vicious cycle that starts with the individual experiencing low self-esteem and high levels of negative affect. In an attempt to influence one of the few aspects of self that are within a person's control, they diet in an attempt to feel better. In the course of this attempt, intake of food is restricted unrealistically, which leads to an inevitable breaking of the diet. This break grows into a binge. Binging behaviour in turn creates a fear of gaining weight, which is alleviated by compensatory behaviours (purging).

These actions relieve some of the anxiety associated with the binging behaviour, but also negatively impact the person's self-esteem, which initiates the vicious cycle again (Fairburn, 1997). Various studies support the link between purging behaviour and anxiety reduction, also explaining the apparent tendency of people diagnosed with bulimia nervosa to binge and purge, particularly during times of stress and emotional difficulties (Johnson, Jarrel, Chupurdia, & Williamson, 1994; Stice, 1998).

The restraint model of binge-eating behaviour is used in cognitive-behavioural interventions with binge-eating disorder. Restraint theory posits that concerns about body weight and shape lead to dietary restraint, which in turn leads to binge eating and ultimately gives rise to a vicious cycle of weight concerns, dietary restraint, and eventual binging (McCuen-Wurst, Ruggieri, & Allison, 2018).

The affect regulation model and escape theory are also explanations offered for the psychological processes involved in binge eating. The affect regulation model views binge-eating behaviour as a coping mechanism that serves to distract from and reduce unpleasant emotions, whereas escape theory explains binge eating as a manoeuvre to avoid self-awareness by shifting focus to the stimulus in the here and now (the eating experience), instead of thoughts and emotions (McCuen-Wurst et al., 2018).

Personality factors

The earlier section on genetics suggested that more general, inherited aspects of personality may be involved in the aetiology of the eating disorders. This section will focus on the more specific personality traits associated with the eating disorders.

Assessment of the personality traits associated with the eating disorders is a difficult undertaking for a number of reasons. For example, the physical semi-starvation associated with an eating disorder can, in itself, impact on personality functioning. This was shown in studies of male conscientious objectors done in the 1940s, which aimed to replicate concentration camp conditions (Keys, Brozek, Hsu, McConoha, & Bolton, 1950). On the other hand, retrospective reports of a person's personality functioning prior to diagnosis are usually collected from the diagnosed person and family members, and could be influenced by pre-existing biases.

The personality aspects that appear to be central to the functioning of individuals with a diagnosis of eating disorders are low self-esteem (Garner, Vitousek, & Pike, 1997), lack of confidence in their personal abilities, and a decreased experience of control over their environment (Bruch, 1985; Dykens & Gerrard, 1986). In addition, particularly negative and distorted views of personal body image characterise these disorders (Klemchuck, Hutchinson, & Frank, 1990). Perfectionism also appears to play a role in these disorders (Pliner & Haddock, 1996) and may be related to the poor body image of people diagnosed with eating disorders (Davis, 1997). Farstad, McGeown, and von Ranson (2016) reviewed a decade of research on eating disorders and personality; these authors concluded that the eating disorder diagnoses are associated with increased perfectionism, neuroticism, avoidance motivation, and sensitivity to social rewards, together with lower self-directedness and extraversion, when compared to control groups.

In terms of relating to others, people diagnosed with eating disorders are usually described as agreeable or compliant, and shy, prior to diagnosis (Vitousek & Manke, 1994). A combination of increased social anxiety and a heightened preoccupation with how others perceive the self, all appear to be at play in causality of the eating disorders (Striegel-Moore, Silberstein, & Rodin, 1993).

Some research has attempted to describe the current personality functioning of people diagnosed with eating disorders utilising personality questionnaires such as the MMPI (Minnesota Multiphasic Personality Inventory) (Vitousek & Manke, 1994). This study reports that people with these diagnoses measure high on neuroticism and anxiety, with low scores on self-esteem. High scores on traditionalism (ascribes strongly to family and social standards) have been reported. Differences between people diagnosed with anorexia nervosa and those diagnosed with bulimia nervosa include high scores for depression, anxiety, and social isolation associated with anorexia nervosa, while a diagnosis of bulimia nervosa was associated with a greater variety of serious psychopathology on MMPI scores (Vitousek & Manke, 1994).

In terms of risk factors for developing an eating disorder identified by prospective studies, low scores on measures of interoceptive awareness (ability to identify one's own physical state) appeared to be predictors of risk for eating disorders (Leon, Fulkerson, Perry, & Early-Zald, 1995).

Aspects of personality functioning that appear to be associated with bulimia nervosa specifically, are qualities such as histrionic traits, affective instability, extraversion, and impulsiveness (Farstad et al., 2016; Vitousek & Manke, 1994). People with a diagnosis of bulimia nervosa can be described as angrier, more impulsive, and more outgoing than those who are anorexic. Dependence on alcohol and other substances, shoplifting, and self-destructive sexual relationships are also associated with the difficulties in impulse control associated with bulimia nervosa (Kaplan et al., 1994).

People with a diagnosis of bulimia nervosa also appear to experience increased anxiety associated with eating, and an experience of intense relief associated with purging. This experience of relief may create a vicious cycle, because it reinforces the binging and purging cycle (Rosen & Leitenberg, 1985). Other studies place less emphasis on the reinforcing effect of anxiety relief, as they emphasise the tendency to restrict food intake and associated negative attitudes towards body image in structuring treatment for bulimia nervosa (Fairburn, Agras, & Wilson, 1992).

Assessments of personality functioning in binge-eating disorder found negative affectivity both as a personality dimension and as an emotional feeling (Dorard & Khorramian-Pour, 2017). Perfectionism has been identified as a vulnerability for binge eating, and perfectionistic concerns appear to predict increased binge-eating behaviour, but not vice versa (Smith et al., 2017).

The way in which personality manifests is also influenced by the comorbid disorders often found with the eating disorders, discussed in an earlier section. Mood disorders and anxiety disorders (specifically obsessive-compulsive disorder), and the personality disorders which are frequently comorbid with the eating disorders, influence the expression of personality in people with this diagnosis (American Psychiatric Association, 2000; Halmi, 2000).

Meta-analysis suggests that avoidant and obsessive-compulsive personality disorders are the most common personality disorder diagnoses with restricting anorexia nervosa and binge-eating disorder, and that paranoid and borderline personality disorder diagnoses are more frequent in binge-eating/purging anorexia nervosa and bulimia nervosa (Farstad et al., 2016). Some researchers posit that the eating disorders are an expression of the mood disorders, while others maintain that depression is a consequence of the eating disorder (Rutter et al., 1990; Vanderlinden, Norré, & Vandereycken, 1992).

Finally, assessments of people diagnosed with an eating disorder in the recovering phases of the disorder continue to show rigid and obsessional thinking patterns, shyness, feelings of insecurity, minimisation of feelings, compliance with convention, and rigid behaviour patterns (Halmi, 2000).

Traumatic childhood experiences

A connection between the eating disorders and traumatic experiences such as sexual and physical abuse in childhood is well established, and higher incidences of reported childhood physical and sexual abuse are found among people diagnosed with eating disorders (Amianto et al., 2018; Everill & Waller, 1995). In particular, childhood sexual abuse among this population has been the focus of research, with some studies indicating higher rates of reported sexual abuse in these people (Deep, Lilenfeld, Plotnicov, Pollice, & Kaye 1999; Welch & Fairburn, 1994).

Schmidt, Evans, Tiller, and Treasure (1995) reported that 22–31% of eating disorder patients included in their study had been sexually abused as children. In a study comparing reported histories of emotional abuse and neglect and sexual abuse in groups with adult obesity, binge-eating disorder, and healthy controls, the overall obese group reported higher levels of emotional abuse and neglect and sexual abuse than the control group (Amianto et al., 2018). Of all three groups, the binge-eating disorder group of patients reported the highest levels of sexual abuse, emotional abuse, and neglect (Amianto et al., 2018).

The suggested causal connection between childhood sexual abuse and the eating disorders has not been confirmed definitively, however (Connors & Morse, 1993; Pope & Hudson, 1992). It should be noted that childhood sexual abuse is associated with a number of diagnostic categories, and that the experience of abuse is a general variable, making it difficult to establish a definite causal link between physical or sexual abuse and the eating disorders.

Role of the family context

The family provides the context for the developmental tasks that face family members. Aetiological aspects that address the role of the family context include family characteristics and the family systems approach. The so-called typical anorexic family and their associated patterns of interaction have been the focus of numerous studies from both the psychodynamic and family systems perspectives.

The following characteristics are associated with a family context where eating disorders may develop: The mothers of the families have the role of being 'society's messengers'. They tend to transmit messages about the desirability of thinness to their daughters and are likely to be dieters themselves (see section on sociocultural factors). The mothers appear to be more 'perfectionistic', and the family as a whole is ambitious and places great emphasis on appearances (Bruch, 1985; Hsu, 1990; Minuchin, Rosman, & Baker, 1978; Pike & Rodin, 1991).

The psychodynamic view on intrapersonal aetiology was discussed in the previous section. The psychodynamic view of the family's involvement is that people with eating disorders often experience their bodies as being under the control of their parents. They regard their mothers as intrusive and unempathic, but are unable to separate from their mothers psychologically. The self-starvation of the anorexic patient is regarded as an attempt to attain a sense of autonomy and selfhood (Kaplan et al., 1994).

It appears likely that differences exist in the enmeshment patterns of families of anorexics and families of bulimics (Evans & Street, 1995). The families of bulimics appear more likely to exhibit high levels of conflict and to be less close than those of anorexics. Bulimia nervosa patients often describe their parents as neglectful and rejecting (Kaplan et al., 1994). Family interaction patterns in families of adolescent patients with binge-eating disorder are more enmeshed, and patients perceive their mothers to be critical, lacking in warmth, and to show high expressed emotion (Schmidt et al., 2015).

A family systems theory view of the eating disorders was formulated by Salvador Minuchin and his co-workers (1978). This view proposes that the symptoms of eating disorders are inseparable from the family context in which they arise. Minuchin is regarded as the father of structural family therapy. In this view, the symptoms of the eating disorder are understood to be related to the dysfunctional structure of the family in which it occurs. The symptoms are regarded as serving a function in the family.

In the case of eating disorders, one possible function of the symptoms is to assist the family in escaping other conflicts and to divert attention from other problems within the family. From this perspective, the families of people diagnosed with an eating disorder are characterised by the following:

- **Enmeshment:** A dynamic characterised by diffuse boundaries within the family, resulting in family members being overly involved with, and responsive to, one another. An example is parents who speak for their children since they believe that they know how their children feel.
- **Overprotectiveness:** Members of the family exhibit excessive concern for one another's well-being. In an overprotective family, criticism is softened by pacifying behaviour. The effect is that children of such a family do not move towards autonomy, and in turn, feel responsible for protecting the family from distress.
- **Rigidity:** Members attempt to maintain balance and try to escape change. During times of normal growth and transition (such as adolescence), they increase their attempts to hold on to their usual patterns.
- **Lack of conflict resolution:** Conflict is avoided, denied, or is engaged in constantly but in an ineffective way. An example is a father who leaves the house every time conflict threatens.

Minuchin and his colleagues describe the family of the future anorexic as being very concerned with diet, appearance, and control. The family is intrusive to the point of scrutinising the adolescent's bodily and psychological functions, with the effect that their autonomy is blocked. Because adolescence is a developmental phase that requires separation, it is a particularly stressful time for the enmeshed family. The identified patient, in response to the stress, responds with self-starvation. This allows the anorexic to remain overtly dependent on the parents, while enabling the patient to engage in covert rebellion (Minuchin et al., 1978).

Once a family member has been diagnosed with an eating disorder, this is also likely to impact negatively on family relationships. Parents may experience high levels of frustration and guilt as a result of their child's symptoms. Levels of conflict can escalate to the point of physical violence when parents have to deal with the struggle to persuade their daughter or son to eat.

 ACTIVITY

The following two quotations by Iruloh (2017) are about the relationship between family distress and eating disorders. Based on these quotations, explain this relationship.

> *'It was shown that maladaptive behaviour of parents or pathology within the family could play an important role in the development of eating disorders.' (p. 76)*

> *'Like any other illness or disease, a loved one's inability to function normally can bring so much anguish, discomfort, or distraction thereby putting the family under perpetual pressure. For example, if a member of the family is hospitalised due to eating disorder disease, other members of the family will be mandated to follow up the victim's medical treatment by frequenting the hospital and spending so much money on drugs to help their person get well.' (p 77)*

 ACTIVITY

Discuss the advantages and disadvantages of the approach outlined below by Adebimpe and Idehen (2015).

Some studies suggest that family-based therapies in which parents assume responsibility for feeding their afflicted adolescent are the most effective in helping a person with anorexia nervosa gain weight and improve eating habits and moods. Shown to be effective in case studies and clinical trials, this particular approach is discussed in some guidelines and studies for treating eating disorders in younger, non-chronic patients.

Sociocultural factors

As mentioned earlier in this chapter, the eating disorders are unique in that they are found most often among one of the most specific population groups, i.e. middle- and upper-class young females from industrialised settings. The specific nature of the population diagnosed with these disorders is thought to have aetiological implications. Aspects of these aetiological implications will be discussed in the following sections.

Sociocultural ideals for physical beauty

The increased incidence of the eating disorders in industrialised settings has been associated with other sociocultural changes in these contexts. Among other aspects, increases in eating disorder incidence occurred simultaneously with changes in the roles of women in Western societies. Sociocultural risk models for the eating disorders mostly emphasise the idealisation of thinness in women. Broad, but indirect, support for this idea is found in historical and cross-cultural trends in eating disorder incidence and prevalence rates in the 20th century, with the simultaneous intensification of the idealisation of thinness and increased anorexia nervosa and bulimia nervosa rates (Culbert et al., 2015). This will be discussed further in the following section.

In industrialised settings, a preoccupation with thinness has emerged, and the ideal for beauty has become increasingly thin over time. There has been an emergence of an entire industry associated with dieting and weight loss (and health and fitness), and all of these aspects have been developing against the background of a population that has been becoming increasingly heavy (Brownell & Fairburn, 1995).

The tension between the cultural ideal and the actual body shape and size of the population has steadily increased as the ideal has become thinner and the population larger. The human species has been becoming bigger in terms of weight and height over a number of centuries. Coupled with better nutrition and availability of food, and a less active lifestyle, the average weight of American females (aged 17–24 years) became 3 kg heavier between 1960 and the early 1980s (Bureau of Census, 1983). The prevalence of obesity in American society has doubled since 1900, with 20–30% of the population being overweight in the mid-1980s (Killen et al., 1986) and by 2004, this rate had reached 32.2% (Ogden et al., 2006). Data for 2015–2016 puts obesity rates at 39.8% and overweight (including obesity) at 71.6% for American adults aged 20 years and older (Centers for Disease Control and Prevention, 2017).

Research focusing on the media found that comparisons between ideals for feminine beauty have shown a steady decrease in size since the 1950s. Compare the iconic Marilyn Monroe with current film stars, for instance (Brownell, 1991). Various studies have investigated the feminine ideal by comparing shifts in the size of the women featured in *Playboy* centrefolds (Wiseman, Gray, Mosimann, & Arhens, 1992) and beauty pageant contestants (Moser, 1989). This trend towards thinness continued into the early 2000s (Seifert, 2005).

Other studies have recorded the number of weight-loss and diet-related articles in women's magazines and have found steady increases in the number of these articles while the cultural ideal has been becoming thinner. Some studies indicate that this tendency has levelled off since the early 2000s (Garner, 1997; Paquette & Raine, 2004; Roberts & Muta, 2017). However, it remains clear that the media plays a role in the transmission of the cultural standards of ideal beauty and in the promotion of thinness (Bessenhof, 2006; Botta, 2003, 2006; Vaughan & Fouts, 2003).

As suggested above, one of the effects of the tension between the cultural ideal and the actual increase in body size has been women's dissatisfaction with their own bodies. Body-image dissatisfaction is understood as the negative evaluation and feelings that an individual experiences towards his or her own body as a result of an interplay of body shape, appearance, attitudes regarding body weight, and cultural perceptions of an ideal body (McGuinness &

Taylor, 2016). The presence of a certain degree of negative body image among women in Western societies is so pervasive that it has come to be labelled as 'normative discontent' (Cash & Henry, 1995).

A systematic review of research found rates of body-image dissatisfaction of 20–70% even among preschool children, and research found that 34% of a group of five-year-old girls engaged in a moderate level of weight-focussed dietary restraint (Damiano, Paxton, Wertheim, McLean, & Gregg, 2015; Tatangelo, McCabe, Mellor, & Mealey, 2016). However, there are some indications that levels of body dissatisfaction among American women may have been gradually decreasing over time since the early 2000s, possibly related to sociocultural changes in diversity and body acceptance that may be countering women's experience of thinness-pressure (Karazsia, Murnen, & Tylka, 2017).

Bessenhof (2006) found that exposure to thin-ideal advertisements was associated with increased body dissatisfaction, negative moods, and depression, as well as lower self-esteem in female undergraduates, confirming the link between the cultural ideal, the media, and body-image dissatisfaction. Similarly, most of the women participants who were exposed to thin-ideal media in a study in an experimental setting reported negative effects on body image (Frederick, Daniels, Bates, & Tylka, 2017).

While decades of research have addressed the detrimental impact of the traditional media on body-image concerns, social media has overtaken traditional media as the most popular sociocultural vehicle to transfer the thin ideal (Fardouly & Vartanian, 2016; Qi & Cui, 2018). Thus, research has begun to investigate the effects of new media formats on body image. Several correlation studies that investigated the relationship between social media usage and body image in pre-teen and teenage females reported that Facebook users experience increased internalisation of the thinness ideal, greater thinness drive, self-objectification, and appearance comparison than non-users (Meier & Gray, 2014; Tiggemann & Slater, 2014).

Increased time spent using Facebook and/or Myspace was related to greater levels of body dissatisfaction, thinness-ideal internalisation, thinness drive, self-objectification, body surveillance and dieting behaviour in female pre-teens, high school students, and undergraduates (Cohen & Blaszczynski, 2015; Fardouly & Vartanian, 2015; Mabe, Forney, & Keel, 2014; Tiggemann & Miller, 2010).

In addition to general social media activity, particular activities such as higher appearance exposure (viewing, posting, and commenting on images) have been noted as especially problematic and associated with more weight dissatisfaction, thinness-ideal internalisation, thinness drive, and self-objectification in female high school students. Similarly, online social grooming (viewing and commenting on peers' profiles) has been linked to drive for thinness in both female and male undergraduates (Kim & Chock, 2015; Meier & Gray, 2014). Generally, the available evidence points to social media effects being similar to those of traditional media and to being related to body image concerns among young people (Fardouly & Vartanian, 2016).

A study investigating the relationships between mass media, self-esteem, body image, and tendencies to disordered eating found that greater exposure to fashion and beauty magazines was related to overall dissatisfaction with appearance and greater eating disorder tendencies in females (Kim & Lennon, 2007). Disturbance of body image is central to the eating disorders, and available research points to the pivotal role that disturbed body image plays in the development of eating disorders, especially in adolescence (Voelker, Reel, &

Greenleaf, 2015). The link between binge-eating disorder and body-image concerns is more oblique than that between body dissatisfaction and attempts to reduce body weight by means of other kinds of disordered eating behaviour. However, it has been speculated that binge-eating behaviour relates to body image concerns as an attempted strategy to avoid negative self-evaluations (Duarte, Pinto-Gouveia, & Ferreira, 2017; McGuinness & Taylor, 2016).

The tripartite influence model is a sociocultural theory of body dissatisfaction that proposes three primary sources of influence, namely parents, peers, and the media, as major contributors to disturbances in body image and eating behaviour. Appearance comparison and internalisation of media influences are thought to be mediating factors between these three influences and the emergence of body and eating disturbances (Van den Berg, Thompson, Obremski-Brandon, & Coovert, 2002).

A longitudinal study among a group of Grade 7 girls in the United States suggests that media ideal internalisation is the precursor and predictor of appearance comparison and later body dissatisfaction. As mentioned above, body dissatisfaction is acknowledged as a key eating disorder risk factor (Rodgers, McLean, & Paxton, 2015). However, the relationship between shape and weight concerns and the clinical manifestations of the eating disorders is complex and variable, and continues to be poorly understood by researchers and clinicians alike (Lydecker, White, & Grilo, 2017).

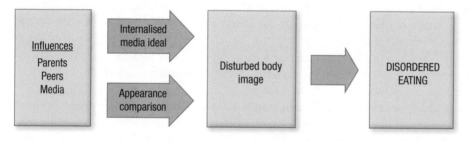

Figure 13.6: The tripartite influence model of body image

Source: Adapted, with permission, from Van den Berg, Thompson, Obremski-Brandon, & Coovert, 2002.

Types of media exposure that are enjoying increasing attention from researchers in terms of impact on body-image concerns and possible promotion of eating disorders are the proliferation of so-called 'thinspiration', 'fitspiration', and pro-ED Internet content. 'Thinspiration' is 'a blend of thin and inspiration (sometimes referred to as thinspo for short), which involves sharing photos/prose intended to inspire eating disorder behaviours' (Lewis & Arbuthnott, 2012, p. 200). Similarly, 'fitspiration' sites claim to promote fit and healthy lifestyles, but offer content that is thematically similar to 'thinspiration' sites (Lewis & Arbuthnott, 2012). Thinspiration content is available not only on platforms designed to promote eating disorders, but also on social media websites and through user-generated content, including open and image-based platforms such as Instagram and video-sharing websites such as YouTube (Ging & Garvey, 2018; Oksanen et al., 2015; Stonebridge, 2011).

In recent years, the rise of Internet websites and online communities that promote anorexia and eating-disordered behaviour, including purging methods (so-called pro-ana sites) have grown into a public health concern (Horie et al., 2016; Oksanen et al., 2015). These websites and communities support and encourage potentially harmful weight control and loss practices by sharing information, emotional content, and social ties. They are easily accessible and often interactive (Oksanen et al., 2015).

BOX 13.2: THE THIN COMMANDMENTS

1. If you aren't thin, then you aren't attractive.
2. Being thin is more important than being healthy.
3. You must buy clothes, cut your hair, take laxatives, starve yourself, and do anything to make yourself look thinner.
4. Thou shall not eat without feeling guilty.
5. Thou shall not eat fattening food without punishing thyself afterwards.
6. Thou shall count calories and restrict intake accordingly.
7. What the scale says is the most important thing.
8. Losing weight is good; gaining weight is bad.
9. You can never be too thin.
10. Being thin and not eating are signs of true willpower and success.

Discussion: The 'Thin Commandments' are published on many of the pro-ana websites and are well known in the extreme communities that regard anorexia nervosa and bulimia nervosa as lifestyle choices rather than psychological disorders. Discuss this statement.

Pro-ana websites typically share 'tips and tricks' for weight loss, 'thinspiration' (quotes and photos that are motivation for weight loss), as well as lifestyle descriptions and advice on concealing symptoms (Harshbarger, Ahlers-Schmidt, Mayans, Mayans, & Hawkins, 2009; Norris, Boydell, Pinhas, & Katzman, 2006). Some of the common themes of the pro-ana websites are concerned with control, success, and perfection (Harshbarger et al., 2009).

However, although pro-eating disorder content is now common, the content is accessed by patients and non-patients alike (Sharpe, Musiat, Knapton, & Schmidt, 2011). In a review study to establish current knowledge of the risks of accessing pro-eating disorder content, Sharpe et al. (2011, p. 34) concluded that despite there being 'evidence for the harmfulness of pro-eating disorder content on the Internet, there is no clear indication that such sites promote the development or maintenance of eating disorders'.

The issue is further clouded by the relative lack of theory-based research on the relationship between social media and the body image and self-perceptions of young women. The interactive and content aspects of social media, including the heavy presence of peers and visual image exchanges, all suggest that social media can significantly impact body-image concerns, body dissatisfaction, and eating disorder, and this should set the research agenda for social media effects on both female and male body image (Perloff, 2014).

BOX 13.3: EXAMPLES OF 'HINTS AND TIPS' FROM PRO-ANA WEBSITES

1. Brush your teeth constantly so you won't be tempted to eat.

2. Put a rubber band around your wrist. Snap it when you feel like eating 'bad' food.

3. Clean something gross (toilet, litter box, boyfriend's closet) when you want to eat. You will not want to eat after cleaning a litter box.

4. Keep your hair in good condition so no one will suspect anything.

5. Get a job so you'll have to work through mealtimes.

6. You don't want food! Food is disgusting, and if you eat it now, you WILL regret it later. You're not even hungry! Don't give in. All it will do is make you bigger and further away from your goal weight. You want to be skinny and beautiful, don't you?

In terms of commerce, the diet industry (selling medication, books, and special foods) has blossomed in relation to the changes in cultural ideals. Similarly, the related health-and-fitness industry has expanded exponentially. The diet industry alone was estimated in the early 1990s to be have been worth about $30 billion per year (about the same amount as the United States' government budget for education, training, social services, and employment at that time) and by 2015, the diet industry in the United States and Europe had a turnover of more than $150 billion (Brownell & Rodin, 1994; Dulloo & Montani, 2015).

Fatness or 'excess' weight is frequently portrayed as potentially fatal and as requiring behavioural intervention, despite considerable evidence and argument to the contrary (Bombak, Monaghan, & Rich, 2018). However, some studies have called into question the possible connections between the economics of the diet industry, the so-called war on obesity, the politics of health, and assumptions of weight/fatness as equating to personal irresponsibility and individuals' unhealthy lifestyles (Bombak et al., 2018; Mollow & McRuer, 2015).

One of the factors associated with the sociocultural value placed on thinness is the meaning attributed to being 'fat' in industrialised societies. 'Fat' is associated with being 'lazy', being 'unsuccessful', and having little self-control. In a study by Silverstein and Perdue (1988), women tended to equate thinness not only with attractiveness, but also with intelligence and professional success. This aspect comes into play when the changing role of women in society is considered.

Gender and the eating disorders

Women appear to internalise the societal ideal of thinness to a greater extent than do men. Evidence exists that physical attractiveness is at the centre of the female sex-role stereotype. This is not the case for the masculine sex-role stereotype. This may be one aspect that explains the fact that fewer males are diagnosed with an eating disorder (Meyer, Blisset, & Oldfield, 2001). Also, males who endorse feminine sex-role characteristics are at greater risk for developing an eating disorder. This is also true for the male homosexual community, where greater emphasis is placed on physical attractiveness (Meyer et al., 2001). In addition, Western cultural norms (that have a greater impact on females) associate more positive attributes (unrelated to body size) with a slim figure. These norms dictate that 'fat' is 'ugly' and 'bad', while 'thin' is 'beautiful', and beautiful is 'good' (Wenar & Kerig, 2006).

On the other hand, the ideal body image portrayed in the media for males emphasises an increasingly muscular appearance. Men may typically strive for more body mass, whereas women attempt to attain thinness (Harvey & Robinson, 2003). While males who experience body dissatisfaction may attempt to exercise weight control, they are also likely to utilise muscle development behaviours such as exercise and the use of anabolic steroids and untested dietary supplements as body-change strategies (Labre, 2002). Male athletes, who are encouraged to maintain low body weights, are considered an at-risk population for eating disorders (Freeman, 2005).

The interplay between body image, disturbance in body image, and body-change strategies is probably different in males. Increased research and clinical attention directed to disordered body-change strategies in males may well result in additional eating disorder diagnoses in future DSM editions.

Some authors suggest that the increased incidence of eating disorders in the latter half of the twentieth century is associated with the changing role of women in Western society (Bemporad, 1997). Traditionally, women were expected to be compliant, unassertive, and respectful (Miller & Pumariega, 2001). Changes in society have resulted in greater opportunities for women, but also in greater demands. These demands are often in conflict with traditional role demands. Women now have to juggle pressures to conform with pressures to compete (Miller & Pumariega, 2001). Examples of these pressures are expectations from professional roles, nurturing demands, and social expectations (Halmi, 2000). Dieting and the eating disorders may represent one way in which women respond to the conflicting demands of success and attractiveness (Miller & Pumariega, 2001)

Feminist theorising has attempted to make sense of the gender differences in the epidemiology of the eating disorders and disordered eating (Myers, 2015). Generally, feminist approaches critique and reject the thin ideal and expectations for women to conform to it, and they link these pressures to the emergence of eating disorders (Myers, 2015). Although diverse, feminist theories typically also link women's experience of sexism to disordered eating and posit that disordered eating is the expression of the hidden challenges that women experience (Myers, 2015). Feminist views on the eating disorders can be summarised in the following four hypotheses:

- Thinness may be a way to attempt to balance demands between traditional femininity and achievement, as discussed above. Western patriarchal society may oppress women through a culture of thinness (Miller & Pumariega, 2001).

- More militant feminist authors have criticised the diet industry as a male strategy to ensure the continued oppression of women (Wolf, 1990). As long as women are starving themselves and are expending their energies on their appearance, they represent no real threat to male power.
- Weight may represent power and control for women. It may constitute the one aspect of their lives that is within their control (Miller & Pumariega, 2001).
- Weight and eating disorders may represent a way for women to establish their own identities and self-definition by using their bodies. The roles of women as 'wife' and 'mother' are devalued by Western society. This may create a situation where women use dieting and weight loss as a means to define an identity (Miller & Pumariega, 2001).

The feminist theories summarised above can be integrated with transcultural theories. In this view, the changing roles of women in Western society represent an example of 'straddling two worlds'. Other examples of this are groups in which acculturation takes place, such as immigrant groups. Research findings of increased incidence of the eating disorders in such groups lend some support to the idea that a situation of cultural change or conflict creates a breeding ground for the eating disorders (Miller & Pumariega, 2001).

A significant aspect of the relationship between gender and the eating disorders is the developmental view. The developmental demands of adolescence (the resolution of issues pertaining to identity, sexuality, achievement, and independence) were discussed in a previous section. These developmental demands intersect with gender in the case of young girls. An increase in body fat due to puberty occurs at a time when attractiveness, popularity, and success become more important to them. If self-worth becomes equated with physical appearance, a preoccupation with weight and dieting may develop (Strober, 1995).

It appears that a preoccupation with thinness emerges in early adolescence in young girls, with some research indicating that many girls between the ages of 10 and 15 years wished for a thinner body shape, but did not report significant body dissatisfaction, and did not regard themselves as fat (Cohn et al., 1987). By their early twenties, women's standards of thinness were much higher than those of young girls, suggesting that the desire to be thin becomes firmly established in women as they move from adolescence to adulthood (Walsh & Devlin, 1998).

CROSS-CULTURAL PERSPECTIVES

Cultural beliefs and attitudes have an effect on how body size and shape are regarded, and these perceptions are significant contributing factors in the development of eating disorders, as is social class. Prevalence rates of eating disorders vary among racial or ethnic groups and nationalities. These rates also shift as cultures undergo change. Eating disorders appear to be prevalent across a greater variety of cultural groups than was believed in the past (Miller & Pumarierga, 2001).

As discussed in the previous section, cultural change itself may be associated with increased risk for developing eating disorders, particularly when values related to physical attractiveness are affected. This change may occur over time within a specific society or may take place within an individual when an immigrant moves to a new culture (Miller & Pumarierga, 2001).

Race and social class previously appeared to be very strongly associated with the incidence of eating disorders. However, anorexia nervosa presents in a range of socially and culturally diverse populations, although there are cross-cultural differences in epidemiology and presentation (American Psychiatric Association, 2013). The frequency of bulimia nervosa occurrence is comparable for most industrialised countries, as is that of binge-eating disorder.

There may be a smaller disparity for binge-eating disorder across gender and ethnic groups, with similar prevalence among African and Hispanic Americans as in non-Hispanic white American individuals (American Psychiatric Association, 2013; Kober & Boswell, 2017). A review of the world-wide epidemiology of eating disorders found that these conditions continue to occur most frequently in young Western females, traditionally the high-risk group. However, they also present in individuals from non-Western countries, in men, and in older women (Hoek, 2016).

In the United States, eating disorders have traditionally been less prevalent among African Americans and other ethnic minority groups (Miller & Pumarierga, 2001). More recent research, however, suggests a trend among African Americans towards an increased risk for eating disorders, as well as among young females in other ethnic minority groups, and eating disorder rates are now similar for African American, Asian American, Hispanic and non-Hispanic whites (Marques et al., 2011).

Outside the United States, a study by Kayano et al. (2008) found disordered eating behaviour among non-Western cultures, but noted the absence of body dissatisfaction as the driver of disordered eating. Culture may have a pathoplastic effect in the eating disorders, particularly anorexia nervosa, and considerable variation in the presentation of eating concerns exists across cultural contexts, particularly the absence of 'fat phobia' (intense fear of weight gain), for instance, in Asian populations (American Psychiatric Association, 2013).

Earlier studies suggested that the prevalence of eating disorders is not significant in cultures where the ideal for attractiveness places less emphasis on being thin (Furnham & Baguma, 1994). In non-Western societies, where plumpness was considered attractive and signified prosperity, success, and fertility, the eating disorders were less prevalent than in Western-oriented countries, where prevalence rates were comparable to those of the United States (Miller & Pumarierga, 2001).

This picture appears to be changing, however. During the 1990s, reports of the increasing presence of eating disorders in the developing world emerged (Rittenbaugh, Shisslak, & Prince, 1992). Outside the United States, research also suggests that women who move from a culture where thinness is not valued, to a culture where it is, are at greater risk of developing an eating disorder (Yates, 1989). Exposure to Western media and Western standards of thinness appear to be associated with increased reporting of body image concerns, occurrence of eating disorders, as well as the more typical Western element of 'fat phobia' as part of the eating disorder presentation in parts of Asia and in Fiji (Lee, Ng, Kwok, & Fung, 2010; Liao et al., 2010).

In addition to the impact of culture and cultural transition, class differences in the incidence of eating disorders appear to be diminishing (Root, 1990). Some recent studies have not supported the link between social class and the eating disorders (Wenar & Kerig, 2006). Indeed, epidemiological surveys do not show a greater distribution of the eating disorders among the upper classes, as was initially thought (Kaplan et al., 1994).

The eating disorders clearly have important variations in their incidence and patterns. Our knowledge of the role of culture remains unclear and is not supported by adequate empirical evidence. The study of the cultural variations, however, may hold one of the keys to understanding the aetiology of these disorders (King, 1993; Sharan & Sundar, 2015). The South African context, which can be regarded as a microcosm involving all the variables above, will be considered in the following section.

South African perspective

As suggested in the introductory section, international research places the prevalence of eating disorders at approximately 1% (anorexia nervosa), 1–4% (bulimia nervosa), and 1.8% (binge-eating disorder) among affected young women. In the South African context, it is to be expected that similar rates will occur amongst young women of settler descent. However, emerging local and international research implies that other ethnic groups, age groups, and social classes are also at risk, in addition to the white, middle-class, young females traditionally associated with the eating disorders (Dirks, 2001).

The South African context provides a backdrop of rapid and dramatic political and social change for the emergence of eating disorders (Szabo & Allwood, 2004). Understanding disorders of eating in South Africa is complicated by ongoing food insecurity, malnutrition, increasing obesity, and decreasing levels of physical activity (Prioreschi et al., 2017). For instance, it seems that the meaning of 'self-starvation', and its related symptoms, may differ for young black females in impoverished circumstances. This emphasises the need for care when conducting cross-cultural research, since a variety of culturally related aspects may change the meaning of standard measures (Le Grange, Louw, Russell, Nel, & Silkstone, 2006).

Elevated rates of overweight and obesity in black South African women have, in part, been ascribed to cultural beliefs and beauty ideals that favour overweight (Puoane et al., 2005). However, Western preferences for the thin ideal appear to be rapidly becoming common in South Africa (Gitau, Micklesfield, Pettifor, & Norris, 2014; Petersen, Norris, Pettifor, & MacKeown, 2006).

Eating disorders have been described in South Africa since the 1970s (Norris, 1979); however, early descriptions related only to white females. In 1995, the first descriptions emerged of eating disorders in black females in South Africa (Szabo, 1999; Szabo, Berk, Tlou, & Allwood, 1995). Subsequent cross-cultural community-based studies of eating attitudes, and behaviours associated with eating disorders, were conducted in mainly urban settings. Eating disorder pathology was found in South African women from a range of ethnic backgrounds, with survey research of a student population finding that black students scored significantly higher than other ethnic groups on measures of the presence and severity of eating disorder pathology (Le Grange, Telch, & Tibbs, 1998; Wassenaar, Le Grange, Winship, & Lachenicht, 2000).

In 2001, eating attitudes were surveyed in a sample of South African schoolgirls from different ethnic backgrounds, who were drawn from five schools in the greater Cape Town area. Findings suggested equal prevalence of disordered attitudes towards eating in schoolgirls from different ethnic backgrounds, although white girls reported greater concerns about body image (Caradas, Lambert, & Charlton, 2001). In summary, these findings implied that prevalence of eating disorders among the black community was on the increase and that eating disorders in other communities would emerge to the same extent as in the white ('settler') community (Szabo & Allwood, 2004).

As predicted, increasing numbers of black women have presented for treatment of eating disorders, although these numbers have not reached equivalence with those presenting for treatment from the white community (Szabo & Allwood, 2004). Survey research appears to have confirmed this trend and indicated that disordered eating is equally common among black female students, white female students, and 'coloured' female students (Le Grange et al., 2004; Le Grange et al., 2006). Le Grange and colleagues (2006) concluded that ethnicity, as such, was not protective against developing disordered eating attitudes and behaviours in black South African women. Similarly, no significant ethnicity-related differences were found in the eating attitudes of a group of 11-year-old urban black and white South African girls surveyed in 2006; this led researchers to conclude that young black girls were experiencing the effects of societal change and were adopting Western notions of thinness and beauty (Petersen et al., 2006).

A more recent study was conducted by Mould, Grobler, Odendaal, and Jager (2011) on the ethnic differences in age of onset and prevalence of disordered eating attitudes and behaviours among girls in a South African school. This research found no differences between white and black schoolgirls on measures of disordered eating attitudes and behaviours between Grades 4 and 6. In Grades 7 to 9, no differences were found, with the notable exception that black students reporting more bulimia-associated behaviours than white students. Ethnic differences in bulimia-associated behaviours disappeared in Grades 10 to 12, with white students emerging with significantly higher drives for thinness, body-image dissatisfaction, and poorer eating attitudes than black students. The Bulimia Scale was the only scale that did not indicate a significant difference between the two groups in grades ten to twelve.

The findings of this study have implications for the development of prevention and early intervention programmes in the South African context (Mould et al., 2011). A survey of abnormal eating attitudes and weight-loss behaviour placed South African female adolescents, who attended a traditionally Jewish school, in the upper range of South African and international reported prevalence rates (Visser, Notelovitz, Szabo, & Fredericks, 2014).

Body-image dissatisfaction is closely linked to the eating disorders. A South African investigation of body-image satisfaction among black female students found that the majority of participants were satisfied with their body image. However, a minority of participants were dissatisfied with their body image and reported engaging in pathological eating behaviours (Mwaba & Roman, 2009). Two studies have compared the body size preferences of South African Zulu migrants to Britain with that of their non-migrant South African counterparts and found that the South African migrants endorsed thinner body size ideals that matched British white participants, whereas South African non-migrants preferred a larger ideal body size (Tovée et al., 2006, 2007).

Earlier South African research found that the rural–urban distinction emerged as a significant factor mediating risk for the eating disorders and for obesity, with increased obesity and eating disorder risk, and higher prevalence of abnormal eating attitudes, found for urban females (Goedecke et al., 2006; Szabo & Allwood, 2004). However, research investigating body-image satisfaction, eating attitudes, and body perception among rural South African adolescents, as well as a study investigating the relationship between body image, eating attitudes, BMI, and physical activity levels among rural and urban young adult South African women, found shifts towards more Western ideals in both settings (Pedro et al., 2016; Prioreschi et al., 2017). It would appear that the urban–rural distinction as a mediating factor for body-image satisfaction, disordered eating, and eating disorders is rapidly shifting in the South African context.

Intriguing research done in the United States on the cultural differences in expressed emotion between white and ethnic minority families found no significant differences, implying that white families and families from other cultural backgrounds may share a number of similarities when it comes to the eating disorders (Hoste & Le Grange, 2008). A South African study found no significant differences in clinical presentation or reported symptoms between white and black participants in a hospital setting. These findings are representative of an increasing body of research suggesting that there are more similarities than differences between patients from different ethnic groups when it comes to the eating disorders (Delport & Szabo, 2008).

Obesity has historically been viewed as a problem typical of high-income countries. However, developing countries have become increasingly affected, and the South African population appears to be especially impacted by the globally increasing prevalence of obesity, with a notable overall trend towards increased BMI and obesity prevalence. Groups with higher obesity risk include those with high socio-economic status, rural dwellers, and young women (Cois & Day, 2015). Obesity and its associated consequences for health are thought to negatively affect the lives of many South Africans and to add to healthcare expenses, both in the private and public sectors (Goedecke et al., 2006).

It seems, then, that neither the eating disorders nor obesity can be typified as problems of high-income countries any longer. South Africa is undergoing a process of rapid epidemiological change (Cois & Day, 2015). Understanding the eating disorders in the South African context is complicated by the tension between pressing public health issues such as HIV/Aids prevention and treatment and the health problems associated with undernutrition and poverty on the one hand, and the increasing prevalence of obesity, coupled with shifting patterns in notions of beauty, body-image satisfaction, and shifting patterns of risk for developing eating disorders, on the other.

BOX 13.4: 'THE EMERGING EATING DISORDERS'

Presentations (phenotypes) of eating disorders that have been emerging in recent literature:

Diabulimia	The purposeful reduction or avoidance of insulin use in patients with type 1 diabetes for the specific reason of controlling or losing weight.
Orthorexia	A severe preoccupation with 'healthy' food and proper nutrition and an associated rigid avoidance of 'unhealthy' or 'contaminated' food.
Muscle dysmorphia	A severe preoccupation with a muscular body appearance, an associated fear of being 'puny', excessive exercise, and increased body size.
Drunkorexia	Restricting food intake before consumption or planned consumption of alcohol to avoid calorie intake and weight gain.
Nocturnal eating disorders	Category proposed to include night-eating syndrome, as described in DSM-5, and sleep-related eating disorder (repeated episodes of eating at the transition from night-time sleep to waking, particularly high-caloric foods).

Source: Volpe et al., 2015.

STRESS, RISK, AND VULNERABILITY

Understanding eating disorder risk factors is complicated by the variable impact of such risk factors in different developmental stages across the lifespan, and by complex interactions between biological, psychological, and socio-environmental risk factors (Bakalar, Shank, Vannucci, Radin, & Tanofsky-Kraff, 2015). Adolescents are at increased risk, although the relative effects of pubertal development (physiological risk factor) and of sociocultural risk factors (such as perception of pressure to be thin and internalisation of the thin ideal in adolescent girls) remain unclear (Bakalar et al., 2015). Similarly, biological sex and gender-role expectations place females at greater risk for eating disorders.

The link between sociocultural risk factors and the eating disorders is well established, as discussed in a previous section. In the first longitudinal study tracking the interactions between risk factors and the eventual onset of an eating disorder, Stice and Desjardins (2018) used diagnostic interview data from three eating disorder prevention interventions. These took place over a three-year period and used classification tree analysis to predict onset of anorexia nervosa, bulimia nervosa, and binge-eating disorder; they found that interactions between risk factors had an amplifying and cumulative effect that was unique to each of the disorders. Specifically, anorexia nervosa was predicted by low body weight, and this was amplified by body dissatisfaction, whereas bulimia nervosa was predicted by overeating and thin-ideal internalisation. Body dissatisfaction was the most powerful predictor of the onset of binge-eating disorder and was amplified by overeating (Stice & Desjardins, 2018). These findings suggest that highly specific sub-populations (adolescent and young adult females) continue to be at high risk from the sociocultural influences that interact to greatly increase their risk for eating disorders.

In addition to broad sociocultural risk factors, more extreme socio-environmental insults elevate eating disorder risk; specifically, exposure to interpersonal physical or emotional trauma increases eating disorder risk (Bakalar et al., 2015). The interpersonal trauma risk factors range from histories of childhood bullying or weight-based teasing to childhood physical or sexual abuse, or emotional abuse (Amianto et al., 2018; Copeland et al., 2015; Groleau et al., 2012; Menzel et al., 2010; Mitchell, Mazzeo, Schlesinger, Brewerton, & Smith, 2012).

Risk factors for the eating disorders remain relatively poorly understood, but at a minimum, they appear to represent a complex interplay of factors cutting across different levels of system to manifest ultimately in eating disorder symptomatology.

CONCLUSION

The eating disorders present us with a puzzling and intriguing aspect of human behaviour. This chapter discussed the variety of disorders that can impact on an aspect of our lives that is essential to our survival, namely eating. The eating disorders represent a divergent range of aetiological factors, including human genetics and human development, as well as human culture and society. These factors play out in the arena of the human body and are further complicated by the constant flux of society and culture.

The eating disorders and obesity represent great costs to individuals and families in terms of distress and suffering, and great costs to society in terms of lost potential. Indeed, the eating disorder mortality rate (especially for anorexia nervosa) is the highest for any psychological disorder (Keel et al., 2003). Obesity (which is not currently a psychological disorder) is associated with high rates of morbidity and lower quality of life, as well as weight-based stigma; this results in deleterious outcomes, particularly for women, in the domains of healthcare, quality of life, and socio-economic status (Fikkan & Rothblum, 2012; Neumark-Stainer & Haines, 2004). This has led to the suggestion that 'feminist scholars need to devote as much attention to the lived experiences of fat women as they have to the "fear of fat" experienced by thin women' (Fikkan & Rothblum, 2012, p. 575). However, rather than opposites, weight bias and 'fear of fat' are part and parcel of the same social phenomena, and the potential threat to human life and quality of life associated with the eating disorders and obesity implies that these conditions are relevant to all members of contemporary human society.

MULTIPLE-CHOICE QUESTIONS

1. What is the literal meaning of the term 'bulimia nervosa'?
   a) ox hunger
   b) nervous loss of appetite
   c) nervousness or fear of fat
   d) split mind
2. Which of the following is the central feature of the eating disorders?
   a) fear of becoming fat
   b) significant and steady weight loss
   c) unrealistically negative body-image
   d) severe restriction of kilojoule intake
3. Which family systems theorist made a significant contribution to our understanding of anorexia nervosa?
   a) Satir
   b) Bruch
   c) Szabo
   d) Minuchin
4. Which psychoanalytic theorist viewed the aetiology of anorexia nervosa and bulimia nervosa as an underdeveloped sense of personal effectiveness and personal power, which the person attempts to rectify by being 'different' and 'independent', in terms of his or her symptoms?
   a) Satir
   b) Bruch
   c) Szabo
   d) Minuchin
5. The main symptom of anorexia nervosa is:
   a) refusal to maintain body weight
   b) food restriction
   c) binging and purging
   d) binging and compensating
6. The 'typical' bulimic family is:
   a) successful and hard driving
   b) chaotic
   c) warm and caring
   d) emotionally distant and controlled
7. The central aspect of a 'binge' in binge-eating disorder is:
   a) consistently eating high calorie and unhealthy foods that lead to weight gain
   b) weight gain as a consequence of episodes of uncontrolled eating
   c) the feeling that one's food consumption is 'out of control' due to dieting failures
   d) eating more food in a discrete time frame than most others would eat in a similar situation and feeling 'out of control'

8. The age, culture, and gender features of the eating disorders are significant because:
   a) they are so variable and diverse
   b) in the eating disorders, these factors are not suggestive of aetiology
   c) they come together in an obviously significant way
   d) the age, culture, and gender features are non-specific

9. Mothers of daughters diagnosed with anorexia nervosa are more likely to be:
   a) obese
   b) focused on their own careers
   c) emotionally distant and uninvolved
   d) on diet themselves

10. Who called on the Nigerian government, educational institutions and parents to 'wake up to their responsibilities' to teach about eating disorders?
   a) Betty-Ruth Iruloh
   b) Rachel Kegethe
   c) Oluwole Fumuyiwa
   d) Frank Njenga

PARAGRAPH AND ESSAY QUESTIONS

1. Compare and contrast the age, culture, and gender features of anorexia nervosa, bulimia nervosa and binge-eating disorder.
2. The courses of anorexia nervosa and bulimia nervosa are characterised by high 'crossover' between the disorders. Discuss this statement.
3. Discuss some of the causative factors of the eating disorders including genetic influences, neurotransmitter imbalances, and psychological stressors.
4. Social media 'thinspiration' sites promote anorexia nervosa and bulimia nervosa as lifestyle choices. Discuss the arguments for and against this statement.

14 | PERSONALITY DISORDERS

Beate von Krosigk

CHAPTER CONTENTS

Introduction
History of personality disorders
Clinical picture
Cluster A personality disorders
  Paranoid personality disorder
  Schizoid personality disorder
  Schizotypal personality disorder
Cluster B personality disorders
  Borderline personality disorder
  Histrionic personality disorder
  Narcissistic personality disorder
  Antisocial personality disorder
Cluster C personality disorders
  Avoidant personality disorder
  Dependent personality disorder
  Obsessive-compulsive personality disorder
Comorbidity
Aetiology
  Biological factors
  Intra- and interpersonal factors
  A holistic perspective for understanding the development of personality functioning/
    dysfunction
Problems and controversies
Conclusion

LEARNING OUTCOMES

After studying this chapter, you should be able to:

- Describe the personality disorders according to the *Diagnostic and Statistical Manual of Mental Disorders* (DSM-5) and the *International Classification of Diseases* (ICD-10) and ICD-11).
- Demonstrate an understanding of the problems with regard to diagnosing personality disorders.
- Demonstrate an understanding of the high degree of overlap between the personality disorders.
- Describe the clinical pictures of the different personality disorders.
- Identify the main aetiological factors for the different personality disorders.

PERSONAL HISTORY CASELET

Dorothy was raised by a subservient mother and disciplined by an authoritarian father. She was taught to respect and defer to her superiors (parents, teachers, other adults). Dorothy was allowed to speak only when she was directly addressed and was taught to model herself on her mother, who was openly considered to be irrational, emotional, and incapable of making decisions on the grounds that she lacked knowledge about the ways of the world.

As a young girl, Dorothy observed how her brothers were allowed to engage in further studies, while she was expected to learn to look after the household by imitating her mother. Dorothy left school at the age of 16 and, when she was about 18, she married a socially acceptable man chosen by her father.

A few years later, Dorothy, who had been totally dependent on her parents, was becoming totally dependent on her husband. After giving birth to three children in quick succession, she lost her husband in a car accident. Without financial backing or education, and with three small children, she was left destitute.

Dorothy's grief following the death of her husband, coupled with a lack of life skills, made her deeply depressed and eventually drove her to move back to her father's house. Her father still considered her to be too inexperienced to manage her financial affairs. As Dorothy had previously allowed her husband to make all her decisions, she now allowed her father to make all the decisions again.

Many years after the death of her husband, Dorothy was even more dependent on her parents than before. She regularly asked her mother to help her make decisions with regard to her three children, her personal life, her personal appearance, and even her choice of friends.

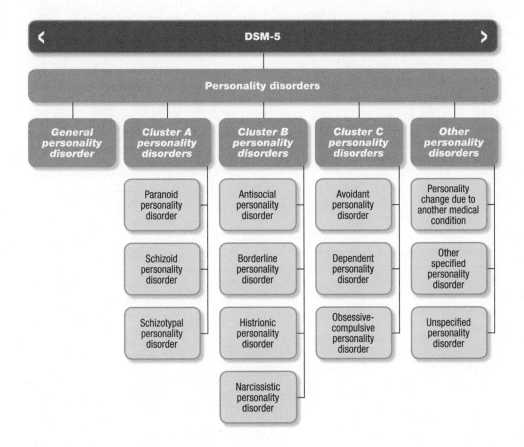

Figure 14.1: The American Psychiatric Association DSM-5 categorises personality disorders as shown above.

Source: Figure created by OUP reflecting information found in *Diagnostic and Statistical Manual of Mental Disorders*, fifth edition (DSM-5), 2013.

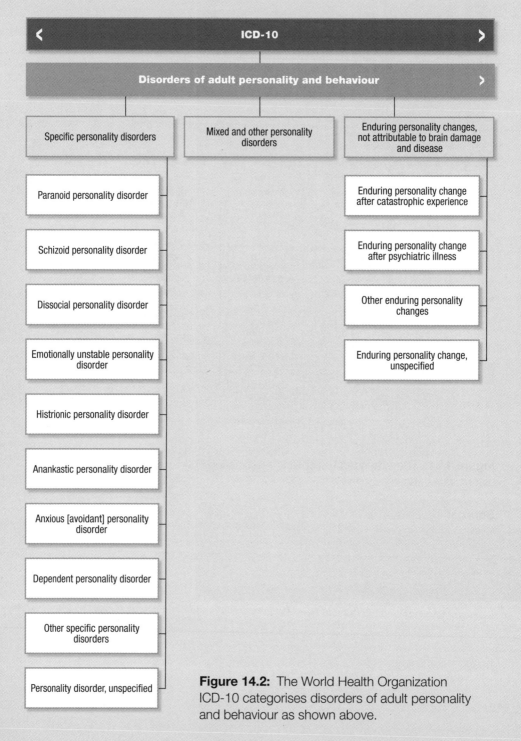

Figure 14.2: The World Health Organization ICD-10 categorises disorders of adult personality and behaviour as shown above.

Source: *International Statistical Classification of Diseases and Related Health Problems*, tenth revision (ICD-10), 2016.

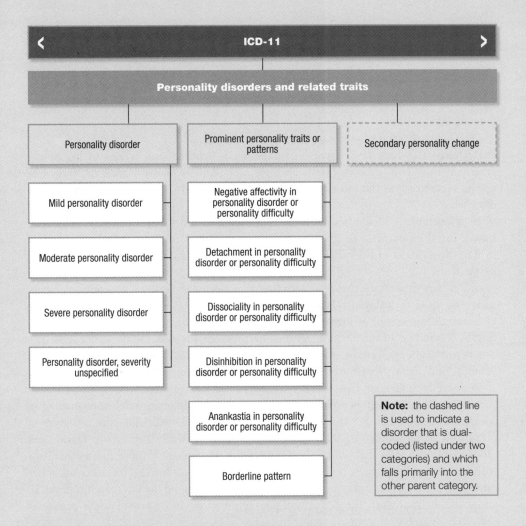

Figure 14.3: The World Health Organization proposed ICD-11 categorises personality disorders and related traits as shown above.

Source: *International Classification of Diseases for Mortality and Morbidity Statistics*, eleventh revision (ICD-11), 2018.

INTRODUCTION

It is thought that each of us has a unique personality made up of traits that come from both our genetic makeup and our life experiences; our personality is a vital part of what makes us who we are and how we interact with others. A person is known through his or her personality.

Personality traits are the characteristics that distinguish someone from others. These characteristics include how a person thinks, feels, behaves, and relates to his or her environment. When someone's traits are rigid, not adaptive to new situations, and cause significant difficulty in their work and social life, then that individual may have a personality disorder.

Individuals may be diagnosed as having a personality disorder if their pattern of behaviour, mood, social interaction, or impulsiveness causes distress to them, or to other people in their lives. Many of these behaviours can cause severe disturbance in the individual's personal and work life. According to the ICD-10 and DSM-5, individuals with personality disorders may experience chronic interpersonal problems in addition to having difficulty sustaining close or intimate relationships. They may also have difficulties in establishing a coherent sense of self or identity. Others may perceive them to be impulsive, irritable, fearful, demanding, hostile, manipulative, or even violent. Problematic alcohol or substance use, mood disorders, certain anxiety or eating disorders, self-harm, suicidal thoughts or attempts, and sexual problems often accompany personality disorders.

In order to understand personality disorders, we have to start with a definition of personality. This, in itself, is problematic as it is extremely difficult to define something as complex as personality. For the purposes of this chapter, we will adopt the definition of personality as formulated by the American psychologists Randy Larsen and David Buss (2002, p. 4), who state that personality 'is the set of psychological traits and mechanisms within the individual that are organised and relatively enduring and that influence his or her interactions with, and adaptation to, the environment (including the intrapsychic, physical, and social environment)'. The elements of this definition can be described briefly as follows (Larsen & Buss, 2002):

- **Psychological traits:** These are the characteristics that describe the way in which people are different from one another; they include aspects such as values, attitudes, motives, styles, sentiments, beliefs, and goals.
- **Psychological mechanisms:** The processes of personality include three essential aspects: inputs, decisions, and outputs. Inputs refer to perception and perceptual biases; that is, people differ in terms of the information that they are sensitive to (input). This information influences the cognitive interpretation of the environment (decisions), which in turn influences the person's behaviour (output).
- **Within the individual:** According to Larsen and Buss (2002), personality is 'something' that people typically sustain over time from one situation to the next; thus, personality refers to the stability and consistency of a person.
- **Organisation:** The psychological traits and mechanisms are not a random collection of elements; rather, they form a coherent whole because the traits and mechanisms are interlinked in an organised way. The personality is organised in the sense that it contains decision rules which determine which traits are activated in given circumstances.

- *Influence:* Personality traits and mechanisms influence people's behaviour, self-image, moods, interpersonal relationships, and goals, as well as their selection of, and adaptation to, their environments.
- *Person-environment interaction:* Interactions with the environment include perception (how a person interprets the environment), selection (the manner in which a person chooses situations, e.g. friends, hobbies, careers, etc.), evocations (the reactions a person elicits from, or produces in, others), and manipulations (the ways in which people attempt to influence others).
- *Adaptation:* Adaptive functioning refers to the way in which people accomplish their goals, as well as the way in which they adjust to and deal with life challenges.
- *Environment:* This refers to a person's physical, social, and intrapsychic environments. All these environments, individually and collectively, pose challenges to people on a continuous basis.

Because of how fundamental personality is to people's functioning in the world, one can assume that, if a person's personality is deemed to be 'disordered', it would imply a relatively pervasive disorder. The DSM-5 (American Psychiatric Association, 2013, p. 645) defines personality disorders 'as enduring patterns of perceiving, relating to, and thinking about the environment and oneself that are exhibited in a wide range of social and personal contexts and are inflexible and maladaptive, and cause significant functional impairment or subjective distress'.

We can expect that a person who is considered to have a personality disorder to experience difficulties in the following areas:

- Self-image
- Relationships with others
- Understanding themselves, others, and the environment
- Impulse control.

Many people may display certain symptoms of a personality disorder; however, it is only individuals who demonstrate enduring personality traits and difficulties as described above who can be diagnosed with a personality disorder. According to the DSM-5 (American Psychiatric Association, 2013) and ICD-10 (World Health Organization, 2016), people can be diagnosed with a personality disorder only if they fulfill certain general criteria (see Table 14.1).

When deciding whether or not a person has a personality disorder, it is imperative to keep two aspects in mind: first, one has to compare the person's behaviour to cultural norms and, second, one has to decide whether the behaviour is extreme enough to warrant such a diagnosis. In terms of extreme behaviour, the judgement is not always clear as many personality disorders represent an extreme form of a personality style (see Table 14.2). It is only once a personality style becomes pervasive and extreme that one can consider a diagnosis of a personality disorder.

Table 14.1: General symptoms of personality disorders from the DSM-5 and the ICD-10

DSM-5	ICD-10
A. An enduring pattern of inner experience and behaviour that deviates markedly from the expectations of the individual's culture. The pattern is manifested in two (or more) of the following areas: (1) Cognition (i.e. ways of perceiving and interpreting self, other people, and events). (2) Affectivity (i.e. the range, intensity, lability, and appropriateness of emotional response). (3) Interpersonal functioning. (4) Impulse control. B. The enduring pattern is inflexible and pervasive across a broad range of personal and social situations. C. The enduring pattern leads to clinically significant distress or impairment in social, occupational, or other important areas of functioning.	■ A personality disorder is a severe disturbance in the characterological constitution and behavioural tendencies of the individual, usually involving several areas of the personality, and nearly always associated with considerable personal and social disruption. A personality disorder tends to appear in late childhood or adolescence and continues to be manifest into adulthood. It is therefore unlikely that the diagnosis of a personality disorder will be appropriate before the age of 16 or 17 years. General diagnostic guidelines applying to all personality disorders are that the condition is not directly attributable to gross brain damage or disease, or to another psychiatric disorder, meeting the following criteria: ▸ Markedly disharmonious attitudes and behaviour, usually involving several areas of functioning, e.g. affectivity, arousal, impulse control, ways of perceiving and thinking, and style of relating to others. ▸ The abnormal behaviour pattern is enduring, of long standing, and not limited to episodes of mental illness. ▸ The abnormal behaviour pattern is pervasive and clearly maladaptive to a broad range of personal and social situations. ▸ The above manifestations always appear during childhood or adolescence and continue into adulthood. ▸ The disorder leads to considerable personal distress but this may only become apparent late in its course. The disorder is usually, but not invariably, associated with significant problems in occupational and social performance. ■ For different cultures it may be necessary to develop specific sets of criteria with regard to social norms, rules, and obligations. For diagnosing most of the subtypes, clear evidence is usually required of the presence of at least three of the traits or behaviours given in the clinical description.

Source: Reprinted with permission from the *Diagnostic and Statistical Manual of Mental Disorders*, fifth edition (DSM-5), American Psychiatric Association (APA), 2013, p. 646, and *International Statistical Classification of Diseases and Related Health Problems*, tenth revision (ICD-10), 2016.

The prevalence of personality disorders may vary according to the specific type of disorder. It is estimated that 9.1% of the general population would meet the criteria for a personality disorder. The prevalence rates of the different clusters of personality disorders differ: 5.7% for disorders in Cluster A, 1.5% for disorders in Cluster B, and 6% for disorders in Cluster C (American Psychiatric Association, 2013). It is, however, difficult to establish the exact prevalence of personality disorders in the general population as these disorders rarely present in isolation to psychiatric and psychological services. In addition, they are frequently associated with alterations of eating behaviour, and alcohol and substance abuse, as well as other mental disorders, antisocial behaviour, and sexual promiscuity.

> **HELPFUL HINT**
> ■ For different cultures it may be necessary to develop specific sets of criteria with regard to social norms, rules, and obligations that may not apply to other cultures.

BOX 14.1: MYTHS ABOUT PERSONALITY DISORDERS

It is commonly believed that people with personality disorders are dangerous. This is probably due to the fact that the term 'psychopath' is often wrongly ascribed to criminals. Board and Fritzon (2005) found in their study of senior business managers that so-called psychopaths can and do function quite effectively in mainstream society. After subjecting the managers to a variety of psychometric tests (e.g. the MMPI), she found evidence of three personality disorder profiles:

1. Histrionic personality disorder: Including superficial charm, insincerity, egocentricity, and manipulation.

2. Narcissistic personality disorder: Including grandiosity, self-focused lack of empathy for others, exploitativeness, and independence.

3. Obsessive-compulsive personality disorder: Including perfectionism, excessive devotion to work, rigidity, stubbornness, and dictatorial tendencies.

When comparing these profiles to incarcerated criminals, she found that the above-mentioned profiles were more common in the managers than in the criminals, thereby dispelling the myth that all psychopaths are necessarily criminals.

HISTORY OF PERSONALITY DISORDERS

In the late 1800s, the German psychiatrist Julius Ludwig August Koch studied people whom he considered morally degenerate, using the term 'psychopathic inferiority' (Gutmann, 2008). This term was then also used in the early 1900s by Emil Kraepelin, who suggested that there were six types within the category of psychopathic inferiority (Ebert & Bär, 2010).

In 1933, the Russian psychiatrist Pyotr Borisovich Gannushkin then published the influential book *Manifestations of Psychopathies: Statics, Dynamics, Systematic Aspects*, where he presented the different personality disorders in nine clusters.

When the ICD-6 was published in 1949, changing from the *International List of Causes of Death* to the *International Statistical Classification of Diseases*, personality disorders were included in the chapter 'Mental, psychoneurotic, and personality disorders' (Clark, Cuthbert, Lewis-Fernández, Narrow, & Reed, 2017). In 1952, when the DSM-I was published, it also included personality disorders. Since the mid-1900s, the category of personality disorders has undergone significant changes in both the ICD and the DSM.

The change in the ICD system from ICD-10 to the proposed ICD-11 is quite substantial. Previous categorical approaches such as the ICD-10 have not yielded diagnoses that assisted with clinical decision-making. Therefore, the WHO has proposed a different model for classifying adult personality disorders for the ICD-11. This is a dimensional model that is treatment oriented and personalised. Five severity levels of personality disturbance have been proposed in ICD-11, which aim to provide an assessment that is more concise, rapid, and precise, and more clinically useful.

The changes in the DSM can be summarised as follows (also see Table 14.2):

- *Changes in the names of the disorders:*
  - In DSM-I, there is reference to an 'emotionally unstable personality trait' disturbance, which changed to hysterical personality disorder in DSM-II, which finally changed to histrionic personality disorder in DSM-III, DSM-IV, and DSM-5.
  - The obsessive-compulsive personality disorder in DSM-5 was initially called a compulsive personality disorder in DSM-I.
  - Antisocial and dyssocial personality disorders in DSM-I have been called different disorders over the years, but are now known as antisocial personality disorder in DSM-IV and DSM-5.
- *Termination of disorders:*
  - Inadequate personality disorder, first described in the DSM-I, was last used in the DSM-II.
  - Passive-aggressive personality disorder was first described in the DSM-I, and appeared in the DSM-II, as well as in the DSM-III. Although it does not appear in the main text in DSM-IV, it was described in the appendix as a disorder that needed further investigation. This personality disorder has disappeared from the DSM altogether and is not mentioned or described in the DSM-5.
- *Inclusion of new disorders:*
  - Schizotypal, borderline, and narcissistic personality disorders first appeared in the DSM-III.
- *Change from Axis II to Axis I:*
  - The cyclothymic personality disorder that appeared in DSM-I and DSM-II was moved to 'Affective/mood disorders' in DSM-III and still appears as such in the DSM-IV and DSM-IV-TR. This disorder is now described in the 'Bipolar and related disorders' section of the DSM-5.
  - The explosive personality disorder, as was described in DSM-II, was a variant of the antisocial personality disorder as described in DSM-I, has subsequently been moved to the impulse control disorders, and is currently referred to as intermittent explosive disorder.

Table 14.2: History of DSM classification of personality disorders

DSM-I (1952)	DSM-II (1968)	DSM-III (1980)	DSM-IV (1994)	DSM-5 (2013)
Personality pattern disturbance Inadequate Paranoid Cyclothymic Schizoid	Inadequate Paranoid Cyclothymic Schizoid	**Cluster A** Paranoid Schizoid Schizotypal	**Cluster A** Paranoid Schizoid Schizotypal	**Cluster A** Paranoid Schizoid Schizotypal
Personality trait disturbance Emotionally unstable Passive-aggressive: ■ Dependent type ■ Aggressive type Compulsive	Hysterical Passive-aggressive Obsessive-compulsive	**Cluster B** Histrionic Antisocial Borderline Narcissistic	**Cluster B** Histrionic Antisocial Borderline Narcissistic	**Cluster B** Histrionic Antisocial Borderline Narcissistic
Sociopathic personality disturbance Antisocial Dyssocial	Asthenic Antisocial Explosive	**Cluster C** Compulsive Avoidant Dependent Passive-Aggressive	**Cluster C** Obsessive-compulsive Avoidant Dependent	**Cluster C** Obsessive-compulsive Avoidant Dependent

Castillo (1998) argues that, although there are many aetiological factors that are shared between personality disorders and other mental disorders, this notion is not reflected in the organisational system of the DSM. According to Castillo (1998), the DSM-IV made some strides towards a more postmodern way of classifying personality disorders, but this move was neither new, nor was it sufficient. This statement is based on the fact that, in both DSM-I and DSM-II, the distinction between different disorders was much more fluid. This is because the DSM-I and DSM-II were based on a psychodynamic paradigm which holds the view that mental illnesses exist on a continuum.

The transition from DSM-II to DSM-III marked a change in the underlying paradigm in the DSM from a psychodynamic to a biopsychosocial paradigm, which was carried through to both the DSM-IV and the DSM-IV-TR. This shift had the following implications (Castillo, 1998):

■ The spectrum, continuum, or dimensional approach to mental illnesses was mostly abandoned.
■ Mental disorders were split into narrow disease entities, each with its own biological causes and narrowly defined symptoms.

- Disorders that were thought to be of a specific kind of pathology with no connection to personality development were placed on Axis I.
- Those disorders that were assumed to be the result of abnormal personality development were placed on Axis II.

It is important to note that, although the spectrum, continuum, or dimensional approach fell out of use, the disorders that were assumed to be the result of abnormal personality development were provided a place on Axis II. These disorders can be seen as occurring along a continuum from normal to maladaptive variants of personality traits. The problem that arose was a practical diagnostic problem. Despite the fact that abnormal personality development is acknowledged as a dimensional process of change, it was diagnosed as a categorical disorder, similar to the way Axis I disorders were conceptualised and diagnosed. Thus, the positive and negative changes of development during the course of childhood, adolescence, and early adulthood were ignored. Instead, personality functioning was classified as if it were a discrete category of a fixed abnormal personality style, rather than a fluid, dimensional, continually evolving way of being and becoming.

The fact that the diagnostic process was based on the biopsychosocial paradigm made this shift away from a dimensional approach even more bewildering, since biological evidence is often intermingled with psychoanalytic/dynamic interpretations within a single explanation of the behavioural aspects of a personality disorder. However, interpretation of a character trait from the psychoanalytic/dynamic perspective should not be a part of an evidence-based diagnostic syndrome required for diagnosing a specific personality disorder.

This is, firstly, because evidence and interpretations are qualitatively different from each other, and secondly, because the psychoanalytic/dynamic approach lacks empirical verification. It was therefore much more difficult than was initially assumed to identify a cluster of specific symptoms (syndrome) together with a certain way of personality functioning that can be recognised as a personality disorder according to the DSM-IV-TR classification system on Axis II.

The DSM-5 introduced a number of paradigmatic and structural changes that impacted on the classification and description of personality disorders in a number of ways. In previous editions of the DSM, a multiaxial diagnostic system was used where a distinction was made between 'clinical disorders' (Axis I) and 'personality disorder' (Axis II). In the DSM-5, there is no longer a distinction between Axis I and Axis II disorders, with the result that personality disorders are coded in the same way as any other disorder. DSM-5 recognises the complexity of these disorders by adopting three different approaches to classifying and describing them:

- Noting some of the personality disorders in the categories where they fit best aetiologically. Schizotypal personality disorder is noted in the category of schizophrenia spectrum disorders, and antisocial personality disorder in the 'disruptive, impulse-control, and conduct disorder' category.
- The 'traditional' categorical description in the personality disorder section where the personality disorders are grouped together in three clusters and described in terms of their clinical pictures.
- A trait approach where personality disorders are described in terms of personality functioning and pathological personality traits (American Psychiatric Association, 2013).

CLINICAL PICTURE

In general, patients with personality disorders have wide-ranging problems in social relationships and mood regulation. These problems have usually been present throughout their adolescent and adult lives (see Table 14.1). These patients' patterns of perception, thought, and behavioural responses are fixed and inflexible, although their behaviour is often unpredictable. These patterns deviate markedly from their specific culture's expectations. To meet the DSM-5 threshold for making a clinical diagnosis, the pattern of symptoms (syndrome) must result in clinically significant distress or impairment in social, occupational, or other important areas of functioning. Note that the disorder should occur in all settings (e.g. social as well as occupational) and is not limited to one sphere of activity.

HELPFUL HINT

General patterns of personality dysfunction

- Patients with personality disorders have problems in social relationships and mood regulation.
- These problems have usually been present throughout their adolescent and adult lives. These patients' patterns of perception, thought, and behavioural responses are fixed and inflexible, although their behaviour is often unpredictable.
- These patterns deviate markedly from their specific culture's expectations.
- The pattern of symptoms (syndrome) must result in clinically significant distress or impairment in social, occupational, or other important areas of functioning.
- The disorder should occur in all settings and spheres of activity (e.g. social as well as occupational).

Note:

- The above-mentioned general patterns of personality dysfunction need to be supplemented by a specific set of diagnostic criteria for each one of the ten specific personality disorders.
- The general and specific patterns of personality dysfunction need to be considered together in order to make a diagnosis.

The above-mentioned general criteria for identifying personality functioning as a possible personality disorder need to be supplemented by another set of diagnostic criteria for each specific personality disorder in order to make a valid clinical diagnosis for a specific personality disorder. Both sets, general and specific, of DSM-5 diagnostic criteria need to be taken into account when the individual's syndrome is compared to the number of required criteria to reach the threshold for making a diagnosis.

However, that process is also fraught with difficulties. According to Meyerson et al. (2009, in Phend, 2009), making a diagnosis requires the presence of general criteria of personality disorders, as well as from two to five (out of eight or nine) specific criteria for the different personality disorders. By applying the above-mentioned freedom of various diagnostic options, 200 to 250 different ways of labelling personality functioning and behaviours are possible, which can all have the possible outcome of diagnosing one individual with more than one personality disorder (Meyerson et al., 2009, in Phend, 2009).

This diversity of symptom manifestation for two individuals diagnosed with personality disorders may in some cases result in two entirely different syndromes, although both individuals are diagnosed with the same disorder. For example, two individuals can each manifest five out of nine different symptoms with one symptom common to both, but will be diagnosed according to the DSM-5 criteria as having the same personality disorder. Theoretically they have the same personality disorder because they manifest five out of nine possible symptoms, despite the fact that their behavioural profiles look like two different disorders. Under such circumstances, it is extremely difficult to identify individuals with personality disorders by observing their symptomatic behaviour.

Another factor that contributes to the difficulty in diagnosing an individual with a personality disorder is the high rate of symptom overlap amongst all the personality disorders, in conjunction with a high rate of comorbidity with other disorders. This is demonstrated by the fact that personality disorders are often misdiagnosed (Gunderson, 2009; Meyerson et al., 2009, in Phend, 2009). Since misdiagnosing leads to administering the wrong kind of medications, which are thus ineffective in assisting the individual to get better, stigmatisation may follow (Oldham, 2009).

For example, if an individual is misdiagnosed several times and treated ineffectively with multiple medications for every incorrect diagnosis, he or she might be reluctant to try further medications upon being given yet another diagnosis (Oldham, 2009). Such an individual might refuse further treatment, and on account of refusing to comply with the clinician's instructions, may be labelled as difficult, uncooperative, or resistant. Indeed, both the patient and the clinician might thus become stigmatised, the individual for being difficult, uncooperative, and resistant, and the clinician for failing to treat his or her clients successfully.

The above-mentioned difficulties involved in diagnosing personality disorders and their high rate of misdiagnosis makes patients and caregivers of almost adult children shy away from taking the arduous road through multiple diagnoses and ineffective treatments. Clinicians, on the other hand, dislike working with clients who are classified with a personality disorder due to the high failure rate in treating these disorders. In addition, these difficulties may lead to a refusal by medical insurance companies to pay for ineffective treatments over long periods of time, sometimes up to five years, according to Kernberg and Michels (2009).

It has been mentioned previously that DSM-5 approaches personality disorders in three different ways, however, for the purposes of this book, we will only focus on the **categorical approach** and not on the aetiologically based approach, nor the personality trait approach to personality disorders. As is the case with other disorders, the personality disorder category is also divided into subcategories. Figure 14.1 illustrates the different clusters and diagnostic categories of personality disorders, according to the DSM-5 classification system.

In comparing the ICD-10 and DSM-5 classifications of personality disorders, quite a few differences are apparent. The DSM-5 distinguishes between ten different personality disorders arranged in three clusters (see Figure 14.1) and one category for personality disorders not otherwise specified. In contrast, the ICD-10 lists eight different personality disorders and one category for personality disorders not otherwise specified (see Figure 14.2).

As illustrated in Figure 14.1, the DSM-5 groups the personality disorders into three clusters, based on their 'descriptive similarities' (American Psychiatric Association, 2013). In addition, DSM-5 has 'general personality disorder' and 'other personality disorder' categories. The main reason for the three clusters is the enormous overlap in the diagnostic criteria for the various personality disorders in the DSM-5. Most people who are diagnosed with one disorder also tend to meet the diagnostic criteria for at least one other disorder, as we discussed above (Nolen-Hoeksema, 2007, 2013; Oldham, 2009; Kernberg & Michels, 2009).

However, the DSM-5 acknowledges that, although the clustering system is useful in some research and educational contexts, it has serious limitations and has not been consistently validated. It also acknowledges that it is possible, in some instances, for individuals to present with symptoms from two different clusters of personality disorders (American Psychiatric Association, 2000; Kernberg & Michels, 2009; Oldham, 2009).

Despite the difficulties with the DSM-5 classification system mentioned above, the cluster system will be used for systematically describing the typical syndromes (clusters of necessary symptoms) for making a diagnosis for each personality disorder in the three clusters.

Table 14.3: Comparison between ICD-10 and DSM-5 categories of personality disorders

Description	ICD-10	DSM-5
Suspicious; believes that other people will treat them wrongly; insists on own rights.	Paranoid PD	Paranoid PD
Shows great social detachment and is restricted in emotional expressions; is indifferent to emotional expressions of others and not interested in social relationships.	Schizoid PD	Schizoid PD
Social and interpersonal deficits marked by acute discomfort with, and reduced capacity for, close relationships.		Schizotypal PD
History of non-compliance with social norms and victimising others.	Dissocial PD	Antisocial PD
Characterised by instability, impulsivity, recklessness, and explosiveness.	Emotionally unstable PD Explosive type Borderline type Aggressive type	Borderline PD
People who show exaggerated emotional expressions and have an extremely strong longing for attention.	Histrionic PD	Histrionic PD

Description	ICD-10	DSM-5
Difficulty in performing work because of an obsession about making everything perfectly right. (Not the same as obsessive-compulsive disorder).	Anankastic PD	Obsessive-compulsive PD
People with a basic fear of being judged; shyness and constant social discomfort (embarrassed; avoid social situations); unwilling to commit themselves to a relationship.	Anxious (avoidant) PD	Avoidant PD
Not able to make day-to-day decisions; afraid of being rejected or abandoned; put aside own wishes and needs, while doing what others want.	Dependent PD	Dependent PD
Strong sense of self-importance; exaggerate own capabilities and achievements.	Other specific PDs Eccentric 'Unstable' type Narcissistic Passive-aggressive Psychoneurotic Immature	Narcissistic PD

Source: http://www.web4health.info, n.d.

CLUSTER A PERSONALITY DISORDERS

This cluster of personality disorders share a common theme of withdrawal from others due to fear and anxiety of people, as well as an indifference to people based on perceptions of the social environment, that differ from cultural or social expectations. Furthermore, these disorders share symptoms with schizophrenia, but without psychotic symptoms, and are often considered to reflect the personality processes that underlie or predispose people to schizophrenia. This cluster includes paranoid, schizoid, and schizotypal personality disorders.

Paranoid personality disorder

The typical symptom that characterises this disorder is a perception that other people, and the world at large, are hostile (American Psychiatric Association, 2013); this leads to extreme distrust and hypervigilance. According to Castillo (1998), typical symptoms include beliefs that:

- Other people want to exploit or deceive them, and that even friends and significant others are untrustworthy.
- All personal information shared with others may be used maliciously.
- There is hidden meaning in remarks or events that others perceive as benign.
- The spouse or partner is unfaithful.

Table 14.4: The relationship between personality style and personality disorders

PERSONALITY STYLE	PERSONALITY DISORDER
Conscientious, diligent	Obsessive-compulsive (**Note:** Obsessive-compulsive PD is not the same as OCD.)
Ambitious, self-confident	Narcissistic
Expressive, emotional	Histrionic
Alert, suspicious	Paranoid
Erratic, spontaneous	Borderline
Affectionate, loyal	Dependent
Independent, secretive, cautious, lonely	Schizoid
Self-critical, careful	Anxious; Avoidant
Full of foreboding, sensitive	Schizotypal
Adventuresome, likely to take risks	Antisocial (diagnosis)

Source: Adapted from: http://www.web4health.info, n.d.

Because of these perceptions, one can generally expect that people with this disorder will be cold and distant in their interpersonal relationships. They tend to react with suspicion to changes in situations and to find hostile and malevolent motives behind other people's trivial, innocent, or even positive acts (Barlow & Durand, 2005). Bernstein, Useda, and Siever (1995) provide an interesting description of the everyday behaviour of people with a paranoid disorder. According to them, these people tend to be either overtly or passively hostile towards others. They tend to be very argumentative, they complain, are very sensitive to criticism, and they have an excessive need for autonomy. The implications are that this type of behaviour will elicit rejection from others, which then reinforces their distrust of others; in this way, their interpersonal style (see Table 14.4), and the disorder, are reinforced.

Castillo (1998) warns that, although paranoid tendencies may develop among people who feel particularly alienated because of physical defects (e.g. deafness) or social factors (e.g. being an immigrant), one should be cautious not to diagnose the disorder too quickly and, as is the case with most other disorders, be mindful of the social context of the person.

There is close congruence between the DSM-5 and ICD-10 criteria for this disorder (see Table 14.5).

HELPFUL HINT
- Although paranoid tendencies may develop among people who feel particularly alienated because of physical defects (e.g. deafness) or social factors (e.g. being an immigrant), one should be cautious not to diagnose the disorder too quickly and be mindful of the social context of the person.

Table 14.5: Diagnostic criteria for paranoid personality disorder from the DSM-5 and the ICD-10

DSM-5	ICD-10
A. A pervasive distrust and suspiciousness of others such that their motives are interpreted as malevolent, beginning by early adulthood and present in a variety of contexts, as indicated by four (or more) of the following: (1) Suspects, without sufficient basis, that others are exploiting, harming, or deceiving him or her. (2) Is preoccupied with unjustified doubts about the loyalty or trustworthiness of friends or associates. (3) Is reluctant to confide in others because of unwarranted fear that the information will be used maliciously against him or her. (4) Reads hidden demeaning or threatening meanings into benign remarks or events. (5) Persistently bears grudges, i.e. is unforgiving of insults, injuries, or slights. (6) Perceives attacks on his or her character or reputation that are not apparent to others and is quick to react angrily or to counterattack.	■ Personality disorder characterised by at least three of the following: ▸ Excessive sensitiveness to setbacks and rebuffs. ▸ Tendency to bear grudges persistently, i.e. refusal to forgive insults and injuries or slights. ▸ Suspiciousness and a pervasive tendency to distort experience by misconstruing the neutral or friendly actions of others as hostile or contemptuous. ▸ A combative and tenacious sense of personal rights out of keeping with the actual situation. ▸ Recurrent suspicions, without justification, regarding sexual fidelity of spouse or sexual partner. ▸ Tendency to experience excessive self-importance, manifest in a persistent self-referential attitude. ▸ Preoccupation with unsubstantiated 'conspiratorial' explanations of events both immediate to the patient and in the world at large. ▸ *Includes:* expansive paranoid, fanatic, querulant, and sensitive paranoid personality (disorder)

DSM-5	ICD-10
(7) Has recurrent suspicions, without justification, regarding fidelity of spouse or sexual partner. B. Does not occur exclusively during the course of schizophrenia, a mood disorder with psychotic features, or another psychotic disorder, and is not due to the direct physiological effects of a general medical condition. **Note:** If criteria are met prior to the onset of schizophrenia, add 'premorbid', e.g. 'paranoid personality disorder (premorbid)'.	▸ ***Excludes:*** delusional disorder, schizophrenia

Source: Reprinted with permission from the *Diagnostic and Statistical Manual of Mental Disorders*, fifth edition (DSM-5), American Psychiatric Association (APA), 2013, p. 649, and ICD-10 *Classification of Mental and Behavioural Disorders: Diagnostic Criteria for Research*, World Health Organization (WHO), Geneva, 2007.

Schizoid personality disorder

One way of describing people with this disorder would be to say that they are extreme introverts; however, this would not be accurate as it is more extreme than 'mere' introversion. According to the American Psychiatric Association (2013), the key features of this disorder include both a pervasive detachment from social relationships, as well as a restricted range of emotions. The American psychologist Richard J. Castillo (1998) describes these people as extremely self-absorbed, with little or no contact with their social or physical environment. They tend to show very little emotional response to events, and they tend to have a lack of emotional motivation for engaging in activities that others seem to enjoy (e.g. intimate relationships, relationships with family and colleagues).

According to Barlow and Durand (2005), other people tend to experience them as being 'cold', 'indifferent', or 'aloof'. Due to their lack of emotional responsiveness, they seem to be untouched by social feedback such as praise or criticism. As is the case with paranoid personality disorder, the DSM and ICD criteria for this disorder are similar (see Table 14.6).

Table 14.6: Diagnostic criteria for schizoid personality disorder from the DSM-5 and the ICD-10

DSM-5	ICD-10
A. A pervasive pattern of detachment from social relationships and a restricted range of expression of emotions in interpersonal settings, beginning by early adulthood and present in a variety of contexts, as indicated by four (or more) of the following: (1) Neither desires nor enjoys close relationships, including being part of a family. (2) Almost always chooses solitary activities. (3) Has little, if any, interest in having sexual experiences with another person. (4) Takes pleasure in few, if any, activities. (5) Lacks close friends or confidants other than first-degree relatives. (6) Appears indifferent to the praise or criticism of others. (7) Shows emotional coldness, detachment, or flattened affectivity. B. Does not occur exclusively during the course of schizophrenia, a mood disorder with psychotic features, another psychotic disorder, or a pervasive developmental disorder and is not due to the direct physiological effects of a general medical condition. **Note:** If criteria are met prior to the onset of schizophrenia, add 'premorbid', e.g. 'schizoid personality disorder (premorbid)'.	■ Personality disorder characterised by at least three of the following: ▸ Few, if any, activities provide pleasure. ▸ Emotional coldness, detachment or flattened affectivity. ▸ Limited capacity to express either warm, tender feelings or anger towards others. ▸ Apparent indifference to either praise or criticism. ▸ Little interest in having sexual experiences with another person (taking age into account). ▸ Almost invariable preference for solitary activities. ▸ Excessive preoccupation with fantasy and introspection. ▸ Lack of close friends or confiding relationships (or having only one) and of desire for such relationships. ▸ Marked insensitivity to prevailing social norms and conventions. ■ Excludes: ▸ Asperger's syndrome ▸ Delusional disorder ▸ Schizoid disorder of childhood ▸ Schizophrenia ▸ Schizotypal disorder

Source: Reprinted with permission from the *Diagnostic and Statistical Manual of Mental Disorders*, fifth edition (DSM-5), American Psychiatric Association (APA), 2013, p. 652, and ICD-10 *Classification of Mental and Behavioural Disorders: Diagnostic Criteria for Research*, World Health Organization (WHO), Geneva, 2007.

Schizotypal personality disorder

This disorder shares some of the characteristics of schizoid personality disorder, such as emotional detachment and social isolation. However, it differs from schizoid personality disorder in that, in addition to anxiety in social relationships, people with this disorder also display eccentricities such as superstitiousness, preoccupation with paranormal phenomena, magical thinking, and rituals (Castillo, 1998). The symptoms of this disorder can be summarised as follows:

- Ideas of reference, that is, the belief that random events have some special meaning for them (Nolen-Hoeksema, 2013).
- Paranoia or extreme suspiciousness, that is, as is the case with paranoid personality disorder, the tendency to view other people as hostile and deceitful (Nolen-Hoeksema, 2013).
- Odd beliefs or magical thinking, for example, believing that they are clairvoyant or telepathic (Barlow & Durand, 2005).
- Illusions, which can be described as the misperception or misinterpretation of real external sensory stimuli (Kaplan, Sadock, & Grebb, 1994). An example of this would be feeling the presence of another person when they are alone (Barlow & Durand, 2005).
- Vague, circumstantial, or stereotyped speech (Nolen-Hoeksema, 2013).

Table 14.7: Diagnostic criteria for schizotypal personality disorder from the DSM-5

DSM-5
A. A pervasive pattern of social and interpersonal deficits marked by acute discomfort with, and reduced capacity for, close relationships as well as by cognitive or perceptual distortions and eccentricities of behaviour, beginning by early adulthood and present in a variety of contexts, as indicated by five (or more) of the following: (1) Ideas of reference (excluding delusions of reference). (2) Odd beliefs or magical thinking that influences behaviour and is inconsistent with subcultural norms (e.g. superstitiousness, belief in clairvoyance, telepathy, or 'sixth sense'; in children and adolescents, bizarre fantasies or preoccupations). (3) Unusual perceptual experiences, including bodily illusions. (4) Odd thinking and speech (e.g. vague, circumstantial, metaphorical, over-elaborate, or stereotyped). (5) Suspiciousness or paranoid ideation. (6) Inappropriate or constricted affect. (7) Behaviour or appearance that is odd, eccentric, or peculiar. (8) Lack of close friends or confidants other than first-degree relatives. (9) Excessive social anxiety that does not diminish with familiarity and tends to be associated with paranoid fears rather than negative judgements about self. B. Does not occur exclusively during the course of schizophrenia, a mood disorder with psychotic features, another psychotic disorder, or a pervasive developmental disorder. **Note:** If criteria are met prior to the onset of schizophrenia, add 'premorbid', e.g. 'schizotypal personality disorder (premorbid)'.

Source: Reprinted with permission from the *Diagnostic and Statistical Manual of Mental Disorders*, fifth edition (DSM-5), American Psychiatric Association (APA), 2013, p. 655.

Some of these symptoms are very similar to those of schizophrenia, but are not severe enough to warrant a diagnosis of schizophrenia. It is for this reason that DSM-5 also notes this disorder in the schizophrenia spectrum disorders. The similarities are such, however, that there is clearly a strong link between this disorder and schizophrenia. The main difference between DSM-5 and ICD-10 is that the ICD-10 does not make provision for a schizotypal personality disorder, and sees this as a variant of schizoid personality disorder.

CLUSTER B PERSONALITY DISORDERS

The core feature of people with personality disorders in this cluster is that they tend to engage in dramatic, impulsive behaviour with little regard for their own safety or the safety of others. They may also act in a hostile and, in some cases, violent way and show very little empathy for others (Nolen-Hoeksema, 2013). This cluster includes borderline, histrionic, narcissistic, and antisocial personality disorders.

Borderline personality disorder

According to Castillo (1998), the core feature of this disorder is a persistent instability in social relationships, self-image, and emotions. It seems as if fear of rejection and abandonment, as well as intense unmet needs for affection and closeness, are central to this instability. It is clear that there is some tension between these two core features: on the one hand, people with this disorder have an intense need for affection; however, on the other hand, they have an intense fear of being rejected or abandoned.

The key clinical features of this disorder include:

- Unstable mood, which is characterised by severe depression, anxiety, and anger, with no obvious environmental triggers (Nolen-Hoeksema, 2007).
- Unstable self-concept, which can range from episodes of extreme self-doubt to episodes of grandiose self-importance (Nolen-Hoeksema, 2007).
- Feelings of emptiness, which are often described as chronic boredom (Barlow & Durand, 2005); however, this may be due to difficulties with their own identities, in other words, a global lack of knowing who or what they are (Nolen-Hoeksema, 2007).
- Impulsive, self-mutilating, and suicidal behaviour (Barlow & Durand, 2005).
- Unstable interpersonal relationships, which are characterised by switching from idealising a person to despising them for no apparent reason (Nolen-Hoeksema, 2007).

This disorder produces significant impairment in social, academic, and occupational functioning. Borderline personality disorder's high comorbidity with other disorders, such as major depression, bipolar disorder, eating, and substance disorders (Barlow & Durand, 2005), and with other personality disorders, makes borderline PD rather difficult to identify and deal with.

Table 14.8: Diagnostic criteria for borderline personality disorder from the DSM-5 and for emotionally unstable personality disorder from the ICD-10

DSM-5 Borderline personality disorder	ICD-10 Emotionally unstable personality disorder
A pervasive pattern of instability of interpersonal relationships, self-image, and affects, and marked impulsivity beginning by early adulthood and present in a variety of contexts, as indicated by five (or more) of the following: (1) Frantic efforts to avoid real or imagined abandonment. **Note:** Do not include suicidal or self-mutilating behaviour covered in Criterion 5. (2) A pattern of unstable and intense interpersonal relationships characterised by alternating between extremes of idealisation and devaluation. (3) Identity disturbance: markedly and persistently unstable self-image or sense of self. (4) Impulsivity in at least two areas that are potentially self-damaging (e.g. spending, sex, substance abuse, reckless driving, binge-eating). **Note:** Do not include suicidal or self-mutilating behaviour covered in Criterion 5. (5) Recurrent suicidal behaviour, gestures, or threats, or self-mutilating behaviour. (6) Affective instability due to a marked reactivity of mood (e.g. intense episodic dysphoria, irritability, or anxiety usually lasting a few hours and only rarely more than a few days). (7) Chronic feelings of emptiness. (8) Inappropriate, intense anger or difficulty controlling anger (e.g. frequent displays of temper, constant anger, recurrent physical fights). (9) Transient, stress-related paranoid ideation or severe dissociative symptoms.	▪ A personality disorder in which there is a marked tendency to act impulsively without consideration of the consequences, together with affective instability. The ability to plan ahead may be minimal, and outbursts of intense anger may often lead to violence or 'behavioural explosions'; these are easily precipitated when impulsive acts are criticised or thwarted by others. Two variants of this personality disorder are specified, and both share this general theme of impulsiveness and lack of self-control. ▪ Impulsive type: The predominant characteristics are emotional instability and lack of impulse control. Outbursts of violence or threatening behaviour are common, particularly in response to criticism by others. ▪ Includes: Explosive and aggressive personality (disorder) ▪ Excludes: Dissocial personality disorder ▪ Borderline type: Several of the characteristics of emotional instability are present; in addition, the patient's own self-image, aims, and internal preferences (including sexual) are often unclear or disturbed. There are usually chronic feelings of emptiness. A liability to become involved in intense and unstable relationships may cause repeated emotional crises and may be associated with excessive efforts to avoid abandonment and a series of suicidal threats or acts of self-harm (although these may occur without obvious precipitants). ▪ Includes: borderline personality (disorder)

Source: Reprinted with permission from the *Diagnostic and Statistical Manual of Mental Disorders*, fifth edition (DSM-5), American Psychiatric Association (APA), 2013, p. 663, and ICD-10 *Classification of Mental and Behavioural Disorders: Diagnostic Criteria for Research*, World Health Organization (WHO), Geneva, 2007.

☑ ACTIVITY

In 2016, the South African psychiatrists Laila Paruk and Albert Janse van Rensburg published an article titled 'Inpatient management of borderline personality disorder at Helen Joseph Hospital, Johannesburg'. Read the extract below from this article, which explains what happened after these patients were discharged, and consider whether this behaviour is what you would expect among people diagnosed with borderline personality disorder.

> On discharge, patients were either referred to continue care as outpatients at Helen Joseph Hospital or were transferred to other facilities. The majority were directed to follow up at the Helen Joseph Hospital Outpatient Department (n = 49, 50.0%), 17 were referred to the Tara Hospital psychotherapy programme (n = 17, 17.7%) and 13 to a community clinic (n = 13, 14.0%). Two patients were placed at a long-term residential facility, whereas 23 were referred to the private sector, or for substance rehabilitation.
>
> The actual movements of patients following discharge were compared to the initially proposed plan. Patients were again split into two groups: those who were supposed to follow up at the Helen Joseph Hospital Psychiatric Outpatient Department (n = 49) and those who were supposed to follow up elsewhere (n = 48).
>
> The electronic outpatient database for 2010 was then scrutinised to track whether these patients did, in fact, present as scheduled. Of the 49 patients meant to be seen as outpatients at Helen Joseph Hospital, only 9 (18.0%) kept their appointments. The data were also cross-referenced against the emergency visits for 2010 while keeping the patients in the same two groups. Seven of the nine patients who were compliant with their outpatient visits also presented as emergency cases during the study period. Thirty-three of the forty (83.0%), who were non-adherent to their outpatient dates, were actually seen as emergency cases.
>
> Of the 48 patients that were given a plan other than following up with Helen Jospeh Hospital outpatients on discharge, 30 (63.0%) presented to the Helen Joseph Hospital Emergency Department anyway, whereas one returned unscheduled to the Helen Joseph Hospital Outpatient Clinic.

Source: Adapted from: Paruk, L., & Janse van Rensburg, A. B. R., 2016. 'Inpatient management of borderline personality disorder at Helen Joseph Hospital, Johannesburg'. In: *South African Journal of Psychiatry*, 22(1). http://dx.doi.org/10.4102/sajpsychiatry.v22i1.678

Histrionic personality disorder

The main characteristics of this disorder include 'excessive' emotionality and attention-seeking (American Psychiatric Association, 2013). Although this seems relatively clear, Castillo (1998) points out that it may be difficult to define 'excessive', as this definition may vary from one culture to another. This definition may also be influenced by gender.

Castillo (1998), Nolen-Hoeksema (2007), and Barlow and Durand (2005) describe the core features of this disorder as follows:

- People with this disorder are overly dramatic, enthusiastic, and flirtatious. Although they may dress and appear to be overtly sexual in social situations, this apparent seductiveness is often not to be taken seriously, as it is often only used to attract attention.
- They show active and purposeful seeking of attention. They constantly want approval and reassurance from others, and if they do not get this, they may get upset or angry.
- They are typically very concerned about their physical appearance.
- They tend to exaggerate medical problems, make more frequent doctor's appointments, and have more suicidal gestures than the average person.
- Other people may experience them as being shallow, self-centred, demanding, and dependent.

Table 14.9: Diagnostic criteria for histrionic personality disorder from the DSM-5 and the ICD-10

DSM-5	ICD-10
A pervasive pattern of excessive emotionality and attention-seeking, beginning by early adulthood and present in a variety of contexts, as indicated by five (or more) of the following: (1) Is uncomfortable in situations in which he or she is not the centre of attention. (2) Interaction with others is often characterised by inappropriate, sexually seductive, or provocative behaviour. (3) Displays rapidly shifting and shallow expression of emotions. (4) Consistently uses physical appearance to draw attention to self. (5) Has a style of speech that is excessively impressionistic and lacking in detail. (6) Shows self-dramatisation, theatricality, and exaggerated expression of emotion. (7) Is suggestible, i.e. easily influenced by others or circumstances. (8) Considers relationships to be more intimate than they actually are.	■ Personality disorder characterised by at least three of the following: ▸ Self-dramatisation, theatricality, exaggerated expression of emotions; ▸ Suggestibility, easily influenced by others or by circumstances; ▸ Shallow and labile affectivity; ▸ Continual seeking for excitement, appreciation by others, and activities in which the patient is the centre of attention; ▸ Inappropriate seductiveness in appearance or behaviour; ▸ Over-concern with physical attractiveness. ▸ Associated features may include egocentricity, self-indulgence, continuous longing for appreciation, feelings that are easily hurt, and persistent manipulative behaviour to achieve own needs. ■ Includes: ▸ hysterical and psychoinfantile personality (disorder)

Source: Reprinted with permission from the *Diagnostic and Statistical Manual of Mental Disorders*, fifth edition (DSM-5), American Psychiatric Association (APA), 2013, p. 667, and ICD-10 *Classification of Mental and Behavioural Disorders: Diagnostic Criteria for Research*, World Health Organization (WHO), Geneva, 2007.

Narcissistic personality disorder

Whereas people with a histrionic personality disorder actively seek attention, people with a narcissistic personality disorder do so in a more passive way. Their whole demeanour tends to portray a quiet sense of knowing that they are more important than others. Nolen-Hoeksema (2007) and Barlow and Durand (2005) describe these people as follows:

- They are preoccupied with thoughts of their self-importance and fantasies of power and success.
- They make unreasonable demands of others.
- They have little empathy, and ignore the needs and wants of others.
- They exploit others to gain power.
- They can be arrogant and demean others.
- They require (and expect) a great deal of special attention.
- When in the presence of truly successful people, they tend to become envious and arrogant.
- They can be very boastful and exaggerate their own talents and accomplishments and, at the same time, downplay, or blame others for, their failures.

Table 14.10: Diagnostic criteria for narcissistic personality disorder from the DSM-5 and the ICD-10

DSM-5	ICD-10
A pervasive pattern of grandiosity (in fantasy or behaviour), need for admiration, and lack of empathy, beginning by early adulthood and present in a variety of contexts, as indicated by five (or more) of the following: (1) Has a grandiose sense of self-importance (e.g. exaggerates achievements and talents, expects to be recognised as superior without commensurate achievements). (2) Is preoccupied with fantasies of unlimited success, power, brilliance, beauty, or ideal love. (3) Believes that he or she is 'special' and unique and can only be understood by, or should associate with, other special or high-status people (or institutions). (4) Requires excessive admiration. (5) Has a sense of entitlement, i.e. unreasonable expectations of especially favourable treatment or automatic compliance with his or her expectations. (6) Is interpersonally exploitative, i.e. takes advantage of others to achieve his or her own ends. (7) Lacks empathy: Is unwilling to recognise or identify with the feelings and needs of others. (8) Is often envious of others or believes that others are envious of him or her. (9) Shows arrogant, haughty behaviours or attitudes.	- While the ICD-10 does not specifically define the characteristics of this personality disorder, it is classified in the category other specific personality disorders. - The ICD-10 states that narcissistic personality disorder is a personality disorder that fits none of the specific criteria of the other personality disorders.

Source: Reprinted with permission from the *Diagnostic and Statistical Manual of Mental Disorders*, fifth edition (DSM-5), American Psychiatric Association (APA), 2013, p. 669, and ICD-10 *Classification of Mental and Behavioural Disorders: Diagnostic Criteria for Research*, World Health Organization (WHO), Geneva, 2007.

Antisocial personality disorder

The essential diagnostic feature of antisocial personality disorder is a pervasive pattern of violation of, and disregard for, the rights of others without showing remorse or guilt for one's behaviour. This pattern of disrespect begins in childhood or early adolescence and continues into adulthood. Antisocial personality disorder is also referred to as 'psychopathy', 'sociopathy', or 'dissocial personality disorder' (ICD-10), and it can only be diagnosed when an individual has reached the age of 18. Because deceit and manipulation are central features of this disorder, it is best to assess the individual systematically by collecting information from collateral sources.

In terms of their personal history, the individual must have had some symptoms of conduct disorder before the age of 15. Conduct disorder involves four groups of persistent and repetitive patterns of behaviour that violate the norms, rules, or basic rights of others, such as aggression towards people and animals, destruction of property, deceit, or theft (see Chapter 15). The pattern of conduct disorder continues into adulthood as antisocial personality disorder and involves an intensification of repetitively performed acts that become grounds for arrest, such as destruction of property, harassing others, stealing, lying, and pursuing illegal occupations.

Table 14.11: Diagnostic criteria for antisocial personality disorder from the DSM-5 and dissocial personality disorder from the ICD-10

DSM-5 Antisocial personality disorder	ICD-10 Dissocial personality disorder
A. A pervasive pattern of disregard for and violation of the rights of others occurring since age 15 years, as indicated by three (or more) of the following: (1) Failure to conform to social norms with respect to lawful behaviours as indicated by repeatedly performing acts that are grounds for arrest. (2) Deceitfulness, as indicated by repeated lying, use of aliases, or conning others for personal profit or pleasure. (3) Impulsivity or failure to plan ahead. (4) Irritability and aggressiveness, as indicated by repeated physical fights or assaults. (5) Reckless disregard for safety of self or others. (6) Consistent irresponsibility, as indicated by repeated failure to sustain consistent work behaviour or honour financial obligations.	■ Personality disorder, usually coming to attention because of a gross disparity between behaviour and the prevailing social norms, and characterised by at least three of the following: ▸ Callous unconcern for the feelings of others. ▸ Gross and persistent attitude of irresponsibility and disregard for social norms, rules, and obligations. ▸ Incapacity to maintain enduring relationships, though having no difficulty in establishing them. ▸ Very low tolerance for frustration and a low threshold for discharge of aggression, including violence. ▸ Incapacity to experience guilt and to profit from experience, particularly punishment. ▸ Marked proneness to blame others, or to offer plausible rationalisations, for the behaviour that has brought the patient into conflict with society.

DSM-5 Antisocial personality disorder	ICD-10 Dissocial personality disorder
(7) Lack of remorse, as indicated by being indifferent to or rationalising having hurt, mistreated, or stolen from another. B. The individual is at least 18 years old. C. There is evidence of conduct disorder with onset before the age of 15. D. The occurrence of antisocial behaviour is not exclusively during the course of schizophrenia or a manic episode.	■ There may also be persistent irritability as an associated feature. Conduct disorder during childhood and adolescence, though not invariably present, may further support the diagnosis. ■ Includes: Amoral, antisocial, asocial, psychopathic, and sociopathic personality (disorder) ■ Excludes: Conduct disorders, emotionally unstable personality disorder

Source: Reprinted with permission from the *Diagnostic and Statistical Manual of Mental Disorders*, fifth edition (DSM-5), American Psychiatric Association (APA), 2013, p. 659, and ICD-10 *Classification of Mental and Behavioural Disorders: Diagnostic Criteria for Research*, World Health Organization (WHO), Geneva, 2007.

The typical clinical picture of people with an antisocial personality disorder includes features such as the following:

■ There is a pattern of impulsive behaviour that indicates their lack of planning ahead; their decision-making is often executed on the spur of the moment without forethought and consideration for the consequences to others and themselves. This impulsivity often leads to sudden changes of job, location, and relationship, and may manifest as irritability and aggressiveness, accompanied by fights and physical assaults on their spouse and/or children.

■ There is a total disregard for their own safety and the safety of others, as displayed by driving recklessly, speeding excessively while intoxicated, and engaging in sexual behaviour or substance use with a high risk of harmful consequences.

■ In order to gain personal profit or pleasure in the form of sex, money, or power, such individuals use manipulative and deceitful means to obtain their desires, often with much charm and by repeatedly lying to and deceiving others.

■ Financial and occupational irresponsibility are indicated by truancy from work without explanation or future planning for the payment of debts, and failure to support their dependants.

■ People with this disorder rarely compensate or make amends for their deliberately harmful behaviour; they frequently lack empathy, and they can be excessively callous, cynical, and contemptuous with regard to the feelings of others.

■ People with this disorder have an inflated and unrealistic self-appraisal.

CLUSTER C PERSONALITY DISORDERS

This cluster includes the avoidant, dependent, and obsessive-compulsive personality disorders. This cluster of personality disorders differs quite significantly from the other personality disorders in that anxiety and fearfulness are quite evident in these disorders. This feature makes it difficult to distinguish these disorders from other disorders and they also have, for this reason, a high comorbidity with anxiety-related disorders.

Avoidant personality disorder

The key features of this disorder are social anxiety, low self-esteem, and hypersensitivity to criticism (Castillo, 1998). People with this disorder are so fearful of social interactions that they actively avoid any social contact that may result in rejection, humiliation, or criticism. Kaplan et al. (1994) highlight the following features shown by people with this disorder:

- They have a need for interpersonal contact. However, their fear of rejection prevents them from establishing interpersonal relationships. They are generally unwilling to enter into relationships unless there is a guarantee of uncritical acceptance.
- In conversations with others, they may express uncertainty and a lack of self-confidence.
- They have a fear of speaking in public or making requests from others.
- They have a tendency to interpret others' comments as derogatory or ridiculing.

This disorder, on face value, is similar to schizoid personality disorder, as people with the latter diagnosis also display patterns of social inhibition, feelings of inadequacy, and hypersensitivity to rejection. However, unlike people with a schizoid personality disorder, people with avoidant personality disorder actually desire relationships with others but are paralysed by their fear and sensitivity into social isolation.

Table 14.12: Diagnostic criteria for avoidant personality disorder from the DSM-5 and the ICD-10

DSM-5	ICD-10
A pervasive pattern of social inhibition, feelings of inadequacy, and hypersensitivity to negative evaluation, beginning by early adulthood and present in a variety of contexts, as indicated by four (or more) of the following: (1) Avoids occupational activities that involve significant interpersonal contact, because of fears of criticism, disapproval, or rejection. (2) Is unwilling to get involved with people unless certain of being liked. (3) Shows restraint within intimate relationships because of the fear of being shamed or ridiculed. (4) Is preoccupied with being criticised or rejected in social situations.	■ Personality disorder characterised by at least three of the following: ▸ Persistent and pervasive feelings of tension and apprehension. ▸ Belief that one is socially inept, personally unappealing, or inferior to others. ▸ Excessive preoccupation with being criticised or rejected in social situations. ▸ Unwillingness to become involved with people unless certain of being liked. ▸ Restrictions in lifestyle because of need to have physical security.

DSM-5	ICD-10
(5) Is inhibited in new interpersonal situations because of feelings of inadequacy. (6) Views self as socially inept, personally unappealing, or inferior to others. (7) Is unusually reluctant to take personal risks or to engage in any new activities because they may prove embarrassing.	‣ Avoidance of social or occupational activities that involve significant interpersonal contact because of fear of criticism, disapproval, or rejection. ‣ Associated features may include hypersensitivity to rejection and criticism.

Source: Reprinted with permission from the *Diagnostic and Statistical Manual of Mental Disorders*, fifth edition (DSM-5), American Psychiatric Association (APA), 2013, p. 672 and ICD-10 *Classification of Mental and Behavioural Disorders: Diagnostic Criteria for Research*, World Health Organization (WHO), Geneva, 2007.

Dependent personality disorder

While many people exhibit dependent behaviours and traits, those with dependent personality disorder have an excessive need to be taken care of, which results in submissive and clinging behaviour, regardless of consequences (American Psychiatric Association, 2013) (see the case study of Dorothy earlier in this chapter). The disorder may be characterised by the following:

■ People with this disorder, because they feel inadequate to cope with the demands of life, may be very passive and indecisive concerning their own lives (Castillo, 1998).

■ As a result, they may become overly dependent on others to make decisions for them and are generally unable to make decisions for themselves without advice and reassurance from others (Kaplan et al., 1994).

■ Because of their dependency on others, they tend to deny their own thoughts, feelings, and needs that may upset others, and ultimately may lead to rejection (Nolen-Hoeksema, 2013).

■ According to Kaplan et al. (1994), these people tend to avoid positions of responsibility and become anxious when asked to take a leadership role.

■ Unlike people with avoidant personality disorder, who cannot function in a relationship, people with dependent personality disorder can *only* function in a relationship (Nolen-Hoeksema, 2013). Kaplan et al. (1994) state that they do not like to be alone and actively seek out others on whom they can depend.

Dependency may be a symptom of other personality disorders. The dependency in other personality disorders may, however, be less evident due to the other, more dramatic, symptoms of such disorders.

Table 14.13: Diagnostic criteria for dependent personality disorder from the DSM-5 and the ICD-10

DSM-5	ICD-10
A pervasive and excessive need to be taken care of that leads to submissive and clinging behaviour and fears of separation, beginning by early adulthood and present in a variety of contexts, as indicated by five (or more) of the following: (1) Has difficulty making everyday decisions without an excessive amount of advice and reassurance from others. (2) Needs others to assume responsibility for most major areas of his or her life. (3) Has difficulty expressing disagreement with others because of fear of loss of support or approval. (Note: Do not include realistic fears of retribution.) (4) Has difficulty initiating projects or doing things on his or her own (because of a lack of self-confidence in judgement or abilities rather than a lack of motivation or energy). (5) Goes to excessive lengths to obtain nurturance and support from others, to the point of volunteering to do things that are unpleasant. (6) Feels uncomfortable or helpless when alone because of exaggerated fears of being unable to care for himself or herself. (7) Urgently seeks another relationship as a source of care and support when a close relationship ends. (8) Is unrealistically preoccupied with fears of being left to take care of himself or herself.	■ Personality disorder characterised by at least three of the following: ▸ Encouraging or allowing others to make most of one's important life decisions. ▸ Subordination of one's own needs to those of others on whom one is dependent, and undue compliance with their wishes. ▸ Unwillingness to make even reasonable demands on the people one depends on. ▸ Feeling uncomfortable or helpless when alone, because of exaggerated fears of inability to care for oneself. ▸ Preoccupation with fears of being abandoned by a person with whom one has a close relationship, and of being left to care for oneself. ▸ Limited capacity to make everyday decisions without an excessive amount of advice and reassurance from others. ■ Associated features may include perceiving oneself as helpless, incompetent, and lacking stamina.

Source: Reprinted with permission from the *Diagnostic and Statistical Manual of Mental Disorders*, fifth edition (DSM-5), American Psychiatric Association (APA), 2013, p. 675, and ICD-10 *Classification of Mental and Behavioural Disorders: Diagnostic Criteria for Research*, World Health Organization (WHO), Geneva, 2007.

Obsessive-compulsive personality disorder

The name of this disorder is problematic in that it often leads to confusion between this disorder and the obsessive-compulsive disorders. It must be noted that these two disorders have very little in common other than their names. In obsessive-compulsive personality disorder, there are neither obsessions nor compulsions (Nolen-Hoeksema, 2013). The key features of this disorder include a marked preoccupation with order, perfection, attention to detail, rules, and control (Castillo, 1998). People with this disorder tend to be inflexible and lack openness, which leads to poor interpersonal relationships (Nolen-Hoeksema, 2013). The characteristics of this disorder include:

- Their preoccupation with rules and procedures interferes with efficiency, according to Castillo (1998), and their dysfunctional belief that things can only be done according to their 'correct' way makes people with this disorder anxious and prone to developing a fear of making mistakes, which prevents them from seeing the 'big picture'.
- They tend to be serious, control their emotions excessively, and lack spontaneity (Millon, Davis, Millon, Escovar, & Meagher, 2000).
- Others experience them as being stubborn, stingy, possessive, moralistic, and officious (Nolen-Hoeksema, 2013).
- They are workaholics and seemingly have very little need for leisure activities or friendships (Nolen-Hoeksema, 2013).
- They are bound by their self-created personal rules that reflect their own rigid standards of control; when they try to transfer these to others in an overly inflexible interpersonal style, this often leads to being ostracised by others.

Table 14.14: Diagnostic criteria for obsessive-compulsive personality disorder from the DSM-5 and for anankastic personality disorder from the ICD-10

DSM-5 Obsessive-compulsive personality disorder	ICD-10 Anankastic personality disorder
A pervasive pattern of preoccupation with orderliness, perfectionism, and mental and interpersonal control, at the expense of flexibility, openness, and efficiency, beginning by early adulthood and present in a variety of contexts, as indicated by four (or more) of the following: (1) Is preoccupied with details, rules, lists, order, organisation, or schedules to the extent that the major point of the activity is lost. (2) Shows perfectionism that interferes with task completion (e.g. is unable to complete a project because his or her own overly strict standards are not met). (3) Is excessively devoted to work and productivity to the exclusion of leisure activities and friendships (not accounted for by obvious economic necessity). (4) Is over-conscientious, scrupulous, and inflexible about matters of morality, ethics, or values (not accounted for by cultural or religious identification).	■ Personality disorder characterised by at least three of the following: ▸ Feelings of excessive doubt and caution. ▸ Preoccupation with details, rules, lists. order, organisation, or schedule. ▸ Perfectionism that interferes with task completion; excessive conscientiousness, scrupulousness, and undue preoccupation with productivity to the exclusion of pleasure and interpersonal relationships. ▸ Excessive pedantry and adherence to social conventions. ▸ Rigidity and stubbornness. ▸ Unreasonable insistence by the patient that others submit to exactly his or her way of doing things, or unreasonable reluctance to allow others to do things. ▸ Intrusion of insistent and unwelcome thoughts or impulses.

DSM-5 Obsessive-compulsive personality disorder	ICD-10 Anankastic personality disorder

(5) Is unable to discard worn-out or worthless objects even when they have no sentimental value.
(6) Is reluctant to delegate tasks or to work with others unless they submit to exactly his or her way of doing things.
(7) Adopts a miserly spending style toward both self and others; money is viewed as something to be hoarded for future catastrophes.
(8) Shows rigidity and stubbornness.
	■ Includes:
	  ▸ compulsive and obsessional personality (disorder).
	  ▸ obsessive-compulsive personality disorder.
	■ Excludes: Obsessive-compulsive disorder

Source: Reprinted with permission from the *Diagnostic and Statistical Manual of Mental Disorders*, fifth edition (DSM-5), American Psychiatric Association (APA), 2013, p. 678, and ICD-10 *Classification of Mental and Behavioural Disorders: Diagnostic Criteria for Research*, World Health Organization (WHO), Geneva, 2007.

COMORBIDITY

Comorbidity is of interest from the viewpoint of a diathesis-stress approach to personality development. The diathesis-stress approach argues that development of a disorder depends on the interaction of an individual's vulnerability due to an innate genetic predisposition and factors in the environment and stressful life experiences (Walker, Downey, & Bergman, 1989). When we apply the diathesis-stress model to the development of personality traits, personality functioning, personality dysfunction, and other disorders, we can see that continuous interactional processes between genetic vulnerabilities and environmental stressors are at work throughout life. These ongoing interactional processes can emerge as a continuous developmental range of personality functioning that manifests as personality functioning/dysfunction or personality traits/disorders.

According to this view, one should find some pre-existing personality disturbance in most clinical disorders, although the manifestations may not always be strong enough to meet the diagnostic criteria for personality disorders. It follows that the pattern of association between particular 'clinical' and personality disorders is not a random one, and clinical disorders are likely to be associated with particular personality disorders or classes of disorders (see Figure 14.4). In clinical practice, the 'clinical' disorders are often, initially, the most evident disorders; however, as these are treated and the symptoms are contained, the underlying personality disorder becomes more evident.

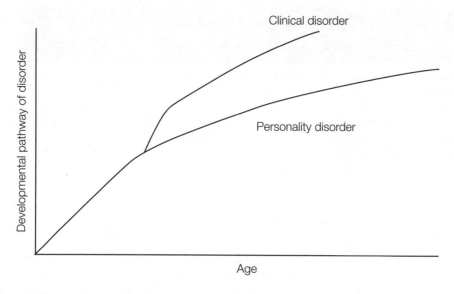

Figure 14.4: Relationship between 'clinical' and personality disorders

Source: Created by author Burke.

AETIOLOGY

It is useful to return to the definition of personality disorders in order to distinguish them from other forms of psychopathology (specifically clinical syndromes). Unlike the clinical syndromes, personality disorders are always defined by enduring, inflexible, and maladaptive patterns of perceiving and responding to the environment and oneself. Individuals with personality disorders are seldom aware of their problematic cognitions and behaviours. The aetiology of personality disorders is unclear; however, a combination of personal history and biology appears to play a role in most personality disorders (see Figure 14.5).

Figure 14.5 illustrates the intricacies of the aetiology of personality disorders, and shows that the factors in the development of a personality disorder may vary from one type of disorder to another or from one individual to another. It is important to remember that one cannot view personality disorders from a purely medical model, as having a sudden onset with a specific trigger.

Rather, they need to be viewed from a developmental perspective, as disorders that develop gradually from an early predisposition. The figure illustrates that there is most likely some genetic or biological vulnerability to a personality disorder, but this will develop into a disorder only if a person is exposed to adverse life events. The main aetiological factors in the personality disorders include biological, and intra- and interpersonal, vulnerabilities. These will be discussed in the following sections.

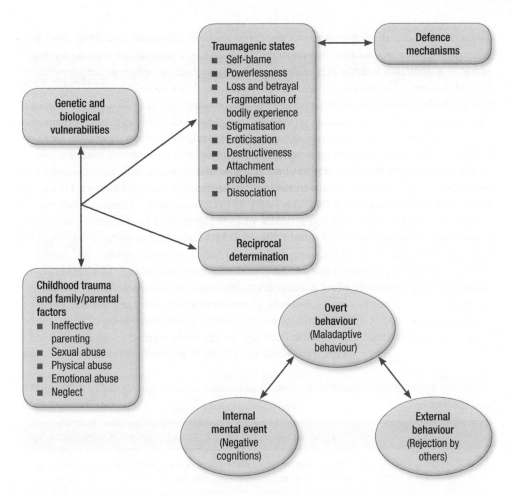

Figure 14.5: Illustration of interaction of causal factors for personality disorders

Source: Created by author Von Krosigk.

Biological factors

Genetic vulnerability

Kaplan et al. (1994) state that the concordance rate for personality disorders is significantly higher in monozygotic than in dizygotic twins, suggesting that genetics play a role in the development of a personality disorder. However, the role of genetic factors in the cause of various personality disorders varies depending on the specific disorder. The role of genetics for the different personality disorders is summarised in Table 14.15.

Table 14.15: Summary of the underlying genetic aetiological factors in personality disorders

Personality disorder	Genetic link
Schizotypal	According to Barlow and Durand (2005), this disorder could be viewed as the phenotype of a schizophrenia genotype. Nolen-Hoeksema (2005) states that family history and adoption and twin studies indicate that this disorder may, to some degree, be transmitted genetically.
Schizoid	Although there is a suspected link between this disorder and schizophrenia, the link is less clear than in the case of schizotypal personality disorder (Kendler, Neale, Kessler, Heath, & Eaves, 1993). Twin studies of personality traits that are associated with this disorder indicate that traits such as low sociability and warmth may be partially inherited.
Paranoid	As in the previous disorders, there may be some link between this disorder and schizophrenia, which suggests that it may be part of the schizophrenia spectrum disorders (Kendler et al., 1993). Genetic studies have not been able to separate the genetic and environmental influences on the development of this disorder.
Antisocial	There is substantial support for genetic influence on antisocial behaviours, particularly criminal behaviour. For example, Cloninger and Gottesman (1987) found in an adoption study that the criminal records of adopted sons are more similar to the records of the biological fathers than their adoptive fathers. Perry (1993) maintains that family history studies show that family members of people with antisocial personality disorder have an increased predisposition for this disorder, alcoholism, and criminality.
Borderline	There are no conclusive findings that this disorder is transmitted genetically. There is an unexplained link between a family history of mood disorder and borderline personality disorder (Nolen-Hoeksema, 2007).
Histrionic	No clear evidence for genetic cause (Barlow & Durand, 2005; Nolen-Hoeksema, 2007).
Narcissistic	No clear evidence for genetic cause (Barlow & Durand, 2005; Nolen-Hoeksema, 2007).
Avoidant	Dahl (1993) states that this disorder is more common in first-degree relatives of people with the disorder than in the relatives of normal control groups. It is, however, not clear whether this is due to genetic or environmental factors.

Personality disorder	Genetic link
Dependent	Dahl (1993) states that this disorder is more common in first-degree relatives of people with the disorder than in the relatives of normal control groups. It is, however, not clear whether this is due to genetic or environmental factors. However, children with histories of separation anxiety or chronic illnesses are more prone to develop this disorder (American Psychiatric Association, 2000).
Obsessive-compulsive	According to Nolen-Hoeksema (2007), no family history, twin or adoption studies have been done for this disorder.

Neurobiological vulnerability

Children with attention-deficit/hyperactivity disorder and/or minimal brain damage have been found to be at risk for personality disorders, particularly for antisocial personality disorder. Central nervous system dysfunction associated with soft neurological signs is particularly common in individuals with antisocial personality disorder and borderline personality disorder (Kaplan & Sadock, 2007). According to Gurvits, Koenigsberg, and Siever (2000), the frontal lobes, which control emotion and planning, show slight abnormalities in some cases of antisocial personality disorder. Low levels of behavioural inhibition may be mediated by serotonergic dysregulation in the septo-hippocampal system. There may also be developmental or acquired abnormalities in the prefrontal brain systems and reduced autonomic activity in antisocial personality disorder. These factors may be the basis for the low levels of arousal, poor fear-conditioning, and decision-making deficits typical of antisocial personality disorder.

Biological factors like neurobiological vulnerability may be intensified or perpetuated by familial interactional styles or broader environmental factors. For example, an unavailable or neglectful parent may not respond to either positive or negative behaviour that the child displays. Thus, there is neither consistent positive reinforcement for positive behaviour nor punishment for destructive behaviour. As a result, the child internalises the belief that any behaviour is acceptable as long as there are external personal gains.

On the other hand, the parent who responds to the child's behaviour inconsistently gives the child mixed messages with regard to which behaviour is acceptable and which is unacceptable. Family factors will be discussed further in the next section. The role of neurobiological factors in the different personality disorders is summarised in Table 14.16.

Table 14.16: Summary of the underlying neurobiological factors in personality disorders

Personality disorder	Neurobiological factors
Schizotypal	According to Nolen-Hoeksema (2007), this disorder shares similar factors with schizophrenia, such as: ■ Problems with sustained attention. ■ Low levels of monoamine oxidase, which could lead to increased levels of dopamine. ■ Similar structural abnormalities of the brain as in schizophrenia.
Schizoid	There seems to be a general lack of information on the causes of this disorder (Phillips, Yen, & Gunderson, 2003). It is postulated that it may share some of the neurobiological factors with autistic spectrum disorders such as a lower density of dopamine receptors (Wolff, 2000).
Paranoid	There is limited evidence of biological causes (Barlow & Durand, 2005).
Antisocial	According to Barlow and Durand (2005), there are two main theories: *Underarousal hypothesis:* According to this hypothesis, people with antisocial personality disorder present with abnormally low levels of cortical arousal (lower skin conductance activity, lower heart rate during rest periods, slow frequency brain wave activity, etc). In order to boost arousal to more optimal levels, these individuals engage in stimulation-seeking behaviour. Furthermore, it has been found that people with antisocial personality disorder frequently have excessive theta waves while awake, like those found in children. It has therefore been hypothesised that people with antisocial personality disorder may have a cerebral cortex that is at an earlier stage of development than in other individuals, thus accounting for certain 'childlike' and impulsive behaviours. *Fearlessness hypothesis:* People with this disorder have a higher threshold for experiencing fear than most other people. Nolen-Hoeksema (2007) also lists the following possible neurobiological causes: ■ Elevated levels of testosterone; however, there is little evidence that ties this in with antisocial personality disorder. ■ Low levels of serotonin, which may lead to impulsive and aggressive behaviour. ■ Deficits in executive functions of the brain, which may also contribute to poor impulse control.
Borderline	Weston and Siever (1993) maintain that impulsive behaviours associated with this disorder could be a result of low levels of serotonin. Further support for this lies in the fact that people with this disorder also show the same abnormalities as people with mood disorders.

Personality disorder	Neurobiological factors
Histrionic	Millon et al. (2000) maintain that people with this disorder were born with high levels of energy and a need for stimulation, which may lead to an intolerance for boredom.
Narcissistic	Halgin and Whitbourne (2003) maintain that this disorder does not have a neurobiological cause and seems to have mainly psychosocial causes.
Avoidant	There are high levels of physical arousal and hypersensitivity to the environment (Millon et al. 2000).
Dependent	There is no evidence of neurobiological causes.
Obsessive-compulsive	There is no evidence of neurobiological causes.

Intra- and interpersonal factors

According to Millon and Everly (1985, p. 18), 'early experiences are not only ingrained more pervasively and forcefully, but their effects tend to persist and are more difficult to modify than the effect of later experiences'. It has been hypothesised that early life experiences are intertwined with biological factors and that these experiences set the structure and tone for subsequent learning throughout the lifespan.

Ineffective parenting, sexual abuse, physical abuse, and emotional abuse and neglect have been extensively researched and found as significant factors with respect to the development of various personality disorders, as well as other forms of psychopathology (Millon et al., 2000). However, not all children who have endured any of the above-mentioned traumas develop personality disorders or other forms of psychopathology. This reminds us that each child experiences, integrates, and copes with trauma uniquely. The trauma cannot be viewed in isolation but should rather be viewed in dynamic interaction with various other factors, such as the biological and other factors already discussed.

Porter (2002) suggests an interesting link between trauma and personality disorders (see Figure 14.5), more specifically antisocial personality disorder. According to him, there is sufficient clinical and empirical evidence supporting the hypothesis that negative childhood experiences can profoundly affect emotional functioning in adulthood. If a person is severely traumatised or disillusioned by significant others, such a person may ultimately learn to cope by 'turning off' their emotions. This could eventually lead to an 'underactive conscience', later emerging as an antisocial personality disorder.

Psychoanalytic theory

In accordance with psychoanalytic theory, many clinicians view personality disorders through the lens of psychological defences. Historically, this is a sign of the time when all individuals who were diagnosed with a personality disorder were treated from the psychoanalytic and/or psychodynamic approach (Gunderson, 2009). According to the psychoanalytic perspective, defences are the 'unconscious mental processes that the ego uses to resolve inner conflicts' (Kaplan & Sadock, 1998, p. 778).

We all use various defences and, in most cases, we have a wide variety of these defence mechanisms at our disposal as ways of coping with our daily lives. Unconsciously, according to the psychoanalytic perspective, we select different defences in different situations, which enables us to adapt to our environments in a 'functional' way. However, individuals with personality disorders use particularly effective, but self-destructive, defence mechanisms in order to abolish anxiety and depression. If they were to abandon these defences, their conscious experience of anxiety and depression would increase, which is why these individuals are often reluctant to alter their behaviour. In addition, these defence mechanisms are considered to be immature and maladaptive by the dominant discourses in society, as the socially constructed myths that parents and/or caregivers have acquired and believe are used to uphold a particular social order (Walker, 2006).

In order to increase our understanding of personality traits with regard to the use of maladaptive defence mechanisms, it is imperative to also consider and integrate theories with brain research findings. Without such integration, there will always be individuals who continue to associate dominant defences with certain personality disorders (see Table 14.17).

Table 14.17: The relationship between coping styles/defence mechanisms and personality disorders

Common coping mechanisms			
Mechanism	**Definition**	**Result**	**Personality disorders involved**
Projection	Attributing one's own feelings or thoughts to others	Leads to prejudice, suspiciousness, and excessive worrying about external dangers	Typical of paranoid and schizotypal personalities. Used by people with borderline, antisocial, or narcissistic personality when under acute stress
Splitting	Use of black-or-white, all-or-nothing thinking to divide people into groups of idealised all-good saviours and vilified all-bad evildoers	Allows a person to avoid the discomfort of having both loving and hateful feelings for the same person, as well as feelings of uncertainty and helplessness	Typical of borderline personality

Common coping mechanisms			
Mechanism	**Definition**	**Result**	**Personality disorders involved**
Acting out	A direct behavioural expression of an unconscious wish or impulse that enables a person to avoid thinking about a painful situation or experiencing a painful emotion	Leads to acts that are often irresponsible, reckless, and foolish Includes many delinquent, promiscuous, and substance-abusing acts, which can become so habitual that the person remains unaware and dismissive of the feelings that initiated the acts	Very common in people with antisocial or borderline personality
Turning aggression against self	Expressing the angry feelings one has toward others by hurting oneself directly (e.g. through self-mutilation) or indirectly (e.g. in body dysmorphic disorder); when indirect, it is called passive aggression	Includes failures and illnesses that affect others more than oneself and silly, provocative clowning	Dramatic in people with borderline personality
Fantasising	Use of imaginary relationships and private belief systems to resolve conflict and to escape from painful realities, such as loneliness	Is associated with eccentricity, avoidance of interpersonal intimacy, and avoidance of involvement with the outside world	Used by people with an avoidant or schizoid personality, who, in contrast to people with psychoses, do not believe (and thus do not act on) their fantasies
Hypochondriasis	Use of health complaints to gain attention	Provides a person with nurturing attention from others May be a passive expression of anger toward others	Used by people with dependent, histrionic, or borderline personality

Source: Grohol, J. D. (2019). 15 common defense mechanisms. Retrieved June 12, 2019, from https://psychcentral.com/lib/15-common-defense-mechanisms/; Ivzāns, I., & Mihailova, S. (2017). Relationship between pathological personality traits and defense mechanisms in the community sample of Russina-speaking adult inhabitants of Latvia. *Acta Psychopathologica*, 3(6), 1–8; Vaillant, G. (1977). *Adaptation to Life*. Cambridge, MA and London: Harvard University Press.

Language as a medium of communication

How do we understand each other? People most commonly use signs and symbols for thinking alone, for trying to understand one another, and for reaching out to and communicating with one another. The signs we make with our body (body language) are as much a way of communicating our thoughts, feelings, motivations, and intentions as using the spoken or written word (language). However, it is not always easy to interpret the body language or spoken words of others correctly, since we do not know for certain what they are thinking, feeling, and doing that motivates them to communicate with us in a certain way about a specific topic.

Indeed, the way we interpret the words or the behaviour of others is often far removed from the internal reality of these individuals. Therefore, there needs to be continual change and reinforcement within the process of communication and feedback in order to assist us to accurately assess the inner landscape of another individual (Tomm & Lannamann, 1988; Watzlawick, Beavin, & Jackson, 1967). Ultimately, we can only assess the thoughts and feelings of others by questioning and verifying the intended meaning of their behavioural or verbal symbols. This facilitates a better understanding of the internal aspects of both individuals, and therefore a better understanding between them (Tomm & Lannamann, 1988).

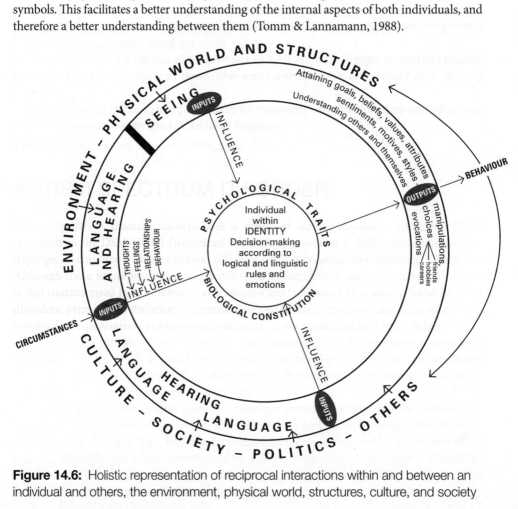

Figure 14.6: Holistic representation of reciprocal interactions within and between an individual and others, the environment, physical world, structures, culture, and society

Source: Created by author Von Krosigk.

In the previous section, we noted how individuals diagnosed with personality disorders tend to use immature and maladaptive defences. However, it does not necessarily follow that they use these kinds of defences when they are not under stress. In addition, their response to stressors might not be consistent and uniform, as the psychoanalytic paradigm suggests; rather, their response may be the result of a complex interactional process between their biological heritage, their present physical health status, and their psychological development and health. All of these exist in the context of the presence (or absence) of a loving support system that practises effective and healthy patterns of communication (see Figure 14.6).

In the outer circle, Figure 14.6 illustrates how all input, output, and interactional processes have to pass through the medium of language; this happens through hearing and/or seeing others speak or by means of reading (seeing the written word in the physical world). Language therefore influences, creates, and shapes our thoughts, feelings, relationships, behaviours, as well as our identity.

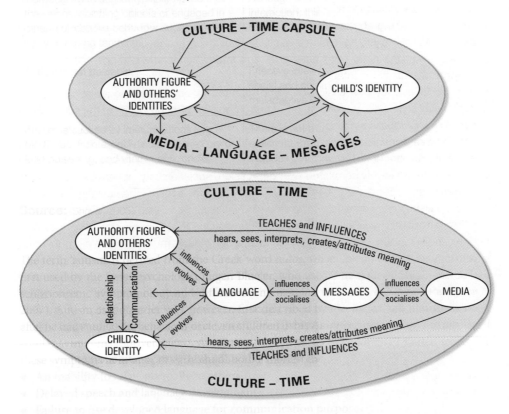

Figure 14.7: The use of language and media in the context of time and culture: Reciprocal processes between authority figure(s) (parents, teachers, adults) and others (peers, friends, enemies, e.g. bullies) and the growing child

Source: Created by author Von Krosigk.

But language and media are also situated within the context of time and culture, which are also critical in the shaping of personality (see Figure 14.7). Note how media, through messages expressed in the language of our culture and within our time, influences, creates, and shapes our and our authority figures' thoughts, feelings, and identity. Note also how the identities of authority figures and other identities, such as peers, friends and enemies, and the growing child, are reciprocally influenced through one another's messages and the messages of the media. These messages are expressed through the medium of the language of the culture, and/or the language of the dominant culture of the time.

 ACTIVITY

In 2006, the American psychologist Catherine Caldwell-Harris and the Turkish psychologist Ayşe Ayçiçegi published an article ' When personality and culture clash: the psychological distress of allocentrics in an individualist culture and idiocentrics in a collectivist culture'. Read the following abstract from this journal, and consider whether the city you know best would be likely to have results similar to Boston or Istanbul.

Because humans need both autonomy and interdependence, persons with either an extreme collectivist orientation (allocentrics) or extreme individualist values (idiocentrics) may be at risk for possession of some features of psychopathology. Is an extreme personality style a risk factor primarily when it conflicts with the values of the surrounding society? Individualism-collectivism scenarios and a battery of clinical and personality scales were administered to non-clinical samples of college students in Boston and Istanbul. For students residing in a highly individualistic society (Boston), collectivism scores were positively correlated with depression, social anxiety, obsessive-compulsive disorder and dependent personality. Individualism scores, particularly horizontal individualism, were negatively correlated with these same scales.

A different pattern was obtained for students residing in a collectivist culture, Istanbul. Here, individualism (and especially horizontal individualism) was positively correlated with scales for paranoid, schizoid, narcissistic, borderline and antisocial personality disorder. Collectivism (particularly vertical collectivism) was associated with low report of symptoms on these scales. These results indicate that having a personality style which conflicts with the values of society is associated with psychiatric symptoms. Having an orientation inconsistent with societal values may thus be a risk factor for poor mental health.

Source: Adapted from: Caldwell-Harris, C. & Ayçiçegi, A. 2006. When personality and culture clash: The psychological distress of allocentrics in an individualist culture and idiocentrics in a collectivist culture. In: *Transcultural Psychology*, 43(3), 331–361. https://doi.org/10.1177/1363461506066982

Family systems theory

Another way of understanding personality disorders is through the lens of family systems theory, in which clinicians direct their focus on the quality of the multiple relationships within the context of nuclear and larger family systems. According to family theorists, the nature of symptoms and the type of behaviours that individuals exhibit under stressful circumstances can only be understood by observing the family members' reciprocal interactions within the context of their family system (Keeney, 1983; Watzlawick et al., 1967; Weakland, Fish, Watzlawick, & Bodin, 1974).

From a family systems perspective, personality traits are internal aspects (that are only part of the whole person) that function in conjunction with the person's external components of functioning within a larger pattern of relationships of reciprocal communication with others. According to Keeney (1983), this can be considered a 'double description' of relationships in which internal personality attributes are conceptualised as the invisible half of a larger pattern of relationships and behaviours, which are seen as fulfilling a function within the interactional and communicational exchanges. The rules of this large interactional pattern of relationships are continually reinforced, changed, revised and adapted, according to the circular patterns of communication and behaviour.

The diathesis-stress model

The diathesis-stress model (see Chapter 2) follows a linear reasoning approach, based on the presupposition that, under conditions of stress, in the absence of support, a pre-existing vulnerability can move towards and/or result in a sudden breakdown of functioning by manifesting as clinical syndromes and/or personality disorders. The diathesis-stress model was developed as an attempt to explain why some individuals under the same environmental conditions develop a disorder while others do not. By presupposing an inherent vulnerability that would lead to a disease or disorder under certain conditions, such as cumulative stress, this model is also based on the assumption that individuals who did not develop a disorder were either free from such vulnerabilities or had sufficient support.

The diathesis-stress model falls into the realm of the biological/medical model, and it has been a part of the dominant scientific discourse throughout the past decades, thus directing our thinking along these same lines of linear reasoning. Since the dominant scientific paradigm was considered to be the only permissible research method for obtaining new insights, our attention was drawn away from theoretical options that could have uncovered other possible solutions for understanding personality functioning.

Unfortunately, new researchers seldom referred back to the original scientific method for data collection. Instead, they built upon the research results of their contemporaries, without questioning the premises and presuppositions upon which these results were based. Had they questioned their contemporaries' philosophical premises, the phenomenological approach to data collection may possibly have emerged as a deep, subjective method for uncovering the internal landscape of diverse ways of human thinking, feeling, behaving, and making decisions. Dialogical exchange with continual feedback could have uncovered the ways in which certain individuals came to be dysfunctional while others seemed to have developed character strengths and resilience (see Chapter 4).

Originally, phenomenology was considered to be the basis for all scientific research, for observing the object/subject of investigation in its natural surroundings, for collecting data (meticulously recording all observations), and particularly for investigating human consciousness (Husserl, 1952/1989; published posthumously). Phenomenological philosophers like Husserl (1859–1938) based their thinking on the presupposition that we can only get to know other individuals by observing and recording what the observed individuals do, feel, and think, without interpreting or judging their thoughts, feelings, and behaviour.

All scientific investigation was built on this process, together with hypothetical reasoning processes, and the testing of hypotheses and conclusions (Husserl, 1952/1989). If the phenomenological method – with its detailed observations, its extensive sets of observational data, and longitudinal research studies – had been employed for understanding the developmental trajectories from functional to dysfunctional behaviour over time, personality disorder research could have yielded rich data.

In addition, personality researchers should have placed the findings of these individual research studies into the context of environmental, social, cultural, and biological factors by means of a grounded research design. A grounded research design refrains from making assumptions with regard to the theoretical basis for the research. Instead, it bases the construction of a theory on the overt aspects of the collected data that forms the ground or basis from which the theory is constructed. Using this approach, this research might have uncovered categories of personality functioning that would have acknowledged all factors in interaction with one another on a dimensional continuum.

Sociocultural influences

As argued above, and as with various other forms of psychopathology, personality disorders are to some extent defined by the context within which they are found. Varying contexts exert differing expectations and pressures on the individual, thus triggering differing vulnerabilities and responses. In addition, there are other possible ways in which the broader context impacts upon the aetiology of personality disorders. Some examples of the role of contextual factors will be given in this section.

Individuals with antisocial personality disorder were found to come from high-risk backgrounds, which may include poor, first-time, and single mothers (Freeman & Reinecke, 2007). Mothers from such backgrounds often have poor parenting skills and may experience poor nutrition themselves. The resulting inadequate pre- and postnatal care of their children in the context of ineffective parental care, discipline, and supervision can lead to delinquency and later conduct disorder and antisocial personality disorder (Dishion & Patterson, 1997). From the perspective of sociocultural norms, antisocial personality disorder can also be the negative outcome of an attempt by an individual to function in a personally meaningful way from within a dysfunctional family and larger sociocultural context.

Individuals with borderline personality disorder tend to report an inordinate number of negative and traumatic events in childhood. These experiences range from abandonment, neglect, separation, rejection, and loss, to physical, emotional, and sexual abuse. Since borderline personality disorder shows a high rate of comorbidity with other disorders such as posttraumatic stress disorder, dissociative disorder, eating disorders, and mood disorders, the possibility exists that socialisation and relational interactions between primary caregivers and these individuals may have been dysfunctional throughout childhood and adolescence, or during critical periods of development.

A holistic perspective for understanding the development of personality functioning/dysfunction

The term 'holism' was coined by the South African general and politician Jan Smuts in the 1920s, who considered it the 'whole-making tendency' in nature (1926). The concept of 'holism' has developed since this time.

Holism is now a concept that is built upon the premise of life's complexity and diversity. It presupposes that the parts of a whole cannot live or exist if separated from that whole. It also presupposes that parts of that whole cannot be understood separately (e.g. if they are detached from the whole). Separate parts can only be understood by viewing them in relation to the whole, and in interaction with all other parts of the whole.

In 2009, Becvar and Becvar observed how one needs to include a person's relationships and communicational patterns, in the light of their circular feedback and reciprocal response patterns. From this perspective, all aspects of the whole should be taken into account in the quest for understanding human functioning and dysfunction.

The five dimensions of human life include the biological, psychological, social, cultural, and environmental dimensions of life and functioning. Some of these dimensions have been involved in the long-standing nature versus nurture debate, which has been ongoing since the inception of psychology and psychotherapy around 1900. Cause-and-effect reasoning processes within the context of dichotomous (either/or) thinking have proved to be of little value in finding a solution to the complex question of whether our naturally inherited biological nature/constitution, or the way we were nurtured/raised and what we learned from our families and communities, determines our functioning or our dysfunction.

However, the linear reasoning inherent in this debate risks severely restricting our view with regard to finding explanations for our functional/dysfunctional development. By assuming that people can only be influenced by either the biological dimension or the psychosocial dimension, but never by both, we exclude other important and available aspects that could also have played a role in our development.

Viewing the same complex question from the holistic perspective yields a more comprehensive way of looking at the possibilities for developing functional and dysfunctional behaviour. Figure 14.8 is a diagrammatic representation of the five dimensions and their possible pathways of reciprocal influence with interactive feedback in a complex, living system.

It is important to note that the system changes and/or adapts to those changes, and initiates new areas of development. It does this by responding over time to coaxing, admonishing, neglecting, or receiving incongruent feedback during the developing years of childhood, adolescence, and early adulthood. This happens in interaction with the dimensions of the self or individual, the family, social community, cultural community, and the environmental aspects that recursively provide input, feedback, mishaps, and misfortunes for individuals, all in the context of their biological vulnerabilities.

We have already described some of the possible factors on the five dimensions that could negatively influence the development of a young person and which could, over time, emerge as one or more difficulties in functioning effectively. Once these difficulties become rigid patterns of behaviour by having been learned and rehearsed, the use of inappropriate thinking and emotional strategies, personality dysfunction, and/or behavioural, cognitive, or emotional dysfunction can appear for a while. If these rigid patterns of behaviour are then changed by learning appropriate thinking and emotional strategies, the personality dysfunction or behavioural, cognitive, or emotional dysfunction may disappear again.

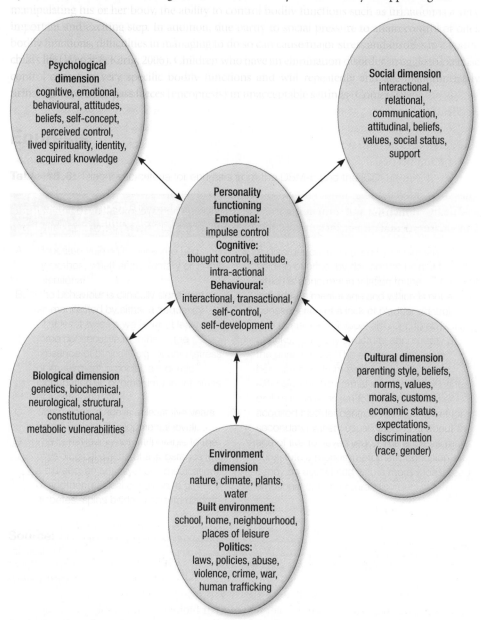

Figure 14.8: The five dimensions and their possible pathways of influence: A holistic process model for understanding the development of personality functioning and personality dysfunction

Source: Created by author Von Krosigk.

PROBLEMS AND CONTROVERSIES

The personality profile of the young woman in the personal history caselet at the start of this chapter would closely resemble the diagnosis of dependent personality disorder according to the DSM-5 criteria. However, as we can see from the case study, this woman was taught to be submissive, dutiful, subservient, and dependent. Between 1900 and 1960, these character traits were highly desirable for Western women in general, while today they are considered to be dysfunctional in many different contexts. Despite changes with regard to what is considered to be desirable and undesirable behaviour as time goes by, the criteria for dependent personality disorder have remained the same for both men and women; however, they reflect a much higher statistical frequency for women than for men. Due to the different socialisation processes for boys and girls, this could have been expected. The statistical frequency for antisocial personality disorder is, however, much higher for men than for women. Could that perhaps also have something to do with child-rearing practices? Or does it perhaps reflect a dysfunctional society?

Although the DSM-5 and ICD-10 distinguish between different personality disorders, and describe each of these in detail, these disorders are not without controversy. One of the main criticisms against the present classification systems regarding personality disorders is the organisation and categorisation of these disorders. Both the DSM and ICD classification systems make a distinction between personality disorders and other mental disorders. According to Castillo (1998), there are three main reasons for this:

- Personality disorders are viewed as being enduring patterns of subjective experience and behaviour.
- They are based on personality development rather than some specific disease entity.
- These disorders generally do not have significant periods of remission, improvement over time, or changes in the type or severity of symptoms.

There seem to be two major schools of thought on the approach to the classification of personality disorders. One is the categorical approach, as reflected in both the DSM and ICD classification system, while the other is a dimensional approach to classification.

The dimensional approach takes the view that personality disorders are maladaptive variants of personality traits that merge with adaptive variants of personality traits. This view sees personality traits as existing on a continuum that allows for a person to function anywhere within the full range from low to high functioning. The attempt to fit the dimensional approach of a personality trait continuum into the qualitatively distinct categories of clinical syndromes (the categorical approach) is like trying to fit every individual person's unique personality traits into a single, predetermined, fixed, and acceptable formal category. This implies that there is a normative or acceptable formal category of personality that requires everybody to think, feel, behave, and respond in the same way to specific situations; however, this discounts ingenuity, creativity, intuitiveness, and new ways of coping.

According to the DSM-5, personality disorders are first diagnosed by applying a set of six general diagnostic criteria for identifying the possibility of the presence of a personality disorder (see Table 14.1), after which another set of diagnostic criteria is applied for diagnosing the particular personality disorder. When we examine the six general diagnostic criteria for a personality disorder, we find that Criterion A refers to a marked deviation from the expectations of a person's culture. Criterion A is manifested as a pattern of behaviour in the areas of cognition, affectivity or emotional response, interpersonal functioning, and impulse control.

On account of the general criteria for personality disorders, everyone who is compared to these theoretical, general diagnostic criteria will necessarily need to fit into the statistical norm of what is considered to be 'normal' (by the clinician) at the time of identifying and classifying the client's symptoms and syndrome. This means that the diagnostic criteria are not differentiated enough for specific disorders to emerge, which increases the possibility of overlapping diagnoses of a number of disorders. It is assumed that we can make a clear, categorical distinction between the presence and absence of a personality disorder, but this assumption is false, due to the poorly differentiated criteria and because of dynamic changes within individual behaviour, as well as changes in society over time.

One of the major challenges that face the classification of personality disorders is the dynamic nature of personality and the factors that influence personality development. If personality is static, or reaches a point of homeostasis, as was initially thought, classification of 'normal' and 'abnormal' personality would be relatively simple. Human development is, however, multifaceted and complex, and occurs on a number of levels simultaneously without a predetermined path.

Recently, genetic vulnerabilities and other biological factors have been found to play a role in the causes of personality disorders such as schizotypal personality disorder. In addition, biological and psychosocial factors have been identified as possible causes for the development of high levels of impulsivity and affective instability, which may lead to a diagnosis of borderline personality disorder in high-risk individuals (Gurvits et al., 2000). A linear cause-effect research strategy unfortunately fails to consider the complex and mutually interactive factors and communications in dysfunctional family systems, for example.

Responses to stressors, including internal and external expectations and limited internal and external resources, often seem dysfunctional from the perspective of society, but they may be functional from the perspective of the dysfunctional environment in which the individual is embedded. When clinicians are evaluating individuals for possible personality disorder diagnoses, they often compare them to the 'ideal' characteristics of a statistically normal personality.

However, in a constantly changing and culturally diverse society, these mutually exclusive categories for personality disorders are problematic for clinicians. Diagnosticians thus find themselves trying to fit their clients, who are dynamically evolving and who are in dynamic reciprocal interaction with their environments, into these static categories.

Misdiagnoses and overlapping symptoms of personality disorders are therefore partly the result of describing such wide variations of what may be idiosyncratic responses to life and its problems, within the confines of a diagnostic system that takes into account only a small number of 'ideal' responses. According to Livesley (2001), no individual can (or will) ever fit the 'ideal' descriptions of personality. This is because many theoretical models of personality, such as the five-factor model of personality, are based on a 'theoretical ideal' of human functioning, which is far removed from the complexity of real-life combinations of personality characteristics, and the pathways and processes of personality development.

In the discussion above, the role of society in the development of personality is emphasised, which brings us to the next dynamic feature of personality. Societies are highly dynamic and, as they change, there will invariably be changes in common practices such as child-rearing. In general, child-rearing practices and expectations for boys differ considerably from those for girls. In the West, between 1900 and 1960, boys were encouraged to learn a trade, to obtain a position in a firm or business, or to aspire to higher learning with the aim of entering a profession such as law, medicine, or scientific research. Western culture, and its social, political, and financial contexts, supported such learning, in conjunction with the division of labour between women and men; in addition, men were remunerated with higher wages than women for the same tasks.

A number of research findings suggest that a dysfunctional personality style is influenced by authoritarian child-rearing practices and social attitudes. Schlachter and Duckitt (2002) found a link between authoritarian social attitudes and prejudice, on the one hand, and a maladjusted personality style, on the other hand. Almajali (2005), in turn, found that an authoritative parenting style, coupled with a child with an internal locus of control, promoted creative thinking in adolescence.

Supporting evidence comes from Langley and Klopper (2005), who found that the establishment of 'trust' was the foundation for therapeutic interventions with patients with borderline personality disorder. This suggests that clients with borderline personality disorder were not able to develop an adequate sense of basic trust with their primary caregiver. Considering the complexity of borderline personality disorder and its associated disorders like alcohol abuse, dysthymia, gender identity disorder, schizotypal personality disorder, posttraumatic stress disorder, and eating disorders, it becomes clear that the client might not have developed these comorbid disorders (or borderline personality disorder) if the individual had developed a sense of basic trust. Thus, one could argue that personality disorders could also be considered to be 'socialisation disorders of childhood'.

If changing societies influence the development of personality disorders, one cannot help but wonder what effect the rapid changes in a society like South Africa will have on the prevalence of personality disorders. Since the advent of democracy in South Africa, women rather than men are preferred as employees, and remuneration for men and women is related to the task rather than their gender. This transformation has impacted both negatively and positively on family structures and socialisation processes for boys and girls.

Both boys and girls are now encouraged to learn domestic, financial, and academic skills. One could thus expect that the high rate of apparent dependent personality disorder in women will diminish while at the same time the rate may increase in the case of men. This would be due to the fact that men might become more financially dependent on their mothers or spouses, as a result of being denied access to the fields of their chosen professions.

The argument for this possible outcome is based on the observed trends in the changes to the classification of personality disorders. When one looks at the history of the classification of these disorders, it is evident how certain personality disorders have 'disappeared' over time, and how others have 'emerged'. The most recent of these changes is the passive-aggressive personality disorder that was moved from the main classification to the appendix of DSM-IV-TR, and the possible inclusion of a new personality disorder, the depressive personality disorder. These disorders have, however, not been included in any way in the DSM-5.

According to Lamiell (2007), we will have ongoing difficulties in categorising and diagnosing personality disorders if we do not interrogate our current understanding of personality research. We need to investigate the inconsistency and fundamental incoherence in thinking that has led to the formulation of a 'trait theory of personality'.

Lamiell's (2007) historical research regarding the development of thought about what a scientific psychology of personality should be has uncovered a false premise on which our present 'trait theory of personality' has been based. Instead of generating knowledge about a single individual, psychological research practices revolved around generating knowledge about attributes in general. According to Lamiell (2007), the fundamental error is that inter-attribute correlations obtained from studies of individual differences have been used for interpreting single individuals.

More recently, person-centred approaches to studying development in context have uncovered the complex nature of parallel pathways and processes in individual and social development (Estell, Farmer, Pearl, Van Acker, & Rodkin, 2003). This complexity of 'being and becoming' makes it extremely difficult to identify and understand the different contributions of inherent personality traits, wilful responses or reactions to social and/or cultural norms, prescriptions and expectations, and complex inner developmental processes, all in the context of a constantly changing multicultural society.

CONCLUSION

When individual behaviour is classified as abnormal by comparing it to what is customary in the culture in which the individual lives, it is quite possible that perfectly adaptive behaviour can be classified as abnormal. By polarising normal and abnormal behaviour on the grounds of comparing it to the individual's culture, the possibility of finding fault with the cultural norms is automatically excluded when viewed from the linear perspective. This problematic state of using culture as a rule by which individual normality and abnormality are determined has been perpetuated since the inception of the first DSM in 1952. However, cultural norms have changed tremendously over the past decades, while the rule of culture as a normative entity has been maintained, even in multicultural societies.

The discussion with regard to the two different diagnostic systems, DSM-5 and ICD-10, demonstrates that the two epistemological systems for communicating knowledge about health and illness differ in their presuppositions about health and illness. The difference between a disease classification (ICD-10) and a psychological disorder classification (DSM-5) constitutes a fundamental difference between a biological aetiology and a psychological and behavioural identification of mental disorders.

This chapter provides a window into the psychologically, socially, politically, and environmentally mediated ways in which disorders develop. From this perspective, personality disorders can ultimately be seen as the interacting outcomes of social practices, within the context of the family and the wider social, political, cultural, and environmental field of values and norms, which are themselves situated within the context of a dominant culture.

The implications of these aetiological findings also throw light on the other issues that have plagued the classification of personality disorders for many years, such as the high rate of overlap between different personality disorders. The 'whole individual' within the context of their environment needs to be considered when possible classifications of personality disorders are made.

MULTIPLE-CHOICE QUESTIONS

1. On which axis of the DSM-5 are personality disorders coded?
   a) I
   b) II
   c) III
   d) DSM-5 does not have a multi-axial diagnostic system
2. The DSM-5 divides personality disorders into how many distinct clusters?
   a) one
   b) two
   c) three
   d) four
3. Which set of adjective pairs correctly describes the clusters into which DSM-5 personality disorders are grouped?
   a) odd/eccentric, dangerous/inconsistent, and shy/withdrawn
   b) shy/withdrawn, anxious/fearful, and dangerous/inconsistent
   c) shy/withdrawn, dramatic/emotional, and bizarre/thought-disordered
   d) odd/eccentric, dramatic/emotional, and anxious/fearful
4. The diagnosis of more than one personality disorder in an individual patient is:
   a) common
   b) impossible unless the person suffers from dissociative identity disorder
   c) rare
   d) only possible for personality disorders in the same DSM-5 cluster
5. One of the influences that has been associated with the development of borderline personality disorder is:
   a) child abuse or neglect
   b) head injuries
   c) parental alcoholism
   d) abnormal dopamine levels
6. Which of the following is a feature associated with anankastic personality disorder, according to the ICD-10?
   a) history of non-compliance with social norms and victimising others.
   b) instability, impulsivity, recklessness, and explosiveness.
   c) exaggerated emotional expressions and an extremely strong longing for attention
   d) difficulty in performing work because of an obsession about making everything perfectly right
7. The following term is one used in the ICD-11 classification:
   a) sociopathy
   b) antisocial personality dissorder
   c) dissocial personality disorder
   d) dissociality in personality disorder or personality difficulty

8. The following coping mechanism has been connected to borderline personality:
   a) splitting
   b) fantasising
   c) distancing
   d) trivialising
9. An individualistic person in a culture that values ubuntu is more likely to be diagnosed with:
   a) avoidant personality disorder
   b) dependent personality disorder
   c) paranoid personality disorder
   d) histrionic personality disorder.
10. Individuals with antisocial personality disorder have been found to:
   a) have an alcoholic or antisocial parent
   b) belong to the female gender
   c) come from a polygamous marriage
   d) develop antisocial behaviour as young adults.

PARAGRAPH AND ESSAY QUESTIONS

1. Describe the three clusters of DSM-5 personality disorders and provide an example of at least one personality disorder that belongs to each cluster. How would you characterise each cluster?
2. Compare and contrast the behaviours, thoughts, and motivations of an individual with avoidant personality disorder against someone with schizoid personality disorder. Make sure to note similarities and differences.
3. Explain what differentiates individuals with schizotypal personality disorder from schizophrenia. What are the similarities observed in individuals diagnosed with schizotypal personality disorder and those diagnosed with schizophrenia?

<table>
<tr><td>15</td><td># NEURODEVELOPMENTAL AND OTHER CHILDHOOD DISORDERS</td></tr>
</table>

Adri Vorster

CHAPTER OUTLINE

Introduction
Developmental psychopathology
History of developmental psychopathology
Contextualising developmental psychopathology in South Africa
Childhood disorders and stigma
The classification of childhood disorders
Intellectual disability (intellectual development disorder)
　　Aetiology of intellectual disability
Autism spectrum disorder
　　Aetiology of autism spectrum disorder
Elimination disorders
　　Enuresis
　　Encopresis
　　Aetiology of elimination disorders
Externalising disorders
　　Attention-deficit/hyperactivity disorder
　　Conduct disorders
　　Aetiology of externalising disorders
Internalising disorders
　　Depression
　　Anxiety
　　Aetiology of internalising disorders
Conclusion

LEARNING OUTCOMES

After studying this chapter, you should be able to:

- Demonstrate knowledge of the key concepts, assumptions, and principles associated with developmental psychopathology.
- Employ a broad range of criteria for differentiating between normal and abnormal development in young people.
- Identify multiple factors and processes associated with the cause and course of a range of disorders experienced by young people.
- Identify risk and protective factors and processes associated with a specific disorder.
- Demonstrate knowledge of factors associated with the development and maintenance of intellectual, autism spectrum, elimination, externalising, and internalising disorders in young people.
- Apply a theoretical model of psychopathology to the development of intellectual, autism spectrum, elimination, externalising, and internalising in young people.

PERSONAL HISTORY CASELET

Sive Ngcobo is eight years old and is in her second term at her special school. She lives with her mother, father and older brother. Both her parents are teachers at the local secondary school. Mrs Ngcobo reported a normal pregnancy and birth. However, before Sive was even one years old, her parents noticed that she was developing very differently to Luniko, her brother. Sive does not make eye contact and uses words sparingly. Her parents also noticed that when she was three, Sive would not play with her toys but would line them up in straight rows, and if one animal was not perfectly in line, she would bang her head on the floor. Her parents realised that given her lack of verbal ability and her behaviour, which could seem aggressive, she would have to go to a school that catered for children with special educational needs. Sive has fitted in well there, although she does not have friends.

It is the Diwali celebrations in her town in two days and her parents are extremely worried about how Sive will react to the fireworks that get set off to celebrate the festival of light. Last year, she had a very traumatic time during the festival, throwing a tantrum and banging her head against the wall in repetitive movements. This year, her parents have approached her teacher Mrs Xaba to help Sive cope with Diwali. Mrs Xaba has suggested to the Ngcobos that they find the quietest place in their house for Diwali and that they use ear plugs for Sive. She has also indicated that she will give a lesson in class before Diwali to tell students all about the festival and its meaning. She feels that if Sive knows more about the festival and what to expect, she will be less traumatised by the sounds on the night.

Source: Written by Joanne Hardman.

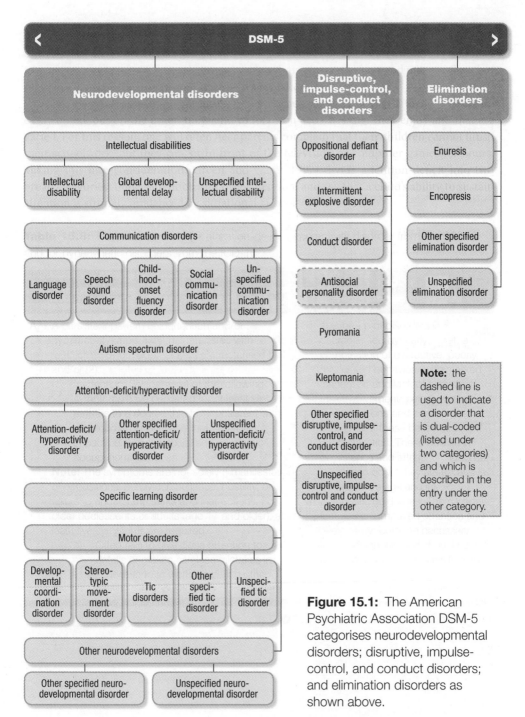

Figure 15.1: The American Psychiatric Association DSM-5 categorises neurodevelopmental disorders; disruptive, impulse-control, and conduct disorders; and elimination disorders as shown above.

Source: Figure created by OUP reflecting information found in *Diagnostic and Statistical Manual of Mental Disorders*, fifth edition (DSM-5), 2013.

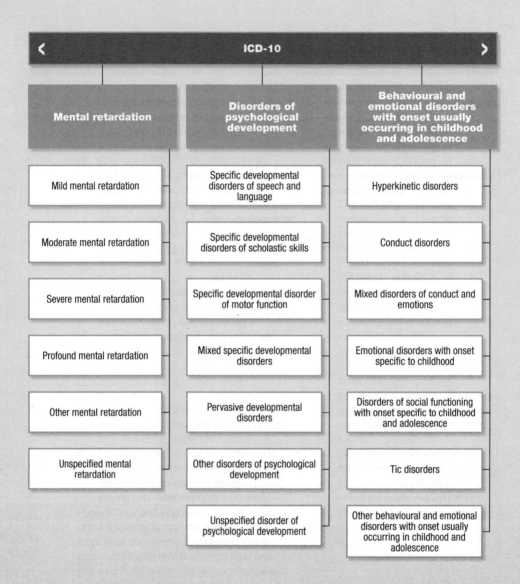

Figure 15.2: The World Health Organization ICD-10 categorises mental retardation; disorders of psychological development; and behavioural and emotional disorders with onset usually occurring in childhood and adolescence, as shown above.

Source: *International Statistical Classification of Diseases and Related Health Problems*, tenth revision (ICD-10), 2016.

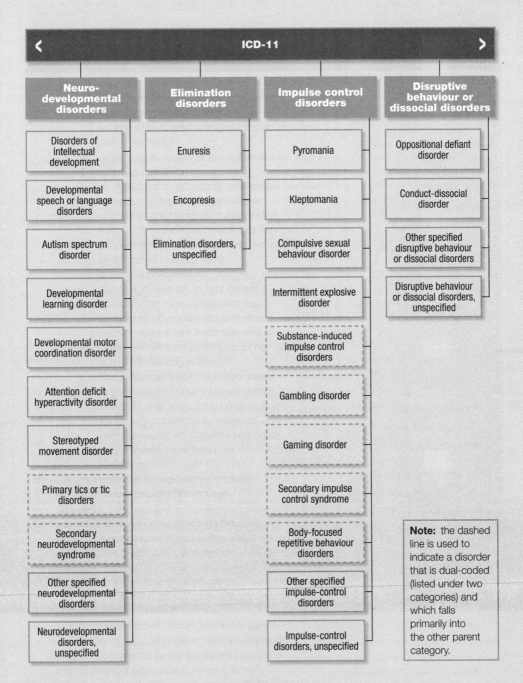

Figure 15.3: The World Health Organization proposed ICD-11 categorises neurodevelopmental disorders, elimination disorders, impulse-control disorders, and disruptive or dissocial disorders as shown above.

Source: *International Classification of Diseases for Mortality and Morbidity Statistics*, eleventh revision (ICD-11), 2018.

INTRODUCTION

Children and adolescents are multifaceted thinking and feeling beings, with a degree of mental complexity that the world has only recently started to truly grasp (World Health Organization, 2005). While children's difficulties were previously treated as downward extensions of adult disorders, clinicians now recognise that there are very important differences between adult and childhood disorders (Comer, 1995).

Although the concept of human development can appear relatively simple, one should be careful not to oversimplify it and to take into consideration the essential characteristics that define development:

- Development refers to specific changes that occur over a person's lifespan. These changes are the result of a person's interactions with biological, psychological, and sociocultural variables, which themselves are constantly changing (Wicks-Nelson & Israel, 2009).
- Over the lifespan, people normally change both quantitatively and qualitatively. Whereas children can initially only speak single words, they can later form sentences (i.e. quantitative changes) and even later add to the quality of their sentences through appropriate adverbs, correct grammar, etc. (i.e. qualitative changes) (Wicks-Nelson & Israel, 2009).
- Children's biological, motor, physical, cognitive, emotional, and social systems follow a common course of development, with early global structures and functions becoming increasingly more differentiated and integrated (Wicks-Nelson & Israel, 2009).
- Added to the above, from a holistic point of view, it is vital to remember that a person's different systems are in continual interaction with one another and, through these interactions, a person's structures become increasingly complex and organised, with new structures emerging out of the ones that came before (Wenar & Kerig, 2006).
- A child's development can be compared to a flight of stairs, with one stage building on the next. This implies that the different developmental stages are connected and that a child's current functioning is connected to both past and future functioning; in addition, a disturbance in one area will affect all of the others (Barlow & Durand, 2009).
- Finally, development implies change; however, change is not always positive (Wicks-Nelson & Israel, 2009).

DEVELOPMENTAL PSYCHOPATHOLOGY

In line with our understanding of development, developmental psychopathology refers to understanding how psychopathology emerges over the course of a person's lifespan and how the person's developing systems, in interaction with the noted variables, contribute to the formation of psychopathology or provide protection against it (Wenar & Kerig, 2006). In addition, developmental psychopathology assumes that psychopathology does not just appear suddenly or unexpectedly. It gradually emerges as a person's systems interact with constantly changing sociocultural, biological, and psychological variables. People differ in their ability to adapt to these changes. If we again consider development as a flight of stairs that follows a specific path, a person's position on the path can at any time be considered either developmentally appropriate or inappropriate. However, one should never think that a person's developmental path is fixed, as new interactions or different reactions to previous circumstances can lead to new directions and either a more appropriate or unfavourable path.

Within the field of developmental psychopathology, developmental disorders are defined as a unique group of disorders that originate in infancy, childhood, or adolescence and that generally impact on specific areas of a person's development. The clinical features of developmental disorders vary with regard to severity and the area of functioning that is affected (Institute of Medicine, 2001). From the different theories of physical, cognitive, language, social, personality, emotional, and moral development, it is evident that childhood is a very important period for neurological changes and the completion of certain developmental tasks and competencies. For this reason, it is important that these disorders are identified and diagnosed as they occur. Not only can this help parents, caregivers, teachers, and other professionals to assist those whose lives are affected by them, but it could also minimise the impact that they have on the young person's developmental course.

HISTORY OF DEVELOPMENTAL PSYCHOPATHOLOGY

As recently as the 1930s and 1940s, children with neurodevelopmental disorders were killed as part of Germany's 'children's euthanasia programme', because the mentally handicapped were seen as useless to society and unworthy of life (Cohen-Arazi, 2003). Since this low point, developmental psychopathology has emerged as a unique field from the fields of developmental psychology, clinical psychology, educational psychology, and psychiatry (Wadsworth, 2005), enabling practitioners to approach childhood mental disorders in a more compassionate and constructive way.

In the 1970s, under the American president John F. Kennedy, the president's panel on mental retardation was given the goal to prevent mental retardation across the globe. This created a structure from which developmental disorders could be defined and treated over the next few decades (Harper, 2008).

From the 1970s to 2000, the definition of developmental disorders changed significantly. While the focus in the 1970 definition fell on defining mental retardation, this was widened in 1975 to incorporate autism, as well as some specific learning disabilities. In 1978, the Developmental Disabilities Act was passed; this provided a detailed explanation of developmental disorders that influenced decision-making, educational interventions, and federal policy for many years to come. The new definitions of developmental disorders became less categorical and placed greater emphasis on the functional limitations that resulted from a specific disorder. In addition, researchers also started to use the term 'impairment' instead of 'disease' (Harper, 2008).

Together with the significant changes that took place in legislation during the 1970s, the dominant diagnostic system of psychopathology, the *Diagnostic and Statistical Manual of Mental Disorders* (DSM), published by the American Psychiatric Association, also went through significant changes as far as developmental psychopathology was concerned. In the early 1970s, the DSM gave almost no attention to developmental psychopathology, mostly because it was assumed that children either did not suffer from psychological disorders or, if they did, they would look much the same as they did in adults (Wadsworth, 2005).

Then, with the publication of Thomas Achenbach's book *Developmental Psychopathology* in 1974, it was proposed that childhood psychopathology should be viewed as a separate and unique branch of psychopathology. In 1983, Rutter and Garmezy took the matter a step further by publishing their chapter on developmental psychopathology in the *Handbook of Child Psychology*. Finally, in 1989 and 1990, the distinction was well cemented as a distinct and unique branch within the broader field of psychopathology when the Rochester Symposium on Developmental Psychopathology brought together a diverse group of students with a specific interest in the field, and the *Journal of Development and Psychopathology* was established (Wadsworth, 2005).

CONTEXTUALISING DEVELOPMENTAL PSYCHOPATHOLOGY IN SOUTH AFRICA

It has long been understood that a person's physical health and well-being can be influenced by genetic and environmental factors. However, healthcare professionals are also acknowledging the adverse impact that these factors can have on a person's mental health and well-being (World Health Organization, 2005). Taking poverty as an example, Petersen (2010) notes that the social conditions associated with poverty (e.g. malnutrition and poorer education) often lead to physical health difficulties (see Figure 15.4).

In addition, however, poverty can also lead to helplessness and shame, which are linked to mental health difficulties such as depression and anxiety. On the other hand, when people are stressed or depressed, they often engage in high-risk health behaviours such as excessive alcohol use and unsafe sex, which can in turn impact on their physical health. Also, continuous stress, anxiety, and depression can compromise a person's immune system and endocrine functioning, exacerbating the risk of infection. Thus, the interrelationship between environmental risk factors and mental and physical health should not be underestimated.

Environmental factors, such as poverty, that can increase the risk of the development of mental health difficulties within a specific context, are called risk factors. The World Health Organization (2005) defines risk factors as those variables that increase the probability of the development and existence of mental health difficulties; protective factors are those variables that moderate the effects of risk exposure and assist in the development of resilience (see Chapter 4).

In understanding and treating developmental disorders, it is essential to understand the risk factors within a specific context that can contribute to the development and prolongation of these disorders. Furthermore, in developing a more proactive approach aimed at preventing developmental disorders, it is important to understand the protective factors within an environment that can enhance mental well-being and resilience in children and adolescents.

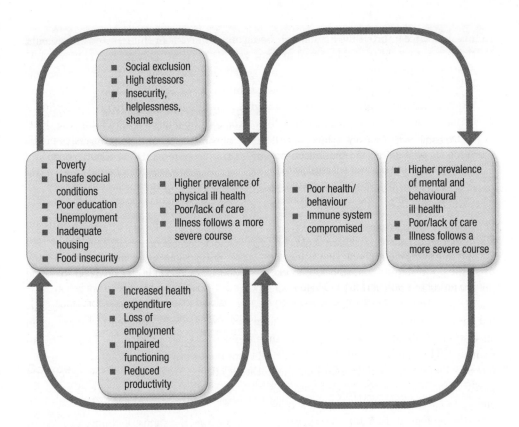

Figure 15.4: The interrelationship between poverty and mental and physical health difficulties

Source: Adapted from Petersen, 2010, p. 8.

From an ecosystemic perspective (see Chapter 4), it is important to understand that risk and protective factors can exist in a child and adolescent's biological, socio-economic, and psychological domains. In the *biological* domain, exposure to toxins, genetic influences, and malnutrition are examples of risk factors, whereas age-appropriate physical development and good intellectual stimulation are examples of protective factors. Within the *psychological* domain, neglect, abuse, and learning disorders are examples of risk factors, whereas good self-esteem and social skills can be considered protective factors. Finally, within the *socio-economic* domain, family factors such as inconsistent parenting, school factors such as academic failure, and community factors such as discrimination and marginalisation, are all considered examples of risk factors. On the other hand, family attachment and opportunities for involvement in one's school and community are considered protective factors (World Health Organization, 2005).

In identifying the risk and protective factors within the South African context it is helpful to adopt a rights-based approach. This not only gives us insight into a wide spectrum of risk factors, but also into the developments that have taken place to expand protective factors and hence improve the mental well-being of South African children and adolescents. Furthermore, in linking child and adolescent well-being with the rights of children, one develops a framework to assess child and adolescent well-being from an ecosystemic perspective that encompasses a concern for the child as a whole (Bray & Dawes, 2007).

According to the South African Human Rights Commission and UNICEF (2011), South Africa has made significant progress since the end of apartheid in 1994 in fulfilling the rights of its children. This has been achieved by passing new laws and through progressive public spending, as well as the reorganisation of administrative systems. However, there are still large disparities: a black child is still, for instance, 18 times more likely to live in poverty and only half as likely to complete secondary education than a white child.

Furthermore, as far as household income is concerned, the poorest 20% of South Africa's households house approximately seven million children, compared to the 1.7 million children living in the richest 20% of households. This is significant when taking into consideration that, compared to a child growing up in the richest quintile, a child growing up in the poorest quintile is only half as likely to experience early childhood developmental programmes and only a third as likely to complete secondary education.

A large number of the risk factors still faced by South African children and adolescents fall within the psychological domain; these violate the rights of children to be protected against all forms of violence, as well as their right to special protection (South African Human Rights Commission & UNICEF, 2011). Some examples are violence and sexual offences against children. In addition, one in three children are exposed to severe corporal punishment, and a 1999 survey found that 36% of children above five years of age were engaged in at least one form of work activity.

In the biological domain, several risk factors show how the rights of children to life, to an adequate standard of living, and to basic health are still being violated (South African Human Rights Commission & UNICEF, 2011). These include problems with hunger and malnutrition, infection with HIV, and lack of immunisation.

Within the socio-economic domain, there are also still several risk factors that violate the rights of children to social security, housing, water and sanitation, education, and family care (South African Human Rights Commission & UNICEF, 2011). These include that only one in three children live with both their biological parents, with many living with a grandparent or other relative.

CHILDHOOD DISORDERS AND STIGMA

In 2010, Zimbabwean epidemiologist Abraham Mukolo and American psychologists Craig Anne Heflinger and Kenneth A. Wallston published a framework for viewing the stigma related to childhood mental disorders. To do this they referred to the definition of stigma given by the Canadian sociologist Erving Goffman, 'in which stigma is an actual/inferred attribute that damages the bearer's reputation and degrades him/her to a socially discredited status' (Mukolo et al., 2010, p. 94). Mukolo and colleagues also use Goffman's term 'courtesy stigma', which describes how being affiliated with a stigmatised person results in secondary stigma.

Mukolo et al. (2010) look at three aspects of stigma in relation to children and mental illness:

- the context of stigma consists of where the stigmatising event takes place: in an institution, in general public life, and/or in the self;
- the dimensions of stigma consist of stereotypes, discrimination, and/or devaluation;
- the targets of stigma consist of the child, the family, and other associates of the child, and the service providers.

Mukolo et al. (2010) observed that younger children are usually thought to be less responsible for their condition (and its outcomes); however, as they develop, the stigma attracted towards the condition becomes associated with the child. The authors noted that this might lead to the whole family being stigmatised. Lastly, Mukolo et al. (2010) also reported that the effect of stigma on the family of the affected child often presents as a barrier to obtaining mental healthcare services.

THE CLASSIFICATION OF CHILDHOOD DISORDERS

With the publication of the fifth edition of the *Diagnostic and Statistical Manual of Mental Disorders* (DSM-5) (American Psychiatric Association, 2013), most of the so-called childhood disorders have been grouped under the category 'neurodevelopmental disorders'. However, others such as oppositional defiant disorder and conduct disorder are grouped under the category 'disruptive, impulse-control and conduct disorders' while enuresis and encopresis have been grouped under 'elimination disorders'.

In addition, certain childhood disorders remain in other categories that have been dealt with earlier in this book. Thus, in terms of the internalising disorders (depression and anxiety), the DSM-5 and the ICD-10 treat these in slightly different ways. DSM-5 places separation anxiety disorder amongst the anxiety disorders; ICD-10 includes it under 'emotional disorders with onset specific to childhood'. The ICD-10 includes childhood depression under its 'mood [affective] disorders', and the DSM-5 includes children in its 'depressive disorders'. For ICD-11, like DSM-5, separation anxiety disorder is placed under 'anxiety or fear-related disorders', and childhood depression is under 'depressive disorders'.

In the ICD-10, the category 'mental retardation' is still used, but this has changed to 'disorders of intellectual development' under the category of 'neurodevelopmental disorders' in the ICD-11; this matches the DSM-5's category of 'intellectual disabilities'. The ICD-10 has the category 'disorders of psychological development', which includes disorders relating to language, scholastic, and motor skills, but in the ICD-11 this category has been merged into the category of 'neurodevelopmental disorders'. In the ICD-10, there is also one category, 'behavioural and emotional disorders with onset usually occurring in childhood and adolescence', which includes disorders relating to hyperactivity, conduct, impulse control, and elimination. However, in the ICD-11 these are dealt with in three separate categories: 'elimination disorders', 'impulse-control disorders', and 'disruptive behaviour or dissocial disorders'. It should be noted that these do not only refer to children, particularly in the case of the impulse-control disorders.

For the purpose of this chapter, the different developmental disorders will be grouped into five categories in the following manner:

- Intellectual disability (intellectual development disorder)
- Autism spectrum disorder
- Elimination disorders (including enuresis and encopresis)
- Externalising disorders (including attention-deficit/hyperactivity disorder, oppositional defiant disorder and conduct disorder)
- Internalising disorders (including depression and separation anxiety disorder).

By grouping the different disorders in this manner, one develops a better understanding of the interrelationship between the different disorders, as well as the underlying risk and protective factors.

INTELLECTUAL DISABILITY (INTELLECTUAL DEVELOPMENT DISORDER)

According to the DSM-5 (American Psychiatric Association, 2013, p. 31), children with an intellectual disability or intellectual developmental disorder, display 'deficits in general mental abilities such as reasoning, problem-solving, planning, abstract thinking, judgement, academic learning, and learning from experience'. The World Health Organization (2016) adds that these abilities/skills contribute to a person's general level of intelligence; thus, individuals with an intellectual disability display deficits in their cognitive, language, motor, and social development. As a result they often struggle to become independent and interact socially at an age-appropriate level.

In the DSM-IV-TR (2000), intellectual disability was termed 'mental retardation' and classified as an Axis II diagnosis. When the multiaxial system fell away with the publication of the DSM-5, mental retardation was grouped under the neurodevelopmental disorders and given a new name: intellectual disability. According to Schalock et al. (2007, as cited in Wicks-Nelson & Israel, 2009), this concept was introduced by the influential American Association of Mental Retardation (AAMR), which later changed its name to the American Association on Intellectual and Developmental Disabilities (AAIDD). The new term was adopted as it appears to better describe the current understanding of intellectual disability, and seems to be in agreement with terms used in Europe. For the purpose of this chapter, the concept 'intellectual disability' will be used, as it appears in the DSM-5.

When examining the diagnostic criteria as stipulated in the DSM-5 (American Psychiatric Association, 2013), it is evident that people with an intellectual disability present with difficulties in both their intellectual and adaptive functioning. As far as their intellectual functioning is concerned, these individuals struggle with the skills noted earlier, i.e. reasoning, problem-solving, planning, abstract thinking, judgement, academic learning, and learning from experience and instruction.

Taking their adaptive functioning into consideration, it is noted that individuals with an intellectual disability display significant restrictions in terms of their adaptive behaviour. They thus struggle to communicate with others, take part in social activities, and live independently.

These intellectual and adaptive difficulties, which first appear during the developmental period, hinder a person's functioning in a variety of environments and can be classified as mild, moderate, severe or profound, depending on the person's level of adaptive functioning. Whereas the DSM-IV-TR (American Psychiatric Association, 2000) distinguished a person's level of functioning based on his or her intellectual abilities as measured on a standardised intelligence test, the DSM-5 shifted the focus to a person's adaptive functioning, as this determines the type and level of support required (see Table 15.2) (American Psychiatric Association, 2013).

Regardless of the focus on adaptive functioning, the diagnosis of an intellectual disability still depends on a clinical assessment and standardised tests of intelligence, specifically as far as the person's difficulties with regard to his or her intellectual functioning are concerned (American Psychiatric Association, 2013). However, the DSM-5 adds a note of caution concerning standardised intelligence tests by advising that the test/s administered should be psychometrically valid and sound, individually administered, and culturally appropriate.

Given the current concerns about the validity and fairness of intelligence tests in a multicultural and multilingual society such as South Africa, it is felt that the diagnosis of an intellectual disability should be made with great caution, and a greater focus on a person's adaptive functioning seems more appropriate. However, there currently do not appear to be any standardised assessments of adaptive functioning in the South African context, although research is being undertaken on the applicability in the South African context of the Vineland Adaptive Behavior Scales 3 (Van der Merwe, 2018)

Table 15.1: Diagnostic criteria for intellectual disability (intellectual developmental disorder) from the DSM-5

DSM-5
Intellectual disability (intellectual developmental disorder) is a disorder with onset during the developmental period that includes both intellectual and adaptive functioning deficits in conceptual, social, and practical domains. The following three criteria must be met:
A. Deficits in intellectual functions, such as reasoning, problem solving, planning, abstract thinking, judgement, academic learning, and learning from experience, confirmed by both clinical assessment and individualised, standardised intelligence testing.
B. Defcits in adaptive functioning that result in failure to meet developmental and sociocultural standards for personal independence and social responsibility. Without ongoing support, the adaptive deficits limit functioning in one or more activities of daily life, such as communication, social participation, and independent living, across multiple environments, such as home, school, work, and community.
C. Onset of intellectual and adaptive deficits during the developmental period.
Note: The diagnostic term *intellectual disability* is the equivalent term for the ICD-11 diagnosis of *intellectual developmental disorders*. Although the term *intellectual disability* is used throughout this manual, both terms are used in the title to clarify relationships with other classification systems. Moreover, a federal statute in the United States (Public Law 111-256, Rosa's Law) replaces the term *mental retardation* with *intellectual disability*, and research journals use the term *intellectual disability*. Thus, *intellectual disability* is the term in common use by medical, educational, and other professions and by the lay public and advocacy groups.

Source: Reprinted with permission from the *Diagnostic and Statistical Manual of Mental Disorders*, fifth edition (DSM-5), American Psychiatric Association (APA), 2013, p. 33.

Table 15.2: Severity levels for intellectual disability (intellectual developmental disorder)

Severity level	Conceptual domain	Social domain	Practical domain
Mild	For preschool children, there may be no obvious conceptual differences. For school-age children and adults, there are difficulties in learning academic skills involving reading, writing, arithmetic, time, or money, with support needed in one or more areas to meet age-related expectations. In adults, abstract thinking, executive function (i.e., planning, strategising, priority setting, and cognitive flexibility), and short-term memory, as well as functional use of academic skills (e.g., reading, money management), are impaired. There is a somewhat concrete approach to problems and solutions compared with age-mates.	Compared with typically developing age-mates, the individual is immature in social interactions. For example, there may be difficulty in accurately perceiving peers' social cues. Communication, conversation, and language are more concrete or immature than expected for age. There may be difficulties regulating emotion and behavior in age-appropriate fashion; these difficulties are noticed by peers in social situations. There is limited understanding of risk in social situations; social judgement is immature for age, and the person is at risk of being manipulated by others (gullibility).	The individual may function age-appropriately in personal care. Individuals need some support with complex daily living tasks in comparison to peers. In adulthood, supports typically involve grocery shopping, transportation, home and child-care organising, nutritious food preparation, and banking and money management. Recreational skills resemble those of age-mates, although judgement related to well-being and organisation around recreation requires support. In adulthood, competitive employment is often seen in jobs that do not emphasise conceptual skills. Individuals generally need support to make healthcare decisions and legal decisions, and to learn to perform a skilled vocation competently. Support is typically needed to raise a family.

Severity level	Conceptual domain	Social domain	Practical domain
Moderate	All through development, the individual's conceptual skills lag markedly behind those of peers. For preschoolers, language and pre-academic skills develop slowly. For school-age children, progress in reading, writing, mathematics, and understanding of time and money occurs slowly across the school years and is markedly limited compared with that of peers. For adults, academic skill development is typically at an elementary level, and support is required for all use of academic skills in work and personal life. Ongoing assistance on a daily basis is needed to complete conceptual tasks of day-to-day life, and others may take over these responsibilities fully for the individual.	The individual shows marked differences from peers in social and communicative behaviour across development. Spoken language is typically a primary tool for social communication but is much less complex than that of peers. Capacity for relationships is evident in ties to family and friends, and the individual may have successful friendships across life and sometimes romantic relations in adulthood. However, individuals may not perceive or interpret social cues accurately. Social judgement and decision-making abilities are limited, and caretakers must assist the person with life decisions. Friendships with typically developing peers are often affected by communication or social limitations. Significant social and communicative support is needed in work settings for success.	The individual can care for personal needs involving eating, dressing, elimination, and hygiene as an adult, although an extended period of teaching and time is needed for the individual to become independent in these areas, and reminders may be needed. Similarly, participation in all household tasks can be achieved by adulthood, although an extended period of teaching is needed, and ongoing supports will typically occur for adult-level performance. Independent employment in jobs that require limited conceptual and communication skills can be achieved, but considerable support from co-workers, supervisors, and others is needed to manage social expectations, job complexities, and ancillary responsibilities such as scheduling, transportation, health benefits, and money management. A variety of recreational skills can be developed. These typically require additional supports and learning opportunities over an extended period of time. Maladaptive behaviour is present in a significant minority and causes social problems.

Severity level	Conceptual domain	Social domain	Practical domain
Severe	Attainment of conceptual skills is limited. The individual generally has little understanding of written language or of concepts involving numbers, quantity, time, and money. Caretakers provide extensive supports for problem solving throughout life.	Spoken language is quite limited in terms of vocabulary and grammar. Speech may be single words or phrases and may be supplemented through augmentative means. Speech and communication are focused on the here and now within everyday events. Language is used for social communication more than for explication. Individuals understand simple speech and gestural communication. Relationships with family members and familiar others are a source of pleasure and help.	The individual requires support for all activities of daily living, including meals, dressing, bathing, and elimination. The individual requires supervision at all times. The individual cannot make responsible decisions regarding well-being of self or others. In adulthood, participation in tasks at home, recreation, and work requires ongoing support and assistance. Skill acquisition in all domains involves long-term teaching and ongoing support. Maladaptive behaviour, including self-injury, is present in a significant minority.

Severity level	Conceptual domain	Social domain	Practical domain
Profound	Conceptual skills generally involve the physical world rather than symbolic processes. The individual may use objects in a goal-directed fashion for self-care, work, and recreation. Certain visuospatial skills, such as matching and sorting based on physical characteristics, may be acquired. However, co-occurring motor and sensory impairments may prevent functional use of objects.	The individual has very limited understanding of symbolic communication in speech or gesture. He or she may understand some simple instructions or gestures. The individual expresses his or her own desires and emotions largely through non-verbal, non-symbolic communication. The individual enjoys relationships with well-known family members, caretakers, and familiar others, and initiates and responds to social interactions through gestural and emotional cues. Co-occurring sensory and physical impairments may prevent many social activities.	The individual is dependent on others for all aspects of daily physical care, health, and safety, although he or she may be able to participate in some of these activities as well. Individuals without severe physical impairments may assist with some daily work tasks at home, like carrying dishes to the table. Simple actions with objects may be the basis of participation in some vocational activities with high levels of ongoing support. Recreational activities may involve, for example, enjoyment in listening to music, watching movies, going out for walks, or participating in water activities, all with the support of others. Co-occurring physical and sensory impairments are frequent barriers to participation (beyond watching) in home, recreational, and vocational activities. Maladaptive behavior is present in a significant minority.

Source: Reprinted with permission from the *Diagnostic and Statistical Manual of Mental Disorders*, fifth edition (DSM-5), American Psychiatric Association (APA), 2013, p. 34.

Aetiology of intellectual disability

In discussing the aetiology of intellectual disabilities, Wicks-Nelson and Israel (2009) and Mash and Wolfe (2010) acknowledge a two-group approach. On the one hand, one finds individuals whose intellectual difficulties have clear underlying organic causes and are more often than not classified with moderate, severe or profound intellectual disabilities. These individuals also often present with other physical disabilities. In the other group, one finds cultural-familial factors, where individuals with intellectual disabilities often have a family member with the same difficulties. These individuals' intellectual difficulties are often mild in nature and can also be attributed to socio-economic factors. They generally display few associated medical or psychical difficulties or disabilities (Wicks-Nelson & Israel, 2009).

Although the distinction between the two groups is helpful in understanding the aetiology of intellectual disabilities, Wicks-Nelson and Israel (2009) caution that multiple factors can play a role. Although a person may for instance have a biomedical vulnerability to develop an intellectual disability, cultural and familial factors may play an important role in the severity of the disability.

The DSM-5 (American Psychiatric Association, 2013) identifies several factors in the prenatal, perinatal, and postnatal period that can contribute to an individual developing an intellectual disability. In the prenatal period, chromosomal disorders, maternal disease, genetic factors, and brain malformations are all potential risk factors. In addition, the use and abuse of alcohol and recreational drugs, as well as the ingestion of other teratogens and toxins, can pose a significant risk to an unborn child.

In the perinatal period, difficulties during the actual birth process that lead to neurological damage in the infant can form the basis of an intellectual disability. In the postnatal period, various diseases, as well as traumatic brain injuries, intoxications, demyelinating disorders, and seizure disorders are all considered potential risk factors that underlie the development of an intellectual disability. With regard to the latter, the influence of socio-economic factors should also not be underestimated as leading causes of intellectual disability (American Psychiatric Association, 2013).

For the purpose of this discussion, these views are combined in understanding the aetiology of intellectual disabilities (see Table 15.3).

Table 15.3: The aetiology of intellectual disabilities

	Organic	Cultural and familial
Prenatal	Factors such as: ■ Chromosomal disorders ■ Brain malformations ■ Genetic abnormalities ■ Multiple congenital anomalies ■ Clear evidence of brain dysfunction ■ Maternal disease	Factors such as: ■ Hereditary influences ■ Maternal recreational drug and alcohol use/abuse ■ Ingestion of teratogens and toxins
Perinatal	Factors such as: ■ Birth difficulties ■ Prematurity ■ Neonatal disorders	Factors such as: ■ Lack of access to birth care ■ Parental abandonment of child ■ Lack of medical interventions upon discharge
Postnatal	Factors such as: ■ Traumatic brain injuries ■ Demyelinating disorders ■ Seizure disorders ■ Various diseases ■ Malnutrition	Factors such as: ■ Inadequate family support ■ Social deprivation ■ Lack of stimulation ■ Poverty

Source: Adapted from Wicks-Nelson & Israel, 2009, p. 308.

Organic factors

In considering the role of organic factors in the development of intellectual difficulties, one acknowledges that biological conditions can pose a significant risk to a person's development (Wicks-Nelson & Israel, 2009). Mash and Wolfe (2010) add that accidents in utero can have a detrimental effect on a child's intellectual development in the prenatal period. In the perinatal period, prematurity and anoxia are considered significant risks, and in the postnatal period, risks arise from head trauma and diseases such as meningitis (Mash & Wolfe, 2010). According to Haugaard (2008), risks include chromosomal and genetic abnormalities such as Down syndrome, fragile X syndrome, phenylketonuria, Williams syndrome, Prader-Willi syndrome, and Angelman syndrome. Haugaard (2008) further acknowledges the detrimental effect of prenatal exposure to alcohol and the comorbidity of intellectual disabilities with foetal alcohol syndrome.

Cultural and familial factors

According to Wicks-Nelson and Israel (2009), twin and adoption studies have shown that there is evidence to suggest that hereditary factors, in combination with other risks, play some role in the development of intellectual disabilities. Other factors that can come into play include psycho-social risks, i.e. low parental education, lack of access to prenatal care, child abuse and neglect, poverty, social deprivation, etc. (Wicks-Nelson & Israel, 2009). Mash and Wolfe (2010) add that undetected organic conditions can also pose a significant risk to the development of intellectual difficulties.

 ACTIVITY

Read the following extract about the stigmatisation of children with intellectual disabilities in Sierra Leone, which comes from a study published in 2016 by Hélène Yoder, Wietse Tol, Ria Reis, and Joop de Jong. How has the framework created by Mukolo et al. helped the writers describe stigma in relation to childhood mental disorders?

'We found examples of the different dimensions of stigma as suggested by Mukolo (stereotypes, discrimination and devaluation), targeting the three groups included in the model: children with mental disorders, families/associates and service providers. The examples we present here are mostly related to children with easily perceptible cognitive limitations.

Stereotypes could be found in the terms used to describe children with mental disorders, e.g. wicked, stubborn, or retarded. *Discrimination* often directly affects the children. A teacher told us how children with mental disorders often face difficulties when taking public transport. Families of children with mental disorders reported being forced to move frequently. On a service level, a teacher told us how she was sometimes discriminated for working at a "Special needs School":

"At times, when they look at me, they can look at me as If I am crazy. Because this is a 'mentally retarded school'."

Discrimination of children with mental disorders frequently results in child abuse or exploitation. Participants told us stories about children being chained or beaten. Girls with mental retardation are believed to be at increased risk of sexual violence. Their cases are not followed-up as the children cannot give evidence. Other children are subjected to child labour; they are given *"filthy jobs to do"* (group interview).

Looking at the context of stigma, we found that discrimination is often brought on by the general public, but also takes place on an institutional level:

"Slow learners are beaten by the teachers and parents withdraw them from school." *(group interview).*

Devaluation was often targeted at the child, e.g.

"People feel they [children with mental disorders] are outcasts. They feel they are not human beings." (Teacher Special Needs School)

"Children with mental health problems are considered a curse." (Group Interview)

"People feel they [children with mental disorders] are not functioning properly. They cannot contribute towards the development of the community." (Teacher Special Needs School)

We did not find examples of self-stigmatisation, but a mother expressed how she wrestled with the public opinion about her child:

"They say, we gave birth to a debul (demon). But it is not true. She got up and she walked. If she were a debul, she'd sit down, she won't walk. But this one, I don't think this is a debul."

Stigma as an obstacle to bring their child for treatment was mentioned by one informant, an MHC [mental health care] Provider in Freetown.'

Source: Yoder, Tol, Reis, & De Jong, 2016, Article ID 48.

AUTISM SPECTRUM DISORDER

Autism spectrum disorder incorporates a group of unique disorders previously listed separately in the DSM-IV-TR (American Psychiatric Association, 2000), including autism, Asperger's, childhood disintegrative disorder, and pervasive developmental disorder. Although these terms are subsequently not used in the DSM-5, autism spectrum disorder is still characterised by a number of overlapping characteristics that were evident in these disorders, primarily in the areas of communication, social interaction, and other distinctive behavioural characteristics (American Psychiatric Association, 2013; Shriver, 2005).

According to the American Psychiatric Association (2012a), the workgroup reviewing the changes for the DSM-5 considered the new name because, although autistic spectrum disorders could be reliably and validly distinguished from typical development, it was often difficult to distinguish between the different disorders. Indeed, it had been found that distinctions amongst the autistic spectrum disorders were often inconsistent and dependent upon time, situational variables, severity, language level, and/or intelligence, rather than the features of the disorder. Also, because these disorders were recognised by a common set of behaviours, they could best be represented by a single diagnostic criterion that is adapted to the individual's clinical presentation by inclusion of specific clinical specifiers and associated features (American Psychiatric Association, 2012a).

Table 15.4: Some common autism myths and facts

MYTH	FACT
'Cold' parenting causes autism.	There are no known types of parenting practices that cause autism.
Autism is seen primarily in families of high socio-economic status.	Autism is found across all socio-economic classes, and across all cultures and races.
Individuals with autism often have exceptional specialised abilities such as adding or memorising geography.	Although some individuals with autism may have specific exceptional abilities, this is uncommon and not a distinguishing characteristic of autism.
Individuals with autism typically spend their time alone, spinning objects or engaged in other maladaptive behaviour such as self-injury or having tantrums.	Although there is qualitative impairment in social interaction, this may present itself in many different ways for the individual.
Autism is not treatable.	Effective interventions are available to teach social and communication skills and reduce maladaptive behaviours.
Autism is caused by immunisations (e.g. MMR), gastrointestinal disorders, mercury or lead poisoning, and vitamin deficiencies.	There is not a specific identifiable cause for autism at this time. It is likely that the cause includes both genetic and environmental variables.

Source: Shriver, 2005.

The term 'autism' is derived from the Greek word *autos*, which means self. It was most likely first used by the Swiss psychologist Eugen Blueler, who used it to describe children who had schizophrenic symptomology and difficulties in engaging with others (Simpson & LaCava, 2007). Autism as a disorder was, however, first described by the doctor Leo Kanner in 1943, after he had studied the behaviour of eleven children in his American practice who all displayed similar symptoms (Shriver, 2005). According to Kanner, these children all started to display these symptoms in infancy or early childhood. Amongst the symptoms he included:

- An inability to relate normally to others
- Delayed speech and language development
- Failure to use developed language for communication purposes
- Speech and language irregularities
- Pronoun reversals and misuse
- Extreme literalness
- Normal physical growth and development
- Obsessive insistence on environmental sameness
- An extreme fascination and preoccupation with objects
- Stereotypic, repetitive, and other self-stimulatory responses (Simpson & LaCava, 2007).

Although these defining characteristics of autism have been refined over the years since Kanner first noticed them, an essential cluster of symptoms has remained. These include difficulties with social interaction and communication, and restrictive behaviours and interests (Shriver, 2005).

In 1944, during the same period in which Kanner first described autism, the German physician Hans Asperger published a paper entitled 'Autistic Psychopathy in Childhood'. In doing this, Asperger became the first person to describe the cluster of symptoms that comprise what we know as Asperger's disorder (Mayes, Calhoun, & Crites, 2001). However, due to the Second World War and a language barrier, it was not until the 1980s that this paper was translated into English. This allowed it to be read more widely, and the disorder to be recognised worldwide (Shriver, 2005; Simpson & LaCava, 2007). As noted earlier, the DSM-5 no longer uses the term Asperger's disorder, most likely because it has always been seen as a milder form of autism (McClaren & Winsler, 2005).

As far as autism spectrum disorder is concerned, the DSM-5 (American Psychiatric Association, 2013) groups a person's difficulties with regard to social interaction and communication into one dimension of symptoms, which includes difficulties with regard to social-emotional reciprocity; deficits in non-verbal communicative behaviours used for social interaction; and deficits in developing, maintaining, and understanding relationships.

This change was recommended as the workgroup (American Psychiatric Association, 2012a) felt that a child's impairments with regard to social interaction and communication are inseparable and can more accurately be considered as symptoms with contextual and environmental specifiers. Furthermore, language delays are not unique to autism spectrum disorders and, by combining these criteria and requiring both to be completely fulfilled, one is contributing to the detail of the diagnosis, without taking anything away from the sensitivity.

The second dimension of symptoms covers the person's restrictive, repetitive behaviours and interests and includes stereotyped or repetitive motor movements; insistence on sameness; an inflexible adherence to routines or ritualised patterns of verbal and non-verbal behaviour; highly restricted, fixated interests; and hypo- or hyper-reactivity to sensory input (American Psychiatric Association, 2013).

These difficulties generally have a significant impact on a person's social, educational, and occupational functioning. In addition, DSM-5 has also added severity specifiers: level 1, level 2 or level 3. People with level 1 autism spectrum disorder require some support, people with level 2 require substantial support, and people with level 3 require very substantial support.

Autism spectrum disorder is generally first diagnosed in infancy or childhood, thus in the early developmental period. Although it was previously said that a child's symptoms are noticeable before the age of three years (Nissenbaum, 2005), the DSM-5 makes provision for the fact that the child's symptoms might only become noticeable when social demands exceed his or her limited capacity (American Psychiatric Association, 2103).

It was previously noted that most children with autism also display some degree of cognitive impairment (Shriver, 2005; Simpson & LaCava, 2007). Although the DSM-5 (American Psychiatric Association, 2013) makes provision for this, it notes that the difficulties experienced by a person with autism spectrum disorder should not be better accounted for by an intellectual disability or global developmental delay.

Depending on the severity of the disorder, it is still believed that children with autism spectrum disorder generally fail to develop suitable peer relationships; in addition, they struggle to share enjoyment with others, and show an appropriate awareness of others. They also present with poor social reciprocity, display great difficulty in pretend or make-believe play, and struggle to understand social relationships. They generally do not like to be touched.

In communicating with others, children with autism spectrum disorder present with language delays, have difficulty in initiating and sustaining conversations, use stereotypical or repetitive language, struggle to maintain eye contact, and present with a poor understanding of non-verbal behaviour (Nissenbaum, 2005; American Psychiatric Association, 2013).

Furthermore, while observing children with autism spectrum disorder, one will notice that they present with stereotypical and repetitive behavioural patterns that include preoccupations, resistance to change, inflexibility, and repetitive motor movements such as rocking. In addition, they also display a need for sameness, a fascination with parts of objects, sensitivity to certain textures, and hand-flapping (Nissenbaum, 2005). Amongst their unusual responses to the environment, children with autism spectrum disorder also occasionally display insensitivity to pain and an over-reactivity or under-reactivity to noise (Boorstein, Fein, & Wilson, 2005). The extent to which they require support with these once again depends on the severity of the disorder.

Table 15.5: Diagnostic criteria for autism spectrum disorder from the DSM-5 and the ICD-10

DSM-5	ICD-10
A. Persistent deficits in social communication and social interaction across multiple contexts, as manifested by all of the following, currently or by history (examples are illustrative, not exhaustive; see text): (1) Deficits in social-emotional reciprocity, ranging, for example, from abnormal social approach and failure of normal back-and-forth conversation to reduced sharing of interests, emotions, or affect, to failure to initiate or respond to social interactions. (2) Deficits in non-verbal communication behaviours used for social interaction, ranging, for example, from poorly integrated verbal and non-verbal communication, to abnormalities in eye contact and body language or deficits in understanding and use of gestures, to total lack of facial expressions and nonverbal communication.	■ A pervasive developmental disorder defined by the presence of abnormal and/or impaired development that is manifest before the age of three years, and by the characteristic type of abnormal functioning in all three areas of social interaction, communication, and restricted, repetitive behaviour. **Diagnostic guidelines:** ▸ Usually there is no prior period of unequivocally normal development but, if there is, abnormalities become apparent before the age of three years. ▸ Qualitative impairments in reciprocal social interaction. These take the form of an inadequate appreciation of socio-emotional cues, as shown by a lack of responses to other people's emotions and/or a lack of modulation of behaviour according to social context. ▸ Poor use of social signals and weak integration of social, emotional, and communicative behaviours, and, especially, a lack of socio-emotional reciprocity.

DSM-5	ICD-10
(3) Deficits in developing, maintaining, and understanding relationships, ranging, for example, from difficulties adjusting behaviour to suit various social contexts, to difficulties in sharing imaginative play or in making friends, to absence of interest in peers.	■ Qualitative impairments in communications, i.e:
	▸ Lack of social usage of whatever language skills are present.
	▸ Impairment in make-believe and social imitative play.
	▸ Poor synchrony and lack of reciprocity in conversational interchange.
B. Restricted, repetitive actions of behaviour, interests, or activities, as manifested by at least two of the following, currently or by history (examples are illustrative, not exhaustive; see text):	▸ Poor flexibility in language expression and a relative lack of creativity and fantasy in thought processes.
	▸ Lack of emotional response to other people's verbal and non-verbal overtures.
(1) Stereotyped or repetitive motor movements, use of objects, or speech (e.g. simple motor stereotypies, lining up toys or flipping objects, echolalia, idiosyncratic phrases).	▸ Impaired use of variations in cadence or emphasis to reflect communicative modulation, and a similar lack of accompanying gesture to provide emphasis or aid meaning in spoken communication.
(2) Insistence on sameness, inflexible adherence to routines, or ritualised patterns of verbal or non-verbal behaviour (e.g. extreme distress at small changes, difficulties with transitions, rigid thinking patterns, greeting rituals, need to take same route or eat same food every day).	■ The condition is also characterised by:
	▸ Restricted, repetitive, and stereotyped patterns of behaviour, interests, and activities.
	▸ In early childhood, particularly, there may be specific attachment to unusual, typically non-soft objects.
(3) Highly restricted, fixated interests that are abnormal in intensity or focus (e.g. strong attachment to or preoccupation with unusual objects, excessively circumscribed or perseverative interests).	▸ The children may insist on the performance of particular routines in rituals of a non-functional character; there may be stereotyped preoccupations with interests such as dates, routes, or timetables.
(4) Hyper- or hyporeactivity to sensory input or unusual interests in sensory aspects of the environment (e.g. apparent indifference to pain/temperature, adverse response to specific sounds or textures, excessive smelling or touching of objects, visual fascination with lights or movement).	■ Often there are:
	▸ Motor stereotypies.
	▸ Specific interest in non-functional elements of objects (such as their smell or feel) is common.
C. Symptoms must be present in the early developmental period (but may not become fully manifest until social demands exceed limited capacities, or may be masked by learned strategies in later life).	▸ There may be a resistance to changes in routine or in details of the personal environment (such as the movement of ornaments or furniture in the family home).

DSM-5	ICD-10
D. Symptoms cause clinically significant impairment in social, occupational, or other important areas of current functioning.	■ A range of other non-specific problems such as fear/phobias, sleeping and eating disturbances, temper tantrums, and
E. These disturbances are not better explained by intellectual disability (intellectual developmental disorder) or global developmental delay. Intellectual disability and autism spectrum disorder frequently co-occur; to make comorbid diagnoses of autism spectrum disorder and intellectual disability, social communication should be below that expected for general developmental level	aggression. Self-injury (e.g. by wrist-biting) is fairly common, especially when there is associated severe mental retardation.
	■ Lack of spontaneity, initiative, and creativity in the organisation of their leisure time and they have difficulty applying conceptualisations in decision-making in work (even when the tasks themselves are well within their capacity).
	■ The specific manifestation of deficits characteristic of autism change as the children grow older, but the deficits continue into and through adult life with a broadly similar pattern of problems in socialisation, communication, and interest patterns.

Source: Reprinted with permission from the *Diagnostic and Statistical Manual of Mental Disorders*, fifth edition (DSM-5), American Psychiatric Association (APA), 2013, p. 50; DSM-5 Update: Supplement to *Diagnostic and Statistical Manual of Mental Disorders*, fifth edition (DSM-5), American Psychiatric Association (APA), 2016, p. 3, and ICD-10 *Classification of Mental and Behavioural Disorders: Diagnostic Criteria for Research*, World Health Organization (WHO), Geneva, 2007.

Aetiology of autism spectrum disorder

The aetiology of autism spectrum disorder is still very unclear, but it is widely assumed to be caused by a convergence of genetic, biological, and environmental variables (Shriver, 2005). In addition, autism spectrum disorder has been associated with a number of medical illnesses, including maternal rubella, phenylketonuria, encephalitis, meningitis, fragile X syndrome, seizure disorder, and tuberous sclerosis (Simpson & LaCava, 2007). The previous assumption that certain familial and parental factors play a role has been widely disproved.

However, research does support the suggestion that there is a genetic component in the development of autism spectrum disorder (Rutter, 2000). Studies of families of those diagnosed with autism spectrum disorder have shown that there is a much higher rate of autism spectrum disorder in monozygotic twins, compared with dizygotic twins. In addition, a family member of a person with autism spectrum disorder has a much higher chance of developing an autism spectrum disorder than do the general population (Simpson & LaCava, 2007). Research has further indicated that parents who have one child with autism spectrum disorder have a 3–5% chance of having another child with the disorder, which is also much higher than the general population (Fritson, 2007).

In the past, there has been speculation that autism spectrum disorder is caused by the MMR (measles-mumps-rubella) vaccination, vitamin deficiencies, and food allergies. This is, however, not supported by scientific research (Nissenbaum, 2007).

ELIMINATION DISORDERS

One of the most important milestones in a child's developmental path is the ability to control bodily functions. As a young child spends the first few years of life exploring, understanding, and manipulating his or her body, the ability to control bodily functions such as urination is a very important and exciting step. In addition, due partly to social pressure to attain control of one's bodily functions, difficulties in managing to do so can cause major stress and distress in a young child's life (Wenar & Kerig, 2006). Children who have an elimination disorder struggle to exercise control over two very specific bodily functions and will repeatedly and age-inappropriately urinate (enuresis) or pass faeces (encopresis) in unacceptable settings (Comer, 1995).

Enuresis

Table 15.6: Diagnostic criteria for enuresis from the DSM-5 and the ICD-10

DSM-5 Enuresis	ICD 10
A. Repeated voiding of urine into bed or clothes, whether involuntary or intentional. B. The behaviour is clinically significant as manifested by either a frequency of at least twice a week for at least three consecutive months or the presence of clinically significant distress or impairment in social, academic (occupational), or other important areas of functioning. C. Chronological age is at least five years (or equivalent developmental level). D. The behaviour is not attributable to the physiological effects of a substance (e.g. a diuretic, an antipsychotic medication) or another medical condition (e.g. diabetes, spina bifida, a seizure disorder).	■ A disorder characterised by involuntary voiding of urine, by day and/or by night, which is abnormal in relation to the individual's mental age and which is not a consequence of a lack of bladder control due to any neurological disorder, to epileptic attacks, or to any structural abnormality of the urinary tract. The enuresis may have been present from birth (i.e. an abnormal extension of the normal infantile incontinence) or it may have arisen following a period of acquired bladder control. The later onset (or secondary) variety usually begins at about the age of five to seven years. The enuresis may constitute a monosymptomatic condition or it may be associated with a more widespread emotional or behavioural disorder.

Source: Reprinted with permission from the *Diagnostic and Statistical Manual of Mental Disorders*, fifth edition (DSM-5), American Psychiatric Association (APA), 2013, p. 355, and ICD-10 *Classification of Mental and Behavioural Disorders: Diagnostic Criteria for Research*, World Health Organization (WHO), Geneva, 2007.

Enuresis comes from the Greek *ouresis* (urination) and refers to how children repeatedly and mostly involuntarily (in some cases intentionally) urinate in inappropriate places, i.e. their bed and/or clothes (American Psychiatric Association, 2000; Haugaard, 2008). For a child to be diagnosed with enuresis, the inappropriate urination takes place after the age at which most children are expected to have learned to urinate in an appropriate place such as a toilet. Although this is dependent upon social norms and customs, a child needs to be at least five years of age, or functioning at an equivalent developmental level, to meet the diagnostic criteria for enuresis (American Psychiatric Association, 2013; Wicks-Nelson & Israel, 2009).

According to the DSM-5 (American Psychiatric Association, 2013), the behaviour becomes clinically significant when it occurs frequently (at least twice weekly for at least three consecutive months) or if it causes significant distress or impairment in social, academic (occupational), or other important areas of functioning.

In addition to the above, the DSM-5 (American Psychiatric Association, 2013) stipulates that the incontinence is not due exclusively to the direct physiological effect of a substance or a general medical condition (such as diabetes, spina bifida, or a seizure disorder).

In order to truly understand enuresis and the different subtypes, it is important to understand that the ability to withhold urination, until it is appropriate to do so, involves the complex coordination between a child's physical and cognitive abilities. On a physical level, the child's bladder needs to develop to the size that it can hold a meaningful amount of urine (Fritz et al., 2004).

However, there is a difference between the actual amount of urine that a child's bladder can hold and the bladder's functional capacity, which refers to the amount of urine that a child's bladder can hold before he or she feels the urge to urinate. A person's functional bladder capacity is always smaller than the actual bladder capacity, which is one of the reasons why we can withhold urination after experiencing the urge to do so (Haugaard, 2008).

Another physical ability that a child needs to develop is the ability to exercise control over the external urinary sphincter so that urine can be voluntarily retained in the bladder. Once in an appropriate place, the child then needs to be able to relax the external urinary sphincter while contracting the muscles of the bladder so that urine can be expelled. In order to do this, the child needs to develop voluntary control of the micturition reflex (Fritz et al., 2004). On a cognitive level, the child needs to develop the ability to recognise the physical sensations indicating that the bladder is full.

Difficulties with any of the stated abilities can contribute to enuresis (Haugaard, 2008). Wenar and Kerig (2006) add that children also require the necessary communication skills to advise their parents that they need to go to the bathroom, as well as the social and emotional knowledge to understand the importance of adhering to social norms.

Based on the above, Von Gontard (1998, in Haugaard, 2008) identifies three different subtypes of enuresis:

- **Urge incontinence** occurs when a child cannot suppress his or her bladder contractions while the bladder fills with urine, resulting in frequent and uncontrollable emptying of the bladder.
- On the other hand, **voiding postponement** occurs when a child does not urinate for long periods on purpose. When the child can then no longer hold the urine, there is a sudden, uncontrollable void of urine. There are several reasons why children might intentionally refuse to urinate, including fear of the bathroom and a desire to continue playing.
- Finally, there is **detrusor-sphincter dyscoordination** where a child cannot relax the external urinary sphincter while contracting the muscles around the bladder, resulting in strained urination and usually only small amounts of urine. Enuresis then occurs when the child's bladder becomes so full that involuntary voiding occurs.

In addition to the noted subtypes, the DSM-5 (American Psychiatric Association, 2013) also distinguishes between nocturnal (night-time) and diurnal (daytime) enuresis. Children may, however, also present with a combination of the two. In addition, enuresis may either be primary or secondary. Primary enuresis indicates that the child has never had a period of urinary continence. Secondary enuresis indicates that the child has had a period of urinary continence, but has returned to wetting incidents (Fritz et al., 2004).

Encopresis

Encopresis, derived from the Greek word *kopros* (excrement) is described as repeated, often involuntary (in some cases voluntary) passing of faeces in inappropriate places that usually starts after the age of four years (Comer, 1995; Haugaard, 2008). To receive a diagnosis of encopresis, a child needs to pass faeces in inappropriate places at least once a month, for at least three months. Therefore, a child who has very rare incidents will not qualify for the diagnosis (Haugaard, 2008).

The most common form of encopresis is the type with constipation and overflow incontinence (Wicks-Nelson & Israel, 2009). In this type, hard faeces blocks the bowel, but liquid faeces leaks past. There are, however, some children who struggle with encopresis without constipation and overflow incontinence (American Psychiatric Association, 2013).

Table 15.7: Diagnostic criteria for encopresis from the DSM-5 and the ICD-10

DSM-5	ICD 10
A. Repeated passage of faeces into inappropriate places (e.g. clothing, floor), whether involuntary or intentional. B. At least one such event occurs each month for at least three months. C. Chronological age is at least four years (or equivalent developmental level). D. The behaviour is not attributable to the physiological effects of a substance (e.g. laxatives) or another medical condition except through a mechanism involving constipation.	Repeated voluntary or involuntary passage of faeces, usually of normal or near-normal consistency, in places not appropriate for that purpose in the individual's own sociocultural setting. The condition may represent an abnormal continuation of normal infantile incontinence, it may involve a loss of continence following the acquisition of bowel control, or it may involve the deliberate deposition of faeces in inappropriate places in spite of normal physiological bowel control. The condition may occur as a monosymptomatic disorder, or it may form part of a wider disorder, especially an emotional disorder or a conduct disorder.

Source: Reprinted with permission from the *Diagnostic and Statistical Manual of Mental Disorders*, fifth edition (DSM-5), American Psychiatric Association (APA), 2013, p. 357, and ICD-10 *Classification of Mental and Behavioural Disorders: Diagnostic Criteria for Research*, World Health Organization (WHO), Geneva, 2007.

Using the same criteria as those applied to enuresis, children can either have diurnal encopresis or nocturnal encopresis or both. Likewise, they can suffer from either primary or secondary encopresis (Haugaard, 2008). Comer (1995) is of the opinion that encopresis usually occurs during the day and seldom at night. Ondersma and colleagues (2001, in Haugaard, 2008) have suggested that there are three different subtypes of encopresis depending on their cause:

- **Retentive encopresis** is similar to encopresis with constipation and overflow incontinence.
- **Manipulative encopresis** where the child purposely expels a stool to achieve some goal (e.g. seeking attention or expressing anger and frustration).
- **Stress-related encopresis** is related to stressful life experiences.

Aetiology of elimination disorders

Early conceptualisations of elimination disorders stated that they were mainly caused by psychological difficulties; however, more recent research has indicated that most cases of elimination disorders are caused by biological difficulties, while the psychological difficulties experienced by children are usually secondary to the elimination difficulties (Haugaard, 2008; Wicks-Nelson & Israel, 2009). According to the ICD-10 criteria (World Health Organization, 2016), elimination disorders may, however, be associated with a more widespread emotional or behavioural disorder. Fritz et al. (2004) agree, but warn that this only accounts for enuresis in a small subgroup of children who develop secondary enuresis in response to a stressful situation.

It is often difficult to be sure which is cause and which is effect, as emotional problems may arise as a result of the elimination difficulties and the distress and stigma attached to them. Haugaard (2008) describes these emotional difficulties; he notes that children with enuresis or encopresis are usually aware that they have not developed the type of physical control that is expected of their developmental level, and that this can impact on their self-worth and self-esteem. In addition, these children often experience negative reactions from those around them and are often teased by others.

On the other hand, elimination difficulties may also develop due to some other emotional or behavioural problems, and one occasionally sees children who expel faeces as an expression of anger. There is generally no straightforward way to decide which problem occurred first, and a clinician also has to take into consideration that enuresis or encopresis may have developed together with emotional or behavioural difficulties as a result of related aetiological factors. The most important rule in making a diagnosis is to consider which difficulty (i.e. the enuresis/encopresis or the emotional/behavioural difficulty) is the most prominent problem (World Health Organization, 2016).

Physiological causes

In the case of enuresis, as noted above, a child's functional bladder capacity is smaller than their actual bladder capacity. Children with nocturnal enuresis tend to urinate automatically when the bladder reaches its functional capacity and the urge to do so arises. As a result, children with a smaller functional capacity may urinate more often during the night than those who have an average capacity (Fritz et al., 2004). Furthermore, according to research by Kawauchi et al. (2003, in Haugaard, 2008), children with nocturnal enuresis have smaller functional bladder capacities during the night than during the day.

Research into children's sleeping patterns and the times at which nocturnal enuresis occurs produced conflicting results. Earlier studies showed that enuresis occurs during all four stages of sleep, while a more recent study indicated that no wetting incidents occur during a normal REM cycle (Haugaard, 2008; Wicks-Nelson & Israel, 2009). The research also indicated that children struggled more with enuresis on nights when they had longer periods of deep sleep, compared to nights where they had shorter periods of stages 3 and 4 sleep. In addition, some research has also indicated that children with enuresis struggle more to wake from sleep than their counterparts who do not experience enuresis. Although there thus appears to be a link between deep sleep and enuresis, more research is required (Haugaard, 2008; Wicks-Nelson & Israel, 2009).

Some research on the physiological causes of nocturnal enuresis has indicated that some children secrete less anginine vasopressin, an antidiuretic hormone that reduces urine production at night. Whereas most people produce more anginine vasopressin during the night than during the day, it would appear that children with nocturnal enuresis secrete less of this hormone and hence produce more urine at night (Haugaard, 2008). According to Wenar and Kerig (2006), evidence in support of the anginine vasopressin hypothesis is questionable as not all the children who struggle with nocturnal enuresis produce excessive urine.

As far as encopresis is concerned, Wicks-Nelson and Israel (2009) state that, as is the case with enuresis, physiological difficulties, for instance with the normal defaecation reflex, may contribute to the development of encopresis.

Genetic factors

Most children with enuresis have a close relative who has experienced the same difficulty, suggesting that there is a genetic link (Comer, 1995). According to Wicks-Nelson and Israel (2009), there are higher concordance rates for enuresis between monozygotic twins than between dizygotic twins. Wenar and Kerig (2006) note that, when both parents have been enuretic as children, there is an estimated 80% risk that their child will also have enuresis. However, when only one parent had enuresis, the child only has an estimated 45% risk. If neither parent had it, the estimated risk is 15%.

According to Haugaard (2008), genes on several chromosomes play a role in the development of enuresis as they influence the child's ability to develop functional bladder capacity. Alternatively, enuresis may be the result of combinations of different genes that impede the maturation needed for urinary continence.

As far as the genetic link in the development of encopresis is concerned, constipation, which can cause encopresis, can be influenced by genetic factors. Genes can either reduce a child's awareness of a full colon and the need for a bowel movement or cause difficulty with normal bowel movements (Haugaard, 2008).

Stool-toilet refusal

One of the causes of constipation can be stool-toilet refusal. This occurs when children refuse to use a toilet for bowel movements despite having learned to urinate in it. As is the case with postponement of urinary voiding, children with stool-toilet refusal withhold bowel movements for as long as they can or until they are given a diaper to wear. This delay in passing faeces can then lead to constipation, which can result in painful bowel movements, making the child even more reluctant to pass a stool. As for voiding postponement, children may avoid passing faeces because of fear of the bathroom or the toilet training that they have received (Haugaard, 2008).

Family factors

Studies on the familial factors involved in enuresis have indicated that the way caregivers manage normal bedwetting during the toilet-training process can play a significant role. One common mistake is to wake children several times during the night to urinate. Not only can this be quite stressful for parents and children, children also learn a pattern of urinating when they are only half awake. They can then continue doing this even when they are in bed and only half aroused or woken by the urge to empty their bladders.

Also, as children are then taught to empty their bladders when they are not yet full, they do not learn to recognise the physical sensations associated with bladders which have reached their functional capacity (Haugaard, 2008). Consequently, children learn to urinate frequently when there are only small amounts of urine in their bladders (Haugaard, 2008).

Some caregivers also tend to limit the amount of fluids that their children take during the evening. However, this might also impede the development of the child's functional bladder capacity, as well as their awareness of the physical sensations associated with it.

Certain caregivers believe that it is helpful to punish children for elimination difficulties. When enuresis or encopresis are involuntary, however, punishment will not resolve the problem. Also, punishment can create stress and fear, which can actually worsen the situation; this can lead to resentment and result in children who intentionally urinate or pass faeces out of anger and frustration (Comer, 1995; Haugaard, 2008).

 ACTIVITY

Josephat Chinawa, Herbert Obu, Pius Manyike, Odetunde Odutola Isreal, and Chinawa Awoere Tamunosiki published a study on encopresis in South East Nigeria in 2015, and had the following to say in this study. Read the paragraph and extract, and consider whether this call to action is something that you might respond to, giving reasons for your answer.

> *While it is important to evaluate and treat all forms of incontinence, encopresis carries the greatest risk of detrimental consequences for the child concerned. These outcomes may include medical issues, as well as factors influencing the child's social and emotional development. This is because those around the child (parents, peers, teachers, etc.) often respond with revulsion and punishment.*

Chinawa et al. go on to say:

> *Evaluation of the pattern of encopresis is a very vital issue often under-reported in pediatric practice, and its importance cannot be overemphasised especially its impact on child health.*

> *The problem of encopresis has also increased due to the apparent lack of interest by researchers and paucity of empirical data especially from this part of the world which made it difficult to ascertain its prevalence especially in Nigeria. Arresting this neglected problem of the child is an important issue in this 21st century.*

EXTERNALISING DISORDERS

Externalising disorders of childhood and adolescence are best described as disorders characterised by behaviours directed outward. The primary difference between these and internalising disorders is in the way in which they are expressed. Unlike internalising disorders, externalising disorders are always expressed outward and become noticeable in the child's or adolescent's interpersonal relations and interactions with others. It is here that we often notice behaviours such as disobedience, defiance, aggression, stubbornness, temper tantrums, fidgetiness, and hyperactivity; these understandably cause a lot of tension and conflict between the child or adolescent and significant others such as parents and teachers (Helm, 2008).

The American research scientist Gerald R. Patterson examined the relationship between antisocial behaviour in young children and antisocial behaviour in later developmental stages. Figure 15.5 below shows how these can be related to each other, although Patterson did not believe that there was inevitable progression between these 'stages'.

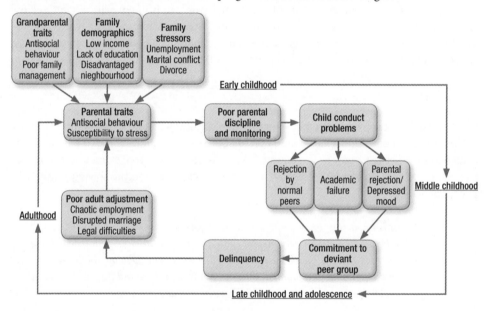

Figure 15.5: Patterson's model of the development of conduct disorder

Source: Wenar & Kerig, 2006, p. 326.

The externalising disorders that will be discussed in this section include attention-deficit/hyperactivity disorder (ADHD), which DSM-5 categorised under 'neurodevelopmental disorders', as well as conduct disorder and oppositional defiant disorder, which have been listed under the category 'disruptive, impulse-control and conduct disorders'. According to the American Psychiatric Association (2013), there was strong evidence to support the categorisation of ADHD as part of the latter category; however, based on the pattern of its symptoms, the underlying risk factors, and the comorbidity of ADHD with a number of other disorders, it was categorised as a 'neurodevelopmental disorder'.

Attention-deficit/hyperactivity disorder

Eight-year-old Eric lives in a dynamic and ever-changing world, a kaleidoscope where sounds, images, and thoughts are constantly moving, shifting, and altering. As his mind manoeuvres him from one thought and activity to the next, frustration has become his companion. Unimportant sounds and sights distract him and he struggles to keep his thoughts on the task at hand. He gets so wrapped up in a collage of thoughts and pictures that he doesn't even realise when people are talking to him. At times, he is not fully aware of what is going on around him. His parents and teachers describe him as disorganised and constantly caught up in a whirlwind of frenzied activities. The difficulty is that there are some days or situations where he appears fine, which makes others believe that he can control his behaviour. Just to put the proverbial cherry on top of it all, all of the above has an enormous impact on his emotional well-being as it disrupts his life, harms his relationships, and damages his self-esteem.

Source: Adapted from The Colorado Personal Growth and Therapy Resources, 1998, p. 2.

History of ADHD

ADHD was first described in 1902 by an English paediatrician, George Still. He noticed that some of the children in his practice, mostly boys, struggled to inhibit their behaviour and adhere to social rules. According to Still, this problem went beyond simple social etiquette; these children were suffering from a lack of 'moral control' (Barkley, 1995; Green & Chee, 1997).

Over the decades following Still's observations, scientists started to study the possible causes of this phenomenon, mostly focusing on the brain. In the early 1960s, the focus shifted to the behaviours associated with the phenomenon (Brochin & Horvath, 1996), which then became known as 'hyperactive child syndrome'. In the 1970s, the focus again shifted, this time to difficulties with impulse control and sustained attention. It was then labelled attention-deficit disorder (with or without hyperactivity).

Clinical picture

According to Anastopoulos, Guevremont, Shelton, and DuPaul (1992), ADHD is a chronic and pervasive developmental condition characterised by problems with sustained attention, impulse control, and activity regulation. Anastopoulos et al. (1992) add that ADHD can be very disruptive to the person and the people around him or her (e.g. parents, teacher, peers, etc.) and has a significant impact on a person's cognitive, emotional, and social functioning and development.

Anastopoulos (1998) maintains that, in diagnosing ADHD, it is always important to consider the child's developmental level. In terms of age of onset, clinicians have started to recognise that ADHD is not only a disorder of childhood, and can also be diagnosed in adulthood (Kieling et al., 2010). Accordingly, the DSM-5 notes that, instead of the symptoms being diagnosed before the age of seven years as in the DSM-IV-TR, ADHD must now be first diagnosed before the age of 12 years.

According to Green and Chee (1997), ADHD contains three essential parts:

- Core behaviours, which include the hyperactive-impulsive and the attention-deficit behaviours
- Secondary behaviours, which include social clumsiness, poor coordination, disorganisation, and poor self-esteem
- Comorbid conditions, which include specific learning disabilities, oppositional defiant disorder, conduct disorder, and depression.

Hyperactive-impulsive behaviours

The DSM-5 describes children who are hyperactive as fidgety and restless. At times, they run or climb excessively in an inappropriate manner given the situation, their age, and developmental level. They may have difficulty playing or taking part in leisure activities quietly. They are often on the go or act as if a motor drives them. During their formal school years, they present with many of the behaviours mentioned in the DSM-5. They generally struggle with situations where they have to make transitions from the classroom to the playground or back again (Brochin & Horvath, 1996).

Anastopoulos (1998) says that hyperactivity is not just displayed through physical restlessness but also verbal restlessness, and parents will regularly describe their children as 'chatterboxes' or 'motor mouths'. Children with ADHD are also hyper-responsive and, compared to other children, they are much more likely to respond to the stimuli in their environments (Barkley, 1995).

ADHD children also tend to be impulsive, behaving 'too quickly' and 'too forcefully'. Thus, they tend to blurt out answers before questions have been completed (American Psychiatric Association, 2013; Green & Chee, 1997). These answers are usually wrong as they have not been well considered. Children with ADHD generally only listen to half of the instructions before they react. They rush through their work, making careless mistakes; they often have difficulty in waiting their turn, and interrupt or intrude on others.

Children with ADHD seldom set out to get into trouble, but they act without thinking of the repercussions and seldom learn from previous experiences. Although they are able to distinguish between right and wrong, this will usually register only after they have reacted to a certain stimulus and, even when the outcome is negative, they tend to repeat the same mistakes. As a result, they tend to be accident-prone, climbing on roofs or running across busy roads without thinking about the consequences.

Attention-deficit behaviours

According to the DSM-5 (American Psychiatric Association, 2013), children who are inattentive have difficulty with sustaining their attention on tasks or other activities, they fail to pay close attention to details and often make careless mistakes. At times it appears as if they do not listen when spoken to. These children subsequently often fail to follow through on instructions and often fail to finish their schoolwork. They also tend to get bored easily and will leave a task after a few minutes as their mind drifts to something new. Attention-deficit children also display problems with short-term memory and will forget something that was mentioned to them two minutes previously, yet remember something that happened two years before.

Children who are inattentive struggle to organise tasks and activities, and often forget or lose things that are necessary to complete tasks. They are easily distracted by sounds and other stimuli in their environments and are forgetful in daily activities. These children tend to avoid tasks, chores, or duties that require a lot of sustained attention and mental effort, but they may give effortless attention to activities that they enjoy.

This creates a confusing picture for parents, because on the one hand, their children are easily bored, but on the other, they tend to focus on activities that they enjoy and that are varied. For this reason, one will often hear parents complain that their children cannot finish their schoolwork, but they can sit in front of the television or computer games for hours. Taking this into consideration, Green and Chee (1997) divide attention-deficit into two broad categories, under-attention and over-attention, and say that a child's ability to sustain attention is strongly influenced by situational factors.

Table 15.8: Diagnostic criteria for attention-deficit/hyperactivity disorder from the DSM-5 and for hyperkinetic disorders from the ICD-10

DSM-5 Attention-deficit/hyperactivity disorder	ICD-10 Hyperkinetic disorders

A. A persistent pattern of inattention and/or hyperactivity-impulsivity that interferes with functioning or development, as characterised by (1) and/or (2):
(1) Inattention: Six (or more) of the following symptoms have persisted for at least six months to a degree that is inconsistent with developmental level and that negatively impacts directly on social and academic/occupational activities:
Note: The symptoms are not solely a manifestation of oppositional behaviour, defiance, hostility, or failure to understand tasks and instructions. For older adolescents or adults (age 17 and older), at least five symptoms are required.
   a) Often fails to give close attention to details or makes careless mistakes in schoolwork, at work, or during other activities (e.g. overlooks or misses details, work is inaccurate).
   b) Often has difficulty sustaining attention in tasks or play activities (e.g. has difficulty remaining focused during lectures, conversations, or lengthy reading).
   c) Often does not seem to listen when spoken to directly (e.g. mind seems elsewhere, even in the absence of any obvious distraction).
	■ This group of disorders is characterised by: early onset; a combination of overactive, poorly modulated behaviour with marked inattention and lack of persistent task involvement; pervasiveness over situations and persistence over time of these behavioural characteristics. These deficits in persistence and attention should be diagnosed only if they are excessive for the child's age and IQ.
	■ Diagnostic guidelines: The cardinal features are impaired attention and overactivity; both are necessary for the diagnosis and should be evident in more than one situation (e.g. home, classroom, clinic).
	■ Impaired attention is manifested by prematurely breaking off from tasks and leaving activities unfinished. The children change frequently from one activity to another, seemingly losing interest in one task because they become diverted to another (although laboratory studies do not generally show an unusual degree of sensory or perceptual distractibility).

DSM-5 Attention-deficit/hyperactivity disorder	ICD-10 Hyperkinetic disorders
d) Often does not follow through on instructions and fails to finish schoolwork, chores, or duties in the workplace (e.g. starts tasks but quickly loses focus and is easily sidetracked). e) Often has difficultly organising tasks and activities (e.g. difficulty managing sequential tasks; difficulty keeping materials and belongings in order; messy, disorganised work; has poor time management; fails to meet deadlines). f) Often avoids, dislikes, or is reluctant to engage in tasks that require sustained mental effort (e.g. schoolwork or homework; for older adolescents and adults, preparing reports, completing forms, reviewing lengthy papers). g) Often loses things necessary for tasks and activities (e.g. school materials, pencils, books, tools, wallets, keys, paperwork, eyeglasses, mobile telephones). h) Is often easily distracted by extraneous stimuli (for older adolescents and adults, may include unrelated thoughts). i) Is often forgetful in daily activities (e.g. doing chores, running errands; for older adolescents and adults, returning calls, paying bills, keeping appointments). (2) Hyperactivity and impulsivity: Six (or more) of the following symptoms have persisted for at least six months to a degree that is inconsistent with developmental level and that negatively impacts directly on social and academic/occupational activities: **Note:** The symptoms are not solely a manifestation of oppositional behaviour, defiance, hostility, or failure to understand tasks and instructions. For older adolescents or adults (age 17 and older), at least five symptoms are required. a) Often fidgets with or taps hands or feet or squirms in seat. b) Often leaves seat in situations when remaining seated is expected (e.g. leaves his or her place in the classroom, in the office or other workplace, or in other situations that require remaining in place).	■ Overactivity implies excessive restlessness, especially in situations requiring relative calm. It may, depending upon the situation, involve the child running and jumping around, getting up from a seat when he or she was supposed to remain seated. ▸ The following associated features are all characteristic of children with this disorder, but they are not sufficient for the diagnosis, or even necessary, but help to sustain it. ▸ Disinhibition in social relationships. ▸ Recklessness in situations involving some danger. ▸ Impulsive flouting of social rules (as shown by intruding on or interrupting others' activities, prematurely answering questions before they have been completed, or difficulty in waiting turns). ▸ Learning disorders and motor clumsiness occur with undue frequency, and should be noted separately when present; they should not, however, be part of the actual diagnosis of hyperkinetic disorder.

DSM-5 Attention-deficit/hyperactivity disorder	ICD-10 Hyperkinetic disorders
c) Often runs about or climbs in situations where it is inappropriate. (Note: In adolescents or adults, may be limited to feeling restless.) d) Often unable to play or engage in leisure activities quietly. e) Is often 'on the go', acting as if 'driven by a motor' (e.g. is unable to be or uncomfortable being still for extended time, as in restaurants, meetings; may be experienced by others as being restless or difficult to keep up with). f) Often talks excessively. g) Often blurts out an answer before a question has been completed (e.g. completes other people's sentences; cannot wait for turn in conversation). h) Often has difficulty waiting his or her turn (e.g. while waiting in line). i) Often interrupts or intrudes on others (e.g. butts into conversations, games, or activities; may start using other people's things without asking or receiving permission; for adolescents and adults, may intrude into or take over what others are doing). B. Several inattentive or hyperactive-impulsive symptoms were present prior to age 12 years. C. Several inattentive or hyperactive-impulsive symptoms are present in two or more settings (e.g. at home, school, or work; with friends or relatives; in other activities). D. There is clear evidence that the symptoms interfere with, or reduce the quality of, social, academic, or occupational functioning. E. The symptoms do not occur exclusively during the course of schizophrenia or another psychotic disorder and are not better explained by another mental disorder (e.g. mood disorder, anxiety disorder, dissociative disorder, personality disorder, substance intoxication or withdrawal).	

Source: Reprinted with permission from the *Diagnostic and Statistical Manual of Mental Disorders*, fifth edition (DSM-5), American Psychiatric Association (APA), 2013, p. 59, and ICD-10 *Classification of Mental and Behavioural Disorders: Diagnostic Criteria for Research*, World Health Organization (WHO), Geneva, 2007.

Secondary symptoms

In addition to the core symptoms that are associated with ADHD, there are also some secondary symptoms that we frequently find in children diagnosed with ADHD. Among these are difficulties with regard to social and motor development, as well as emotional worries (American Psychiatric Association, 2013):

- *Social clumsiness:* Many children with ADHD are socially 'clumsy' despite the fact that they can be very sensitive and caring. According to Brochin and Horvath (1996), children with ADHD are often rejected by their peers, because they tend to misinterpret social cues and will say and do things that are quite inappropriate within a specific situation. They also tend to be bossy (Green & Chee, 1997).
- *Poor coordination:* Children with ADHD tend to experience problems with fine and gross motor skills. They have particular problems with their handwriting, and some of them are very clumsy and have difficulty coordinating a sequence of movements or doing two things at once, for example, simultaneously moving their arms and their legs. However, this does not apply to all children with ADHD, as some of them turn out to be exceptional athletes (Green & Chee, 1997).
- *Disorganisation:* Often, children with ADHD are highly disorganised. A school bag will be left somewhere, and books are forgotten at school. They also have difficulty getting started on a particular project and can be very untidy (Green & Chee, 1997).
- *Poor self-esteem:* Children who are diagnosed with ADHD often present with low self-esteem (Johnson & Bunce, 2008). They are constantly faced with failure and rejection at school and at home; they may feel as if they can never do anything right, no matter how hard they try.

Comorbid conditions

According to Green and Chee (1997) and Brochin and Horvath (1996), more than half of the children who are diagnosed with ADHD also display symptoms of one or more comorbid conditions. This has important implications for the treatment of the conditions. The following are the most common conditions that co-exist with ADHD:

- *Specific learning disability:* Approximately half the children with ADHD will also have some kind of learning disability, which differs from the academic problems directly related to the ADHD. When children have a specific learning disability, they present with a significant discrepancy between their intellectual potential and their academic performance. This may be due to, for instance, a specific reading disability (Green & Chee, 1997).
- *Oppositional defiant disorder (ODD):* Between 40% and 60% of the children who display ADHD symptoms will also display symptoms of ODD, which creates quite a volatile mixture. Children with ADHD may act before they think, but they are still remorseful and caring towards others. This will not be the case with ADHD children who have ODD, who think that their behaviour is totally justified (Green & Chee, 1997).
- *Conduct disorder (CD):* Children with ADHD and CD are also more likely to use alcohol and other illegal recreational drugs than children with just ADHD (Brochin & Horvath, 1996).
- *Depression:* Many children with ADHD feel inadequate as they are unable to behave or perform well or be accepted by others. This can lead to a low self-esteem and comorbid

depression and anxiety. Children with a comorbid depressive disorder will often appear moody, sad, socially withdrawn, and preoccupied (Colorado Personal Growth and Therapy Resources, 1998; Green & Chee, 1997). It is important to determine the source of the depression as this will have very important implications for treatment.

Conduct disorders

Most children and adolescents are occasionally non-compliant in that they defy their parents or refuse to comply with their parents' requests (Erickson, 1998). However, when there is continuous defiance or non-compliance, this has a significant impact on the child and family's well-being. The more serious forms of this behaviour are classified in the DSM-5 as oppositional defiant disorder (ODD) and conduct disorder (CD) (American Psychiatric Association, 2013).

Oppositional defiant disorder

Children and adolescents with ODD display a recurrent and repetitive pattern of negative and antagonistic behaviour that significantly impacts on their academic and family functioning, as well as their social and emotional well-being (Halgin & Whitbourne, 2003; Masse & McNeil, 2008). Although some children and adolescents occasionally display rebellious and non-compliant tendencies, the behaviour of children and adolescents with ODD is more extreme.

This behaviour differs from the behaviour of others of the same developmental age such that it is considered to be much more than 'just a phase' that will pass in time (Erickson, 1998). However, although their behaviour can be verbally aggressive and hurtful towards others, children and adolescents with ODD are generally not physically aggressive, and they do not become involved in serious criminal acts (Joyce, 2007).

Children and adolescents with ODD often lose their temper, are generally angry, irritable and argumentative, tend to be resentful, actively defy or refuse to comply with adults' requests or social rules and norms, and are easily annoyed. They will also purposefully and deliberately annoy others, blame others for their wrongdoings and mistakes, often swear and use obscene language, and are often self-righteous, spiteful, or vindictive (American Psychiatric Association, 2013; Erickson, 1998; Halgin & Whitbourne, 2003). What often starts as ODD may develop into the more serious pattern of non-compliance typical of conduct disorder (CD) (Barrett, 2004).

No major changes were recommended for the diagnostic criteria of oppositional defiant disorder for the DSM-5 (American Psychiatric Association, 2012a); however, a severity index was developed, based on the cross-situation pervasiveness of the symptoms. Consequently, the DSM-5 distinguishes between mild, moderate, and severe ODD. Children with mild ODD display challenging behaviour in only one setting, whereas children with moderate ODD do so in at least two settings, and children with severe ODD do so in three or more settings.

The DSM-5 also removed the exclusionary criteria for conduct disorder, but added that children cannot be diagnosed with ODD if they have been diagnosed with disruptive mood dysregulation disorder (see Chapter 7).

In addition, the DSM-5 organises the symptoms of ODD so that one can distinguish between emotional and behavioural symptoms, hence the division of symptoms as part of one of the following three categories: angry/irritable mood, argumentative/defiant behaviour, and vindictiveness. The latter category describes children who are considered to be spiteful and vindictive. Finally, the DSM-5 also provides standard and objective definitions for the frequency of ODD symptoms (American Psychiatric Association, 2013) (see Table 15.9).

Table 15.9: Diagnostic criteria for oppositional defiant disorder from the DSM-5 and the ICD-10

DSM-5	ICD-10

A. A pattern of angry/irritable mood, argumentative/defiant behaviour, or vindictiveness lasting at least six months as evidenced by at least four symptoms from any of the following categories, and exhibited during interaction with at least one individual who is not a sibling.
 	
Angry/irritable mood
(1) Often loses temper.
(2) Is often touchy or easily annoyed.
(3) Is often angry and resentful.
Argumentative/defiant behaviour
(4) Often argues with authority figures or, for children and adolescents, with adults.
(5) Often actively defies or refuses to comply with requests from authority figures or with rules.
(6) Often deliberately annoys others.
(7) Often blames others for his or her mistakes or misbehaviour.
Vindictiveness
(8) Has been spiteful or vindictive at least twice within the past six months.
Note: The persistence and frequency of these behaviours should be used to distinguish a behaviour that is within normal limits from a behaviour that is symptomatic. For children younger than five years, the behaviour should occur on most days for a period of at least six months unless otherwise noted (Criterion A8). For individuals five years and older, the behaviour should occur at least once a week for at least six months, unless otherwise noted (Criterion A8). While these frequency criteria provide guidance
	■ This type of conduct disorder is characteristically seen in children below the age of nine or ten years.
	■ It is defined by the presence of markedly defiant, disobedient, provocative behaviour, and by the absence of more severe dissocial or aggressive acts that violate the law or the rights of others.
	■ The disorder requires that the overall criteria be met; even severely mischievous or naughty behaviour is not in itself sufficient for diagnosis.
	■ The essential feature of this disorder is a pattern of:
	  ▸ Persistently negativistic, hostile, defiant, provocative, and disruptive behaviour, which is clearly outside the normal range of behaviour for a child of the same age in the same sociocultural context, and which does not include the more serious violations of the rights of others as reflected in the aggressive and dissocial behaviour specified for categories.
	  ▸ Frequently and actively defy adult requests or rules and deliberately act to annoy other people.
	  ▸ Usually, they tend to be angry, resentful, and easily annoyed by other people, whom they blame for their own mistakes or difficulties.
	  ▸ Low frustration tolerance and readily lose their temper.
	  ▸ Typically, their defiance has a provocative quality, so that they initiate confrontations and generally exhibit excessive levels of rudeness, uncooperativeness, and resistance to authority.

DSM-5	ICD-10
on a minimal level of frequency to define symptoms, other factors should also be considered, such as whether the frequency and intensity of the behaviours are outside a range that is normal for the individual's developmental level, gender, and culture. B. The disturbance in behaviour is associated with distress in the individual or others in his or her immediate social context (e.g. family, peer group, work colleagues), or it impacts negatively on social, educational, occupational, or other important areas of functioning. C. The behaviours do not occur exclusively during the course of a psychotic, substance use, depressive, or bipolar disorder. Also, the criteria are not met for disruptive mood dysregulation disorder.	▸ Frequently, this behaviour is most evident in interactions with adults or peers whom the child knows well, and signs of the disorder may not be evident during a clinical interview. ▪ The key distinction from other types of conduct disorder is the absence of behaviour that violates the law and the basic rights of others, such as theft, cruelty, bullying, assault, and destructiveness. The definite presence of any of the above would exclude the diagnosis. However, oppositional defiant behaviour, as outlined in the paragraph above, is often found in other types of conduct disorder. ▪ Excludes: Conduct disorders including overtly dissocial or aggressive behaviour.

Source: Reprinted with permission from the *Diagnostic and Statistical Manual of Mental Disorders*, fifth edition (DSM-5), American Psychiatric Association (APA), 2013, p. 462, and ICD-10 *Classification of Mental and Behavioural Disorders: Diagnostic Criteria for Research*, World Health Organization (WHO), Geneva, 2007.

Conduct disorder

Juvenile delinquency is a legal term that is used to describe antisocial and criminal behaviours that are committed by persons younger than a specified statutory age and that are in direct violation of a country's laws and cultural norms (Erickson, 1998). Upon investigation, most juvenile delinquents present with symptoms associated with conduct disorder (CD).

The most common characteristic of CD is a repetitive and persistent violation of the rights of others. In addition, adolescents with CD also tend to defy societal norms and rules, and they often perform illegal acts against others (Erickson, 1998). The typical behaviours associated with CD are mentioned below. Many adolescents with CD are also addicted to alcohol or other recreational drugs. As is the case with ODD, adolescents with CD tend to blame others for their misbehaviour, refuse to accept responsibility, and display a lack of remorse for their behaviours and the consequences thereof (Halgin & Whitbourne, 2003).

Although CD is often diagnosed in adolescents, a differentiation is often made between CD with childhood onset (at least one symptom characteristic of CD before the age of ten years); CD with adolescent onset (no symptoms characteristic of CD before the age of ten years); and unspecified onset (not enough information available on the presentation of symptoms before or after the age of ten years) (American Psychiatric Association, 2013).

One should also differentiate between more severe cases and moderate or mild cases. Severe cases usually result in arrest and include a pattern of delinquent behaviour, where the symptoms are in excess of those required to make the diagnosis and the child's difficulties cause major harm to others. In moderate cases, the individual's symptoms and the harm this causes to others are somewhere in between the mild and severe categories, whereas mild cases include pranks, insignificant lying, and/or group mischief, which cause only mild harm to others (American Psychiatric Association, 2013; Halgin & Whitbourne, 2003).

According to Erickson (1998), there are four types of conduct disorders, varying in terms of degree of socialisation and aggression. The four types are:

- Undersocialised aggressive
- Undersocialised non-aggressive
- Socialised aggressive
- Socialised non-aggressive.

Those adolescents with CD who are undersocialised commonly have superficial, one-sided relationships. They do not have normal patterns of affection and are generally considered to be egocentric. They will manipulate others for their own advantage without feeling guilt or remorse. Although people with the socialised types are generally more attached to others, they are also manipulative and they show little remorse in their interactions with people to whom they are not attached. These adolescents are often part of gangs where they join others in performing illegal acts.

People with the aggressive types often violate the rights of others and tend to become involved in physical acts of violence outside of the home. These include assault, physical harm to animals, sexual violence, and direct confrontation with their victims, for instance, during a hijacking. Non-aggressive adolescents with conduct disorder tend to avoid violence, but constantly violate rules and become involved in activities such as truancy and running away from home, constant lying both in and out of home, vandalism, fire-setting, property damage or loss, deceitfulness, and theft (Erickson, 1998).

As far as conduct disorder in the DSM-5 is concerned, no major revisions were recommended. However, an additional specifier for 'with limited prosocial emotions' has been included (American Psychiatric Association, 2013). Included in this are individuals who show a lack of remorse or guilt, a callous lack of empathy, a lack of concern about performance, and/or shallow or deficient affect (American Psychiatric Association, 2013).

Table 15.10: Diagnostic criteria for conduct disorder from the DSM-5 and the ICD-10

DSM-5	ICD-10
A. A repetitive and persistent pattern of behaviour in which the basic rights of others or major age-appropriate societal norms or rules are violated, as manifested by the presence of at least three of the following 15 criteria in the past 12 months from any of the categories below, with at least one criterion present in the past six months:	■ Diagnostic guidelines: Judgements concerning the presence of conduct disorder should take into account the child's developmental level. ▸ Temper tantrums, for example, are a normal part of a three-year-old's development and their mere presence would not be grounds for diagnosis.

DSM-5	ICD-10

Aggression to people or animals
(1) Often bullies, threatens, or intimidates others.
(2) Often initiates physical fights.
(3) Has used a weapon that can cause serious physical harm to others (e.g. a bat, brick, broken bottle, knife, gun).
(4) Has been physically cruel to people.
(5) Has been physically cruel to animals.
(6) Has stolen while confronting a victim (e.g. mugging, purse snatching, extortion, armed robbery).
(7) Has forced someone into sexual activity.
Destruction of property
(8) Has deliberately engaged in fire-setting with the intention of causing serious damage.
(9) Has deliberately destroyed others' property (other than by fire-setting).
Deceitfulness or theft
(10) Has broken into someone else's house, building, or car.
(11) Often lies to obtain goods or favours or to avoid obligations (i.e. "cons" others).
(12) Has stolen items of non-trivial value without confronting a victim (e.g. shoplifting, but without breaking and entering; forgery).
Serious violations of rules
(13) Often stays out at night despite parental prohibitions, beginning before age 13 years.
(14) Has run away from home overnight at least twice while living in the parental or parental surrogate home, or once without returning for a lengthy period.
(15) Is often truant from school, beginning before age 13 years.
B. The disturbance in behaviour causes clinically significant impairment in social, academic, or occupational functioning.
C. If the individual is age 18 or older, criteria are not met for antisocial personality disorder.
	▸ Equally, the violation of other people's civic rights (as by violent crime) is not within the capacity of most seven-year-olds and so is not a necessary diagnostic criterion for that age group.
	■ Examples of the behaviours on which the diagnosis is based include the following:
	  ▸ Excessive levels of fighting or bullying.
	  ▸ Cruelty to animals or other people.
	  ▸ Severe destructiveness to property.
	  ▸ Fire-setting.
	  ▸ Stealing.
	  ▸ Repeated lying.
	  ▸ Truancy from school and running away from home.
	  ▸ Unusually frequent and severe temper tantrums.
	  ▸ Defiant provocative behaviour.
	  ▸ Persistent severe disobedience.
	■ Exclusion criteria include uncommon but serious underlying conditions such as schizophrenia, mania, pervasive developmental disorder, hyperkinetic disorder, and depression.
	■ This diagnosis is not recommended unless the duration of the behaviour described above has been six months or longer.

Source: Reprinted with permission from the *Diagnostic and Statistical Manual of Mental Disorders*, fifth edition (DSM-5), American Psychiatric Association (APA), 2013, p. 469, and ICD-10 *Classification of Mental and Behavioural Disorders: Diagnostic Criteria for Research*, World Health Organization (WHO), Geneva, 2007.

Comorbid disorders

The most common disorders that occur in conjunction with the conduct disorders include ADHD, substance abuse disorders, mood disorders such as depression, anxiety, poor self-esteem, adjustment disorders, and learning difficulties or academic underachievement (Masse & McNeil, 2008). It is very difficult to establish whether these disorders led to the development of the conduct disorder, or whether they exist as a result of the child or adolescent's severe behavioural difficulties (Acosta & Rosen, 2008). However, it is important to remember that, when a conduct disorder co-exists with another disorder, it is important that both are identified and treated.

Aetiology of externalising disorders

When considering the aetiology of all of the externalising disorders, clinicians will find it valuable to take a multidimensional approach and recognise that externalising disorders are not caused by a single identifiable factor. It is through the interaction of several factors that externalising disorders are developed and maintained.

Genetic factors

Twin and adoption studies confirm the presence of a genetic influence in the development of ADHD (Johnson & Bunce, 2008; Whitman, 1991). A 1989 twin study found a 51% concordance for ADHD between monozygotic twins and a 31% concordance between dizygotic twins (Bennett, 2003). More recent studies found a higher concordance between monozygotic twins, ranging between 58% and 83% (Bennett, 2003). As far as dizygotic twins are concerned, Bennett (2003) describes research indicating concordance ranges between 31% and 47%.

As is the case with ADHD, research conducted through twin and adoption studies has shown that a child's risk of developing a conduct disorder increases significantly if a parent has been diagnosed with a substance use disorder, a mood disorder, schizophrenia, ADHD, antisocial personality disorder, or conduct disorder (Joyce, 2007).

Neurological factors

According to Green and Chee (1997), children with ADHD display an unusual imbalance in their neurotransmitters. Dopamine and noradrenalin are the two chemicals involved (Bennett, 2003). These neurotransmitters are either produced in lower volumes by the pre-synaptic cell, or picked up less efficiently by the post-synaptic cell. These neurotransmitters have different functions. Amongst other effects, dopamine prevents our own thoughts or outside activities from distracting us. Low levels of dopamine explain why children with ADHD are easily distracted. Noradrenalin helps us to focus on what is important and to act appropriately. Children whose noradrenalin levels are low tend to become withdrawn. When these levels are too high, these children are hyperactive and impulsive (Green & Chee, 1997).

An imbalance in the functioning of certain neurotransmitters is not the only neurological factor contributing to ADHD. Although the central nervous system is, out of necessity and for survival purposes, equipped to deal with all external stimuli (e.g. visual, auditory, kinaesthetic, etc.), it is impossible for the brain to attend to all stimuli. In order to deal effectively with external stimuli, the central nervous system prioritises stimuli and, in order to formulate a coordinated response, filters out less important stimuli before these stimuli are relayed to the cortex (Green & Chee, 1997). It is suggested that, in the case of ADHD children, stimuli are not filtered properly, which leads to a stimulus overload and uncoordinated responses to these stimuli.

Family factors

People are always influenced by, and influence, other people, groups, organisations, and the environment (Donald, Lazarus, & Lolwana, 1997). People and groups in a specific context form interdependent, dynamic, and interacting relationships with the people around them and with their physical environment. Given these relationships, Barkley (1995) suggests that ADHD is not caused by poor parenting or other environmental factors. On the contrary, it is usually the children with ADHD who place substantial stress on their parents and others in their environment. Parents may start to see themselves as less skilled and knowledgeable than others, and they may start to doubt their own parenting style (Anastopoulos, 1998).

However, despite the fact that poor parenting does not cause ADHD, it can make the situation worse (Barkley, 1995; Green & Chee, 1997). According to Johnson and Bunce (2008), the parents of children with ADHD often experience problems with parenting, parent-child relationships, and parental stress. Not only are their relationships with their children marked by conflict, but they also tend to use more harsh and punitive methods of discipline.

Likewise, parents of children and adolescents who have been diagnosed with a conduct disorder are also more likely to make fewer positive and more negative statements towards their children. They are also more likely to fail to supervise or monitor their children on a regular basis, or to perceive the behavioural problems of their children to be intentional. In addition, they present with poor problem-solving skills and tend to abuse or neglect their children. Children and adolescents who have been diagnosed with a conduct disorder also often do not receive adequate support from their parents (Barrett, 2004). In addition to these factors, Acosta and Rosen (2008) have identified that family break-up, single parent homes, and even large family size place the family context under huge pressure, and these often precede the development of serious behavioural difficulties in some of the family members.

Socio-economic factors

In South Africa, there are many children and adolescents who survive in very poor socio-economic circumstances; although not all of these children will develop a conduct disorder, it is important to note that low socio-economic status and high rates of crime have been associated with the development of conduct disorders (Acosta & Rosen, 2008; Barrett, 2004).

School and academic factors

According to Barrett (2004), children and adolescents with a conduct disorder often attend schools where there is little emphasis on academic work. In addition, educators in these schools may spend less time on lessons and show little appreciation for good school work. In addition, there is little emphasis placed on individual responsibility, and there are very poor working conditions for learners.

Personal and emotional factors

According to Joyce (2007), children and adolescents who are diagnosed with a conduct disorder generally display a lack of self-evaluative insight. For this reason, they struggle to take responsibility for their own behaviour and, as mentioned earlier, will often blame others for their wrongdoings. In addition, they tend to become involved impulsively in high-risk behaviour without considering the consequences for either themselves or others (Masse & McNeil, 2008).

They are also highly reactive to emotional situations or perceived injustices and display a very low tolerance for frustration. Research has found that children and adolescents with serious behavioural difficulties have very poor emotional self-regulation, and it has been hypothesised that their emotional self-control is either delayed or poorly developed (Joyce, 2007).

In addition to poor emotional self-control, researchers such as Kenneth Dodge have noted that these children and adolescents have poor communication patterns and tend to misinterpret ambiguous social cues (Joyce, 2007). This not only leads to poor social relations but also tends to escalate hostility (Acosta & Rosen, 2008; Joyce, 2007).

Another personal and emotional risk factor for developing a conduct disorder is temperament (Joyce, 2007). Temperament involves the relatively consistent and stable personality characteristics that influence a person's behaviour. The Swiss psychiatrist Carl Jung was the first to explain temperament in terms of opposites, including extraversion and introversion, and sensing and intuition.

In the studies of Joyce and Oakland (Joyce, 2007), it has been noted that children and adolescents with conduct disorders generally show a preference for extraversion and sensing functions. The latter implies that, in learning new information, individuals with conduct disorders place a lot of emphasis on facts as perceived by them, and not on concepts. This could explain why they tend to be argumentative about rules and struggle to generalise behaviour expectations across different circumstances.

The American psychiatrists Alexander Thomas and Stella Chess took the concept of temperament further in describing the concept of goodness-of-fit. According to this concept, conflict often arises (and increases) when a parent and child's temperaments are dramatically different, and there is thus less understanding and tolerance for the child's behaviour (Joyce, 2007).

Diet

In 1973, the American doctor Benjamin Feingold suggested that there might be a relationship between a child's diet and his or her hyperactive behaviour (Green & Chee, 1997). According to Barkley (1995), a substantial amount of research has been done; however, no support for this claim has been found. According to Green and Chee (1997), aspects of diet never cause ADHD; however, some foods can make some children more active and irritable.

INTERNALISING DISORDERS

Internalising disorders of childhood and adolescence are best described as disorders that occur within the child. As a result of their difficulties, these children and adolescents often appear shy, withdrawn, and fearful. Unlike externalising disorders, these disorders are usually within the child, rather than being acted out externally in the environment (Helm, 2008). The internalising disorders that will be described in this chapter include depression and anxiety. It is important to note that these disorders should be read in conjunction with the disorders described in Chapter 6 and Chapter 7.

Table 15.11: Diagnostic criteria for emotional disorders with onset specific to childhood, according to the ICD-10

ICD-10
In child psychiatry, a differentiation has traditionally been made between emotional disorders specific to childhood and adolescence, and adult-type neurotic disorders. There have been four main justifications for this differentiation. 1. First, research findings have been consistent in showing that the majority of children with emotional disorders go on to become normal adults; only a minority show neurotic disorders in adult life. Conversely, many adult neurotic disorders appear to have an onset in adult life without significant psychopathological precursors in childhood. Hence, there is considerable discontinuity between emotional disorders occurring in these two age periods. 2. Second, many emotional disorders in childhood seem to constitute exaggerations of normal developmental trends rather than phenomena that are qualitatively abnormal in themselves. 3. Third, related to the last consideration, there has often been the theoretical assumption that the mental mechanisms involved in emotional disorders of childhood may not be the same as for adult neuroses. 4. Fourth, the emotional disorders of childhood are less clearly demarcated into supposedly specific entities such as phobic disorders or obsessional disorders. The third of these points lacks empirical validation, and epidemiological data suggest that, if the fourth is correct, it is a matter of degree only (with poorly differentiated emotional disorders quite common in both childhood and adult life). Accordingly, the second feature (i.e. developmental appropriateness) is used as the key diagnostic feature in defining the difference between the emotional disorders with an onset specific to childhood and the neurotic disorders. The validity of this distinction is uncertain, but there is some empirical evidence to suggest that the developmentally appropriate emotional disorders of childhood have a better prognosis.

Source: Reprinted with permission from the ICD-10 *Classification of Mental and Behavioural Disorders: Diagnostic Criteria for Research*, World Health Organization, Geneva, 2007.

Depression

EXAMPLE CASE

John is sixteen years old and lives with his mother in a lower middle-class area. He has his own bedroom. His mother is a nurse at a private hospital.

John has a sister who is eighteen months younger than him. John's parents divorced when he was nine years old. His father got custody of his younger sister and his mother got custody of him. His father and sister live in Zimbabwe and he seldom gets to see them.

Although the divorce happened almost ten years ago, his mother is still extremely bitter and often says terrible things about his father to him. John cannot tell his mother that these things upset him because he doesn't want to hurt her feelings.

Recently, his mother has been under a lot of stress at work and while she used to drink a glass of wine after work, she has now taken to drinking a bottle of wine a night. She becomes a different person when she drinks. She is no longer sweet and kind but becomes bitter and often bursts into tears, asking John why his father left her. John feels as if he must be the adult in the household now.

His marks at school have started to drop from As to Cs and he has been feeling extremely tired all the time. He cannot wake up for school on time and is now getting detention almost every week for late-coming.

John cannot see much in life to look forward to. He has thought about committing suicide. He has located a rope in the garage that he thinks will be good for hanging himself.

Source: Written by Joanne Hardman.

Depression, currently one of the most common psychiatric diagnoses, impacts on the child or adolescent's cognitive, emotional, and physical functioning. It is of great concern that depression often goes undetected in childhood and adolescence. Thus, instead of being diagnosed as a major disorder with a significant impact on the child's development, it is often interpreted as part of a normal pattern of mood swings. Also, as the externalising disorders often attract more attention, children's internal sufferings often go undetected (Mash & Wolfe, 2005).

It is also said that professionals are often reluctant prematurely to diagnose and label a young person with depression (Knox & Lichtenberg, 2005). The danger, however, is that if the disorder goes undiagnosed and hence untreated, it not only has a major impact on the child's current functioning, but also on his or her future development and functioning.

For a child or adolescent to be diagnosed with a major depressive disorder, he or she not only needs to present with the symptoms of major depressive disorder (see Chapter 7), but other possible disorders also need to be excluded. According to the DSM-5 (American Psychiatric Association, 2013), adults with a major depressive disorder often present with depressed mood, whereas children and adolescents might rather appear irritable, agitated, angry, and hostile. Other symptoms noted in children and adolescents who have been diagnosed with depression include, amongst others:

- Persistent sadness and crying or outbursts of shouting and complaining
- Loss of interest in activities that were once enjoyed (e.g. social gatherings, play dates, and sport)
- Social isolation
- Alcohol and/or substance use/abuse
- An increase or decrease in appetite with subsequent weight loss or gain
- Sleeping difficulties
- Loss of energy, lethargy, and fatigue
- Feelings of worthlessness and guilt without reason
- Extreme sensitivity to rejection or failure
- Talk of running away, or even efforts to run away, from home, or truancy
- Difficulty in sustained attention and concentration, and poor school performance
- Fear of death
- Frequent, non-specific physical complaints such as headaches, stomach pains, and muscle aches
- Boredom and/or reckless behaviour.

These symptoms are expressed in a variety of ways, based on the child or adolescent's developmental level and ability to express emotions.

Anxiety

Anxiety is typically characterised by two key features – strong negative emotion and a state of fear (see Chapter 6). In addition, it is also accompanied by bodily symptoms of tension. When children and adolescents experience excessive and debilitating anxieties, they are often diagnosed with an anxiety disorder (Mash & Wolfe, 2005). Although there are several types of anxiety disorders, this chapter will focus only on separation anxiety disorder, as it is the one most commonly experienced by children and adolescents. However, it is important to note that the different anxiety disorders all share common characteristics, which include (Lopez & Silverman, 2004):

- Maladaptive thoughts or cognitions of harm to self or loved ones
- Physiological arousal or reactions
- Avoidance of, or attempts to avoid, certain situations, objects or events
- The presence of anxiety, fear, and/or worry that is developmentally inappropriate
- Significant distress and impact on the child or adolescent's normal functioning
- Prolonged periods of anxiety, stress, and/or worry.

Anxiety may also manifest through behavioural symptoms that include motor restlessness, difficulty sitting still, and attempts to escape the source of the anxiety (Lowe & Raad, 2007). In addition, children and adolescents who experience anxiety may also present with the following cognitive symptoms: excessive worry, concentration difficulties, attention difficulties, and memory problems. Finally, the physiological symptoms of anxiety include muscle tension, increased perspiration, rapid heartbeat, headaches, and stomach aches.

Although fear and anxiety can be considered normal human responses to danger or threat, they are clinically significant if they are persistent, cause significant functional impairment, or interfere with the child or adolescent's quality of life. In children and adolescents, it is often difficult to diagnose anxiety as it is often considered normal depending on their developmental stage. For instance, children around the age of three years are often afraid of the dark or monsters (Arnold et al., 2003; Lowe & Raad, 2007). However, when the anxiety experienced by a child or adolescent persists past what is expected of a certain developmental stage, causes significant impairment in their daily functioning, and interferes with their quality of life, further diagnosis and intervention are required.

Separation anxiety disorder

Separation anxiety often occurs during childhood. It refers to an excessive, age-inappropriate, and unrealistic worry in response to separation from home or a caregiver; it is often accompanied by physical symptoms such as headaches, stomach aches, heart palpitations, sweating, shortness of breath, or nausea. Nightmares and sleeping difficulties are also quite common (Lowe & Raad, 2007). As children with this anxiety disorder are scared to separate from home or their caregivers, this disorder has a significant impact on their daily functioning at home and school. In addition, it also has an impact on their social development as they tend to avoid camps, school, or even sleepovers at a friend's house (Lee, 2005).

Table 15.12: Diagnostic criteria for separation anxiety disorder from the DSM-5 and the ICD-10

DSM-5	ICD-10
A. Developmentally inappropriate and excessive fear or anxiety concerning separation from those to whom the individual is attached, as evidenced by at least three of the following: (1) Recurrent excessive distress when anticipating or expecting separation from home or from major attachment figures. (2) Persistent and excessive worry about losing major attachment figures or about possible harm to them, such as illness, injury, disasters, or death. (3) Persistent and excessive worry about experiencing an untoward event (e.g. getting lost, being kidnapped, having an accident, becoming ill) that causes separation from a major attachment figure.	■ The key diagnostic feature is a focused, developmentally inappropriate, excessive anxiety concerning separation from those individuals to whom the child is attached (usually parents or other family members), that is not merely part of a generalised anxiety about multiple situations. The anxiety may take the form of: ▸ An unrealistic, preoccupying worry about possible harm befalling major attachment figures or a fear that they will leave and not return.

DSM-5	ICD-10
(4) Persistent reluctance or refusal to go out, away from home, to school, to work, or elsewhere because of fear of separation. (5) Persistent and excessive fear of or reluctance about being alone or without major attachment figures at home or in other settings. (6) Persistent reluctance or refusal to sleep away from home or to go to sleep without being near a major attachment figure. (7) Repeated nightmares involving the theme of separation. (8) Repeated complaints of physical symptoms (e.g. headaches, stomach aches, nausea, vomiting) when separation from major attachment figures occurs or is anticipated. B. The fear, anxiety or avoidance is persistent, lasting at least four weeks in children and adolescents and typically six months or more in adults. C. The disturbance causes clinically significant distress or impairment in social, academic, occupational, or other important areas of functioning. D. The disturbance is not better explained by another mental disorder, such as refusing to leave home because of excessive resistance to change in autism spectrum disorder; delusions or hallucinations concerning separation in psychotic disorders; refusal to go outside without a trusted companion in agoraphobia; worries about ill health or other harm befalling significant others in generalised anxiety disorder; or concerns about having an illness in illness anxiety disorder.	▸ An unrealistic, preoccupying worry that some untoward event, such as the child being lost, kidnapped, admitted to hospital, or killed, will separate him or her from a major attachment figure. ▸ Persistent reluctance or refusal to go to school because of fear about separation (rather than for other reasons such as fear about events at school). ▸ Persistent reluctance or refusal to go to sleep without being near or next to a major attachment figure.

Source: Reprinted with permission from the *Diagnostic and Statistical Manual of Mental Disorders*, fifth edition (DSM-5), American Psychiatric Association (APA), 2013, p. 191, and ICD-10 *Classification of Mental and Behavioural Disorders: Diagnostic Criteria for Research*, World Health Organization (WHO), Geneva, 2007.

Aetiology of internalising disorders

Depression and anxiety are often the result of interdependent physiologically and genetically based causes that can be triggered by certain life events; these include familial discord or parental divorce and personal stresses such as academic problems, grief, or the end of a significant relationship. Other risk factors include attention difficulties, conduct problems, learning disabilities, chronic illness, abuse or neglect, and trauma (Fried, 2004; Knox & Lichtenberg, 2005).

Genetic and family factors

As far as genetic influences are concerned, children and adolescents who develop symptoms associated with a major depressive disorder and anxiety disorders will most likely have a parent with, or a family history of, depression (Fried, 2004; Knox & Lichtenberg, 2005). Twin and family studies have suggested a genetic vulnerability to the development of affective disorders in childhood and adolescence.

However, the influence of familial factors extends far beyond that of genetics. As we have seen in Chapter 7 and will be explained in more detail below, depression and anxiety are often associated with certain negative thinking patterns. It is believed that depressed parents or caregivers may model these to their children and that this, rather than the genetic vulnerability, may explain why children with depressed parents also often develop depression (Sander & McCarty, 2005; Wicks-Nelson & Israel, 2006).

In addition, this negative parental cognitive style may result in children developing lower self-worth, a negative attributional style, and feelings of hopelessness, all of which may contribute to the development of depression and anxiety. Furthermore, research has indicated that parental depression may result in disruption in effective parenting, as it can lead to a lower frustration tolerance, hostility, irritation, withdrawal, and/or a lack of nurturance (Jewell & Stark, 2003; Wicks-Nelson & Israel, 2006). Although there thus appears to be a genetic link in the development of emotional disorders, the influence of parental styles should not be underestimated.

Personal and emotional factors

Quite recently, researchers have begun to look at the role that emotional processing plays in the development of internalising developmental disorders and, more specifically, paediatric affective disorders. The results of a study conducted by Ladouceur et al. (2005) suggest that children and adolescents with depression and anxiety, which are often comorbid, seemed to process emotional information differently from those from their normative sample. For instance, children and adolescents with major depressive disorder and comorbid anxiety tend to spend more time processing negative emotional information than their peers.

In addition, anxiety and depression are also associated with an attentional bias towards negative or even threatening information. Therefore, although further research in this area is required, it would appear that children and adolescents with depression and/or anxiety disorders tend to pay more attention to negative and threatening emotions and linger on these for longer periods than other children and adolescents (Ladouceur et al., 2005).

This idea links to the theory of the American psychiatrist Aaron Beck (see Chapter 7), which stated that children and adolescents develop depression as a result of the fact that they use negative and biased filters for processing information and interpreting events (Mash & Wolfe, 2005). As far as their biased filters are concerned, Beck stipulated that depressive children and adolescents display negative automatic thoughts that include thoughts of physical and social threat, personal failure, and hostility. As they are biased in the processing of information, they selectively attend to negative information and ignore positive information.

Beck further stipulated that adolescents and children with depression also display a negative cognitive triad (Mash & Wolfe, 2005). This implies that they have negative thoughts and feelings about themselves, the world, and the future. Finally, as far as cognitions are concerned, Beck stipulated that children and adolescents with depression present with negative cognitive schemata.

Schemata are stable structures in the child's memory that are used to process information. When these are negative, children and adolescents will tend to filter information in a negative manner. Also, when these are rigid and resistant to change, children and adolescents will be more prone to depression. In addition, these children and adolescents have negative thought patterns about themselves and their environment, which influences their mood. These are called depressogenic (depression-causing) cognitions.

A variety of negative attributions, misperceptions, and deficiencies in cognitive problem-solving skills are also related to depression. According to Mash and Wolfe (2005), children and adolescents with depression often display internal, stable, and global attributions to explain the causes of negative events. Thus, when something bad happens, they will often attribute this to something that they have done and hold themselves responsible (internal). Also, the reason that they are to blame will not change over time (stable). Finally, bad things happen because this applies to most things they do (global). In contrast to this, they tend to attribute positive things to something outside of themselves (external) and believe that they are not likely to happen again (unstable). Finally, they also tend to think that positive events are unique (specific), and will not happen to them.

Learning, conditioning and attachment

In terms of anxiety disorders, learned behaviour is often considered significant in the development of the disorder. According to the behaviourists, anxiety is a learned behaviour that is both acquired and maintained through operant conditioning, and/or a combination of operant and classical conditioning, and/or modelling. For instance, when a neutral stimulus like a dog is paired repeatedly with an aversive stimulus such as a loud noise (e.g. barking) to produce a conditioned response such as a startled reaction, anxiety problems can develop, and the presence of a dog may evoke the startled response. This will result in the avoidance of the dog, which will relieve the anxiety.

According to operant conditioning, the avoidance behaviour will be maintained because the reduction of the anxiety is a negative reinforcement. In modelling, a child or adolescent develops an anxiety disorder through the observation and modelling of the behaviour of a significant other. For instance, when a mother avoids snakes for which she has a phobia, a child may develop a similar phobia through simply modelling her mother's behaviour (Lowe & Raad, 2007; Mash & Wolfe, 2005).

As far as depression is concerned, the behaviourists emphasise the importance of learning, environmental consequences, and skills and deficits during the onset and maintenance of depression. Thus, they propose that depression in childhood and adolescence is often related to a lack of response-contingent positive reinforcement (Mash & Wolfe, 2005). According to this theory, a lack of positive reinforcement may occur for three reasons. First, a child may not be able to experience positive reinforcement due to interfering anxiety. Second, changes in the child's environment, such as a divorce or the loss of a significant other, may result in a lack of availability of reward. Finally, a child may not have the skills or ability to have rewarding and satisfying social relationships. When a child continuously experiences a lack of positive reinforcement, he or she may be vulnerable to the development of depression.

Another theory in the development of anxiety and depression is the theory of attachment conceived by the British psychologist John Bowlby (Sander & McCarty, 2005). According to this theory, fearfulness in children and adolescents is biologically rooted in the emotional attachment that is needed for survival. For instance, for an infant to survive, it needs to be emotionally and physically attached to its parents. When infants are not near their parents, they tend to display attachment behaviours such as crying, 'clinging', and fear of strangers, in an effort to maintain or restore proximity to their caregivers.

Separation will generally become more tolerable as the child matures. However, when children are separated from their significant caregivers too early, are treated harshly, are abused, or do not have their primary needs met, they will react differently from their peers to separation and reunion. Also, when children view their environment as unpredictable or hostile, they tend to develop anxieties and fears (Mash & Wolfe, 2005). Furthermore, children and adolescents who are often confronted with unresponsive and emotionally unavailable caregivers go through a typical set of emotions that include despair, protest, and detachment. In addition, these children will start to feel unworthy and unloved, which places them at a greater risk of developing depression (Mash & Wolfe, 2005).

CONCLUSION

One of the biggest challenges facing most developing countries is not only the extent of the developmental disorders experienced by their children and adolescents, and the constant increase in prevalence, but also the treatment of such disorders. It is extremely costly to manage developmental disorders effectively, as this involves intervention on many different levels of the social context. Not only does this require individual intervention and/or therapy, but also teacher training and support, community education, school-based interventions, parental training and support, and hospital-based interventions.

In addition, it urgently requires a national strategy to assist children in dealing with the challenges that they face every day, including broader socio-economic and political problems. Indeed, should we ever succeed in effectively addressing these, the benefits of reduced dependency and improved productivity and quality of life will be immense (Institute of Medicine, 2001).

MULTIPLE-CHOICE QUESTIONS

1. The main reason why it is so important to identify children with developmental disorders as early as possible is that:
   a) medications are most effective when administered at an early stage of the disorder
   b) skill deficits can be identified and addressed before they impact on later development
   c) family functioning often declines as the developmental disorder progresses
   d) children are more receptive to therapy when they are young
2. An individual diagnosed with attention-deficit/hyperactivity disorder will always present with:
   a) hyperactive behaviour that alternates with periods of distraction
   b) patterns of inattention OR hyperactivity/impulsivity
   c) both patterns of inattention AND hyperactivity/impulsivity
   d) periods of distraction that lead to hyperactive/impulsive behaviour
3. The inattention cluster of attention-deficit/hyperactivity disorder symptoms is characterised by:
   a) careless mistakes
   b) not seeming to listen when spoken to directly
   c) not waiting one's turn to answer questions
   d) all of these
4. One of the most characteristic patterns for children with autism spectrum disorder is that they are generally:
   a) uninterested in people
   b) very intelligent
   c) extremely talkative
   d) hyperactive
5. The two-group approach to the development of intellectual disabilities states that the following factors are possible causes of these disabilities:
   a) organic/genetic-familial factors
   b) MMR and tuberculosis vaccinations
   c) German measles and mumps
   d) authoritarian parenting
6. Which one of the following is not considered a subtype of enuresis?
   a) urge incontinence
   b) voiding postponement
   c) voiding obstruction
   d) detrusor-sphincter dyscoordination
7. Which one of the following is not considered a subtype of encopresis?
   a) voiding encopresis
   b) manipulative encopresis
   c) retentive encopresis
   d) stress-related encopresis

8. 'Courtesy stigma' can affect the treatment of children because:
   a) the children do not want to go for treatment to a mental healthcare provider
   b) the parents do not want to take children to a mental healthcare provider
   c) mental healthcare providers do not want to label children
   d) governments do not want healthcare providers to label children.
9. Which of the following is not one of the seven categories of neurodevelopmental disorder in the DSM-5?
   a) communication disorders
   b) specific learning disorder
   c) motor disorders
   d) kleptomania
10. Oppositional defiant disorder is categorised under which of the following in the ICD-11?
   a) Neurodevelopmental disorders
   b) Elimination disorders
   c) Impulse-control disorders
   d) Disruptive behaviour or dissocial disorders

PARAGRAPH AND ESSAY QUESTIONS

1. Most models of developmental psychology suggest that normal childhood development progresses as a series of steps, with each new achievement building on prior development. Given this model, select any childhood developmental disorder and describe how it can influence current and future deficits for the individual.
2. Explain the statement: 'We are not sure whether academic difficulties of children with attention-deficit/hyperactivity disorder are a result of the disorder or a result of the symptoms of the disorder.'
3. Describe the causes of intellectual disabilities using the two-group approach as explained by Wicks-Nelson and Israel (2009).
4. Describe the different subtypes of enuresis and encopresis and how they differ from one another given their underlying causes.

ANSWERS TO MULTIPLE-CHOICE QUESTIONS

Chapter	Question	Answer
1	1	c
	2	d
	3	d
	4	d
	5	d
	6	c
	7	a
	8	a
	9	d
	10	a
2	1	b
	2	b
	3	a
	4	b
	5	b
3	1	d
	2	d
	3	d
	4	a
	5	a
4	1	c
	2	b
	3	c
	4	b
	5	a
5	1	b
	2	a
	3	c
	4	d
	5	c
6	1	c
	2	b
	3	e
	4	b
	5	b

Chapter	Question	Answer
7	1	d
	2	c
	3	d
	4	a
	5	c
	6	d
8	1	d
	2	c
	3	d
	4	d
	5	b
	6	c
	7	d
	8	d
	9	c
	10	b
9	1	a
	2	b
	3	a
	4	c
	5	a
	6	a
	7	b
	8	a
	9	d
	10	c
10	1	b
	2	c
	3	b
	4	d
	5	c
11	1	d
	2	a
	3	b
	4	d
	5	b

Chapter	Question	Answer
12	1	c
	2	d
	3	c
	4	d
	5	a
13	1	a
	2	a
	3	d
	4	b
	5	a
	6	b
	7	d
	8	c
	9	d
	10	a
14	1	b
	2	c
	3	d
	4	a
	5	a
	6	d
	7	d
	8	a
	9	c
	10	a
15	1	b
	2	b
	3	c
	4	a
	5	a
	6	c
	7	a
	8	b
	9	d
	10	d

REFERENCES

Aakre, J. M., Brown, C. H., Benson, K. M., Drapalski, A. L., & Gearon, J. S. (2014). Trauma exposure and PTSD in women with schizophrenia and coexisting substance use disorders: Comparisons to women with severe depression and substance use disorders. Psychiatry Research, 220(3), 840–845. doi:10.1016/j.psychres.2014.10.004

Abdel-Khalek, A. M. (2012). Associations between religiosity, mental health, and subjective wellbeing among Arabic samples from Egypt and Kuwait. *Mental Health, Religion & Culture*, 15(8), 741–758. doi: 10.1080/13674676.2011.624502

Abdussalam-Bali, W. (2004). *Sword against black magic and evil magicians.* London: Al-Firdous Books.

Academy of Science of South Africa (ASSAf). (2015). *Diversity in human sexuality: Implications for policy in Africa. Consensus study report* (May). Pretoria: ASSAf.

Acosta, S. J., & Rosen, L. A. (2008). Conduct disorder. *Encyclopedia of counseling.* Retrieved March 20, 2009, from http://www.sage-ereference.com/counseling/Abstract_n30.html

Adamis, D., Treloar, A., Martin, F. C., & Macdonald, A. J. (2007). A brief review of the history of delirium as a mental disorder. *History of Psychiatry*, 18(4), 459–469.

Adams, G. L. (1984). *Normative Adaptive Behavior Checklist.* San Antonio, TX: The Psychological Corporation.

Adebimpe, O. A., & Idehen, E. E. (2015). Cognitive Behaviour Therapy in the Management of Eating Disorder among Female Undergraduates of Obafemi Awolowo University Ile-Ife. *Gender & Behaviour*, 13(1). Retrieved August 12, 2019, from https://www.questia.com/library/journal/1P3-3907908551/cognitive-behaviour-therapy-in-the-management-of-eating

Adebimpe, V. (1981). Overview: White norms and psychiatric diagnosis of black patients. *American Journal of Psychiatry*, 138(3), 279–285.

Afara, A. E. & Senosy, S. A. (2018). Female sexual dysfunction in Egyptian women with anxiety: Prevalence and patterns. *Journal of Public Health*, 26(5), 545–549.

Affleck, G., & Tennen, H. (1996). Constructing benefits from adversity: Adaptational significance and dispositional underpinnings. *Journal of Personality*, 64, 899–902.

African News Agency. (2018, September 18). Buying and selling dagga remains a crime, says court. *IOL News.* Retrieved from https://www.iol.co.za/news/south-africa/western-cape/buying-and-selling-dagga-remains-a-crime-says-court-17128161

Aggarwala, N. K., Nicasio, A. V., DeSilva, R., Boiler, M., & Lewis-Fernández, R. (2013). Barriers to implementing the DSM-5 Cultural Formulation Interview: A qualitative study. *Culture, Medicine and Psychiatry*, 37(3), 505–533. doi:10.1007/s11013-013-9325-z

Agras, W. S. (1987). *Eating disorders: Management of obesity, bulimia, and anorexia nervosa.* New York, NY: Elmsford.

Ahmed, R., & Pretorius-Heuchert, J. W. (2001). Notions of social community psychology: Issues and challenges. In M. Seedat, N. Duncan, & S. Lazarus (Eds.), *Community psychology: Theory, method and practice. South African and other perspectives.* Cape Town: Oxford University Press, 67–85.

Aiyelero, O. M., Kwanashie, H. O., Sheikh, T. L., & Hussaini, I. M. (2011). Some socio-demographic features of mood disorders presented by patients attending a northern Nigerian tertiary health institution clinic. *Journal of Applied Pharmaceutical Science*, 1(06), 92–95.

Akbarian, S., Kim, J. J., Potkin, S. G., Hagman, J. O., Tafazzoli, A., Potkin, S. G., Bunney, W. E., & Jones, E. G. (1995). Gene expression for glutamic acid decarboxylase is reduced without loss of neurons in prefrontal cortex of schizophrenics. *Archives of General Psychiatry*, 52, 258–266.

Akst, D. (2011). *Procrastination, problematic internet addiction and resilience*. The Resilience Institute Newsletter. Retrieved March 10, 2012, from http://www.resiliencei.com

Alarcon, R. (2001). Hispanic psychiatry: From margin to mainstream. *Transcultural Psychiatry*, 38(1), 5–25.

Alcoholics Anonymous World Services, Inc. (2012). *Welcome to Alcoholics Anonymous*. Retrieved March 10, 2012, from www.aa.org/

Al-Issa I. (2000). *Mental illness in the Islamic World*. Madison, CT: International Universities Press.

Al-Krenawi, A., Elbedour, S., Parsons, J. E., Onwuegbuzie, A. J., Bart, W. M., & Ferguson, A. (2011). Trauma and war: Positive psychology/strengths approach. *Arab Journal of Psychiatry*, 23(2), 103–112.

Allan, A. (1997). *The law for psychotherapists and counsellors*. Somerset West: Inter-Ed Publishers.

Allen, D. F., Postel, J., & Berrios, G. E. (2000). The Ganser Syndrome. In G. H. Berrios (Ed.), *Memory disorders in psychiatric practice*. Cambridge, UK: Cambridge University Press, 443–454.

Allison, K. C., Lundgren, J. D., & Wadden, T. A. (2016). Albert J. Stunkard: His research on obesity and its psychological impact. *Current Obesity Reports*, 5(1), 140–144. doi:10.1007/s13679-016-0199-6

Ally, Y., & Laher, S. (2008). South African Muslim faith healers' perceptions of mental illness: Understanding, aetiology and treatment. *Journal of Religious Health*, 47(1), 45–46. http://dx.doi.org/10.1007/s10943-007-9133-2

Almajali, H. K. (2005). *The influence of family upbringing style and locus of control on the creative thinking of preparatory school learners in the United Arab Emirates* (Unpublished doctoral thesis). University of South Africa, Pretoria, South Africa.

Alvesson, M., & Sköldberg, K. (2000). *Reflexive methodology: New vistas for qualitative research*. London: Sage Publications Inc.

Alzheimer's Disease International. (2017). Dementia in sub-Saharan Africa: Challenges and opportunities. Retrieved from https://www.alz.co.uk/news/dementia-in-sub-saharan-africa-challenges-and-opportunities

Ambrose, M., & Deisler, V., 2010. *Investigating eating disorders (anorexia, bulimia, and binge-eating): Real facts for real lives*. Berkeley Heights, NJ: Enslow Publishing, LLC.

American Psychiatric Association. (1980). *Diagnostic and statistical manual of mental disorders* (3rd ed.) (DSM-III). Washington, DC: American Psychiatric Association.

American Psychiatric Association. (1987). *Diagnostic and statistical manual of mental disorders* (3rd ed. – revised) (DSM–III–R). Washington, DC: American Psychiatric Association.

American Psychiatric Association. (1994). *Diagnostic and statistical manual of mental disorders* (4th ed.) (DSM-IV). Washington, DC: American Psychiatric Association.

American Psychiatric Association. (2000). *Diagnostic and statistical manual of mental disorders* (4th ed. – Text Revision) (DSM-IV-TR). Washington, DC: American Psychiatric Association.

American Psychiatric Association. (2012a). *DSM-5 development*. Retrieved February 10, 2012, from, http://www.dsm5.org/Pages/Default.aspx

American Psychiatric Association. (2012b). *Highlights of changes from DSM-IV-TR to DSM-5*. Washington, DC: American Psychiatric Association. Retrieved from https://dsm.psychiatryonline.org/doi/10.1176/appi.books.9780890425596.changes

American Psychiatric Association. (2013). *Diagnostic and statistical manual of mental disorders* (5th ed.) (DSM-5). Washington DC: American Psychiatric Association.

American Psychiatric Association. (2016). *DSM-5 Update: Supplement to Diagnostic and Statistical Manual of Mental Disorders, fifth edition* (DSM-5). Washington, DC: American Psychiatric Association.

American Psychological Association. (2011). *Practice guidelines for LGB clients*. Washington, DC: American Psychological Association. Retrieved from http://www.apa.org/pi/lgbt/

American Society of Addiction Medicine. (2011). *Public policy statement: Definition of addiction*. Adopted by the ASAM Board of Directors April 12, 2011. Retrieved March 10, 2012 from https://www.asam.org/advocacy/find-a-policy-statement/view-policy-statement/public-policy-statements/2011/12/15/the-definition-of-addiction

Amianto, F., Spalatro, A. V., Rainis, M., Andriulli, C., Lavagnino, L., Abbate-Daga, G., & Fassino, S. (2018). Childhood emotional abuse and neglect in obese patients with and without binge eating disorder: Personality and psychopathology correlates in adulthood. *Psychiatry Research*, 269, 692–699. doi:10.1016/j.psychres.2018.08.089

Anastasi, A. (1988). *Psychological testing* (6th ed.). New York, NY: Oxford University Press.

Anastasi, A., & Urbina, S. (1997). *Psychological testing* (7th ed.). Chicago, IL: Prentice Hall.

Anastopoulos, A. D. (1998). A training program for parents of children with Attention Deficit Hyperactivity Disorder. In J. M. Briesmeister & C. E. Schaefer (Eds), *Handbook of parent training* (2nd ed.). New York, NY: John Wiley & Sons, Inc.

Anastopoulos, A. D., Guevremont, D. C., Shelton, T. L., & DuPaul, G. J. (1992). Parenting stress among families of children with Attention Deficit Hyperactivity Disorder. *Journal of Abnormal Child Psychology*, 20(5), 503–520.

Andersen, B. L., & Cyranowski, J. C. (1994). Women's sexual self-schema. *Journal of Personality and Social Psychology*, 67, 1079–1100.

Andersen, B. L., Cyranowski, J. C., & Espindle, D. (1999). Men's sexual self-schema. *Journal of Personality and Social Psychology*, 76, 645–661.

Andrasik, F. (2000). Biofeedback. In D. I. Motofsky & D. H. Barlow (Eds), *The management of stress and anxiety in medical disorders*. Needham Heights, MA: Allyn & Bacon, 66–83.

Andreasen, N. C., Olsen, S. A., Dennert, J. W., & Smith, M. R. (1982). Ventricular enlargement in Schizophrenia: Relationship to positive and negative symptoms. *American Journal of Psychiatry*, 139, 297–302.

Andreasen, N. C., Rezai, K., Alliger, R., Swayze, V. W, Flaum, M., Kirchner, P., Cohen, G, & O'Leary, D. S. (1992). Hypofrontality in neuroleptic-naive patients and in patients with chronic Schizophrenia: Assessment with xenon 133 single-photon emission computed tomography with the Tower of London. *Archives of General Psychiatry*, 49, 943–958.

Andreasen, N. C. & Swayze, V. W. (1993). Neuroimaging. In J. A. Costa e Silva, & C. C. Nadelson (Eds), *International review of psychiatry* (Vol. 1). Washington, DC: American Psychiatric Press.

Andreasen, N. C., Swayze, V. W., Flaum, M., Yates, W. R., Arndt, S., & McChesney, C. (1990). Ventricular enlargement in Schizophrenia evaluated with computed tomographic scanning: Effects of gender, age, and stage of illness. *Archives of General Psychiatry*, 47, 1008–1015.

Andrèasson, S., Engström, A., Allebeck, P., & Rydberg, U. (1987). Cannabis and Schizophrenia: A longitudinal study of Swedish conscripts. *Lancet*, 330(8574), 1483–1486.

Angleitner, A., & Ostendorf, F. (1994). Temperament and the Big Five factors of personality. In C. F. Halverson, Jr., G. A. Kohnstamm, & R. P. Martin (Eds), *The developing structure of temperament from infancy to adulthood*. Hillsdale, NJ: Lawrence Erlbaum, 69–90.

Anonymous. (2016, May 14). My secret life as a high-functoning drug user. *The Guardian*. Retrieved from https://www.theguardian.com/society/2016/may/14/secret-life-high-functioning-drug-user

Ansumana, J. (n.d.). The Black Consciousness Movement and Steve Biko. *South African history online – Toward a people's history*. Retrieved April 15, 2019, from https://www.sahistory.org.za/archive/black-consciousness-movement-and-steve-biko-jonathan-ansumana

Anupama, M., Nagaraja Rao, K., & Dhananjaya, S. (2006). Ganser syndrome and lesion in the temporoparietal region. *Indian Journal of Psychiatry*, 48(2), 123–125, 2006. doi:10.4103/0019-5545.31605

Arciniegas, D. B. (2015). Psychosis. *Behavioral Neurology and Neuropsychiatry*, 21(3), 715–736. doi:10.1212/01.CON.0000466662.89908.e7

Arnold, P., Bhandan, S. P., Lorch, E., Ivey, J., Rose, M., & Rosenberg, D. R. (2003). Childhood anxiety disorders and developmental issues in anxiety. *Current Psychiatry Reports*, 5, 252–265.

Asefzadeh, S., & Sameefar F. (2001). Traditional healers in the Qazvin region of the Islamic Republic of Iran: A qualitative study. *Eastern Mediterranean Health Journal*, 7(3), 544–550.

Ashworth, A. (2000). *Sentencing and criminal justice* (3rd ed.). Oxford: Oxford University Press.

Asmal, L., Kilian, S., du Plessis, S., Scheffler, F., Chiliza, B., Fouche, J. P., Seedat, S., Dazzan, P., & Emsley, R. (2018). Childhood trauma associated white matter abnormalities in first-episode schizophrenia. *Schizophrenia Bulletin*, 45(2), 369–376. doi:oi.org/10.1093/schbul/s

Asuni, T., Schoenberg, F., & Swift, C. (1994). *Mental health and disease in Africa*. Ibadan: Spectrum Books.

Austin, D. W., & Richards, J. C. (2001). The catastrophic misinterpretation model of panic disorder. *Behaviour Research & Therapy*, 39, 1277–1291.

Austin, E. J., Saklofske, D. H., & Egan, V. (2005). Personality, well-being and health correlates of trait emotional intelligence. *Personality and Individual Differences*, 38, 547–558.

Automobile Association of South Africa. (2016). Graph prepared from RTMC Calendar report, 2016.

Ayano, G. (2016). Schizophrenia: A concise over view on etiology epidemiology diagnosis and management: review on literature. *Journal of Schizophrenia Research*, 3(2), 2–7. Retrieved from https://www.researchgate.net/profile/Getinet_Ayano/publication/318012024

Bakalar, J. L., Shank, L. M., Vannucci, A., Radin, R. M., & Tanofsky-Kraff, M. (2015). Recent advances in developmental and risk factor research on eating disorders. *Current Psychiatry Reports*, 17(6), 42. doi:10.1007/s11920-015-0585-x.

Baker, J. H., Janson, L., Trace, S. F., & Bulik, C. M. (2015). Genetic risk factors for eating disorders. In L. Smolak & M. P. Levine (Eds.), *The Wiley handbook of eating disorders*. Chichester, West Sussex, UK: John Wiley & Sons, 367–378.

Bakhshi, K., & Chance, S. A. (2015). The neuropathology of schizophrenia: A selective review of past studies and emerging themes in brain structure and cytoarchitecture. *Neuroscience*, 303, 82–102. doi:10.1016/j.neuroscience.2015.06.028

Balaban, C. D., & Jacob, R. G. (2001). Background and history of the interface between anxiety and vertigo. *Journal of Anxiety Disorders*, 15(1–2), 27–51.

Baldwin, G. (2003). *Ties that bind: The SM/Leather/Fetish erotic style* (2nd ed.). Los Angeles, CA: Daedalus Publishing Company.

Baloyi, L. J. (2008). *Psychology and psychotherapy redefined from the viewpoint of the African experience* (Unpublished doctoral dissertation). University of South Africa, Pretoria, South Africa.

Bandelow, B., Baldwin, D., Abelli, M., Altamura, C., Dell'Osso, B., Domschke, K., … Riederer, P. (2016). Biological markers for anxiety disorders, OCD and PTSD: A consensus statement. Part I: Neuroimaging and genetics. *World Journal of Biological Psychiatry*, 17(5), 321–365. doi:10.1080/15622975.2016.1181783

Barkley, R. A. (1995). *Taking charge of ADHD: The complete authoritative guide for parents*. London: Guilford Press.

Barlow, D. H. (2005). What's new about evidence-based assessment? *Psychological Assessment*, 17, 308–311.

Barlow, D. H., & Durand, V. M. (2005). *Abnormal psychology: An integrative approach* (4th ed.). London: Cengage.

Barlow, D. H. & Durand, V. M. (2009). *Abnormal psychology: An integrative approach* (5th ed.). Belmont, CA: Wadsworth Cengage Learning.

Barlow, D. H. & Durand, V. M. (2011). *Abnormal psychology: An integrative approach* (6th ed.). Belmont, C.A.: Wadsworth.

Barlow, D. H., Durand, V. M., Du Plessis, L. M., & Visser, C. (2017). *Abnormal psychology: An integrative approach*. London: Cengage Learning.

Barrantes-Vidal, N., Grant, P., & Kwapil, T. R. (2015). The role of schizotypy in the study of the etiology of schizophrenia spectrum disorders. *Schizophrenia Bulletin*, 41(suppl_2), S408–S416. doi:10.1093/schbul/sbu191

Barrett, J. G. (2004). Conduct disorders. *Encyclopedia of applied developmental science*. Retrieved March 20, 2009, from http://www.sage–ereference.com/applieddevscience/Article_n111.html

Bartlett, P., & Sandland, R. (2003). *Mental health law: Policy and practice*. Oxford: Oxford University Press.

Bartol, C. R. (2002). *Criminal behavior: A psychosocial approach* (6th ed.). Upper Saddle River, NJ: Prentice Hall.

Bartol, C. R., & Bartol, A. M. (2005). *Criminal behavior: A psychosocial approach* (7th ed.). Upper Saddle River, NJ: Pearson.

Bartol, C. R., & Bartol, A. M. (2008). *Criminal behavior: A psychosocial approach* (8th ed.). Upper Saddle River, NJ: Pearson.

Bartol, C. R., & Bartol, A. M. (2011). *Criminal behavior: A psychosocial approach* (9th ed.). Upper Saddle River, NJ: Pearson.

Bartol, C. R., & Bartol, A. M. (2017). *Criminal behavior: A psychosocial approach* (11th ed.). Upper Saddle River, NJ: Pearson.

Bateson, G. (1959). Cultural problems posed by a study of schizophrenic process. In A. Auerback (Ed.), *Schizophrenia: An integrated approach*. New York: Ronald Press, 122–148.

Batson, C. D., Ahmad, N., Lishner, D. A., & Tsang, J. (2005). Empathy and altruism. In C. R. Snyder & S. J. Lopez (Eds), *Handbook of positive psychology*. Oxford: Oxford University Press, 485–498.

Baumeister, R. F., & Vohs, K. D. (2002). The pursuit of meaningfulness in life. In C. R. Snyder & S. J. Lopez (Eds), *Handbook of positive psychology*. Oxford: Oxford University Press, 608–617.

Baumeister, R. F., Vohs, K. D., & Tice, D. M. (2007). The strength model of self-control. *Current Directions in Psychological Science*, 16(6), 351–355.

Baumgardner, S. R., & Crothers, M. K. (2009). *Positive psychology*. Upper Saddle River, NJ: Pearson.

Beards, S., Gayer-Anderson, C., Borges, S., Dewey, M. E., Fisher, H. L., & Morgan, C. (2013). Life events and psychosis: A review and meta-analysis. *Schizophrenia Bulletin*, 39(4), 740–747. doi:10.1093/schbul/sbt065

Bechdolf, A., Thompson, A., Nelson, B., Cotton, S., Simmons, M.B., Amminger, G.P., … Sidis, A. (2010). Experience of trauma and conversion to psychosis in an ultra-high-risk (prodromal) group. *Acta Psychiatrica Scandinavica*, 121(5), 377–384. doi:10.1111/j.1600-0447.2010.01542.x

Beck, A. T. (1972). *Depression: Causes and treatment*. Philadelphia, PA: University of Pennsylvania Press.

Beck, A. T. (1976). *Cognitive therapy and the emotional disorders*. New York, NY: International Universities Press.

Beck, A. T., & Clark, D. A. (1988). Anxiety and depression: An information-processing perspective. *Anxiety Research*, 1, 23–26.

Beck, A. T., & Emery, G. (1985). *Anxiety disorders and phobias*. New York, NY: Basic Books.

Becker, D., & Marecek, J. (2008). Dreaming the American dream: Individualism and positive psychology. *Social and Personality Psychology Compass*, 2(5), 1767–1780. http://dx.doi.org/10.1111/j.1751-9004.2008.00139.x

Becker, L. C. (1992a). Places for pluralism. *Ethics*, 102(4), 707–719.

Becvar, D. S., & Becvar, R. J. (2009). *Family therapy: A systemic integration* (7th ed.). Boston, MA: Allyn & Bacon/Pearson.

Bello, N. T., & Hajnal, A. (2010). Dopamine and binge eating behaviors. *Pharmacology Biochemistry and Behavior*, 97(1), 25–33. doi:10.1016/j.pbb.2010.04.016

Bemporad, J. R. (1997). Cultural and historical aspects of eating disorders. *Theoretical Medicine*, 18, 401–420.

Bennett, P. (2003). *Abnormal and clinical psychology: An introductory textbook*. Maidenhead, UK: Open University Press.

Berk, L. E. (2000). *Child development* (5th ed.) Boston, MA: Allyn & Bacon.

Bernstein, D. P., Useda, D., & Siever, L. J. (1995). Paranoid personality disorder. In W. J. Livesley (Ed.), *The DSM-IV personality disorders*. New York, NY: Guilford Press, 45–57.

Berrios, G. E., Luque, R., & Villagrán, J. M. (2003). Schizophrenia: A conceptual history. *International Journal of Psychology and Psychological Theory*, 3(2), 111–140.

Berry, C. (2015). *Mastering compliance newsletters: Practising POPI*. Retrieved August 8, 2018 from https://www.masthead.co.za/newsletter/practising-popi/

Berry, J. W., Poortinga, Y. H., Segall, M. H., & Dasen, P. R. (2002). *Cross-cultural psychology: Research and applications* (2nd ed.). Cambridge: Cambridge University Press.

Bersoff, D. N. (2002). Some contrarian concerns about law, psychology, and public policy. *Law and Human Behavior*, 26(5), 565–574.

Bessenhof, G. R. (2006). Can media affect us? Social comparison, self-discrepancy, and the thin ideal. *Psychology of Women Quarterly*, 30, 239–251.

Bevilacqua, L., & Goldman, D. (2009). Genes and addictions. *Clinical Pharmacology & Therapeutics*, 85, 359–361.

Bezuidenhout, C., & Klopper, H. (2011). Crimes of a violent nature. In C. Bezuidenhout (Ed.), *A Southern African perspective on fundamental criminology*. Cape Town: Pearson.

Bhamjee, S. (2010). Is the right to die with dignity constitutionally guaranteed? Baxter v Montana and other developments in patient autonomy and physician assisted suicide. *Obiter*, 31(2), 333–352.

Bhardwaj, V. (2018, February 8). South Africans are not the world's highest alcohol consumers. *AfricaCheck*. Retrieved from https://africacheck.org/reports/south-africans-not-worlds-biggest-alcohol-consumers/

Bhana, D. (2008). Beyond stigma? Young children's responses to HIV and AIDS. *Culture, Health & Sexuality*, 10(7), 725–738.

Bhana, D. (2012) Understanding and addressing homophobia in schools: A view from teachers. *South African Journal of Education*, 32, 307–318.

Bhorat, H. (2015, September 30). *South Africa the most unequal society in the world?* Retrieved from https://mg.co.za/article/2015-09-30-is-south-africa-the-most-unequal-society-in-the-world

Bhugra, D. (1997). *Psychiatry and religion: Context, consensus and controversies*. London: Routledge.

Bhugra D., & Bhui, K. (2001). African-Caribbeans and schizophrenia: Contributing factors. *Advances in Psychiatric Treatment* 2001(7), 288–293.

Bhugrah, D., & Bhui, K. (Eds.). (2007). *Textbook of cultural psychiatry*. Cambridge: Cambridge University Press.

Bilker, W., Hansen, J., Brensinger, C., Richard, J., Gur, R., & Gur, R. (2012). Development of abbreviated nine-item forms of the Raven's standard progressive matrices test. *Assessment*, 354–369.

Birley, J., & Brown, G. W. (1970). Crisis and life changes preceding the onset or relapse of acute Schizophrenia: Clinical aspects. *British Journal of Psychiatry*, 16, 327–333.

Black, D. S. (2004). Conversion hysteria: Lessons from functional imaging. *Journal of Neuropsychiatry and Clinical Neurosciences*, 16(3), 245–251.

Blackburn, R. (1993). *The psychology of criminal conduct: Theory, research and practice*. New York, NY: Wiley & Sons.

Blashfield, R. K. (1984). *The classification of psychopathology. Neo-Kraepelinian and quantitative approaches*. New York, NY: Plenum.

Bleueler, E. (1911/1950) *Dementia praecox or the group of schizophrenias*. New York, NY: International Universities Press.

Board, B. J., & Fritzon, K. (2005). Disordered personalities at work. *Psychology, Crime and Law*, 11(1), 17–32.

Bojuwoye, O. (2003). Mental health care delivery practices among traditional African cultures – nature, process and virtues. In N. S. Madu (Ed.), *Contributions to psychotherapy conference in Africa*. Turfloop: University of the North, 188–206.

Bojuwoye, O. & Sodi, T. (2010). Challenges and opportunities to integrating traditional healing into counselling and psychotherapy. *Counselling Psychology Quarterly*, 23(3), 283–296. doi:10.1080/095150 70.2010.505750

Boll, T. J. (1985). Developing issues in clinical neuropsychology. *Journal of Clinical and Experimental Neuropsychology*, 7(5), 473–485.

Bombak, A., Monaghan, L. F., & Rich, E. (2018). Dietary approaches to weight-loss, Health At Every Size® and beyond: Rethinking the war on obesity. *Social Theory & Health*, 17(1), 89–108. doi:10.1057/s41285-018-0070-9

Boog, G. (2004). Obstetrical complications and subsequent Schizophrenia in adolescent and young adult offspring: Is there a relationship? *European Journal of Obstetrics & Gynaecology and Reproductive Biology*, 114(2), 130–136.

Bookwalter, J. T. (2012). Living the good life: An economic view of happiness in South Africa. In H. Selin & G. Davey (Eds), *Happiness across cultures: Views of happiness and quality of life in non-Western cultures*. Dordrecht: Springer, 329–344.

Boorstein, H. C., Fein, D. A., & Wilson, L. B. (2005). Pervasive developmental disorders. *Encyclopedia of Human Development*. Retrieved March 20, 2009, from http://www.sage-ereference.com/humandevelopment/ Article_n477.html

Bornman, J. (2017). Life Esidimeni: The greatest cause of human right violations since democracy. *Mail & Guardian*, 9 October 2017. Retrieved August 9, 2019, from https://mg.co.za/article/2017-10-09-life-esidimeni-the-greatest-cause-of-human-right-violations-since-democracy

Boss, L. (1997). Epidemic hysteria: A review of the published literature. *Epidemiologic Reviews*, 19(2), 233–243.

Boswell, R. G., & Kober, H. (2016). Food cue reactivity and craving predict eating and weight gain: A meta-analytic review. *Obesity Reviews*, 17(2), 159–177. doi:10.1111/obr.12354

Botha, K. F. H. (2013). Self-regulation as psychological strength in South Africa: A review. In M. O. Wissing (Ed.), *Well-being research in South Africa: Cross-cultural advancements in positive psychology*. Springer: Dordrecht, 501–516.

Botha, U. A., Koen, L., Joska, J., Parker, J. S., Horn, N., Hering, L. M., & Oosthuizen, P. P. (2010). The revolving door phenomenon in psychiatry: Comparing low-frequency and high-frequency users of psychiatric inpatient services in a developing country. *Social Psychiatry and Psychiatric Epidemiology*, 45(4), 461–468. doi:10.1007/s00127-009-0085-6.

Botta, R. A. (2003). For your health? The relationship between magazine reading and adolescents' body image and eating disturbances. *Sex Roles*, 48, 389–399.

Botta, R. A. (2006). Television images and adolescent girls' body image disturbance. *Journal of Communication*, 49, 22–41.

Bowie, M. J., & Schaffer, R. M. (2014). *Understanding ICD-10-CM and ICD-10-PCS: A worktext* (2nd ed.). Boston, MA: Cengage.

Bowlby, J. (1980). *Attachment and loss: Loss, sadness and depression*. New York, NY: Basic.

Brandtstädter, J., & Rothermund, K. (2002). The life-course dynamics of goal pursuit and goal adjustment: A two-process framework. *Developmental Review*, 22, 117–150.

Bray, R., & Dawes, A. (2007). A rights-based approach to monitoring the well-being of children in South Africa. In A. Dawes, R. Bray, & A. van der Merwe (Eds), *Monitoring child well-being: A South Africa rights-based approach*. Cape Town: HSRC Press, 29–52.

Brett-Jones, J., Garety, P., & Hemsley, D. (1987). Measuring delusional experiences: A method and its application. *British Journal of Clinical Psychology*, 26, 257–265.

Briggs, H. (2012). *Web addicts have brain changes, research suggests*. Retrieved January 15, 2012, from BBC News website.

Brochin, H. A., & Horvath, J. A. (1996). Attention Deficit Hyperactivity Disorder. In G. M. Blau & T. P. Gullotta (Eds), *Adolescent dysfunctional behaviour: Causes, interventions and prevention*. Thousand Oaks, CA: Sage, 37–60.

Brockmeyer, T., Skunde, M., Wu, M., Bresslein, E., Rudofsky, G., Herzog, W., & Friederich, H. C. (2014). Difficulties in emotion regulation across the spectrum of eating disorders. *Comprehensive Psychiatry*, 55(3), 565–571. doi:10.1016/j.comppsych.2013.12.001

Brodrick, K. (2002). Correlation between scores on two screening tools for dementia in Xhosa women. *South African Journal of Occupational Therapy*, 32(3), 8–13.

Bronfenbrenner, U. (1979). *The ecology of human development: Experiments by nature and design*. Cambridge, MA: Harvard University Press.

Bronfenbrenner, U. (1989). Ecological systems theory. In R. Vasta (Ed.), *Annals of child development* (Vol. 6). London, UK: Jessica Kingsley Publishers, 187–249.

Brooks, S., Prince, A., Stahl, D., Campbell, I. C., & Treasure, J. (2011). A systematic review and meta-analysis of cognitive bias to food stimuli in people with disordered eating behaviour. *Clinical Psychology Review*, 31(1), 37–51. doi:10.1016/j.cpr.2010.09.006

Brotto, L. A., & Klein, C. (2007). Sexual and gender-identity disorders. In M. Hersen, S. M. Turner, & D. Beidel (Eds), *Adult psychopathology and diagnosis* (5th ed.) Hoboken, NJ: John Wiley & Sons, 504–570.

Brown, G. W., Birley, J. L. T., & Wing, J. K. (1972). The influence of family life on the course of schizophrenic disorders: A replication. *British Journal of Psychiatry*, 121, 241–58.

Brown, G. W., Bone, M., Dalison, B., & Wing, J.K. (1966). *Schizophrenia and social care*. London: Oxford University Press.

Brown, S. (1997). Excess mortality of Schizophrenia: A meta-analysis. *British Journal of Psychiatry*, 171, 502–508.

Brownell, K. D. (1991). Dieting and the search for the perfect body: Where physiology and culture collide. *Behaviour Therapy*, 22, 1–12.

Brownell, K. D., & Fairburn, C. G. (Eds). (1995). *Eating disorders and obesity: A comprehensive handbook*. New York, NY: Guilford Press.

Brownell, K. D., & Rodin, J. (1994). The dieting maelstrom: Is it possible and advisable to lose weight? *American Psychologist*, 49(9), 781–791.

Bruch, H. (1985). Four decades of eating disorders. In D. M. Garner & P. E. Garfunkel (Eds), *Handbook of psychotherapy for anorexia nervosa and bulimia*. New York, NY: Guilford Press, 7–18.

Buhrman, M. V. (1984). *Living in two worlds: Communication between a white healer and her black counterparts*. Cape Town: Human & Rosseau.

Buickians, A., Miklowitz, D. J., & Kim, E. Y. (2007). Behavioral activation, inhibition and mood symptoms in early-onset bipolar disorder. *Journal of Affective Disorders*, 97, 71–76.

Bulbulia, T., & Laher, S. (2013). Exploring the role of Islam in perceptions of mental illness in a sample of Muslim psychiatrists based in Johannesburg. *South African Journal of Psychiatry*, 19(2), 52–54. https://sajp.org.za/index.php/sajp/article/view/396/403

Bulhan, H. A. (1985). *Frantz Fanon and the psychology of oppression*. New York, NY: Plenum Press.

Bulhan, H. A. (2015). *Frantz Fanon – the revolutionary psychiatrist*. New York, NY: Plenum.

Bureau of Census. (1983). *Statistical abstract of the United States*. Washington, DC: US Government Printing Office.

Burke, A. (Ed.). (2009). *Abnormal psychology: A South African perspective*. Cape Town: Oxford Press.

Burke, A. (2010). The abuse of social science research results for political gain: The apartheid system as case study. *Journal of Public Administration*, 45(3), 403–419.

Burke, A., Harper, M., Rudnick, H., & Kruger, G. (2007). Moving beyond statutory ethical codes: Practitioner ethics as a contextual, character-based enterprise. *South African Journal of Psychology*, 37(1), 107–120.

Burns, J. K. (2009). Dispelling a myth: Developing world poverty, inequality, violence and social fragmentation are not good for outcome in Schizophrenia. *African Journal of Psychiatry*, 12, 200–205.

Burns, J. K., Jhazbhay, K., Esterhuizen, T., & Emsley, R. (2010). Exposure to trauma and the clinical presentation of first-episode psychosis in South Africa. *Journal of Psychiatric Research*, 45(2), 179–184.

Businesstech. (2018). South Africa crime stats 2018: Everything you need to know. Businesstech, 11 September 2018. Retrieved from https://businesstech.co.za/news/government/270689/south-africa-crime-stats-2018-everything-you-need-to-know/

Butcher, J. N. (2000). Revising psychological tests: Lessons learned from the revision of the MMPI. *Psychological Assessment*, 12, 263–271.

Butcher, J. N., Graham, J. R., Williams, C. L., & Ben-Porath, Y. S. (1990). *Development and use of the MMPI–2 content scales*. Minneapolis, MN: University of Minnesota Press.

Butcher, J. N., Mineka, S., & Hooley, J. M. (2010). *Abnormal psychology* (14th ed.). Boston, MA: Allyn & Bacon.

Caelers, D., & Bailey, C. (2006, September 29). How tik scourge fuels gang violence. *IOL News*. Retrieved from https://www.iol.co.za/news/south-africa/how-tik-scourge-fuels-gang-violence-295663

Caico, C. (2014). Sexually risky behavior in college-aged students. *Open Journal of Preventive Medicine*, 4, 354–364.

Caldwell-Harris, C., & Ayçiçegi, A. (2006). When personality and culture clash: The psychological distress of allocentrics in an individualist culture and idiocentrics in a collectivist culture. *Transcultural Psychology*, 43(3), 331–361. https://doi.org/10.1177/1363461506066982

Callard, F. (2006). Understanding agoraphobia: Women, men, and the historical geography of urban anxiety. In C. Berkin, J. Pinch, & C. Appel (Eds), *Exploring women's studies: Looking forward, looking back*. New York, NY: Prentice Hall, 201–217.

Campbell, M. M., Artz, L., & Stein, D. J. (2015). Sexual disorders in DSM-5 and ICD-11: A conceptual framework. *Current Opinion in Psychiatry*, 28(6), 435–439.

Campbell, M. M., Sibeko, G., Mall, S., Baldinger, A., Nagdee, M., Susser, E., & Stein, D. J. (2017). The content of delusions in a sample of South African Xhosa people with schizophrenia. *BMC Psychiatry*, 17(1), 41–50. doi:10.1186/s12888-017-1196-3

Campbell, M. M., & Stein D. J. (2014). Sexual dysfunction: A systematic review of South African research. *South African Medical Journal*, 106(6), 440–444.

Camprodon, J. A., Rausch, S. L., Greenberg, B. D., & Dougherty, D. D. (Eds). (2016). *Psychiatric neurotherapeutics: Contemporary surgical and device-based treatments*. New York, NY: Springer Publishing Company.

Cannon, T. D., Barr, C. E., & Mednick, S.A. (1991). Genetic and perinatal factors in the etiology of schizophrenia. In E. F. Walker (Ed.), *Schizophrenia: A life-course developmental perspective*. New York, NY: Academic Press, 9–31.

Canter, M. B., Bennett, B. E., Jones, S. E., & Nagy, T. F. (1994). *Ethics for psychologists: A commentary on the APA ethics code*. Washington, DC: American Psychological Association.

Caradas, A. A., Lambert, E. V., & Charlton, E. (2001). An ethnic comparison of eating attitudes and associated body image concerns in adolescent South African schoolgirls. *Journal of Human Nutrition and Dietetics*, 14, 111–120.

Carbonell, D. (n. d.). *Claire Weekes: Float through anxiety*. Retrieved from https://www.anxietycoach.com/claire-weekes.html

Cardeña, E. (1994). The domain of dissociation. In S. J. Rhue (Ed.), *Dissociation, clinical and theoretical perspectives*. New York, NY: Guilford Press, 15–31.

Carpenter, W. T. (1992).The negative symptom challenge. *Archives of General Psychiatry*, 49(3), 236–237.

Carrey, N., & Ungar, M. (2007). Resilience theory and the diagnostic and statistical manual: Incompatible bed fellows? *Child and Psychiatric Clinics of North America*, 16, 497–513.

Carson, R. C. (1985). The schizophrenias. In H. E. Adams & P. B. Sutker (Eds), *Comprehensive textbook of psychopathology*. New York, NY: Plenum, 411–434.

Carson, R. C., Butcher, J. N., & Coleman, J. C. (1988). *Abnormal psychology and modern life*. Glenview, IL: Scott, Foresman & Co.

Cartwright, D. (2008). Psychopathology. In L. Swartz, C. de la Rey, N. Duncan, & L. Townsend (Eds), *Psychology: An introduction*. Cape Town: Oxford University Press.

Cartwright, D. (2016). Psychopathology. In L. Swartz, C. de la Rey, N. Duncan, & L. Townsend (Eds), Psychology: An introduction (4th ed). Cape Town: Oxford University Press.

Carver, C. S. (2004). Self-regulation of action and affect. In R. F. Baumeister & K. D. Vohs (Eds), *Handbook of self-regulation: Research, theory, and applications*. London: Guilford Press, 13–39.

Carver, C. S., & Scheier, M. F. (2005). Optimism. In C. R. Snyder & S. J. Lopez (Eds), *Handbook of positive psychology*. Oxford: Oxford University Press, 231–243.

Cash, T. F., & Henry, P. E. (1995). Women's body images: The results of a national survey in the USA. *Sex Roles*, 33(1–2), 19–28. doi:10.1007/BF01547933

Casino Association of South Africa. (2011). *Problem gambling and responsible gambling*. Retrieved December 15, 2011, from www.casasa.org.za

Castellini, G., Mannucci, E., Mazzei, C., Sauro, C. L., Faravelli, C., Rotella, C. M., Maggi, M., & Ricca, V., (2010). Sexual function in obese women with and without binge eating disorder. *Journal of Sexual Medicine*, 7(12), 3969–3978. doi:10.1111/j.1743-6109.2010.01990.x

Castillo, R. J. (Ed.). (1998). *Meanings of madness*. Pacific Grove, CA: Brooks/Cole.

Castro, M. (2006). The world's most dangerous drug. *National Geographic*. Retrieved from watchdocumentaries.com/worlds-most-dangerous-drug

Cauce, A. M. (2011). Is multicultural psychology a-scientific? Diverse methods for diversity research. *Cultural Diversity and Ethnic Minority Psychology*, 17(3), 228–233.

Centers for Disease Control and Prevention. (2017). *Overweight and obesity. Data and statistics.* Retrieved from https://www.cdc.gov/obesity/data/index.html

Centres for Disease Control and Prevention. (2018, March 7). *Does marijuana use lead to other drug use?* Retrieved from https://www.cdc.gov/marijuana/faqs/does-marijuana-lead-to-other-drugs.html

Chamorro-Premuzic, T., Bennett, E., & Furnham, A. (2007). The happy personality: Meditational role of trait emotional intelligence. *Personality and Individual Differences*, 42, 1633–1639.

Charney, D. S., Deutsch, A. V., Krystal, J. H., Southwick, A. M., & Davis, M. (1993). Psychobiologic mechanisms of post-traumatic stress disorder. *Archives of General Psychiatry*, 50, 295–305.

Cherki, A. (2017). Foreword. In F. Fanon, *Psychiatry and politics*. London: Rowman & Littlefield.

Chhagan, U., & Burns, J. K. (2017). The clinical value of brain computerised tomography in a general hospital psychiatric service. *South African Journal of Psychiatry*, 23.

Chinawa, J. M., Obu, H. A., Manyike, P., Isreal, O. O., & Tamunosiki, C. A. (2015). Prevalence of encopresis in children aged 5–12 years attending government primary schools in South East Nigeria. *African Journal of Medical and Health Sciences*, 14(1), 13–17.

Chou, D., Cottler, S., Khosla, R., Reed, G. M., & Say, L. (2015). Sexual health in the International Classification of Diseases (ICD): Implications for measurement and beyond. *Reproductive Health Matters*, 23(46), 185–192. http://dx.doi.org/10.1016/j.rhm.2015.11.008 pmid: 26719010

Christensen, A.L. (1979). *Luria's neuropsychological investigation* (2nd ed.). Copenhagen: Munksgaard.

Christopher, J. C., & Hickinbottom, S. (2008). Positive psychology, ethnocentrism, and the disguised ideology of individualism. *Theory & Psychology*, 18(5), 563–589. http://dx.doi.org/10.1177/0959354308093396

Chua, S. E., & McKenna, P. J. (1995). Schizophrenia – a brain disease? A critical review of structural and functional cerebral abnormality in the disorder. *British Journal of Psychiatry*, 166, 563–582.

Churcher, F. P., Mills, J. F., & Forth, A. E. (2016). The predictive validity of the Two-Tiered Violence Risk Estimates Scale (TTV) in a long-term follow-up of violent offenders. *Psychological Services*, 13(3), 232–245.

Cicchetti, D., & Rogosch, F. A. (1996). Equifinality and multifinality in developmental psychopathology. *Development and Psychopathology*, 8(4), 597–600. http://dx.doi.org/10.1017/S0954579400007318

Clark, D. M. (1986). A cognitive approach to panic. *Behaviour Research and Therapy*, 24(4), 461–470. http://dx.doi.org/10.1016/0005-7967(86)90011-2

Clark, L. A., Cuthbert, B, Lewis-Fernández, R., Narrow, W. E., & Reed, G. M. (2017). Three approaches to understanding and classifying mental disorder: ICD-11, DSM-5, and the National Institute of Mental Health's Research Domain Criteria (RDoC). *Psychological Science in the Public Interest*, 18(2), 72–145. https://journals.sagepub.com/doi/full/10.1177/1529100617727266

Clausen, J. A. (1957). Social and psychological factors in narcotics addiction. *Law and Contemporary Problems*, 22, 34–51.

Cleghorn, J. M., Franco, S., Szechtman, B., Kaplan, R. D, Szechtman, H., Brown, G. M., Nahmias, G. M., & Garnett, E. S. (1992). Toward a brain map of auditory hallucinations. *American Journal of Psychiatry*, 149, 1062–1069.

Cloitre, C., Courtois, C. A., Charivastra, A., Carapezza, R., Stolbach, B., & Green, B. L. (2011). Treatment of complex PTSD: Results of the ISTSS expert clinical survey on best practices. Journal of Traumatic Stress, 24(6), 615-627. DOI: 10.1002/kts.20697.

Cloninger, C. R., & Gottesman, I. I. (1987). Genetic and environmental factors in antisocial behavior disorders. In S. A. Mednick, T. E. Moffitt, & S. A. Stack (Eds), *The cause of crime: New biological approaches.* New York, NY: Cambridge University Press, 92–109.

Cloninger, C., & Yutzy, S. (1993). Somatoform and dissociative disorders: A summary of changes for DSM–IV. In D. L. Dunner (Ed.), *Current psychiatric therapy.* Philadelphia, PA: W. B. Saunders, 310–313.

Cohen, R., & Blaszczynski, A. (2015). Comparative effects of Facebook and conventional media on body image dissatisfaction. *Journal of Eating Disorders,* 3(1), 23–34. doi:10.1186/s40337-015-0061-3

Cohen-Arazi, J. (2003). *The euthanasia program and nurses' participation.* Retrieved from http://www.history.ucsb.edu/faculty/marcuse/classes/33d/projects/euth/EuthanasiaNurses.htm

Cohn, L. D., Adler, N. E., Irwin, C. E., Millstein, S. G., Kegeles, S. G., & Stone, G. (1987). Body-figure preferences in male and female adolescents. *Journal of Abnormal Psychology,* 96, 276–279.

Cois, A., & Day, C. (2015). Obesity trends and risk factors in the South African adult population. *BMC Obesity,* 2(1), 42–52. doi:10.1186/s40608-015-0072-2

Colorado Personal Growth and Therapy Resources (1998). Retrieved January 15, 1998, from http://www.telosnet.com

Comer, R. J. (1995). *Abnormal psychology* (2nd ed.). New York, NY: W.H. Freeman and Company.

Compton, W. C. (2005). *An introduction to positive psychology.* Belmont, CA: Wadsworth/Cengage Learning.

Compton, W. M., Jones, C. M., & Baldwin, G. T. (2016). Relationship between nonmedical prescription opiod use and heroin use. *New England Journal of Medicine,* 374, 154–163.

Compulsive gambling. (2012). Retrieved March 10, 2012 from http://www.miph.org/projects/gambling-problems-resource-center

Conard, M. A. (2006). Aptitude is not enough: How personality and behaviour predict academic performance. *Journal of Research in Personality,* 339–346.

Connors, M. E., & Morse, W. (1993). Sexual abuse and eating disorders: A review. *International Journal of Eating Disorders,* 13, 1–11.

Conus, P., Cotton, S., Schimmelmann, B. G., McGorry, P. D., & Lambert, M. (2010). Pretreatment and outcome correlates of sexual and physical trauma in an epidemiological cohort of first-episode psychosis patients. *Schizophrenia Bulletin,* 36(6), 1105–1114. doi:10.1093/schbul/sbp009

Cooper, D. (1967). *Psychiatry and anti-psychiatry.* London: Tavistock Publications.

Copeland, W. E., Bulik, C. M., Zucker, N., Wolke, D., Lereya, S. T., & Costello, E. J. (2015). Does childhood bullying predict eating disorder symptoms? A prospective, longitudinal analysis. *International Journal of Eating Disorders,* 48(8), 1141–1149. doi:10.1002/eat.22459

Corey, G., Nicholas, L. J., & Bawa, U. (2017). *Theory and practice of counselling and psychotherapy.* Andover, Hampshire: Cengage Learning EMEA.

Cornblatt, B., & Erlenmeyer-Kimling, L. E. (1985). Global attention deviance in children at risk for schizophrenia: Specificity and predictive validity. *Journal of Abnormal Psychology,* 94, 470–486.

Costa e Silva, J. A. (1998). The public health impact of anxiety disorders: A WHO perspective. *Acta Psychiatrica Scandinavica,* 373, 2–5.

Costello, E. J., Pine, D. S., Hammen, C., March, J. S., Plotsky, P. M., Weissman, M. M., … Leckman, J. F. (2002). Development and natural history of mood disorders. *Biological Psychiatry,* 52, 529–542.

Coulacoglou, C., & Saklofske, D. H. (2017). Executive Functoin, Theory of Mind and Adaptive Behavior. In *Psychometrics and Psychological Assessment.* Amsterdam: Elsevier.

Council of Europe. (2015). *Human rights and intersex people.* Retrieved from https://book.coe.int/eur/en/commissioner-for-human-rights/6683-pdf-human-rightsand-intersex-people.html

Cranco, R., & Lehman, H. E. (2000). Schizophrenia: Clinical features. In B. J. Sadock & V. A. Sadock (Eds), *Kaplan & Sadock's comprehensive textbook of psychiatry* (Vol. 7). Philadelphia, PA: Williams & Wilkins, 1663–1676.

Crosson, B., & Warren, R. L. (1982). Use of the Luria–Nebraska Neuropsychological Battery in aphasia: A conceptual critique. *Journal of Consulting and Clinical Psychology*, 50, 22–31.

Crossroads Recovery Centre. (2019). *Cocaine addiction*. Retrieved from http://crossroadsrecovery.co.za/types-of-addiction/drug-addiction/cocaine-addiction/

Crow, T. J. (1985). The two-syndrome concept: Origins and current status. *Schizophrenia Bulletin*, 11, 471–486.

Csikszentmihalyi, M. (1990). *Flow: The psychology of optimal experience*. New York, NY: Harper & Row.

Culbert, K. M., Racine, S. E., & Klump, K. L. (2015). Research review: What we have learned about the causes of eating disorders – a synthesis of sociocultural, psychological, and biological research. *Journal of Child Psychology and Psychiatry*, 56(11), 1141–1164. doi:10.1111/jcpp.12441

Cunnien, A. J. (1997). Psychiatric and medical syndromes associated with deception. In R. Rogers (Ed.), *Clinical assessment of malingering and deception*. New York, NY: Guilford, 23–46.

Dahl, A. A. (1993). The personality disorders: A critical review of family, twin, and adoption studies. *Journal of Personality Disorders*, Suppl. 1, 86–99.

Dahlgren, C. L., Wisting, L., & Rø, Ø. (2017). Feeding and eating disorders in the DSM-5 era: A systematic review of prevalence rates in non-clinical male and female samples. *Journal of Eating Disorders*, 5(1), 56–66. doi:10.1186/s40337-017-0186-7

Damiano, S. R., Paxton, S. J., Wertheim, E. H., McLean, S. A., & Gregg, K. J. (2015). Dietary restraint of 5-year-old girls: Associations with internalization of the thin ideal and maternal, media, and peer influences. *International Journal of Eating Disorders*, 48(8), 1166–1169. doi.org/10.1002/eat.22432

Dana, R. H. (2000). *Handbook of cross-cultural personality assessment*. Mahwah, NJ: Lawrence Erlbaum Associates.

Dangaremba, T. (1991). *Nervous conditions*. London: The Women's Press.

Danner, U. N., Sternheim, L., & Evers, C. (2014). The importance of distinguishing between the different eating disorders (sub) types when assessing emotion regulation strategies. *Psychiatry Research*, 215(3), 727–732. doi:10.1016/j.psychres.2014.01.005

Daubenton, F., & Van Rensburg, P. (2001). Schizophrenia and other psychotic disorders. In B. Robertson, C. W. Allwood, & C. Gagiano (Eds), *Textbook of psychiatry for Southern Africa*. Cape Town: Oxford University Press, 92–110.

Davidson, L. L., & Heinrichs, R. W. (2003). Quantification of frontal and temporal lobe brain imaging findings in Schizophrenia: A meta-analysis. *Psychiatry Research*, 122(2), 69–87.

Davidson, M., Keefe, R. S. E., Mohs, R. C., Siever, L. J., Losonczy, M. E, Horvath, T. B., & Davis, K. L. (1987). L-Dopa challenge and relapse in Schizophrenia. *American Journal of Psychiatry*, 144, 934–938.

Davis, C. (1996). The interdependence of obsessive-compulsiveness, physical activity, and starvation: A model for anorexia nervosa. In W. F. Epling & W. D. Pierce (Eds), *Activity nervosa: Theory, research, and treatment*. Mahwah, NJ: Erlbaum, 209–218.

Davis, K. L., Kahn, R. S., Ko, G., & Davidson, M. (1991). Dopamine and schizophrenia: A review and reconceptualization. *American Journal of Psychiatry*, 148, 1474–1486.

Deep, A. L., Lilenfeld, L. R., Plotnicov, K. H., Pollice, C., & Kaye, W. H. (1999). Sexual abuse in eating disorder subtypes and control women: The role of comorbid substance dependence in bulimia nervosa. *International Journal of Eating Disorders*, 25(1), 1–10.

De Haan, S., Rietveld, E., Stokhof, M., & Denys, D. (2013). The phenomenology of Deep Brain Stimulation-induced changes in OCD: An enactive affordance-based model. *Frontiers in Human Neuroscience*, 7(653), 1–14.

DeGrandpre, R. (2006). *The cult of pharmacology: How America became the world's most troubled drug culture*. Durham, NC: Duke University Press.

De Lange, C. (2013, May 5). Sherry Turkle: 'We're losing the raw human part of being with each other'. *The Guardian*. Retrieved from https://www.theguardian.com/science/2013/may/05/rational-heroes-sherry-turkle-mit

De la Rey, C., & Eagle, G. (1997). Gender and mental health policy development. In D. Foster, M. Freeman, & Y. Pillay (Eds), *Mental health policy issues for South Africa*. Cape Town: MASA Multimedia, 143–165.

De Leon, J., Diaz, F. J., Rogers, T., Browne, D., & Dinsmore, L. (2002). Initiation of daily smoking and nicotine dependence in Schizophrenia and mood disorders. *Schizophrenia Research*, 56(1), 47–54.

Dell'Osso, L., Shear, M. K., Carmassi, C., Rucci, P., Maser, J. D., Frank, E., … Cassano, G. B. (2008). Validity and reliability of the Structured Clinical Interview for the Trauma and Loss Spectrum (SCI-TALS). *Clinical Practice & Epidemiology in Mental Health*, 4, 2.

Delphi Health Group. (2019). *Cocaine and its influence on a person's sex drive*. Retrieved from https://addictionresource.com/drugs/cocaine-and-crack/cocaine-and-sex/

Delport, I., & Szabo, C. P. (2008). Eating disorders in South Africa: An inter-ethnic comparison of admission data. *SAMJ: South African Medical Journal*, 98(4), 272–274. Retrieved from https://hdl.handle.net/10520/EJC69229

DementiaTalk. (2017, July 12). *History of dementia – when did it all start?* Retrieved April 3, 2019, from http://dementiatalk.net/history-of-dementia-when-did-it-all-start/

De Shazer, S., & Berg, I. K. (1997). What works? Remarks on research aspects of solution-focused brief therapy. *Journal of Family Therapy*, 19, 121–124.

Dewan, M. C., Rattani, A., Gupta, S., Baticulon, R. E., Hung, Y.-C., Punchak, M., … Park, K. B. (2018). Estimating the global incidence of traumatic brain injury. *Journal of Neurosurgery*, 27, 1–18 doi:10.3171/2017.10.JNS17352

Diener, E. (2000). Subjective well-being: The science of happiness and a proposal for a national index. *American Psychologist*, 55, 34–44.

Diener, E., & Biswas-Diener, R. (2008). *Happinesss: Unlocking the mysteries of psychological wealth*. Malden, MA: Blackwell Publishing.

Di Nuovo, S., & Castellano, S. (2016). Validity indices of the Rorschach test and Personality Assessment Inventory; a comparison in pathological and healthy subjects. *Mediterranean Journal of Clinical Psychology*, 4(2).

Dirks, B. (2001). Eating disorders. In B. Robertson, C. W. Allwood, & C. Gagiano (Eds), *Textbook of Psychiatry for Southern Africa*. Cape Town: Oxford University Press.

Dishion, T. J., & Patterson, G. R. (1997). The timing and severity of antisocial behavior: Three hypotheses within an ecological framework. In D. M. Stoff, J. Breiling, & J. D. Maser (Eds), *Handbook of Antisocial Personality Disorder*. New York, NY: Wiley, 205–217.

Doer, P., Fichter, M., Pirke, K. M., & Lund, R. (1980). Relationship between weight gain and hypothalamic–pituitary–adrenal function in patients with anorexia nervosa. *Journal of Steroid Biochemistry*, 13, 529–537.

Dolan, M., & Doyle, M., (2000). Violence risk prediction: Clinical and actuarial measures and the role of the Psychopathy Checklist. *British Journal of Psychiatry*, 177(4), 303–311.

Donald, D., Lazarus, S., & Lolwana, P. (1997). *Educational psychology in social context: Challenges of development, social issues and special need in southern Africa*. Cape Town: Oxford University Press.

Dorard, G., & Khorramian-Pour, M. (2017). Binge eating disorder: Links with personality and emotionality. *L'Encephale*, 43(2), 114–119. doi:10.1016/j.encep.2016.05.005

Drake, R. E., Mueser, K. T., & Brunette, M. F. (2007). Management of persons with co-occurring severe mental illness and substance use disorder: Program implications. *World Psychiatry*, 6(3), 131–136.

Dreger, A. D. (2006). Intersex and human rights: The long view. In S. Sytsma (Ed.), *Ethics and intersex*. New York, NY: Springer, 73–86.

Drug Policy Alliance. (2019). *What is heroin and what does it feel like?* Retrieved from http://www.drugpolicy.org/drug-facts/what-is-heroin

Duarte, C., Pinto-Gouveia, J., & Ferreira, C. (2017). Ashamed and fused with body image and eating: Binge eating as an avoidance strategy. *Clinical Psychology & Psychotherapy*, 24(1), 195–202. doi:10.1002/cpp.1996

Duffy, A. (2015). Early identification of recurrent mood disorders in youth: The importance of a developmental approach. *Evidence-Based Mental Health*, 18(1), 7–9.

Dulloo, A. G., & Montani, J. P. (2015). Pathways from dieting to weight regain, to obesity and to the metabolic syndrome: An overview. *Obesity Reviews*, 16, 1–6. doi:10.1111/obr.12250

Du Plessis, L. (2003). *An investigation into models for the assessment of malingering in criminal forensic evaluations: A focus on malingering of mental illness* (Unpublished Master of Arts dissertation). University of South Africa, Pretoria, South Africa.

Du Preez, M. (2018, August 25). History of dagga in SA shows its decriminalisation is overdue. *News 24*. Retrieved from https://www.news24.com/Columnists/MaxduPreez/history-of-dagga-in-sa-shows-its-decriminalisation-is-overdue-20180925

Du Toit, M. M., Wissing, M. P., & Khumalo, I. P (2014). Positive relationships. In M. P. Wissing (Ed.), *Towards flourishing: Contextualising positive psychology*. Pretoria: Van Schaik.

Dutton, J. (2018, July 8). Why psychedelics could be the new class of antidepressant. *The Independent UK*. Retrieved July 28, 2018, from https://www.independent.co.uk/news/long_reads/psychedelic-drugs-new-class-antidepressant-albert-hofmann-lsd-a8437201.html

Dvir, Y., Ford, J. D., Hill, M., & Frazier, J. A. (2014). Childhood maltreatment, emotional dysregulation, and psychiatric comorbidities. *Harvard Review of Psychiatry*, 22(3), 149–161. doi:10.1097/HRP.0000000000000014

Dvorak, J. C. (2015, December 2). *Smartphone addiciton is a plague*. Retrieved from https://www.pcmag.com/commentary/340014/smartphone-addiction-is-a-plague

Dwork, A. J. (1997). Postmortem studies of the hippocampal formation in Schizophrenia. *Schizophrenia Bulletin*, 23, 385–402.

Dworkin, R. H., Lenzenwenger, M. F., & Moldin, S. O. (1987). Genetics and the phenomenology of schizophrenia. In P. D. Harvey & E. F. Walker (Eds), *Positive and negative symptoms of psychosis*. Hillsdale, NJ: Erlbaum, 258–288.

Dworkin, S. F., & Wilson, L. (1993). Somatoform Pain Disorder and its treatment. In D. D. Dunner (Ed.), *Current psychiatric therapy*. Philadelphia, PA: W. B. Saunders Company, 321–237.

Dwyer, J., & Reid, R. (2004). Ganser's Syndrome. *The Lancet*, 364(9432), 471–473.

Dykens, E. M., & Gerrard, M. (1986). Psychological profiles of purging bulimics, repeat dieters and controls. *Journal of Consulting and Clinical Psychology*, 54(3), 283–288. doi: 10.1027/0022-006X.54.3.283

Eagles, J. M. (1991).The relationship between Schizophrenia and immigration. Are there alternatives to psychosocial hypothesis? *The British Journal of Psychiatry*, 159, 783–789.

Eabon, M. F., & Abrahamson, D. (2019). Understanding psychological testing and assessment. Retrieved from American Psychological Association: https://www.apa.org/helpcenter/assessment

Eaton, W. W., Bienvenu, O. J., & Miloyan, B. (2018). Specific phobias. *Lancet Psychiatry*, 5(8), 678–686.

Ebata, A. T., Peterson, A. C., & Conger, J. J. (1990). The development of psychopathology in adolescence. In J. Rolf, A. S. Masten, D. Cicchetti, K. H. Nuechterlein, & S. Weintraub (Eds), *Risk and protective factors in the development of psychopathology*. Cambridge, UK: Cambridge University Press, 308–333.

Ebert, A., & Bär, K-J. (2010). Emil Kraepelin: A pioneer of scientific understanding of psychiatry and psychopharmacology. *Indian Journal of Psychiatry*, 52(2), 191–192. doi:10.4103/0019-5545.64591

Edwards, S.D. (1998). The Zululand community psychology story. South Africa beyond transition: Psychological well-being. Proceedings of the Third Annual Congress of the Psychological Society of South Africa (pp. 79–81). Johannesburg: Psychological Society of South Africa.

Edwards, S. D. (2010). A Rogerian perspective on empathic patterns in Southern African Healing. *Journal of Psychology in Africa*, 20(2), 321–326.

Egan, A. (2008). Should the state support the 'right to die'? *South African Journal of Bioethics and Law*, 1(2), 47–52.

Eggers, C., & Bunk, D. (1997). The long-term course of childhood onset Schizophrenia: A 42-year follow up. *Schizophrenia Bulletin*, 23, 105–116.

Eisenberg, L. (1995). The social construction of the human brain. *American Journal of Psychiatry*, 152, 1563–1575.

Eisenberg, L. A. (1959). A clinical study of Gilles de la Tourette's Disease (Maladie des Tics) in children. *American Journal of Psychiatry*, 115, 715–723.

Eisenberg, N., & Ota Wang, V. (2003). Toward a positive psychology: Social development and cultural contributions. In L. G. Aspinwall & U. M. Staudinger (Eds), *A psychology of human strengths. Fundamental questions and future directions for a positive psychology*. Washington, DC: American Psychological Association, 117–129.

Ekman, P. (1993). Facial expression and emotion. *American Psychologist*, 48, 384–392.

Elhai, J. D., Carvalho, L. F., Miguel, F. K., Palmieri, P. A., Primi, R., & Frueh, B. C. (2011). Testing whether Posttraumatic Stress Disorder and Major Depressive Disorder are similar or unique constructs. *Journal of Anxiety Disorders*, 25(3), 404–410.

Eliason, M. J. (1996). *Who cares? Institutional barriers to health care for lesbian, gay, and bisexual people*. New York: National League for Nursing Press.

Ellis, A. (1995). Changing rational-emotive therapy (RET) to rational emotive behavior therapy (REBT). *Journal of Rational-Emotive and Cognitive-Behavior Therapy*, 13, 85–89.

Ellis, A. (2004). How my theory and practice of psychotherapy has influenced and changed other psychotherapies. *Journal of Rational-Emotive and Cognitive-Behavior Therapy*, 22(2), 79–83.

Ellison, J. M. (n.d.). *The history of Alzheimer's Disease*. Retrieved April 3, 2019, from https://www.brightfocus.org/alzheimers/article/history-alzheimers-disease

Elneil, S. (2016). Female sexual dysfunction in female genital mutilation. *Tropical Doctor*, 46(1), 2–11. doi:10.1177/0049475515621644

Eloff, I., Achoui, M., Chireshe, R., Mutepfa, M., & Ofovwe, C. (2008). Views from Africa on Positive Psychology. *Journal of Psychology in Africa*, 18(1), 189–194. doi:10.1080/14330237.2008.10820185

Emsley, R. A., Niehaus, D. J. H., Mbanga, N. I., Oosthuizen, P. P., Stein, D. J., … Mallet, J. (2001). The factor structure for positive and negative symptoms in South African Xhosa patients with Schizophrenia. *Schizophrenia Research*, 47, 149–157.

England, M. J., & Sim, L. J. (2009). *Depression in parents, parenting, and children: Opportunties to improve identification, treatment, and prevention.* Washington, DC: National Academies Press.

Ensink, K. R. (1996). Indigenous categories of distress and dysfunction in South African Xhosa children and adolescents as described by indigenous healers. *Transcultural Psychiatry*, 33(2), 137–172.

Ensink, K. R. & Robertson, B. (1999). Patient and family experiences of psychiatric services and African indigenous healers. *Transcultural Psychiatry*, 36(1), 23–43.

Ephrahim, A. (2014, July 4). Nyaope's deadly, and addictive, mix. *Mail & Guardian*. Retrieved from https:// mg.co.za/article/2014-07-03-hook-line-and-sinker-thats-nyaope

Erickson, M. T. (1998). *Behaviour disorders of children and adolescents: Assessment, etiology and intervention.* Upper Saddle River, NJ: Prentice Hall.

Escobar, J. (2004). Transcultural aspects of dissociative and somatoform disorders. *Psychiatric Times*, 21(5). Retrieved from https://www.psychiatrictimes.com/transcultural-aspects-dissociative-and-somatoform-disorders

Escobar, J. I., Gara, M., Silver, R. C., Waitzkin, H., Holman, A., & Compton, W. (1998). Somatisation disorder in primary care. *British Journal of Psychiatry*, 173, 262–266.

Esplen, E. & Jolly, S. (2006). *Gender and sex: A sample of definitions.* Brighton: Bridge Development – Gender.

Estell, D. B., Farmer, T. W., Pearl, R., Van Acker, R., & Rodkin, P. C. (2003). Heterogeneity in the relationship between popularity and aggression: Individual, group, and classroom influences. *New Directions for Child and Adolescent Development*, 101, 75–85.

Evans, C., & Street, E. (1995). Possible differences in family patterns in anorexia nervosa and bulimia nervosa. *Journal of Family Therapy*, 17, 115–131.

Evans, J. (2017, March 31). Dagga can be used in the home, Western Cape High Court rules. *News24*. Retrieved from https://www.news24.com/SouthAfrica/News/dagga-can-be-used-in-the-home-western-cape-high-court-rules-20170331

Everill, J. T., & Waller, G. (1995). Reported sexual abuse and eating psychopathology: A review of the evidence for a causal link. *International Journal of Eating Disorders*, 18, 1–11.

Exner, J. E. (2002). *The Rorschach: Basic foundations and principles of interpretation.* Hoboken, NJ: Wiley.

Fairburn, C. G. (1997). Eating disorders. In D. M. Clark & C.G. Fairburn (Eds), *The science and practice of cognitive behaviour therapy.* Oxford: Oxford University Press, 209–241.

Fairburn, C. G., Agras, W. S., & Wilson, G. T. (1992). The research on the treatment of bulimia nervosa: Practical and theoretical implications. In G. H. Anderson & S. H. Kennedy (Eds), *The biology of fast and famine: Relevance to eating disorders.* New York, NY: Academic Press, 317–340.

Fairburn, C. G., Shafran, R., & Cooper, Z. (1999). A cognitive behavioural theory of anorexia nervosa. *Behaviour Research and Therapy*, 37, 1–13.

Fajewonyomi, B. A., Orji, E. O., & Adeyemo, A. O. (2007). Sexual dysfunction among female patients of reproductive age in a hospital setting in Nigeria. *Journal of Health, Population and Nutrition*, 25(1), 101–106.

Famuyiwa, O. O. (1988). Anorexia nervosa in two Nigerians. *Acta Psychiatrica Scandinavica*, 78(5), 550–554.

Fanon, F. (1967a). *Toward the African revolution.* New York, NY: Grove Press.

Fanon, F. (1967b). *Black skin, white masks.* London: Pluto Press

Fardouly, J., & Vartanian, L. R. (2015). Negative comparisons about one's appearance mediate the relationship between Facebook usage and body image concerns. *Body Image*, 12, 82–88. doi:10.1016/j.bodyim.2014.10.004

Fardouly, J., & Vartanian, L. R. (2016). Social media and body image concerns: Current research and future directions. *Current Opinion in Psychology*, 9, 1–5. doi:10.1016/j.copsyc.2015.09.005

Farstad, S. M., McGeown, L. M., & Von Ranson, K. M. (2016). Eating disorders and personality, 2004–2016: A systematic review and meta-analysis. *Clinical Psychology Review*, 46, 91–105. doi:10.1016/j.cpr.2016.04.005

Fava, G. A. (1992). Morselli's legacy: Dysmorphophobia. *Psychotherapy and Psychosomatics*, 58, 117–118.

Fava, M., & Kendler, K. S. (2000). Major depressive disorder. *Neuron*, 28, 335–341.

Fazel, S., Gulati, G., Linsell, L., Geddes, J. R., & Grann, M. (2009). Schizophrenia and violence: Systematic review and meta-analysis. *PLoS Medicine*, 6(8), e1000120–e1000135. doi:10.1371/journal.pmed.1000120

Feighner, J. P., Robins, E., Guze, S. B., Woodruff, R. A., Winokur, G., & Munoz, R. (1972). Diagnostic criteria for use in psychiatric research. *Archives of General Psychiatry*, 26, 57–63.

Ferracuti, S. S. (1996). Dissociative Trance Disorder: Clinical and Rorschach findings in ten persons reporting demon possession and treated by exorcism. *Journal of Personality Assessment*, 66, 525–539.

Fichter, M. M., & Naegel, R. (1990). Concordance for bulimia nervosa in twins. *International Journal of Eating Disorders*, 9, 425–436.

Fichter, M. M., & Quadflieg, N. (1997). Six-year course of bulimia nervosa. *International Journal of Eating Disorders*, 22(4), 361–384.

Fichter, M. M. & Quadflieg, N. (1999) Six-year course and outcome of Anorexia Nervosa. *International Journal of Eating Disorders*, 26(4), 359–385.

Fichter, M. M., Quadflieg, N., & Gnutzmann, A. (1998). Binge eating disorder: Treatment outcome over a 6-year course. *Journal of Psychosomatic Research*, 44(3–4), 385–405. doi:10.1016/S0022-3999(97)00263-8

Fikkan, J. L., & Rothblum, E. D. (2012). Is fat a feminist issue? Exploring the gendered nature of weight bias. *Sex Roles*, 66(9–10), 575–592. doi:10.1007/s11199-011-002205

Filatova, S., Koivumaa-Honkanen, H., Hirvonen, N., Freeman, A., Ivandic, I., Hurtig, T., … Miettunen, J. (2017). Early motor developmental milestones and schizophrenia: a systematic review and meta-analysis. *Schizophrenia Research*, 188, 13–20. doi:10.1016/j.schres.2017.01.029

Flensborg-Madsen, T., Tolstrup, J., Sørensen, H. J., & Mortensen, E. L. (2012). Social and psychological predictors of onset of anxiety disorders: Results from a large prospective cohort study. *Social Psychiatry and Psychiatric Epidemiology*, 47, 711–721.

Flint, J., & Kendler, K. S. (2014). The genetics of major depression. *Neuron*, 81(3), 484–503. doi:10.1016/j.neuron.2014.01.027.

Folstein, M. F., Folstein, S. E., & McHugh, P. R. (1975). 'Mini-mental state'. A practical method for grading the cognitive state of patients for the clinician. *Journal of Psychiatric Research*, 12(3), 189–198.

Fontenelle, L. F., & Grant, J. E. (2014). Hoarding disorder: A new diagnostic category in ICD-11? *Brazilian Journal of Psychiatry*, 36(Suppl), 28–39.

Ford, C. V. (1985). Conversion Disorders: An overview. *Psychosomatics*, 26, 371–385.

Forgus, R. H., & DeWolfe, A. S. (1974). Coding of cognitive input in delusional patients. *Journal of Abnormal Psychology*, 83, 278–284.

Foster, D. (1993). On racism: Virulent mythologies and fragile threads. In L. Nicholas (Ed.), *Psychology and oppression: Critiques and proposals*. Johannesburg: Skotaville, pp. 55–80

Foster, D., Freeman, M., & Pillay, Y. (1997). *Mental health policy issues for South Africa*. Pinelands, Cape Town: Medical Association of South Africa.

Foulks, E. F. (1996). Culture and personality disorders. In J. E. Mezzich, A. Kleinman, H. Fabrega, Jr., & D. L. Parron (Eds), *Culture and psychiatric diagnosis: A DSM-IV perspective*. Washington, DC: American Psychiatric Press, 243–252.

Fowler, J. S., Volkow, N. D., Kassed, C. A., & Chang, L. (2007). Imaging the addicted human brain. *NIDA Science & Practice Perspectives*, 3(2), 4–15.

Francoeur, R. T. (Ed.) (2001). *The international encyclopedia of sexuality*. New York, NY: Continuum Publishing Company. Retrieved November 24, 2006, from http:// www2.hu-berlin.de/sexology/IES/index.html.

Frankl, V. E. (1959). *The will to meaning: Foundations and applications of logotherapy*. New York, NY: World Publishing House.

Frankl, V. E. (1976). *Man's search for meaning. An introduction to Logotherapy* (3rd ed.). New York, NY: Pocket.

Frederick, D. A., Daniels, E. A., Bates, M. E., & Tylka, T. L. (2017). Exposure to thin-ideal, media affect most, but not all, women: Results from the Perceived Effects of Media Exposure Scale and open-ended responses. *Body Image*, 23, 188–205. doi.org/10.1016/j.bodyim.2017.10.006

Fredrickson, B. L. (2013). Positive Emotions Broaden and Build. *Advances in Experimental Social Psychology*, 47, 1–53.

Frederiksen, N. (1986). Toward a broader conception of human intelligence. *American Psychologist*, 41(4), 445–452.

Freeman, A. C. (2005). Eating disorders in males: A review. *South African Psychiatry Review*, 8, 58–64.

Freeman, A. & Reinecke, M. A. (Eds). (2007). *Personality disorders in childhood and adolescence*. Hoboken, NJ: John Wiley & Sons.

Freeman, M. (1992). *Providing mental health care for all in South Africa – structure and strategy*. Johannesburg: Centre for Health Policy.

Fried, A. (2004). Depression in adolescence. *Encyclopedia of applied developmental science*. Sage Publications. Retrieved March 20, 2009, from http://www.sage–ereference.com/applied devscience/Article_n15.html

Fritson, K. K. (2007). Autism. 21st century psychology: A reference handbook. *Encyclopedia of counseling*. Retrieved March 20, 2009, from http://www.sage–ereference.com/psychology/Article_n57.html

Fritz, G., Rockney, R., Bernet, W., Arnold, V., Beitchman, J., Benson, R. S., ... & Academy of Child and Adolescent Psychiatry. (2004). Practice parameter for the assessment and treatment of children and adolescents with enuresis. *American Academy of Child and Adolescent Psychiatry*, 43(12), 1540–1550.

Fromm-Reichmann, F. (1948). Notes on the development of treatment of schizophrenics by psychoanalytic psychotherapy. *Psychiatry*, 11, 263–273.

Frude, N. (1998). *Understanding abnormal psychology*. Oxford: Blackwell.

Frydenburg, E. (1997). *Adolescent coping: Theoretical and research perspectives*. London: Routledge.

Frydenburg, E. (2008). *Adolescent coping: Advances in theory, research and practice*. London: Routledge.

Furnham, A., & Baguma, P. (1994). Cross-cultural differences in the evaluation of male and female body shapes. *International Journal of Eating Disorders*, 15, 81–89.

Fusar-Poli, P., Tantardini, M., De Simone, S., Ramella-Cravaro, V., Oliver, D., Kingdon, J., ... Galderisi, S. (2017). Deconstructing vulnerability for psychosis: Meta-analysis of environmental risk factors for psychosis in subjects at ultra high-risk. *European Psychiatry*, 40, 65–75. doi:10.1016/j.eurpsy.2016.09.003

Gaebel, W., & Zielasek, J. (2015). Focus on psychosis. *Dialogues in Clinical Neuroscience*, 17(1), 9–18. Retrieved from https://www.ncbi.nlm.nih.gov/pmc/articles/PMC4421906/

Gallagher III, B. J., Jones, B. J., & Pardes, M. (2016). Stressful life events, social class and symptoms of schizophrenia. *Clinical Schizophrenia & Related Psychoses*, 10(2), 101–108. doi: oi.org/10.3371/1935-1232-10.

Ganasen, K. A., Finchama, D., Smit, J., Seedat, S., & Stein, D. (2007). Utility of the HIV Dementia Scale (HDS) in identifying HIV dementia in a South African sample. *Journal of the Neurological Sciences*, 269(1–2), 62–64.

Garety, P. (1991). Reasoning and delusions. *British Journal of Psychiatry*, 159, 14–18.

Garner, D. M. (1997). The body image survey. *Psychology Today*, 30, 30–45. Retrieved from https://www.psychologytoday.com/us/articles/199702/body-image-in-america-survey-results

Garner, D. M., Vitousek, K. M., & Pike, K. M. (1997). Cognitive-behavioral therapy for anorexia nervosa. In D. M. Garner & P. E. Garfinkel (Eds), *Handbook of treatment for eating disorders*. New York, NY: Guilford Press, 94–144.

Gates, G. J. (2011). *How many people are lesbian, gay, bisexual and transgender?* Los Angeles, CA: The Williams Institute, UCLA School of Law.

GenderdynamiX. (n.d.). Retrieved March 6, 2012, from http://www.genderdynamix.org.za

Genetic Science Learning Center, University of Utah. (2013, August 30). *Genes and addiction*. Retrieved July 28, 2018, from https://learn.genetics.utah.edu/content/addiction/

George, A. A. (2009). *Risk and resilience in adolescent suicidal ideation* (Unpublished doctoral dissertation). University of the Free State, Bloemfontein, South Africa.

Gibson, K., & Swartz, L. (2008). Putting the 'heart' into community psychology: Some South African examples. *Psychodynamic Practice*, 14(1), 59–75.

Gibson, L. E., Alloy, L. B., & Ellman, L. M. (2016). Trauma and the psychosis spectrum: A review of symptom specificity and explanatory mechanisms. *Clinical Psychology Review*, 49, 92–105. doi:10.1016/j.cpr.2016.08.003

Gibson, N. C., & Beneduce, R. (2017). *Frantz Fanon, psychiatry and politics*. London: Rowman & Littlefield.

Ging, D., & Garvey, S. (2018). 'Written in these scars are the stories I can't explain': A content analysis of pro-ana and thinspiration image sharing on Instagram. *New Media & Society*, 20(3), 1181–2000. doi:10.1177/1461444816687288

Gitau, T. M., Micklesfield, L. K., Pettifor, J. M., & Norris, S. A. (2014). Ethnic differences in eating attitudes, body image and self-esteem among adolescent females living in urban South Africa. *Journal of Psychiatry*, 17(1), 468–474. doi:10.4172/Psychiatry.1000101

Glasser, W. (1984). *Control theory*. New York, NY: Harper & Row.

Gobodo-Madikizela, P., & Foster, D. (2005). Psychology and human rights abuses. In C. Tredoux, D. Foster, A. Allan, A. Cohen, & D. Wassenaar (Eds), *Psychology and law*. Pretoria: Juta Legal and Academic Publishers, 343–383.

Godow, A. (1982). *Human sexuality*. St Louis, IL: Mosby.

Goedecke, J. H., Jennings, C. L., & Lambert, E. V. (2006). Obesity in South Africa. In K. Steyn, J. Fourie, & N. Temple (Eds), *Chronic diseases of lifestyle in South Africa: 1995–2005*. Cape Town: South African Medical Research Council, 65–79.

Goff, D. C., Cather, C., Evins, A. E., Henderson, D. C., Freudenreich, O., Copeland, P. M., Bierer, M., Duckworth, K., & Sacks, F. M. (2005). Medical morbidity and mortality in Schizophrenia. Guidelines for psychiatrists. *Journal of Clinical Psychiatry*, 66(2), 183–194.

Golden, C. J., Purisch, A. D., & Hammeke, T. A. (1985). *Luria-Nebraska Neuropsychological Battery: Forms I & II*. Los Angeles, CA: Western Psychological Services.

Goldfried, M. R. (2001). Integrating gay, lesbian, and bisexual issues into mainstream psychology. *American Psychologist*, 56, 975–988.

Goldsmith, S. K., Shapiro, R. N., & Joyce, J. N. (1997). Disrupted pattern of D2 dopamine receptors in the temporal lobe in Schizophrenia. A postmortem study. *Archives of General Psychiatry*, 54, 649–658.

Goldstein, S. B. (2000). *Cross-cultural explorations: Activities in culture and psychology*. Boston, MA: Allyn & Bacon.

Golub, D. (1995). Cultural variations in multiple personality disorder. In L. Cohen, J. Berzoff, & M. Elin (Eds), *Dissociative Identity Disorder*. Northvale, NJ: Jason Aronson, 285–326.

Gonchar, M. (2017, October 14). Does technology make us more alone? *New York Times*. Retrieved from https://www.nytimes.com/2016/10/14/learning/does-technology-make-us-more-alone.html

Gone, J. P. (2011). Is psychological science a-cultural? *Cultural Diversity and Ethnic Minority Psychology*, 17(3), 234–242.

Gonsiorek, J. C. (1988). Mental health issues of gay and lesbian adolescents. *Journal of Adolescent Health Care*, 9, 114–122.

Gonsiorek, J. C., & Weinrich, J. D. (1991). *Homosexuality: Research implications for public policy*. Newbury Park, CA: Sage Publications.

Goodsitt, A. (1997). Eating disorders: A self-psychological perspective. In D. M. Garner & P. E. Garfinkel (Eds), *Handbook of treatment for eating disorders*. New York, NY: Guilford Press, 205–228.

Goodwach, R. (2005). Sex therapy: Historical evolution, current practice. Part 1. *Anzjft*, 26(3), 155–164.

Gottesman, I. I. (1991). *Schizophrenia genesis*. New York, NY: W. H. Freeman & Co.

Gould, S. J. (1981). *The mismeasure of man*. New York, NY: W. W. Norton.

Grabe, H. R. (2000). The relationship between dimensions of alexithymia and dissociation. *Psychotherapy and Psychosomatics*, 69, 128–131.

Grant, J. E., & Chamberlain, S. R. (2016). Trichotillomania. *American Journal of Psychiatry*, 173(9), 868–874.

Grant, J. E., Potenza, M. N., Weinstein, A., & Gorelick, D. A. (2010). Introduction to behavioural addictions. *American Journal of Drug and Alcohol Abuse*, 36(5), 233–241.

Greeff, A. P. (2012). Aspects of family resilience in various groups of South African families. In M. P. Wissing (Ed.), *Well-being research in South Africa*. Dordrecht: Springer, 273–291.

Green, C., & Chee, K. (1997). *Understanding ADHD* (2nd ed.). London: Vermilion.

Green, H. (2018). Why does the diagnosis of schizophrenia persist? *Philosophy, Psychiatry, & Psychology*, 25(3), 197–207. doi:10.1353/ppp.2018.0029

Greene, R. W., & Ollendick, T. H. (2000). Behavioral assessment of children. In G. Goldstein & M. Hersen (Eds), *Handbook of psychological assessment* (3rd ed.). Oxford: Elsevier Science (Pergamon), 453–470.

Groleau, P., Steiger, H., Bruce, K., Israel, M., Sycz, L., Ouellette, A. S., & Badawi, G. (2012). Childhood emotional abuse and eating symptoms in bulimic disorders: An examination of possible mediating variables. *International Journal of Eating Disorders*, 45(3), 326–332. doi:10.1002/eat.20939

Gross, J. J., & Jazaieri, H. (2014). Emotion, emotion regulation, and psychopathology: An affective science perspective. *Clinical Psychological Science*, 2(4), 387–401. doi:10.1177/2167702614536164

Gross, R. (2010). *Psychology: The science of mind and behaviour* (6th ed). London: Hodder Education.

Groth-Marnat, G. (1999). *Handbook of psychological assessment* (3rd ed. Revised). New York, NY: John Wiley & Sons.

Groth-Marnat, G., & Jordan Wright, A. (2016). *Handbook of psychological assessment* (6th ed.). Hoboken, NJ: Wiley.

Grupe, D. W., & Nitschke, J. B. (2013). Uncertainty and anticipation in anxiety: An integrated neurobiological and psychological perspective. *Nature Reviews Neuroscience*, 14, 488–501.

Guarnaccia, P. J., Martinez, I., Ramirez, R., & Canino, G. (2005). Are *ataques de nervios* in Puerto Rican children associated with psychiatric disorder? *Journal of the American Academy of Child and Adolescent Psychiatry*, 44, 1184–1192.

Guerdjikova, A. I., Mori, N., Casuto, L. S., & McElroy, S. L. (2017). Binge eating disorder. *Psychiatric Clinics*, 40(2), 255–266. doi:10.1016/j.psc.2017.01.003

Guerdjikova, A. I., O'Melia, A. M., Mori, N., McCoy, J., & McElroy, S. L. (2012). Binge eating disorder in elderly individuals. *International Journal of Eating Disorders*, 45(7), 905–908. doi:10.1002/eat.22028

Guloksuz, S., & Van Os, J. (2018). The slow death of the concept of schizophrenia and the painful birth of the psychosis spectrum. *Psychological Medicine*, 48(2), 229–244. doi:10.1017/S0033291717001775

Gumbiner, J. (2010). *What causes addiction? Psychoanalytic theories of addiction.* Retrieved March 20, 2011, from http://www.psychologytoday.com

Gunderson, J. G. (2009). Borderline personality disorder: Ontogeny of a diagnosis. *American Journal of Psychiatry*, 166(5), 530–539.

Gureje, O., & Reed, M. G. (2016). Bodily distress disorder in ICD-11: Problems and prospects. *World Psychiatry*, 15(3), 291–292.

Gurvits, I. G., Koenigsberg, H. W., & Siever, L. J. (2000). Neurotransmitter dysfunction in patients with borderline personality disorder. *Psychiatric Clinics of North America*, 23, 27–40.

Guterres, A. (2012). Positive lessons from the Arab Spring. *Forced Migration Review*, 39, 3. Retrieved from https://www.fmreview.org/north-africa/guterres

Gutmann, P. (2008). Julius Ludwig August Koch (1841–1908): Christian, philosopher and psychiatrist. *History of Psychiatry*, 19(2), 202–214. doi:10.1177/0957154X07080661

Hales, R. E., Yudofsky, S. C., & Gabbard, G. O. (Eds). (2008). *The American Psychiatric Publishing Textbook of Psychiatry* (5th ed.). Arlington, VA: American Psychiatric Publishing.

Halgin, R. P., & Whitbourne, S. K. (2003). *Abnormal psychology: Clinical perspectives on psychological disorders.* New York, NY: McGraw-Hill.

Hall, G. R. (1994). Caring for people with Alzheimer's disease using the conceptual model of progressively lowered stress threshold in the clinical setting. *The Nursing Clinics of North America*, 29(1), 129–141.

Halmi, K. A. (2000). Eating disorders. In B. J. Sadock & V. A. Sadock (Eds), *Kaplan & Sadock's comprehensive textbook of psychiatry* (7th ed.). Philadelphia, PA: Williams & Wilkins, 1663–1676.

Hammond, W. E., & Richeson, R. L. (2012). Standards development and the future of research data sources, interoperability, and exchange. In R. L. Richeson & J. Andrews (Eds), *Clinical research informatics.* London: Springer, 335–366.

Hanson, C., & Modiba, W. (2017). Overview and management of anxiety disorders. *South African Pharmaceutical Journal*, 84(5), 43–50.

Harper, D. C. (2008). Developmental disorders. *Encyclopedia of counseling.* Retrieved March 20, 2009, from http://www.sage–ereference.com/counseling/Article_n50.html

Harrell, S. P. (2014). A psychoecocultural perspective on positive psychology and well-being. *The California Psychologist*, 47(2), 8–11.

Harrison, A., Sullivan, S., Tchanturia, K., & Treasure, J. (2009). Emotion recognition and regulation in anorexia nervosa. *Clinical Psychology & Psychotherapy: An International Journal of Theory & Practice*, 16(4), 348–356. doi:10.1002/cpp.628

Harrison, G. (1990). Searching for the causes of Schizophrenia: The role of migrant studies. *Schizophrenia Bulletin*, 16(4), 663–671.

Harshbarger, J. L., Ahlers-Schmidt, C. R., Mayans, L., Mayans, D., & Hawkins, J. H. (2009). Pro-anorexia websites: What a clinician should know. *International Journal of Eating Disorders*, 42, 367–370.

Harvey, J. A., & Robinson, J. D. (2003). Eating disorders in men: Current considerations. *Journal of Clinical Psychology in Medical Settings*, 10(4), 297–306.

Hashim, I. H. (2003). Cultural and gender differences in perceptions of stressors and coping skills: A study of Western and African college students in China. *School Psychology International*, 24(2), 182–203.

Haslam, J. (1809/1976). *Observations on madness and melancholy.* New York, NY: Arno Press.

Haugaard, J. J. (2008). *Child Psychopathology.* New York, NY: McGraw-Hill.

Hayes, J. F., Osborn, D. P., Lewis, G., Dalman, C., & Lundin, A. (2017). Association of late adolescent personality with risk for subsequent serious mental illness among men in a Swedish nationwide cohort study. *JAMA Psychiatry*, 74(7), 703–711. doi:10.1001/jamapsychiatry.2017.0583

Haynes, S. N. (2000). Behavioural assessment of adults. In G. Goldstein & M. Hersen (Eds), *Handbook of psychological assessment*. New York, NY: Pergamon Press, 471–502.

Haynos, A. F., & Fruzzetti, A. E. (2011). Anorexia nervosa as a disorder of emotion dysregulation: Evidence and treatment implications. *Clinical Psychology: Science and Practice*, 18(3), 183–202. doi:10.1111/j.1468-2850.2011.01250.x

Haysam, S. (2019). *Hiding in plain sight*. Enhancing Africa's Response to Transnational Organised Crime (ENACT). Retrieved from https://enactafrica.org/research/policy-briefs/hiding-in-plain-sight-heroins-stealthy-takeover-of-south-africa

Health24. (2014, April 11). *Is nyaope South Africa's worst drug?* Retrieved July 29, 2018, from https://www.health24.com/Lifestyle/Street-drugs/News/Street-drug-nyaope-classified-as-illegal-20140403

Health Professions Council of South Africa (HPCSA). (2007). *Guidelines for good practice in the health care professions*. Ethical and professional rules of the health professions council of South Africa as promulgated in Government Gazette r717/2006. (2nd ed.). Booklet 2 (29 May 2007). Pretoria: HPCSA.

Health Professions Council of South Africa (HPCSA). (2017/2018). *Annual Report 2017/2018*. Retrieved April 15, 2019, from https://www.hpcsa.co.za/Uploads/editor/UserFiles/downloads/publications/annual_reports/hpcsa_annual_report_2017_2018.pdf

Health Professions Council of South Africa (HPCSA). (2008). Guidelines for good practice in the health care professions: General ethical guidelines for the health care professions. Pretoria: HPCSA.

Heap, M. R. (1991). The quest for wholeness: Health care strategies among the residents of council-built hostels in Cape Town. *Social Science and Medicine*, 32, 117–126.

Hecker, T., Barnewitz, E., Stenmark, H., & Iversen, V. (2016). Pathological spirit possession as a culural interpretation of trauma-related symptoms. *Psychological Trauma: Theory, Research, Pratice and Policy*, 8(4), 468–476.

Heckers, S. (1997). Neuropathology of schizophrenia: Cortex, basal ganglia, and neurotransmitter-specific projection systems. *Schizophrenia Bulletin*, 23, 403-421.

Hefferon, K., & Boniwell, I. (2011). *Positive psychology: Theory, research and applications*. London: McGraw-Hill.

Hekma, G. (2009). *ABC van perversies*. Amsterdam: J. M. Meulenhoff.

Helm, H. M. (2008). Externalizing problems of childhood. *Encyclopedia of counseling*. Retrieved March 20, 2009, from http://www.sage-ereference.com/counseling/Article_n64.html

Henquet, C., Murray, R., Linszen, D., & Van Os, J. (2005). The environment and Schizophrenia: The role of cannabis use. *Schizophrenia Bulletin*, 31(3), 608–612.

Hepworth, D. H., Rooney, R. R., Dewberry Rooney, G., Strom-Gottfried, K., & Larsen, J. A. (2010). *Direct social work practice: Theory and skills* (8th ed.).Pacific Grove, CA: Brooks/Cole/

Herbert, P. B., & Young, K. A. (2002). Tarasoff at twenty-five. *Journal of the American Academy of Psychiatry and Law*, 30, 275–81.

Herman, A. A., Stein, D. J., Seedat, S., Heerings, S. G., Moomal, H., & Williams, D. R. (2009). The South African stress and health (SASH) study: 12-month and lifetime prevalence of common mental disorders. *South African Medical Journal*, 99(5), 339–344.

Hersen, M., Turner, S. M., & Beidel, D. (2007). *Adult psychopathology and diagnosis* (5th ed.). Hoboken, NJ: John Wiley & Sons.

Hinton, D., Nathan, M., Bird, B., & Park, L. (2002). Panic probes and the identification of panic: A historical and cross-cultural perspective. *Culture, Medicine and Psychiatry*, 26(2), 137–153.

Hirschfeld, R. M. A., & Weissman, M. M. (2002). Risk factors for major depression and bipolar disorder. In K. L. Davis, D. Charney, J. T. Coyle, & C. Nemaroff (Eds), *Neuropsychopharmacology: The fifth generation of progress*. Brentwood, TN: American College of Neuropsychopharmacology, 1017–1025.

Hoebel, B. G., & Teitelbaum, P. (1966). Weight regulation in normal and hypothalamic hyperphagic rats. *Journal of Comparative and Physiological Psychology*, 61, 189–193.

Hoek, H. W. (2017). Epidemiology of eating disorders. In K. D. Brownell & B. T. Walsh (Eds), *Eating disorders and obesity: A comprehensive handbook* (3rd ed.). New York, NY: Guilford, 237–242.

Hofmann, A. (1980). *LSD: My problem child*. New York, NY: McGraw Hill.

Hofmann, S. G., Dozois, D. J. A., & Smits, J. A. J. (2014). *The Wiley handbook of cognitive behavioural therapy*. Oxford, UK: Wiley-Blackwell.

Hoffmann, W. A., Myburgh, C., & Poggenpoel, M. (2010). The lived experiences of late-adolescent female suicide survivors: 'A part of me died'. *Journal of Interdisciplinary Health Sciences*, 15(1), 1–9.

Holdstock, T. L. (1981). Psychology in South Africa belongs to the colonial era: Arrogance or ignorance. *South African Journal of Psychology*, 11, 123–129.

Holland, A. J., Hall, A., Murray, R., Russell, G. F. M., & Crisp, A. H. (1984). Anorexia nervosa: A study of 34 twin pairs and one set of triplets. *British Journal of Psychiatry*, 145, 414–419.

Holtzman, N. A., & Marteau, T. M. (2000). Will genetics revolutionize medicine? *New England Journal of Medicine*, 342, 141–144.

Holzinger, A. (2014). *Biomedical informatics: Discovering knowledge in big data*. Heidelberg: Springer.

Hook, D. (2001). Critical psychology in South Africa: Applications, limitations, possibilities. *Psychology in Society*, 27, 3–17.

Hook, D. (2002). The other side of language: The body and the limits of signification. *Psychoanalytic Review*, 89(5), 681–713.

Hor, K., & Taylor, M. (2010). Review of 'Suicide and Schizophrenia: A systematic review of rates and risk factors'. *Journal of Psychopharmachology*, 24(4), 81–90.

Hoste, R. R., & Le Grange, D. (2008). Expressed emotion among white and ethnic minority families of adolescents with Bulimia Nervosa. *European Eating Disorders Review*, 16(5), 395–400.

Horie, T., Harashima, S., Yoneda, R., Hiraide, M., Inada, S., Otani, M., & Yoshiuchi, K. (2016). A series of patients with purging type anorexia nervosa who do "tube vomiting". *BioPsychoSocial Medicine*, 10(1), 32–36. doi:10.1186/s13030-016-0083-3

How 143 mentally ill South Africans were sent to their deaths. What a horrifying scandal reveals about the rotting of the state under Jacob Zuma. (2018). *The Economist*. Retrieved August 8, 2018 from https://www.economist.com/middle-east-and-africa/2018/01/11/how-143-mentally-ill-south-africans-were-sent-to-their-deaths

Howard, R. (1992). Folie a deux involving a dog. *American Journal of Psychiatry*, 149, 414.

Howes, O., McCutcheon, R., & Stone, J. (2015). Glutamate and dopamine in schizophrenia: An update for the 21st century. *Journal of Psychopharmacology*, 29(2), 97–115. doi:10.1177/0269881114563634

Hsu, L. K. G. (1990). *Eating disorders*. New York, NY: Guilford Press.

Hugo, C. J., Boshoff, D. E. L., Traut, A., Zungu-Dirwayi, N., & Stein, D. J. (2003). Community attitudes toward and knowledge of mental illness in South Africa. *Social Psychiatry and Psychiatric Epidemiology*, 38, 715–719.

Hussain, A. F., & Cochrane, R. (2002). Depression in South Asian women: Asian women's beliefs on causes and cures. *Mental Health, Religion & Culture*, 5(3), 285–311.

Hussein Rassool, G. (2019). *Evil eye, jinn possession, and mental health issues: An Islamic perspective.* Abingdon: Routledge. Retrieved from https://www.researchgate.net/publication/328124453_Evil_Eye_Jinn_Possession_and_Mental_Health_Issues_An_Islamic_Perspective

Husserl, E. G. A. (1952/1989). Ideas pertaining to a pure phenomenology and to a phenomenological philosophy – Second book: Studies in the phenomenology of constitution (R. Rojcewicz, & A. Schuwer, Trans.). *Collected works* (Vol. 3). The Hague, Netherlands: Kluwer.

Ineichen, B. (2000). The epidemiology of dementia in Africa: A review. *Social Science & Medicine*, 50(11), 1673–1677.

Infantolino, Z. P., Crockers, L. D., Heller, W., Yee, C. M., & Miller, G. A. (2016). Psychophysiology in pursuit of psychopathology. In J. T. Cacioppo, L. G. Tassinary, & G. G. Berntson (eds). *Handbook of psychophysiology* (4th ed.). Cambridge: Cambridge University Press. Retrieved from Illinois Experts.

Institute of Medicine: Committee on Nervous System Disorders in Developing Countries, Board on Global Health. (2001). *Neurological, psychiatric and developmental disorders: Meeting the challenge in the developing world.* Washington, DC: National Academy Press. Retrieved March 23, 2009, from http://books.nap.edu/openbook/0309071925/gifmid/112.gif.

Iruloh, B. N. (2017). Family distress and eating disorders among undergraduate students of University of Port Harcourt, Rivers State, Nigeria. *Journal of Education and Practice*, 8(5), 76–80.

Janoff-Bulman, R. (1992). *Shattered assumptions.* New York, NY: Free Press.

Janse van Rensburg, A. B. R. (2009). A changed climate for mental health care delivery in South Africa. *Psychiatry*, 12, 157–165.

Jarvis, E. (1998). Schizophrenia in British immigrants: Recent findings, issues and implications. *Transcultural Psychiatry*, 35(1), 39–74.

Jaspers, K. (1962). *General psychopathology.* Manchester, United Kingdom: Manchester University Press.

Jewell, J. D., & Stark, K. D. (2003). Comparing the family environments of adolescents with conduct disorder or depression. *Journal of Child and Family Studies*, 12(1), 77–89.

Jimerson, D. C., Wolfe, B. E., Metzger, E. D., Finkelstein, D. M., & Cooper, T. B. (1997). Decreased serotonin function in bulimia nervosa. *Archives of General Psychiatry*, 54(6), 529–536.

Jinabhai, C. C., Taylor, M., Rangongo, M. F., Mkhize, N., Anderson, S., Pillay, B. J., & Sullivan, K. R. (2004). Investigating the mental abilities of rural Zulu primary school children in South Africa. *Ethnicity and Health*, 9(1), 17–36.

Johnson, B. D., & Bunce, R. (2008). Attention Deficit/Hyperactivity Disorder. *Encyclopedia of counseling.* Retrieved March 20, 2009, from. http://www.sage-ereference.com/counseling/Article_n11.html

Johnson, D. M., Zlotnick, C., & Perez, S. (2011). Cognitive-behavioral treatment of PTSD in residents of battered women's shelters: Results of a randomised clinical trial. *Journal of Consulting and Clinical Psychology*, 79(4), 542–551.

Johnson, J. C. (2006). Dissociative disorders among adults in the community, impaired functioning, and axis I and II comorbidity. *Journal of Psychiatric Research*, 40(2), 131–140.

Johnson, W. G., Jarrell, M. P., Chupurdia, K. M., & Williamson, D. A. (1994). Repeated binge/purge cycles in bulimia nervosa: Role of glucose and insulin. *International Journal of Eating Disorders*, 15(4), 331–341. doi:10.1002/eat.2260150404

Johnstone, L. (2000). *Users and abusers of psychiatry: A critical look at psychiatric practice* (2nd ed.). London: Routledge.

Jones, B. E., & Gray, B. A. (1986). Problems in diagnosing Schizophrenia and affective disorders in Blacks. *Hospital and Community Psychiatry*, 37, 61–65.

Jones, D. J., Fox, M. M., Babigan, H. M., & Hutton, H. E. (1980). Epidemiology of anorexia nervosa in Monroe County, New York: 1960–1976. *Psychosomatic Medicine*, 42, 551–558.

Jordan, K. D., & Okifuji, A. (2011). Anxiety disorders: Differential diagnosis and their relationship to chronic pain. *Journal of Pain and Palliative Care Pharmacotherapy*, 25, 231–245.

Jorge, J., & Adams, S. (2019, April 14). Flying high – Weed in the workplace. *The South African Labour Guide*. Retrieved from https://www.labourguide.co.za/latest-news-1/2455-flying-high-weed-in-the-workplace

Joseph, M. (2017, May 4). The poor are getting poorer. *Huffington Post*. Retrieved from https://www.huffpost.com/entry/the-poor-are-getting-poor_b_9830104

Joseph, S. & Linley, P. A. (2004). Positive therapy: A positive psychological theory of therapeutic practice. In P. A. Linley & S. Joseph (Eds), *Positive psychology in practice*. Hoboken, NJ: John Wiley, 354–368.

Joyce, D. (2007). Conduct disorders. *Encyclopedia of school psychology*. Sage Publications. Retrieved March 9, 2009, from http://www.sage-ereference.com/educationalpsychology/Article_n47.html

Junginger, J., Barker, S., & Coe, D. (1992). Mood theme and bizarreness of delusions in Schizophrenia and mood psychosis. *Journal of Abnormal Psychology*, 101, 287–292.

Kabat-Zinn, J. (1990). *Full catastrophe living: Using the wisdom of your body and mind to face stress, pain and illness*. New York, NY: Delacourt.

Kahn, M. S., & Kelly, K. (2001). Cultural tensions in psychiatric nursing: Managing the interface between Western mental health care and Xhosa traditional healing in South Africa. *Transcultural Psychiatry*, 38, 35–50.

Kahn, R. S., Davidson, M., Knott, P., Stern, R. G., Apter, S., & Davis, K. L. (1993). Effect of neuroleptic medication on cerebrospinal fluid monoamine metabolite concentrations in Schizophrenia: Serotonin-dopamine interactions as a target for treatment. *Archives of General Psychiatry*, 50, 599–605.

Kale, R. (1995). New South Africa's mental health. *British Medical Journal*, 310(6989), 1254–1256.

Kaliski, S. Z. (2006). The criminal defendant. In S. Z. Kaliski (Ed.), *Psycholegal assessment in South Africa*. Cape Town: Oxford University Press, 93–112.

Kaminer, D., Grimsrud, A., Myer, L., Stein, D. J., & Williams, D. R. (2008). Risk for post-traumatic stress disorder associated with different forms of interpersonal violence in South Africa. *Social Science & Medicine*, 67, 1589–1595.

Kaplan, H. I., & Sadock, B. J. (1998). *Kaplan & Sadock's synopsis of psychiatry: Behavioral sciences clinical psychiatry* (8th ed.). Baltimore, MD: Lippincott Williams and Wilkins.

Kaplan, H. I., & Sadock, B. J. (2007). *Kaplan & Sadock's synopsis of psychiatry: Behavioral sciences clinical psychiatry* (10th ed.). Baltimore, MD: Lippincott Williams & Wilkins.

Kaplan, H. I., Sadock, B. J., & Grebb, J. A. (1994). *Kaplan & Sadock's synopsis of psychiatry: Behavioral sciences/clinical psychiatry* (7th ed.). Baltimore, MD: Lippincott Williams & Wilkins.

Kaplan, H. I., Sadock, B. J., & Grebb, J. A. (1996). *Synopsis of psychiatry: Behavioral sciences, clinical psychiatry*. Baltimore: Williams & Wilkins.

Kaplan, H. S. (1979). *Disorders of sexual desire*. New York, NY: Brunner/Mazel.

Karayiorgou, M., & Gogos, J.A. (2011). *Human genetic approaches*. Retrieved November 30, 2011, from http://schizophreniaresearch.columbia.edu/content/research-program-0

Karazsia, B. T., Murnen, S. K., & Tylka, T. L. (2017). Is body dissatisfaction changing across time? A cross-temporal meta-analysis. *Psychological Bulletin*, 143(3), 293–320. doi:10.1037/bul0000081

Karim, S., Saeed, K., Rana, M. H., Mubbashar, M., & Jenkins, R. (2004). Pakistan mental health country profile. *International Review of Psychiatry*, 16, 83–92.

Karunakara, U. K., Neuner, F. Schauer, M., Singh, K., Hill, K., Elbert, T., & Burnha, G. (2004). Traumatic events and symptoms of post-traumatic stress disorder amongst Sudanese nationals, refugees and Ugandans in the West Nile. *African Health Sciences*, 4(2), 83–93. Retrieved from https://www.ncbi.nlm. nih.gov/pmc/articles/PMC2141616/

Kasayira, J. M., & Chireshe, R. (2010). Poverty and HIV/AIDS in sub-Saharan Africa: Implications for psychological well-being. *Journal of Psychology in Africa*, 20(2), 203–208.

Kavanagh, D. J. (1992). Recent developments in expressed emotion in Schizophrenia. *British Journal of Psychiatry*, 160, 601–620.

Kayano, M., Yoshiuchi, K., Al-Adawi, S., Viernes, N., Dorvlo, A. S., Kumano, H., Kuboki, T., & Akabayashi, A. (2008). Eating attitudes and body dissatisfaction in adolescents: Cross-cultural study. *Psychiatry and Clinical Neurosciences*, 62(1), 17–25. doi:10.1111/j.14401819.2007.01772.x

Kaye, W. H. (2008). Neurobiology of anorexia and bulimia nervosa. *Physiology & Behavior*, 94(1), 121–135. doi:10.1016/j.physbeh.2007.11.037

Kaye, W. H., Barbarich, B. S., Putnam, B. S., Gendall, K. A., Fernstrom, J., Fernstrom, M., McConaha, C. W., & Kishore, A. (2003). Anxiolytic effects of acute tryptophan depletion in anorexia nervosa. *International Journal of Eating Disorders*, 33, 825–838.

Kaye, W. H., Weltzin, T. E., Hsu, L. K. G., McConaha, C. W., & Bolton, B. (1993). Amount of calories retained after binge eating and vomiting. *American Journal of Psychiatry*, 150(6), 969–971.

Kazadi, N. J. B., Moosa, M. Y. H., & Jeenah, F. Y. (2008). Factors associated with relapse in Schizophrenia. *South African Journal of Psychiatry*, 14(2), 52–62.

Keane, T. M., & Barlow, D. H. (2002). Post-traumatic stress disorder. In D. H. Barlow (Ed.), *Anxiety and its disorders: The Nature and Treatment of Anxiety and Panic* (2nd ed.). New York, NY: Guilford Press, 418–453.

Keane, T. M., Marshall, A. D., & Taft, C. T. (2006). Posttraumatic stress disorder: Etiology, epidemiology, and treatment outcome. *Annual Review of Clinical Psychology*, 2(18) 161–197.

Keel, P. K., Doer, D. J., Eddy, K. T., Franko, D., Charatan, D. L., & Herzog, D. B. (2003). Predictors of mortality in eating disorders. *Archives of General Psychiatry*, 60, 179–183.

Keeney, B. P. (1983). *Aesthetics of change*. New York, NY: Guilford.

Keith, S. J., Regier, D. A., & Rae, D. S. (1991). Schizophrenic disorders. In L. N. Robins & D. A. Regier (Eds.), *Psychiatric disorders in America*. New York, NY: Free Press, 33–52.

Kendler, K. S., MacLean, C., Neale, M., Kessler, R., Heath, A., & Eaves, L. (1991). The genetic epidemiology of bulimia nervosa. *American Journal of Psychiatry*, 148, 1627–1637.

Kendler, K. S., Neale, M. C., Kessler, R. C., Heath, A. C., & Eaves, L. J. (1993). A test of the equal-environment assumption in twin studies of psychiatric illness. *Archives of General Psychiatry*, 49, 257–266.

Kernberg, O. F., & Michels, R. (2009). Borderline personality disorder. *American Journal of Psychiatry*, 166, 505–508.

Kessler, R. C., Aguilar-Gaxiola, S., Alonso, J., Chatterji, S., Lee, S., Ormel, J., Üstün, T. B., & Wang, P. S. (2009). The global burden of mental disorders: An update from the WHO World Mental Health (WMH) Surveys. *Epidemiologia e Psichiatria Sociale*, 18(1), 23–33.

Kessler, R. C., Avenevoli, S., & Merikangas, K. R. (2001). Mood disorders in children and adolescents: An epidemiologic perspective. *Biological Psychiatry*, 49(12), 1002–1014.

Kessler, R. M., Hutson, P. H., Herman, B. K., & Potenza, M. N. (2016). The neurobiological basis of binge-eating disorder. *Neuroscience & Biobehavioral Reviews*, 63, 223–238. doi:10.1016/j.neubiorev. 2016.01.013

Kety, S. S., Wender, P. H., Jacobsen, B., Ingraham, L. T., Jansson, L., Faber, B., & Kinney, D. K. (1994). Mental illness in the biological and adoptive relatives of schizophrenic adoptees: Replication of the Copenhagen study in the rest of Denmark. *American Journal of Psychiatry*, 144, 934–938.

Keyes, C. L. M. (1998). Social well-being. *Social Psychology Quarterly*, 61, 121–140.

Keyes, C. L. M. (2002). The mental health continuum: From languishing to flourishing in life. *Journal of Health and Social Behavior*, 43, 207–222.

Keyes, C. L. M., & Lopez, S. J. (2005). Toward a science of mental health: Positive directions in diagnosis and interventions. In C. R. Snyder & S. J. Lopez (Eds), *Handbook of positive psychology*. Oxford: Oxford University Press, 45–62.

Keys, A., Brozek, J., Hsu, L. K. G., McConoha, C. E., & Bolton, B. (1950). *The biology of human starvation*. Minneapolis, MN: University of Minnesota Press.

Khumalo, I. P. (2014). Well-being: Societies, nations and cultures. In M. P. Wissing (Ed.), *Towards flourishing: Contextualising positive psychology*. Pretoria: Van Schaik, 263–288.

Khumalo, I. P., Temane, Q. M., & Wissing, M. P. (2013). Further validation of the General Psychological Well-Being Scale among a Setwana-speaking group. In M. P. Wissing (Ed.), *Well-being research in South Africa: Cross-cultural advancements in positive psychology*. Springer: Dordrecht, 199–224.

Khumalo, I. P., Wissing, M. P., & Temane, Q. M. (2008). Exploring the validity of the VIA-Inventory of Strengths in an African Context. *Journal of Psychology in Africa*, 18(1), 133–142.

Khumalo, T., & Plattner, I. E. (2019). The relationship between locus of control and depression: A cross-sectional survey with university students in Botswana. *South African Journal of Psychiatry*, 25, a1221. https://www.ajol.info/index.php/sajpsyc/article/viewFile/184128/173497

Kieling, C., Kieling, R. R., Rohde, L. A., Frick, P. J., Moffitt. T., Nigg, J. T., Tannock, R., & Castellanos, F. X. (2010). The age at onset of Attention-deficit/Hyperactivity Disorder. *American Journal of Psychiatry*, 167, 14–16.

Kilian, S., Burns, J. K., Seedat, S., Asmal, L., Chiliza, B., Du Plessis, S., ... Emsley, R. (2017). Factors moderating the relationship between childhood trauma and premorbid adjustment in first-episode schizophrenia. *PLoS One*, 12(1), e0170178–e01710193. doi:10.1371/journal.pone.0170178

Killen, J. D., Taylor, C. B., Telch, M. J., Saylor, K. E., Maron, D. J., & Robinson, T. N. (1986). Self-induced vomiting and laxative and diuretic use among teenagers: Precursors of the binge–purge syndrome. *Journal of the American Medical Association*, 255, 1447–1449.

Kim, M. (2016). Understanding the etiology and treatment approaches of Schizophrenia: Theoretical perspectives and their critique. *Open Journal of Psychiatry*, 6(4), 253–261. doi:10.4236/ojpsych.2016.64030

Kim, J. H., & Lennon, S. J. (2007). Mass media and self-esteem, body image, and eating disorder tendencies. *Clothing and Textiles Research Journal*, 25(1), 3–23.

Kim, J. W., & Chock, T. M. (2015). Body image 2.0: Associations between social grooming on Facebook and body image concerns. *Computers in Human Behavior*, 48, 331–339. doi:10.1016/j.chb.2015.01.009

Kim-Prieto, C., & Diener, E. (2009). Religion as a source of variation in the experience of positive and negative emotions. *Journal of Positive Psychology*, 4(6), 447–460. doi:10.1080/17439760903271025

King, M. B. (1993). Cultural aspects of eating disorders. *International Review of Psychiatry*, 5, 205–216.

Kinsey, A. C., Pomeroy, W. R., & Martin, C. E. (1948). *Sexual behavior in the human male*. Philadelphia, PA: W. B. Saunders Company.

Kinsey, A. C., Pomeroy, W. R., Martin, C. E., & Gebhart, P. H. (1953). *Sexual behavior in the human female*. Philadelphia, PA: W. B. Saunders Company.

Kleinman, A. (1977). Culture, and illness: A question of models. *Culture, Medicine and Psychiatry*, 1, 229–231.

Klemchuk, H. P., Hutchinson, C. B., & Frank, R. I. (1990). Body dissatisfaction and eating-related problems on the college campus: Usefulness of the Eating Disorder Inventory with a nonclinical population. *Journal of Counseling Psychology*, 37(3), 297–305. doi:10.1037/0022-0167.37.3.297

Klimidis, S., & Tokgoz, A. (n.d.). *A transcultural perspective on the Mini Mental State Examination.* Victorian Transcultural Psychiatry Unit. Retrieved October 27, 2008, from http://www.tpu.org.au/docs/mmse/mini_mental_document.pdf

Klonsky, E. D., & May, A. M. (2013). Differentiating suicide attempters from suicide ideators: A critical frontier for suicidology research. *Suicide & Life-Threatening Behavior*, 44(1), 1–5. doi:10.1111/sltb.12068

Knox, P. L., & Lichtenberg, J. W. (2005). Depression. Encyclopedia of school psychology. Retrieved March 20, 2009, from http://www.sage-ereference.com/schoolpsychology/Article_n76.html

Kober, H., & Boswell, R. G. (2017). Potential psychological and neural mechanisms in binge eating disorder: Implications for treatment. *Clinical Psychology Review*, 60, 32–44. doi:10.1016/j.cpr.2017.12.004

Koen, L., Niehaus, D. J. H., De Jong, G., Muller, J. E., & Jordaan, E. (2006). Morphological features in a Xhosa Schizophrenia population. *BMC Psychiatry*, 6(1), 47.

Kosidou, K., & Lindholm, S. (2007). A rare case of dissociative with unusually prolonged amnesia succesfully resolved by ECT. European Psychiatry, 22(Supp. 1), S264–S265. doi:https://doi.org/10.1016/j.eurpsy.2007.01.889

Krahn, L. B. (2008). Looking toward DSM-V: Should Factitious Disorder become a subtype of Somatoform Disorder? *Psychosomatics*, 49, 277–282.

Kramer, P. D. (1999, February 1). Freud vs. God: *How psychiatry lost its soul and Christianity lost its mind.* Retrieved from https://ajp.psychiatryonline.org/doi/full/10.1176/ajp.156.2.327

Krassoievitch, M., Perez-Rincon, H., & Suarez, P. (1982). Correlation entre les hallucinations visuelles et auditives dans une population de schophrenes Mexicains. *Confrontations Psychiatriques*, 15, 149–162.

Kreek, M. J., Nielsen, D. A., Butelman, E. R., & Laforge, K. S. (2005). Genetic influences on impulsivity, risk taking, stress responsivity and vulnerability to drug use and addiction. *Nature Neuroscience*, 8(11), 1451–1457.

Kruger, C. S. (2007). Dissociation – a preliminary contextual model. *South African Journal of Psychiatry*, 13(1), 13–17, 20–21.

Kua, E. S. (1986). A cross-cultural study of the possession-trance in Singapore. *Australia and New Zealand Journal of Psychiatry*, 20(3), 361–364.

Kuepper, R., Van Os, J., Lieb, R., Wittchen, H. U., Höfler, M., & Henquet, C. (2011). Continued cannabis use and risk of incidence and persistence of psychotic symptoms: 10-year follow-up cohort study. *BMJ Research*, 342, d738. doi:https://doi.org/10.1136/bmj.d738

Kuhl, J., Kazén, M., & Koole, S. L. (2006). Putting self-regulation into practice: A user's manual. *Applied Psychology: An International Review*, 55(3), 408–418.

Kwizera, A., Nakibuuka, J., Ssemogerere, L., Sendikadiwa, C., Obua, D., Kizito, S., … Nakasujja, N. (2015). Incidence and risk factors for delirium among mechanically ventilated patients in an African intensive care setting: An observational multicenter study. *Critical Care Research and Practice*, 2015, 491780. doi:10.1155/2015/491780

Labre, M. P. (2002). Adolescent boys and the Muscular Male Body ideal. *Journal of Adolescent Health*, 30(4), 233–242.

Lachenmeier, D. W., & Rehm, J. (2015). Comparative risk assessment of alcohol, tobacco, cannabis and other illicit drugs using the margin of exposure approach. *Scientific Reports*, 1–7, 8126. doi:10.1038/srep08126

Ladouceur, C. D., Dahl, R. E., Williamson, D. E., Birmaher, B., Ryan, N. D., & Casey, B. J. (2005). Altered emotional processing in pediatric anxiety, depression and comorbid anxiety-depression. *Journal of Abnormal Child Psychology*, 33(2), 165–177.

Laher, S., & Khan, S. (2011). Exploring the influence of Islam on the perceptions of mental illness of volunteers in a Johannesburg community-based organisation. *Psychology and Developing Societies*, 23(1), 63–84. http://dx.doi.org/10.1177/097133361002300103

Laing, R. D. (1969). *The divided self*. New York, NY: Pantheon.

Laing, R. D. (1976). A critique of Kallmann's and Slater's henetic theory of Schizophrenia. In R. I. Evans & R. D. Laing (Eds), *The man and his ideas*. New York, NY: Dutton.

Laing, R. D., & Esterson, A. (1964). *Sanity, madness, and the family*. London: Tavistock.

Lake, A., Staiger, P., & Glowinski, H. (2000). Effect of Western culture on women's attitudes to eating and perceptions of body shape. *International Journal of Eating Disorders*, 27, 83–89.

Lambley, P. (1980). *The psychology of apartheid*. London: Secker & Warburg.

Lamiell, J. T. (2007). On sustaining critical discourse with mainstream personality investigators: Problems and prospects. *Theory & Psychology*, 17(2), 169–185.

Langer, E. (2005). Well-being: Mindfulness versus positive evaluation. In C. R. Snyder & S. J. Lopez (Eds), *Handbook of positive psychology*. Oxford: Oxford University Press, 214–230.

Langley, G. C., & Klopper, H. (2005). Trust as a foundation for the therapeutic intervention for patients with borderline personality disorder. *Journal of Psychiatric and Mental Health Nursing*, 12(1), 23–32.

Larsen, R. J., & Buss, D. M. (2002). *Personality psychology*. Boston, MA: McGraw-Hill.

Latalova, K., Kamaradova, D., & Prasko, J. (2014). Violent victimization of adult patients with severe mental illness: a systematic review. *Neuropsychiatric Disease and Treatment*, 10, 1925–1939. doi:10.2147/NDT. S68321

Laumann, E. O., Paik, A., Glasser, D. B., Kang, J. H., Wang, T., & Levinson, B. (2006). A cross-national study of subjective sexual well-being among older women and men: Findings from the global study of sexual attitudes and behaviors. *Archives of Sexual Behavior*, 35(2), 145–161.

Launer, J. (2016). Epigenetics for dummies. *Postgraduate Medical Journal*, 92(1085), 183–184. doi:10.1136/postgradmedj-2016-133993

Laurens, K. R., Luo, L., Matheson, S. L., Carr, V. J., Raudino, A., Harris, F., & Green, M. J. (2015). Common or distinct pathways to psychosis? A systematic review of evidence from prospective studies for developmental risk factors and antecedents of the schizophrenia spectrum disorders and affective psychoses. *BMC Psychiatry*, 15(1), 205–225. doi:10.1186/s12888-015-0562-2

Laursen, T. M., Munk-Olsen, T., & Vestergaard, M. (2012). Life expectancy and cardiovascular mortality in persons with schizophrenia. *Current Opinion in Psychiatry*, 25(2), 83–88. doi:10.1097/YCO.0b013e32835035ca

Lavender, J. M., Wonderlich, S. A., Peterson, C. B., Crosby, R. D., Engel, S. G., Mitchell, J. E., ... Berg, K. C. (2014). Dimensions of emotion dysregulation in bulimia nervosa. *European Eating Disorders Review*, 22(3), 212–216.

Lawler, K., Mosepele, M., Ratcliffe, S., Seloilwe, E., Steele, K., Nthobatsang, R., & Steenhoff, A. (2010). Neurocognitive impairment among HIV-positive individuals in Botswana: A pilot study. *Journal of the International Aids Society*, 13, 15. doi:10.1186/1758-2652-13-15

Lazarus, R. S., & Folkman, S. (1984). *Stress, appraisal and coping*. New York, NY: Springer.

Lazarus, S. (1988). *The role of the psychologist in South African society: In search of an appropriate community psychology* (Unpublished doctoral thesis). University of Cape Town, Cape Town, South Africa.

Learn.Genetics. (2013, August 30). *Genes and addiction.* Genetic Science Learning Centre, University of Utah. Retrieved July 28, 2018, from https://learn.genetics.utah.edu/content/addiction/genes/

Leavey, G. (2010). The appreciation of the spiritual in mental illness: A qualitative study of beliefs among clergy in the UK. *Transcultural Psychiatry, 47*(4), 571–590. https://doi.org/10.1177/1363461510383200

Lechner, S. (2009). Benefit finding. In S. Lopez (Ed.), *The encyclopedia of positive psychology.* Chichester: Blackwell, 99–102.

Lee, C. J. (2011). Decolonization of a special type: Rethinking Cold War history in Southern Africa. *Kronos,* 37(1). Retrieved from http://www.scielo.org.za/scielo.php?script=sci_arttext&pid=S0259-01902011000100001

Lee, S., Ng, K. L., Kwok, K., & Fung, C. (2010). The changing profile of eating disorders at a tertiary psychiatric clinic in Hong Kong (1987–2007). *International Journal of Eating Disorders, 43*(4), 307–314. doi:10.1002/eat.20686

Lee, S. W. (2005). Separation Anxiety Disorder. *Encyclopedia of school psychology.* Sage Publications. Retrieved March 20, 2009, from http://www.sage-ereference.com/schoolpsychology/Article_n123.html

Lee, Y., & Lin, P. Y. (2010). Association between serotonin transporter gene polymorphism and eating disorders: A meta-analytic study. *International Journal of Eating Disorders, 43*(6), 498–504. doi:10.1002/eat.20732

Leehr, E. J., Krohmer, K., Schag, K., Dresler, T., Zipfel, S., & Giel, K. E. (2015). Emotion regulation model in binge eating disorder and obesity – a systematic review. *Neuroscience & Biobehavioral Reviews, 49,* 125–134. doi:10.1016/j.neubiorev.2014.12.008

Leff, J., Wig, N. N., Bedi, H., Menon, D. K., Kuipers, L., Korten, A., … Jablenski, A. (1990). Relatives' expressed emotion and the course of schizophrenia in Chandigarh. *British Journal of Psychiatry, 156,* 351–356.

Le Grange, D., Louw, J., Breen, A., & Katzman, M. A. (2004). The meaning of 'self-starvation' in impoverished black adolescents in South Africa. *Culture, Medicine and Psychiatry, 28,* 439–461.

Le Grange, D., Louw, J., Russell, B., Nel, T., & Silkstone, C. (2006). Eating attitudes and behaviours in South African adolescents and young adults. *Transcultural Psychiatry, 43*(3), 401–417. doi:10.1177/1363461506066984

Le Grange, D., Telch, C. F., & Tibbs, J. (1998). Eating attitudes and behaviours in 1,435 South African Caucasian and non–Caucasian college students. *American Journal of Psychiatry, 155,* 250–254.

Lemonick, M. D., & Alice, P. (2007, July 16). The science of addiction. *Time, 170*(3), 42.

Lenger, V., De Villiers, C., & Louw, S. J. (1996). Informant questionnaires as screening measures to detect dementia. A pilot study in the South African context. *South African Medical Journal, 86*(6), 737–741.

Leon, G. R., Fulkerson, J. A., Perry, C. L., & Early-Zald, M. B. (1995). Prospective analysis of personality and behavioural vulnerabilities and gender influences in the later development of disordered eating. *Journal of Abnormal Psychology, 104,* 140–149.

Lerner, R. M. (2006). Resilience as an attribute of the developmental system: Comments on the papers of Professors Masten & Wachs. *Annals of the New York Academy of Sciences, 1094,* 40–51.

Lesolang-Pitje, N. (2003). African traditional healing and psychotherapy. In N. S. Madu (Ed.), *Contributions to psychotherapy conference in Africa.* Turfloop: University of the North, 207–213.

Levine, M. P., & Troiden, R. R. (1988). The myth of sexual compulsivity. *Journal of Sex Research, 25,* 347–363.

Lewis, C. M., Levinson, D. F., Wise, L. H., DeLisi, L. E., Straub, R. E., Hovatta, I. … Helgason, T. (2003). Genome scan meta-analysis of Schizophrenia and Bipolar Disorder, Part II: Schizophrenia. *American Journal of Genetics, 73*(1), 34–48.

Lewis, D. A. & Levitt, P. (2002). Review of Schizophrenia as a disorder of neurodevelopment. *Annual Review of Neuroscience, 25,* 409–432.

Lewis, R., & Frydenburg, E. (2002). Concomitants of failure to cope: What we should teach adolescents about coping. *British Journal of Educational Psychology*, 72, 419–431.

Lewis, S. P., & Arbuthnott, A. E. (2012). Searching for thinspiration: The nature of internet searches for pro-eating disorder websites. *Cyberpsychology, Behavior, and Social Networking*, 15(4), 200–204. doi:10.1002/eat.22403

Lewis-Fernández, R. (2009). Editorial: The Cultural Formulation. *Transcultural Psychiatry*, 46(3), 379–382.

Lewis-Fernández, R., & Kleinman, A. (1995). Cultural psychiatry: Theoretical, clinical, and research issues. *The Psychiatric Clinics of North America*, 18(3), 433–448.

Lezak, M. D. (1995). *Neuropsychological assessment* (3rd ed.). New York, NY: Oxford University Press.

Liao, Y., Knoesen, N. P., Castle, D. J., Tang, J., Deng, Y., Bookun, R., … Liu, T. (2010). Symptoms of disordered eating, body shape, and mood concerns in male and female Chinese medical students. *Comprehensive Psychiatry*, 51(5), 516–523. doi:10.1016/j.comppsych.2009.11.007

Lidz, T., Fleck, S., & Cornelison, A. R. (1965). *Schizophrenia and the family*. New York, NY: International Universities Press.

Liebowitz, S. F. (1983). Brain neurotransmitters and appetite regulation. *Psychopharmacology Bulletin*, 21(3), 412–418.

Linden, D. E., & Fallgatter, A. J. (2009). Neuroimaging in Psychiatry: From Bench to Bedside. *Frontiers in Human Neuroscience*, 3, 1–7.

Lindquist, P., & Allebeck, P. (1990). Schizophrenia and crime: A longitudinal follow-up of 644 schizophrenics in Stockholm. *British Journal of Psychiatry*, 157, 345–350.

Lindsey, K. P., & Paul, G. L. (1989). Involuntary commitments to public mental institutions: Issues involving the overrepresentation of blacks and assessment of relevant functioning. *Psychological Bulletin*, 106, 171–183.

Linley, P. A., Joseph, S., Harrington, S., & Wood, A. M. (2006). Positive psychology: Past, present, and (possible) future. *Journal of Positive Psychology*, 1(1), 3–16.

Lipowski., Z. J. (1987). Delirium (acute confusional states). *Journal of the American Medical Association*, 258(13), 1789–1792.

Lippi, G., Smit, D. J., Jordaan, J. C., & Roos, J. L. (2009). Suicide risk in Schizophrenia – a follow-up study after 20 years Part 1: Outcome and associated social factors. *South African Journal of Psychology*, 15(3), 56–62.

Littlewood, R. (1990). The new cross-cultural psychiatry. *British Journal of Psychiatry*, 157, 775–776.

Littlewood, R., & Lipsedge, M. (1997). *Aliens and alienists: Ethnic minorities and psychiatry* (3rd ed.). London: Routledge.

Livesley, W. J. (2001). Conceptual and taxonomic issues. In W. J. Livesley (Ed.), *Handbook of personality disorders: Theory, research, and treatment*. New York, NY: Guilford, 3–38.

Lock, J., La Via, M. C., & American Academy of Child and Adolescent Psychiatry (AACAP) Committee on Quality Issues (CQI). (2015). Practice parameter for the assessment and treatment of children and adolescents with eating disorders. *Focus*, 14(1), 75–89. doi:10.1016/j.jaac.2015.01.018

Lock, J., & Le Grange, D. (2015). *Treatment manual for anorexia nervosa: A family-based approach* (2nd ed.). New York, NY: Guilford Publications.

Lopez, B., & Silverman, W. K. (2004). Anxiety disorders in children. *Encyclopedia of applied developmental science*. Retrieved March 20, 2009, from http://www.sage-ereference.com/applieddevscience/Article_n35.html

Lopez, S. J., Floyd, R. K., Ulven, J. C., & Snyder, C. R. (2000). Hope therapy: Helping clients build a house of hope. In C. R. Snyder (Ed.), *Handbook of hope: Theory, measures, and applications.* San Diego, CA: Academic Press, 123–150.

Lopez, S. R., Nelson, K. A., Snyder, K. S., & Mintz, J. (1999). Attributions and affective reactions of family members and course of Schizophrenia. *Journal of Abnormal Psychology*, 108, 307–317.

Louw, D. A., & Allan, A. (1996). Forensic psychology in South Africa. *American Journal of Forensic Psychology*, 14, 1–13.

Louw, D. A. & Edwards, D. J. A. (1993). *Psychology: An introduction for students in Southern Africa.* Johannesburg: Lexicon.

Louw, D., & Louw, A. (2019). *Human development for students in Southern Africa.* Haga Haga: Psychology Publications.

Louw, J. (1997a). Regulating professional conduct. Part I: Codes of ethics of national psychology associations in South Africa. *South African Journal of Psychology*, 27(3), 183–188.

Louw, J. (1997b). Regulating professional conduct. Part II: The professional board for psychology in South Africa. *South African Journal of Psychology*, 27(3), 189–195.

Love, B. (1995). *Encyclopedia of unusual sex practices.* Fort Lee, NJ: Barricade Books.

Lowe, P. A., & Raad, J. M. (2007). Anxiety. *Encyclopedia of educational psychology.* Sage Publications. Retrieved March 20, 2009, from http://www.sage–ereference.com/educationalpsychology/Article_n12.html

Lucas, A. R., Beard, C. M., O'Fallon, W. M., & Kurlan, L. T. (1991). 50-year trends in the incidence of anorexia nervosa in Rochester Minn.: A population-based study. *American Journal of Psychiatry*, 148, 917–922.

Luciano, M. (2015). The ICD-11 beta draft is available online. *World Psychiatry*, 14(3), 375–376. doi:10.1002/wps.20262

Ludwig, A. (1972). Hysteria: A neurobiological theory. *Archives of General Psychiatry*, 27, 771–777.

Lund, C., Kleintjes, S., Kakuma, R., Flisher, A. J., & the MHaPP Research Programme Consortium. (2010). Public sector mental health systems in South Africa: Interprovincial comparisons and policy implications. *Social Psychiatry and Psychiatric Epidemiology*, 45(3), 393–404.

Luria, A. R. (1966). *Higher cortical functions in man.* New York, NY: Basic Books.

Lydecker, J. A., & Grilo, C. (2017). Parents with binge-eating disorder, obesity, and healthy-weight: Associations with children's eating behavior disturbance. *Journal of Adolescent Health*, 60(2), S48. doi.org/10.1016/j.jadohealth.2016.10.278

Lydecker, J. A., White, M. A., & Grilo, C. M. (2017). Form and formulation: Examining the distinctiveness of body image constructs in treatment-seeking patients with binge-eating disorder. *Journal of Consulting and Clinical Psychology*, 85(11), 1095–1103. doi:10.1037/ccp0000258

Lynch, M. (2013). Nonmedical use of prescription opioids: What is the real problem? *Pain Research and Management*, 18(2), 67–68.

Maatz, K. R. (2005). The alcoholic offender – significance for determination of guilt. A legal view. *Nervenarzt*, 76(11), 1389–1401.

Mabe, A. G., Forney, K. J., & Keel, P. K. (2014). Do you "like" my photo? Facebook use maintains eating disorder risk. *International Journal of Eating Disorders*, 47(5), 516–523. doi.org/10.1002/eat.22254

MacDonald, A. W., & Schulz, S. C. (2009). What we know: Findings that every theory of Schizophrenia should explain. *Schizophrenia Bulletin*, 35(3), 493–508.

Madden, S., Miskovic-Wheatley, J., Clarke, S., Touyz, S., Hay, P., & Kohn, M. R. (2015). Outcomes of a rapid refeeding protocol in adolescent Anorexia Nervosa. *Journal of Eating Disorders*, 3(1), 8–16. doi:10.1186/s40337-015-0047-1

Maddux, J. E. (2005). Stopping the 'madness'. Positive psychology and the deconstruction of the illness ideology and the DSM. In C. R. Snyder & S. J. Lopez (Eds), *Handbook of positive psychology*. Oxford: Oxford University Press, 13–25.

Maddux, J. E. (2008). Positive psychology and the illness ideology: Toward a positive clinical psychology. *Applied Psychology: An International Review*, 57, 54–70. doi:10.1111/j.1464–0597.2008.00354.x

Maes, S., & Karoly, P. (2005). Self-regulation and intervention in physical health and illness: A review. *Applied Psychology: An International Review*, 54(2), 267–299.

Mailis-Gagnon, A., & Israelson, D. (2003). *Beyond pain: Making the mind–body connection*. Toronto: Viking Canada/Penguin Books.

Majuri, J., Joutsa, J., Johansson, J., Voon, V., Parkkola, R., Alho, H., Arponen, E., & Kaasinen, V. (2017). Serotonin transporter density in binge eating disorder and pathological gambling: A PET study with [11C] MADAM. *European Neuropsychopharmacology*, 27(12), 1281–1288. doi:10.1016/j.euroneuro.2017.09.007

Makgoba, M. W. (2017). The Report into the 'Circumstances Surrounding the Deaths of Mentally Ill Patients: Gauteng Province'. Pretoria: Office of the Health Ombud. Retrieved August 9, 2019, from https://www.sahrc.org.za/home/21/files/Esidimeni%20full%20report.pdf

Makhubela, M. (2016). 'From psychology in Africa to African psychology': Going nowhere slowly. *Psychology in Society*, 52, 1–18. http://dx.doi.org/10.17159/2309-8708/2016/n52a1

Malindi, J. M., & Theron, L. C. (2010). The hidden resilience of street youth. *South African Journal of Psychology*, 40(3), 318–326.

Manderscheid R. W., Ryff, C. D., Freeman, E. J., McKnight-Eily, L. R., Dhingra, S., & Strine, T. W. (2010). Evolving definitions of mental illness and wellness. *Preventing Chronic Disease*, 7(1), A19.

Manji, H. K., Quiroz, J. A., Payne, J. L., Sinh, J., Lopes, B. P., Viegas, J. S., & Zarate, C. A. (2003). The underlying neurobiology of bipolar disorder. *World Psychiatry*, 2(3), 136–146.

Mann, L., Radford, M., Burnett, P., Ford, S., Bond, M., Leung, K., … Yang, K. (1998). Cross-cultural differences in self-reported decision-making style and confidence. *International Journal of Psychology*, 33(5), 325–335.

Marcus, J., Hans, S. L., Nagier, S., Auerbach, J. G., Mirsky, A., & Aubrey, A. (1987). Review of the NIMH Israeli Kibbutz-City and the Jerusalem infant development study. *Schizophrenia Bulletin*, 13, 425–438.

Marder, S. R., & Galderisi, S. (2017). The current conceptualization of negative symptoms in schizophrenia. *World Psychiatry*, 16(1), 14–24. doi:10.1002/wps.20385

Maree, D. J. F., Maree, M., & Collins, C. (2008). The relationship between hope and goal achievement. *Journal of Psychology in Africa*, 18(1), 65–74.

Markel, H. (2007, March 20). Tracing the cigarettes path from sexy to deadly. *The New York Times*. Retrieved from https://www.nytimes.com/2007/03/20/health/20essay.html

Markov, I. S., & Berrios, G. E. (1992).The meaning of insight in clinical psychiatry. *British Journal of Psychiatry*, 160, 850–860.

Marneros, A., Angst, J. (2007). Bipolar disorders: Roots and revolution. In A. Marneros & J. Angst (Eds), *Bipolar disorders: 100 years after manic-depressive insanity*. New York, NY: Kluwer, 1–35.

Marques, L., Alegria, M., Becker, A. E., Chen, C. N., Fang, A., Chosak, A., & Diniz, J. B. (2011). Comparative prevalence, correlates of impairment, and service utilization for eating disorders across US ethnic groups: Implications for reducing ethnic disparities in health care access for eating disorders. *International Journal of Eating Disorders*, 44(5), 412–420. doi:10.1002/eat.20787

Marrazzi, M. A., & Luby, E. D. (1986). An auto-addiction model of chronic anorexia nervosa. *International Journal of Eating Disorders*, 5, 191–208.

Martinez-Pilkington, A. (2007). Shame and guilt: The psychology of sacramental confession. *The Humanistic Psychologist*, 35(2), 203–218. http://dx.doi.org/10.1080/08873260701274272

Marujo, H. A., & Neto, L. M. (2014). Felicitas Publica and community well-being: Nourishing relational goods through dialogic conversations between deprived and privileged populations. *Journal of Psychology in Africa*, 24(1), 161–181.

Maseko, N. (2015, March 18). South African townships' addictive drug cocktail. *BBC News*. Retrieved from https://www.bbc.com/news/world-africa-31620569

Mash, E. J., & Wolfe, D. A. (2010). *Abnormal child psychology* (4th ed.). Belmont, CA: Wadsworth Cengage Learning.

Masinga, L. (2017). *Life Esidimeni transfers caused at 'least 118 deaths'*. Retrieved August, 8, 2018, from https://www.iol.co.za/news/south-africa/gauteng/life-esidimeni-transfers-caused-at-least-118-deaths-11528935.

Masipa, N. (2015, February 10). Mbamba madness. *Daily Sun*. Retrieved from https://www.dailysun.co.za/News/National/MBAMBA-MADNESS-20150210

Maslow, A. (1987). *Motivation and personality* (3rd ed.). New York, NY: Harper & Row.

Maslowski, J., Janse van Rensburg, D., & Mthoko, N. (1998). A polydiagnostic approach to the differences in the symptoms of schizophrenia in different cultural and ethnic populations. *Acta Psychiatrica Scandinavica*, 98(1), 41–46.

Masse, J. J., & McNeil, C. B. (2008). Oppositional Defiant Disorder. *Encyclopedia of counseling*. Retrieved March 20, 2009, from http://www.sage-ereference.com/counseling/Article_n105.html

Masten, A. S. (2001). Ordinary magic: Resilience processes in development. *American Psychologist*, 56, 227–238.

Masten, A. S., & Obradovic, J. (2006). Competence and resilience in development. *Annals of the New York Academy of Sciences*, 1094, 13–27.

Masters, W. H., & Johnson, V. E. (1970). *Human sexual inadequacy*. Boston, MA: Little, Brown and Company.

Masters, W. H., & Johnson, V. E. (1976). Principles of the new sex therapy. *American Journal of Psychiatry*, 133(5), 548–554.

Mayer, J. D., Caruso, D., & Salovey, P. (1999). Emotional intelligence meets traditional standards for an intelligence. *Intelligence*, 27, 267–298.

Mayes, S. D., Calhoun, S. L., & Crites, D. L. (2001). Does DSM-IV Asperger's disorder exist? *Journal of Abnormal Child Psychology*, 29(3), 263–271.

Mayhew, A. J., Pigeyre, M., Couturier, J., & Meyre, D. (2018). An evolutionary genetic perspective of eating disorders. *Neuroendocrinology*, 106(3), 292–306. doi:10.1159/000484525

Mayo, D., Corey, S., Kelly, L. H., Yohannes, S., Youngquist, A. L., Stuart, B. K., Niendam, T. A., & Loewy, R. L. (2017). The role of trauma and stressful life events among individuals at clinical high risk for psychosis: A review. *Frontiers in Psychiatry*, 8, 55–73. doi:10.3389/fpsyt.2017.00055

Mbanga, N. I., Niehaus, D. J., Mzamo, N. C., Wessels, C. J., Allen, A., Emsley, R. A., & Stein, D. J. (2002). Attitudes towards and beliefs about Schizophrenia in Xhosa families with affected probands. *Curationis*, 25, 69–73.

McCann, U. D. (2014). *Learn more about MDMA: Effects of MDMA on the human nervous system*. *ScienceDirect*. Retrieved from https://www.sciencedirect.com/topics/neuroscience/mdma

McCarthy-Jones, S. (2017). The concept of schizophrenia is coming to an end – here's why. *The Conversation*. Retrieved from https://theconversation.com/the-concept-of-schizophrenia-is-coming-to-an-end-heres-why-82775

McClaren, E., & Winsler, A. (2005). Asperger syndrome. *Encyclopedia of human development.* Retrieved March 20, 2009, from http://www.sage–ereference.com/humandevelopment/Article_n53.html

McConaghy, N. (2005). Time to abandon the gay/heterosexual dichotomy? *Archives of Sexual Behavior,* 34(1), 1–2.

McCuen-Wurst, C., Ruggieri, M., & Allison, K. C. (2018). Disordered eating and obesity: Associations between binge-eating disorder, night-eating syndrome, and weight-related comorbidities. *Annals of the New York Academy of Sciences,* 1411(1), 96–105. doi:10.1111/nyas.13467

McCullough, M. E., & Van Oyen Witvliet, C. (2005). The psychology of forgiveness. In C. R. Snyder & S. J. Lopez (Eds), *Handbook of positive psychology.* Oxford: Oxford University Press, 446–458.

McFarlane, C. (2015). South Africa: The rise of traditional medicine. *Insight on Africa,* 7(1), 60–70.

McFarlane, W. R. (2016). Family interventions for schizophrenia and the psychoses: A review. *Family Process,* 55(3), 460–482. doi:10.1111/famp.12235

McGlashan, T. H., & Fenton, W. S. (1991). Classical subtypes for Schizophrenia: Literature review for DSM-III. *Schizophrenia Bulletin,* 17, 609–622.

McGrath, J., Saha, S., Welham, J., Saadi, O. E., MacCauley, C., & Chant, D. (2004). A systematic review of the incidence of Schizophrenia: The distribution of rates and the influence of sex, urbanicity, migrant status and methodology. *BMC Medicine,* 2, 13.

McGue, M. (1993) From proteins to cognitions: The behavioral genetics of alcoholism. In R. Plomin & G. E. McClearn (Eds). *Nature, nurture, and psychology.* Washington, DC: APA Press, 245–268.

McGuffin, P., & Katz, R. (1993) Genes, adversity, and depression. In R. Plomin & G. E. McClearn (Eds). Nature, nurture, and psychology. Washington, DC: APA Press, 217–230.

McGuffin, P., & Martin, N. (1999). Behaviour and genes. *British Medical Journal,* 3(19), 37–40.

McGuinness, S., & Taylor, J. E. (2016). Understanding body image dissatisfaction and disordered eating in midlife adults. *New Zealand Journal of Psychology,* 45(1), 4–12. Retrieved from https://pdfs.semantics cholar.org/020c/a9f44071d20e0bc48a7b4d810257eca534e5.pdf

McGuire, P. K., Shah, G. M. S., & Murray, R. M. (1993). Increased blood flow in Broca's area during auditory hallucinations in Schizophrenia. *Lancet,* 342, 703–706.

McLachlan, C. (2019). Editorial: Que(e)ring trans and gender diversity. *South African Journal of Psychology,* 49(1), 10–13.

Medical marijuana given green light in South Africa: Report. (2017, February 20). *BusinessTech.* Retrieved from https://businesstech.co.za/news/lifestyle/158633/medical-marijuana-given-green-light-in-south-africa-report/

Mednick, S. A., Huttonen, M. O., & Machon, R. A. (1994). Prenatal influenza infections and adult Schizophrenia. *Schizophrenia Bulletin,* 20, 263–268.

Mednick, S. A., & Schulsinger, F. (1968). Some premorbid characteristics related to breakdown in children with schizophrenic mothers. *Journal of Psychiatric Research,* 6, 267–291.

Meehl, P. E. (1962). Schizotaxia, schizotypia, schizophrenia. *American Psychologist,* 17, 827–838.

Mehrabi, A., Mohammadkhani, P., Dolatshahi, B., Pourshahbaz, A., & Mohammadi, A. (2014). Emotion regulation in depression: An integrative review. *Research Papers,* 2(3), 181–193.

Meier, E. P., & Gray, J. (2014). Facebook photo activity associated with body image disturbance in adolescent girls. *Cyberpsychology, Behavior, and Social Networking,* 17(4), 199–206. doi:10.1089/cyber.2013.0305

Menezes, N. M., Georgiades, K., & Boyle, M. H. (2011). The influence of immigrant status and concentration on psychiatric disorder in Canada: A multi-level analysis. *Psychological Medicine,* 41, 2221–2231.

Menzel, J. E., Schaefer, L. M., Burke, N. L., Mayhew, L. L., Brannick, M. T., & Thompson, J. K. (2010). Appearance-related teasing, body dissatisfaction, and disordered eating: A meta-analysis. *Body Image*, 7(4), 261–270.doi:10.1016/j.bodyim.2010.05.004

Merskey, H., & Bogduk, N. (Eds). (1986). Pain terms: A current list with definitions and notes on usage. *Classification of chronic pain* (2nd ed.). Seattle, WA: IASP Press, 209–214.

Meyer, A. (1951/2). In E. Winters (Ed.), *The collected papers of Adolf Meyer*. Baltimore, MD: Johns Hopkins Press.

Meyer, C., Blisset, J., & Oldfield, C. (2001). Sexual orientation and eating psychopathology: The role of masculinity and femininity. *International Journal of Eating Disorders*, 29, 413–318.

Meyer, I. H., Teylan, T., & Schwartz, S. (2014). The role of help-seeking in preventing suicide attempts among lesbians, gay men, and bisexuals. *Suicide and Life-threatening Behavior*, 45(1), 25–36. doi:10.1111/sltb.12104 1-12

Meyer, W. F., Moore, C., & Viljoen, H. G. (1993). *Personality theories – from Freud to Frankl*. Johannesburg: Lexicon.

Meyer, W. F., Moore, C., & Viljoen, H. G. (2002). *Personology: From individual to ecosystem*. Cape Town: Heinemann Publishers.

Meyerbröker, K., & Powers, M. B. (2015). Panic disorder and agoraphobia across the lifespan. *International Encyclopedia of the Social & Behavioral Sciences*, 17(2), 474–481.

Mezzich, J., Kleinman, A., Fabrega, H., Jr., & Parron, D. (Eds) (1996). *Culture and psychiatric diagnosis: A DSM-IV perspective*. Washington, DC: American Psychiatric Press.

Mianji, F., & Semnani, Y. (2015). Zār spirit possession in Iran and African countries: Group distress, culture-bound syndrome or cultural concept of distress? *Iran Journal of Psychiatry*, 10(4), 225–232.

Micali, N., Hagberg, K. W., Petersen, I., & Treasure, J. L. (2013). The incidence of eating disorders in the UK in 2000–2009: Findings from the General Practice Research Database. *BMJ Open*, 3(5), e002646. doi:10.1136/bmjopen-2013-002646

Michael, T., Zetsche, U., & Margraf, J. (2007). Epidemiology of anxiety disorders. *Epidemiology and Psychopharmacology*, 6(4), 136–142. doi10.1016/j.mppsy.2007.01.007

Miller, C. A., & Golden, N. H. (2010). An introduction to eating disorders: Clinical presentation, epidemiology, and prognosis. *Nutrition in Clinical Practice*, 25, 110–115.

Miller, M. N., & Pumarierga, A. J. (2001). Culture and eating disorders: A historical and cross-cultural review. *Psychiatry*, 64, 93–110.

Millon, T. (1969). *Modern psychopathology: A biosocial approach to maladaptive learning and functioning*. Philadelphia, PA: W.B. Saunders.

Millon, T. (2004). *Personality disorders in modern life* (2nd ed.). New York, NY: Wiley.

Millon, T., & Davis, R. D. (1996). *Disorders of personality: DSM-IV and beyond*. New York, NY: Wiley.

Millon, T., Davis, R. D., Millon, C., Escovar, L., & Meagher, S. (2000). *Personality disorders in modern life*. New York, NY: Wiley.

Millon, T. & Everly, G. S., Jr. (1985). *Personality and its disorders*. New York, NY: Wiley.

Mills, J., & Gray, A. (2013). Two-tiered violence risk estimates: A validation study of an integrated-actuarial risk assessment instrument. *Psychological Services*, 10(4), 361–371.

Mineka, S., & Zinbarg, R. (2006). A contemporary learning theory perspective on the etiology of anxiety disorders. *American Psychologist*, 61(1), 10–26.

Ministerial Advisory Committee on Gay and Lesbian Health. (2002). *Gay, lesbian, bisexual, transgender and intersex community consultations: Stage one. Introductory paper to accompany issues papers on major health issues affecting GLBTI Victorians, Australia*. Retrieved from http://www.dhs.vic.gov.au/phd/ macglh/ index.htm.

Minuchin, S., Rosman, B. L., & Baker, L. (1978). *Psychosomatic families: Anorexia nervosa in context*. Cambridge, MA: Harvard University Press.

Miric, A. (2015). The rollercoaster journey with bipolar mood disorder. *Mental Health Matters*, 2(4), 18–20.

Misiak, B., & Frydecka, D. (2016). A history of childhood trauma and response to treatment with antipsychotics in first-episode schizophrenia patients: Preliminary results. *Journal of Nervous and Mental Disease*, 204(10), 787–792. doi:10.1097/NMD.0000000000000567

Mitchell, K. S., Mazzeo, S. E., Schlesinger, M. R., Brewerton, T. D., & Smith, B. N. (2012). Comorbidity of partial and subthreshold PTSD among men and women with eating disorders in the national comorbidity survey-replication study. *International Journal of Eating Disorders*, 45(3), 307–315. doi:10.1002/eat.20965

Mitchell, Y., & Nel, J. A. (2017). *The hate and bias crimes monitoring form project: January 2013 to September 2017*. Johannesburg: The Hate Crimes Working Group.

Mokgothu, M. C., Du Plessis, E., & Koen, M. P. (2015). The strengths of families in supporting mentally-ill family members. *Curationis*, 38(1). http://dx.doi.org/10.4102/curationis.v38i1.1258

Mokolobate, K. (2017, October 27). Effects of alcohol consumption in South Africa: From the cradle to the grave. *Mail & Guardian*. Retrieved from https://mg.co.za/article/2017-10-27-00-effects-of-alcohol-consumption-in-south-africa-from-the-cradle-to-the-grave

Moldin, S. O. (1997). The maddening hunt for madness genes. *Nature Genetics*, 17, 127–129.

Moletsane, M. (2004). *The efficacy of the Rorshach among black learners in South Africa* (Unpublished PhD thesis). University of Pretoria, Pretoria, South Africa.

Moletsane, M. K. (2004). *The efficacy of the Rorschach among black learners in South Africa* (Unpublished Phd thesis). University of Pretoria, Pretora, South Africa. Retrieved from https://repository.up.ac.za/ bitstream/handle/2263/27930/Complete.pdf?sequence=4&isAllowed=y

Moletsane, M. K. (2011). *Indigenous African personality and health theories*. Paper presented at a seminar, at the University of Western Cape, Department of Psychology.

Mollow, A., & McRuer, R. (2015). Fattening austerity. *Body Politics: Zeitschrift für Körpergeschichte*, 5, 25–49. Retrieved from https://www.dbthueringen.de/servlets/MCRFileNodeServlet/dbt_derivate_00033041/ Heft_5_03_McRuer_Mollow_Fattening-Austerity.pdf

Money, J. (1984). Paraphilias: Phenomenology and classification. *American Journal of Psychotherapy*, 38(2), 164–179.

Money, J. (1988). *Venuses penuses: Sexology, sexosophy, and exigency theory*. New York, NY: Prometheus Books.

Monosson, E. (2015). *Unnatural selection: How we are changing life gene by gene*. Washington, DC: Island Press.

Moodley, R., & Sutherland, P. (2010). Psychic retreats in other places: Clients who seek healing with traditional healers and psychotherapists. *Counselling Psychology Quarterly*, 23(3), 267–282. doi:10.108 0/09515070.2010.505748

Moosa, M. Y. H., & Jeenah, F. Y. A. (2010). A review of the applications for involuntary admissions made to the Mental Health Review Boards by institutions in Gauteng in 2008. *South African Journal of Psychology*, 16(4), 125–130.

Morgan, W. G. (1995). Origin and history of the Thematic Apperception Test images. *Journal of Personality Assessment*, 65, 237–252.

Moseneke, D. (2018). *Award in the arbitration between: Families of mental health care users affected by the Gauteng Mental Marathon Project (Claimants) and National Minister of Health of the Republic of South Africa, Government of the province of Gauteng, member of the Executive Council of Health: Province of Gauteng (Respondents).* Retrieved March 19, 2019, from. http://www.gauteng.gov.za/government/ departments/office-of-the-premier/Life%20Esidimeni%20Documents/Life%20Esidimeni%20 arbitration%20award%20by%20retired%20Deputy%20Chief%20Justice%20Dikgang%20Mosenke.pdf

Moser, C. (1999). Health care without shame. A handbook for the sexually diverse and their caregivers. San Francisco, CA: Greenery Press.

Moser, P. W. (1989). Double vision: Why do we never match up to our mind's ideal? *Self Magazine*, January, 51–52.

Mosotho, L., Louw, D., & Calitz, F. J. W. (2011a). Schizophrenia among Sesotho speakers in South Africa. *African Journal of Psychiatry*, 14, 50–55.

Mosotho, L., Louw, D. A., & Calitz, F. J. W. (2011b). The manifestation of anxiety among Sesotho speakers. *South African Journal of Psychology*, 41(4), 437–450.

Motlana, N. (1988). The tyranny of superstition. *Nursing SA*, 3(1), 17–18.

Motsi, R. G., & Masango, M. J. (2012). Redefining trauma in an African context: A challenge to pastoral care. *HTS Teologiese Studies/Theological Studies*, 68(1), Article 955. http://dx.doi.org/10.4102/hts.v68i1.955

Mould, J., Grobler, A. A., Odendaal, D. C., & De Jager, L. (2011). Ethnic differences in age of onset and prevalence of disordered eating attitudes and behaviours: A school-based South African study. *South African Journal of Clinical Nutrition*, 24(3), 137–141.

Moynihan, R. (2003). The making of a disease: Female sexual dysfunction. *British Medical Journal*, 326, 45–47.

Mueser, K., Yarnold, P., & Levinson, D. (1990). Prevalence of substance abuse in schizophrenia: demographic and clinical correlates. *Schizophrenia Bulletin*, 16, 31–56.

Mukolo, A., Heflinger, C. A., & Wallston, K. A. (2010). The stigma of childhood mental disorders: A conceptual framework. *Journal of the American Academy of Child and Adolescent Psychiatry*, 49(2), 92–103.

Mulders-Jones, B., Mitchison, D., Girosi, F., & Hay, P. (2017) Socioeconomic correlates of eating disorder symptoms in an Australian population-based sample. *PloS One*, 12(1), 1–17. doi:10.1371/journal. pone.0170603

Murphy, A., & Janeke, H. C. (2009). The relationship between thinking styles and emotional intelligence: An exploratory study. *South African Journal of Psychology*, 39(3), 357–375.

Murray, C. J. L., & Lopez, A. D. (1996). *The global burden of disease: A comprehensive assessment of mortality and disability from disease, injuries and risk factors in 1990 and projected to 2020.* Cambridge, MA: Harvard University Press.

Murray, R. M. (2017). Mistakes I have made in my research career. *Schizophrenia Bulletin*, 43(2), 253–256. doi: 10.1093/schbul/sbw165

Murstein, B. I. (1972). A thematic test and the Rorschach in predicting marital choice. *Journal of Personality Assessment*, 36(3), 213–217.

Musisi, S. (2004). Mass trauma and mental health in Africa. *African Health Sciences*, 4(2), 80–82.

Mwaba, K., & Roman, N. V. (2009). Body image satisfaction among a sample of black female South African students. *Social Behavior and Personality: An International Journal*, 37(7), 905–909. doi:10.2224/ sbp.2009.37.7.905

Myers, T. A. (2015). Feminist theories of eating disorders. In L. Smolak & M. P. Levine (Eds), *The Wiley handbook of eating disorders*. Chichester, UK: John Wiley & Sons, 238–252.

Naidoo, A. V. (1996). Challenging the hegemony of Eurocentric Psychology. *Journal of Community and Health Sciences*, 2(2), 9–16.

Narcotics Anonymous, Inc. (2012). *Narcotics anonymous world services*. Retrieved July 21, 2012, from www.NA.org/

National Academies of Sciences, Engineering and Medicine (NAP). (1999). *Marijuana and medicine: Assessing the Science Base*. Washington, DC: National Academies Press.

National Department of Health, South Africa. (2012). *National mental health policy framework and strategic plan 2013–2020*. Pretoria: National Department of Health.

National Geographic. (2017). Gender revolution. *National Geographic*, 231(1), 1–154.

National Institute on Drug Abuse (NIDA). (2016, February). *DrugFacts: Genetics and epigenetics of addiction*. Retrieved from https://www.drugabuse.gov/publications/drugfacts/genetics-epigenetics-addiction

National Institute on Drug Abuse (NIDA). (2017). *Marijuana*. Retrieved from https://www.drugabuse.gov

National Institute on Drug Abuse (NIDA). (2018, July). *Drugs, brains and behaviour: The science of addiction (Revised)*. Retrieved from https://www.drugabuse.gov/publications/drugs-brains-behavior-science-addiction/preface

Ndetei, D. M., Khasakhala, L., Kuria, M., Mutiso, V., Ongecha, F. A., & Kokonya, D. (2009). The prevalence of mental disorders in adults in different level general medical facilities in Kenya: A cross-sectional study. *Annals of General Psychiatry*, 8(1). Retrieved from http://www.annals-general-psychiatry.com/content/8/1/1

Ndetei, D. M., & Singh, A. (1983). Hallucinations in Kenyan schizophrenic patients. *Acta Psychiatrica Scandinavica*, 67, 144–147.

Ndetei, D. M., & Vadher, A. (1984). A cross-cultural study of the frequencies of Schneider's first-rank symptoms of Schizophrenia. *Acta Psychiatrica Scandinavica*, 70, 540–544.

Negash, A. (2009). *Bipolar disorder in rural Ethiopia: Community-based studies in Butajira for screening, epidemiology, follow-up, and the burden of care* (Unpublished doctoral dissertation). University of Umeå, Umeå, Sweden.

Nel, J. A. (1999). Sexual and gender identity disorders. In A. Novello (Ed.), *Abnormal psychology: An integrative approach: A workbook for South African Students*. Johannesburg: Thomson, 117–125.

Nel, J. A. (2005a). Hate crimes: A new category of vulnerable victims for a new South Africa. In L. Davis & R. Snyman (Eds), *Victimology in South Africa*. Pretoria: Van Schaik, 240–256.

Nel, J. A. (2005b). Moving from rhetoric to creating the reality: Empowering South Africa's lesbian and gay community. In M. van Zyl & M. Steyn (Eds), *Performing queer: Shaping sexualities 1994–2004*. Cape Town: Kwela Books, 281–300.

Nel, J. A. (2007). Counteracting heterosexism and introducing LGBTI-affirmative stance in the psychology curriculum: A roundtable discussion. Retrieved February 25, 2008, from http://uovs.ac.za/faculties/documents/01/163/conference2007.

Nel, J. A. (2009). Same-sex sexuality and health: Current psycho-social scientific research in South Africa. In V. Reddy, T. Sandfort, & L. Rispel (Eds), *Same-sex sexuality, HIV & AIDS and gender in South Africa*. Proceedings of an international conference on gender, same-sex sexuality and HIV/ AIDS, 9–11 May 2007. Pretoria: HSRC Press.

Nel, J. A., & Lake, M. (2005). Sexual and gender identity disorders. In A. Burke (Ed.), *Abnormal Psychology in South Africa*. Cape Town: Oxford University Press.

Neumark-Stainer, D., & Haines, J. (2004). Psychological and behavioural consequences of obesity. In J. K. Thompson (Ed.), *Handbook of eating disorders and obesity*. New York, NY: John Wiley, 349–371.

Ng, L., & Davis, C. (2013). Cravings and food consumption in binge eating disorder. *Eating Behaviors*, 14(4), 472–475. doi:10.1016/j.eatbeh.2013.08.011

Ngcobo, M., & Pillay, B. J. (2008). Depression in African women presenting for psychological services at a general hospital. *African Journal of Psychiatry*, 11(2), 133–137.

Nicholas, L., Daniels, P., & Hurwitz, M. (2001). Part 1: A perspective on the people of color. In R. T. Francoeur (Ed.). *International Encyclopedia of Sexuality* (4). London: Continuum International.

Niehaus, D. O. (2004). A culture-bound syndrome 'amafufunyana' and a culture-specific event 'ukuthwasa': Differentiated by a family history of Schizophrenia and other psychiatric disorders. *Psychopathology*, 37(2), 59–63.

Nielsen, E. B., Lyon, M., & Ellison, G. (1983). Apparent hallucinations in monkeys during around-the-clock amphetamine for seven to fourteen days. *Journal of Nervous Mental Disorder*, 171, 222–233.

Nissenbaum, M. S. (2005). Autism. *Encyclopedia of human development*. Retrieved March 20, 2009, from http://www.sage-ereference.com/humandevelopment/Article_n67.html

Njenga, F. G., & Kangethe, R. N. (2004). Anorexia nervosa in Kenya. *East African Medical Journal*, 1(4), 188–193.

Nock, M. K., Wedig, M. M., Holmberg, E. B., & Hooley, J. M. (2008). The emotion reactivity scale: Development, evaluation, and relation to self-injurious thoughts and behaviors. *Behavior Therapy*, 39(2), 107–116. doi:10.1016/j.beth.2007.05.005

Nolen-Hoeksema, S. (2007). *Abnormal psychology* (3rd ed.). Boston, MA: McGraw-Hill.

Nolen-Hoeksema, S. (2013). *Abnormal psychology* (6th ed.). New York, NY: McGraw-Hill Education.

Nolen-Hoeksema, S., & Davis, C. G. (2002). Positive responses to loss: Perceiving benefits and growth. In C. R. Snyder & S. J. Lopez (Eds), *Handbook of positive psychology*. Oxford: Oxford University Press, 598–607.

Nopoulos, P., Flaum, M., & Andreasen, N. C. (1997). Sex differences in brain morphology in Schizophrenia. *American Journal of Psychiatry*, 154(12), 1648–1654.

Norris, D. L. (1979). Clinical diagnostic criteria for primary anorexia nervosa. *South African Medical Journal*, 56, 987–993.

Norris, M. L., Boydell, K. M., Pinhas, L., & Katzman, D. K. (2006). Ana and the Internet: A review of pro-anorexia websites. *International Journal of Eating Disorders*, 39, 443–447.

Nzimande, B. (1986). Industrial psychology and the study of black workers in South Africa: A review and critique. *Psychology in Society*, 2, 54–91.

Obesity and food addiction summit. (2011). Retrieved 2012, from http://www.foodaddictionsummit.org.

Occhiogrosso, M. (2008). 'Gourmandizing', gluttony and oral fixations. Perspectives on overeating in the American Journal of Psychiatry 1844 to present. In L. C. Rubin (Ed.), *Food for thought: Essays of eating and culture*. Jefferson, NC: MacFarland & Company, 265–290.

Ogden, C. L., Carroll, M. D., Curtin, L. R., McDowell, M. A., Tabak, C. J., & Flegal, K. M. (2006). Prevalence of overweight and obesity in the United States, 1999–2004. *Journal of the American Medical Association*, 295, 1549–1555.

Okasha, A. (2001). Egyptian contributions to the concept of mental health. *Eastern Mediterranean Health Journal*, 7(3), 377–380.

Oksanen, A., Garcia, D., Sirola, A., Näsi, M., Kaakinen, M., Keipi, T., & Räsänen, P. (2015). Pro-anorexia and anti-pro-anorexia videos on YouTube: Sentiment analysis of user responses. *Journal of Medical Internet Research*, 17(11), e256. doi:10.2196/jmir.5007

Oldham, J. M. (2009). Borderline Personality Disorder comes of age. *American Journal of Psychiatry*, 166(5), 509–511.

Olfson, M., Gerhard, T., Huang, C., Crystal, S., & Stroup, T. S. (2015). Premature mortality among adults with schizophrenia in the United States. *JAMA Psychiatry*, 72(12), 1172–1181. doi:10.1001/jamapsychiatry.2015

Olivier, I., Curfs, I., & Viljoen, D. (2016). Fetal alcohol spectrum disorders: Prevalence rates in South Africa. *South African Medical Journal*, 106(6 Suppl 1), S103–S106.

Orford, J. (1992). *Community psychology: Theory and practice*. Chichester: Wiley.

O'Shaughnessy, R., & Dallos, R. (2009). Review of attachment research and eating disorders: A review of the literature. *Clinical Child Psychology and Psychiatry*, 14(4), 559–574.

Otte, C., Gold, S. M., Penninx, B. W., Pariante, C. M., Etkin, A., Fava, M., Mohrm, D. C., & Schatzberg, A. F. (2016). Major depressive disorder. *Nature Reviews. Disease Primers*, 15(2), 16065. doi:10.1038/nrdp.2016.65.

Pai, A., Suris, A. M., & North, C. S. (2017). Posttraumatic stress disorder in the DSM-5: Controversy, change and conceptual considerations. *Behavioural Sciences*, 7(7), e7. doi:10.3390/bs7010007

Painter, D., & TerreBlanche, M. (2004). *Critical psychology in South Africa: Looking back and looking forwards*. Retrieved from http://www.criticalmethods.org/collab/critpsy.htm

Pan-American Health Organization and World Health Organization. (2000). *Promotion of sexual health: Recommendations for action*. Antigua Guatemala: PAHO. Promotion of sexual health: Recommendations for action. Proceedings of a regional consultation convened by Pan-American Health Organisation (PAHO) and World Health Organisation (WHO), in collaboration with the World Association for Sexology (WAS), Antigua, Guatemala, May 19–22, 2000, pp. 37–38.

Paquette, M. C., & Raine, K. (2004). Sociocultural context of women's' body image. *Social Science and Medicine*, 59, 1047–1058.

Park, N., Peterson, C., & Seligman, M. E. P. (2004). Strengths of character and well-being. *Journal of Social and Clinical Psychology*, 23(5), 603–619.

Parker, J. D. A., Summerfeldt, L. J., Hogan, M. J., & Majeski, S. A. (2004). Emotional intelligence and academic success: Examining the transition from high school to university. *Personality and Individual Differences*, 36, 163–172.

Parle, J. (2003). Witchcraft or madness? The Amandiki of Zululand, 1894–1914. *Journal of Southern African Studies*, 29(1), 105–132.

Paruk, L., & Janse van Rensburg, A. B. R. (2016). Inpatient management of borderline personality disorder at Helen Joseph Hospital, Johannesburg. *South African Journal of Psychiatry*, 22(1), a678. http://dx.doi.org/10.4102/sajpsychiatry.v22i1.678

Paxton, S. J., Schutz, H. K., Wertheim, E. H., & Muir, S. L. (1999). Friendship clique and peer influences on body image concerns, dietary restraint, extreme weight-loss behaviors, and binge eating in adolescent girls. *Journal of Abnormal Psychology*, 108, 255–264.

Pedro, T. M., Micklesfield, L. K., Kahn, K., Tollman, S. M., Pettifor, J. M., & Norris, S. A. (2016). Body image satisfaction, eating attitudes and perceptions of female body silhouettes in rural South African adolescents. *PLoS One*, 11(5), e0154784. doi:10.1371/journal.pone.0154784

Peltzer, K. ((2009). *Traditional health practitioners in South Africa*. Retrieved April 15, 2019, from http://www.hsrc.ac.za/uploads/pageContent/1550/25aug09lancetpeltzer.pdf

Peltzer, K., Davids, A., & Njuho, P. (2010). Alcohol use and problem drinking South Africa: findings from a national population based survey. *African Journal of Psychiatry*, 14(1), 30–37.

Peltzer, K., & Phaswana-Mafuya, N. (2018). Drug use among youth and adults in a population-based survey in South Africa. *South African Journal of Psychiatry*, 24, 1608–1614.

Pérez-Edgar, K., & Fox, N. A. (2005). Temperament and anxiety disorders. *Child and Adolescent Psychiatric Clinics*, 14, 681–786.

Perkins, D. O., Gu, H., Boteva, K., & Lieberman, J. A. (2005). Relationship between duration of untreated psychosis and outcome in first-episode Schizophrenia: A critical review and meta-analysis. *American Journal of Psychiatry*, 162(10), 1785–1804.

Perloff, R. M. (2014). Social media effects on young women's body image concerns: Theoretical perspectives and an agenda for research. *Sex Roles*, 71(11–12), 363–377. doi:10.1007/s11199-014-0384-6

Perry, J. C. (1993). Longitudinal studies of personality disorders. *Journal of Personality Disorders*, Suppl. 1, 63–85.

Petchesky, R. (2008). Introduction: Sexual rights policies across countries and cultures: Conceptual frameworks and minefields. In R. Parker, R. Petchesky, & R. Sembler (Eds), *SexPolitics. Reports from the front lines*. Sexuality Policy Watch, 9–25. Retrieved February 9, 2012, from http://www.siyanda.org/docs/sexpolitics.pdf

Peters, M. E., & Chisolm, M. S. (2017). *The perspectives approach to psychiatry*. Retrieved from https://www.hopkinsguides.com/hopkins/view/Johns_Hopkins_Psychiatry_Guide/787008/all/The_Perspectives_Approach_to_Psychiatry

Petersen, C., Norris, S., Pettifor, J., & MacKeown, J. (2006). Eating attitudes in a group of 11-year old urban South African girls. *South African Journal of Clinical Nutrition*, 19(2), 80–85. doi:10.1080/16070658.2006.11734096

Petersen, I. (2010). At the heart of development: An introduction to mental health promotion and the prevention of mental health disorders in scarce-resource contexts. In I. Petersen, A. Bhana, A. J. Flisher, L. Swartz, & L. Richter (Eds), *Promoting mental health in scare-resource contexts*. Cape Town: Human Sciences Research Council, 3–36.

Petersen, I., & Lund, C. (2011). Mental health service delivery in South Africa from 2000 to 2010: One step forward, one step back. *South African Medical Journal*, 101, 751–757.

Peterson, C. (2006). *A primer in positive psychology*. New York, NY: Oxford University Press.

Pettifor, J. L., & Sawchuk, T. R. (2006). Psychologists' perceptions of ethically troubling incidents across international borders. *International Journal of Psychology*, 41(3), 216–225.

Phan, T. (2006). Resilience as coping mechanism: A common story of Vietnamese refugee women. In P. Wong & L. Wong (Eds), *Handbook of multicultural perspectives on stress and coping*. New York NY: Springer, 427–437.

Phend, C. (2009). APA: Borderline Personality Disorder often missed first time around. *MedPage Today*, 22, 1–3.

Philen, R. M., Kilbourne, E. M., McKinley, T. W., & Parrish, R. G. (1989). Mass sociogenic illness by proxy: Parentally reported epidemic in an elementary school. *Lancet*, 9(2), 1372–1376.

Philipps, D. (2016, November 29). F.D.A. agrees to new trials for Ecstasy as relief for PTSD patients. *The New York Times*. Retrieved from https://www.nytimes.com/2016/11/29/us/ptsd-mdma-ecstasy.html

Phillips, K. A., Yen, S., & Gunderson, J. G. (2003). Personality disorders. In R. E. Hales & S. C. Yudofsky (Eds), *Textbook of clinical psychiatry* (4th ed.). Washington, DC: American Psychatric Publishing, 804–832.

Picchioni, M. M., & Murray, R. (2008). Schizophrenia. *Scholarpedia*, 3(4), 4132. Retrieved from *www.scholarpedia.org/article/Schizophrenia*

Pigg, S. L., & Adams, V. (2005). Introduction: The moral object of sex. In V. Adams & S. L. Pigg (Eds), *Development science, sexuality and morality in global perspective*. Durham, NC: Duke University Press, 1–38.

Pike, K. M., Hoek, H. W., & Dunne, P. E. (2014). Cultural trends and eating disorders. *Current Opinion in Psychiatry*, 27(6), 436–442. doi:10.1097/YCO.0000000000000100

Pike, K. M., & Rodin, J. (1991). Mothers, daughters, and disordered eating. *Journal of Abnormal Psychology*, 100(2), 198–204.

Pillay, B. J. (1996). A model of help-seeking behaviour for urban Africans. *South African Journal of Psychology*, 1, 4–9.

Pillay B. J. (2000). Providing mental health services to survivors: A KwaZulu-Natal perspective. *Ethnicity and Health*, 5(3), 269–272.

Pillay, J. (2003). 'Community psychology is all theory and no practice': Training educational psychologists in community practice within the South African context. *South African Journal of Psychology*, 33(4), 261–268.

Pincus, A., & Krueger, R. F. (2015). Theodore Millon's Contributions to Conceptualizing Personality Disorders. *Journal of Personality Assessment*, 97(6), 1–4.

Pinel, P. (1801/1962). *A Treatise of Insanity*. New York, NY: Hafner.

Pliner, P., & Haddock, G. (1996). Perfectionism in weight-concerned and unconcerned women: An experimental approach. *International Journal of Eating Disorders*, 19, 381–389.

Polders, L. A. (2006). *Factors affecting vulnerability to depression among gay men and lesbian women* (Unpublished master's dissertation). University of South Africa, Pretoria, South Africa.

Pope, H. G., Jr., & Hudson, J. I. (1992). Is childhood sexual abuse a risk factor for bulimia nervosa? *American Journal of Psychiatry*, 149, 455–463.

Pope, K. S., & Vasques, M. (2007). *Ethics in psychotherapy and counseling: A practical guide* (3rd ed.). San Francisco, CA: Jossey-Bass.

Porter, R. (2002). *Madness: A brief history*. Oxford: Oxford University Press.

Priest, J. B. (2015). A Bowen family systems model of generalized anxiety disorder and romantic relationship distress. *Journal of Marital and Family Therapy*, 41(3), 340–353.

Prinsloo, J. F. & Louw, D. A. (1989). Selfmoord. In D. A. Louw, (Ed.), *Suid-Afrikaanse handboek van abnormale gedrag*. Pretoria: Kagiso Tertiary.

Prioreschi, A., Wrottesley, S. V., Cohen, E., Reddy, A., Said-Mohamed, R., Twine, R., … Norris, S. A. (2017). Examining the relationships between body image, eating attitudes, BMI, and physical activity in rural and urban South African young adult females using structural equation modeling. *PloS One*, 12(11), e0187508. doi:10.1371/journal.pone.0187508

Psychological Society of South Africa (PsySSA). (1994). A new-look psychological society for South Africa. Newsletter of the Psychological Society for South Africa (PsySSA), 1(1), 1.

Psychological Society of South Africa (PsySSA). (2017). *Practice guidelines for psychology professionals working with sexually and gender-diverse people*. Johannesburg: Psychological Society of South Africa.

Puoane, T., Fourie, J. M., Shapiro, M., Rosling, L., Tshaka, N. C., & Oelefse, A. (2005). 'Big is beautiful' – an exploration with urban black community health workers in a South African township. *South African Journal of Clinical Nutrition*, 18(1), 6–15. doi:10.1080/16070658.2005.11734033

Qi, W., & Cui, L. (2018). Being successful and being thin: The effects of thin-ideal social media images with high socioeconomic status on women's body image and eating behaviour. *Journal of Pacific Rim Psychology*, 12, e8. doi.org/10.1017/prp.2017.16

Rab, F., Mamdou, R., & Nasir, S. (2008). Rates of depression and anxiety among female medical students in Pakistan. *Eastern Mediterranean Health Journal*, 14, 126 133.

Rachman, S. (2000). Obituaries: Joseph Wolpe (1915–1997). *American Psychologist*, 55(4), 441–442.

Ramlall, S., Chipps, J., & Mars, M. (2010). Impact of the South African Mental Health Care Act No. 17 of 2002 on regional and district hospitals designated for mental health care in KwaZulu-Natal. *South African Medical Journal*, 100(10), 667–670.

Rao, M. A., Donaldson, S. I., & Doiron, K. M. (2015). Positive psychology research in the Middle East and North Africa. *Middle East Journal of Positive Psychology*, 1(1), 60–76.

Ratnasuriya, R. H., Eisler, I., Szmukler, G. I., & Russell, G. F. M. (1991). Anorexia Nervosa: Outcome and prognostic factors after 20 years. *British Journal of Psychiatry*, 158(4), 495–502. doi:10.1192/bjp.158.4.495

Reed, G. M., Drescher, J., Krueger, R. B., Atalla, E., Cochran, S. D., First, M. B., … Saxena, S. (2016). Disorders related to sexuality and gender identity in the ICD-11: Revising the ICD-10 classification based on current scientific evidence, best clinical practices, and human rights considerations. *World Psychiatry*, 15, 205–221.

Reed, G. M., First, M. B., Kogan, C. S., Hyman, S. E., Gureje, O., Gaebel, W., … Claudino, A. (2019). Innovations and changes in the ICD-11 classification of mental, behavioural and neurodevelopmental disorders. *World Psychiatry*, 18(1), 3–19. doi:10.1002/wps.20611

Regier, D. A., Kuhl, E. A., & Kupfer, D. J. (2013). The DSM-5: Classification and criteria changes. *World Psychiatry*, 12(2): 92–98. doi:10.1002/wps.20050

Reid, G., & Dirsuweit, T. (2002). Understanding systemic violence. *Urban Forum*, 31(3), 99–126.

Reid, J. A. (2011). Crime and Personality: Personality Theory and Criminality Examined. *Inquiries*, 3(1).

Reid, H. K., & Sheeby, N. (1990). The grand unification theory of alcohol abuse: It's time to stop fighting each other and start working together. In R. C. Engs (Ed.), *Controversies in the addiction field*. Dubuque, IA: Kendall-Hunt, 2–9.

Reineke, M. A. (2006). Problem-solving: A conceptual approach to suicidality and psychotherapy. In F. M. Dattilio & A. Freeman (Eds), *Cognitive behavioural strategies in crisis intervention* (3rd ed.). New York, NY: Guilford Press, 25–67.

Republic of South Africa. (2003). *Alteration of Sex Description and Sex Status Act, 2003*, Act No. 49 of 2003. Retrieved from http://www.gov.za/documents/index.php?term=alteration+of+sex&dfrom=&dto=&yr=0&tps%5B%5D=1&subjs%5B%5D=0

Resick, P. A., Monson, C. M., & Chard, K. M. (2017). *Cognitive Processing Therapy for PTSD: A Comprehensive Manual*. The Guilford Press: New York.

Revelas, A. (2013). Eating disorders are real treatable medical illnesses. *South African Family Practice*, 55(3), 252–255. doi:10.1080/20786204.2013.10874346

Reynolds, G. P. (1989). Beyond the dopamine hypothesis. The neurochemical pathology of schizophrenia. *British Journal of Psychiatry*, 155, 305–316.

Ritchie, K., & Fuhrer, R. (1992). A comparative study of the performance of screening: Tests for senile dementia using receiver operating characteristics analysis. *Journal of Clinical Epidemiology*, 45(6), 627–637.

Ritchie, K., & Fuhrer, R. (1994). The development and validation in France of a screening test for senile dementia. *Revue Geriatric*, 19, 223–242.

Rittenbaugh, C., Shisslak, C., & Prince, R. (1992). A cross-cultural review in regard to the DSM-IV. In J. E. Mezzich, H. Fabrega, A. Kleinman, & D. Perron (Eds), *Culture and psychiatric diagnosis: A DSM-IV perspective*. Washington, DC: American Psychiatric Association Press, 171–186.

Robinson, M., & Wilson, G. (2011). *Toss your textbooks: Docs redefine sexual behaviour addictions*. Retrieved January 15, 2012, from http://www.psychologytoday.com

Roberts, A., & Muta, S. (2017). Representations of female body weight in the media: An update of Playboy magazine from 2000 to 2014. *Body Image*, 20, 16–19. doi.org/10.1016/j.bodyim.2016.08.009

Robertson, L. J., Janse van Rensburg, B., Talatala, M., Chambers, C., Sunkel, C., Patel, B., & Stevenson, S. (2018). Unpacking Recommendation 16 of the Health Ombud's report on the Life Esidimeni tragedy. *SAMJ: South African Medical Journal*, 108(5), 362–363. doi:10.7196/samj.2018.v108i5.13223

Rodgers, J. E. (1994). Addiction: A whole new view. *Psychology Today*. Retrieved August, 13, 2012, from https://www.psychologytoday.com/us/articles/199409/addiction-whole-new-view

Rodgers, R. F., McLean, S. A., & Paxton, S. J. (2015). Longitudinal relationships among internalization of the media ideal, peer social comparison, and body dissatisfaction: Implications for the tripartite influence model. *Developmental Psychology*, 51(5), 706–713. doi:10.1037/dev0000013

Rodseth, D. (2011). Dealing with bipolar disorder in general practice. *South African Family Practice*, 53(6), 549–552.

Roff, J. D., & Knight, R. (1981). Family characteristics, childhood symptoms, and adult outcome in schizophrenia. *Journal of Abnormal Psychology*, 90, 510–520.

Rogers, R. (1988). *Clinical assessment of deception and malingering*. New York, NY: Guilford Press.

Rogers, R., Salekin, R. T., Sewell, K. W., Goldstein, A., & Leonard, K. (1998). A comparison of forensic and nonforensic malingerers: A prototypical analysis of explanatory models. *Law and Human Behavior*, 22(4), 353–367.

Rome, H. P. (2000). Limbically augmented pain syndrome (LAPS): Kindling, corticolimbic sensitization, and the convergence of affective and sensory symptoms in chronic pain disorders. *Pain Medicine*, 1(1), 7–23.

Roos, V., Chigeza, S., & Van Niekerk, D. (2012). Relational coping strategies of older adults in a rural African context. In M. P. Wissing (Ed.), *Well-being research in South Africa: Cross-cultural advancements in positive psychology*. Dordrecht: Springer, 375–388.

Root, M. P. (1990). Disordered eating in women of color. *Sex Roles*, 22, 525–536.

Ropper, A. H. (2001). Deafness, dizziness and disorders of equilibrium. In A. H. Ropper (Ed.), *Adams and Victor's principles of neurology* (7th ed.). New York, NY: McGraw-Hill, 301–328.

Rosen, J. C., & Leitenberg, H. (1985). Exposure plus response prevention treatment of bulimia. In D. M. Gamer & P. E. Garfinkel (Eds), *Handbook of psychotherapy for anorexia nervosa and bulimia*. New York, NY: Guilford Press, 193–209.

Rosenfeld, B., Foellmi, M., Khadivi, A., Wijetunga, C., Howe, J., Nijdam-Jones, A., Grover, S., & Rotter, M. (2017). Determining when to conduct a violence risk assessment: Development and initial validation of the Fordham Risk Screening Tool (FRST). *Law and Human Behavior*, 41(4), 325–332. doi:10.1037/lhb0000247

Rosenhan, D. L. (1973). On being sane in insane places. *Science*, 179(70), 250–258.

Rouleau, I., Salmon, D. P., Butters, N. (1996). Longitudinal analysis of clock drawing in Alzheimer's disease patients. *Brain Cognition*, 31, 17–34.

Roy, A. (2001). Consumers of mental health services. *Suicide and Life-Threatening Behaviour*, 31, 60–83.

Roy, A. K., Lopes, V., & Klein, R. G. (2014). Disruptive mood dysregulation disorder (DMDD): A new diagnostic approach to chronic irritability in youth. *American Journal of Psychiatry*, 171(9), 918–924.

Rudaz, M., Ledermann, T., Margraf, J., Becker, E. S., & Craske, M. G. (2017). The moderating role of avoidance behaviour on anxiety over time: Is there a difference between social anxiety disorder and specific phobia? *PLoS One*, 12(7), e0180298. doi: 10.1371/journal.pone.0180298.

Ruini, C., & Fava, G. A. (2004). Clinical applications of well-being therapy. In P. A. Linley & S. Joseph (Eds), *Positive psychology in practice*. Hoboken, NJ: John Wiley, 371–389.

Rutherford, J., McGuffin, P., Katz, R. J., & Murray, R. M. (1993). Genetic influences on eating attitudes in a normal female twin population. *Psychological Medicine*, 23, 425–436.

Rutter, M. (2000). Genetic studies of Autism: From the 1970s into the millennium. *Journal of Abnormal Child Psychology*, 28(1), 3–14.

Rutter, M., Macdonald, H., Le Couteur, A., Harrington, R., Bolton, P., & Bailey, A. (1990). Genetic factors in child psychiatric disorders – II. Empirical findings. *Journal of Child Psychology and Psychiatry*, 31(1), 39–83. doi:10.1111/j.1469-7610.1990.tb02273.x

Ryan, C., Nielssen, O., Paton, M., & Large, M. (2010). Clinical decisions in psychiatry should not be based on risk assessment. *Australasian Psychiatry* 18(5), 398–403.

Ryan, R. M., & Deci, E. L. (2000). Self-determination theory and the facilitation of intrinsic motivation, social development, and well-being. *American Psychologist*, 55(1), 68–78.

Ryff, C. D., & Keyes, C. L. (1995). The structure of psychological well-being revisited. *Journal of Personality and Social Psychology*, 69, 719–727.

Ryff, C. D., & Singer, B. (1998). The contours of positive human health. *Psychological Inquiry*, 9, 1–8.

Ryff, C. D., & Singer, B. (2003). Flourishing under fire: Resilience as a prototype of challenged thriving. In C. L. M. Keyes & J. Haidt (Eds), *Flourishing: Positive psychology and the life well-lived*. Washington, DC: American Psychological Association, 15–36.

Saban, A., Flisher, A. J., Grimsrud, A., Morojele, N., London, L., Williams, D. R., & Stein, D. J. (2014). The association between substance use and common mental disorders in young adults: Results from the South African Stress and Health (SASH) survey. *Pan African Medical Journal*, 17 Suppl 1, 11. doi: 10.11694/pamj.supp.2014.17.1.3328.

SADAG Conference. (April 2011). South African Depression and Anxiety Group (SADAG). 34 Key SA journalists attend SADAG conference on mental health reporting. *African Journal of Psychiatry*, 164–166.

Sadock, B. J., & Sadock, V. A. (2000). *Kaplan & Sadock's comprehensive textbook of psychiatry* (7th ed.). Philadelphia, PA: Lippincott Williams & Wilkins.

Sadock, B. J., & Sadock, V. A. (2007). *Kaplan and Sadock's synopsis of psychiatry: Behavioral sciences/clinical psychiatry* (10th ed.). Philadelphia, PA: Lippincott, Williams & Wilkins.

Sadock, B. J., Sadock, V. A., & Ruiz, P. (2015). *Kaplan and Sadock's synopsis of psychiatry: Behavioral sciences/ clinical psychiatry* (11th ed.). Philadelphia: Wolters Kluwer.

Sadock, B. J., Sadock, V. A., & Ruiz, P. (2017). *Kaplan and Sadock's comprehensive textbook of psychiatry*. Philadelphia: Wolters Kluwer.

Şahin, S., Yüksel, Ç., Güler, J., Karadayı, G., Akturan, E., Göde, E., Özhan, A. A., & Üçok, A. (2013). The history of childhood trauma among individuals with ultra high risk for psychosis is as common as among patients with first-episode schizophrenia. *Early Intervention in Psychiatry*, 7(4), 414–420. doi:10.1111/eip.12022

SA History Online. 2008. *SAHO Classroom: Grades 4–12*. Retrieved from *https://www.sahistory.org.za/classroom*

Salovey, P., Bedell, B. T., Detweiler, J. B., & Mayer, J. D. (1999). Coping intelligently: Emotional intelligence and the coping process. In C. R. Snyder (Ed.), *Coping: The psychology of what works*. New York, NY: Oxford University Press, 141–164.

Salovey, P., & Mayer, J. D. (1990). Emotional intelligence. *Imagination, Cognition and Personality*, 9, 185–211.

Salovey, P., Mayer, J. D., & Caruso, D. (2002). The positive psychology of emotional intelligence. In C. R. Snyder & S. J. Lopez (Eds), *Handbook of positive psychology*. Oxford: Oxford University Press, 159–171.

Salovey, P., Stroud, L. R., Woolery, A., & Epel, E. S. (2002). Perceived emotional intelligence, stress reactivity, and symptom reports: Further explorations using the trait meta-mood scale. *Psychology & Health*, 17, 611–627.

Samelius, L., & Wägberg, E. (2005). *Sexual orientation and gender identity issues in development*. Stockholm: Swedish International Development Co-operation Agency Health Division.

Sander, J. B., & McCarty, C. A. (2005). Youth depression in the family context: Familial risk factors and models of treatment. *Clinical Child and Family Psychology Review*, 8(3), 203–219.

Sarason, I. G. & Sarason, B. R. (1993). *Abnormal psychology: The problem of maladaptive behavior* (7th ed.). Englewood Cliffs, NJ: Prentice Hall.

Sartorius, N., Shapiro, R., & Jablonsky, A. (1974). The international pilot study of Schizophrenia. *Schizophrenia Bulletin*, 2, 21–35.

Saunders, E. (2008). *Assessment in South Africa: Finding method in madness*. Retrieved May 31, 2008, from http://www.workinfo.com/free/Downloads/36.htm

Schafer, W. (2000). *Stress management for wellness* (4th ed.). Belmont, CA: Thomson.

Scherrer, R., Louw, D. A., & Möller, A. T. (2002). Ethical complaints and disciplinary action against South African psychologists. *South African Journal of Psychology*, 32(1), 54–64.

Schlachter, A., & Duckitt, J. (2002). Psychopathology, authoritarian attitudes and prejudice. *South African Journal of Psychology*, 32(2), 1–8.

Schmidt, R., Tetzlaff, A., & Hilbert, A. (2015). Perceived expressed emotion in adolescents with binge-eating disorder. *Journal of Abnormal Child Psychology*, 43(7), 1369–1377. doi:10.1007/s10802-015-0015-x

Schmidt, U., Evans, K., Tiller, J., & Treasure, J. (1995). Puberty, sexual milestones and abuse: How are they related in eating disorder patients? *Psychological Medicine*, 25, 413–417.

Schneider, K. (1959). *Clinical psychopathology*. New York, NY: Grune & Stratton.

Schneier, F., & Goldmark, J. (2015). Social anxiety disorder. In D. J. Stein & B. Vythilingum (Eds), *Anxiety disorders and gender*. Cham, Switzerland: Springer International Publishing, 49–67. http://dx.doi.org/10.1007/978-3-319-13060-6_3

Schwartz, C. C., & Myers, J. K. (1977). Life events and Schizophrenia: I. Comparison of schizophrenics with a community sample. *Archives of General Psychiatry*, 34, 1238–1241.

Schwartz, M. B., & Brownell, K. D. (2007). Actions necessary to prevent childhood obesity: Creating the climate for change. *Journal of Law, Medicine, & Ethics*, 35, 1, 78–89.

Secades-Villa, R., Garcia-Rodriguez, O., Jin, C. J., Wang, S., & Blanco, C. (2015). Probability and predictors of the cannabis gateway effect: A national study. *International Journal of Drug Policy*, 26(2), 135–142.

Seedat, M., Duncan, N., & Lazarus, S. (2001). *Community psychology: Theory, method and practice – South African and other perspectives*. Cape Town: Oxford University Press.

Seedat, S. (2013). Social anxiety disorder (social phobia). *South African Journal of Psychiatry*, 19(3), 192–196.

Seifert, T. (2005). Anthropomorphic characteristics of centerfold models: Trends towards slender figures over time. *International Journal of Eating Disorders*, 37, 271–274.

Seiffge-Krenke, I. (2006). Coping with relationship stressors: The impact of different working models of attachment and links to adaptation. *Journal of Youth and Adolescence*, 35(1), 23–39.

Seligman, M. E. P. (1975). *Helplessness: On depression, development, and death*. San Francisco, CA: W.H. Freeman.

Seligman, M. E. P. (2005). Positive psychology, positive prevention, and positive therapy. In C. R. Snyder & S. J. Lopez (Eds), *Handbook of positive psychology*. Oxford: Oxford University Press, 3–12.

Seligman, M. E. P. (2006). Afterword. In M. Csikszentmihalyi & I. S. Csikszentmihalyi (Eds), *A life worth living. Contributions to positive psychology*. Oxford: Oxford University Press, 230–236.

Seligman, M. E. P. (2008). Positive health. *Applied Psychology: An International Review*, 57, 3–18 doi:10.1111/j.1464-0597.2008.00351.x

Seligman, M. E. P., & Rosenhan, D. L. (1998). *Abnormality*. New York, NY: W.W. Norton Publishers.

Selye, H. (1956). *The stress of life*. New York, NY: McGraw-Hill.

Setlalentoa, B. M., Pisa, P. T., Thekisho, G. R., & Loots, D. T. (2009). The social aspect of alcohol misuse/abuse in Soth Africa. *South African Journal of Clinical Nutrition*, 22(5), 511–515.

Sewell, A. R., Poling, J., & Sofuoglu, M. (2009). The effect of cannabis compared with alcohol on driving. *American Journal of Addiction*, 18(3), 185–193.

Sharan, P., & Sundar, A. S. (2015). Eating disorders in women. *Indian Journal of Psychiatry*, 57(2), S286–295. doi:10.4103/0019-5545.161493

Sharpe, H., Musiat, P., Knapton, O., & Schmidt, U. (2011). Pro-eating disorder websites: Facts, fictions and fixes. *Journal of Public Mental Health*, 10(1), 34–44. doi:10.1108/17465721111134538

Sheldon, K. M., & King, L. (2001). Why positive psychology is necessary. *American Psychologist*, 56, 216–217.

Shiang, R. R. (1993). Mutations in the 1 subunit of the inhibitory glycine receptor cause the dominant neurologic disorder, hyperekplexia. *Nature Genetics*, 5, 351–358.

Shidlo, A., & Schroeder, M. (2002). Changing sexual orientation: A consumers' report. *Professional Psychology: Research and Practice*, 33(3), 249–259.

Shimada-Sugimoto, M., Otowa, T., & Hettema, J. M. (2015). Genetics of anxiety disorders: Genetic epidemiological and molecular studies in humans. *Psychiatry and Clinical Neurosciences*, 69, 388–401.

Shipton, E. (2008). The chronic pain experience. *New Zealand Medical Journal*, 121(1270), 9–11.

Shiromani, P., Keane, T., & Le Doux, T. (Eds) (2009). *Post-traumatic stress disorder: Basic science and clinical practice*. New York, NY: Springer-Verlag.

Shriver, M. (2005). Autism spectrum disorders. *Encyclopedia of school psychology*. Retrieved March 20, 2009, from http://www.sage–ereference.com/schoolpsychology/Article_n20.html

Siegel, D., & Hartzell, M. (2004). *Parenting from the inside out*. New York, NY: Penguin.

Sierra, M. B. (1998). Depersonalization: Neurobiological perspectives. *Biological Psychiatry*, 44, 898–908.

Sifile, L. (2017, August 8). Bluetooth drug high 'impossible'. *IOL News*. Retrieved from https://www.iol.co.za/news/bluetooth-drug-high-impossible-10686212.

Silver, N. C. (2017). Legalising recreational marijuana: Another Pandora's box opened? *Social Behaviour Research and Practice Open Journal*, 2(1), e4–e6. doi:10.17140/

Silverstein, B., & Perdue, L. (1988). The relationship between role concern, preference of slimness, and symptoms of eating problems among college women. *Sex Roles*, 18, 101–160.

Simpson, R. L., & LaCava, P. G. (2007). Autism spectrum disorders. *Encyclopedia of educational psychology*. Retrieved March 20, 2009, from http://www.sage-ereference.com/educationalpsychology/Article_n23.html

Singh, A., Mattoo, S. K., & Grover, S. (2016). Stigma associated with mental illness: Conceptual issues and focus on stigma perceived by the patients with schizophrenia and their caregivers. *Indian Journal of Social Psychiatry*, 32(2), 134–142. doi:10.4103/0971-9962.181095

Sinnott, A., Jones, B., & Fordham, A. S. (1981). Agoraphobia: A situational analysis. *Journal of Clinical Psychology*, 37(1), 123–127.

Skårderud, F. (2009). Bruch revisited and revised. *European Eating Disorders Review: The Professional Journal of the Eating Disorders Association*, 17(2), 83–88. doi:10.1002/erv.923

Skinner, B. F. (1953). *Science and human behavior*. New York, NY: Macmillan.

Slater, E. (1965). Diagnosis of hysteria. *British Medical Journal*, 1, 1395–1399.

Slavin-Mulford, J., & Hilsenroth, M. J. (2012). Evidence-based psychodynamic treatments for anxiety disorders: A view. In R. A. Levy, J. S. Ablon, & H. Kachele (Eds), *Psychodynamic psychotherapy research: Evidence-based practice and practice-based evidence*. Ottawa, NJ: Humana Press – Springer, 117–137.

Small, G. P. (1991). Mass hysteria among student performers: Social relationship as a symptom predictor. *American Journal of Psychiatry*, 148, 1200–1205.

Smink, F. R., Van Hoeken, D., & Hoek, H. W. (2012). Epidemiology of eating disorders: Incidence, prevalence and mortality rates. *Current Psychiatry Reports*, 14(4), 406–414. doi:10.1007/s11920-012-0282-y

Smit, F., Bolier, L., & Cuijpers, P. (2004). Cannabis use and the risk of later Schizophrenia: A review. *Addiction*, 99(4), 425–430.

Smith, K. A., Fairburn, C. G., & Cowen, P. J. (1999). Symptomatic relapse in bulimia nervosa following tryptophan depletion. *Archives of General Psychiatry*, 56, 171–176.

Smith, M. M., Sherry, S. B., Gautreau, C. M., Stewart, S. H., Saklofske, D. H., & Mushquash, A. R. (2017). Are perfectionistic concerns an antecedent of or a consequence of binge eating, or both? A short-term four-wave longitudinal study of undergraduate women. *Eating Behaviors*, 26, 23–26. doi.org/10.1016/j.eatbeh.2017.01.001

Smith, R. C., Singh, A., Infante, M., Khandat, A., & Kloos, A. (2002). Effects of cigarette smoking and nicotine nasal spray on psychiatric symptoms and cognition in Schizophrenia. *Neuropsychopharmachology*, 27, 479–497.

Smolak, L., & Levine, M. P. (2015). Body image, disordered eating and eating disorders: Connections and disconnects. In L. Smolak & M. P. Levine (Eds), *The Wiley handbook of eating disorders*. Chichester, UK: John Wiley & Sons, 3–10.

Smuts, J. C. (1926). *Holism and evolution*. New York, NY: Macmillan.

Sneiderman, B., & McQuoid-Mason, D. (2000). Decision-making at the end of life: The termination of life-prolonging treatment, euthanasia (mercy-killing), and assisted suicide in Canada and South Africa. *Comparative and International Law Journal of Southern Africa*, 33(2), 193–204.

Snyder, C. R., Rand, K. L., & Sigmon, D. R. (2005). Hope theory: A member of the positive psychology family. In C. R. Snyder & S. J. Lopez (Eds), *Handbook of positive psychology*. Oxford: Oxford University Press, 257–276.

Sodi, T. (2011). Cultural embeddedness of health, illness and healing: Prospects for integrating indigenous and western healing practices. *Journal of Psychology in Africa*, 21(3), 349–356.

Soltan, M., & Girguis, J. (2017). How to approach the mental state examination. *BMJ*. Retrieved from https://www.bmj.com/content/357/sbmj.j1821.full

Sommer, R. (2011). The etymology of psychosis. *American Journal of Orthopsychiatry*, 81, 162–166.

Sontheimer, H. (2015). *Diseases of the nervous system*. Cambridge, MA: Academic Press.

South Africa worst in the world for drunk driving. (2015, October 19). *BusinessTech*. Retrieved from https://businesstech.co.za/news/lifestyle/101626/south-africa-worst-in-the-world-for-drunk-driving/

South African Human Rights Commission & UNICEF (2011). *South Africa's children — a review of equity and child rights*. Retrieved March 5, 2012, from http://www.health-e.org.za/uploaded/fe94f5f04583baf7585f6701946b5ac9.pdf

South African National AIDS Council. (2018). *National strategic plan on HIV, TB and STIs 2017–2022*. Pretoria. Retrieved from https://sanac.org.za//wp-content/uploads/2017/06/NSP_FullDocument_FINAL-1.pdf.

Southern African Sexual Health Association (SASHA). (2015). *Definitions*. Retrieved from http://sexualhealth.org.za/home/sexologist-medical-sexologist-sex-therapist-sex-educator-and-sex-counsellor-definitions/

Spence, C. H. (2000). Discrete neurophysiological correlates in prefrontal cortex during hysterical and feigned disorder of movement. *Lancet*, 355(9211), 1243–1244.

Spiegel, D. L. (1997). Dissociated cognition and disintegrated experience. In D. Stein (Ed.), *Cognitive science and the unconscious*. Washington, DC: American Psychiatric Publishing, 177–188.

Spitzer, C. B. S. (2006). Recent developments in the theory of dissociation. *World Psychiatry*, 5(2), 82–86.

Spreen, O., & Strauss, E. (1991). *A Compendium of neuropsychological tests: Administration, norms, and commentary*. New York, NY: Oxford

Statistics South Africa. (2018). *Mid-year population estimates 2018. Statistical Release P0302*. Pretoria: Statistics South Africa. Retrieved from https://www.statssa.gov.za/publications/P0302/P03022018.pdf

Staniloiu, A., Borsutzky, S., & Markowitsch, H. J. (2010). Dissociative memory disorders and immigration. *ASCS09: Proceedings of the 9th Conference of the Australasian Society for Cognitive Science*. North Ryde, NSW: Macquarie Centre for Cognitive Science.

Steadman, H. J., & Ribner, S. A. (1980). Changing perceptions of the mental health needs of inmates in local jails. *American Journal of Psychiatry*, 137, 1115-1116.

Steffens, M. C., & Eschmann, B. (2001). Fighting psychologists' negative attitudes and prejudices towards lesbians, gay men and bisexuals. In M. C. Steffens & U. Biechele (Eds), *Annual review of lesbian, gay and bisexual issues in European psychology*. Trier, Germany: ALGBP, 7–30.

Steffens, M., Meyhöfer, I., Fassbender, K., Ettinger, U., & Kambeitz, J. (2018). Association of schizotypy with dimensions of cognitive control: A meta-analysis. *Schizophrenia Bulletin*, 44(Suppl. 2), S512–S524.

Stein, D. J. (2008). Is disorder X in category or spectrum Y? General considerations and application to the relationship between obsessive-compulsive disorder and anxiety disorders. *Depression and Anxiety*, 25, 330–335.

Stein, D. J. (2013). What is a mental disorder: A perspective from cognitive-affective science. *Canadian Journal of Psychiatry*, 58, 656–662.

Stein, D. J., Phillips, K. A, Bolton, D, Fulford, K. W., Sadler, J. Z., & Kendler, K. S. (2010). What is a mental/psychiatric disorder: From DSM-IV to DSM-V. *Psychological Medicine*, 20, 1–7.

Stein, D. J., Seedat, S., Herman, A. A., Heeringa, S. G., Moomal, H., Myer, L., & Williams, D. (2007). *Findings from the first South African Stress and Health Study*. South African Medical Research Council. Retrieved from http://www.mrc.co.za/policybriefs/stresshealth.pdf

Steiner, H. & Lock, J. (1998). Anorexia nervosa and bulimia nervosa in children and adolescents: A review of the past 10 years. *Journal of the American Academy of Child and Adolescent Psychiatry*, 37, 352–359.

Stice, E. (1998). Relations of restraint and negative affect to bulimic pathology: A longitudinal test of three competing models. *International Journal of Eating Disorders*, 23, 243–260.

Stice, E., & Desjardins, C. D. (2018). Interactions between risk factors in the prediction of onset of eating disorders: Exploratory hypothesis generating analyses. *Behaviour Research and Therapy*, 105, 52–62. doi:10.1016/j.brat.2018.03.005

Stice, E., Marti, C. N., & Rohde, P. (2013). Prevalence, incidence, impairment, and course of the proposed DSM-5 eating disorder diagnoses in an 8-year prospective community study of young women. *Journal of Abnormal Psychology*, 122(2), 445–457. doi:10.1037/a0030679

Stonebridge, V. (2011). *Thinspiration: New media's influence on girls with eating disorders* (Unpublished master's dissertation). Rowan University, Glassboro, NJ, United States. Retrieved from https://rdw.rowan.edu/etd/29

Stones, C. (1996). Attitudes toward psychology, psychiatry and mental illness in the central Eastern Cape of South Africa. *South African Journal of Psychology*, 26, 221–225.

Striegel-Moore, R. H., Silberstein, L. R., & Rodin, J. (1993). The social self in bulimia nervosa: Public self-consciousness, social anxiety, and perceived fraudulence. *Journal of Abnormal Psychology*, 102(2), 297–303.

Strober, M. (1995). Family-genetic perspectives on anorexia nervosa and bulimia nervosa. In K. Brownell & C. G. Fairburn (Eds), *Eating disorders and obesity: A comprehensive casebook*. New York, NY: Guilford, 212–218.

Strober, M., & Bulik, C. M. (2002). Genetic epidemiology of the eating disorders. In C. G. Fairburn & K. D. Brownell (Eds), *Eating disorders and obesity: A comprehensive handbook*. New York, NY: Guilford, 238–242.

Strober, M., Freeman, R., Lampert, C., Diamond, J., & Kaye, W. (2000). Controlled family study of anorexia nervosa and bulimia nervosa: Evidence of shared liability and transmission of partial syndromes. *American Journal of Psychiatry*, 157(3), 393–401. doi:10.1176/appi.ajp.157.3.393

Strong, A., Bancroft, J., Carnes, L., Davis, L., & Kennedy, J. (2005). The impact of sexual arousal on sexual risk-taking: A qualitative study. *Journal of Sex Research*, 42(3), 185–191.

Strümpfer, D. J. W. (1995). The origin of health and strength: From 'salutogenesis' to 'fortigenesis'. *South African Journal of Psychology*, 25, 81–89.

Stutz, S. J., Anastasio, N. C., & Cunningham, K. A. (2015). The role of serotonin 2A (5-HT2A) and 2C (5-HT2C) receptors in the association between binge eating and impulsive action. *Drug & Alcohol Dependence*, 156, e215. doi:10.1016/j.drugalcdep.2015.07.580

Struwig, W., & Pretorius, P. J. (2009). Quality of psychiatric referrals to secondary-level care. *South African Journal of Psychology*, 15(20), 33–36.

Suddath, R. L., Christison, G. W, Torrey, E. F., Casanova, M. F., & Weinberger, D. R. (1990). Anatomical abnormalities in the brains of monozygotic twins discordant for Schizophrenia. *New England Journal of Medicine*, 322, 789–794.

Sue, D., Sue, D., & Sue, S. (2006). Understanding abnormal behaviour. Boston: Houghton Mifflin.

Sue, S., & Morishima, J. K. (1982). *The mental health of Asian-Americans*. San Francisco: Jossey-Bass.

Sullivan, P. F., Kendler, K. S., & Neale, M. C. (2003). Schizophrenia as a complex trait: Evidence from a meta-analysis of twin studies. *Archives of General Psychiatry*, 60(12), 1187–1192. Doi:10.1001/archpsyc.60.12.1187

Sumathipala, A., Siribadanna, S. H., & Bhugra, D. (2004). Culture bound syndromes: The story of dhat syndrome. *British Journal of Psychiatry*, 184, 200–209.

Summers, F. (2014). *Object relations theory and psychopathology: A comprehensive text* (2nd ed.). New York, NY: Psychology Press.

Svaldi, J., Griepenstroh, J., Tuschen-Caffier, B., & Ehring, T. (2012). Emotion regulation deficits in eating disorders: A marker of eating pathology or general psychopathology? *Psychiatry Research*, 197(1–2), 103–111. doi:10.1016/j.psychres.2011.11.009

Swanepoel, M. (2010). Ethical decision-making in forensic psychology. *Koers*, 75(4), 851–872.

Swartz, L. (1987). Transcultural Psychiatry in South Africa. *Transcultural Psychiatric Research Review*, 24, 273–303.

Swartz, L. (1998). *Culture and mental health: A southern African view*. Cape Town: Oxford University Press.

Swartz, L., & Lund, C. (1998). Xhosa-Speaking Schizophrenic patients' experience of their condition: Psychosis and Amafufunyana. *South African Journal of Psychology*, 28(2), 62–70. https://journals.sagepub.com/doi/10.1177/008124639802800202

Szabo, C. J. (2005). Dissociative trance disorder associated with major depression and bereavement in a South African female adolescent. *Australian and New Zealand Journal of Psychiatry*, 39(5), 423. doi:10.1111/j.1440-1614.2005.01593.x

Szabo, C. P. (1998). Eating disorders and adolescence. *South African Journal of Child and Adolescent Mental Health*, 10, 117–125.

Szabo, C. P. (1999). Eating attitudes among black South Africans. *American Journal of Psychiatry*, 156, 981–982.

Szabo, C. P., & Allwood, C. W. (2004). A cross-cultural study of eating attitudes in adolescent South African females. *World Psychiatry*, 3, 41–44.

Szabo, C. P., Berk, M., Tlou, E., & Allwood, C. W. (1995). Eating disorders in black female South Africans: A series of cases. *South African Medical Journal*, 85, 588–590.

Szasz, T. S. (1961). *The myth of mental illness*. New York, NY: Hoeber-Harper.

Szasz, T. S. (1970). *The manufacture of madness: A comparative study of the inquisition and the mental health movement*. London: Routledge.

Szasz, T. S. (1974). *The myth of mental illness: Foundations of a theory of personal conduct*. New York, NY: Harper & Row.

Szasz, T. S. (1976). 'Anti-psychiatry': The paradigm of a plundered mind. *New Review*, 3, 3–14.

Tafet, G. E., & Nemeroff, M. D. (2016). The links between stress and depression: Psychoneuroendocrinological, genetic, and environmental interactions. *Journal of Neuropsychiatry and Clinical Neuroscience*, 28(2), 77–88.

Talmadge, L. D., & Talmadge, W. C. (1986). Relational sexuality: An understanding of low sexual desire. *Journal of Sex and Marital Therapy*, 12(1), 3–21.

Tangney, J. P. (2005). Humility. In C. R. Snyder & S. J. Lopez (Eds), *Handbook of positive psychology*. Oxford: Oxford University Press, 411–422.

Tanner, C. C. (2001). Latah in Jakarta, Indonesia. *Movement Disorders*, 16(3), 526–529.

Tatangelo, G., McCabe, M., Mellor, D., & Mealey, A. (2016). A systematic review of body dissatisfaction and sociocultural messages related to the body among preschool children. *Body Image*, 18, 86–95. doi:10.1016/j.bodyim.2016.06.003

Taylor, S. F., & Tso, I. F. (2015). GABA abnormalities in schizophrenia: A methodological review of in vivo studies. *Schizophrenia Research*, 167(1–3), 84–90. doi:10.1016/j.schres.2014.10.011

Tennen, H., & Affleck, G. (2002). Benefit-finding and benefit-reminding. In C. R. Snyder & S. J. Lopez (Eds), *Handbook of positive psychology*. Oxford: Oxford University Press, 584–597.

Thomas, E., & Seedat, S. (2018). The diagnosis and management of depression in the era of the DSM-5. *South African Family Practice*, 60(1), 22–28.

Thombs, D. (2006). *Introduction to addictive behaviours*. New York, NY: Guilford Press.

Thompson, J., Coovert, M. D., Richards, K. J., Johnson, S., & Cattarin, J. (1995). Development of body image, eating disturbance, and general psychological functioning in female adolescents: Covariance structure modeling and longitudinal investigations. *International Journal of Eating Disorders*, 18, 221–236.

Thoreson, R. (2013). Beyond equality: The post-apartheid counternarrative of trans and intersex movements in South Africa. *African Affairs*, 112(449), 646-665.

Tiggemann, M., & Miller, J. (2010). The Internet and adolescent girls' weight satisfaction and drive for thinness. *Sex Roles*, 63(1–2), 79–90. doi:10.1007/s11199-010-9789-z

Tiggemann, M., & Slater, M. A. (2014). NetTweens: The internet and body image concerns in preteenage girls. *Journal of Early Adolescence*, 34(5), 606–620. doi:10.1177/0272431613501083

Tiliouine, H. (2017). Algeria's children and the history of wellbeing in MENA nations. *Middle East Journal of Positive Psychology*, 3(1) https://middleeastjournalofpositivepsychology.org/index.php/mejpp/article/view/51/49

Tomita, A., & Moodley, Y. (2016). The revolving door of mental, neurological, and substance use disorders re-hospitalization in rural KwaZulu-Natal province, South Africa. *African Health Sciences*, 16(3), 817–821. doi:10.4314/ahs.vl6i3.23

Tomlinson, M., Grimsrud, A. T., Stein, D. J., Williams, D. R., & Myer, L. (2009). The epidemiology of depression in South Africa: Results from the South African Stress and Health Study. *South African Medical Journal*, 99(5), 367–373.

Tomm, K., & Lannamann, J. (1988). Questions as interventions. *The Family Therapy Networker*, 12(5), 38–41.

Torrey, E. F. (2011). Stigma and violence: Isn't it time to connect the dots? *Schizophrenia Bulletin*, 37(5), 892–896. doi:10.1093/schbul/sbr057

Tortelli, A., Errazuriz, A., Croudace, T., Morgan, C., Murray, R. M., Jones, P. B., Szoke, A., & Kirkbride, J. B. (2015). Schizophrenia and other psychotic disorders in Caribbean-born migrants and their descendants in England: Systematic review and meta-analysis of incidence rates, 1950–2013. *Social Psychiatry and Psychiatric Epidemiology*, 50(7), 1039–1055. doi:10.1007/s00127-015-1021-6

Tovée, M. J., Furnham, A., & Swami, V. (2007). Healthy body equals beautiful body? Changing perceptions of health and attractiveness with shifting socioeconomic status. In A. Furnham & V. Swami (Eds), *The body beautiful: Evolutionary and socio-cultural perspectives*. Basingstoke, UK: Palgrave Macmillan, 108–128.

Tovée, M. J., Swamib, V., Furnham, A., & Mangalparsad, R. (2006). Changing perceptions of attractiveness as observers are exposed to a different culture. *Evolution and Human Behavior*, 27, 443–456.

Townsend, M. C. (2014). *Essentials of psychiatric mental health nursing: Concepts of care in evidence-based practice* (6th ed.). Philadelphia, PA: F. A. Davis Co.

Treasure, J. (2013). *Anorexia Nervosa: A survival guide for families, friends and sufferers*. Hove, UK: LP Press.

Triplett, K. N., Tedeschi, R. G., Cann, A., Calhoun, L. G., & Reeve, C. L. (2011). Posttraumatic growth, meaning in life and satisfaction in response to trauma. *Psychological Trauma: Theory, Research, Practice, and Policy*, 4(4), 400–410. doi:10.1037/a0024204

Tsaousis, I., & Nikolaou, I. (2005). Exploring the relationship of emotional intelligence with physical and psychological health functioning. *Stress and Health*, 21, 77–86.

Tseng, W. S. (2001). *Handbook of cultural psychiatry*. San Diego, CA: Academic Press.

Tshehla, B. (2015). The Traditional Health Practitioners Act 22 of 2007: A perspective on some of the statute's strengths and weaknesses. *Indilinga African Journal of Indigenous Knowledge Systems*, 14(1), 42–51.

Tsuang, M. T., Stone, W. S., & Faraone, S. V. (2000). Toward reformulating the diagnosis of schizophrenia. *American Journal of Psychiatry*, 157, 1041–1050.

Tully, C. (2000). *Lesbians, gays, & the empowerment perspective*. New York, NY: Columbia University Press.

Tulsky, D. S., Zhu, J., & Prifitera, A. (2000). Assessment of adult intelligence with the WAIS–III. In G. Goldstein & M. Hersen (Eds), *Handbook of psychological assessment* (3rd ed.). Oxford: Elsevier Science (Pergamon), 453–470.

Turner, M. (1997). Malingering. *British Journal of Psychiatry*, 171, 409–411.

Ubell, E. (1989, December 3). They're closing in on mental illness. *Parade Magazine*, 6–7.

UNAIDS. (2018). UNAIDS Data 2018. Retrieved from https://www.unaids.org/sites/default/files/media_asset/unaids-data-2018_en.pdf, pp. 56–57.

UNAIDS. (2019). *Fact Sheet – Global AIDS Update 2019*. Retrieved from https://www.unaids.org/sites/default/files/media_asset/UNAIDS_FactSheet_en.pdf

UNAIDS/WHO. (2006). *AIDS epidemic update*. Geneva: WHO. Retrieved from data.unaids.org/pub/epireport/2006/2006_epiupdate_en.pdf

Urban, K. R., & Gao, W.-J. (2014). Performanc enhancement at the cost of potential brain plasticity: Neural ramifications of nootropic drugs in the healthy developing brain. *Fronteirs in Systems Neuroscience*. Retrieved July 15, 2018, from https://doi.org/10.3389/fnsys.2014.00038

Ussher, J. M. (1991). *Women's madness: Misogyny or mental illness?* New York, NY: Harvester Wheatsheaf.

Van den Berg, P., Thompson, J. K., Obremski-Brandon, K., & Coovert, M. (2002). The tripartite influence model of body image and eating disturbance: A covariance structure modeling investigation testing the mediational role of appearance comparison. *Journal of Psychosomatic Research*, 53(5), 1007–1020. doi:10.1016/S0022-3999(02)00499-3

Vandereycken, W. (2002). History of anorexia nervosa and bulimia nervosa. In C. G. Fairburn & K. D. Brownell (Eds), *Eating disorders and obesity: A comprehensive handbook* (2nd ed.). New York, NY: Guilford, 151–154.

Vandereycken, W., & Van Deth, R. (1989). Who was the first to describe anorexia nervosa: Gull or Lasègue? *Psychological Medicine*, 19(4), 837–845. doi:10.1017/S0033291700005559

Vanderlinden, J., Norré, J., & Vandereycken, W. (1992). *A practical guide to the treatment of bulimia nervosa*. New York, NY: Brunner/Mazel.

Van der Merwe, M. (2018). *Evidence-based assessment: Adaptive behaviour*. Pretoria: Clinic for High-risk Babies seminar, University of Pretoria. Retrieved from https://www.up.ac.za/media/shared/67/2018/maria-van-der-merwe-vineland-compatibility-mode.zp161152.pdf

Van der Spuy, H. I. J., & Shamley, D. A. F. (1978). *The psychology of apartheid*. Washington, DC: University Press of America.

Van der Vijver, A. J., & Rothmann, S. (2004). Assessment in Multicultural Groups: The South African Case. *SA Journal of Industrial Psychology*, 30(4), 1–7.

Van der Zee, K., Thijs, M., & Schakel, S. F. (2002). The relationship of emotional intelligence with academic intelligence and the Big Five. *European Journal of Personality*, 16, 103–125.

Van Dyk, A. J. (2008). Forgiveness and the well-being of members of the South African National Defence Force: A process for discussion. *Journal of Psychology in Africa*, 18(4), 669–674.

Van Kammen, D. P., Docherty, J. P., & Bunney, W. E. (1982). Prediction of early relapse after pimozide discontinuation by response to d-amphetamine during pimozide treatment. *Biological Psychiatry*, 17, 223–242.

Van Meter, A. R., & Youngstrom, E. A. (2012). Cyclothymic disorder in youth: Why is it overlooked, what do we know and where is the field headed? *Neuropsychiatry*, 2(6), 509–519.

Van Onselen, C. (1982). *New Babylon, new Nineveh*. Cape Town: Jonathan Ball.

Van Schalkwyk, I., & Wissing, M. P. (2010). Psychosocial well-being in a group of South African adolescents. *Journal of Psychology in Africa*, 20(1), 53–60.

Van Snellenberg, J. X., Torres, I. J., & Thornton, A. E. (2006). Functional neuroimaging of working memory in Schizophrenia: Task performance as a moderating variable. *Neuropsychology*, 20(5), 497–510.

Vaughan, K. K., & Fouts, G. T. (2003). Changes in television and magazine exposure and eating disorder symptomatology. *Sex Roles*, 49, 1573–2762.

Veenhoven, R. (2012). Does happiness differ across cultures? In H. Selin & G. Davey (Eds), *Happiness across cultures: Views of happiness and quality of life in non-Western cultures*. Dordrecht: Springer, 451–472.

Vemuri, M., & Steiner, H. (2007). Historical and current conceptualizations of eating disorders: A developmental perspective. In T. Jaffa & B. McDermott (Eds), *Eating disorders in children and adolescents*. New York, NY: Cambridge University Press, 3–18.

Ventriglio, A., Gentile, A., Bonfitto, I., Stella, E., Mari, M., Steardo, L., & Bellomo, A. (2016). Suicide in the early stage of schizophrenia. *Frontiers in Psychiatry*, 7, 16–225. doi:10.3389/fpsyt.2016.00116

Ventura, J., Nuechterlein, K. H., Lukoff, D., & Hardesty, J. P. (1989). A prospective study of stressful life events and Schizophrenia relapse. *Journal of Abnormal Psychology*, 98, 407–411.

Verhaak, P., Kerssens, J., Dekker, J., Sorbi, M., & Bensing, J. (1998). Prevalence of chronic benign pain disorder among adults: A review of the literature. *Pain*, 77, 231–239.

Verhaege, P. (1998). *Love in a time of loneliness: Three essays on drive and desire*. New York, NY: Other Press.

Victor, C. J., Nel, J. A., Lynch, I., & Mbatha, K. (2014). The Psychological Society of South Africa sexual and gender diversity position statement: Contributing towards a just society. *South African Journal of Psychology*, 44(3), 292–302.

Visser, J., Notelovitz, T., Szabo, C. P., & Fredericks, N. (2014). Abnormal eating attitudes and weight loss behaviour of adolescent girls attending a 'traditional' Jewish high school in Johannesburg, South Africa. *South African Journal of Clinical Nutrition*, 27(4), 208–216. doi:10.1080/16070658.2014.11734511

Viswanath, B., & Chaturvedi, S. K. (2012). Cultural aspects of major mental disorders: A critical review from an Indian perspective. *Indian Journal of Psychological Medicine*, 34(4): 306–312. doi:10.4103/0253-7176.108193

Vitousek, K. M., & Gray, J. A. (2005). Eating disorders. In G. O. Gabbard, J. S. Beck, & J. Holmes (Eds), *Oxford textbook of psychotherapy*. Oxford: Oxford University Press, 177–202.

Vitousek, K. M. & Manke, F. (1994). Personality variables and disorders in anorexia nervosa and bulimia nervosa. *Journal of Abnormal Psychology*, 103, 137–147.

Voelker, D. K., Reel, J. J., & Greenleaf, C. (2015). Weight status and body image perceptions in adolescents: Current perspectives. *Adolescent Health, Medicine and Therapeutics*, 6, 149–158. doi:10.2147/AHMT.S68344

Vohs, K. D., & Baumeister, R. F. (2004). Understanding self-regulation: An introduction. In R. F. Baumeister & K. D. Vohs (Eds), *Handbook of self-regulation: Research, Theory, and Applications*. London: Guilford Press, 1–12.

Volpe, U., Atti, A. R., Cimino, M., Monteleone, A. M., De Ronchi, D., Fernández-Aranda, F., & Monteleone, P. (2015). Beyond anorexia and bulimia nervosa: What's 'new' in eating disorders. *Journal of Psychopathology*, 21, 415–423.

Von Hausswolff-Juhlin, Y., Brooks, S. J., & Larsson, M. (2015). The neurobiology of eating disorders – a clinical perspective. *Acta Psychiatrica Scandinavica*, 131(4), 244–255. doi:10.1111/acps.12335

Von Krosigk, B. (2012). Personality disorders. In A. Burke (Ed.), *Abnormal psychology: A South African perspective* (2nd ed.). Cape Town: Oxford University Press.

Wadsworth, M. E. (2005). Developmental psychopathology. *Encyclopedia of human development*. Retrieved March 20, 2009, from http://www.sage-ereference.com/humandevelopment/Article_n190.html

Walker, E. E, Downey, G., & Bergman, A. (1989). The effects of parental psychopathology and maltreatment on child behavior: A test of the diathesis-stress model. *Child Development*, 60, 15–24.

Walker, M. T. (2006). The social construction of mental illness and its implication for the recovery model. *International Journal of Psychosocial Rehabilitation*, 10(1), 71–87.

Walker, S. P. (1996). The criminal upperworld and the emergence of a disciplinary code in the early chartered accountancy profession. *Accounting History*, 1(2), 7–35.

Wallace, J. M. (1999). The social ecology of addiction: Race, risk and resilience. *Pediatrics*, 103, 1122–1127.

Walsh, B., & Devlin, M. J. (1998). Eating disorders: Progress and problems. *Science*, 280, 1387–1390.

Walsh, S., Ismaili, E., Naheed, B., & O'Brien, S. (2015). Diagnosis, pathophysiology and management of premenstrual syndrome. *The Obstetrician and Gynaecologist*, 17, 99–104.

Wan Hazmy, C. H., Zainur, R. Z., & Hussaini, R. (2003*). Islamic medicine and code of medical ethics*. Sembilan, Malaysia: Islamic Medical Association of Malaysia.

Wassenaar, D., Le Grange, D., Winship, J., & Lachenicht, L. (2000). The prevalence of eating disorder pathology in a cross-ethnic population of female students in South Africa. *European Eating Disorder Review*, 8, 225–236.

Watkins, C. E., Campbell, V. L., Nieberding, R., & Hallmark, R. (1995). Contemporary practice of psychological assessment by clinical psychologists. *Professional Psychology: Research and Practice*, 26, 54–60.

Watzlawick, P., Beavin, J. B., & Jackson, D. D. (1967). *Pragmatics of human communication: A study of interactional patterns, pathologies, and paradoxes*. New York, NY: Norton.

Weakland, J., Fisch, R., Watzlawick, P., & Bodin, A. B. (1974). Brief therapy: Focused problem resolution. *Family Process*, 13, 141–168.

Webster, E. (1986). Excerpt from 'Servants of Apartheid'. *Psychology in Society*, 6, 6–12.

Weiner, I. B. (1994). The Rorschach Inkblot Method (RIM) is not a test: Implications for theory and practice. *Journal of Personality Assessment*, 62, 498–504.

Weintraub, M. J., Hall, D. L., Carbonella, J. Y., Weisman de Mamani, A., & Hooley, J. M. (2017). Integrity of literature on expressed emotion and relapse in patients with schizophrenia verified by ap-curve analysis. *Family Process*, 56(2), 436–444. doi:10.1111/famp.12208

Weisman, A. G., Nuechterlein, M. J., Goldstein, M. J., & Snyder, K. S. (1998). Expressed emotion, attributions, and Schizophrenia symptom dimensions. *Journal of Abnormal Psychology*, 107, 355–359.

Weiss, M. G., & Somma, D. (2007). Explanatory models in psychiatry. In D. Bhugrah & K. Bhui (Eds), *Text book of cultural psychiatry*. Cambridge: Cambridge University Press, 127–141.

Weiten, W. (2007). *Psychology: Themes and variations* (7th ed.). Belmont, CA: Thomson.

Welch, S. L, & Fairburn, C. G. (1994). Sexual abuse and bulimia nervosa: Three integrated case-control comparisons. *American Journal of Psychiatry*, 151, 402–407.

Wenar, C., & Kerig, P. (2006). *Developmental psychopathology: From infancy to adolescence* (5th ed.). New York, NY: McGraw-Hill.

Wertham, F. (1950). *Dark legend*. New York, NY: Doubleday and Company.

Westergaard, T., Mortensen, P. B., Pedersen, C. B., Wohlfahrt, J., & Melbye, M. (1999). Exposure to prenatal and childhood infections and the risk of Schizophrenia. *Archives of General Psychiatry*, 56, 993–998.

Westerhof, G. J., & Keyes, C. L. M. (2010). Mental illness and mental health: The two continua model across the lifespan. *Journal of Adult Development*, 17, 110–119.

Weston, S. C., & Siever, L. J. (1993). Biologic correlates of personality disorders. NIMH Conference: Personality disorders (1990, Williamsburg, Virginia). *Journal of Personality Disorders*, Suppl. 1, 129–148.

Whiteford, H. A., Degenhardt, L., Rehm, J., Baxter, A. J., Ferrari, A. J., Erskine, H. E., …, Vos, T. (2013). Global burden of disease attributable to mental and substance use disorders: Findings from the Global Burden of Disease Study 2010. *Lancet*, 389(9904), 1575–1586.

Whitfield, C. L., Dube, S. R., Felitti, V. J., & Anda, R. F. (2005). Adverse childhood experiences and hallucinations. *Child Abuse & Neglect*, 29(7), 797–810. doi:10.1016/j.chiabu.2005.01.004

Whitman, B. Y. (1991). The roots of organicity: genetics and genograms. In P. J. Accardo, T. A. Blondis, & B. Y. Whitman (Eds), *Attention deficits and hyperactivity in children*. New York, NY: Marcel Dekker, 37–86.

Wicks-Nelson, R. & Israel, A. C. (2006). *Behavior disorders of childhood* (6th ed.). Englewood Cliffs, NJ: Prentice Hall.

Wicks-Nelson, R., & Israel, A.C. (2009). *Abnormal child and adolescent psychology* (7th ed.). Englewood Cliffs, NJ: Pearson Education.

Wig, N. N. (1983). DSM III: Its strengths and weaknesses – a perspective from the Third World. In R. L. Spitser, I. B. W. Williams, & A. E. Skodol (Eds), *International perspectives on the DSM III*. Washington, DC: American Psychiatric Press, 79–89.

Wildgust, H. J. & Beary, M. (2010). Review of 'Are there modifiable risk factors which will reduce the excess mortality in Schizophrenia?'. *Journal of Psychopharmacology*, 24(4), 37–50.

Wilkinson, K. (2017). #5facts: The sad extent of suicide in South Africa. Retrieved August 1, 2018, from https://africacheck.org/reports/5facts-sad-extent-suicide-south-africa/

Willi, J., & Grossman, S. (1983). Epidemiology of anorexia nervosa in a defined region of Switzerland. *American Journal of Psychiatry*, 140, 564–567.

Wilson, G. T. (1991). The addiction model of eating disorders: A critical analysis. *Advances in Behavior Research and Therapy*, 13, 27–72.

Wilson, M. (1993). DSM-III and the transformation of American psychiatry: A history. *American Journal of Psychiatry*, 150, 399–410.

Wirz-Justice, A. (2008). Biological rhythms and depression: Treatment opportunities. *WPA Bulletin on Depression*, 13(36), 2–4.

Wise, E. A., Streiner, D. L., & Walfish, S. (2009). A Review and Comparison of the Reliabilities of the MMPI-2, MCMI-III and PAI Presented in Their Respective Test Manuals. *Measurement and Evaluation in Counseling and Development*, 42(4), 246–254.

Wiseman, C. V., Gray, J. J., Mosimann, J. E., & Arhens, A. H. (1992). Cultural expectations of thinness in women: An update. *International Journal of Eating Disorders*, 11, 85–89.

Wissing, M. P., Claassens, E., & du Toit, M. M. (1998). The dynamics of cognitive styles, coping and psychological well-being in youths. In L. Schlebusch (Ed.), *South Africa beyond transition: Psychological well-being*. Proceedings of the Third Annual Congress of the Psychological Society of South Africa. Pretoria: PsySSA, 375–379.

Wissing, M. P., & Temane, Q. M. (2008). The structure of psychological well-being in cultural context: Towards a hierarchical model of psychological health. *Journal of Psychology in Africa*, 18(1), 45–56.

Wissing, M. P., & Van Eeden, C. (1997). *Psychological well-being: A fortigenic conceptualization and empirical clarification*. Paper presented at the Annual Congress of the Psychological Society of South Africa (PsySSA), Durban, South Africa.

Wissing, M. P., & Van Eeden, C. (2002). Empirical clarification of the nature of psychological well-being. *South African Journal of Psychology*, 32(1), 32–44

Wittchen, H. U., Gloster, A. T., Beesdo-Baum, K., Fava, G. A., & Craske, M. G. (2010). Agoraphobia: A review of the diagnostic classificatory position and criteria. *Depression and Anxiety*, 27, 13–133.

Wittstock, B. R. (1991). Mass phenomena at a black South African primary school. *Hospital and Community Psychiatry*, 1(42), 851–853.

Wolf, N. (1990). *The beauty myth*. New York, NY: HarperCollins.

Wolff, S. (2000). Schizoid personality in childhood and Asperger syndrome. In A. Klin, F. R. Volkmar, & S. S. Sparrow (Eds), *Asperger syndrome*. New York, NY: Guilford Press, 278–305.

Wolitzky, D. L., & Eagle, M. N. (1997). Psychoanalytic theories of psychotherapy. In P. L. Wachtel & S. B. Messer (Eds), *Theories of psychotherapy: Origins and evolution*, 39–96. (Reprinted in modified form from D. K. Freedheim (Ed.), *History of psychotherapy: A century of change*. Washington, DC: American Psychological Association, 109–158).

Wonderlich, S. A., Gordon, K. H., Mitchell, J. E., Crosby, R. D., & Engel, S. G. (2009). The validity and clinical utility of binge-eating disorder. *International Journal of Eating Disorders*, 42, 687–705.

Wong, P. T. P. (2011). Positive psychology 2.0: Towards a balanced interactive model of the good life. *Canadian Psychology*, 52(2), 69–81.

Wong, P. T. P., Reker, G. T., & Peacock, E. J. (2006). A resource-congruence model of coping and the development of the coping schema inventory. In P. Wong & L. Wong (Eds), *Handbook of multicultural perspectives on stress and coping*. New York, NY: Springer, 223–283.

Wood, A. M., & Tarrier, N. (2010). Positive clinical psychology: A new vision and strategy for integrated research and practice. *Clinical Psychology Review*, 30, 819–829. doi:10.1016/j.cpr.2010.06.003

Wood, J. M., Nezworski, M. T., Lilienfeld, S. O., & Garb, H. N. (2003). *What's wrong with the Rorschach? Science confronts the controversial inkblot test*. New York, NY: Wiley.

World Health Organization. (1992). *International statistical classification of diseases and related health problems* (10th ed). Geneva: World Health Organization.

World Health Organization. (1993). *The ICD-10 classification of mental and behavioural disorders.* Geneva: World Health Organization.

World Health Organization. (2002). *Defining sexual health: Report of a technical consultation on sexual health.* Geneva: World Health Organization.

World Health Organization. (2004). *Global Burden of Disease.* Retrieved March 7, 2012, from http://www.who.int/topics/global_burden_of_disease/en/

World Health Organization. (2005). *Mental health policy and service guidance package.* Retrieved from *https://www.who.int/mental_health/policy/essentialpackage1/en/*

World Health Organization. (2007). *International classification of diseases and related health problems, 10th revision.* Geneva, Switzerland: World Health Organisation.

World Health Organization. (2010). *Mental health and development: Targeting people with mental health conditions as a vulnerable group.* Geneva: World Health Organization.

World Health Organization. (2012). *Risks to mental health: An overview of vulnerabilities and risk factors.* Retrieved May 3, 2019, from https://www.who.int/mental_health/mhgap/risks_to_mental_health_EN_27_08_12.pdf

World Health Organization. (2014a). *Global status report on alcohol and health 2014: Country profile: South Africa.* Geneva: World Health Organization. Retrieved August 20, 2018, from http://www.who.int/substance_abuse/publications/global_alcohol_report/profiles/zaf.pdf?ua=1

World Health Organization. (2014b). *Preventing suicide: A global imperative.* Luxembourg: WHO Press.

World Health Organization. (2016). *The ICD-10 classification of mental and behavioural disorders.* Geneva: World Health Organization. Retrieved from https://icd.who.int/browse10/2016/en

World Health Organization. (2018a). *Global health observatory (GHO) data.* Geneva: World Health Organization. Retrieved August 20, 2018, from http://www.who.int/gho/alcohol/en/

World Health Organization. (2018b). *Obesity.* Retrieved from https://www.who.int/topics/obesity/en/

World Health Organization. (2018c). *ICD-11 is here!* Retrieved from https://www.who.int/classifications/icd/en/

World Health Organization. (2018d). ICD-11 for Mortality and Morbidity Statistics. Retrieved from https://icd.who.int/browse11/l-m/en#/http://id.who.int/icd/entity/1136473465

World Health Organization. (2018e). Global status report on alcohol and health 2018. Retrieved September 26, 2018, from https://apps.who.int/iris/bitstream/handle/10665/274603/9789241565639-eng.pdf?ua=1

World Professional Association for Transgender Health (WPATH). (2011). *Standards of care for the health of transsexual, transgender and gender nonconforming people* (7th ed.). Retrieved February 9, 2012, from www.wpath.org/Documents2/ socv7.pdf

Worthen, V. (1974). Psychotherapy and Catholic confession. *Journal of Religion and Health*, 13(4), 275–284

Wouters, A. R. (1993). *Relevant psychological help in the South African context: A personal empowerment model* (Unpublished PhD thesis). Vista University, Soweto, South Africa.

Wright, B. A., & Lopez, S. J. (2005). Widening the diagnostic focus: A case for including human strengths and environmental resources. In C. R. Snyder & S. J. Lopez (Eds), *Handbook of positive psychology*. Oxford: Oxford University Press, 26–44.

Wynne, L. C., Ryckoff, I. M., Day, J., & Hirsch, S. I. (1958). Pseudomutuality in the family relations of schizophrenics. *Psychiatry*, 21, 205–220.

Xu, B., Woodroffe, A., Rodrigues-Murillo, L., Roos, J. L., Van Rensburg, E. J., Abecasis, G. R., Gogos, J. A., & Karayiorgou, M. (2009). Elucidating the genetic architecture of familial Schizophrenia using rare copy number variant and linkage scans. *Proceedings of the National Academy of Sciences of the United States of America*, 106(39), 16746–16751.

Yates, A. (1989). Current perspectives on the eating disorders. *Journal of the American Academy of Child and Adolescent Psychiatry*, 28, 813–828.

Yatham, L. N., & Maj, M. (2010). *Bipolar disorder: Clinical and neurobiological foundations*. Chichester, UK: Wiley-Blackwell.

Yilmaz, Z., Hardaway, J. A., & Bulik, C. M. (2015). Genetics and epigenetics of eating disorders. *Advances in Genomics and Genetics*, 5, 131–151. doi:10.2147/AGG.S55776

Yoder, H. N., Tol, W. A., Reis, R., & De Jong, J. T. (2016). Child mental health in Sierra Leone: A survey and exploratory qualitative study. *International Journal of Mental Health Systems*, 10(1), Article ID 48. doi:10.1186/s13033-016-0080-8.

Zabow, L. (2008). Competence and decision-making: Ethics and clinical psychiatric practice. *South African Journal of Bioethics and Law*, 1(2), 61–63.

Zabow, T. (2007). Traditional healers and mental health in South Africa. *African Journal of Psychiatry*, 4(4), 81–82.

Zabow, T., & Kaliski, S. Z. (2006). Ethical considerations In S. Z. Kaliski (Ed.), *Psycholegal assessment in South Africa*. Cape Town: Oxford University Press, 357–375.

Zhiguo, W. U., & Fang, Y. (2014). Comorbidity of depressive and anxiety disorders: Challenges in diagnosis and assessment. *Shanghai Archives of Psychiatry*, 26(4), 227–231.

Zilesnick, S. (2014). Managing bipolar disorder. *Mental Health Matters*, 1(2), 7–10.

Zuma, T., Wight, D., Rochat, T., & Moshabela, M. (2016). The role of traditional health practitioners in rural KwaZulu-Natal, South Africa: Generic or mode specific? *BMC Complementary and Alternative Medicine*, 16, 304. doi:10.1186/s12906-016-1293-8

Zungu, L. I., & Malungu, N. G. (2011). *Post Traumatic Stress Disorder in the South African Mining Industry*. Draft final report phase 2. Turfloop: University of Limpopo (Medunsa Campus).

GLOSSARY

Abstract thinking: Thinking characterised by the ability to grasp the essentials of a whole, to break a whole into its parts and to discern common properties. To think symbolically.

Acting out: Behavioural response to an unconscious drive or impulse that brings about temporary partial relief of inner tension; relief is attained by reacting to a present situation as if it were the situation that originally gave rise to the drive or impulse. Common in borderline states.

Acute stress disorder: Syndrome closely related to posttraumatic stress disorder characterised by anxiety and dissociative symptoms after exposure to extreme stress. The only major distinctions are in duration and point of onset. By definition, ASD has an onset within one month after the traumatic event and does not persist beyond four weeks after the event.

Addiction: Refers to a dependence on a behaviour or substance that a person is powerless to stop. The term has been partially replaced by the word dependence for substance abuse. Addiction has been extended, however, to include mood-altering behaviours or activities. Some researchers speak of two types of addictions: substance addictions (for example alcoholism, drug abuse, and smoking) and process addictions (for example gambling, spending, shopping, eating, and sexual activity). There is a growing recognition that many addicts, such as polydrug abusers, are addicted to more than one substance or process.

Adjustment disorder: A disorder found in the DSM-5 that refers to the development of symptoms in relation to a particular stressor.

Adolescence: The period between the onset of puberty and the attainment of adulthood. Determined by cultural factors that define behaviour expected of the adolescent, and in the length of time spent in this period.

Aetiology: The causes, origins, evolution, and implications of disease and other phenomena.

Affect: The subjective and immediate experience of emotion attached to ideas or mental representations of objects. Affect has outward manifestations that may be classified as restricted, blunted, flattened, broad, labile, appropriate, or inappropriate.

Aggression: Forceful, goal-directed action that may be verbal or physical; the motor counterpart of the affect of rage, anger, or hostility. Seen in neurological deficit, temporal lobe disorder, impulse-control disorders, mania, schizophrenia.

Agitation: Severe anxiety associated with motor restlessness.

Agnosia: Impaired ability to recognise objects or people.

Agonist: Chemical substance that effectively increases the activity of a neurotransmitter by imitating its effects.

Alogia: Inability to speak (e.g., talks very little or gives brief, empty replies to questions) because of a mental deficiency such as dementia or schizophrenia. It involves a speech disturbance in which the individual displays a general lack of additional, unprompted content seen in normal speech.

Amnesia: Loss or lack of memory.

Anterograde amnesia: Loss of memory for events subsequent to the onset of the amnesia common after trauma.

Retrograde amnesia: Loss of memory for events preceding the onset of the amnesia.

Anhedonia: Loss of interest in and withdrawal from all regular and pleasurable activities. Often associated with depression.

Anorexia: Loss of or decrease in appetite. In anorexia nervosa appetite may be reserved but patient refuses to eat.

Anorexia nervosa: Syndrome characterised by a refusal of the person to maintain a minimally normal body weight, an intense fear of being overweight, and a misperception of one's own body size or shape.

Antagonist: A chemical substance that decreases or blocks the effects of a neurotransmitter.

Antidiuretic: Chemical that reduces urination.

Anti-psychiatry: A socio-political movement that rejects the methodologies, medical practices and underlying assumptions of psychiatry.

Anxiety: Feeling of apprehension caused by anticipation of danger, which may be internal or external./The emotion of fear linked to the anticipation of future danger or misfortune.

Anxiolytic: Drug used to reduce anxiety.

Apathy: Dulled emotional tone associated with detachment or indifference; observed in certain types of schizophrenia and depression.

Aphasia: Impairment or loss of language skills resulting from brain damage caused by a stroke, Alzheimer's disease, or other illness or trauma.

Atherosclerosis: Process by which a fatty substance or plaque builds up in the arteries to form an obstruction.

Attention: Concentration; the aspect of consciousness that relates to the amount of effort exerted in focusing on certain aspects of an experience, activity, or task. Usually impaired in anxiety and depressive disorders.

Attributional style: How people explain the events of their lives, either positively or negatively.

Avolition: A common symptom associated with schizophrenia involving the inability to begin and sustain goal-directed activity.

Behaviour: Sum total of the psyche that includes impulses, motivations, wishes, drives, instincts, and cravings, as expressed by a person's behaviour or motor activity. Also called conation.

Bereavement: Feeling of grief or desolation, especially at the death or loss of a loved one.

Biomedical model: A perspective in psychopathology that claims that all mental illnesses have a biological cause.

Biopsychosocial approach: A perspective in psychopathology that attempts to integrate biological, psychological and social factors to gain a better understanding of why mental disorders occur.

Biopsychosocial paradigm: The view that mental disorders are reactions of the personality to a combination of biological, psychological, and social factors.

Bipolar disorders: Syndromes characterised by the presence of manic, hypomanic, or mixed episodes, including bipolar I disorder, bipolar II disorder, and cyclothymic disorder.

Bipolar I disorder: A mood disorder found in the DSM-5 that refers to manic and depressive mood swings. Syndrome characterised by the presence of one or more manic or mixed episodes.

Bipolar II disorder: Syndrome characterised by the presence of at least one major depressive episode accompanied by at least one hypomanic episode.

Blackout: Amnesia experienced by alcoholics about behaviour during drinking bouts. Usually indicates reversible brain damage.

Blocking: Abrupt interruption in train of thinking before a thought or idea is finished; after a brief pause, person indicates no recall of what was being said or was going to be said (also known as thought deprivation). Common in schizophrenia and severe anxiety.

Blunted affect: Disturbance of affect manifested by a severe reduction in the intensity of externalised feeling tone.

Body dysmorphic disorder: Syndrome characterised by a persistent belief that the person's appearance is somehow seriously defective. Complaints commonly involve perceived defects in the face or head, but can involve any body part.

Brief psychotic disorder: Syndrome characterised by a psychotic disturbance that lasts more than one day, but less than one month.

Bulimia nervosa: Syndrome characterised by binge eating and inappropriate methods of preventing weight gain including vomiting, misuse of laxatives, diuretics, or enemas.

Cannabinoids: Chemical compounds that act directly or indirectly on the cannabinoid receptors; they have a similar effect to those produced by cannabis

Cataplexy: Temporary sudden loss of muscle tone, causing weakness and immobilisation. Can be precipitated by a variety of emotional states and is often followed by sleep. Commonly seen in narcolepsy.

Catatonic behaviour: A common symptom associated with schizophrenia involving marked motor abnormalities such as bizarre postures, purposeless repetitive movements and an extreme degree of unawareness.

Cathinone: A monoamine alkaloid that is chemically similar to ephedrine; acts as a stimulant

Choreiform: Occasional jerking or writhing movements which appear to be minor problems with coordination. These movements, which are absent during sleep, worsen over time and progress to random, uncontrollable and often violent twitchings. It is a common symptom of Huntington's disease, which usually appears between the ages of 35 and 50 and worsens over time.

Cisnormative: Assumption that a person's gender identity matches his or her biological sex.

Cognition: Mental process of knowing and becoming aware. Function closely associated with judgement.

Cognitive schemas: Learned structures of cognition used by an individual to make sense of and construct to some extent their subjective experience of the world.

Coma: State of profound unconsciousness from which a person 'cannot' be roused, with minimal or no detectable responsiveness to stimuli. Seen in injury or disease of the brain, in such systemic conditions as diabetic ketoacidosis and uraemia, and in intoxications with alcohol and other drugs. Coma may also occur in severe catatonic states and in conversion disorder.

Comorbidity: Refers to the simultaneous existence of two or more disorders in the same individual/more than one disorder or disease in the same individual at the same time.

Concordance rate: A quantitative statistical expression for the agreement of a given genetic trait, especially in pairs of twins in genetic studies.

Confabulation: Unconscious filling of gaps in memory by imagining experiences or events that have no basis in fact. Commonly seen in amnestic syndromes. Should be differentiated from lying.

Control: False belief that a person's will, thoughts, or feelings are being controlled by external forces.

Conversion disorder: Syndrome characterised by pseudoneurological (somatoform and dissociative) symptoms such as amnesia, paralysis, impaired coordination or balance, localised anaesthesia, blindness, deafness, double vision, hallucinations, tremors, or seizures without medical explanation.

Convulsion: An involuntary, violent muscular contraction or spasm.

Culture: The sum total of knowledge passed on from generation to generation within any given society. This body of knowledge includes language, forms of art and expression, religion, social and political structures, economic systems, legal systems, norms of behaviour, ideas about illness and healing, and so on.

Culture-bound syndromes: Mental illnesses structured by indigenous sets of cultural schemas. Some of the mental illnesses are in fact cultural entities; they exist primarily in particular cultural contexts or are responses to certain precipitants in the indigenous meaning systems.

Culture-fair test: A psychological test that is designed to be free of cultural bias.

Culture-free test: A psychological test that attempts to minimise the effects that culture may have on a person's performance on the test.

Cupping: An ancient therapy in which small cups are placed on the skin and suction created. This can be used for problems with pain and inflammation, as well as for deep massage.

Cyclothymic disorder: Syndrome characterised by numerous hypomanic symptoms alternating with numerous depressive symptoms not severe enough to warrant a diagnosis of a major depressive episode occurring over a two-year period.

Delirium: Acute reversible mental disorder characterised by confusion and some impairment of consciousness; generally associated with emotional lability, hallucinations or illusions, and inappropriate, impulsive, irrational, or violent behaviour.

Delirium tremens: Acute and sometimes fatal reaction to withdrawal from alcohol – usually occurring 72 to 96 hours after the cessation of heavy drinking. Distinctive characteristics are marked autonomic hyperactivity (tachycardia, fever, hyperhidrosis, dilated pupils), usually accompanied by tremulousness, hallucinations, illusions, and delusions.

Delusion: A common symptom associated with schizophrenia which involves false belief, based on incorrect inference about external reality, that is firmly held despite objective and obvious contradictory proof or evidence and despite the fact that other members of the culture do not share the belief.

Bizarre delusion: False belief that is patently absurd or fantastic (e.g., invaders from space have implanted electrodes in a person's brain). Common in schizophrenia. In non-bizarre delusion content is usually within range of possibility.

Delusional disorder: Syndrome characterised by at least one month of non-bizarre delusions, without other psychotic symptoms.

Delusion of grandeur: Exaggerated conception of one's importance, power, or identity.

Delusion of persecution: False belief of being harassed or persecuted. Often found in litigious patients who have a pathological tendency to take legal action because of imagined mistreatment. Most common delusion.

Delusion of reference: False belief that the behaviour of others refers to oneself; that events, objects, or other people have a particular and unusual significance, usually of a negative nature. Derived from idea of reference, in which persons falsely feel that others are talking about them (e.g., belief that people on television or radio are talking to or about the person).

    Mood-congruent delusion: Delusion with content that is mood appropriate (e.g., depressed patients who believe they are responsible for the destruction of the world).

    Mood-incongruent delusion: Delusion based on incorrect reference about external reality, with content that has no association to mood or is mood inappropriate (e.g., depressed patients who believe that they are the new Messiah).

    Paranoid delusion: Includes persecutory delusions and delusions of reference, control, and grandeur.

Dementia: Mental disorder characterised by general impairment in intellectual functioning without clouding of consciousness. Characterised by failing memory, difficulty with calculations, distractibility, alterations in mood and affect, impaired judgement and abstraction, reduced facility with language, and disturbance of orientation. Although irreversible because of underlying progressive degenerative brain disease, dementia may be reversible if the cause can be treated.

Denial: A psychological defence mechanism whereby individuals refuse to acknowledge what has happened, is happening, or will happen, i.e., keeping any aspects of external reality out of conscious awareness because if it was acknowledged, it would produce anxiety.

Depersonalisation: Mental condition based in divided consciousness characterised by a persistent or recurrent feeling of being detached from one's mental processes or body.

Depersonalisation disorder: Syndrome characterised by depersonalisation accompanied by clinically significant emotional distress or impairment.

Depression: Mental state characterised by feelings of sadness, loneliness, despair, low self-esteem, and self-reproach. Accompanying signs include psychomotor retardation or at times agitation, withdrawal from interpersonal contact, and vegetative symptoms such as insomnia and anorexia. The term refers to either a mood that is so characterised or a mood disorder.

Derealisation: An alteration in the perception or experience of the external world so that it seems strange or unreal. Other symptoms include feeling as though one's environment is lacking in spontaneity, emotional colouring and depth. It is a dissociative symptom of many conditions, such as psychiatric and neurological disorders, and not a standalone disorder. It is also a transient side effect of acute drug intoxication, sleep deprivation, and stress.

Detachment: Characterised by distant interpersonal relationships and lack of emotional involvement.

Determinism: The belief that states or events are determined by previously existing causes.

Diabetes: Diabetes mellitus (sometimes called 'sugar diabetes'). A condition that occurs when the body cannot use glucose (a type of sugar) normally, resulting in high levels of blood sugar

Diathesis-stress model: A perspective in psychopathology that proposes that some people inherit or develop predispositions (diathesis) to psychopathology, although mental disorders will not emerge until stressors become intense enough to convert predispositions into actual psychological disorders.

Differential diagnosis: The process of distinguishing between two or more disorders with similar or overlapping signs and symptoms.

Direct observation: A method in which a researcher observes and records behaviour while something is happening.

Disease: A medical syndrome or cluster of symptoms, or a physiological disease that manifests in parts of the body. In medical terminology this refers to the diagnosis of the doctor. It is the clinician's definition of the patient's problem, always taken from the paradigm of disease in which the clinician was trained.

Disorganised behaviour: A common symptom associated with schizophrenia involving both an inability to persist in goal-directed activity and the performance of very inappropriate behaviours in public.

Disorganised speech: A common symptom associated with schizophrenia where speech is incomprehensible and related only remotely to the subject under discussion.

Disorientation: Confusion; impairment of awareness of time, place, and person (the position of the self in relation to other persons). Characteristic of cognitive disorders.

Dissociation: Mental condition characterised by a loss of the integration of faculties or functions that are normally integrated in consciousness. Can affect memory, sensory modalities, motor functions, cognitive functions, and personal identity or sense of self./ Unconscious defence mechanism involving the segregation of any group of mental or behavioural processes from the rest of the person's psychic activity. May entail the separation of an idea from its accompanying emotional tone, as seen in dissociative and conversion disorders.

Dissociative amnesia: Syndrome characterised by divided consciousness in which there is an inability to recall important information that is held in a separate part of consciousness.

Dissociative disorders: Syndromes characterised by divided consciousness including dissociative amnesia, dissociative fugue, dissociative identity disorder (formerly multiple personality disorder), depersonalisation disorder, dissociative trance disorder, and dissociative disorder not otherwise specified.

Dissociative fugue: Syndrome based in divided consciousness characterised by sudden, unexpected travel away from home or one's customary place of work, accompanied by an inability to recall one's past, and also a confusion about personal identity.

Dissociative hallucinations and delusions: Psychotic-type symptoms based on the mental processes of trance.

Dissociative identity disorder: Syndrome characterised by the presence of two or more distinct identities or personality states in consciousness that recurrently take control of the individual's behaviour, accompanied by dissociative amnesia.

Dissociative trance disorder: New diagnostic category included as a disorder which is described in the 'other specified dissociative disorder' section to accommodate dissociative syndromes, characterised by trance or possession trance symptoms.

Diuretic: Anything that promotes the formation of urine by the kidney.

Dopaminergic: Activated or transmitted by dopamine. Pertaining to tissues or organs affected by dopamine.

Dysarthria: Speech that is characteristically slurred, slow, and difficult to produce (difficult to understand). The person with dysarthria may also have problems controlling the pitch, loudness, rhythm, and voice qualities of his or her speech.

Dyspareunia: Syndrome characterised by genital pain before, during, or after sexual intercourse. Closely related to sexual aversion disorder, hypoactive sexual desire disorder, and vaginismus.

Dysphoria: Feeling of unpleasantness or discomfort; a mood of general dissatisfaction and restlessness. Occurs in depression and anxiety.

Dysthymic disorder: Syndrome characterised by a chronically depressed mood lasting for at least two years. Differs from major depressive disorder in that dysthymic disorder is a chronic illness with generally less severe depressive symptoms.

Eating disorders: Syndromes characterised by obsessive-compulsive or addictive type behaviour involving food. Persons are obsessed with ingesting or not ingesting food.

Echolalia: Psychopathological repeating of words or phrases of one person by another. Tends to be repetitive and persistent. Seen in certain kinds of schizophrenia, particularly the catatonic types.

Egocentric: Refers to personal identity centred in the self. Persons perceive themselves as autonomous individuals with personal choices, desires, and rights, and see dependence as undesirable. In an egocentric society the 'self' becomes the primary object of interest, and personal freedom and power become the supreme values.

Elation: Mood consisting of feelings of joy, euphoria, triumph, and intense self-satisfaction, or optimism. Occurs in mania when not grounded in reality.

Elevated mood: Air of confidence and enjoyment. A mood more cheerful than normal but not necessarily pathological.

Emotion: A mental and physiological state associated with a wide variety of feelings, thoughts, and behaviour. Emotions are subjective experiences, or experienced from an individual point of view. Emotion is often associated with mood, temperament, personality, and disposition.

Endocrine system: The system in the body comprising all the glands that produce hormones; chemical messenger system comprising feedback loops of hormone action.

Epidemiology: The study of incidence, distribution, and control of diseases.

Ethnocentrism: Refers to judging other people from within one's own cultural perspective.

Euphoria: An affective state of exaggerated well-being or elation.

Exhibitionism: Syndrome characterised by a compulsion to expose one's genitals to a stranger. The typical case is a young man exposing his erect penis to unsuspecting females.

Explanatory model: Refers to the ways a set of cultural schemas explains the cause of mental illness, why the onset occurred when it did, the effects of the illness, what course the illness will take, and which treatments are appropriate. These meanings dramatically affect the lived experiences of mental patients, in many ways structuring their subjective experiences.

Expressed emotion: Refers to criticism, hostility, and emotional over-involvement directed at a mental patient by their family members.

Factitious disorder: A disorder found in the DSM-5 that refers to the intentional production of symptoms in order to assume the 'sick role'.

False negatives: Test results that indicate no problem when a problem does exist.

False positives: Test results that indicate a problem when no problem is present.

Female orgasmic disorder: Syndrome characterised by a persistent absence of orgasm after normal sexual arousal that causes marked distress or interpersonal difficulty.

Female sexual arousal disorder: Syndrome characterised by an inability of a woman to maintain sexual arousal during coitus. This typically results in pleasureless lovemaking, painful intercourse, avoidance of sexual activity, and marital or relationship problems.

Fetishism: Syndrome involving the use of inanimate objects (the fetish) for sexual arousal. This is typically a male disorder. Commonly used fetishes are objects associated with females, for example women's undergarments, stockings, shoes, or other articles of clothing.

Flashbacks: Sudden, intense re-experiencing of a previous, usually traumatic, event.

Flat affect: A common symptom associated with schizophrenia involving the lack of emotional responsiveness in gesture, facial expression and/or tone of voice.

Frotteurism: Syndrome characterised by a compulsion to rub against or touch a non-consenting person in a sexual way. It usually occurs in crowded public spaces such as buses or train carriages.

Gender:
1. The behavioural, cultural, or psychological traits typically associated with one sex.
2. Sexual identity, especially in relation to society or culture.
3. The condition of being female or male; sex.
4. Females or males considered as a group.
5. Traditionally, the word 'gender' has been used primarily to refer to the grammatical categories of 'masculine', 'feminine', and 'neuter', but in recent years the word has become well established in its use to refer to sex-based categories, as in phrases such as 'gender gap' and 'the politics of gender'. This usage is supported by the practice of many anthropologists, who reserve the word 'sex' for reference to biological categories, while using the word 'gender' to refer to social or cultural categories. According to this rule, one would say, 'The effectiveness of the medication appears to depend on the sex [not gender] of the patient', but 'In peasant societies, gender [not sex] roles are likely to be more clearly defined'. This distinction is useful in principle, but it is by no means widely observed, and considerable variation in usage occurs at all levels.

Gender identity: The private subjective cognition of one's gender.

Gender identity disorder: Syndrome characterised by an intense and persistent sense of identity as someone of the opposite gender, causing significant emotional distress and social or occupational impairment.

Gender role behaviour: The gender-specific activities that are expected in any given society. This can include such things as wearing gender-specific clothing; having a gender-specific occupation; using gender-specific forms of speech, mannerisms, hairstyles, jewellery, accessories, and cosmetics; performing gender-specific recreational activities, sexual behaviour, and household duties; and holding gender-specific socio-politico-religious offices.

Generalised anxiety disorder: Syndrome characterised by excessive anxiety, restlessness, inability to concentrate, and worry occurring more days than not for period of at least six months.

Hallucination: False sensory perception occurring in the absence of any relevant external stimulation of the sensory modality involved. It is symptom that is commonly associated with Schizophrenia.

Auditory hallucination: False perception of sound, usually voices but also other noises such as music. Most common hallucination in psychiatric disorders.

Gustatory hallucination: Hallucination primarily involving taste.

Mood-congruent hallucination: Hallucination with content that is consistent with either a depressed or manic mood (e.g., depressed patients hearing voices telling them that they are bad persons; manic patients hearing voices telling them that they have inflated worth, power, or knowledge).

Mood-incongruent hallucination: Hallucination not associated with real external stimuli, with content that is not consistent with either depressed or manic mood (e.g., in depression, hallucinations not involving such themes as guilt, deserved punishment, or inadequacy; in mania, not involving such themes as inflated worth or power).

Olfactory hallucination: Hallucination primarily involving smell or odours. Most common in medical disorders, especially in the temporal lobe.

Somatic hallucination: Hallucination involving the perception of a physical experience localised within the body.

Tactile (haptic) hallucination: Hallucination primarily involving the sense of touch.

Hallucinogen: Psychoactive agent that causes perceptual distortions, including hallucinations, as well as changes in thinking and emotions.

Hebephrenia: Complex of symptoms, considered a form of schizophrenia, characterised by wild or silly behaviour or mannerisms, inappropriate affect, and delusions and hallucinations that are transient and unsystematised. Hebephrenic schizophrenia is now called disorganised schizophrenia.

Hyperactivity: Increased muscular activity. The term is commonly used to describe a disturbance found in children that is manifested by constant restlessness, overactivity, distractibility, and difficulties in learning.

Hyperprolactinaemia: An elevated level of prolactin in the blood.

Hypersomnia: Excessive time spent asleep. May be associated with underlying medical or psychiatric disorder (e.g., mood disorders or narcolepsy), or be primary.

Hypertension: Abnormally high blood pressure (the force of blood pushing against the walls of arteries as it flows through them). It is a major risk for stroke and heart and kidney disease that is intimately related to psychological factors.

Hyperthyroidism: Overactive thyroid gland, which produces too much thyroxine (thyroid hormone); speeds up the body's metabolism potentially causing weight loss, anxiety, and irregular heartbeat.

Hypervigilance: Excessive attention to, and focus on, all internal and external stimuli. Usually seen in delusional or paranoid states.

Hypnotic: Drugs that induce sleep; used as a sedative, and for insomnia and anaesthesia.

Hypoactive sexual desire disorder: Syndrome characterised by the absence of the desire for sexual activity resulting in emotional distress or interpersonal difficulty.

Hypochondriasis: Exaggerated concern about health that is based not on real medical pathology but on unrealistic interpretations of physical signs or sensations as abnormal. Hypochondriasis is a syndrome characterised by persistent and unfounded fears of having a serious disease based on a misinterpretation of normal bodily functions or minor symptoms.

Hypoglycaemia: Low blood sugar.

Hypogonadism: A condition in which decreased production of gonadal hormones leads to below-normal function of the gonads and to retardation of sexual growth and development. (The gonads are the ovaries and testes and the hormones they normally produce include estrogen, progesterone, and testosterone.)

Hypomania: Mood abnormality with the qualitative characteristics of mania but somewhat less intense. Seen in cyclothymic disorder. A hypomanic episode is a period of at least four days in which the person experiences an abnormal and persistently elevated, expansive, or irritable mood, with at least three additional symptoms such as: non-delusional grandiosity, decreased need for sleep, pressure of speech, flight of ideas, distractibility, increased involvement in goal-directed activities. Differs from a manic episode in that a hypomanic episode does not cause social or occupational impairment, and there are no hallucinations or delusions.

Hypotheses: The lowest level, most specific testable explanations for unanswered scientific problems.

Hypothyroidism: Underactive thyroid gland so that too little thyroxine (thyroid hormone) is produced; leads to symptoms of slowed metabolism (e.g. weight gain, constipation).

Hypotonia: Diminished tone of the skeletal muscles.

Hysteria: Obsolete diagnostic category used commonly in the latter half of the nineteenth century characterised by extreme anxiety, somatoform, depressive, and dissociative symptoms such as paralyses, anaesthesias, blindness, seizures, and head and body aches, with no medical explanation, as well as dysphoria, hallucinations and multiple personalities.

Iatrogenic: Referring to a physical or mental condition caused by a physician or healthcare provider that may be due to exposure to pathogens, toxins or injurious treatment or procedures.

Illness: In medical anthropology, this refers to the subjective experience of being sick, including the experience of symptoms, suffering, help seeking, side effects of treatment, social stigma, explanations of causes, diagnosis, prognosis, and personal consequences in family life and occupation.

Illusion: Perceptual misinterpretation of a real external stimulus.

Impulse control: Ability to resist an impulse, drive, or temptation to perform some action.

Inappropriate affect: Emotional tone out of harmony with the idea, thought, or speech accompanying it.

Incoherence: Communication that is disconnected, disorganised, or incomprehensive. See also 'word salad'.

Infection: Invasion and multiplication of microorganisms in body tissues.

Insomnia: Difficulty in falling asleep or difficulty in staying asleep. It can be related to a mental disorder, can be related to a physical disorder or an adverse effect of medication, or can be primary (not related to a known medical factor or another mental disorder).

Hypersomnia: An inability to stay awake; excessive sleeping.

Terminal insomnia: Early morning awakening or waking up at least two hours before planning to.

Intellectualisation: A psychological defence mechanism whereby individuals remove all emotion from their emotional experiences.

Intelligence: Capacity for learning and ability to recall, integrate constructively, and apply what one has learned. The capacity to understand and think rationally.

Intoxication: Mental disorder caused by recent ingestion or presence in the body of an exogenous substance producing maladaptive behaviour by virtue of its effects on the central nervous system. The most common psychiatric changes involve disturbances of perception, wakefulness, attention, thinking, judgement, emotional control, and psychomotor behaviour. The specific clinical picture depends on the substance ingested.

Irritability: Abnormal or excessive excitability, with easily triggered anger, annoyance, or impatience.

Irritable mood: State in which one is easily annoyed and provoked to anger. See also 'Irritability'.

Labile affect: Affective expression characterised by rapid and abrupt changes, unrelated to external stimuli.

Labile mood: Oscillations in mood between euphoria and depression or anxiety.

Magical thinking: Thinking similar to that of the preoperational phase in children (Jean Piaget), in which thoughts, words, or actions assume power (e.g., to cause or prevent events).

Major depressive disorder: Syndrome characterised by one or more major depressive episodes without a history of manic, mixed, or hypomanic episodes.

Major depressive episode: At least two weeks of depressed mood with at least four additional symptoms of depression which can include changes in appetite, weight, sleep, or psychomotor activity, fatigue, feelings of worthlessness or guilt, difficulty thinking, and recurrent thoughts of suicide or suicide attempts.

Maladaptiveness: One way of defining psychopathology that, in order to determine what is abnormal, uses the extent to which certain behaviours or experiences are maladaptive to the self or others.

Male erectile disorder: Syndrome characterised by a persistent inability to attain or maintain an erection sufficient for the completion of coitus.

Male orgasmic disorder: Syndrome characterised by a failure or delay to achieve orgasm during coitus.

Malingering: Feigning disease to achieve a specific goal, for example to avoid an unpleasant responsibility. Compare factitious disorder.

Mania: Mood state characterised by an abnormally elevated, euphoric, or irritable mood lasting at least one week, or less if hospitalisation is required, with at least three additional manic symptoms, which can include grandiosity, decreased need for sleep, pressure of speech, flight of ideas, distractibility, increased goal-directed activity, and excessive involvement in pleasurable activity with a high potential for painful consequences. There may be grandiose delusions and hallucinations. Seen in bipolar I disorder.

Mannerism: Ingrained, habitual involuntary movement.

MDA/MDMA (3.4-Methylenedioxyamphetamine; Ecstasy): Psychostimulant drug related to amphetamines.

Melancholia: Severe depressive state.

Memory: Process whereby what is experienced or learned is established as a record in the central nervous system (registration), where it persists with a variable degree of permanence (retention) and can be recollected or retrieved from storage at will (recall).

Mental disorder: Psychiatric illness or disease whose manifestations are primarily characterised by behavioural or psychological impairment of function, measured in terms of deviation from some normative concept. Associated with distress or disease, not just an expected response to a particular event or limited to relations between a person and society.

Mental retardation: Sub-average general intellectual functioning that originates in the developmental period and is associated with impaired maturation and learning, and social maladjustment. Retardation is commonly defined in terms of intelligence quotient: mild (50–55 to 70), moderate (35–40 to 50–55), severe (20–25 to 35–40) and profound (below 20–25).

Metaphor: Figure of speech; not meant literally (e.g. 'a rolling stone gathers no moss').

Methcathinone: A monoamine alkaloid; substitute for cathinone; has powerful stimulant and euphoric effects.

Mixed episode: Episode characterised by a period of at least one week in which diagnostic criteria are met for both a manic episode and a major depressive episode.

Models: General theories that explain a large part of the field of inquiry within a scientific discipline.

Mood: Pervasive and sustained feeling tone that is experienced internally and that, in the extreme, can markedly influence virtually all aspects of a person's behaviour and perception of the world. Distinguished from affect, the external expression of the internal feeling tone. For types of mood, see the specific term.

Mood disorders: Syndromes that have depressive or manic symptoms as their primary feature.

Mood episodes: Episodes of emotional illness and distress characterised by depression, mania, or hypomania, or some combination of these, including major depressive episode, manic episode, mixed episode, or hypomanic episode.

Morbid/morbidity: Symptom or sign which is indicative of disease.

Negativism: Verbal or non-verbal opposition or resistance to outside suggestions and advice. Commonly seen in catatonic schizophrenia in which the patient resists any effort to be moved or does the opposite of what is asked.

Neologism: New word or phrase whose derivation cannot be understood. Often seen in schizophrenia. It has also been used to mean a word that has been incorrectly constructed but whose origins are nonetheless understandable (e.g., 'headshoe' to mean 'hat'), but such constructions are more properly referred to as 'word approximations'.

Neurasthenia: A disorder referring to 'tired nerves' and including symptoms of fatigue, anxiety, and various somatic complaints. Originated in the United States, but is no longer a part of the DSM classification system. A very common diagnosis in China.

Neurogenic: Starting with or having to do with the nerves or the nervous system.

Neuropeptide: Small molecules (similar to proteins) used in communications between neurons.

Neuroses: Mental disorders presumed to have psychodynamic origins existing towards the mild to moderate end of a spectrum of mental illnesses in the biopsychosocial paradigm.

Neurotransmitters: Chemical substances in the brain that are responsible for the communication of nerve impulses among the brain cells.

Nociception: A typical sensory experience that may be described as the unpleasant awareness of a noxious (harmful to life or health, especially by being poisonous) stimulus or bodily harm.

Nociceptive: Relating to the sensation or perception of pain.

Nosology: Branch of medicine that deals with classification of diseases.

Obsession: Persistent and recurrent idea, thought, or impulse that cannot be eliminated from consciousness by logic or reasoning; obsessions are involuntary and ego-dystonic.

Obsessive-compulsive disorder: Syndrome characterised by persistent thoughts or impulses that are experienced as intrusive and inappropriate (obsessions), and repetitive behaviours (compulsions) that are performed to reduce the emotional distress associated with obsessions.

Opiate/opioid: Drug derived from opium; alkaloid compounds found in nature in the poppy plant; provides an intense 'high'.

Orientation: State of awareness of oneself and one's surroundings in terms of time, place, and person.

Paedophilia: Syndrome characterised by a person sixteen years or older having recurrent sexual activity with a prepubescent child (legally this is generally thirteen years or younger).

Panic: Acute, intense attack of anxiety associated with personality disorganisation; the anxiety is overwhelming and accompanied by feelings of impending doom.

Panic attacks: Experiences characterised by a discrete period of intense fear with at least four additional somatic or cognitive symptoms including: palpitations, sweating, trembling, shortness of breath, feelings of choking, chest pain, nausea or abdominal distress, dizziness, depersonalisation, derealisation, fear of going crazy, fear of dying, tactile sensations (paresthesias), and chills or hot flushes.

Panic disorder: Syndrome characterised by recurrent and unexpected panic attacks.

Paradigm: The highest, most general level in a hierarchy of scientific intellectual structures. A paradigm is a generally accepted view of the nature of a scientific discipline.

Paranoia: Rare psychiatric syndrome marked by the gradual development of a highly elaborate and complex delusional system, generally involving persecutory or grandiose delusions, with few other signs of personality disorganisation or thought disorder.

Paraphilias: Syndromes characterised by recurrent sexual fantasies and behaviours involving objects, persons, or situations that are considered deviant in the prevailing cultural meaning system, causing significant emotional distress and/or social impairment.

Pathoplastic: Of or pertaining to factors (i.e., culture) that exert an influence on the final presentation of a disorder.

Perception: Conscious awareness of elements in the environment by the mental processing of sensory stimuli. Sometimes used in a broader sense to refer to the mental process by which all kinds of data, intellectual, emotional, and sensory, are meaningfully organised.

Perseveration: Pathological repetition of the same response to different stimuli, as in a repetition of the same verbal response to different questions. Persistent repetition of specific words or concepts in the process of speaking. Seen in cognitive disorders, schizophrenia, and other mental illness.

Personal distress: Distress and suffering experienced by a person.

Personality: The set of psychological traits and mechanisms within the individual that are organised and relatively enduring and that influence the individual's interactions with, and adaptation to, the environment (including the intrapsychic, physical, and social environment).

Personality disorders: Enduring patterns of pathological subjective experience and behaviour based in personality development, rather than in some specific disease entity.

Antisocial personality disorder: Personality characterised by a persistent pattern of victimising others through theft or destruction of property, physical assault (including spouse or child abuse), or deceit to gain personal profit or pleasure.

Avoidant personality disorder: Personality characterised by extreme social anxiety, low self-esteem, and hypersensitivity to criticism to the point that the person purposely avoids interpersonal contact.

Borderline personality disorder: Personality characterised by a persistent instability in social relationships, self-image, and emotions. Central to this instability is fear of abandonment and rejection.

Dependent personality disorder: Personality characterised by an excessive need to be taken care of, associated with submissive, clinging behaviour, and fear of independence.

Histrionic personality disorder: Personality characterised by excessive emotionality and attention-seeking behaviour.

Narcissistic personality disorder: Personality characterised by an obsession with grandiosity, an intense need for admiration, and a lack of empathy for others.

Obsessive-compulsive personality disorder: Personality characterised by a persistent preoccupation with order, perfection, attention to detail, rules, and control.

Paranoid personality disorder: Personality characterised by a pervasive distrust of other people such that others are virtually always perceived as threatening or hostile.

Schizoid personality disorder: Personality characterised by a pervasive detachment from social relationships and a restricted range of emotions.

Schizotypal personality disorder: Personality characterised by anxiety in social relationships accompanied by eccentricities of behaviour such as superstitiousness, preoccupation with paranormal phenomena, magical thinking, or use of rituals in everyday situations.

Phencyclidine (PCP): Psychoactive drug which distorts perception and may lead to hallucinations.

Phenomenology: The study of phenomena, i.e., the mental construction of cognition out of raw sensory data. A phenomenon is an experience of an object by a subject. In phenomenology, it is the experience of the object that is the focus of study, not the object itself.

Phobia: Persistent, pathological, unrealistic, intense fear of an object or situation. The phobic person may realise that the fear is irrational but, nonetheless, cannot dispel it. For types of phobias, see the specific term.

Agoraphobia: Syndrome characterised by anxiety about being in places in which a panic attack or other anxiety reaction might occur, resulting in a pervasive avoidance of a variety of situations./Morbid fear of open places or leaving the familiar setting of the home. May be present with or without panic attacks.

Social phobia: Syndrome characterised by a persistent fear of social situations in which extreme embarrassment may occur. Exposure to these situations provokes an anxiety response.

Specific phobia: Syndrome characterised by a persistent fear of specific objects or situations, exposure to which almost invariably evokes an anxiety response.

Polyneuropathy: A neurological disorder that occurs when many peripheral nerves throughout the body malfunction simultaneously.

Posttraumatic stress disorder: Syndrome characterised by prominent anxiety and dissociative symptoms following exposure to an extreme traumatic stressor.

Posturing: Strange, fixed, and bizarre bodily positions held by a patient for an extended time.

Poverty of speech: Restriction in the amount of speech used; replies may be monosyllabic.

Praxis: The ability to have interpersonal relationships and perform actions.

Premature ejaculation: Syndrome characterised by persistent ejaculation after minimal sexual stimulation and before the person or the person's sexual partner wishes it.

Proband: A term used most often in medical genetics and other medical fields to denote a particular subject (person or animal) being studied or reported on.

Prodromal: Symptomatic of the onset of an attack or a disease. Of or pertaining to the early symptoms of a disease; as, the prodromal stage of a disease.

Projection: A psychological defence mechanism whereby individuals take something of themselves and place it outside themselves, onto others.

Psychoanalysis: A means of treating patients who suffer from hysterical and neurotic conditions based on Freud's theory that psychopathology is largely caused by the repression of forbidden wishes or instinctual drives.

Psychodynamic approaches: Approaches to psychopathology that believe that the way we relate to others and ourselves is largely influenced by internal forces that exist outside consciousness.

Psychogenic illness: Physical illness for which no physical cause has yet been found; thought to arise from psychological or emotional stressors/disorders.

Psychological disorder: A mental abnormality that manifests on the level of thinking, feeling or behaving.

Psychomotor agitation: Physical and mental overactivity that is usually non-productive and is associated with a feeling of inner turmoil, as seen in agitated depression.

Psychomotor retardation: Physical and mental underactivity that is typically characterised by stooped posture, very little spontaneous movement, poor eye contact, impaired coordination, slow speech, and difficulties with articulation.

Psychosis: Mental disorder in which the thoughts, affective response, ability to recognise reality, and ability to communicate and relate to others are sufficiently impaired to interfere grossly with the capacity to deal with reality. The classical characteristics of psychosis are impaired reality testing, hallucinations, delusions, and illusions.

Psychotic: The presence of delusions, prominent hallucinations, disorganised speech, and disorganised or catatonic behaviour.

Psychotic disorders: Syndromes characterised by a loss of reality testing, including schizophrenia, schizophreniform disorder, schizoaffective disorder, delusional disorder, brief psychotic disorder, and shared psychotic disorder.

Reaction-formation: A psychological defence mechanism whereby individuals turn painful or threatening reactions into their opposite.

Reality testing: Fundamental ego function that consists of tentative actions that test and objectively evaluate the nature and limits of the environment. Includes the ability to differentiate between the external world and the internal world and to judge the relation between the self and the environment accurately. The loss of reality testing leads to a disturbance in the experience of self and one's relationship with the external physical and social environments. The presence of hallucinations and/or delusions is usually viewed as a loss of reality testing.

Reliability: The ability of separate clinicians or researchers to diagnose the same disorder consistently after observing the same pattern of symptoms in patients.

Repression: A psychological defence mechanism whereby individuals unconsciously put painful thoughts and memories out of their minds.

Ritual: In a 'normal' sense, this refers to a ceremonial activity of cultural origin. In an abnormal context it refers to a formalised activity practised by a person to reduce anxiety, as in obsessive-compulsive disorder.

Rumination: Constant preoccupation with thinking about a single idea or theme, as in obsessive-compulsive disorder.

Schema: Pattern of thought (mental structure) used to organise information.

Schizoaffective disorder: Syndrome characterised by a combination of psychotic and mood symptoms in which psychotic symptoms occur in conjunction with either a manic or depressive episode, followed by at least two weeks of psychotic symptoms without prominent mood symptoms.

Schizophrenia: Syndrome characterised by the presence of psychotic symptoms for a significant portion of the time during a one-month period, and some signs of the disorder for at least a six-month period.

Schizophreniform disorder: Syndrome characterised by a psychotic disturbance that lasts for at least one month, but for less than six months.

Secondary gain: Any benefit a person receives as an indirect result of having a disorder.

Sedative: Drug taken to induce calmness or sleep.

Seizure: Also referred to as a fit, is a transient symptom of abnormal neuronal activity in the brain. There are different types of seizures, including grand mal, absence, myoclonic, clonic, tonic, and atonic seizures.

Sensorium: Hypothetical sensory centre in the brain that is involved with clarity of awareness about oneself and one's surroundings, including the ability to perceive and process ongoing events in the light of past experiences, future options, and current circumstances. Sometimes used interchangeably with 'consciousness'.

Serological: Of or pertaining to the science that deals with the properties and reactions of serums, especially blood serum. It is the characteristics of a disease or organism shown by study of blood serums.

Sexual aversion disorder: Syndrome characterised by an aversion to and active avoidance of genital contact with a sexual partner. The typical case is a female who experiences anxiety, fear, or disgust from genital or other explicitly sexual contact.

Sexual dysfunctions: Syndromes characterised by psychophysiological problems impacting on one's ability to have satisfying sexual relations, causing marked emotional distress and interpersonal difficulties.

Sexual masochism: Syndrome characterised by sexual arousal resulting from being humiliated, beaten, or bound, or from other forms of corporal punishment.

Sexual preference: The gender(s) that an individual finds sexually arousing.

Sexual sadism: Syndrome characterised by sexual arousal resulting from inflicting physical or psychological punishment on another person.

Shared psychotic disorder: Syndrome characterised by a delusional belief in an individual who is influenced by someone else who has an established delusion.

Statistical deviance: One way of defining psychopathology that uses statistical norms of behaviour and experience to determine what is 'normal', and therefore what is abnormal.

Straw man: An argument that intentionally misrepresents the opponent's argument, making it easier to defeat.

Stroke: Blood flow to the brain stops, resulting in death of brain cells.

Sublimation: A psychological defence mechanism whereby individuals redirect emotions into more positive activities.

Substance: As a scientific term, an element, compound or mixture. In psychology this would refer to any chemical that is ingested, inhaled or injected that leads to a change in affect, perception, cognition or behaviour.

Substance abuse: Syndrome associated with repeated negative consequences resulting from a maladaptive pattern of substance use, such as multiple legal, social, and occupational problems.

Substance intoxication: Condition characterised by clinically significant maladaptive behavioural or psychological changes resulting from ingestion of a specific substance, such as social or occupational impairment, mood instability, cognitive impairment, or belligerence.

Substance-related disorders: Syndromes associated with substance intoxication, substance abuse, substance dependence, or substance withdrawal.

Substance withdrawal: Condition characterised by negative cognitive, physiological, and behavioural changes that occur when bodily concentrations of a substance decline after cessation of prolonged use.

Suicidal ideation: Thoughts or the act of taking one's own life.

Suppression: A psychological defence mechanism whereby individuals consciously try to put painful thoughts and memories out of their minds.

Symbol: A sign that has no logical connection to the thing it represents – an arbitrary sign. It is used simply out of convention, and its use results primarily out of historical accident.

Tachycardia: Rapid heartbeat.

Tangentiality: Oblique, digressive or even irrelevant manner of speech in which the central idea is not communicated.

Tension: Physiological or psychic arousal, uneasiness, or pressure toward action. An unpleasurable alteration in mental or physical state that seeks relief through action.

Teratogen: Agent or factor causing malformation of an embryo.

Theories: Specific explanations for large unanswered scientific problems.

Thought disorder: Any disturbance of thinking that affects language, communication, or thought content. The hallmark feature of schizophrenia. Manifestations range from simple blocking and mild circumstantiality to profound loosening of associations, incoherence, and delusions. Characterised by a failure to follow semantic and syntactic rules that is inconsistent with the person's education, intelligence, or cultural background.

Thought broadcasting: Feeling that one's thoughts are being broadcast or projected into the environment.

Thought insertion: Delusion that thoughts are being implanted in one's mind by other people or forces.

Thought withdrawal: Delusion that one's thoughts are being removed from one's mind by other people or forces.

Trance: Mental condition based on a narrowed focus of attention such that what is outside attention is lost to consciousness.

Transvestic fetishism: Syndrome characterised by males deriving sexual pleasure by intermittently wearing female clothing.

Tumescence: A swelling or enlarging.

Tumour: A mass of abnormal tissue.

Unipolar mood disorder: A mood disorder characterised by episodes of depression only.

Vaginismus: Syndrome characterised by recurrent involuntary contraction of the muscles surrounding the vagina whenever vaginal penetration is attempted.

Validity: Refers to the reality of diagnostic categories. A diagnostic category (e.g., schizophrenia) is valid when it refers to a real clinical entity independent of diagnosis, and is an appropriate means of naming that entity.

Vegetative states: In depression, denoting characteristic symptoms such as sleep disturbance (especially early morning awakening), decreased appetite, constipation, weight loss, and loss of sexual response.

Volatile solvents: Liquids that evaporate at room temperature; can be used for psychoactive effects (e.g. glue, paint thinners, aerosols).

Voyeurism: Syndrome characterised by a compulsion to achieve sexual arousal by observing unsuspecting persons who are getting undressed, naked, or engaged in sexual activities.

Waxy flexibility: Condition in which person maintains the body position in which they are placed. Also called catalepsy.

Word salad: Incoherent, essentially incomprehensible mixture of words and phrases commonly seen in far advanced cases of schizophrenia.

INDEX

Page numbers in italics refer to Figures, Tables and Examples; those in bold refer to Boxes and Case studies

A

abnormal behaviour 46–50, **47**
    definition of terms **47**
acetylcholine *10*
acute stress disorder 189, *189–90*
adaptation 533
addiction 446 *see also under* substance
Adjusted Rorschach Comprehensive System 92
admission to psychiatric hospital 130
adrenaline 8, *8*, 10
advertising 142
aetiology 5
affective disorders *see* mood disorders
African Traditional Religion 25, 25–8
agnosia 296
agoraphobia 174, *174–5*
alarm response 168
alcohol, South Africa 460–1, *461*
alcoholic dementia 289
alienation 339
alogia 248
altruism 116–7
Alzheimer's disease 289
amafufunyane 23, 347–8
amenorrhea 492
American Psychological Association 136, 137
amino acid neurotransmitters *10*
amnestic disorders 305
    aetiology 306–7
    assessment of 308–11, *308–11*
    clinical picture 305, *306*
    epidemiology 306
    treatment and management of 307
amok 349
amphetamines 262
amygdala 193, *194*
anal character 183

ancestors *23*, 25–6
anhedonia 248
anorexia nervosa 479–81, **485, 488**
    binge-eating/purging type 488
    clinical picture 484–7
    cultural, gender, age features 484
    and DSM-5, ICD-10 *484–5*
    in Kenya **488–9**
    outcomes *496*
    prevalence and course 483–4
    restricting type 488
anti-psychiatry 55–6, 274
antidepressants 222
antipsychotic drugs 263
    atypical 9
antisocial personality disorder 553–4, *553–4*
anxiety and panic disorders, history 168–9
anxiety disorders **162**, 166–7, 199
    agoraphobia 174, *174–5*
    anxiety 166, 167–8
    biopsychosocial model 199
    cross-cultural, African perspectives 190–1
    and depressive disorders 166
    and DSM *163–5*
    epidemiology 192
    fear 167
    generalised anxiety disorder 178–9, *179*
    panic disorder 172–3, *173–4*
    separation anxiety disorder 170
    social anxiety disorder (social phobia) 175–7, *176–8*
    specific phobias 170–1, *171–2*

    stress, worry 168
anxiety disorders, aetiology 192
    integrated perspectives 199
anxiety disorders, aetiology; biological processes 192–3
    brain structure, functioning 193, *194*
    genetics 194
    neurochemistry 193
anxiety disorders, aetiology; psychological perspectives
    behavioural models 195–6
    cognitive models 196
    developmental perspectives 197
    family systems theory 197
    humanistic and existential models 197
    psychodynamic models 194–5
anxiety disorders, aetiology; psychosocial stressors 198
apartheid 18–9
    and children 590
    mental healthcare during 19, 54
    and sexuality 428, 429
aphasia 296
aphonia 359
appearance and behaviour in assessment 81
aromatic amino acids 8
asociality 248
Asperger's disorder 602
assessment *see* psychological testing
asylums 51
attachment theory 14
attention-deficit/hyperactivity disorder **613**
    attention-deficit behaviours 614–5
    clinical picture 613–4
    comorbid conditions 618–9

and DSM-5, ICD-10 615–7
history of 613
hyperactive-impulsive behaviours 614
positive features 99
secondary symptoms 618
atypical antipsychotic medication 9
auditory hallucinations 244–5
autism spectrum disorder 600–3
aetiology 605
and DSM-5, ICD-10 603–5
myths and facts 601
autonomy 104
impaired 108
avoidance 113–4
avoidant personality disorder 555, 555–6
avoidant/restrictive food intake disorder 482–3
avolition 249, 249

B

Beck, Aaron 196
behavioural assessment 82–3, 83
behaviour-rating scales 83
behavioural theories of addiction 449
behavioural/learning perspectives 14–5
behaviourism 53, 633
Benjamin, Harry 399
Bertillon Classification of Causes of Death 67
bewitchment 22–3, 28, 347
biases, psychological 15
binge-eating 490–1
binge-eating disorder 481, 494, **494**
clinical picture 495–6
and DSM-5 495
outcomes 497
prevalence and course 494–5
binge-eating/purging type anorexia nervosa 488
biomedical perspectives 7
abnormal functioning of neurotransmitters 8–9, 8–9, 10

and DSM 59
endocrine dysregulation 11, 11
genetic predisposition 7–8
structural abnormalities 12
biopsychiatry 59
biopsychosocial model 31, 39–40, 73
and anxiety disorders 537–8
and personality disorders 199
bipolar and related disorders 203, 216, 218
cyclothymic disorder 218–9
bipolar I and bipolar II disorders 216, 218
hypomanic episode and DSM-5 217–8
manic episode and DSM-5 216–7
Bleuler, Eugen 238
Bloch, Iwan 398
body dysmorphic disorder 182–3
Body Mass Index 486
borderline personality disorder 548–50, 549
brain function
and anxiety disorder 193, 194
measuring 85–6
brain plasticity 12
brain structure 85, 85
and functioning and anxiety disorder 193, 194
and schizophrenia 260–1
brief psychotic disorder 253
Bronfenbrenner, Urie 37, 37–8
bulimia nervosa 479–80, 481, **489**
clinical picture 490–3
culture-, gender-related diagnostic issues 490
and DSM-5, ICD-10 491–2
outcomes 496
prevalence and course 490
burnout 105–6

C

cannabis 447
and schizophrenia 267
South Africa 462–3
caffeine 456
carbon monoxide 10
catastrophic cognition 168
catatonic behaviour 247–8
catatonic schizophrenia 250, 252
category fallacy 40
character strengths 108
chemical imbalance 9
childhood disorders see neurodevelopmental, other childhood disorders
China 349
Christianity 29–30
chromosomes 7
chronic pain see persistent somatoform pain disorder
chronosystem 37, 37–8
civic strengths 109, 109
classification of mental disorders 56–8, 73–5
classical view 74–5, 75
critical perspective 74–5, 75
fuzziness, usefulness, problematic aspects 71
integrative perspective 74–5, 75
philosophical questions 74–5, 75
problems in nosology 72–3
and South Africa 74–5
clinical assessment and diagnosis 79, 96
definitions 79
steps in diagnostic process 79–80
value of assessments 79
see also interviewing and observations; physiological assessments; psychological testing
clinical interview 80–1, 81
Clock Drawing Test 309, 309–10
cocaine, South Africa 465
cognitive ability and risk 33
cognitive disorders see neurocognitive disorders (dementia)

cognitive dissonance 324
cognitive mechanisms, schizophrenia 266
cognitive or emotional vulnerability 73
cognitive strengths 109, *109*
cognitive structuring 91
cognitive theory of depression 16
cognitive-behavioural perspective 15–6
colonial psychiatry 54
colonialism 19, 39, 40
committing a client 154–5
community and well-being 104–5
community protective factors 35, *35*
community psychology 17–8, *18*, 53
comorbidity 60
compartmentalisation 324–6, *325–6*
competence 142
Comprehensive System 91
Computerised Tomography (CT) scan 85, *85*
conditioning 15, 195–6, 633
conduct disorders 619
    comorbid disorders 624
    conduct disorder 621–2
    and DSM-5, ICD-10 *620–1*, 622–3
    oppositional defiant disorder 619–20
confession 30
confidentiality
    breaches of 142
    dilemmas 145–6
    and forensic reports 142
conscience 13
consciousness, levels of 290, *290*
Constitution of South Africa 129, *129–30*, 130
conversion disorder 353
    aetiology, pathogenesis 354–6
    diagnosis, clinical presentation, course *356–7*, 356–60
    differential diagnosis 360
    epidemiology 354
    history 353–4
courage 109, *109*
critical psychology 19

cross-cultural psychology perspectives 19–22, *22–3*, 24
cultural context 17–8
    and 'normal' behaviour 48
    see also under sociocultural
cultural identity and wellness 104–5
cultural insensitivity 21
cultural psychology, cross-cultural psychology perspectives 19–22, *22–3*, 24
cultural transition and risk *33*
culture
    and assessment 88
    and coping 114
    and nosology 39
    see also under sociocultural
culture-fair, -free tests 88
cyclothymic disorder 218–9

D

dangerousness 147–52, *151–2*
    actuarial risk assessment 150–1
    case study **147–8**
    clinical risk assessment 150–1
    defined 138
    and ethics 147–52, *151–2*
    risk assessment 150–2
    risk factors *151–2*
de-institutionalisation 275
deceit 373
delirium 289–90
    aetiology 292, *292*
    clinical picture 290, *290*
    and DSM-5 and ICD-10 *291*
    epidemiology 291
    treatment and management 292–3
delusional disorder 253
delusions 233, 245–6, **246**
    types of 245–6
dementia *see* neurocognitive disorders
denial *13*, 487
dependent personality disorder 556, *557*
depersonalisation/derealisation disorder 339–40

aetiology, pathogenesis 340, *341*
    diagnosis, clinical features, course 341–3
    differential diagnosis 343–4
    and DSM-5, ICD-10 *342*
    epidemiology 340
depression; children **628**, 628–9
depression, positive features 99
depressive disorders 210
    disruptive mood dysregulation disorder 214, *214–5*, 215
    and DSM-5 *203*, 210
    due to another medical condition 215
    major depressive disorder 211, *211–2*, 212–3
    persistent depressive disorder (dysthymia) 213
    premenstrual dysphoric disorder 213
    substance/medication-induced 215
detachment 326–8, *327*
Deterioration Cognitive Observee 310, *311*
developmental psychopathology 586–7
deviant behaviours defined 138
Deviant Verbalisations scale 91
diagnosis **78**, 79–80
    definition 79
    see also clinical assessment and diagnosis
Diagnostic and Statistical Manual of Mental Disorders (DSM) 57
    background and history 58, *59–60*, 61–2, *62–6*
    criticism of 61
    development of classification system *59–60*
    and ICD, comparison and critique 71–3
    see also under DSM
diagnostic systems
    fuzziness in 71
    helpfulness of 71
    problematic aspects 71

diathesis-stress model 224
differential diagnosis 95, *96*
dimensional model 72
direct observation 82–3
discrimination and risk *33*
disease 72
  vs illness 46–7
disease model of addiction 448
disorders
  macro/micro
    understandings of 5
  medical and
    psychological
    explanations 5
  social factors 5–6
disorganised behaviour 247–8,
247
  and speech 233
displacement 13, 370
disruptive mood dysregulation
disorder 214, *214–5*, 215
  and bipolar mood
    disorder *215*
  and DSM-5 *214*
dissociation, somatising, stress
  causes of dissociation
    323–4
  compartmentalisation
    324–6, *325–6*
  detachment 326–8, *327*
  dissociation 322, *323*
  early adversity, future
    pathology *328*, 328–9
dissociation, somatoform,
related disorders **318**, 322
  dissociation, somatising,
    stress 322–9
  and DSM *319–21*,
    329–30
  pathogenesis 382
  as symptom dimensions
    383
  symptom expression
    382, *382–3*
  see also factitious
    disorder and malingering;
    somatoform disorders
dissociative amnesia 331–2,
332
  aetiology, pathogenesis
    333
  diagnosis, clinical
    features, course 333–4,
    334
  differential diagnosis
    333–5

and DSM-5, ICD-10 *333*
  epidemiology 332
dissociative anaesthesia *357*,
358
dissociative convulsions *357*,
358
dissociative disorders,
comparative nosology 329–30,
329–30
  depersonalisation/
    derealisation disorder
    339–44
  dissociative amnesia
    331–5
  dissociative fugue 335–6,
    336
  dissociative identity
    disorder 336–9
  epidemic hysteria 350–2
  Ganser's syndrome
    345–6, **346**
  related conditions, other
    cultures 348–50
  related conditions, South
    Africa 347–8
  trance and possession
    disorders 344–5, *345*
dissociative fugue 335
  diagnosis, clinical
    presentation, course
    335–6, *336*
  differential diagnosis 336
  epidemiology, aetiology,
    pathogenesis 335
dissociative identity disorder
336–7
  diagnosis, clinical
    presentation, course
    337–9, *338*
  differential diagnosis 339
  epidemiology, aetiology,
    pathogenesis 337
dissociative motor disorder
357, 358
distressing behaviours defined
138
domestic violence 431
dopamine 9, *9*, *10*
  and eating disorders 502
dopamine hypothesis 261–3
  of schizophrenia 9
dopaminergic pathways *262*
double-bind theory 267–8
DSM-5 39, 40, 57, *60*, 61
  and aetiology 57

categorisation of mental
  disorders *66*
and clinical practice 57
Cultural Formulation
  Interview 62–5
incremental advances
  in 61
problems with 57–8
DSM-I *59*
DSM-II *59*
DSM-III 57, 58, *59*
  criticism of 61
DSM-IV 39, 40, 58, *60*, 61
  criticism of 60
DSM-IV-TR *60*
dysfunctional behaviours
  defined 138
dysthymia 213

E

early trauma/deprivation 14
eating and feeding disorders
476, 479–80, 524
  avoidant/restrictive food
    intake disorder 482–3
  comparison of *493*
  cross-cultural
    perspectives 518–22
  and DSM *477–8*, 498
  emerging eating
    disorders **523**
  history of 480–2
  other specified 497, *498*
  pica 482
  rumination disorder 482
  South African
    perspective 520–2
  stress, risk, vulnerability
    523–4
  unspecified 498
  see also anorexia
    nervosa; binge-eating
    disorder; bulimia nervosa
eating and feeding disorders;
aetiology, biological factors 499
  genetic factors 499–500
  neurobiological factors
    500–3
eating and feeding disorders;
aetiology; psychological factors
503
  developmental factors
    503–4
  emotion reactivity and
    dysregulation 504–5

family context 509–11
personality factors 507–9
psychological theories 505–7
traumatic childhood experiences 509
eating and feeding disorders; aetiology, sociocultural factors 511
    and gender 517–8
    ideals for physical beauty 512–6, *514*, **515**, **516**
ecological systems theory 20, *37*, 37–8
ecstasy (MDMA) 466
ego 13
elimination disorders 606
    aetiology 609–11
    encopresis *608*, 608–9
    enuresis *606*, 606–8
    family factors 611
    genetic factors 610
    physiological causes 609–10
    stool-toilet refusal 610
Ellis, Havelock *398*
emotion reactivity and dysregulation 504–5
emotion regulation 224
emotion-focused coping 113
emotional intelligence 89
emotional strengths 109, *109*
emotions and wellness 111
empathy 116–7
empowerment 27
    and psychiatric nurses **120–1**
encopresis *608*, 608–9
endocannabinoids *10*
endogenous opioid peptides 502
endorphins 366–7
engaged life 103
enmeshment 510
enuresis *606*, 606–8
environmental mastery 104
    impaired 108
epidemic hysteria 350–2, **351**
epigenetics 500
epilepsy 334–5
epinephrine 8, *8*, 10
equifinality 6, *6*
ethical behaviour 138–9, 157
    case study **144**
    challenges to 142–5

consequences of unethical conduct 155–6, **156**
statutory control over 139–40, *140*, 141, *141*, 142
ethical dilemmas 145
    committing a client 154–5
    confidentiality and reporting to third parties 145–6, **146**
    dangerousness **147–8**, 147–52, *151–2*
    suicide and euthanasia 152–4
ethical issues 127
    core values, standards 127–8
    history of SA ethical code 136–8
    see also legal perspective
ethnocentrism 22
eudaimonic well-being 103
euthanasia 153
evil eye 28
excoriation disorder 184
exhibitionism *426*
existential perspectives 16, 197, 597
Exner Scoring System 91
exorcism 344, 351
exosystem *37*, 37–8
expressed emotion 269–70, **270**
externalising disorders 612, *612*
    aetiology 624–6
    family, socio-economic factors 625
    genetic factors 624
    neurological factors 624–5
    personal and emotional, diet factors 626
    school, academic factors 625
    see also attention-deficit/hyperactivity disorder; conduct disorder

F

factitious disorder and malingering 373–4

aetiology, pathogenesis, epidemiology 374
diagnosis, clinical presentation, and course 374–5
differential diagnosis 375
and DSM-5 *375*
factitious disorder 373–6, 376
malingering 376–81
false positives, false negatives, malingering 95
family and risk *33*
family murders 154
family protective factors 35, *35*
family systems approach 267–9
Fanon, Frantz 19, 24, 53, *53*
fear 167
fees 142
female genital mutilation 416
fetishism *425*
'fight-or-flight' reaction 167, 168
floundering/flourishing *106*, 106–7
foetal alcohol spectrum disorders 460
Forced Choice test 95
forgiveness 117
Frankl, Viktor 115
Freud, Sigmund 12–3, 46, 52, *52*, 183
frontotemporal neurocognitive disorder 300, *300*
frotteurism *426*
functional MRI (fMRI) 86

G

G-aminobutyric acid (GABA) *10*, 263
gambling disorder 458–9, *459*
Ganser's syndrome 345–6, **346**
gender
    and anorexia nervosa 484
    and coping 114
    and eating disorders 484, 490, 494, 517–8
    and mood disorders 209
    and risk *33*
    and schizophrenia 239
    and stress 114
    and suicide 152
    see also sexual health and paraphilic disorders;

sexuality and gender, medicalisation of
gender dysphoria/gender incongruence 416–8
  and DSM-5, ICD-10 418–9
  issues with gender identity 420–2
General Adaptation Syndrome 168
generalised anxiety disorder 179
genes 7
genome-wide association studies 71
Glasgow Coma Scale 309
global mental health 55
glossolalia 350
glutamate hypothesis 263
glutamic acid 10
goals 112, 112
growth hormone axes 11, 11

H

habituation 14
hair-pulling disorder 184
hallucinations 233, 244, 244–5
Halstead-Reitan Neuropsychological Battery 94
happiness 103, 105, 122
harmful dysfunction 50
health disparities 54
Health Professions Council of South Africa 137, 139–40,146
  and unethical conduct 155–6
hebephrenic schizophrenia 249, 251–2
hedonic well-being 103
helplessness, theories of 15–6
hemi-neglect 355
heroin, South Africa 465
Hirschfeld, Magnus 398
histrionic personality disorder 551, 551
HIV Dementia Scale 310
HIV/Aids and sexuality 430, 431–3
  and neurocognitive disorders 301–2, 302
hoarding disorder 183
holism 573
holistic model 72
homosexuality 50, 396–7, 517
hope 110

hope psychotherapy 119
hopelessness, theories of 15–6
hormonal messaging axes 11, 11
human rights
  in SA 128, 129–30, 130, 590
  and sexual rights 431, **432**
  violations of 54
humanistic and existential perspectives 16, 197, 597
humanity 109, 109
humility 117
Huntington's disease 299, 300
hyperactivity see under attention-deficit/hyperactivity disorder
hypochondriacal disorder see illness anxiety disorder
hypomania 208
hypomanic episode 217–8
Hypothalamic-Pituitary- axes 11, 11
hysteria 353–4

I

iatrogenic effects 9, 365
id 13
illness anxiety disorder 369–72
  diagnosis, clinical presentation, course 370–2
  differential diagnosis 372
  and DSM-5, ICD-10 371
  epidemiology, aetiology, pathogenesis 370
illness explanatory models 40
illness vs disease 46–7
incomplete mental health 107
India 55, 364, 430
indigenous knowledge, African 22, 22–3 see also under traditional
individual protective factors 35, 35
inequality and well-being 105
insulin axes 11, 11
integrated perspectives 30
  biopsychosocial model 31, 31
  diathesis-stress model 31, 31–2
  ecological systems theory 37, 37–8

protective factors 35, 35
risk and vulnerability 32, 32–4, 34
stress and coping 36
universal schema in context of globalisation 38–40
intellectual disability 592–3
  aetiology 597–9, 598
  and DSM-5 593
  organic, cultural, familial factors 599
  severity levels 594–7
intellectual functioning in assessment 82
intellectualisation 13
intelligence tests 88–9
interconnectedness, principle of 27
internal objects 14
internalising disorders 627
  aetiology 631–4
  anxiety disorders 629–30
  depression **628**, 628–9
  genetic, family factors 632, 627
  learning, conditioning, attachment 633–4
  personal, emotional factors 632–3
  separation anxiety disorder 630, 630–1
International Classification of Diseases (ICD) 39, 57
  and aetiology 57
  background and history 67, 67–8, 68–9, 69–70
  categories 70
  and DSM 68–9
internet gaming disorder 459
interpersonal strengths 109, 109
  altruism and empathy 116–7
  humility and forgiveness 117
intersectionality 429
intersex 422
interviewing and observations
  behavioural assessment 82–3, 83
  clinical interview 80–1, 81
  Mental Status Examination 81–2

inyangas 133
    and schizophrenia 257
Islam 28–9
Israeli–Palestinian conflict
105–6

J

jinn 313
Johns Hopkins model 72
Jumper Disease of Maine 349
justice 109, *109*

K

Kenya, anorexia nervosa in
488–9
Keyes' Mental Health
Continuum *106*, 106–7
Kinsey, Alfred *398*
Kraepelin, Emil 52, 208, 238

L

L-dopa 262
la belle indifférence 355, 358
labelling 274–5
Laing, R. D. 56, 269
language, communication
568–9, 568–70
languishing *106*, 106–7
latah 349
legal perspective 128
    human rights in SA 129,
129–30, 130
    Mental Health Care Act
and Amendment Act
131, *131–3*, 133
    statutory control over
ethical behaviour 139–
40, *140*, 141, *141*, 142
    Traditional Health
Practitioners Act 133–4,
134–5, 135–6
Lewy body disease 301, *301*
LGBTIQA+ 427–30
libido 408–9, *409*
Life Esidimeni **126**, 128, 130,
607
life events and risk *33*
limbic system 12, 193, *194*
Luria-Nebraska
Neuropsychological Battery
93–4
lysergic acid diethylamide
(LSD) 447

M

macro/micro understandings of
disorders 5
macrosystem *37*, 37–8
Magnetic Resonance Imaging
(MRI) 85
major depressive disorder
211–2, 211–3
maladaptiveness 49
malingering 376–7
    and DSM-5 *377*
    epidemiology,
clinical presentation,
assessment 377
    Expert Model for
detection of *378–81*,
379–81
    and false positives, false
negatives 95
mania 208
manic episode *216–7*
marital schism 268
marital skew 268
Maslow, Abraham 16, 102
Maslow's hierarchy of needs
101, **120–1**
Masters and Johnson *399*, 404
MDMA 466
meaning strengths 109, *109*
meaningful life 116
medical and psychological
explanations 5
medical examination 80
medical metaphors 74
medication-induced depressive
disorders 215
medication-induced psychotic
disorders 453, *454*
medications and addiction 466
melatonin axes 11, *11*
mental disorders 46
    attitudes towards **51**
    criteria for 47–50
    definitions **47**
    and harmful dysfunction
50
    and maladaptiveness 49
    myths about *48*
    and personal distress
49–50
    specificity vs universality
of 50
    and statistical deviance
47–8
    terminology 46–7

and understanding
strengths 100
Mental Health Care Act and
Amendment Act 131–3, *131–3*
mental health continuum
see Keyes' Mental Health
Continuum
Mental Status Examination
81–2
mental wellness perspective
99, 100–1, 123
    brief history 101–2,
101–2, 103
    individual perspectives
103–4
    sociocultural and
sociopolitical
perspectives 104–5
    see also strengths and
wellness; well-being
perspective
mental wellness perspective,
treatment
    family of mentally ill
person 119, **120–1**
    of mentally ill person
118–9
    promoting well-being,
communities 121–2
micro/mesosystem *37*, 37–8
migrant status and
schizophrenia 271–2
mindfulness 110–1
Mini Mental Status Examination
308, *308*
minority status and risk *33*
modelling 15
monoamine neurotransmitters
8
mood and affect 82
mood disorders **202**, 206–7,
206–7, 225
    bipolar and related
disorders 216–9
    clinical picture 209–10
    cross-cultural, African
perspectives 220
    depressive disorders
210–5
    and DSM *203–5*
    epidemiology 208–9
    history of 207–8
    life course 209
    symptoms of mania and
depression 219

terms used in relation to
mood 206
terms used in relation to
mood disorders 206–7
mood disorders, aetiology 221
biological factors 222
genetics 222–3
integrative model 224–5
stress and environmental
factors 221
mood-altering drugs 53–4
moral metaphors 74
moral theory of addiction 448
moral therapy 51–2
motor vehicle accidents 303,
303
multicultural assessment
21 see also cross-cultural
psychology perspectives
multifinality 6, 6
muscle dysmorphia 183

N

narcissistic personality disorder
552, 552
negative affective
communication 269
neighbourhood and risk 32
neuro-endocrine axes 11, 11
neuroanatomy **284**
neurocognitive disorders
(dementia) **280**, 284–5, 293–4,
313
amnestic disorders
305–7
anatomical terms of
direction **285**
basic neuroanatomy **284**
classification of 286,
286–8, 289
clinical picture 294–6
cultural and contextual
factors 311–3
delirium 290–3
and DSM 281, 283,
286–8, 294–6
epidemiology 297–8
history of 289–90
and ICD 283, 286–8,
294–5
treatment and
management of 304
neurocognitive disorders
(dementia), aetiology 298
Alzheimer's disease 298

frontotemporal
neurocognitive disorder
300, 300
and HIV infection 301–2,
302
Huntington's disease
299, 300
Lewy body disease 301,
301
Parkinson's disease 299
and Prion disease 301,
301
and substance/
medication use 304
and traumatic brain injury
303–4, 303–4
vascular disease 298–9
neurodevelopmental, other
childhood disorders **582**, 586,
634
classification of 591–2
developmental
psychopathology 586–7
and DSM 583–5
history of 587–8
in South Africa 588–90,
589
and stigma 590–1
see also autism
spectrum disorder;
elimination disorders;
externalising disorders;
intellectual disability;
internalising disorders
neuroleptic drugs 9
neurological examination 80
neuropeptides 10
neuropsychological
assessment 93–4
Halstead-Reitan
Neuropsychological
Battery 94
Luria-Nebraska
Neuropsychological
Battery 93–4
neuroscience and DSM 58, 61
neurotransmitters 8–10, 8–10
and anxiety disorders
193
and mood disorders 222
nitric oxide 10
non-judging 110
non-striving 111
non-substance-related
disorders 458–9

non-Western countries, myths
about mental illness in 18, 18
norepinephrine (noradrenaline)
8, 8, 10
nosology, problems in 72–3
normality and abnormality
47–50, 100, 274
novel neurotransmitters 10
number, duration of symptoms
95, 96
nyaope 464

O

obesity 479, 522
object-relations theories 14
obsessive-compulsive and
related disorders 180
and anorexia nervosa
487
body dysmorphic
disorder 182–3
and DSM-5 163
excoriation disorder 184
hoarding disorder 183
obsessive-compulsive
disorder 180, 181–2
positive features 99
trichotillomania 184
obsessive-compulsive
personality disorder 557–8,
558–9
operant conditioning 15, 438
and anxiety disorders
195, 633
oppositional defiant disorder
619–20
optimism, pessimism 110
overprotectiveness 197, 510
oxytocin axes 11, 11

P

paedophilic disorder 427
panic disorder 172–3, 173–4
paranoid personality disorder
543–4, 544–5
paranoid schizophrenia 249,
251
paraphilic disorders 422–4,
425–7
Parkinson's disease 299
pathways thinking 110, 119
patience 110–1
patient vs client 46
Pavlov, Ivan 53

persistent somatoform pain disorder 365–6, **367**
aetiology, pathogenesis 366–7
diagnosis, clinical presentation, course 368
differential diagnosis 368–9, *369*
epidemiology 366
person-environment interaction 533
personal growth 104
impaired 108
personality 13
personality disorders **528**, 532–5, 578
aetiology 560–74
clinical picture 539–42
comorbidity 559, *560*
and culture 20, 535
and DSM 529–31, *534*, 536–9, *541–2*
history of 535–8
and ICD *534*, *536*, *541*, *541–2*
myths about **535**
problems, controversies 575–8
personality disorders: aetiology; biological factors 560, *561*
diathesis-stress model 571–2
family systems theory 570–1
genetic vulnerability 561, *562–3*
intra-, interpersonal 565
and language, communication *568–9*, 568–70
neurobiological vulnerability 563, *564–5*
psychoanalytic theory 565–6, *566–7*
sociocultural influences 572
personality disorders: cluster A 542–8
personality disorders: cluster B 548–54
personality disorders: cluster C 555–9
personality functioning/ dysfunction; holistic perspective 573–4, *574*
personality inventories 89–90

Millon Clinical Multiaxial Inventory-IV (MCMI-IV) 90
Minnesota Multiphasic Personality Inventory-2 (MMPI-2) 89–90
personality model, African *25*, 25–6
perspectival model 72
phenomenal field 16
phenomenology 571–2
phenothiazines 262
phobias, specific 170–1, *171–2*
physiological assessments
neuro-imaging *85*, 85–6
physical examination 84
psycho-physiological assessment 86
pica 482
Pinel, Phillipe 51–2, 207
pituitary insufficiency 481
playing dead 325
political ideology and well-being 105–6
political perspective 19
polygenetic models of inheritance 7
positive and negative behaviours 48
positive psychology 102–3
definition 102
and social justice 103
see also mental wellness perspective
positive psychotherapy 119
Positron Emission Tomography (PET) scan 85–6
post-schizophrenic depression 250
post-traumatic growth 115–6
posttraumatic stress disorder 186, *186–8*
community psychology perspective 18
and conditioning 15
and psychosocial stressors 198
poverty
and mental, physical health 588, *589*
and risk *32*
and well-being 105
prejudice and risk 33
presenting problem 79
Prion disease 301, *301*

privacy, confidentiality, and records *140*
problem-focused coping 113
Professional Board for Psychology 137, 139, 140
registered practitioners *141*
professional competence *140*
professional disrespect 142
professional relations *140*
projection *13*
projective tests 90–3
Rorschach Inkblot Test *91*, 91–2
Thematic Apperception Test 93
prolactin axes 11, *11*
Protection of Personal Information Act 141–2
elements of potential liability 142
protective factors 35, *35*
pseudo-hostility, -mutuality 268
psychiatric vs psychological disorders 46–7
psychiatric nurses and family support **120–1**
psychoanalysis 12–3, 52, 58
psychoanalytic theories of addiction 449
psychodynamic approaches 12–4, *13–4*, 59
psychological arousal 27
Psychological Association of South Africa 136–7
psychological defence mechanisms 13, *13–4*
psychological disorder defined **47**
psychological mechanisms 532
psychological perspectives 12
behavioural/learning perspectives 14–5
cognitive-behavioural perspective 15–6
humanistic and existential perspectives 16
psychodynamic approaches 12–3, *13–4*, 14
Psychological Society of South Africa 137, 391, 421
psychological testing 86–7
arriving at a diagnosis 95–6, *96*

culture and assessment 88
ethics of *140*
false positives, false negatives, malingering 95
intelligence tests 88–9
neuropsychological assessment 93–4
personality inventories 89–90
projective tests 90–3
use of diagnostic classification systems 95–6, *96*
who can administer them? 87
psychological traits 532
psychologists registered per ethnic group *135*
psychometrists 87
psychopathology **4**, 5–6
limited and narrows focus 100
macro/micro understandings of 5
medical and psychological explanations 5
social factors 5–6
as socially constructed 55–6
psychopathology defined **47**
psychopathology, brief history
critical perspectives 55–6
global perspectives 55
in South Africa 54
in the West 51–4
psychopathology, origins and causes 5–6
cquifinality, multifinality 6, *6*
psychopharmacological treatment 53–4
psychosis and psychotic disorders 233–4
definition of terms 233
psychotropic drugs 9, 53–4
purging 491–2
purpose in life 104
impaired 108

R
rational-emotive theory 16
Raven's Standard Progressive Matrices 89
reaction-formation *14*
reactivity 83
registered psychologists 87
reinforcement 15
and childhood depression 633
relationships with clients, inappropriate 142
relations with others, impaired 108
reliability of assessments 79
religiosity and spirituality 117–8
religious perspectives *25*, 25–8
repression 12–3, *13*
Research Domain Criteria 72
residual schizophrenia 250
resilience 114–5
respect for persons 127
Rey 15-item test 95
right to die 153
risk
and family 33
and life events 33
and prejudice 33
and resiliency 115
and socioeconomic status 32
and suicide 152–3
violence risk, mortality risk 254–6
see also under dangerousness
risk and vulnerability 32
factors *34*
risk factors 32, *32–3*, 588
and settings 34
ritualistic support 27
Rorschach Comprehensive System 92
Rosenhan experiment **65**, 274
rumination disorder 482
Ryff, Carol 103–4

S
sangomas 133
and schizophrenia 257
schemata 633
schizoaffective disorder 253
schizoid personality disorder 545, *546*

schizophrenia
case study **241**
clinical picture 241–3, *242–3*
and culture 20, 256–8
and DSM-5, ICD-10 *242–3*
history of 238–9
prevalence and course 239, *239–40*, 240
and suicide 152, 255
and *ukuthwasa* 17–8, 257
violence risk, mortality risk 254–6
schizophrenia spectrum and other psychotic disorders **228**, 232, 253–4, 275
cross-cultural, South African perspectives 256–8
diagnosing 234–5, *235–7*, 237
and DSM *229–31*, *236–7*
psychosis and psychotic disorders 233–4
schizophrenia subtypes in ICD-10 249–51, *251–2*
schizophrenia; aetiological factor integration 272
schizophrenia; aetiology, biological factors 258
brain structure 260–1
genetics 259–60
neurochemistry 261, *262*, 262–4
neurodevelopmental factors 264
schizophrenia; aetiology, psychological factors 265
family influences 267–70
individual factors 265–7
schizophrenia; aetiology, sociocultural factors
effects of migrant status 271–2
effects of social class 270–1
schizophrenia; controversies 273
'normality' vs 'abnormality' 274
classification systems 273
de-institutionalisation 275

labelling 274–5
schizophrenia; negative symptoms 248
anhedonia, asociality 248
avolition 249
blunted affect, alogia 248
schizophrenia; positive symptoms 244
delusions 245, *245–6*, 246
disorganised or catatonic behaviour 247–8
disorganised thinking, speech 247
hallucinations *244*, 244–5
schizophreniform disorder 253
schizophrenogenic mother 267
schizotypal personality disorder 253, *547*, 547–8
secondary gain 95
seizures; dissociative disorders 358–9
selective serotonin reuptake inhibitors 222, *223*
self-acceptance 104
impaired 107
self-control strengths 109, *109*
self-monitoring 83
self-regulation 112–3
senile dementia 289
sense-making 116
sensitisation 15
sensorium in assessment 82
separation anxiety disorder 170, 630, *630–1*
serotonin 9, *9*, 222, *223*
and eating disorders 501, *503*
role of in disorders 10
sexology 395, 431
sexual health and paraphilic disorders **386**, 390–6, **392**, 438–9
clinical picture 400
cultural and African perspectives 427–33
and DSM *387–9, 402, 409*
paraphilic disorders 422–4, *425–7*
sexual health and paraphilic disorders; aetiology 434
biological factors 434–5
psychological factors 435–7

social and interpersonal factors 437–8
sexual health, conditions related to 400
male, female sexual dysfunctions **403**, 403–4, **416**
sexual dysfunctions 401–3
sexual pain disorders 414–6
sexual interest/arousal disorders
delayed ejaculation 413, *414*
and DSM-5, ICD-10 *405–6, 409, 410, 411*
erectile disorder 410–1
female, and male hypoactive sexual desire disorder 405–8, *407*
male hypoactive sexual desire disorder **408**, 408–9
orgasmic disorders 411, *411–2*
premature ejaculation 412, *413*
sexual aversion disorder 409, *409*
sexual masochism *425*
sexual pain disorders 414–5, *415–6*
sexual rights **432**
sexual sadism *425*
sexuality and gender, medicalisation of 396–7, *397–400*, 400
Single Photon Emission Computed Tomography (SPECT) 86
skin-picking disorder 184
Skinner, B. F. 53
social anxiety disorder (social phobia) 175–7, *176–8*
social class
and eating disorders 518, 519, 520
and schizophrenia 270–1
social contact, African principle of 27
social control, psychiatry as 55, 73, 274
social drift and risk *32*
social factors 5–6
social justice 103

social learning theory 20
social perspectives
and 'normal' behaviour 48
community psychology perspective 17–8, *18*
social protective factors 35, *35*
social selection theory 271
socio-economic factors
and mood disorders 224
and risk *32*
sociocultural and sociopolitical perspectives 104–5
sociocultural factors
and anxiety 191
and conversion disorder 354
and eating disorders 499, 511–8, 523–4
and personality disorders 572
and schizophrenia 270
and sexual health 403, 428
sociogenic hypothesis 270–1
sociopolitical context 16
solution-focused therapy 119
somatic symptom disorder 360–1
aetiology, pathogenesis 361–2
diagnosis, clinical presentation, course *362–3*, 362–5
differential diagnosis 365
and DSM-5, ICD-10 *362–3*
epidemiology 361
somatoform disorders 252
conversion disorder 353–60
and DSM-5, ICD-10 352, *352–3*
illness anxiety disorder 369–72
persistent somatoform pain disorder 365–9
psychological factors affecting other medical conditions 372
somatic symptom disorder 360–5
South African Psychological Association 136–7
South African Stress and Health Study 166

spirit *25*, 25–8
spirit possession 257, 313, 344, *351*
spiritual illnesses
 African perspective 26–7
 Christian perspective 29–30
 Islamic perspective 28
standardisation of assessments 79
state anxiety 166
stigma 254
 and childhood disorders 590–1
stool-toilet refusal 610
strengths and wellness 110
 cognitive strengths 110–1
 coping 113–4
 interpersonal strengths 116–7
 mental illness and 108–9, *109*
 mindfulness 110–1
 optimism 110
 positive affect, emotional intelligence 111
 post-traumatic growth 115–6
 religiosity and spirituality 117–8
 resilience 114–5
 self-regulation *112*, 112–3
stress
 disorders specifically associated with *165*
 severe, and adjustment disorders *164*
 social and risk 32
 and worry 168
structured clinical/professional judgement 151
struggling *106*, 106–7
sublimation *13*
substance use disorder 455–6, *456–7*
substance-induced disorders 452
 substance intoxication, withdrawal 452–3, *452–3*
 substance/medication-induced psychotic disorder 453, *454*

substance-related and addictive disorders **442**, 446, 472
 addiction defined 446
 clinical picture 451–2
 and DSM *443–5*
 historical perspective 447
 non-substance-related disorders 458–9
 South Africa, specific substances 460–6
 theories of addiction 448–9
 types of addiction 449, *450–1*
substance-related and addictive disorders; aetiology 467
 biological factors 467–70
 brain structures *468*, 468–9
 genetic predisposition 467–8
 neurotransmitters 469–70
 psychological, social factors 470–2
substance/medication-induced depressive disorders 215
suicide
 assisted suicide 153
 and beneficence, non-maleficence 153
 extended suicide 154
 risk factors 152–3
superego 13
supernatural, the 29, 51
suppression *14*
symptom dimensions 369
synapses 8, *8*
syphilis 52
systems theory 197
Szasz, Thomas 56, 274

T

Tarasoff Case **147–8**
target behaviour 83
temperament and risk *33*
temperance 109, *109*
terminology 46–7, **47**
therapeutic activities, ethics of *140*
thought processes in assessment 82

tik 462–3
tobacco 447
traditional healers 22, *22–3*, 24, 133–6
 healthcare delivery approaches 27–8, 55
 Islamic 28–9
 see also under indigenous knowledge
traditional health practitioner defined 133
Traditional Health Practitioners Act 133–4, *134–5*, 135–6
trait anxiety 166
traits 89
trance and possession disorders 344–5, *345*
Transactional Model of Stress and Coping 36
transcendence 109, *109*
transgender 417–8, 420, 421
 rights 433
transsexualism 420
transvestic fetishism *425*
transvestites 417
trauma- and stressor-related disorders 184–5
 acute stress disorder 189, *189–90*
 disinhibited social engagement disorder 185
 and DSM-5 *163*
 posttraumatic stress disorder 186, *186–8*
 reactive attachment disorder 185
traumatic brain injury 303–4, *303–4*
triangulation in diagnostic process *81*
trichotillomania 184
tripartite influence model of body image *514*
twin studies 7
 and schizophrenia 259–60
two-continuum model 106

U

ubuntu 116
ubuthakathi 22, 312
ukufa kwabantu 312
ukuphonsa **312**

ukuthwasa 17–8, *23*, 312
  and dissociative
  disorders 347–8
  and schizophrenia 17–8,
  257
unconscious thoughts and
feelings, assessing 90–3
unconscious, the 12–3
under-diagnosis and over-
diagnosis 74
undifferentiated schizophrenia
250–1, *252*
Universal Declaration of Human
Rights 128
unspecified schizophrenia 250
unspecified schizophrenia
spectrum disorders 254

V

validity of assessments 79
validity of psychiatric
diagnoses **65**
Values in Action Classification
of Strengths 108–9, *109*
violence 303, 622
  domestic 431
  and ethics 149–51
  political 105–6
  and risk *151–2*, 254
  and trauma 18
violent crime 303, **303**
voyeurism *426*

W

Watson, John 53
Wechsler Adult Intelligence
Scale 89

well-being perspective
  Keyes' Mental Health
  Continuum *106*, 106–7
  mental illness and
  psychological strengths
  108–9, *109*
  mental illness as
  impaired psychological
  well-being 107–8
well-being therapy 107, 119
wellness *see* mental wellness
perspective
wisdom 109, *109*
witchcraft *22–3*
World Health Organization
(WHO) 57, 67–9
worry 168